CONTINUED ON REVERSE ⟶

The Little, Brown Handbook

Instructor's Annotated Edition

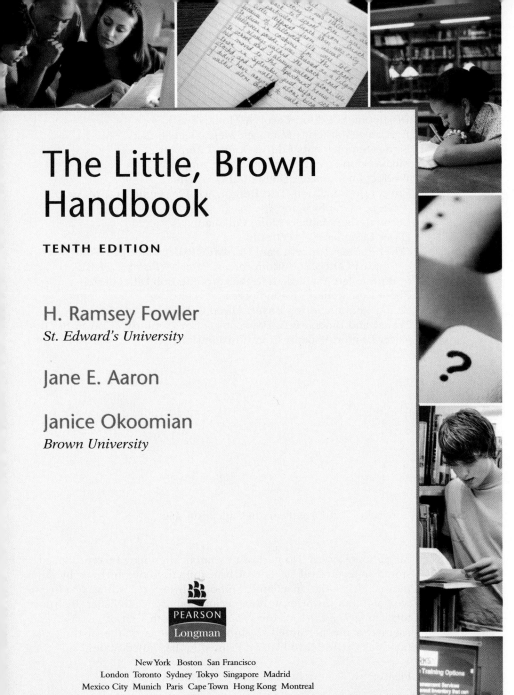

The Little, Brown Handbook

TENTH EDITION

H. Ramsey Fowler
St. Edward's University

Jane E. Aaron

Janice Okoomian
Brown University

PEARSON
Longman

New York Boston San Francisco
London Toronto Sydney Tokyo Singapore Madrid
Mexico City Munich Paris Cape Town Hong Kong Montreal

Publisher: Joseph Opiela
Acquisitions Editor: Brandon Hight
Development Manager: Mary Ellen Curley
Development Editor: Carol M. Hollar-Zwick
Executive Marketing Manager: Megan Galvin-Fak
Senior Supplements Editor: Donna Campion
Media Supplements Editor: Jenna Egan
Production Manager: Donna DeBenedictis
Project Coordination, Text Design, and Electronic Page Makeup:
    Nesbitt Graphics, Inc.
Cover Design Manager: John Callahan
Cover Designer: Kay Petronio
Cover Photos: Top left: Paul Hardy/CORBIS. Top right: Tom
    Stewart/CORBIS. Bottom center: Peter M. Fisher/CORBIS.
    Bottom left: Picturequest. Background: Bob Diffenderfer
Photo Researcher: Vivette Porges
Senior Manufacturing Buyer: Alfred C. Dorsey
Printer and Binder: R.R. Donnelley & Sons Company/Crawfordsville
Cover Printer: Phoenix Color Corporation

Please visit us at *www.ablongman.com/littlebrown*

ISBN 0-321-41986-3

1 2 3 4 5 6 7 8 9 10—DOC—09 08 07 06

Designing and Teaching Composition Courses

These chapters appear only in this *Instructor's Annotated Edition.*

Brief Contents of the Student Edition

The complete student edition of *The Little, Brown Handbook*, Tenth Edition, with its detailed table of contents, follows the six chapters appearing only in this instructor's edition. The annotations in the margins of this instructor's edition—which include answers to the exercises and tips for presenting the material—do not appear in the student edition.

Designing
and Teaching
Composition Courses

CHAPTER 1
Teaching Writing as a Process

Writing as a *how*

Drawing on the results of three decades of research into the composing processes of writers, most writing instructors now emphasize the *how* of writing. While theorists such as Lester Faigley and Susan Miller have pointed out the limitations of trying to define systematically what happens when a writer sits down to compose a work, most writing teachers and their students have effectively adapted a focus on the processes through which students generate and revise their writing, rather than focusing solely on a final product. This book is designed to support that focus on the *hows* of writing.

Most writers agree that at least three components contribute to the processes they use most of the time: *prewriting*, the finding and exploring of ideas and the construction of plans for expressing them (in classical terminology, *invention*); *drafting*, getting the ideas down on paper and generating sentences about them; and *revising*, reconsidering the ideas, the treatment they receive, the plans for expressing them, and the ways they are expressed (in classical terminology, *arrangement, style,* and to some extent, *delivery*).

Theories about the writing process have focused on the ways in which writers do the following:

- perceive and explore themselves and their worlds through the medium of language;
- consider their subject matter as the occasion for interpretive analysis and as the testing ground for ideas and hypotheses;
- respond to, understand, and to some degree, invent their audiences; and
- position themselves in relation to writerly conventions, to institutional restraints, and to communities within and outside of the classroom.

These assumptions are based on the theories outlined below.

Writing as an expressive process

Many theories of the writing process from the 1960s and 1970s focused on its expressive content, the attempts of writers to use language to capture and articulate the unique vision of the writer. For instance, D. Gordon Rohman and Albert O. Wlecke argue that techniques such as meditative exercises, journal keeping, and the composition of analogies (called "existential sentences") help writers find a personal truth in even the most abstract of subjects. They argue that such "prewriting" techniques lead in a smooth and linear fashion to drafting and revision as writers refine the expression of the truth they tell. This privileging of self-discovery, what is sometimes called the *expressionistic* or *romantic* view of composing, is also held by Peter Elbow, Ken Macrorie, William Coles, and Donald Murray, to name a few of its most influential proponents. Elbow argues for the efficacy of freewriting and drafting in helping writers explore ideas before worrying about structure and presentation. Macrorie encourages students to use "case histories" of past experiences and to work from direct observation in order to go beyond the obvious clichés, which he calls "Engfish" (because they stink of insincerity). Coles values prewriting because it allows students to explore multiple relationships to readers and subjects (what he calls "plural I's"). Murray emphasizes aspects of prewriting that cultivate surprise, originality, and new combinations of ideas which lead to personal discovery.

The expressionistic theory gives discovery of ideas primacy in the writing process and sees the writer's personal vision as more important than conventions and codes; its emphasis on pre- and freewriting is an attempt to give writers the power to control or even exploit conventions and expectations in the interests of conveying an original vision. These beliefs have thus attracted criticism from those who believe that the teacher's responsibility is to show writers how to become part of a community, not how to put themselves outside it. However, the expressionists' contributions to our understanding of the formative stages of prewriting and drafting and their respect for students as writing colleagues have benefited many teachers and theorists. Ann Berthoff's work is an interesting example of that influence; she draws on the expressionistic emphasis by stressing the power of the imagination to create relationships between ideas, but in "Recognition, Representation and Revision" she also develops an understanding of revision as a nonlinear part of the composing process, an ongoing reconsideration of those relationships. Where many expressionists might insist that prewriting generates the ideas, that revision is the process of getting them right, and that editing is the radically separate task of adjusting the etiquette of presentation (spelling, punctuation, and the like), Berthoff and others view revision as a recursive process, as the meaningful reconsideration and development of ideas articulated through the grammar of the paragraph and the sentence.

Writing as a cognitive process

A second school of theories about the writing process is deeply rooted in psychology, particularly in studies of cognition. For such *cognitive* theorists, "protocols" (detailed descriptions of how a document is produced) and draft analyses play a key role. One of the earliest such cognitive studies is Janet Emig's. In *The Composing Process of Twelfth Graders* (1971), she studies writing behaviors: how student writers find and develop their ideas. Drawing on James Britton's terminology, she finds that these processes differ with the audience: if students write for themselves (expressively), they are concerned with the presentation of ideas, but if students write for teachers (transactionally), they are concerned (even obsessed) with mechanical correctness. Emig's technique of asking writers to compose out loud has also been used by Sondra Perl in her studies of unskilled writers and by Carol Berkenkotter in her study of a professional writer's composing processes. Nancy Sommers's comparisons of student and experienced adult writers show that experienced writers come to value the development of ideas far more than mechanical correctness, whereas student writers' concern with correctness and with the demands of the writing situation often impedes the development of ideas.

Richard Young, Alton Becker, and Kenneth Pike also developed a cognitive theory of the writing process; however, theirs depends on the writer's knowledge not of the audience but of the subject. Their "tagmemics" theory models cognitive efforts to know a subject; it focuses on how writers perceive a subject's individuality, variability, and place in a larger system. These cognitive efforts should help writers find and develop new combinations of ideas. Like the romantic theories, tagmemics emphasizes prewriting and only discusses drafting or revision as it manifests writers' developing understanding of their subject matter.

The cognitivist position has been most fully expanded by Linda Flower, John Hayes, and their graduate students and colleagues at Carnegie-Mellon University. They view the composing process as a series of decision-making strategies: planning texts, translating those plans into sentences, and revising the texts produced to bring them in line with the original (or reshaped) plans. Although Emig first suggested it, Flower and Hayes and their collaborators have done most to demonstrate the recursive and hierarchical levels of writing processes, especially in the planning and revising stages of writing activities.

Cognitivists find linear expressionist models too simplistic; they argue that writers continually move back and forth between stages to adjust their plans. Like the expressionists, the cognitivists value personal expression highly, claiming it represents most validly an individual's way of thinking. Cognitivists spend little time discussing the finished forms writing may take; it's rare to see an entire piece of discourse reproduced in their discussions. More recently, they have been giving slightly more emphasis to the audience's role in the cognitive workings of writers. But for cognitivists, the writer's "brain work" and reflections on it remain paramount. This position has been challenged as an attempt to systematize the complex cognitive processes of writers and their varying situations. However, cognitive studies have arguably helped teachers to become more attentive to the varied composing processes of individuals and better able to respond to the particular challenges faced by student writers.

Writing as a social process

Most recently, as theorists have focused on the social functions of, and constraints on, writing, studies of the writing process have broadened to examine the contexts in which writing occurs, to define the discourse communities in which particular writing processes participate. This broadening has also been influenced by the changing demographics of college populations. As more and more nontraditional students—older or returning, working class, of non-European origin, international—have entered the academy, teachers have been forced to change their expectations about the kinds of knowledge students bring with them. No longer can a teacher take for granted that students know what an essay looks like, or what "thesis and support" are, or how academics think. (Indeed, research conducted by Robert Connors and Andrea Lunsford suggests that an unfamiliarity with the look of the printed page may be responsible for many student "errors.")

Because of the traditional link between writing programs and English departments, one response to this situation has been to teach students the kinds of discourse that scholars trained in literature and its criticism value: journals, poetry, fiction, and literary analysis. But the "social-epistemic" theorists, as James Berlin called them, have argued that the role of writing programs is to prepare students to read and respond to the various specialized languages—academic, legal, governmental—that they might encounter.

Such social theories of the writing process have two current focuses. According to the political focus, represented by David Bartholomae and Anthony Petrosky, Patricia Bizzell, and others influenced to some extent by the Brazilian theorist Paolo Freire, awareness of the constraints of a discourse community is politically liberating, potentially enabling, and revolutionary. If students can understand the constraints of that community and master them, they can come to control and change the community through their own discourse. For theorists who believe this, discovery of the contexts in which students write and the constraints that govern those contexts comes before any other part of the writing process. In terms of classroom practice such theories emphasize a problem-solving format in which students often work with discursive academic prose in peer-group settings and use revision and rereading to establish articulate positions within and against those discourses. A number of contemporary writing texts now employ this multicultural and overtly political approach to collegiate writing.

Another socially focused theory sees writing as a fundamental tool for learning in all communities and at all curricular levels and attempts to foster the teaching of writing beyond the limits of traditional writing programs. In particular, this focus is apparent in "writing-across-the-curriculum" and "writing-across-the-disciplines" movements, which have achieved increasing success in the colleges where they have been implemented. Toby Fulwiler and Barbara Walvoord, two noted proponents of the movement, have both argued convincingly for the benefits of writing instruction beyond the first-year courses. Related "social construction" theories make the case that knowledge is achieved as a consensus among communities rather than as a hierarchical transfer of information from teacher to student. In *Collaborative Learning: Higher Education, Interdependence, and the Authority of Knowledge*, Kenneth Bruffee argues for collaborative student learning as the process through which students become members in their college communities and in communities of knowledge. While social constructionism has been critiqued for its goal of consensus on the grounds that it erases vital differences and competing discourses within communities, collaborative work has become an invaluable part of most classrooms (see for instance the criticisms of Stewart and the recent review by Sullivan).

Ultimately, most teachers adapt the theories and methods that make the most sense given the needs of their students and the shape of their institutional setting. The key effort of this book is to support a range of pedagogical emphases on the composing processes of writers and to help students understand rhetorical forms as flexible frameworks rather than as rigid formulas—as essential parts of a creative composing process.

Resources for teaching writing

Bartholomae, David. "A Conversation with Peter Elbow." *College Composition and Communication* 46 (1995): 62–71.

———. "Inventing the University." In *When a Writer Can't Write: Studies in Writer's Block and Other Composing Process Problems*. Ed. Mike Rose. New York: Guilford, 1985. 134–65.

Beach, Richard, and Lillian S. Bridwell, eds. *New Directions in Composition Research.* New York: Guilford, 1984.

Berkenkotter, Carol. "Decisions and Revisions: The Planning Strategies of a Publishing Writer." *College Composition and Communication,* 34 (1983), 156–69.

Berlin, James. "Rhetoric and Ideology in the Writing Class." *College English* 50 (1988): 477–94.

Berthoff, Ann. *The Making of Meaning: Metaphors, Models, and Maxims for Writing Teachers.* Upper Montclair: Boynton/Cook, 1981.

———. *Reclaiming the Imagination: Philosophical Perspectives for Writers and Teachers of Writing.* Upper Montclair: Boynton/Cook, 1984.

———. "Recognition, Representation and Revision." *Rhetoric and Composition.* Ed. Richard L. Graves. Upper Montclair: Boynton/Cook, 1984.

Bizzell, Patricia. *Academic Discourse and Critical Consciousness.* Pittsburgh: U of Pittsburgh P, 1992.

Bloom, Lynn Z., Donald A. Daiker, and Edward M. White, eds. *Composition in the Twenty-First Century: Crisis and Change.* Carbondale: Southern Illinois UP, 1996.

Britton, James. "Theories of the Disciplines and a Learning Theory." *Writing, Teaching, and Learning in the Disciplines.* Ed. Anne Herrington and Charles Moran. New York: MLA, 1992. 47–60.

Bruffee, Kenneth. *Collaborative Learning: Higher Education, Interdependence, and the Authority of Knowledge.* Baltimore: Johns Hopkins UP, 1993.

Clifford, John, and John Schilb, eds. *Writing Theory and Critical Theory: Research and Scholarship in Composition.* New York: MLA, 1994.

Coles, William E., Jr. *The Plural I: The Teaching of Writing.* New York: Holt, 1978.

Connors, Robert J., and Andrea A. Lunsford. "Frequency of Formal Errors in Current College Writing, or Ma and Pa Kettle Do Research." *College Composition and Communication* 39 (1988): 395–409.

Corbett, Edward P. J., et al., eds. *The Writing Teacher's Sourcebook,* 4th ed. New York: Oxford UP, 2000.

Elbow, Peter. "Reflections on Academic Discourse: How It Relates to Freshmen and Colleagues." *College English* 53 (1991): 135–55.

Emig, Janet. *The Composing Processes of Twelfth Graders.* Urbana: NCTE, 1971.

———. *The Web of Meaning.* Upper Montclair: Boynton/Cook, 1983.

Faigley, Lester. *Fragments of Rationality: Postmodernity and the Subject of Composition.* Pittsburgh: U of Pittsburgh P, 1992.

Flower, Linda. *The Construction of Negotiated Meaning: A Social Cognitive Theory of Writing.* Carbondale: Southern Illinois UP, 1994.

Flower, Linda, and John R. Hayes. "A Cognitive Process Theory of Writing." *College Composition and Communication* 32 (1981): 365–87.

———. "The Construction of Purpose in Writing and Reading." *College English* 50 (1988): 528–50.

Fulwiler, Toby, and Art Young, eds. *Language Connections: Writing and Reading Across the Curriculum.* Urbana: NCTE, 1978.

———. *Programs That Work: Models and Methods for Writing Across the Curriculum.* Portsmouth, NH: Boynton/Cook (Heineman), 1990.

Hairston, Maxine. "Different Products, Different Processes: A Theory About Writing." *College Composition and Communication* 37 (1986): 442–52.

———. "The Winds of Change: Thomas Kuhn and the Revolution in the Teaching of Writing." *College Composition and Communication* 33 (1982): 76–88.

Hayes, John R., and Linda S. Flower. "Writing Research and the Writer." *American Psychologist* 41:10 (1986): 1106–13.

Jarratt, Susan C., and Lynn Worsham, eds. *Feminism and Composition Studies: In Other Words.* New York: MLA, 1998.

Lindquist, Julie. "Class Ethos and the Politics of Inquiry: What the Barroom Can Teach Us about the Classroom." *College Composition and Communication* 51 (1999): 225–47.

Macrorie, Ken. *Searching Writing.* Upper Montclair: Boynton/Cook, 1980.

Miller, Susan. *Textual Carnivals: The Politics of Composition.* Carbondale: Southern Illinois UP, 1991.

———. "Writing Theory: Theory Writing." In *Methods and Methodology in Composition Research.* Ed. Gesa Kirsch and Patrick A. Sullivan. Carbondale: Southern Illinois UP, 1992: 62–83.

Moffett, James. *Teaching the Universe of Discourse.* Boston: Houghton, 1968.

Murray, Donald M. *The Craft of Revision.* New York: Harcourt Brace, 1991.

————. *Expecting the Unexpected: Teaching Myself—and Others—to Read and Write.* Portsmouth, NH: Heinemann, 1989.

Newkirk, Thomas. *The Performance of Self in Student Writing.* Portsmouth, NH: Boynton/Cook (Heinemann), 1997.

North, Steven. *The Making of Knowing in Composition: Portrayal of an Emerging Field.* Portsmouth, NH: Heineman, 1987.

Odell, Lee, ed. *Theory and Practice in the Teaching of Writing: Rethinking the Discipline.* Carbondale: Southern Illinois UP, 1993.

Pemberton, Michael A. "Modeling Theory and Composing Process Models." *College Composition and Communication* 44:1 (1993): 40–58.

Perl, Sondra. "The Composing Process of Unskilled College Writers." *College Composition and Communication* 31 (1980): 389–401.

Perelman, Les. "The Context of Classroom Writing." *College English* 48 (1986): 471–79.

Reither, James A. "Writing and Knowing: Toward Redefining the Writing Process." *College English* 47 (1985): 620–28.

Robinson, Jay L. "Literacy in the Department of English." *College English* 47 (1985): 482–98.

Rohman, D. Gordon, and Alberto O. Wlecke. *Pre-Writing: The Construction and Application of Models for Concept-Formation in Writing.* USOE Cooperative Research Project No. 2174. East Lansing: Michigan State UP, 1964.

Rose, Mike. "Rigid Rules, Inflexible Plans, and the Stifling of Language: A Cognitivist Analysis of Writer's Block." *College Composition and Communication* 31 (1980): 389–401.

Russell, David P. *Writing in the Academic Disciplines: A Curricular History.* Carbondale: Southern Illinois UP, 1991.

Sommers, Nancy. "Revision Strategies of Student Writers and Experienced Adult Writers." *College Composition and Communication* 31 (1980): 378–88.

Sternglass, Marilyn. *Time to Know Them: A Longitudinal Study of Writing and Learning at the College Level.* Mahwah, NJ: Lawrence Erlbaum Associates, 1997.

Stewart, Donald. "Collaborative Learning and Composition: Boon or Bane?" *Rhetoric Review* 7 (1988): 58–85.

Sullivan, Patricia A. "Social Constructionism and Literacy Studies." *College English* 57 (1995): 950–959.

Walvoord, Barbara E. "The Future of WAC." *College English* 58:1 (1996): 58–79.

Yagelski, Robert P. "The Ambivalence of Reflection: Critical Pedagogies, Identity, and the Writing Teacher." *College Composition and Communication* 51 (1999): 32–50.

Yancey, Kathleen Blake. *Reflection in the Writing Classroom.* Logan: Utah State UP, 1998.

Young, Richard E., Alton L. Becker and Kenneth L. Pike. *Rhetoric: Discovery and Change.* New York: Harcourt, 1970.

CHAPTER 2
Using *The Little, Brown Handbook*

In many writing courses, the writing done by the students in that class serves as the core. The text or texts the instructor chooses should serve as resources to encourage and improve that writing. And the instructor's choice should be based on a clear understanding of the assumptions on which each text is founded.

Assumptions shaping *The Little, Brown Handbook*

It would be foolish to suggest that all composition instructors who emphasize the composing process are in agreement over specific teaching strategies—or that they ought to be. Two teachers who share a belief in the importance of revision or who encourage students to discover ideas and information through freewriting may also disagree strongly about the purposes for writing. Yet it is possible to identify some generally agreed-upon elements of a process paradigm.

The process paradigm of *The Little, Brown Handbook* is based on the following assumptions:

- Writing consists of a variety of activities including *developing* (exploring, gathering, focusing, organizing); *drafting* (finding and expressing meaning, establishing relationships); and *revising* (rethinking, rewriting, editing, proofreading).
- The activities that make up the writing process are recursive, not fixed in order. For example, revising often includes the discovery of fresh insights, and the drafting of one part of a paper may occur at the same time the writer is gathering materials for another part.
- Writing often is a process of discovering ideas, arriving at knowledge of the self, and selecting effective ways to present concepts and information.

- Knowledge of the conventions of expression and of stylistic options is an important part of the writer's repertoire, but a premature striving for correctness and for grace and clarity often can impede the free flow of ideas and the discovery of appropriate form. Thus, activities such as editing and proofreading, which pay considerable attention to style, grammar, and mechanics, are generally best left until relatively late in the composing of an essay.
- Skilled writers (in contrast to unskilled writers) are characterized by the range of strategies they know and employ in developing, drafting, and revising—strategies that can be both taught and learned.
- Effective writing is the product of interaction among the four elements of the writing situation: author, subject, language, and audience.

These assumptions shape the advice offered throughout *The Little, Brown Handbook,* not only in the discussions of the writing process (Part 1) and of reading and writing in college (Part 2), but also in treatments of research writing (Part 9), writing in the academic disciplines (Part 10), special writing situations (Part 11), strategies for clear and effective sentences (Parts 4 and 5), and diction (Part 8). Even the discussions of grammatical sentences (Part 3), punctuation (Part 6), and mechanics (Part 7) mix firm and relatively conservative advice with an awareness of the demands of various audiences and of the difference between an early draft and a final, carefully edited draft.

At the same time, discussions in the handbook point out that different writing situations may call for different composing processes and that the knowledge of forms for expression—the *what* of writing—is an important companion to an awareness of the *how*. In this the handbook agrees with the work of theorists and teachers such as

Maxine Hairston, James Reither, Patricia Bizzell, and Arthur Applebee. These writers share a belief that the process paradigm needs to be augmented by:

- an awareness of the ways the writing process varies according to the writer's purpose and the social context;
- a recognition of the important roles knowledge of form and convention can play in guiding the composing process; and
- an acknowledgment of the extent to which communities of readers and writers are bound together by specific expectations governing the form and content of discourse.

The handbook recognizes that the processes of composing are "strategies that writers employ for particular purposes" (Applebee 106) and emphasizes this perspective in:

- the writing process (Chapters 1–5)
- reading and writing in college (Chapters 6–11)
- discussions of specialized forms of writing:

  research writing (Chapters 42–48)
  writing in the academic disciplines (Chapters 49–53)
  public writing (Chapter 55)
  oral presentations (Chapter 56)

The emphasis throughout is on seeing the forms as the shared expectations of readers and writers and using these expectations to guide the discovery and expression of ideas so as not to constrain creativity.

New features of the tenth edition

The tenth edition of *The Little, Brown Handbook* has been revised to meet the needs of today's students, providing a solid foundation in the goals and requirements of college writing and research. Listed below are highlights of the new edition.

- A new Part 2, "Reading and Writing in College," offers coverage of academic writing; study skills and essay exams; critical thinking, reading, and writing about texts and images; reading arguments critically; writing arguments; and reading, and using visual arguments.
- Part 9, "Research Writing," continues to emphasize using the library as Web gateway while keeping pace

with the methods and challenges of research in an electronic environment. New coverage includes preparing an annotated bibliography, searching library subscription services (with annotated examples), using Web logs as possible sources requiring careful evaluation and documentation, and using images as research sources.

- Chapter 47, on MLA documentation, includes new annotated sample pages from key source types. Other documentation chapters reflect each style's latest version.
- Key computer material is more fully integrated into the text. Managing files, using a spelling checker, and other computer skills are discussed in the context of editing in Chapter 3. Document design, now Chapter 5, concludes the chapters on the writing process and includes more help with using illustrations and a section on designing for readers with disabilities. Other forms of electronic writing—e-mail, Web compositions, and online colaboration—are gathered in Chapter 54, "Writing Online."
- The handbook has a fresh design, with annotations on visual and verbal examples that connect principles and illustrations directly.
- The handbook's many exercises are available in Word format at *ablongman.com/littlebrown*.

For more information about the revisions to the tenth edition, see "Preface for Instructors" on pp. vii–xiii.

Familiarizing students with the handbook

Many students have little experience with a comprehensive handbook like *The Little, Brown Handbook*, so it is well worth your time and theirs to review where they can find material, how the book is organized, and how they might use it. Encourage students to personalize the book by marking sections that are particularly useful to them and by keeping an ongoing list of the sections they find themselves returning to for reference or that correspond to their identified patterns of error. The Editing Checklist (pp. 58–59) is a useful place to begin discussions about recognizing common errors, and it also provides a touchstone for your responses to student papers. It is equally important to make handbook usage part of the continuing conversation of the classroom, with frequent, in-class index and content searches, so that the handbook becomes a familiar resource. Such exercises can be a useful accompaniment to group or class-wide revision work on student papers.

Several users of previous editions of this handbook have successfully used a quiz as a means of orienting students to the material it contains. We offer this one with thanks to George Meese of Eckerd College, Florida.

■ Quiz for Handbook Users

Your goal is to show me that you can find answers to common writing questions by using your handbook. For instance, if the question is how to paraphrase material from a book in your research paper, you would need to turn to 44d (pp. 617–23). For each question below, list the page or section you would consult to answer this question. For extra credit, answer the question itself.

1. You need to cite an article in the *New York Times* using the MLA system of citations.
2. You can't decide whether to use *that* or *which* in a sentence.
3. You need pointers for writing the introduction for your essay.
4. You can't decide whether to use *rise* or *raise* as the verb in your sentence.
5. You need to know how to type a business letter.
6. You're confused about the difference between *affect* and *effect*.
7. You need to know whether to put a comma before *and* in the phrase *environment, politics and society*.
8. You need to know if the period goes before or after the quotation marks at the end of a direct quote.
9. You have trouble narrowing the topic for your essay.
10. You need to know how to fix a comma splice in your essay.

Organizing a composition course

Organizing a composition course means choosing to emphasize those aspects of writing or kinds of texts that the instructor or the department considers most important and that meet the students' needs. Each institution will set its own goals and standards for what students are expected to achieve in a required writing course, and your class must help students meet those goals. This discussion may be particularly useful for inexperienced teachers who are planning a course for the first time.

In recent years, composition teaching has followed several general patterns for organizing a course, including emphasis on:

- patterns of expression and thought,
- the writing process,
- content and ideas, and
- academic writing (writing across the curriculum).

Each approach can be successful if it meets the needs of a particular group of students and if the instructor pays some attention to all aspects of composing.

■ Emphasis on patterns of expression and thought

Many instructors believe that a composition course ought to give students a chance to understand and practice basic patterns of expression and thought. Such courses may vary widely in the patterns they emphasize:

- rhetorical and logical patterns, such as classification, comparison-contrast, and deduction;
- general essay structures, such as thesis and support or general to specific;
- types of essays, such as informative and argumentative;
- patterns of paragraph development;
- sentence patterns.

Courses designed in this fashion are often used as basic writing courses, designed to meet the needs of students who enter college with limited experience in reading and writing. These courses emphasize the writing skills and patterns of thought essential to success in college courses. Although courses of this kind have their roots in "current-traditional rhetoric," an approach that tended to emphasize product over process, they can be adapted to take students' composing processes into consideration. The course might begin with sentence and paragraph construction, moving to longer essay forms as students become more comfortable with different kinds of paragraphs. A process approach would vary the focus from sentence-level constructions to considerations of the student's overall project in the paragraph and in the essay in order to emphasize their interrelated functions.

Organizing the course

In organizing a skills course, you might begin with a unit on sentence structure, drawing on Chapters 12–16 of the handbook ("Grammatical Sentences"), and you might stress an understanding of phrases, clauses, basic sentence types, and verb forms and tenses. Along with this, you might require paragraph-length writing that helps students to understand the functions of those sentence structures, and make use of the extensive discussion in Chapter 4 ("Writing and Revising Paragraphs"). Paragraph- and essay-length writing can continue through the semester, accompanied by work in Chapters 17–22 ("Clear Sentences") and 23–26 ("Effective Sentences"). Chapters on punctuation, mechanics, diction, and usage can be assigned whenever they meet the needs of the class or of individual students. Students might also use the Editing Checklist to keep track of the patterns of error that recur in their writing. In-class sessions can reinforce this practice by focusing on identifying errors in order to create meaningful revisions.

Teaching suggestions

Start paragraphs as early in the semester as possible to give students a sense of accomplishment and a chance to put into practice what they are learning in the sentence units. Also early on, you can incorporate essay-length writings into the course by requiring students to keep a writing journal with a specific number of pages to be devoted to a single topic at least once a week. You can integrate the journals into the class work by having them serve as topics for the students' paragraph and sentence constructions. This helps students to understand the relationship between the function of individual sentences and paragraphs and the overall purpose of an essay.

Other considerations

Although an effective basic course, often planned for developmental students, can focus on sentence, paragraph, and essay patterns, it also needs to pay attention to the writing process and to audience (see Chapters 1, 2, and 3 in the handbook). Students who have trouble mastering the basic forms of expression are also likely to underestimate the importance of planning and revising and to have difficulty shaping their writing to the needs of an audience. Collaborative revision work can help by providing students with immediate feedback from an identified audience of their peers. These matters can also be reinforced throughout the course with assignments that require planning, drafting, and revising and also create realistic audiences and situations for students to address in their writing. For example, the exercises in sections 1d and 1e on audience and purpose can be developed into group projects on which students work collaboratively to create directed appeals to the campus newspaper, to local government, or to a defined public organization.

■ Emphasis on patterns of development

Rhetorically oriented courses use standard essay types or patterns of development (for instance, comparison-contrast or process analysis) as a means of probing subjects and developing and organizing essays. Instructors who use such approaches share the belief that helping students understand these patterns and practice them in their writing will enable them to use the patterns in a variety of writing tasks. Most of these instructors would also agree that each pattern of development directs attention to a different aspect of a subject and thus the patterns can be seen as shaping the way we think about a subject and as affecting a reader's attitudes. Instructors of rhetorically oriented courses often rely on a reader or rhetoric to provide examples of essay types and patterns of development.

Organizing the course

If you wish to give your course a rhetorical orientation, you may want to begin with Parts 1 and 2 ("The Writing Process" and "Reading and Writing in College") as a way of showing students how to develop, write, revise, and edit an essay and to adapt it to an audience. Later in the course, you may want to return to this material to remind students how important the stages of the writing process are, particularly planning and revising. You can also point out that Chapters 2 and 4 treat the rhetorical patterns as answers to questions about aspects of a topic as well as ways of organizing and developing essays and paragraphs. You might include a unit on essay types or patterns of essay and paragraph development (Chapters 1–4) with assignments that give students a chance to use the forms. The chapters on sentence emphasis, coordination and subordination, parallelism, and variety (Chapters 23–26, "Effective Sentences") can be introduced later in the course to add variety and style to students' writing. The Editing Checklist and the chapters on common sentence errors, punctuation, mechanics, diction, and usage can be assigned according to the needs of individuals or of the class and may also be used for reference. The course might culminate in a research paper (Chapters 42–48) or oral presentations (Chapter 56) or business and community-based writing projects (Chapter 55).

Teaching suggestions

The risk in a rhetorically oriented course is that students will come to regard the various forms as ends in themselves and ignore the role they play in viewing experience and in shaping communication to an audience or situation. For this reason, many instructors emphasize throughout the course the process of exploring subjects and revising the plan for an essay, and they encourage students to create specific audiences and situations to address in their writing. Collaborative work in which students debate topics in class and/or through a Web site can be enormously useful in helping students to work toward particular audiences and purposes. Students also become aware that the forum of the computer link, the face-to-face discussion, and the revised results (which can be "published" for the class) powerfully affects the choices they make as writers.

■ Emphasis on the writing process

Some instructors choose to orient their courses around an exploration of the writing process, so that students become aware of the range of strategies and choices available to them as writers and become confident in their ability to respond to future writing tasks. In such courses,

- students are taught to respond to writing situations with a full awareness of the importance of discovering, focusing, planning, drafting, revising, and editing;
- students are given the opportunity to adapt the process to the demands of different kinds of writing;
- forms of expression are presented as strategies best learned in the context of a particular writing task; and
- grammar, punctuation, and mechanics are introduced when necessary for effective communication in an essay.

Organizing the course

In organizing a course that emphasizes the writing process, you might begin by having students look over the discussion of the process in the handbook (Chapter 1, "Assessing the Writing Situation," Chapter 2, "Developing and Shaping Ideas," Chapter 3, "Drafting and Revising," Chapter 6, "Writing in Academic Situations," and Chapter 8, "Forming a Critical Perspective"). You will have to review briefly the writing process as part of each assignment, both to remind students that each of the elements of composing is important and to show how the kinds of planning and revising a writer must do will vary slightly depending on the subject, the aim of the writing task, and the audience for the essay. You may wish to include personal writing as a way to enhance students' awareness of the range of approaches and personas available to them as writers. When you move to more public kinds of writing, however, section 10f ("Reaching Your Readers") will help alert students to the need to take their readers into account as they shape what they have to say and decide how to say it.

Teaching suggestions

Assignments in a process-oriented course should stress planning and revising in all writing tasks and also suggest a range of writing strategies that students can use to deal with a subject and meet the needs of a reader.

If the assigned essay requires particular attention to paragraphing—a persuasive paper, for example—then students might be required to look at Chapter 4 ("Writing and Revising Paragraphs"). Chapters 23–26 ("Effective Sentences") will also help introduce students to useful strategies, and Chapters 42–48 ("Research Writing") and Chapters 54–56 ("Special Writing Situations") can be good resources when students are asked to write for a business or professional audience or to prepare oral presentations. Coverage of matters of grammar, punctuation, diction, and usage will depend on the needs of the class and of individual students.

Since many problems in student writing stem from a lack of effective planning or revising, a composition course that emphasizes process can have a significant effect on student writing. But students need to be aware that word choice, sentence structure, paragraph development, and essay organization also contribute to the effectiveness of writing. Therefore a course that emphasizes the writing process needs to introduce students to the options made possible by formal proficiency (the flexibility that semicolon usage can add to a writer's repertoire, for example—see Chapter 29). Collaborative peer-group revision work supported by the handbook can help student writers to understand the usefulness of formal strategies in communicating the purpose of an essay to an audience.

■ Emphasis on content and ideas (thematic courses)

In some writing courses, the writing grows out of the students' strong need to communicate about significant ideas and issues. Such courses focus on ideas and issues, whether personal (family life, education, social relationships) or public policy (pornography, the American legal system). The source for content may be an anthology, a lecture series, films, or the students' own research and experience. Although the handbook uses many examples that are thematically organized around the subject of the environment, students working with this or any other thematic content could be encouraged to draw examples from their own writing to consider in conjunction with those offered by the handbook. Instructors looking for a theme around which to organize their own courses may wish to add to the environment-oriented examples in the handbook with a supplemental collection of readings on the environment, or with other locally available material, so that students get more exposure to extended pieces of discourse on this topic. Because students may be unused to working interpretively with discursive prose, exercises that encourage them to practice responding to quotations, individually and in groups, will be particularly useful. See Exercises 44.5 and 44.10 in Chapter 44, especially sections c and d, for exercises that help students to position themselves in relation to the other authors they are using. Depending on the kinds of material that students are reading, the chapters in Part 10 ("Writing in the Academic Disciplines") encourage students to recognize relationships between formal, discipline-based strategies and thematic content. The chapters in Part 2 ("Reading and Writing in College") help students to read and write in academic situations.

Organizing the course

Since instructors who teach such courses generally value the content of a piece of writing most, they cover the forms of writing and the writing process primarily to help students communicate ideas and feelings clearly and effectively. If you choose to emphasize the content of essays in your composition course, you may wish to begin by introducing students to the writing process and the basic forms of the essay with Chapters 1–5 ("The Writing Process"). These chapters suggest ways students can develop their ideas and organize them into paragraphs and whole essays. Chapters 6–11 on academic writing; study skills; critical thinking, reading, and writing; and reading and writing text-based and visual arguments can also help students to analyze the strategies of the writers they are reading and to respond effectively.

Teaching suggestions

As students struggle to express their ideas, you may wish to assign Chapters 37–41 ("Effective Words") to help them communicate more precisely and Chapters 23–26 ("Effective Sentences") to help them add variety, clarity, and style to their writing. The Editing Checklist can be a useful touchstone in helping students to identify patterns of error that recur in their work; students can often use the recognized error (such as comma splices, fused sentences, ambiguous pronoun references) as the occasion for substantive revision. Chapters on punctuation, mechanics, grammar, and usage can be assigned to the class or to individual students according to need. Whether or not students are required to use research in their writing, the discussion of differences among summary, paraphrase, and analysis in Chapter 44 ("Working with Sources") can help students to work effectively with their quoted sources.

■ Emphasis on writing about literature

Writing about literature in a writing course

In a writing class that includes literature, many sections of *The Little, Brown Handbook* will be relevant. Students can begin by reviewing the chapters in Part 2 on academic writing; critical thinking, reading, and writing; and argument, as well as the material in Part 1 about beginning a writing project, and then move on to Chapter 50, "Reading and Writing About Literature," which shows how those general skills translate into questions and strategies for reading and writing about fiction, poetry, and drama. Thorough coverage of MLA documentation in Chapter 47 will also be useful, as will the strategies for conducting research in Chapters 42–45. And the high standards of editing usually found in literary texts can profitably be tied to the discussions of sentence-construction problems in Chapters 17–22 and to matters of punctuation in Chapters 27–32.

Writing about literature in literature courses

Many college and university literature courses now stress writing as well as reading, and *The Little, Brown Handbook* can play a vital role in such courses. The guide to writing about literature in Chapter 50 stresses the interplay of critical thinking, reading, and writing as discussed in Part 2, and it shows students how to transfer those skills to the literature classroom. The thorough coverage of style (Chapters 23–26 on fluid and effective sentences, Chapters 37–40 on diction) can be used not only to help students analyze the works of literature they read but also to help them write more effectively about those works. And the material in Chapter 50 on drafting, writing, and revising a literary analysis, along with the sample student paper and thorough coverage of MLA documentation, will prove invaluable to students and teachers in any literature course.

Teaching suggestions

Because of the pressure to cover content issues, many literature classes underemphasize the role of drafting and revision. Assignments that foreground these processes, such as prewriting in response to quotes, in-class work with student drafts, and group revisions of selected paragraphs and single sentences by student writers, will help students to develop and gain confidence in their writing skills.

■ Emphasis on academic writing

Writing across the curriculum in a writing course

Chapters 49–53 ("Writing in the Academic Disciplines") cover much of the territory appropriate for a course emphasizing writing across the curriculum. Such a course may ask students to write papers in each of the areas covered by these chapters—literature, the humanities, the social sciences, and the natural and applied sciences—and may ask students to become acquainted with the research tools in each area (also discussed in detail in the chapters). The treatment of the writing process in Chapters 1–3; of paragraphing in Chapter 4; of academic

writing, essay exams, critical thinking, and argument in Chapters 6–11; and of the functions of sentence structure in Chapters 23–26 can also be important elements of a course built around the varieties of academic writing.

Writing across the curriculum in the disciplines

In many writing-across-the-curriculum programs, writing instruction is part of content courses, employed both as a tool for learning and as a way of sharing knowledge in forms appropriate to a discipline. Because it is designed as a reference tool and therefore does not impose a particular design on a course, the handbook can be a useful resource for content courses emphasizing writing. It provides discussions of the writing process and of research and documentation in specific disciplines as well as resources for editing style, grammar, and mechanics. Whatever the particular uses of writing in a course, the handbook's advice about the process of writing (Chapters 1–3) is likely to prove valuable.

Using the handbook with other texts

Although the handbook can be used as the only text in a course, many instructors also adopt a reader, a rhetoric, or a workbook such as *The Little, Brown Workbook*. Each kind of text enables you to emphasize different elements of the course and also provides activities to help students develop their writing.

■ Readers

Readers are generally of three kinds: rhetorical, thematic, or cross-curricular.

Rhetorical readers

Rhetorical readers illustrate different aims and patterns of writing with selections by professional authors and sometimes by students. Readers of this type frequently begin with writing patterns that students find most accessible—narration, description, exemplification—and move on to patterns that students find more difficult to use—classification, comparison-contrast, inductive and deductive argument. Many readers provide extensive introductions to the rhetorical patterns, discussing their uses in writing and the aspects of a subject that they focus on. Some recent rhetorical readers go beyond the basic rhetorical patterns to discuss common forms of nonfiction writing—such as the problem-solution report, the personal essay, the evaluation, and the proposal—that combine the basic patterns in a number of ways. The questions accompanying the essays in most rhetorical readers direct students' attention to the most important features of the models and suggest ways students can incorporate such features in their own writing.

Thematic readers

Thematic readers illustrate and explore a number of themes, such as the stages of personal growth or family relationships, or topics of general interest, such as capital punishment or the impact of technology. The readings may include fiction or poetry as well as essays. If the main purpose for using the reader is to provide subject matter for essays, a thematic reader may be preferable because, as a rule, readers of this type provide several perspectives on a subject and more background information to get class discussion started and give students material to use in their writing.

Some readers are both rhetorical and thematic in organization and coverage, providing a table of contents for each emphasis. Both types of readers can be used to generate class discussion and topics for student writing. Some readers even provide questions to stimulate discussion and include lists of possible topics for papers, as well as bibliographies for further reading and research.

Cross-curricular readers

Cross-curricular readers typically provide examples of writing in a variety of disciplines and cover a range of topics. Some include essays directed to general readers as well as specialists. Others focus on the kinds of writing expected from students or professionals in a discipline. Readers of this kind often emphasize writing as a social process and are designed to help students participate actively within specialized discourse communities. While the primary aim of readers of this type is to provide models of academic and professional prose, some also arrange readings in thematic clusters designed to encourage discussion and suggest subjects for students to pursue in their own writing. Instructors often choose a problem-posing approach to the readings by encouraging students to work on an essay individually and in groups, identify-

ing difficult passages and terms and creating interpretive responses. Classroom practice focuses on student responses to texts, and particularly on the revision process as the means to create meaningful positions in relation to those readings.

Integrating *The Little, Brown Handbook* with a reader

Instructors who adopt a reader typically make discussion of its essays a major activity in the course, yet they also tend to make significant use of a handbook. If the reader chosen for a course does not provide a rhetorical framework for students' essays or a thorough coverage of writing and reasoning processes, instructors using *The Little, Brown Handbook* may wish to direct students to the coverage of these matters in Chapters 1–3 and 6–11. As students begin working with quotation and citation, Chapter 44 on working with sources can become a useful resource, even outside of the research context. The handbook provides explanations and examples of other matters frequently not covered in readers, such as the revision and editing checklists (Chapter 3); paragraphing (Chapter 4); sentence structure, grammar, and style (Chapters 12–26); diction and usage (Chapters 37–40 and the Glossary of Usage); research writing (Chapters 42–48); and writing in the disciplines (Chapters 49–53). In addition, the handbook can be used as a reference guide for punctuation and mechanics, as an aid in marking student papers, and as a guide for revision. Some instructors who use a reader like to devote one period each week to subjects covered in the handbook; others like to set aside part of each day.

■ **Rhetorics**

Rhetorics and handbooks

Rhetorics cover many of the same topics as handbooks—discovering, planning, drafting, revising, rhetorical patterns, and paragraphing—but do so in greater depth, at the same time giving less coverage to grammar, punctuation, mechanics, and usage. A rhetoric usually embodies a particular perspective toward writing and the teaching of writing—a theoretical bias, perhaps, or an emphasis on thesis-and-support essays, personal writing, academic writing, argumentation, critical thinking, or tone and style. Since a rhetoric helps determine the emphasis within a course, it provides less flexibility for the teacher than the handbook does, especially if the rhetoric has been chosen by a department rather than by the instructor.

Integrating *The Little, Brown Handbook* with a rhetoric

Because rhetorics provide full coverage in some areas at the expense of others, instructors frequently adopt a handbook as a supplement. Used in this way, *The Little, Brown Handbook* can provide treatment of sentence style (Chapters 23–26), research writing (Chapters 42–46), and writing in the disciplines (Chapters 49–53) for rhetorics that give only brief attention to these matters. It can also provide discussion and exercises for sentence structure and grammar (Chapters 12–22), punctuation and mechanics (Chapters 27–36), and diction and usage (Chapters 37–40 and the Glossary of Usage). The discussions of the writing process, paragraphs, academic writing study skills and essay exams, critical thinking, and argument (Chapters 1–11) can supplement the material in a rhetoric and provide useful exercises.

When the handbook is used with a rhetoric, instructors often assign its chapters and exercises along with those in the rhetoric, and they devote class time to discussing both texts and reviewing the exercises. They also use the handbook as a reference for students, as an aid to grading papers, and as a guide for revision.

■ The handbook's ancillary publications

In addition to its companion Web site (see p. IAE-50), the handbook comes with an instructional package that will meet the needs of many classes.

For students

■ *CompSolutions Plus Interactive E-Book for The Little, Brown Handbook* offers a complete, searchable version of the handbook, video and audio clips on key topics, interactive exercises, writing-related Web links, and links through an access code to the *Comp-Solutions* Web site.

■ *CompSolutions* Web site offers one convenient portal to several of Longman's most popular multimedia resources for composition (described below). An access card comes with the interactive e-book CD featuring the entire contents of the handbook.

Longman Writer's Warehouse for Composition provides guided assistance through the writing process, access to Web-based journals and writing portfolios, diagnostic tests, exercises, and video-based writing assignments.

Avoiding Plagiarism Tutorial consists of interactive modules on plagiarism, common knowledge, paraphrase, and summary. The tutorial also covers both MLA and APA documentation.

Research Navigator provides access to a database of thousands of academic journals and general-interest periodicals, *The New York Times* online archives, and several online research tools.

Longman ExerciseZone offers diagnostic tests to help students identify where they need help along with more than 2500 exercises on grammar, style, usage, and punctuation.

The Student Bookshelf is an online library of brief e-books in PDF format, including *Public Literacy*, *Academic Literacy*, *Workplace Literacy*, *Visual Communication*, *Analyzing Literature*, and *Reading Critically*.

■ *The Little, Brown Workbook* parallels the handbook's organization but provides briefer instructional text and many more exercises.

■ *ESL Worksheets* provide nonnative speakers with extra practice in especially troublesome areas.

■ *Research Navigator Guide for English* teaches students how to conduct high-quality online research and to document it properly, provides discipline-specific academic resources and helpful tips on the writing process, and links through an access code to the *Research Navigator* on *CompSolutions*.

■ *Take Note!* is a cross-platform CD-ROM that integrates note taking, outlining, and bibliography management in one easy-to use package.

■ A separate answer key provides answers to all the exercises in the handbook. It is available both in print and online (password-protected).

■ *Course Compass* is a proprietary version of *Blackboard*, the course-management resource, augmented with Longman's *CompSolutions*. For instructors already using *Blackboard* or *WebCT*, the *CompSolutions* resources are available as content cartridges for either platform.

For instructors

- On the handbook's companion Web site, instructors can download the password-protected instructor's manual and answer key as well as more than a hundred transparency masters and *PowerPoint* slides that reproduce key boxes and lists from the text.
- *Teaching Online: Internet Research, Conversation, and Composition* is an accessible introduction to Internet resources for teaching writing.
- *Diagnostic Editing Tests and Exercises* helps instructors assess students' standard American English for placement or to gauge progress. The package is available on reproducible sheets or on TestGen EQ, Longman's online testing program.
- An extensive assessment package includes TASP and CLAST exams. All items are keyed to the handbook. The tests are available on reproducible sheets or on TestGen EQ, Longman's online testing program.
- The Longman resources for instructors include six valuable works: *Teaching in Progress: Theories, Practices, and Scenarios*; *Using Portfolios*; *Comp Tales*, writing teachers' reports on their teaching experiences; and the videos *Writing, Teaching, and Learning* and *Writing Across the Curriculum: Making It Work*

■ Sentence combining with the handbook

During the past decade, extensive research has shown that having students work with the elements of sentences—manipulating, combining, and altering—leads not only to a greater understanding of sentence structure but also to a greater willingness to experiment stylistically, leading to more flexible, expressive syntax characteristic of mature writing. However, teachers and students can get carried away with sentence combining. Doing exercises with someone else's prose can be fun; students seem to enjoy the activities, but they are no substitute for the students' writing their own sentences and applying the techniques to their own sentences as part of a larger writing assignment.

What sentence combining is

Sentence combining arose from applications of transformational-generative grammar principles to classroom practices. Researchers such as Kellogg Hunt and Frank O'Hare determined that encouraging students to expand sentences by coordinating (adding on), deleting (eliminating repeated words), and embedding (inserting new information into a main clause) enables them to write complex, fluent sentences without having to master elaborate grammatical terminology. The practice they recommend is to give students a base sentence and several other sentences of information to incorporate in the base sentence then have students experiment with various ways to combine the information.

In most sentence-combining instruction, students learn various kinds of combinations, starting with relatively simple coordination and subordination using conjunctions. Then they progress to removing repeated elements and embedding information such as adjectives and phrases, culminating in "advanced" structures such as adverbials and absolutes. After they control the structures, they are introduced to the punctuation conventions the new sentences require. Students are encouraged to practice not only on the words of other writers but on their own sentences in their drafts as they master new stylistic patterns.

A sequence for sentence combining

Chapter 12 introduces students to basic sentence structures, and Chapters 21 and 28 introduce modifying clauses and phrases along with their primary focus on grammar and punctuation. Chapters 28 and 29 present strategies of coordination as well as of punctuation, and Chapters 24 and 25 introduce progressively more sophisticated sentence strategies. In Chapters 23 and 26 students encounter sentence patterns characteristic of mature writing, and in Chapter 4 they get a chance to combine all the strategies in paragraphs.

The handbook exercises you might stress in teaching sentence combining are these:

Chapter 4, Exercises 4.4, 4.11
Chapter 12, Exercises 12.8, 12.10, 12.12, 12.13, 12.15, 12.16, 12.17, 12.21
Chapter 13, Exercise 13.4
Chapter 18, Exercise 18.3
Chapter 21, Exercise 21.7
Chapter 23, Exercises 23.2, 23.6
Chapter 24, Exercises 24.1, 24.3, 24.6
Chapter 25, Exercises 25.3, 25.4
Chapter 26, Exercises 26.1, 26.2, 26.3, 26.6
Chapter 28, Exercises 28.2, 28.4, 28.6
Chapter 29, Exercises 29.2, 29.4

Tutoring with the handbook

Writing centers and tutoring programs can make good use of the handbook to set common goals and to develop a common language that will sustain the diverse relationships among students, tutors, and teachers. For example, the handbook provides a reference point for teachers' responses to student papers, which can then become the basis for tutoring sessions on the identified points of difficulty in student work: paragraphing, interpretive work with quotes, particular patterns of error. Students are also able to refer to explanations and exercises in the tutor's absence, to keep a journal of their error patterns and sample revisions, and to refer back to the handbook to reinforce what they have learned in tutoring sessions. The handbook can also become a primary reference for the tutoring center or lab by providing advice and practice exercises for targeted areas. Tutors should encourage students to bring the handbook along with their work-in-progress. Once tutor and student together have identified revision areas or targeted patterns of error, they might review the relevant sections of the handbook together; the tutor might then give the student a chance to revise a targeted area on his or her own. As a resource tool for the lab or tutoring center, the handbook can help resolve conflicts over points of grammar and usage, becoming a primary reference or arbiter in debates. It can be a training manual for new tutors, providing simple and clear explanations of problems they will encounter every day. In particular, the revision worksheets included in the chapter on collaborative learning (pp. IAE-34 to IAE-45) can be used as the basis for tutorial sessions. And the handbook can be a reference for students who are working on a paper in the writing center without direct supervision by a tutor.

The Little, Brown Workbook and the *ESL Worksheets* can provide the "raw material" of tutoring—sample sentences, exercises, and brief explanations—to be used in discussion with the student or for independent work. The workbook can be particularly effective for tutoring if students are taking a composition course that uses the handbook, because the language, rules, and exercises encountered in tutoring will be consistent with those encountered in the classroom.

Sample syllabi

Syllabus for a ten-week course with four graded papers:

Week	Goals
1	Introduction and course description; diagnostic writing sample. Begin discussion of essay development (Chapter 1); assign first essay. Academic writing (Chapter 6) and critical thinking, reading, and writing (Chapter 8).
2	Developing ideas (Chapter 2), drafting and revising essays (Chapter 3); first peer-response workshop. Preparing a manuscript (Chapter 5).
3	Writing and revising paragraphs (Chapter 4); conferences with students to discuss drafts and journals. Review common errors seen in drafts (Parts 4–6).
4	First essay due. Assign second essay. Repeat emphasis on prewriting (Chapters 1 and 2); discuss correction symbols and grading.
5	Return first essay; discuss clear sentences (Part 4). Peer-response workshop for second paper.
6	Effective words (Part 8); conferences to discuss drafts and journals. If needed, discuss with the class common errors or problems.
7	Second essay due; assign third essay. Work on invention strategies in small groups.
8	Return second essay; peer-group workshop in class; work on effective sentences (Part 5). Introduce basics of argument (Chapters 9–11).
9	Third essay due; assign last essay, which may be a revision of an earlier piece of writing, an essay from another course, or an essay exam. Peer-group activities. If students are keeping portfolios (pp. IAE-29 to IAE-31), final copies of first two papers are due this week. Journals due.
10	Return third essay. Final essay due; individual conferences and course evaluations; last two papers for portfolio due.

Syllabus for a fifteen-week course with five graded papers, including a research paper:

Week	Goals
1	Course introduction and requirements; writing sample. Discuss Chapters 1 and 2. Introduce journals.
2	Assign first paper. Begin draft work. Peer-response session for first paper. Review Chapter 54 if appropriate. Discuss Chapter 3 and Part 4.
3	Conferences about drafts. Discuss Chapter 4.
4	Take up journals. Second peer-response session for first paper. Review Chapter 5. Discuss Chapters 28 and 29.
5	First paper due. Assign second paper. Discuss Chapter 3 again; discuss Chapters 24 and 25.
6	Return first paper. Discuss evaluation criteria and correction symbols. If appropriate, discuss Chapter 55. Draft work on second paper. Peer-response session for second paper.
7	Discuss Chapter 37. Discuss Chapters 23 and 26. Second peer-response session for second paper.
8	Second paper due. Assign third paper. Take up journals. Reemphasize developing the essay (Chapter 2) and conduct microclinics on problem areas with small groups of students. Conferences to discuss drafts and journals.
9	Return second paper. Assign fourth paper (research paper). Discuss Chapter 42. Peer-response session for third paper. Assign each student an appropriate chapter from Part 10.
10	Research week. Library tour (if available). Chapter 43.
11	Return third paper. Documentation week. Chapters 47–50, and appropriate sections of the chapters in Part 10. Miniconferences to address specific research problems.
12	Fourth paper due. Discuss Chapter 48 and appropriate sections of the chapters in Part 10. Discuss Chapter 5.
13	Return fourth paper. Assign fifth paper. Discuss Chapters 9–11. Journals due.
14	Draft work for fifth paper. If students are keeping portfolios (pp. IAE-29 to IAE-31), edited copies of first four papers are submitted this week.
15	Finished copy of fifth paper due. Individual conferences and course evaluations.

Resources for designing a writing course

Applebee, Arthur N. "Problems in Process Approaches: Toward a Reconceptualization of Process Instruction." In *The Teaching of Writing*. Chicago: National Society for the Study of Education, 1986. 95–113.

Bartholomae, David, and Anthony Petrosky. *Facts, Counterfacts, Artifacts: Theory and Method for a Reading and Writing Course*. Upper Montclair: Boynton/Cook, 1986.

Dawkins, John. "Teaching Punctuation as a Rhetorical Tool." *College Composition and Communication* 46:4 (1995): 533–48.

Eble, Kenneth E. *The Craft of Teaching: A Guide to Mastering the Professor's Art*. 2nd ed. San Francisco: Jossey-Bass, 1988.

Enos, Theresa, ed. *A Sourcebook for Basic Writing Teachers*. New York: Random, 1987.

Farber, Jerry. "Learning to Teach: A Progress Report." *College English* 52 (1990): 135–41.

Fishman, Stephen M., and Lucille McCarthy. *John Dewey and the Challenge of Classroom Practice*. New York: Teachers College P, 1998.

Foster, David. *A Primer for Writing Teachers: Theories, Theorists, Issues, Problems*. Upper Montclair: Boynton/Cook, 1983.

Gebhardt, Richard C. "Unifying Diversity in the Training of Writing Teachers." In *Training the New Teacher of College Composition*. Ed. Charles W. Bridges. Urbana: NCTE, 1986. 1–12.

George, Diana. "Who Teaches the Teacher? A Note on the Craft of Teaching College Composition." *College English* 51 (1989): 418–23.

Graves, Richard L., ed. *Rhetoric and Composition: A Sourcebook for Teachers and Writers*. Upper Montclair: Boynton/Cook, 1st ed. 1976; 2nd ed. 1983; 3rd ed. 1990.

Hashimoto, Irvin Y. *Thirteen Weeks: A Guide to Teaching College Writing*. Portsmouth NH: Boynton/Cook, 1991.

Herzberg, Bruce. "Composition and the Politics of the Curriculum." *The Politics of Writing Instruction: Postsecondary*. Ed. Richard Bullock and John Trimbur. Portsmouth NH: Boynton/Cook (Heineman) 1991.

Hoffman, Eleanor M., and John P. Schifsky. "Designing Writing Assignments." *English Journal* 66 (1977): 41–45.

Hunt, Kellogg. *Grammatical Structures Written at Three Grade Levels.* Urbana: NCTE, 1965.

Irmscher, William. *Teaching Expository Writing.* New York: Holt, 1979.

Lindemann, Erika. *A Rhetoric for Writing Teachers,* 2nd ed. New York: Oxford UP, 1987.

———. "Teaching as a Rhetorical Art," *CEA Forum* 15:2 (1985): 9–12.

Lindemann, Erika, and Gary Tate, eds. *An Introduction to Composition Studies.* New York: Oxford UP, 1991.

O'Hare, Frank. *Sentence Combining: Improving Student Writing Without Formal Grammar Instruction.* Urbana: NCTE, 1973.

Passmore, John. *The Philosophy of Teaching.* London: Duckworth, 1980.

Ponsot, Marie, and Rosemary Deen. *Beat Not the Poor Desk! Writing: What to Teach, How to Teach It, and Why.* Upper Montclair: Boynton/Cook, 1982.

Rankin, Elizabeth. "From Simple to Complex: Ideas of Order in Assignment Sequences." *Journal of Advanced Composition* 10:1 (1990): 126–35.

Ronald, Kate, and Hephzibah Roskelly. *Reason to Believe: Romanticism, Pragmatism, and the Possibility of Teaching.* Albany: State U of New York P, 1998.

Scott, Patrick, and Bruce Castner. "Reference Sources for Composition Research: A Practical Survey." *College English* 45 (1983): 756–68.

Shaughnessy, Mina. *Errors and Expectations: A Guide for the Teacher of Basic Writing.* New York: Oxford UP, 1977.

Tarvers, Josephine Koster. *Teaching Writing: Theories and Practices.* 4th ed. New York: HarperCollins, 1993.

Tobin, Lad. "Reading Students, Reading Ourselves: Revising the Teacher's Role in the Writing Class." *College English* 53 (1991): 333–48.

CHAPTER 3
Working with Student Writing

Nothing we do as composition teachers—not lecturing, setting up peer critique groups, leading discussions, or preparing activities—has as much potential for helping students improve their writing as do our efforts to respond as sensitive and thorough readers. Moreover, as readers we can play several roles, some of them simultaneously. We can respond to a work in progress, acting as editors and critics with suggestions for revision or as ordinary readers whose reactions students can take into account as they shape the final product. Or we can be judges of a finished work, justifying a grade (as evaluators) or pointing out strengths and weaknesses (as teachers), encouraging students to build on one and avoid the other.

At some time, of course, all the work that you and students put into the course has to be judged—and in the final analysis, you'll be the one who has to make the judgments and assign the grade. This is one of the hardest parts of your job as a writing teacher, yet it's also one of the most essential. But you needn't go it alone; students can collaboratively do a good deal of the preliminary work for you and set standards that enable you and your students to agree upon grades.

The roles of response

It takes more than an efficient correction system to bring about improvement in writing. How we respond and when are most important. In addition, the correction system we choose needs to be consistent with our purposes for responding and the roles we play as readers.

■ Responses to papers in progress

Responses directed toward a paper in progress often need to focus as much on the way the writer approaches the task as on the evolving text. On the one hand, it makes little sense to comment on detailed matters of punctuation in a draft full of helter-skelter ideas, thereby drawing attention away from advice about strategies the writer can employ to develop focus and discover purpose. On the other hand, helpful comments on agreement or mechanics coming at later stages in the writing of an essay can enable students to understand the importance of editing and can provide knowledge for later use.

Responses to a paper in progress ought to focus to a considerable extent on the writer's behaviors. Novice writers generally need to pay as much attention to learning how to discover ideas or draft an entire paper as to using topic sentences and effective patterns of paragraph development. Much of the advice in the handbook, especially in Chapters 1, 2, and 3, is directed toward strategies for writing. Other discussions, such as the treatment of paragraphs in Chapter 4, pay more attention to the specific features of essays, though they do not ignore the process of composition.

In commenting on drafts of an essay, we can assume the role of a general reader, noting points of interest or confusion, expressing an interest in more information or requesting stronger support, sharing feelings of pleasure and surprise—but always recognizing that at this point a paper belongs primarily to the writer, not yet to the reader. When a draft of an essay has a clear purpose and structure, however, we can read as editors or critics, identifying particular options for paragraphing or expression the writer might consider during revision or suggesting areas of grammar and style that need attention.

■ Responses to final drafts

Response to a final draft ought to provide a clear evaluation and the justification for it yet at the same time look toward future efforts. Student writers need to recognize and consolidate their successes; they need as well to understand what steps they can take in later essays. The essentially supportive tone of explanations in the handbook can help create this kind of understanding even when comments or the number-and-letter codes are used to identify outright errors.

When as evaluators we comment on a graded final draft, we need to provide a clear justification for the judgment on one or more of the following grounds:

- the paper's success in achieving its goals
- the requirements set by the assignment
- the standards established for the course

Comments that refer students to a particular section of the handbook, perhaps to specific sets of exercises, can provide a bridge to future writing efforts.

■ Composing comments: praise

Most students will give you an honest effort. They will use the strategies they know to complete an assignment well and to win your approval in the form of a high grade. But effort notwithstanding, students will have differing degrees of success with an assignment. And your reactions will have to differ accordingly.

Any writing effort will have strengths, even if they are few and sometimes hard to find. It's essential to identify them; not only do they show what goals have been attained, but they also help the students see which competencies they can apply to different situations. Even when you praise a very minor feature or an insight that could be developed more, the student has something to start from in a revision or in the next paper. It is also important to remember that critique can be either ego-crushing or empowering for the writer. Encouragement through praise can help keep your students, especially those with the weakest skills, from despairing about their capacity for improving their writing. Of course, the strengths sometimes outweigh the weaknesses; then the only problem is deciding what to praise. No matter what the level of skill in the paper, however, your goal is to help each student recognize and learn to capitalize on her strengths in future papers. The role of encouragement is often underestimated, seen as the "positive spin" tacked onto the "real" message of critique. Instead, it should be seen as an integral part of critique and a powerful tool for improvement. Students need to know when they have revised even one paragraph effectively, when they have gained control over a single pattern of error, when they have successfully used a quotation, even if their overall argument fell apart in the process. You may want to review your comments on a set of papers before handing them back to your students, in order to make sure that you have included some positive commentary on each paper.

■ Composing comments: critique

What about the weaknesses? The weaknesses are what most of us first see when we read a student paper. We feel compelled to alert our students to these problems so that their writing can improve. But the method of identifying such weaknesses must be constructive and goal-oriented. Ideally, students will be able to read our responses and focus on the one substantive issue or skill that will move their writing forward. As Nancy Sommers discovered in her research on teachers' responses, many teachers try to mark every error (often idiosyncratically and elliptically), leaving students with the confused sense that the paper is "all wrong" but with no sense of revision priorities. The effect of such comments is to superimpose the grid of an "ideal" paper against the actual project that the student writer was trying to accomplish. Sommers proposes instead a carefully selected and focused comment that enters into the student's own project and suggests a way to move it forward. The teacher might also identify a single pattern of error, mark several instances, ask the student to find several more instances and then to hand in revised versions of all those sentences. In some cases, the pattern of error and the substantive comment are linked, as for example a pattern of fused sentences manifesting the writer's tendency to rush cryptically through ideas rather than slowing down to think them through. In those cases, recognition of the error can lead the student to the points in the paper that are most rushed and become the basis for an effective revision (see Richard Straub's useful review article for a discussion of Sommers, Brannon/Knoblauch, and styles of teacher response).

Mina Shaughnessy, in her book *Errors and Expectations*, did all of us a great service by reminding us that the intentionality of student texts is quite different from that of literary works. In a literary work the writer is in control; he or she adheres to or violates conventions based on deliberate decisions. But when students violate the etiquette of syntax or spelling or punctuation, Shaughnessy reminds us, we assume that they did so with the same kind of artistic control experience that writers wield (or with a studied carelessness). And this is not the case. Students rarely if ever make deliberate errors; they are trying to succeed. Often, however, they attempt syntactic structures or make linguistic choices over which they have imperfect control. And so we must not regard their errors and weaknesses as intentions to fail; rather, we must determine at what they were trying to succeed. We must not just identify and criticize their errors; we must analyze them and try to help students fulfill their true intentions.

David Bartholomae, applying some of Shaughnessy's observations to basic writers, argues that such error analysis can be a valuable diagnostic technique for instructors. "By investigating and interpreting the patterns of error in [students'] writing, we can help them begin to see those errors as evidence of hypotheses or strategies they have formed and, as a consequence, put them in a position to change, experiment, imagine other strategies. Studying their own writing puts students in a position to see themselves as language users, rather than as victims of a language that uses them" (258).

Many times, in fact, errors and weaknesses signal growth. Often student papers submitted after sentence-combining practices are plagued with comma splices, as students struggle to master new syntactic patterns. The students are courageously trying new techniques; penalizing them for failing on the first try to master the punctuation etiquette required may defeat your attempts to help them grow. Sometimes, of course, there will be careless errors: a word transposed or omitted in copying, the phonetic mishearing of a term (such as Freud's "edible complex"), an embarrassing or amusing typo (such as "Shakespeare's play of love and punishment, *Romeo and Joliet*"). These represent failures of editing skills, language performance rather than language competence, and can be treated as such.

Finally, remember that exposing their work to the critique of others can make writers feel intensely vulnerable. It is essential to be delicate in your tone when you identify weaknesses so as not to arouse feelings of shame in your students. Especially when you are trying to move through a stack of papers efficiently, you may find yourself falling into a kind of terseness in your comments that may seem harsh to your students. Try drafting your comments in pencil and then reviewing them before handing the papers back to your students; in this way you can fine-tune any comments whose tone is too negative.

Commenting on papers

Composition instructors have developed innovative and useful ways of evaluating student writing, including conferences, tape-recorded commentary, and peer evaluation. The handbook can be a useful aid for all these approaches, particularly peer evaluation (see "Using Collaborative Learning with the Handbook," pp. IAE-34 to IAE-45). Many teachers, however, still prefer to respond to student essays through marginal and summary comments. These responses take three general forms: a correction code, correction symbols, and written comments. Each method has advantages and disadvantages; some teachers choose to combine them to draw on the strengths of each while others feel that correction codes and symbols undercut students' individualized projects. Some teachers use a correction code method accompanied by student conferences in which they give more personalized feedback; other teachers use written comments and establish feedback sessions, during which students respond to those comments and outline a revision plan or a goal for the next paper. The important thing is that your students understand your method and are able to work productively from your comments.

■ Using the correction code

To use the correction code, an instructor simply writes in the margin of a paper the number and letter of the section of the handbook a student should consult for help with a particular problem or error, for example, 15b (pronoun and antecedent agreement), 18a (comma splice), or 2b (problem with thesis). The code for each section of the handbook is listed inside the front cover; after a short time, most instructors find they have memorized the codes for common problems and seldom have to consult the list. Here is a section of a student paper marked using the correction code:

Parents have become more lenient with regard to television
watching. For example, allowing their children to watch cartoons
(17) in the early morning before school. As soon as they come home
(39) from school they sit before the set again, completely ingrossed
(28b) with a soap opera or a talk show. Some parents actually allow (41a)
(38c) their children to watch television while they are at the supper
table. Of course, the latter part of the evening, the prime time, (19b)
(21c) is solely set aside for the purpose of watching a special show or a
favorite series. In some ways, parents are using the television as a
substitute for personal communication with the child. The
(41d) days then, remain a never ending chain of program after program.
(28c)

When students get their graded papers back, they
need only turn to the front of the handbook to understand
what the instructor's notations mean and then refer to the
appropriate section of the text for a full explanation (the
code for each section appears in colored boxes at the sides
of the pages). Students, too, quickly learn to recognize the
notations for common errors and problems. An important
follow-up to this method is to ask students to identify several more instances of one kind of error and to revise those
sentences using the handbook. The goal is to help students
identify the kinds of errors that commonly occur in their
writing so that they can look for those errors on the next
draft. As a helpful accompaniment to this method you
might ask students to keep a list or journal of the errors
that you have marked and that they have revised as a
resource for future revisions. That journal can also become
the basis for an individual conference, in which you and
the student discuss a pattern of error and its significance
for revision (a pattern of vague pronoun references that
manifests the student's difficulty in defining and working
with key terms, for instance).

■ **Using the correction symbols**

Correction symbols work in much the same way as
the number-and-letter code. An instructor locates the
appropriate symbol in the list inside the back cover of the
handbook (e.g., *dev, log, agr, coh*) and writes it in the margin of the essay, often drawing a line to indicate the location and extent of the problem. Students reverse the

procedure, looking up symbols on the list, which also
gives the name of the problem and a reference to the
appropriate section of the text: for example, *dm*—Dangling modifier, 21h. Here is the passage from above
marked in this way:

Parents have become more lenient with regard to television
watching. For example, allowing their children to watch cartoons
          frag   *rep*
in the early morning before school. As soon as they come home
                                      sp
from school, they sit before the set again, completely ingrossed
ww
with a soap opera or a talk show. Some parents actually allow
                            ref
their children to watch television while they are at the supper
table. Of course, the latter part of the evening, the prime time,
      mm
is solely set aside for the purpose of watching a special show or a
favorite series. In some ways, parents are using the television as a
p substitute for personal communication with the child. The
days then, remain a never ending chain of program after program.
                   hyph

Because correction symbols are easier to remember
than the number-and-letter code, both students and teachers can spend less time turning away from a paper to consult the list of symbols than they might do with the code.
Yet symbols are less specific than the code; *shift*, for
instance, covers a variety of problems—20a (person and
number), 20b (tense and mood), and 20c (subject and
voice). Moreover, instead of being able to turn directly
from the paper to a discussion in the handbook, students
may need to consult the list of symbols to find the appropriate section of the text. Most of the symbols, however,
also appear in the colored boxes in the margins of the
pages. It becomes increasingly important, then, to aug-
ment the symbol method with comments or conferences
that help students create revision priorities. For instance,
you might write a marginal comment next to the first
instance of a sentence fragment, then put the symbol
(*frag*) next to three other occasions of the same error. An
end comment or conference would direct the student to
Chapter 17 of the handbook, would ask the student to
locate several more instances of the error in the paper,
and would ask for revisions. Once students understand
that the fragment is often an undeveloped thought, they

are able to use their recognition of the error to create substantive revisions, not only of sentences but of paragraphs and papers as well.

■ Using written comments

Written comments can appear in two places: in the margins and at the paper's end. Each does a different job, and students need to learn what those jobs are. Marginal comments generally note specific areas of strength or weakness in student papers. As Nancy Sommers reminds us, marginal comments focus a student's attention on a particular draft, often causing the student to ignore the possibilities of revision and moving on in new drafts. Students sometimes become so overwhelmed by marginal comments that they want only to "fix" what's "wrong" with a particular draft. Sparing use of marginal comments may make students look to the end comments for your directions. Carefully phrased marginal comments can also direct students to revise. Often in such a system, the marginal comments that identify weaknesses are questions or statements that lead students to examine the text more carefully: "Can you give a more precise description of the hotel than 'nice' and 'rad'?" "What's your evidence for this claim?" "Does your reader know what a 'buydown mortgage' is?" Or they can describe your reaction as a reader ("I can't see the connection between these two ideas. Did you leave a step out?"). Occasionally you may want to refer the student to a particular reference source ("Your citations should be in MLA form; see Chapter 47").

Checks in the margin can direct a student's attention to mechanical, grammatical, or stylistic weaknesses. Such individual problems should be summed up as part of your end comment: "Often you provide a quotation to support your assertions, but you rarely analyze the quotations to show how they fit into your argument. Where you do this, as on p. 3, it really strengthens your argument. Where you leave it out, your argument is less persuasive—you make your readers guess the connections you see." "A lot of the check marks have to do with where commas go in complex sentences. Review Chapter 28 to correct these problems."

The second kind of comment, usually at the end of the paper, should direct students to new writing goals. Whether you rely on a single method or a combination of methods to mark students' papers, it is usually important to provide students with a comment at the end of their papers to explain the grade and to tie together the marginal commentary, emphasizing the key points. This is also a good place to assign exercises in the handbook and to remind students what they need to do in future essays. The discussion "Evaluating Essays for a Grade" later in this chapter contains several examples of summary comments. Your end comments need to give clear rhetorical response and guidance to your students: "Your careful examination of King's religious language gives your paper a great deal of credibility. In your subsequent papers you can use this sensitivity to language to support your own assertions." Every writer likes to know he or she has succeeded; tell your students what competencies they show, and give them goals to strive for. Your end comment needs a context just like the student papers do; don't neglect it.

■ Establishing priorities for the students

When commenting on students' papers, try to be selective about the issues you address. Two, or at most three, weaknesses are enough for a student to focus on for the next paper. Focus on the largest issues first; if the writer can't address an audience or formulate a thesis, spelling and colon placement are trivial problems. And often, as in the cases discussed above, the weaknesses are signs of growth. Even if a student has not yet learned to analyze evidence, he's learned to provide it; even if a student continues to make comma splices, she's learning to write more complex sentences. Your comments can be phrased to reflect these tentative steps of growth: "I'm glad you tried some of the sentence combining we practiced. Now that you've learned the patterns, take a close look at where the punctuation goes so that you can use those elaborate sentences to their best effect." "You've picked really sharp quotations to back up your points. Next time follow up each of those quotes with a sentence or two of comment to help your audience see how they fit into your argument."

Finally, your response should help the writer set and reach new goals. These will usually involve mastering skills that were not used effectively in the current text or moving on to apply those skills in new contexts. Here is where the critical teaching in comments takes place: you want the student to move to a new level of achievement. The goals should be clearly expressed: "Now that you've mastered simple and compound sentences, it's time to move to complex ones." "It's clear you can persuade an audience that basically agrees with you. Next time why don't you aim to persuade a mildly hostile audience?" And your comments should suggest clear strategies for achieving those goals: "Try brainstorming and using the journalist's questions to generate more details about your subject. Then you can choose which ones you want to use." "Write down all the arguments opposed to your position that you can think of, and try to find reasonable answers to those objections." You may even need to offer a small reward to encourage timorous students to take risks: "Try to write some different kinds of sentence patterns; I won't 'mark off' if you don't quite master the punctuation next time." Your response can also encourage students to reconsider their writing processes: "The drafts of this paper show you just changed a few words; you didn't revise much. Next time, once you've got your ideas down, allow yourself to move paragraphs around, change sentences, scratch out! Revision is the chance to improve the problems mentioned above; make your organization clearer, smooth sentences, add details. Let your drafts be messy."

In sum, your end comments should encourage the student not only to go back into this paper but to move forward to the next. If you keep the tripartite structure in mind—praise strengths, identify weaknesses, set goals— you'll find it relatively easy to write a coherent, goal-oriented end comment. Encourage students to discuss those comments with you before they submit their next paper; often a word or two of reinforcement or clarification can lead to quantum leaps in writing performance.

Making sure students understand your comments

▦ Dealing with codes and symbols

Perhaps the most common reason students fail to understand our comments is that they do not understand the symbols or terms we use. If you were to ask a class what a fused sentence is, some students might answer in this vein: "a sentence where everything seems to run together and gets confused or awkward." Such terms as *reference*, *development*, and *parallelism* are also likely to draw puzzled or incorrect responses, though a few students might be able to give general explanations. Asking students the meaning of such common symbols as *pass, cs, dm,* and [*agr*] will produce similar results.

Telling students to look up correction marks on the front or back endpapers of the handbook can help, as can alerting them to the Glossary of Grammatical Terms or handing out a list of terms you plan to use in written comments. A lot of students, however, are likely to put off learning the symbols or terms until they absolutely have to, perhaps several papers into the semester, when they realize how much help they need to improve their writing. One technique that can speed the process is to foreground student papers in group work and in revision exercises with the entire class. For example, you might hand out a paper that has two sentence fragments and a comma splice in a key paragraph. After asking students to use the Editing Checklist and the relevant sections from the handbook to identify and "correct" the errors, have them work in groups to revise the errors substantively and in doing so to develop the content of the paragraph. In a follow-up class you might hand out the revised paragraphs created in the groups and ask students to compare the different analytical and grammatical choices that were made. Such exercises help students to understand the reasons for seemingly arbitrary codes.

▦ Discussing a graded paper

Another good way to help students understand your comments is to discuss a graded paper with them. Chapter 3 of the handbook (pp. 55–57 and 63–65) contains two student papers that you may wish to "grade" and then use as the basis of class discussion. In addition, the paragraphs presented earlier in this chapter contain many errors of the kind likely to turn up on student papers. The paragraphs can be distributed in class with either or both of the marking systems or with some other system you prefer. If you choose to distribute the paragraphs without markings, you can ask the students to work with you in identifying errors and choosing appropriate symbols or comments.

Evaluating essays for a grade

A grade can carry several messages: it can describe the overall quality of a paper; it can indicate how close the essay comes to achieving the goals for writing set forth in the course; and it can help tell a student writer what elements to work on in the next assignment. But unless grading standards are clear, the grades we assign will have little value for teaching beyond establishing a final grade for the course.

To help establish clear evaluation standards, many instructors discuss grading criteria with students and distribute sample papers, either already graded or to be graded in class. Another method is to attach to each paper a comment sheet reflecting the goals for the assignment. Preparing a comment sheet for each assignment can be taxing, however, so many instructors prepare a sheet that can be used for all assignments. Here is a sample:

These are the areas in which your paper is	
strong	weak
thesis	
development	
paragraphs	
sentences	
word choice	
punctuation	
style	
Comment/grade:	

If you do not like to use comment sheets, you may prefer to hand out grading criteria at the beginning of the course. Sometimes a department or program provides its own set of criteria for grading papers; if yours does not, you may wish to adapt for your own use the following set that reflects the major areas of emphasis in the handbook:

> Thesis:
>
> Organization:
>
> Development:
>
> Grammar and
>
>   punctuation:
>
> Style:
>
> Comment/grade:

- *A* (superior). An A paper meets the standards in all these areas and excels in one or more of them:

  The *paper as a whole* presents a fresh subject or main idea or treats it in an interesting or original manner, displaying unusual insight and taking appropriate account of the audience. The *paragraphs* are fully developed with detail that supports the main idea; sentences within the paragraphs are clearly linked, forming an appropriate pattern; transitions are effective. *Sentences* are varied and imaginative in style, concise and creative in wording. The paper contains few errors in *grammar and punctuation* or errors only in sophisticated matters, and few *spelling* errors.

- *B* (strong). A B paper meets the standards in all these areas:

  The *paper as a whole* presents an interesting subject or main idea and approaches it in a consistent and careful manner, displaying good insight, though without the freshness or originality characteristic of the *A* paper. The writing makes use of consistent rhetorical strategies and a tone appropriate to the audience. *Paragraphs* are, with only a few exceptions, adequately developed and generally successful in supporting the main idea; transitions are clear, and sentences within the paragraphs are, for the most part, clearly related. *Sentences* are generally clear and correct in structure and style and are not excessively wordy. Word choice is usually appropriate. *Grammar, punctuation,* and *spelling* follow accepted conventions, except for a few minor errors.

- *C* (adequate). A *C* paper is seriously deficient in one of these areas:

  The *paper as a whole* presents a clearly defined subject or main idea, but the treatment may be trivial, uninteresting, or too general and the insight adequate but not marked by independent thought. The plan and purpose are clear but inconsistently or incompletely carried out; tone may be inconsistent. Some paragraphs may lack adequate supporting detail or may be only loosely linked to the main idea. Sentences within paragraphs may be only loosely related, and some transitions may be missing. *Sentences* are generally correct in structure but may be excessively wordy, vague, or, at times, even incorrect. Style and word choice may be flat, inconsistent, or not entirely appropriate to the audience. The paper may display isolated serious errors in *grammar and punctuation* or frequent minor errors that do not interfere substantially with meaning or that do not greatly distract the reader; the paper may contain occasional *misspellings*.

- *D* (weak). A D paper is seriously deficient in any one of these areas:

The *paper as a whole* presents a poorly defined or inconsistently treated subject or central idea and displays little insight or development. The tone is inappropriate to the audience. *Paragraphs* contain little supporting detail. Sentences within paragraphs are often unrelated to the main idea and transitions are lacking. *Sentences* are frequently incorrect in structure, vague, wordy, and distracting. Style and word choice are inappropriate, incorrect, or inconsistent. The paper may contain serious and distracting errors in *grammar and punctuation* as well as numerous irritating minor errors and frequent *misspellings*.

- *F* (unacceptable/no credit). An F paper is unacceptable in any one of these areas:

The *paper as a whole* does not have a clear subject or main idea and has no apparent purpose or plan; or the subject and main idea are defined and treated in a way that clearly does not meet the requirements of the assignment. *Paragraphs* are not related to the main idea; sentences within paragraphs are unrelated, and transitions are missing. *Sentences* are so faulty in structure and style that the essay is not readable. Frequent serious errors in *grammar, punctuation,* and *spelling* indicate an inability to handle the written conventions; there are excessive minor errors or misspellings.

These criteria need to be adapted to the level of students in a particular course or institution and to the goals set for the course. For example, admirable organization or style may differ markedly for a student in a two-year technical program and a student in a four-year school that stresses the arts and humanities.

Evaluating for revision

■ Revision in composition teaching

In recent years the process of revision has come to be viewed as increasingly important in composition instruction. Instructors who make revision a regular part of their composition classes argue that writers should be judged not (or not only) on the early version of an essay but on what they are able to make of the essay after they have had a chance to revise it and, perhaps, to take into account the comments of readers.

Composition instructors have long viewed revision as an important process for student writers to learn. What is new is the extent to which revision is being made a regular part of instruction, an emphasis reflected in the extensive treatment of both revision and editing in Chapter 3 of the handbook. In addition, many instructors have begun structuring their classes around collaborative learning groups that provide audiences for papers in progress and advice for revision. This method is reinforced in Chapter 3, which contains checklists for students' giving and receiving criticism. The chapter "Using Collaborative Learning with the Handbook," which follows this discussion, contains suggestions for handouts to help students analyze their peers' work. Furthermore, students' increasing access to computers and the availability of computer classrooms have made possible a range of new approaches to the revision process (see Daniel Anderson's chapter on pp. IAE-46 to IAE-64).

■ Commenting on drafts for revision

The distinction made in Chapter 3 of the handbook between revision and editing is important for instructors to keep in mind when responding to a student paper in progress. For essays whose perspective, form, and content are well enough developed to require only editing, your role may be simply to call attention to errors or to suggest ways to polish sentences and paragraphs. Many of the techniques already discussed for commenting on papers can be used to aid editing, particularly those that refer students to sections of the handbook for advice on improving a passage or correcting a problem. In addition, you may wish to refer students to the editing checklist in Chapter 3 (pp. 58–59).

Evaluation for revision, however, is more likely to suggest extensive changes in a paper, often encouraging the writer to adopt a different perspective on a topic. Since revision may and often should involve substantial changes in the direction of an essay, however, you should be wary of comments that impose your view of what a paper should do or how it should be accomplished. Instead, try to identify a problem clearly and offer some possible solutions but at the same time leave the student writers free to make their own choices. Such comments as "Your thesis statement needs to focus more sharply on the specific government toxic-waste regulations to which you object" may be helpful in cases where the student's intentions and the direction of a paper are quite clear. But when a writer is still struggling with subject and intention, such statements may limit the process of revision rather than encourage it. A comment like the following, however, leaves the eventual direction of the essay up to the student:

> I'm not sure which specific regulations you object to most. Is this a place in the essay where you want to focus your concerns sharply for readers? From the detailed evidence you present later about the struggles of small businesses to pay for state-of-the-art pollution equipment, I suspect that one of your main purposes is to have readers understand the hard times these ordinary people are facing. What do you care most about in this subject, and what do you most want your audience to understand and feel?

In commenting on papers for revision, you should call attention to any serious errors. At the same time, however, keep in mind this maxim: "Don't spend time improving a sentence that ought to be dropped from the paper." Remember, too, that awkward and confused sentences are often signs of confusion about the overall direction of an essay, and problems at the sentence level may disappear as the writer resolves the larger problems.

> You shift pronouns often in this passage, sometimes addressing the reader as "you," sometimes using "one" or "we." I think the root of the problem is that you are not sure of your relation to your readers. Since you are talking about a situation that you face along with most readers, you might choose "we" and stick to it.

In addition, most students need more than advice about what sections of a paper need to be revised; they need advice about the process of revision itself. By focusing your comments on how to go about revising rather than solely on the direction of possible changes, you can avoid doing the students' work for them and can instead help them develop an effective writing/revising process.

Coping with the paper load

At this point you may well be asking, "How am I supposed to do all these things—run groups, intervene in processes, hold conferences, analyze errors, write long comments—and remain sane?" That's a good question, probably the most vexing one writing teachers face. You can't avoid it: grading papers takes time, lots of it, time that you'd often rather spend reading or working on your own scholarship or having a personal life or just enjoying fresh air and natural light. The best way to speed up the grading process, then, is to reduce the amount of grading you have to do. Several techniques will help you achieve this goal.

■ Grading the paper

Evaluating student papers can be time-consuming: instructors often report spending fifteen to twenty minutes on each paper, making marginal notes, writing summary comments, and deciding on a grade. Many set aside hours of office time for individual conferences. To help make the job of marking papers somewhat easier and quicker, *The Little, Brown Handbook* provides a number of aids:

- a list of correction symbols keyed to discussions in the text;
- a number-and-letter correction code that refers students to appropriate sections of the handbook; and
- a thorough index and glossary of terms directing students to explanations of grammatical and rhetorical terms used in an instructor's written comments.

Some practical tips will help you speed the grading process:

1. Start with carefully designed assignments and give students enough time to complete the assignment successfully. The clearer the assignment, the fewer variables will be left for you to cope with; the more adequate the time, the fewer hasty or careless errors you should have to contend with.
2. Be realistic when telling students when they'll get papers back. Many authorities insist that teachers return papers at the first class meeting after the

assignments are submitted. Two class meetings—or a week—is more realistic. The students also need at least one class meeting to review your comments and suggestions on one paper before submitting their next effort—and more time is helpful if they need a conference to discuss those comments with you. Schedule papers far enough apart to let you grade them carefully, and don't make promises you can't keep.

3. Not all papers must be new assignments. Students often profit from revising and reshaping an earlier paper, either one of their own choosing or one that you suggest they revise. Such assignments teach students the crucial importance of revising while giving you time to hold conferences, attend to individual problems, and design subsequent assignments.

4. Set a schedule for your grading and keep it. If you must grade fifty papers in five days, that's ten a day. At half an hour for each paper (a good beginner's rate), that's five hours of grading a day (you'll need a break or two to maintain your concentration).

5. Set reasonable time limits. Buy a timer and be ruthless about paying attention to it. Allow yourself a maximum time per paper—as a beginner, twenty-five or thirty minutes for an average (500–700 word) paper; as you get more experienced, fifteen to twenty minutes. Read the paper through once in its entirety before you mark anything, even minor mechanical errors. This allows you to assess the biggest strengths and weaknesses, to target your attention. Reread the paper, making your minimal marks and marginal comments. Then skim it one more time and compose your end comments. Sometimes the end comments written by beginning teachers are a page or longer; you'll learn to control this with experience. Again, using the three-part formula—strengths, a few weaknesses, and goals and strategies—can help you compose a response quickly.

Although you may find yourself calling on stock phrases to compose your end comments, it will help to refer back to specific marginal comments and moments in the paper as well. For example, you might say, "One of the strongest things about this paper is your use of quotations to support your opinions. On p. 2, for example, I've noted a particularly well-chosen quote and suggested ways that you might further develop your response to it." The relationship that you develop between your marginal comments and your end comment can be particularly helpful in guiding students from their global priorities for revision to local examples of where they might begin (or may already have begun) to develop the paper further.

6. Write a good end comment. If you have clear grading standards, put a letter grade on the paper after you've written your end comment; if not, sort all the papers into roughly defined piles—the good ones, the okay ones, the problem ones—and go back to assign grades later. If your time runs out, finish your note immediately and move on; you're probably asking the student to address too many issues. If you finish early, take a quick stretch and keep going; you'll want that time later. If a paper is very weak, set it aside; you'll want time to write a thoughtful note later. Don't turn the end comment into a justification or apology for a low grade; use it as a chance to teach the student ways to improve. If you think that assigning a very low grade would be detrimental to the student's progress, you can always mark the paper "No grade pending conference," discuss the paper with the student, and grade it after the student has revised it further. This solution works best when used sparingly and privately; otherwise you'll have B+ students clamoring for a chance to rewrite papers to get an A. (You can choose to allow such students to do so, of course, but be prepared to fight accusations of grade inflation.)

7. Keep good records. Don't just put the grade on the paper; record it in your grade book or progress folder immediately. If you're keeping a progress chart in the student's folder, make a few sketchy notes now; you can go back and elaborate later if necessary. If you forget to record grades now, you'll eventually find yourself in the position of returning a set of papers without having recorded the grades; then you have to go through all sorts of contortions to get the papers back to record the grades. Such a time-consuming annoyance can be avoided by keeping records carefully from the beginning.

■ Portfolios

You can reduce the number of assignments you actually give letter grades by allowing students to select some of their papers to submit as a portfolio for the class. Usually students submit drafts at an early point in the semester for your comments, then revise them and choose which ones to submit for their final grade in the course. Such an approach grants them more autonomy and may heighten their desire to achieve. Portfolios also encourage students to see writing as a process, enabling their growth as writers; for this reason, many colleges and universities are using portfolios not only in first-year writing but throughout a student's academic career; these portfolios become substantially more than just an evaluation method.

Portfolio grading, at its best, empowers students and spurs revision; thus it has drawn a great deal of attention in recent years as programs struggle with the whole question of evaluation. Several fine collections of perspectives on the portfolio question have appeared in recent years, including *Portfolios: Process and Product*, edited by Pat Belanoff and Marcia Dickson; *Portfolios and Beyond: Collaborative Assessments in Reading and Writing* by Susan Mandel Glazer and Carol Smullen Brown; *Process and Portfolios in Writing Instruction*, edited by Ken Gill and the Committee on Classroom Practices; and *Portfolio Resource Guide: Creating and Using Portfolios in the Classroom* by Judith C. Gilbert. However, some studies (particularly in Vermont) have questioned how well portfolios function in measuring students' writing ability over time. Others have pointed to the fact that while many people claim portfolios' virtues, very few studies have demonstrated either the practical use of handling them in the classroom or their effectiveness in helping students become better writers over the course of their college careers. Portfolio theory is still in its infancy, and much research remains to be done to understand how portfolios can best be used. Thus, this method will certainly continue to draw critical scrutiny.

If you choose to use portfolios in your classes, you'll need to make choices about scheduling them, grading them, and about the process of selecting what should go in them. You may want to experiment with the following options before settling on the arrangements you think work best for you and your students:

- Structuring portfolio assignments over the course of the semester takes some logistical planning. One issue is the pace of your own workload. Consider: if you have four classes of 25 students each, and each student turns in a portfolio of four papers at the end of the term, you'll have 400 papers to grade all at once. Students too may have difficulty managing an unbalanced workload. Moreover, students benefit most from getting feedback throughout the semester—your comments on one paper may help them not only with the revision of that paper but with the first draft of their next paper. To balance the workload for yourself and your students, you may want to require that some of the portfolio revisions be turned in for comments midway through the semester. Alternatively, you can make sure to give back first drafts well enough in advance of the portfolio due date that students will have ample time to work on revisions. Another option is to give very thorough critique on first drafts and minimal comments on the revisions in the portfolio. If you choose the latter option, you may want to have your students write you a memo about each revised paper, or even annotate the paper, to show what changes they made from the first draft, so that you will have a focus for your comments. Or you could have them resubmit the first draft of each paper along with the revised version; in this way you can review your comments on the draft and more quickly evaluate the success of the revision.

- You'll need to give some thought to developing a grading system for portfolios in your courses. You may want to give only comments (no grades) on first drafts, and then give a grade for each revised paper and another for the portfolio as a whole. Alternatively, you can give grades on individual first drafts and then one overall grade for the portfolio. You can give all papers equal weight in determining the overall grade or allow students to choose which papers they'd like to have weighed more heavily. You may want to give credit for degree of improvement, but if you do so you'll need to take care not to end up with inflated grades.

- Students should decide for themselves what to include in the portfolio, but it can be very productive for them to discuss their decisions with you and/or their classmates. You can meet with students to discuss which papers they think they'd like to revise and why. You may want to ask your students to prepare for these conferences by filling out self-assessment forms identifying the strengths and weaknesses of each paper and setting goals for revision. Or have students work in small groups to help one another select which papers should be revised. If you have all your students bring their portfolios to class and pass them around, so that each student looks at fifteen or more, they will quickly get a feeling for what makes a good portfolio.

■ Conference

You can also work individually with students on the development of their papers, looking at rough drafts of either portions or complete versions of their texts. You could "evaluate" some papers in one-to-one conferences, assigning verbal grades of "excellent," "very good," "fair," and the like. Since these grades will likely be high, reflecting your evaluation of the project at many stages, you might then assign letter grades only to papers students produce independently, alternating conference and independent papers. This strategy reduces by half the number of written comments you must produce; its drawback is the amount of time such conference teaching requires. Some teachers address the time issue by meeting with selected groups of students for intensive revision discussions focused on those students' particular needs. An additional advantage of conferences is that you can work through relevant sections of the handbook with students, so that they have specific places to look for information as they revise their papers. A good rule of thumb in planning conferences is to set a defined agenda in advance so that students come to the conference with a particular piece of writing, a list of questions, or a revision plan, and with a mutually understood goal for the session.

■ Collaborating

A different kind of workload reduction can be achieved by letting your students do some of the work for you collaboratively. When students work effectively in small and large groups, they can identify writing problems at the draft stage and help their fellow students remedy weaknesses. Group proofreading sessions likewise can find and solve many mechanical problems before they reach your desk. If you train the groups to look for the kinds of problems students are having, they can do a great deal of the diagnostic work for each other. You'll occasionally have to correct a faulty diagnosis, but you will save yourself a little time while promoting students' inde-

pendent revision and editing skills. If all students have access to computer facilities, you can encourage them to use spelling checker programs, and perhaps to create networked revision groups or e-mail chat groups to support each other's editing processes. See the chapter on "Collaborative Learning" (pp. IAE-34 to IAE-45).

■ Student-set standards

You can also encourage students to set the standard for achievement in the class, perhaps using a model such as the description of letter grades given above. Or, using that model as a general criterion, you might ask students to derive a more specific set of criteria from a particular assignment. Such an exercise might ask: "What kinds of things does this assignment ask for? What might be a minimal (C-level) response to this assignment? What kinds of strategies might an excellent (B- to A-level paper) adopt in responding to this assignment?" Or, early in the semester, you can have students develop sets of criteria that characterize above-average, average, and below-average writing; then hold them to these criteria in assigning grades. Duplicate the criteria and distribute them to the class members; use them to develop goals in assignments, to develop heuristics for group work, and to support your comments.

Evaluation *cans* and *can'ts*

Some teachers, particularly beginning ones, have an extremely idealistic view of evaluation: they see it as a cure-all for all the writer's problems. To gain these results, they write comments that may approach (or exceed) the original paper in length. The overwhelmed student may try to respond but is usually daunted by all the advice and suggestions—and subsequent papers sometimes are disasters. It's particularly crucial to remember that students can rarely learn a new skill or learn to recognize and correct even a single pattern of error overnight. It takes an enormous amount of practice and consideration for a student to locate sentence fragments in his or her own writing—about as much time as it takes to create well-developed paragraphs. Although it can be frustrating to see recurring errors of exactly the same type that you have carefully marked in previous papers, those errors are rarely a sign of carelessness; more often they suggest that the student needs more personalized support (a conference, a tutoring session, an assigned task using the handbook).

Evaluating individual written products is a matter of seeing how well students have reached intermediate goals in the course. It can't be done on the bell curve; writing progress is too individual a process for that. While you'll want to apply the same standards to all students, you'll probably have to allow some leeway in measuring achievement. Students who quickly master narrow competencies (such as mechanics or syntactic variety) should receive credit for these successes but should probably be judged more on how well they master more open matters—audience manipulation, voice, development, and so on. Students who have a great deal of difficulty mastering the narrow skills—those who come from particularly weak backgrounds or who have dialect interference problems, for example—may have excellent ideas but difficulty in presenting them. They should be rewarded for the content of their papers but encouraged to master the conventions of academic discourse as well. Make it clear to students that you're not evaluating how well they compete against other students—or against your ideals—but how much progress they're making in achieving the goals set for all students.

Likewise, you may be tempted to reward a student's effort on a paper rather than the product he or she actually produces ("This just doesn't hold together, but he worked so hard; look at all these drafts!"); such sympathy may be human, but it's not going to help the student. Giving good grades for effort rather than for results provides students with false assessments of their achievements. It's dishonest. Better in such cases to withhold a grade pending a conference and revision than to inflate students' expectations artificially.

Resources for response and evaluation

Bartholomae, David. "Released into Error: Errors, Expectations and the Legacy of Mina Shaughnessy." *The Territory of Language*. Ed. Donald A. McQuade. Carbondale: Southern Illinois UP, 1986.

———. "The Study of Error." *College Composition and Communication* 31 (1980): 253–69.

Belanoff, Pat, and Marcia Dickson, eds. *Portfolios: Process and Product*. Portsmouth: Boynton/Cook, 1991.

———. "Toward an Ethics of Grading." *Foregrounding Ethical Awareness in Composition and English Studies*. Ed. Sheryl I. Fontaine and Susan M. Hunter. Portsmouth: Boynton/Cook, 1998. 174–96.

Black, Laurel Johnson. *Between Talk and Teaching: Reconsidering the Writing Conference*. Logan: Utah State UP, 1998.

Boynton, Victoria. "Collaborative Power Sharing." *Composition Chronicle* 6:1 (February 1993): 6–8.

Brannon, Lil, and C. H. Knoblauch. "On Students' Rights to Their Own Texts: A Model of Teacher Response." *College Composition and Communication* 33 (1982): 157–66.

Conners, Robert J., and Andrea Lunsford. "Teachers' Rhe-torical Comments on Student Papers." *College Composition and Communication* 44:2 (May 1993): 200–233.

Cooper, Charles R., and Lee Odell, eds. *Evaluating Writing: Describing, Measuring, Judging*. Urbana: NCTE, 1977.

Faigley, Lester. "Judging Writing, Judging Selves." *College Composition and Communication* 40 (1989): 395–412.

Ford, James E., and Gregory Larkin. "The Portfolio System: An End to Backsliding Writing Standards." *College English* 39 (1978): 950–55.

Freedman, Sarah Warshauer. *Responses to Student Writing*. Urbana: NCTE, 1987.

Freedman, Sarah Warshauer, and Melanie Sperling. "Teacher–Student Interaction in the Writing Conference: Response and Teaching." In *The Acquisition of Written Language: Response and Revision*. Ed. Sarah Warshauer Freedman. Norwood: Ablex, 1985.

Garrison, Roger. *One-to-One: Making Writing Instruction Effective*. Instructor's Manual to Accompany Garrison's *How a Writer Works*. New York: Harper & Row, 1981.

———. "One-to-One: Tutorial Instruction in Freshman Composition." *New Directions for Community Colleges* 2 (Spring 1974): 55–84.

Gere, Ann Ruggles, and Robert Stevens. "The Language of Writing Groups: How Oral Response Shapes Revision." In *The Acquisition of Written Language: Response and Revision*. Ed. Sarah Warshauer Freedman. Norwood: Ablex, 1985. 85–105.

Gilbert, Judith C. *Portfolio Resource Guide: Creating and Using Portfolios in the Classroom.* Ottawa, KS: The Writing Conference, 1993.

Gill, Ken, and the Committee on Classroom Practices, eds. *Process and Portfolios in Writing Instruction.* Urbana: NCTE, 1993.

Glazer, Susan Mandel, and Carol Smullen Brown. *Portfolios and Beyond: Collaborative Assessments in Reading and Writing.* Norwood: Christopher-Gordon, 1993.

Hamp-Lyons, Liz. "Uncovering Possibilities for a Constructivist Paradigm for Writing Assessment." Review in *College Composition and Communication* 46:3 (Oct. 1995): 446–55.

Hillocks, George. "The Interaction of Instruction, Teacher Comment, and Revision in Teaching the Composing Process." *Research in the Teaching of English* 16 (1982): 261–78.

Hunter, Susan, and Ray Wallace. *The Place of Grammar in Writing Instruction, Past, Present, Future.* Portsmouth: Boynton/Cook, 1995.

Larson, Bruce, Susan Stern Ryan, and Ross Winterowd, eds. *Encountering Student Texts: Interpretive Issues in Reading Student Writing.* Urbana: NCTE, 1990.

McDonald, W. U., Jr. "The Revising Process and the Marking of Student Papers." *College Composition and Communication* 29 (1978): 167–70.

Miller, Linda P. "A Conference Methodology for Freshman Composition." *Teaching English in the Two-Year College* 7 (1980): 23–26.

Noguchi, Rei R. *Grammar and the Teaching of Writing: Limits and Possibilities.* Urbana: NCTE, 1991.

Olsen, Gary A. "Beyond Evaluation: The Recorded Response to Essays." *Teaching English in the Two-Year College* 8 (1982): 121–23.

Prendergast, Catherine. "Race: The Absent Presence in Composition Studies." *College Composition and Communication* 50 (1998): 36–53.

Purves, Alan. "The Teacher as Reader: An Anatomy." *College English* 46 (1984): 259–65.

Schiff, Peter. "Responding to Writing: Peer Critiques, Teacher-Student Conferences, and Essay Evaluations." In *Language Connections: Writing and Reading Across the Curriculum.* Urbana: NCTE, 1982. 153–65.

Shaughnessy, Mina. *Errors and Expectations: A Guide for the Teacher of Basic Writing.* New York: Oxford UP, 1977.

Shaw, Margaret L. "What Students Don't Say: An Approach to the Student Text." *College Composition and Communication* 42 (1991): 45–54.

Sommers, Nancy. "Responding to Student Writing." *College Composition and Communication* 33 (1982): 148–56.

Speck, Bruce. *Grading Student Writing: An Annotated Bibliography.* Westport, CT: Greenwood, 1998.

Stanford, Gene, ed. *How to Handle the Paper Load.* Urbana: NCTE, 1978.

Straub, Richard. "The Concept of Control in Teacher Response: Defining the Varieties of 'Directive' and 'Facilitative' Commentary." *College Composition and Communication* 47:2 (May 1996): 223–51.

Tarvers, Josephine Koster. *Teaching Writing: Theories and Practices.* 4th ed. New York: HarperCollins, 1993.

Yancey, Katherine Blake, ed. *Portfolios in the Writing Classroom: An Introduction.* Urbana: NCTE, 1992.

Zak, Frances, and Christopher C. Weaver, eds. *The Theory and Practice of Grading Writing.* Albany: State U of New York P, 1998.

CHAPTER 4
Using Collaborative Learning with the Handbook

Collaborative learning activities provide effective ways to get students to write to a tangible audience of their peers, to practice their revision skills in a supportive, non-intimidating environment, and to experience the reality of alternative perspectives and approaches to writing and to the course readings. Group work also shifts classroom learning to an ongoing conversation between students rather than as a constant deferral to the teacher's greater authority. Kenneth Bruffee, a key proponent of collaborative learning, argues that because knowledge itself is the result of consensus among members of a community, and is produced by collaborative activity, "interdependent" student groups offer the ideal learning tool (3). They become "transition communities or support groups that students can rely on as they go through the risky process of becoming new members of the knowledge communities" (4). While Bruffee argues for a long history of informal cooperation and support systems among students as the natural basis for collaborative classroom assignments, others have pointed to the difficulty of grafting collaborative procedures into institutions that base their standards on individual performance and reward individual excellence (Gergits and Schramer). Still others have countered Bruffee's model of consensus as one that overlooks or erases the powerful differences between groups and individuals, differences that are the basis for continual collaborative negotiation (Trimbur and Spellmeyer, for example).

As these theoretical models suggest, it is important to be aware of potentially contradictory messages when setting up collaborative activities. For instance, students may not readily embrace a collaborative revision exercise if the grading system for the class, the teacher's responses on papers, and other classroom practices are all focused on individual performance. Conversely, the more collaborative work that students do, and the more that work is supported by surrounding classroom practices, the more students will understand the goals of group activities and feel confident in negotiating group dynamics. It also helps to remember that collaborative groups are part of a complex social process; as students work to overcome the social awkwardness of organizing and starting the task, they are also finding some common ground, finding ways to communicate across (sometimes) enormous ideological and conceptual differences (see *Singular Texts/Plural Authors*, Andrea Lunsford and Lisa Ede).

Forming groups for collaboration

Inexperienced teachers who are considering collaborative activities may find the following suggestions useful. Collaborative groups can vary in size and configuration depending on the activity—from pairs to groups of four or five. For example, if the task is to choose a passage from the reading and come up with an interpretive response to present to the class, a larger group is useful in producing energetic debates (especially if each student is responsible for presenting some of the material). If you are having students work with the handbook to identify and revise particular problems, groups of three allow for both a range of skills and attention to individual difficulties. Students might begin with the revision checklist (p. 51) or the editing checklist (pp. 58–59) to identify recurrent problem patterns in each other's work, then revise using the relevant sections from the handbook. If your revision groups of three or four are becoming careless in their suggestions for each other's papers, you might pair students in groups of two and ask them to respond in writing and at length to another student's paper.

Some teachers always allow students to choose their own groups; the advantage here is that students generally establish a working dynamic and continue to choose the same group throughout the course. Other teachers select groups in order to mix or isolate skill levels or to create productive environments for silent or outspoken students. Again, you might make this decision based on the particular task and on group dynamics. If the task you have assigned is to revise a sentence or a paragraph in a student essay, you might streamline the process by asking students to work with the person next to them. If you notice a larger revision group veering into discussions of movies or a sociology exam, you might sit in with them for that session to listen to the group dynamic, then make an effort to reorganize groups for the next session (see Brook, Mirtz, and Evans for further discussion of small group dynamics).

One way to reinforce collaborative goals in a course in which grades depend upon individual performance is to incorporate peer-review suggestions into your final graded comments on each student's paper. After reading the student's paper and scanning the peer-review worksheets or marked drafts, you might say, for example, "You have effectively made use of Jeffrey D's suggestion about developing paragraphs 5–8. Audrey F's question about your transitions on pages 4 and 5 might have led you to strengthen your argument—look out for those transitional movements next time!" Another way to reinforce those goals is to assign one or two collaboratively written and graded projects.

Many instructors assign students in pairs or small teams to collaborate on papers; for certain kinds of writing, especially research writing, such strategies can be very effective and will prepare students well for the kinds of writing they may do in their careers. Many of the exercises in Chapters 42–45 can be adapted for collaborative projects. Such projects can be combined with individually produced and evaluated papers as well. For example, you might have students work in pairs to write out the different sides of a debate, then ask each student to produce an individually written paper that takes the other student's perspective into account. "Collaborative Learning" exercises in Chapters 9, 10, and 11 suggest various ways for students to produce arguments and to analyze each other's claims.

Developing skills in collaboration

As with any other process, collaborative work is a slowly developed skill. New teachers will sometimes report that they tried it once and it "didn't work" so they're hesitant to try it again. Remember that groups might not seem highly productive at first; students can be unsure of their revision skills, hesitant about showing their work, and dependent on the teacher's greater authority. One way to make group work more productive from the start is to give students shorter, highly directed tasks at first; for example, each group might read and discuss Chapter 4, section c, on developing paragraphs, then work together to revise a student writer's paragraph. It also helps to model the assigned activity within the class as a whole before moving to smaller groups. For example, you might bring in a sample student paper, have each student come up with a revision suggestion or practice revising a sample sentence, then share the results with the class. Then, when students undertake a similar activity in smaller groups, you can refer back to the previous class-wide activity. Also, in many cases in which group work appears to "fail," students are simply confused about the assigned activity. It helps to be extremely clear about what you want each group to accomplish—even to provide a written handout or worksheet (sample worksheets follow this discussion). It's also important that students recognize the relationship between the group activity and their personal goals as writers; many teachers preface group work with a discussion of those goals in relation to the group task.

The crucial thing to remember is that working in revision or writing groups is as much a skill to be demonstrated and learned as any other. In working with a sample paper, for example, you might start with basic questions that help students to look globally at pieces of discourse as a teacher (evaluator) looks at it. "What's the point of this paper? Who are the readers supposed to be? What are some things this writer does well?" Then you might ask students to look more specifically at the construction of the paper: the places where assertions are backed up by evidence and the places where more evidence is needed; the indications of strong organizational control and the places where the text seems choppy and disorganized; the clear definition with supporting examples and the terms of the essay that need further clarification and development. The sample worksheets that accompany this chapter can be modified to guide students through particular tasks. For example, you might ask each student writer to create a self-evaluation of the paper (Form G), then compare it to her or his group's suggestions (Form A, B, or C). If students seem to be supplying vague responses to larger questions about audience and argument, Forms D, E, and F suggest ways to focus the groups on specific areas of the essay.

In addition to identifying strengths and problem areas, collaborative groups can go on to help each writer begin the work of revision. If, for instance, the text seems choppy or disorganized, they can experiment with organizational tools (using Exercise 2.9 in 2c, for example) or look for transition problems (using Exercise 4.9, 4b). If the thesis is underdeveloped, they might apply the questions in 10i, Exercise 10.11, to suggest places where new examples or analysis would help. Or, if the essay seems to lack a directed purpose, Exercises 1.6 and 1.9 in 1d and 1e offer specific and effective practice in thinking about audience and purpose. Many of the other exercises in *The Little, Brown Handbook* are well suited to such collaborative work.

Customizing collaborative materials

Many teachers like to modify the worksheets and exercises for the uses of a particular class. For instance, worksheet questions can be adapted to focus on a particular reading or essay assignment. Some teachers begin the course with detailed revision worksheets, then gradually taper off as group members become familiar with each other and confident about their revision skills. Teachers working in a computer classroom can supplement these exercises by creating networked revision groups, e-mail chat groups, and virtual-reality publications that help students experience various audience responses to their work (see Barrett, for example, and Daniel Anderson's chapter on pp. IAE-46 to IAE-64).

While some teachers are active participants in group activities, other teachers try not to intervene directly in groups unless students have questions or have ceased to address the task (for more on this topic see "A Conversation About Small Groups" in Brook et al.). The teacher's primary role in a collaborative classroom is to plan group tasks that are effectively designed and that take the varying needs of students into account. For example, highly skilled students may not always trust their peers to give them revision advice. For those students it is important to emphasize that in learning to critique another writer's work in a way that encourages a productive revision they are honing their own revision skills as well. Conversely, less skilled writers occasionally feel overwhelmed by the group's advice and may seek to deflect attention from the paper by protesting that it's not a real draft or that it's not ready to be read. Here it helps to emphasize that active revision can begin from a sketchy paragraph or from notes. In some cases, the most effective task for a group might be to help the writer pinpoint useful passages in the readings, or to ask the writer to describe verbally where he or she intends to go with the project. In this sense, collaborative work can be flexibly attuned to the needs of various writers at different stages of a project. In a process-oriented class, this emphasis on the way different writers work can be a useful focus for class-wide discussions—and a way to encourage students to take themselves and each other seriously as writers.

Since students may profit from having specific guidelines for collaboration, we've prepared the following worksheets that will help you guide collaborative activities in your classroom.

■ **Worksheets for collaborative activities**

FORM A

General Guidelines for Peer Readers Commenting
Directly on a Writer's Work

Author: _____   Reader: _____

As a reader, you are going to comment directly on a photocopy of a classmate's paper. Read the paper through carefully before making any comments. Then follow the guidelines below. If the writer has submitted a self-evaluation sheet, read it after answering question 1.

1. Consider the thesis, purpose, and audience for the paper. Are they indicated clearly? Are they consistent? If not, ask the writer questions to help clarify these essential elements of writing.

2. Skim the paper to see how it is organized. Are there any breaks in the organization? If so, try to explain why you feel that a gap exists. Whenever possible, phrase your comments as questions, not judgments. If you think that the organization needs to be revised significantly, skip to question 7 after answering this question.

3. Now go back and look at each paragraph. Is it unified, coherent, and developed? If not, ask the writer a question to help focus or complete the paragraph.

4. Are the paragraphs connected to one another smoothly and logically? If there are any logical gaps between the paragraphs, ask the writer how one paragraph is linked to the next. If you think that most of the paragraphs need to be revised significantly, skip to question 7 after answering this question.

5. Now look at sentences. Do any sentences confuse you? If so, try to describe your confusion or ask the writer a question about the sentence.

6. Are there any mechanical or grammatical problems in the paper? If so, point them out to the writer, but do not correct them.

7. Decide what the paper's two most important strengths are. Point them out to the writer.

FORM B

Reader Response Sheet for a Descriptive Critique

Author: _____   Reader: _____

Answer the questions below, being as specific as possible.

1. Read the first paragraph and then pause. Write down what you expect will be the topic, purpose, and audience of the paper.

2. Now finish reading the paper. Were your expectations for the paper's topic, purpose, and audience fulfilled? If not, what do you now think the topic, purpose, and audience are?

3. What do you think the main idea, or thesis, of the paper is?

4. What sort of evidence is used to develop or support this main idea?

5. Summarize the paper, devoting one sentence to each paragraph.

FORM C

Reader Response Sheet for an Evaluative Critique

Author: _____   Reader: _____

Answer the questions below, being as specific as possible. If the author has included a self-evaluation sheet, do not read it until you have answered questions 1 through 6.

1. Read the first paragraph and then pause. Write down what you expect will be the topic, purpose, and audience of the paper.

2. Now finish reading the paper. Were your expectations for the paper's topic, purpose, and audience fulfilled? If not, what do you now think the topic, purpose, and audience are?

3. What do you think the main idea, or thesis, of the paper is?

4. What sort of evidence is used to develop or support this main idea?

5. Summarize the paper, devoting one sentence to each paragraph.

6. What did you like best about the paper?

7. Did anything in the paper surprise you?

8. What two features of the paper most need improvement?

9. Please respond to the author's questions on the back of this sheet.

To the author: Before giving this sheet to your reader, list on the back the three questions that you would like your reader to answer about this paper.

FORM D

Reader Response Sheet for a Thorough Critique

Author: —————————————— Reader: ——————————————

Answer the questions below, being as specific as possible. If the author has included a self-evaluation sheet, do not read it until you have answered questions 1 through 3.

1. Read the first paragraph and then pause. Write down what you expect will be the topic, purpose, and audience of the paper.

2. Now finish reading the paper. Were your expectations for the paper's topic, purpose, and audience fulfilled? If not, what do you now think the topic, purpose, and audience are?

3. Summarize the paper, devoting one sentence to each paragraph.

4. What do you think the main idea, or thesis, of the paper is? Do you agree with this thesis? Why or why not? What is your position on this topic?

5. What sort of evidence is used to develop or support this main idea? Is this evidence appropriate? Is there sufficient evidence? If not, what sort of evidence should the writer consider?

6. Does the author take into account different points of view about the thesis of the paper? Does the author consider counterarguments?

7. Are there counterarguments that the author does not consider, but should?

8. What did you like best about this paper?

9. What two features of the paper most need improvement?

10. Please respond to the author's questions on the back of this sheet.

_____

To the author: Before giving this sheet to your reader, list on the back the three questions that you would like your reader to answer about this paper.

FORM E

Author's and Reader's Responses in the Second Round of a Thorough Critique

Author: _____   Reader: _____

Author's section. Please attach a revision of your original paper to this form and answer the following questions.

1. What do you think is your reader's point of view on this subject? Do you share that point of view?

2. What assumptions does your reader make about the topic? Do you agree with these assumptions? Why or why not?

3. What two comments by the reader were the most useful? Why were they helpful?

4. What are the two most important changes that you have made in this revision?

5. What do you like best about the essay?

6. What two questions would you like your reader to answer about this revision?

Reader's section. Please respond to the questions below.

1. Please summarize the author's revision, devoting one sentence to each paragraph.

2. How do you think that the author has improved the essay?

3. Has the author changed your feeling about the topic?

4. What is the strongest argument against the revised essay?

5. What two features most need improvement?

6. Respond to the author's questions.

FORM F

Reader Response Sheet for an Essay Assignment Stressing Paragraphing
(Handbook, Chapter 4)

Author: _____   Reader: _____

Answer the questions below, being as specific as possible. If the author has included a self-evaluation sheet, do not read it until you have answered questions 1 through 6.

1. Read the first paragraph and then pause. Write down what you expect will be the topic, purpose, and audience of the paper.

2. Now finish reading the paper. Were your expectations for the paper's topic, purpose, and audience fulfilled? If not, what do you now think the topic, purpose, and audience are?

3. What do you think the main idea, or thesis, of the paper is?

4. What sort of evidence is used to develop or support this main idea?

5. Number the paragraphs. Are the author's paragraphs unified, coherent, and developed? If so, note them. Also indicate any that confuse you, and explain why.

6. Do the paragraphs follow a logical order? Describe how the argument does or does not flow from the first to the second, from the second to the third, and so on.

7. What did you like best about the paper?

8. What two features of the paper most need improvement?

FORM G

Self-Evaluation Sheet to Accompany an Essay for Peer Response or Instructor's Evaluation

Author: In order to help your instructor or peer reader evaluate this essay, you should explain where you are in the writing process. Be as specific as possible in answering the following questions.

1. What are you trying to say in this paper? What is your main idea?

2. Who might be interested in reading this paper?

3. What do you like best in the paper?

4. What do you like least in the paper?

5. What would you work on if you had twenty-four hours more to spend on the project?

6. What three questions would you like to ask your reader? How can your reader help you develop the paper further?

Resources for collaborative learning and peer criticism

Arkin, Marian, and Barbara Shollar. *The Writing Tutor.* New York: Longman, 1982.

Barrett, Edward. "Collaboration in the Electronic Classroom." *Technology Review* 96:2 (Feb./March 1993): 51–55.

Bishop, Wendy. "Helping Peer Writing Groups Succeed." *Teaching English in the Two-Year College* 15 (1988): 120–25.

Bizzaro, Patrick, and Stuart Werner. "Collaboration of Teacher and Counselor in Basic Writing." *College Composition and Communication* 38 (1987): 397–425.

Bormann, Ernest. *Small-Group Communication: Theory and Practice.* New York: Harper, 1990.

Brook, Robert, Ruth Mirtz, and Rick Evans, eds. *Small Groups in Writing Workshops.* Urbana: NCTE, 1994.

Bruffee, Kenneth. *Collaborative Learning: Higher Education, Interdependence, and the Authority of Knowledge.* Baltimore: Johns Hopkins UP, 1993.

Clark, Beverly Lyon. *Talking About Writing: A Guide for Tutor and Teacher Conferences.* Ann Arbor: U of Michigan P, 1985.

Clarke, Irene L. "Portfolio Evaluations, Collaboration, and Writing Centers." *College Composition and Communication* 44 (1993): 515–24.

Corder, Jim W. "Tribes and Displaced Persons: Some Observations on Collaboration." In *Theory and Practice in the Teaching of Writing: Rethinking the Discipline.* Ed. Lee Odell. Carbondale: Southern Illinois UP, 1993. 271–88.

Elbow, Peter. "Reflecting on Academic Discourse: How It Relates to Freshmen and Colleagues." *College English* 53 (Feb. 1991): 135–55.

Fontaine, Sheryl L. "The Unfinished Story of the Interpretative Community." *Rhetoric Review* 7 (1988): 86–96.

Forman, Janis, ed. *New Visions of Collaborative Writing.* Portsmouth, NH: Cook/Boynton, 1992.

Fraser, Scott C., et al. "Two, Three, or Four Heads Are Better Than One: Modification of College Performance by Peer Monitoring." *Journal of Educational Psychology* 69 (1977–78): 101–08.

Gebhardt, Richard. "Team Work and Feedback: Broadening the Base of Collaborative Writing." *College English* 42 (1980): 69–74.

Gergits, Julia M., and James J. Schramer. "The Collaborative Classroom as the Site of Difference." *Journal of Advanced Composition* 14:1 (Winter 1994): 187–202.

George, Diana. "Working with Peer Groups in the Composition Classroom." *College Composition and Communication* 35 (1984): 320–26.

Gere, Anne Ruggles. *Writing Groups: History, Theory, and Implications.* Carbondale: Southern Illinois UP, 1987.

———, and Robert D. Abbott. "Talking About Writing: The Language of Writing Groups." *Research in the Teaching of English* 19 (1985): 362–86.

———, and Ralph Stevens. "The Language of Writing Groups: How Oral Response Shapes Revision." In *The Acquisition of Written Language: Response and Revision.* Ed. Sarah Warshauer Freedman. Norwood: Ablex, 1985. 85–105.

Golub, Jeff, and the Committee on Classroom Practices, eds. *Focus on Collaborative Learning.* Urbana: NCTE, 1988.

Haring-Smith, Tori. *Writing Together: Collaborative Learning in the Classroom.* New York: HarperCollins, 1994.

Harris, Joseph. "The Idea of Community in the Study of Writing." *College Composition and Communication* 40 (1989): 11–22.

Harris, Muriel. "Peer Tutoring: How Tutors Learn." *Teaching English in the Two-Year College* 15 (1988): 28–33.

Hillocks, George. "Environments for Active Learning." In *Theory and Practice in the Teaching of Writing: Rethinking the Discipline.* Ed. Lee Odell. Carbondale: Southern Illinois UP, 1993. 244–70.

Kail, Harvey. "Collaborative Learning in Context: The Problem with Peer Tutoring." *College English* 45 (1983): 817–23.

Knox-Zuinn, Carolyn. "Collaboration in the Writing Classroom: An Interview with Ken Kesey." *College Composition and Communication* 41 (1990): 309–17.

Lunsford, Andrea, and Lisa Ede. "Rhetoric in a New Key: Women and Collaboration." *Rhetoric Review* 8 (1990): 234–41.

————. *Singular Texts/Plural Authors: Perspectives on Collaborative Writing.* Carbondale: Southern Illinois UP, 1992.

Lyon, Arabella. "Re-presenting Communities: Teaching Turbulence." *Rhetoric Review* 10 (1992): 279–90.

Madden-Simpson, Janet. "A Collaborative Approach to the Research Paper." *Teaching English in the Two-Year College* 16 (1989): 113–15.

Reither, James A., and Douglas Vipond. "Writing as Collaboration." *College English* 51 (1989): 855–67.

Roskelly, Hephzibah. "The Risky Business of Group Work." *The Writing Teacher's Sourcebook,* 4th ed. Ed. Edward P. J. Corbett et al. New York: Oxford UP, 2000. 123–28.

Smit, David W. "Some Difficulties with Collaborative Learning." *Journal of Advanced Composition* 9 (1989): 45–58.

Spear, Karen. *Sharing Writing: Peer Response Groups in English Classes.* Portsmouth: Heinemann, 1988.

Speck, Bruce, et al., eds. *Collaborative Writing: An Annotated Bibliography.* Westport, CT: Greenwood, 1999.

Spellmeyer, Kurt. "On Conventions and Collaboration: The Open Road and the Iron Cage." In *Writing Theory and Critical Theory.* Ed. John Clifford and John Schilb. New York: MLA, 1994.

Spigelman, Candace. "Habits of Mind: Historical Configurations of Textual Ownership in Peer Writing Groups." *College Composition and Communication* 49 (1998): 234–55.

Stewart, Donald. "Collaborative Learning and Composition: Boon or Bane?" *Rhetoric Review* 7 (1988): 58–85.

Stygall, Gail. "Women and Language in the Collaborative Writing Classroom." *Feminism and Composition Studies: In Other Words.* Ed. Susan C. Jarratt and Lynn Worsham. New York: MLA, 1998.

Teich, Nathaniel, ed. *Rogerian Perspectives: Collaborative Rhetoric for Oral and Written Communication.* Norwood: Ablex, 1992.

Trimbur, John. "Collaborative Learning and Teaching Writing." In *Perspectives on Research and Scholarship in Composition.* Ed. Ben W. McClelland and Timothy R. Donovan. New York: MLA, 1985. 87–109.

————. "Consensus and Difference in Collaborative Learning." *College English* 51 (1989): 602–16.

Tobin, Lad. *Writing Relationships: What Really Happens in the Composition Class.* Portsmouth: Boynton/Cook, 1993.

Wiener, Harvey S. "Collaborative Learning in the Classroom: A Guide to Evaluation." *College English* 48 (1986): 52–61.

Yancey, Kathleen Blake, and Michael Spooner. "A Single Good Mind: Collaboration, Cooperation, and the Writing Self." *College Composition and Communication* 49 (1998): 45–62.

CHAPTER **5**
Using Computers to Teach Writing

By Daniel Anderson

Information technologies continue to make dramatic alterations in the educational landscape, and many writing teachers are finding themselves called upon to use technological tools in their teaching. Administrators may be asking that curricula adapt to serve the changing demands of constituents. Students may arrive at school either already equipped with information skills or insistent that these skills be included as part of their learning. This chapter helps instructors meet the challenges of this transformational moment in education. The chapter provides an overview of some of the opportunities made possible by information technology, discusses concerns likely to arise as teachers adapt information technologies to teaching, and offers practical advice for using instructional technologies critically. (*The Little, Brown Handbook* also serves to illuminate the use of information technologies. Chapter 3 offers advice on managing files, using spelling and grammar checkers, and other computer skills in the context of revising and editing; Chapter 5 treats document design; Chapters 43 and 44 offer specific information about electronic research; and Chapter 54 focuses on the rhetorical issues of writing online, including e-mail, collaboration, and Web composition, and computer tips appear throughout the text.)

Imagining the possibilities for teaching with technology

Information technologies offer new modes of learning and avenues for research and collaboration. Word processors and basic computing skills help students enhance and strengthen their writing process. Electronic discussions enable them to converse with one another as they explore issues and ideas about writing. File-sharing functions and collaboration programs allow students to work together on projects. Electronic library resources provide students with extended opportunities for research. And students who compose Web pages and other electronic documents can develop and sharpen their writing skills as they participate in emergent forms of communication and literacy.

What makes this range of possibilities exciting for writing instructors is the way all of these activities build upon what we know to be useful methodologies for helping students to become better writers. Here are some ideas about the pedagogical uses of computers:

- You can use computers to foreground the process-oriented nature of successful writing. The fluid nature of electronic text and the capacity to write multiple drafts and revisions can help convey an understanding of the ongoing and evolving nature of successful writing. You can teach your students the difference between surface-level revision and deep or structural revision by having them use advanced word-processing features to track the changes they make to documents. You can also help them master the elements of format and document design.

- Electronic discussion tools can stimulate thinking and provide a space in which students can practice writing. You can create opportunities for students to express their ideas freely in writing using e-mail, blogs, or chat, and you can coordinate discussion activities with class readings or projects. You can further authorize student ideas by making public the transcripts of conversations or encouraging the citation of peer comments in formal class documents. If you appoint discussion moderators or provide credit for productive participation in any of these conversations, you will be enabling your students to take charge of their learning. These activities can also help your students evaluate the ways that conventions and media affect communication, and they can promote writing within a social context by showing students how to interact conversationally with groups outside of the classroom.

- Computers can promote collaboration and student-centered learning in numerous ways. You might employ file-sharing to simplify the logistics of group projects and peer review. You can teach students to use the comment and change-tracking functions of word processors to amplify their ability to conduct peer reviews. Web-based collaboration options can be used to create work spaces for small groups and to conduct peer-to-peer activities. You can even capitalize upon the different levels of computer literacy among your students, allowing the more skilled to mentor their peers about information technologies.

- Students can develop their research skills and information literacy by using computers. When you give research assignments to your students, you have an opportunity to help them learn to think and use resources critically. You can emphasize the ways that library and Internet research complement one another. At the same time, you can ask students to consider the relative advantages and disadvantages of print and electronic resources, and to evaluate electronic resources for credibility. You can show students how to find, manage, and document electronic research. You can learn to supplement your own courses by finding and providing appropriate learning resources for students (the most exciting of which may be related to ways of conducting primary research using Internet communications).

- One of the greatest advantages of information technologies is that they promote new forms of literacy. You'll need to teach your students to read electronic compositions critically and to look at elements of interactivity and design in terms of purpose and audience. You might conduct some comparisons between print and electronic compositions to explore the larger rhetorical issues addressed by each. You might also assign Web or other multimedia compositions to allow students to practice working with visual and hypertextual rhetoric, or you could craft Web composition assignments that ask students to manage and tap into selected Web resources. If you assign some Web pro-

jects, you can highlight the importance of audience and issues of publication as they relate to writing.

Computer technology in and out of the classroom

For many years the only practical way of integrating technology-related activities into your classes was through full or part-time use of a computer-assisted classroom. Today you may have a number of options when it comes to integrating technology into teaching, including the use of supplemental Internet resources, the use of a companion course Web site or blog, or the use of a computer-assisted classroom or lab.

The key to choosing the best option for integrating computer technology into your teaching is to take time to investigate the resources already available at your institution and to identify others which it might be feasible to develop. Begin by talking with your colleagues in technology support. Ideally, your institution will offer support in the form of technical infrastructure and instructional planning and design. Once you have established a good working relationship with people knowledgeable about the resources at your school, you can consider and choose among the numerous opportunities to adapt information technologies to the teaching of writing. Before leaping into the breach, however, you should acquaint yourself with some of the challenges associated with using instructional technologies and develop strategies that can make your efforts more successful.

The list below details some of those challenges and offers suggestions for how to address them.

- **Access**

You may find that your school has no computer-assisted lab or classroom facilities—or that the equipment in these facilities is outdated. Students may also have inadequate access to technology outside of class. Some students may own the latest computers, others may have three-year-old machines, and still others will have to use the computers in a lab or library. You may not be able to improve or equalize your students' access, but you can work to adapt to whatever level of access they have. If you will be working in a computer-assisted classroom, investigate the capabilities of the environment. If you will be asking students to do Internet work or to interact with a course Web site outside of class, check to make sure your students will have adequate access and make clear to your students what your expectations for participation are. It can be difficult to anticipate every contingency, but you should try to find out ahead of time what access problems are likely to arise and plan accordingly.

■ Skills and training

Once you've made sure that your students have access to adequate technological resources, the next step is to make sure that they have the skills necessary to accomplish technology-related work. Again, you'll need to investigate the options available to you and your students. Many institutions offer workshop training courses in computer basics and other aspects of technology. There are also many resources available online which can provide advice for learning about computer technologies (see the handbook's companion Web site). You could even make learning about technology a central focus of your course, something that you and your students do together. Allow knowledgeable students to take the lead in helping one another learn computer-related tasks: by "deputizing" them, you will not only relieve yourself of the burden of having to solve every technical problem, but you'll also foster collaborative work in your classroom.

■ Time demands

It is a cruel misconception that technology makes teaching and learning more efficient. If anything, you will find that using information technologies places heavy demands on your time. Not only must you devote yourself to learning new skills, but you must also invest energy into reconceiving the ways that you teach. The best strategy for protecting your time as you integrate new technologies into your teaching is to take small bites. Don't try to implement every option available to you for every class. In fact, you can build a highly successful semester around exploring a single computer-assisted activity. Additionally, rather than conducting or monitoring all computer-related work yourself, you can allow students to take charge of some of the class activities, appointing them to moderate class e-mail discussions or to spearhead class research expeditions.

■ Distractions

One of the most powerful aspects of instructional technology is its capacity to enable student-centered activities. There are some drawbacks, however. You may find that the computers become a distraction when you are trying to conduct a face-to-face discussion or present information to your class, or you may notice students drifting away from the task at hand or behaving inappropriately when interacting in electronic forums. A good way to address these potential distractions is to develop rules of decorum as a class. Early in the semester, talk over these concerns and decide upon conventions that you will follow during class activities. You may also want to build those rules right into your course requirements. For problems related to computers in the classroom, ask students to turn off their monitors or close the lids of their laptops when distractions become overwhelming.

■ Institutional culture

Not only does instructional technology place new demands on your time and energy, but it also prompts you to work in ways that may not be familiar to your colleagues or fit in with traditional categories used for promotion and reward. A related problem some teachers have is that they are isolated from other colleagues in the department, who may not actively be pursuing instructional technologies. Again, explore the context at your school as you consider how the technology-related work you do will fit in with your institution's culture. Ask administrators about their expectations for and ways of evaluating computer-related work. It may also help to establish contact with other members of your institution who use computers in their teaching and/or with Internet communities devoted to technology-based pedagogies (see the links at the end of this chapter).

Incorporating *The Little, Brown Handbook* into the wired classroom

Many instructors wonder how textbooks fit into the computer-assisted learning environment. At present, it is impossible to predict how soon, or if, the dominant medium for instructional publishing will shift from the bound book to an electronic medium. Remembering that access to computers may vary greatly, the tenth edition of

The Little, Brown Handbook and its ancillaries provide resources for teaching all phases of the writing process for instructors working in both electronic and traditional classroom environments. Additionally, the book design facilitates quick reference while working online through checklists and other emphasized material set aside in quickly identifiable tinted boxes, a list of which appears in the endpapers. Throughout the handbook are specific strategies for working with computers, and the companion Web site offers video tutorials, Web-only exercises, exercises from the handbook in Word format, and links to relevant Web sites.

■ Basic computer skills for writers

Basic computer skills for writers—organizing with a word processor, revising on screen versus on paper, and so on—are covered throughout Part 1 on the writing process. In addition, Chapter 3 emphasizes how computers can help break down the boundaries between prewriting and drafting and support collaborative work. Chapter 3 includes discussions of how students can use file management techniques to work on multiple drafts of papers, which will help them develop the understanding that successful writing results from an evolving and recursive process of prewriting, drafting, and revision. Students can also use file management and naming conventions to share and review one another's papers more easily; this will enable them to strengthen their writing based upon feedback and interaction with their peers. Chapter 3 also instructs students in the use of advanced word-processing features, such as Comment and Track Changes. Teaching students to use just one or two of these advanced functions is an easy way to promote process-oriented writing in a collaborative context.

Later in the book, Chapter 54 discusses options for using computers in the service of collaboration. Students are shown how to collaborate with classmates using e-mail and the Web (including Web-based courseware such as *Blackboard*, *WebCT*, or a Web log). The coverage includes strategies for interacting in class discussions, sharing files, and using online collaboration tools.

■ Editing and other sentence-level activities

Teaching grammar, mechanics, punctuation, and other sentence-level concerns with computers is a double-edged sword. While functions like spelling and style checkers offer powerful assistance in many situations, they can also lull a student into a false sense of security when it comes to editing her work. Furthermore, they can prove distracting, focusing undeserved attention on surface errors at times when deeper revision or drafting deserves the writer's full attention. Chapter 3 discusses these concerns in detail in order to help students develop a critical understanding of the value of spelling and grammar functions. It also offers instruction in how to customize spelling and grammar functions to maximize their usefulness.

Opportunities for using spelling and style checkers are noted throughout the handbook. These notations also warn students about problems that may arise from uncritical reliance on computer-based editing tools. Links to Web sites that offer additional exercises and instruction on sentence-level writing problems are given on the companion Web site.

■ Research-based writing

The research chapters cover the use of computers in the research process. Beginning with Chapter 42, "Planning a Research Project," the handbook distinguishes between online and print sources and explains how to find bibliographic information for online sources. Chapter 43, "Finding Sources," emphasizes using the library as Web gateway and includes coverage of keyword searches for both library and Internet sources, and the use of electronic catalogs, indexes, abstracts, and subscription services. Chapters 44 and 45, "Working with Sources" and "Avoiding Plagiarisim," discuss ways of evaluating and managing electronic materials, and warn about online plagiarism and explain how plagiarism can be detected by online tools. In addition, the four documentation sections—MLA, Chicago, APA, and CSE—provide the most up-to-date models for citing electronic sources in each style.

■ Document design

Chapter 5 shows students how to use computers to design academic papers and also provides guidance in the principles of electronic document design (including the role of flow, spacing, emphasis, color, fonts, and illustrations). Chapter 5 also includes guidelines on designing for readers with disabilities.

■ **Online communication and electronic documents**

Chapters 54–56 cover a range of opportunities for writing and communicating online. Chapter 54, "Writing Online," focuses on the rhetorical issues of writing e-mail, working in online collaborative writing environments, and composing online papers and original Web sites. Chapter 55, "Public Writing," contains guidelines for preparing an electronic, scannable résumé and a student sample. Chapter 56, "Oral Presentations," provides tips for working with PowerPoint and sample slides from a student presentation.

■ **Ancillaries to** *The Little, Brown Handbook*

For more ideas on using Internet resources in the writing classroom, Longman offers *Teaching Online: Internet Research, Conversation, and Composition*, prepared by Daniel Anderson, Bret Benjamin, Chris Busiel, and Bill Paredes-Holt. Instructors with little online experience will find basic definitions, numerous examples, and detailed information about using Internet resources in each chapter. Those more familiar with online resources can learn more about using e-mail and discussion lists to foster a workshop atmosphere in the classroom and using the Web to begin a research project. Chapter-end case studies and a sample research paper show numerous applications of online composition, conversation, and research.

Several other important ancillaries can benefit students and instructors alike, most notably the interactive e-book and the *MyCompLab* Web site. See page IAE-15 for a description. In addition, the handbook's companion Web site, besides offering the student features described on pp. IAE-51 to IAE-62, also provides a password-protected copy of this manual as well as transparency masters and *PowerPoint* slides.

■ **Other software programs: Computer learning environments and grammar programs**

Although you can incorporate technology into writing instruction with only a word processor, an e-mail program, and a Web browser, most instructors also have the option of teaching in a computer classroom or using an online learning package. Several software applications have been developed for use in a writing classroom, such as *WebCT* and *Blackboard*. These applications can assist instructors in structuring classroom activities and assignments and provide students and instructors with the opportunity to combine individual writing assignments with collaboration at any point in the writing process. Generally, these learning packages provide a chat option, file-sharing features, a class e-mail system or discussion forum, and the ability to post and collect assignments online. (A proprietary version of *Blackboard*, *Course Compass*, is available to adopters of the handbook, and the *MyCompLab* online resources are available as content cartridges for instructors who are already using *Blackboard* or *WebCT*.)

Applications devoted to issues of grammar, mechanics, and punctuation generally fall into one of two categories—tutorials or style checkers. Tutorials contain sets of questions (multiple choice, true/false, short answer) on various topics. They may also contain various levels of description and explanation of the topics covered, as well as diagnostic or proficiency tests. Tutorials currently available on the market include *Grammar-ROM*, *The Grammar Tree*, *The Grammar Key*, and *Easy English Grammar*, the last designed for ESL and EFL students. Grammar/style checkers examine writing for potential grammatical problems. *Microsoft Word* and *WordPerfect* include style checkers, and others available include *Grammar Slammer*, *Correct Grammar*, and *Grammatik*. Though occasionally useful in helping students spot specific flaws in their work, these applications should never be viewed as a substitute for careful and thorough editing. (For more information on using word-processor grammar and style checkers, see Chapter 3.)

■ **The companion Web site**

The accompanying companion Web site for *The Little, Brown Handbook* serves as an additional teaching tool for instructors, and a studying and practice tool for students. Here students will be able to practice their grammar skills with exercises, watch video tutorials to guide them through the writing process, and link to resources on the Web. Following is an outline of what can be found on the companion Web site:

5 Designing Documents

Video Tutorials

Working with illustrations on a word processor
Formatting documents on a word processor

Web Links

Good overall sites on document design
Color
Tables, figures, and images
Document and Web page design for readers with
    disabilities

6 Writing in Academic Situations

Exercises

Web-only Exercises
6.1   Revising in academic writing

Exercises from *The Little, Brown Handbook*
6.1   Using academic language *134*

Web Links

Academic writing

7 Studying Effectively and Taking Exams

Exercises

Web-only Exercises
7.1   Reading main points and supporting ideas
7.2   Summarizing

Web Links

Good overall sites for study skills and essay exams
Time management and organization
Taking notes
Reading
Summary
Essay exams

8 Forming a Critical Perspective

Exercises

Web-only Exercises
8.1   Reading a Web site critically

Exercises from *The Little, Brown Handbook*
8.3   Thinking critically *163–64*
8.9   Responding to critical writing *177–78*

Checklists from *The Little, Brown Handbook*

Guidelines for analysis, interpretation, and synthesis *158*
Guidelines for evaluation *163*

Web Links

Good overall sites on critical thinking
Reading journal
Summary
Analysis, interpretation, synthesis, and evaluation
Working with images
Critical writing

9 Reading Arguments Critically

Video Tutorial

Investigating assumptions

Exercises

Web-only Exercise
9.1   Identifying fallacies

Exercise from *The Little, Brown Handbook*
9.3   Identifying and revising fallacies *198*

Checklist from *The Little, Brown Handbook*

Questions for critically reading an argument *181*

Web Links

Good overall sites on reading arguments
Claims
Evidence
Assumptions
Fallacies

10 Writing an Argument

Video Tutorials

Finding subjects for argument
Answering opposing views

Exercises

Web-only Exercises
10.1   Choosing a suitable subject for argument
10.2   Evaluating thesis statements for argument

Exercises from *The Little, Brown Handbook*
10.1   Finding a subject for argument *200*
10.4   Reasoning inductively *206*
10.5   Reasoning deductively *206–07*
10.7   Identifying appeals *211*
10.11 Critically reading an argument *218*

Exercises

Web-only Exercises

17.1   Sentence fragments
17.2   Subordinate clauses as sentence fragments
17.3   Other sentence fragments

Exercises from *The Little, Brown Handbook*

17.1   Identifying and revising sentence fragments *337–38*
17.2   Revising: Sentence fragments *340–41*
17.3   Revising: Sentence fragments *341*

Web Links

Sentence fragments

18 Comma Splices and Fused Sentences

Video Tutorial

Recognizing comma splices

Exercises

Web-only Exercises

18.1   Comma splices and fused sentences
18.2   Comma splices and fused sentences: Main clauses without *and, but,* etc.
18.3   Comma splices and fused sentences: Main clauses with *however, for example,* etc.

Exercises from *The Little, Brown Handbook*

18.1   Identifying and revising comma splices *347*
18.2   Identifying and revising fused sentences *348–49*
18.3   Sentence combining: Comma splices and fused sentences *349*
18.4   Revising: Comma splices and fused sentences *349*

Web Links

Comma splices and fused sentences

19 Pronoun Reference

Video Tutorial

Recognizing pronoun reference problems

Exercises

Web-only Exercises

19.1   Pronoun reference: Clear and close reference
19.2   Pronoun reference: Specific reference [Indefinite *it, they, you*]

Exercises from *The Little, Brown Handbook*

19.1   Revising: Ambiguous and remote pronoun reference *352–53*

19.2   Revising: Indefinite and inappropriate pronoun reference *356*
19.3   Revising: Pronoun reference *356–57*

Web Links

Pronoun reference

20 Shifts

Exercises

Web-only Exercises

20.1   Shifts in person and number
20.2   Shifts in tense and mood
20.3   Shifts in subject and voice
20.4   Shifts in quotations and questions

Exercises from *The Little, Brown Handbook*

20.1   Revising: Shifts in person and number *359*
20.2   Revising: Shifts in tense and mood *360–61*
20.3   Revising: Shifts in subject and voice *361*
20.4   Revising: Shifts in direct and indirect quotations and questions *362–63*
20.5   Revising: Shifts *363*

Web Links

Shifts

21 Misplaced and Dangling Modifiers

Video Tutorial

Repairing misplaced modifiers

Exercises

Web-only Exercises

21.1   Misplaced modifiers: Unclear placement
21.2   Misplaced modifiers: Awkward placement
21.3   Position of adverbs and adjectives
21.4   Dangling modifiers

Exercises from *The Little, Brown Handbook*

21.1   Revising: Misplaced phrases and clauses *365*
21.2   Using limiting modifiers *366*
21.3   Revising: Squinting modifiers *366*
21.4   Revising: Separated sentence parts *368*
21.5   Revising: Placement of adverbs and adjectives *370*
21.6   Revising: Dangling modifiers *372–73*
21.7   Sentence combining: Placing modifiers *373*
21.8   Revising: Misplaced and dangling modifiers *373*

31 Quotation Marks

Exercises

Web-only Exercise
31.1 Quotation Marks

Exercises from *The Little, Brown Handbook*
31.1 Using double and single quotation marks *471*
31.2 Quoting titles *473*
31.3 Revising: Quotation marks *475–76*
31.4 Revising: Quotation marks *476*

Web Links
Quotation marks

32 Other Punctuation Marks

Exercises

Web-only Exercises
32.1 Colons, dashes, parentheses
32.2 The ellipsis mark

Exercises from *The Little, Brown Handbook*
32.1 Revising: Colons *479*
32.2 Revising: Dashes *481–82*
32.3 Revising: Parentheses *483*
32.4 Using ellipsis marks *486–87*
32.5 Revising: Colons, dashes, parentheses, brackets, ellipsis marks, slashes *487–88*

Review
27–32 Revising: Punctuation *488*

Web Links
Other punctuation marks

33 Capitals

Exercises

Web-only Exercise
33.1 Capitals

Exercise from *The Little, Brown Handbook*
33.1 Revising: Capitals *495–96*

Web Links
Capitals

34 Underlining or Italics

Exercises

Web-only Exercise
34.1 Underlining or italics

Exercise from *The Little, Brown Handbook*
34.1 Revising: Underlining or italics *499–500*

Web Links
Underlining or italics

35 Abbreviations

Exercises

Web-only Exercise
35.1 Abbreviations

Exercise from *The Little, Brown Handbook*
35.1 Revising: Abbreviations *503–04*

Web Links
Abbreviations

36 Numbers

Exercises

Web-only Exercise
36.1 Numbers

Exercise from *The Little, Brown Handbook*
36.1 Revising: Numbers *506–07*

Review
33–36 Revising: Mechanics *507–08*

Web Links
Numbers

37 Using Appropriate Language

Video Tutorial
Using appropriate language

Exercises

Web-only Exercises
37.1 Standard American English
37.2 Unbiased and gender-neutral language

Exercise from *The Little, Brown Handbook*
37.1 Revising: Appropriate words *517–18*

Web Links
Good overall sites
Colloquial language
Slang
Standard American English
Unbiased and gender-neutral language

38 Using Exact Language

Exercises

Web-only Exercises
38.1   Denotation and connotation
38.2   Idioms

Exercises from *The Little, Brown Handbook*
38.1   Revising: Denotation *520*
38.2   Considering the connotations of words *521*
38.3   Revising: Concrete and specific words *522–23*
38.4   Using concrete and specific words *523*
38.5   Using prepositions in idioms *525*
38.6   Analyzing figurative language *527*
38.7   Using figurative language *527*
38.8   Revising: Trite expressions *528–29*

Web Links
Clichés
Denotation and connotation
Idioms

39 Writing Concisely

Video Tutorial
Sentence combining

Exercises

Web-only Exercises
39.1   Focusing on subject and verb
39.2   Cutting empty words and repetition

Exercises from *The Little, Brown Handbook*
39.1   Revising: Subjects and verbs; empty words and phrases *532*
39.2   Revising: Unnecessary repetition *533–34*
39.3   Revising: Conciseness *535–36*
39.4   Revising: Conciseness *536*

Web Links
Good overall sites
Sentence combining

40 Using Dictionaries

Exercise from *The Little, Brown Handbook*
40.1   Using a dictionary *541–42*

Web Links
Using dictionaries

41 Spelling and the Hyphen

Exercises

Web-only Exercises
41.1   Spelling
41.2   The hyphen

Exercises from *The Little, Brown Handbook*
41.1   Distinguishing between *ie* and *ei* *546*
41.2   Keeping or dropping a final *e* *547*
41.3   Keeping or dropping a final *y* *547*
41.4   Doubling consonants *548*
41.5   Forming plurals *549*
41.6   Using hyphens in compound words *556*

Web Links
Good overall sites
Commonly misspelled words
Hyphens in compound words

42 Planning a Research Project

Video Tutorial
Finding source information

Exercises

Web-only Exercise
42.1   Finding source information

Checklists from *The Little, Brown Handbook*
Scheduling steps in research writing *560*
Information for a working bibliography *569*

Web Links
Research journal
Finding a subject and question
Research strategy

43 Finding Sources

Video Tutorial
Using keywords with a search engine

Exercises

Web-only Exercise
43.1   Searching electronically

Exercise from *The Little, Brown Handbook*
43.1   Using the library *597–98*

Web Links
Good overall sites
Keyword searches

Web Links
> Business writing
> Reports and proposals
> Designing flyers, newsletters, brochures, and other
>   public documents
> Writing for community and service learning projects

56 Oral Presentations

Video Tutorial
> Designing a *PowerPoint* presentation

Web Links
> Oral presentations
> Using *PowerPoint*
> Collections of effective speeches

Usage Flashcards

Instructor Resources
> Transparency Masters
> Web Links

Sample schedule for a first-year composition course

The following schedule represents one possible way of structuring a composition course using *The Little, Brown Handbook* and relying on computer-assisted activities. The schedule assumes that you use a course Web site, blog, or e-mail to supplement class activities and that your students have access to computers and support resources. Students will complete four major projects during the course; these may either be graded individually or collectively in a portfolio, depending on your institution's requirements.

In the objectives-and-requirements portion of your syllabus, be sure to explain fully any requirements involving technology as you would any others. For example:

- Require that students back up all their work. Make it known that technical difficulties such as lost or damaged files are unacceptable excuses for not turning in assignments.
- Clarify requirements for participation in online components of the course, while taking into account that some students may need to participate as "lurkers" for a week or two before involving themselves in conversations.

- If you expect students to attend computer-related workshops or complete computer-related tasks such as obtaining e-mail accounts, provide them with handouts and schedules that will help them do so.

Week 1
General course introduction, including objectives; discussion of requirements—assignments, participation, attendance. Complete writing sample, if desired. Introduction to course Web site. Make sure students have e-mail accounts and can check them regularly. Make sure students have access to computers for class activities. Establish conventions for online behavior. Assign Chapter 1.

Week 2
Discussions of purpose and audience in writing, using various examples from online and printed sources. Assign first essay. Discuss invention techniques and have students apply to first assignment. Have students begin using online class discussion e-mail list for brainstorming or to discuss class readings. Assign Chapters 2–4.

Week 3
Draft of first essay due. Discuss and model peer response techniques. Have students review each other's work. Review drafts yourself, focusing on scope and suitability to objectives of the assignment. Establish small groups for semester activities. Conduct peer responses using the Comment and Track Changes functions on a word processor or embedded comments in e-mail or forum postings of papers. Review peer responses, focusing on attention to deepest levels of revision. Continue online discussion exchanges to brainstorm topics or discuss revision strategies.

Week 4
Discuss problem areas individually or in small groups with students, or e-mail suggestions on drafts, focusing on larger organization and meaning problems and one or two sentence-level concerns, and referring students to appropriate handbook chapters. Assign Chapter 5. Continue online discussions to brainstorm topics, discuss class readings, or plan final revision strategies. First essay due.

Week 5
Assign second essay. Employ small groups for prewriting and invention work using e-mail or class Web

tools. Assign Chapter 54. Begin drafting essays. Continue Web forum or class e-mail exchanges to brainstorm topics, discuss class readings, or converse about issues of collaboration.

Week 6

Model successful peer responses using samples from the first essay. Conduct peer response exercise using word-processing Comment and Track Changes functions, embedded comments in e-mail, or forum postings of papers. Revise drafts.

Week 7

Second essay due. Assign third essay (research-based). Assign Chapters 42–43. In-class introduction to research techniques. Continue online discussions to brainstorm topics, discuss class readings, or converse about research issues and strategies.

Week 8

Online discussions of research projects: work in class to compile working bibliography of online and print sources. Discuss bibliographic tools and conventions. Browse discussion-group archives to explore topics. Continue online discussions to brainstorm topics, explore class readings, or discuss assignment.

Week 9

Assign Chapters 44–46. Continue browsing discussion-group archives. Working bibliography due. Begin drafting essay. Continue online discussions to brainstorm topics, explore class readings, or discuss assignment.

Week 10

Individual conferences during class with students on their projects. Model successful integration of quotation, paraphrase, and summary. Continue online discussions to brainstorm topics, explore class readings, or discuss research assignment.

Week 11

Peer response to research projects. Final revisions. Research projects due. Continue online discussions to brainstorm topics, explore class readings, or discuss research assignment.

Week 12

Assign fourth project—a problem/solution proposal, based on research essay, for students not in computer-

assisted classrooms, or a Web site exploring the research topic for students in computer-assisted classrooms. Assign Chapter 54 for Web projects. Continue online discussions to brainstorm topics, explore class readings, or discuss final assignment.

Week 13

Web-building workshop for Web project. Additional research and modeling of formats for proposal project. Continue online discussions to brainstorm topics, explore class readings, or discuss research assignment.

Week 14

Drafts due. Discuss and implement uploading of Web projects. Peer reviews in small groups. Continue online discussions to brainstorm topics, explore class readings, or discuss research assignment.

Week 15

In-class editing. Final drafts due. Course evaluations. Final online discussions to evaluate course and assignments.

Resources for using computers to teach writing

Books

Bolter, Jay David, and Richard Grusin. *Remediation: Understanding New Media.* Cambridge: MIT, 1999.

Borgman, Albert. *Holding on to Reality: The Nature of Information at the Turn of the Millennium.* Chicago: U of Chicago P, 1999.

Hawisher, Gail, and Cynthia Selfe, eds. *Passions, Pedagogies and 21st Century Technologies.* Logan: Utah State UP, 1999.

Hobson, Eric. *Wiring the Writing Center.* Logan: Utah State UP, 1998.

Joyce, Michael. *Of Two Minds: Hypertext, Pedagogy, and Poetics.* Ann Arbor: U of Michigan P, 1995.

Kalmbach, James R. *The Computer and the Page: Publishing, Technology, and the Classroom.* Norwood, NJ: Ablex, 1997.

Kiesler, Sara. *Culture of the Internet.* Mahwah, NJ: Erlbaum, 1997.

Landow, George. *Hypertext 2.0: The Convergence of Contemporary Critical Theory and Technology.* Baltimore: Johns Hopkins, 1997.

Nardi, Bonnie A., and Vicki L. O'Day. *Information Ecologies: Using Technology with Heart.* Cambridge: MIT, 1999.

O'Donnell, James J. *Avatars of the Word: From Papyrus to Cyberspace.* Cambridge: Harvard UP, 1997.

Porter, James E., and Patricia Sullivan. *Opening Spaces: Writing Technologies and Critical Research.* Norwood, NJ: Ablex, 1997.

Reiss, Donna, and Dickie Self, eds. *Electronic Communication Across the Curriculum.* Urbana: National Council of Teachers of English, 1998.

Snyder, Ilana, and Michael Joyce, eds. *Page to Screen: Taking Literacy into the Electronic Era.* London and New York: Routledge, 1998.

Taylor, Todd W., and Irene Ward, eds. *Literacy Theory in the Age of the Internet.* New York: Columbia UP, 1998.

Tyner, Kathleen. *Literacy in a Digital World: Teaching and Learning in the Age of Information.* Mahwah, NJ: Erlbaum, 1998.

Welch, Kathleen. *Electric Rhetoric: Classical Rhetoric, Oralism and a New Literacy.* Cambridge: MIT, 1999.

Journals

CCC
College English
Computers and Composition
Currents in Electronic Literacy
Journal of Advanced Composition
Kairos

Listservs

Rhetnt-L
    Devoted to issues of electronic publishing and composition.
    web.missouri.edu/~rhetnet/roadmap.html

TESL-L
    For educators interested in issues related to teaching English as a second language.
    www.hunter.cuny.edu/~tesl-l/
WPA-L
    Geared toward issues of teaching writing as they relate to writing centers.
    www.english.ilstu.edu/Hesse/listserv.htm

MOOs

Lingua MOO
    lingua.utdallas.edu
Diversity University
    www.du.org

Web sites

Writing@CSU: For Teachers
    writing.colostate.edu/instructors.cfm
Computer Teaching Tips
    www.emunix.emich.edu/~krause/Tips
MyCompLab
    www.ablongman.com/mycomplab
Computer Writing and Research Lab
    www.cwrl.utexas.edu
CourseCompass
    www.coursecompass.com
Courses in Cyberculture
    www.com.washington.edu/rccs/courselist.asp
SITES Instructional Tool Resources
    sites.unc.edu/tools
SITES Teaching Pages
    sites.unc.edu
Traci's Lists of Ten
    www.tengrrl.com/tens/index.shtml
The World Lecture Hall
    web.austin.utexas.edu/wlh

CHAPTER **6**

Teaching Writing to ESL Students

By Jocelyn Steer and Dawn Schmid

The composition instructor's reaction to having ESL students in a class of native speakers can be a mixture of pleasure and apprehension. On the one hand, students using English as a second language can introduce a fresh perspective to class discussions and in their written work. Competing with this positive response to the richness of cultural diversity, however, may be a feeling of trepidation at entering into the syntactical and lexical labyrinth of the ESL student's written world. There is no question about it: ESL writers struggle with a number of language problems that do not beset native speakers and for which writing instructors may not have quick solutions. However, encouraging ESL writers to become outspoken members of the class and shaping the overall goals of the class to include ESL needs provides benefits for native and nonnative speakers alike.

This chapter is intended to help instructors find their way within that ESL labyrinth. It presents a profile of ESL students, an overview of how culture shapes their notions about learning and composing, a description of effective approaches to teaching writing to ESL students, and some guidelines for evaluating their writing. A cursory look at the most common grammatical errors found in ESL writing and a list of print and online resources for teaching ESL students are also included.

Profile of ESL students

The ESL label indicates that a student's first language is not English, but it says nothing about the student's country of origin or reasons for being at college and very little about specific language problems. In fact, ESL students are a remarkably heterogeneous group, about which it is often difficult to make any generalizations. One of the first and most important distinctions to make is between international and permanent resident students.

Generally speaking, international students (also referred to as foreign students) reside permanently in another country and obtain student (F-1) visas in order to study in a school in the United States. Their stay in the United States is usually funded by their families, their place of employment, their government, or their own savings. Their countries of origin vary; they come to the United States in waves, affected by global political and economic events.

Most likely these international students have had previous formal English language instruction in their home country or in the United States. Students trained in their home countries have probably had heavy doses of grammar, vocabulary, and reading, with some translation. Although they will be proficient readers with good command of grammar, they may lack ease and confidence in speaking up in class. Their written work may be mechanically accurate but lack fluency and appropriate organization. International students who have learned English at a language institute in this country will have a higher degree of oral fluency and some basic notions about the conventions of higher education in the United States.

Unlike international students, permanent residents usually do not plan to return to their home country. Their reasons for staying in the United States are varied and may include the need for political asylum, economic advancement, and family ties.

Most students admitted to the United States with refugee status have come for political, not economic, reasons. Refugee students have come from places such as Cambodia, Vietnam, Laos, Eastern Europe, Latin America, Haiti, Ethiopia, and Somalia. Many came to the United

States as children and went through the public school system here; others are adults who have decided to return to school to get a better job. Students who graduate from a high school in the United States and who are permanent residents are usually admitted to universities and colleges without submitting a Test of English as a Foreign Language (TOEFL) score, which is required of international students.

Not all permanent residents are refugees seeking political asylum. Many have come to the United States for family or employment reasons. Immigrants are given a resident alien card (a "green card"), which does not grant them citizenship but does allow them to reside permanently in the United States and to work here legally. After a number of years, green card holders may apply for citizenship and become naturalized citizens. Immigrants are given permanent resident status for many reasons; for example, they may have married a US citizen or have been sponsored by a family member. Immigrant students usually acquire English informally, so their spoken English is quite fluent, but their written English requires more formal instruction to achieve the same fluency and accuracy.

Obviously, ESL students have varying degrees of language ability in speaking, reading, and writing. You can also expect to see wide gaps in socioeconomic status among ESL students in the same class, even among those from the same country, and such differences may create friction. ESL students may also hold varying attitudes toward the United States, ranging from open anti-American hostility to a Pollyanna-like view of the United States as the epitome of freedom and opportunity. This range of attitudes can provide an interesting basis for in-class discussions by including a variety of perspectives and by stimulating native speakers to rethink their cultural assumptions.

Cross-cultural issues

Some ESL students will freely admit to being in a mild state of confusion much of the time during their academic experience. Clearly, a large portion of this confusion may be attributed to having to read and write at a very sophisticated level in a language that they have not yet mastered. There are also cultural factors less visible to the student and the instructor: the unwritten, but well-entrenched, conventions of the academy. These range from the acceptable forms of compiling a research paper to the appropriate ways of addressing an instructor. Because of their prior experience and training, native speakers may be somewhat familiar with these academic conventions, while ESL students may not even know that they exist. However, one advantage in having ESL writers as active participants in a class is that their questions can propel the class as a whole to discover the reasons for conventions that often seem puzzlingly arbitrary. In some cases ESL students know the "rules" of grammar far better than the native speakers and can be called upon to share that expert knowledge.

■ Ideas about learning

ESL students may approach the learning situation from a schema formed largely by their experiences in their first culture. For example, many Latin cultures foster more cooperative learning, whereas Japan adheres to a hierarchical, teacher-dominated model. While these cultural generalities cannot be presumed to apply to individual students, they can be useful in sensitizing us to our own cultural assumptions. The situation in a college classroom may well shock ESL students—the informality of instructors who sit on the desk, classmates who openly disagree with or interrupt their professors. Such students are not comfortable with the open discussion format in which American students feel free to express their opinions, whether or not those opinions align with the professor's. Instructors may view their more quiet ESL students as resistant or unprepared, when in fact these students are showing respect by remaining silent.

In some cultures, professors are expected to mentor and guide students to a greater extent than they do in the United States. Thus, many ESL students may feel that their professors do not do enough for them. It is not unusual for an ESL student to bring in a piece of writing for another class and ask the composition instructor to correct it. Or some students may attempt to negotiate grades because they "need" that grade for a scholarship or admission to a school, and they may be visibly disappointed when an instructor refuses to change a grade. While a teacher in the United States may interpret such behavior as impertinent, the student may view it as a chance for the instructor to use his or her power to further the student's career. And while ESL students may find the informality of the classroom surprising, many find constant testing, penalties for absences, and general surveillance on the part of the instructor to be offensive to their sense of maturity. Many ESL students have attended foreign universities that do not monitor student behavior so closely.

Cross-cultural discussions in which students trace how basic assumptions result in varying styles of learning behavior may be useful for both ESL and native-speaking students. Many ESL students benefit from such discussions because they wish to conform to the conventions of their school in order to enjoy academic success. Similarly, such explorations can help native speakers develop sensitivity to these cross-cultural issues.

■ Contrastive rhetoric

Cross-cultural analyses of ESL student writing can also be fruitful. Cultures express ideas using different organizational patterns and types of support, and the written and unwritten rules governing what is considered appropriate writing in the culture are transmitted to children in school. It is not surprising, therefore, that ESL students use these first-language writing strategies when they compose in English. The result may be a grammatically correct piece of writing with an idiosyncratic development.

Instructors need to apply the principles of contrastive rhetoric cautiously. Although it is not necessary to undertake an extensive study of the rhetorics of all languages, it is important to recognize how a culture shapes its members' expectations of good writing. An instructional approach that places too much emphasis on contrastive rhetoric, on the other hand, is reductionistic. Such an approach would fail to account for a specific writer's process, potentially misinterpreting a writer's lack of experience as interference from first-language writing strategies. (For a detailed discussion of contrastive rhetoric, consult Ilona Leki's *Understanding ESL Writers: A Guide for Teachers*.)

■ Levels of support and specificity

One important feature of ESL writing that varies among cultures is the level of support and specificity required for assertions. It is not always obvious to ESL writers that facts and statistics are usually considered to be the strongest method of support in English and that when a student makes an assertion, that assertion must be supported with specific examples or quantifiable measures. Other cultures may rely on the hierarchical, rather than the scientific, model of proof. It is not unusual, for example, to have ESL students use quotes from the Koran or statements made by a political leader as evidence for their assertions. Students will need practice in identifying and supplying the kinds of support expected in academic writing in English.

Another central issue in cross-cultural analyses of texts is the level of explicitness expected in academic writing. English is a "writer-responsible" language: the onus is on the writer to present ideas clearly and succinctly. If the reader has difficulty with a text, the blame usually rests with the writer and not the reader. We expect to have the main points stated directly and clearly in a piece of writing, which may help to explain some of our frustration at reading a piece of writing by an ESL student who does not share the same expectation.

This distinction is especially pertinent to native writers of Japanese and Chinese, which are "reader-responsible" languages. Japanese and Chinese readers do not expect the writer to link information and draw conclusions; they expect to do that as readers (Cowie). A Japanese student explained this when asked why she used transitions so sparingly and never seemed to tie up her examples with a general statement: she said that doing so would be insulting to Japanese readers, who are expected to be informed and sensitive enough to be able to make those inferences on their own.

■ Attitudes toward plagiarism

American students who commit plagiarism have a sense that it is an academic offense. ESL students, however, may come from countries where plagiarism, although not completely ethical, is more easily overlooked or accepted. Research and writing in the United States is prized for its originality, but this is not the case in all cultures. Some ESL students may have been taught to incorporate great writing from their culture into their own work out of respect for those scholars. For some students, plagiarism may be a way of coping with their uncertainty about their own lexical abilities (Currie). Other students may be too modest to believe that they can paraphrase the writing of a respected author.

Of course, many ESL students copy for the same reasons American students do—because it's easier, faster, and sure to be more fluent. Whether or not your students are guilty, they need to be warned that plagiarism is unacceptable in a college in the United States. Be sure to discuss the issue of plagiarism early in the semester and invite students to share their understanding of the differences between quoting, paraphrasing, and plagiarizing. Students will benefit from explicit classroom discussion of different cultural attitudes toward what constitutes plagiarism, instruction in how to distinguish between borrowing of words and borrowing of ideas, and plenty of practice with paraphrasing, summarizing, and citing sources. Chapter 45 can be particularly useful here in showing students examples of unacceptable writing with plagiarized sections.

■ **Topic selection**

Topics that seem to be extremely pertinent to the lives of your native speakers may be inappropriate or difficult for ESL writers. An essay on breaking away from family or living on one's own, for example, may have no meaning for those ESL students who expect to live with their families until they get married. In fact, you may find that your ESL students are more comfortable writing about impersonal subjects than those designed to facilitate self-discovery. Other topics may offend certain groups of students because of their religious beliefs—living together before marriage, gay rights, evolution. We have assigned what seemed to be an innocuous topic—"superstitions in my culture"—only to find out that the Islamic religion does not tolerate superstitions. At the same time, some topics will be more appealing to ESL students, who are often better informed about and more interested in topics dealing with global issues than are American students.

Issues in working with ESL writing

The above discussion of cross-cultural differences in organization, style, and topic selection underscores the need to provide ESL students with guidelines and models of academic writing so that they can function smoothly and successfully in the college culture. Yet there is a danger—as there is in any acculturation process—of placing too great a value on the expected and accepted form of the writing and too little value on the writer's discovery of voice.

■ **Process versus product approach to writing**

This dilemma between emphasizing the product over the process of writing is not a new one but one that takes on a slightly different slant when applied to teaching writing to ESL students. An approach that emphasizes the conventions of academic discourse provides ESL students with models of discipline-specific writing that they can emulate, along with guidelines for operating within that discipline. It has been our experience that ESL students welcome this type of instruction. Since they lack the cultural and linguistic schema of native speakers, they benefit from explicit instruction in how to complete academic tasks. Essay-test prompts are an excellent example of this: native speakers have a better notion than ESL students of what is meant by "discuss," for example. By the same token, when ESL students feel free to raise questions about the wording of assignments, the whole class often benefits from the discussion. Assignments that allow students to practice writing essay exams, critical reviews, laboratory reports, case reports, and so on will also help to equip students with the necessary tools for their academic careers.

The danger in such an approach is that students may begin to rely more on the imposed model of academic communication than on their own voice and expression. The result may be mimicry rather than inspiration. This is especially true for ESL students who enter the writing process haltingly. An approach that emphasizes the process of brainstorming, sharing ideas, and collaborating on a topic nurtures ESL students' wavering self-confidence as writers in a second language. By engaging students in the discovery of ideas, this approach also distracts them from ruminating over potential surface errors.

Since a process approach to writing does not outline a single "accepted" product, it encourages students to identify their own personal style first before reconciling that with the models of writing endorsed by the academic community. Yet we would be remiss if we failed to provide our ESL students with those models. Clearly, a combination of the two approaches, without overreliance on product or neglect of process, will serve your ESL students best. As with any student it is important to focus on the strengths of an ESL writer's work and to suggest one or two issues for revision rather than to view the paper as a minefield of errors.

▪ Attitudes toward errors

While research indicates that ESL students need more work with actual composing than with language development (Zamel, "Composing"), it may be difficult persuading your ESL students of this. They may believe that good writing means producing grammatically correct sentences. They see errors as obstacles to good writing, and unlike many native speakers, they do not perceive them as symbols of personal failure. They expect to make mistakes since they are learning a second language, and they expect those errors to be corrected. Leki's survey on student perceptions of teacher feedback supports what any ESL teacher might have predicted: students believe that error correction is important. Out of 100 ESL college students surveyed, 91 percent believed that it was very important to have as few errors as possible in their writing, and 93 percent stated that it was important to have the teachers correct the errors.

It was once thought that errors in a second language were the result of interference from the first language. For example, if writers had problems with word order in English, this was because they were applying first-language rules of word order to the second language. Now, however, it is largely believed that most ESL errors are the result of an "interlanguage," a system for communicating in the second language that the student has developed based on what he or she knows about the second language.

Theoretically, this interlanguage is constantly changing as the learner mentally reorganizes what is known about the language. This is an important point and a distinction between the native English and ESL writers. During the course of a semester, your ESL students will probably make a great deal of progress in English because their language-acquisition process is still activated. Their improvement will result not only from your class but also from exposure to other sources of language input. The more that students write, the more likely they are to improve their writing. According to Cowie, the act of writing and revising itself is key to improving student writing at both surface and global levels.

Viewing ESL errors as temporary edifices supporting an ESL writer's ideas lends credence to the argument against correcting every single error in an ESL composition. These errors will disappear as students gain more control over the second language. Errors that seem to be careless mistakes to the reader may not be that at all. They may be the student's individual system for organizing English structure, which will change as the student acquires more language. Nor is it uncommon for advanced ESL students to regress temporarily in their language accuracy as they struggle with new forms and constructions.

You may have some students in your class who have been in the United States for quite some time and who for some reason may have reached a plateau; second-language researchers say that these students' errors are "fossilized." It is not clear why fossilization occurs, but it is clear that working with fossilized errors can be difficult. Distinguishing between errors that occur as the result of fossilization and those that occur because of interlanguage is important; unlike interlanguage errors, which remit spontaneously with increased exposure to the language, fossilized errors require more explicit and direct treatment.

▪ Techniques for responding to ESL writing

As an experienced composition instructor, you have probably developed a variety of techniques and strategies for providing effective feedback to your students. (In this manual, "Working with Student Writing" on pp. IAE-20 to IAE-33 provides guidelines for responding to student work.) Below are some suggested techniques and strategies that may be especially helpful in providing feedback to your ESL students.

Sometimes students are confused about what to do with feedback. Research (Conrad and Goldstein) suggests that students have difficulty revising when asked to develop their points by being more explicit, explaining, or analyzing. Providing students with training in how to respond to feedback will enable them to produce better revisions (Currie; Conrad and Goldstein). Moreover, if you use peer feedback in your class, you may find that students from cultures where the teacher is considered the source of knowledge and truth do not take into account their peers' feedback when revising. In this case, it is important to train students in how to give effective peer feedback as well as how to receive it (Cowie; Nelson and Carson).

In general, it is best to provide feedback on grammar, punctuation, and spelling in earlier drafts so that students can incorporate those corrections into subsequent drafts.

Students are not as likely to benefit from feedback that is offered on a final draft; they will often look at the grade, read the comments quickly, and file the paper away. However, you can encourage attention to final drafts by asking for localized revisions of a particular pattern of error or of a paragraph. Students can also be encouraged to make note of their common patterns of error and to keep revised examples as a resource for the next paper.

There is no one method for drawing students' attention to sentence-level errors, but generally it is best to locate the error for the student and have the student correct the error on a subsequent draft. Leki's survey found that students like to be given a clue regarding the nature of the error. A numbering system for the most basic errors (for example, verb tense, number agreement, word order, spelling, punctuation, and word form) works well because students seem to respond better to numbers than to abbreviations or words (for example, *sp*, *awk*), and they become familiar with the errors they tend to make often. The correction code in the handbook is easy to use; it includes a number-and-letter system that directs students to the appropriate section in the handbook that deals with the error. (See pp. IAE-22 to IAE-24 for a more detailed description of the correction code.) It is most useful to identify one or two significant patterns of error (subject-verb problems and misused articles, for example) rather than correct every example of error.

Some errors—often those pertaining to sentence boundaries, clause structure, and choice of words—cannot be identified by circling and numbering. When the writer's meaning is unclear, avoid the temptation to rewrite the sentence for the student. You may find your interpretation to be quite different from what the student intended. It's best to ask the student to rewrite the passage.

A concern that continues to surface when dealing with ESL writing is knowing what and how much to correct. As noted earlier, students make many errors; some of them may be careless mistakes, but more likely the sentences were carefully constructed using the students' still-developing knowledge of English structure and vocabulary. Correcting ESL work seems to be more an art than a science because the instructor needs to gauge the particular student's threshold for error correction and identify the errors that the student will benefit from knowing about.

We have also found that students are very receptive to and benefit a great deal from immediate, oral feedback, especially when they solicit it. Students often ask for help with grammar and vocabulary during in-class writing, and they almost always incorporate those revisions into their writing.

Some teachers and students find it helpful to keep track of repeated errors. Using a numbering system such as the one mentioned above can facilitate this process. (See p. 69 in the handbook for a model that can be used to track errors.) In any case, it is very important to recommend or require that students consult the handbook. Not only will it help clarify a confusing grammatical point, but it will also teach students to edit their work independently, an extremely important skill for the ESL student.

■ Evaluation

The question of evaluation is a thorny one in composition classes comprising both native and nonnative speakers. Some of the questions that come up are: How do I compare the two? Will I need to lower my standards? Should I expect error-free writing from my ESL students? Should I give a grade to each draft? How many revisions should I allow before assigning a grade?

Keep a few points in mind when deciding how to evaluate ESL writers. First, the ESL student is writing in a second (or third or fourth) language. It is next to impossible to achieve native fluency and accuracy in a second language, especially when the learner began acquisition as an adult. Thus, we need to consider whether it is realistic to expect ESL students to produce error-free writing.

Research (Santos) has indicated that college professors in disciplines other than English tend to be more forgiving of ESL-type errors than of native speakers' errors, which they regard as careless. In addition, although ESL students may not always produce fluent English, their prior training and knowledge in their field of study may far exceed that of their native-speaker classmates. Professors may be delighted to have their input, both in writing and in class discussions, because of the value of their comments and diverse points of view for the class. In such cases, the standards of these professors and their discipline may be less stringent than those maintained in the composition class.

When assigning grades to ESL students, consider a few guidelines that may make the situation more equitable for ESL writers. If at all possible, allow students the opportunity to write multiple drafts that are not graded. This will permit ESL writers the opportunity to refine a piece of writing to their satisfaction. A split grade for the content (for example, organization, development, exemplification) and form (for example, the grammar, spelling, and punctuation) sometimes proves beneficial, especially when ESL students have many good ideas but still struggle with expression. Such a grading system helps students focus on the specific areas in which their writing needs improvement (Song and Caruso). Other solutions include assigning a satisfactory/unsatisfactory grade for work done during the semester and requiring a portfolio of the student's best work at the end of the class. (See pp. IAE-29 to IAE-31 for a discussion of portfolios.) The final grade is based on the final portfolio and not the individual assignments.

A final, very important consideration is the time it takes for ESL students to complete written work. It may seem obvious that ESL writers need more time to complete their assignments, but even after many years of teaching ESL students, we are still surprised at the amount of time they actually do need. All writers need help getting started, but ESL writers seem more frightened of that first sentence than native speakers do. It's almost as if they believe that once they put that first sentence down, they are wed to it forever. As Ann Raimes has said, "The first sentence restricts them before they have begun to develop their ideas" (261). This need for more time also has implications for in-class and timed writing assignments. Research (Polio, Fleck, and Leder) has shown that ESL students can self-correct their papers when given extra time, even without feedback from the teacher. If at all possible, allow students a flexible schedule of deadlines.

Sentence-level errors in ESL writing

English composition instructors know a great deal about grammar and punctuation, but many who have not worked extensively with ESL students are puzzled by the errors such students make. Below are a few areas of grammar that are especially troublesome to many ESL students. All these trouble spots are discussed and illustrated in *The Little, Brown Handbook*. For more detailed explanations, consult Marianne Celce-Murcia and Diane Larsen-Freeman's *Grammar Book*, Second Edition, a specialized ESL reference grammar for the instructor, Jocelyn Steer and Karen Carlisi's *Advanced Grammar Book*, Second Edition, an ESL grammar textbook with an accompanying workbook by Jocelyn Steer and Dawn Schmid, or *Teaching English as a Second or Foreign Language,* Third Edition, edited by Marianne Celce-Murcia.

■ Verb tenses

ESL students have difficulty with verb tenses and forms of helping verbs. Some tenses in English are straightforward and usually have a direct translation in most languages. These include the past tense, the future tense, and in some cases the present tense. However, other tenses (for example, present progressive and the present perfect) do not have equivalent forms in some languages. (See handbook section 14g.)

■ Helping verbs

Students often have difficulty choosing the appropriate form of the helping verb in a sentence. You may encounter sentences like *He should has been gone* rather than *He should have gone*. (See handbook section 14d.)

■ Verb endings

ESL students often leave off the *-ed* endings on verbs used in the passive (*It was return*) and in the past perfect tense (*I had return it*). One explanation may be that they do not hear the *-ed* ending in spoken English. (See handbook sections 14c and 14d.) They also often forget to add the *-s* or *-es* ending on present-tense verbs in the third-person singular (*He go; it don't work*) but can correct this error immediately when it is pointed out. It's a good idea to have your ESL students check their papers for subject-verb agreement before handing them in to you. (See handbook section 15a.)

■ Verbs with gerunds or infinitives

One particularly difficult area for ESL students to master is the use of a gerund or an infinitive after a verb. Some English verbs may be followed by a gerund (*He recommended going*). Others may be followed by an infinitive (*I want to go*). Some may be followed by either a gerund or an infinitive with no change in meaning (*I continued eating; I continued to eat*). Finally, some verbs may be followed by either form, but with a change in meaning (*I stopped smoking yesterday; I stopped to smoke*). (See handbook section 14e.)

◼ Count and noncount nouns

The distinction between count and noncount nouns in English is especially troublesome for ESL students because correct choice of article or quantifier and agreement with the verb depend on the differences. When ESL students first learn about count and noncount nouns, they are told that count nouns (*book/books; girl/girls*) are easily divided and counted, whereas noncount nouns are not. This rule is fine for the clear-cut examples such as *water*, *cheese*, or *love*. However, when students learn that *money* is a noncount noun, the rule seems to fall apart: who hasn't counted money easily and successfully? (See handbook section 16h.)

◼ Articles

Choosing an appropriate article is extremely trying for ESL students, especially students whose native language (e.g., Japanese, Chinese) does not have articles. It is equally trying for ESL teachers to explain why a definite article is used instead of an indefinite one. Once again, students learn rules to guide them in their choices. (See handbook section 16h.)

◼ Verbs with particles

Students often complain about prepositions in English. These combinations of verbs and so-called particles (some of them adverbs) are particularly confusing: what may seem to be a simple construction of two (or three) words has a specific meaning that cannot be discerned from the meanings of the specific verb and preposition. There are literally hundreds of these idiomatic constructions. (See handbook section 14f.)

Conclusion

Initially, you may feel overwhelmed by the number of errors your ESL students make, and you may even harbor some resentment that you have to spend so much time correcting them. In such cases, it's important to remember that these students are still learning the language as well as writing skills. Don't feel compelled to correct every single mistake. Help students instead to develop and organize their ideas. And keep in mind that it may take your

ESL students a long time before they write without making a lot of errors.

As you can see, ESL students—regardless of the cultural or socioeconomic group they may be from—confront a number of obstacles in their daily college lives. Most of these students spend an enormous amount of energy simply listening to lectures and trying to understand the language and the cultural content of what the instructor is saying. Anyone who has lived in a foreign country and listened to a foreign language continuously knows how exhausting negotiating simple tasks in the foreign culture can be. As their instructor, you have a chance to assist your students in this process of acculturation to the academic community and to give them the encouragement they need to succeed in their academic endeavors.

Print and online resources for teaching ESL students

Print resources

Auerbach, Elsa Roberts. "The Politics of the ESL Classroom: Issues of Power in Pedagogical Choices." In *Power and Inequality in Language Education.* Ed. James Tollefson. Cambridge: Cambridge UP, 1995. 99–133.

Braine, George. "ESL Students in First-Year Writing Courses: ESL Versus Mainstream Classes." *Journal of Second Language Writing* 5 (1996): 91–107. Includes examples of rubrics for evaluating compositions.

Celce-Murcia, Marianne, and Diane Larsen-Freeman. *The Grammar Book.* 2nd ed. Boston: Heinle and Heinle, 1999. The updated edition of an excellent reference book on ESL grammar for instructors.

Connor, Ulla. *Contrastive Rhetoric: Cross-Cultural Aspects of Second-Language Writing.* New York: Cambridge UP, 1996.

Conrad, Susan M., and Lynn M. Goldstein. "ESL Student Revision after Teacher-Written Comments: Text, Contexts, and Individuals." *Journal of Second Language Writing* 8 (1999): 147–79.

Cowie, Neil. "Students of Process Writing Need Appropriate and Timely Feedback on Their Work, and in Addition, Training in Dealing With That Feedback." *Saitama University Review* 31 (1995): 181–94. ERIC

Document ED 417581. Includes a summary of the research and practical suggestions for giving effective feedback on student papers.

Currie, Pat. "Staying Out of Trouble: Apparent Plagiarism and Academic Survival." *Journal of Second Language Writing* 7 (1998): 1–18.

Klein, Deborah. "Iago Lives in the Panopticon, or, Teaching Resistance, Granting Respect." *College English* 62 (1999): 169–91.

Kroll, Barbara, ed. *Second Language Writing: Research Insights for the Classroom.* New York: Cambridge UP, 1990. An interesting and often-cited collection of articles by distinguished researchers in second-language writing.

Leki, Ilona. "The Preferences of ESL Students for Error Correction in College Level Writing Classes." *Foreign Language Annals* 24 (1991): 203–14.

———. *Understanding ESL Writers: A Guide for Teachers.* Portsmouth, NH: Boynton/Cook/Greenwood-Heinemann, 1992. An often-cited text.

Matsuda, Paul. "Composition Studies and ESL Writing: A Disciplinary Division of Labor." *College Composition and Communication* 50 (1999): 699–721. A history of the development of ESL instruction as a profession separate from composition instruction; includes a helpful listing of titles of several second-language and composition-study journals.

Mlynarczyk, Rebecca Williams. *Conversations of the Mind: The Uses of Journal Writing for Second-Language Learners.* Mahwah, NJ: Erlbaum, 1998.

Nelson, Gayle L., and Joan G. Carson. "ESL Students' Perceptions of Effectiveness in Peer Response Groups." *Journal of Second Language Writing* 7 (1998): 113–31.

Polio, Charlene, Catherine Fleck, and Nevin Leder. "If I Had More Time: ESL Learners' Changes in Linguistic Accuracy on Essay Revisions." *Journal of Second Language Writing* 7 (1998): 43–68.

Raimes, Ann. "Anguish as a Second Language? Remedies for Composition Teachers." *Composing in a Second Language.* Ed. Sandra McKay. Rowley: Newbury, 1984.

———. "Out of the Woods: Emerging Traditions in the Teaching of Writing." *TESOL Quarterly* 25 (1991): 407–30.

Reid, Joy M. *Teaching ESL Writing.* White Plains, NY: Pearson Education ESL, 1993. A comprehensive text with an overview of native speaker and ESL composition; includes specific information for syllabus and course development, responding to and evaluating student writing, and classroom activities.

Santos, Tony. "Professors' Reactions to the Academic Writing of Nonnative-Speaking Students." *TESOL Quarterly* 22 (1988): 69–90.

Song, Bailin, and Isabella Caruso. "Do English and ESL Faculty Differ in Evaluating the Essays of Native English-Speaking and ESL Students?" *Journal of Second Language Writing* 5 (1996): 163–82. Includes a sample writing assessment test, evaluation scale, and analytic assessment sheet for rating ten essay components.

Steer, Jocelyn, and Karen Carlisi. *The Advanced Grammar Book.* 2nd ed. Boston: Heinle and Heinle, 1998. Presents grammar principles in context for ESL students.

Steer, Jocelyn, and Dawn Schmid. *The Advanced Grammar Book 2nd ed. Workbook.* Boston: Heinle and Heinle, 1998. Highly contextualized practice of grammar principles for ESL students.

Zamel, Vivian. "The Composing Process of Advanced ESL Students: Six Case Studies." *TESOL Quarterly* 17 (1983): 165–87.

———. "Strangers in Academia: The Experiences of Faculty and ESL Students Across the Curriculum." *The Writing Teacher's Sourcebook.* 4th ed. Ed. Edward P. J. Corbett et al. New York: Oxford UP, 2000. 100–12.

Online resources

The ESL Links Site

www.esldesk.com/esl-links/index.htm

A list of online ESL resources. Provides access to grammar resources, online quizzes, games, English dictionaries, and dictionaries that translate from English to other languages. Lists writing, reading, and listening resources. Includes links to related sites.

Purdue University Writing Lab

owl.english.purdue.edu/handouts/esl/eslstudent.html

A directory of Web sites about ESL resources for students, compiled by the Purdue University Writing Lab. Includes links to information about online courses, grammar, vocabulary, quizzes, listservs, and games.

Dave's ESL Cafe

eslcafe.com/

A collection of ESL resources for students and teachers. Includes chat rooms and discussion forums, mailing lists, and an ESL quiz center with questions on current news, grammar, idioms and slang, reading comprehension, writing, and world culture. Includes phrasal verbs arranged in a complete list, by meanings and examples, and by random phrasal verbs from the collection. Contains a FAQ section.

The Little, Brown Handbook

TENTH EDITION

H. Ramsey Fowler
St. Edward's University

Jane E. Aaron

PEARSON
Longman

New York   Boston   San Francisco
London   Toronto   Sydney   Tokyo   Singapore   Madrid
Mexico City   Munich   Paris   Cape Town   Hong Kong   Montreal

Publisher: Joseph Opiela
Acquisitions Editor: Brandon Hight
Development Manager: Mary Ellen Curley
Development Editor: Carol M. Hollar-Zwick
Executive Marketing Manager: Megan Galvin-Fak
Senior Supplements Editor: Donna Campion
Media Supplements Editor: Jenna Egan
Production Manager: Donna DeBenedictis
Project Coordination, Text Design, and Electronic Page Makeup: Nesbitt
    Graphics, Inc.
Cover Design Manager: John Callahan
Cover Designer: Kay Petronio
Cover Photos: Top left: Paul Hardy/CORBIS. Top right: Tom Stewart/
    CORBIS. Bottom center: Peter M. Fisher/CORBIS. Bottom left:
    Picturequest. Background: Bob Diffenderfer
Photo Researcher: Vivette Porges
Senior Manufacturing Buyer: Alfred C. Dorsey
Printer and Binder: R.R. Donnelley & Sons Company/Crawfordsville
Cover Printer: Phoenix Color Corporation

The authors and publisher are grateful to the many students who allowed
their work to be reprinted here and to the copyright holders who are listed
on pages 905–06, which are hereby made part of this copyright page.

Library of Congress Cataloging-in-Publication Data

Fowler, H. Ramsey (Henry Ramsey)
  The Little, Brown handbook / H. Ramsey Fowler, Jane E. Aaron.-- 10th ed.
    p. cm.
  Includes index.
  ISBN 0-321-38951-4
  1. English language--Grammar--Handbooks, manuals, etc. 2. English
language--Rhetoric--Handbooks, manuals, etc. 3. Report writing--
Handbooks, manuals, etc. I. Aaron, Jane E. II. Title.
PE1112.F64 2006
808'.042--dc22

                                                              2005037704

Copyright © 2007 by Pearson Education, Inc.

Please visit us at *ablongman.com/littlebrown.*

ISBN 0-321-38951-4

1 2 3 4 5 6 7 8 9 10—DOC—09 08 07 06

Preface for Students: Using This Book

The Little, Brown Handbook is a basic resource that will answer almost any question you have about writing. Here you can find how to get ideas, punctuate quotations, search the Internet, cite sources, or write a résumé. The handbook can help you not only in writing courses but also in other courses and outside school.

Don't let the size of the handbook put you off. You need not read the whole book to get something out of it, and no one expects you to know everything included. Primarily a reference tool, the handbook is written and arranged to help you find the answers you need when you need them, quickly and easily.

Using this book will not by itself make you a good writer; for that, you need to care about your work at every level, from finding a subject to spelling words. But learning how to use the handbook and its information can give you the means to write *what* you want in the *way* you want.

■ Reference aids

You have many ways to find what you need in the handbook:

- **Use the directory.** "Plan of the Book," inside the front cover, displays the book's entire contents.
- **Use a glossary.** "Glossary of Usage" (pp. 864–80) clarifies more than 275 words that are commonly confused and misused. "Glossary of Terms" (pp. 881–904) defines more than 350 words used in discussing writing.
- **Use the index.** Beginning on page 907, the extensive index includes every term, concept, and problem word or expression mentioned in the book.
- **Use a list.** Three helpful aids fall inside the book's back cover: (1) "CULTURE LANGUAGE Guide" pulls together all the book's material for students using standard American English as a second language or a second dialect. (2) "Editing Symbols" explains abbreviations often used to comment on papers. And (3) "Useful Lists and Summaries" indexes topics that students frequently ask about.
- **Use the elements of the page.** As shown in the illustration on the next page, the handbook constantly tells you where you are and what you can find there.

The handbook's page elements

Running head (header) and page tab showing the topic being discussed on this page, its section code (**15b**), and its editing symbol (**pn agr**)

Section heading, a main convention or topic labeled with the section code, **15b**: chapter number (**15**) and section letter (**b**)

Examples, always indented, with underlining and annotations highlighting sentence elements and revisions

Summary or checklist box providing key information in accessible form

Web box linking to the handbook's companion Web site

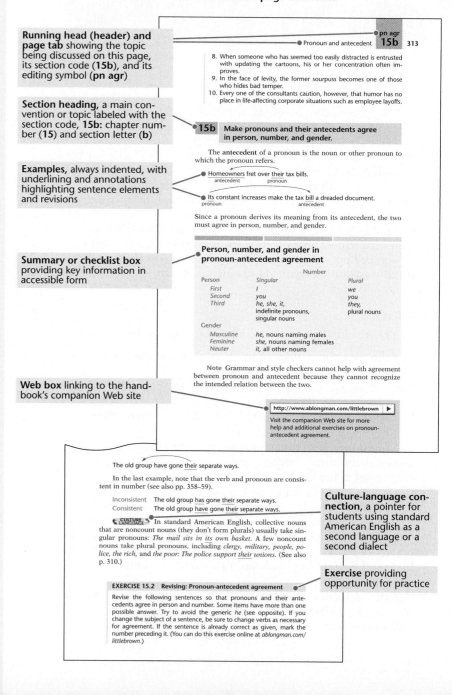

pn agr
15b 313

Pronoun and antecedent

8. When someone who has seemed too easily distracted is entrusted with updating the cartoons, his or her concentration often improves.
9. In the face of levity, the former sourpuss becomes one of those who hides bad temper.
10. Every one of the consultants caution, however, that humor has no place in life-affecting corporate situations such as employee layoffs.

15b **Make pronouns and their antecedents agree in person, number, and gender.**

The **antecedent** of a pronoun is the noun or other pronoun to which the pronoun refers.

Homeowners fret over their tax bills.
  antecedent   pronoun

Its constant increases make the tax bill a dreaded document.
pronoun   antecedent

Since a pronoun derives its meaning from its antecedent, the two must agree in person, number, and gender.

Person, number, and gender in pronoun-antecedent agreement

Person	Number Singular	Plural
First	I	we
Second	you	you
Third	he, she, it, indefinite pronouns, singular nouns	they, plural nouns

Gender	
Masculine	he, nouns naming males
Feminine	she, nouns naming females
Neuter	it, all other nouns

Note Grammar and style checkers cannot help with agreement between pronoun and antecedent because they cannot recognize the intended relation between the two.

http://www.ablongman.com/littlebrown ▶

Visit the companion Web site for more help and additional exercises on pronoun-antecedent agreement.

The old group have gone their separate ways.

In the last example, note that the verb and pronoun are consistent in number (see also pp. 358–59).

| Inconsistent | The old group has gone their separate ways. |
| Consistent | The old group have gone their separate ways. |

CULTURE LANGUAGE In standard American English, collective nouns that are noncount nouns (they don't form plurals) usually take singular pronouns: *The mail sits in its own basket.* A few noncount nouns take plural pronouns, including *clergy, military, people, police, the rich,* and *the poor: The police support their unions.* (See also p. 310.)

EXERCISE 15.2 Revising: Pronoun-antecedent agreement

Revise the following sentences so that pronouns and their antecedents agree in person and number. Some items have more than one possible answer. Try to avoid the generic *he* (see opposite). If you change the subject of a sentence, be sure to change verbs as necessary for agreement. If the sentence is already correct as given, mark the number preceding it. (You can do this exercise online at *ablongman.com/littlebrown.*)

Culture-language connection, a pointer for students using standard American English as a second language or a second dialect

Exercise providing opportunity for practice

■ Content and organization

An overview of the handbook's contents appears inside the front cover. Briefly, the book divides into the following sections:

- **Chapters 1–5:** The big picture, including the writing process, paragraphs, and document design.
- **Chapters 6–11:** Reading and writing in college, with chapters on academic writing, study skills and exams, critical reading and writing, reading arguments, writing arguments, and reading and using visual arguments.
- **Chapters 12–26:** Sentence basics, including the conventions of English grammar, errors that affect clarity, and techniques of effective sentences.
- **Chapters 27–36:** Punctuation and mechanics (capital letters, underlining, and the like).
- **Chapters 37–41:** Words—how to use them appropriately and precisely, how to look them up, how to spell them.
- **Chapters 42–48:** Research writing, from planning through revising, with detailed help on finding and evaluating electronic sources, a complete guide to citing sources, and two sample papers.
- **Chapters 49–53:** Writing in the academic disciplines, including literature, the other humanities, the social sciences, and the natural and applied sciences.
- **Chapters 55–56:** Practical information about online writing, business and other public writing, and oral presentations.

■ Recommended usage

The conventions described and illustrated in this handbook are those of standard American English—the label given the dialect used in higher education, business, and the professions. (See also pp. 132–33.) The handbook stresses written standard English, which is more conservative than the spoken dialect in matters of grammar and usage. A great many words and constructions that are widely spoken remain unaccepted in careful writing.

When clear distinctions exist between the language of conversation and that of careful writing, the handbook provides examples of each and labels them *spoken* and *written*. When usage in writing itself varies with the level of formality intended, the handbook labels examples *formal* and *informal*. When usage is mixed or currently changing, the handbook recommends that you choose the more conservative usage because it will be acceptable to all readers.

■ Companion Web site

The companion Web site offers many resources to help you use the handbook and improve your writing. You can use the site on your own (it is not password protected), or your instructor may direct you to portions of it as part of his or her course assignments.

Go to *ablongman.com/littlebrown,* and click on *The Little, Brown Handbook,* Tenth Edition. You'll see further directions to the following:

- Downloadable checklists and other material from the book.
- The book's exercises in electronic format.
- More than a thousand additional electronic questions.
- Video tutorials that supplement the book's explanations.
- Hundreds of links to other Web sites providing help on the book's topics.
- Sample research papers from various academic disciplines.
- Usage flashcards allowing you to test yourself on tricky words and phrases.

Preface for Instructors

The Little, Brown Handbook always aims to address both the current and the recurrent needs of writing students and teachers. This tenth edition is no exception. Writing and its teaching are changing dramatically, and the handbook has changed in response. At the same time, much about writing does not change, and the handbook remains a comprehensive, clear, and accessible guide to a host of writing situations and challenges.

The Little, Brown Handbook is actually many books in one, and each is stronger in this edition. The revisions—highlighted below with New—affect most pages.

■ A guide to academic writing

The handbook gives students a solid foundation in the goals and requirements of college writing.

- New Part 2 now covers the skills needed for academic success, beginning with a new chapter that helps students analyze and compose in academic writing situations.
- New A chapter provides practical tips for effective study skills, including time management, reading for comprehension, and preparing for and taking exams.
- Four chapters detail techniques of critical reading and writing, reading arguments critically, writing arguments, and reading and using visual arguments.
- Later chapters discuss the emphases and methods of writing about literature and writing in other humanities, the social sciences, and the natural and applied sciences. Extensive, specially highlighted sections cover documentation and format in MLA, Chicago, APA, and CSE styles.

■ A guide to research writing

With detailed advice and two sample MLA papers, the handbook always attends closely to research writing, keeping pace with changes in its methods and challenges.

- The discussion emphasizes using the library as Web gateway, managing information, evaluating and synthesizing sources, integrating source material, and avoiding plagiarism.
- New Guidelines and samples explain how to prepare an annotated bibliography, whether descriptive or evaluative.

- **New** Library subscription services receive even greater emphasis. In addition to a detailed, annotated sample search, the text now provides help with choosing databases and brainstorming keywords.
- **New** Web logs are covered as possible sources requiring careful evaluation and documentation.
- **New** Using images as research sources receives close attention, including a guide to image banks.
- **New** An expanded discussion of evaluating Web sites includes tips for distinguishing scholarly, personal, commercial, and other kinds of sites.
- **New** MLA documentation now includes annotated samples of key source types, showing students how to find the bibliographical information needed to cite each type.
- **New** The extensive coverage of documentation in four styles—MLA, Chicago, APA, and CSE—reflects each style's latest version and includes more electronic sources, such as Web logs and multimedia.

A guide to visual literacy

The handbook helps students process visual information and use it effectively in their writing.

- **New** An expanded section on using illustrations includes annotated examples.
- **New** An expanded discussion of viewing images critically uses diverse examples to demonstrate identifying and analyzing visual elements.
- **New** A student paper illustrates a critique of an image.
- **New** A chapter on reading and using visual arguments focuses on images' claims, evidence, assumptions, appeals, and fallacies.
- **New** Illustrations in many of the handbook's student papers show various ways in which visual information can support written ideas.

A guide to the writing process

The handbook takes a practical approach to assessing the writing situation, generating ideas, writing the thesis statement, revising, and other elements of the writing process.

- Numerous examples, including a student work-in-progress on Internet communication, illustrate every stage.
- **New** A student paper shows techniques for achieving whole-essay unity and coherence.
- **New** Managing files, using a spelling checker, and other computer skills are now integrated into discussions of revision and editing.

- New The extensive material on document design, now concluding the chapters on the writing process, includes more help with using illustrations and a section on designing for readers with disabilities.

■ A guide for culturally and linguistically diverse writers

At notes and sections labeled ⟨ **CULTURE LANGUAGE** ⟩, the handbook provides extensive rhetorical and grammatical help for writers whose first language or dialect is not standard American English.

- Fully integrated coverage, instead of a separate section, means that students can find what they need without having to know which problems they do and don't share with native SAE speakers.
- New "⟨ **CULTURE LANGUAGE** ⟩ Guide," inside the back cover, orients students with advice on mastering SAE and pulls all the integrated coverage together in one place.

■ A guide to usage, grammar, and punctuation

The handbook's core reference material continues to be reliable and accessible.

- Concise text explains all basic concepts and common errors.
- Annotated examples from across the curriculum represent college writers and writing.
- Frequent exercises in connected discourse include end-of-part exercises that combine several kinds of problems. The exercises are also available on the book's companion Web site.

■ An accessible reference guide

The handbook is designed to be easy to use.

- New A clean, uncluttered page design uses color and type clearly to distinguish elements.
- New Annotations on both visual and verbal examples directly connect principles and illustrations.
- New Dictionary-style headers in the index make it easy to find entries.
- Helpful endpapers offer several paths to the book's content.
- More than 150 boxes provide summaries and checklists of key information.
- A preface just for students outlines the book's contents, details reference aids, and explains the page layout.

■ A reference for college and beyond

With chapters on document design, study skills, academic and cross-curricular writing, online writing, public writing, and oral presentations, the handbook is a resource that students keep. With a hard cover and sturdy binding, it is a book that lasts.

- New A chapter on writing online focuses on the rhetorical issues of e-mail, collaboration, and Web composition.
- New A chapter on public writing covers writing for business and for community work, with annotated samples of letters, résumés, and a memo, report, proposal, flyer, newsletter, and brochure.
- New The chapter on oral presentations now includes a discussion and illustrations of *PowerPoint* slides.

■ An integrated text and Web site

At the start of every handbook chapter, a Web box links students to the book's companion Web site, a powerful online resource for students and teachers.

- New Most of the handbook's exercises can now be completed online. A cross-reference to the Web site appears in the instruction of each dual-format exercise.
- More than a thousand additional self-study questions, keyed to the handbook, provide immediate feedback for every answer.
- Fifteen of the handbook's checklists are available for students to copy and use in generating ideas and revising their work.
- More than thirty video tutorials provide explanations, examples, and tips to help students understand concepts and techniques.
- Hundreds of Web links direct students to helpful sites on the writing process, critical thinking, argument, grammar, research, writing in the disciplines, and more.
- Ten documented student research papers provide examples of writing across the curriculum.
- Usage flashcards allow students to test their knowledge and practice usage.
- The "Instructor's Resources" section provides links to material from the print *Instructor's Resource Manual* and *Instructor's Annotated Edition*, including teaching tips and answers to the handbook's exercises. It also provides lists and summaries from the handbook in transparency and *PowerPoint* format and links to Web sites that are useful to writing teachers.

■ Supplements

In addition to the companion Web site, an extensive package of supplements accompanies *The Little, Brown Handbook* for both students and instructors.

For students

An asterisk precedes every supplement that is free to students when it is packaged with *The Little, Brown Handbook.*

- **MyCompLab* with the E-book of *The Little, Brown Handbook* offers comprehensive online resources in grammar, writing, and research in one dynamic, accessible place:

  Grammar resources include *ExerciseZone,* with more than three thousand self-grading practice questions on sentences and paragraphs; and *ESL ExerciseZone,* with more than seven hundred self-grading questions.

  Writing resources include a hundred writing activities involving videos, images, and Web sites; guided assistance through the writing process, with worksheets and exercises; and an extensive collection of sample papers from across the disciplines.

  Research resources include *ResearchNavigator,* which provides help with the research process, the *AutoCite* bibliography maker, and access to *ContentSelect* by EBSCOhost and the subject-search archive of the *New York Times;* and *Avoiding Plagiarism,* which offers tutorials in recognizing plagiarism, paraphrasing, documenting sources in MLA or APA style, and other topics.

  Other student features of *MyCompLab* include *Grade Tracker,* a system for tracking work on the site, and access to *Longman's English Tutor Center,* offering live help from qualified writing teachers.

- *The Little, Brown Workbook,* by Donna Gorrell, parallels the handbook's organization but provides many more exercises and briefer instructional text. A separate answer key is available.

- **ESL Worksheets,* by Jocelyn Steer and Dawn Schmid, provides nonnative speakers with extra practice in typical problem areas.

- **Longman Grammar and Documentation Study Card* is a laminated eight-page guide to key writing skills.

- Many supplements help students in and out of writing courses: **10 Practices of Highly Successful Students; *The Longman Writer's Portfolio and Student Planner; *The Longman Writer's Journal; *The Longman Researcher's Journal; *Peer-Evaluation Manual; *Analyzing Literature: A Guide for Students; *Visual Communication;* and the Literacy Library, consisting of **Academic Literacy, *Workplace Literacy,* and **Public Literacy.*

- Four references are available: **The New American Webster Handy College Dictionary; *The Oxford American Desk Dictionary and Thesaurus; *The Oxford Essential Thesaurus;* and *The Oxford American College Dictionary.*

- Two programs provide resources at deep discounts: any Penguin title can be packaged with the handbook; and *Newsweek* magazine is available to students in twelve-week subscriptions.

For instructors

All of the following supplements are free to confirmed adopters of *The Little, Brown Handbook*.

- *MyCompLab* offers a wealth of teaching resources:

  MyCompLab Faculty Teaching Guide helps instructors make the most of this extensive resource.

  Online course-management versions are available in *Course Compass, Blackboard,* and *WebCT.*

  MyDropBox, a leading online plagiarism detection service, is available to instructors who adopt the handbook in a Value Pack.

- *Instructor's Annotated Edition* of *The Little, Brown Handbook* provides a complete teaching system in one book. Integrated with the student text are essays on teaching, updated reading suggestions, specific tips for class discussions and activities, and answers to the handbook's exercises.

- *Instructor's Resource Manual to Accompany The Little, Brown Handbook* is a freestanding, two-color paperback that includes all the teaching material and exercise answers from the *Instructor's Annotated Edition.*

- *The Little, Brown Handbook Answer Key* provides answers to the handbook's exercises.

- *Diagnostic and Editing Tests and Exercises* are cross-referenced to the handbook and are available on reproducible sheets or on CD.

- *Longman's Teaching Resource Library* includes works on both theory and practice.

Acknowledgments

The Little, Brown Handbook stays fresh and useful because instructors talk with Longman's sales representatives and editors, answer questionnaires, write detailed reviews, and send us personal notes.

For the tenth edition, we are especially grateful to the many instructors who communicated with us directly or through reviews, drawing on their rich experience to offer insights into the handbook and suggestions for its improvement: Dale T. Adams, Lee College; Jonathan Ausubel, Chaffey College; Mark Bernier, Blinn College; Jacqueline A. Blackwell, Thomas Nelson Community College; Winfred P. Bridges, Arkansas State University; Daniel Brigham, University of Colorado, Boulder; Lynnda L. Brown, Tulsa Community College; Melania Rosen Brown, St. Johns River Community College; Michael Burke, Southern Illinois University, Edwardsville; Mary Joanne de Falla, Miami Dade College, InterAmerican; Suzanne Gitonga, North Lake College; Kyle S. Glover, Lindenwood University; Maurice A. Hunt, Baylor University; Lori Kanitz, Oral Roberts University; Patricia Kramer, Rock Valley College; William J. Kupinse, University of Puget Sound; Judith H. McKibbon, Jacksonville State University; Susan T. Peters, East Central College; Ingrid Schreck, College of Marin; Annette Olsen-Fazi, Louisiana State University, Alexandria; Rita Wade Perkins, Camden County College; R. G. Rader, Passaic County Community College; Elizabeth L. Rambo, Campbell University; Gardner Rogers, University of Illinois, Urbana-Champaign; John Schaffer, Blinn College; Eric G. Waggoner, West Virginia Wesleyan College; and Pavel Zemliansky, James Madison University.

In responding to the ideas of these thoughtful critics, we had the help of many creative people. Carol Hollar-Zwick, development editor and sine qua non, is our ideal for can-do attitude, smart thinking, and gentle encouragement. Brooke Hessler, Oklahoma City University, served invaluably as a consultant on visual literacy and research writing; her ideas infuse this edition. Caroline Crouse, University of Minnesota, guided us through the labyrinth of the contemporary library. Susan Smith Nash, Excelsior College, advised us on disabilities issues and new technologies. And Sylvan Barnet, Tufts University, continued to lend his expertise in the chapter "Reading and Writing About Literature," which is adapted from his *Short Guide to Writing About Literature* and *Introduction to Literature* (with William Burto and William E. Cain).

A superb team helped us make this book. At Longman, Brandon Hight, the book's sponsor, offered perceptive insights into instructors' and students' needs. He and Rebecca Gilpin, assistant editor, responded enthusiastically to our many needs. Megan Galvin-Fak, marketing manager, provided helpful ideas at key moments in development. Donna DeBenedictis applied a long view and a sharp eye to overseeing production. At Nesbitt Graphics, Jerilyn Bockorick created both the striking new design and the clear page layouts, and Susan McIntyre worked her now-customary miracles of scheduling and management to produce the book. We are grateful to all these collaborators.

Contents

PART 1

The Writing Process

HIGHLIGHTS

Teachers know that writing is *not* easy, but students, especially beginning writers, often have the misconception that writing comes easily to experienced writers and is hard only for the untalented or inexperienced. This chapter begins by recognizing the difficulties faced by all writers, experienced and inexperienced alike. Next, the chapter alerts students to the various elements of the writing situation and the writing process and discusses ways to discover and limit subjects. The concluding sections explore flexible strategies for considering audience and defining a purpose for writing. Special features of this chapter are the attention paid to the role of audience and purpose throughout the composition process and the list of "Questions About Audience" (p. 11).

Although Chapters 1 and 2 look at activities typical of the early stages of composing and Chapter 3 treats drafting and revising, the text does not endorse a strictly linear view of the composing process. Instead, all three chapters emphasize the writer's many options and the flexibility of the composing process. They point out that writing is a way of thinking and discovering: that in the middle of drafting an essay a writer may recognize the need to develop new supporting ideas, to make major changes in the organization, or to shift the purpose of the essay and modify the thesis.

COMPANION WEB SITE

See page IAE-51 for companion Web site content description.

CHAPTER 1

Assessing the Writing Situation

"Writing is easy," snarled the late sportswriter Red Smith. "All you do is sit down at the typewriter and open a vein." Most writers would smile in agreement, and so might you. Like anything worthwhile, writing well takes hard work. This chapter and the next two will show you some techniques that successful writers use to ease the discomfort of writing and produce effective compositions.

1a Understanding how writing happens

Every time you sit down to write, you embark on a **writing process**—the term for all the activities, mental and physical, that go into creating what eventually becomes a finished piece of work. Even for experienced writers the process is usually messy, which is one reason that it is sometimes difficult. Though we may get a sense of ease and orderliness from a well-crafted magazine article, we can safely assume that the writer had to work hard to achieve those qualities, struggling to express half-formed thoughts, shaping and reshaping paragraphs to make a point convincingly.

There is no *one* writing process: no two writers proceed in the same way, and even an individual writer adapts his or her process to the task at hand. Still, most experienced writers pass through overlapping stages:

- **Analyzing the writing situation:** considering subject, purpose, audience, and other elements of the project (pp. 4–15).
- **Developing or planning:** gathering information, focusing on a central theme, and organizing material (pp. 16–43).
- **Drafting:** expressing and connecting ideas (pp. 44–48).
- **Revising and editing:** rethinking and improving structure, content, style, and presentation (pp. 48–65).

http://www.ablongman.com/littlebrown ▶

Visit the companion Web site for more help and additional exercises on the writing situation and the writing process.

The writing process

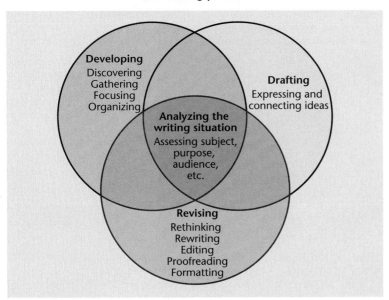

With experience, as you complete varied assignments and try the varied techniques described in this book, you will develop your own basic writing process.

Note Like many others, you may believe that writing is only, or even mainly, a matter of correctness. True, any written message will find a more receptive audience if it is correct in grammar, spelling, and similar matters. But these concerns should come late in the writing process, after you've allowed yourself to discover what you want to say, freeing yourself to make mistakes along the way. As one writer put it, you need to get the clay on the potter's wheel before you can shape it into a bowl, and you need to shape the bowl before you can perfect it. So get your clay on the wheel, and work with it until it looks like a bowl. Then worry about correctness.

AT EASE

Students often bring their apprehensions about writing (and writing instructors) with them to class. To create a positive atmosphere for your course, you may wish to establish a setting in which students feel at ease about acknowledging and sharing their apprehensions. One way to do this is to ask them to *list* what they dislike (and like) about writing without worrying about the form or correctness of entries in their lists. Voluntary sharing of the entries can help reduce the isolation many students feel and help you (and them) set priorities for instruction.

EXERCISE 1.1   Starting a writing journal

Recall several writing experiences that you have had—a letter you had difficulty composing, an essay you enjoyed writing, an all-nighter spent happily or miserably on a term paper, a posting to an online newsgroup that received a surprising response. What do these experiences reveal to you about writing, particularly your successes and problems with it? Consider the following questions:

ANSWERS: EXERCISE 1.1

Individual response.

RESOURCES AND IDEAS

Ball, Kevin and Amy Goodburn. "Composition Studies and Service Learning: Appealing to Communities?" *Composition Studies* 28.1 (2000): 79–94. The authors are critical of service learning pedagogy which too often excludes the voices of community participants; they offer suggestions for writing assignments that would include the perspectives of community participants.

Bartholomae, David. "Inventing the University." In *When a Writer Can't Write: Studies in Writer's Block and Other Composing Process Problems.* Ed. Mike Rose. New York: Guilford, 1985. 134–65. Bartholomae argues persuasively that many student writers, especially those with little writing experience, need to be taught explicitly the discourse standards of an academic community in order to write successfully for it.

Berlin, James A. "Contemporary Composition: The Major Pedagogical Theories." *College English* 44 (1982): 765–77. Berlin points out that various process approaches have consequences instructors must consider.

Blakeslee, Ann M. "Bridging the Workplace and the Academy: Teaching Professional Genres Through Classroom-Workplace Collaborations." *Technical Communication* 10.2 (2001): 169–92. Using case studies, Blakeslee shows how student writing improves when students work on projects provided by professionals in business and industry.

Deans, Thomas. *Writing Partnerships: Service-Learning in Composition.* Urbana: NCTE, 2000. Deans provides an excellent introduction to the theoretical and pedagogical issues of community writing initiatives.

Durst, Russel K. *Collision Course: Conflict, Negotiation, and Learning in College Composition.* Urbana: NCTE, 1999. Durst advocates that teachers use a "reflective instrumentalism" in order to reconcile students' practical goals with their own desire to teach critical awareness and reflection.

Flower, Linda, and John R. Hayes. "A Cognitive Process Theory of Writing." *College Composition and Communication* 32 (1981): 365–87. This classic article contains what is probably the best-known and most widely accepted discussion of the components of the writing process, though its model is more theoretical than practical.

Do you like to experiment with language?
Are some kinds of writing easier than others?
Do you have trouble getting ideas or expressing them?
Do you worry about grammar and spelling?
Do your readers usually understand what you mean?

Record your thoughts as part of continuing journal entries that track your experiences as a writer. (See pp. 17–19 on keeping a journal, and see the exercises titled "Considering your past work" in Chapters 1–4.) As you complete writing assignments for your composition course and other courses, keep adding to the journal, noting especially which procedures seem most helpful to you. Your aim is to discover your feelings about writing so that you can develop a dependable writing process of your own.

1b Analyzing the writing situation

Any writing you do for others occurs in a context that both limits and clarifies your choices. You are communicating something about a particular subject to a particular audience of readers for a specific reason. You may need to conduct research. You'll be up against a length requirement and a deadline. And you may be expected to present your work in a certain format.

These are the elements of the **writing situation,** and analyzing them at the very start of a project can tell you much about how to proceed. (For more information about these elements, refer to the page numbers given in parentheses.)

Context

- **What is your writing for?** A course in school? Work? Something else? What do you know of the requirements for writing in this context?
- **Will you present your writing on paper, online, or orally?** What does the presentation method require in preparation time, special skills, and use of technology?
- **How much leeway do you have for this writing?** What does the stated or implied assignment tell you?

Subject (pp. 6–9)

- **What does your writing assignment require you to write about?** If you don't have a specific assignment, what subjects might be appropriate for this situation?
- **What interests you about the subject?** What do you already know about it? What questions do you have about it?
- **What does the assignment require you to do with the subject?**

Audience (pp. 9–13)

- **Who will read your writing?**
- **What do your readers already know and think about your subject?** What characteristics—such as education or political views—might influence their response?
- **What is your relationship to your readers?** How formal or informal should your writing be?
- **What do you want readers to do or think after they read your writing?**

Purpose (pp. 13–15)

- **What aim does your assignment specify?** For instance, does it ask you to explain something or argue a point?
- **Why are you writing?**
- **What do you want your work to accomplish?** What effect do you intend it to have on readers?
- **How can you best achieve your purpose?**

Research (pp. 558–638)

- **What kinds of evidence will best suit your subject, audience, and purpose?** What combination of facts, examples, and expert opinions will support your ideas?
- **Does your assignment require research?** Will you need to consult sources or conduct interviews, surveys, or experiments?
- **Even if research is not required, what information do you need to develop your subject?** How will you obtain it?
- **What documentation style should you use to cite your sources?** (See pp. 637–38 on source documentation in the academic disciplines.)

Deadline and length

- **When is the assignment due?** How will you apportion the work you have to do in the time available?
- **How long should your writing be?** If no length is assigned, what seems appropriate for your subject, audience, and purpose?

Document design

- **What organization and format does the assignment require?** (See pp. 111–12 on format in the academic disciplines and pp. 839–54 on format in public writing.)
- **How might you use margins, headings, and other elements to achieve your purpose?** (See pp. 116–20.)
- **How might you use graphs, photographs, or other images to support ideas and engage readers?** (See pp. 120–25, 225–29.)

Lindemann, Erika. "Three Views of English 101." *College English* 57 (1995): 287–302. This article lays out the opposing claims and assumptions of the "process," "product," and "system of social action" approaches to the writing classroom.

McComiskey, Bruce. *Teaching Composition as a Social Process*. Logan: Utah State University Press, 2000. McComiskey extends composition theory beyond a discussion of the writing process, re-examining product, in the context of cultural theory, as a cycle of production, distribution, and consumption.

Sherman, Linda K., and Beverly Wall. "The Things that Go Without Saying in Composition Studies: A Colloquy." *Journal of Advanced Composition* 15 (1995): 281–320. The authors assemble a many-voiced critique of some of the current assumptions of composition pedagogy, including the process paradigm.

Tobin, Lad, and Thomas Newkirk, eds. *Taking Stock: The Writing Process Movement in the '90's*. Portsmouth, NH: Boynton, 1994. This collection of essays analyzes the goals of the writing process movement, its application in particular institutions, and the ways in which a focus on the writing process can be adapted for the classrooms of the future.

Yagelski, Robert P. *Literacy Matters: Writing and Reading the Social Self*. New York: Teachers College Press, 2000. Yagelski supports changes to writing curricula to account for the seminal influence of social context on the production and composition of written texts.

COMPUTER ACTIVITY

WEB MODELS

Ask students to locate articles or other material on the World Wide Web that can serve as models (having clear subjects, audiences, and purposes) or as negative models (having unclear subjects, purposes, or audiences). Students can share what they find with the rest of the class by e-mailing the URLs to their classmates.

COLLABORATIVE LEARNING

GROUP ANALYSIS

Break students into small groups and ask them to work together to analyze a writing situation using the questions on pp. 4–5 as a guideline.

ANSWERS: EXERCISE 1.2

The assignment specifies the subject (the combinations of client, therapist, and theory that tend to make psychotherapy successful), the audience (the instructor and a "discussion group" of classmates), and the purpose (to explain and support a conclusion about the subject). It requires research into studies of psychotherapy. It specifies a length range and a deadline. It does not specify a format, but APA format could be assumed because the course is in psychology.

RESOURCES AND IDEAS

Brady, Laura. "Overcoming Resistance: Computers in the Writing Classroom." *Computers and Composition* 7:2 (1990): 21–33. Brady found that word processing in the first-year composition classroom increased the volume of student writing, prompted new ways of thinking about topics, encouraged collaboration, and fostered a positive workshop atmosphere.

Brooke, Rupert, Ruth Mirtz, and Rick Evans, eds. *Small Groups in Writing Workshops: Invitations to a Writer's Life.* Urbana: NCTE, 1994. This collection of essays offers many strategies for using collaborative group work to create an active learning situation.

TRANSPARENCY MASTER 1.1

Flower, Linda S., and John R. Hayes. "The Cognition of Discovery: Defining a Rhetorical Problem." *College Composition and Communication* 31 (1980): 21–32. This article reports on a detailed study of how good writers and poor writers conceive of writing tasks as they begin to compose.

Golub, Jeff. *Activities for an Interactive Classroom.* Urbana: NCTE, 1994. Golub provides a number of hands-on suggestions for creating an effective workshop environment.

Hillocks, George, Jr. "Environments for Active Learning." In *Theory and Practice in the Teaching of Writing: Rethinking the Discipline.* Ed. Lee Odell. Carbondale: Southern Illinois UP, 1993. 244–70. Hillocks' essay is part case study and part analysis of a classroom structure based on student interactions with each other and with texts.

EXERCISE 1.2   Analyzing a writing situation

The following assignment was given in a survey course in psychology. What does the assignment specify about the elements of the writing situation? What does it imply? Given this assignment, how would you answer the questions on the previous two pages? (You can do this exercise online at *ablongman.com/littlebrown*.)

When is psychotherapy most likely to work? That is, what combinations of client, therapist, and theory tend to achieve good results? In your paper, cite studies supporting your conclusions. Length: 1500 to 1800 words. Post your paper online to me and to your discussion group by March 30.

1c   Discovering and limiting a subject

For most college and public writing, you will write in response to an assignment. The assignment may specify your subject, or it may leave the choice to you. (If you're stuck, you can use the discovery techniques on pp. 16–26 to think of subjects.) Whether the subject is assigned or not, it will probably need some thought if it is to achieve these aims:

- **The subject should be suitable for the assignment.**
- **It should be neither too general nor too limited** for the length of project and deadline assigned.
- **It should be something you care about.**

1   Responding to a specific assignment

Many assignments will set boundaries for your subject. For instance, you might be asked to discuss what makes psychotherapy effective, to prepare a lab report on a physics experiment, or to analyze a character in a short story.

Such assignments may seem to leave little room for you to move around, but in fact you'll have several questions to answer:

- **What's wanted from you?** Writing assignments often contain words such as *discuss, describe, analyze, report, interpret, explain, define, argue,* and *evaluate.* These words specify the way you are to approach your subject, what kind of thinking is expected of you, and what your general purpose is. (See pp. 13–15 for more on purpose.)
- **For whom are you writing?** Many assignments will specify or imply your readers, but sometimes you will have to figure out for yourself who your audience is and what it expects from you. (For more on analyzing audience, see pp. 9–13.)
- **What kind of research is required?** Sometimes an assignment specifies the kinds of sources you are expected to consult, and

you can use such information to choose your subject. (If you are unsure whether research is required, check with your instructor.)

- **How can you narrow the assigned subject to do it justice in the length and time required?** (See below.)

2 Responding to a general assignment

Some assignments specify features such as length or amount of research, but they leave the choice of subject entirely to you. Others are somewhat more focused—for instance, "Respond to a reading assigned in this course" or "Discuss a proposal for solving a local social problem"—but still give you much leeway in choosing a particular reading or a particular proposal. To find your approach, consider your experiences, interests, or curiosities:

- **What subject do you already know something about or have you been wondering about?** Athletic scholarships? Unemployment in your town?
- **Have you recently disagreed with someone over a substantial issue?** The change in relations between men and women? The methods being used to fight terrorism?
- **What have you read or seen lately?** A shocking book? A violent or funny movie? An effective television commercial?
- **What topic in the reading or class discussion for a course has intrigued you?** An economic issue such as taxes? A psychological problem such as depression?
- **What makes you especially happy or especially angry?** A hobby? The behavior of your neighbors?
- **Which of your own or others' dislikes and preferences would you like to understand better?** The demand for sport-utility vehicles? A taste for vegetarian cuisine?

Once you have a subject, you'll also need to answer the questions in the bulleted list opposite.

3 Narrowing a subject to a question

Let's say you've decided to write about communication on the Internet or about a particular character in a short story. You've got a subject, but it's still broad, worthy of a lengthy article if not a whole book. For a relatively brief paper, you'll need a narrow focus in order to provide the specific details that make writing significant and interesting—all within the length and deadline specified by the assignment.

One helpful technique for narrowing a subject is to ask focused questions about it, seeking one that seems appropriate for your assignment and that promises to sustain your interest through the writing process. The following examples illustrate how questioning

Summerfield, Judith. "Is There a Life in This Text? Reimagining Narrative." In *Writing Theory and Critical Theory: Research and Scholarship in Composition.* Ed. John Clifford and John Schilb. NY: MLA, 1994. 179–194. Summerfield examines the role of student narratives in the composition class, especially the extent to which they can provoke and sustain students' "authentic" voices.

Tedlock, David. "The Case Approach to Composition." *College Composition and Communication* 32 (1981): 253–61. Tedlock argues for the use of cases—detailed, self-contained descriptions of a writing situation—as a basis for assignments and instructions.

COMPUTER ACTIVITY

If your classroom is linked to the Internet, ask your students to do a subject search on a broad topic, like the "environment," and to note the successive points at which they will be able to narrow the topic by choosing among lists of subheadings. At a later stage you might ask students to create their own hypertext document in which a broad subject heading leads the user to information on more specific topics.

NARROWING SUBJECTS TO TOPICS

Clustering (2a-5) and asking the journalist's questions (2a-6) can also help narrow subjects to topics. For example, the broad subject "Islam" can be the center point of a cluster, and students can write related topic ideas such as "theology of Islam," "Western attitudes toward Muslims and Islam," and "women in Islam" in branches radiating from the center. "Islam" can also be narrowed by asking such questions as "*Who* are major figures in Islam?," "*What* do Muslims believe?," "*How* are Muslims and Islam viewed in the United States?," "*Where* is Islam practiced?," and "*How* and *Why* are women and men treated differently in Islamic tradition?"

Other good subject areas that give students practice in narrowing topics are movies, cars, television programs, and academic fields (for example, sociology, geology).

RESOURCES AND IDEAS

Guiher-Huff, Susan. "Involvement in a Current Problem as a Basis for Writing." *Teaching English in the Two-Year College* 17 (1990): 187–88. Guiher-Huff describes how students used a range of essay formats, made a cause-and-effect oral presentation, and wrote persuasive letters around the topic of pollution. The sustained topic seemed to make the writing meaningful for the students.

Schreffler, Peter H. "'Where All the Children Are Above Average': Garrison Keillor as a Model for Personal Narrative Assignments." *College Composition and Communication* 40 (1989): 82–85. Schreffler discusses the delightful experience personal narrative writing can be as students delve into themselves as well as into the world around them.

Seabury, Marcia Bundy. "The Abstraction Ladder in Freshman Composition." *College Composition and Communication* 40 (1989): 89–92. Seabury has found that teaching S. I. Hayakawa's abstraction ladder can benefit first-year composition students in their thinking through and writing about their topics.

Wallace, David. "From Intention to Text: Articulating Initial Intentions for Writing." *Research in the Teaching of English* 30 (1996): 182–219. This essay explores the relationship between the planning and composing stages of writing. Wallace's study found that students who were most able to articulate their initial intentions for a writing task were also most able to complete the task effectively.

On limiting subjects

Coe, Richard M. "If Not to Narrow, Then How to Focus: Two Techniques for Focusing." *College Composition and Communication* 32 (1981): 272–77. Coe describes ways to get students to focus on a particular aspect of a topic as an alternative to the usual approach of narrowing a topic.

Tucker, Amy. *Decoding ESL: International Students in the American College Classroom.* Portsmouth, NH: Boynton, 1995. This book explores the larger issues of how to read and respond to ESL writers, and includes (particularly in Chapter 8) strategies for using readings as the prompts for writing assignments.

can scale down broad subjects to specific subjects that are limited and manageable:

Broad subjects	Specific subjects
Communication on the Internet	What are the advantages of online communication?
	How, if at all, should the government regulate Internet content?
	How might the Internet contribute to social and economic equality?
Mrs. Mallard in Kate Chopin's "The Story of an Hour"	What changes does Mrs. Mallard undergo?
	Why does Mrs. Mallard respond as she does to news of her husband's death?
	What does the story's irony contribute to the character of Mrs. Mallard?
Lincoln's weaknesses as President	What was Lincoln's most significant error as commander-in-chief of the Union army?
	Why did Lincoln delay emancipating the slaves?
	Why did Lincoln have difficulties controlling his cabinet?
Federal aid to college students	Which students should be entitled to federal aid?
	How adequate are the kinds of federal aid available to college students?
	Why should the federal government aid college students?

As these examples illustrate, your questions should not lend themselves to yes-or-no answers but should require further thinking.

Here are some guidelines for posing questions:

- **Reread the assignment.** Consider what it tells you about purpose, audience, sources, length, and deadline.
- **Pursue your interests.** If questions don't come easily, try freewriting or brainstorming (pp. 20–22) or use a tree diagram (pp. 34–35).
- **Ask as many questions as you can think of.**
- **Test the question that seems most interesting and appropriate by roughly sketching out the main ideas.** Consider how many paragraphs or pages of specific facts, examples, and other details you would need to pin those ideas down. This thinking should give you at least a vague idea of how much work you'd have to do and how long the resulting paper might be.
- **Break a too-broad question down further, and repeat the previous step.**

The Internet can also help you limit a general subject. On the Web, browse a directory such as *BUBL LINK* (*bubl.ac.uk*). As you pursue increasingly narrow categories, you may find a suitably limited topic.

Don't be discouraged if the perfect question does not come easily or early. You may find that you need to do some planning and writing, exploring different facets of the general subject and pursuing your specific interests, before you hit on the best question. And the question you select may require further narrowing or may shift subtly or even dramatically as you move through the writing process.

EXERCISE 1.3   Narrowing subjects

Following are some general writing assignments. Use the given information and your own interests to pose specific questions for three of these assignments. (You can do this exercise online at *ablongman.com/ littlebrown*.)

1. For a writing course, consider how the World Wide Web could alter the experience of popular culture. Length: three pages. Deadline: one week.
2. For a course in sociology, research and analyze the dynamics of a particular group of people. Length: unspecified. Deadline: four weeks.
3. For a writing course, read and respond to an essay in a text you are using. Length: three pages. Deadline: two weeks.
4. For a government course, consider possible restrictions on legislators. Length: five pages. Deadline: two weeks.
5. For a letter to the editor of the town newspaper, describe the effects of immigration on your community. Length: two pages. Deadline: unspecified.

**EXERCISE 1.4   Considering your past work:
Discovering and limiting a subject**

Think of something you've recently written—perhaps an application essay, a business report, or a term paper. How did your subject evolve from beginning to end? In retrospect, was it appropriate for your writing situation? How, if at all, might it have been modified?

EXERCISE 1.5   Finding and narrowing a subject for your essay

As the first step in developing a three- to four-page essay for the instructor and the other students in your writing course, choose a subject and narrow it. Use the guidelines in the previous section to come up with a question that is suitably interesting, appropriate, and specific.

1d   Considering the audience

- Who are my readers?
- Why will they read my writing?
- What will they need from me?
- What do I want them to think or do after they read my writing?

Have students work in groups to find specific topics for the assignments in Exercise 1.3, and then share their conclusions with the class. Students benefit from realizing the numerous and varied options for narrowing a broad subject.

ANSWERS: EXERCISE 1.3

Possible answers

1. How has direct distribution of popular music on the Web affected consumers' choices?
2. How does slang help to bind members of the college community?
3. How does X's theory about math anxiety apply to me?
4. How might term limits affect the House of Representatives?
5. How has immigration affected food choices?

SHARING PAST WRITING

Sharing past work can help students connect the writing they are doing in your class to their broader experience as writers, a connection that helps them to gain greater awareness of their own progress as writers. Have students bring in a piece of previous work and present it to their group, describing the context in which that piece was written, their purpose in writing it, what they learned from writing it, and how it differs from other kinds of writing they have done. Ask groups to report on the interesting or unexpected moments that occurred in the group presentations.

ANSWERS: EXERCISE 1.4

Individual response.

ANSWERS: EXERCISE 1.5

Individual response.

As part of the process of developing their topics for Exercise 1.5, have students verbally articulate their ideas in small groups and receive suggestions for further development and focus.

AUDIENCE INVENTORY

Ask students to choose a possible topic for an essay and to list the kinds of people who might be interested in the topic. Tell students that if they wish they may employ the "Questions About Audience" on page 11. (In theory, the lists might be very long. In practice, students soon run out of ideas, but not until they have begun to visualize the audience for their essays.) To extend the exercise, ask students what part of the potential audience they would most like to address or what kinds of people would be most interested in the topic. Then ask them to list either (1) what the restricted audience probably already knows about the topic and what it needs to know or (2) what its attitudes are and what kinds of arguments will be needed to change them.

COLLABORATIVE LEARNING

AUDIENCE INVENTORY

Ask students to compare the lists they developed for the audience inventory and suggest changes, additions, or deletions.

COLLABORATIVE LEARNING

AUDIENCE ASSESSMENT

Distribute to your class an article from a special-interest magazine, a newspaper feature or editorial, an article from the Internet, or another brief essay whose appeal to a particular audience students will be able to recognize fairly easily. Ask students to read the essay and then to work together to identify the characteristics and attitudes of the intended audience as they think the author viewed it. Ask them also to identify the tone of the essay and to decide whether or not it is appropriate to the subject, the intended audience, and the publication in which the essay appeared. Tell them to be ready to point out what evidence in the essay they used to identify the intended audience and the tone. Rather than bring articles to class yourself, ask students either individually or as teams to bring in a variety of essays or writings aimed at particular audiences. Some target audiences you might pick are consumers, sports fans, parents, businesspeople, patients, and health-care workers.

These questions are central to any writing project, and they will crop up again and again. Except in writing meant only for yourself, you are always trying to communicate with readers—something about a particular subject, for a particular purpose.

Your audience will often be specified or implied in a writing assignment. When you write an editorial for the student newspaper, your audience consists of fellow students. When you write a report on a physics experiment, your audience consists of your physics instructor and perhaps other physicists or your classmates. (See pp. 129–30 for more on audience in academic writing.) Whatever the audience, considering its needs and expectations can help you form or focus a question about your subject, gather answers to the question, and ultimately decide what to say and how to say it.

1 Knowing what readers need

As a reader yourself, you know what readers need:

- **Context:** a link between what they read and their own knowledge and experiences.
- **Predictability:** an understanding of the writer's purpose and how it is being achieved.
- **Information:** the specific facts, examples, and other details that make the subject clear, concrete, interesting, and convincing.
- **Respect:** a sense that the writer respects their values and beliefs, their background, and their intelligence.
- **Voice:** a sense that the writer is a real person.
- **Clarity and correctness:** writing free of unnecessary stumbling blocks and mistakes.

For much academic and public writing, readers have definite needs and expectations. Thus Chapter 6 discusses academic writing in general, Chapters 49–53 discuss writing in various disciplines, and Chapter 55 discusses public writing. Even in these areas, you must make many choices based on audience. In other areas where the conventions of structure and presentation are vaguer, the choices are even more numerous. The box opposite contains questions that can help you define and make these choices.

2 Pitching your writing to your audience

Your sense of your audience will influence three key elements of what you write:

- **The specific information you use to gain and keep the attention of readers and to guide them to accept your conclusions.** This information may consist of concrete details, facts, examples,

Questions about audience

Identity and expectations

- **Who *are* my readers?**
- **What are my readers' expectations for the kind of writing I'm doing?** Do readers expect features such as a particular organization and format, distinctive kinds of evidence, or a certain style of documenting sources?
- **What do I want readers to know or do after reading my work?** How should I make that clear to them?
- **What is my relationship to my readers?** How formal or informal will they expect me to be? What role and tone should I assume?

Characteristics, knowledge, and attitudes

- **What characteristics of readers are relevant for my subject and purpose?** For instance:

  Age and sex
  Occupation: students, professional colleagues, etc.
  Social or economic role: subject-matter experts, voters, car buyers, potential employers, etc.
  Economic or educational background
  Ethnic background
  Political, religious, or moral beliefs and values
  Hobbies or activities

- **How will the characteristics of readers influence their attitudes toward my subject?**
- **What do readers already know and *not* know about my subject?** How much do I have to tell them?
- **How should I handle any specialized terms?** Will readers know them? If not, should I define them or avoid them?
- **What ideas, arguments, or information might surprise, excite, or offend readers?** How should I handle these points?
- **What misconceptions might readers have of my subject and/or my approach to it?** How can I dispel these misconceptions?

Uses and format

- **What will readers do with my writing?** Should I expect them to read every word from the top, to scan for information, to look for conclusions? Can I help by providing a summary, headings, illustrations, or other aids? (See pp. 111–26 on document design.)

You can download these questions from *ablongman.com/littlebrown*. Save them in a file of their own, duplicate the file for each writing project, and insert appropriate answers between the questions. Print your answers for reference as you develop your paper.

TRANSPARENCY MASTER 1.2

COMPUTER ACTIVITY

COLLABORATIVE POSTINGS

Have your students work together to compose a posting for an Internet newsgroup in which they practice pitching their writing to a nonspecific audience. In their postings they should try to include sufficient (or even extra) information, to assume the role of an equal in the conversation they are entering, and to write in a level tone.

RESOURCES AND IDEAS

Bacon, Nora. "Building a Swan's Nest for Instruction in Rhetoric." *College Composition and Communication* 51.4 (2000): 589–609. Bacon shows how cummunity-based writing assignments help students understand how purpose and style must change as a result of rhetorical context.

Ong, Walter J., S. J. "The Writer's Audience Is Always a Fiction," *PMLA* 90 (1975): 9–21. Ong argues that writers must construct audiences in their imaginations as an essential part of the act of writing and that readers must play the role defined for them by the writer's act of imagination. Of course, students are probably aware that in many writing circumstances, such as writing for a professor or a manager at work, the audience is real, not fictional. It's worth discussing how a writer's task can be shaped by his or her knowledge of actual readers.

Vandenberg, Peter. "Pick Up This Cross and Follow: (Ir)responsibility and the Teaching of 'Writing for Audience.'" *Composition Studies: Freshman English News* 20 (Fall 1992): 84–97. Vandenberg reviews debates over the changing concept of audience and pinpoints some of the contradictions that students face as they try to write for particular audiences.

COLLABORATIVE LEARNING

Have students work in groups to critique and revise one of their paragraph-length responses to Exercise 1.6. In networked classrooms, students can "publish" the revised paragraphs for the class.

ANSWERS: EXERCISE 1.6

Possible answers

1. *For elementary school students:* physical effects in simple terms; statistics in simple figures; difficulty of quitting once addicted; importance of resisting peer pressure.

    Role: combined teacher and parent. Tone: warm, slightly admonitory.

    For adult smokers: graphic depiction of physical effects; detailed statistics; influence on children; effect on smoker's appearance, odor, breath.

    Role: combined friend and lecturer. Tone: no-nonsense.

or other evidence that makes your ideas clear, supports your assertions, and suits your readers' background, biases, and special interests.

- **The role you choose to play in relation to your readers.** Depending on your purpose and your attitude toward your topic, you will want readers to perceive you in a certain way. The possible roles are many and varied—for instance, scholar, storyteller, lecturer, guide, reporter, advocate, inspirer.
- **The tone you use. Tone** in writing is like tone of voice in speaking: words and sentence structures on the page convey some of the same information as pitch and volume in the voice. Depending on your writing situation and what you think your readers will expect and respond to, your tone may be formal or informal. The attitude you convey may be serious or light, forceful or calm, irritated or cheerful.

Even when you're writing on the same subject, your information, role, and tone may change substantially for different audiences. Both memos below were written by a student who worked part-time in a small company and wanted to get the company to conserve paper. But the two memos address different readers.

To coworkers

Ever notice how much paper collects in your trash basket every day? Well, most of it can be recycled with little effort, I promise. Basically, all you need to do is set a bag or box near your desk and deposit wastepaper in it. I know, space is cramped in these little cubicles. But what's a little more crowding when the earth's at stake? . . .

Information: how employees could handle recycling; no mention of costs

Role: cheerful, equally harried colleague

Tone: informal, personal (*Ever notice; Well; you; I know, space is cramped; what's*)

To management

In my four months here, I have observed that all of us throw out baskets of potentially recyclable paper every day. Considering the drain on our forest resources and the pressure on landfills that paper causes, we could make a valuable contribution to the environmental movement by helping to recycle the paper we use. At the company where I worked before, employees separate clean wastepaper from other trash at their desks. The maintenance staff collects trash in two receptacles, and the trash hauler (the same one we use here) makes separate pickups. I do not know what the hauler charges for handling recyclable material. . . .

Information: specific reasons; view of company as a whole; reference to another company; problem of cost

Role: serious, thoughtful, responsible employee

Tone: formal, serious (*Considering the drain; forest resources; valuable contribution;* no *you* or contractions)

Typically for business writing, the information grows more specific and the tone more formal as the rank and number of readers rise.

If you are writing online—for instance, to an Internet news-group—you may not know enough about your audience to pitch your writing to particular expectations and needs. Consider, then, providing more information than you otherwise might, assuming the role of an equal (perhaps a colleague), and using a level tone (neither hostile nor chummy, neither very formal nor very informal).

EXERCISE 1.6   Considering audience

Choose one of the following subjects, and, for each audience speci-fied, ask the questions on page 11. Decide on four points you would make, the role you would assume, and the tone you would adopt for each audience. Then write a paragraph for each based on your deci-sions. (You can do this exercise online at *ablongman.com/littlebrown*.)

1. The effects of smoking: for elementary school students and for adult smokers
2. Your opposition to a proposed law requiring adult bicyclists to wear helmets: for cyclists who oppose the law and for people who favor it
3. Why your neighbors should remove the wrecked truck from their front yard: for your neighbors and for your town zoning board

---

EXERCISE 1.7   Considering your past work:
Writing for a specific audience

How did audience figure in a piece of writing you've done in the re-cent past—perhaps an essay for an application or a paper for a course? Who were your readers? How did your awareness of them influence your choice of information, your role, and your tone? At what point in the writing process did you find it most productive to consider your readers consciously?

EXERCISE 1.8   Analyzing the audience for your essay

Use the questions on page 11 to determine as much as you can about the probable readers of your essay-in-progress (see Exercise 1.5). What does your analysis reveal about the specific information your readers need? What role do you want to assume, and what tone will best con-vey your attitude toward your topic?

1e   Defining a purpose

When you write, your **purpose** is your chief reason for commu-nicating something about a topic to a particular audience. Purpose thus links both the specific situation in which you are working and the goal you hope to achieve. It is your answer to a potential reader's question, "So what?"

2. *For cyclists who also oppose the law:* status of law; reasons for opposition; need for ac-tion; suggested actions.
   Role: peer, motivator. Tone: informal, urgent.
   For people who favor the law: acknowl-edgment of pro-law position; disadvantages of helmets; lack of proven need; infringe-ment of cyclists' rights.
   Role: fellow citizen. Tone: informative, reasonable, appealing to shared values.
3. *For your neighbors:* feelings of neighbor-hood residents; dangers to children and pets; lowered property values; threat of peti-tion to zoning board.
   Role: peer. Tone: direct, a bit angry.
   For the zoning board: violation of zoning regulations; length of time the wrecked truck has been present; number of unsuc-cessful appeals to neighbors; dangers to children and pets.
   Role: plaintiff. Tone: serious, reasonable.

ANSWERS: EXERCISE 1.7

Individual response.

COLLABORATIVE LEARNING

Students can often experience difficulty in identifying the implied readers of their own work. Have students work in small groups to compare their responses to Exercise 1.8, to help one another identify the probable readers of their essays-in-progress, and to note places in each es-say where too much or too little information is supplied.

ANSWERS: EXERCISE 1.8

Individual response.

IDENTIFYING PURPOSE

Use paragraphs drawn from magazine arti-cles, essays in a reader, or student papers as the basis for class discussion of the purposes of writ-ing. You may ask students to work individually or in groups to compare the aims of individual paragraphs with the overall purpose of the essay from which they are taken and to decide what role the paragraphs play within the essay.

RESOURCES AND IDEAS

Ede, Lisa, and Andrea Lunsford. "Audience Addressed/Audience Invoked: The Role of Audience in Composition Theory and Pedagogy." *College Composition and Communication* 35 (1984): 155–71. The authors suggest a negotiated balance between the writer's desires and the audience's needs. See also their "Representing Audience: 'Successful' Discourse and Disciplinary Critique" in *College Composition and Communication* 47 (1996): 167–79.

Kirsch, Gesa, and Duane H. Roen. *A Sense of Audience in Written Communication.* Newbury Park: Sage, 1990. Sixteen interdisciplinary essays on audience treat the subject from a number of critical perspectives.

Park, Douglas B. "Analyzing Audiences." *College Composition and Communication* 37 (1986): 478–88. Understanding the social context of a writing act helps students define their audiences.

Rieff, Mary Jo. "Rereading 'Invoked' and 'Addressed' Readers Through a Social Lens: Towards a Recognition of Multiple Audiences." *Journal of Advanced Composition* 16 (1996): 407–24. Reiff reviews ways in which the term *audience* has been evoked by composition theorists and examines ways that writing teachers and students can take multiple audience perspectives into account.

Trimbur, John. "Composition and the Circulation of Writing." *College Composition and Communication* 52 (December 2000): 188-219. Trimbur suggests that teachers should enrich composition instruction by alerting students to the effects a broader circulation of students' work would have on the manner of its composition.

Wells, Susan. "Rogue Cops and Health Care: What Do We Want from Public Writing?" *College Composition and Communication* 47 (1996): 325–41. Wells explores the problems of addressing a "general public" audience in student assignments.

Willey, R. J. "Audience Awareness: Methods and Madness." *Freshman English News* 18:2 (1990): 20+. Willey found that when rhetorical, informational, and social perspectives on audience awareness were considered in the composition classroom, the social perspective was the most productive because of its transactional nature.

The general purposes for writing

- To entertain readers
- To express your feelings or ideas
- To explain something to readers (exposition)
- To persuade readers to accept or act on your opinion (argument)

1 Defining a general purpose

Your purpose may fall into one of four general categories: entertainment, self-expression, explanation, or persuasion. These purposes may overlap in a single piece of writing, but usually one predominates. And the dominant purpose will influence your particular slant on your topic, the supporting details you choose, even the words you use.

In college or public writing, by far the most common purposes are explanation and persuasion:

- **Writing that is mainly explanatory is often called** *exposition* (from a Latin word meaning "to explain or set forth"). Using examples, facts, and other evidence, you present an idea about your subject so that readers understand it as you do. Almost any subject is suitable for exposition: how to pitch a knuckleball, why you want to major in business, the implications of a new discovery in computer science, the interpretation of a short story, the causes of an economic slump. Exposition is the kind of writing encountered most often in newspapers, magazines, and textbooks.

- **Writing that is primarily persuasive is often called** *argument.* Using examples, facts, and other evidence, you support your position on a debatable subject so that readers will at least consider your view and perhaps agree with it or act on it. A newspaper editorial favoring city council reform, a business proposal for a new personnel policy, a student paper recommending more required courses or defending a theory about human psychological development—all these are arguments. (Chapters 9–11 discuss argument in some detail and provide examples.)

2 Defining a specific purpose

Purpose can be conceived more specifically, too, in a way that incorporates your particular subject and the outcome you intend—what you want readers to do or think as a result of reading your writing. Here are some examples of specific purposes:

> To explain how Annie Dillard's "Total Eclipse" builds to its climax so that readers appreciate the author's skill

To explain the methods and results of an engineering experiment so that readers understand and accept your conclusions

To explain why the county has been unable to attract new businesses so that readers better understand the local economic slump

To persuade readers to support the college administration's plan for more required courses

To argue against additional regulation of health-maintenance organizations so that readers perceive the disadvantages for themselves

To argue for additional gun-control laws so that readers agree on their necessity

Often, a writing assignment will specify or imply both a general and a specific purpose. Say, for instance, that a psychology teacher assigns a review of the research on infants' perception of color. You know that the purpose is generally to explain, more specifically to summarize and analyze the established findings on the subject. You want readers to come away understanding the current state of the investigation into the subject. In addition, you want your instructor to see that you can competently read others' work and write about it. (See p. 130 for more on purpose in academic writing.)

With any writing assignment, try to define your specific purpose as soon as you have formed a question about your subject. Don't worry, though, if you feel uncertain of your purpose at the start. Sometimes you may not discover your purpose until you begin drafting, or you may find that your initial sense of purpose changes as you move through the writing process.

EXERCISE 1.9   Finding purpose in assignments

For each of your questions from Exercise 1.3 (p. 9), suggest a likely general purpose (entertainment, self-expression, explanation, persuasion) and try to define a specific purpose as well. Make audience part of your suggestions: What would you want readers to do or think in each case? (If you completed Exercise 1.3 online, you can add these suggestions to that file.)

EXERCISE 1.10   Considering your past work: Defining a purpose

Look over two or three things you've written in the past year or so. What was your specific purpose in each one? How did the purpose influence your writing? Did you achieve your purpose?

EXERCISE 1.11   Defining a purpose for your essay

For your essay-in-progress, use your thinking so far about topic (Exercise 1.5, p. 9) and audience (Exercise 1.8, p. 13) to define a general and specific purpose for your writing.

ANSWERS: EXERCISE 1.9

Possible answers

1. *How has direct distribution of popular music on the web affected consumers' choices?* Explain how the ability to connect directly with musicians on the Web results in more music choices for consumers. Introduce readers to a benefit of the Web.
2. *How does slang help to bind members of the college community?* Explain how the community's unique slang contributes to a sense of belonging. Show readers the value of their slang.
3. *How does X's theory about math anxiety apply to me?* Explain the way X's theory reflects your own experience. Demonstrate to readers the truth of the theory.
4. *How might term limits affect the House of Representatives?* Argue against term limits for legislators. Lead readers to agree that term limits are unnecessary and potentially harmful.
5. *How has immigration affected food choices?* Explain how immigrants have vastly increased the variety of foods available. Help readers appreciate this benefit of immigration.

ANSWERS: EXERCISE 1.10

Individual response.

ANSWERS: EXERCISE 1.11

Individual response.

mycomplab 2.0

Please visit MyCompLab at *www.myco[...]* for more on the writing process.

HIGHLIGHTS

Continuing the discussion of th[...] process begun in Chapter 1, this cha[...] students generate and shape their ide[...] sion of strategies for exploration, incl[...] nal writing, observing, freewriting, li[...] tering, using the journalist's questi[...] patterns of development, reading, an[...] critically, begins the chapter (2a). Th[...] tion focuses on conceiving, drafting, a[...] thesis statements (2b). Students then [...] how to organize their essays: disting[...] general and the specific, using org[...] tools such as outlines and tree diagrams, and choosing an appropriate structure for an essay (2c). The chapter concludes by addressing unity and coherence and how to check for them.

The exercises for this chapter ask students to reflect on how they have generated ideas for writing in the past and to try out some new techniques as they work on an essay-in-progress.

[Handwritten note:]
Process Writing
Chapt. 2
Pre-writing
Thesis statement
Organizing
Editing

...eloping and *...haping Ideas*

Once you have assessed [y]our writing situation, or even while you're assessing it, you'll begin answering the question you posed about your subject (pp. 7–8). As you generate ideas and information, they in turn may cause you to rephrase your lead question, which will open up new areas to explore. Throughout this stage, you'll bring order to your thoughts, eventually focusing and organizing them so that readers will respond as you intend.

2a Discovering ideas

For some writing projects, you may have little difficulty finding what you have to say about your subject: possible answers to your starting question will tumble forth as ideas on paper or screen. But when you're stuck for what to say, you'll have to coax answers out. Instead of waiting around for inspiration to strike, use a technique to get your mind working. Anything is appropriate: if you like to make drawings or take pictures, for instance, then try that.

The following pages describe some strategies for discovering ideas. These strategies are to be selected from, not followed in sequence: some may help you during early stages of the writing process, even before you're sure of your topic; others may help you later on; and one or two may not help at all. Experiment to discover which strategies work best for you.

Note **Whatever strategy or strategies you use, do your work in writing, not just in your head.** Your work will be retrievable, and the act of writing will help you concentrate and lead you to fresh, sometimes surprising, insights. If you participate in online collaboration to develop subjects, your activities will probably be stored electronically so that you can review and use the work. Ask your instructor how to reach the online files.

COMPANION WEB SITE

See page IAE-51 for companion Web site content description.

http://www.ablongman.com/littlebrown ▶

Visit the companion Web site for more help with discovering and shaping ideas.

Techniques for developing a subject

- Keep a journal (below).
- Observe your surroundings (p. 19).
- Freewrite (p. 20).
- Make a list or brainstorm (p. 21).
- Cluster (p. 23).
- Use the journalist's questions (p. 23).
- Use the patterns of development (p. 24).
- Read (p. 25).
- Think critically (p. 26).

CULTURE LANGUAGE The discovery process encouraged here rewards rapid writing without a lot of thinking beforehand about what you will write or how. If your first language is not standard American English, you may find it helpful initially to do this exploratory writing in your native language or dialect and then to translate the worthwhile material for use in your drafts. This process can be productive, but it is extra work. You may want to try it at first and gradually move to composing in standard American English.

1 Keeping a journal

A place to record thoughts and observations, a **journal** can be a good source of ideas for writing. It is a kind of diary, but one more concerned with ideas than with day-to-day events. *Journal* comes from the Latin for "daily," and many journal keepers do write faithfully every day; others make entries less regularly, when the mood strikes or an insight occurs or they have a problem to work out.

Advantages of a journal

Writing in a journal, you are writing to yourself. That means you don't have to worry about main ideas, organization, correct grammar and spelling, or any of the other requirements of writing for others. You can work out your ideas and feelings without the pressure of an audience "out there" who will evaluate your thinking and expression. The freedom and flexibility of a journal can be liberating. Like many others, you may find writing easier, more fun, and more rewarding than you thought possible.

You can keep a journal either on paper (such as a notebook) or on a computer. If you write in the journal every day, or almost, even just for a few minutes, the routine will loosen up your writing muscles and improve your confidence. Indeed, journal keepers often become dependent on the process for the writing practice it gives

KEEPING JOURNALS

Students may have mixed feelings about journal keeping, so it's important to explain to them why writers find keeping journals so valuable. Make clear how journals differ from diaries and how many (and what kind of) entries you expect per week or term. Giving some guidelines or prompts for students to follow helps them get started. Students can also add clippings, photocopies, pictures, and cartoons and even use tapes and videos in their journals as a way of expanding their horizons. (These other media will have to be submitted separately if you have students hand their journals in.)

It's important to make the journal a productive tool, not just make-work. Encourage students to plumb their journals for essay topics and samples of strategies they might use in more formal pieces of writing. You can also make journals productive by encouraging students to write journal entries as letters to you or classmates, then incorporate your or their classmates' answers into the journal as well.

Most instructors react to issues raised or comment on attempts to try new strategies without actually grading the journal. Students will often include very personal material in their journals, so they should be encouraged to fold over, staple, or secure (but not remove) personal material before they show it to you; and they must trust that you will respect their confidentiality.

COMPUTER JOURNALS

If your students keep their journals on their computers, the Cut-and-Paste function will make it easy for them to mine their journal entries for appropriate material to copy to the document in which they are drafting their paper.

WRITING PROCESS AS CULTURAL VALUE

Students who have not previously been schooled in the process approach to writing may be surprised by classroom activities that focus on discrete elements of the process. They may be surprised that you as the instructor are interested in the entire process, rather than just the end product, and that you may be reviewing their work on early stages of the process. You may want to spend some time discussing what an original idea is; what a draft is supposed to be; the responsibilities of the teacher and student respectively at various stages of the writing process; and how to determine where the line is between appropriate and inappropriate use of the help of the instructor, peer reviewers, or tutors.

RESOURCES AND IDEAS

On keeping journals

Fulwiler, Toby, ed. *The Journal Book.* Portsmouth: Boynton/Cook, 1987. The essays in this collection describe the uses of journals for discovering and exploring ideas and as an important strategy for writing and learning in various subject areas.

Gannett, Cinthia. *Gender and the Journal: Diaries and Academic Discourse.* Albany: State U of New York P, 1992. Gannett discusses the development of the genre and how it has been "feminized," with consideration of the pedagogical implications of this history.

White, Fred D. "Releasing the Self: Teaching Journal-Writing to Freshmen." *The Writing Instructor* 1 (1982): 147–54. White offers practical advice on the use of journals: kinds of journals and entries, professional samples, exercises, and a summary of supporting research.

Whitehill, Sharon. "Using the Journal for Discovery: Two Devices." *College Composition and Communication* 38 (1987): 472–74. Whitehill argues that journal assignments calling for lists and for imaginary dialogues can help generate ideas and alleviate writing blocks, and she provides detailed examples of each strategy.

them, the concentrated thought it encourages, and the connection it fosters between personal, private experience and public information and events.

Usually for the same reasons, teachers of writing and other subjects sometimes require students to keep journals. The teachers may even collect students' journals to monitor progress, but they read the journals with an understanding of purpose (in other words, they do not evaluate work that was not written to be evaluated), and they usually just credit rather than grade the work.

CULTURE LANGUAGE A journal can be especially helpful if your first language is not standard American English. You can practice writing to improve your fluency, try out sentence patterns, and experiment with vocabulary words. Equally important, you can experiment with applying what you know from experience to what you read and observe.

■ Uses of a journal

Two uses of a journal are discussed elsewhere in this book: a reading journal, in which you think critically (in writing) about what you read (pp. 152–53, 736–37); and a research journal, in which you record your activities and ideas while you pursue a research project (pp. 559–60). But you can use a journal for other purposes as well. Here are just a few:

- **Prepare for or respond to a course you're taking** by puzzling over a reading or a class discussion.
- **Build ideas for specific writing assignments.**
- **Sketch possible designs for a Web composition.**
- **Explore your reactions to events, trends, or the media.**
- **Confide your hopes.**
- **Write about your own history:** an event in your family's past, a troubling incident in your life, a change you've seen.
- **Analyze a relationship that disturbs you.**
- **Practice various forms or styles of writing**—for instance, poems or songs, reviews of movies, or reports for TV news.

The writing you produce in your journal will help you learn and grow, and even the personal and seemingly nonacademic entries can supply ideas when you are seeking a subject to write about or are developing an essay. A thought you recorded months ago about a chemistry lab may provide direction for a research paper on the history of science. Two entries about arguments with your brother may suggest what you need to anchor a psychology paper on sibling relations. If you keep your journal on a computer, you can even copy passages from it directly into your drafts.

The following student samples give a taste of journal writing for different purposes. In the first, Charlie Gabnes tries to work out a personal problem with his child:

> Will's tantrums are getting worse—more often, more intense. Beginning to realize it's affecting my feelings for him. I feel resentment sometimes, and it's not as easy for me to cool off afterward as for him. Also I'm afraid of him sometimes for fear a tantrum will start, so treat him with kid gloves. How do we break this cycle?

In the next example Megan Polanyis ponders something she learned from her biology textbook:

> Ecology and economics have the same root—Greek word for house. Economy = managing the house. Ecology = studying the house. In ecology the house is all of nature, ourselves, the other animals, the plants, the earth, the air, the whole environment. Ecology has a lot to do with economy: study the house in order to manage it.

In the next example Sara Ling responds to an experience. (We'll follow Ling's writing process in this chapter and the next.)

> Had an exchange today on the snowboarding forum with a woman who joined the forum a while ago. She says she signed on at first with a screen name that didn't give away her gender, and she didn't tell anyone she was a woman. She was afraid the guys on the forum might shout her down. She waited until she'd established herself as an experienced snowboarder. Then she revealed her gender, and no one reacted badly. She asked me about my experiences, since my screen name says Sara. Had to admit I'd had problems of the what-does-a-girl-know sort. Wish I'd taken her approach.

2 Observing your surroundings

Sometimes you can find a good subject or good ideas by looking around you, not in the half-conscious way most of us move from place to place in our daily lives but deliberately, all senses alert. On a bus, for instance, are there certain types of passengers? What seems to be on the driver's mind? On campus, which buildings stand out? Are bicyclists and pedestrians at peace with each other?

To get the most from observation, you should have a handheld computer or a notepad and pen handy for taking notes and making sketches. If you have a camera, you may find that the lens sees things your unaided eyes do not notice. (When observing or photographing people, though, keep some distance, take photographs quickly, and avoid staring. Otherwise, your subjects will feel uneasy.) Back at your desk, study your notes, sketches, or photographs for oddities or patterns that you'd like to explore further.

In some academic writing, you'll be expected to formalize observation with surveys, interviews, or experiments. See pages 596 and 778.

ACTIVITIES THAT SUGGEST TOPICS AND IDEAS

1. Ask students to take a notebook with them to some place likely to be filled with activity and vivid sense impressions—a laundromat, the center of the campus, a busy restaurant. They can record their impressions of the scene in the notebook, later turning those impressions into a structured description or using the material in some other form of writing.

2. Ask students to look at a variety of magazines and to bring in a list of the topics covered in the articles. These topics may in turn suggest topics for student essays. The exercise can be extended by asking students to summarize the contents of one or more of the articles and to indicate how the content might appeal to a particular audience.

3. Check with your media center or a film rental service for short films that deal with values or controversies. The films or the ensuing discussions can become the basis of student papers.

4. Set up class presentations or debates on an issue in order to provide information and sharpen the focus for papers dealing with the issue or related topics.

PLACES TO WRITE

To help students discover interesting topics and ideas through freewriting, you might give them some places to begin. For essays focusing on events:

> sports, contests, camping, accidents, storms, childhood experiences, giving a speech, getting lost in a department store, robberies, fires

For writing about a scene or character:

> outdoors—woods, seashore, mountains, fields, city streets, parks
> indoors—dorm rooms, laundromats
> scenes—family gatherings, football games, funerals, a snowy morning
> people—parents, grandparents, uncles, aunts, childhood friends, people in a public place, teachers, unpleasant people, cartoon characters

For informative or explanatory writing:

> hobbies, jobs, investments, fields of study, recent scientific discoveries, places to visit, ways to save money, fishing, gardening, study habits, car repair, canoeing, audio equipment, magazines

For persuasive writing:

> campus issues, environmental concerns, automobile or airline safety, support for education, cost of medical care, regulation of new drugs, specialized education versus liberal arts education, rights of minorities and women, gun control, divorce and child rearing, school prayer, censorship, proposals to improve campus or local services, ways of dealing with a social problem

3 Freewriting

■ **Writing into a subject**

Many writers find subjects or discover ideas by **freewriting:** writing without stopping for a certain amount of time (say, ten minutes) or to a certain length (say, one page). The goal of freewriting is to generate ideas and information from *within* yourself by going around the part of your mind that doesn't want to write or can't think of anything to write. You let words themselves suggest other words. *What* you write is not important; that you *keep* writing is. Don't stop, even if that means repeating the same words until new words come. Don't go back to reread, don't censor ideas that seem dumb or repetitious, and above all don't stop to edit: grammar, punctuation, vocabulary, spelling, and the like are irrelevant at this stage.

The physical act of freewriting may give you access to ideas you were unaware of. For example, the following freewriting by a student, Robert Benday, drew him into the subject of writing as a disguise:

> Write to write. Seems pretty obvious, also weird. What to gain by writing? never anything before. Writing seems always—always—Getting corrected for trying too hard to please the teacher, getting corrected for not trying hard enuf. Frustration, nail biting, sometimes getting carried away making sentences to tell stories, not even true stories, esp. not true stories, that feels like creating something. Writing just pulls the story out of me. The story lets me be someone else, gives me a disguise.

(A later phase of Benday's writing appears on p. 23.)

If you write on a computer, try this technique for moving forward while freewriting: turn off your computer's monitor, or turn its brightness control all the way down so that the screen is dark. The computer will record what you type but keep it from you and thus prevent you from tinkering with your prose. This **invisible writing** may feel uncomfortable at first, but it can free the mind for very creative results. When you've finished freewriting, simply turn the monitor on or turn up the brightness control to read what you've written, and then save or revise it as appropriate. Later, you may be able to transfer some of your freewriting directly into your draft.

⟨ **CULTURE LANGUAGE** ⟩ Invisible writing can be especially helpful if you are uneasy writing in standard American English and you tend to worry about errors while writing. The blank computer screen leaves you no choice but to explore ideas without giving attention to the way you are expressing them. If you choose to write with the monitor on, concentrate on *what* you want to say, not *how* you are saying it.

■ **Focused freewriting**

Focused freewriting is more concentrated: you start with your question about your subject and answer it without stopping for, say, fifteen minutes or one full page. As in all freewriting, you push to bypass mental blocks and self-consciousness, not debating what to say or editing what you've written. With focused freewriting, though, you let the physical act of writing take you into and around your subject.

An example of focused freewriting can be found in the work of Sara Ling, whose journal entry appears on page 19. In a composition course, Ling's instructor had distributed "Welcome to Cyberbia," an essay by M. Kadi about communication on the Internet. The instructor then gave the following assignment:

> M. Kadi's "Welcome to Cyberbia" holds that the Internet will do little to bridge differences among people because its users gravitate toward other users who are like themselves in most respects. More than a decade later, do Kadi's concerns seem valid? Can the Internet serve as a medium for positive change in the way people of diverse backgrounds relate to each other? If so, how? If not, why not? In an essay of 500–700 words, respond to Kadi's essay with a limited and well-supported opinion of your own. The first draft is due Monday, October 31, for class discussion.

On first reading Kadi's essay, Ling had been impressed with its tight logic but had found unconvincing its pessimistic view of the Internet's potential. She reread the essay and realized that some of Kadi's assertions did not correspond to her own Internet experiences. This discovery led Ling to a question: *How might the Internet help to break down barriers between people?* Her focused freewriting began to develop an answer:

> Kadi says we only meet people like ourselves on the Internet, but I've met lots who have very different backgrounds and interests—or "turned out to have" is more like it, since I didn't know anything about them at first. There's the anonymity thing, but Kadi ignores it. You can be anyone or no one. People can get to know me and my ideas without knowing I'm female or Asian American or a student. Then they can find out the facts about me, but the facts will be less likely to get in the way of communication. Communication without set identity, especially physical appearance. This could make for more tolerance of others, of difference.

With this freewriting, Ling moved beyond her initial response to Kadi's essay into her own views of how anonymity on the Internet could improve communication among diverse groups.

4 Making a list

Like focused freewriting, list making requires opening yourself to everything that seems even remotely connected to your topic, without concern for order or repetition or form of expression. You can let your topic percolate for a day or more, recording thoughts on it whenever they occur. (For this approach to work, you need to keep paper or a computer with you at all times.) Or, in a method more akin to freewriting, you can **brainstorm** about the topic—that is, focus intently on

---

COLLABORATIVE LEARNING

TEAMED FREEWRITING

A good variation on freewriting is to make it collaborative: have students write freely for five or ten minutes, then pass their freewriting to the students sitting next to them. Students should read the freewriting, then reflect on it in another freewriting session. This encourages not only more perspectives on a topic but the notion that writing is a dialogue between writer and reader— and it teaches the value of feedback and audience awareness in writing as well.

COMPUTER ACTIVITY

FREEWRITING IN CYBERSPACE

Have students freewrite on the computer using the "invisible writing" technique if desired. During the next class period ask students to revise their freewriting into a paragraph, then e-mail that paragraph to another student in the class for a further critique and for revision suggestions. After a final revision, students might "publish" the resulting paragraphs on the network or hand them in for the teacher's evaluation.

RESOURCES AND IDEAS

On generative strategies

Flower, Linda S., and John R. Hayes. "Problem-Solving Strategies and the Writing Process." *College English* 39 (1977): 449–61. Flower and Hayes describe techniques for discovering and developing ideas, including cue words, nutshelling, idea trees, and brainstorming.

Hunter, Susan. "Oral Negotiations in a Textual Community: A Case for Pedagogy and Theory." *Writing Instructor* 8 (1989): 105–10. Hunter states that validating oral communication during the composing process is theoretically sound and helpful in generalizing successful oral communication to successful written communication.

Lackey, Kris. "Amongst the Awful Subtexts: Scholes, The *Daily Planet*, and Freshman Composition." *College Composition and Communication* 38 (1987): 88–93. In this thought-provoking piece, Lackey suggests encouraging and enabling students to tease out the binary oppositions in texts as a way of discovering various subtexts that suggest topics for students' own writing.

Perrin, Robert. "10:00 and 2:00: A Ten-Paragraph Defense of the Five-Paragraph Theme." *Teaching English in the Two Year College* 22 (March 2000): 312–314. Perrin defends assigning the infamous five-paragraph essay, showing that it does not necessarily stifle creativity.

Qualley, Donna. *Turns of Thought: Teaching Composition as Reflexive Inquiry.* Portsmouth: Boynton/Cook (Heinemann), 1997. Qualley advocates "essayism"—a mode of writing in which students reflect upon and reconsider their own claims in response to an encounter with a new idea or text.

Ratcliffe, Krista. "Rhetorical Listening: A Trope for Interpretive Invention and a 'Code of Cross-Cultural Conduct.'" *College Composition and Communication* 51 (1991): 195–224. Ratcliffe advocates a form of listening (as distinct from reading) in combination with rhetorical invention as a way of creating productive cross-cultural discourse.

Wesley, Kimberly. "The Ill Effects of the Five Paragraph Theme." *English Journal* 90 (September 2000): 57–60. Wesley argues that students' ability to think critically is stifled when a writing assignment is too prescribed.

the topic for a fixed amount of time (say, fifteen minutes), pushing yourself to list every idea and detail that comes to mind.

Like freewriting, brainstorming requires turning off your internal editor so that you keep moving ahead instead of looping back over what you have already written to correct it. It makes no difference whether the ideas and details are expressed in phrases or complete sentences. It makes no difference if they seem silly or irrelevant. Just keep pushing. If you are working on a computer, the technique of invisible writing, described on page 20, can help you move forward.

Here is an example of brainstorming by a student, Johanna Abrams, answering *What can a summer job teach?*

> summer work teaches—
>
>> how to look busy while doing nothing
>> how to avoid the sun in summer
>> seriously: discipline, budgeting money, value of money
>
> which job? Burger King cashier? baby-sitter? mail-room clerk?
> mail room: how to sort mail into boxes: this is learning??
> how to survive getting fired—humiliation, outrage
> Mrs. King! the mail-room queen as learning experience
> the shock of getting fired: what to tell parents, friends?
> Mrs. K was so rigid—dumb procedures
> Mrs. K's anger, resentment: the disadvantages of being smarter than your boss
> The odd thing about working in an office: a world with its own rules for how to act
> what Mr. D said about the pecking order—big chick (Mrs. K) pecks on little chick (me)
> probably lots of Mrs. Ks in offices all over—offices are all barnyards
> Mrs. K a sad person, really—just trying to hold on to her job, preserve her self-esteem
> a job can beat you down—destroy self-esteem, make you desperate enough to be mean to other people
> how to preserve/gain self-esteem from work??
> if I'd known about the pecking order, I would have been less show-offy, not so arrogant

(A later phase of Abrams's writing appears on pp. 34–35.)

When you think you've exhausted the ideas on your topic, you can edit and shape the list into a preliminary outline of your paper (see pp. 32–35). Working on a computer makes this step fairly easy: you can delete weak ideas, expand strong ones, and rearrange items with a few keystrokes. You can also freewrite from the list if you think some items are especially promising and deserve more exploration.

5 Clustering

Like freewriting and list making, **clustering** draws on free association and rapid, unedited work. But it also emphasizes the *rela-*

tions between ideas by combining writing and nonlinear drawing. When clustering, you radiate outward from a center point—your topic. When an idea occurs, you pursue related ideas in a branching structure until they seem exhausted. Then you do the same with other ideas, staying open to connections, continuously branching out or drawing arrows.

The example of clustering below shows how Robert Benday used the technique for ten minutes to expand on the topic of creative writing as a means of disguise, an idea he arrived at through freewriting (see p. 20). Though he ventured into one dead end, Benday also circled into the interesting possibility (at the bottom) that the fiction writer is like a god who forgives himself by creating characters that represent his good and bad qualities.

TOPIC CLUSTERS

The topic cluster we show in 2a-5 is very well developed; students need to know it's acceptable to develop smaller or messier clusters. You might ask students to work on topic clusters in groups. If your classroom permits, you might also want to try doing clusters on overhead transparencies or the blackboard, so that students can add to and change their contents more easily.

Clustering

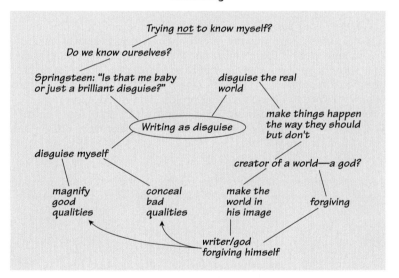

---

6 Using the journalist's questions

Asking yourself a set of questions about your subject—and writing out the answers—can help you look at the subject objectively and see fresh possibilities in it. Asking questions can also provide some structure to the development of ideas.

One such set of questions is that posed by a journalist with a story to report:

- Who was involved?
- What happened and what were the results?
- When did it happen?

USING QUESTIONS AND PATTERNS

To help students discover the power of sets of questions or the patterns of development for exploring topics, begin by giving them a list of general subjects—music, sports, guns, multiculturalism, the environment—and then ask them to explore each, looking for limited aspects that might make good topics for essays. Do not encourage students to use either the questions or the patterns in probing the topics. Class discussion can focus on how to limit the topics and can indicate how an audience might respond to them.

Following the discussion, ask students to explore the same topics using either the journalist's questions (2a-6) or the patterns of development (2a-7). Ask students to direct their attention to as many different aspects of the topic as they can and at the same time to suggest ways of developing it and organizing an essay around it. Discussion should focus on differences between the "guided" and "unguided" approaches to developing a topic.

RESOURCES AND IDEAS

On freewriting

Dunn, Patricia. *Talking, Sketching, Moving: Multiple Literacies in the Teaching of Writing.* Portsmouth, NH: Boyton/Cook, 2001. Dunn encourages us to motivate students to write and improve their attitude to writing through pre-writing assignments that include oral and visual presentations.

Elbow, Peter. *Writing Without Teachers.* New York: Oxford UP, 1973. In this classic work, Elbow discusses freewriting and other techniques for tapping imagination and creativity during the writing process.

Price, Gayle B. "A Case for a Modern Commonplace Book." *College Composition and Communication* 31 (1980): 175–82. This article reviews freewriting and other techniques for helping students generate ideas and tells how students can use a notebook to record ideas.

Reynolds, Mark. "Make Free Writing More Productive." *College Composition and Communication* 39 (1988): 81–82. Reynolds offers twenty "questions, activities, and guidelines" for drawing useful ideas and promising topics from the often jumbled material provided by freewriting.

On clustering

Frye, Bob. "Artful Compositions, Corder's 'Laws of Composition,' and the Weekly Letter: Two Approaches to Teaching Invention and Arrangement in Freshman English." *Journal of Teaching Writing* 8 (1989): 1–14. Frye argues that having students write replies to the instructor's weekly letters allows them to experience genuine rhetorical invention rather than experiencing closure, often the product of structure.

Rico, Gabriele Lusser. *Writing the Natural Way.* Los Angeles: Tarcher, 1983. Rico draws on research about brain functions as the basis for advice about strategies—especially clustering—that encourage creativity in expression.

- Where did it happen?
- Why did it happen?
- How did it happen?

These questions can also be useful in probing an essay subject, especially if you are telling a story or examining causes and effects. (See also the facing page.)

7 Using the patterns of development

The **patterns of development**—such as narration, definition, comparison and contrast, and classification—are ways we think about and understand a vast range of subjects, from our own daily experiences to the most complex scientific theories. They also serve as strategies and patterns for writing about these subjects, as illustrated by the discussions and paragraph-length examples on pages 91–100.

To see your subject from many angles and open up ideas about it, you can ask the following questions based on the patterns of development. Not all these questions will be productive, but at least a few should open up new possibilities. (You can download these questions from *ablongman.com/littlebrown*. Save the list in a file of its own, duplicate it for each writing project, and insert appropriate answers between the questions. Print your answers so they're handy as you develop your paper. You can also move passages from the answers directly into your draft.)

How did it happen?

In **narration** you develop the subject as a story, with important events usually arranged chronologically (as they occurred in time): for instance, an exciting basketball game or the steps leading to a war.

How does it look, sound, feel, smell, taste?

In **description** you use sensory details to give a clear impression of a person, place, thing, or feeling, such as a species of animal, a machine, a friend, a building, or an experience.

What are examples of it or reasons for it?

The pattern of **illustration** or **support** suggests development with one or more examples of the subject (one couple's efforts to adopt a child, say, or three states that outlaw Internet gambling) or with the reasons for believing or doing something (three reasons for majoring in English, four reasons for increasing federal aid to college students).

What is it? What does it encompass, and what does it exclude?

These questions lead to **definition**: specifying what the subject is and is not to give a precise sense of its meaning. Abstract terms—such as *justice, friendship,* and *art*—especially need defining (see p. 183).

What are its parts or characteristics?

Using the pattern of **division** or **analysis,** you separate a subject such as a bicycle or a short story into its elements and examine the relations between elements. The first step in critical thinking, analysis is also discussed on pages 158–59.

What groups or categories can it be sorted into?

Classification involves separating a large group (such as cars) into smaller groups (subcompact, compact, and so on) based on the characteristics of the individual items (the sizes of the cars). Another example: academic, business, personal, literary, and other types of writing.

How is it like, or different from, other things?

With **comparison and contrast** you point out the similarities and differences between ideas, objects, people, places, and so on: the differences between two similar computer systems, for instance, or the similarities between two opposing political candidates.

Is it comparable to something that is in a different class but more familiar to readers?

This question leads to **analogy,** an extended comparison of unlike subjects. Analogy is often used to explain a topic that may be unfamiliar to readers (for instance, the relation of atoms in a molecule) by reference to a familiar topic (two people slow dancing).

Why did it happen, or what results did it have?

With **cause-and-effect analysis,** you explain why something happened or what its consequences were or will be, or both: the causes of cerebral palsy, the effects of a Supreme Court decision, the causes and effects of a gradual change in the climate.

How do you do it, or how does it work?

In **process analysis** you explain how the subject happens (how a plant grows, how a robot works) or how it is accomplished (how to write an essay).

8   Reading

Many assignments require reading. To respond to M. Kadi's essay about the Internet, for instance, Sara Ling had to digest Kadi's work. Essays on literary works as well as research writing also demand reading. But even when reading is not required by an assignment, it can help you locate or develop your subject by introducing you to ideas you didn't know or expanding on what you do know.

Say you were writing in favor of amateur athletics, a subject to which you had given a lot of thought. You might be inclined to proceed entirely on your own, drawing on facts, examples, and opinions already in your head. But a little digging in sources might open up

On heuristics

Kneupper, Charles W. "Revising the Tagmemic Heuristic: Theoretical and Pedagogical Considerations." *College Composition and Communication* 31 (1980): 160–68. Kneupper offers a simplified version of the powerful question system introduced by Young, Becker, and Pike in their text, *Rhetoric: Discovery and Change* (New York: Harcourt, 1970).

Washington, Eugene. "WH-Questions in Teaching Composition." *College Composition and Communication* 28 (1977): 54–56. Washington suggests using what, why, where, and how questions to increase density of information in essays and clarify structure.

On patterns of development

D'Angelo, Frank J. *A Conceptual Theory of Rhetoric.* Cambridge: Winthrop, 1975. D'Angelo argues that rhetorical patterns of organization (e.g., analysis, classification, and description) are also patterns of thought and invention and can be used to probe experience as part of the composing process. See also D'Angelo's "Topoi and Form in Composition," in *The Territory of Language.* Ed. Donald A. McQuade. Carbondale: Southern Illinois UP, 1986. 114–22.

Podis, Leonard A. "Teaching Arrangement: Defining a More Practical Approach." *College Composition and Communication* 31 (1980): 197–204. Podis describes a teaching sequence designed to make students aware of the basic principles of organization, and he reviews some standard patterns of arrangement useful for academic and professional writing.

Wilcox, Lance. "Time Lines in the Composing of Narratives: A Graphic Aid to Organization." *The Writing Instructor* 6 (1987): 162–73. Wilcox describes in detail the use of time lines to help develop and organize narrative essays.

more. For instance, an article in *Time* magazine could introduce you to an old rule for amateur status, or a comment on a Web log could suggest a pro-amateurism argument that hadn't occurred to you.

People often read passively, absorbing content like blotters, not interacting with it. To read for ideas, you need to be more active, probing text and illustrations with your mind, nurturing any sparks they set off. Always write while you read, taking notes on content and—just as important—on what the content makes you *think*. (See pp. 138–42 for specific guidelines on the process of active reading.)

Note Whenever you use the information or ideas of others in your writing, you must acknowledge your sources in order to avoid the serious offense of plagiarism. (See Chapter 45.)

9   Thinking critically

Even if you do not read for information and ideas on your subject, you can still think critically about it. Critical thinking (discussed on pp. 157–63) can produce creative ideas by leading you to see what is not obvious. It can also lead you systematically to conclusions about your subject.

Sara Ling, writing about communication on the Internet, used the operations of critical thinking to explore her topic:

- **Analysis: What are the subject's elements or characteristics?** Ling looked at the ways Internet users can communicate because of their anonymity.
- **Interpretation: What is the meaning or significance of the elements?** Ling saw that the anonymity of Internet users could help them transcend their physical differences.
- **Synthesis: How do the elements relate to each other, or how does this subject relate to another one?** Ling perceived important and hopeful differences between anonymous Internet communication and face-to-face interaction.
- **Evaluation: What is the value or significance of the subject?** Ling concluded that by making people more tolerant of one another, the Internet could help build community out of diversity.

EXERCISE 2.1   Considering your past work: Developing a topic

In the past how have you generated the ideas for writing? Have you used any of the techniques described on the preceding pages? Have you found the process especially enjoyable or difficult? If some writing tasks were easier than others, what do you think made the difference?

EXERCISE 2.2   Keeping a journal

If you haven't already started a journal on your own or in response to Exercise 1.1 (pp. 3–4), try to do so now. Every day for at least a week, write for at least fifteen minutes about anything on your mind—or consult the list on page 18 for ideas of what to write about. At the end of the week, write about your experience. What did you like about journal writing? What didn't you like? What did you learn about yourself or the world from the writing? How can you use this knowledge?

EXERCISE 2.3 Using freewriting, brainstorming, or clustering

If you haven't tried any of them before, experiment with freewriting, brainstorming, or clustering. Continue with the subject you selected in Exercise 1.5 (p. 9), or begin with a new subject. Write or draw for at least ten minutes without stopping to reread and edit. (Try using invisible writing as described on p. 20 if you're freewriting or brainstorming on a computer.) When you finish your experiment, examine what you have written for ideas and relationships that could help you develop the subject. What do you think of the technique you tried? Did you have any difficulties with it? Did it help you loosen up and generate ideas?

EXERCISE 2.4 Sending an online query

When you have spent some time developing your subject, consider any doubts you may have or any information you still need. Send an online message to your classmates posing your questions and asking for their advice and insights.

EXERCISE 2.5 Developing your subject

Use at least two of the discovery techniques discussed on the preceding pages to develop the subject you selected in Exercise 1.5 (p. 9). (If you completed Exercise 2.3 above, then use one additional technique.) Later exercises for your essay-in-progress will be based on the ideas you generate in this exercise.

2b Developing a thesis

Your readers will expect an essay you write to be focused on a central idea, or **thesis**, to which all the essay's paragraphs, all its general statements and specific information, relate. The thesis is the controlling idea, the main point, the conclusion you have drawn about the evidence you have accumulated. It is the answer to the question you have been posing about your subject.

A thesis will probably not leap fully formed into your head. You may begin with an idea you want to communicate, but you will need to refine that idea to fit the realities of the paper you write. And often you will have to write and rewrite before you come to a conclusion about what you have. Still, it's wise to try to pin down your thesis when you have a fairly good stock of ideas. Then the thesis can help you start drafting, help keep you focused, and serve as a point of reference when changes inevitably occur.

IMPLICIT THESIS VERSUS EXPLICIT THESIS

Students need to understand that all good writing has a controlling idea (an implied thesis) but that some good writing doesn't have an explicit thesis. Asking students to look for theses in various kinds of writing (from textbooks to novels to travel articles to junk mail) is one way of showing them that a writer must decide whether to use an explicit thesis based on his or her purpose and audience.

1 Conceiving a thesis statement

A thesis is an idea. Spelling out the idea in a **thesis statement** gives you something concrete to work with. Eventually you may place your thesis statement or (more likely) a revised version in the introduction of your final essay as a promise to readers of what they can expect.

As an expression of the thesis, the thesis statement serves three crucial functions and one optional one.

Functions of the thesis statement

- The thesis statement **narrows your subject** to a single, central idea that you want readers to gain from your essay.
- It **claims something specific and significant** about your subject, a claim that requires support.
- It **conveys your purpose**, your reason for writing.
- It often concisely **previews the arrangement of ideas.**

Here are some examples of questions and answering thesis statements. As assertions, the thesis statements each consist of a topic (usually naming the general subject) and a claim about the topic.

Question	Thesis statement
1. What are the advantages of direct distribution of music via the Web?	Because artists can now publish their music directly via the Web, consumers have many more choices than traditional distribution allows. [**Topic:** consumers. **Claim:** have many more choices.]
2. How did Home Inc. survive the scandal over its hiring practices?	After Home Inc.'s hiring practices were exposed in the media, the company avoided a scandal with policy changes and a well-publicized outreach to employees and consumers. [**Topic:** the company. **Claim:** avoided a scandal in two ways.]
3. What steps can prevent juvenile crime?	Juveniles can be diverted from crime by active learning programs, full-time sports, and intervention by mentors and role models. [**Topic:** juveniles. **Claim:** can be diverted from crime in three ways.]
4. Why did Abraham Lincoln delay in emancipating the slaves?	Lincoln delayed emancipating any slaves until 1863 because his primary goal was to restore and preserve the Union, with or without slavery. [**Topic:** Lincoln's delay. **Claim:** was caused by his goal of preserving the Union.]

5. Which college students should be entitled to federal aid?	As an investment in its own economy, the United States should provide a tuition grant to any college student who qualifies academically. [**Topic:** United States. **Claim:** should provide a tuition grant to any college student who qualifies academically.]
6. Why should strip-mining be controlled?	Strip-mining should be tightly controlled in this region to reduce its pollution of water resources, its destruction of the land, and its devastating effects on people's lives. [**Topic:** strip-mining. **Claim:** should be tightly controlled for three reasons.]

Notice that statements 3 and 6 clearly predict the organization of the essay that will follow. Notice, too, that every statement conveys the purpose of its writer. Statements 1 to 4 announce that the writers mainly want to explain something to readers: music choices for consumers, a company's success in avoiding a scandal, and so on. Statements 5 and 6 announce that the authors mainly want to convince readers of something: the federal government should aid qualified college students; strip-mining should be controlled.

◆ CULTURE LANGUAGE ◆ In some cultures it is considered rude or unnecessary for a writer to state his or her main idea outright or to state it near the beginning. When writing in American schools or workplaces, you can assume that your readers expect a clear and early idea of what you think.

2 Drafting and revising a thesis statement

To draft a thesis statement, begin with your question about your subject. If you have updated the question as you generated ideas and information, answering it can get you started.

Question   Why did Lincoln delay in emancipating the slaves?
Answer   Lincoln's goal was primarily to restore and preserve the Union.

Question   How might the Internet help to break down barriers between people?
Answer   Anonymous Internet communication can bypass physical differences.

The next step is to spell out the answer in a sentence that names the topic and makes a claim about it. Creating this sentence may require several drafts.

Sara Ling went through a common process in writing and revising her thesis statement on Internet communication. She first answered her starting question, as shown in the second pair of examples above. Then she tried a statement derived from her answer:

ORAL PROGRESS REPORTS

Have students report orally to the class or to their peer writing groups on topics and thesis statements for a coming paper. Giving an oral presentation forces students to focus their ideas and adopt a stance. As they speak, moreover, students may sense difficulties with the topic or thesis. Comments from classmates can help identify strengths and weaknesses and suggest an appropriate tone for the essay.

CONDENSING THE ARGUMENT

Often the exercise of condensing the main ideas of a paper in a separate forum can help writers recognize and articulate their thesis. Ask students to set their paper-in-progress aside and write a short (three sentences to one paragraph) abstract summarizing its central argument.

STUDENT MODELS

You may wish to copy effective thesis statements from student papers to use in class discussion or small-group work. The statements will provide positive models and may suggest topics for future essays. You can vary this exercise by copying ineffective statements and discussing how they may be revised. Be sure to keep the discussion of ineffective statements positive in tone, however.

SUPPLYING AN OMITTED THESIS STATEMENT

Ask students to read their papers to the class or to a peer group, deliberately leaving out the thesis statement. Ask the other students to supply a thesis for the essay. If the original thesis and the one supplied by the students match, fine. If not, the thesis a student has chosen may be inappropriate for the paper and the discussion that follows can suggest possible revisions.

COLLABORATIVE LEARNING

AGREEMENT ON THESIS

Ask students to read an essay from a collection or a fellow student's paper and then to state its thesis in their own words. Divide students into small groups and ask the group members to come up with a thesis statement together. Next have the groups try to identify a thesis statement in the essay. If the essay has an explicit thesis statement, ask if they consider it effective or if the thesis statement they produced would be more effective. If the thesis is implicit, ask students whether or not the essay would benefit from an explicit thesis statement.

TRANSPARENCY MASTER 2.2

COLLABORATIVE LEARNING

THESIS CHECKLIST

Divide students into pairs or small groups and ask them to use the Checklist for revising the thesis statement as a tool for peer review. They can trade essays and use the checklist to evaluate one another's thesis statements.

> Internet communication that is anonymous can bypass physical differences.

Ling saw that this statement focused on her starting topic (*Internet communication*) but somewhat buried the crucial quality of anonymity. And the claim lacked significance: So what? Ling first tried to emphasize her intended subject:

> The anonymity of Internet communication . . .

Then she worked on her claim:

> . . . can bypass physical differences, and it could build diversity into community.

This statement said why the subject was significant (*it could build diversity into community*) but the idea was tacked on with *and.* Ling tried again, emphasizing cause and effect:

> Through bypassing physical differences, the unique anonymity of Internet communication could build diversity into community.

For her final revision, Ling responded to a friend's comment that *bypassing physical differences* was too vague. She spelled out her meaning:

> By lowering the barriers of physical appearance, the unique anonymity of Internet communication could build diversity into community.

When you are writing and revising your thesis statement, check it against the following questions:

Checklist for revising the thesis statement

- How well does the **subject** of your statement capture the subject of your paper?
- What **claim** does your statement make about your subject?
- What is the **significance** of the claim? How does it answer "So what?" and convey your purpose?
- How can the claim be **limited** or made more **specific**? Does it state a single idea and clarify the boundaries of the idea?
- How **unified** is the statement? How does each word and phrase contribute to a single idea?

Here are other examples of thesis statements revised to meet these requirements:

Original	Revised
Seat belts can save lives, but now carmakers are installing air bags. [Not unified: how do the two parts of the sentence relate?]	If drivers had used lifesaving seat belts more often, carmakers might not have needed to install air bags.

This new product brought in over $300,000 last year. [A statement of fact, not a claim about the product: what is significant about the product's success?]

This new product succeeded because of its innovative marketing campaign, including widespread press coverage, in-store entertainment, and a consumer newsletter.

People should not go on fad diets. [A vague statement that needs limiting with one or more reasons: what's wrong with fad diets?]

Fad diets can be dangerous when they deprive the body of essential nutrients or rely excessively on potentially harmful foods.

Televised sports are different from live sports. [A general statement: how are they different, and why is the difference significant?]

Although television cannot transmit all the excitement of a live game, its close-ups and slow-motion replays reveal much about the players and the strategy of the game.

Note You may sometimes need more than one sentence for your thesis statement, particularly if it requires some buildup:

Modern English, especially written English, is full of bad habits that interfere with clear thinking. Getting rid of these habits is a first step to political regeneration. —Adapted from George Orwell, "Politics and the English Language"

However, don't use this leeway to produce a wordy, general, or disunified statement. The two (or more) sentences must build on each other, and the final sentence must present the key assertion of your paper.

EXERCISE 2.6 Evaluating thesis statements

Evaluate the following thesis statements, considering whether each one is sufficiently significant, specific, and unified. Rewrite the statements as necessary to meet these goals.

1. Aggression usually leads to violence, injury, and even death, and we should use it constructively.
2. The religion of Islam is widely misunderstood in the United States.
3. Manners are a kind of social glue.
4. One episode of a radio talk show amply illustrates both the appeal of such shows and their silliness.
5. The poem is about motherhood.

EXERCISE 2.7 Considering your past work: Developing a thesis

Have you been aware in the past of focusing your essays on a central idea, or thesis? Have you found it more efficient to try to pin down your idea early or to let it evolve during drafting? To what extent has a thesis helped or hindered you in shaping your draft?

ANSWERS: EXERCISE 2.6

1. The statement lacks unity because the two halves do not seem to relate to each other.
   Possible revision: We should channel our natural feelings of aggression toward constructive rather than destructive ends.
2. The statement needs to be more specific and significant: How is Islam misunderstood? So what?
   Possible revision: Americans' misconceptions about Islam—especially that it is fanatical and oppressive—contribute to global instability.
3. The statement needs to be more specific: How do manners work as "social glue"?
   Possible revision: Manners are a kind of social glue, binding people together by regulating the interctions of acquaintances and strangers alike.
4. Good thesis statement: significant, specific, and unified.
5. The statement simply states a fact.
   Possible revision: The poem depicts motherhood as a saintly calling.

ANSWERS: EXERCISE 2.7

Individual response.

ANSWERS: EXERCISE 2.8

Individual response.

RESOURCES AND IDEAS

Liszka, Thomas R. "Formulating a Thesis for Essays Employing Comparison." *College Composition and Communication* 38 (1987): 474–77. Liszka offers a method that helps students to generate theses and guides them in organizing and developing their essays; the method appears to be adaptable to various kinds of essays.

COLLABORATIVE LEARNING

ASSESSING STRUCTURES

Ask students to find (in newspapers or magazines) essays that use a general-to-specific, specific-to-general, or problem-solution structure. Working in pairs, they can discuss the appropriateness and effectiveness of each essay's structure.

COMPUTER ACTIVITY

BOLD HIGHLIGHTS

Ask students to use the Bold function or particular fonts to highlight general ideas and distinguish them from specific ideas.

EXERCISE 2.8   Drafting and revising your own thesis statement

Continuing from Exercise 2.5 (p. 27), write a significant, specific, and unified thesis statement for your essay-in-progress.

2c   Organizing ideas

An effective essay has a recognizable shape—an arrangement of parts that guides readers, helping them see how ideas and details relate to each other and contribute to the whole. You may sometimes let an effective organization emerge over one or more drafts. But many writers find that organizing ideas to some extent before drafting can provide a helpful sense of direction, as a map can help a driver negotiate a half-familiar system of roads. If you feel uncertain about the course your essay should follow or have a complicated topic with many parts, devising a shape for your material can clarify your options.

Before you begin organizing your material, look over all the writing you've done so far—freewriting, notes from reading, whatever. Either on paper or on a computer, pull together a master list of all the ideas and details you think you might want to include. You can add to or subtract from the list as you think about shape.

1 Distinguishing the general and the specific

To organize material for an essay, you need to distinguish general and specific ideas and see the relations between ideas. **General** and **specific** refer to the number of instances or objects included in a group signified by a word. The "ladder" below illustrates a general-to-specific hierarchy.

Most general
↑ life form
  plant
  flowering plant
  rose
  American Beauty rose
↓ Uncle Dan's prize-winning American Beauty rose
Most specific

Here are some tips for arranging the ideas in your preliminary writing:

- **Underline, boldface, or circle the most general ideas.** These are the ideas that offer the main support for your thesis statement. They will be more general than the evidence that in turn supports them.

- **Make connections between each general idea and the more specific details that support it.** On paper, start with a fresh sheet, write each general idea down with space beneath it, and add specific information in the appropriate spaces. On a computer, rearrange supporting information under more general points. Your word processor may include a Comment function that allows you to add notes about connections.
- **Respect the meanings of ideas.** Think through the implications of ideas as you sort them. Otherwise, your hierarchies could become jumbled, with *rose,* for instance, illogically subordinated to *animal,* or *life form* somehow subordinated to *rose.*
- **Remove information that doesn't fit.** If you worry about losing deleted information, transfer the notes to a separate sheet of paper or word-processing file.
- **Fill holes where support seems skimpy.** If you recognize a hole but don't know what to fill it with, try using a discovery technique such as freewriting or clustering, or go back to your research sources.
- **Experiment with various arrangements of general ideas and supporting information.** Seek an order that presents your material clearly and logically. On paper, you can cut the master list apart and paste or tape each general idea and its support on a separate piece of paper. Then try different orders for the pages. On a computer, first save the master list and duplicate it. To move material around, select a block of text and either copy and then paste it where you want it or (a little quicker) drag the selected text to where you want it.

2 Choosing an organizing tool

Some writers view outlines as chores and straitjackets, but they need not be dull or confining. There are different kinds of outlines, some more flexible than others. All of them can enlarge and clarify your thinking, showing you patterns of general and specific, suggesting proportions, and highlighting gaps or overlaps in coverage.

Many writers use outlines not only before but also after drafting—to check the underlying structure of the draft when revising it (see p. 49). No matter when it's made, though, an outline can change to reflect changes in your thinking. View any outline you make as a tentative sketch, not as a fixed paint-by-numbers diagram.

■ A scratch or informal outline

For many essays, especially those with a fairly straightforward structure, a simple listing of ideas and perhaps their support may provide adequate direction for your writing.

A **scratch outline** lists the key points of the paper in the order they will be covered. Here is Sara Ling's scratch outline for her essay on Internet communication:

Thesis statement

By lowering the barriers of physical appearance, the unique anonymity of Internet communication could build diversity into community.

Scratch outline

No fear of prejudgment
    Physical attributes unknown—age, race, gender, etc.
    We won't be shut out because of appearance
Inability to prejudge others
    Assumptions based on appearance
    Meeting of minds only
    Finding shared interests and concerns

Ling put more into this outline than its simplicity might imply, not only working out an order for her ideas but also sketching their implications.

An **informal outline** is usually more detailed than a scratch outline, including key general points and the specific evidence for them. A student's informal outline appears below.

Thesis statement

After Home Inc.'s hiring practices were exposed in the media, the company avoided a scandal with policy changes and a well-publicized outreach to employees and consumers.

Informal outline

Background on scandal
    Previous hiring practices
    Media exposure and public response (brief)
Policy changes
    Application forms
    Interviewing procedures
    Training of personnel
Outreach to employees
    Signs and letters
    Meetings and workshops
Outreach to consumers
    Press conference
    Store signs
    Advertising—print and radio

■ A tree diagram

In a **tree diagram,** ideas and details branch out in increasing specificity. Like any outline, the diagram can warn of gaps, overlaps, and digressions. But unlike more linear outlines, it can be supplemented and extended indefinitely, so it is easy to alter for new ideas and arrangements discovered during drafting and revision.

Below is a tree diagram by Johanna Abrams, based on her earlier brainstorming about a summer job (p. 22) and the following thesis statement:

Thesis statement

Two months working in a large government agency taught me that an office's pecking order should be respected.

Tree diagram

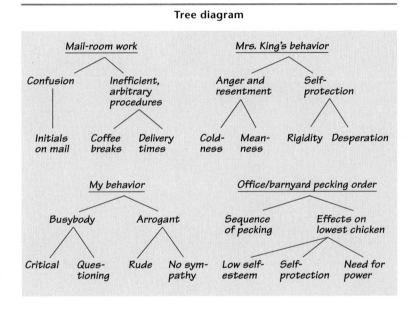

Each main part of the four-part diagram represents a different general idea about the summer-job experience. Within each part, information grows more specific as it branches downward.

A tree diagram or other visual map can be especially useful for planning a project for the World Wide Web. The diagram can help you lay out the organization of your project and its links and then later can serve as a site map for your readers. (For more on composing for the Web, see pp. 832–38.)

■ A formal outline

For complex topics requiring complex arrangements of ideas and support, you may want or be required to construct a **formal outline.** More rigidly arranged and more detailed than other outlines,

CUT-AND-PASTE OUTLINES

The flexibility of a computer's Cut-and-Paste feature allows students to arrange ideas in various order and then to consider the result. As a follow-up to Exercises 2.9 and 2.10, pose a thesis statement (such as one of the revised examples from Exercise 2.6), then have students brainstorm on the computer to come up with a related list of ideas and organize them into several possible outlines.

a formal outline not only lays out main ideas and their support but also shows the relative importance of all the essay's elements and how they connect with one another.

Note Because of its structure, a formal outline can be an excellent tool for checking the arrangement of a draft before revising it (see p. 49).

On the basis of her scratch outline (p. 34), Sara Ling prepared this formal outline for her essay on the Internet:

Thesis statement

By lowering the barriers of physical appearance, the unique anonymity of Internet communication could build diversity into community.

Formal outline

I. No fear of being prejudged
    A. Unknown physical attributes
        1. Gender
        2. Age
        3. Race
        4. Style
    B. Freer communication
    C. No automatic rejection
II. Inability to prejudge others
    A. No assumptions based on appearance
        1. Body type
        2. Physical disability
        3. Race
    B. Discovery of shared interests and concerns
        1. Sports and other activities
        2. Family values
        3. Political views
    C. Reduction of physical bias

Ling's outline illustrates several principles of outlining that can help ensure completeness, balance, and clear relationships. (These principles largely depend on distinguishing between the general and the specific. See pp. 32–33.)

Principles of the formal outline

- Labels and indentions indicate order and relative importance.
- Sections and subsections reflect logical relationships.
- Topics of equal generality appear in parallel headings.
- Each subdivision has at least two parts.
- Headings are expressed in parallel grammatical form.
- The introduction and conclusion may be omitted (though not, of course, from the essay).

- **All the outline's parts are systematically indented and labeled.** Roman numerals (I, II) label primary divisions of the essay, indented capital letters (A, B) label secondary divisions, and farther indented Arabic numerals (1, 2) label principal supporting points and examples. A fourth level would be indented farther still and labeled with small letters (a, b). Each succeeding level contains more specific information than the one before it.

- **The outline divides the material into several groups.** An uninterrupted listing of ideas like the one following would indicate a need for tighter, more logical relationships among ideas. (Compare this example with part II of Ling's actual outline.)

  II. Inability to prejudge others
      A. Body type
      B. Physical disability
      C. Race
      D. Sports and other activities
      E. Family values
      F. Political views
      G. Reduction of physical bias

- **Within each part of the outline, distinct topics of equal generality appear in parallel headings,** with the same indention and numbering or lettering. In the following example, points B, C, and D are more specific than point A, not equally general, so they should be subheadings 1, 2, and 3 under it. (See section IIA of Ling's outline.)

      A. No assumptions based on appearance
      B. Body type
      C. Physical disability
      D. Race

- **All subdivided headings in the outline break into at least two parts** because a topic cannot logically be divided into only one part. The following example violates this principle:

      B. Discovery of shared views
          1. Interests and concerns

  Any single subdivision should be combined with the heading above it (as in section IIB of Ling's actual outline), matched with another subdivision, or rechecked for its relevance to the heading above it.

- **All headings are expressed in parallel grammatical form** (see pp. 405–09 on parallelism). Ling's is a **topic outline,** in which the headings consist of a noun (*fear, attributes, gender,* and the like) with modifiers (*no, unknown physical, no automatic,* and the like). In a **sentence outline** all headings are expressed as full sentences, as in the following rewrite of part II of Ling's outline.

II. On the Internet, we are unable to prejudge others.
   A. We cannot make common assumptions based on physical appearance.
      1. People with athletic builds must be unintelligent.
      2. People in wheelchairs must be unapproachable or pathetic.
      3. People of other races must hold views different from our own.
   B. We discover shared interests and concerns.
      1. We find common ground in sports and other activities.
      2. We see that we all feel much the same about our families.
      3. We learn the similarities in each other's political views.
   C. The Internet could reduce physical bias in the world.

See pages 692–93 for a complete sentence outline.

- **The outline covers only the body of the essay, omitting the introduction and the conclusion.** The beginning and the ending are important in the essay itself, but you need not include them in the outline unless you are required to do so or anticipate special problems with their organization.

3 Choosing a structure

Introduction, body, and conclusion

Most essays share a basic shape:

- **The *introduction*, usually a paragraph or two, draws readers into the world of the essay.** At a minimum, it announces and clarifies the topic. Often, it ends with the thesis statement, making a commitment that the rest of the essay delivers on. (See pp. 102–06 for more on introductions.)
- **The *body* of the essay develops the thesis and thus fulfills the commitment of the introduction.** The paragraphs in the body develop the general points that support the thesis—the items that would be labeled with Roman numerals and capital letters in a formal outline like the one on page 36. These general points are like the legs of a table supporting the top, the thesis. Each general point may take a paragraph or more, with the bulk of the content providing the details, examples, and reasons (the wood of the table) to support the general point and thus the thesis.
- **The *conclusion* gives readers something to take away from the essay**—a summary of ideas, for instance, or a suggested course of action. (See pp. 106–09 for more on conclusions.)

This basic shape applies mainly to traditional essays. A composition for the World Wide Web probably will have a more flexible structure and will lack a formal conclusion. See pages 832–38 for more on composing for the Web.

    CULTURE & LANGUAGE If you are not used to reading and writing American academic prose, its pattern of introduction-body-conclusion and the particular schemes discussed below may seem unfamiliar. For instance, instead of introductions that focus quickly on the topic and thesis, you may be used to openings that establish personal connections with readers or that approach the thesis indirectly. And instead of body paragraphs that first emphasize general points and then support those points with specific evidence, you may be used to general statements without support (because writers can assume that readers will supply the evidence themselves) or to evidence without explanation (because writers can assume that readers will infer the general points themselves). When writing American academic prose, you need to take into account readers' expectations for directness and for the statement and support of general points.

■ Organizing the body by space or time

Two organizational schemes—spatial and chronological—grow naturally out of the topic. A **spatial organization** is especially appropriate for essays that describe a place, an object, or a person. Following the way people normally survey something, you move through space from a chosen starting point to other features of the subject. Describing a building, for instance, you might begin with an impression of the whole, then scan exterior details from top to bottom, and then describe interior spaces.

A **chronological organization** reports events as they occurred in time, usually from first to last. This pattern, like spatial organization, corresponds to readers' own experiences and expectations. It suits an essay in which you do one of the following:

- **Recount a sequence of events,** such as a championship baseball game or the Battle of Gettysburg.
- **Explain a process from beginning to end**—for instance, how to run a marathon or how a tree converts carbon dioxide to oxygen.
- **Explain the causes that led to an effect,** such as the lobbying that helped to push a bill through the legislature. Alternatively,

CULTURE LANGUAGE

WRITING PATTERNS

In some cultures, expository writing patterns are circular rather than linear: students will repeat or restate the topic sentence before going on to the next topic. As a result, students seem to be "writing in circles" when they are simply following the pattern they have been taught. Explain to students that in American expository writing development is linear; that transitions, not restated topics, link ideas together in a paper; and that the conclusion is the point at which ideas are restated or summarized.

I. Introduction with thesis
    A. Idea 1
        1. Support
    B. Idea 2 (with transition)
        1. Support
II. Conclusion
    A. Summarize ideas
    B. Restate thesis in a fresh way

Schemes for organizing ideas in an essay

- Space
- Time
- Emphasis

General to specific	Increasing importance (climax)
Specific to general	Decreasing familiarity
Problem-solution	Increasing complexity

PURPOSE OUTLINES

Some students have trouble maintaining unity of purpose and coherent organization even after they have outlined an essay because the outline describes the content of the essay but does not indicate the function of each part. To help students overcome this problem, ask them to add a statement of purpose to each major section of their outlines and to indicate how the section will carry out the purpose of the paper, as in this example:

> In this section I plan to explain how much money industries lose by failing to treat industrial waste to recover precious metals like chromium, gold, silver, and platinum. This will be the second of the three little-known costs of pollution that my thesis statement promises the paper will discuss.

Statements of purpose can alert students to potential problems in the organization or unity of an essay, and they can provide instructors with a quick way to spot the problems. Some instructors even ask students to submit "purpose outlines" in place of formal outlines:

> In this section of the paper, I plan to show that there is a real need for this university to provide more funds for the library. To support my point, I plan to explore three serious effects of underfunding—lack of basic reference materials, lack of staff to shelve books properly and check for missing volumes, and poor maintenance of the library building.

USING VISUAL CUES

Some students find it handy to write their purpose statement or thesis on squares of stick-on paper and post these on their drafts, over their desks, or on the monitor of their word processors, in order to keep these ideas clearly in mind.

explain how a cause, such as a flood or a book, had multiple effects.

- **Tell a story about yourself or someone else.**
- **Provide background**—for instance, the making of a film you are analyzing or the procedure used in an experiment you are reporting.

■ Organizing the body for emphasis

Some organizational schemes must be imposed on ideas and information to aid readers' understanding and achieve a desired emphasis.

General to specific

Two ways of organizing essays depend on the distinction between the general and the specific, discussed on pages 32–33. The **general-to-specific scheme** is common in expository and argumentative essays that start with a general discussion of the main points and then proceed to specific examples, facts, or other evidence. The following thesis statement forecasts a general-to-specific organization:

> As an investment in its own economy, the United States should provide a tuition grant to any college student who qualifies academically.

The body of the essay might first elaborate on the basic argument and then provide the supporting data.

Specific to general

Sometimes you may anticipate that readers will not appreciate or agree with your general ideas before they see the support for them—for instance, in an expository essay that presents a unique way of looking at common experience, or in an argumentative essay that takes an unpopular view. In these cases a **specific-to-general scheme** can arouse readers' interest in specific examples or other evidence, letting the evidence build to statements of more general ideas. The following thesis statement could be developed in this way:

> Although most of us are unaware of the public relations campaigns directed at us, they can significantly affect the way we think and live.

The writer might devote most of the essay to a single specific example of a public relations campaign and then explain more generally how the example typifies public relations campaigns.

Problem-solution

Many arguments use a **problem-solution scheme:** first outline a problem that needs solving; then propose a solution. (If the solution involves steps toward a goal, it may be arranged chronologically.) The following thesis statement announces a problem-solution paper:

To improve workflow and quality, the data-processing department should add one part-time staffer and retrain three others in the new systems.

Climax

A common scheme in both explanations and arguments is the **climactic organization,** in which ideas unfold in order of increasing drama or importance to a climax. For example, the following thesis statement lists three effects of strip-mining in order of their increasing severity, and the essay would cover them in the same order:

Strip-mining should be tightly controlled in this region to reduce its pollution of water resources, its destruction of the land, and its devastating effects on people's lives.

As this example suggests, the climactic organization works well in arguments because it leaves readers with the most important point freshest in their minds. In exposition such an arrangement can create suspense and thus hold readers' attention.

Familiarity or complexity

Expository essays can also be arranged to take account of reader's knowledge of the subject. An essay on the effects of air pollution might proceed from **most familiar to least familiar**—from effects readers are likely to know to ones they may not know. Similarly, an explanation of animals' nervous systems might proceed from **simplest to most complex,** so that the explanation of each nervous system provides a basis for readers to understand the more difficult one following.

4   Checking for unity and coherence

In conceiving your organization and writing your essay, you should be aware of two qualities of effective writing that relate to organization: unity and coherence. When you perceive that someone's writing "flows well," you are probably appreciating these two qualities. An essay has **unity** if all its parts relate to and support the thesis statement. Check for unity with these questions:

- Is each main section relevant to the main idea (thesis) of the essay?
- Within main sections, does each example or detail support the principal idea of that section?

An essay has **coherence** if readers can see the relations among parts and move easily from one thought to the next. Check for coherence with these questions:

- Do the ideas follow in a clear sequence?
- Are the parts of the essay logically connected?
- Are the connections clear and smooth?

A unified and coherent outline will not necessarily guide you to a unified and coherent essay, because so much can change during drafting. Thus you shouldn't be too hard on your outline, in case a seemingly wayward idea proves useful. But do cut obvious digressions and rearrange material that clearly needs moving.

■ Sample essay

The following essay illustrates some ways of achieving unity and coherence (highlighted in the annotations).

MODELS OF STUDENT WRITING

While "A Picture of Hyperactivity" is included here for its ways of achieving unity and coherence, its argument and tone are also worthy of consideration. If your students have had any experience with ADHD themselves, they may have a lot to say about the argument of this essay. If they knew nothing about ADHD before reading Linda Devereaux's essay, they might want to do additional research about learning disabilities. You might also want to ask your students to discuss how well the emotional tone of the piece advances its argument, and this might lead to a more general discussion of how to write about emotionally laden topics.

RESOURCES AND IDEAS

On organizational strategies

Lotto, Edward. "Utterance and Text in Freshman English." *College English* 51 (1989): 677–87. Lotto analyzes the differences between spoken and written language as they relate to the difficulties students have in supporting generalizations with concrete examples. He makes suggestions for helping students become aware of text and concrete expression.

Perdue, Virginia. "The Politics of Teaching Detail." *Rhetoric Review* 8 (1990): 280–88. Perdue provides methods for using detail to arrive at broader thoughts in the composing process.

Walvoord, Barbara, Virginia Johnson Anderson, John R. Breihan, Lucille Parkinson McCarthy, Susan Miller Robinson, and A. Kimbrough Sherman. "Functions of Outlining Among College Students in Four Disciplines." *Research in the Teaching of English* 29 (1995): 390–421. The authors demonstrate the varying functions served by outlining across the disciplines and explore the strategies that students use in different situations.

On unity and coherence

Sloan, Gary. "The Frequency of Transitional Markers in Discursive Prose." *College English*

A Picture of Hyperactivity

Introduction establishing subject of essay

A hyperactive committee member can contribute to efficiency. A hyperactive salesperson can contribute to profits. When children are hyperactive, though, people—even parents—may wish they had never been born. **[Thesis statement]** A collage of those who must cope with hyperactivity in children is a picture of frustration, anger, and loss.

Paragraph idea, linked to thesis statement

The first part of the collage is the doctors. In their terminology, the word hyperactivity has been replaced by ADHD, attention-deficit hyperactivity disorder. **[Paragraph developed with evidence supporting its idea]** They apply the term to children who are abnormally or excessively busy. But doctors do not fully understand the problem and thus differ over how to treat it. Some recommend a special diet, others recommend behavior-modifying drugs, and still others, who do not consider ADHD a medical problem, recommend psychotherapy. The result is a merry-go-round of tests, confusion, and frustration for the children and their parents.

Paragraph idea, linked to thesis statement

As the mother of an ADHD child, I can say what the disorder means to the parents who form the second part of the collage. **[Paragraph developed with evidence supporting its idea]** It means worry that is deep and enduring. It means despair that is a constant companion. It means a mixture of frustration, guilt, and anger. And finally, since there are times when parents' anger goes out of control and threatens the children, it means self-loathing.

Transition

Paragraph idea, linked to thesis statement

The weight of ADHD, however, does not rest on the doctors and parents. The darkest part of the collage belongs to the children. **[Paragraph developed with evidence supporting its idea]** From early childhood they may be dragged from doctor to doctor, attached to machines, medicated until they feel numb, and tested or discussed by physicians, teachers, neighbors, and strangers on the street. They may be highly intelligent, but they'll still do poorly in school because of their short attention spans. Their playmates dislike them because of their temper and their unwillingness to follow rules. Even their pets mistrust them because of their erratic behavior. As time goes on, the children see their parents more and more in tears and anger, and they know they are the cause.

The collage is complete, and it is dark and somber. ADHD, as applied to children, is a term with uncertain, unattractive, and bitter associations. The picture does have one bright spot, however, for inside every ADHD child is a lovely, trusting, calm person waiting to be recognized.

—Linda Devereaux (student)

> Conclusion echoing thesis statement, summarizing, and looking ahead

■ Unity and coherence within paragraphs

The unity and coherence of writing begin in its paragraphs, so the two concepts are treated in greater detail in Chapter 4. You may want to consult several sections in particular before you begin drafting:

- ■ **The topic sentence and unity** (pp. 72–75)
- ■ **Transitions and coherence** (pp. 77–88, 108)
- ■ **Linking paragraphs in the essay** (pp. 109–10)

■ Unity and coherence on the Web

Unity and coherence may seem unimportant in compositions for the World Wide Web, in which entire documents are linked to each other so that it's easy to move among them. However, precisely because the Web is such a fluid medium, you risk losing or confusing your readers if you don't consider unity and coherence. Your project should have a clear purpose and clear ideas relating to that purpose, and the connections between ideas should be spelled out to orient readers. (For more on composing for the Web, see pp. 832–38.)

EXERCISE 2.9   Organizing ideas

The following list of ideas was extracted by a student from freewriting he did for a brief paper on soccer in the United States. Using his thesis statement as a guide, pick out the general ideas and arrange the relevant specific points under them. In some cases you may have to infer general ideas to cover specific points in the list. (You can do this exercise online at *ablongman.com/littlebrown.*)

Thesis statement

Despite increasing interest within the United States, soccer may never be the sport here that it is elsewhere because both the potential fans and the potential backers resist it.

List of ideas

Sports seasons are already too crowded for fans.
Soccer rules are confusing to Americans.
A lot of kids play soccer in school, but the game is still "foreign."
Sports money goes where the money is.
Backers are wary of losing money on new ventures.
Fans have limited time to watch.
Fans have limited money to pay for sports.
Backers are concerned with TV contracts.

---

46 (1984): 158–79. Sloan shows how infrequently explicit transition markers are used by either professional or student writers.

Smith, Rochelle. "Paragraphing for Coherence: Writing as Implied Dialogue." *College English* 46 (1984): 8–21. Smith uses reader-response theory and the notion of author-reader dialogue to improve paragraph cohesion.

Witte, Stephen P., and Lester Faigley. "Coherence, Cohesion, and Writing Quality." *College Composition and Communication* 32 (1981): 189–204. Students need to learn the features of coherence that extend across sentence boundaries; the article stresses ways to make them aware of coherence strategies.

COLLABORATIVE LEARNING

Ask students to compare their responses to Exercise 2.9 and then to work in pairs to create the formal outline described in Exercise 2.10. The discussions necessitated by this collaborative project encourage students to think through and articulate an organizational logic.

ANSWERS: EXERCISES 2.9 & 2.10

Possible answer

I. Fans resist [new general idea].
  A. Sports seasons are already too crowded for fans.
    1. Baseball, football, hockey, and basketball seasons already overlap.
    2. Fans have limited time to watch.
    3. Fans have limited money to pay for sports.
  B. Soccer is unfamiliar [new general idea].
    1. A lot of kids play soccer in school, but the game is still "foreign."
    2. Soccer rules are unfamiliar.
II. Backers resist [new general idea].
  A. Sports money goes where the money is.
    1. Soccer fans couldn't fill huge stadiums.
    2. Backers are concerned with TV contracts.
    3. TV contracts almost matter more than live audiences.
    4. American soccer fans are too few for TV interest.
  B. Backers are wary of losing money on new ventures.
    1. Failure of the US Football League was costly.
    2. Previous attempts to start a pro soccer league failed.

Previous attempts to start a pro soccer league failed.
TV contracts almost matter more than live audiences.
Failure of the US Football League was costly.
Baseball, football, hockey, and basketball seasons already overlap.
Soccer fans couldn't fill huge stadiums.
American soccer fans are too few for TV interest.

EXERCISE 2.10   Creating a formal outline

Use your arrangement of general ideas and specific points from Exercise 2.9 as the basis for a formal topic or sentence outline. Follow the principles given on pages 36–38. (If you completed Exercise 2.9 online, you can use that file to create this outline.)

EXERCISE 2.11   Considering your past work: Organizing ideas

What has been your experience with organizing your writing? Many writers find it difficult. If you do, too, can you say why? What kinds of outlines or other organizing tools have you used? Which have been helpful and which have not?

EXERCISE 2.12   Organizing your own essay

Continuing from Exercise 2.8 (p. 32), choose an appropriate organization for your essay-in-progress. Then experiment with organizing tools by preparing a tree diagram or other visual map or a scratch, informal, or formal outline.

ANSWERS: EXERCISE 2.11

Individual response.

ANSWERS: EXERCISE 2.12

Individual response.

mycomplab 2.0

Please visit MyCompLab at *www.mycomplab.com* for more on the writing process.

HIGHLIGHTS

This chapter continues the exploration, begun in Chapters 1 and 2, of writing as a flexible process and looks in detail at strategies for drafting, revising, editing, and proofreading. The journey from initial draft to finished essay may involve many decisions and changes of direction for which there are no firm rules. To alert student writers to the options available to them, the chapter provides lists of strategies for drafting an essay and check-

COMPANION WEB SITE

See page IAE-51 for companion Web site content description.

CHAPTER 3

Drafting and Revising

The separation of drafting and revising from the planning and development discussed in Chapters 1 and 2 is somewhat artificial because the stages almost always overlap during the writing process. Indeed, if you compose on a computer, you may not experience

http://www.ablongman.com/littlebrown ▶

Visit the companion Web site for more help with drafting, revising, collaborating, and preparing a writing portfolio.

any boundaries between stages at all. Still, your primary goal during the writing process will usually shift from gathering and shaping information to forming connected sentences and paragraphs in a draft and then restructuring and rewriting the draft.

3a Writing the first draft

The only correct drafting style is the one that works for you. Generally, though, the freer and more fluid you are, the better. Some writers draft and revise at the same time, but most let themselves go during drafting and *especially* do not worry about errors. Drafting is the occasion to find and convey meaning through the act of writing. If you fear making mistakes while drafting, that fear will choke your ideas. You draft only for yourself, so errors do not matter. Write freely until you have worked out what you want to say; *then* focus on any mistakes you may have made.

Starting to draft sometimes takes courage, even for seasoned professionals. Students and pros alike find elaborate ways to procrastinate—rearranging shelves, napping, lunching with friends. Such procrastination may actually help you if you let ideas for writing simmer at the same time. At some point, though, enough is enough: the deadline looms; you've got to get started. If the blankness still stares back at you, then try one of the following techniques for unblocking.

Ways to start drafting

- **Read over what you've already written**—notes, outlines, and so on. Immediately start your draft with whatever comes to mind.
- **Freewrite** (see p. 20).
- **Write scribbles or type nonsense** until words you can use start coming.
- **Pretend you're writing to a friend about your subject.**
- **Describe an image that represents your subject**—a physical object, a facial expression, two people arguing over something, a giant machine gouging the earth for a mine, whatever.
- **Write a paragraph.** Explain what you think your essay will be about when you finish it.
- **Skip the opening and start in the middle.** Or write the conclusion.
- **Start writing the part that you understand best or feel most strongly about.** Using your outline, divide your essay into chunks—say, one for the introduction, another for the first point, and so on. One of these chunks may call out to be written.

lists for revising (p. 51) and editing (p. 58). It also provides concrete advice for the stages of composing that many writers find the most difficult: getting started and completing the initial draft.

Students who view revision as an expendable stage in the writing process may benefit from following, draft by draft, the development of Sara Ling's essay (begun in Chapter 2) on Internet communication. Like most initial efforts, Ling's early draft can benefit from revisions in organization, content, tone, and approach to clarify the essay's purpose and the relationships among its ideas and also to make it easier for readers to share Ling's perspective. The revised draft, in turn, needs editing for clarity, style, and correction of errors in grammar, usage, punctuation, and spelling—changes that appear in the final version of the essay. Ling's paper can provide material for small-group discussion and evaluation, and the section on benefiting from criticism (3g) can help students learn to work effectively in peer critique groups. "Commenting on others' writing" and "Benefiting from comments on your writing" on pages 67 and 68 clarify peer review in a helpful list format.

TRANSPARENCY MASTER 3.1

A WRITER'S PERSPECTIVE

I've never thought of myself as a good writer; anyone who wants reassurance of that should read one of my first drafts. But I'm one of the world's great rewriters.

—JAMES MICHENER

How can I know what I think until I see what I say?

—E. M. FORSTER

OVERCOMING WRITING BLOCKS

Many students have a hard time writing first drafts because they try to get everything right the first time. They end up writing sentences and then crossing out what they have written so often that they have no time left to revise their thoughts in a second draft. Sometimes the pressure of perfection is so great that students become blocked writers, unable to finish even a single draft before the deadline. Here are four ways to help students get started and to help them develop flexibility and self-confidence in their approach to the task:

1. Show them copies of your own first and final drafts to indicate that you were not afraid to make mistakes in the initial draft because you had a chance to correct them in the later versions.

2. Give students a time limit for the first draft, perhaps an hour and a half or two hours, depending on the length of the assignment. Require them to hand in the draft with the final paper so that you can see how they approached the task of writing.

3. Have students start writing in class, where you can encourage them to get ideas down on paper before they try to perfect the wording.

4. Require students to spend some time either jotting down ideas and phrases or freewriting so that they will be loosened up before tackling the initial draft.

COMPUTER ACTIVITY

KEEPING TRACK OF IDEAS

Writers can often become anxious about adding in or losing track of ideas that don't seem to fit as they write out a rough draft. Students who are composing on the computer might keep a notebook nearby to scrawl down extra ideas that occur as they write. If your students' computer programs have a Versions feature, you can also encourage students to shift quickly to a second document to note ideas that don't seem to fit into the document they're composing.

You should find some momentum once you've started writing. If not, however, or if your energy flags, try one or more of the following techniques to keep moving ahead.

Ways to *keep* drafting

- **Set aside enough time for yourself.** For a brief essay, a first draft is likely to take at least an hour or two.
- **Work in a quiet place.**
- **Make yourself comfortable.**
- **If you must stop working, write down what you expect to do next.** Then you can pick up where you stopped with minimal disruption.
- **Be as fluid as possible, and don't worry about mistakes.** Spontaneity will allow your attitudes toward your subject to surface naturally in your sentences, and it will also make you receptive to ideas and relations you haven't seen before. Mistakes will be easier to find and correct later, when you're not also trying to create.
- **Keep going.** Skip over sticky spots; leave a blank if you can't find the right word; put alternative ideas or phrasings in brackets so that you can consider them later without bogging down. If an idea pops out of nowhere but doesn't seem to fit in, quickly jot it down on a separate sheet, or write it into the draft and bracket or boldface it for later attention. You can use an asterisk (*) or some other symbol to mark places where you feel blocked or uncertain. (With a word processor, you can later return to these places by using the Find command to locate the symbol.)
- **Resist self-criticism.** Don't worry about your style, grammar, spelling, punctuation, and the like. Don't worry about what your readers will think. These are very important matters, but save them for revision. On a word processor, help yourself resist self-criticism by turning off automatic spelling- or grammar-checking functions or by trying invisible writing (p. 20).
- **Use your thesis statement and outline** to remind you of your planned purpose, organization, and content.
- **But don't feel constrained by your thesis and outline.** If your writing leads you in a more interesting direction, follow.

If you write on a computer, frequently save the text you're drafting—at least every five or ten minutes and every time you leave the computer. See pages 52–53 for tips on saving documents.

Whether you compose on paper or on a computer, you may find it difficult to tell whether a first draft is finished. The distinction between drafts can be significant because creating text is different from rethinking it and because your instructor may ask you and your classmates to submit your drafts, either on paper or over a computer network, so that others can give you feedback on them. For your own revision or others' feedback, you might consider a draft finished for any number of reasons: perhaps you've reached the assigned length and have run out of ideas; perhaps you find yourself writing the conclusion; perhaps you've stopped adding content and are just tinkering with words.

■ Sample first draft

Sara Ling's first draft on Internet communication appears below. As you read the draft, mark the thesis statement and each key idea developing the thesis. Note places where you think the ideas could be clearer or better supported.

Title?

In "Welcome to Cyberbia," written in 1995, M. Kadi predicts that the Internet will lead to more fragmentation in society because people just seek out others like themselves. But Kadi fails to foresee how the unique anonymity of Internet communication could actually build diversity into community by lowering the barriers of physical appearance.

Anonymity on the Internet. It's one of the best things about technology. Most people who communicate online use an invented screen name to avoid revealing personal details such as age, gender, and ethnic background. No one knows whether you're fat or thin or neat or sloppy. What kind of clothes you wear. (Maybe you're not wearing clothes at all). People who know you personally don't even know who you are with an invented screen name.

We can make ourselves known without first being prejudged because of our physical attributes. For example, I participate in a snowboarding forum that has mostly men. I didn't realize what I was getting into when I used my full name as my screen name. Before long, I had received unfriendly responses such as "What does a girl know?" and "Why don't you go back to knitting?" I guess I had run into a male prejudice against female snowboarders. However, another woman on the forum had no such problems. At first she signed on with a screen name that did not reveal her gender, and no one responded negatively to her messages. When she had contributed for a while, she earned respect from the other snowboarders. When she revealed that she was a woman at that point, no one responded negatively in the way I had experienced. She posed at first as someone different from who she really was and could make herself heard.

We also cannot prejudge others because of their appearance. Often in face-to-face interaction we assume we know things about people just because of the way they look. Assumptions prevent people from discovering their shared interests and concerns, and this is particularly true where race is concerned. The anonymity of

MODELS OF STUDENT WRITING

Sara Ling essay

Sara Ling's essay is the first of several models of student writing that appear throughout *The Little, Brown Handbook*. Reading these examples of student writing may give your students a better idea of what you expect from their writing. Even when your students are not yet able to produce papers as strong as these sample papers, they may find it helpful to have concrete examples to emulate.

The inclusion of multiple drafts of Sara Ling's essay is intended to help students understand the process by which a paper is formulated, developed, and polished. Several of this chapter's exercises ask students to evaluate drafts of the paper; you might want to supplement these exercises by asking your students what they think about the final draft. If your students are well versed in the five-paragraph essay, they may be particularly interested to see how Ling's essay departs from that structure while still maintaining a coherent organization and a measure of fluidity.

You may also find the topic of this essay and its argument about the Internet to be very interesting to students. The essay might be a springboard for class debate on the topic; you could ask students to compose a rebuttal to Ling's essay, or you could allow them to use it to begin to formulate their own research projects.

RESOURCES AND IDEAS

On writer's block

Bartholomae, David. "Inventing the University." In *When a Writer Can't Write: Studies in Writer's Block and Other Composing Process Problems.* Ed. Mike Rose. New York: Guilford, 1985. 134–65. Bartholomae points out that one of the factors causing blocks or writing anxiety may be an unfamiliarity with the community for which the writer is writing, and he suggests ways to familiarize writers with the discourse expectations of academic writing.

Bloom, Lynn Z. "Research on Writing Blocks, Writing Anxiety, and Writing Apprehension." In *Research in Composition and Rhetoric.* Ed. Michael G. Moran and Ronald F. Lunsford. Westport: Greenwood, 1984. 71–91. Bloom surveys research on the fears and blocks that many writers encounter and examines strategies, similar to those presented in this chapter, for overcoming the difficulties.

Rose, Mike. *Writer's Block: The Cognitive Dimension.* Carbondale: Southern Illinois UP, 1984. The case studies of student writers that Rose discusses demonstrate that blocked writers often follow rigid, absolute rules about the forms and process of writing, whereas fluent writers use flexible, enabling strategies.

- - - . "Writing Around Rules." *Patterns in Action,* 2nd ed. Ed. Robert A. Schwegler. Glenview: Scott, 1988. 473–80. As an illustration of the kinds of rules that block writing and the kinds of strategies that enable it, Rose tells of the difficulties he encountered in titling a poem.

ANSWERS: EXERCISE 3.1

Possible answers

Some significant differences between Ling's outline and her first draft:

- In paragraph 1, Ling explicitly addressed the essay by M. Kadi.
- In paragraph 2, she added an explanation of how the Internet allows anonymity.
- In paragraph 3, she added a long example from her experience.
- In paragraph 4, she omitted planned examples and focused on working out her larger ideas. (Her readers objected to the lack of examples. See page 54 in the handbook.)

ANSWERS: EXERCISE 3.2

Individual response.

ANSWERS: EXERCISE 3.3

Individual response.

COLLABORATIVE LEARNING

Ask students to work in groups to complete Exercise 3.1 and to use that exercise as the occasion to discuss their own drafting processes (Exercise 3.2). Students can benefit a great deal both from articulating their habits, choices, and difficulties throughout the writing process and hearing how other writers work.

the Internet makes physical barriers irrelevant, and only people's minds meet. Because of this, the Internet could create a world free of physical bias.

Logged on to the Internet we can become more tolerant of others. We can become a community.

EXERCISE 3.1 Analyzing a first draft

Compare Ling's draft with the previous step in her planning (her formal outline) on page 36. List the places in the draft where the act of drafting led Ling to rearrange her information, add or delete material, or explore new ideas. (You can do this exercise online at *ablongman.com/littlebrown*.)

EXERCISE 3.2 Considering your past work: Drafting

Think back over a recent writing experience. At what point in the writing process did you begin drafting? How did drafting go—smoothly, haltingly, painfully, painlessly? If you had difficulties, what were they? If you didn't, why do you think not?

EXERCISE 3.3 Drafting your essay

Prepare a draft of the essay you began in Chapters 1 and 2. Use your thesis statement and your outline as guides, but don't be unduly constrained by them. Concentrate on opening up options, not on closing them down. Do not, above all, worry about mistakes.

3b Revising the first draft

Revision literally means "re-seeing"—looking anew at ideas and details, their relationships and arrangement, the degree to which they work or don't work for the thesis. While drafting, you focus inwardly, concentrating on pulling your topic out of yourself. In revising, you look out to your readers, trying to anticipate how they will see your work. You adopt a critical perspective toward your work (see Chapter 8), examining your draft as a pole-vaulter or dancer would examine a videotape of his or her performance. (Writing teachers often ask students to read each other's drafts partly to train the students in using and benefiting from this critical perspective. See p. 66 for more on such collaboration.)

1 Gaining distance from your work

Reading your own work critically requires that you create some distance between it and yourself—not always an easy task. The following techniques may help.

Ways to gain distance from your work

- **Take a break after finishing the draft.** A few hours may be enough; a whole night or day is preferable. The break will clear your mind, relax you, and give you some objectivity.
- **Ask someone to read and react to your draft.** Many writing instructors ask their students to submit their first drafts so that the instructor and, often, the other members of the class can serve as an actual audience to help guide revision. (See also pp. 68–69 on receiving and benefiting from comments.)
- **Type a handwritten draft.** The act of transcription can reveal gaps in content or problems in structure.
- **Print out a word-processed draft.** You'll be able to view all pages of the draft at once, and the different medium can reveal weaknesses you didn't see on screen.
- **Outline your draft.** Highlight the main points supporting the thesis, and write these sentences down separately in outline form. (If you're working on a word processor, you can copy and paste these sentences.) Then examine the outline you've made for logical order, gaps, and digressions. A formal outline can be especially illuminating because of its careful structure. (See pp. 33–38 for a discussion of outlining.)
- **Listen to your draft.** Read the draft out loud to yourself or a friend or classmate, read it into a tape recorder and play the tape, or have someone read the draft to you. Experiencing your words with ears instead of eyes can alter your perceptions.
- **Ease the pressure.** Don't try to re-see everything in your draft at once. Use a checklist like the one on p. 51, making a separate pass through the draft for each item.

2 Revising, then editing

Strictly speaking, revision includes editing—refining the manner of expression to improve clarity or style or to correct errors. In this chapter, though, revision and editing are treated separately to stress their differences: in revision you deal with the underlying meaning and structure of your essay; in editing you deal with its surface. By making separate drafts beyond the first—a revised one and then an edited one—you'll be less likely to waste time tinkering with sentences that you end up cutting, and you'll avoid the temptation to substitute editing for more substantial revision.

The temptation to edit while revising can be especially attractive on a word processor because it's easy to alter copy. Indeed, writers sometimes find themselves editing compulsively, spinning their wheels with changes that cease to have any marked effect on meaning or clarity and that may in fact sap the writing of energy. Planning to revise and then to edit encourages you to look beyond

REVISION ACTIVITIES

Here are a few revision activities for students working on their own or in groups:

Making out an inventory. After students have written an initial draft, ask them to complete a brief version of the audience inventory described in Chapter 1 (p. 11). Their completed inventory can help guide the choices they make during revision. Students may wish to share drafts and inventories with other students.

Using dialog. For narrative writing, ask students to circle every use of "He said that" and "She thought that" or similar phrases in their own or someone else's paper. Then ask them to consider replacing the indirect discourse with dialogue and direct quotations to make the writing more vivid and realistic.

Using the senses. For narrative and descriptive writing, ask students to check how many of the senses they have drawn on: then ask them to consider making use of the other senses.

Adding other arguments. For argumentative essays, have students list all the arguments they could use but have not yet included in the paper; they may wish to turn to other students for advice about including these arguments.

Soliciting class suggestions. For argument essays, ask students to summarize their theses and supporting arguments for their classmates. Then ask the other students to suggest more supporting arguments and opposing arguments the writer might consider during revision.

Answering more questions. For expository essays, ask students to answer these questions for their own or someone else's paper: What five things do you know about this topic that are not included in the draft? Which ones could be put into the essay without harming its unity or coherence? What three things are readers most likely to find interesting, useful, or surprising about this topic? Could these three things be given more emphasis without disrupting the organization or clarity of the essay?

QUESTIONING TABOOS

A good way to emphasize the distinction between revising and editing is to ask students to brainstorm a list of the taboos they've been taught about writing: "Don't begin sentences with I"; "Don't end sentences with prepositions"; "Never use contractions"; and so on. Then discuss the possible reasons for these rules and the occasions when they would apply. Once students understand the reasons for the rules they are much more able to check for usage errors in the editing process and to avoid allowing such taboos to hamper their revision processes.

ENCOURAGING REVISION

The only way to get students to revise regularly is to require it. You may need some ingenuity; one strategy that works is to require students to revise each graded essay and return it to you. Only when the essay is revised do you formally record a grade. Then students who don't revise won't get credit for their papers. Another method for encouraging revision efforts is to focus your written comments on the areas that students have revised effectively or failed to revise. Later in the semester it can also be useful to ask students to choose one of their own earlier papers to revise in the light of further reading or increased skills. This practice helps students to gain confidence in their own revision skills.

COLLABORATIVE LEARNING

CHOOSING TITLES

Ask students to work with their revision group to create several possible titles for each other's revised drafts. This kind of discussion often helps the writer of each paper to reconsider and articulate the central aims of the piece.

the confines of the screen so that deeper issues of meaning and structure aren't lost to surface matters such as word choice and sentence arrangement.

3 Titling your essay

The revision stage is a good time to consider a title. After drafting, you have a clearer sense of your direction, and the attempt to sum up your essay in a title phrase can help you focus sharply on your topic, purpose, and audience.

Here are suggestions for titling an essay:

- *A descriptive title* **is almost always appropriate and is often expected for academic writing.** It announces the topic clearly, accurately, and as briefly as possible. The final title of Sara Ling's essay—"The Internet: Fragmentation or Community?"—is an example, as are "Images of Lost Identity in *North by Northwest*," "An Experiment in Small-Group Dynamics," "Why Lincoln Delayed Emancipating the Slaves," and "Food Poisoning Involving *E. coli* Bacteria: A Review of the Literature."
- *A suggestive title*—**the kind often found in popular magazines—may be appropriate for more informal writing.** Examples include "Making Peace" (for an essay on the Peace Corps) and "Anyone for Soup?" (for an essay on working in a soup kitchen). For a more suggestive title, Ling might have chosen "What We Don't Know Can Help Us" or "Secrets of the Internet." Such a title conveys the writer's attitude and main concerns but not the precise topic, thereby pulling readers into the essay to learn more. A source for such a title may be a familiar phrase, a fresh image, or a significant expression from the essay itself.
- **A title tells readers how big the topic is.** For Ling's essay, the title "The Internet" or "Anonymity" would have been too broad, whereas "Lose Your Body" or "Discovering Common Ground" would have been too narrow because each deals with only part of the paper's content.
- **A title should not restate the assignment or the thesis statement**, as in "The Trouble with M. Kadi's Picture of the Internet" or "What I Think About Diversity on the Internet."

For more information on essay titles, see page 354 (avoiding reference to the title in the opening of the paper), 491 (capitalizing words in a title), and 687–88 (the format of a title in the final paper).

4 Using a revision checklist

Set aside at least as much time to revise your essay as you took to draft it. Plan on going through the draft several times to answer the questions in the checklist opposite and to resolve any problems.

(If you need additional information on any of the topics in the checklist, refer to the page numbers given in parentheses.) Note that the checklist can also help you if you have been asked to comment on another writer's draft (see p. 67).

Checklist for revision

See also specific revision checklists for arguments (pp. 213–14), research papers (p. 645), and literary analyses (p. 749).

Purpose

What is the essay's purpose? Does that purpose conform to the assignment? Is it consistent throughout the paper? (See pp. 13–15.)

Thesis

What is the thesis of the essay? Where does it become clear? How well do thesis and paper match: Does the paper stray from the thesis? Does it fulfill the commitment of the thesis? (See pp. 27–31.)

Structure

What are the main points of the paper? (List them.) How well does each support the thesis? How effective is their arrangement for the paper's purpose? (See pp. 32–33, 38–42.)

Development

How well do details, examples, and other evidence support each main point? Where, if at all, might readers find support skimpy or have trouble understanding the content? (See pp. 16–26, 90–91.)

Tone

What is the tone of the paper? How appropriate is it for the purpose, topic, and intended readers? Where is it most and least successful? (See p. 12.)

Unity

What does each sentence and paragraph contribute to the thesis? Where, if at all, do digressions occur? Should these be cut, or can they be rewritten to support the thesis? (See pp. 41–43, 72–75.)

Coherence

How clearly and smoothly does the paper flow? Where does it seem rough or awkward? Can any transitions be improved? (See pp. 41–43, 77–78.)

Title, introduction, conclusion

How accurately and interestingly does the title reflect the essay's content? (See opposite.) How well does the introduction engage and focus readers' attention? (See pp. 102–06.) How effective is the conclusion in providing a sense of completion? (See pp. 106–09.)

You can download this checklist from *ablongman.com/littlebrown*. Save the list in a file of its own, duplicate the file for each writing project, and insert appropriate answers between the questions along with ideas for changes. Print the expanded list so it's handy as you revise.

RESOURCES AND IDEAS

On revision generally

Bishop, Wendy, ed. *Elements of Alternate Style: Essays on Writing and Revision.* Portsmouth: Boynton/Cook (Heinemann), 1997. A collection of essays offering hands-on approaches to recovering play and joy in the writing and revision processes.

Elbow, Peter. *Writing with Power: Techniques for Mastering the Writing Process.* New York: Oxford UP, 1981. Elbow's book offers detailed, practical, and often innovative advice on drafting, revising, shaping for an audience, and making use of feedback, including several chapters on revising ("Quick Revising," "Thorough Revising," "Revising with Feedback," and "Cut and Paste Revising and the Collage").

Harris, Muriel. "Composing Behaviors of One- and Multi-Draft Writers." *College English* 51 (1989): 174–91. Harris emphasizes the differences in revision techniques and success of student writers.

Laib, Nevin. "Conciseness and Amplification." *College Composition and Communication* 41 (1990): 443–59. Laib argues for a balance between brevity and abbreviation.

Schwartz, Mimi. "Revision Profiles: Patterns and Implications." *College English* 45 (1983): 549–58. Schwartz maintains that revisers can be grouped by the revision strategies they use.

Sommers, Nancy. "Revision Strategies of Student Writers and Experienced Adult Writers." *College Composition and Communication* 31 (1980): 378–88. According to Sommers, students see revision as changes in small units—words and sentences. Experienced writers see it as a recursive process directed at larger units of the text and the meaning it conveys.

Welch, Nancy. *Getting Restless: Rethinking Revision in Writing Instruction.* Portsmouth: Boynton/Cook (Heinemann), 1997. Welch looks at what student writers have to say about their own attempts at revision. She concludes that revision engages the domain of the emotional/personal, a domain which makes most academics uncomfortable.

On computers and the revision process

Many writers find that the computer facilitates their composing and revision processes without realizing the extent to which the medium

5 Revising on a word processor

Word processors have removed the mechanical drudgery of revising by hand or on a typewriter, but they have also complicated the process: you must conscientiously save your changes and manage the files you create, both discussed below. At the same time, like the more cumbersome revision methods, word processors allow you to display changes as you make them.

■ Saving changes

Computers malfunction frequently. You can avoid losing your work by taking two precautions:

- **Save your work every five to ten minutes.** Most word processors have an Auto Save function that will save your work automatically as you type, at the interval you specify. Still, get in the habit of saving manually whenever you make major changes.
- **After doing any major work on a project, create a backup version of the file.** Use a second hard drive, a removable disk, or a removable "flash" drive. If you need to share files but have difficulty e-mailing them, or if you need to save large multimedia files, you can also store backups on a drive accessed through the Internet. XDrive, for example, offers storage space for a reasonable price (*xdrive.com*).

The following screen shot illustrates the essentials of a word processor's File menu, the key to saving and organizing drafts.

Save menu

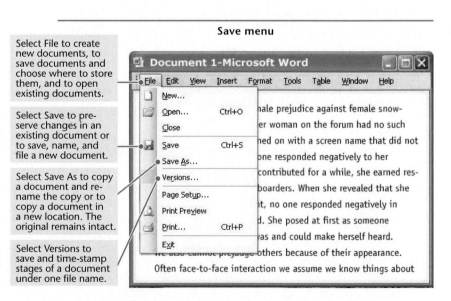

Select File to create new documents, to save documents and choose where to store them, and to open existing documents.

Select Save to preserve changes in an existing document or to save, name, and file a new document.

Select Save As to copy a document and rename the copy or to copy a document in a new location. The original remains intact.

Select Versions to save and time-stamp stages of a document under one file name.

■ Managing files

With the Save As option in the File menu, you can organize your work for a course or the drafts of a paper by giving each file a name that indicates the content, the date, and (if you're sharing work with others) the author. The following screen shot shows Sara Ling saving a document she named *Sara.NetcomD1.10-28-05.doc* in a new folder titled *English 120*. In addition to her name and the date, the file name includes an identifier for the paper (*Netcom*) and the draft number (*D1*).

Save As screen

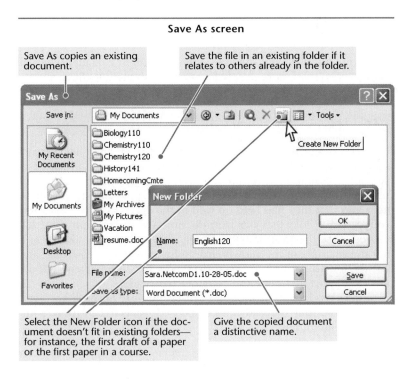

Save As copies an existing document.

Save the file in an existing folder if it relates to others already in the folder.

Select the New Folder icon if the document doesn't fit in existing folders—for instance, the first draft of a paper or the first paper in a course.

Give the copied document a distinctive name.

■ Displaying changes

You can keep track of the revisions you make in a document with an option often called Track Changes and usually found under the Tools or File menu. The function highlights additions and deletions so they're easy to spot (see the screen shot on the next page). Tracking changes may encourage you to revise more freely because you can always revert to your original text. You can weigh the original and revised versions as you view them side by side. You can also evaluate the kinds of changes you are making. For instance, if during revision you see only minor surface alterations (word substitutions,

has changed the way we think and write. In "The Metaphor of Collage: Beyond Computer Composition," Russel Wiebe and Robert S. Dornsife, Jr., argue that computers are not simply an addition to the classroom; rather, they revolutionize the way we and our students write and think about texts. The authors use the metaphor of a multimedia collage to describe the best pedagogical approach to these changes (*Journal of Advanced Composition* 15 (1995): 131–37). See also, Cynthia Selfe and Susan Hilligoss, *Literacy and Computers: the Complications of Teaching and Learning with Technology* (New York: MLA, 1994).

On collaborative revision

Peer editing and collaborative learning have become regular features of many composition courses over the past two decades, and these approaches are particularly well suited to drafting and revising activities. Section 3g coaches students in giving and receiving criticism. And the chapter "Using Collaborative Learning with the Handbook" on pages IAE 34–45 offers detailed advice about designing collaborative activities and preparing students to work in groups. It also provides sample reader response forms, which you may wish to copy and use in your class.

Much has been written recently about collaborative learning and peer writing groups. See, for example, the *Journal of Advanced Composition* 14:1 (1994); the entire issue is devoted to issues of collaboration. The following two works offer good starting points for someone interested in examining both the opportunities offered by this approach and the controversies that it has created:

Gere, Anne Ruggles. *Writing Groups: History, Theory, and Implications.* Carbondale: Southern Illinois UP, 1987. Gere reviews the history, theory, and practice of writing groups and collaborative learning; she also provides a useful annotated bibliography of research and pedagogy.

Trimbur, John. "Collaborative Learning and Teaching Writing." In *Perspectives on Research and Scholarship in Composition.* Ed. Ben W. McClelland and Timothy R. Donovan. New York: MLA, 1985. 87–109. Trimbur offers a compact survey of the history and theories behind collaborative learning and raises important questions about the roles of response and evaluation in a student- (rather than teacher-) centered classroom.

On independent revision

Even though you encourage students to revise and offer them detailed advice about what and when to revise, you may still find that their revisions are limited to superficial changes. Part of the problem may be that students have not yet become good enough readers of their own texts to identify features that might be altered or dropped and to identify places where something might be added. Here are some resources for helping students to become active readers and writers, aware of what they have written and how it might be changed:

Beck, James P. "Asking Students to Annotate Their Own Papers." *College Composition and Communication* 33 (1982): 322–26. Beck asks students to identify specific techniques they have used in their writing (including features of structure, detail, argument, and style) and to evaluate how well they have used those techniques.

Sommers, Jeffrey. "The Effects of Tape-Recorded Commentary on Student Revision: A Case Study," *Journal of Teaching Writing* 8 (1989): 49–75. Sommers argues that students can misunderstand instructor response to their writing and demonstrates how tape-recorded responses led one student through a series of successive revisions.

Straub, Richard. "The Concept of Control in Teacher Response: Defining the Varieties of 'Directive' and 'Facilitative' Commentary." *College Composition and Communication* 47 (1996): 223–51. Straub reviews the influential studies on teacher response in an effort to identify the kinds of comments that encourage students to produce effective independent revisions.

Track Changes function

Use Save As from the File menu to copy and rename the original document. Here, *D2* indicates the second draft.

Deleted copy is crossed out.

Added copy appears in blue.

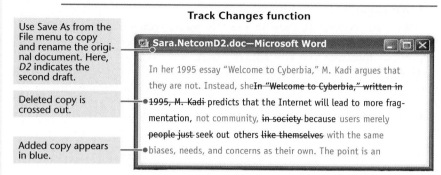

added punctuation, and the like), then you might consider whether and where to read more deeply for more fundamental changes.

3c Examining a sample revision

In revising her first draft, Sara Ling had the help of her instructor and several of her classmates, to whom she showed the draft as part of her assignment. Based on the revision checklist, she thought that she wanted to stick with her initial purpose and thesis statement and that they had held up well in the draft. But she also knew without being told that her introduction and conclusion were too hurried, that the movement between paragraphs was too abrupt, that the example of the snowboarding forum went on too long, and that the fourth paragraph was thin: she hadn't supplied enough details to support her ideas and convince her readers.

Ling's readers confirmed her self-evaluation. Several, however, raised points that she had not considered, reflected in these comments by classmates:

Comment 1

Why do you say (par. 2) that most people use invented screen names? I don't, and I know other people who don't either. Do you have evidence of how many people use invented names or why they do?

Comment 2

I would have an easier time agreeing with you about the Internet if you weren't quite so gung-ho. For instance, what about the dangers of the Internet, as when adults prey on children or men prey on women? In par. 3, you don't acknowledge that such things can and do happen. Also, is a bias-free world (par. 4) really such a sure thing? People will still meet in person, after all.

At first Ling was tempted to resist these comments because the writers seemed to object to her ideas. But eventually she understood that the comments showed ways she could make the ideas convincing to more readers. The changes took some time, partly because Ling decided to conduct a survey of students in order to test her assumption about people's use of invented screen names.

The following revised draft shows the survey results and Ling's other changes. Ling used the Track Changes function on her word processor, so that deletions are crossed out and additions are in blue. Marginal annotations highlight the main revisions.

The Internet: Fragmentation or Community?

~~Title?~~

We hear all sorts of predictions about how the Internet will enrich our lives and promote equality, tolerance, and thus community in our society. But are these promises realistic? In her 1995 essay "Welcome to Cyberbia," M. Kadi argues that they are not. Instead, she~~In "Welcome to Cyberbia," written in 1995, M. Kadi~~ predicts that the Internet will lead to more fragmentation, not community, ~~in society~~ because users merely ~~people just~~ seek out others ~~like themselves~~ with the same biases, needs, and concerns as their own. The point is an interesting one, ~~B~~but Kadi fails to foresee that ~~how~~ the unique anonymity of Internet communication could actually build diversity into community by lowering the barriers of physical appearance.

Internet communication can be anonymous on at least two levels. ~~Anonymity on the Internet. It's one of the best things about technology. Most people who communicate online use an invented screen name to avoid revealing personal details such as age, gender, and ethnic background. No one knows~~ The people who communicate with you do not know your age. ~~w~~Whether you're fat or thin or neat or sloppy. What kind of clothes you wear. (Maybe you're not wearing clothes at all). Or anything else about physical appearance. ~~People who know you personally don't even know who you are with an invented screen name.~~ If you use an invented screen name instead of your real name, readers don't even know whatever your name says about you, such as gender or ethnic background.

Internet anonymity seems a popular option, judging by the numbers of invented user names seen in online forums. But I thought it would be a good idea to determine the extent of invented user names as well as the reasons for them, so I surveyed seventy-eight students with two questions: (1) Do you ever write with an invented user name when contributing to chat rooms, newsgroups, blogs, and so on? (2) If yes, why do you use an invented name: to protect your privacy, to avoid revealing personal

Descriptive title names topic and forecasts approach.

Expanded introduction draws readers into Ling's question and summarizes Kadi's essay.

New transition relates paragraph to thesis statement and smoothes flow.

Blanket assertion is deleted in favor of survey results added later.

Addition clarifies use of invented screen names.

Largest revision presents results of survey conducted to support use of invented screen names.

information, or for some other reason? Fig. 1 shows that most of the students do use invented names online. And most do so to protect their privacy or to avoid revealing personal details.

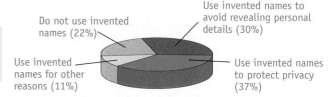

Fig. 1. Use of invented screen names among seventy-eight Internet users.

New pie graph presents survey results in an easy-to-read format.

New paragraph summarizes survey results and adds examples.

Users of the Internet clearly value the anonymity it can give them. Twenty students said that they use invented names to mask personal details because they think the details might work against them. One said she is able to participate in a physics discussion list without fear of being ignored by the group's professional physicists. Another said he thinks he can contribute more freely to a political forum because no one knows he's African American. I learned the benefits of anonymity myself when I joined a snowboarding forum using my full name and received hostile

Revisions condense overly long example from Ling's experience.

~~With invented screen names, we can make ourselves known without first being prejudged because of our physical attributes. For example, I participate in a snow-boarding forum that has mostly men. I didn't realize what I was getting into when I used my full name as my screen name. Before long, I had received unfriendly~~ responses such as "What does a girl know?" and "Why don't you go back to knitting?" I guess I had run into a male prejudice against female snowboarders. However, another woman on the forum had no such problems. ~~At first she signed on with a screen name that did not reveal her gender, and no one responded negatively to her messages. When~~ when she ~~had~~ contributed for a while~~,~~ before revealing her gender. ~~she earned respect from the other snowboarders. When she revealed that she was a woman at that point, no one responded negatively in the way I had experienced. She posed at first as someone different from who she really was and could make herself heard.~~

New paragraph acknowledges complexities that were previously ignored.

Granted, concealing or altering identities on the Internet can be a problem, as when adults pose as children to seduce or harm them. These well-publicized occurrences say a great deal about the need to monitor the use of the Internet by children and to be cautious about getting together with Internet correspondents. However, they do not undermine the value of people being able to make themselves heard in situations where normally (in the real world) they would be shut out.

The Internet's anonymity has a flip side too. We cannot be prejudged and ~~W~~we also cannot prejudge others because of their appearance. Often in face-to-face interaction we assume we know things about people just because of the way they look. Someone with an athletic build must be dumb. Someone who is heavy must be uninteresting. Perhaps most significant, someone of another race must have fixed or contrary views about family values, crime, affirmative action, and all sorts of other issues as well. Assumptions like these prevent people from discovering their shared interests and concerns~~,~~. But with ~~and this is particularly true where race is concerned. T~~the anonymity of the Internet~~,~~ ~~makes~~ such physical barriers to understanding are irrelevant~~., and only people's minds meet. Because of this, the Internet could create a world free of physical bias.~~

~~Logged on to the Internet we can become more tolerant of others. We can become a community.~~

A world free of physical bias is a long way off, but the more we communicate with just our minds the more likely it is that our minds will find common ground. Logged on, we can become more accepted and accepting, more tolerated and tolerant. We can become a community.

Work Cited

Kadi, M. "Welcome to Cyberbia." Utne Reader Mar.-Apr. 1995: 57-59.

Margin annotations:

New transition clarifies shift to second main point.

New examples support general statement.

New conclusion qualifies and spells out previously rushed ideas.

New work-cited entry. (See p. 656 on MLA style.)

COLLABORATIVE LEARNING

Exercise 3.4 works well as a small-group project. Encourage students to discuss their differing ideas for further revisions and then have each group present their conclusions to the class.

EXERCISE 3.4 Analyzing a revised draft

Compare Ling's revised draft with her first draft on pages 47–48. Can you see the reasons for most of her changes? Where would you suggest further revisions, and why? (You can do this exercise online at *ablongman.com/littlebrown*.)

EXERCISE 3.5 Considering your past work: Revising

In the past, have you usually revised your drafts extensively? Do you think your writing would benefit from more revision of the sort described in this chapter? Why or why not? Many students who don't revise much explain that they lack the time. Is time a problem for you? Can you think of ways to resolve the problem?

EXERCISE 3.6 Revising your own draft

Revise your own first draft from Exercise 3.3 (p. 48). Use the checklist for revision on page 51 as a guide. Concentrate on purpose, content, and organization, leaving smaller problems for the next draft.

ANSWERS: EXERCISE 3.4

Answers will vary.

ANSWERS: EXERCISE 3.5

Individual response.

ANSWERS: EXERCISE 3.6

Individual response.

3d   Editing the revised draft

Editing for style, clarity, and correctness may come second to more fundamental revision, but it is still very important. A carefully developed essay will fall flat with readers if you overlook awkwardness and errors.

1   Discovering what needs editing

Try these approaches to spot possible flaws in your work:

Ways to find what needs editing

- **Take a break,** even fifteen or twenty minutes, to clear your head.
- **Read the draft** *slowly,* **and read what you** *actually see.* Otherwise, you're likely to read what you intended to write but didn't.
- **Read as if you are encountering the draft for the first time.** Put yourself in the reader's place.
- **Have a classmate, friend, or relative read your work.** Make sure you understand and consider the reader's suggestions, even if eventually you decide not to take them.
- **Read the draft aloud or, even better, record it.** Listen for awkward rhythms, repetitive sentence patterns, and missing or clumsy transitions.
- **Learn from your own experience.** Keep a record of the problems that others have pointed out in your writing. (See p. 69 for a suggested format.) When editing, check your work against this record.

In your editing, work first for clarity and a smooth movement among sentences and then for correctness. Use the questions in the following checklist to guide your editing, referring to the page numbers in parentheses as needed.

Checklist for editing

Clarity

How well do words and sentences convey their intended meanings? Which words and sentences are confusing? Check especially for these:

Exact language (pp. 518–28)
Parallelism (pp. 405–11)
Clear modifiers (pp. 364–72)
Clear reference of pronouns (pp. 350–56)
Complete sentences (pp. 334–40)
Sentences separated correctly (pp. 342–48)

Effectiveness

How well do words and sentences engage and focus readers? Where does the writing seem wordy, choppy, or dull? Check especially for these:

Emphasis of main ideas (pp. 384–93)
Smooth and informative transitions (pp. 85–88, 108)
Variety in sentence length and structure (pp. 412–19)
Appropriate language (pp. 510–17)
Concise sentences (pp. 529–35)

Correctness

How little or how much do surface errors interfere with clarity and effectiveness? Check especially for these:

Spelling (pp. 542–54)
Pronoun forms, especially subjective (*he, she, they, who*) vs. objective (*him, her, them, whom*) (pp. 267–74)
Verb forms, especially *-s* and *-ed* endings, correct forms of irregular verbs, and appropriate helping verbs (pp. 275–92)
Verb tenses, especially consistency (pp. 292–98, 359–60)
Agreement between subjects and verbs, especially when words come between them or the subject is *each, everyone,* or a similar word (pp. 305–12)
Agreement between pronouns and antecedents, especially when the antecedent contains *or* or the antecedent is *each, everyone, person,* or a similar word (pp. 131–17)
Sentence fragments (pp. 334–40)
Commas, especially with comma splices (pp. 342–47), with *and* or *but* (432), with introductory elements (433–34), with nonessential elements (435–38), and with series (441–42)
Apostrophes in possessives but not plural nouns (*Dave's/witches*) and in contractions but not possessive personal pronouns (*it's/its*) (pp. 461–66)

You can download this checklist from *ablongman.com/littlebrown.* Save the list in a file of its own, duplicate the file for each writing project, and insert appropriate answers between the questions along with notes on specific changes to make.

INDIVIDUALIZED CHECKLISTS

Since most students' work demonstrates patterns of repeated error, have them keep ongoing lists of their recurring editing errors and stylistic problems. Ask them to bring their lists to class for in-class revision and editing sessions and to have their revision group help them look particularly for those errors.

The second paragraph of Sara Ling's edited draft appears below. One change Ling made throughout the essay shows up here: she resolved an inconsistency in references to *you, people,* and *we,* settling on a consistent *we.* In addition, Ling corrected several sentence fragments in the middle of the paragraph.

Internet communication can be anonymous on at least two levels. The people we~~you~~ communicate with do not know our ~~your~~ age~~.~~, ~~W~~whether we're~~you're~~ fat or thin or neat or sloppy~~.~~, ~~W~~what kind of clothes we~~you~~ wear~~.~~ (~~Maybe you're not~~ if we're wearing clothes at all)., Θor anything else about physical appearance. If weyou use an invented screen names instead of ouryour real names, readers don't even know whatever ouryour names may reveal or suggest says about usyou, such as gender or ethnic background.

2 Editing on a word processor

When you work on a word processor, consider these additional approaches to editing:

- **Don't rely on your word processor's spelling or grammar and style checker to find what needs editing.** See the discussion of these checkers below.
- **If possible, work on a double-spaced paper copy.** Most people find it much harder to spot errors on a computer screen than on paper.
- **Use the Find command to locate and correct your common problems**—certain misspellings, overuse of *there is*, wordy phrases such as *the fact that*, and so on.
- **Resist overediting.** The ease of editing on a computer can lead to rewriting sentences over and over, stealing the life from your prose. If your grammar and style checker contributes to the temptation, consider turning it off.
- **Take special care with additions and omissions.** Make sure you haven't omitted needed words or left in unneeded words.

3 Working with spelling and grammar/style checkers

The spelling checker and grammar and style checker that may come with your word processor can be helpful *if* you work within their limitations. The programs miss many problems and may even flag items that are actually correct. Further, they know nothing of your purpose and your audience, so they cannot make important decisions about your writing. Always use these tools critically:

- **Read your work yourself to ensure that it's clear and error-free.**
- **Consider a checker's suggestions carefully, weighing each one against your intentions.** If you aren't sure whether to accept a checker's suggestion, consult a dictionary, writing handbook, or other source. Your version may be fine.

Using a spelling checker

Your word processor's spelling checker can be a great ally: it will flag words that are spelled incorrectly and usually suggest alternative spellings that resemble what you've typed. However, this ally also has the potential to undermine you because of its limitations:

COMPUTER ACTIVITIES

AN ARCHIVE FOR REJECTED PASSAGES

Having labored so hard to produce a first draft, writers are sometimes reluctant to cut passages when revising their drafts. Your students may find it easier to make cuts if they paste the cut passages into a blank document, saving that document as part of their own personal writing archive. They can choose to replace the cut passages later or use them for a different piece of writing altogether.

EDITING VEHICLES

To help students explore how editing on a computer may produce different results from editing hard copy, ask students to edit a sample paper, but ask half of them to edit it on the computer and half to edit it by hand. Then, in small groups, have them compare their edits and discuss the differences.

HUMAN VERSUS MACHINE

Have a contest between student proofreaders and the spell check or grammar check program of their word processing software, to see which method produces the cleanest copy.

- **The checker may flag a word that you've spelled correctly,** just because the word does not appear in its dictionary.
- **The checker may suggest incorrect alternatives.** In providing a list of alternative spellings for your word, the checker may highlight the one it considers most likely to be correct. You need to verify that this alternative is actually what you intend before selecting it. Consult an online or printed dictionary when you aren't sure of the checker's recommendations.
- **Most important, a spelling checker will not flag words that appear in its dictionary but you have misused.** The jingle in the following screen shot has circulated widely as a warning about spelling checkers (we found it in the *Bulletin of the Missouri Council of Teachers of Mathematics*).

Spelling checker

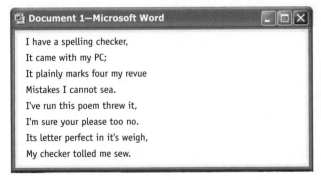

I have a spelling checker,
It came with my PC;
It plainly marks four my revue
Mistakes I cannot sea.
I've run this poem threw it,
I'm sure your please too no.
Its letter perfect in it's weigh,
My checker tolled me sew.

A spelling checker failed to catch any of the thirteen errors in this jingle. Can you spot them?

Using a grammar and style checker

Word processors' grammar and style checkers can flag incorrect grammar or punctuation and wordy or awkward sentences. However, these programs can call your attention only to passages that *may* be faulty. They miss many errors because they are not yet capable of analyzing language in all its complexity (for instance, they can't accurately distinguish a word's part of speech when there are different possibilities, as *light* can be a noun, a verb, or an adjective). And they often question passages that don't need editing, such as an appropriate passive verb or a deliberate and emphatic use of repetition. The screen shot on the next page illustrates the limitations.

You can customize a grammar and style checker to suit your needs and habits as a writer. (Select Options under the Tools menu.) Most checkers allow you to specify whether to check grammar only or grammar and style. Some style checkers can be set to the level of writing you intend, such as formal, standard, and informal. (For

Grammar/style checker

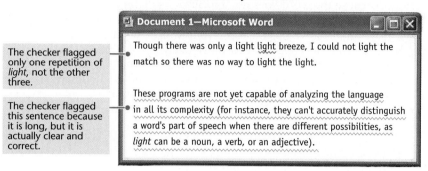

The checker flagged only one repetition of *light*, not the other three.

The checker flagged this sentence because it is long, but it is actually clear and correct.

> Though there was only a light light breeze, I could not light the match so there was no way to light the light.
>
> These programs are not yet capable of analyzing the language in all its complexity (for instance, they can't accurately distinguish a word's part of speech when there are different possibilities, as *light* can be a noun, a verb, or an adjective).

academic writing choose formal.) You can also instruct the checker to flag specific grammar and style problems that tend to occur in your writing, such as mismatched subjects and verbs, apostrophes in plural nouns, overused passive voice, or a confusion between *its* and *it's*.

EXERCISE 3.7   Considering your past work: Editing

How do you find what needs editing in your drafts? What kinds of changes do you make most often? Have you tried focusing on particular kinds of changes, such as correcting mistakes you made in previous writing? If your readers often comment on editing concerns in your work, what can you do to reduce such comments?

EXERCISE 3.8   Editing your own draft

Use the checklist for editing and your own sense of your essay's needs to edit the revised draft of your essay-in-progress.

3e   Preparing and proofreading the final draft

After editing your essay, retype or print it once more for submission to your instructor. You may be required to use one of the following formats: MLA (pp. 687–89), Chicago (pp. 775–77), APA (pp. 800–03), or CSE (p. 820). If no format is specified, consult the document-design guidelines in Chapter 5. If you've composed on a word processor, use the Print Preview function under the File menu to check for formatting problems that may not otherwise show up on your screen.

Be sure to proofread the final essay several times to spot and correct errors. To increase the accuracy of your proofreading, you may need to experiment with ways to keep yourself from relaxing into the rhythm and the content of your prose. The box below gives a few tricks, including some used by professional proofreaders.

Techniques for proofreading

- **Read printed copy,** even if you will eventually submit the paper electronically. Most people proofread more accurately when reading type on paper than when reading it on a computer screen. (At the same time, don't view the printed copy as necessarily error-free just because it's clean. Clean-looking copy may still harbor errors.)
- **Read the paper aloud.** Slowly and distinctly pronounce exactly what you see.
- **Place a ruler under each line as you read it.**
- **Read "against copy."** Compare your final draft one sentence at a time against the edited draft you copied it from.
- **Ignore content.** To keep the content of your writing from distracting you while you proofread, read the essay backward, end to beginning, examining each sentence as a separate unit. Or, taking advantage of a computer, isolate each paragraph from its context by printing it on a separate page. (Of course, reassemble the paragraphs before submitting the paper.)

3f Examining a final draft

Sara Ling's final essay begins below, typed in MLA format except for page breaks. Comments in the margins point out key features of the essay's content.

Sara Ling

Professor Nelson

English 120A

4 November 2005

The Internet:

Fragmentation or Community?

We hear all sorts of predictions about how the Internet will enrich our individual lives and promote communication, tolerance, and thus community in our society. But are these promises realistic? In her 1995 essay "Welcome to Cyberbia," M. Kadi argues that they are not. Instead, she predicts that the Internet will lead to more fragmentation, not community, because users merely seek out others with the same biases, concerns, and needs as their own. The point is an interesting one, but Kadi fails to foresee that the unique anonymity of Internet communication could actually build diversity into community by lowering the barriers of physical appearance.

Margin notes:
- Descriptive title
- Introduction
- Question to be addressed
- Summary of Kadi's essay
- Thesis statement

Explanation of Internet's anonymity

Internet communication can be anonymous on at least two levels. The people we communicate with do not know our age, whether we're fat or thin or neat or sloppy, what kind of clothes we wear (if we're wearing clothes at all), or anything else about physical appearance. If we use invented screen names instead of our real names, readers don't even know whatever our names may reveal or suggest about us, such as gender or ethnic background.

Presentation of survey conducted to gauge use of invented screen names

Explanation of survey method

Summary of survey results

Internet anonymity seems a popular option, judging by the numbers of invented user names seen in online forums. To determine the extent of invented user names as well as the reasons for them, I surveyed seventy-eight students. I asked two questions: (1) Do you ever write with an invented user name when contributing to chat rooms, newsgroups, Web logs, and so on? (2) If yes, why do you use an invented name: to protect your privacy, to avoid revealing personal information, or for some other reason? The results are shown in fig. 1. A large majority of the students (seventy-eight percent) do use invented names online. And most of them do so to protect their privacy (thirty-seven percent) or to avoid revealing personal details (thirty percent).

Graph displaying survey results, with self-explanatory labels and caption

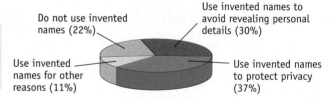

Fig. 1. Use of invented screen names among seventy-eight Internet users.

First main point: We are not prejudged by others.

Examples of first point

Users of the Internet clearly value the anonymity it can give them. This anonymity allows users to communicate freely without being prejudged because of physical attributes. In follow-up interviews, twenty students said that they use invented names to mask personal details because they think the details might work against them in online communication. One said she is able to participate in a physics discussion list without fear of being ignored by the group's professional physicists. Another said he thinks he can contribute more freely to a political forum because no one knows he's African American. I learned the benefits of anonymity myself when I joined a snowboarding forum using my full name and received hostile responses such as "What does a girl know?" and "Why don't you go back to knitting?" I assumed I had run into a male prejudice against female snowboarders. However, another woman on the forum had no such problems when she contributed for a while before revealing her gender.

Granted, concealing or altering identities on the Internet can be a problem, as when adults pose as children to seduce or harm them. These well-publicized occurrences say much about the need to monitor children's use of the Internet and to be cautious about meeting Internet correspondents. However, they do not undermine the value of being able to make ourselves heard in situations where normally (in the real world) we would be shut out.

The Internet's anonymity has a flip side, too: just as we cannot be prejudged, so we cannot prejudge others because of their appearance. Often in face-to-face interaction, we assume we know things about people just because of the way they look. Someone with an athletic build must be unintelligent. Someone who is heavy must be uninteresting. Perhaps most significant, someone of another race must have fixed and contrary views about all kinds of issues, from family values to crime to affirmative action. Assumptions like these prevent us from discovering the interests and concerns we share with people who merely look different. But with the anonymity of the Internet, such physical barriers to understanding are irrelevant.

A world without physical bias may be an unreachable ideal. However, the more we communicate with just our minds, the more likely it is that our minds will find common ground and put less emphasis on physical characteristics. Logged on, we can begin to become more accepted and more accepting, more tolerated and more tolerant. We can begin to become a community.

	Qualification of first point
	Conclusion of first point
	Second main point: We cannot prejudge others.
	Clarification of second point
	Examples of second point
	Effects of assumptions
	Conclusion of second point
	Conclusion, summarizing essay

Work Cited

Kadi, M. "Welcome to Cyberbia." Utne Reader Mar.-Apr. 1995: 57-59.

Work cited in MLA style (see p. 656)

EXERCISE 3.9 Proofreading

Proofread the following passage, using any of the techniques listed on page 63 to bring errors into the foreground. There are thirteen errors in the passage: missing and misspelled words, typographical errors, and the like. If you are in doubt about any spellings, consult a dictionary. (You can do this exercise online at *ablongman.com/littlebrown*.)

An envirnmental group, Natural Resources Defense Council, has estimated that 5500 to 6200 children who are preschool today may contract cancer durng there lives becuase of the pesticides they

ANSWER: EXERCISE 3.9

An environmental group, Natural Resources Defense Council, has estimated that 5,500 to 6,200 children who are in preschool today may contract cancer during their lives because of the pesticides they consume in their food. In addition, these children will be at greater risk for kidney damage, problems with immunity, and other serious impairments. The government bases its pesticide-safety standards on adults, but children consume many more of the fruits and fruit products likely to contain pesticides.

consume in there food In addition, these children will be at greater risk for kidney damage, problems with immunity, and other serious imparments. The government bases it's pesticide-safety standards on adults, but childen consume many more the fruits and fruit products likely too contain pestcides.

EXERCISE 3.10 Preparing your final draft

Prepare the final draft of the essay you have been working on throughout Chapters 1–3. Proofread carefully and correct all errors before submitting your essay for review.

3g Giving and receiving comments

1 Working collaboratively

Almost all the writing you do in college will generate responses from an instructor. In courses that stress writing, you may submit early drafts as well as your final paper, and your readers may include your classmates as well as your instructor. Like Sara Ling's, such courses may feature **collaborative learning,** in which students work together on writing, from completing exercises to commenting on each other's work to producing whole papers. (At more and more schools this group work occurs over a computer network. See pp. 829–32.)

Whether you participate as a writer or as a writing "coach," collaboration can give you experience in reading written work and in reaching readers through writing. You may at first be anxious about criticizing others' work or sharing your own rough drafts, but you'll soon grow to appreciate the interaction and the confidence it gives you in your own reading and writing.

CULTURE LANGUAGE In some cultures writers do not expect criticism from readers, or readers do not expect to think critically about what they read. If critical responses are uncommon in your native culture, collaboration may at first be uncomfortable for you. As a writer, consider that readers are responding to your draft or even your final paper more as an exploration of ideas than as the last word on your subject; then you may be more receptive to readers' suggestions. As a reader, allow yourself to approach a text skeptically, and know that your tactful questions and suggestions will usually be considered appropriate.

2 Responding to the writing of others

If you are the reader of someone else's writing, keep the following principles in mind:

ANSWERS: EXERCISE 3.10

Individual response.

RESOURCES AND IDEAS

Harrington, Jane. "Editing: the Last Step in the Process." In *Nuts and Bolts: A Practical Guide to Teaching.* Ed. Thomas Newkirk. Portsmouth, NH: Boynton, 1993. 151–178. Harrington defines the editing process and provides practical suggestions for making editing a familiar part of classroom practice.

Harris, Jeanette. "Proofreading: A Reading/Writing Skill." *College Composition and Communication* 38 (1987): 464–66. Harris argues that proofreading is a reading skill, a process of looking at each word and punctuation mark rather than of paying attention to the meaning of the text; and she suggests teaching students strategies like those outlined in this chapter—using a pointer (finger, pencil), reading aloud, reading in reverse order, and letting time elapse between writing and proofreading—in order to develop the specialized skill of proofreading.

Horner, Bruce. "Rethinking the 'Sociality' of Error: Teaching Editing as Negotiation." *Rhetoric Review* 11 (1992): 172–99. Horner argues for a consideration of editing as a process of social exchange best supported by peer groups and one-on-one conferences.

Commenting on others' writing

- **Be sure you know what the writer is saying.** If necessary, summarize the paper to understand its content. (See pp. 140–42.)
- **Address only your most significant concerns with the work.** Use the revision checklist on p. 51 as a guide to what is significant. Unless you have other instructions, ignore mistakes in grammar, punctuation, spelling, and the like. (The temptation to focus on such errors may be especially strong if the writer is less experienced than you are with standard American English.) Emphasizing mistakes will contribute little to the writer's revision.
- **Remember that you are the reader, not the writer.** Don't edit sentences, add details, or otherwise assume responsibility for the paper.
- **Phrase your comments carefully.** Avoid misunderstandings by making sure comments are both clear and respectful. If you are responding on paper or online, not face to face with the writer, remember that the writer has nothing but your written words to go on. He or she can't ask you for immediate clarification and can't infer your attitudes from gestures, facial expressions, and tone of voice.
- **Be specific.** If something confuses you, say *why*. If you disagree with a conclusion, say *why*.
- **Be supportive as well as honest.** Tell the writer what you like about the paper. Word comments positively: instead of *This paragraph doesn't interest me,* say *You have an interesting detail here that I almost missed.* Comment in a way that emphasizes the effect of the work on you, the reader: *This paragraph confuses me because. . . .* And avoid measuring the work against a set of external standards: *This essay is poorly organized. Your thesis statement is inadequate.*
- **While reading, make your comments in writing.** Even if you will be delivering your comments in person later on, the written record will help you recall what you thought.
- **Link comments to specific parts of a paper.** Especially if you are reading the paper on a computer, be clear about what part of the paper each comment relates to. You can embed your comments directly into the paper, distinguishing them with highlighting or color. Or you can use the Comment function of a word processor (see below).

If you are reviewing others' drafts on a word processor, its Comment function will allow you to add comments without inserting words into the document's text. Usually found on the Insert menu, the function creates something like a sticky Post-it note that pops up when readers move their cursors across words you have highlighted. The following screen shot shows one such comment.

CONSTRUCTIVE CRITICISM

Students sometimes initially think of "criticizing" as a negative activity rather than a supportive practice. These "suggestions for commenting" on each other's writing can help set a supportive tone for collaborative revision groups. Criticism that is given in a helpful and careful manner is perhaps the easiest kind of criticism to benefit from. You can also encourage student writers to take an active role by bringing in questions and concerns about their own papers and by probing their peers' comments for specific examples and explanations: "Can you show me the places where my organization starts to break down?" See the chapter "Using Collaborative Learning with the Handbook" on pages IAE 34–45 for a detailed discussion on preparing students to provide and receive peer criticism. You may wish to draw on this discussion as a way of helping your students learn how to benefit from criticism and learn how to offer their classmates advice that can lead to real improvements in expression.

ELECTRONIC FEEDBACK

If students have easy access to e-mail, it's possible to post drafts or sample essays on a bulletin board or class account to receive comments and feedback. See Daniel Anderson's essay on "Using Computers to Teach Writing" on pages IAE 46–64 for more information on working in a computer classroom.

Comment function

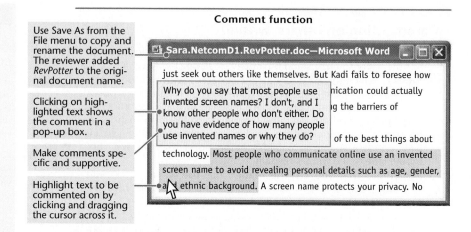

Use Save As from the File menu to copy and rename the document. The reviewer added *RevPotter* to the original document name.

Clicking on highlighted text shows the comment in a pop-up box.

Make comments specific and supportive.

Highlight text to be commented on by clicking and dragging the cursor across it.

3 Responding to comments on your own writing

When you *receive* comments from others, whether your classmates or your instructor, you will get more out of the process if you follow the guidelines below.

Benefiting from comments on your writing

- **Think of your readers as counselors or coaches.** They can help you see the virtues and flaws in your work and sharpen your awareness of readers' needs.
- **Read or listen to comments closely.**
- **Know what the critic is saying.** If you need more information, ask for it, or consult the appropriate section of this handbook.
- **Don't become defensive.** Letting comments offend you will only erect a barrier to improvement in your writing. As one writing teacher advises, "Leave your ego at the door."
- **Revise your work in response to appropriate comments.** Whether or not you are required to act on comments, you will learn more from actually revising than from just thinking about it.
- **Remember that you are the final authority on your work.** You should be open to suggestions, but you are free to decline advice when you think it is inappropriate.
- **Keep track of both the strengths and the weaknesses others identify.** Then in later assignments you can build on your successes and give special attention to problem areas.

As the last item in the preceding box indicates, you'll gain the most from collaboration if you carry your learning from one assignment into the next. To keep track of things to work on, try a chart like the one below, with a vertical column for each assignment (or draft) and a horizontal row for each weakness. Check marks indicate how often the problem occurs in each essay. The chart also provides a convenient place to keep track of words you misspell so that you can master their spellings.

Record of errors

Weaknesses	Assignment		
	1	2	3
not enough details for readers	✓	✓	✓
unity—wanders away from thesis	✓		
subject-verb agreement	✓		✓
comma splice	✓✓	✓	✓
misspellings	among deceive	rebel seize	omission cruelty

3h Preparing a writing portfolio

Your writing teacher may ask you to assemble samples of your writing into a portfolio, or folder, once or more during the course. Such a portfolio gives you a chance to consider all your writing over a period and to showcase your best work.

Teachers' requirements for portfolios vary. For instance, some teachers ask students to choose their five or so best papers and to submit final drafts only. Others ask for final papers illustrating certain kinds of writing—say, one narrative, one critique, one argument, one research paper, and so on. Still others ask for notes and drafts along with selected papers. If your class is using online writing tools, your work may be archived as part of the course site and you may be asked to submit your portfolio electronically.

Just as teachers' requirements differ, so do their purposes. But most are looking for a range of writing that demonstrates your progress and strengths as a writer. You, in turn, see how you have advanced from one assignment to the next, as you've had time for new knowledge to sink in and time for practice. Teachers often allow students to revise papers before placing them in the portfolio, even if the papers were submitted earlier. In that case, every paper in the portfolio can benefit from all your learning.

when instructors expect students to think critically and to question dominant cultural values.

Johnson, T. R. "School Sucks." *College Composition and Communication* 52 (June 2001): 620–630. Johnson explains why so many students dislike writing classes and provides advice on improving students' attitudes.

McKendy, Thomas F. "Legitimizing Peer Response: A Recycling Project for Placement Essays." *College Composition and Communication* 41 (1990): 89–91. McKendy found that when students in a remedial writing course holistically scored placement essays, their scoring correlated closely with that of trained readers. This exercise led to the students' being more accepting of their placement in the course and more trusting of each others' responses to their writing.

Simmons, Robin L. *http://www.chompchomp.com* Because it is interactive, this is an especially good Web site to send students to for help with a variety of writing problems.

Sirc, Geoffrey, and Tom Reynolds. "The Face of Collaboration in the Networked Writing Classroom." *Computers and Composition* 7 (1990): 53–70. Sirc and Reynolds discuss the use of networked classrooms in peer response to compositions.

Sperling, Melanie. "Constructing the Perspective of Teacher as Reader: A Framework for Studying Response to Student Writing." *Research in the Teaching of English* 28 (1994): 175–223. This article studies one teacher's responses to student papers in order to evaluate the impact of teacher comments on student writing.

Weissberg, Bob. "Speaking of Writing: Some Functions of Talk in the ESL Composition Class." *Journal of Second Language Writing* 3 (1994): 1121–39. This essay examines class discussion and peer input as learning factors, particularly in the ESL context.

Welch, Nancy. "Sideshadowing Teacher Response." *College English* 60 (1998): 374–95. Welch suggests the technique of "sideshadowing," in which students make marginal comments on their own drafts.

Yancey, Kathleen Blake and Irwin Weiser, eds. *Situating Portfolios: Four Perspectives.* Logan: Utah State UP, 1996. This collection of essays explores the issues of power and authority in portfolio evaluation.

PORTFOLIO PRESENTATION

Ask students to prepare to hand in their portfolios by making an oral presentation to their regular revision group. Each student can briefly describe the pieces she has chosen to include in her portfolio and explain how each piece has contributed to her progress. Revision group members can often remind writers of noticeable overall strengths that they might have overlooked.

mycomplab^20

Please visit MyCompLab at *www.mycomplab.com* for more on the writing process.

HIGHLIGHTS

The writing some American high school students do is no more than a paragraph in length, and even older or nontraditional students may have had little writing experience. So learning to think of paragraphs as units in larger pieces of discourse may be a challenge for your students. If they have written longer essays, these probably have been in the familiar "five-paragraph theme" pattern of introduction, three paragraphs of development, and conclusion. ESL students may conceptualize and shape paragraphs differently or may not be used to writing in paragraphs at all. Don't be surprised, then, if learning to use paragraphs in different ways presents a challenge for your students.

Here we present a strategy of developing paragraphs as mini-essays, each with a general-

See page IAE-51 for companion Web site content description.

An assignment to assemble a writing portfolio will probably also provide guidelines for what to include, how the portfolio will be evaluated, and how (or whether) it will be weighted for a grade. Be sure you understand the purpose of the portfolio and who will read it. For instance, if your composition teacher will be the only reader and her guidelines urge you to show evidence of progress, you might include a paper that took big risks but never entirely succeeded. In contrast, if a committee of teachers will read your work and the guidelines urge you to demonstrate your competence as a writer, you might include only papers that did succeed.

Unless the guidelines specify otherwise, provide error-free copies of your final drafts, label all your samples with your name, and assemble them all in a folder. Add a cover letter or memo that lists the samples, explains why you've included each one, and evaluates your progress as a writer. The self-evaluation involved should be a learning experience for you and will help your teacher assess your development as a writer.

CHAPTER 4

Writing and Revising Paragraphs

A **paragraph** is a group of related sentences set off by a beginning indention or, sometimes, by extra space. For you and your readers, paragraphs provide breathers from long stretches of text and indicate key changes in the development of your thesis. They help to organize and clarify ideas.

In the body of an essay, you may use paragraphs for any of these purposes:

- **To introduce and give evidence for a main point supporting your essay's central idea (its thesis).** See pages 27–31 for a discussion of an essay's thesis.

http://www.ablongman.com/littlebrown ▶

Visit the companion Web site for more help and additional exercises on paragraphs.

- **Within a group of paragraphs centering on one main point,** to develop a key example or other important evidence.
- **To shift approach**—for instance, from pros to cons, from problem to solution, from questions to answers.
- **To mark movement in a sequence,** such as from one reason or step to another.

In addition, you will use paragraphs for special purposes:

- **To introduce or to conclude an essay.** See pages 102 and 106.
- **To emphasize an important point or to mark a significant transition between points.** See page 108.
- **In dialog, to indicate that a new person has begun speaking.** See pages 108–09.

The following paragraph illustrates simply how an effective body paragraph works to help both writer and reader. The thesis of the essay in which this paragraph appears is that a Texas chili championship gives undue attention to an unpleasant food.

> Some people really like chili, apparently, but nobody can agree how the stuff should be made. C. V. Wood, twice winner at Terlingua, uses flank steak, pork chops, chicken, and green chilis. My friend Hughes Rudd of CBS News, who imported five hundred pounds of chili powder into Russia as a condition of accepting employment as Moscow correspondent, favors coarse-ground beef. Isadore Bleckman, the cameraman I must live with on the road, insists upon one-inch cubes of stew beef and puts garlic in his chili, an Illinois affectation. An Indian of my acquaintance, Mr. Fulton Batisse, who eats chili for breakfast when he can, uses buffalo meat and plays an Indian drum while it's cooking. I ask you.
>
> —Charles Kuralt, *Dateline America*

General statement relating to thesis: announces topic of paragraph

Four specific examples, all providing evidence for general statement

While you are drafting, conscious attention to the requirements of the paragraph may sometimes help pull ideas out of you or help you forge relationships. But don't expect effective paragraphs like Kuralt's to flow from your fingertips while you are grappling with what you want to say. Instead, use the checklist on the next page to guide your revision of paragraphs so that they work to your and your readers' advantage.

Note On the Web the paragraphing conventions described here do not always apply. Web readers sometimes skim text instead of reading word for word, and they are accustomed to embedded links that may take them from the paragraph to another page. Writing

ization (topic sentence) supported by limitations and evidence. Practicing these essays-in-miniature can help students develop longer essays as they gain more skill. Of course, not all paragraphs in professional writing conform in length, structure, or purpose to the models this chapter provides.

The chapter reviews strategies for improving paragraph unity, achieving paragraph coherence, developing paragraph content, and writing special-purpose paragraphs. It concludes by showing how paragraphs can be linked within the larger context of the essay. Helping students learn and practice the standard paragraphing strategies elaborated in this chapter can be a good way to help them improve their writing. The annotations provided for sample paragraphs help students see the strategies explained in the chapter "in practice."

A WRITER'S PERSPECTIVE _____

The purpose of paragraphing is to give the reader a rest. The writer is saying [. . .] : "Have you got that? If so, I'll go on."

—H. W. FOWLER

TRANSPARENCY MASTER 4.1

COMPUTER ACTIVITY

Have students print out Web pages and bring them into class. Individually or as a class, they can evaluate the paragraphs for unity, coherence, and development. Students can make suggestions for how to revise each page's paragraphs and for where to position links to other pages.

RESOURCES AND IDEAS

Rhetorical scholarship is split on a number of the "givens" of paragraphing: whether paragraphs are self-contained units or building blocks of larger discourses, whether topic sentences are needed, and so on. These references offer you a fairly mainstream view of research into paragraphing.

Knoblauch, C. H. "The Rhetoric of the Paragraph." *Journal of Advanced Composition* 2 (1981): 53–61.

Stern, Arthur A. "When Is a Paragraph?" *College Composition and Communication* 27 (1976): 253–57. Stern argues for the rhetorical flexibility of paragraphs as development devices.

HIGHLIGHTS

Section 4a of this chapter addresses the need for a paragraph to focus on a topic and to make the focus clear to the reader through an explicit statement in the form of a topic sentence. It introduces the basic form of the expository paragraph—topic sentence, illustrations, and details—and indicates how this pattern can be varied to suit a writer's purpose and to fit within the context created by the surrounding paragraphs.

The concept of a clearly stated and variously placed topic sentence that controls the shape of a paragraph is an oversimplification. But it ap-

Checklist for revising paragraphs

- **Is the paragraph unified?** Does it adhere to one general idea that is either stated in a topic sentence or otherwise apparent? (See below.)
- **Is the paragraph coherent?** Do the sentences follow a clear sequence? Are the sentences linked as needed by parallelism, repetition or restatement, pronouns, consistency, and transitional expressions? (See p. 77.)
- **Is the paragraph developed?** Is the general idea of the paragraph well supported with specific evidence such as details, facts, examples, and reasons? (See p. 90.)

for the Web, you may want to write shorter paragraphs than you would in printed documents, and save embedded links for the ends of paragraphs lest readers miss important information. (For more on composing for the Web, see pp. 832–38.)

CULTURE LANGUAGE Not all cultures share the paragraphing conventions of American academic writing. The conventions are not universal even among users of standard American English: for instance, US newspaper writers compose very short paragraphs that will break up text in narrow columns. In some other languages, writing moves differently from English—not from left to right, but from right to left or down rows from top to bottom. Even in languages that move as English does, writers may not use paragraphs at all. Or they may use paragraphs but not state the central ideas or provide transitional expressions to show readers how sentences relate. If your native language is not English and you have difficulty with paragraphs, don't worry about paragraphing during drafting. Instead, during a separate step of revision, divide your text into parts that develop your main points. Mark those parts with indentions.

4a   Maintaining paragraph unity

Readers generally expect a paragraph to explore a single idea. They will be alert for that idea and will patiently follow its development. In other words, they will seek and appreciate paragraph **unity:** clear identification and clear elaboration of one idea and of that idea only.

In an essay the thesis statement often asserts the main idea as a commitment to readers (see p. 27). In a paragraph a **topic sentence** often alerts readers to the essence of the paragraph by asserting the central idea and expressing the writer's attitude toward it. In a brief essay each body paragraph will likely treat one main point supporting the essay's thesis statement; the topic sentences simply elaborate on parts of the thesis. In longer essays paragraphs tend to work in groups, each group treating one main point. Then the topic sentences will tie into that main point, and all the points together will support the thesis.

1 Focusing on the central idea

Like the thesis sentence, the topic sentence is a commitment to readers, and the rest of the paragraph delivers on that commitment. Look again at Kuralt's paragraph on chili on page 71: the opening statement conveys the author's promise that he will describe various ways to make chili, and the following sentences keep the promise. But what if Kuralt had written this paragraph instead?

> Some people really like chili, apparently, but nobody can agree how the stuff should be made. C. V. Wood, twice winner at Terlingua, uses flank steak, pork chops, chicken, and green chilis. My friend Hughes Rudd, who imported five hundred pounds of chili powder into Russia as a condition of accepting employment as Moscow correspondent, favors coarse-ground beef. He had some trouble finding the beef in Moscow, though. He sometimes had to scour all the markets and wait in long lines. For any American used to overstocked supermarkets and department stores, Russia can be quite a shock.

Topic sentence: general statement

Two examples supporting statement

Digression

By wandering off from chili ingredients to consumer deprivation in Russia, the paragraph fails to deliver on the commitment of its topic sentence.

You should expect digressions while you are drafting: if you allow yourself to explore ideas, as you should, then of course every paragraph will not be tightly woven, perfectly unified. But spare your readers the challenge and frustration of repeatedly shifting focus to follow your rough explorations: revise each paragraph so that it develops a single idea.

While revising your paragraphs for unity, you may want to highlight the central idea of each paragraph to be sure it's stated and then focus on it. On paper you can bracket or circle the idea. On a computer you can format the idea in color or highlight it with a color background. Just be sure to remove the color or highlighting before printing the final draft.

2 Placing the topic sentence

The topic sentence of a paragraph and its supporting details may be arranged variously, depending on how you want to direct

pears to help students a great deal to think of the paragraph as a unit dominated and controlled by an expressly stated generalization. Students can see the topic sentence as a commitment they make to the reader, with the rest of the paragraph following through on the commitment. Seeing the obvious parallel between the paragraph's topic sentence and the essay's thesis statement is also helpful to many students. Finally, stating a central point in a single sentence and marshaling support for it enables students to see more clearly what is required for unity.

The exercises for this section ask students to identify the central idea in unified paragraphs, to revise paragraphs, to build a paragraph by combining and revising kernel sentences, and to write their own paragraphs. These exercises can be easily adapted to small-group work: in coming to understand how others view paragraphs, students may more readily understand the influence of paragraph structure and unity on readers.

USING STUDENT WRITING

Ask students to choose key paragraphs from their work-in-progress and read them aloud to their groups. The listeners should take notes on the effectiveness of the various unity strategies they hear in each paragraph. If students have trouble responding without seeing a written text, you can have them work in pairs to critique and revise the unity of each other's paragraphs.

COLORING PARAGRAPHS

Bring in copies of sample paragraphs and felt-tipped pens or pencils in two colors. Split the class into groups and ask each group to underline topic sentences in one color and examples and details in another color. Students should then be able to discover the arrangement of each paragraph, the placement of the topic sentence, and the way the parts fit together to form a unified whole. Students working in a computer classroom can use the Bold feature and designated fonts instead of pens to identify each of these elements.

USING STUDENT WRITING

Ask students to bring in paragraphs from writings in other classes or other disciplines to use in the "coloring paragraphs" activity. They will find it instructive to note how different writers decide to place, emphasize, or omit topic sentences. They can also perform this exercise on the paragraphs in their drafts.

SEEING PARAGRAPHS

Visually, students may find it easier to understand topic sentence placement and paragraph arrangement by using these diagrams as guides:

Topic sentence at the beginning: △
Topic sentence at the
  beginning and in the middle: △
Topic sentence at the end: ▽
Topic sentence at the
  beginning and the end: ◇

TOPIC SENTENCE OMISSION

Some research suggests that the necessity of a topic sentence is determined by the author's relation

readers' attention and how complex your central idea is. In the most common arrangements, the topic sentence comes at the beginning of the paragraph, comes at the end, or is not stated at all but is nonetheless apparent. The advantages of each approach are described on these two pages. If you write on a computer, you can easily experiment with the position of the topic sentence by moving the sentence around (or deleting it) to see the effect. (The sentence will probably take some editing to work smoothly into various positions.)

■ Topic sentence at the beginning

When the topic sentence appears first in a paragraph, it can help you select the details that follow. For readers, the topic-first model establishes an initial context in which all the supporting details can be understood. Reading Kuralt's paragraph on page 71, we easily relate each detail or example back to the point made in the first sentence.

The topic-first model is common not only in expository paragraphs, such as Kuralt's, but also in argument paragraphs, such as the one following:

> It is a misunderstanding of the American retail store to think we go there necessarily to buy. Some of us shop. There's a difference. Shopping has many purposes, the least interesting of which is to acquire new articles. We shop to cheer ourselves up. We shop to practice decision-making. We shop to be useful and productive members of our class and society. We shop to remind ourselves how much is available to us. We shop to remind ourselves how much is to be striven for. We shop to assert our superiority to the material objects that spread themselves before us.
> —Phyllis Rose, "Shopping and Other Spiritual Adventures"

Topic sentence: statement of misconception

Correction of misconception

■ Topic sentence at the end

In some paragraphs the central idea may be stated at the end, after supporting sentences have made a case for the general statement. Since this model leads the reader to a conclusion by presenting all the evidence first, it can prove effective in argument. And because the point of the paragraph is withheld until the end, this model can be dramatic in exposition, too, as illustrated by the following example from an essay about William Tecumseh Sherman, a Union general during the US Civil War:

Sherman is considered by some to be the inventor of "total war": the first general in human history to carry the logic of war to its ultimate extreme, the first to scorch the earth, the first to consciously demoralize the hostile civilian population in order to subdue its army, the first to wreck an economy in order to starve its soldiers. He has been called our first "merchant of terror" and seen as the spiritual father of our Vietnam War concepts of "search and destroy," "pacification," "strategic hamlets," and "free-fire zones." As such, he remains a cardboard figure of our history: a monstrous arch-villain to unreconstructed Southerners, and an embarrassment to Northerners.

> Information supporting and building to topic sentence

> Topic sentence

—Adapted from James Reston, Jr.,
"You Cannot Refine It"

Expressing the central idea at the end of the paragraph does not eliminate the need to unify the paragraph. The idea in the topic sentence must still govern the selection of all the preceding details.

■ Central idea not stated

Occasionally, a paragraph's central idea will be stated in the previous paragraph or will be so obvious that it need not be stated at all. The following is from an essay on the actor Humphrey Bogart:

Usually he wore the trench coat unbuttoned, just tied with the belt, and a slouch hat, rarely tilted. Sometimes it was a captain's cap and a yachting jacket. Almost always his trousers were held up by a cowboy belt. You know the kind: one an Easterner waiting for a plane out of Phoenix buys just as a joke and then takes a liking to. Occasionally, he'd hitch up his slacks with it, and he often jabbed his thumbs behind it, his hands ready for a fight or a dame.

> Details adding up to the unstated idea that Bogart's character could be seen in his clothing

—Peter Bogdanovich, "Bogie in Excelsis"

Paragraphs in descriptive writing (like the one above) and in narrative writing (relating a sequence of events) often lack stated topic sentences. But a paragraph without a topic sentence still should have a central idea, and its details should develop that idea.

EXERCISE 4.1 Finding the central idea

What is the central idea of each of the following paragraphs? In what sentence or sentences is it expressed? (You can do this exercise online at *ablongman.com/littlebrown*.)

to his or her readers; a writer writing to less expert or more expert readers is more likely to use a topic sentence than one writing for peers, for instance. Ask students to work in groups to collect examples of topic sentence use and omission, then analyze the different author-reader relationships implied in each example. Encourage students to collect samples from their own journals and papers, but also from various kinds of published writing, to get the best results from this survey.

COMPUTER ACTIVITY

REORGANIZING PARAGRAPHS

For students working on computers, the reorganization of paragraphs is particularly easy. Encourage students to select one or two paragraphs from their drafts and reorganize them with the controlling idea at the end, as Reston does. Then ask them to judge whether they gain any rhetorical advantage from such a rearrangement. Leonard A. Podis suggests some other exercises of this nature in "Teaching Arrangement: Defining a More Practical Approach," *College Composition and Communication* 31 (1980): 197–204, and JoAnne M. Podis and Leonard A. Podis present more exercises in "Identifying and Teaching Rhetorical Plans for Arrangement," *College Composition and Communication* 41 (1990): 430–42.

COLLABORATIVE LEARNING

Ask students to work in groups to complete Exercise 4.1. Ask each group to discuss what effect the particular placement of each topic sentence has, and then report back to the class on the sentences that best express the central idea of each paragraph.

ANSWERS: EXERCISE 4.1

1. The central idea is sentence 8: The black bourgeoisie feel a sense of shame about their own identity.
2. The central idea is sentence 1: Scientists know something about the song of the humpback whale.

COLLABORATIVE LEARNING

Have students work in groups to complete Exercise 4.2. Ask groups to consider how they might revise and expand the deleted material to include it in a follow-up paragraph.

ANSWERS: EXERCISE 4.2

The topic sentence is sentence 1. Unrelated are sentences 4 and 7.

ANSWERS: EXERCISE 4.3

Individual response.

1.   Today many black Americans enjoy a measure of economic security beyond any we have known in the history of black America. But if they remain in a nasty blue funk, it's because their very existence seems an affront to the swelling ranks of the poor. Nor have black intellectuals ever quite made peace with the concept of the black bourgeoisie, a group that is typically seen as devoid of cultural authenticity, doomed to mimicry and pallid assimilation. I once gave a talk before an audience of black academics and educators, in the course of which I referred to black middle-class culture. Afterward, one of the academics in the audience, deeply affronted, had a question for me. "Professor Gates," he asked rhetorically, his voice dripping with sarcasm, "what *is* black middle-class culture?" I suggested that if he really wanted to know, he need only look around the room. But perhaps I should just have handed him a mirror: for just as nothing is more American than anti-Americanism, nothing is more characteristic of the black bourgeoisie than the sense of shame and denial that the identity inspires.
        —Henry Louis Gates, Jr., "Two Nations . . . Both Black"

2.   Though they do not know why the humpback whale sings, scientists do know something about the song itself. They have measured the length of a whale's song: from a few minutes to over half an hour. They have recorded and studied the variety and complex arrangements of low moans, high squeaks, and sliding squeals that make up the song. And they have learned that each whale sings in its own unique pattern.   —Janet Lieber (student), "Whales' Songs"

EXERCISE 4.2   Revising a paragraph for unity

The following paragraph contains ideas or details that do not support its central idea. Identify the topic sentence in the paragraph and delete the unrelated material. (You can do this exercise online at *ablongman.com/littlebrown*.)

In the southern part of the state, some people still live much as they did a century ago. They use coal- or wood-burning stoves for heating and cooking. Their homes do not have electricity or indoor bathrooms or running water. The towns they live in don't receive adequate funding from the state and federal governments, so the schools are poor and in bad shape. Beside most homes there is a garden where fresh vegetables are gathered for canning. Small pastures nearby support livestock, including cattle, pigs, horses, and chickens. Most of the people have cars or trucks, but the vehicles are old and beat-up from traveling on unpaved roads.

EXERCISE 4.3   Considering your past work: Paragraph unity

For a continuing exercise in this chapter, choose a paper you've written in the past year. Examine the body paragraphs for unity. Do they have clear topic sentences? If not, are the paragraphs' central ideas still clear? Are the paragraphs unified around their central ideas? Should any details be deleted for unity? Should other, more relevant details be added in their stead?

EXERCISE 4.4   Writing a unified paragraph

Develop the following topic sentence into a unified paragraph by using the relevant information in the supporting statements. Delete each statement that does not relate directly to the topic, and then rewrite and combine sentences as appropriate. Place the topic sentence in the position that seems most effective to you. (You can do this exercise online at *ablongman.com/littlebrown.*)

Topic sentence

Mozart's accomplishments in music seem remarkable even today.

Supporting information

Wolfgang Amadeus Mozart was born in 1756 in Salzburg, Austria.
He began composing music at the age of five.
He lived most of his life in Salzburg and Vienna.
His first concert tour of Europe was at the age of six.
On his first tour he played harpsichord, organ, and violin.
He published numerous compositions before reaching adolescence.
He married in 1782.
Mozart and his wife were both poor managers of money.
They were plagued by debts.
Mozart composed over six hundred musical compositions.
His most notable works are his operas, symphonies, quartets, and piano concertos.
He died at the age of thirty-five.

EXERCISE 4.5   Turning topic sentences into unified paragraphs

Develop three of the following topic sentences into detailed and unified paragraphs. (You can do this exercise online at *ablongman.com/littlebrown.*)

1. Men and women are different in at least one important respect.
2. The best Web search engine is [*name*].
3. Fans of ———— music [*country, classical, rock, rap, jazz, or another kind*] come in [*number*] varieties.
4. Professional sports have [*or have not*] been helped by extending the regular season with championship play-offs.
5. Working for good grades can interfere with learning.

4b   Achieving paragraph coherence

A paragraph is unified if it holds together—if all its details and examples support the central idea. A paragraph is **coherent** if readers can see *how* the paragraph holds together—how the sentences relate to each other—without having to stop and reread.

Incoherence gives readers the feeling of being yanked around, as the following example shows.

ANSWERS: EXERCISE 4.4

Delete statements not pertaining to Mozart's accomplishments: when he was born, where he lived, when he married, his debts. Possible paragraph:

Mozart's accomplishments in music seem remarkable even today. At the age of six he made his first concert tour of Europe, playing harpsichord, organ, and violin. He had begun composing music at the age of five, and by adolescence he had published numerous musical compositions. When he died at thirty-five, his work included over six hundred compositions, most notably operas, symphonies, quartets, and piano concertos.

COMPUTER ACTIVITY

REARRANGING PARAGRAPHS

Exercises 4.4 and 4.5 work well in a computer classroom because students have the flexibility to rearrange sentences multiple times without retyping them. Students can print out the results in order to compare their differing responses in groups. Students might also e-mail their responses to a partner in the class, or you could post several volunteer responses on the class Web site for the whole class to read and discuss.

ANSWERS: EXERCISE 4.5

Individual response.

RESOURCES AND IDEAS

Becker, A. L. "A Tagmemic Approach to Paragraph Analysis." *College Composition and Communication* 16 (1965): 237–42. Becker observes that expository paragraphs generally follow a variation of one of two patterns: topic-restriction-illustration (TRI) or problem-solution (PS).

Wiener, Harvey S. "The Single Narrative Paragraph and College Remediation." *College English* 33 (1972): 660–69. Wiener suggests using paragraph-length narrative themes to help students develop both paragraph and essay skills.

HIGHLIGHTS

This section of the chapter deals with paragraph coherence, addressing it from the reader's perspective as well as the writer's. Students are shown how the devices they use to achieve paragraph coherence help readers to follow the arguments or information being presented.

The discussion emphasizes the need to maintain a clear organizational pattern as one of the principal ways to ensure coherence, and it presents examples of two basic ways of organizing paragraphs: organizing by space or time and organizing for emphasis. Students who have difficulty organizing their own writing can usually see the pattern of organization in a well-made example from another writer's work.

Following the discussion of patterns, the section takes up and illustrates other methods of achieving coherence: parallelism; repetition of words; careful use of pronouns; consistency in person, tense, and number; and transitional expressions. Analysis of paragraphs can help students understand these explicit and implicit means by which individual sentences are held together so that the reader effortlessly follows the flow of ideas and information. As in the preceding section, the exercises move from analysis to revision to production and are useful in small-group activities as well as in individual work.

Ways to achieve paragraph coherence

- Organize effectively (p. 79).
- Repeat or restate key words and word groups (p. 83).
- Use parallel structures (p. 83).
- Use pronouns (p. 84).
- Be consistent in nouns, pronouns, and verbs (p. 84).
- Use transitional expressions (p. 85).

> The ancient Egyptians were masters of preserving dead people's bodies by making mummies of them. Mummies several thousand years old have been discovered nearly intact. The skin, hair, teeth, finger- and toenails, and facial features of the mummies were evident. One can diagnose the diseases they suffered in life, such as smallpox, arthritis, and nutritional deficiencies. The process was remarkably effective. Sometimes apparent were the fatal afflictions of the dead people: a middle-aged king died from a blow on the head, and polio killed a child king. Mummification consisted of removing the internal organs, applying natural preservatives inside and out, and then wrapping the body in layers of bandages.

— Topic sentence

Sentences related to topic sentence but disconnected from each other

The paragraph as it was actually written appears below. It is much clearer because the writer arranged information differently and also built links into his sentences so that they would flow smoothly:

- After stating the central idea in a topic sentence, the writer moves to two more specific explanations and illustrates the second with four sentences of examples.
- (Circled) words repeat or restate key terms or concepts.
- [Boxed] words link sentences and clarify relationships.
- Underlined phrases are in parallel grammatical form to reflect their parallel content.

> The ancient Egyptians were masters of preserving dead people's bodies by (making mummies) of them. [Basically,] (mummification) consisted of removing the internal organs, applying natural preservatives inside and out, and then wrapping the body in layers of bandages. [And] (the process) was remarkably effective.

— Topic sentence

Explanation 1: What mummification is

Indeed, (mummies) several thousand years old
have been discovered nearly intact. (Their) skin,
hair, teeth, finger- and toenails, and facial features are still evident. (Their) diseases in life, such
as smallpox, arthritis, and nutritional deficiencies, are still diagnosable. Even (their) fatal afflic-
tions are still apparent: a middle-aged king died
from a blow on the head; a child king died from
polio.

— Mitchell Rosenbaum (student),
"Lost Arts of the Egyptians"

> Explanation 2: Why the Egyptians were masters

> Specific examples of explanation 2

Though some of the connections in this paragraph were added in revision, the writer attended to them while drafting as well. Not only superficial coherence but also an underlying clarity of relationships can be achieved by tying each sentence to the one before—generalizing from it, clarifying it, qualifying it, adding to it, illustrating it. Each sentence in a paragraph creates an expectation of some sort in the mind of the reader, a question such as "How was a mummy made?" or "How intact are the mummies?" or "What's another example?" When you recognize these expectations and try to fulfill them, readers are likely to understand relationships without struggle.

1 Organizing the paragraph

The paragraphs on mummies illustrate an essential element of coherence: information must be arranged in an order that readers can follow easily and that corresponds to their expectations. The common organizations for paragraphs correspond to those for entire essays: by space, by time, and for emphasis. (In addition, the patterns of development also suggest certain arrangements. See pp. 91–100.)

Note On a computer you can experiment with different paragraph organizations and emphases. Copy a paragraph, paste the copy into your document, and then try moving sentences around. To evaluate the versions, you'll need to edit each one so that sentences flow smoothly, attending to repetition, parallelism, transitions, and the other techniques discussed in this section.

▪ Organizing by space or time

A paragraph organized **spatially** focuses readers' attention on one point and scans a person, object, or scene from that point. The movement usually parallels the way people actually look at things, from top to bottom, from side to side, from near to far. Virginia Woolf follows the last pattern in the following paragraph:

PICTURING THE PARAGRAPH

A good metaphor to use with students is that of cinematography and film. Remind them how in movies the camera can give wide shots, pan in for close-ups, or sweep across a scene for effect. A writer chooses similar "shots" (i.e., positions from which to view the material) in order to organize paragraphs.

PARAGRAPH PATTERNS I

Give students a topic sentence and a set of assertions, facts, and details in undeveloped form. Tell them to use the material to write a coherent paragraph, following one of the patterns described in the handbook: spatial, chronological, general-to-specific, specific-to-general, problem-solution, climactic, most familiar to least familiar, or simplest to most complex. Students can manipulate the material however they wish to achieve an effect that is appropriate to the pattern. You may want to ask for several paragraphs, each using the same content but a different pattern.

PARAGRAPH PATTERNS II

Write a paragraph following one of the basic organizational schemes discussed in 4b-1. Leave the subject and content of the paragraph up to the individual student. If they wish, students may make up information, as long as they keep it plausible. Students can compare results in group, then work together to revise one of those responses into a paragraph to be "published" on the class computer network or printed out and distributed.

EXTRA EXAMPLES

The following examples illustrate the specific-to-general pattern in a sentence and may be extended to short sample paragraphs:

(specific) + good study habits
(specific) + consistent effort
(specific) + curiosity
(general) = good grades

Good study habits, consistent effort, and intellectual curiosity will result in good grades.

(specific) + seeds
(specific) + soil
(specific) + sunlight
(specific) + water
(general) = good vegetable crop

A combination of fresh seeds, well-balanced soil, and adequate sunlight and water results in a good vegetable crop.

Spatial organization

The sun struck straight upon the house, making the white walls glare between the dark windows. Their panes, woven thickly with green branches, held circles of impenetrable darkness. Sharp-edged wedges of light lay upon the window-sill and showed inside the room plates with blue rings, cups with curved handles, the bulge of a great bowl, the criss-cross pattern in the rug, and the formidable corners and lines of cabinets and bookcases. Behind their conglomeration hung a zone of shadow in which might be a further shape to be disencumbered of shadow or still denser depths of darkness.
—Virginia Woolf, *The Waves*

> Description moving from outside (closer) to inside (farther)

> Unstated central idea: Sunlight barely penetrated the house's secrets.

Another familiar way of organizing the elements of a paragraph is **chronologically**—that is, in order of their occurrence in time. In a chronological paragraph, as in experience, the earliest events come first, followed by more recent ones.

Chronological organization

Nor can a tree live without soil. A hurricane-born mangrove island may bring its own soil to the sea. But other mangrove trees make their own soil—and their own islands—from scratch. These are the ones which interest me. The seeds germinate in the fruit on the tree. The germinated embryo can drop anywhere—say, onto a dab of floating muck. The heavy root end sinks; a leafy plumule unfurls. The tiny seedling, afloat, is on its way. Soon aerial roots shooting out in all directions trap debris. The sapling's networks twine, the interstices narrow, and water calms in the lee. Bacteria thrive on organic broth; amphipods swarm. These creatures grow and die at the tree's wet feet. The soil thickens, accumulating rainwater, leaf rot, seashells, and guano; the island spreads.
—Annie Dillard, "Sojourner"

> Topic sentence

> Details in order of their occurrence

■ Organizing for emphasis

Some organizational schemes are imposed on paragraphs to achieve a certain emphasis. The most common is the **general-to-specific** scheme, in which the topic sentence often comes first and then the following sentences become increasingly specific. The paragraph on mummies (pp. 78–79) illustrates this organization: each sentence is either more specific than the one before it or at the same level of generality. Here is another illustration:

General-to-specific organization

> Perhaps the simplest fact about sleep is that individual needs for it vary widely. — **Topic sentence**
>
> Most adults sleep between seven and nine hours, but occasionally people turn up who need twelve hours or so, while some rare types can get by on three or four. Rarest of all are those legendary types who require almost no sleep at all; respected researchers have recently studied three such people. One of them—a healthy, happy woman in her seventies—sleeps about an hour every two or three days. The other two are men in early middle age, who get by on a few minutes a night. One of them complains about the daily fifteen minutes or so he's forced to "waste" in sleeping. — **Supporting examples, increasingly specific**
>
> —Lawrence A. Mayer,
> "The Confounding Enemy of Sleep"

In the less common **specific-to-general** organization, the elements of the paragraph build to a general conclusion:

Specific-to-general organization

> It's disconcerting that so many college women, when asked how their children will be cared for if they themselves work, refer with vague confidence to "the day care center" as though there were some great amorphous kiddie watcher out there that the state provides. — **Common belief**
>
> But such places, adequately funded, well run, and available to all, are still scarce in this country, particularly for middle-class women. And figures show that when she takes time off for family-connected reasons (births, child care), a woman's chances for career advancement plummet. In a job market that's steadily tightening and getting more competitive, these obstacles bode the kind of danger ahead that can shatter not only professions, but egos. — **Actual situation**
>
> A hard reality is that there's not much more support for our daughters who have family-plus-career goals than there was for us; there's simply a great deal more self and societal pressure. — **General conclusion: topic sentence**
>
> —Judith Wax,
> *Starting in the Middle*

As its name implies, the **problem-solution** arrangement introduces a problem and then proposes or explains a solution. The next paragraph explains how to gain from Internet newsgroups despite their limitations:

PARAGRAPH SCRAMBLES

These activities are suitable for students working individually; when assigned to small groups, however, the activities work even better by encouraging considerable discussion and discovery.

1. Take a good paragraph, by either a student or a professional, and rearrange the sentences. Then ask students to unscramble the sentences and make a clear, coherent paragraph. This exercise will make students aware of the flow of a coherent paragraph and will alert them to the number of examples and details found in a well-developed paragraph.

2. Choose a paragraph that lacks coherence and rearrange the sentences. Tell students to unscramble the sentences to form a coherent paragraph. Indicate that students are free to add any transitions, sentences, illustrations, or details they feel are necessary to make the paragraph both coherent and well developed. Students will quickly spot any coherence problems in the original paragraph, and unless the topic of the paragraph is quite unusual, they will be able to add any necessary content.

DRAMATIC EXAMPLES

Climactic order is a form of structuring that moves from least to most important. To help explain this strategy you may wish to draw examples from drama, particularly from the structure of tragedy. Othello provides an obvious example of structuring that moves from least dramatic/tension-filled to most dramatic/tension-filled.

Least dramatic—Othello marries Desdemona
More dramatic—Othello suspects Desdemona of infidelity
More dramatic—Desdemona defends her chastity and argues for her life
Most dramatic (climax)—Othello kills Desdemona and then realizes that she has been faithful to him

Problem-solution organization

Even when you do find a newsgroup with apparently useful material, you have no assurance of a correspondent's authority because of e-mail's inherent anonymity. Many people don't cite their credentials. Besides, anyone can pose as an expert. _[Topic sentence and clarification: statement of the problem]_ The best information you can get initially is apt to be a reference to something of which you were not aware but can then investigate for yourself. Internet newsgroups can be valuable for that alone. I have been directed to software-problem solutions, owners of out-of-print books, and important people who know nothing about communicating through electronic communities. It is best to start with the assumption that you are conversing with peers, people who know things that you don't, while you probably know things that they don't. Gradually, by trading information, you develop some virtual relationships and can assess the relative validity of your sources. Meanwhile, you will probably have learned a few things along the way. _[Solution to the problem]_

—Adapted from John A. Butler,
Cybersearch

When your details vary in significance, you can arrange them in a **climactic** order, from least to most important or dramatic:

Climactic organization

Nature has put many strange tongues into the heads of her creatures. _[Topic sentence]_ There is the frog's tongue, rooted at the front of the mouth so it can be protruded an extra distance for nabbing prey. _[Least dramatic example]_ There is the gecko lizard's tongue, so long and agile that the lizard uses it to wash its eyes. But the ultimate lingual whopper has been achieved in the anteater. The anteater's head, long as it is, is not long enough to contain the tremendous tongue which licks deep into anthills. Its tongue is not rooted in the mouth or throat: it is fastened to the breastbone. _[Most dramatic example]_

—Alan Devoe, "Nature's Utmost"

In other organizations, you can arrange details according to how you think readers are likely to understand them. In discussing the virtues of public television, for instance, you might proceed from **most familiar to least familiar,** from a well-known program your readers have probably seen to less well-known programs they may not have seen. Or in defending the right of government employees to strike, you might arrange your reasons from **simplest to most complex,** from the employees' need to be able to redress grievances to more subtle consequences for relations between employers and employees.

2 Repeating or restating key words

Repeating or restating the important words in a paragraph binds the sentences together and keeps the paragraph's topic uppermost in readers' minds. In the next example, notice how the circled words relate the sentences and stress the important ideas of the paragraph:

> Having listened to both (Chinese) and (English,) I also tend to be suspicious of any (comparisons) between the two (languages.) Typically, one (language)—that of the person doing the (comparing)—is often used as the standard, the benchmark for a logical form of expression. And so the (language) being (compared) is always in danger of being judged deficient or superfluous, simplistic or unnecessarily complex, melodious or cacophonous. (English) speakers point out that (Chinese) is (extremely difficult) because it relies on variations in tone barely discernible to the human ear. By the same token, (Chinese) speakers tell me (English) is (extremely difficult) because it is inconsistent, a language of too many broken rules, of Mickey Mice and Donald Ducks.
>
> —Amy Tan, "The Language of Discretion"

This paragraph links sentences through their structure, too, because the subject of each one picks up on key words used earlier:

Sentence 1: Having listened to both (Chinese) and (English,) I tend to be suspicious of any comparisons between the two (languages.)
Sentence 2: Typically, one (language). . .
Sentence 3: And so the (language). . .
Sentence 4: (English speakers). . .
Sentence 5: (Chinese speakers). . .

In many incoherent paragraphs, such as the one on mummification on page 78, each sentence subject introduces a topic new to the paragraph so that readers have trouble following the thread. (See pp. 386–87 for more on linking sentences through their subjects.)

3 Using parallel structures

Another way to achieve coherence is through **parallelism**—the use of similar grammatical structures for similar elements of meaning

Sloan, Gary. "The Frequency of Transitional Markers in Discursive Prose." *College English* 46 (1984): 158–79. Sloan shows how infrequently explicit transition markers are used by either professional or student writers.

Smith, Rochelle. "Paragraphing for Coherence: Writing as Implied Dialogue." *College English* 46 (1984): 8–21. Smith uses reader-response theory and the notion of author-reader dialogue to improve paragraph cohesion.

Witte, Stephen, and Lester Faigley. "Coherence, Cohesion, and Writing Quality." *College Composition and Communication* 32 (1981): 189–204. Students need to learn the features of coherence that extend across sentence boundaries; the article stresses ways to make them aware of coherence strategies.

Winterowd, W. Ross. "The Grammar of Coherence." *College English* 31 (1971): 828–35. This article describes the kinds of relations that link sentence to sentence and paragraph to paragraph.

HE'S ON SECOND

To illustrate the importance of clear pronoun reference in paragraphs, try to locate a recording or transcript of the famous Abbott and Costello skit, "Who's on First." While humorous, this skit demonstrates the frustration a reader can feel when encountering a series of pronouns with unclear antecedents. Keep in mind that students' use of unclear pronoun antecedents may signal a larger difficulty in defining or expanding on their subject matter.

within a sentence or among sentences. (See Chapter 25 for a detailed discussion of parallelism.) Parallel structures help tie together the last three sentences in the paragraph on mummies (p. 79). In the following paragraph, underlining highlights the parallel structures linking sentences. Aphra Behn (lived 1640–89) was the first Englishwoman to write professionally.

> In addition to her busy career as a writer, Aphra Behn also found time to briefly marry and spend a little while in debtor's prison. She found time to take up a career as a spy for the English in their war against the Dutch. She made the long and difficult voyage to Suriname [in South America] and became involved in a slave rebellion there. She plunged into political debate at Will's Coffee House and defended her position from the stage of the Drury Lane Theater. She actively argued for women's rights to be educated and to marry whom they pleased, or not at all. She defied the seventeenth-century dictum that ladies must be "modest" and wrote freely about sex.
> —Angeline Goreau, "Aphra Behn"

Note Though planned repetition can be effective, careless or excessive repetition weakens prose (see pp. 532–33).

4 Using pronouns

Pronouns such as *she, he, it, they,* and *who* refer to and function as nouns (see p. 237). Thus pronouns naturally help relate sentences to one another. In the following paragraph the pronouns and the nouns they refer to are circled:

> After dark, on the warrenlike streets of Brooklyn where I live, I often see women who fear the worst from me. They seem to have set their faces on neutral, and with their purse straps strung across their chests bandolier-style, they forge ahead as though bracing themselves against being tackled. I understand, of course, that the danger they perceive is not a hallucination. Women are particularly vulnerable to street violence, and young black males are drastically overrepresented among the perpetrators of that violence. Yet these truths are no solace against the kind of alienation that comes of being ever the suspect, a fearsome entity with whom pedestrians avoid making eye contact.
> —Brent Staples, "Black Men and Public Space"

5 Being consistent

Being consistent is the most subtle way to achieve paragraph coherence because readers are aware of consistency only when it is absent. Consistency (or the lack of it) occurs primarily in the tense of verbs and in the number and person of nouns and pronouns (see

Chapter 20). Although some shifts will be necessary to reflect your meaning, inappropriate shifts, as in the following passages, will interfere with a reader's ability to follow the development of ideas:

Shifts in tense

In the Hopi religion, water <u>is</u> the driving force. Since the Hopi <u>lived</u> in the Arizona desert, they <u>needed</u> water urgently for drinking, cooking, and irrigating crops. Their complex beliefs <u>are</u> focused in part on gaining the assistance of supernatural forces in obtaining water. Many of the Hopi kachinas, or spirit essences, <u>were</u> directly concerned with clouds, rain, and snow.

Shifts in number

<u>Kachinas</u> represent the things and events of the real world, such as clouds, mischief, cornmeal, and even death. A <u>kachina</u> is not worshiped as a god but regarded as an interested friend. <u>They</u> visit the Hopi from December through July in the form of men who dress in kachina costumes and perform dances and other rituals.

Shifts in person

Unlike the man, the Hopi <u>woman</u> does not keep contact with kachinas through costumes and dancing. Instead, <u>one</u> receives a small likeness of a kachina, called a *tihu*, from the man impersonating the kachina. <u>You</u> are more likely to receive a tihu as a girl approaching marriage, though a child or older woman sometimes receives one, too.

Note The grammar checker on a word processor cannot help you locate shifts in tense, number, or person among sentences. Shifts are sometimes necessary (as when tenses change to reflect actual differences in time). Furthermore, a passage with needless shifts may still consist of sentences that are grammatically correct, as all the sentences are in the preceding examples. The only way to achieve consistency in your writing is to review it yourself.

6 Using transitional expressions

Specific words and word groups, called **transitional expressions,** can connect sentences whose relationships may not be instantly clear to readers. Notice the difference in the following two versions of the same paragraph:

> Medical science has succeeded in identifying the hundreds of viruses that can cause the common cold. It has discovered the most effective means of prevention. One person transmits the cold viruses to another most often by hand. An infected person covers his mouth to cough. He picks up the telephone. His daughter picks up the telephone. She rubs her eyes. She has a

Paragraph is choppy and hard to follow

READING ALOUD

Often students can spot a lack of transitions in their own writing if they read their papers aloud. If you ask students to read one another's papers aloud, the student writers will often be able to recognize missing or unclear transitions at those points where the readers stumble over a passage or have to stop to puzzle out the meaning.

Ask students to work in groups to analyze what happens when they substitute another transition from the same group into one of the sentences from Kathleen LaFrank's paragraph. How can a transitional word affect the meaning of that sentence and of the relationships between sentences?

HIGHLIGHTING TRANSITIONS

Encourage students to use highlighting pens or the Highlighting feature on a word processor to mark where transitional expressions appear in their texts; if they think too few "highlights" show up, students can add more.

cold. It spreads. To avoid colds, people should wash their hands often and keep their hands away from their faces.

Medical science has ⟨thus⟩ succeeded in identifying the hundreds of viruses that can cause the common cold. It has ⟨also⟩ discovered the most effective means of prevention. One person transmits the cold viruses to another most often by hand. ⟨For instance,⟩ an infected person covers his mouth to cough. ⟨Then⟩ he picks up the telephone. ⟨Half an hour later,⟩ his daughter picks up the ⟨same⟩ telephone. ⟨Immediately afterward,⟩ she rubs her eyes. ⟨Within a few days,⟩ she, ⟨too,⟩ has a cold. ⟨And thus⟩ it spreads. To avoid colds, ⟨therefore,⟩ people should wash their hands often and keep their hands away from their faces.

—Kathleen LaFrank (student),
"Colds: Myth and Science"

> Transitional expressions (boxed) remove choppiness and spell out relationships

There are scores of transitional expressions on which to draw. The box below shows many common ones, arranged according to the relationships they convey.

Transitional expressions

To add or show sequence
again, also, and, and then, besides, equally important, finally, first, further, furthermore, in addition, in the first place, last, moreover, next, second, still, too

To compare
also, in the same way, likewise, similarly

To contrast
although, and yet, but, but at the same time, despite, even so, even though, for all that, however, in contrast, in spite of, nevertheless, notwithstanding, on the contrary, on the other hand, regardless, still, though, yet

To give examples or intensify
after all, an illustration of, even, for example, for instance, indeed, in fact, it is true, of course, specifically, that is, to illustrate, truly

To indicate place

above, adjacent to, below, elsewhere, farther on, here, near, nearby, on the other side, opposite to, there, to the east, to the left

To indicate time

after a while, afterward, as long as, as soon as, at last, at length, at that time, before, earlier, formerly, immediately, in the meantime, in the past, lately, later, meanwhile, now, presently, shortly, simultaneously, since, so far, soon, subsequently, then, thereafter, until, when

To repeat, summarize, or conclude

all in all, altogether, as has been said, in brief, in conclusion, in other words, in particular, in short, in simpler terms, in summary, on the whole, that is, therefore, to put it differently, to summarize

To show cause or effect

accordingly, as a result, because, consequently, for this purpose, hence, otherwise, since, then, therefore, thereupon, thus, to this end, with this object

   Note Draw carefully on the preceding list of transitional expressions because the ones in each group are not interchangeable. For instance, *besides, finally,* and *second* may all be used to add information, but each has its own distinct meaning.

   To see where transitional expressions might be needed in your paragraphs, examine the movement from each sentence to the next. (On a computer or on paper, you can highlight the transitional expressions already present and then review the sentences that lack them.) Abrupt changes are most likely to need a transition: a shift from cause to effect, a contradiction, a contrast. You can smooth and clarify transitions *between* paragraphs, too. See pages 108 and 109–10.

    If transitional expressions are not common in your native language, you may be tempted to compensate when writing in English by adding them to the beginnings of most sentences. But such explicit transitions aren't needed everywhere, and in fact too many can be intrusive and awkward. When inserting transitional expressions, consider the reader's need for a signal: often the connection from sentence to sentence is already clear from the context, or it can be made clear by relating the content of sentences more closely (see pp. 83–84). When you do need transitional expressions, try varying their positions in your sentences, as shown in the sample paragraph on the facing page.

Punctuating transitional expressions

   A transitional expression is usually set off by a comma or commas from the rest of the sentence:

CROSS-CULTURAL COMMUNICATION

   Pan-cultural examples lend themselves to collaborative discussion; students might collect and discuss examples of mistranslations from other languages to English or from English to other languages. For instance, the Chevy Nova was a failure when it was introduced in Puerto Rico because *No va* means "It doesn't run" in Spanish. Students for whom English is a second language can contribute many examples of idioms that give them trouble.

COMPUTER ACTIVITY

SCRAMBLING SENTENCES

   The computer makes scrambling exercises particularly viable. Ask each student to scramble the sentence order deliberately in one of their own paragraphs and then present that exercise in "unscrambling" to their group. It can be very useful for each writer to hear their own coherence "clues" being analyzed and debated.

Immediately afterward, she rubs her eyes. Within a few days, she, too, has a cold.

See page 438 for more on this convention and its exceptions.

7 Combining devices to achieve coherence

The devices for achieving coherence rarely appear in isolation in effective paragraphs. As any example in this chapter shows, writers usually combine sensible organization, parallelism, repetition, pronouns, consistency, and transitional expressions to help readers follow the development of ideas.

EXERCISE 4.6   Analyzing paragraphs for coherence

Study the paragraphs by Janet Lieber (p. 79), Hillary Begas (p. 91), and Freeman Dyson (p. 93) for the authors' use of various devices to achieve coherence. Look especially for organization, parallel structures and ideas, repetition and restatement, pronouns, and transitional expressions.

EXERCISE 4.7   Arranging sentences coherently

After the topic sentence (sentence 1), the sentences in the student paragraph below have been deliberately scrambled to make the paragraph incoherent. Using the topic sentence and other clues as guides, rearrange the sentences in the paragraph to form a well-organized, coherent unit. (You can do this exercise online at *ablongman.com/littlebrown.*)

We hear complaints about the Postal Service all the time, but we [1] should not forget what it does *right*. The total volume of mail de- [2] livered by the Postal Service each year makes up almost half the total delivered in all the world. Its 70,000 employees handle [3] 140,000,000,000 pieces of mail each year. And when was the last [4] time they failed to deliver yours? In fact, on any given day the Postal [5] Service delivers almost as much mail as the rest of the world combined. That huge number means over 2,000,000 pieces per employee [6] and over 560 pieces per man, woman, and child in the country.

EXERCISE 4.8   Eliminating inconsistencies

The following paragraph is incoherent because of inconsistencies in person, number, or tense. Identify the inconsistencies and revise the paragraph to give it coherence. (You can do this exercise online at *ablongman.com/littlebrown.*) For further exercises in eliminating inconsistencies, see pages 359, 360–61, and 363.

The Hopi tihu, or kachina likeness, is often called a "doll," but its owner, usually a girl or woman, does not regard them as a plaything. Instead, you treated them as a valued possession and hung them out of the way on a wall. For its owner the tihu represents a connection

---

ANALYZING FOR COHERENCE

Exercise 4.6 works well as a group exercise because students have more opportunity to debate and explore options. Have each group report back to the class on the different methods each writer uses to achieve coherence.

ANSWERS: EXERCISE 4.6

1. Lieber paragraph (p. 76): Organization: general to specific. Parallelism after first sentence: *They have measured . . . recorded and studied . . . learned.* Repetition: *whale, sings, song.* Pronoun: *they.* Transitional expression: *And.*

2. Begas paragraph (p. 91): Organization: chronological. Parallelism: *They persuaded . . . they deprived; Jill became . . . she dropped out.* Repetition: *lonely, college/school.* Pronouns: *Jill/she; men and women/they.* Transitional expressions: *Between . . . , increasingly, Before long, too.*

3. Dyson paragraph (p. 93): Organization: climactic. Parallelism and repetition: *reason is the need . . . reason is the need . . . reason is our spiritual need.* Further repetition: *space, earth/this planet.* Pronouns: *we, our, us.* Transitional expressions: *first, second, third.*

ANSWERS: EXERCISE 4.7

Possible answer

The coherent order would be 1, 2, 5, 3, 6, 4.

ANSWERS: EXERCISE 4.8

The Hopi *tihu,* or kachina likeness, is often called a "doll," but its owner, usually a girl or woman, does not regard it as a plaything. Instead, she treats it as a valued possession and hangs it out of the way on a wall. For its owner the *tihu* represents a connection with the kachina's spirit. It is considered part of the kachina, carrying a portion of the kachina's power.

with the kachina's spirit. They are considered part of the kachina, carrying a portion of the kachina's power.

EXERCISE 4.9   Using transitional expressions

Transitional expressions have been removed from the following paragraph at the numbered blanks. Fill in each blank with an appropriate transitional expression (1) to contrast, (2) to intensify, and (3) to show effect. Consult the list on pages 86–87 if necessary. (You can do this exercise online at *ablongman.com/littlebrown*.)

All over the country, people are swimming, jogging, weightlifting, dancing, walking, playing tennis—doing anything to keep fit. ____(1)____ this school has consistently refused to construct and equip a fitness center. The school has ____(2)____ refused to open existing athletic facilities to all students, not just those playing organized sports. ____(3)____ students have no place to exercise except in their rooms and on dangerous public roads.

EXERCISE 4.10   Considering your past work:
Paragraph coherence

Continuing from Exercise 4.3 (p. 76), examine the body paragraphs of your essay to see how coherent they are and how their coherence could be improved. Do the paragraphs have a clear organization? Do you use repetition and restatement, parallelism, pronouns, and transitional expressions to signal relationships? Are the paragraphs consistent in person, number, and tense? Revise two or three paragraphs in ways you think will improve their coherence.

EXERCISE 4.11   Writing a coherent paragraph

Write a coherent paragraph from the following information, combining and rewriting sentences as necessary. First, begin the paragraph with the topic sentence given and arrange the supporting sentences in a climactic order. Then combine and rewrite the supporting sentences, helping the reader see connections by introducing repetition and restatement, parallelism, pronouns, consistency, and transitional expressions. (You can do this exercise online at *ablongman.com/littlebrown*.)

Topic sentence
Hypnosis is far superior to drugs for relieving tension.

Supporting information
Hypnosis has none of the dangerous side effects of the drugs that relieve tension.
Tension-relieving drugs can cause weight loss or gain, illness, or even death.
Hypnosis is nonaddicting.
Most of the drugs that relieve tension do foster addiction.
Tension-relieving drugs are expensive.
Hypnosis is inexpensive even for people who have not mastered self-hypnosis.

ANSWERS: EXERCISE 4.9
Possible answers

1. *Yet, However, Even so,* or *Nevertheless*
2. *even, also,* or *further*
3. *As a result, Consequently,* or *Therefore*

TRANSITIONAL EXPRESSIONS

Ask students to compare answers to Exercise 4.9 and discuss the effects of each student's choices on the meaning of the sentences and of the paragraph.

ANSWERS: EXERCISE 4.10

Individual response.

ANSWERS: EXERCISE 4.11
Possible paragraph

Hypnosis is far superior to drugs for relieving tension. It is inexpensive even for people who have not mastered self-hypnosis, whereas drugs are expensive. It is nonaddictive, whereas drugs foster addiction. And most important, hypnosis has none of the dangerous side effects of drugs, such as weight loss or gain, illness, and even death.

COMPUTER ACTIVITY

REARRANGING SENTENCES

Exercise 4.11 is particularly feasible on the computer since students can rearrange the information in multiple ways without retyping.

COHERENT PARAGRAPHS

The kind of coherence achieved in Exercises 4.11 and 4.12 will depend a great deal on each individual's choice of connective strategies. When students compare their responses to Exercises 4.11 and 4.12 in groups, it is beneficial for them to note the results of other writers' differing choices.

ANSWERS: EXERCISE 4.12

Individual response.

HIGHLIGHTS

Section 4c looks at ways to convey the central idea of a paragraph fully and convincingly to the reader. Developing paragraphs and essays fully is often difficult for students. One of the important differences between casual conversation and formal writing is the degree to which ideas must be concretely developed in writing. Because students are more experienced in conversation than in writing, they find generalizations much easier to come by than the details, examples, and reasons to support them.

All of us must grapple with the student essay or single paragraph that is largely a succession of generalizations without support or explanation. Part of the solution to such problem paragraphs is to make students aware of readers as a special kind of audience for ideas. Another part is to make them aware of different strategies for developing paragraphs or essays.

The ways to develop ideas are infinite, but this section focuses on a limited number. The initial emphasis falls on the use of details, examples, and reasons, which are essential to any more specific method of development. Students are encouraged to follow the standard methods or patterns of development by posing questions about an idea, event, or object in order to uncover concrete information about it.

You may wish to ask students to spend time in class or in groups working with sample topics to discover how the methods of development can be used to probe a topic and how the questions reveal different aspects of a topic. This discus-

---

EXERCISE 4.12 **Turning topic sentences into coherent paragraphs**

Develop three of the following topic sentences into coherent paragraphs. Organize your information by space, by time, or for emphasis, as seems most appropriate. Use repetition and restatement, parallelism, pronouns, consistency, and transitional expressions to link sentences. (You can do this exercise online at *ablongman.com/littlebrown*.)

1. The most interesting character in the book [or movie] was _____.
2. Of all my courses, _____ is the one that I think will serve me best throughout life.
3. Although we in the United States face many problems, the one we should concentrate on solving first is _____.
4. The most dramatic building in town is the _____.
5. Children should not have to worry about the future.

4c Developing the paragraph

In an essay that's understandable and interesting to readers, you will provide plenty of solid information to support your general statements. You work that information into the essay through the paragraph, as you build up each point relating to the thesis.

A paragraph may be unified and coherent but still be inadequate if you skimp on details. Take this example:

> Untruths can serve as a kind of social oil when they smooth connections between people. In preventing confrontation and injured feelings, they allow everyone to go on as before.

General statements needing examples to be clear and convincing

This paragraph lacks **development,** completeness. It does not provide enough information for us to evaluate or even care about the writer's assertions.

1 Using specific information

If they are sound, the general statements you make in any writing will be based on what you have experienced, observed, read, and thought. Readers will assume as much and will expect you to provide the evidence for your statements—sensory details, facts, statistics, examples, quotations, reasons. Whatever helps you form your views you need, in turn, to share with readers.

Here is the actual version of the preceding sample paragraph. With examples, the paragraph is more interesting and convincing.

> Untruths can serve as a kind of social oil when they smooth connections between people. Assuring a worried friend that his haircut is

flattering, claiming an appointment to avoid an aunt's dinner invitation, pretending interest in an acquaintance's children—these lies may protect the liar, but they also protect the person lied to. In preventing confrontation and injured feelings, the lies allow everyone to go on as before.
—Joan Lar (student), "The Truth of Lies"

> Examples specifying kinds of lies and consequences

If your readers often comment that your writing needs more specifics, you should focus on that improvement in your revisions. Try listing the general statements of each paragraph on lines by themselves with space underneath. Then use one of the discovery techniques discussed on pages 16–26 (freewriting, brainstorming, and so on) to find the details to support each sentence. Write these into your draft. If you write on a computer, you can do this revision directly on your draft. First create a duplicate of your draft, and then, working on the copy, separate the sentences and explore their support. Rewrite the supporting details into sentences, reassemble the paragraph, and edit it for coherence.

2 Using a pattern of development

If you have difficulty developing an idea or shaping your information, then try asking yourself questions derived from the patterns of development. (The same patterns can help with essay development, too. See pp. 24–25.)

You can download the following questions from *ablongman .com/littlebrown*. When you're having difficulty with a paragraph, you can duplicate the list and explore answers. You may be able to import what you write directly into your draft.

■ How did it happen? (Narration)

Narration retells a significant sequence of events, usually in the order of their occurrence (that is, chronologically):

> Jill's story is typical for "recruits" to religious cults. She was very lonely in college and appreciated the attention of the nice young men and women who lived in a house near campus. They persuaded her to share their meals and then to move in with them. Between intense bombardments of "love," they deprived her of sleep and sometimes threatened to throw her out. Jill became increasingly confused and dependent, losing touch with any reality besides the one in the group. She dropped out of school and refused to see or communicate with her family. Before long she, too, was preying on lonely college students.
> —Hillary Begas (student),
> "The Love Bombers"

> Important events in chronological order

sion may help students see how the process of development can be an act of discovery. You will probably want to stress, however, that the methods of development covered in the handbook are not the only ones writers can use and that most paragraphs use more than a single method.

The exercises for this section range from analyzing paragraphs to producing them, and whether used in groups or by students working individually, they encourage students to treat the patterns of development as different ways of viewing a topic.

WHAT AND WHY

Students from non-Western cultures may be unaccustomed to analysis that involves critical thinking. They may know how to describe an item or text by listing component parts, for instance, but they may not be accustomed to including discussion of why the thing or text is important. A quick way to help these students learn to distinguish between "what" a thing is and "why" it is important is to ask them the following series of questions about a flag:

What is the object attached to the tall pole in the quad? (Describe its appearance, give its name, discuss the component colors and shapes.)

How does the object work? (How is it attached? How is it raised and lowered? When is it raised and lowered?)

Why does it get flown? (This question will lead students into a discussion of the symbolism and meaning of the flag and of its being flown on campus.)

As this paragraph illustrates, a narrator is concerned not just with the sequence of events but also with their consequence, their importance to the whole. Thus a narrative rarely corresponds to real time; instead, it collapses transitional or background events and focuses on events of particular interest. In addition, writers sometimes rearrange events, as when they simulate the workings of memory by flashing back to an earlier time.

▪ How does it look, sound, feel, smell, taste? (Description)

Description details the sensory qualities of a person, place, thing, or feeling. You use concrete and specific words to convey a dominant mood, to illustrate an idea, or to achieve some other purpose. Some description is **subjective:** the writer filters the subject through his or her biases and emotions. In the subjective description by Virginia Woolf on page 80, the *glare* of the walls, the *impenetrable darkness,* the *bulge of a great bowl,* and the *formidable corners and lines* all indicate the author's feelings about what she describes.

In contrast to subjective description, journalists and scientists often favor description that is **objective,** conveying the subject without bias or emotion:

> The two toddlers, both boys, sat together for half an hour in a ten-foot-square room with yellow walls (one with a two-way mirror for observation) and a brown carpet. The room was unfurnished except for two small chairs and about two dozen toys. The boys' interaction was generally tense. They often struggled physically and verbally over several toys, especially a large red beach ball and a small wooden fire engine. The larger of the two boys often pushed the smaller away or pried his hands from the desired object. This larger boy never spoke, but he did make grunting sounds when he was engaging the other. In turn, the smaller boy twice uttered piercing screams of "No!" and once shouted "Stop that!" When he was left alone, he hummed and muttered to himself.
> —Ray Mattison (student),
> "Case Study: Play Patterns of Toddlers"

Objective description: specific record of sensory data without interpretation

▪ What are examples of it or reasons for it? (Illustration or support)

Some ideas can be developed simply by **illustration or support**—supplying detailed examples or reasons. The writer of the paragraph on lying (pp. 90–91) developed her idea with several specific examples of her general statements. You can also supply a single extended example:

THE SUBJECT-OBJECT BOUNDARY

Students may find that the subjective-objective boundary is sometimes fuzzy. Even the objective paragraph has judgmental language like "piercing" in it. Perhaps a way of solving this dilemma is to say that in *subjective* description, the writer's intention is to interpret experience for readers, while in *objective* description, the writer's intention is to allow the audience to interpret the reported experiences themselves.

The language problem that I was attacking loomed larger and larger as I began to learn more. When I would describe in English certain concepts and objects enmeshed in Korean emotion and imagination, I became slowly aware of nuances, of differences between two languages even in simple expression. *(Topic sentence (assertion to be illustrated))* The remark "Kim entered the house" seems to be simple enough, yet, unless a reader has a clear visual image of a Korean house, his understanding of the sentence is not complete. When a Korean says he is "in the house," he may be in his courtyard, or on his porch, or in his small room! If I wanted to give a specific picture of entering the house in the Western sense, I had to say "room" instead of house—sometimes. I say "sometimes" because many Koreans entertain their guests on their porches and still are considered to be hospitable, and in the Korean sense, going into the "room" may be a more intimate act than it would be in the English sense. Such problems! *(Single detailed example)*
—Kim Yong Ik, "A Book-Writing Venture"

Sometimes you can develop a paragraph by providing your reasons for stating a general idea:

There are three reasons, quite apart from scientific considerations, that mankind needs to travel in space. *(Topic sentence)* The first reason is the need for garbage disposal: we need to transfer industrial processes into space, so that the earth may remain a green and pleasant place for our grandchildren to live in. The second reason is the need to escape material impoverishment: the resources of this planet are finite, and we shall not forgo forever the abundant solar energy and minerals and living space that are spread out all around us. The third reason is our spiritual need for an open frontier: the ultimate purpose of space travel is to bring to humanity not only scientific discoveries and an occasional spectacular show on television but a real expansion of our spirit. *(Three reasons arranged in order of increasing drama and importance)*
—Freeman Dyson, "Disturbing the Universe"

■ **What is it? What does it encompass, and what does it exclude? (Definition)**

A **definition** says what something is and is not, specifying the characteristics that distinguish the subject from the other members of its class. You can easily define concrete, noncontroversial terms

PARAGRAPH COHERENCE

Students sometimes have the idea that "next to" means "connected to" as far as coherence goes; this is emphatically not the case. Take a paragraph like this one and have students mark the coherence devices used; or sabotage a paragraph by removing or disguising the coherence devices, and ask students to put them back in.

Students might complete the draft of their paragraphs and e-mail them to a revision partner for comments and suggestions before reworking them. It is important for students to recognize that a well-developed paragraph generally emerges from successive drafts. You can dramatize this process by posting student paragraphs at various stages of revision on the class network and holding discussions about strategies for developing each example further.

in a single sentence: *A knife is a cutting instrument* (its class) *with a sharp blade set in a handle* (the characteristics that set it off from, say, scissors or a razor blade). But defining a complicated or controversial topic often requires extended explanation, and you may need to devote a whole paragraph or even an essay to it. Such a definition may provide examples to identify the subject's characteristics. It may also involve other methods of development discussed here, such as classification or comparison and contrast.

The following definition of the word *quality* comes from an essay asserting that "quality in product and effort has become a vanishing element of current civilization":

> In the hope of possibly reducing the hail of censure which is certain to greet this essay (I am thinking of going to Alaska or possibly Patagonia in the week it is published), let me say that quality, as I understand it, means investment of the best skill and effort possible to produce the finest and most admirable result possible. Its presence or absence in some degree characterizes every man-made object, service, skilled or unskilled labor—laying bricks, painting a picture, ironing shirts, practicing medicine, shoemaking, scholarship, writing a book. You do it well or you do it half-well. Materials are sound and durable or they are sleazy; method is painstaking or whatever is easiest. Quality is achieving or reaching for the highest standard as against being satisfied with the sloppy or fraudulent. It is honesty of purpose as against catering to cheap or sensational sentiment. It does not allow compromise with the second-rate.

— General definition

— Activities in which quality may figure

— Contrast between quality and nonquality

> —Barbara Tuchman,
> "The Decline of Quality"

▧ What are its parts or characteristics? (Division or analysis)

Division and **analysis** both involve separating something into its elements, the better to understand it. Here is a simple example:

> A typical daily newspaper compresses considerable information into the top of the first page, above the headlines. The most prominent feature of this space, the newspaper's name, is called the *logo* or *nameplate*. Under the logo and set off by rules is a line of small type called the *folio line*, which contains the date of the issue, the volume and issue numbers, copyright information, and the price. To the right of the logo is a block of small type called a *weather ear*, a summary of the day's forecast. And above

— The subject being divided

— Elements of the subject, arranged spatially

EXTRA EXAMPLE

Division: Face

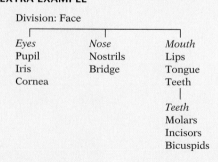

Eyes	Nose	Mouth
Pupil	Nostrils	Lips
Iris	Bridge	Tongue
Cornea		Teeth

		Teeth
		Molars
		Incisors
		Bicuspids

the logo is a *skyline*, a kind of advertisement in which the paper's editors highlight a special feature of the issue.

—Kansha Stone (student),
"Anatomy of a Paper"

Generally, analysis goes beyond simply identifying elements. Often used as a synonym for *critical thinking*, analysis also involves interpreting the elements' meaning, significance, and relationships. You identify and interpret elements according to your particular interest in the subject. (See pp. 157–63 for more on critical thinking and analysis.)

The following paragraph comes from an essay about soap operas. The analytical focus of the whole essay is the way soap operas provide viewers with a sense of community missing from their own lives. The paragraph itself has a narrower focus related to the broader one.

The surface realism of the soap opera conjures up an illusion of "liveness." The domestic settings and easygoing rhythms encourage the viewer to believe that the drama, however ridiculous, is simply an extension of daily life. The conversation is so slow that some have called it "radio with pictures." (Advertisers have always assumed that busy housewives would listen, rather than watch.) Conversation is casual and colloquial, as though one were eavesdropping on neighbors. There is plenty of time to "read" the character's face; close-ups establish intimacy. The sets are comfortably familiar: well-lit interiors of living rooms, restaurants, offices, and hospitals. Daytime soaps have little of the glamour of their prime-time relations. The viewer easily imagines that the conversation is taking place in real time.

> Topic and focus: how "liveness" seems an extension of daily life
>
> Elements:
> Slow conversation
>
> Casual conversation
>
> Intimate close-ups
> Familiar sets
>
> Absence of glamour
> Appearance of real time

—Ruth Rosen,
"Search for Yesterday"

■ **What groups or categories can it be sorted into? (Classification)**

Classification involves sorting many things into groups based on their similarities. Using the pattern, we scan a large group composed of many members that share at least one characteristic—office workers, say—and we assign the members to smaller groups on the basis of some principle—salary, perhaps, or dependence on computers. Here is an example:

In my experience, the parents who hire daytime sitters for their school-age children tend to fall into one of three groups. The first group

> — Topic sentence

CLASSIFICATION PRACTICE

Other topics to be classified might include car models, job categories, types of music, and local restaurants. (You might want to bring in the Yellow Pages for the last topic.)

EXTRA EXAMPLE

Classification:

Great Dane, Terrier
\ /
DOGS

Siamese, Tabby
\ /
CATS

Morgan, Arabian
\ /
HORSES

Guernsey, Holstein
\ /
COWS

QUADRUPEDS
|
MAMMALS

includes parents who work and want someone to be at home when the children return from school. These parents are looking for an extension of themselves, someone who will give the care they would give if they were at home. The second group includes parents who may be home all day themselves but are too disorganized or too frazzled by their children's demands to handle child care alone. They are looking for an organizer and helpmate. The third and final group includes parents who do not want to be bothered by their children, whether they are home all day or not. Unlike the parents in the first two groups, who care for their children whenever and however they can, these parents are looking for a permanent substitute for themselves.

—Nancy Whittle (student),
"Modern Parenting"

> Three groups:
> Alike in one way (all hire sitters)
>
> No overlap in groups (each has a different attitude)
>
> Classes arranged in order of increasing drama

■ **How is it like, or different from, other things? (Comparison and contrast)**

Asking about similarities and differences leads to **comparison and contrast:** comparison focuses on similarities, whereas contrast focuses on differences. The two may be used separately or together to develop an idea or to relate two or more things. Commonly, comparisons are organized in one of two ways. In the first, **subject by subject,** the two subjects are discussed separately, one at a time:

Consider the differences also in the behavior of rock and classical music audiences. At a rock concert, the audience members yell, whistle, sing along, and stamp their feet. They may even stand during the entire performance. The better the music, the more active they'll be. At a classical concert, in contrast, the better the performance, the more *still* the audience is. Members of the classical audience are so highly disciplined that they refrain from even clearing their throats or coughing. No matter what effect the powerful music has on their intellects and feelings, they sit on their hands.

—Tony Nahm (student),
"Rock and Roll Is Here to Stay"

> Subjects: rock and classical audiences
>
> Rock audience
>
> Classical audience

In the second comparative organization, **point by point,** the two subjects are discussed side by side and matched feature for feature:

The first electronic computer, ENIAC, went into operation just over fifty years ago, yet the differences between it and today's personal computer are enormous. ENIAC was enormous

> Subjects: ENIAC and personal computer

itself, consisting of forty panels, each two feet wide and four feet deep. Today's notebook PC or Macintosh, by contrast, can fit easily on one's lap. ENIAC had to be configured by hand, with its programmers taking up to two days to reset switches and cables. Today, the average user can change programs in an instant. And for all its size and inconvenience, ENIAC was also slow. In its time, its operating speed of 100,000 pulses per second seemed amazingly fast. However, today's notebook can operate at more than 1 billion pulses per second.

> Size: ENIAC, personal computer

> Ease of programming: ENIAC, personal computer

> Speed: ENIAC, personal computer

—Shirley Kajiwara (student),
"The Computers We Deserve"

The following examples show the two organizing schemes in outline form. The one on the left corresponds to the point-by-point paragraph about computers. The one on the right uses the same information but reorganizes it to cover the two subjects separately: first one, then the other.

Point by point	Subject by subject
I. Size	I. ENIAC
A. ENIAC	A. Size
B. Personal computer	B. Ease of programming
II. Ease of programming	C. Speed
A. ENIAC	II. Personal computer
B. Personal computer	A. Size
III. Speed	B. Ease of programming
A. ENIAC	C. Speed
B. Personal computer	

■ **Is it comparable to something that is in a different class but more familiar to readers? (Analogy)**

Whereas we draw comparisons and contrasts between elements in the same general class (audiences, computers), we link elements in different classes with a special kind of comparison called **analogy**. Most often in analogy we illuminate or explain an unfamiliar, abstract class of things with a familiar and concrete class of things:

> We might eventually obtain some sort of bedrock understanding of cosmic structure, but we will never understand the universe in detail; it is just too big and varied for that. If we possessed an atlas of our galaxy that devoted but a single page to each star system in the Milky Way (so that the sun and all its planets were crammed on one page), that atlas would run to more than ten million volumes of ten thousand pages each. It would take a library the size of

> Abstract subject: the universe, specifically the Milky Way

> Concrete subject: an atlas

COMBINING FOR EMPHASIS

Put together a group of sentences or bits of information about a topic, perhaps drawing the material from an essay in a reader or a magazine article. Ask students, working individually or in groups, to combine the material into a paragraph that has a distinct point of view. You might, for example, provide information about a recent controversial incident and ask for a paragraph emphasizing one perspective toward the incident or one perspective on its causes and effects.

Harvard's to house the atlas, and merely to flip through it, at the rate of a page per second, would require over ten thousand years.

—Timothy Ferris,
Coming of Age in the Milky Way

◼ Why did it happen, or what results did it have? (Cause-and-effect analysis)

When you use analysis to explain why something happened or what is likely to happen, then you are determining causes and effects. **Cause-and-effect analysis** is especially useful in writing about social, economic, or political events or problems. In the next paragraph the author looks at the causes of Japanese collectivism, which he elsewhere contrasts with American individualism:

> The *shinkansen* or "bullet train" speeds across the rural areas of Japan giving a quick view of cluster after cluster of farmhouses surrounded by rice paddies. This particular pattern did not develop purely by chance, but as a consequence of the technology peculiar to the growing of rice, the staple of the Japanese diet. The growing of rice requires the construction and maintenance of an irrigation system, something that takes many hands to build. More importantly, the planting and the harvesting of rice can only be done efficiently with the cooperation of twenty or more people. The "bottom line" is that a single family working alone cannot produce enough rice to survive, but a dozen families working together can produce a surplus. Thus the Japanese have had to develop the capacity to work together in harmony, no matter what the forces of disagreement or social disintegration, in order to survive.
>
> —William Ouchi, *Theory Z*

Effect: pattern of Japanese farming

Causes: Japanese dependence on rice, which requires collective effort

Effect: working in harmony

Cause-and-effect paragraphs tend to focus either on causes, as Ouchi's does, or on effects, as this paragraph does:

> At each step, with every graduation from one level of education to the next, the refrain from bystanders was strangely the same: "Your parents must be so proud of you." I suppose that my parents were proud, although I suspect, too, that they felt more than pride alone as they watched me advance through my education. They seemed to know that my education was separating us from one another, making it difficult to resume familiar intimacies. Mixed with the instincts of parental pride, a certain hurt

Cause: education

Effects:
Pride

Separation
Loss of intimacies
Hurt

also communicated itself—too private ever to be adequately expressed in words, but real nonetheless.

> —Richard Rodriguez, "Going Home Again"

- **How does one do it, or how does it work? (Process analysis)**

When you analyze how to do something or how something works, you explain the steps in a **process.** Paragraphs developed by process analysis are usually organized chronologically, as the steps in the process occur. Some process analyses tell the reader how to do a task:

> As a car owner, you waste money when you pay a mechanic to change the engine oil. The job is not difficult, even if you know little about cars. *[Process: changing oil]* All you need is a wrench to remove the drain plug, a large, flat pan to collect the draining oil, plastic bottles to dispose of the used oil, and fresh oil. *[Equipment needed]* First, warm up the car's engine so that the oil will flow more easily. When the engine is warm, shut it off and remove its oil-filler cap (the owner's manual shows where this cap is). Then locate the drain plug under the engine (again consulting the owner's manual for its location) and place the flat pan under the plug. Remove the plug with the wrench, letting the oil flow into the pan. When the oil stops flowing, replace the plug and, at the engine's filler hole, add the amount and kind of fresh oil specified by the owner's manual. Pour the used oil into the plastic bottles and take it to a waste-oil collector, which any garage mechanic can recommend. *[Steps in process]*
>
> —Anthony Andreas (student), "Do-It-Yourself Car Care"

Other process analyses explain how processes are done or how they work in nature. Annie Dillard's paragraph on mangrove islands (p. 80) is one example. Here is another:

> What used to be called "laying on of hands" is now practiced seriously by nurses and doctors. *[Process: therapeutic touch]* Studies have shown that therapeutic touch, as it is now known, can aid relaxation and ease pain, two effects that may in turn cause healing. *[Benefits]* A "healer" must first concentrate on helping the patient. Then, hands held a few inches from the patient's body, the healer moves from head to foot. Healers claim that they can detect energy disturbances in the patient that indicate tension, pain, or sickness. With further hand movements, the healer tries to redirect the *[Steps in process]*

COLLABORATIVE LEARNING

PRACTICAL INSTRUCTIONS

The most hilarious process exercise is one of the oldest: bring the ingredients for peanut butter and jelly sandwiches to class. Have each group write instructions for making a peanut butter and jelly sandwich. Then have the groups exchange instructions and make the sandwich exactly according to instructions they receive. (Typically, students' instructions will omit using a knife to spread the fillings, or putting together the sides with fillings.) The results are usually hilarious—and messy—but prove the point that process paragraphs must be complete to be effective.

IMITATING PARAGRAPHS

Choose a successful paragraph (student or professional) with a clear pattern, and discuss it in class. Then ask students to write paragraphs imitating the pattern but not the content of the model paragraph.

DEVELOPING PARAGRAPHS

Take underdeveloped paragraphs on subjects likely to be familiar to students and ask them to develop the paragraphs fully by drawing on their own knowledge. Student paragraphs often provide good material for this exercise. Students can work collaboratively in groups of two or three to develop each person's paragraph. Alternatively, groups can supply a list of questions for each paragraph based on the questions provided in this chapter. Then each student can brainstorm responses to the questions and use that material to revise his or her own paragraph.

COLLABORATIVE LEARNING

ANALYZING PARAGRAPHS

When students work together to analyze the paragraphs in Exercise 4.13 they benefit by discovering a broader range of interpretive responses. Those discoveries can be put to work in revising the underdeveloped paragraphs in Exercise 4.14 either individually or in groups.

ANSWERS: EXERCISE 4.13

1. Gates paragraph (p. 76): Patterns of development: cause-and-effect analysis and illustration. Supporting information: mainly the example in sentences 4–8.
2. Wax paragraph (p. 81): Pattern of development: cause-and-effect analysis. Supporting information: first three sentences.

energy. Patients report feeling heat from the healer's hands, perhaps indicating an energy transfer between healer and patient.
⎤
⎥ How process works
⎦

—Lisa Kuklinski (student),
"Old Ways to Noninvasive Medicine"

Diagrams, photographs, and other figures can do much to clarify process analyses. See pages 120–25 for guidelines on creating and clearly labeling figures.

■ Combining patterns of development

Whatever pattern you choose as the basis for developing a paragraph, other patterns may also prove helpful. Combined patterns have appeared often in this section: Dyson analyzes causes and effects in presenting reasons (p. 93); Tuchman uses contrast to define *quality* (p. 94); Nahm uses description to compare (p. 96); Ouchi uses process analysis to explain causes (p. 98).

3 Checking length

The average paragraph contains between 100 and 150 words, or between four and eight sentences. The actual length of a paragraph depends on the complexity of its topic, the role it plays in developing the thesis of the essay, and its position in the essay. Nevertheless, very short paragraphs are often inadequately developed; they may leave readers with a sense of incompleteness. And very long paragraphs often contain irrelevant details or develop two or more topics; readers may have difficulty following, sorting out, or remembering ideas.

When you are revising your essay, reread the paragraphs that seem very long or very short, checking them especially for unity and adequate development. If the paragraph wanders, cut everything from it that does not support your main idea (such as sentences that you might begin with *By the way*). If it is underdeveloped, supply the specific details, examples, or reasons needed, or try one of the methods of development we have discussed here.

EXERCISE 4.13   Analyzing paragraph development

Examine the paragraphs by Henry Louis Gates, Jr. (p. 76), and Judith Wax (p. 81) to discover how the authors achieve paragraph development. What pattern or patterns of development does each author use? Where does each author support general statements with specific evidence?

EXERCISE 4.14   Analyzing and revising skimpy paragraphs

The following paragraphs are not well developed. Analyze them, looking especially for general statements that lack support or leave questions in your mind. Then rewrite one into a well-developed paragraph, supplying your own concrete details or examples. (You can do this exercise online at *ablongman.com/littlebrown*.)

1. One big difference between successful and unsuccessful teachers is the quality of communication. A successful teacher is sensitive to students' needs and excited by the course subject. In contrast, an unsuccessful teacher seems uninterested in students and bored by the subject.

2. Gestures are one of our most important means of communication. We use them instead of speech. We use them to supplement the words we speak. And we use them to communicate some feelings or meanings that words cannot adequately express.

3. I've discovered that a word processor can do much—but not everything—to help me improve my writing. I can easily make changes and try out different versions of a paper. But I still must do the hard work of revising.

EXERCISE 4.15   Considering your past work:
Paragraph development

Continuing from Exercises 4.3 (p. 76) and 4.10 (p. 89), examine the development of the body paragraphs in your writing. Where does specific information seem adequate to support your general statements? Where does support seem skimpy? Revise the paragraphs as necessary to make your ideas clearer and more interesting. It may help you to pose the questions on pages 91–99.

EXERCISE 4.16   Writing with the patterns of development

Write at least three unified, coherent, and well-developed paragraphs, each one developed with a different pattern. Draw on the topics provided here, or choose your own topics.

1. **Narration**
    An experience of public
        speaking
    A disappointment
    Leaving home
    Waking up
2. **Description (objective or
    subjective)**
    Your room
    A crowded or deserted
        place
    A food
    An intimidating person
3. **Illustration or support**
    Why study
    Having a headache
    The best sports event

    Usefulness or uselessness
        of a self-help book
4. **Definition**
    Humor
    An adult
    Fear
    Authority
5. **Division or analysis**
    A television news show
    A barn
    A Web site
    A piece of music
6. **Classification**
    Factions in a dispute
    Styles of playing poker
    Types of Web sites
    Kinds of teachers

ANSWERS: EXERCISE 4.14
Possible answers

1. Sentence 1 requires some expansion to explain *quality of communication*. Each of the next two sentences needs to be supported with specific examples of the two qualities named.
2. Sentences 2, 3, and 4 should each be followed by at least two specific examples of gestures to make the writer's meaning concrete.
3. Sentences 2 and especially 3 require specific support: examples of easy changes, advantages of trying out different versions, and clarification of *the hard work of revising*. What does it involve? Why is it *hard*? Why is it different from what a word processor can do?

ANSWERS: EXERCISE 4.15

Individual response.

ANSWERS: EXERCISE 4.16

Individual response.

COLLABORATIVE LEARNING

DEVELOPING PARAGRAPHS

   In exercises like 4.15 and 4.16, where students may find it difficult to develop their own paragraphs, they can work initially with their revision groups to pinpoint unsupported statements, highlight unclear claims, and create a list of specific questions to aid each writer in a further revision.

RESOURCES AND IDEAS

Cohan, Carol. "Writing Effective Paragraphs." *College Composition and Communication* 27 (1976): 363–65. Cohan suggests encouraging paragraph development by treating topic sentences as questions to be answered by the paragraph that follows.

Eden, Rick, and Ruth Mitchell. "Paragraphing for the Reader." *College Composition and Communication* 37 (1986): 416–30. The authors suggest that judgments about length and paragraph decisions should be made with the readers in mind.

Lanham, Richard. *Analyzing Prose.* New York: Scribner, 1983. Lanham offers extensive advice on revising paragraphs for stylistic effect.

Witte, Stephen, and Lester Faigley. "Coherence, Cohesion, and Writing Quality." *College Composition and Communication* 32 (1981): 189–204. Students need to learn the features of coherence that extend across sentence boundaries; the article stresses ways to make them aware of coherence strategies.

HIGHLIGHTS

This section addresses introductory and concluding paragraphs, the occasionally useful transitional and short emphatic paragraphs, and the conventions of paragraphing in dialogue. The emphasis you give to introductory and concluding paragraphs may vary with the experience of your students. For some, writing a straightforward introductory paragraph that simply sets the stage for the essay and presents a thesis statement will be an accomplishment. Others will benefit from experimenting with some of the variations illustrated. Most, however, will appreciate the list of don'ts for introductory paragraphs.

Because concluding paragraphs often present a special problem, you may wish to highlight the common inept endings that trap students and then suggest satisfactory alternatives.

USING JOURNALS

Encourage students to collect a repertoire of introduction strategies in their journals. They can draw these strategies from class readings, other courses, and their outside reading. They might also make a log of the ways television news or tabloid shows introduce various subjects, and add them to this repertoire. This strategy can also be applied to conclusions.

7. **Comparison and contrast**
Surfing the Web and watching TV
AM and FM radio DJs
High school and college football
Movies on TV and in a theater

8. **Analogy**
Paying taxes and giving blood
The US Constitution and a building's foundation
Graduating from high school and being released from prison

9. **Cause-and-effect analysis**
Connection between tension and anger
Causes of failing or acing a course
Connection between credit cards and debt
Causes of a serious accident

10. **Process analysis**
Preparing for a job interview
Setting up a Web log
Protecting your home from burglars
Making a jump shot

4d Writing special kinds of paragraphs

Several kinds of paragraphs do not always follow the guidelines for unity, coherence, development, and length because they serve special functions. These are the essay introduction, the essay conclusion, the transitional or emphatic paragraph, and the paragraph of spoken dialog.

1 Opening an essay

Most of your essays will open with a paragraph that draws readers from their world into your world. A good opening paragraph usually satisfies several requirements:

- It focuses readers' attention on your subject and arouses their curiosity about what you have to say.
- It specifies what your topic is and implies your attitude.
- Often it provides your thesis statement.
- It is concise and sincere.

The box on the facing page provides a range of options for achieving these goals.

Note If you are composing on the World Wide Web, you'll want to consider the expectations of Web readers. Your opening page may take the place of a conventional introduction, providing concise text indicating your site's subject and purpose, a menu of its contents, and links to other pages. (See pp. 832–38 for more on composing for the Web.)

CULTURE LANGUAGE The requirements and options for essay introductions may not be what you are used to if your native language is not English. In other cultures, readers may seek familiarity or reassur-

Some strategies for opening paragraphs

- Ask a question.
- Relate an incident.
- Use a vivid quotation.
- Offer a surprising statistic or other fact.
- State an opinion related to your thesis.
- Outline the argument your thesis refutes.
- Provide background.

- Create a visual image that represents your subject.
- Make a historical comparison or contrast.
- Outline a problem or dilemma.
- Define a word central to your subject.
- In some business or technical writing, summarize your paper.

ance from an author's introduction, or they may prefer an indirect approach to the subject. In academic and business English, however, writers and readers prefer concise, direct expression.

- **The funnel introduction**

One reliably effective introduction forms a kind of funnel:

Funnel introduction

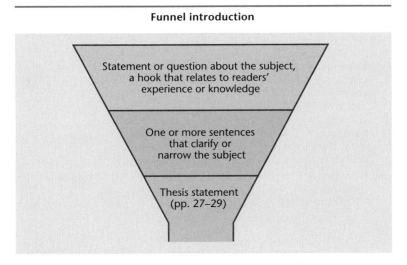

Statement or question about the subject, a hook that relates to readers' experience or knowledge

One or more sentences that clarify or narrow the subject

Thesis statement (pp. 27–29)

Here are two examples of the funnel introduction:

Can your home or office computer make you sterile? Can it strike you blind or dumb? The answer is: probably not. Nevertheless, reports of side effects relating to computer use should be examined, especially in the area of birth defects, eye complaints, and postural difficulties.

— Questions about subject

— Clarification of subject: bridge to thesis statement

MAGAZINE MODELS

Magazines like *Time, Glamour, Outdoor Life, Ebony,* and *Self* contain a variety of informative articles. The authors of these articles and students writing expository essays face a similar problem—how to get readers interested enough to keep reading. Have students collect effective openings and bring them to class for discussion. Students can also comb editorials and magazine articles for openings of argumentative essays.

LEARNING STRATEGIES

To help students learn effective strategies for writing opening paragraphs, give the class outlines of well-known essays and ask students to construct opening paragraphs based on the information provided. Compare students' opening paragraphs with those of the essays. This exercise will expose students to the numerous possibilities for creating good opening paragraphs and will promote discussion of the relative merits of different techniques for a specific subject, essay, or audience.

IMITATING OPENINGS AND CLOSINGS

When experienced writers have trouble beginning or ending essays, they usually turn to strategies that have been successful on other occasions. To help student writers develop similar resources, distribute opening and closing paragraphs that demonstrate particularly effective strategies and ask students to write their own paragraphs using the same strategies but containing different content.

Although little conclusive evidence exists to establish a causal link between computer use and problems of this sort, the circumstantial evidence can be disturbing.
— Thomas Hartmann, "How Dangerous Is Your Computer?"

| Thesis statement

The Declaration of Independence is so widely regarded as a statement of American ideals that its origins in practical politics tend to be forgotten. Thomas Jefferson's draft was intensely debated and then revised in the Continental Congress. Jefferson was disappointed with the result. However, a close reading of both the historical context and the revisions themselves indicates that the Congress improved the document for its intended purpose.
— Ann Weiss (student), "The Editing of the Declaration of Independence"

| Statement about subject

| Clarification of subject: bridge to thesis statement

| Thesis statement

■ Other effective introductions

Several other types of introduction can be equally effective, though they are sometimes harder to invent and control.

Quotation leading into the thesis statement

"It is difficult to speak adequately or justly of London," wrote Henry James in 1881. "It is not a pleasant place; it is not agreeable, or cheerful, or easy, or exempt from reproach. It is only magnificent." Were he alive today, James, a connoisseur of cities, might easily say the same thing about New York or Paris or Tokyo, for the great city is one of the paradoxes of history. In countless different ways, it has almost always been an unpleasant, disagreeable, cheerless, uneasy and reproachful place; in the end, it can only be described as magnificent.
— *Time*

| Quotation

| Bridge to thesis statement

| Thesis statement

Incident or image setting up the thesis statement

Canada is pink. I knew that from the map I owned when I was six. On it, New York was green and brown, which was true as far as I could see, so there was no reason to distrust the map maker's portrayal of Canada. When my parents took me across the border and we entered the immigration booth, I looked excitedly for the pink earth. Slowly it dawned on me: this foreign, "different" place was not so different.

| Incident from writer's experience

I discovered that the world in my head and the world at my feet were not the same.
—Robert Ornstein, *Human Nature*

⎱ Thesis statement

Startling opinion or question

Caesar was right. Thin people need watching. I've been watching them for most of my adult life, and I don't like what I see. When these narrow fellows spring at me, I quiver to my toes. Thin people come in all personalities, most of them menacing. You've got your "together" thin person, your mechanical thin person, your condescending thin person, your tsk-tsk thin person. All of them are dangerous.
—Suzanne Britt,
"That Lean and Hungry Look"

— Opinion

⎱ Thesis statement

Background, such as a historical comparison

Throughout the first half of this century, the American Medical Association, the largest and most powerful medical organization in the world, battled relentlessly to rid the country of quack potions and cure-alls; and it is the AMA that is generally credited with being the single most powerful force behind the enactment of the early pure food and drug laws. Today, however, medicine's guardian seems to have done a complete about-face and become one of the pharmaceutical industry's staunchest allies—often at the public's peril and expense.
—Mac Jeffery, "Does Rx Spell Rip-off?"

— Historical background

— Thesis statement

An effective introductory paragraph need not be long, as the following opener shows:

I've often wondered what goes into a hot dog. Now I know and I wish I didn't.   —William Zinsser, *The Lunacy Boom*

■ Ineffective introductions

When writing and revising an introductory paragraph, avoid the following approaches that are likely to bore readers or make them question your sincerity or control:

Openings to avoid

- **A vague generality or truth.** Don't extend your reach too wide with a line such as *Throughout human history . . .* or *In today's world. . . .* Readers can do without the warm-up.

(continued)

RESOURCES AND IDEAS

Fulkerson, Richard. "Composition at the Turn of the Twenty-First Century." *College Composition and Communication* 56 (June 2005): 654–687. Fulkerson provides an excellent introduction to current key issues in composition theory and pedagogy, including the influence on curriculum of critical/cultural studies and genre analysis and the continuing popularity of expressive approaches to teaching writing.

McClish, Glen. "Of Attention-Getting Openers and Contracts: A Reassessment of an Introductory Dilemma." *Journal of Teaching Writing* 13: 1 (1996): 197–207. McClish discusses the metaphor of the "contract" as a way to teach students about the rhetorical impact of introductions without prompting clichés.

Platz, Judith. "Revision and Process: 'Round Robin' Group Writing." *Teaching English in the Two Year College* 22 (March 2000): 342. Platz shows how a collaborative writing activity can improve the structure and content of student writing.

Openings to avoid
(continued)

- **A flat announcement.** Don't start with *The purpose of this essay is . . . , In this essay I will . . .* , or any similar presentation of your intention or topic.
- **A reference to the essay's title.** Don't refer to the title of the essay in the first sentence—for example, *This is a big problem* or *This book is about the history of the guitar.*
- *According to Webster. . . .* Don't start by citing a dictionary definition. A definition can be an effective springboard to an essay, but this kind of lead-in has become dull with overuse.
- **An apology.** Don't fault your opinion or your knowledge with *I'm not sure if I'm right, but . . . ; I don't know much about this, but . . . ;* or a similar line.

COMPARING CLOSINGS

Using the same essays gathered for the preceding activity, ask students to read all but the conclusions. Then have them underline the thesis statement and the main ideas of each paragraph. Finally, have students write their own conclusions. This exercise will help students to recognize the structure, effectiveness, and importance of concluding paragraphs and will provide diverse examples of how key information may be arranged for variety and emphasis.

TRANSPARENCY MASTER 4.5

2 Closing an essay

Most of your compositions will end with a closing statement or conclusion, a signal to readers that you have not simply stopped writing but have actually finished. The conclusion completes an essay, bringing it to a climax while assuring readers that they have understood your intention.

Note Compositions for the Web usually do not provide the kind of closure featured in essays. In fact, you'll need to ensure that your Web pages don't dead-end, leaving the reader stranded without options for moving backward or forward through your material. (For more on Web composition, see pp. 832–38.)

- **Effective conclusions**

An essay conclusion may consist of a single sentence or a group of sentences, usually set off in a separate paragraph. The conclusion may take one or more of the following approaches:

Some strategies for closing paragraphs

- Recommend a course of action.
- Summarize the paper.
- Echo the approach of the introduction.
- Restate your thesis and reflect on its implications.
- Strike a note of hope or despair.
- Give a symbolic or powerful fact or other detail.
- Give an especially compelling example.
- Create an image that represents your subject.
- Use a quotation.

The following paragraph concludes the essay on the Declaration of Independence (the introduction appears on p. 104):

> The Declaration of Independence has come to be a statement of this nation's political philosophy, but that was not its purpose in 1776. Jefferson's passionate expression had to bow to the goals of the Congress as a whole to forge unity among the colonies and to win the support of foreign nations.
>   —Ann Weiss (student), "The Editing
>   of the Declaration of Independence"

Echo of introduction: contrast between past and present

Restatement and elaboration of thesis

Maxine Hong Kingston uses a different technique—a vivid image—to conclude an essay about an aunt who committed suicide by drowning:

> My aunt haunts me—her ghost drawn to me because now, after fifty years of neglect, I alone devote pages of paper to her, though not origamied into houses and clothes. I do not think she always means me well. I am telling on her, and she was a spite suicide, drowning herself in the drinking water. The Chinese are always very frightened of the drowned one, whose weeping ghost, wet hair hanging and skin bloated, waits silently by the water to pull down a substitute.
>   —Maxine Hong Kingston,
>   "No Name Woman"

Summary

Image

In the next paragraph the author concludes an essay on environmental protection with a call for action:

> Until we get the answers, I think we had better keep on building power plants and growing food with the help of fertilizers and such insect-controlling chemicals as we now have. The risks are well known, thanks to the environmentalists. If they had not created a widespread public awareness of the ecological crisis, we wouldn't stand a chance. But such awareness by itself is not enough. Flaming manifestos and prophecies of doom are no longer much help, and a search for scapegoats can only make matters worse. The time for sensations and manifestos is about over. Now we need rigorous analysis, united effort and very hard work.
>   —Peter F. Drucker, "How Best to
>   Protect the Environment"

Summary and opinion

Call for action

■ **Ineffective conclusions**

The preceding examples illustrate ways of avoiding several pitfalls of conclusions:

COLLABORATIVE LEARNING

OPENING AND CLOSINGS

Students can work together effectively to analyze the introductory and concluding paragraphs of the student essay in Chapter 3, the openings and closings of published essays, and the opening and closing paragraphs from their own papers. Ask each group of students to create their own list of effective opening and concluding strategies accompanied by quoted examples from these various readings.

PAIRS OF IDEAS

Students may hone their skills with transitional paragraphs by being given pairs of seemingly unrelated ideas and being asked to link them. For example, using the topic of global sweatshop labor, have students create a transitional paragraph linking the discussion of legal implications to the discussion of moral implications.

ONE-SENTENCE PARAGRAPHS

Students may be confused about the use of one-sentence paragraphs. Take time to discuss publicly the uses of such paragraphs and to make them aware of any taboos or restrictions you place on such paragraphs; this will save you and your students time and grief later.

COMPUTER ACTIVITY

NAVIGATION MARKERS

Ask students to locate sample Web pages and bring them to class. Together, the class can evaluate the effectiveness of the navigational markers in the text of each Web page and discuss how to use paragraphing to optimize the reader's ease of navigation.

Closings to avoid

- **A repeat of the introduction.** Don't simply replay your introduction. The conclusion should capture what the paragraphs of the body have added to the introduction.
- **A new direction.** Don't introduce a subject different from the one your essay has been about. If you arrive at a new idea, this may be a signal to start fresh with that idea as your thesis.
- **A sweeping generalization.** Don't conclude more than you reasonably can from the evidence you have presented. If your essay is about your frustrating experience trying to clear a parking ticket, you cannot reasonably conclude that *all* local police forces are tied up in red tape.
- **An apology.** Don't cast doubt on your essay. Don't say, *Even though I'm no expert* or *This may not be convincing, but I believe it's true* or anything similar. Rather, to win your readers' confidence, display confidence.

3   Using short emphatic or transitional paragraphs

A short emphatic paragraph can give unusual stress to an important idea, in effect asking the reader to pause and consider before moving on.

> In short, all those who might have taken responsibility ducked it, and catastrophe was inevitable.

A transitional paragraph, because it is longer than a word or phrase and is set off by itself, moves a discussion from one point to another more slowly or more completely than does a single transitional expression or even a transitional sentence attached to a larger paragraph.

> These, then, are the causes of the current contraction in hospital facilities. But how does this contraction affect the medical costs of the government, private insurers, and individuals?

> So the debates were noisy and emotion-packed. But what did they accomplish? Historians have identified at least three direct results.

Use transitional paragraphs only to shift readers' attention when your essay makes a significant turn. A paragraph like the following one betrays a writer who is stalling:

> Now that we have examined these facts, we can look at some others that are equally central to an examination of this important issue.

4   Writing dialog

When recording a conversation between two or more people, start a new paragraph for each person's speech. The paragraphing establishes for the reader the point at which one speaker stops talk-ing and another begins.

> The dark shape was indistinguishable. But once I'd flooded him with light, there he stood, blinking.
> "Well," he said eventually, "you're a sight for sore eyes. Should I stand here or are you going to let me in?"
> "Come in," I said. And in he came.
> —Louise Erdrich, *The Beet Queen*

Though dialog appears most often in fictional writing (the source of the preceding example), it may occasionally freshen or en-liven narrative or expository essays. (For guidance in using quo-tation marks and other punctuation in passages of dialog, see pp. 444–46 and 471–72.)

EXERCISE 4.17   Analyzing an introduction and conclusion

Analyze the introductory and concluding paragraphs in the first and fi-nal drafts of the student essay in Chapter 3, pages 47–48 and 63–65. What is wrong with the first-draft paragraphs? Why are the final-draft paragraphs better? Could they be improved still further?

**EXERCISE 4.18   Considering your past work:
                   Introductions and conclusions**

Examine the opening and closing paragraphs of the essay you've been analyzing in Exercises 4.3, 4.10, and 4.15. Do the paragraphs fulfill the requirements and avoid the pitfalls outlined on pages 102–08? Revise them as needed for clarity, conciseness, focus, and interest.

4e   Linking paragraphs in the essay

Your paragraphs do not stand alone: each one is a key unit of a larger piece of writing. Though you may draft paragraphs or groups of paragraphs almost as mini-essays, you will eventually need to stitch them together into a unified, coherent, well-developed whole. The techniques parallel those for linking sentences in para-graphs:

- **Make sure each paragraph contributes to your thesis.**
- **Arrange the paragraphs in a clear, logical order.** See pages 32–43 for advice on essay organization.
- **Create links between paragraphs.** Use repetition and restate-ment to stress and connect key terms, and use transitional ex-pressions and transitional sentences to indicate sequence, di-rection, contrast, and other relationships.

ANSWERS: EXERCISE 4.17
Possible answers

The introduction in the first draft rushes to Kadi's essay without first securing the reader's interest, and it summarizes and dismisses Kadi's point too tersely. In contrast, the final introduc-tion approaches readers with a statement and question of general interest, more fully explains Kadi's point, and grants it some value.

The conclusion in the first draft is abrupt, does not pick up both of the essay's main points (becoming more tolerated as well as more toler-ant), and does not clearly link tolerance to com-munity. The final conclusion solves these prob-lems (especially with the addition of common ground) and finishes strongly.

ANSWERS: EXERCISE 4.18

Individual response.

COMPUTER ACTIVITY

Ask your students to visit each other's Web sites (for those who already have them) and give feedback on the smoothness of the page-to-page transitions.

The essay "A Picture of Hyperactivity" on pages 42–43 illustrates the first two of these techniques. The following passages from the essay illustrate the third technique, with (circled) repetitions and restatements, [boxed] transitional expressions, and transitional sentences noted in annotations.

Introduction establishing subject and stating thesis	A (hyperactive) committee member can contribute to efficiency. A hyperactive salesperson can contribute to profits. When (children) are hyperactive, though, people— even parents—may wish they had never been born. A
Thesis statement	(collage) of those who must cope with hyperactivity in children is a picture of frustration, anger, and loss.
Transitional topic sentence relating to thesis statement	The [first] part of the (collage) is the (doctors.) In their terminology, the word (hyperactivity) has been replaced by (ADHD,) attention-deficit hyperactivity disorder. They apply the term to (children) who are abnormally or excessively busy. . . .
Transitional topic sentence relating to thesis statement	As the mother of an (ADHD) (child,) I can say what the disorder means to the (parents) who form the [second] part of the (collage.) . . .
Transitional sentence	The weight of (ADHD,) [however,] does not rest on the
Topic sentence relating to thesis statement	(doctors) and (parents.) The darkest part of the (collage) belongs to the (children.) . . .
Transitional sentence into conclusion, restating thesis statement	The (collage) is complete, and it is dark and somber. (ADHD,) as applied to (children,) is a term with uncertain, unattractive, and bitter associations. The (picture) does have one bright spot, [however,] for inside every (ADHD) (child) is a lovely, trusting, calm person waiting to be recognized.

EXERCISE 4.19   Analyzing paragraphs in an essay

Analyze the ways in which paragraphs combine in the student essay in Chapter 3, pages 63–65. What techniques does the writer use to link paragraphs to the thesis statement and to each other? Where, if at all, does the writer seem to stray from the thesis or fail to show how paragraphs relate to it? How would you revise the essay to solve any problems it exhibits?

EXERCISE 4.20   Considering your past work: Paragraphs in the essay

Examine the overall effect of the essay you've been analyzing in Exercises 4.3, 4.10, 4.15, and 4.18. Do all the paragraphs relate to your

ANSWERS: EXERCISE 4.19

Possible answer

Throughout the essay the author repeats or restates her key terms: *communication/interaction, community, anonymous/anonymity, physical barriers/physical appearance/the way they look/physical bias, prejudged/prejudge, tolerance/tolerated/tolerant,* and so on. For each main point, the opening sentence specifically connects to the thesis statement. The pronouns *we, us,* and *our* appear consistently. Transitional expressions (*Instead, Because of . . . , For example, Granted, However,* and many others) explicitly link sentences and paragraphs. And parallelism links sentences in the second, third, and fifth paragraphs (for instance, *The people we communicate with do not know* and *readers don't even know* in the second paragraph). (Further analysis of this essay appears in Chapter 3 of the handbook and in the answers to Exercise 4.17 on page 109.)

ANSWERS: EXERCISE 4.20

Individual response.

thesis? Are they arranged clearly and logically? How do repetition and restatement, transitional expressions, or transitional sentences connect the paragraphs? Can you see ways to improve the essay's unity, coherence, and development?

CHAPTER 5

Designing Documents

Imaginehowharditwouldbetoreadandwriteiftextlookedlikethis. To make reading and writing easier, we place a space between words. This convention and many others—such as page margins, page numbers, and paragraph breaks—have evolved over time to help writers communicate clearly with readers.

5a Designing academic papers and other documents

The design guidelines offered in this chapter apply to all types of documents, including academic papers, Web sites, business reports, flyers, and newsletters. Each type has specific requirements as well, covered elsewhere in this book.

1 Designing academic papers

Many academic disciplines prefer specific formats for students' papers. This book details four such formats:

- **MLA,** used in English, foreign languages, and some other humanities (pp. 687–89).
- **Chicago,** used in history, art history, religion, and some other humanities (pp. 775–77).

http://www.ablongman.com/littlebrown ▶

Visit the companion Web site for more help with document design.

Please visit MyCompLab at *www.mycomplab.com* for more on the writing process.

HIGHLIGHTS

Document design is increasingly important to the creation of written documents, as technology gives the individual computer user access to increasingly powerful design tools. If the courses you teach include diverse forms of writing, or if you teach journalism, technical writing, or business writing, you may wish to ask your students to put together a smart-looking newsletter, report, or brochure, and they will need to know how to design their projects. Even if you are teaching a course strictly focused on argument and academic prose, your students can benefit from understanding how to design their documents.

The chapter begins by referencing various academic formatting styles that will probably be useful to your student. Section 5b explains the principles of good document design: creating flow, using good spacing techniques, grouping related elements, emphasizing important elements, and standardizing the appearance of elements. Section 5c covers application of design principles using specific tools and features, including print quality, margins, text, lists, headings, tables, figures, images, and color. Section 5d has an expanded treatment of using illustrations, with examples of tables, figures, and photographic or other images. A new section (5e) on considering readers who have vision disabilities ends the chapter.

COMPANION WEB SITE

See page IAE-52 for companion Web site content description.

A WRITER'S PERSPECTIVE

[After revising,] nothing should then remain that offends the eye.

—Robert Graves

RESOURCES AND IDEAS

Connors, Robert J. "Actio: A Rhetoric of Manuscripts." *Rhetoric Review* 2 (1983): 64–73. Connors discusses the rhetorical effect of typefaces, paper, and format on readers.

Flammia, Madelyn. "Avoiding Desktop Disasters: Why Technical Communication Students Should Learn About Mechanical Paste Up Techniques." *Journal of Technical Writing and Communication* 23 (1993): 287–95. Flammia discusses a group of assignments intended to make students more aware of the principles of page design and layout.

Harris, Jeanette. "Proofreading: A Reading/Writing Skill." *College Composition and Communication* 38 (1987): 464–66. Harris discusses why students have proofreading problems and how they can improve their editing skills.

Henry, Mathew. "Advertising and Interpretive Analysis: Developing Reading, Thinking, and Writing Skills in the Composition Course." *Teaching English in the Two-Year College* 31 (May 2002): 355–366. Henry explains how he helps students develop critical thinking, writing, and reading skills by having them analyze advertisements.

Madroso, Jan. "Proofreading: The Skill We've Neglected to Teach." *English Journal* 82.2 (1993): 32–41. Madroso suggests ways to make this activity more productive for students.

Norton, Robert. "Commentary: Graphic Excellence for the Technical Communicator." *Journal of Technical Writing and Communication* 23 (1993): 1–6. Norton reminds students how good visuals can contribute to a better understanding of difficult concepts.

PACKAGING SELLS

Students who have written résumés probably understand how important formatting is to a résumé (both because of the multilayered nature of résumé text and because hiring decisions are at

- **APA,** used in the social sciences (pp. 800–03).
- **CSE,** used in some natural and applied sciences (p. 820).

Other academic formats can be found in the style guides listed on pages 764, 784, and 812.

The design guidelines in this chapter extend the range of elements and options covered by most academic styles. Your instructors may want you to adhere strictly to a particular style or may allow some latitude in design. Ask them for their preferences.

2 Writing online

In and out of school, you are likely to do a lot of online writing—certainly e-mail and possibly Web logs and other Web sites. The purposes and audiences for online writing vary widely, and so do readers' expectations for its design. Chapter 54 details the approaches you can take in different online writing situations.

3 Designing business documents and other public writing

When you write outside your college courses, your audience will have certain expectations for how your documents should look and read. Guidelines for such writing appear in the following chapters:

- **Chapter 55 on public writing:** letters, job applications, reports, proposals, flyers, newsletters, brochures.
- **Chapter 56 on oral presentations:** *PowerPoint* slides and other visual aids.

5b Considering principles of design

Most of the principles of design respond to the ways we read. White space, for instance, relieves our eyes and helps to lead us through a document. Groupings or lists help to show relationships. Type sizes, images, and color add variety and help to emphasize important elements.

The sample documents on pages 114–15 illustrate quite different ways of presenting a report for a marketing course. Even at a glance, the revised document is easier to scan and read. It makes better use of white space, groups similar elements, uses bullets and fonts for emphasis, and more successfully integrates and explains the chart.

As you design your own documents, think about your purpose, the expectations of your readers, and how readers will move through your document. Also consider the following general principles of design, noting how they overlap and support each other.

Principles of document design

- **Create flow** to conduct the reader through the document.
- **Space elements** to give the reader's eye a rest and to focus the reader's attention.
- **Group related elements** in lists or under similar headings.
- **Standardize elements** to match appearance with content and to minimize variations.
- **Emphasize important elements.**

1 Creating flow

Many of the other design principles work in concert with the larger goal of conducting the reader through a document by establishing flow, a pattern for the eye to follow. In text-heavy documents like that on page 115, flow may be achieved mainly with headings, lists, and illustrations. In more visual documents, flow will come from the arrangement and spacing of information as well as from headings.

2 Spacing

The white space on a page eases crowding and focuses readers' attention. On an otherwise full page, just the space indicating paragraphs (an indention or a line of extra space) gives readers a break and reassures them that ideas are divided into manageable chunks.

In papers, reports, and other formal documents, spacing appears mainly in paragraph breaks, in margins, and around headings and lists. In publicity documents, such as flyers and brochures, spacing is usually more generous between elements and helps boxes, headings, and the like pop off the page.

3 Grouping

Grouping information shows relationships visually, reinforcing the sense of the text itself. Here in this discussion, we group the various principles of design under visually identical headings to emphasize them and their similar importance. In the revised design on page 115, the bulleted list details statistics about students' computer use. The list uses similar wording for each item to reinforce

stake), but they may not be used to thinking about college papers as having comparable requirements. A moment's reflection will probably produce the realization that almost all of the written material they encounter in their daily lives, from cereal-box blurbs to the newspaper, is formatted in some way.

TRANSPARENCY MASTER 5.1

COMPUTER ACTIVITY

PREVIOUS WORK

Students who have already written papers using one of the academic formats can send their old papers as e-mail attachments to the rest of the class. Ask them to write a cover note explaining why the document format standards are useful within the discipline.

NEWSLETTER CRITIQUE

If any student organization on your campus produces a newsletter, bring in copies of one issue and ask the class to critique it from a document design standpoint.

ALTERNATIVE FORMATS

Demonstrate to students the effect of different arrangements and presentations of the same text. Comparing formats in this way teaches them the importance of good manuscript presentation. You might handwrite, type, and print out a simple passage on several types of computer printers (with and without corrected errors), then display these on overhead transparencies for class discussion.

DESIGN ANALYSIS

Have students bring to class a brochure, advertisement, or announcement. In small groups, ask them to discuss each document and evaluate it for flow, spacing, grouping, emphasis, and standardization of elements. Each group might also write up a report of their analysis and present it to the class.

CAMPUS FLYER SERVICE I

Set up a flyer designing service for your campus, perhaps located at the college writing center. Campus groups that need a flyer designed for an event can bring content and ideas to your students, the designers. As a first step, have teams of students use the "Principles of document design" list on p. 113 to plan the flyer they will be designing. (A sample flyer appears on p. 852.)

REVISING DESIGN

Have students locate a brochure, ad, or announcement that they think has an ineffective design. On their computers, they can redesign the document, using the comment function of their wordprocessing software to insert notes about what they changed and why.

Original design

> Runs title and subtitle together. Does not distinguish title from text.

> Crowds the page with minimal margins.

> Downplays paragraph breaks with small indentions.

> Buries statistics in a paragraph. Obscures relationships with non-parallel wording.

> Does not introduce the figure, leaving readers to infer its meaning and purpose.

> Overemphasizes the figure with large size and excessive white space.

> Presents the figure un-dynamically, flat on.

> Does not caption the figure to explain what it shows, offering only a figure number and a partial text explanation.

Ready or Not, Here They Come: College Students and the Internet

College life once meant classrooms of students listening to teachers or groups of students talking over lunch in the union. But the reality today is more complex: students interact with their peers and professors by computer as much as face to face. As these students graduate and enter the workforce, all of society will be affected by their experience.

According to the Pew Internet Research Center (2005), today's college students are practiced computer and Internet users. The Pew Center reports that 20 percent of students in college today started using computers between ages five and eight. By age eighteen all students were using computers. Almost all college students, 86 percent, rely on the Internet, with 66 percent of students using more than one e-mail address. Computer ownership among this group is also very high: 85 percent have purchased or have been given at least one computer.

Students are eager to tap into the Internet's benefits and convenience.

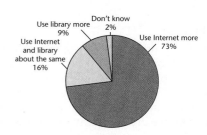

Figure 1

The Internet has eclipsed the library as the site of college students' research, as shown in Figure 1 from the Pew Report. In fact, a mere 9 percent of students

---

the similarities in the data. Thinking of likely groups as you write can help you organize your material so that it makes sense to you and your readers.

4 Standardizing

As we read a document, the design of its elements quickly creates expectations in us. We assume, for instance, that headings in the same size and color signal information of the same importance or that a list contains items of parallel content. Just as the design creates expectations, so it should fulfill them, treating similar elements similarly. Anticipating design standards as you write a document can help you treat its elements consistently and emphasize the elements you want to draw attention to.

Standardizing also creates clear, uncluttered documents. Even if they are used consistently, too many variations in type fonts and

Revised design

Ready or Not, Here They Come

College Students and the Internet

College life once meant classrooms of students listening to teachers or groups of students talking over lunch in the union. But the reality today is more complex: students interact with their peers and professors by computer as much as face to face. As these students graduate and enter the workforce, all of society will be affected by their experience.

According to the Pew Internet Research Center (2005), today's college students are practiced computer users and Internet users.

- They started young: 20 percent were using computers between ages five and eight, and all were using them by age eighteen.
- They rely on the Internet: 86 percent have used the network, and 66 percent use more than one e-mail address.
- They own computers: 85 percent have purchased or have been given at least one computer.

Students are eager to tap into the Internet's benefits and convenience. Figure 1, from the Pew Report, shows that the Internet has eclipsed the library as the site of college students' research.

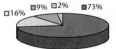

□16% □9% □2% ■73%   ■ Use Internet more
□ Use Internet and library about the same
■ Use library more
□ Don't know

Figure 1. College students' use of the Internet and the library for research

---

Distinguishes title from subtitle and both from text.

Provides adequate margins.

Emphasizes paragraph breaks with white space.

Groups statistics in a bulleted list set off with white space. Uses parallel wording for parallel information.

Introduces the figure to indicate its meaning and purpose.

Reduces white space around the figure.

Presents the figure to emphasize the most significant segment.

Captions the figure so that it can be read independently from the text.

---

sizes, colors, indentions, and the like overwhelm readers as they try to determine the significance of the parts. Most formal documents, such as papers and reports, need no more than a single type font for text and headings, with type size and highlighting (such as CAPITAL LETTERS, **boldface,** or *italics*) distinguishing the levels of headings. Publicity documents, such as flyers and brochures, generally employ more variation to arrest readers' attention.

5 Emphasizing

Part of a critical reader's task is to analyze and interpret the meaning of a document, and design helps the reader by stressing what's important. Type fonts and sizes, headings, indentions, color, boxes, white space—all of these establish hierarchies of information, so that the reader almost instinctively grasps what is crucial, what is less so, and what is merely supplementary. In this book, for example, the importance of headings is clear from their size and from the use of decorative elements, such as the boxes around 5c and the heading below; and boxes like the one on page 113 clearly mark summaries and other key information. As you design a document, considering where and how to emphasize elements can actually help you determine your document's priorities.

5c Using the elements of design

Applying the preceding principles involves margins, text, lists, headings, color, and illustrations. You won't use all these elements for every project, and in many writing situations you will be required to follow a prescribed format (see pp. 111–12). If you are addressing readers who have vision disabilities, consider as well the points discussed on pages 125–26.

Note Your word processor may provide wizards or templates for many kinds of documents, such as letters, memos, reports, agendas, résumés, and brochures. **Wizards** guide you through setting up and writing complicated documents. **Templates** are preset forms to which you add your own text, headings, and other elements. Wizards and templates can be helpful, but not if they lead you to create cookie-cutter documents no matter what the writing situation. Always keep in mind that a document should be appropriate for your subject, audience, and purpose.

1 Setting margins

Margins at the top, bottom, and sides of a page help to prevent the pages from overwhelming readers with unpleasant crowding. Most academic and business documents use a minimum one-inch margin on all sides. Publicity documents, such as flyers and brochures, often use narrower margins, compensating with white space between elements.

2 Creating readable text

A document must be readable. You can make text readable by attending to line spacing, type fonts and sizes, highlighting, word spacing, and line breaks.

■ Line spacing

Most academic documents are double-spaced, with an initial indention for paragraphs, while most business documents are single-spaced, with an extra line of space between paragraphs. Double or triple spacing sets off headings in both. Web sites and publicity documents, such as flyers and brochures, tend to use more line spacing to separate and group distinct parts of the content.

▨ Type fonts and sizes

The readability of text also derives from the type fonts (or faces) and their sizes. For academic and business documents, generally choose a type size of 10 or 12 points, as in these samples:

```
10-point Courier      10-point Times New Roman
12-point Courier      12-point Times New Roman
```

Fonts like these and the one you're reading have **serifs**—the small lines finishing the letters, such as the downward strokes on the top of this T. Serif fonts are appropriate for formal writing and are easier for most people to read on paper. **Sans serif** fonts (*sans* means "without" in French) include this one found on many word processors:

10-point Arial   12-point Arial

Sans serif fonts are usually easier to read on a computer screen and are clearer on paper for readers with some vision disabilities (see p. 126).

Your word processor probably offers many decorative fonts as well:

10-point Bodega Sans	10-point Tekton
10-POINT STENCIL	10-point Ruzicka Freehand
10-point Lucinda Sans	10-point Park Avenue

Decorative fonts are generally inappropriate in academic and business writing, where letter forms should be conventional and regular. But on some Web sites and in publicity documents, decorative fonts can attract attention, create motion, and reinforce a theme.

Note The point size of a type font is often an unreliable guide to its actual size, as the decorative fonts above illustrate: all the samples are 10 points, but they vary considerably. Before you use a font, print out a sample to be sure it is the size you want.

▨ Highlighting

Within a document's text, underlined, *italic*, **boldface,** or even color type can emphasize key words or sentences. Underlining is rarest these days, having been replaced by italics in all but a few disciplines. (It remains called for in MLA style. See p. 660.) Both academic and business writing sometimes use boldface to give strong emphasis—for instance, to a term being defined—and publicity documents often rely extensively on boldface to draw the reader's eye. Neither academic nor business writing generally uses color

COLLABORATIVE LEARNING

CLASS NEWSLETTERS

Have each peer group put together a short newsletter for the rest of the class. Each student should write a different part of the copy, and then all can work together on the document design.

COLLABORATIVE LEARNING

CURRENT ISSUE REPORTS

Have groups of students work together to write a brief report on a current campus issue. Reports should include summary, statement of problem, and solution, and their design features should be appropriate to the topic.

COMPUTER ACTIVITY

CAMPUS FLYER SERVICE III

As a follow-up to the previous "flyer service" exercise in 5c, have your students create a mock-up of a flyer on their computers. They should plan to revise it based upon feedback from you, the class as a whole, and the campus group that commissioned the flyer.

COLLABORATIVE LEARNING

OVERKILL

Some students use underlining, boldface, or italics liberally without being aware that the more highlights they use, the less each one will mean, and that highlighting is no substitute for choosing the right words. To help convey this, have them print out two versions of the same paper, one version with multiple highlights and the other with only one highlight. Then have their peer groups read the papers and respond.

within passages of text. In Web and publicity documents, however, color may be effective if the color is dark enough to be readable. (See p. 120 for more on color in document design.)

No matter what your writing situation, use highlighting selectively to complement your meaning, not merely to decorate your work. Many readers consider type embellishments to be distracting.

■ Word spacing

In most writing situations, follow these guidelines for spacing within and between words:

- **Leave one space between words.**
- **Leave one space after all punctuation, with these exceptions:**

Dash (two hyphens or the so-called em dash on a computer)	book- -its	book—its
Hyphen	one-half	
Apostrophe within a word	book's	
Two or more adjacent marks	book.")	
Opening quotation mark, parenthesis, or bracket	("book	[book

- **Leave one space before and after an ellipsis mark.** In the examples below, ellipsis marks indicate omissions within a sentence and at the end of a sentence. See pages 484–86 for additional examples.

  book . . . in
  book. . . . The

■ Line breaks

Your word processor will generally insert appropriate breaks between lines of continuous text: it will not, for instance, automatically begin a line with a comma or period, and it will not end a line with an opening parenthesis or bracket. However, you will have to prevent it from breaking a two-hyphen dash or a three-dot ellipsis mark by spacing to push the beginning of each mark to the next line.

When you instruct it to do so (usually under the Tools menu), your word processor will also automatically hyphenate words to prevent very short lines. If you must decide yourself where to break words, follow the guidelines on page 556.

3 Using lists

Lists give visual reinforcement to the relations between like items—for example, the steps in a process or the elements of a proposal. A list is easier to read than a paragraph and adds white space to the page.

When wording a list, work for parallelism among items—for instance, all complete sentences or all phrases (see also p. 408). Set the list with space above and below. Number the items, or mark them with bullets: centered dots or other devices, such as the squares used in the list below about headings. On most word processors you can format a numbered or bulleted list automatically using the Format menu.

4 Using headings

Headings are signposts: they direct the reader's attention by focusing the eye on a document's most significant content. In Web and publicity documents, headings may be decorative as well as functional, capturing the reader's attention with large sizes, lots of white space, and unconventional fonts. In academic and much business writing, however, headings are more purely functional. They break the text into discrete parts, create emphasis, and orient the reader.

When you use headings in academic and business writing, follow these guidelines:

- **Use one, two, or three levels of headings** depending on the needs of your material and the length of your document. Some level of heading every two or so pages will help keep readers on track. (A three-page paper or a one-page letter probably will not need headings.)
- **Create an outline of your document to plan where headings should go.** Reserve the first level of heading for the main points (and sections). Use a second and perhaps a third level of heading to mark subsections of supporting information.
- **Keep headings as short as possible** while making them specific about the material that follows.
- **Word headings consistently**—for instance, all questions (*What Is the Scientific Method?*), all phrases with *-ing* words (*Understanding the Scientific Method*), or all phrases with nouns (*The Scientific Method*).
- **Indicate the relative importance of headings** with type size, positioning, and highlighting, such as capital letters or boldface.

First-Level Heading

Second-Level Heading

Third-Level Heading

Generally, you can use the same type font and size for headings as for the text.

- **Don't break a page immediately after a heading.** Push the heading to the next page.

Note Document format in psychology and some other social sciences requires a particular treatment of headings. See pages 800–03.

5 Using color

With a color printer, most word processors and desktop publishers can produce documents that use color for bullets, headings, borders, boxes, illustrations, and other elements. Web and publicity documents almost always use color, whereas academic and business documents consisting only of text and headings may not need color. (Ask your instructor or supervisor for his or her preferences.) If you do use color, follow these guidelines:

- **Employ color to clarify and highlight your content.** Too much color or too many colors on a page will distract rather than focus readers' attention.
- **Make sure that color type is readable.** For text, where type is likely to be relatively small, use only dark colors. For headings, lighter colors may be readable if the type is large and boldfaced.
- **Stick to the same color for all headings at the same level**—for instance, red for primary headings, black for secondary headings.
- **Use color for bullets, lines, and other nontext elements.** But use no more than a few colors to keep pages clean.
- **Use color to distinguish the parts of illustrations**—the segments of charts, the lines of graphs, and the parts of diagrams. Use only as many colors as you need to make your illustration clear. (See below.)

See also page 126 on the use of color for readers who have vision disabilities.

EXERCISE 5.1   Redesigning a paper

Save a duplicate copy of a recent paper or one you are currently working on. Then format the duplicate using appropriate elements of design, such as type fonts, lists, and headings. (For a new paper, be sure your instructor will accept your new design.) When you have finished the redesign, share the work with your instructor.

5d   Using illustrations

Illustrations can often make a point for you more efficiently than words can. Tables present data. Figures (such as graphs and charts) usually recast data in visual form. Diagrams, drawings, photographs, and clip art can explain processes, represent what something looks like, add emphasis, or convey a theme.

Note The Web is an excellent resource for photographs (see pp. 594–96), and you can edit the images with a program such as

---

ANSWERS: EXERCISE 5.1

Individual response.

INSTRUCTIONS FOR MAKING A HOT FUDGE SUNDAE

Have students create an instructional document on how to "build" a hot fudge sundae (or other dessert of their choice). They should apply elements of design appropriately and create the document on their computer. They can include illustrations, color, highlighting, numbered lists, or other elements they think will make for a well-designed document. The goal is for the document to be visually appealing and easy to read.

Adobe Photoshop or *Corel Paint Shop*. Your word processor may include a program for creating tables, graphs, diagrams, and other illustrations, or you can work with specialized software such as *Excel* or *Quattro Pro* (for graphs and charts) or *Adobe Illustrator* or *CorelDRAW* (for diagrams, maps, and the like). Use *PowerPoint* or a similar program for visuals in oral presentations (see pp. 860–62).

1 Using illustrations appropriately for the writing situation

Academic and many business documents tend to use illustrations differently from publicity documents. In the latter, illustrations generally attract attention, enliven, or emphasize, and they may not be linked directly to the document's text. In academic and business writing, however, illustrations directly reinforce and amplify the text. Follow these guidelines for academic and most business writing:

- **Focus on a purpose for your illustration**—a reason for including it and a point you want it to make. Otherwise, readers may find it irrelevant or confusing.
- **Provide a source note whenever the data or the entire illustration is someone else's independent material** (see p. 633). Each discipline has a slightly different style for such source notes: those in the illustrations on the next four pages reflect MLA style for English and some other humanities. See also Chapters 47 and 51–53.
- **Number figures, photographs, and other images together,** and label them as figures: Fig. 1, Fig. 2, and so on.
- **Number and label tables separately:** Table 1, Table 2, and so on.
- **Refer to each illustration in your text**—for instance, "See fig. 2." Place the text reference at the point(s) in the text where readers will benefit by consulting the illustration.
- **Determine the placement of illustrations.** The social sciences and some other disciplines require each illustration to fall on a page by itself immediately after the text reference to it (see p. 803). You may want to follow this rule in other situations as well if you have a large number of illustrations. Otherwise, you can place them on your text pages just after their references.

2 Using tables

Tables usually present raw data, making complex information accessible to readers. The data may show how variables relate to one another, how two or more groups contrast, or how variables change over time. The table on the following page emphasizes the last two functions.

Some tables use rows and columns to present related textual information rather than data. An example appears on page 145.

Table

Table 1
Percentage of Young Adults Living at Home, 1960-2000

	1960	1970	1980	1990	2000
Males					
Age 18-24	52	54	54	58	57
Age 25-34	9	9	10	15	13
Females					
Age 18-24	35	41	43	48	47
Age 25-34	7	7	7	8	8

A self-explanatory title falls above the table.

Self-explanatory headings label horizontal rows and vertical columns.

The layout of rows and columns is clear: headings align with their data, and numbers align vertically down columns.

Source: Data from United States, Dept. of Commerce, Census Bureau, Census 2000 Summary Tables, 1 July 2002 <http:www.census.gov/servlet/QTTTable?_ts=30543101060>.

3 Using figures

Figures represent data or show concepts visually. They include charts, graphs, and diagrams.

▪ Pie charts

Pie charts show the relations among the parts of a whole. The whole totals 100 percent, and each pie slice is proportional in size to its share of the whole. Use a pie chart when shares, not the underlying data, are your focus.

Pie chart

Color distinguishes segments of the chart. Use distinct shades of gray, black, and white if your paper will not be read in color.

Segment percentages total 100.

Every segment is clearly labeled. You can also use a key, as in the chart on p. 115.

Self-explanatory caption falls below the chart.

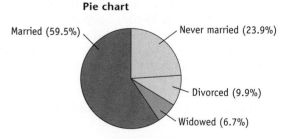

Fig. 1. Marital status in 2004 of adults aged eighteen and over. Data from United States, Dept. of Commerce, Census Bureau, Statistical Abstract of the United States, 2004-05 (Washington, GPO, 2005) no. 30.

▪ Bar charts

Bar charts compare groups or time periods on a measure such as quantity or frequency. Use a bar chart when relative size is your focus.

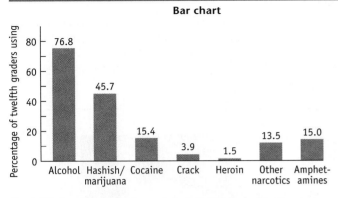

Bar chart

Vertical scale shows and clearly labels the values being measured. Zero point clarifies values.

Horizontal scale shows and clearly labels the groups being compared.

Fig. 2. Lifetime prevalence of use of alcohol, compared with other drugs, among twelfth graders in 2004. Data from Monitoring the Future: A Continuing Study of American Youth, U of Michigan, 12 May 2005, 10 Oct. 2005 <http://www.monitoringthefuture.org/data/data.html>.

Self-explanatory caption falls below the chart.

▓ Line graphs

Line graphs show change over time in one or more subjects. They are an economical and highly visual way to compare many points of data.

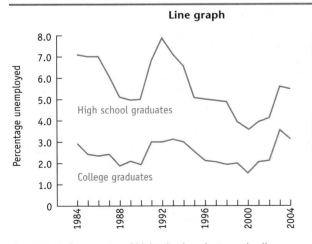

Line graph

Vertical scale shows and clearly labels the values being measured. Zero point clarifies values.

Color and labels distinguish the subjects being compared. Use dotted and dashed black lines if your paper will not be read in color.

Horizontal scale shows and clearly labels the range of dates.

Fig. 3. Unemployent rates of high school graduates and college graduates, 1984-2004. Data from Antony Davies, The Economics of College Tuition, 3 Mar. 2005, 26 June 2005 <http://www.mercatus.org/capitalhill/php?id=420>.

Self-explanatory caption falls below the graph.

Diagrams

Diagrams show concepts visually, such as the structure of an organization, the way something works or looks, or the relations among subjects. Often, diagrams show what can't be described economically in words. For other examples of diagrams, see pages 3, 103, and 833.

Diagram

Diagram makes concept comprehensible.

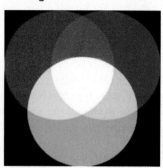

Self-explanatory caption falls below the diagram.

Fig. 4. RGB color theory, applied to televisions and computer monitors, in which all possible colors and white are created from red, green, and blue. From "Color Theory," Wikipedia, 16 July 2005, 2 Aug. 2005 <http://en.wikipedia.org/wiki/Color_theory>.

Photographs and other images

Sometimes you may focus an entire paper on an image such as a photograph, painting, or advertisement (see pp. 175–77). But most commonly you'll use images to add substance to ideas or to enliven them. You might clarify an astronomy paper with a photograph of Saturn (see opposite), add information to an analysis of a novel with a drawing of the author, or capture the theme of a brochure with a cartoon. Images grab readers' attention, so use them carefully to explain, reinforce, or enhance your writing.

One kind of image rarely appears in academic writing: **clip art,** consisting of icons and drawings such as those below from the free site *Barry's Clipart Server* (*http://www.barrysclipart.com/index.php*):

Clip art

A THOUSAND WORDS

Students who are not strong writers may like the idea of allowing a visual image to speak for them in their own papers. You may need to show them that, while images can add to readers' understanding of your writing, they are not a substitute for clear, developed prose.

WEB SITE RECOMMENDATIONS

Ask students to evaluate the photographs and illustrations on your college's Web site and to make recommendations for additional illustrations where appropriate. You might even have the class present their top three recommendations to your campus computer services department for consideration when the college Web site is next updated.

Photograph

Photograph shows subject more economically and dramatically than words could.

Fig. 5. View of Saturn from the Cassini spacecraft, showing the planet and its rings. From United States, National Atmospheric and Space Administration, Jet Propulsion Laboratory, Cassini-Huygens: Mission to Saturn and Titan, 24 Feb. 2005, 26 Apr. 2005 <http://saturn.jpl.nasa.gov/multimedia/images/ image-details.cfm?imageID=1398>.

Self-explanatory caption falls below the image.

Many word processors provide files of clip art, and they are also available from CD-ROMs and Web sites (links appear on this book's Web site at *ablongman.com/littlebrown*). Be selective in using these resources: clip art is mostly decorative (which is why it seldom appears in academic and business documents), and an overdecorated document is not only cluttered but unemphatic. In a Web or publicity document, use only clip art that is relevant to your theme and content, directing readers' attention to elements you want to stress.

Note When using an image prepared by someone else—for instance, a photograph or an item of clip art downloaded from the Web —you must verify that the source permits reproduction of the image before you use it. In most documents but especially academic papers, you must also fully cite the source of any borrowed image. See pages 635–37 on copyright issues with Internet sources.

5e   Considering readers with disabilities

Your audience may include readers who have low vision, problems with color perception, or difficulties processing visual information. If so, consider adapting your design to meet these readers' needs. Here are a few pointers:

- **Use large type fonts.** Most guidelines call for 14 points or larger.

RESOURCES AND IDEAS

Draga, Sam and Van Doss. "Cruel Pies: The Inhumanity of Technical Illustrations." *Technical Communication* 48.3 (2001): 265–74. The authors' review of the research on the ethics of visual communication suggests that visual information is not always presented accurately and honestly; they suggest ways of correcting the problem.

Williams, Robin. *The Non-Designer's Design Book*, 2nd Ed. Berkeley, CA, 2003. This is an accessible beginner's guide to modern document design.

COMPUTER ACTIVITY

Take your students on a tour of Web sites and ask them to evaluate each site in terms of its accessibility to vision-impaired readers.

- **Use standard type fonts.** Many people with low vision find it easier to read sans serif fonts such as Arial than serif fonts (see p. 117). Avoid decorative fonts with unusual flourishes, even in headings.
- **Avoid words in ALL-CAPITAL LETTERS.**
- **Avoid relying on color alone to distinguish elements.** Label elements, and distinguish them by position or size.
- **Use red and green selectively.** To readers who are red-green colorblind, these colors will appear in shades of gray, yellow, or blue.
- **Use contrasting colors.** To make colors distinct, choose them from opposite sides of the color spectrum—violet and yellow, for instance, or orange and blue.
- **Use only light colors for tints behind type.** Make the type itself black or a very dark color.

PART **2**

Reading and Writing in College

Writing in Academic Situations

CHAPTER **7**
Studying Effectively and Taking Exams

CHAPTER **8**
Forming a Critical Perspective

CHAPTER **9**
Reading Arguments Critically

CHAPTER **10**
Writing an Argument

CHAPTER **11**
Reading and Using Visual Arguments

mycomplab 2.0

Please visit MyCompLab at *www.mycomplab.com* for more on the writing process.

HIGHLIGHTS

Chapter 6 is new to the 10th edition of *The Little, Brown Handbook*. Because beginning students often have difficulty assuming an academic writing stance, this chapter begins with a detailed discussion of how students can make the transition. The "tips for becoming an academic writer" checklist can give students strategies that will help prepare them for academic writing. Subsequent chapter sections cover analyzing audience, determining purpose, choosing structure and content, and use of academic language.

RESOURCES AND IDEAS

Rose, Shirley K. "The Voice of Authority: Developing a Fully Rhetorical Definition of Voice in Writing." *Writing Instructor* 8 (1989): 111–18. Rose argues that voice, or authority over one's texts, is a measure of effective writing, and shows how this quality can be developed in students' writing in a fifteen-week time period.

Valarie-Gold, Maria and Mary P. Demming. "Reading, Writing, and the College Developmental Student." In *Handbook of College Reading and Study Strategy Research*. Ed. Rona F. Flippo and David C. Caverly. Mahwah NJ: Lawrence Erlbaum, 2000: 149–57. The authors show how focused, critical reading can benefit student writing.

COMPANION WEB SITE

See page IAE-52 for companion Web site content description.

CHAPTER 6

Writing in Academic Situations

When you write in college, you work within a community of teachers and students who have specific aims and expectations. The basic aim of this community—whether in English, psychology, biology, or some other discipline—is to contribute to and build knowledge through questioning, research, and communication. The differences among disciplines lie mainly in the kinds of questions asked, the kinds of research done to find the answers, and the ways of communicating the answers.

Academic writers communicate using conventional forms, such as case studies, research reports, and reviews of others' writings on a particular subject. Both a discipline's concerns and the kind of writing create the writing situation, which in turn shapes a writer's choice of subject, conception of audience, definition of purpose, choice of structure and content, and even choice of language. This chapter introduces academic writing situations in general. Chapters 50–53 detail the particular goals and expectations of the humanities, the social sciences, and the natural and applied sciences.

6a   Becoming an academic writer

As an academic writer, you participate in a discipline community first by studying a subject, acquiring its vocabulary, and learning to express yourself in its ways. As you gain experience and knowledge, you begin to contribute to the community by asking questions and communicating your answers. Such a contribution may seem beyond you at first, as you try to grasp the content of assigned reading and identify important ideas. In any discipline, making the transition to academic writing will be easier if you practice the strategies outlined in the box on the facing page.

http://www.ablongman.com/littlebrown ▶

Visit the companion Web site for more help with academic writing.

Tips for becoming an academic writer

- **Study the syllabus for each course.** This outline lays out the instructor's expectations as well as the course topics, assignments, and deadlines.
- **Do the assigned reading.** You'll gain experience with the discipline's terms and ideas, and you'll become familiar with the kinds of writing expected of you.
- **Attend and participate in class.** Make class attendance a priority, whether or not the instructor checks the roll. Listen carefully, take notes (see p. 137 for tips), ask questions, and join in discussions.
- **Ask questions.** Instructors, advisers, tutors, other students—all can help you.
- **Understand the writing situation posed by each assignment.** Knowing your audience, purpose, options for subjects, and other elements of the situation will help you meet the assignment's expectations. (See pp. 6–7 on analyzing assignments.)

6b Analyzing audience

Some of your writing assignments may specify an identifiable group of readers—for instance, fellow students, the city council, or the editors of a newspaper. Such readers' needs and expectations vary widely; the discussion on pages 9–13 can help you discover what they might be. Many assignments will specify or assume an educated audience or an academic audience. This more general group of readers looks for writing that is clear, balanced, well organized, and well reasoned, among other qualities discussed on page 131. Still other assignments will specify or assume an audience of experts on your subject, readers who look in addition for writing that meets the subject's requirements for claims and evidence, organization, language, format, and other qualities discussed in Chapters 49–53.

Of course, much of your academic writing will have only one reader besides you: the instructor of the course for which you are writing. Instructors fill two main roles as readers:

- **They represent the audience you are addressing.** They may actually be members of the audience, as when you address academic readers or subject experts. Or they may imagine themselves as members of your audience—reading, for instance, as if they sat on the city council. In either case, they're interested in how effectively you write for the audience.
- **They serve as coaches,** guiding you toward achieving the goals of the course and, more broadly, toward the academic aims of building and communicating knowledge.

BUILDING THE ROLE

Students may be surprised to find that becoming an academic writer is dependent upon these collateral activities. Share with them the analogy of an actor who does background work to prepare for a role. The actor might read historical works about the time period; might work with a dialect coach to understand the meaning of lines and how to say them; might visit the place in which the play takes place to absorb the atmosphere; might become familiar with their character's profession by shadowing a real professional in that field. These activities take place before rehearsals begin and help the actor to make the role believable.

CROSSOVER WRITERS

Many academic professionals write successfully for different audiences. Stephen Jay Gould, Carl Sagan, and Deborah Tannen are well known for their crossover writings, but there are many others as well. Show your students two samples of a single author's writing on the same subject but pitched to different audiences, to help them see the differences.

CLASSROOM AUDIENCES

The members of your classroom, including the students and you, constitute an educated or academic audience (albeit less specialized or sophisticated than an audience composed of academic professionals). Asking students to read their papers aloud in class, standing at the front of the class or a podium, can be a way to establish a more formal atmosphere. The experience of making a formal oral presentation may help them get a better feeling for the formal qualities of academic writing.

Like everyone else, instructors have preferences and peeves, but you'll waste time and energy trying to anticipate them. Do attend to written and spoken directions for assignments, of course. But otherwise view your instructors as representatives of the community you are writing for. Their responses will be guided by the community's aims and expectations and by a desire to teach you about them.

6c Determining purpose

For most academic writing, your general purpose will be mainly explanatory or mainly argumentative. That is, you will aim to clarify your subject so that readers understand it as you do, or you will aim to gain readers' agreement with a debatable idea about the subject. (See p. 14 for more on general purposes and Chapters 9–11 for more on argument.) Although the general purpose for writing may not be stated outright in an assignment, it will probably be implied, as you can see in these two abbreviated assignments:

Explanation

Compare the depiction of war in two films viewed this semester, considering plots, characters, dialog, battle scenes, production designs, and other elements of the films.

Argument

What ideology do you see informing the movies of director Steven Spielberg? What beliefs about the world do his choices convey, whether explicitly or implicitly, intentionally or unintentionally? Support your claim with evidence from at least four of Spielberg's movies, considering plots, characters, dialog, production designs, and other elements.

Your specific purpose—including your subject and how you hope readers will respond—depends on the kind of writing you're doing. In a biology lab report, for instance, you want your readers to understand why you conducted your study, how you conducted it, what the results were, and what their significance is. Not coincidentally, these topics correspond to the major sections of a biology lab report. In following the standard format, you both help to define your purpose and begin to meet the discipline's (and thus your instructor's) expectations.

Your specific purpose will be more complex as well. You take a course to learn about a subject and the ways experts think about it. Your writing, in return, contributes to the discipline through the knowledge you uncover and the lens of your perspective. At the same time, as a student you want to demonstrate your competence with research, evidence, format, and other requirements of the discipline.

6d Choosing structure and content

Many academic writing assignments will at least imply how you should organize your paper and even how you should develop your ideas. Like the biology lab report mentioned earlier, the type of paper required will break into discrete parts, each with its own requirements for content. A common academic writing assignment, the analysis, does not predict definite content but still implies certain requirements: you are asked to make a claim about your subject's meaning or significance, to support the claim with specific evidence, and, often, to show that you understand what others think about the subject. (See Chapter 8 for more on analysis.)

No matter what type of paper an assignment specifies, the broad academic aims of building and exchanging knowledge determine features that are common across disciplines. Follow these general guidelines for your academic writing, supplementing them as indicated with others elsewhere in this book:

- **Develop a central idea or claim, called a *thesis*.** Everything in the paper should relate clearly to this claim. For more on theses, see pages 27–31.
- **State your thesis,** usually near the beginning of the paper.
- **Support the thesis with evidence,** drawn usually from research and sometimes from your own experience. The kinds of evidence will depend on the discipline you're writing in and the type of paper you're doing. For more on evidence in the disciplines, see pages 743 (literature), 759–60 (other humanities), 778–79 (social sciences), and 807–08 (natural and applied sciences).
- **Interact with sources.** Do not merely summarize sources but evaluate and synthesize them from your own perspective. For more on using sources, see pages 599–611.
- **Acknowledge sources fully,** using the documentation style appropriate to the discipline. See pages 764, 784, and 812 for lists of disciplines' style guides and pages 648–86 (MLA style for English and some other humanities), 764–75 (Chicago style for history, philosophy, and some other humanities), 784–800 (APA style for the social sciences), and 812–19 (CSE style for the natural and applied sciences).
- **Balance your presentation.** Discuss evidence and opposing views fairly, and take a serious and impartial approach.
- **Organize clearly within the framework of the type of writing you're doing.** Develop your ideas as simply and directly as your purpose and content allow. Clearly relate sentences, paragraphs, and sections so that readers always know where they are in the paper's development.

CULTURE **LANGUAGE** These features are far from universal. In other cultures, academic writers may be indirect, may expect readers to discover the thesis, or may assume that readers do not require acknowledgment of well-known sources. Recognizing such differences between practices in your native culture and in the United States can help you adapt to US academic writing.

6e   Using academic language

American academic writing relies on a dialect called standard American English. The dialect is also used in business, the professions, government, the media, and other sites of social and economic power where people of diverse backgrounds must communicate with one another. It is "standard" not because it is better than other forms of English, but because it is accepted as the common language, much as the dollar bill is accepted as the common currency.

You'll recognize standard American English as the dialect used in this handbook, in magazines and newspapers, and on television news. But you might also notice that the dialect varies a lot, from the formal English of a President's State of the Union address through the middle formality of this handbook to the informal chitchat between anchors on morning TV. Even in academic writing, standard American English allows much room for the writer's own tone and voice, as these passages on the same topic show:

More formal

Using the technique of "color engineering," manufacturers and advertisers can heighten the interest of consumers in a product by adding color that does not contribute to the utility of the product but appeals more to emotions. In one example from the 1920s, manufacturers of fountain pens, which had previously been made of hard black rubber, dramatically increased sales simply by producing the pens in bright colors.	Two complicated sentences, one explaining the technique and one giving the example
	Drawn-out phrasing, such as *interest of consumers* instead of *consumers' interest*
	Formal vocabulary, such as *heighten, contribute,* and *utility*

Less formal

A touch of "color engineering" can sharpen the emotional appeal of a product or its ad. New color can boost sales even when the color serves no other use. In the 1920s, for example, fountain pen makers introduced brightly colored pens along with the familiar ones of hard black rubber. Sales shot up.	Four sentences, two each explaining the technique and giving the example
	More informal phrasing, such as *Sales shot up*
	More informal vocabulary, such as *boost* and *ad*

As different as they are, both examples illustrate several common features of academic language:

- **It follows the conventions of standard American English for grammar and usage.** These conventions are detailed in guides to the dialect, such as this handbook.

- **It uses a standard vocabulary,** not one that only some groups understand, such as slang, an ethnic or regional dialect, or another language. (See pp. 510–13 for more on specialized vocabularies.)

- **It creates some distance between writer and reader with the third person** (*he, she, it, they*). The first person (*I, we*) is sometimes appropriate to express personal opinions or invite readers to think along, but not with a strongly explanatory purpose (*I discovered that "color engineering" can heighten . . .*). The second person (*you*) is appropriate only in addressing readers directly (as in this handbook), and even then it may seem condescending or too chummy (*You should know that "color engineering" can heighten . . .*).

- **It is authoritative and neutral.** In the examples on the facing page, the writers express themselves confidently, not timidly (as in *One possible example of color engineering that might be considered in this case is . . .*). They also refrain from hostility (*Advertisers will stop at nothing to achieve their goals*) and enthusiasm (*Color engineering is genius at work*).

At first, the diverse demands of academic writing may leave you groping for an appropriate voice. In an effort to sound fresh and confident, you may write too casually:

> Too casual
>
> "Color engineering" is a great way to get at consumers' feelings. . . . When the guys jazzed up the color, sales shot through the roof.

In an effort to sound "academic," you may produce wordy and awkward sentences:

> Wordy and awkward
>
> The emotions of consumers can be made more engaged by the technique known as "color engineering." . . . A very large increase in the sales of fountain pens was achieved by the manufacturers of the pens as a result of this color enhancement technique. [The passive voice in this example, such as *increase . . . was achieved* instead of *the manufacturers achieved,* adds to its wordiness and indirection. See pp. 302–03 for more on voice.]

A cure for writing too informally or too stiffly is to read academic writing so that the language and style become familiar and to edit your writing (see pp. 58–59).

CULTURE & LANGUAGE If your first language is not English or is an English dialect besides standard American, you know well the power of communicating with others who share your language. Learning to write standard American English in no way requires you to abandon your first language. Like most multilingual people, you are probably already adept at switching between languages as the situation demands—speaking one way with your relatives, say, and another way with an employer. As you practice academic writing, you'll develop the same flexibility with it.

ANSWERS: EXERCISE 6.1

Possible revision:

The stereotype that women talk more on cell phones than men do turns out to be false. In a five-year survey of 1021 cell phone owners, a major wireless company found that men spend 35 percent more time on their phones, talking an average of 571 minutes a month compared to womens' average of 424 minutes a month. Women do talk more on home phones than men do, but that difference is declining.

EXERCISE 6.1 Using academic language

Revise the following paragraph to make the language more academic while keeping the factual information the same. (You can do this exercise online at *ablongman.com/littlebrown*.)

If you buy into the stereotype of girls chatting away on their cell phones, you should think again. One of the major wireless companies surveyed 1021 cell phone owners for a period of five years and—surprise!—reported that guys talk on cell phones more than girls do. In fact, guys were way ahead of girls, using an average of 571 minutes a month compared to 424 for girls. That's 35 percent more time on the phone! The survey also asked about conversations on home phones, and while girls still beat the field, the guys are catching up.

ANSWERS: EXERCISE 6.2

Individual response.

EXERCISE 6.2 Considering your past work: Writing in academic situations

Look back at a paper you wrote for a course in high school or college. To what extent does it share the features of academic writing discussed in this chapter? How does it differ? Write a revision plan for making the paper more academic.

ANSWERS: EXERCISE 6.3

Individual response.

EXERCISE 6.3 Considering your native language or dialect

CULTURE & LANGUAGE What main similarities and differences do you notice between writing in your native language or dialect and writing for US college courses? Consider especially audience, purpose, content, structure, and the expression of ideas. Which differences do you think are easiest to bridge? Which are most difficult? Why?

CHAPTER **7**

Studying Effectively and Taking Exams

Academic success depends on active, involved learning. If you haven't already, read the previous chapter on academic writing. Use the principles there along with this chapter's practical tips for managing your time, getting the most from your classes and your reading, and taking exams.

As a first step, become familiar with your school's resources and procedures:

Campus know-how

Learn the answers to the following questions from your school's Web site, its catalog, or, best yet, an orientation session.

- **Where are the important buildings and offices?** Locate the library, classrooms, registrar, financial-aid office, health center, gym, and other facilities.
- **What support services are available for students?** Investigate your options for getting help when you need it. Most schools provide advisers and counselors, writing centers, tutoring centers, computer assistance, library tours, and other services.
- **What are the key procedures for students?** Learn how to register for classes, drop or add a class, declare or change your major, request a transcript, or pay tuition bills.

7a   Managing your time

Planning and pacing your schoolwork and other activities will help you study more efficiently with less stress.

http://www.ablongman.com/littlebrown ▶

Visit the companion Web site for more help with studying effectively and taking exams.

---

mycomplab²·⁰

Please visit MyCompLab at *www.mycomplab.com* for more on the writing process.

HIGHLIGHTS

Chapter 7 is new to the 10th edition of *The Little, Brown Handbook.* The first three sections cover successful study methods, from time management and organization to reading and writing, including discussion of summary and note-taking techniques. Section 7d contains a discussion, expanded in this edition of the handbook, of how to prepare for and take essay examinations. The sample instruction chart on p. 145 provides hypothetical essay questions and strategies for answering them. There are also two sample answers (successful and unsuccessful) to an essay question, with marginal annotations for each.

ADD & TIME MANAGEMENT

Students with attention deficit disorder often have difficulty with time management. For these students, time management strategies (alarm clocks or other external cueing devices, planners, and study schedules) are essential. Most campuses have a learning center or academic assistance office that can provide additional support to these students.

COMPANION WEB SITE

See page IAE-52 for companion Web site content description.

WRITING CHUNKS

Remind your students that paper-writing usually requires multiple sessions, with time for incubating thoughts in between. So when they are planning their weekly work schedule, they will do best to break a paper assignment into chunks, such as brainstorming, outlining, drafting, and revising. Chunks can be spread out over several days or longer.

1 Surveying your activities

How do you spend your days? For a week, keep track of all your activities and the time they absorb. How many of the week's 168 hours do you spend eating, sleeping, watching television, talking on the phone, attending classes, studying, working at a job, attending religious services, exercising, commuting, caring for children, doing laundry, socializing, and so on? How much time can you realistically devote to studying?

2 Scheduling your time

One way to organize your time is to use a calendar that divides each day into waking hours. Block out your activities that occur regularly and at specific times, such as commuting, attending classes, and working. Then fill in the other activities (such as exercise, eating, and studying) that do not necessarily occur at fixed times. Be sure to leave time for relaxing: an unrealistic schedule that assigns all available time to studying will quickly prove too difficult to live by. If you use a computer regularly, consider keeping your schedule online using a calendar program. Set it to remind you of important due dates.

3 Organizing your workload

Use the syllabuses for your courses to estimate the amount of weekly study time required for each course. Generally, plan on two hours of studying for each hour in class—that is, about six hours for a typical course. Block out study periods using these guidelines:

- **Schedule study time close to class time.** You'll study more productively if you review notes, read assigned material, or work on projects shortly after each class period.
- **Pace assignments.** Plan to start early and work regularly on projects requiring extensive time, such as research papers, so that you will not be overwhelmed near the deadline. (See pp. 559–60 for advice on scheduling research projects.)
- **Adjust the weekly plan as needed to accommodate changes in your workload.** Before each week begins, examine its schedule to be sure you've built in enough time to study for an exam, finish a paper, or meet other deadlines and commitments.

4 Making the most of study time

When you sit down to study, use your time efficiently:

- **Set realistic study goals.** Divide your study sessions into small chunks, each with a short-term goal, such as previewing a textbook chapter or drafting three paragraphs of a paper. Plan breaks, too, so that you can clear your mind, stretch, and refocus on your goals.

- **Tackle difficult homework first.** Resist any urge to put off demanding jobs, such as working on papers, reading textbooks, or doing math problems. Save easy tasks for when you're less alert.
- **Evaluate how you use your study time.** At the end of each week, ask yourself whether you were as productive as you needed to be. If not, what changes can you make to accomplish your goals for the coming week?

7b Listening and taking notes in class

When you begin each class, push aside other concerns so that you can focus and listen. Either on paper or on a computer, record what you hear as completely as possible while sorting out the main ideas from the secondary and supporting ones. (See the box below.) Such active note taking will help you understand the instructor's approach to the course and provide you with complete material for later study.

Tips for taking class notes

- **Use your own words.** You will understand and retain the material better if you rephrase it. But use the speaker's words if necessary to catch everything.
- **Leave space in your notes if you miss something.** Instructors usually welcome questions about content but not requests for simple repetition, and it's not fair to distract fellow students during class. Ask someone for the missing information as soon as possible after class.
- **Include any reading content mentioned by your instructor.** Use the notes to integrate all the components of the course—your instructor's views, your own thoughts, and the assigned reading, even if you've already read it.
- **Review your notes shortly after class.** Reinforce your new knowledge when it is fresh by underlining key words and ideas, adding headings and comments in the margins, converting your notes to questions, or outlining the lecture based on your notes. If you don't understand something in the notes, consult a classmate for his or her version.

COLLABORATIVE LEARNING

READING NOTES

Have students read a short article in class and take reading notes on it. Then ask them to use their reading notes to discuss the article in small groups.

PRACTICE PREVIEWING

Give your students practice in previewing techniques by bringing a collection of books to class (one per student) and asking them each to preview one. Then ask them to present the book to the rest of the class.

7c   Reading for comprehension

The assigned reading you do for college courses—such as textbooks, journal articles, and works of literature—requires a greater focus on understanding and retention than does the reading you do for entertainment or for practical information. The process discussed here may seem time consuming, but with practice you'll become efficient at it.

Note   The following process stresses ways of understanding what you read. In critical reading, covered in the next chapter, you extend this process to analyze and evaluate what you read and see.

1   Writing while reading

Reading for comprehension is an *active* process. Students often believe they are reading actively when they roll a highlighter over the important ideas in a text, but truly engaged reading requires more than that. If you take notes while reading, you "translate" the work into your own words and reconstruct it for yourself.

The substance of your reading notes will change as you preview, read, and summarize. At first, you may jot quick, short notes in the margins, on separate pages, or on a computer. (Use the last two for material you don't own or are reading online.) As you delve into the work, the notes should become more detailed, restating important points, asking questions, connecting ideas. (See p. 154 for an example of a text annotated in this way by a student.) For in-depth critical reading, you may want to keep a reading journal that records both what the work says and what you think about it. (See p. 154.)

2   Previewing

For most course reading, you should **skim** before reading word for word. Skimming gives you an overview of the material that will help you understand any part of it. Your goal is not to comprehend all the details or even the structure of the author's argument. Rather, working as outlined below, aim for a general sense of the length and difficulty of the material, its organization, and its principal ideas.

- **Gauge length and level.** Is the material brief and straightforward enough to read in one sitting, or do you need more time?
- **Examine the title and introduction.** The title and first couple of paragraphs will give you a sense of the topic, the author's approach, and the main ideas. As you read them, ask yourself what you already know about the subject so that you can integrate new information with old.

- **Move from heading to heading.** Viewing the headings as headlines or as the levels of an outline will give you a feeling for which ideas the author sees as primary and which subordinate.
- **Note highlighted words.** You will likely need to learn the meanings of terms in **bold**, *italic*, or color.
- **Slow down for pictures, diagrams, tables, graphs, and other illustrations.** They often contain concentrated information.
- **Read the summary or conclusion.** These paragraphs often recap the main ideas.
- **Think over what you've skimmed.** Try to recall the central idea, or thesis, and the sequence of ideas.

3 Reading

After previewing a text, you can settle into it to learn what it has to say.

First reading

The first time through new material, read as steadily and smoothly as possible, trying to get the gist of what the author is saying.

- **Read in a place where you can concentrate.** Choose a quiet environment away from distractions such as music or talking.
- **Give yourself time.** Rushing yourself or worrying about something else you have to do will prevent you from grasping what you read.
- **Try to enjoy the work.** Seek connections between it and what you already know. Appreciate new information, interesting relationships, forceful writing, humor, good examples.
- **Make notes sparingly during this first reading.** Mark major stumbling blocks—such as a paragraph you don't understand—so that you can try to resolve them before rereading.

CULTURE LANGUAGE If English is not your first language and you come across unfamiliar words, don't stop and look up every one. You will lose more in concentration than you will gain in understanding. Instead, try to guess the meanings of unfamiliar words from their contexts, circle them, and look them up later.

Rereading

After the first reading, plan on at least one other. This time read *slowly*. Your main concern should be to grasp the content and how it is constructed. That means rereading a paragraph if you didn't get the point or using a dictionary to look up words you don't know.

A WRITER'S PERSPECTIVE

Those who fail to reread are obliged to read the same story everywhere.

—Roland Barthes

READING GOALS

Reading with a goal in mind can help students focus their reading process. You could give students a list of study questions before they read to help them focus their reading to extract key ideas. Alternatively, you could ask each student to bring to class one discussion question based on the reading.

Use your pen, pencil, or keyboard freely to highlight and distill the text:

- **Distinguish main ideas from supporting ideas.** Look for the central idea, or thesis, for the main idea of each paragraph or section, and for the evidence supporting ideas.
- **Learn key terms.** Understand both their meanings and their applications.
- **Discern the connections among ideas.** Be sure you see why the author moves from point A to point B to point C and how those points relate to support the central idea. It often helps to outline the text or summarize it (see below).
- **Add your own comments.** In the margins or separately, note links to other readings or to class discussions, questions to explore further, possible topics for your writing, points you find especially strong or weak. (This last category will occupy much of your time when you are expected to read critically. See pp. 157–63.)

4   Summarizing

A good way to master the content of a text is to **summarize** it: reduce it to its main points, in your own words. Some assignments call for brief summaries, as when you summarize the plot in a critical essay about a novel (p. 747). Summary is also an essential tool in research papers and other writing that draws on sources (p. 617). Here, though, we're concerned with summarizing for yourself—for your own enlightenment.

A summary should state in as few words as possible the main ideas of a passage. When you need to summarize a few paragraphs or a brief article, your summary should not exceed one-fifth the length of the original. For longer works, such as chapters of books or whole books, your summary should be quite a bit shorter in proportion to the original. A procedure for drafting a summary appears in the following box.

Writing a summary

- **Understand the meaning.** Look up words or concepts you don't know so that you understand the author's sentences and how they relate to one another.
- **Understand the organization.** Work through the text to identify its sections—single paragraphs or groups of paragraphs focused on a single topic. To understand how parts of a work relate to one another, try drawing a tree diagram or creating an outline (pp. 34–38).

- **Distill each section.** Write a one- or two-sentence summary of each section you identify. Focus on the main point of the section, omitting examples, facts, and other supporting evidence.
- **State the main idea.** Write a sentence or two capturing the author's central idea.
- **Support the main idea.** Write a full paragraph (or more, if needed) that begins with the central idea and supports it with the sentences that summarize sections of the work. The paragraph should concisely and accurately state the thrust of the entire work.
- *Use your own words.* By writing, you re-create the meaning of the work in a way that makes sense for you.

Summarizing even a passage of text can be tricky. Below is one attempt to summarize the following material from an introductory biology textbook.

Original text

As astronomers study newly discovered planets orbiting distant stars, they hope to find evidence of water on these far-off celestial bodies, for water is the substance that makes possible life as we know it here on Earth. All organisms familiar to us are made mostly of water and live in an environment dominated by water. They require water more than any other substance. Human beings, for example, can survive for quite a few weeks without food, but only a week or so without water. Molecules of water participate in many chemical reactions necessary to sustain life. Most cells are surrounded by water, and cells themselves are about 70–95% water. Three-quarters of Earth's surface is submerged in water. Although most of this water is in liquid form, water is also present on Earth as ice and vapor. Water is the only common substance to exist in the natural environment in all three physical states of matter: solid, liquid, and gas.
—Neil A. Campbell and Jane B. Reece, *Biology*

Draft summary

Astronomers look for water in outer space because life depends on it. It is the most common substance on Earth and in living cells, and it can be a liquid, a solid (ice), or a gas (vapor).

This summary accurately restates ideas in the original, but it does not pare the passage to its essence. The work of astronomers and the three physical states of water add color and texture to the original, but they are asides to the key concept that water sustains life because of its role in life. The following revision narrows the summary to this concept:

Revised summary

Water is the most essential support for life, the dominant substance on Earth and in living cells and a component of life-sustaining chemical processes.

CASUAL SUMMARIZING

You can point out to students that they summarize all the time when telling friends about movies they've seen or books they've read. Have them summarize a favorite book from memory, and then revise the summary to make sure it's comprehensive and succinct.

Note Do not count on the AutoSummarize function on your word processor for summarizing texts that you may have copied onto your computer. The summaries are rarely accurate, and you will not gain the experience of interacting with the texts on your own.

7d Preparing for and taking exams

Examinations give you a chance to demonstrate what you have learned from listening, reading, and writing. Studying for an exam involves three main steps, each requiring about a third of the preparation time: reviewing the material, organizing summaries of the material, and testing yourself. Your main goals are to strengthen your understanding of the subject, making both its ideas and its details more memorable, and to increase the flexibility of your new knowledge so that you can apply it in new contexts.

The procedure outlined here works for any exam, no matter how much time you have, what material you're studying, or what kind of test you'll be taking. Because an essay exam requires a distinctive approach during the exam itself, it receives special attention on pages 144–49.

Note Cramming for an exam is about the least effective way of preparing for one. It takes longer to learn under stress, and the learning is shallower, more difficult to apply, and more quickly forgotten. Information learned under stress is even harder to apply in stressful situations, such as taking an exam. And the lack of sleep that usually accompanies cramming makes a good performance even more unlikely. If you must cram for a test, face the fact that you can't learn everything. Spend your time reviewing main concepts and facts.

1 Reviewing and memorizing the material

Divide your class notes and reading assignments into manageable units. Reread the material, recite or write out the main ideas and selected supporting ideas and examples, and then skim for an overview. Proceed in this way through all the units of the course, returning to earlier ones as needed to refresh your memory or to relate ideas.

During this stage you should be memorizing what you don't already know by heart. Try these strategies for strengthening your memory:

- **Link new and known information.** For instance, to remember a sequence of four dates in twentieth-century African history, link the dates to simultaneous and more familiar events in the United States.

- **Create groups of ideas or facts that make sense to you.** For instance, memorize French vocabulary words in related groups, such as words for parts of the body or parts of a house. Keep the groups small: research has shown that we can easily memorize about seven items at a time but have trouble with more.
- **Create narratives and visual images.** You may recall a story or a picture more easily than words. For instance, to remember how the economic laws of supply and demand affect the market for rental housing, you could tie the principles to a narrative about the aftermath of the 1906 San Francisco earthquake, when half the population was suddenly homeless. Or you could visualize a person who has dollar signs for eyes and is converting a spare room into a high-priced rental unit, as many did after the earthquake to meet the new demand for housing.
- **Use *mnemonic devices*, or tricks for remembering.** Say the history dates you want to remember are separated by five years, then four, then nine. By memorizing the first date and recalling $5 + 4 = 9$, you'll have command of all four dates.

2   Organizing summaries of the material

Allow time to reorganize the material in your own way, creating categories that will help you apply the information in various contexts. For instance, in studying for a biology exam, work to understand a process, such as how a plant develops or how photosynthesis occurs. Or in studying for an American government test, explain the structures of the local, state, and federal levels of government. Other useful categories include causes/effects and advantages/disadvantages. Such analytical thinking will improve your mastery of the course material and may even prepare you directly for specific essay questions.

3   Testing yourself

Convert each heading in your lecture notes and course reading into a question. Answer in writing, going back to the course material to fill in what you don't yet know. Be sure you can define and explain all key terms. For subjects that require solving problems (such as mathematics, statistics, or physics), work out a difficult problem for every type on which you will be tested. For all subjects, focus on the main themes and questions of the course. In a psychology course, for example, be certain you understand principal theories and their implications. In a literature course, test your knowledge of literary movements and genres or the relations among specific works.

STUDY GROUP QUESTIONS

A good way for a study group to review material together is for each member of the group to come up with some study questions to ask the other members.

When you are satisfied with your preparation, stop studying and get a good night's sleep.

4 Taking essay exams

In writing an essay for an examination, you summarize or analyze a topic, usually in several paragraphs or more and usually within a time limit. An essay question not only tests your knowledge of a subject (as short-answer and objective questions do) but also tests your ability to think critically about what you have learned.

■ Planning your time and your answer

When you first receive an exam, take a few minutes to get your bearings and plan an approach. The time spent will not be wasted.

- **Read the exam all the way through at least once.** Don't start answering any questions until you've seen them all.
- **Weigh the questions.** Determine which questions seem most important, which ones are going to be most difficult for you, and approximately how much time you'll need for each question. (Your instructor may help by assigning a point value to each question as a guide to its importance or by suggesting an amount of time for you to spend on each question.)

Planning continues when you turn to an individual essay question. Resist the temptation to rush right into an answer without some planning, for a few minutes can save you time later and help you produce a stronger essay.

- **Read the question at least twice.** You will be more likely to stick to the question and answer it fully.
- **Examine the words in the question and consider their implications.** Look especially for words such as *describe, define, explain, summarize, analyze, evaluate,* and *interpret,* each of which requires a different kind of response. Here, for example, is an essay question whose key term is *explain:*

  Question

  Given humans' natural and historical curiosity about themselves, why did a scientific discipline of anthropology not arise until the 20th century? Explain, citing specific details.

  See the box opposite, and consult other discussions of such terms on pages 24–25 and 91–100.
- **Make a brief outline of the main ideas you want to cover.** Use the back of the exam sheet or booklet for scratch paper. In the brief outline on page 146, a student planned her answer to the anthropology question above.

Sample instructions for essay examinations

Sample instructions	Key terms	Strategies for answers	Examples of wrong answers
Define *dyslexia* and compare and contrast it with two other learning disabilities.	Define	Specify the meaning of *dyslexia*—distinctive characteristics, ways the impairment works, etc.	Feelings of children with dyslexia. Causes of dyslexia.
	Compare and contrast	Analyze similarities and differences (severity, causes, treatments, etc.).	Similarities without differences, or vice versa.
Analyze the role of Horatio in *Hamlet*.	Analyze	Break Horatio's role into its elements (speeches, relations with other characters, etc.).	Plot summary of *Hamlet*. Description of Horatio's personality.
Explain the effects of the drug Thorazine.	Explain	Set forth the facts and theories objectively.	Argument for or against Thorazine.
	Effects	Analyze the consequences.	Reasons for prescribing Thorazine.
Discuss term limits for elected officials.	Discuss	Explain and compare the main points of view on the issue.	Analysis of one view. Argument for or against one view.
Summarize the process that resulted in the Grand Canyon.	Summarize	Distill the subject to its main points, elements, or steps.	Detailed description of the Grand Canyon.
How do you evaluate the Laffer curve as a predictor of economic growth?	Evaluate	Provide your opinion of significance or value, supported with evidence.	Explanation of the Laffer curve, without evaluation. Comparison of the Laffer curve and another predictor, without evaluation.

Outline

1. Unscientific motivations behind 19th-c anthro.

   Imperialist/colonialist govts.
   Practical goals
   Nonobjective and unscientific (Herodotus, Cushing)

2. 19th-c ethnocentricity (vs. cultural relativism)

3. 19th-c anthro. = object collecting

   20th-c shift from museum to univ.
   Anthro. becomes acad. disc. and professional (Boas, Malinowski)

■ **Write a thesis statement for your essay that responds directly to the question and represents your view of the topic.** (If you are unsure of how to write a thesis statement, see pp. 27–31.) Include key phrases that you can expand with supporting evidence for your view. The thesis statement of the student whose outline appears above concisely previews a three-part answer to the sample question:

Thesis statement

Anthropology did not emerge as a scientific discipline until the 20th century because of the practical and political motivations behind 19th-century ethnographic studies, the ethnocentric bias of Western researchers, and a conception of culture that was strictly material.

■ **Starting the essay**

An essay exam does not require a smooth and inviting opening. Instead, begin by stating your thesis immediately and giving an overview of the rest of your essay. Such a capsule version of your answer tells your reader (and grader) generally how much command you have and also how you plan to develop your answer. It also gets you off to a good start.

The opening statement should address the question directly and exactly, as it does in the successful essay answer beginning on the facing page. In contrast, the opening of the unsuccessful essay (pp. 148–49) restates the question but does not answer it, nor does the opening provide any sense of the writer's thesis.

■ **Developing the essay**

Develop your essay as you would develop any piece of sound academic writing:

■ **Observe the methods, terms, or other special requirements of the discipline in which you are writing.**
■ **Support your thesis statement with solid generalizations,** each one perhaps the topic sentence of a paragraph.
■ **Support each generalization with specific, relevant evidence.**

If you observe a few *don't*s as well, your essay will have more substance:

- **Avoid filling out the essay by repeating yourself.**
- **Avoid other kinds of wordiness that pad and confuse,** whether intentionally or not. (See pp. 529–35.)
- **Avoid resorting to purely subjective feelings.** Keep focused on analysis or whatever is asked of you. (It may help to abolish the word *I* from the essay.)

The following essays illustrate a successful and an unsuccessful answer to the sample essay question on page 144 about anthropology. Both answers were written in the allotted time of forty minutes. Marginal comments on each essay highlight their effective and ineffective elements.

Successful essay answer

Anthropology did not emerge as a scientific discipline until the 20th century because of the practical and political motivations behind 19th-century ethnographic studies, the ethnocentric bias of Western researchers, and a conception of culture that was strictly material.

Introduction stating thesis

Direct answer to question and preview of three-part response

Before the 20th century, ethnographic studies were almost always used for practical goals. The study of human culture can be traced back at least as far as Herodotus's investigations of the Mediterranean peoples. Herodotus was like many pre-20th-century "anthropologists" in that he was employed by a government that needed information about its neighbors, just as the colonial nations in the 19th century needed information about their newly conquered subjects. The early politically motivated ethnographic studies that the colonial nations sponsored tended to be isolated projects, and they aimed less to advance general knowledge than to solve a specific problem. Frank Hamilton Cushing, who was employed by the American government to study the Zuni tribe of New Mexico, and who is considered one of the pioneers of anthropology, didn't even publish his findings. The political and practical aims of anthropologists and the nature of their research prevented their work from being a scholarly discipline in its own right.

First main point: practical aims

Example

Example

Anthropologists of the 19th century also fell short of the standards of objectivity needed for truly scientific study. This partly had to do with anthropologists' close connection to imperialist governments. But even independent researchers were hampered by the prevailing assumption that Western cultures were inherently superior. While the modern anthropologist believes that a culture must be studied in terms of its own values, early ethnographers were ethnocentric: they judged "primitive" cultures by their own "civilized" values. "Primitive" peoples were seen as uninteresting in their own right. The reasons to study them, ultimately, were to satisfy curiosity, to exploit them, or to prove their inferiority. There was even some debate as to whether so-called savage peoples were human.

Second main point: ethnocentricity

WHAT WORKS AND WHAT DOESN'T

Comparing these sample "successful" and "unsuccessful" essay exam answers should help students get a better idea of what to strive for in their own essay exam answers. The successful answer is direct, substantive, and well structured. You may also want to have students take a closer look at the use of transitions in the successful essay; they provide coherence within and among paragraphs, giving the reader essential information about how the various pieces of information in the essay are interrelated.

ACHIEVABLE STANDARDS

Both of the sample essay answers here (successful and unsuccessful) are clearly written and correct in grammar and usage. Your students may think they set a standard impossible to achieve. You can reinforce the idea that content and structure are the most important elements in a good essay exam answer and that they should not waste valuable exam time trying to perfect grammar, sentence structure, or mechanics. If they leave time at the end they can do a quick clean-up to catch any egregious errors.

Third main point (with transition *Finally*): focus on objects

Finally, the 19th century tended to conceive of culture in narrow, material terms, often reducing it to a collection of artifacts. When not working for a government, early ethnographers usually worked for a museum. The enormous collections of exotica still found in many museums today are the legacy of this 19th-century object-oriented conception of anthropology, which ignored the myths, symbols, and rituals the objects related to. It was only when the museum tradition was broadened to include all aspects of a culture that anthropology could come into existence as a scientific discipline. When anthropologists like Franz Boas and Bronislaw Malinowski began to publish their findings for others to read and criticize and began to move from the museum to the university, the discipline gained stature and momentum.

Examples

Conclusion, restating thesis supported by essay

In brief, anthropology required a whole series of ideological shifts to become modern. Once it broke free of its purely practical bent, the cultural prejudices of its practitioners, and the narrow conception that limited it to a collection of objects, anthropology could grow into a science.

Unsuccessful essay answer

Introduction, not answering question

No thesis statement or sense of direction

Irrelevant information

Cliché added to language of question without answering question

Wheel spinning, positioning contemporary anthropology as a scientific discipline

Not *Another reason* but the first reason given

Assertion without support

Next three paragraphs: discussion of pioneers showing familiarity with their work but not answering question

The discipline of anthropology, the study of humans and their cultures, actually began in the early 20th century and was strengthened by the Darwinian revolution, but the discipline did not begin to take shape until people like Franz Boas and Alfred Kroeber began doing scientific research among nonindustrialized cultures. (Boas, who was born in Germany but emigrated to the US, is the father of the idea of historical particularism.)

Since the dawn of time, humans have always had a natural curiosity about themselves. Art and literature have always reflected this need to understand human emotions, thought, and behavior. Anthropology is yet another reflection of this need. Anthropologists have a different way of looking at human societies than artists or writers. Whereas the latter paint an individualistic, impressionistic portrait of the world they see, anthropologists study cultures systematically, scientifically. They are thus closer to biologists. They are *social scientists*, with the emphasis on both words.

Another reason why anthropology did not develop until the 20th century is that people in the past did not travel very much. The expansion of the automobile and the airplane has played a major role in the expansion of the discipline.

Cushing's important work among the Zuni Indians in New Mexico is a good example of the transition between 19th-century and 20th-century approaches to anthropology. Cushing was one of the first to develop the method of *participant observation*. Instead of merely coming in as an outsider, taking notes, and leaving, Cushing actually lived among the Zuni, dressing like them and following their customs. In this way, he was able to build a relationship of trust with his informants, learning much more than someone who would have been seen as an outsider.

Franz Boas, as mentioned earlier, was another anthropology pioneer. A German immigrant, Boas proposed the idea of *historical particularism* as a response to the prevailing theory of *cultural evolution*. Cultural evolution is the idea that cultures gradually evolve toward higher levels of efficiency and complexity. Historical particularism is the idea that every culture is unique and develops differently. Boas developed his theory to counter those who believed in cultural evolution. Working with the Kwakiutl Indians, he was also one of the first anthropologists to use a native assistant to help him gain access to the culture under study.

| Padding with repetition |
| Irrelevant information |

A third pioneer in anthropology was Malinowski, who developed a theory of *functionalism*—that culture responds to biological, psychological, and other needs. Malinowski's work is extremely important and still influential today.

| Vague assertion without support |

Anthropologists have made great contributions to society over the course of the past century. One can only hope that they will continue the great strides they have made, building on the past to contribute to a bright new future.

| Irrelevant and empty conclusion |

■ Rereading the essay

The time limit on an essay examination does not allow for the careful rethinking and revision you would give an essay or research paper. You need to write clearly and concisely the first time. But try to leave yourself a few minutes after finishing the entire exam for rereading the essay (or essays) and doing touch-ups.

- **Correct mistakes:** illegible passages, misspellings, grammatical errors, and accidental omissions.
- **Verify that your thesis is accurate**—that it is, in fact, what you ended up writing about.
- **Ensure that you have supported all your generalizations.** Cross out irrelevant ideas and details, and add any information that now seems important. (Write on another page, if necessary, keying each addition to the page on which it belongs.)

COMPUTER ACTIVITY

ONLINE EXAMS

If your students are going to compose and submit their essay exams using a computer, have them do a dry run with a practice document to make sure they know how to save, format, and submit it according to your specifications.

mycomplab²·⁰

Where writing and research help is just a click away!

Please visit MyCompLab at *www.mycomplab.com* for more on the writing process.

HIGHLIGHTS

Becoming explicitly aware of their critical powers, and then learning to use them, may seem an overwhelming task to students who are already coping with other changes brought on by the first year of college. However, developing a critical awareness is one of the most important things first-year students need to do to make the transition to college.

This chapter begins with the sometimes challenging concept of being critical without being negative. Thomas Sowell's provocative essay, "Student Loans," models truly academic critical reading. The essay is printed in full, and it is also used as an example throughout the chapter's coverage of active reading, summarizing, and constructing a critical response with the use of analysis, interpretation, synthesis, and evaluation.

An expanded section on "Viewing images critically" discusses writing while reading an image; previewing, interpreting, analyzing, and evaluating an image; and synthesizing ideas about an image. Several illustrations provide examples for this section.

Finally, the chapter covers ways of communicating the results of critical thinking and reading to an audience through critical writing. Two annotated student papers, one responding to Sowell's essay and the other responding to the *Time* magazine advertisement, provide models of how to shape and produce a coherent critical response.

COMPANION WEB SITE

See page IAE-52 for companion Web site content description.

CHAPTER **8**

Forming a Critical Perspective

Throughout college and beyond, you will be expected to think, read, and write critically. **Critical** here means "skeptical," "exacting," "creative." When you operate critically, you question, test, and build on what others say and what you yourself think. The word *critical* does not mean "negative" in this context: you can think critically about something you like, don't like, or just view neutrally.

You already operate critically every day of your life, as when you probe a friendship ("What did she mean by that?") or when you discuss a movie you just saw ("Don't you think the bad guy was too obvious?"). Such questioning helps you figure out why things happen to you or what your experiences mean.

This chapter introduces more formal methods for thinking and reading critically (opposite), viewing images critically (p. 164), and writing critically (p. 172). Learning and applying these methods will both engage you in and prepare you for school courses, career, and life in a democratic society:

- **Teachers and employers will expect you to think critically.** In every field, you will need to assess what you read, see, and hear and to make a good case for your own ideas.
- **Critical thinking helps you understand and express yourself.** With it, you gain insight into your actions and ideas, can weigh them against opposing views, and can persuasively articulate your reasoning and motivations.
- **Your very independence and freedom depend on your ability to think, read, and write critically.** An open democracy allows as much play for stupid and false claims as for sound ones, and the claims that seem sound often conflict with each other. Critical thinking empowers you to decide for yourself what's useful, fair, and wise—and what's not.

http://www.ablongman.com/littlebrown ▶

Visit the companion Web site for more help and additional exercises on critical thinking, reading, and writing.

There's no denying that critical thinking, reading, and writing require discipline and hard work. Besides channeling your curiosity, paying attention, and probing, you will often need to consult experts, interpreting and evaluating their ideas. Such an approach also requires a healthy tolerance for doubt or uncertainty—that feeling you may have when the old rules don't seem to apply or when a change is frightening but still attractive. Out of uncertainty, though, comes creativity—the capacity to organize and generate knowledge, to explain, resolve, illuminate, play. Compared to passive, rote learning, creative work is more involving, more productive, and more enjoyable.

8a Thinking and reading critically

In college much of your critical thinking will focus on written texts (a short story, a journal article, a Web log) or on visual objects (a photograph, a chart, a film). Like all subjects worthy of critical consideration, such works operate on at least three levels: (1) what the creator actually says or shows, (2) what the creator does not say or show but builds into the work (intentionally or not), and (3) what you think. Discovering the first of these levels—reading for comprehension—is discussed in the preceding chapter as part of effective study skills (see pp. 138–40). This chapter builds on the earlier material to help you discover the other two levels. The box below summarizes the reading techniques involved.

The techniques of critical reading are not steps in a firm sequence. You will not use all of them for all the reading you do. On some occasions, even when a close, critical reading is required, you

Techniques of critical reading

For reading a work of literature, which requires a somewhat different approach, see pp. 735–43.

- **Writing:** making notes on your reading throughout the process (next page)
- **Previewing:** getting background; skimming (p. 153)
- **Reading:** interacting with and absorbing the text (pp. 153–54)
- **Summarizing:** distilling and understanding content (p. 157)
- **Forming your critical response** (pp. 157–63)

  Analyzing: separating into parts
  Interpreting: inferring meaning and assumptions
  Synthesizing: reassembling parts; making connections
  Evaluating: judging quality and value

THE MEANING OF *CRITICAL*

One of the greatest difficulties in teaching critical strategies is the problems students have with the negative connotations of the word *critical*. Brainstorm all the meanings and uses of the word they know; beyond those implying value judgments, some students will come up with "critical temperature," "critical mass," "critical condition," "critical point of the game," and so on. By showing how these terms connect to discernment, or important stages of development, you can demonstrate that the word need not always have negative overtones and thus help students to study these techniques with a better attitude.

TRANSPARENCY MASTER 8.1

MATTHIESSEN'S MISTAKE

One good anecdote to share with students concerns F. O. Matthiessen's classic work of literary criticism, *American Renaissance*. When it first appeared in 1941, it contained a passage praising the irony in Herman Melville's metaphor "the soiled fish of the sea" (describing an eel). When readers rushed to read the Melville passage in question, however, they found that "soiled" was actually a typographical error; the correct reading was "coiled." Matthiessen's brilliant critique of Melville's irony was founded on a typesetter's mistake. Students find it comforting to know that great critics can make mistakes, too; you can point out that it was, in fact, people employing critical reading who found Matthiessen's misreading!

CHALLENGING TEXTS

Critical activities may provide an additional hurdle for students whose first language is not English or who come from cultures outside the United States. In many cultures, students are taught not to challenge ideas in print; such questions may be considered disrespectful by some who see print as an indication of authority and value. (This is especially true if the text refers to religious beliefs.) Other students, especially those who grew up in nondemocratic societies, may know from experience how dangerous it can be to challenge the "party line" espoused in school. And depending on the area of the United States you teach in, you may find students who believe in the "inerrancy of the word," even if the text is not biblical. Discuss the students' right to ask questions about, respond to, and challenge printed works, whether in published texts or in personal manuscripts.

may simply lack the time to preview, read, and reread. (But if your reading time is continually squeezed by your schedule, you may need to rethink your schedule.) On other occasions your reason for reading (your purpose) will determine which techniques you use.

Even a publication like *People* magazine is open to different methods of reading for different purposes:

Purpose	Learn some gossip while filling time in the dentist's office.
Kind of reading	Quick, uncritical
Purpose	Examine *People* as an artifact of our popular culture that reflects and perhaps even molds contemporary values.
Kind of reading	Close, critical

Course assignments, too, differ in their requirements. A book report may require writing, previewing, reading, and summarizing but not intense critical reading. An evaluation of a journal article, in contrast, requires all the techniques discussed here.

CULTURE LANGUAGE The idea of reading critically may require you to make some adjustments if readers in your native culture tend to seek understanding or agreement more than engagement from what they read. Readers of English use texts for all kinds of reasons, including pleasure, reinforcement, information, and many others. But they also read skeptically, critically, to see the author's motives, test their own ideas, and arrive at new knowledge.

1 Writing while reading

Reading a work for comprehension and then for a critical approach is an *active* process. Making notes on what you read involves you by helping you understand how the text works, why, and what you think about it. The notes help you bring to the work your own experiences, knowledge, and questions.

If you own the material you're reading (a book, a photocopy, or a printout), you can make notes in the margins (see p. 154 for an example). If you don't own the material or if your notes won't fit in the margins, make notes separately using pen and paper or your computer. Many readers keep a **reading journal** in which they regularly work out questions and thoughts about what they read. One technique for keeping such a journal is to divide a page or computer screen into two vertical columns, the left side for the work itself, such as summary and questions, and the right side for what the work makes you think, such as agreements or doubts based on your own experiences, comparisons with other works, and ideas for writing. A two-column journal can encourage you to go beyond summarizing what you read to interacting critically with it because the blank right column will beckon you to respond. See the next page for an example of this technique.

Note Whenever you photocopy or download a document or take notes separately from the text you're reading, be sure to record all necessary information about the text's location so that you can find it again and cite it fully if you use it. See page 569 for a list of information to record.

2 Previewing the material

When you're reading a work of literature, such as a story or a poem, it's often best to plunge right in (see pp. 736–37). But for critical reading of other works, it's worthwhile to skim before reading word for word, forming expectations and even preliminary questions. The preview will make your reading more informed and fruitful.

Use the questions in the box below as a guide to previewing a text.

Questions for previewing a text

- **What is the work's subject and structure?** Following the steps outlined on pages 138–39, gauge length and level, read the title and introduction for clues to the topic and main ideas, read the headings, note highlighted words (defined terms), examine illustrations, and read the summary or conclusion.
- **What are the facts of publication?** Does the date of publication suggest currency or datedness? Does the publisher or publication specialize in a particular kind of material—scholarly articles, say, or popular books? For a Web site, who or what sponsors the site: an individual? a nonprofit organization? an academic institution? a corporation? a government body? (See pp. 672 and 675 on locating the authors of online sources.)
- **What do you know about the author?** Does a biography tell you about the author's publications, interests, biases, and reputation in the field? For an online source, which may be posted by an unfamiliar or anonymous author, what can you gather about the author from his or her words? If possible, trace unfamiliar authors to learn more about them.
- **What is your preliminary response?** What do you already know about the author's topic? What questions do you have about either the topic or the author's approach to it? What biases of your own might influence your reception of the work—for instance, curiosity, boredom, or an outlook similar or opposed to the author's?

3 Reading

Reading is itself more than a one-step process. You want to understand the first level on which the text operates—what the author actually says—and begin to form your impressions.

TRANSPARENCY MASTER 8.2

COLLABORATIVE LEARNING

GROUP PRACTICE

Even after they work through the materials in this chapter, students will need to practice critical reading until it becomes a familiar process. Having students work in groups to answer previewing questions or to create questions for rereading can make the critical approach to reading more accessible, and it will result in a broader range of interpretive responses.

COMPLEX TEXTS

Choose a relatively complex essay from your reader or another published collection. Ask students to work through various sections of the essay in small groups, then present their findings to the class. After those presentations, students might reread the essay and write an interpretive response to a short passage from it, which they again can share and critique in groups. Students can also use the essay as the basis for the appropriate exercises in this chapter. This will give them further confidence in their critical skills.

A procedure for this stage appears in the preceding chapter (pp. 139–40). To recap: Read once through fairly smoothly, trying to appreciate the work and keeping notes to a minimum. Then read again more carefully, this time making detailed notes, to grasp the ideas and their connections and to pose questions.

Following are examples of active reading from a student, Charlene Robinson. She was responding to Thomas Sowell's "Student Loans," reprinted on the next two pages. First Robinson annotated a photocopy of the essay (the first four paragraphs appear below):

> The first lesson of economics is scarcity: There is never enough of anything to fully satisfy all those who want it. *— Basic contradiction between economics and politics*
>
> The first lesson of politics is to disregard the first lesson of economics. When politicians discover some group that is being vocal about not having as much as they want, the "solution" is to give them more. Where do politicians get this "more"? They rob Peter to pay Paul. *← biblical reference?*
>
> After a while, of course, they discover that Peter doesn't have enough. Bursting with compassion, politicians rush to the rescue. Needless to say, they do not admit that robbing Peter to pay Paul was a dumb idea in the first place. On the contrary, they now rob Tom, Dick, and Harry to help Peter. *← ironic and dismissive language*
>
> The latest chapter in this long-running saga is that politicians have now suddenly discovered that many college students graduate heavily in debt. To politicians it follows, as the night follows the day, that the government should come to their rescue with the taxpayers' money. *politicians = fools? or irresponsible*

After reading the text, Robinson wrote about it in the journal she kept on her computer. She divided the journal into two columns, one each for the text and her responses. Here is the portion pertaining to the paragraphs above:

Text	Responses
Economics teaches lessons (1), and politics (politicians) and economics are at odds	Is economics truer or more reliable than politics? More scientific?
Politicians don't accept econ. limits—always trying to satisfy "vocal" voters by giving them what they want (2)	Politicians do spend a lot of our money. Is that what they're elected to do, or do they go too far?
"Robbing Peter to pay Paul" (2)— from the Bible (the Apostles)?	
Politicians support student loan program with taxpayer funds bec. of "vocal" voters (2-4): another ex. of not accepting econ. limits	I support the loan program, too. Are politicians being irresponsible when they do? (Dismissive language underlined on copy.)

You should try to answer the questions about meaning that you raise in your annotations and your journal, and that may take another reading or some digging in other sources, such as dictionaries and encyclopedias. Recording in your journal what you think the author means will help you build an understanding of the text, and a focused attempt to summarize will help even more (see pp. 140–42 and 157). Such efforts will resolve any confusion you feel, or they will give you the confidence to say that your confusion is the fault of the author, not the reader.

EXERCISE 8.1   Reading

Reprinted below is an essay by Thomas Sowell on the federal government's student-loan program. An economist, Sowell is also a newspaper columnist and the author of many books on economics, politics, and education. This essay appeared in Sowell's collection *Is Reality Optional?*

Read this essay at least twice, until you think you understand what the author is saying. Either on these pages or separately, note your questions and reactions in writing.

Student Loans

1 The first lesson of economics is scarcity: There is never enough of anything to fully satisfy all those who want it.

2 The first lesson of politics is to disregard the first lesson of economics. When politicians discover some group that is being vocal about not having as much as they want, the "solution" is to give them more. Where do politicians get this "more"? They rob Peter to pay Paul.

3 After a while, of course, they discover that Peter doesn't have enough. Bursting with compassion, politicians rush to the rescue. Needless to say, they do not admit that robbing Peter to pay Paul was a dumb idea in the first place. On the contrary, they now rob Tom, Dick, and Harry to help Peter.

4 The latest chapter in this long-running saga is that politicians have now suddenly discovered that many college students graduate heavily in debt. To politicians it follows, as the night follows the day, that the government should come to their rescue with the taxpayers' money.

5 How big is this crushing burden of college students' debt that we hear so much about from politicians and media deep thinkers? For those students who graduate from public colleges owing money, the debt averages a little under $7,000. For those who graduate from private colleges owing money, the average debt is a little under $9,000.

6 Buying a very modestly priced automobile involves more debt than that. And a car loan has to be paid off faster than the ten years that college graduates get to repay their student loans. Moreover, you have to keep buying cars every several years, while one college education lasts a lifetime.

7 College graduates of course earn higher incomes than other people. Why, then, should we panic at the thought that they have to

WEARING THE FILM CRITIC'S HAT

To help students understand the concept of "misreading," try the "movie critic" exercise: a movie critic writes that a film is "one of the really great awful films of the decade." An ad for the film that claims "Critic So-and-So calls this 'one of the really great . . . films of the decade'" is a deliberate misreading. Ask students to construct deliberate misreadings of reviews or critiques as a way of teaching them what not to do in their own summaries.

COLLABORATIVE LEARNING

COMPARING SUMMARIES

Ask students to compare their summaries in groups and list points that are similar and different among the summaries in their group. Then, as a way of deciding how much information is needed to create an effective summary, have each student defend the places where his or her summary differs from the group consensus.

SUMMARY STRATEGIES

Students learning standard American English may find synonyms for some key words in the sentences that express the main points of a source, but they may feel insecure about using other sentence structures. Encourage students to change the sentence structure as well as the vocabulary of the original in writing summaries. Working collaboratively on summaries helps students see alternative ways to express ideas; in addition, stronger students (and native speakers) can help the weaker students and, in so doing, reinforce their own writing skills. Alice Oshima and Ann Hogue, in *Writing Academic English*, 3rd ed. (New York: Longman, 1999), include useful exercises for students who need additional practice in summarizing.

RESOURCES AND IDEAS

On approaches to teaching critical thinking

Anson, Chris M., ed. *Writing and Response: Theory, Practice, and Research*. Urbana: NCTE, 1989. A collection of essays that explore the practical and theoretical issues involved in reading and commenting on student texts.

repay loans for the education which gave them their opportunities? Even graduates with relatively modest incomes pay less than 10 percent of their annual salary on the loan the first year—with declining percentages in future years, as their pay increases.

Political hysteria and media hype may focus on the low-income [8] student with a huge debt. That is where you get your heart-rending stories—even if they are not at all typical. In reality, the soaring student loans of the past decade have resulted from allowing high-income people to borrow under government programs.

Before 1978, college loans were available through government [9] programs only to students whose family income was below some cut-off level. That cut-off level was about double the national average income, but at least it kept out the Rockefellers and the Vanderbilts. But, in an era of "compassion," Congress took off even those limits.

That opened the floodgates. No matter how rich you were, it still [10] paid to borrow money through the government at low interest rates. The money you had set aside for your children's education could be invested somewhere else, at higher interest rates. Then, when the student loan became due, parents could pay it off with the money they had set aside—pocketing the difference in interest rates.

To politicians and the media, however, the rapidly growing loans [11] showed what a great "need" there was. The fact that many students welshed when time came to repay their loans showed how "crushing" their burden of debt must be. In reality, those who welsh typically have smaller loans, but have dropped out of college before finishing. People who are irresponsible in one way are often irresponsible in other ways.

No small amount of the deterioration of college standards has [12] been due to the increasingly easy availability of college to people who are not very serious about getting an education. College is not a bad place to hang out for a few years, if you have nothing better to do, and if someone else is paying for it. Its costs are staggering, but the taxpayers carry much of that burden, not only for state universities and city colleges, but also to an increasing extent even for "private" institutions.

Numerous government subsidies and loan programs make it possible [13] for many people to use vast amounts of society's resources at low cost to themselves. Whether in money terms or in real terms, federal aid to higher education has increased several hundred percent since 1970. That has enabled colleges to raise their tuition by leaps and bounds and enabled professors to be paid more and more for doing less and less teaching.

Naturally all these beneficiaries are going to create hype and hysteria [14] to keep more of the taxpayers' money coming in. But we would be fools to keep on writing blank checks for them.

When you weigh the cost of things, in economics that's called [15] "trade-offs." In politics, it's called "mean-spirited." Apparently, if we just took a different attitude, scarcity would go away.

—Thomas Sowell

4 Summarizing

Summarizing a text—distilling it to its essential ideas, in your own words—is an important step for comprehending it and is discussed in detail in the previous chapter (pp. 140–42). Here, we'll look at how Charlene Robinson summarized paragraphs 1–4 of Thomas Sowell's "Student Loans." She first drafted this sentence:

> Draft summary
>
> As much as politicians would like to satisfy voters by giving them everything they ask for, the government cannot afford a student loan program.

Rereading the sentence and Sowell's paragraph, Robinson saw that this draft misread the text by asserting that the government cannot afford student loans. She realized that Sowell's point is more complicated than that and rewrote her summary:

> Revised summary
>
> As their support of the government's student loan program illustrates, politicians ignore the economic reality that using resources to benefit one group (students in debt) involves taking the resources from another group (taxpayers).

Note Using your own words when writing a summary not only helps you understand the meaning but also constitutes the first step in avoiding plagiarism. The second step is to cite the source when you use it in something written for others. See Chapter 45.

EXERCISE 8.2 Summarizing

Start where Robinson's summary of Thomas Sowell's essay ends (at paragraph 5) to summarize the entire essay. Your summary, in your own words, should not exceed one paragraph. For additional exercises in summarizing, see pp. 622–23.

---

5 Developing a critical response

Once you've grasped the content of what you're reading—what the author says—then you can turn to understanding what the author does not say outright but suggests or implies or even lets slip. At this stage you are concerned with the purpose or intention of the author and with how he or she carries it out. Depending on what you are reading and why, you may examine evidence, organization, attitude, use of language, and other elements of the text.

Critical thinking and reading consist of four operations: analyzing, interpreting, synthesizing, and (often) evaluating. Although we'll look at them one by one, these operations interrelate and overlap. Indeed, the first three are often combined under the general label *analysis,* and evaluation is sometimes taken for granted as a result of the process.

Brookfield, Stephen D. *Developing Critical Thinkers.* San Francisco: Jossey-Bass, 1987. Brookfield encourages connections between critical skills developed in school and their applications in daily life.

Chambers, Marilyn J. "Text Cues and Strategies Successful Readers Use to Construct the Gist of Lengthy Written Arguments." *Reading Research Quarterly* 30 (1995): 778–807. Chambers examines students' strategies for identifying argument structure, claim, and evidence in lengthy texts.

Elbow, Peter. "Ranking, Evaluating, and Liking: Sorting Out Three Forms of Judgment." *College English* 55 (1993): 187–206. Elbow's essay is largely concerned with these three activities as part of teacher assessment of student writing, but it gives many ideas that can be translated into classroom practice.

Fiske, John. *Introduction to Communication Studies.* New York: Routledge, 1990. Fiske provides *(continued on p. 158)*

COLLABORATIVE LEARNING

Make Exercise 8.2 collaborative by asking each group of students to write a collective summary; then switch summaries among groups and have the readers decide how effective the other group's effort is in conveying the essential information in Sowell.

ANSWERS: EXERCISE 8.2

Possible answer

As their support of the government's student loan program illustrates, politicians ignore the economic reality that using resources to benefit one group (students in debt) involves taking the resources from another group (taxpayers). Students' average debt is not even that high, and college graduates can afford to pay it off. The greatest attention is paid to the graduate with a large debt, but the law also allows affluent students to borrow, even if their parents profit and the students drop out of school or waste time there. Funded by taxpayers, the loan program has contributed to declining educational standards, rising tuitions, and rising professors' salaries. Taxpayers should balk at funding the program further.

COLLABORATIVE LEARNING

MAGAZINE COLLECTION

Encourage students to bring magazines of various kinds to class. Have students work in groups to brainstorm lists similar to the one shown here for each magazine they collected. Each group might present their most surprising or revealing findings to the class.

(*continued*)

a general overview (for students and teachers) of the methods of cultural criticism, with explicit connections to the teaching of writing.

Foehr, Regina Paxton, and Susan A. Schiller, eds. *The Spiritual Side of Writing: Releasing the Learner's Whole Potential.* Portsmouth: Boynton/Cook (Heinemann), 1997. Essays exploring how writing, learning, and teaching may be experiences that lead to spiritual and ethical awareness and growth.

Golub, Jeff, and the NCTE Committee on Classroom Practices, eds. *Activities to Promote Critical Thinking.* Urbana: NCTE, 1986. The authors have compiled a collection of essays focusing on practical advice and teaching strategies.

Jenseth, Richard. "Understanding Hiroshima: An Assignment Sequence for Freshman English." *College Composition and Communication* 40 (1989): 215–19. Jenseth describes a course wherein students focus on one work (or theme) for an entire semester, considering and reconsidering issues from various critical perspectives.

Jones, Libby Falk. "Exploring Beliefs Through Dialectical Thinking." In *The Critical Writing Workshop: Designing Writing Assignments to Foster Critical Thinking.* Ed. Toni-lee Capossella. Portsmouth: Boynton, 1993. 17–34. This essay and the collection as a whole offer general discussion and practical examples of how to structure thought-provoking assignments.

Kline, Nancy. "Intertextual Trips: Teaching the Essay in the Composition Class." *Journal of Teaching Writing* 8 (1989): 15–37. Kline describes an "active and playful" strategy used by writers of essays and suggests ways to help students detect and appreciate it.

Guidelines for analysis, interpretation, and synthesis

- **What is the purpose of your reading?**
- **What questions do you have about the work,** given your purpose?
- **What elements does the most interesting question highlight?** What elements might you ignore as a result?
- **How do you interpret the meaning and significance of the elements?** What are your assumptions about the work? What do you infer about the author's assumptions?
- **What patterns can you see in (or synthesize from) the elements?** How do the elements relate? How does this whole work relate to other works?
- **What do you conclude about the work?** What does this conclusion add to the work?

You can download these guidelines from *ablongman.com/littlebrown.* Create a copy each time you're reading a work critically, and use the questions to prompt your written responses.

In the following pages, we use two quite different examples to show how critical reading can work: *People* magazine and Sowell's "Student Loans."

■ Analyzing

Analysis is the separation of something into its parts or elements, the better to understand it. To see these elements in what you are reading, begin with a question that reflects your purpose in analyzing the text: why you're curious about it or what you're trying to make out of it. This question will serve as a kind of lens that highlights some features and not others.

Here are some questions you might ask about *People* magazine, listed along with the elements of the magazine that each question highlights:

Questions for analysis	Elements
Does *People* challenge or perpetuate stereotypes?	Stereotypes: explicit and implicit stereotypes or challenges in the magazine
Does the magazine offer positive role models for its readers?	Role models: text and photographs presenting positive or negative role models
Does the magazine's editorial material (articles and accompanying photographs) encourage readers to consume goods and entertainment?	Encouragement of consumption: references to goods and entertainment, focus on consumers, equation of consumption with happiness or success

As these examples show, a question for analysis concentrates your attention on relevant features and eliminates irrelevant features. To answer the question about *People*'s encouragement of consumption, you would focus on items that feature consumption and the products consumed: photographs of designer clothes and celebrities' well-appointed homes, articles on the authors of best-selling books and the stars of new movies. At the same time, you would skip over items that have little or no relevance to consumption, such as uplifting stories about families or the physically challenged.

Analyzing Thomas Sowell's "Student Loans" (pp. 155–56), you might ask these questions:

Questions for analysis	Elements
What is Sowell's attitude toward politicians?	References to politicians: content, words, tone
How does Sowell support his assertions about the loan program's costs?	Support: evidence, such as statistics and examples

A difference in the kinds of questions asked is a key distinction among academic disciplines. A sociologist neatly outlined three disciplines' approaches to poverty:

> Political science does a wonderful job looking at poverty as a policy issue. Economics does an equally wonderful job looking at it from an income-distribution perspective. But sociology asks how people in poverty live and what they aspire to.

Even within disciplines, approaches may differ. The sociologist quoted above may focus on how people in poverty live, but another may be more interested in the effects of poverty on cities or the changes in the poor population over the last fifty years. (See Chapters 49–53 for more on the disciplines' analytical questions.)

■ Interpreting

Identifying the elements of something is of course only the beginning: you also need to interpret the meaning or significance of the elements and of the whole. Interpretation usually requires you to infer the author's **assumptions,** opinions or beliefs about what is or what could or should be. (**Infer** means to draw a conclusion based on evidence.)

The word *assumption* here has a more specific meaning than it does in everyday usage, where it may stand for expectation ("I assume you'll pay"), speculation ("It was a mere assumption"), or error ("The report was riddled with assumptions"). Defined more strictly as what a person *supposes* to be true, assumptions are unavoidable. We all adhere to certain values and beliefs; we all form opinions. We live our lives by such assumptions.

Marzano, Robert J. *Cultivating Thinking in English: The Language Arts*. Urbana: NCTE, 1991. Marzano explores strategies for enhancing student learning, emphasizing ways in which students can analyze their own values and responses to class texts and discussions.

Matthews, Mitford M. "The Freshman and His Dictionary." In *About Language*. Ed. William H. Roberts and Gregoire Turgeon. Boston: Houghton, 1986. Matthews outlines three categories of information students can find in dictionaries; useful on inference.

McLeod, Susan H. "Cultural Literacy, Curricular Reform, and Freshman Composition." *Rhetoric Review* 8 (1990): 270–78. McLeod argues that students can move beyond personal experience in writing essays by reading scholarly materials and responding to them.

(continued on p. 160)

COMPUTER ACTIVITIES

WEB THREADS

Have students visit an online discussion group and follow a "thread" of conversation. Ask them to list some of the assumptions made by individual writers, make inferences about those writers' beliefs, and then evaluate whether or not most of the participants seem to share those beliefs.

NETWORKED INFERENCES

Having students summarize and draw inferences from one another's work can be a useful exercise for both reader and writer. Have students work in pairs (either on the computer or on printed copy) to summarize, then practice reasonable and deliberately faulty inferences of passages from each other's work. In each case, the writer of the passage can argue for his or her intention in writing the passage and evaluate the effectiveness of the summary, while the reader can point to evidence or lack of evidence for the inference. Particularly in a networked classroom, each student pair can send two passages with attached summary and inferences to another group for evaluation, and/or the instructor can post one or two examples for the entire class.

Mirskin, Jerry. "Writing as a Process of Valuing." *College Composition and Communication* 46 (1995): 387–410. Mirskin argues that because values shape meaning, teachers must learn to recognize students' systems of value in order to best help them make meaningful connections within an academic environment.

Nelson, Jennie. "Reading Classrooms as Text: Exploring Student Writers' Interpretive Practices." *College Composition and Communication* 46 (1995): 411–429. Nelson examines four case studies to show students' strategies for reading and responding to assignments, grading practices, and teacher comments.

Odell, Lee. "Strategy and Surprise in the Making of Meaning." In *Theory and Practice in the Teaching of Writing: Rethinking the Discipline.* Ed. Lee Odell. Carbondale: Southern Illinois UP, 1993. 213–243. This essay explores the debates over fostering spontaneity and intuitive insights in the teaching of writing as opposed to teaching conscious control, and identifies several approaches that work to do both.

Qualley, Donna. "Using Reading in the Writing Classroom." In *Nuts and Bolts: A Practical Guide to Teaching College Composition.* Ed. Thomas Newkirk. Portsmouth: Boynton, 1993. Qualley lays out strategies for integrating critical reading and writing using journals, reading conferences, and small group discussions.

Robertson, Julie Fisher, and Donna Rane Szotstak. "Using Dialogues to Develop Critical Thinking Skills: A Practical Approach." *Journal of Adolescent and Adult Literacy* 39 (April 1996): 552–56. Robertson and Szotstak describe how students can write, analyze, and perform dialogues in order to develop critical thinking skills.

Shaughnessy, Mina. *Errors and Expectations: A Guide for the Teacher of Basic Writing.* New York: Oxford UP, 1977. This pathbreaking study of the challenges faced by basic writers reveals the connections between student error and issues of critical thinking.

Shor, Ira. *Empowering Education: Critical Teaching for Social Change.* Chicago: U of Chicago P, 1992. Shor promotes critical thinking as a part of a pedagogy designed to empower students and citizens.

Tierney, Robert J., John E. Readence, and Ernest K. Dishner, eds. *Reading Strategies and Practices: A Compendium,* 3rd ed. Boston: Allyn and Bacon, 1990. This textbook approach to reading offers a number of exercises and work-

Though pervasive, assumptions are not always stated outright. Speakers and writers may judge that their audience already understands and accepts their assumptions; they may not even be aware of their assumptions; or they may deliberately refrain from stating their assumptions for fear that the audience will disagree. That is why your job as a critical thinker is to interpret what the assumptions are.

Reasonable inferences

Like an author deciding what to say in an article, the publishers of *People* magazine make assumptions that guide their selection of content for the magazine. One set of assumptions, perhaps the most important, concerns what readers want to see: as a for-profit enterprise, the magazine naturally aims to maintain and even expand its readership (currently about 3.4 million each week). If your analysis of the magazine's editorial material reveals that much of it features consumer products, you might infer the following:

Reasonable   **The publishers of *People* assume that the magazine's readers are consumers who want to see and hear about goods and entertainment.**

Nowhere in *People* will you find a statement of this assumption, but the evidence implies it.

Similarly, Thomas Sowell's "Student Loans" (pp. 155–56) is based on certain assumptions, some obvious, some not so obvious. If you were analyzing Sowell's attitude toward politicians, as suggested earlier, you would focus on his statements about them. Sowell says that they "disregard the first lesson of economics" (paragraph 2), which implies that they ignore important principles (knowing that Sowell is an economist himself makes this a reasonable assumption on your part). Sowell also says that politicians "rob Peter to pay Paul," are "[b]ursting with compassion," "do not admit . . . a dumb idea," are characters in a "long-running saga," and arrive at the solution of spending taxes "as the night follows the day"—that is, inevitably (paragraphs 2–4). From these statements and others, you can infer the following:

Reasonable   **Sowell assumes that politicians become compassionate when a cause is loud and popular, not necessarily just, and they act irresponsibly by trying to solve the problem with other people's (taxpayers') money.**

Unreasonable inferences

Interpreting assumptions gives you greater insight into an author's intentions. But it's crucial that inferences fit the evidence of the text, as those above about *People* and Sowell's essay do. Sometimes it's tempting to read too much into the text, as in the next examples:

| Faulty | *People*'s publishers deliberately skew the magazine's editorial material to promote products on which they receive kickbacks. [The inference is far-fetched, even absurd. It would be reasonable only if there were hard evidence of kickbacks.] |
| Faulty | Sowell thinks that politicians should not be entrusted with running the country. [The inference misreads Sowell. Although he does not outline a solution for politicians' irresponsibility, there's no evidence that he would overhaul our democratic political system.] |

Faulty inferences like these are often based on the reader's *own* assumptions about the text or its subject. When thinking and reading critically, you need to look hard at *your* ideas, too.

■ Synthesizing

If you stopped at analysis and interpretation, critical thinking and reading might leave you with a pile of elements and possible meanings but no vision of the whole. With **synthesis** you make connections among parts *or* among wholes. You create a new whole by drawing conclusions about relationships and implications.

The following conclusion pulls together the earlier analysis of *People* magazine's editorial content and the interpretation of the publisher's assumptions about readers:

| Conclusion | *People* magazine appeals to its readers' urge to consume by displaying, discussing, and glamorizing consumer goods. |

The statement below about Thomas Sowell's essay "Student Loans" connects his assumptions about politicians to a larger idea also implied by the essay:

| Conclusion | Sowell's view that politicians are irresponsible with taxpayers' money reflects his overall opinion that the laws of economics, not politics, should drive government. |

Synthesis may involve working within the text, as in the preceding examples, or it may take you outside the text to the surroundings. (This emphasis is important in research writing, as discussed on pp. 610–11.) The following questions can help you investigate the context of a work:

- **How does the work compare with works by others?** For instance, how does *People*'s juxtaposition of articles and advertisements compare with that in similar magazines, such as *Us Weekly, Entertainment Weekly,* and *Interview*? Or how have other writers responded to Sowell's views on student loans?
- **How does the work fit into the context of other works by the same author or group?** What distinguishes *People* from the

sheets that help to focus students on particular aspects of the reading process.

Toulmin, Stephen, Richard Rieke, and Allan Janik. *An Introduction to Reasoning*, 2nd ed. New York: Macmillan, 1984. Toulmin et al. detail the reasoning processes involved in making claims, supplying evidential backing, and preparing for rebuttal.

Tripp, Ellen L. "Speak, Listen, Analyze, Respond: Problem-Solving Conferences." *Teaching English in the Two-Year College* 17 (1990): 183–86. Tripp suggests collaborative and individual activities to be completed before students write final papers proposing solutions.

Wiley, Mark. "How to Read a Book: Reflections on the Ethics of Book Reviewing." *Journal of Advanced Composition* 13 (1993): 477–92. Wiley discusses communities of inquiry and why we grant some readers more authority over texts than others.

On writing and critical reading

Berrent, Howard I. "Open to Suggestion: OH RATS—A Note-taking Technique." *Journal of Reading* 27 (1984): 548–50. This essay outlines a useful note-taking strategy to complement critical reading.

Berthoff, Ann E. "A Curious Triangle and the Double-Entry Notebook: Or, How Theory Can Help Us Teach Reading and Writing." *The Making of Meaning: Metaphors, Models, and Maxims for Writing Teachers*. Upper Montclair: Boynton/Cook, 1981. Berthoff shows how use of a double-entry journal can help students improve critical reading skills.

Emig, Janet. "Writing as a Mode of Learning." *College Composition and Communication* 28 (1977): 122–28. A seminal analysis of the ways in which writing facilitates mental processes like intuition, reformulation, and the construction of meaningful relationships between ideas.

Greene, Stuart, and John M. Ackerman. "Expanding the Constructivist Metaphor: A Rhetorical Perspective on Literary Research and Practice." *Review of Educational Research* 65 (Winter 1995): 383–420. This review essay evaluates a number of constructivist explanations of the relationship between reading and writing as a learning model.

Price, Gayle B. "A Case for a Modern Commonplace Book." *College Composition and Communication* 31 (1980): 175–82. Price suggests using classic techniques for commonplace books in conjunction with other journal activities.

Walsh, John A. "Circle Diagrams for Narrative Essays." *Journal of Reading* 32 (1989): 366–68. Use of a graphic technique of concentric circles (similar to Venn diagrams) helps students comprehend and analyze narrative events, relationships, and significance.

On discourse communities

Carter, Duncan. "Critical Thinking for Writers: Transferable Skills or Discipline-Specific Strategies?" *Composition Studies: Freshman English News* 21 (1993): 86–93. Carter explores the question of whether critical thinking skills are transferable across discourse communities.

Killingsworth, M. Jimmie. "Discourse Communities—Global and Local." *Rhetoric Review* 11 (Fall 1992): 110–22. Killingsworth makes readers aware that they are members of both kinds of communities, and he suggests ways to negotiate the bridge(s) between the two.

Morris, Barbara S. *Disciplinary Perspectives on Thinking and Writing.* Ann Arbor: U of Michigan English Composition Board, 1989. This essay collection demonstrates different modes of inquiry and acceptable responses among various disciplines.

Williams, James D., David Huntley, and Christine Hanks. *The Interdisciplinary Reader: A Collection of Student Writing.* New York: HarperCollins, 1992. The editors provide a collection of student essays from various disciplines, accompanied by critiques of their effectiveness in writing critically for particular discourse communities.

On summaries

Carella, Michael J. "Philosophy as Literacy: Teaching College Students to Read Critically and Write Cogently." *College Composition and Communication* 34 (1983): 57–61. Carella argues that students can be taught not only to summarize complex arguments but to respond critically to them.

Lambert, Judith R. "Summaries: A Focus for Basic Writers." *Journal of Developmental Education* 8 (1984): 10+. Lambert reviews advantages of teaching students to summarize.

Sherrard, Carol. "Summary Writing: A Topographical Study." *Written Communication* 3 (1986): 324–43. Sherrard shows that assigning longer summaries forces students to use their own words instead of copying from the source.

many other magazines published by Time Inc., such as *Time* magazine, *Sports Illustrated, Family Circle,* and *Fortune*? How do Sowell's views on student loans typify, or not, the author's other writings on political and economic issues?

- **What cultural, economic, or political forces influence the work?** Why, for instance, are *People* and other celebrity magazines increasingly popular with readers? What other examples might Sowell have given to illustrate his view that economics, not politics, should determine government spending?
- **What historical forces influence the work?** What changes does *People* reflect in the ways readers choose magazines? How has the indebtedness of college students changed over the past four decades?

To create links among the elements of a work or between a work and its context, it helps (again) to write while reading and thinking. The active reading recommended earlier is the place to start, as you note your questions and opinions about the text. You can also create connections with a combination of writing and drawing: start with your notes, expand them as needed to take account of context, and draw connections between related thoughts with lines and arrows. (On a word processor you can use the Highlight function or different colors to link related ideas, or use the Comment function to annotate connections.) You want to open up your thinking, so experiment freely.

With synthesis, you create something different from what you started with. To the supermarket shopper reading *People* while standing in line, the magazine may be entertaining and inconsequential. To you—after a critical reading in which you analyze, interpret, and synthesize—the magazine is (at least in part) a significant vehicle of our consumer culture. The difference depends entirely on the critical reading.

■ Evaluating

Many critical reading and writing assignments end at analysis, interpretation, and synthesis: you explain your understanding of what the author says and doesn't say. Only if you are expected to **evaluate** the work will you state and defend the judgments you've made about its quality and its significance.

You'll inevitably form judgments while reading the work: *What a striking series of images* or *That just isn't enough evidence.* In evaluating, you collect your judgments, determine that they are generally applicable and are themselves not trivial, and turn them into assertions: *The poet creates fresh, intensely vivid images. The author does not summon the evidence to support his case.* And you support these statements with citations from the text.

Evaluation takes a certain amount of confidence. You may think that you lack the expertise to cast judgment on another's writing, especially if the text is difficult or the author well known. True, the more informed you are, the better a critical reader you are. But conscientious reading and analysis will give you the internal authority to judge a work *as it stands* and *as it seems to you*, against your own unique bundle of experiences, observations, and attitudes.

The box below gives questions that can help you evaluate many kinds of works. There's more on evaluation (including evaluation of online sources) on pages 599–609. For arguments and in academic disciplines, you'll require additional, more specific criteria. See Chapters 9, 11, and 49–53.

Guidelines for evaluation

- **What are your reactions to the work?** What in the work are you responding to?
- **How sound are the work's central idea and evidence?**
- **How well does the author achieve his or her purpose?** How worthwhile is the purpose?
- **How authoritative, trustworthy, and sincere is the author?**
- **How unified and coherent is the work?** Do its parts all support a central idea and clearly relate to one another?
- **What do color, graphics, or (online) sound or video contribute to the work?** Do such elements add meaning or merely decoration?
- **What is the overall quality and significance of the work?**
- **Do you agree or disagree with the work?** Can you support, refute, or extend it?

You can download these guidelines from *ablongman.com/littlebrown*. Create a copy each time you're evaluating a work, and use the questions to prompt your written responses.

EXERCISE 8.3 Thinking critically

Following are some statements about the communications media. Use systematic critical thinking to understand not only what the statement says but also why its author might have said it. As in the example, do your thinking in writing: the act of writing will help you think, and your notes will help you discuss your ideas with your classmates. (You can do this exercise online at *ablongman.com/littlebrown*.)

Example:

Statement: Every year sees the disappearance of more book publishers because the larger companies gobble up the smaller ones.

Analysis: Why did the author make this statement? Certain words reveal the author's purpose: *disappearance of <u>more</u> book publishers; because; larger companies <u>gobble up</u> smaller ones.*

ANSWERS: EXERCISE 8.3

Possible answers

1. *Analysis:* What is the basis for the author's comparison of print and televised journalism? The key words are *demand reading, not just viewing.*

    Interpretation: Are better . . . than implies a value judgment. *Demand reading, not just viewing* reveals the author's assumption that viewing is somehow less worthy than reading, perhaps because viewing is more passive.

    Synthesis: This author prefers print journalism and disparages television journalism because of the different activities needed to partake of them.

    Evaluation: This statement shows the author's bias in favor of written news and implies some contempt for TV news. The author's reasons for preferring reading over viewing are not evident and require explanation. Some other questions: Are people who get their news from TV less well-informed than those who get it from reading? Even if television news is inferior, isn't it better than no news at all (for those who won't or can't read)? Might television news be preferable for its immediacy?

2. *Analysis:* What is the author's purpose? The key words are *true, democratic, giving voice to,* and *people of all persuasions.*

    Interpretation: Democratic means "of or for the people." *True democratic forum* means that there are competing, perhaps misleading, forums. *Giving voice to people* appeals to a sense of fair play and belief in free speech, while *all persuasions* implies open-mindedness. The author assumes that people need a public forum where they can voice their opinions. Because it is immediate, radio gives people the freedom to say what they want. Other forums may censor or restrict who can say what.

Synthesis: The writer values radio call-in shows for affording all kinds of people a chance to express themselves without censorship.

Evaluation: This writer evidently believes that radio is somehow freer than other places for people to speak their minds. What other forums for free speech are there? Does radio censor or alter the opinions expressed? (What about the time delays for objectionable language?) Are "people of all persuasions" really calling such shows, or just some kinds of people? Are unedited, inexpert opinions a democratic necessity?

3. *Analysis:* What is the author's attitude toward online communication? The key words are *threaten, undermine, ability,* and *interact face to face.*

Interpretation: Threaten and *undermine* imply danger; *ability* and *interact face to face* imply that face-to-face communication is a kind of skill or talent. Together the words imply that the skill or talent is vulnerable, subject to some kind of destruction. The author's assumptions: Online and face-to-face communication are different. Face-to-face interaction has an intrinsic value. Online communication does not have this value. Communicating online diminishes this value.

Synthesis: The author believes that something valuable will be lost to online communication.

Evaluation: This statement indicates a preference for face-to-face interaction over online communication and a concern about the latter overwhelming the former. But what exactly is special about face-to-face interaction? What does it provide that online communication doesn't? Won't people continue to meet face to face even if they also communicate online? Will online communication necessarily undermine face-to-face interaction? Might online communication also contribute something positive of its own, adding to rather than subtracting from the ways people interact?

ANSWERS: EXERCISE 8.4

Individual response.

ANSWERS: EXERCISE 8.5

Individual response.

Interpretation: *More* book publishers means others have disappeared. *Because* specifies cause. *Gobble up* implies consumption, predator to prey. Author's assumptions: Large publishers behave like predators. The predatory behavior of large companies causes the disappearance of small companies. The more publishing companies there are, the better.

Synthesis: The author objects to the predatory behavior of large publishing companies, which he or she holds responsible for eliminating small companies and reducing the total number of companies.

Evaluation: This biased statement against large publishers holds them responsible for the shrinking number of book publishers. But are the large companies solely responsible? And why is the shrinking necessarily bad?

1. Newspapers and newsmagazines are better news sources than television because they demand reading, not just viewing.
2. Radio call-in shows are the true democratic forum, giving voice to people of all persuasions.
3. Online communication threatens to undermine our ability to interact face to face.

EXERCISE 8.4   Reading an essay critically

Reread Thomas Sowell's "Student Loans" (pp. 155–56) in order to form your own critical response to it. Follow the guidelines for analysis, interpretation, synthesis, and evaluation in the boxes on pages 158 and 163. Focus on any elements suggested by your question about the text: possibilities are assumptions, evidence, organization, use of language, tone, authority, vision of education or students. Be sure to write while reading and thinking; your notes will help your analysis and enhance your creativity, and they will be essential for writing about the selection (Exercise 8.10, p. 178).

EXERCISE 8.5   Reading a magazine critically

Do your own critical reading of *People* or another magazine. What do you see beyond the obvious? What questions does your reading raise? Let the guidelines on pages 158 and 163 direct your response, and do your work in writing.

8b   Viewing images critically

Every day we are bombarded with images—pictures on billboards, commercials on television, graphs and charts in newspapers and textbooks, to name just a few examples. Most images slide by without our noticing them, or so we think. But images, sometimes even more than text, can influence us covertly. Their creators have purposes, some worthy, some not, and understanding those purposes requires critical reading. The method parallels that in the previous section for reading text critically: write while reading, preview, read for comprehension, analyze, interpret, synthesize, and (often) evaluate.

1 Writing while reading an image

Writing as you read an image helps you view it deliberately and allows you to record your impressions precisely. If possible, print a copy of the image or scan it into your reading journal, and write your comments in the image margins or separately. The example on the next page shows how one student annotated an image he was reading.

2 Previewing an image

Your first step in exploring an image is to form initial impressions of the work's origin and purpose and to note distinctive features. This previewing process is like the one for previewing a text (p. 153):

Questions for previewing an image

- **What do you see?** What is most striking about the image? What is its subject? What is the gist of any text or symbols? What is the overall effect of the image?
- **What are the facts of publication?** Where did you first see the image? Do you think the image was created especially for that location or for others as well? What can you tell about when the image was created?
- **What do you know about the person or group that created the image?** For instance, was the creator an artist, scholar, news organization, or corporation? What seems to have been the creator's purpose?
- **What is your preliminary response?** What about the image interests, confuses, or disturbs you? Are the form, style, and subject familiar or unfamiliar? How might your knowledge, experiences, and values influence your reception of the image?

3 Reading an image

Reading an image requires the same level of concentration as reading a text. Plan to spend more than one session working with the image to absorb its meaning and purpose and then to analyze and maybe challenge its message.

Try to answer the following questions about the image. If some answers aren't clear at this point, skip the question until later.

- **What is the purpose of the image?** Is it mainly explanatory, conveying information, or is it argumentative, trying to convince readers of something or persuade them to act? What information or point of view does it seem intended to get across?

- **Who is the intended audience for the image?** What does the source of the image, including its publication facts, tell about the image creator's expectations for readers' knowledge, interests, and attitudes? What do the features of the image itself add to your impression?
- **What do any words or symbols add to the image?** Whether located on the image or outside it (such as in a caption), do words or symbols add information, focus your attention, or alter your impression of the image?
- **What people, places, things, or action does the image show?** Does the image tell a story? Do its characters or other features tap into your knowledge, or are they unfamiliar?
- **What is the form of the image?** Is it a photograph, advertisement, painting, graph, diagram, cartoon, or something else? How do its content and apparent purpose and audience relate to its form?

The following notes by a student, John Latner, illustrate the results of asking questions like those above. Reading an advertisement for *Time* magazine, Latner first annotated a copy of the image and then filled out his ideas in his reading journal.

Annotation of an image

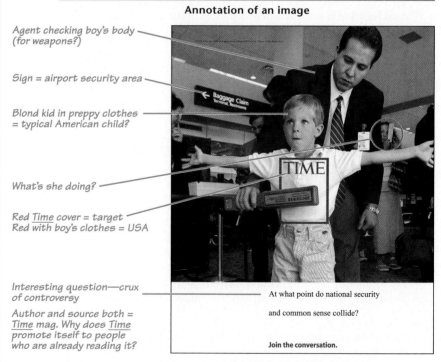

Agent checking boy's body (for weapons?)

Sign = airport security area

Blond kid in preppy clothes = typical American child?

What's she doing?

Red <u>Time</u> cover = target
Red with boy's clothes = USA

Interesting question—crux of controversy

Author and source both = <u>Time</u> mag. Why does <u>Time</u> promote itself to people who are already reading it?

At what point do national security and common sense collide?

Join the conversation.

Advertisement appearing in *Time* magazine, October 7, 2002

Image details	**Responses**
Red Time border positioned over boy's chest and around scanning wand	The framing of the wand makes this clearly a story about airport (and homeland) security, not about the boy or the guard.
Boy with blond hair and blue eyes, USA colors in clothes and Time border	The boy is a stereotyped all-American kid, almost doll-like. Most American kids don't look like this, though. How would the ad be different if the kid looked different?
Caption asking "At what point do national security and common sense collide?"	The position of the wand seems to imply that the point of collision is in the middle of the boy or maybe the moment when an innocent-looking kid is treated as a security threat. (But aren't there lots of kids throughout history who have become soldiers or were used by adults as weapons? Is it completely illogical to consider kids as potentially dangerous?) "Common sense" seems to mean taking things at face value. Is that the view of people who read Time? Wouldn't it be just the opposite—people buy the mag. because they know there's more to the story than meets the eye? Confusing.

4 | Analyzing an image

■ Elements for analysis

As when analyzing a written work, you analyze an image by identifying its elements. The image elements you might consider appear in the box below. Keep in mind that an image is a visual *composition* whose every element likely reflects a deliberate effort to communicate. Still, few images include all the elements, and you can narrow the list further by posing a question about the image you are reading, as illustrated on the next page.

Elements of images

- **Emphasis:** Most images pull your eyes to certain features: a graph line moving sharply upward, a provocative figure, bright color, thick lines, light against shadow, and so on. The cropping of a photograph or, say, the date range in a chart will also reflect what the image creator considers most important.
- **Narration:** Most images tell stories, whether in a sequence (a TV commercial or a graph showing changes over time) or at a single moment (a photograph, a painting, or a pie chart). Sometimes dialog or a title or caption contributes to the story.

(continued)

SUGGESTED READINGS

George, Diana. "From Analysis to Design: Visual Communication in the Teaching of Writing." *College Composition and Communication* 54 (2002): 11–39. Excellent explanation of how instruction in visual literacy can inform the composition curriculum.

Soleil, Naome. "Reflective Reading: A Study in (Tele)literacy." *Journal of College Reading and Learning* 30 (Fall 1999): 5–16. Soleil shows how a reflective reading of television texts can provide a bridge to link oracy and literacy.

TRANSPARENCY MASTER 8.5

COMPARING IMAGES

To give students practice in analyzing elements of images, give them several images and ask them to compare a single element in all the images. By focusing on one element at a time, you can help students develop their ability to analyze that element. You could also ask them to find examples of images that have a distinctive use of an element, such as an image with an unusual point of view, a compelling narration, or a good use of tension or allusion.

Elements of images
(continued)

- **Point of view:** The image creator influences responses by taking account of both the viewer's physical relation to the image subject—for instance, whether it is seen head-on or from above—and the viewer's assumed attitude toward the subject.
- **Arrangement:** Patterns among colors or forms, figures in the foreground and background, and elements that are juxtaposed or set apart contribute to the image's meaning and effect.
- **Color:** An image's colors can direct the viewer's attention and convey the creator's attitude toward the subject. Color may also suggest a mood, an era, a cultural connection, or another frame for viewing the image.
- **Characterization:** The figures and objects in an image have certain qualities—sympathetic or not, desirable or not, and so on. Their characteristics reflect the roles they play in the image's story.
- **Context:** The source of an image or the background in an image affects its meaning, whether it is a graph from a scholarly journal or a photo of a car on a sunny beach.
- **Tension:** Images often communicate a problem or seize attention with features that seem wrong, such as misspelled or misaligned words, distorted figures, or controversial relations between characters.
- **Allusions:** An **allusion** is a reference to something the audience is likely to recognize and respond to. Examples include a cultural symbol such as a dollar sign, a mythological figure such as a unicorn, or a familiar movie character such as Darth Vader from *Star Wars*.

▪ Question for analysis

As discussed on pages 158–59, you can focus your analysis of elements by framing your main interest in the image as a question. John Latner concentrated his analysis of the *Time* ad with the question *Does the ad challenge readers to view airport security differently, or does it just reinforce common perceptions?* The question led Latner to focus on certain elements of the ad and to ignore others, as seen in the following entry from his reading journal:

Image elements	Responses
Emphasis	The ad foregrounds the boy (especially his eyes looking upward), the security agent, and the familiar Time cover over a scanner like a target around a bull's-eye.
Point of view	We identify with the boy—so innocent and uncomfortable. We identify even more because we're positioned at his eye level. The security agent almost hovers over us, too.

Narration	The collision point of the caption ("At what point do national security and common sense collide?") seems to be the bull's-eye of the scanning wand—treating a boy as a security threat. The ad's commonsense opinion seems to be that airport security procedures are flawed, unfair. But the caption's question mark and "Join the conversation" imply that there may be other views, too.
Color	The boy is much the brightest figure in the image, and his brightness emphasizes his fairness. His clothes are in patriotic colors (white shirt, blue and white pants, red tag on the pants). The Time cover adds more red to the flag colors.
Allusions	The familiar Time cover and the security checkpoint stand out. Also, is there Christian symbolism in the boy's outstretched arms, open hands, and upward gaze—like Christ on the cross?
Characterization	The boy plays the role of unlikely terrorist, maybe even a victim. He is the stereotyped all-American kid, blond, blue-eyed, wholesome. The security agent is the boy's "interrogator"—serious, dark, even menacing.
Tension	The security agent hovering over the boy is disturbing. So are what they're doing and the whole busy scene behind them—bound to evoke a negative response from anyone who's experienced air travel in recent years.

▨ Sample images for analysis

The following images give you a chance to analyze selective elements in two kinds of images, a painting and a Web page. Questions in the annotations can help to open up your thinking.

Elements in a painting

Emphasis: What does light emphasize? Where does the painting guide your eyes next, and how?

Narration: What story does the painting tell? How does it tell the story?

Color: What mood do the colors create? How do they relate to the subject?

Characterization: What role does the central figure play in the story? What other characters can you identify?

Tension: What elements are unexpected, even disturbing?

Liberty's Children, 2002, painting by Ron Oden

COMPUTER ACTIVITIES

VIEWS OF THE WEB

The Web, so abundant in visual images, is an ideal place to practice critical viewing. You can create a guided tour for your students through some choice Web pages. As they follow the links in order, students can answer worksheet questions or just record their interpretations of the images they see.

PERSONAL WEB PAGES

Some of your students may have their own Web pages with graphics or other visual images. Ask for volunteers to have their Web pages viewed and evaluated by the rest of the class. Alternatively, if your students are building their own Web pages, you can ask them to experiment with images and try them out on their classmates.

CLAIMS AND EVIDENCE

These examples of reasonable and faulty inferences should be familiar to students who have been writing thesis and topic sentence claims supported by evidence. Some students may be adept at interpreting images but less so at interpreting the written word. If so, have them practice first on images. If they can understand how to draw reasonable inferences from an image, they may be able to apply that understanding to interpretations of written texts.

Elements of a Web page

Narration: What story is being told by the Web page as a whole and by the chart? Who is telling the story, and why?

Arrangement: How are the bars in the chart organized? What does their arrangement contribute to the story?

Point of view: What can you tell about the intended audience? What is the audience's interest in the story?

Context: How do the CNN source and the page's banner and titles affect the story being told by the chart?

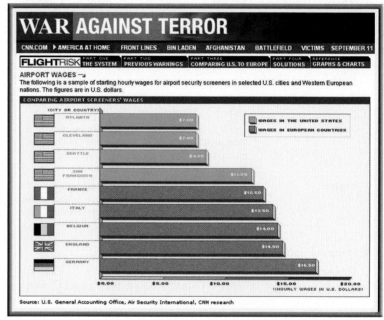

Web page from *CNN.com*, 2001

5 Interpreting an image

The strategies for interpreting an image parallel those for interpreting a written text (pp. 159–61). In this process you look more deeply at the elements, considering them in relation to the image creator's likely assumptions and intentions. You aim to draw reasonable inferences about *why* the image looks as it does. Here's a reasonable inference about the *Time* advertisement on page 166:

Reasonable The creators of the *Time* ad assume that the magazine's readers are concerned about both national security and the treatment of air travelers.

This inference is supported by the ad's text and photograph: the caption specifically mentions national security, and the photograph clearly emphasizes the experience of air travelers. In contrast, the next inference is *not* reasonable because it leaps to a conclusion that is not supported by the ad:

Faulty   The creators of the *Time* ad assume that the magazine's readers believe airport security checkpoints are unnecessary.

The ad implies that readers may object to some checkpoint procedures, not that they believe the checkpoints themselves are unnecessary.

6 Synthesizing ideas about an image

As discussed on pages 161–62, with synthesis you take analysis and interpretation a step further to consider how a work's elements and underlying assumptions mesh: How do the elements and assumptions relate to one another? What is the overall message of the image? You may also expand your synthesis to view the whole image in a larger context: How does the work compare with works by others? How does the work fit into the context of other works by the same author or group? What cultural, economic, political, or historical forces influence the work?

Placing an image in its context often requires research. For instance, to learn more about the assumptions underlying the *Time* advertisement, John Latner investigated data on the backgrounds and perceptions of the magazine's readers. And to understand the marketing strategies at work in the image, he consulted a book on advertising campaigns that, like the *Time* ad, promote products to people who already use them. The following entry from his reading journal shows the ideas resulting from his synthesis:

Social and political context
The emphasis on the boy plays to two views often held by travelers and Time readers: airport searches needlessly inconvenience people who are highly unlikely to be terrorists, and the better alternative may be profiling, treating people differently on the basis of physical characteristics such as skin and hair color.

"Common sense"
The ad implies certain understandings of readers' "common sense" about national security and airport security: security is a serious issue, many airport procedures are unreasonably broad based and time consuming, and profiling might be used to focus on people who look like terrorists. The ad doesn't challenge these perceptions, but with "Join the conversation" it does suggest that the problem is open to interpretation.

Marketing context
The provocative photograph seems to promise an unconventional perspective on the subject, but the ad mostly reinforces the views assumed to be held by readers. Time's strategy reflects marketing studies: people are more likely to purchase a product that reflects their own opinions and values, even when they're acquiring it to broaden their understanding.

RESOURCES AND IDEAS

Zeller, Robert. "Developing the Inferential Reasoning of Basic Writers." *College Composition and Communication* 38 (1987): 343–46. Zeller suggests that asking students to make connections between visual prompts like photographs and writing helps their critical thinking skills.

7　Evaluating an image

If your critical reading moves on to evaluation, you'll form judgments about the quality and significance of the image. Questions to ask for evaluation appear in the box on page 163. Briefly: Is the message of the image accurate and fair, or is it distorted and biased? Can you support, refute, or extend the message? Does the image achieve its apparent purpose, and is the purpose worthwhile? How does the image affect you?

See John Latner's paper on pages 175–77 for an evaluation of the *Time* advertisement.

EXERCISE 8.6　Viewing an image critically

Review the list of visual elements on pages 167–68 and then take another close look at the *Time* advertisement on page 166. Using the guidelines on the preceding pages, draw your own conclusions about the ad. Write while reading and thinking to help yourself concentrate and develop ideas. A writing suggestion based on this activity appears in Exercise 8.11, page 178.

EXERCISE 8.7　Viewing an image critically

Select either the painting *Liberty's Children* (p. 169) or the CNN Web page (p. 170) to examine in more detail. Using the guidelines on the preceding pages, read the image methodically and critically. Write down your ideas. A writing suggestion based on this activity appears in Exercise 8.12, page 178.

EXERCISE 8.8　Comparing images critically

Each image in this section—the advertisement, the painting, and the Web page—communicates a perspective on the causes or effects of terrorism in the United States. Using the guidelines on the preceding pages, read these three images as a group, focusing on the story they tell together and on their relative effectiveness in contributing to that story. Write down your responses. A writing suggestion based on this activity appears in Exercise 8.13, page 178.

8c　Writing critically

Critical writing, often called *critique*, is largely influenced by the discipline or profession in which it occurs. Thus the topic is covered more extensively in Chapters 10–11 (argument), 50 (literature), 51 (other humanities), 52 (social sciences), and 53 (natural and applied sciences). In this introduction, we'll look at two illustrations, one on a written work and the other on an image.

Note Critical writing is *not* summarizing. You may write a summary to clarify for yourself what an author says or what an image shows, and you may briefly summarize a work in your own larger piece of writing. But your job in critical writing is not just to report; it is to transmit your analysis, interpretation, synthesis, and perhaps evaluation of the text.

1 Writing critically about a text

The following essay by the student Charlene Robinson responds to Thomas Sowell's "Student Loans." Robinson arrived at her response through the process of critical reading outlined in this chapter and then by gathering and organizing her ideas, developing her own central idea (or thesis) about Sowell's text, and drafting and revising until she believed she had supported her central idea.

Robinson does not assume that her readers see the same things in Sowell's essay or share her views, so she offers evidence of Sowell's ideas in the form of direct quotations, summaries, and paraphrases (restatements in her own words). (See pp. 617–22 for more on these techniques.) Robinson then documents these borrowings from Sowell using the style of the Modern Language Association (MLA): the numbers in parentheses are page numbers in the book containing Sowell's essay, listed at the end as a "work cited." (See Chapter 47 for more on MLA style.)

Weighing the Costs

In his essay "Student Loans," the economist Thomas Sowell challenges the US government's student-loan program for several reasons: a scarce resource (taxpayers' money) goes to many undeserving students, a high number of recipients fail to repay their loans, and the easy availability of money has led to both lower academic standards and higher college tuitions. Sowell wants his readers to "weigh the costs of things" (133) in order to see, as he does, that the loan program should not receive so much government funding. But does he provide the evidence of cost and other problems to lead the reader to agree with him? The answer is no, because hard evidence is less common than debatable and unsupported assumptions about students, scarcity, and the value of education.

Sowell's portrait of student-loan recipients is questionable. It is based on averages, some statistical and some not, but averages are often deceptive. For example, Sowell cites college graduates' low average debt of $7,000 to $9,000 (131) without acknowledging the fact that many students' debt is much higher or giving the full range of statistics. Similarly, Sowell dismisses "heart-rending stories" of "the low-income student with a

Annotations (right of essay):
- Introduction
- Summary of Sowell's essay
- Robinson's critical question
- Thesis statement
- First main point
- Evidence for first point: paraphrases and quotations from Sowell's text

POLLING STUDENTS

Have each student solicit critical responses to Sowell's article from their roommates or friends. Then have students work in pairs to compare the responses of their friends to that of Robinson. This exercise will help students get a sense of the range of responses a written argument can engender.

MODELS OF STUDENT WRITING

Charlene Robinson essay

Charlene Robinson's essay is an excellent example of critical writing, combining a well-developed critique with good organization, effective transitions, and balanced tone. Particularly if they are not strong writers, your students may feel that their own efforts (in Exercises 8.4 and 8.10) do not measure up. In order to emphasize for your students that Robinson's approach is but one possible way of critiquing Sowell, you might want to spend some time as a class developing alternative critiques. For instance, you might point out to your students that Robinson does not provide statistical evidence of her own, and ask them to test her assertions by doing some further research on student loans.

ILLUSTRATED ARGUMENTS

Ask your students to find or create a visual image (photograph, graphic, drawing, etc.) that could accompany Robinson's essay. They can compare the image they chose with members of their small group, and this could prompt discussion of the different merits of written and visual critiques.

SUMMARY TO ARGUMENT

On your class Web site or through e-mail, post a summary of a course reading of your choice. Then ask students to begin the process of converting the summary to a written critical response. They can begin with some online discussion and then propose arguments that would form the basis of a response essay.

huge debt" as "not at all typical" (132), yet he invents his own exaggerated version of the typical loan recipient: an affluent slacker ("Rockefellers" and "Vanderbilts") for whom college is a "place to hang out for a few years" sponging off the government, while his or her parents clear a profit from making use of the loan program (132). Although such students (and parents) may well exist, are they really typical? Sowell does not offer any data one way or the other—for instance, how many loan recipients come from each income group, what percentage of loan funds go to each group, how many loan recipients receive significant help from their parents, and how many receive none.

Evidence for first point: Sowell's omissions

Another set of assumptions in the essay has to do with "scarcity": "There is never enough of anything to fully satisfy all those who want it," Sowell says (131). This statement appeals to readers' common sense, but does the "lesson" of scarcity necessarily apply to the student-loan program? Sowell omits many important figures needed to prove that the nation's resources are too scarce to support the program, such as the total cost of the program, its percentage of the total education budget and the total federal budget, and its cost compared to the cost of defense, Medicare, and other expensive programs. Moreover, Sowell does not mention the interest paid by loan recipients, even though the interest must offset some of the costs of running the program and covering unpaid loans.

Transition to second main point

Second main point

Evidence for second point: Sowell's omissions

The most fundamental and most debatable assumption underlying Sowell's essay is that higher education is a kind of commodity that not everyone is entitled to. In order to diminish the importance of graduates' average debt from education loans, Sowell claims that a car loan will probably be higher (131). This comparison between education and an automobile implies that the two are somehow equal as products and that an affordable higher education is no more a right than a new car is. Sowell also condemns the "irresponsible" students who drop out of school and "the increasingly easy availability of college to people who are not very serious about getting an education" (132). But he overlooks the value of encouraging education, including education of those who don't finish college or who aren't scholars. For many in the United States, education has a greater value than that of a mere commodity like a car. And even from an economic perspective such as Sowell's, the cost to society of an uneducated public needs to be taken into account.

Third main point

Evidence for third point: paraphrases and quotations of Sowell's text

Sowell writes with conviction, and his concerns are valid: high taxes, waste, unfairness, declining educational standards, obtrusive government. However, the essay's flaws make it unlikely that Sowell could convince

Conclusion

Acknowledgment of Sowell's concerns

readers who do not already agree with him. He does not support his portrait of the typical loan recipient, he fails to demonstrate a lack of resources for the loan program, and he neglects the special nature of education compared to other services and products. Sowell may have the evidence to back up his assumptions, but by omitting it he himself does not truly weigh the costs of the loan program.

Work Cited

Sowell, Thomas. "Student Loans." Is Reality Optional? and Other Essays. Stanford: Hoover, 1993. 131-33.

—Charlene Robinson (student)

2 Writing critically about an image

The essay below, by the student John Latner, responds to the *Time* magazine advertisement. As you've seen earlier in this chapter, Latner examined the image over several stages, each time discovering more in it and gradually developing his own ideas. In his paper Latner takes pains to be sure that readers will see the image as he does: he reproduces the ad, captions it, and clearly describes its features. He cites his sources using the style of the Modern Language Association (Chapter 47). (All but one of Latner's text citations lack page numbers because the sources themselves are not numbered.)

Note An image is a source just as a written work is, and like a written source it must be acknowledged. Latner cites the *Time* ad both in the image caption and in the list of works cited. If he published his paper online, he would also need to seek the copyright owner's permission to use the image. See pages 633–34 for more about acknowledging sources and pages 635–37 for more about permissions for online publication.

Playing It Safe

At first glance, the "Boy at Security" advertisement for Time magazine (fig. 1) is both a humorous and a provocative depiction of a troubling subject: airport security since September 11, 2001. A boy with an angelic face and a nervous expression stands obediently as a security agent passes a large scanner over his chest. The familiar red border and banner of a Time cover surround the scanner, making it the bull's-eye of a target. The caption reads, "At what point do national security and common sense collide?" and then "Join the conversation." This eye-catching ad implies that by reading Time magazine consumers will gain alternative perspectives on important issues. However, a close examination of the ad reveals that it actually reinforces public opinion instead of challenging it.

RESOURCES AND IDEAS

Cheville, Julie. "Automated Scoring Technologies and the Rising Influence of Error." *English Journal* 93 (March 2004): 47–52. Cheville cautions that automated assessment can shape a writing curriculum that may benefit private industry but is at odds with current composition theory and research.

Herrington, Ann and Charles Moran. "What Happens When Machines Read Our Students' Writing?" *College English* 63 (March 2001): The authors are highly critical of software programs that claim they can grade students' essays accurately for both style and content.

Jones, Billie J. "Learning with, through and about Computers: Students' Best Friend or Worst Nightmare?" *Teaching English in the Two-Year College* 30 (2003): 286–95. The author reports on students' responses to her computer-based writing class, noting that some students were intimidated by computers while others thrived.

Koerber, Amy. "Toward a Feminist Rhetoric of Technology." *Journal of Business and Technical Communication* 14.1 (2000): 58–73. Koerber argues that the rhetoric of technology must evolve to account for feminist concerns, including the gender inequities that technology fosters.

Langer, Judith A. "Learning Through Writing: Study Skills in the Content Area." *Journal of Reading* 29 (1986): 400–06. Langer contends that students learn more effectively by writing full essays about their reading than by just taking notes or answering questions.

Lent, Robin. "'I Can Relate to That . . .': Reading and Responding in the Writing Classroom." *College Composition and Communication* 44 (1993): 232–40. Lent demonstrates how using short, informal response papers can deepen students' interpretations of assigned readings.

Moran, Charles. "Computers and Composition 1983–2002: What We Have Hoped For." *Computers and Composition* 20.4 (2003): 343–358. Moran provides a practical and comprehensive review of the literature on the question: Do computers improve student writing?

Salvatori, Mariolina. "Conversations with Texts: Reading in the Teaching of Composition." *College English* 58 (1996): 440–54. Salvatori

At what point do national security and common sense collide?

Join the conversation.

Caption giving the ad's main idea and source

Fig. 1. "Boy at Security," an advertisement appearing in Time magazine, promotes the magazine as a source of challenging views on current events. From Time 7 Oct. 2002: 42.

First main point

Evidence for first point: news article (Sharkey) and Latner's interpretation of image details

The awkward stance of the boy evokes the common complaint that airport security is intrusive and time consuming (Sharkey). This attitude is encouraged by the cropping of the photograph, which puts the boy at our eye level (increasing our empathy with him) and makes the looming security agent seem intimidating. As the agent does his work, the boy waits uncomfortably and travelers mill around in the background. The ad represents a travel experience that is familiar to the target audience: according to a recent survey, the typical Time reader is a white, middle-income adult who takes commercial flights at least yearly (Schulman, Ronca, and Bucuvalas).

Evidence for first point: survey of magazine's readers

Second main point

Evidence for second point: news article

Evidence for second point: Latner's interpretation of image details

The advertisement also taps into a dilemma and debate about airport security. Everyone wants terrorists stopped from boarding airplanes, but many people believe that security procedures go too far by treating all travelers as potential threats, even those who aren't the least bit suspicious (Sharkey). The boy in the ad is a most unlikely terrorist. Besides being quite young, he looks like the stereotype of the all-American child: blond, blue-eyed, neatly dressed in patriotic colors (white shirt and blue and white pants with a red tag). With such a figure at its center, the ad implies and appeals to a preference for profiling travelers—singling people out for suspicion solely because of nationality or physical traits such as skin and hair color. Judging from the public comments in the news media, many Americans, reluctantly or not, favor profiling over the discomfort and inconvenience caused by searching everyone.

Why would a news magazine print a seemingly provocative ad that actually does little more than appeal to beliefs that its readers already hold? An answer can be found in the research of marketing analyst Marc Gobe, who has found that customers prefer to build long-term relationships with companies that represent their views (32). The intended audience for the Time ad is people who are already reading the magazine. The ad attempts to reinforce the loyalty of these customers by flattering their eagerness for "conversation." The attention-getting image communicates a cutting-edge approach—something to make this magazine seem more interesting than its competitors—but the ad doesn't risk challenging and thus alienating readers.

Latner's critical question

Evidence for answer: findings of an analyst

Latner's interpretation of source and application to the image

If Time truly wanted to demonstrate that it offers rich and diverse opinions on airport security and other issues, it might have juxtaposed two different passengers receiving the same treatment: the seemingly innocent child and someone fitting the profile of a terrorist. Or, to challenge readers' assumptions, the existing photograph might have shown the boy looking defiantly into the camera, raising doubts about his innocence. Either image would have been more thought provoking, but at the risk of disturbing consumers instead of attracting them to the magazine. Ultimately, the Time advertisement achieves its apparent purpose because it creates the illusion of daring without actually taking readers outside their comfort zone.

Conclusion

Possible alternatives to ad's safe approach

Summary and restatement of thesis

Works Cited

List of works cited (in MLA style)

Gobe, Marc. Citizen Brand. New York: Allworth, 2002.

Schulman, Ronca, and Bucuvalas, Inc. "Time Magazine/SRBI—March 15-17, 2005, Survey." 18 Mar. 2005. 27 May 2005 <http://www.srbi.com/TimePoll-3-18-05b.pdf>.

Sharkey, Joe. "Pants and Profiling: Life on the Front Lines of Checkpoint Security at the Nation's Airports." New York Times on the Web 9 Jan. 2003. 20 May 2005 <http://travel2.nytimes.com/mem/travel/article-page.html?res=9D07E2DE1239>.

Time magazine. Advertisement. Time 7 Oct. 2002: 42.

—John Latner (student)

EXERCISE 8.9   Responding to critical writing

Read Charlene Robinson's and John Latner's essays carefully. Do you think the authors' critiques are accurate and fair? Are they perceptive? Do the authors provide enough evidence to convince you of their

examines the theoretical basis for the argument that critical reading and writing are linked learning activities.

Tuzi, Frank. "The Impact of E-feedback on the Revisions of L2 Writers in an Academic Writing Course." *Computers and Composition* 21.2 (2004): 217–235. Tuzi's study suggests that ESL students benefit more from electronic feedback than oral feedback.

Wilson, Smokey. "When Computers Come to English Class." *Teaching English in the Two-Year College* 27 (May 2000): 387–399. Wilson's study shows that students who took English in computer-based classrooms were more likely to pass the course and less likely to drop out compared to students in non–computer-based classrooms.

COLLABORATIVE LEARNING

Have students form a networked chatgroup (or work in small groups) to discuss the questions for Exercise 8.9 and come up with a number of responses to each question. Then ask each student to revise those responses individually into a brief essay. When students exchange the completed essays in their group they are often surprised by the varying interpretations developed by the individual essays.

If time and your classroom situation permit, you might put students into groups to compare their answers to these questions, and post the group's consensus on the class Web site so that students can compare their responses with those of their classmates. Encourage students to focus not only on points on which they agree but on their disagreements. Such differences of opinion indicate where their analytical frameworks and assumptions vary, even though they may consider themselves all part of the same "audience."

ANSWERS: EXERCISE 8.9

Individual response.

COLLABORATIVE LEARNING

Exercises 8.10 and 8.11 may be particularly difficult for students if their perspectives are similar to Charlene Robinson's or John Latner's. Beginning students especially may find it difficult to define a distinct perspective of their own in the face of a well-argued example they have just read. You might work with them as a group to brainstorm some alternative (but not too dissimilar) perspectives.

ANSWERS: EXERCISE 8.10

Individual response.

ANSWERS: EXERCISE 8.11

Individual response.

ANSWERS: EXERCISE 8.12

Individual response.

ANSWERS: EXERCISE 8.13

Individual response.

points? Do they miss anything you would have mentioned? Write your responses to one of the essays in a brief critique of your own. (You can do this exercise online at *ablongman.com/littlebrown*.)

EXERCISE 8.10   Writing critically about a text

Write an essay based on your own critical reading of Thomas Sowell's "Student Loans" (Exercise 8.4, p. 164). Your critique may be entirely different from Charlene Robinson's, or you may have developed some of the same points. If there are similarities, they should be expressed and supported in your own way, in the context of your own critical perspective.

EXERCISE 8.11   Writing critically about an image

Write an essay based on your own critical reading of the *Time* advertisement (Exercise 8.6, p. 172). Your critique may be entirely different from John Latner's, or you may have developed some of the same points. If there are similarities, they should be expressed and supported in your own way, in the context of your own critical perspective.

EXERCISE 8.12   Writing critically about an image

Write an essay based on your critical reading of the painting *Liberty's Children* or the CNN Web page (Exercise 8.7, p. 172).

EXERCISE 8.13   Writing critically about several images

Write an essay based on your critical reading and comparison of the three images in this chapter (Exercise 8.8, p. 172).

CHAPTER 9

Reading Arguments Critically

Argument is writing that attempts to open readers' minds to an opinion, change readers' own opinions, or move readers to action. A good argument is neither a cold exercise in logic nor an attempt to beat others into submission. It is a work of negotiation and problem solving in which both writer and reader search for the knowledge that will create common ground between them.

Of course, not all arguments are "good." Whether deliberately or not, some are unclear, incomplete, misleading, or downright false. The negotiation fails; the problem remains unsolved. This chapter will help you read written arguments critically, and the next chapter will help you write effective arguments. After that, in Chapter 11, you'll see how to read and use visual arguments.

CULTURE LANGUAGE The ways of reading and writing arguments described in this chapter and the next may be uncomfortable to you if your native culture approaches such writing differently. In some cultures, for example, a writer is expected to begin indirectly, to avoid asserting his or her opinion outright, or to establish a compromise rather than argue a position. In American academic and business settings, readers and writers look or aim for a well-articulated opinion, evidence gathered from many sources, and a direct and concise argument for the opinion.

9a Recognizing the elements of argument

Few arguments are an easy read. Most demand the attentive critical reading discussed in the previous chapter. (If you haven't read pp. 151–63, you should do so before continuing.) As a reader of argument, your purpose will almost always be the same: you'll want to know whether you should be convinced by the argument. This

> **http://www.ablongman.com/littlebrown** ▶
>
> Visit the companion Web site for more help and additional exercises on reading arguments critically.

mycomplab

Please visit MyCompLab at *www.mycomplab.com* for more on the writing process.

HIGHLIGHTS

This chapter presents a discussion of reading arguments critically. The first section describes the elements of arguments: assertions, evidence, and assumptions (9a). The next section offers techniques for testing assertions; for identifying fact, opinion, belief, and prejudice; and for looking at a writer's definition of terms, use of evidence, and appeals to beliefs or needs (9b). Discussions of weighing evidence, analyzing underlying assumptions, attending to language and tone, and judging reasonableness round out the first part of this chapter. Ways for students to recognize logical fallacies—various kinds of evasions and oversimplifications—constitute the second half of this chapter.

The need to read arguments critically is becoming ever more important as argumentation proliferates online. Web sites and online discussion groups are breeding grounds for arguments based on poor evidence, prejudice, or false authority. Exercises and teaching tips offer suggestions for helping students become more critical users of cyberspace.

This chapter assumes that students have read Chapter 8, "Forming a Critical Perspective," and are familiar with its terminology and research.

A WRITER'S PERSPECTIVE

> *A great many people think they are thinking when they are merely rearranging their prejudices.*
>
> —WILLIAM JAMES

COMPANION WEB SITE

See page IAE-52 for companion Web site content description.

COMPUTER ACTIVITIES

HIGHLIGHTING THE ELEMENTS

Create an electronic version of an assigned reading, or ask students to find an argument-based text of their own. Using the shading function of their word processor, students can highlight the elements of argument in the text, using different colors for claims, evidence, and assumptions.

MISSING ELEMENTS

On your class Web site or via e-mail, post an essay from which you have deleted necessary evidence. Then ask your students to insert comments into their copy of the essay where they think evidence is necessary, and send their commented versions back to you.

RESOURCES AND IDEAS

Bator, Paul. "Aristotelian and Rogerian Rhetoric." *College Composition and Communication* 31 (1980): 427–32. Bator describes the differences between the two schools of argument and helps students understand when each strategy is most appropriate.

Brent, Doug. "Young, Becker, and Pike's 'Rogerian' Rhetoric: A Twenty-Year Reassessment." *College English* 53 (1991): 452–66. Brent reassesses the usefulness of argument based on common views and values in a culturally diverse world.

Ferris, Dana R. "Rhetorical Strategies in Student Persuasive Writing: Differences Between Native and Non-native Speakers." *Research in the Teaching of English* 28 (1994): 45–65. Ferris analyzes sixty persuasive essays by first-year composition students to show the particular difficulties that nonnative speakers can encounter in formulating claims, using data, and anticipating counterarguments.

Katula, Richard A., and Richard W. Roth. "A Stock-Issues Approach to Writing Arguments." *College Composition and Communication* 31 (1980): 183–96. The authors use problem-solving strategies as ways to build arguments.

Maxley, John M. "Reinventing the Wheel or Teaching the Basics: College Writers' Knowledge of Argumentation." *Composition Studies:*

purpose focuses your attention on the elements that make an argument convincing, or not.

In a scheme adapted from the work of the British philosopher Stephen Toulmin, an argument has three main elements:

- **Claims:** positive statements that require support. In a written argument the central claim is stated outright in a **thesis statement** (see p. 27). This central claim is what the argument is about. For instance:

  In both its space and its equipment, the college's chemistry laboratory is outdated.

  Several minor claims, such as that the present equipment is inadequate, will contribute to the central assertion.

- **Evidence:** the facts, examples, expert opinions, and other information that support the claims. (Toulmin calls evidence *data* or *grounds*, terms that indicate both its specificity and its work as an argument's foundation.) Evidence to support the preceding claim might include the following:

  The present lab's age and square feet
  An inventory of equipment
  The testimony of chemistry professors

  Like the claims, the evidence is always stated outright.

- **Assumptions:** the writer's underlying (and often unstated) beliefs, opinions, principles, or inferences that tie the evidence to the claims. (Toulmin calls these assumptions *warrants:* they justify making the claims on the basis of the evidence provided.) For instance, the following assumption might connect the evidence of professors' testimony with the claim that a new lab is needed:

  Chemistry professors are the most capable of evaluating the present lab's quality.

In the following pages, we'll examine each of these elements along with several others: tone and language, reasonableness, and common errors in reasoning. Charlene Robinson's "Weighing the Costs" in the previous chapter (pp. 173–75) provides a good example of critically reading an argument for its claims, evidence, and assumptions.

9b Testing claims

The claims or assertions in an argument will likely be statements of opinion, fact, belief, or prejudice. It's important to distinguish between the kinds of statements and to analyze the definitions of terms.

Questions for critically reading an argument

- What **claims** does the writer make?
- What kinds and quality of **evidence** does the writer provide to support the claims?
- What **assumptions** underlie the argument, connecting evidence to claims?
- What is the writer's **tone?** How does the writer use **language?**
- Is the writer **reasonable?**
- Is the argument logical? Has the writer committed any **fallacies?**
- Are you convinced? Why or why not?

You can download these questions from *ablongman.com/littlebrown*. Create a copy for each argument you are reading, and use the questions to prompt your written responses.

1 Recognizing opinions

An **opinion** is a judgment based on facts and arguable on the basis of facts. Reasonable people could and probably do disagree over opinions, and they are potentially changeable: with more facts, a writer might change opinions partly or wholly.

The thesis statement of an effective argument is an opinion, often one of the following:

- **A claim about past or present reality:**

  In both its space and its equipment, the college's chemistry laboratory is outdated.

  Academic cheating increases with students' economic insecurity.

- **A claim of value:**

  The new room fees are unjustified given the condition of the dormitories.

  Computer music pirates undermine the system that encourages the very creation of music.

- **A recommendation for a course of action,** often a solution to a perceived problem:

  The college's outdated chemistry laboratory should be replaced incrementally over the next five years.

  Schools and businesses can help to resolve the region's traffic congestion by implementing car pools and rewarding participants.

The backbone of an argument consists of specific claims that support the thesis statement. These may be statements of opinion, too, or they may state facts or beliefs.

TRANSPARENCY MASTER 9.1

Freshman English News 21 (1993): 3–15. Maxley reviews various approaches to teaching argument, including the "Toulmin model," in an effort to identify the most effective strategies.

Rapkins, Angela A. "The Uses of Logic in the College Freshman English Classroom." *Activities to Promote Critical Thinking: Classroom Practices in Teaching English.* Urbana: NCTE, 1986. Rapkins argues that students should be introduced to logic early in the semester, even if writing arguments comes later.

Toulmin, Stephen, Richard Rieke, and Allan Janik. *An Introduction to Reasoning.* New York: Macmillan, 1979. This is a classic textbook exposition of reasoning.

COLLABORATIVE LEARNING

"STUMP THE CLASS" GAME SHOW

Students can benefit from lots of practice in distinguishing between facts, opinions, beliefs, and prejudices. Divide your class into two teams and give each team a set of statements. The team members have to decide on whether the statement is a fact, opinion, belief, or prejudice. The team that gets the most right answers in the shortest amount of time wins.

COMPUTER ACTIVITY

WEB CLAIMS

Ask students to locate and visit an online discussion group on an assigned topic (environmentalism, for instance) and follow a thread of conversation. Have them make a list of claims they find and then evaluate whether each claim is one of fact, opinion, belief, or prejudice. Students may find that opinion statements rely upon facts presented in earlier entries by other thread participants, so they should make sure to look beyond a single entry or writer for facts.

DEFINING ARGUMENT

Some students may need instruction on the technical meaning of argument, since their view of this rhetorical mode may include only vehement disagreement. Ask students to look up *argument* in various dictionaries and bring a number of definitions of this word to share with their group. Have them discuss how all come into play in persuasive writing.

COLLABORATIVE LEARNING

CUT AND PASTE

Ask groups of students to identify an issue, collect newspaper or magazine articles on it, and bring the articles to class (in photocopied form, if possible). Then ask them to work in groups to identify what the articles say on the different sides of the issue and to cut out the assertions and paste them in columns (or simply write them out) according to the particular perspective on the argument they represent.

ANALYZING ISSUES

Break students into groups to discuss a campus issue such as residential policies, parking arrangements, or library or computer services. The goal of students' discussion should be to identify the assertions and supporting evidence on each side of the argument. As each group reports back on their findings, list the assertions and evidence on the board so that students can distinguish fact from opinion and identify terms that need defining. If students know enough about issues of public policy (such as gun control, capital punishment, or nuclear disarmament), these topics, too, can be used for discussion.

Opinions do not make arguments by themselves. As a critical reader, you must satisfy yourself that the writer has specified the evidence for the opinions and that the assumptions linking claims and evidence are clear and believable.

2 Recognizing facts

A **fact** may be a verifiable statement—that is, one that can be proved as true:

> Last year tuition increased 16 percent.

Or it may be an inference from verifiable facts:

> Over their lifetimes, four-year college graduates earn almost twice as much as high school graduates.

A claim of fact does not work as the thesis of an argument. Although people often dispute facts, they are not fundamentally arguable because ultimately they can be verified. Facts have another important role in argument, providing crucial evidence for other claims (see p. 184).

3 Recognizing beliefs

A **belief** is a conviction based on cultural or personal faith, morality, or values:

> Abortion is legalized murder.
> Capital punishment is legalized murder.
> The primary goal of government should be to provide equality of opportunity for all.

Such statements are often called opinions because they express viewpoints, but they are not based on facts and other evidence. Since they cannot be disproved by facts or even contested on the basis of facts, they cannot serve as the central or supporting claims of an argument. Statements of belief do figure in argument, however: they can serve as a kind of evidence, and they often form the assumptions that link claims and evidence (see pp. 185 and 187–88).

4 Recognizing prejudices

One kind of assertion that has no place in argument is a **prejudice**, an opinion based on insufficient or unexamined evidence:

> Women are bad drivers.
> Fat people are jolly.
> Teenagers are irresponsible.

Unlike a belief, a prejudice is testable: it can be contested and disproved on the basis of facts. Very often, however, we form prejudices or accept them from others—parents, friends, the communications media—without questioning their meaning or testing their truth. Writers who display prejudice do not deserve the confidence and agreement of readers. Readers who accept prejudice are not thinking critically.

When reading arguments that appear online, you should be especially vigilant for claims of belief or prejudice that pose as considered opinions. Anyone with a computer and an Internet connection can post anything on the Internet, without passing it through an editorial screening like that undergone by books and articles in journals and magazines. The filtering of such material is entirely up to the reader.

5 Looking for defined terms

In any argument, but especially in arguments about abstract ideas, clear and consistent definition of terms is essential. In the following claim, the writer is not clear about what she means by the crucial term *justice*:

> Over the past few decades, justice has deteriorated so badly that it almost does not exist anymore.

The word *justice* is **abstract:** it does not refer to anything specific or concrete and in fact has varied meanings. (The five definitions in *The American Heritage Dictionary* include "the principle of moral rightness" and "the administration and procedure of law.") When the writer specifies her meaning, her assertion is much clearer:

> If by *justice* we mean treating people fairly, punishing those who commit crimes, and protecting the victims of those crimes, then justice has deteriorated badly over the past few decades.

Writers who use highly abstract words such as *justice, equality, success,* and *maturity* have a responsibility to define them. If the word is important to the argument, such a definition may take an entire paragraph. As a reader you have the obligation to evaluate the writer's definitions before you accept his or her assertions. (See pp. 93–94 for more on definition and a paragraph defining the abstract word *quality*.)

9c Weighing evidence

In argument, evidence demonstrates the validity of the writer's claims. If the evidence is inadequate or questionable, the claims are at best doubtful.

REASSEMBLING AN ARGUMENT

Select a short text that contains claims and evidence. Put each claim or item of evidence on a separate slip of paper and shuffle them. Give a set of randomized slips to each small group of students and ask them to sort the slips into two piles: one pile of claims and another of evidence. If they like, they can then try to match each claim with its appropriate supporting evidence.

COLLABORATIVE LEARNING

PEER REVIEW FOR UNDEFINED TERMS

Ask students to work with their peer review partner to identify abstract terms in their own essays. They can work collaboratively on creating or revising definitions for those key terms.

COMPUTER ACTIVITY

TERMS NEEDING DEFINITIONS

Ask students to go online to locate op-ed articles that contain abstract terms. If the author has provided the definition, the student can highlight the definition and insert a comment evaluating the usefulness of the definition. If the author has not defined the term, the student can propose a definition they think would be appropriate in context.

COLLABORATIVE LEARNING

EDITORIAL EVIDENCE

Distribute copies of newspaper editorials and ask students, in groups, to examine the evidence the editorials contain in order to (1) identify facts, statistics, examples, and expert opinions and (2) evaluate the evidence for accuracy, relevance, representativeness, adequacy, and reliability. Then ask the groups to compare the results of their analysis and evaluation.

COMPUTER ACTIVITY

FACT CHECKING

Students can locate a Web site (commercial, educational, or informational) that presents evidence and then go to an authoritative source to verify that the evidence is true and quoted accurately. Together, the class can start a collection of Web sites that present false or misleading evidence.

EXPERT OPINION?

A common variation of the expert opinion is a celebrity endorsement. Students should be asked to decide what various celebrities' credentials are for offering their opinions and why the persuaders thought celebrities were the best people to endorse their respective products.

1 Recognizing kinds of evidence

Writers draw on several kinds of evidence to support their claims.

Evidence for argument

- **Facts:** verifiable statements
- **Statistics:** facts expressed in numbers
- **Examples:** specific cases
- **Expert opinions:** the judgments of authorities
- **Appeals to readers' beliefs or needs**

■ Facts

Facts are statements whose truth can be verified or inferred (see p. 182). Facts employing numbers are **statistics:**

> Of those polled, 62 percent stated a preference for a flat tax.
>
> In 2005 there were 1,370,237 men and women on active duty in the US armed forces.
>
> The average American household consists of 2.58 persons.

Numbers may be implied:

> Earth is closer to the sun than Saturn is.
> The cost of medical care is rising.

Or a fact may involve no numbers at all:

> The city council adjourned without taking a vote.
> The President vetoed the bill.

■ Examples

Examples are specific instances of the point being made, including historical precedents and personal experiences. The passage below uses a personal narrative as partial support for the claim in the first sentence:

> Besides broadening students' knowledge, required courses can also introduce students to possible careers that they otherwise would have known nothing about. Somewhat reluctantly, I enrolled in a psychology course to satisfy the requirement for work in social science. But what I learned in the course about human behavior has led me to consider becoming a clinical psychologist instead of an engineer.

■ Expert opinions

Expert opinions are the judgments formed by authorities on the basis of their own examination of the facts. In the following passage the writer cites the opinion of an expert to support the claim in the first sentence:

> Despite the fact that affirmative action places some individuals at a disadvantage, it remains necessary to right the wrongs inflicted historically on whole groups of people. Howard Glickstein, a past director of the US Commission on Civil Rights, maintains that "it simply is not possible to achieve equality and fairness" unless the previous grounds for discrimination (such as sex, race, and national origin) are now considered as grounds for admission to schools and jobs (26).

As this passage illustrates, a citation of expert opinion should always refer the reader to the source, here indicated by author's name and the page number in parentheses, "(26)." Such a citation is also generally accompanied by a reference to the expert's credentials. See pages 626–27 and 637–38.

CULTURE LANGUAGE In some cultures a person with high standing in government, society, or organized religion may be considered an authority on many different subjects. In American academic and business settings, authority tends to derive from study, learning, and experience: the more knowledge a person can demonstrate about a subject, the more authority he or she has. See the next page on relevant evidence.

■ Appeals to beliefs or needs

An **appeal to beliefs or needs** asks readers to accept an assertion in part because they already accept it as true without evidence or because it coincides with their needs. Each of the following examples combines such an appeal (second sentence) with a summary of factual evidence (first sentence).

> Thus the chemistry laboratory is outdated in its equipment. In addition, its shabby, antiquated appearance shames the school, making it seem a second-rate institution. [Appeals to readers' belief that their school is or should be first-rate.]

> That police foot patrollers reduce crime has already been demonstrated. Such officers might also restore our sense that our neighborhoods are orderly, stable places. [Appeals to readers' need for order and stability.]

(For more on beliefs, see p. 182. For more on appeals to emotion, see pp. 208–09).

2 Judging the reliability of evidence

To support claims and convince readers, evidence must be reliable. The tests of reliability for appeals to readers' beliefs and needs are specific to the situation: whether they are appropriate for the argument and correctly gauge how readers actually feel (see p. 209).

ATTITUDES TOWARD SOURCES

The ideas that some sources are more authoritative than others and that part of the reader's job is to evaluate the accuracy and veracity of evidence may be counterintuitive to students from Asian or Middle Eastern countries. You may want to spend some time discussing your students' attitudes toward various kinds of sources.

SURVEYING PERSUASION

Assign students to keep track of all the persuasive communications they are exposed to in the course of one day and to share that list with their groups. (Examples may include advertisements, conversations, television programs, junk mail, songs on the radio, Internet ads, and so on.) Then ask each group to classify and weigh the kinds of evidence used to support each of these persuasive appeals. Which kinds are used most and least often?

With the other kinds of evidence, the standards are more general, applying to any argument.

Criteria for weighing evidence

- Is it **accurate**: trustworthy, exact, undistorted?
- Is it **relevant**: authoritative, pertinent, current?
- Is it **representative**: true to context?
- Is it **adequate**: plentiful, specific?

▨ Accuracy

Accurate evidence is true:

- **It is drawn from trustworthy sources.**
- **It is quoted exactly.**
- **It is presented with the original meaning undistorted.**

In an essay favoring gun control, a writer should not rely exclusively on procontrol sources, which are undoubtedly biased. Instead, the writer should also cite anticontrol sources (representing the opposite bias) and neutral sources (attempting to be unbiased). If the writer quotes an expert, the quotation should present the expert's true meaning, not just a few words that happen to support the writer's argument. (As a reader you may have difficulty judging the accuracy of quotations if you are not familiar with the expert's opinions.)

Not just opinions but also facts and examples may be misinterpreted or distorted. Suppose you were reading an argument for extending a three-year-old law allowing the police to stop vehicles randomly as a means of apprehending drunk drivers. If the author cited statistics showing that the number of drunk-driving accidents dropped in the first two years of the law but failed to note that the number rose back to the previous level in the third year, then the evidence would be distorted and thus inaccurate. You or any reader would be justified in questioning the entire argument, no matter how accurate the rest seemed.

▨ Relevance

Relevant evidence pertains to the argument:

- **It comes from sources with authority on the subject.**
- **It relates directly to the point the writer is making.**
- **It is current.**

In an argument against a method of hazardous-waste disposal, a writer should not offer his church minister's opinion as evidence unless she is an authority on the subject and her expertise is up to date. If she is an authority on Method A and not Method B, the writer should not use her opinion as evidence against Method B. Similarly, the writer's own experience of living near a hazardous-waste site may be relevant evidence *if* it pertains to his thesis. His authority in this case is that of a close observer and a citizen. (See also p. 194 on the fallacy of false authority.)

■ Representativeness

Representative evidence is true to its context:

- **It reflects the full range of the sample from which it is said to be drawn.**
- **It does not overrepresent any element of the sample.**

In an essay arguing that dormitories should stay open during school holidays, a writer might say that "the majority of the school's students favor leaving the dormitories open." But that writer would mislead you and other readers if the claim were based only on a poll of her roommates and dormitory neighbors. A few dormitory residents could not be said to represent the entire student body, particularly the nonresident students. To be representative, the poll would have to take in many more students in proportions that reflect the numbers of resident and nonresident students on campus.

■ Adequacy

Adequate evidence is sufficient:

- **It is plentiful enough to support the writer's assertions.**
- **It is specific enough to support the writer's assertions.**

A writer arguing against animal abuse cannot hope to win over readers solely with statements about her personal experiences and claims of her opinions. Her experience may indeed be relevant evidence if, say, she has worked with animals or witnessed animal abuse. And her opinions are indeed important to the argument, so that readers know what she thinks. But even together these are not adequate evidence: they cannot substitute entirely for facts, nonpersonal examples, and the opinions of experts to demonstrate abuse and describe the scope of the problem.

9d   Discovering assumptions

Assumptions connect evidence to claims: they are the opinions or beliefs that explain why a particular piece of evidence is relevant to a particular claim. As noted in the preceding chapter on critical thinking, assumptions are not flaws in arguments but necessities:

we all acquire beliefs and opinions that shape our view of the world. Here are some examples that you, or people you know, may hold:

> Criminals should be punished.
> Hard work is virtuous.
> Teachers' salaries are too low.

Assumptions are inevitable in argument, but they aren't neutral. For one thing, an assumption can weaken an argument. Say that a writer claims that real estate development should be prevented in your town. As evidence for this claim, the writer offers facts about past developments that have replaced older buildings. But the evidence is relevant to the claim only if you accept the writer's extreme assumptions that old buildings are always worthy and new development is always bad.

In such a case, the writer's bias may not even be stated. Hence a second problem: in arguments both sound and unsound, assumptions are not always explicit. Following are a claim and evidence forming a reasonable argument. What is the unstated assumption?

> Claim
>
> The town should create a plan to manage building preservation and new development.

> Evidence
>
> Examples of how such plans work; expert opinions on how and why both preservation and development are needed.

In this instance the assumption is that neither uncontrolled development nor zero development is healthy for the town. If you can accept this assumption, you should be able to accept the writer's claim (though you might still disagree over particulars).

Here are some tips for dealing with assumptions:

Guidelines for analyzing assumptions

- **What are the assumptions underlying the argument?** How does the writer connect claims with evidence?
- **Are the assumptions believable?** Do they express your values? Do they seem true in your experience?
- **Are the assumptions consistent with one another?** Is the argument's foundation solid, not slippery?

9e Watching language, hearing tone

Tone is the expression of the writer's attitudes toward himself or herself, toward the subject, and toward the reader (see p. 12 for a

ADVERTISING TONE

People who have something to sell provide examples of subtle or not-so-subtle tone. Have students evaluate print advertisements, commercial Web sites, television ads, even junk mail. How does each solicitor try to persuade the reader to buy/use/subscribe to his or her product?

discussion). Tone can tell you quite a bit about the writer's intentions, biases, and trustworthiness. For example:

> Some women cite personal growth as a reason for pursuing careers while raising children. Of course, they are equally concerned with the personal growth of the children they relegate to "child-care specialists" while they work.

In the second sentence this writer is being **ironic,** saying one thing while meaning another. The word *relegate* and the quotation marks with *child-care specialists* betray the writer's belief that working mothers may selfishly neglect their children for their own needs. Irony can sometimes be effective in argument, but here it marks the author as insincere in dealing with the complex issues of working parents and child care.

When reading arguments, you should be alert for the author's language. Look for words that **connote,** or suggest, certain attitudes and evoke certain responses in readers. (Notice your own responses to these word pairs with related meanings but different connotations: *daring/foolhardy, dislike/detest, glad/joyous, angry/rabid, freedom/license.*) Connotative language is no failure in argument; indeed, the strongest arguments use it skillfully to appeal to readers' hearts as well as their minds (see pp. 208–09). But be suspicious if the language runs counter to the substance of the argument.

Look also for evasive words. **Euphemisms,** such as *attack of a sexual nature* for "rape" or *peace-keeping force* for a war-making army, are supposedly inoffensive substitutes for words that may frighten or offend readers (see pp. 513–14). In argument, though, they are sometimes used to hide or twist the truth. An honest, forthright arguer will avoid them.

Finally, watch carefully for sexist, racist, and other biased language that reveals deep ignorance or, worse, entrenched prejudice on the part of the writer. Obvious examples are *broad* for woman and *fag* for homosexual. (See pp. 514–17 for more on such language.)

9f Judging reasonableness

The **reasonableness** of an argument is the sense you get as a reader that the author is fair and sincere. The reasonable writer does not conceal or distort facts, hide prejudices, mask belief as opinion, manipulate you with language, or resort to any of dozens of devices used unconsciously by those who don't know better and deliberately by those who do.

Reasonableness involves all the elements of argument examined so far: claims, evidence, assumptions, and language. In addition, the fair, sincere argument always avoids so-called fallacies (covered in the next section), and it acknowledges the opposition.

COLLABORATIVE LEARNING

Students will benefit from working together on Exercise 9.1. In discussing possible responses and debating the evidence for each response they will learn even more about how each argument is crafted and its effects on different readers. Since the skill of analyzing arguments in these terms is a crucial and challenging one, you might expand on Exercise 9.1 by bringing in other examples of persuasive argumentation and asking students to analyze further examples using these terms.

ANSWERS: EXERCISE 9.1

Possible answers

Kirkpatrick Sale essay

Claims: Thesis (paragraph 5): Individuals' conservation efforts do not raise the consciousness necessary to solve the ecological crisis. Supporting claims: Individuals' conservation does not make a significant dent in energy consumption dominated by industry and government (1, 2). The ecological crisis requires a *drastic overhaul of this civilization,* not individual *life-style solutions* (3). Such solutions divert individuals from the hard truths and hard choices of truly changing consciousness (4).

Evidence: Statistics and other facts: 2–5. Examples: 1, 3–5. Appeals to beliefs or needs: mainly, we should do what's necessary to solve the ecological crisis (throughout).

Assumptions: Notably: There is an environmental crisis. It must be solved. Ozone depletion and rain forest destruction are *corporate crimes* (2). Industry and government are powerful and self-protective. They will not respond appropriately to the ecological crisis unless forced to do so by the people. The people are unwilling to make more than life-style changes to solve the crisis.

Tone: No-nonsense (*I don't . . . believe that I am saving the planet*), unrestrained (*patently corporate crimes; truly pernicious*), sardonic (*"all of us"; "our" control; life-style solutions; write-your-congressperson solutions*).

Reasonableness: Sale is obviously biased, so his reasonableness will probably reside in the eye of the beholder. He does offer evidence for his key assertion about the environmental responsibility of industry and government, and his examples show him to be familiar with the mentality

Judging whether a writer deals adequately with his or her opposition is a fairly simple matter for the reader of argument. By definition, an arguable issue has more than one side. Even if you have no preconceptions about a subject, you will know that another side exists. If the writer pretends otherwise or dismisses the opposition too quickly, you are justified in questioning the honesty and fairness of the argument. (For the more complicated business of *writing* an acknowledgment of opposing views, see pp. 210–11.)

EXERCISE 9.1 Reading arguments critically

Following are two brief arguments. Though not directly opposed, the two arguments do represent different stances on environmental issues. Read each argument critically, following the process outlined in the previous chapter (pp. 152–63) and answering the questions in the box on page 181 (questions about claims, evidence, assumptions, and the other elements of argument). Develop your responses in writing so that you can refer to them for later exercises and class discussion.

The Environmental Crisis Is Not Our Fault

I am as responsible as most eco-citizens: I bike everywhere; I don't own a car; I recycle newspapers, bottles, cans, and plastics; I have a vegetable garden in the summer; I buy organic products; and I put all vegetable waste into my backyard compost bin, probably the only one in all of Greenwich Village. But I don't at the same time believe that I am saving the planet, or in fact doing anything of much consequence about the various eco-crises around us. What's more, I don't even believe that if "all of us" as individuals started doing the same it would make any but the slightest difference. 1

Leave aside ozone depletion and rain forest destruction—those are patently corporate crimes that no individual actions can remedy to any degree. Take, instead, energy consumption in this country. In the most recent figures, residential consumption was 7.2 percent of the total, commercial 5.5 percent, and industrial 23.3 percent; of the remainder, 27.8 percent was transportation (about one-third of it by private car) and 36.3 percent was electric generation (about one-third for residential use). Individual energy use, in sum, was something like 28 percent of total consumption. Although you and I cutting down on energy consumption would have some small effect (and should be done), it is surely the energy consumption of industry and other large institutions such as government and agribusiness that needs to be addressed first. And it is industry and government that must be forced to explain what their consumption is for, what is produced by it, how necessary it is, and how it can be drastically reduced. 2

The point is that the ecological crisis is essentially beyond "our" control, as citizens or householders or consumers or even voters. It is not something that can be halted by recycling or double-pane insulation. It is the inevitable by-product of our modern industrial civilization, dominated by capitalist production and consumption and serviced and protected by various institutions of government, federal to 3 local. It cannot possibly be altered or reversed by simple individual actions, even by the actions of the millions who take part in Earth Day —even if they all go home and fix their refrigerators and from then on walk to work. Nothing less than a drastic overhaul of this civilization and an abandonment of its ingrained gods—progress, growth, exploitation, technology, materialism, anthropocentricity, and power —will do anything substantial to halt our path to environmental destruction, and it's hard to see how life-style solutions will have an effect on that.

What I find truly pernicious about such solutions is that they get |4| people thinking they are actually making a difference and doing their part to halt the destruction of the earth: "There, I've taken all the bottles to the recycling center and used my string bag at the grocery store; I guess that'll take care of global warming." It is the kind of thing that diverts people from the hard truths and hard choices and hard actions, from the recognition that they have to take on the larger forces of society—corporate and governmental—where true power, and true destructiveness, lie.

And to the argument that, well, you have to start somewhere to |5| raise people's consciousness, I would reply that this individualistic approach does not in fact raise consciousness. It does not move people beyond their old familiar liberal perceptions of the world, it does nothing to challenge the belief in technofix or write-your-Congressperson solutions, and it does not begin to provide them with the new vocabulary and modes of thought necessary for a true change of consciousness. We need, for example, to think of recycling centers not as the answer to our waste problems, but as a confession that the system of packaging and production in this society is out of control. Recycling centers are like hospitals; they are the institutions at the end of the cycle that take care of problems that would never exist if ecological criteria had operated at the beginning of the cycle. Until we have those kinds of understandings, we will not do anything with consciousness except reinforce it with the same misguided ideas that created the crisis.

—Kirkpatrick Sale

Myths We Wouldn't Miss

There are tall tales and legends. There are fables and apocryphal |1| stories. And there are myths—a number of which we would like to see disappear. Here are some myths that would not be missed:

MYTH: Offshore drilling would be an ecological disaster. |2|

Truth is, there hasn't been a serious spill in US waters resulting |3| from offshore drilling operations in more than thirty years—and even that one, in Santa Barbara Channel in 1969, caused no permanent damage to the environment.

This is why we always have such a problem with the reasoning of |4| those who call for moratoriums or outright bans on such activity while the nation continues to import foreign oil. The fact is, oil industry offshore drilling operations cause less pollution than urban runoff, atmospheric phenomena, municipal discharges or natural seeps.

Why this nation would choose *not* to drill for oil and *not* to |5| provide the jobs, profits and taxes such activity would mean for the

of most recyclers (a group he even includes himself in). He acknowledges the opposition most clearly in paragraph 5, where he rebuts the claim that the individualistic approach is at least a start on consciousness raising.

Fallacies: See the answer to Exercise 9.4.

Evaluation: Answers will vary.

Oil corporation advertisement

Claims: Thesis (paragraphs 2, 6, 10, 13): Myths about oil exploration, waste, and conservation do not address America's true energy needs. Supporting claims: Offshore drilling is necessary and does not unduly pollute (4). Though heavy, America's energy use is appropriate for the nation's size and productivity (7, 9). Favoring conservation over exploration would increase oil imports or stop economic growth (12).

Evidence: Statistics and other facts: 3–4, 7–9, 12. Examples: 3. Appeals to beliefs or needs: Mainly, America is a strong country whose economic health is crucial for all (throughout).

Assumptions: Notably: Policy needs to be guided by truths, not myths. Importing foreign oil is undesirable. Some pollution is inevitable and acceptable. America is justified in using energy proportionate to its size and productivity. Conservation is desirable. Economic growth is essential.

Tone: Sincere (*a mystery we hope puzzles others as much as it does us; We probably can—and should—do more*), candid (*Truth is; The fact is; In fact; Let's face it; No doubt about it*), perplexed (*We always have such a problem; where is the waste*).

Reasonableness: Like Sale's essay, the ad is strongly biased, but the statistics and other facts and the sincere tone contribute to a sense of reasonableness. So do the several bows to the opposition, including the statements of the objectionable myths themselves and the support for conservation.

Fallacies: See the answer to Exercise 9.4.

Evaluation: Answers will vary.

American economy when there are no better alternatives is a mystery we hope puzzles others as much as it does us.

MYTH: America is a profligate waster of energy. 6

The myth makers like to throw around numbers that read like this: 7 with only 5 percent of the world's population, the US uses about 25 percent of the world's energy. But ours is a big country—three thousand miles from one ocean to the next. Transportation accounts for more than 60 percent of US oil use. We could probably cut down if we moved everybody into one corner of the country, but where is the waste?

It certainly isn't the automobiles that are inefficient. They are 8 twice as efficient as the ones we used thirty years ago. If American drivers use more gasoline than their counterparts in Europe and Japan, it may just have something to do with the country's size.

In fact, proof of the country's size may be in our economic out- 9 put—and may also hold a clue as to why we use the energy we do. Despite having only 5 percent of the world's population, America may indeed use 25 percent of the world's energy. However, according to the latest statistics, we also produce about 25 percent of the world's goods and services. Again, where's the waste?

MYTH: Conservation is *the answer* to America's energy problems. 10

No doubt about it, we all need to be careful of the amount of 11 energy we use. But as long as this nation's economy needs to grow, we are going to need energy to fuel that growth.

For the foreseeable future, there are no viable alternatives to petro- 12 leum as the major source of energy, especially for transportation fuels. Let's face it. Over the past thirty years we *have* learned to conserve—in our factories, our homes, our cars. We probably can—and should—do more. But conservation and new exploration should not be mutually exclusive, because even without an increase in energy consumption, we are using up domestic reserves of oil and gas and must replace them. For the good of the economy, those reserves should be replaced with new domestic production, to the extent economically possible. Otherwise, the only solutions would be additional imports or no growth. And stifling growth would be a gross disservice to the people for whom such growth would provide the opportunity for a better life.

Simply put, America is going to need more energy for all its people. 13
And that is no myth. 14

—Oil corporation advertisement

9g Recognizing fallacies

Fallacies—errors in argument— fall into two groups. Some evade the issue of the argument. Others treat the argument as if it were much simpler than it is.

1 Recognizing evasions

The central claim of an argument defines an issue or question: Should real estate development be controlled? Should drug testing be mandatory in the workplace? An effective argument faces the

Checklist of fallacies

Evasions

- **Begging the question:** treating an opinion that is open to question as if it were already proved or disproved.
- **Non sequitur** ("it does not follow"): drawing a conclusion from irrelevant evidence.
- **Red herring:** introducing an irrelevant issue to distract readers.
- **False authority:** citing as expert opinion the views of a person who is not an expert.
- **Inappropriate appeals:**

  Appealing to readers' fear or pity.
  Snob appeal: appealing to readers' wish to be like those who are more intelligent, famous, rich, and so on.
  Bandwagon: appealing to readers' wish to be part of the group.
  Flattery: appealing to readers' intelligence, taste, and so on.
  Argument ad populum ("to the people"): appealing to readers' general values, such as patriotism or love of family.
  Argument ad hominem ("to the man"): attacking the opponent rather than the opponent's argument.

Oversimplifications

- **Hasty generalization (jumping to a conclusion):** asserting an opinion based on too little evidence.
- **Sweeping generalization:** asserting an opinion as applying to all instances when it may apply to some, or to none. **Absolute statements** and **stereotypes** are variations.
- **Reductive fallacy:** generally, oversimplifying causes and effects.
- **Post hoc fallacy:** assuming that *A* caused *B* because *A* preceded *B*.
- **Either/or fallacy (false dilemma):** reducing a complicated question to two alternatives.
- **False analogy:** exaggerating the similarities in an analogy or ignoring key differences.

central issue squarely with relevant opinions, beliefs, and evidence. An ineffective argument dodges the issue.

▪ Begging the question

A writer **begs the question** by treating an opinion that is open to question as if it were already proved or disproved. (In essence, the writer begs readers to accept his or her ideas from the start.)

> The college library's expenses should be reduced by cutting subscriptions to useless periodicals. [Begged questions: Are some of the library's periodicals useless? Useless to whom?]

> The fact is that the welfare system is too corrupt to be reformed. [Begged questions: How corrupt is the welfare system? Does corruption, even if extensive, put the system beyond reform?]

COMPUTER ACTIVITIES

FALLACY HUNTING

To sharpen student sensitivity to fallacies, tell your students to go "fallacy hunting" on the Web. Each student should try to collect at least one example of each fallacy on the checklist. You can prepare a "dictionary of fallacies" to be posted on your class Web site.

KEEPING THE FALLACIES STRAIGHT

Students can keep a copy of the "Checklist of fallacies" on their computers, and refer to it when they are writing their own papers. If they find they have made a fallacious statement in a draft of their paper, they can paste it into the "Checklist" document to keep as an example.

▪ Non sequitur

A **non sequitur** occurs when no logical relation exists between two or more connected ideas. In Latin *non sequitur* means "it does not follow." In the sentences below, the second thought does not follow from the first:

> She uses a wheelchair, so she must be unhappy. [The second clause does not follow from the first.]

> Kathleen Newsome has my vote for mayor because she has the best-run campaign organization. [Shouldn't one's vote be based on the candidate's qualities, not the campaign's organization?]

▪ Red herring

A **red herring** is literally a kind of fish that might be drawn across a path to distract a bloodhound from a scent it's following. In argument, a red herring is an irrelevant issue intended to distract readers from the relevant issues. The writer changes the subject rather than pursue the argument.

> A campus speech code is essential to protect students, who already have enough problems coping with rising tuition. [Tuition costs and speech codes are different subjects. What protections do students need that a speech code will provide?]

> Instead of developing a campus speech code that will infringe on students' First Amendment rights, administrators should be figuring out how to prevent another tuition increase. [Again, tuition costs and speech codes are different subjects. How would the code infringe on rights?]

▪ False authority

Arguments often cite as evidence the opinions of people who are experts on the subject (see pp. 184–85). But writers use **false authority** when they cite as an expert someone whose expertise is doubtful or nonexistent.

> Jason Bing, a recognized expert in corporate finance, maintains that pharmaceutical companies do not test their products thoroughly enough. [Bing's expertise in corporate finance bears no apparent relation to the testing of pharmaceuticals.]

> According to Helen Liebowitz, the Food and Drug Administration has approved sixty dangerous drugs in the last two years alone. [Who is Helen Liebowitz? On what authority does she make this claim?]

▪ Inappropriate appeals

Appeals to readers' emotions are common in effective arguments. But such appeals must be relevant and must supplement rather than substitute for facts, examples, and other evidence.

Writers sometimes ignore the question with **appeals to readers' fear or pity.**

By electing Susan Clark to the city council, you will prevent the city's economic collapse. [Trades on people's fears. Can Clark singlehandedly prevent economic collapse? Is collapse even likely?]

She should not have to pay taxes, because she is an aged widow with no friends or relatives. [Appeals to people's pity. Should age and loneliness, rather than income, determine a person's tax obligation?]

Sometimes writers ignore the question by appealing to readers' sense of what other people believe or do. One approach is **snob appeal**, inviting readers to accept an assertion in order to be identified with others they admire.

As any literate person knows, James Joyce is the best twentieth-century novelist. [But what qualities of Joyce's writing make him a superior novelist?]

Barry Bonds has an account at Big City Bank, and so should you. [A celebrity's endorsement of course does not automatically guarantee the worth of a product, a service, an idea, or anything else.]

A similar tactic invites readers to accept an assertion because everybody else does. This is the **bandwagon approach.**

As everyone knows, marijuana use leads to heroin addiction. [What is the evidence?]

Yet another diversion involves **flattery** of readers, in a way inviting them to join in a conspiracy.

We all understand campus problems well enough to see the disadvantages of such a policy. [What are the disadvantages of the policy?]

The **argument ad populum** ("argument to the people") asks readers to accept a conclusion based on shared values or even prejudices and nothing else.

Any truly patriotic American will support the President's action. [But why is the action worth taking?]

One final and very common kind of inappropriate emotional appeal addresses *not* the pros and cons of the issue itself but the real or imagined negative qualities of the people who hold the opposing view. This kind of argument is called **ad hominem**, Latin for "to the man."

One of the scientists has been treated for emotional problems, so his pessimism about nuclear waste merits no attention. [Do the scientist's previous emotional problems invalidate his current views?]

2   Recognizing oversimplifications

To **oversimplify** is to conceal or ignore complexities in a vain attempt to create a neater, more convincing argument than reality allows.

RESOURCES AND IDEAS

Moore, Vincent. "Using Role Playing in Argument Papers to Deconstruct Stereotypes." *Teaching English in the Two-Year College* 22 (1995): 190–96. Moore argues for the efficacy of role-playing to help students gain flexibility in seeing multiple perspectives when developing an argument.

Rapkins, Angela A. "The Uses of Logic in the College Freshman English Curriculum." In *Activities to Promote Critical Thinking*. Ed. Jeff Golub. Urbana: NCTE, 1986. 130–35. Rapkins suggests emphasizing logic in all the papers in a course and describes in detail the use of ads in a final argumentation unit, a strategy that expands awareness of the logical fallacies students have been developing throughout the course.

▪ Hasty generalization

A **hasty generalization**, also called **jumping to a conclusion**, is a claim based on too little evidence or on evidence that is unrepresentative. (See also p. 187.)

> It is disturbing that several of the youths who shot up schools were users of violent video games. Obviously, these games can breed violence, and they should be banned. [A few cases do not establish the relation between the games and violent behavior. Most youths who play violent video games do not behave violently.]

> From the way it handled this complaint, we can assume that the consumer protection office has little intention of protecting consumers. [One experience with the office does not demonstrate its intention or overall performance.]

▪ Sweeping generalization

Whereas a hasty generalization comes from inadequate evidence, a **sweeping generalization** probably is not supportable at all. One kind of sweeping generalization is the **absolute statement** involving words such as *all, always, never,* and *no one* that allow no exceptions. Rarely can evidence support such terms. Moderate words such as *some, sometimes, rarely,* and *few* are more reasonable.

Another common sweeping generalization is the **stereotype**, a conventional and oversimplified characterization of a group of people.

> People who live in cities are unfriendly.
> Californians are fad-crazy.
> Women are emotional.
> Men can't express their feelings.

(See also pp. 514–17 on sexist and other biased language.)

▪ Reductive fallacy

The **reductive fallacy** oversimplifies (or reduces) the relation between causes and their effects. The fallacy (sometimes called **oversimplification**) often involves linking two events as if one caused the other directly, whereas the causes may be more complex or the relation may not exist at all. For example:

> Poverty causes crime. [If so, then why do people who are not poor commit crimes? And why aren't all poor people criminals?]

> The better a school's athletic facilities are, the worse its academic programs are. [The sentence assumes a direct cause-and-effect link between athletics and scholarship.]

▪ Post hoc fallacy

Related to the reductive fallacy is the assumption that because *A* preceded *B*, then *A* must have caused *B*. This fallacy is called in

Latin *post hoc, ergo propter hoc,* meaning "after this, therefore because of this," or the **post hoc fallacy** for short.

> In the two months since he took office, Mayor Holcomb has allowed crime in the city to increase 12 percent. [The increase in crime is probably attributable to conditions existing before Holcomb took office.]
>
> The town council erred in permitting the adult bookstore to open, for shortly afterward two women were assaulted. [It cannot be assumed without evidence that the women's assailants visited or were influenced by the bookstore.]

■ Either/or fallacy

In the **either/or fallacy** (also called **false dilemma**), the writer assumes that a complicated question has only two answers, one good and one bad, both bad, or both good.

> City police officers are either brutal or corrupt. [Most city police officers are neither.]
>
> Either we permit mandatory drug testing in the workplace or productivity will continue to decline. [Productivity is not necessarily dependent on drug testing.]

■ False analogy

An **analogy** is a comparison between two essentially unlike things for the purpose of definition or illustration. In arguing by analogy, a writer draws a likeness between things on the basis of a single shared feature and then extends the likeness to other features. For instance, the "war on drugs" equates a battle against a foe with a program to eradicate (or at least reduce) sales and use of illegal drugs. Both involve an enemy, a strategy of overpowering the enemy, a desired goal, officials in uniform, and other similarities.

Analogy can only illustrate a point, never prove it: just because things are similar in one respect, they are not *necessarily* alike in other respects. In the fallacy called **false analogy,** the writer assumes such a complete likeness. Here is the analogy of the war on drugs taken to its false extreme:

> To win the war on drugs, we must wage more of a military-style operation. Prisoners of war are locked up without the benefit of a trial by jury, and drug dealers should be, too. Soldiers shoot their enemy on sight, and officials who encounter big drug operations should, too. Military traitors may be executed, and corrupt law enforcers could be, too.

EXERCISE 9.2   Analyzing advertisements

Leaf through a magazine or watch commercial television for half an hour, looking for advertisements that attempt to sell a product not on the basis of its worth but by snob appeal, flattery, or other inappropriate appeals to emotions. Be prepared to discuss the advertisers'

Have students work in groups to list and analyze the fallacies found in Exercise 9.2. Ask each group to present the advertisement with the most blatant or surprising fallacy to the class.

Ask students to work in groups on Exercise 9.4. After completing the exercise, each group might go on to compose an advertisement in which the argument for the product contains each of these fallacies.

ANSWERS: EXERCISE 9.2

Individual response.

ANSWERS: EXERCISE 9.3
Possible answers

1. Begged question, argument ad populum, and false analogy.
   A revision: The fact that individuals in the United States cannot legally sell nuclear technology to nonnuclear nations, which the government can, points up a disturbing limit on individual rights.
2. Sweeping generalization and begged question.
   A revision: A successful marriage demands a degree of maturity.
3. Hasty generalization and non sequitur.
   A revision: Students' persistent complaints about the unfairness of the grading system should be investigated.
4. Either/or fallacy and hasty generalization.
   A revision: People watch television for many reasons, but some watch because they are too lazy to talk or read or because they want mindless escape from their lives.
5. Reductive fallacy and begged question.
   A revision: Racial tension may occur when people with different backgrounds live side by side.

ANSWERS: EXERCISE 9.4

Possible answers

Though free of the most egregious appeals, the Sale essay and the advertisement both demonstrate several basic fallacies. Most notably:

Kirkpatrick Sale essay

Either/or: Either we achieve a *drastic overhaul of our civilization* or the environment will be destroyed (paragraph 3).

Begged question: The individualistic approach to environmental problems does not *challenge the belief in technofix or write-your-Congressperson solutions* [Do these not work?] or achieve an essential, fundamental change in thinking [Is the change essential?] (5).

False analogy: The analogy between recycling centers and hospitals (5) implies that a preventive approach (*ecological criteria* for packaging and production; preventive medicine) would eliminate the need for the institution. This isn't true of hospitals (people would still get sick), so how is it true of recycling centers?

Oil corporation advertisement

Begged question: The fact is, oil industry offshore drilling operations cause *less pollution* than other sources of pollution (4). [But how much pollution do the drilling operations cause?]

Either/or: Either we move everyone to one place or we continue to use a disproportionate amount of the world's energy (7).

Either/or: Either we find more energy or the economy will not grow; either we find more energy or we will have to increase imports (2).

Begged question: Despite good conservation efforts, we still need petroleum exploration (12). [But why can't conservation be improved to eliminate the need for risky exploration?]

ANSWERS: EXERCISE 9.5

Individual response.

techniques. (See Chapter 11, p. 229, if you need help analyzing the appeals in images.)

EXERCISE 9.3 Identifying and revising fallacies

Fallacies tend to appear together, as each of the following sentences illustrates. Identify at least one fallacy in each sentence. Then revise the sentences to make them more reasonable. (You can do this exercise online at *ablongman.com/littlebrown*.)

1. The American government can sell nuclear technology to non-nuclear nations, so why can't individuals, who after all have a God-given right to earn a living as they see fit?
2. A successful marriage demands a maturity that no one under twenty-five possesses.
3. Students' persistent complaints about the grading system prove that it is unfair.
4. People watch television because they are too lazy to talk or read or because they want mindless escape from their lives.
5. Racial tension is bound to occur when people with different backgrounds are forced to live side by side.

EXERCISE 9.4 Identifying fallacies in arguments

Analyze the two arguments on pages 190–92 for fallacies. To what extent do any fallacies weaken either argument? Explain.

EXERCISE 9.5 Identifying fallacies online

At *groups.yahoo.com*, find a conversation about drug testing in the workplace, environmental pollution, violence in the media, or any other subject that interests you and that is debatable. Read through the arguments made in the conversation, noting the fallacies you see. List the fallacious statements as well as the types of fallacies they illustrate, keeping in mind that a given statement may illustrate more than a single type.

CHAPTER 10

Writing an Argument

In composing an argument, you try to clarify an issue or solve a problem by finding the common ground between you and your readers. Using critical thinking, you develop and test your own ideas. Using a variety of techniques, you engage readers in an attempt to narrow the distance between your views and theirs.

This chapter introduces the process and techniques of composing a written argument. The next chapter discusses the use of images, such as photographs and charts, as an effective tool for argument.

10a   Finding a subject

An argument subject must be arguable—that is, reasonable people will disagree over it and be able to support their positions with evidence. This sentence implies the *do*s and *don't*s listed below.

Tests for an argument subject

A good subject:

- Concerns a matter of opinion—a conclusion drawn from evidence.
- Can be disputed: others might take a different position.
- *Will* be disputed: it is controversial.
- Is something you care about and know about or want to research.
- Is narrow enough to argue in the space and time available.

A bad subject:

- Cannot be disputed because it concerns a fact, such as the distance to Saturn or the functions of the human liver.
- Cannot be disputed because it concerns a personal preference or belief, such as a liking for a certain vacation spot or a moral commitment to vegetarianism.
- *Will not* be disputed because few if any disagree over it—the virtues of a secure home, for instance.

---

http://www.ablongman.com/littlebrown   ▶

Visit the companion Web site for more help
and additional exercises on writing arguments.

---

mycomplab 2.0

Please visit MyCompLab at *www.mycomplab.com* for more on the writing process.

HIGHLIGHTS

This chapter introduces students to the process of conceiving their own written arguments. Discussions of subject, thesis, purpose, and audience are considered before the chapter turns to the concepts of inductive and deductive argumentation. As they construct their own arguments, students will consider their own use of evidence, the most effective kinds of appeals to readers, how to deal with opposing views, how to organize their arguments, and how to revise their arguments. A helpful checklist for revising an argument appears on p. 213. The chapter concludes with an annotated sample argument written by a student.

The Internet can be particularly useful for the novice argument-builder. A series of exercises in this chapter's annotations asks students to work with Internet discussion list postings to evaluate subjects, theses, purposes, and audience. You could create an extended project in which students mine an Internet discussion list for the elements of argument and then construct one of their own.

TRANSPARENCY MASTER 10.1

LISTING PRIORITIES AND VALUES

Ask groups of students first to list the five (or ten) issues they consider most worth arguing about and then to record their different opinions about the top two or three.

RESTRICTED LISTS

Ask students to prepare lists as above, but to restrict the list to a specific area, such as sports, the economy, or drugs. In so doing, you will create a situation in which students will need to go beyond obvious issues and opinions to complete their lists.

COMPANION WEB SITE

See page IAE-52 for companion Web site content description.

Additional help on subjects for writing appears earlier in this book:

- **Working with a specific assignment,** pages 6–7.
- **Working with a general assignment,** page 7.
- **Narrowing a subject to a question,** pages 7–9.

CULTURE LANGUAGE Choosing a subject for argument may seem difficult if you're not familiar with what people in the United States find debatable. One way to find a subject is to scout online discussion groups, such as those listed at *groups.yahoo.com,* for subjects on which there is a range of opinion. Another approach is to read a newspaper every day for at least a week, looking for issues that involve or interest you. Following the development of the issues in articles, editorials, and letters to the editor will give you a sense of how controversial they are, what the positions are, and what your position might be.

EXERCISE 10.1 Finding a subject for argument

Explain why each subject below is or is not appropriate for argument. Refer to the box on the previous page if you need help. (You can do this exercise online at *ablongman.com/littlebrown.*)

1. Granting of athletic scholarships
2. Care of automobile tires
3. Censoring the Web sites of hate groups
4. History of the town park
5. Housing for the homeless
6. Billboards in urban residential areas or in rural areas
7. Animal testing for cosmetics research
8. Cats versus dogs as pets
9. Ten steps in recycling wastepaper
10. Benefits of being a parent

10b Conceiving a thesis statement

The **thesis** is the main idea of your paper (see pp. 27–31). In an argument the **thesis statement** makes the claim that you want your readers to accept or act on. Here are two thesis statements on the same subject:

The new room fees are unjustified given the condition of the dormitories.

The administration should postpone the new room fees at least until conditions in the dormitories are improved.

Your thesis statement must satisfy the same requirements as your subject (see the box on p. 199). But it must also specify the basis for your claim. In both of the preceding thesis statements, the basis for protesting the room fees is that the dormitories are in poor condition.

Note that the writer of either of these arguments must clarify the definition of *condition(s)* if the argument is to be clear and reasonable. Always take pains to define abstract and general terms that are central to your argument, preferably in or just after the thesis statement. (See p. 183.)

EXERCISE 10.2 Conceiving a thesis statement

For each subject in Exercise 10.1 that you deemed arguable, draft a tentative thesis statement that specifies the basis for an argument. If you prefer, choose five arguable subjects of your own and draft a thesis statement for each one. One thesis statement should interest you enough to develop into a complete argument in later exercises.

10c Analyzing your purpose and your audience

Your purpose in argument is, broadly, to engage readers in order to convince them of your position or persuade them to act. But arguments have more specific purposes as well, such as the following:

To strengthen the commitment of existing supporters
To win new supporters from the undecided or uninformed
To get the opposition to reconsider
To inspire supporters to act
To deter the undecided from acting

It's no accident that each of these purposes characterizes the audience (*existing supporters, the undecided,* and so on). In argument, even more than in other kinds of writing, achieving your purpose depends on the response of your readers, so you need a sense of who they are and where they stand. The "Questions About Audience" on page 11 can help you identify readers' knowledge, beliefs, and other pertinent information. In addition, you need to know how readers stand on your subject—not only whether they agree or disagree generally, but also which specific assertions they will find more or less convincing.

Your purpose can help you fill in this information. If you decide to address supporters or opponents, you essentially select readers with certain inclinations and ignore other readers who may tune in. If you decide to win new supporters from those who are undecided on your topic, you'll have to imagine skeptical readers who will be convinced only by an argument that is detailed, logical, and fair. Like you when you read an argument critically, these skeptical readers seek to be reasoned with, not manipulated into a position or hammered over the head.

> **EXERCISE 10.3 Analyzing purpose and audience**
>
> Specify a purpose and likely audience for the thesis statement you chose to develop in Exercise 10.2. What do purpose and audience suggest about the way you should develop the argument?

10d Using reason

As a reader of argument, you seek evidence for the writer's claims and clear reasoning about the relationship of evidence to claims. As a writer of argument, you seek to provide what the reader needs in a way that furthers your case.

The thesis of your argument is a conclusion you reach by reasoning about evidence. Two common processes of reasoning are induction and deduction—methods of thinking that you use all the time even if you don't know their names. You can think of induction and deduction as two different ways of moving among claims, evidence, and assumptions—the elements of argument derived from Stephen Toulmin's work and discussed on pages 180–81.

1 Reasoning inductively

When you're about to buy a used car, you consult friends, relatives, and consumer guides before deciding what kind of car to buy. Using **inductive reasoning**, you make specific observations about cars (your evidence) and you induce, or infer, a **generalization** (or claim) that Model X is the most reliable. Writing a paper on the effectiveness of print advertising, you might also use inductive reasoning:

> First analyze statistics on advertising in print and in other media (evidence).
> Then read comments by advertisers and publishers (more evidence).
> Finally, form a conclusion that print is the most cost-effective advertising medium (generalization).

This reasoning builds from the evidence to the claim, with assumptions connecting evidence to claim. By predicting something about the unknown based on what you know, you create new knowledge out of old.

The more evidence you accumulate, the more probable it is that your generalization is true. Note, however, that absolute certainty is not possible. At some point you must *assume* that your evidence

Inductive reasoning

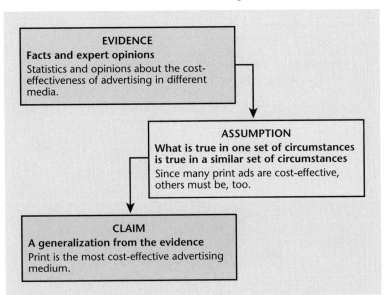

justifies your generalization, for yourself and your readers. Most errors in inductive reasoning involve oversimplifying either the evidence or the generalization. See pages 192–97 on fallacies.

2 Reasoning deductively

You use **deductive reasoning** when you proceed from your generalization that Model X is the most reliable used car to your own specific circumstances (you want to buy a used car) to the conclusion (or claim) that you should buy a Model X car. Like induction, deduction uses the elements of argument—claims, evidence, and assumptions—but with it you apply old information to new.

◼ The deductive syllogism

The conventional way of displaying a deductive argument is in a **syllogism:**

> **Premise:** All human beings are mortal. [A generalization, fact, principle, or belief that you assume to be true.]
> **Premise:** I am a human being. [New information: a specific case of the first premise.]
> **Conclusion:** Therefore, I am mortal.

As long as the premises of a syllogism are true, the conclusion derives logically and certainly from them. If you want the school

TRANSPARENCY MASTER 10.2

COLLABORATIVE LEARNING

CHECKING THE LOGIC

Ask students to work in pairs to evaluate each other's use of logic in an assigned essay. Each partner can read the other's paper and use the "Tests for inductive and deductive reasoning" list (p. 205) to evaluate the paper's use of logic. For inductive reasoning, the reader can list the evidence, assumption, and claim. For deductive reasoning, the reader can construct a syllogism. After readers have had a chance to evaluate the logic, they can share their findings with their partner, the writer.

RESOURCES AND IDEAS

Kasterly, James L. "From Formalism to Inquiry: A Model of Argument in *Antigone.*" *College English* 62 (1999): 222–41. Kasterly takes an anti-formalist (non-Toulminian) approach to argument, presenting a reading of *Antigone* as a case in point.

Kneupper, Charles W. "Teaching Argument: An Introduction to the Toulmin Model." *College Composition and Communication* 29 (1978): 237–41. Kneupper provides a brief review of Stephen Toulmin's simplified, practical logic, a system based primarily on three elements: data, claim, and warrant.

Lamb, Catherine E. "Beyond Argument in Feminist Composition." *College Composition and Communication* 42 (1991): 11–24. Lamb finds that the oral discourse modes of negotiation and mediation can be effectively used in conceiving the purpose and audience of a written argument. She says, "Argument still has a place, although now as a means, not an end. The end—a resolution of conflict that is fair to both sides—is possible even in the one-sidedness of written communication."

Deductive reasoning

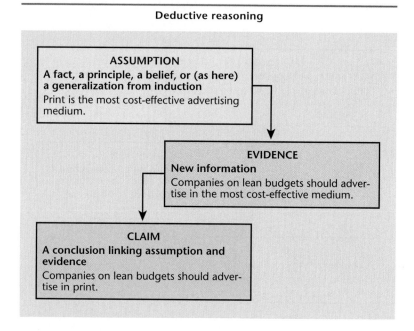

administration to postpone new room fees for one dormitory, your deductive argument might be expressed in this syllogism:

> **Premise:** The administration should not raise fees on dorm rooms in poor condition.
> **Premise:** The rooms in Polk Hall are in poor condition.
> **Conclusion:** Therefore, the administration should not raise fees on the rooms in Polk Hall.

The force of deductive reasoning depends on the reliability of the premises and the care taken to apply them in drawing conclusions. The reasoning process is **valid** if the premises lead logically to the conclusion. It is **true** if the premises are believable.

Problems with syllogisms

Sometimes the reasoning in a deductive argument is true because the premises are believable, but it is *not* valid because the conclusion doesn't derive logically from the premises:

> **Premise:** The administration should not raise fees on dorm rooms in poor condition.
> **Premise:** Tyler Hall is a dormitory.
> **Conclusion:** Therefore, the administration should not raise fees on the rooms in Tyler Hall.

Tests for inductive and deductive reasoning

Induction

- Have you stated your evidence clearly?
- Is your evidence complete enough and good enough to justify your claim? What is the assumption that connects evidence and claim? Is it believable?
- Have you avoided fallacies?

Deduction

- What are the premises leading to your conclusion? Look especially for unstated premises.
- What does the first premise assume? Is the assumption believable?
- Does the first premise necessarily apply to the second premise?
- Is the second premise believable?
- Have you avoided fallacies?

Both premises may be true, but the first does not *necessarily* apply to the second, so the conclusion is invalid.

Sometimes, too, deductive reasoning is valid but *not* true:

Premise: All college administrations are indifferent to students' needs.
Premise: The administration of Central State is a college administration.
Conclusion: Therefore, the administration of Central State is indifferent to students' needs.

This syllogism is valid but useless: the first premise is an untrue assumption, so the entire argument is untrue. Invalid and untrue syllogisms underlie many of the fallacies discussed on pages 192–97.

A particular hazard of deductive reasoning is the **unstated premise:** the basic assumption linking evidence and conclusion is not stated but implied. Here the unstated premise is believable and the argument is reasonable:

Ms. Stein has worked with drug addicts for fifteen years, so she knows a great deal about their problems. [Unstated premise: Anyone who has worked fifteen years with drug addicts knows about their problems.]

But when the unstated premise is wrong or unfounded, the argument is false. For example:

Since Jane Lightbow is a senator, she must receive money illegally from lobbyists. [Unstated premise: All senators receive money illegally from lobbyists.]

To avoid such false conclusions, you may be tempted to make your claims sound more reasonable. But even a conclusion that

Students can work effectively together on Exercises 10.4 and 10.5. To foster a more active discussion of likely inferences and deductions, ask each group to note places where individuals disagree and to pose those cases to the class as a whole.

ANSWERS: EXERCISE 10.4

The unreasonable generalizations from the given evidence are statements 2 (can't be inferred from the facts), 3 (contradicted by the facts), and 5 (can't be inferred from the facts).

ANSWERS: EXERCISE 10.5

Possible answers

1. *Premise:* Anyone who has opposed pollution controls may continue to do so.
   Premise: The mayor has opposed pollution controls.
   Conclusion: The mayor may continue to do so.
   The statement is valid and true.
2. *Premise:* Corporate Web sites are sponsored by for-profit entities.
   Premise: Information from for-profit entities is unreliable.
   Conclusion: Information on corporate Web sites is unreliable.
   The statement is untrue because the second premise is untrue.
3. *Premise:* Many good artists trained at Parsons.
   Premise: Schroeder trained at Parsons.
   Conclusion: Schroeder is a good artist.
   The statement is invalid because the first premise does not necessarily apply to the second.
4. *Premise:* Those who use their resources to help others deserve our particular appreciation.
   Premise: Some wealthy athletes use their resources to help others.
   Conclusion: Some wealthy athletes deserve our particular appreciation.
   The statement is valid and, if the first premise is accepted, true.
5. *Premise:* Any employer who has hired only one woman is sexist.
   Premise: Jimson is an employer who has hired only one woman.
   Conclusion: Jimson is sexist.

sounds reasonable must be supportable. For instance, changing *must* to *might* modifies the unstated assumption about Senator Lightbow:

> Since Jane Lightbow is a senator, she might receive money illegally from lobbyists. [Unstated premise: *Some* senators receive money illegally from lobbyists.]

But it does not necessarily follow that Senator Lightbow is one of the "some." The sentence, though logical, is not truly reasonable unless evidence demonstrates that Senator Lightbow should be linked with illegal activities.

EXERCISE 10.4 Reasoning inductively

Study the facts below and then evaluate each of the numbered conclusions following them. Which of the generalizations are reasonable given the evidence, and which are not? Why? (You can do this exercise online at *ablongman.com/littlebrown*.)

In 2004–05 each American household viewed an average of 50 hours and 12 minutes of television, DVDs, or videos weekly.

Each individual viewed an average of 30 hours and 23 minutes per week.

Those viewing the most television per week (43 hours and 6 minutes) were women over age 55.

Those viewing the least television per week (19 hours and 17 minutes) were children ages 6 to 11.

Households earning under $30,000 a year watched an average of 53 hours and 19 minutes a week.

Households earning more than $60,000 a year watched an average of 48 hours and 7 minutes a week.

1. Households with incomes under $30,000 tend to watch more television than average.
2. Women watch more television than men.
3. Nonaffluent people watch less television than affluent people.
4. Women over age 55 tend to watch more television than average.
5. Children watch less television than critics generally assume.

EXERCISE 10.5 Reasoning deductively

Convert each of the following statements into a syllogism. (You may have to state unstated assumptions.) Use the syllogism to evaluate both the validity and the truth of the statement. (You can do this exercise online at *ablongman.com/littlebrown*.)

Example:
DiSantis is a banker, so he does not care about the poor.

Premise: Bankers do not care about the poor.
Premise: DiSantis is a banker.
Conclusion: Therefore, DiSantis does not care about the poor.

The statement is untrue because the first premise is untrue.

1. The mayor opposed pollution controls when he was president of a manufacturing company, so he may not support new controls or vigorously enforce existing ones.
2. Information on corporate Web sites is unreliable because the sites are sponsored by for-profit entities.
3. Schroeder is a good artist because she trained at Parsons, like many other good artists.
4. Wealthy athletes who use their resources to help others deserve our particular appreciation.
5. Jimson is clearly a sexist because she has hired only one woman.

10e Using evidence

Whether your argument is reasonable or not depends heavily on the evidence you marshal to support it. The kinds of evidence and the criteria for evaluating evidence are discussed in detail on pages 183–87. Finding evidence is discussed under research writing on pages 571–97. Evaluating sources of evidence, including online sources, is discussed under research writing on pages 599–609.

The kind and quantity of evidence you use should be determined by your purpose, your subject, and the needs of your audience. Some arguments, such as an appeal for volunteer help in a soup kitchen, will rely most heavily on examples (including perhaps a narrative of your own experience) and on appeals to readers' beliefs. Other arguments, such as a proposal for mandatory side air bags in cars, will rely much more on statistics and expert opinions. Most arguments, including these, will mingle facts, examples, expert opinions, and appeals to readers' beliefs and needs.

In using evidence for argument, you'll need to be especially wary of certain traps that carelessness or zeal can lure you into. These are listed in the following box.

Responsible use of evidence

- **Don't distort.** You mislead readers when you twist evidence to suit your argument—for instance, when you claim that crime in your city occurs five times more often than it did in 1955, without mentioning that the population is also seven times larger.

(continued)

The statement is untrue because the first premise is not true: there may be other reasons besides sexism for hiring only one woman.

RESOURCES AND IDEAS

Corrigan, Dagmar Stuehrk and Chidsey Dickson. "Ezines and Freshman Composition." *Kairos* (Summer 2002). http://english.ttu.edu/kairos7.2binder.html?sectiontwo/corrigan/description.html. The authors show how course content is enriched with the addition of assignments that ask students to contribute to electronic magazines.

Gage, John T. "Teaching the Enthymeme: Invention and Arrangement." *Rhetoric Review* 2 (1983): 38–50. Gage argues that students can gain awareness and control over the context, logic, and structure of their arguments by stating their reasoning in enthymemic fashion, as a sentence containing an assertion and a because clause.

George, Diana. "From Analysis to Design: Visual Communication in the Teaching of Writing." *College Composition and Communication* 54 (September 2002): 11–39. In this review of current theory and research and the pedagogical history of visual literacy, George provides an excellent introduction for writing teachers who want to include instruction in visual literacy in their curricula.

Geisler, Cheryl, et al. "Itext: Future Directions for Research on the Relationship between Information Technology and Writing." *Journal of Business and Technical Communication* 15.3 (2001): 269–309. The authors argue that Itexts such as e-mail are altering the nature of written communication and recommend a variety of ways to monitor such changes and to assess their social impact.

Porter, Jeffrey. "The Reasonable Reader: Knowledge and Inquiry in Freshman English." *College English* 49 (1987): 332–44. Porter argues that enthymemes organize readers' "participation in the text."

INTERNET EVIDENCE

As a follow-up to the "Internet debates", "Internet theses," "Internet purposes and audiences," and "Internet logic" exercises suggested for 10a, 10b, and 10d, ask your students to find examples of good and poor use of evidence in the Internet discussion groups they have been shadowing.

After students have drafted an argument as suggested in Exercise 10.6, ask them to work in groups to help one another to test and to develop the evidence for each argument further. Then ask each student to revise his or her argument using the group's comments.

ANSWERS: EXERCISE 10.6

Individual response.

COLLECTING APPEALS

Ask students to read, on their own, a relatively long and complex argumentative essay from a reader or a magazine of political or social opinion. In class, assign students to groups and ask each group (1) to identify purely logical appeals, purely emotional appeals, and mixed appeals in the essay and (2) to describe, if they can, the effect of each appeal on average readers (like the members of the group).

Responsible use of evidence

(continued)

- **Don't stack the deck.** Ignoring damning evidence is like cheating at cards. You must deal forthrightly with the opposition. (See pp. 210–11.)
- **Don't exaggerate.** Watch your language. Don't attempt to manipulate readers by characterizing your own evidence as *pure* and *rock-solid* and the opposition's as *ridiculous* and *half-baked*. Make the evidence speak for itself.
- **Don't oversimplify.** Avoid forcing the evidence to support more than it can. (See also p. 196.)
- **Don't misquote.** When you cite experts, quote them accurately and fairly.

EXERCISE 10.6 Using reason and evidence in your argument

Develop the structure and evidence for the argument you began in Exercises 10.2 and 10.3 (pp. 201 and 202). (You may want to begin drafting at this stage.) Is your argument mainly inductive or mainly deductive? Use the box on page 205 to test the reasoning of the argument. Use the boxes on page 186 and above to test your evidence.

10f Reaching your readers

To reach your readers in argument, you appeal directly to their reason and emotions, you present yourself as someone worth heeding, and you account for views opposing your own.

1 Appealing to readers

In forming convictions about arguable issues, we generally interpret the factual evidence through the filter of our values, beliefs, tastes, desires, and feelings. You may object to placing the new town dump in a particular wooded area because the facts suggest that the site is not large enough and that prevailing winds will blow odors back through the town. But you may also have fond memories of playing in the wooded area as a child, feelings that color your interpretation of the facts and strengthen your conviction that the dump should be placed elsewhere. Your conviction is partly rational, because it is based on evidence, and partly emotional, because it is also based on feelings.

■ Rational and emotional appeals

In most arguments you will combine **rational appeals** to readers' capacities for reasoning logically between evidence and claims with **emotional appeals** to readers' beliefs and feelings. The following passages, all arguing the same view on the same subject, illustrate how either a primarily rational or a primarily emotional appeal may be weaker than an approach that uses both:

Rational appeal

Advertising should show more physically challenged people. The millions of disabled Americans have considerable buying power, yet so far advertisers have made no attempt to tap that power. [Appeals to the logic of financial gain.]

Emotional appeal

Advertising should show more physically challenged people. By keeping the physically challenged out of the mainstream depicted in ads, advertisers encourage widespread prejudice against disability, prejudice that frightens and demeans those who hold it. [Appeals to the sense of fairness, open-mindedness.]

Rational and emotional appeals

Advertising should show more physically challenged people. The millions of disabled Americans have considerable buying power, yet so far advertisers have made no attempt to tap that power. Further, by keeping the physically challenged out of the mainstream depicted in ads, advertisers encourage widespread prejudice against disability, prejudice that frightens and demeans those who hold it.

The third passage, in combining both kinds of appeal, gives readers both rational and emotional bases for agreeing with the writer.

For an emotional appeal to be successful, it must be appropriate for the audience and the argument:

- **It must not misjudge readers' actual feelings.**
- **It must not raise emotional issues that are irrelevant to the claims and the evidence.** See pages 194–95 for a discussion of specific inappropriate appeals, such as the bandwagon approach.

One further caution: Photographs and other images can reinforce your claims with a strong emotional appeal, but they must be relevant to your claims, and you must explain their relevance in your text and captions. See page 299 for more on the appeals in images.

▪ Ethical appeal

A third kind of approach to readers, the **ethical appeal,** is the sense you give of being a competent, fair, trustworthy person. A sound argument backed by ample evidence—a rational appeal—will convince readers of your knowledge and reasonableness. (So will your acknowledging the opposition. See the next page.) Appropriate emotional appeals will demonstrate that you share readers' beliefs

ANTICIPATING OPPOSITION

A good strategy for teaching students to anticipate opposition is to have them generate "yes, but" lists. Ask them to list all the strong points supporting their argument, then think of a counterargument for each point. (Sometimes they will be able to overcome these counterarguments; at other times they may have to concede the point.) For instance, if their thesis is "Raising the tuition at Golden College will reduce enrollment," they might produce a "yes, but" list like this:

SUPPORTING POINT	"YES, BUT" OBJECTION
Tuition rose 3 percent last year, and enrollment dropped by 2 percent.	Yes, but the recession and the lack of financial aid may also have contributed to lower enrollment.
There are cheaper schools in the area.	Yes, but Golden College is rated in the top ten of small schools in the area.
Students can't afford higher tuition costs.	Yes, but they seem to afford all the clothes, cars, and CDs they want to buy. Where are their priorities?

COLLABORATIVE LEARNING

DEVIL'S ADVOCATE

Group work is particularly useful in helping students to anticipate opposition to an argument. Ask the groups to play devil's advocate in order to test each writer's reasoning processes and use of evidence. To ensure that this is a supportive experience, remind groups to frame their questions about each writer's argument as a series of productive revision suggestions.

RESOURCES AND IDEAS

Winder, Barbara E. "The Delineation of Values in Persuasive Writing." *College Composition and Communication* 29 (1978): 55–58. Winder asks writers to spell out both sides of an argument to make them sensitive to their own values and those of their readers.

and needs. An argument that is concisely written and correct in grammar, spelling, and other matters will underscore your competence. In addition, a sincere and even tone will assure readers that you are a balanced person who wants to reason with them.

A sincere and even tone need not exclude language with emotional appeal—words such as *frightens* and *demeans* at the end of the third example on the previous page. But avoid certain forms of expression that will mark you as unfair:

- **Insulting words,** such as *idiotic* or *fascist*.
- **Biased language,** such as *rednecks* or *fags*. (See pp. 514–17.)
- **Sarcasm**—for instance, using the phrase *What a brilliant idea* to indicate contempt for the idea and its originator.
- **Exclamation points!** They'll make you sound shrill!

See also pages 188–89 on tone.

2 Answering opposing views

A good test of your fairness in argument is how you handle possible objections. Assuming your thesis is indeed arguable, then others can marshal their own evidence to support a different view or views. You need to find out what these other views are and what the support is for them. Then, in your argument, you need to take these views on, refute those you can, grant the validity of others, and demonstrate why, despite their validity, the opposing views are less compelling than your own.

The following paragraph illustrates this approach:

The athletic director argues against reducing university support for athletic programs on the grounds that they make money that goes toward academic programs.	Statement of opposing view
It is true that here at Springfield the surpluses from the football and basketball programs have gone into the general university fund, and some of that money may have made it into academic departments (the fund's accounting methods make it impossible to say for sure).	Concession that opposing view is partly valid
But the athletic director misses the point. The problem is not that the athletic programs may cost more than they take in but that they demand too much to begin with. For an institution that hopes to become first-rate academically, too many facilities, too much money, too much energy, and too many people are tied up in the effort to produce championship sports teams.	Demonstration that opposing view is irrelevant

—William Hoving (student),
"Scholarship Versus Gamesmanship"

Before or while you draft your essay, list for yourself all the opposing views you can think of. You'll find them in your research, by talking to friends and classmates, and by critically thinking about your own ideas. You can also look for a range of views in a discussion group that deals with your subject. A place to start is the archive at *groups.yahoo.com*.

To deal with opposing views, figure out which ones you can refute (do more research if necessary), and prepare to concede those views you can't refute. It's not a mark of weakness or failure to admit that the opposition has a point or two. Indeed, by showing yourself to be honest and fair, you strengthen your ethical appeal and thus your entire argument.

EXERCISE 10.7 Identifying appeals

Identify each passage below as primarily a rational appeal or primarily an emotional appeal. Which passages make a strong ethical appeal as well? (You can do this exercise online at *ablongman.com/littlebrown*.)

1. Web surfing may contribute to the global tendency toward breadth rather than depth of knowledge. Using those most essential of skills—pointing and clicking—our brightest minds may now never encounter, much less read, the works of Plato, Shakespeare, and Darwin.
2. Thus the data collected by these researchers indicate that a mandatory sentence for illegal possession of handguns may lead to reduction in handgun purchases.
3. Most broadcasters worry that further government regulation of television programming could breed censorship—certainly, an undesirable outcome. Yet most broadcasters also accept that children's television is a fair target for regulation.
4. Anyone who cherishes life in all its diversity could not help being appalled by the mistreatment of laboratory animals. The so-called scientists who run the labs are misguided.
5. Many experts in constitutional law have warned that the rule violates the right to free speech. Yet other experts have viewed the rule, however regretfully, as necessary for the good of the community as a whole.

EXERCISE 10.8 Reaching your readers

Continuing your argument-in-progress from Exercise 10.6 (p. 208), analyze whether your claims are rational or emotional and whether the mix is appropriate for your audience and argument. Analyze your ethical appeal, too, considering whether it can be strengthened. Then make a list of possible opposing views. Think freely at first, not stopping to censor views that seem far-fetched or irrational. When your list is complete, decide which views must be taken seriously and why, and develop a response to each one.

ANSWERS: EXERCISE 10.7

Possible answers

1. Primarily emotional appeal. Ethical appeal: knowledgeable, concerned, reasonable (at least in the two uses of *may*), slightly sarcastic (*most essential of skills*).
2. Primarily rational appeal. Ethical appeal: knowledgeable, reasonable.
3. Primarily rational appeal. Ethical appeal: knowledgeable, fair, willing to acknowledge opposing views.
4. Primarily emotional appeal. Ethical appeal: sympathetic toward animals (but perhaps unfair to *so-called scientists*).
5. Primarily rational appeal. Ethical appeal: knowledgeable, fair, willing to acknowledge opposing views.

ANSWERS: EXERCISE 10.8

Individual response.

10g   Organizing your argument

All arguments include the same parts:

- The *introduction* establishes the significance of the subject and provides background. The introduction generally includes the thesis statement. However, if you think your readers may have difficulty accepting your thesis statement before they see at least some support for it, then it may come later in the paper. (See pp. 102–06 for more on introductions.)
- The *body* states and develops the claims supporting the thesis. In one or more paragraphs, support each claim with clearly relevant evidence. See below for more on organizing the body.
- The *response to opposing views* details and addresses those views, either demonstrating your argument's greater strengths or conceding the opponents' points. See below for more on organizing this response.
- The *conclusion* completes the argument, restating the thesis, summarizing the supporting claims, and making a final appeal to readers. (See pp. 106–08 for more on conclusions.)

The arrangement of the body and the response to opposing views depends on your subject, purpose, audience, and form of reasoning. The box below shows several possibilities.

Organizing an argument's body and response to opposing views

The traditional scheme

Claim 1 and evidence
Claim 2 and evidence
Claim X and evidence
Response to opposing views

The problem-solution scheme

The problem: claims and evidence
The solution: claims and evidence
Response to opposing views

Variations on the traditional scheme

Use a variation if you believe your readers will reject your argument without an early or intermittent response to opposing views.

Response to opposing views
Claim 1 and evidence
Claim 2 and evidence
Claim X and evidence

Claim 1 and evidence
Response to opposing views
Claim 2 and evidence
Response to opposing views
Claim X and evidence
Response to opposing views

You may want to experiment with various organizations—for instance, trying out your strongest claims first or last in the body, stating claims outright or letting the evidence build to them, answering the opposition near the beginning or near the end or claim by claim. You can do this experimentation on paper, of course, but it's easier on a computer. Try rearranging your outline as described on page 33. Or try rearranging your draft (work with a copy) by cutting and pasting parts of it for different emphases.

EXERCISE 10.9   Organizing your argument

Continuing from Exercise 10.8 (p. 211), develop a structure for your argument. Consider especially how you will introduce it, how you will arrange your claims, where you will place your responses to opposing views, and how you will conclude.

10h   Revising your argument

When you revise your argument, do it in at least two stages— revising underlying meaning and structure, and editing more superficial elements. The checklists on pages 51 and 58–59 can be a guide. Supplement them with the checklist below, which encourages you to think critically about your own argument.

Checklist for revising an argument

Thesis
- What is your thesis? Where is it stated?
- In what ways is your thesis statement an arguable claim?

Reasoning
- If your thesis derives from induction, where have you related the evidence to your generalization?
- If your thesis derives from deduction, is your syllogism both true and valid?
- Have you avoided fallacies in reasoning?

Evidence
- Where have you provided the evidence readers need?
- Where might your evidence not be accurate, relevant, representative, or adequate? (Answer this question from the point of view of a neutral or even skeptical reader.)

Appeals
- Where have you considered readers' probable beliefs and values?
- How are your rational appeals and emotional appeals appropriate for your readers?
- What is your ethical appeal? How can you improve it?

(continued)

ANSWERS: EXERCISE 10.9

Individual response.

PEER OUTLINING

Making an outline of a draft of a paper is challenging to do, but is a very powerful tool for revision. To make it easier for students, have them work with a partner to construct an outline of the draft. Then, the writer can revise the outline before writing the next draft.

TRANSPARENCY MASTER 10.5

COMPUTER ACTIVITY

Revision tools like the "Checklist for revising an argument" can be saved for easy access during the revision process.

COLLABORATIVE LEARNING

Students can work effectively together using the questions about Holbrook's essay in Exercise 10.11 to critique each other's final arguments. If students have worked continuously with the same group throughout the process of developing their arguments, you might rearrange the groups for this exercise so that each writer experiences a fresh set of responses to his or her argument.

ANSWERS: EXERCISE 10.10

Individual response.

MODELS OF STUDENT WRITING

Craig Holbrook's essay "TV Can Be Good for You" is a strong example of student writing featuring an introductory hook, a tight structure (with topic sentence claims at the ends of some paragraphs), extensive research, and effective appeals to reason. It may serve as a model of writing as engagement in reasoned debate, especially for students whose own writing overuses emotional appeals. It may also serve as a model of writing that goes against the grain of received wisdom, and does so persuasively.

To help your students formulate their own responses to the paper (especially in Exercise 10.11, questions 6 and 7), you might begin with classroom discussion or debate on the topic of television's effects on viewers. Students generally love to talk about television, although they may have an emotional stake in believing that their own watching habits are not harmful. You might compile some anecdotal data about class members and their families, and then discuss whether the evidence provided by the class seems to confirm or refute Holbrook's findings. On the basis of this discussion, you might also introduce the concept of evidence gathered in controlled studies versus anecdotal evidence.

Checklist for revising an argument

(continued)

Opposing views

- What opposing views have you answered?
- How successfully have you refuted opposing views? (Again, consider the neutral or skeptical reader.)

Organization

- How clearly does your argument move from one point to the next?
- How appropriate is your organization given your readers' likely views?

You can download this checklist from *ablongman.com/littlebrown*. Create a copy and answer the questions for each argument you write.

EXERCISE 10.10 Writing and revising your argument

Draft and revise the argument you have developed in the exercises in this chapter. Use the revision checklists on page 51 and above to review your work.

10i Examining a sample argument

The following essay by the student Craig Holbrook illustrates the principles discussed in this chapter. As you read the essay, notice especially the organization, the relation of claims and supporting evidence (including illustrations), the kinds of appeals Holbrook makes, and the ways he responds to opposing views.

TV Can Be Good for You

Introduction	Television wastes time, pollutes minds, destroys brain cells, and turns some viewers into murderers. Thus runs the prevailing talk
Identification of prevailing view	about the medium, supported by serious research as well as simple belief. But television has at least one strong virtue, too, which helps
Disagreement with prevailing view	to explain its endurance as a cultural force. It provides replacement voices that ease loneliness, spark healthful laughter, and even edu-
Thesis statement making three claims for television	cate young children.
Background for claim 1: effects of loneliness	Most people who have lived alone understand the curse of silence, when the only sound is the buzz of unhappiness or anxiety inside one's own head. Although people of all ages who live alone can experience intense loneliness, the elderly are especially vulnerable to solitude. For example, they may suffer increased confusion or
Evidence for effects of loneliness	depression when left alone for long periods but then rebound when they have steady companionship (Bondevik and Skogstad 329-30).

A study of elderly men and women in New Zealand found that television can actually serve as a companion by assuming "the role of social contact with the wider world," reducing "feelings of isolation and loneliness because it directs viewers' attention away from themselves" ("Television Programming"). (See fig. 1.) Thus television's replacement voices can provide comfort because they distract from a focus on being alone.

> Evidence for effects of television on loneliness

> Statement of claim 1

Fig. 1. Television can be a source of companionship for people whose living situations and limited mobility leave them lonely. Photograph by Jean Michel Foujols, Corbis image 42-15243193, 13 June 2005 <http://pro.corbis.com>.

> Illustration supporting claim 1

The absence of real voices can be most damaging when it means a lack of laughter. Here, too, research shows that television can have a positive effect on health. Laughter is one of the most powerful calming forces available to human beings, proven in many studies to reduce heart rate, lower blood pressure, and ease other stress-related ailments (Burroughs, Mahoney, and Lippman 172; Griffiths 18). (See fig. 2.) Television offers plenty of laughter: the recent listings for a single Friday night included more than twenty comedy programs running on the networks and on basic cable.

> Background for claim 2: effects of laughter

> Evidence for effects of laughter

> Evidence for comedy on television

A study reported in a health magazine found that laughter inspired by television and video is as healthful as the laughter generated by live comedy. Volunteers laughing at a video comedy routine "showed significant improvements in several immune functions, such as natural killer-cell activity" (Laliberte 78). Further, the effects of the comedy were so profound that "merely anticipating watching a funny video improved mood, depression, and anger as

> Evidence for effects of laughter in response to television

Illustration supporting healthful effects of laughter

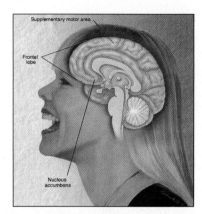

Fig. 2. According to the Society for Neuroscience, the process of understanding and being amused by something funny stimulates at least three main areas of the brain. The society makes no recommendation about TV watching, but other studies show the healthful effects of the activity. Illustration by Lydia Kibiuk from Society for Neuroscience, Brain Briefings, Dec. 2001, 12 June 2005 <http://apu.sfn.org/BrainBriefings/bb_humor.htm>.

Statement of claim 2

much as two days beforehand" (Laliberte 79). Even for people with plenty of companionship, television's replacement voices can have healthful effects by causing laughter.

Background for claim 3: educational effects

Television also provides information about the world. This service can be helpful to everyone but especially to children, whose natural curiosity can exhaust the knowledge and patience of their parents and caretakers. While the TV may be baby-sitting children, it can also enrich them. For example, educational programs such as those on the Discovery Channel, the Disney Channel, and PBS offer a steady stream of information at various cognitive levels. (See fig. 3.) Even many cartoons, which are generally dismissed as mindless or worse, familiarize children with the material of literature, including strong characters enacting classic narratives.

Evidence for educational programming on television

Evidence for educational effects of television on children

Two researchers studying children and television found that TV is a source of creative and psychological instruction, inspiring children "to play imaginatively and develop confidence and skills" (Colman and Colman 9). Instead of passively watching, children "interact with the programs and videos" and "sometimes include the fictional characters in reality's play time" (Colman and Colman 8). Thus television's voices both inform young viewers and encourage exchange.

Statement of claim 3

Fig. 3. Educational television programs such as <u>Sesame Street</u> are an important source of learning for children. Characters such as Elmo (shown here) promote reading, learning, and healthy behaviors. Photograph from United Nations Children's Fund, <u>The State of the World's Children</u>, 2002, 12 June 2005 <http://www.unicef.org/sowc02/feature10.htm>.

The value of these replacement voices should not be oversold. For one thing, almost everyone agrees that too much TV does no one any good and may cause much harm. Many studies show that excessive TV watching increases violent behavior, especially in children, and can cause, rather than ease, other antisocial behaviors (Reeks 114; Walsh 34). In addition, human beings require the give and take of actual interaction. Steven Pinker, an expert in children's language acquisition, warns that children cannot develop language properly by watching television. They need to interact with actual speakers who respond directly to their needs (282). Replacement voices are not real voices and in the end can do only limited good.

But even limited good is something, especially for those who are lonely or neglected. Television is not an entirely positive force, but neither is it an entirely negative one. Its voices stand by to provide company, laughter, and information whenever they're needed.

Illustration supporting claim 3

Anticipation of objection: harm of television

Anticipation of objection: need for actual interaction

Qualification of claims in response to objections

Conclusion

Works Cited

Bondevik, Margareth, and Anders Skogstad. "The Oldest Old, ADL, Social Network, and Loneliness." <u>Western Journal of Nursing Research</u> 20.3 (1998): 325-43.

Burroughs, W. Jeffrey, Diana L. Mahoney, and Louis G. Lippman. "Attributes of Health-Promoting Laughter: Cross-Generational Comparison." <u>Journal of Psychology</u> 136.2 (2004): 171-81.

Colman, Robyn, and Adrian Colman. "Inspirational Television." <u>Youth Studies in Australia</u> 21.3 (2003): 8-10.

ANSWERS: EXERCISE 10.11

Possible answers

1. *Claims* related to the thesis statement: the last sentences of paragraphs 3, 5, and 7; the first and last sentences of paragraph 8; and the conclusion. *Evidence:* studies cited in paragraphs 2, 3, 4, 5, 7, and 9; evidence gathered by the author in paragraphs 4 (comedy programming) and 6 (educational programming).

2. *Appeals to reason:* mainly, the use of studies as evidence (pars. 2, 3, 4 5, 7), the tempered claim (pars. 8, 9), and the deductive argument (replacement voices can be helpful; television provides replacement voices; therefore, television can be helpful). *Appeals to emotion:* sympathy for the lonely (par. 2), appreciation of children (par. 6). The argument is mainly rational.

3. The ethical appeal is that of a fair-minded, reasonable person.

4. *Appeals made by the illustrations:* Responses about the effectiveness of the illustrations will vary. Some of the appeals:

   Fig. 1 backs up the claim that TV can ease loneliness (rational appeal), shows the man enjoying himself (emotional appeal), and conveys the writer's competence in choosing an appropriate image (ethical appeal).

   Fig. 2 strengthens the claim that laughter is healthful with information from a reliable source (rational appeal), arouses curiosity with an unusual combination of photograph and diagram (emotional appeal), and proves the writer trustworthy and fair with the caption's acknowledgment that the source does not mention TV watching (ethical appeal).

   Fig. 3 supports the claim that TV can educate children by showing children with a character from a respected educational program (rational appeal), depicts a familiar, comfortable character and cute, smiling children (emotional appeal), and shows sensitivity to readers' probable knowledge as well as seriousness.

5. The objections are raised and answered in paragraph 8: too much TV is harmful, and replacement voices are not enough. Both objections are accepted as valid.

6. Individual response.

7. Individual response.

Foujouls, Jean Michel. Photograph. Corbis image 42-15243193. 13 June 2005 <http://pro.corbis.com>.

Griffiths, Joan. "The Mirthful Brain." Omni Aug. 1996: 18-19.

Kibiuk, Lydia. Illustration. Society for Neuroscience. Brain Briefings. Dec. 2001. 12 June 2005 <http://apu.sfn.org/BrainBriefings/bb_humor.htm>.

Laliberte, Richard W. "The Benefits of Laughter." Shape Sept. 2003: 78-79.

Pinker, Steven. The Language Instinct: How the Mind Creates Language. New York: Harper, 1994.

Reeks, Anne. "Kids and TV: A Guide." Parenting Apr. 2005: 110-15.

"Television Programming for Older People: Summary Research Report." NZ on Air. 25 July 2004. 15 Oct. 2005 <http://www.nzonair.gov.nz/media/oldpeoplesreport.pdf>.

United Nations Children's Fund. Photograph. The State of the World's Children. 2002. 12 June 2005 <http://unicef.org/sowc02/features10.htm>.

Walsh, Teri. "Too Much TV Linked to Depression." Prevention Feb. 2001: 34-36.

—Craig Holbrook (student)

EXERCISE 10.11   Critically reading an argument

Analyze the construction and effectiveness of the preceding essay by answering the following questions. (You can do this exercise online at *ablongman.com/littlebrown*.)

1. Where does Holbrook make claims related to his thesis statement, and where does he provide evidence to support the claims?
2. Where does Holbrook appeal primarily to reason, and where does he appeal primarily to emotion? What specific beliefs and values of readers does he appeal to?
3. How would you characterize Holbrook's ethical appeal?
4. How effective do you find the illustrations as support for Holbrook's claims? What appeals do they make? (For an analysis of Holbrook's first illustration, see p. 229.)
5. What objections to his argument does Holbrook anticipate? How does he respond to them?
6. How effective do you find this argument? To what extent does Holbrook convince you that television has virtues? Do some claims seem stronger or weaker than others? Does Holbrook respond adequately to objections?
7. Write a critical evaluation of "TV Can Be Good for You." First summarize Holbrook's views. Then respond to those views by answering the questions posed in number 6 above.

CHAPTER **11**

Reading and Using Visual Arguments

A **visual argument** uses images to engage and convince readers. Advertisements often provide the most vivid and memorable examples, but writers in almost every field—from astronomy to music to physiology—support their claims with images. In this chapter you'll learn how to read visual arguments critically (below) and how to use images to strengthen your own arguments (p. 225).

Note This chapter builds on the previous three, which discuss forming a critical perspective (including viewing images critically), reading an argument critically, and writing an argument. If you haven't already done so, read those chapters before this one.

11a   Reading visual arguments critically

Chapter 9 explains the three main elements of any argument: claims, evidence, and assumptions. To read visual arguments critically, you'll analyze all three elements.

1   Testing claims

Claims are positive statements that require support (see pp. 180, 181–83). In a visual argument, claims may be made by composition as well as by content, with or without accompanying words. Here are a few examples of visual claims:

Image	A magnetic sticker shaped like a ribbon and decorated with the colors and symbols of the American flag, positioned prominently on a car.
Claim	I support American troops overseas, and you should, too.
Image	A photograph framing hundreds of chickens crammed into small cages, resembling familiar images of World War II concentration camps.
Claim	Commercial poultry-raising practices are cruel and unethical.

http://www.ablongman.com/littlebrown ▶

Visit the companion Web site for more help
with reading and using visual arguments.

HIGHLIGHTS

This chapter is new to the 10th edition of *The Little, Brown Handbook*. Its coverage of visual argument should be very timely for students who are bombarded with visual images on television, in the print media, and online. The first half of the chapter teaches students how to read images for their underlying claims; how to evaluate the kinds of evidence used by a visual argument; how to identify the underlying assumptions upon which the image's claims are based; and how to recognize fallacies in visual arguments. The chapter's second half focuses on to how to use visual arguments to optimum effect. Students are shown how to choose images, how to use them as evidence, and how to evaluate their appeal to readers. Throughout the chapter, examples of visual arguments are provided as concrete illustrations of the concepts presented in each section.

IMAGE CAPTIONING

Collect a group of magazine ads that make claims visually. Cover the captions or text of each image so only the image is visible. Then have your students try to guess what the caption is by looking at the image alone. This exercise might produce hilarious results, and you can use it to help students understand how text and picture work together.

COMPANION WEB SITE

See page IAE-53 for companion Web site content description.

Image	A chart with dramatically contrasting bars that represent the optimism, stress, and weight reported by people before and after they participated in a program of daily walking.
Claim	Daily exercise leads to a healthier and happier life.

Image	A cartoon featuring affluent-looking young adults on an affluent-looking college campus, conversing and frowning sadly as they gaze downhill at rough-looking teens in a dilapidated schoolyard. The caption reads, "Yes, it's sad what's happening to schools today. But everyone knows that throwing money at the problem isn't the solution."
Claim	Better funding makes for better schools.

The following image is one of a series of advertisements featuring unnamed but well-known people as milk drinkers. The celebrity here is Oscar de la Hoya, a boxing champion. The advertisement makes several claims both in the photograph and in the text.

GET MORE MILK

The celebrity milk ads are so abundant that students may know of many additional examples. Ask them to bring those in and compare their claims to that of the Oscar de la Hoya example provided in this section. Most will be similar, but subtle differences in claims may be enlightening to students. They can also find many of the ads at whymilk.com/celebrity_archive.htm.

Claims in an image

Image claim: Cool, tough men drink milk.

Image claim: Attractive people drink milk.

Image claim: Athletes drink milk.

Text claim: Milk is a good source of nutrition, helping to build muscles.

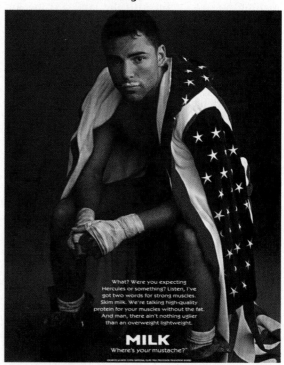

Advertisement by the Milk Processor
Education Program

2 Weighing evidence

The kinds of evidence provided in images parallel those found in written arguments (see pp. 183–85):

- **Facts** can be verified by observation or research. In visual arguments they may be data, as in a graph showing a five-year rise in oil prices. Or they may be inferences drawn from data, as in the statement in the preceding ad that milk provides "high-quality protein for your muscles without the fat." Sometimes images serve as facts themselves, objects that are analyzed in accompanying writing, as the milk ad is examined by this text or as the ad from *Time* magazine is examined by John Latner in the essay on pages 175–77.
- **Examples** illustrate and reinforce a point. Visual arguments often focus on an instance of the argument's claims, as Oscar de la Hoya does in the milk ad. Another ad might feature multiple images as examples: a Sizzler TV commercial, for instance, shows a sequence of luscious-looking foods to be had at the restaurant. An image might also illustrate a claim made in accompanying writing, as, again, the milk ad does in this text.
- **Expert opinions** are the findings of subject-matter authorities based on their research and experience. A visual argument might present a chart from an expert showing a trend in, say, unemployment among high school graduates. The familiar TV ad that features a doctor recommending a particular medicine to a patient offers the doctor as an expert.
- **Appeals to beliefs or needs** reinforce readers' values or truths. Many visual arguments make such appeals by depicting how things clearly ought to be (an antidrug ad featuring a teenager who is confidently refusing peer pressure) or, in contrast, by showing how things clearly should not be (a Web site for an antihunger campaign featuring images of emaciated children).

The evidence in a visual argument should be judged by the same criteria as that in a written argument (pp. 185–87):

- **Is the evidence accurate?** Images can be manipulated just as words can, and like words they should be analyzed for their fairness, precision, and trustworthiness. For example, a graph claiming to show changes in college living expenses between 1995 and 2005 should identify the source and purpose of the research, supply data for all the years, and clarify the definition of *living expenses* (the cost of room and board only, or transportation, recreation, and other expenses as well?).
- **Is the evidence relevant and adequate?** An image should pertain to the claims made in the larger argument and should sufficiently demonstrate its own claims. In an article on eating

FASHION DESIGN EXAMPLES

If your students are interested in fashion, you could ask them to bring in flyers or catalogs from their favorite designers or stores. Photographic examples of clothing can be compared from designer to designer or store to store.

PSEUDO-EXPERTS

Students are often very savvy about advertising claims. Ask them to locate an image using an expert opinion that they find suspect, and to explain to the rest of the class why they think the "expert" may not be credible.

COMPUTER ACTIVITY

GALLERY OF APPEALS

Ask students to look around on the Web and collect visual appeals that reinforce readers' values. They can provide links to the Web site and a brief analysis on your class Web site of the values to which the images appeal.

COLLABORATIVE LEARNING

RIIS'S IMAGES

Jacob Riis, the famous photojournalist, provides an excellent example of using visual images to advance an argument in his classic text *How the Other Half Lives* (New York: Charles Scribner's Sons, 1890). Have students work together to evaluate selected images and the accompanying data and text.

disorders, for instance, relevant and adequate images might include a medical diagram showing the liver damage from malnutrition and a photograph of a frail-bodied person suffering from anorexia. However, a photograph of a skinny model or actor would be neither relevant nor adequate, merely sensationalistic, unless the subject had publicly confirmed that his or her low weight resulted from an eating disorder.

■ **Does the evidence represent the context?** Representative visual evidence reflects the full range of the sample it's drawn from and does not overrepresent or hide important elements of the subject. For example, a photographic essay claiming to document the poor working conditions of migrant farm workers might reasonably include images of one worker's scarred hands and another worker suffering from heat prostration. But to be representative, the essay would also need to illustrate the full range of migrant workers' experiences.

The annotations on the following pie chart demonstrate a way to analyze the evidence in a visual argument—even when, as in this case, the image comes from a highly reputable source. (The Social Science Data Analysis Network is a scholarly organization.)

Evidence in a visual argument

Accuracy: Trustworthy because based on data from the US Census, but perhaps somewhat distorted by the census's reliance on information volunteered by respondents

Relevance and adequacy: Shows incomes, as claimed, but the data are not immediately current because the US Census is conducted only every ten years

Representativeness: Fully representative of the census sample, with no distortion of particular segments (e.g., by emphasizing some pie slices over others)

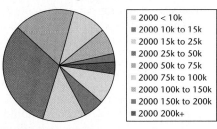

Fig. 1. Household incomes in the United States, based on data from the 2000 US Census, from Social Science Data Analysis Network, CensusScope, 15 Oct. 2005 <http://www.censusscope.org/us/chart_income.html>.

3 Discovering assumptions

Like a written argument, a visual argument is based on **assumptions**—the creator's ideas, often unstated, about why the evidence relates to the claims (see pp. 187–88). In visual arguments many assumptions involve the creator's beliefs about the audience, as detailed on the facing page. The examples analyze the milk ad on page 220, featuring the boxer Oscar de la Hoya.

- **Who readers are and where they will see the argument.** The de la Hoya ad first appeared in sports magazines, so the advertiser could assume readers who are interested in sports and athletes.
- **What readers already know about the subject.** To sports fans, de la Hoya would be a familiar subject. The advertiser presumably considers readers less familiar with the benefits of milk or with its appeal to celebrities like de la Hoya.
- **How familiar readers are with the purpose, format, and style of the argument.** With nearly two hundred print and TV ads since 1994, the milk-mustache campaign has become a fixture of US popular culture. Each new ad fits into the framework established by its predecessors.
- **Whether readers are likely to lean toward the argument's claims.** The advertiser clearly assumes that the endorsement of a sports star like de la Hoya will carry weight with readers. At the same time, it seems to assume that the benefits of milk still need selling to readers.
- **What kinds of information, ideas, and images readers will find persuasive.** The advertiser seems to assume that a strictly factual claim about the health benefits of milk would not be persuasive enough to readers, so it shows that admirable people like de la Hoya consume milk. The photograph of de la Hoya emphasizes qualities that the advertiser presumably thinks will appeal to readers: fitness, toughness, directness, and even (in the robe draped over the boxer's shoulders) patriotism.

4 Recognizing fallacies

Fallacies, or errors in argument, are sometimes accidental, but they are often used deliberately to manipulate readers' responses. All the fallacies of written arguments discussed on pages 192–97 appear in visual arguments as well. Here we'll focus on examples of the two main categories.

- **Evasions attempt to deflect the reader from the central claim of the argument.** One evasion is **snob appeal,** inviting readers to think or be like someone they admire. Look again at the de la Hoya milk ad on page 220. Like all celebrity ads in the milk-mustache campaign, this one appeals to the reader's wish to emulate a famous person. If you drink milk, the ad says subtly, you too may become fit, skillful, and direct (notice that de la Hoya looks unguardedly into the camera). The ad does have some substance in its specific and verifiable claim that milk contains "high-quality protein for your muscles without the fat," but de la Hoya himself, with his milk mustache, makes a stronger claim.

■ **Oversimplifications imply that subjects are less complex than they are.** Two examples are the **either/or fallacy,** which asserts that a complicated situation has only two sides worth considering, and the **sweeping generalization,** which asserts that a single view applies to all instances when it may apply only to some, or to none. Both fallacies appear in the map below, which represents the Electoral College vote in the 2004 US Presidential election: red for states won by Republican George W. Bush, blue for states won by Democrat John F. Kerry. The colors represent majority votes and Electoral College, not popular, votes. Still, the colors have been used to characterize the political and social preferences of each state's entire population and to reinforce stereotypes about rural vs. urban, heartland vs. coastal, and conservative vs. liberal citizens.

Fallacies in a visual argument

Either/or fallacy: Solid colors implying that all of the voters in each state chose either the Republican or the Democratic candidate, when every state had voters for both candidates and for candidates from other political parties

Sweeping generalization: Strong contrast implying that voters' concerns were unconflicted and were represented by a single vote

The Electoral College vote in the 2004 US Presidential election: red states for Bush, blue states for Kerry

ANSWERS: EXERCISE 11.1

Possible answers:

1. The audience seems to be people who are serving or might serve as Big Brothers or Big Sisters (primarily the latter since the people depicted are female). The happiness and togetherness of the subjects would reinforce the commitment of current volunteers and invite the participation of others.
2. The organization fosters pairings of adults and children and emphasizes togetherness and having fun.
3. The main claim is in the large text: "Time spent with you is like a day at the beach." In other words, the relationship of volunteer and child is carefree, invigorating, fun.
4. The photograph provides the evidence for the claim: the beach is inviting, the subjects are happy, lively, and affectionate.
5. Some assumptions: Happy, affectionate relationships are good for adults and children. The smiling subjects are in fact a volunteer and her "little sister." A day at the beach is an appealing prospect and a desirable parallel for a relationship.
6. The most noticeable elements of the image are subjects' feet, the subjects' smiles and windblown hair, and the bright background, all conveying beach fun. The foregrounded bare feet, especially, emphasize freedom and playfulness. The large type across the woman's feet further focuses attention on them.
7. Individual response.

EXERCISE 11.1 Reading a visual argument critically

The image on the facing page is an e-card found on the Web site of Big Brothers Big Sisters of America, a community organization that brings children and mentors together. The organization invites site visitors to send its cards "to encourage friends and family members to support Big Brothers Big Sisters." Examine the card's visual argument closely, and jot down your answers to the following questions. (You can do this exercise online at *ablongman.com/littlebrown*.)

1. Who appears to be the intended audience? What aspects of the text and photograph seem best suited to that audience?
2. What can you tell about Big Brothers Big Sisters from this e-card?
3. What claims does the image make?
4. What evidence supports the claims? How effective is it?
5. What assumptions underlie the argument, connecting evidence to claims?

6. How does the visual organization (cropping of the photograph, placement of the text) make the argument more or less effective?
7. Is the argument persuasive to you? Why or why not?

E-card from the Web site of
Big Brothers Big Sisters of America

EXERCISE 11.2 Identifying fallacies in visual arguments

Locate a current or historical source with extreme views on a subject, such as the Web site of an outspoken political commentator, a sensationalist tabloid newspaper, or a collection of wartime propaganda (from any nation or era). Photocopy or print an image that seems especially ripe with fallacies and, referring to the complete list of fallacies on p. 193, find as many as possible in the image. The following sites can help you begin your search:

Political commentators

Al Franken: *shows.airamericaradio.com/alfrankenshow*
Rush Limbaugh: *rushlimbaugh.com/home/today.guest.html*

Tabloids

National Enquirer (US): *nationalenquirer.com*
Daily Mail (Great Britain): *http://www.dailymail.co.uk/pages/live/dailymail/ home.html?in_page_id=1766*

World War II propaganda

Northwestern University library (American images): *http://www.library .northwestern.edu/govpub/collections/wwii-posters*
Calvin College (German images): *http://www.calvin.edu/academic/cas/ gpa*

CONTEMPORARY PROPAGANDA

The propaganda sources listed in Exercise 11.2 are for World War II, but propaganda has arguably been used by the United States in more recent wars (Vietnam, Persian Gulf, Iraq). The validity of these wars and the US role in them are matters highly contested by the American public. Students may hold strong opinions that impair their ability to evaluate US documents about these wars or to entertain the notion that the US might have engaged in propaganda activities. However, if your students are able to handle such controversial issues, it could be productive to bring in some examples of government-produced images about these wars.

ANSWERS: EXERCISE 11.2

Individual response.

11b Using visual arguments effectively

Chapter 10 explains how you can use written argument to convince readers of your claims and perhaps move them to take action. Weaving images into an argument can strengthen it *if* the images are well chosen to provide evidence and make appropriate appeals.

Note Any visual you include in a paper requires the same detailed citation as a written source. If you plan to publish your argument online, you will also need to seek permission from the author. See pages 633–37 for more on acknowledging sources and obtaining permissions.

1 Choosing images

You can wait until you've drafted an argument before concentrating on what images to include. This approach keeps your focus on the research and writing needed to craft the best argument from sources. But you can also begin thinking visually at the beginning of a project, as you might if your initial interest in the subject was sparked by a compelling image. Either way, ask yourself some basic questions as you consider visual options:

- **Which parts of your argument can use visual reinforcement?** What can be explained better visually than verbally? Can a graph or chart present data compactly and interestingly? Can a photograph appeal effectively to readers' beliefs and values?
- **What are the limitations or requirements of your writing situation?** What do the type of writing you're doing and its format allow? Look through examples of similar writing to gauge the kinds of illustrations readers will expect. And consider the medium you're writing in: a short animation sequence might be terrific in a *PowerPoint* presentation or on the Web, but a printed document requires photographs, drawings, and other static means of explanation.
- **What kinds of visuals are readily available on your subject?** As you researched your subject, what images seemed especially effective? What sources have you not yet explored? Tips for locating images, whether printed or online, appear on pages 594–96.
- **Should you create original images tailored to your argument?** Instead of searching for existing images, would your time be better spent taking your own photographs or using computer software to compose visual explanations, such as diagrams, charts, and graphs? Tips for creating images appear on pages 120–25.

2 Using images as evidence

An image can attract readers' attention, but if it stops there it will amount to mere decoration or, worse, it will distract readers from the substance of your argument. When you use images as *evidence* for your argument, you engage readers both intellectually and visually.

The images used as evidence in visual arguments fall into four general categories:

- **Artifacts serving as the subject of the argument,** such as a painting or advertisement you are analyzing. (See pp. 175–77 for an example.)
- **Visual records of a subject or incident,** such as a historical photograph or a seismic record of an earthquake tremor.
- **Visual explanations of a concept or trend,** such as a diagram of the human respiratory system or a graph of financial data.
- **Visual examples of claims made in the argument,** such as a photograph of a school building abandoned after funding shortfalls or a screen shot of a Web pop-up advertisement.

To make an image work hard as evidence, be sure it relates directly to a point in your argument, adds to that point, and gives readers something to think about. Always include a caption that explicitly ties the image to your text, so that readers don't have to puzzle out your intentions, and that provides source information. Number images in sequence (Fig. 1, Fig. 2, and so on), and refer to them by number at the appropriate points in your text. (See Chapter 5, pp. 120–25, for more on captioning and numbering illustrations.)

The images below and on the next page illustrate approaches to using visual evidence in an argument with the following thesis: *Television shows focusing on cosmetic procedures are encouraging women to opt for such procedures in order to conform to a particular standard of beauty.*

Image as evidence

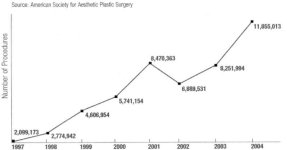

Graph from a reputable source providing a visual explanation of the overall increase in cosmetic procedures

Fig. 1. Numbers of cosmetic procedures performed in the United States, 1997-2004. In 2004 such procedures increased 44 percent. Graph from American Society for Aesthetic Plastic Surgery, 2004 Cosmetic Surgery National Data Bank: Statistics, 3 June 2005 <http://www.surgery.org/press/statistics-2004.php>.

Caption explaining the graph and highlighting the 2004 increase, the most relevant to the paper's claims

SEARCHING FOR VISUALS

Some search engines, such as *Google*, allow users to limit a search to images only, which can help students search more efficiently.

SUGGESTED READINGS

Langrehr, Don. "From a Semiotic Perspective: Inference Formation and the Critical Comprehension of Television Advertising." *Reading Online* 9 (May 2003). Langrehr illustrates the difficulty students have "reading" television advertisements and offers advice on improving this dimension of visual literacy.

Sellen, Mary. "Information Literacy in the General Education: A New Requirement for the 21st Century." *Journal of General Education* 51 (2002): 115–126. Sellen suggests that there is a need for instruction in multimedia literacy because students can now incorporate visual and aural information into their texts.

Stroupe, Craig. "Visualizing English: Recognizing the Hybrid Literacy of Visual and Verbal Authorship on the Web." *College English* 62 (May 2000): 607–632. Stroupe presents a method for combining verbal and nonverbal features in student texts, made possible by the advances in visual digitality.

Images as evidence

A decorative image that sensationalizes but does not illuminate the argument

An uninformative caption that neither tells how to view the image nor links the image to the argument's claims

Fig. 2. A participant on the television show Extreme Makeover, from Walt Disney Internet Group, ABC, Extreme Makeover, 2005, 30 May 2005 <http://abc.go.com/primetime/extrememakeover/index.html>.

Before and after images providing both a visual record and visual examples of the argument's claims

Caption explaining the images and the woman's cosmetic treatments, tying the images to the text of the paper

Fig. 2. Before and after images of a participant on the television show Extreme Makeover. In addition to the change in personal style implied by the change in clothes, hairdo, and body language, this participant also underwent nose surgery, a brow lift, eye surgery, dental work, liposuction, and breast augmentation. Photographs from Walt Disney Internet Group, ABC, Extreme Makeover, 2005, 30 May 2005 <http://abc.go.com/primetime/extrememakeover/index.html>.

3 Considering images' appeals to readers

Images can help to strengthen your argument's appeals to readers. The appeals are discussed in detail on pages 208–10. The summary below suggests how they apply to images:

- **Rational appeals target readers' capacity for reasoning logically.** Images can strengthen the evidence for an argument if they come from reliable sources, present information fairly and accurately, and relate clearly to the paper's claims.
- **Emotional appeals tap into readers' beliefs and feelings.** Images can appeal to a host of ideas and emotions, including patriotism, curiosity, moral values, sympathy, and anger. Any such appeal should correctly gauge readers' beliefs and feelings and should be clearly relevant to the argument.
- **Ethical appeals show readers that you are a competent, fair, and trustworthy source of information.** Images make ethical appeals largely by making appropriate rational and emotional appeals. In addition, they can show awareness of readers' knowledge, prove your seriousness, and demonstrate your neutrality.

To see how all three appeals can work in images, look again at a photograph used in the sample argument paper on pages 214–18. This image illustrates the writer's claim that television can ease loneliness.

Appeals in an image

Rational appeal: Backs up the writer's claim that TV can ease loneliness: the man appears to live alone (only one chair is visible) and is interacting enthusiastically with the TV

Emotional appeal: Reinforces the benefits of TV watching: the man's isolation may be disturbing, but his excitement is pleasing

Ethical appeal: Conveys the writer's competence through the appropriateness of the image for the point being made

Fig. 1. Television can be a source of companionship for people whose living situations and limited mobility leave them lonely. Photograph by Jean Michel Foujols, Corbis image 42-15243193, 13 June 2005 <http://pro.corbis.com>.

2. Images somewhat helpful; photographs of people gathered in building entrances or other places where smokers congregate, emphasizing variety of people and obvious interactions.
3. Images essential: Military recruitment ads targeted to certain kinds of people.
4. Images helpful: photograph of solid-waste landfill; chart showing current and proposed volume of campus waste; diagram showing proposed recycling process.
5. Images not helpful unless data demonstrate relation of music listening and information retention.

ANSWERS: EXERCISE 11.4

Additional images might include a graph showing the increase in viewers watching TV makeover shows (to complement the graph showing an increase in cosmetic procedures) and additional before and after photographs of women having makeovers on such shows (to reinforce the claim that the shows encourage a "particular beauty standard."

COMPUTER ACTIVITY

As a follow-up to Exercise 11.4, ask students to conduct a Web search to find additional images to support the argument about cosmetic procedures.

ANSWERS: EXERCISE 11.5

Individual response.

ANSWERS: EXERCISE 11.6

Individual response.

ANSWERS: EXERCISE 11.7

Individual response.

COLLABORATIVE LEARNING

DAILY SHOWS

Television comedians like Jon Stewart often use visual images in a deliberately bad way to expose ironies and poke fun at public figures. As a follow-up to Exercise 11.6, have your class create and perform its own daily news spoof show, juxtaposing images and text for satirical effect.

EXERCISE 11.3   Brainstorming images for a visual argument

Working on your own or with others in a small group, apply the four questions for choosing images (p. 226) to the argument subjects below. Which subject would most likely benefit from images? Which would be most difficult to illustrate? Why? (You can do this exercise online at *ablongman.com/littlebrown*.)

1. A program to help senior citizens adopt and care for a pet would improve seniors' lives and benefit the community.
2. Smoking cigarettes is a good way to meet interesting people.
3. Today's military-recruitment advertising targets certain kinds of people more than others.
4. Our campus needs a better recycling program.
5. Listening to music while studying helps one retain information.

EXERCISE 11.4   Filling gaps in a visual argument

Take another look at the graph and the paired photographs on pages 227–28, taken from a paper claiming that TV makeover shows encourage women to have cosmetic procedures in order to conform to a particular beauty standard. What additional images might bolster the argument? Consider especially how you might supplement the graph to connect the increase in cosmetic procedures with the growing popularity of TV makeover shows that feature such procedures.

EXERCISE 11.5   Revising an oversimplified visual argument

The red and blue map on page 224 comes from *Maps and Cartograms of the 2004 US Presidential Election Results* at www-personal.umich.edu/ ~mejn/election. Visit the site to see illustrations that capture more of the complexity of the 2004 election. Then write a brief visual argument based on one of the other images. Alternatively, write a brief argument about the original red and blue map, explaining its flaws. (Remember to include and cite in your paper any image you discuss.)

EXERCISE 11.6   Creating a deliberately bad visual argument

Purposely breaking the rules of argument can be fun and illuminating, building your knowledge about what works best and why. Using one of the topics listed in Exercise 11.3 or a new one, create a visual argument and an accompanying paragraph of text that deliberately antagonize readers instead of appealing to them. Do your best to do your worst: instead of demonstrating logic, use flawed reasoning or confusing examples; instead of appealing to readers' values and emotions, let your argument be boring or hostile; instead of communicating your credibility and expertise, display ignorance or ineptness.

EXERCISE 11.7   Revising an ineffective visual argument

Locate an ineffective visual argument, and use the guidelines on page 229 to improve its likely appeal to readers. If your classmates completed Exercise 11.6, you could revise another student's deliberately bad argument.

HIGHLIGHTS

In this chapter, students will encounter a brief descriptive grammar that can serve as a reference for explanations of basic grammatical terms and as a guide to how sentences are constructed and their major elements punctuated. The chapter builds cumulatively from the simplest sentence to increasingly complex expansions rather than compartmentalizing grammar into parts of speech and kinds of phrases, clauses, and sentences. Moreover, it treats punctuation in context, as part of the discussion of word groups and syntactic relationships that may require it.

Because of its whole sentence approach and because of the many sentence-combining and -modeling exercises it contains, this chapter can be useful for a wide range of students. Those whose writing displays fundamental problems with sentences will benefit from its clear treatment of sentence parts and structure and from the exercises that require manipulation of sentence elements. Those who have mastered basic sentence strategies will be able to develop many options for expression through sentence-combining exercises that introduce elements like verbal phrases, absolute phrases, and appositives. And all students will gain a greater understanding of punctuation when they see how it grows out of and communicates a sentence's structure and meaning.

This chapter uses almost entirely traditional terminology because such terminology, despite its weaknesses, is still the most widely used and most likely to be familiar to students and instructors. The overall description largely reflects a structural view of English grammar. It is as simple as possible while still including all the word classes and syntactic structures needed by the student to understand the twenty successive chapters on sentences and punctuation.

You may wish to emphasize or de-emphasize the chapter, depending in part on the preparation of your students and on how much you think an understanding of grammar can contribute to

COMPANION WEB SITE

See page IAE-53 for companion Web site content description.

CHAPTER **12**

Understanding Sentence Grammar

Grammar describes how language works. Following the rules of standard English grammar is what allows you to communicate with others across barriers of personality, region, class, or ethnic origin. If you are a native English speaker, you follow these rules mostly unconsciously. But when you're trying to improve your ability to communicate, it can help to make the rules conscious and learn the language used to describe them.

Grammar reveals a lot about a sentence, even if you don't know the meanings of all the words:

The rumfrums prattly biggled the pooba.

You don't know what this sentence means, but you can infer that some things called *rumfrums* did something to a *pooba*. They *biggled* it, whatever that means, in a *prattly* way. Two grammatical cues, especially, make this sentence like *The students easily passed the test:*

- **Word forms.** The ending *-s* means more than one *rumfrum*. The ending *-ed* means that *biggled* is an action that happened in the past. The ending *-ly* means that *prattly* probably describes *how* the *rumfrums biggled.*
- **Word order.** *Rumfrums biggled pooba* resembles a common sequence in English: something (*rumfrums*) performed some action (*biggled*) to or on something else (*pooba*). Since *prattly* comes right before the action, it probably describes the action.

This chapter explains how such structures work and shows how practicing with them can help you communicate more effectively.

Note Grammar and style checkers can both offer assistance and cause problems as you compose sentences. Look for the cautions and tips for using such checkers in this and the next five parts

http://www.ablongman.com/littlebrown ▶

Visit the companion Web site for more help and additional exercises on sentence grammar.

of this book. For more information about grammar and style checkers, see pages 60–62.

12a Understanding the basic sentence

The **sentence** is the basic unit of thought. Its grammar consists of words with specific forms and functions arranged in specific ways.

1 Identifying subjects and predicates

Most sentences make statements. First the **subject** names something; then the **predicate** makes an assertion about the subject or describes an action by the subject.

Subject	Predicate
Art	thrives.

The **simple subject** consists of one or more nouns or pronouns, whereas the **complete subject** also includes any modifiers. The **simple predicate** consists of one or more verbs, whereas the **complete predicate** adds any words needed to complete the meaning of the verb plus any modifiers.

Sometimes, as in the short example *Art thrives,* the simple and complete subject and predicate are the same. More often, they are different:

Subject   Predicate
———complete———   ———complete———
     simple   simple
Some contemporary **art**   **stirs** controversy.
———complete———   ———complete———
  — simple —   — simple —
Critics and the **media** **discuss** and **dispute** its value.

In the second example, the simple subject and simple predicate are both **compound:** in each, two words joined by a coordinating conjunction (*and*) serve the same function.

Note If a sentence contains a word group such as *that makes it into established museums* or *because viewers finally agree about its quality,* you may be tempted to mark the subject and verb in the word group as the subject and verb of the sentence. But these word groups are subordinate clauses, made into modifiers by the words they begin with: *that* and *because.* See pages 252–53 for more on subordinate clauses.

CULTURE LANGUAGE The subject of an English sentence may be a noun (*art*) or a pronoun that refers to the noun (*it*), but not both. (See p. 235.)

Faulty	Some art it stirs controversy.
Revised	Some art stirs controversy.

their writing. As may be obvious, this chapter of the handbook was prepared in the belief that a clear understanding of the essential structure of English sentences and of the uses of syntactic groups and compound structures can help many students not only to punctuate correctly but also to gain greater control of subordination and emphasis within their sentences. This process will take place only if students get a chance to put knowledge into action through exercises that ask them to manipulate and create sentences. In this regard, the sentence-combining exercises in the chapter can be coordinated with those in other chapters of the text to create a program of sentence combining designed to complement instruction in essay and paragraph writing.

RESOURCES AND IDEAS

Grammar instruction

Does grammar instruction help? The effectiveness of grammar instruction in improving writing and in helping students achieve correctness in their prose is still a hotly debated issue. The essays in *The Place of Grammar in Writing Instruction: Past, Present, Future*, edited by Susan Hunter and Ray Wallace, explore the various possibilities for integrating grammar into writing instruction, including Eric H. Hobson's "Taking Computer-Assisted Grammar Instruction to New Frontiers" (Portsmouth, NH: Boynton, 1995). A recent issue of *English Journal* (85: 7, Nov. 1996) is devoted to considerations surrounding the teaching of grammar. These essays range from historical overviews like Martha Kolln's "Rhetorical Grammar: A Modification Lesson" to the debates surrounding grammar instruction in Ed Vavra's "On Not Teaching Grammar" to specific discussions of how best to teach pronoun and verb usage.

Other useful works on grammar instruction include the following:

Connors, Robert, J. "The Erasure of the Sentence." *College Composition and Communication* 52 (September 2001): 96–128. Connors suggests that sentence combining and imitation exercises, which fell out of favor after the paradigm shift in composition theory, remain useful for improving student writing.

Enos, Teresa, ed. *A Sourcebook for Basic Writing Teachers.* New York: Random, 1987. This collection of essays explores the debates over the efficacy of grammar instruction for standard and for nonstandard dialect speakers. The collection includes Sarah D'Eloia's "The Uses —and Limits—of Grammar," which suggests ways to integrate instruction in writing and grammar, including dictation, paraphrase and conversion, imitation, follow-ups to writing assignments, and exercises that ask students to "discover" a rule from examples of it in operation (373–416).

Farr, Marcia, and Harvey Daniels. *Language Diversity and Writing Instruction.* New York: ERIC Clearinghouse on Urban Education, 1986. Though the issue is clearly far from resolved, the perspective offered in this work is promising. The authors look at standard and nonstandard dialects in the context of linguistic research and provide suggestions for shaping writing instruction as a whole (including

Tests to find subjects and predicates

The tests below use the following example:

> Art that makes it into museums has often survived controversy.

Identify the subject.

- **Ask *who* or *what* is acting or being described in the sentence.**

Complete subject	art that makes it into museums

- **Isolate the sample subject by deleting modifiers**—words or word groups that don't name the actor of the sentence but give information about it. In the example, the word group *that makes it into museums* does not name the actor but modifies it.

Simple subject	art

Identify the predicate.

- **Ask what the sentence asserts about the subject:** what is its action, or what state is it in? In the example, the assertion about *art* is that it *has often survived controversy.*

Complete predicate	has often survived controversy

- **Isolate the verb, the simple predicate, by changing the time of the subject's action.** The simple predicate is the word or words that change as a result.

Example	Art . . . has often survived controversy.
Present	Art . . . often <u>survives</u> controversy.
Future	Art . . . often <u>will survive</u> controversy.
Simple predicate	has survived

2 Identifying the basic words: Nouns and verbs

The following five simple sentences consist almost entirely of two quite different kinds of words:

Subject	Predicate
The earth	trembled.
The earthquake	destroyed the city.
The result	was chaos.
The government	sent the city aid.
The citizens	considered the earthquake a disaster.

The words in the subject position name things, such as *earth, earthquake,* and *government.* In contrast, the words in the predicate position express states or actions, such as *trembled, destroyed,* and *sent.*

These two groups of words work in different ways. *Citizen* can become *citizens,* but not *citizened. Destroyed* can become *destroys,*

The parts of speech

Nouns name persons, places, things, ideas, or qualities: *Roosevelt, girl, Kip River, coastline, Koran, table, strife, happiness.* (See below.)

Pronouns usually substitute for nouns and function as nouns: *I, you, he, she, it, we, they, myself, this, that, who, which, everyone.* (See p. 237.)

Verbs express actions, occurrences, or states of being: *run, bunt, inflate, become, be.* (See the next page.)

Adjectives describe or modify nouns or pronouns: *gentle, small, helpful.* (See p. 242.)

Adverbs describe or modify verbs, adjectives, other adverbs, or whole groups of words: *gently, helpfully, almost, really, someday.* (See p. 242.)

Prepositions relate nouns or pronouns to other words in a sentence: *about, at, down, for, of, with.* (See p. 245.)

Conjunctions link words, phrases, and clauses. **Coordinating conjunctions** and **correlative conjunctions** link words, phrases, or clauses of equal importance: *and, but, or, nor; both . . . and, not only . . . but also, either . . . or.* (See pp. 259–60.) **Subordinating conjunctions** introduce subordinate clauses and link them to main clauses: *although, because, if, whenever.* (See p. 253.)

Interjections express feeling or command attention, either alone or in a sentence: *hey, oh, darn, wow.*

but not *destroyeds*. Grammar reflects such differences by identifying the **parts of speech** or **word classes** shown in the box above. Except for *the* and *a*, which simply point to and help identify the words after them, the five sentences about the earthquake consist entirely of nouns and verbs.

■ Nouns

Meaning

Nouns name. They may name a person (*Hilary Duff, Jesse Jackson, astronaut*), a thing (*chair, book, Mt. Rainier*), a quality (*pain, mystery, simplicity*), a place (*city, Washington, ocean, Red Sea*), or an idea (*reality, peace, success*).

Form

Most nouns form the **possessive** to indicate ownership or source. Singular nouns usually add an apostrophe plus *-s* (*Auden's poems*); plural nouns usually add just an apostrophe (*citizens' rights*).

Nouns also change form to distinguish between singular (one) and plural (more than one). Most nouns add *-s* or *-es* for the plural: *earthquake, earthquakes; city, cities.* Some nouns have irregular plurals: *woman, women; child, children.*

DICTATION

Read to your class the words in the list below (or in a similar one) and then go through the list again, giving students a minute or two to write sentences using the words in as many different roles (parts of speech) as they can. The word *good*, for example, can be an adjective or a noun.

well	post
set	bill
that	needle
while	bit
turn	

instruction in formal grammar) in ways that are likely to benefit speakers of nonstandard dialects.

Gorrell, Donna. "Controlled Composition for Basic Writers," *College Composition and Communication* 32 (1981): 308–16. Gorrell argues that students who learn to correct the grammar of their peers become more skilled in producing their own error-free sentences.

Newman, Michael. "Correctness and Its Conceptions: The Meaning of Language Form for Basic Writers." *Journal of Basic Writing* 15 (Summer 1996): 23–38. Newman discusses changing views on "correctness" and "error" since Mina Shaughnessy's pathbreaking *Errors and Expectations*.

Noguchi, Rei. R. *Grammar and the Teaching of Writing: Limits and Possibilities*. Urbana: NCTE, 1991. Noguchi has made an important contribution in helping teachers conceive of grammar instruction as a conceptual issue, and of student errors as an inseparable part of the larger concerns with meaning-making in writing instruction.

Online Writing Center of the University of Wisconsin at Madison. *http://www.wisc.edu/writing*. This site is especially helpful to students with grammar problems.

Purdue University Online Writing Lab. *http://owl.english.purdue.edu* This is one of our profession's most respected OWLs.

Sams, Lynn. "How to Teach Grammar, Analytical Thinking, and Writing: A Method That Works." *English Journal* 92 (January 2003): 57–65.

Sams rejects instruction in prescriptive grammar and in-context grammar instruction in favor of a sequenced approach to grammar instruction designed to build students' competence gradually.

Dealing with error

Bartholomae, David. "The Study of Error." *College Composition and Communication* 31 (1980): 253–69. Bartholomae suggests that asking basic writers to read their papers aloud helps identify sources of error and can contribute to improvement in writing.

Horner, Bruce. "Discoursing Basic Writing." *College Composition and Communication* 47 (1996): 199–222. Horner discusses the larger trends in the basic writing movement since the 1970s, including changing approaches to error.

Shaughnessy, Mina P. *Errors and Expectations: A Guide for the Teacher of Basic Writing*. New York: Oxford UP, 1977. This valuable book focuses on basic writing but is also an important work for teachers of writing at all levels. It provides a detailed analysis of the causes of student errors as well as useful strategies for dealing with writing problems.

Viera, Carroll. "Helping Students to Help Themselves: An Approach to Grammar." *College Composition and Communication* 37 (1986): 94–96. Viera suggests having students analyze their own grammatical problems, do research in their handbooks, and present mini-lessons in small groups.

ARTICLES AND LANGUAGES

Students who are native speakers of such languages as Russian, Korean, and Japanese may have difficulty understanding the concept of the article, and you may need to work on this basic concept before moving on to the distinction between definite and indefinite articles. Students who are native speakers of Spanish or Italian may have difficulty hearing the difference between "this" and "these" because of the way "i" is pronounced in those languages.

CULTURE LANGUAGE Some useful rules for forming noun plurals appear on pages 548–49. The irregular plurals must be memorized. Note that some nouns (noncount nouns) do not form plurals in English—for instance, *equality, anger, oxygen, equipment*. (See p. 237.)

Nouns with *the, a,* and *an*

Nouns are often preceded by *the* or *a* (*an* before a vowel sound: *an apple*). These words are usually called **articles** or **determiners** and always indicate that a noun follows.

CULTURE LANGUAGE See pages 326–30 for the rules governing the use of *the, a/an,* or no article at all before a noun.

Verbs

Meaning

Verbs express an action (*bring, change, grow*), an occurrence (*become, happen*), or a state of being (*be, seem*).

Form

Most verbs can be recognized by two changes in form:

- **Most verbs add -*d* or -*ed* to indicate a difference between present and past time:** *They play today. They played yesterday.* Some verbs indicate past time irregularly: *eat, ate; begin, began* (see pp. 278–80).
- **Most present-time verbs add -*s* or -*es* with subjects that are singular nouns:** *The bear escapes. It runs. The woman begins. She sings.* The exceptions are *be* and *have,* which change to *is* and *has.*

(See Chapter 14, pp. 275–92, for more on verb forms.)

Helping verbs

Certain forms of all verbs can combine with other words such as *do, have, can, might, will,* and *must.* These other words are called **helping verbs** or **auxiliary verbs.** In verb phrases such as *could run, will be running,* and *has escaped,* they help to convey time and other attributes. (See Chapter 14, pp. 276–77, 283–87.)

A note on form and function

In different sentences an English word may serve different functions, take correspondingly different forms, and belong to different word classes. For example:

> The government sent the city aid. [*Aid* functions as a noun.]
> Governments aid citizens. [*Aid* functions as a verb.]

Because words can function in different ways, we must always determine how a particular word works in a sentence before we can identify what part of speech it is. **The *function* of a word in a sentence always determines its part of speech in that sentence.**

■ Pronouns

Most **pronouns** substitute for nouns and function in sentences as nouns do. In the following sentence all three pronouns—*who, they, their*—refer to *nurses*:

Some nurses <u>who</u> have families prefer the night shift because <u>they</u> have more time with <u>their</u> children.

The most common pronouns are the **personal pronouns** (*I, you, he, she, it, we, they*) and the **relative pronouns** (*who, whoever, which, that*). Most of these change form to indicate their function in the sentence—for instance, *He called <u>me</u>. I called <u>him</u> back.* (See Chapter 13 for a discussion of these form changes.)

EXERCISE 12.1   Identifying subjects and predicates

In the following sentences, insert a slash between the complete subject and the complete predicate. Underline each simple subject once and each simple predicate twice. Then use each sentence as a model to create a sentence of your own. (You can do this exercise online at *ablongman.com/littlebrown*.)

Example:
The <u>pony</u>, the light <u>horse</u>, and the draft <u>horse</u> | <u><u>are</u></u> three types of domestic horses.
Sample imitation: Toyota, Honda, and Nissan are three brands of Japanese cars.

1. The leaves fell.
2. October ends soon.
3. The orchard owners made apple cider.
4. They examined each apple carefully before using it.
5. Over a hundred people will buy cider at the roadside stand.

EXERCISE 12.2   Identifying nouns, verbs, and pronouns

In the following sentences identify all words functioning as nouns with *N*, all words functioning as verbs with *V*, and all pronouns with *P*. (You can do this exercise online at *ablongman.com/littlebrown*.)

Example:
  P   V   N   N
<u>They</u> <u>took</u> the <u>tour</u> through the <u>museum</u>.

1. The trees died.
2. They caught a disease.
3. The disease was a fungus.
4. It ruined a grove that was treasured.
5. Our great-grandfather planted the grove in the last century.

ANSWERS: EXERCISE 12.1

        SUBJECT|PREDICATE
1. The leaves|fell.
   Sample imitation: The kite soared.

        SUBJECT|PREDICATE
2. October|ends soon.
   Sample imitation: My class begins soon.

        SUBJECT|PREDICATE
3. The orchard owners|made apple cider.
   Sample imitation: The couple grew summer squash.

  SUBJECT|PREDICATE
4. They|examined each apple carefully before using it.
   Sample imitation: They dried each glass gingerly after washing it.

        SUBJECT|PREDICATE
5. Over a hundred people|will buy cider at the roadside stand.
   Sample imitation: Few pool owners will swim at the public beach.

ANSWERS: EXERCISE 12.2

      N   V
1. The <u>trees</u> <u>died</u>.

    P   V   N
2. <u>They</u> <u>caught</u> a <u>disease</u>.

       N   V   N
3. The <u>disease</u> <u>was</u> a <u>fungus</u>.

  P   V   N   P   V   V
4. <u>It</u> <u>ruined</u> a <u>grove</u> <u>that</u> <u>was</u> <u>treasured</u>.

  P   N   V   N
5. <u>Our great-grandfather</u> <u>planted</u> the <u>grove</u> in
                    N
   the last <u>century</u>.

ANSWERS: EXERCISE 12.3
Possible answers

1. Noun and verb.
   Blow out the candles and make a <u>wish</u>. [Noun.] The child <u>wished</u> for a new bicycle. [Verb.]
2. Noun and verb.
   Many people purchase <u>ties</u> as Father's Day presents. [Noun.] <u>Tie</u> the rope into a square knot. [Verb.]
3. Noun and verb.
   The <u>swing</u> hung from a large oak tree. [Noun.] Ted picked up his niece and <u>swung</u> her around and around. [Verb.]
4. Noun and verb.
   The <u>mail</u> does not come on national holidays. [Noun.] <u>Mail</u> the package to her home address. [Verb.]
5. Verb.
   He <u>spends</u> his free time doing volunteer work.
6. Noun and verb.
   The <u>label</u> bore a poison warning. [Noun.] The companies must <u>label</u> their products. [Verb.]
7. Noun.
   The <u>door</u> flew open by itself.
8. Noun.
   My younger sister was good <u>company</u>.
9. Noun and verb.
   The <u>whistle</u> released us from work. [Noun.] We <u>whistle</u> all the way home. [Verb.]
10. Noun and verb.
    The <u>glue</u> stuck to my hands. [Noun.] We <u>glue</u> our models together. [Verb.]

EXERCISE 12.3 Using nouns and verbs

Identify each of the following words as a noun, as a verb, or as both. Then create sentences of your own, using each word in each possible function. (You can do this exercise online at *ablongman.com/littlebrown*.)

Example:
fly
Noun and verb.
The <u>fly</u> sat on the meat loaf. [Noun.] The planes <u>fly</u> low. [Verb.]

1. wish
2. tie
3. swing
4. mail
5. spend
6. label
7. door
8. company
9. whistle
10. glue

3 Forming sentence patterns with nouns and verbs

English builds all sentences on the five basic patterns shown in the box on the facing page. As the diagrams indicate, the patterns differ in their predicates because the relation between the verb and the remaining words is different.

CULTURE LANGUAGE The word order in English sentences may not correspond to word order in the sentences of your native language. English, for instance, strongly prefers subject first, then verb, then any other words, whereas some other languages prefer the verb first. The main exceptions to the word patterns discussed below appear on pages 263–64. See also pages 364–70 on positioning modifiers in sentences.

■ Pattern 1: The earth trembled.

In the simplest pattern the predicate consists only of the verb. Verbs in this pattern do not require following words to complete their meaning and thus are called **intransitive** (from Latin words meaning "not passing over").

Subject	Predicate
	Intransitive verb
The earth	trembled.
The hospital	may close.

■ Pattern 2: The earthquake destroyed the city.

In pattern 2 the predicate consists of a verb followed by a noun that identifies who or what receives the action of the verb. This noun is a **direct object**. Verbs that require direct objects to complete their meaning are called **transitive** ("passing over"): the verb transfers the action from subject to object.

The five basic sentence patterns

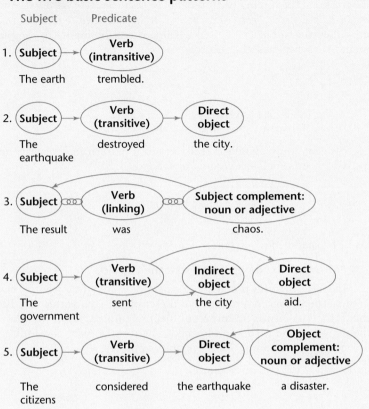

Subject	Predicate
	Transitive verb

Subject	Predicate	
	Transitive verb	*Direct object*
The earthquake	destroyed	the city.
Education	opens	doors.

  The distinction between transitive verbs and intransitive verbs like those in pattern 1 is important because only transitive verbs may be used in the passive voice (*The city was destroyed*). (See p. 302.) Your dictionary says whether a verb is transitive or intransitive. Some verbs (*begin, learn, read, write,* and others) are both.

▤ Pattern 3: The result was chaos.

In pattern 3 the predicate also consists of a verb followed by a noun, but here the noun renames or describes the subject. We could

---

CULTURE LANGUAGE

TRANSITIVE AND INTRANSITIVE VERBS

Remind students that intransitive verbs *cannot* be followed by a direct object. Transitive verbs, in contrast, *must* have a direct object to complete the meaning of a sentence. Some transitive verbs can have both a direct object and an indirect object. For students who need additional practice with transitive and intransitive verbs and passive voice, Jocelyn Steer and Karen Carlisi include useful exercises in Chapters 5 and 11 of *The Advanced Grammar Book* (Boston: Heinle, 1991).

write the sentence *The result = chaos.* The verb serving as an equal sign is a **linking verb** because it links the subject and the following description. The linking verbs include *be, seem, appear, become, grow, remain, stay, prove, feel, look, smell, sound,* and *taste.* The word that describes the subject is called a **subject complement** (it complements, or completes, the subject).

Subject	Predicate	
	Linking verb	*Subject complement*
The result	was	chaos.
The man	became	an accountant.

Subject complements in this sentence pattern may also be adjectives, words such as *tall* and *hopeful* (see p. 242):

Subject	Predicate	
	Linking verb	*Subject complement*
The result	was	chaotic.
The apartments	seem	expensive.

■ Pattern 4: The government sent the city aid.

In pattern 4 the predicate consists of a verb followed by two nouns. The second noun, *aid,* is a direct object (see pattern 2). But the first noun, *city,* is an **indirect object**, identifying to or for whom the action of the verb is performed. The direct object and indirect object refer to different things, people, or places.

Subject	Predicate		
	Transitive verb	*Indirect object*	*Direct object*
The government	sent	the city	aid.
One company	offered	its employees	bonuses.

A number of verbs can take indirect objects, including those above and *allow, bring, buy, deny, find, get, leave, make, pay, read, sell, show, teach,* and *write.*

CULTURE LANGUAGE With some verbs expressing action done to or for someone, the indirect object must be turned into a phrase beginning with *to* or *for.* These verbs include *admit, announce, demonstrate, explain, introduce, mention, prove, recommend, say,* and *suggest.* The *to* or *for* phrase then falls after the direct object.

Faulty	The manual explains <u>workers</u> the new procedure.
Revised	The manual explains the new procedure <u>to workers</u>.

■ Pattern 5: The citizens considered the earthquake a disaster.

In pattern 5, as in pattern 4, the predicate consists of a verb followed by two nouns. But in pattern 5 the first noun is a direct

---

TO BE TEST

Advise students that one way to determine whether a sentence fits into pattern 5 is to insert the words *to be* between the first noun and the following noun or adjective: *The citizens considered the earthquake to be a disaster.*

object and the second noun renames or describes it. Here the second noun is an **object complement** (it complements, or completes, the object):

Subject	Predicate		
	Transitive verb	*Direct object*	*Object complement*
The citizens	considered	the earthquake	a disaster.
The class	elected	Joan O'Day	president.

Like a subject complement (pattern 3), an object complement may be a noun or an adjective, as below:

Subject	Predicate		
	Transitive verb	*Direct object*	*Object complement*
The citizens	considered	the earthquake	disastrous.
Success	makes	some people	nervous.

EXERCISE 12.4 Identifying sentence patterns

In the following sentences, identify each verb as intransitive, transitive, or linking. Then identify each direct object (DO), indirect object (IO), subject complement (SC), and object complement (OC). (You can do this exercise online at *ablongman.com/littlebrown*.)

Example:

transitive
verb   IO   DO   DO
Children give their parents both headaches and pleasures.

1. Many people find New York City exciting.
2. Tourists flock there each year.
3. Often they visit Times Square first.
4. The square's lights are astounding.
5. The flashing signs sell visitors everything from TVs to underwear.

EXERCISE 12.5 Creating sentences

Create sentences by using each of the following verbs in the pattern indicated. (For the meanings of the abbreviations, see the directions for Exercise 12.4.) You may want to change the form of the verb. (You can do this exercise online at *ablongman.com/littlebrown*.)

Example:

give (S-V-IO-DO)
Sam gave his brother a birthday card.

1. laugh (S-V)
2. elect (S-V-DO-OC)
3. steal (S-V-DO)
4. catch (S-V-DO)
5. bring (S-V-IO-DO)
6. seem (S-V-SC)
7. call (S-V-DO-OC)
8. become (S-V-SC)
9. buy (S-V-IO-DO)
10. study (S-V)

ANSWERS: EXERCISE 12.4

1. Find is transitive.
                          DO   OC
   Many people find New York City exciting.
2. Flock is intransitive.
   No objects or complements.
3. Visit is transitive.
                              DO
   Often they visit Times Square first.
4. Are is linking.
                              SC
   The square's lights are astounding.
5. Sell is transitive.
                          IO   DO
   The flashing signs sell visitors everything
                  DO
   from TVs to underwear.

ANSWERS: EXERCISE 12.5

Possible answers

1. The audience laughed.
2. The town elected Flynn mayor.
3. Pip stole the pie.
4. Josie caught the ball.
5. My uncle brought me a cake.
6. Marilou seems unhappy.
7. One candidate called the other a crook.
8. We became reckless.
9. We bought ourselves a television set.
10. No one studied.

12b   Expanding the basic sentence with single words

Most of the sentences we read, write, or speak are more complex and also more informative and interesting than those examined so far. Most sentences contain one or more of the following: (1) modifying words (discussed here); (2) word groups, called phrases and clauses (p. 244); and (3) combinations of two or more words or word groups of the same kind (p. 258).

1   Using adjectives and adverbs

The simplest expansion of sentences occurs when we add modifying words to describe or limit the nouns and verbs. Modifying words add details:

> <u>Recently</u>, the earth trembled.
> The earthquake <u>nearly</u> destroyed the <u>old</u> city.
> The <u>federal</u> government <u>soon</u> sent the <u>city</u> aid.
> The grant was a <u>very generous</u> one but disappeared <u>too quickly</u>.

The underlined words represent two different parts of speech:

- **Adjectives** describe or modify nouns and pronouns. They specify which one, what quality, or how many.

  old   city   generous one   two pears
  adjective noun   adjective pronoun   adjective noun

- **Adverbs** describe or modify verbs, adjectives, other adverbs, and whole groups of words. They specify when, where, how, and to what extent.

  nearly destroyed   too quickly
  adverb   verb   adverb adverb

  very generous   Unfortunately, taxes will rise.
  adverb adjective   adverb   word group

An *-ly* ending often signals an adverb, but not always: *friendly* is an adjective; *never, not,* and *always* are adverbs. The only way to tell whether a word is an adjective or an adverb is to determine what it modifies.

Adjectives and adverbs appear in three forms:

- The **positive** form is the basic form, the one listed in the dictionary: *good, green, angry; badly, quickly, angrily.*
- The **comparative** form indicates a greater degree of the quality named by the word: *better, greener, angrier; worse, more quickly, more angrily.*

- The **superlative** form indicates the greatest degree of the quality named: *best, greenest, angriest; worst, most quickly, most angrily.*

(For further discussion of these forms, see p. 322.)

2 Using other words as modifiers

Nouns and special forms of verbs may sometimes serve as modifiers of other nouns. In combinations such as *office buildings, Thanksgiving prayer,* and *shock hazard,* the first noun modifies the second. In combinations such as *singing birds, corrected papers,* and *broken finger,* the first word is a verb form modifying the following noun. (These modifying verb forms are discussed in more detail on pp. 247–50.) Again, the part of speech to which we assign a word always depends on its function in a sentence.

EXERCISE 12.6   Identifying and using adjectives and adverbs

Identify the adjectives and adverbs in the following sentences. Then use each sentence as a model for creating a sentence of your own. (You can do this exercise online at *ablongman.com/littlebrown.*)

Example:

    adjective   adverb   adjective
The red barn sat uncomfortably among modern buildings.

Sample imitation: The little girl complained loudly to her busy mother.

1. The blue water glistened in the hot afternoon sunlight.
2. Happily, children dipped their toes in the cool lake.
3. Excitedly, some of the children hopped into the water.
4. Cautious parents watched from their shady porches.
5. The children played contentedly until the day finally ended.

EXERCISE 12.7   Using verb forms as modifiers

Use each of the following verb forms to modify a noun in a sentence of your own. (You can do this exercise online at *ablongman.com/littlebrown.*)

Example:
smoking
Only a smoking cigar remained.

1. scrambled   5. painted   8. ripened
2. twitching   6. written   9. known
3. rambling   7. charging   10. driven
4. typed

ANSWERS: EXERCISE 12.6

1. The blue [ADJ] water glistened in the hot [ADJ] afternoon [ADJ] sunlight.
   Sample imitation: The blue bird perched on a thin leafy branch.
2. Happily [ADV], children dipped their toes in the cool [ADJ] lake.
   Sample imitation: Quietly, we peeked into the silent cathedral.
3. Excitedly [ADV], some of the children hopped into the water.
   Sample imitation: Impatiently, two of the children howled for the candy.
4. Cautious [ADJ] parents watched from their shady [ADV] porches.
   Sample imitation: Ambitious runners train for every marathon.
5. The children played contentedly [ADV] until the day finally [ADV] ended.
   Sample imitation: The babies lay still while the singer quietly crooned.

ANSWERS: EXERCISE 12.7
Possible answers

1. Jack woke up craving scrambled eggs.
2. The twitching limb relaxed when the sedative took effect.
3. The treasurer's rambling speech covered more topics than I can remember.
4. The typed manuscript contained many errors.
5. Painted birds decorate the window.
6. He wanted to know the origins of the written word.
7. The man escaped the charging animal.
8. We picked the ripened fruit.
9. All the known facts contradict his theory.
10. Driven people may have hypertension.

Students can work effectively in pairs or small groups on Exercise 12.8. Encourage the groups to be imaginative about combining each sentence in more than one way, and to report back to the class on their most innovative combinations.

ANSWERS: EXERCISE 12.8

Possible answers

1. The turn of the <u>twentieth</u> century ushered in <u>improved</u> technology and new materials.
2. A <u>sturdy steel</u> skeleton made the construction of skyscrapers possible.
3. By 1913 the <u>towering</u> Woolworth Building, with its <u>Gothic</u> ornaments, stood 760 feet (55 stories).
4. At 1450 feet the Sears Tower in Chicago <u>now</u> doubles the <u>relatively puny</u> height of the Woolworth Building.
5. Skyscrapers would not have been practical if Elisha Graves Otis had not built the <u>first safe passenger</u> elevator in 1857.

RESOURCES AND IDEAS

Bushman, Donald, and Elizabeth Ervin. "Rhetorical Contexts of Grammar: Some Views from Writing Emphasis Instructors." *The Place of Grammar in Writing Instruction: Past, Present, Future.* Ed. Susan Hunter and Ray Wallace. Portsmouth, NH: Boynton, 1995. 136–58. This essay explains strategies for teaching grammar in cross-disciplinary rhetorical contexts.

Hashimoto, I. "Sentence Variety: Where Theory and Practice Meet and Lose." *Composition Studies: Freshman English News* 21 (Spring 1993): 66–77. Hashimoto explores the contradictions between the common injunctions to students about sentence variation and stylistic choices of professional writers.

Herriman, Jennifer, and Aimo Seppänen. "What is an Indirect Object?" *English Studies* 77 (1996): 484–500. This essay contrasts the consensus on defining and teaching the "direct object" with the vaguer approaches to the indirect object.

Herrington, Anne J. "Grammar Recharted: Sentence Analysis for Writing." In *Writing Exercises from "Exercise Exchange."* Ed. Charles R. Duke, vol. 2. Urbana: NCTE, 1984. 276–87.

EXERCISE 12.8 Sentence combining: Single-word modifiers

To practice expanding the basic sentence patterns with single-word modifiers, combine each group of sentences below into one sentence. You will have to delete and rearrange words. (You can do this exercise online at *ablongman.com/littlebrown*.)

Example:

Paris offers tourists food. Paris offers food proudly. The food is delicious.

Paris <u>proudly</u> offers tourists <u>delicious</u> food.

1. The turn of the century ushered in technology and materials. The century was the twentieth. The technology was improved. The materials were new.
2. A skeleton made the construction of skyscrapers possible. The skeleton was sturdy. It was made of steel.
3. By 1913 the Woolworth Building, with its ornaments, stood 760 feet (55 stories). The building was towering. The ornaments were Gothic.
4. At 1450 feet the Sears Tower in Chicago doubles the height of the Woolworth Building. The doubling is now. The Woolworth height is puny. The puniness is relative.
5. Skyscrapers would not have been practical if Elisha Graves Otis had not built the elevator in 1857. It was the first elevator. The elevator was safe. It served passengers.

12c Expanding the basic sentence with word groups

Most sentences we read or write contain whole word groups that serve as nouns and modifiers. Such word groups enable us to combine several bits of information into one sentence and to make the relations among them clear, as in the following sentence:

subject
When the experiment succeeded, the <u>researchers</u>, excited by the re-
verb   object
sults, <u>expanded</u> the <u>study</u> to enroll more patients.

Attached to *researchers expanded the study,* the skeleton of this sentence, are three groups of words that add related information: *When the experiment succeeded, excited by the results, to enroll more patients.* These constructions are phrases and clauses:

■ A *phrase* is a group of related words that lacks either a subject or a predicate or both: *excited by the results, to enroll more patients.*
■ A *clause* contains both a subject and a predicate: *When the experiment succeeded* and *the researchers expanded the study* are both clauses, though only the second can stand alone as a sentence.

1 Using prepositional phrases

Prepositions are connecting words. Unlike nouns, verbs, and modifiers, which may change form, prepositions never change form. As the box below shows, many prepositions signal relationships of time or space; others signal relationships such as addition, comparison or contrast, cause or effect, concession, condition, opposition, possession, and source. Notice that some prepositions consist of more than one word.

Common prepositions

Time or space (position or direction)			Other relationships (addition, comparison, etc.)	
about	by	out of	according to	in spite of
above	down	outside	as	instead of
across	during	over	as for	like
after	for	past	aside from	of
against	from	since	because of	on account of
along	in	through	concerning	regarding
along with	inside	throughout	despite	regardless of
among	inside of	till	except	unlike
around	into	to	except for	with
at	near	toward	excepting	without
before	next to	under	in addition to	
behind	off	underneath		
below	on	until		
beneath	onto	up		
beside	on top of	upon		
between	out	within		
beyond				

A preposition connects a noun or pronoun to another word in the sentence: *Robins nest in trees*. The noun or pronoun so connected (*trees*) is the **object of the preposition**. The preposition plus its object and any modifiers is a **prepositional phrase**:

Preposition	Object
on	the surface
upon	entering the room
from	where you are standing
except for	ten employees

Prepositional phrases function as adjectives (modifying nouns) or as adverbs (modifying verbs, adjectives, or other adverbs). As modifiers, they add details that make sentences clearer and more interesting for readers.

Herrington suggests using a five-column chart to analyze sentence patterns and help make students aware of syntax. The five columns in the chart—Preceding Subject, Subject, Between Subject and Verb, Verb, and Following Verb—allow the system to account for both relatively simple sentences and those to which considerable information has been added. The columns can be layered as well to account for compound sentences.

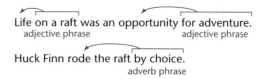

Life on a raft was an opportunity for adventure.
adjective phrase   adjective phrase

Huck Finn rode the raft by choice.
adverb phrase

 CULTURE LANGUAGE The meanings and idiomatic uses of English prepositions can be difficult to master; most must be memorized or looked up in a dictionary. (A list of dictionaries for English as a second language appears on p. 537.) See pages 291–92 for the uses of prepositions in two-word verbs such as *look after* and pages 523–25 for the uses of prepositions in idioms.

Punctuating prepositional phrases

Since a prepositional phrase lacks a subject and a predicate, it should not be punctuated as a complete sentence. If it is, the result is a **sentence fragment** (Chapter 17):

> Fragment   Toward the sun.

The phrase must be attached to another group of words containing both a subject and a predicate:

> Revised   The plane turned toward the sun.

A prepositional phrase that introduces a sentence is set off with punctuation, usually a comma, unless it is short (see pp. 433–34):

> According to the newspaper and other sources, the governor has reluctantly decided to veto the bill.
>
> In 1865 the Civil War finally ended.

A prepositional phrase that interrupts or concludes a sentence is *not* set off with punctuation when it is essential to the meaning of the word or words it modifies (see p. 435):

> The announcement of a tuition increase surprised no one.
>
> Students expected new fees for the coming year.

When an interrupting or concluding prepositional phrase is *not* essential to meaning, but merely adds information to the sentence, then it *is* set off with punctuation, usually a comma or commas (see p. 435):

> The governor, according to the newspaper and other sources, has reluctantly decided to veto the bill.

As all the preceding examples illustrate, a preposition and its object are not separated by a comma.

CULTURE LANGUAGE

PREPOSITIONS AND DIALECTS

Regional and social dialects may contribute to prepositional confusion; for instance, students may become sick *in, on,* or *to* their stomachs. In parts of the Northeast, people stand *on,* not *in,* line. This issue is given full coverage in 38c.

PREPOSITION PROBLEMS

Prepositions follow few specific rules, and, because of idiomatic usage, often cannot be translated directly into students' first languages. As a result, even advanced ESL students find prepositions difficult. Refer students who need additional practice to Unit 6 of Len Fox, *Focus on Editing: A Grammar Workbook for Advanced Writers* (White Plains: Longman, 1992), and to Alan Meyers, *Writing with Confidence* (6th ed., New York: Longman, 2000).

EXERCISE 12.9 Identifying prepositional phrases

Identify the prepositional phrases in the following passage. Indicate whether each phrase functions as an adjective or as an adverb, and name the word that the phrase modifies. (You can do this exercise online at *ablongman.com/littlebrown*.)

Example:

┌─adverb─┐   ┌─adverb─┐┌─adjective─┐
After an hour I finally arrived at the home of my professor.

   On July 3, 1863, at Gettysburg, Pennsylvania, General Robert E. Lee gambled unsuccessfully for a Confederate victory in the American Civil War. Called Pickett's Charge, the battle was one of the most disastrous conflicts of the war. Confederate and Union forces faced each other on parallel ridges separated by almost a mile of open fields. After an artillery bombardment of the Union position, about 12,000 Confederate infantry marched toward the Union ridge. The Union guns had been silent but suddenly roared, mowing the approaching Confederates. Within an hour, perhaps half of the Confederate soldiers lay wounded or dead.

EXERCISE 12.10 Sentence combining: Prepositional phrases

To practice writing sentences with prepositional phrases, combine each group of sentences below into one sentence that includes one or two prepositional phrases. You will have to add, delete, and rearrange words. Some items have more than one possible answer. (You can do this exercise online at *ablongman.com/littlebrown*.)

Example:
I will start working. The new job will pay the minimum wage.
I will start working <u>at a new job</u> <u>for the minimum wage</u>.

1. The slow loris protects itself well. Its habitat is Southeast Asia. It possesses a poisonous chemical.
2. To frighten predators, the loris exudes the chemical. The chemical comes from a gland. The gland is on the loris's upper arm.
3. The loris's chemical is highly toxic. The chemical is not like a skunk's spray. Even small quantities of the chemical are toxic.
4. A tiny dose can affect a human. The dose would get in the mouth. The human would be sent into shock.
5. Predators probably can sense the toxin. They detect it at a distance. They use their nasal organs.

2 Using verbals and verbal phrases

   Verbals are special verb forms such as *smoking* or *hidden* or *to win* that can function as nouns (*smoking is dangerous*) or as modifiers (*the hidden money, the urge to win*).

   Note A verbal *cannot* stand alone as the complete verb in the predicate of a sentence. For example, *The man smoking* and *The*

ANSWERS: EXERCISE 12.9

┌──ADVERB──┐ ┌────────ADVERB────────┐
On July 3, 1863, at Gettysburg, Pennsylvania,
                                    ┌─ADVERB─┐
Robert E. Lee gambled unsuccessfully for a Con-
                        ┌──────ADJECTIVE──────┐
federate victory in the American Civil War.

Called Pickett's Charge, the battle was one
┌────────ADJECTIVE────────┐ ┌─ADJECTIVE─┐
of the most disastrous conflicts of the war. Con-

federate and Union forces faced each other
┌───ADVERB───┐   ┌──────ADVERB──────┐
on parallel ridges separated by almost a mile
┌─ADJECTIVE─┐ ┌──────ADVERB──────┐
of open fields. After an artillery bombardment of

the Union position, about 12,000 Confederate in-
            ┌──────ADVERB──────┐
fantry marched toward the Union ridge. The

Union guns had been silent but suddenly roared,
                                    ┌ADVERB┐
mowing the approaching Confederates. Within

an hour, perhaps half of the Confederate soldiers

lay wounded or dead.

ANSWERS: EXERCISE 12.10

Possible answers

1. The slow loris of Southeast Asia protects itself well with a poisonous chemical.
2. To frighten predators, the loris exudes the chemical from a gland on its upper arm.
3. Unlike a skunk's spray, the loris's chemical is highly toxic even in small quantities.
4. A tiny dose in the mouth can send a human into shock.
5. Predators probably can sense the toxin at a distance with their nasal organs.

money hidden are not sentences but sentence fragments (see p. 334). Any verbal must combine with a helping verb to serve as the predicate of a sentence: *The man was smoking. The money is hidden.*

Because verbals cannot serve alone as sentence predicates, they are sometimes called **nonfinite verbs** (in essence, they are "unfinished"). **Finite verbs,** in contrast, can make an assertion or express a state of being without a helping verb (they are "finished"). Either of the two tests below can distinguish finite and nonfinite verbs.

Tests for finite and nonfinite verbs (verbals)

Test 1 Does the word require a change in form when a third-person subject changes from singular to plural?

> Yes Finite verb: *It sings. They sing.*
>
> No   Nonfinite verb (verbal): *bird singing, birds singing*

Test 2 Does the word require a change in form to show the difference in present, past, and future?

> Yes Finite verb: *It sings. It sang. It will sing.*
>
> No   Nonfinite verb (verbal): *The bird singing is/was/will be a robin.*

There are three kinds of verbals: participles, gerunds, and infinitives.

■ Participles

All verbs have two participle forms, a present and a past. The **present participle** consists of the dictionary form of the verb plus the ending *-ing: beginning, completing, hiding.* The **past participle** of most verbs consists of the dictionary form plus *-d* or *-ed: believed, completed.* Some common verbs have an irregular past participle, such as *begun* or *hidden.* (See pp. 278–80.)

Both present and past participles function as adjectives to modify nouns and pronouns:

Shopping malls sometimes frustrate shoppers.

Shoppers may feel trapped.

CULTURE LANGUAGE For English verbs expressing feeling, the present and past participles have different meanings: *It was a boring lecture. The bored students slept.* See pages 325–26.

■ Gerunds

Gerund is the name given to the *-ing* form of the verb when it serves as a noun:

GRAMMAR TERMS

Terminology like *gerund* is one reason many students are convinced they can't "do" grammar, despite the fact that they construct sophisticated sentences every day. You may want to use a synonym like *verbal noun* or *-ing noun* to help students become more comfortable with this term.

subject

Strolling through stores can exhaust the hardiest shopper.

object

Many children learn to hate shopping.

Present participles and gerunds can be distinguished *only* by their function in a sentence. If the *-ing* form functions as an adjective (a *teaching* degree), it is a present participle. If the *-ing* form functions as a noun (*Teaching is difficult*), it is a gerund.

CULTURE LANGUAGE In English, always use a gerund, not any other verb form, as the object of a preposition: *Diners are prohibited from smoking.* See also the culture-language note below.

▥ Infinitives

The **infinitive** is the *to* form of the verb, the dictionary form preceded by the infinitive marker *to: to begin, to hide, to run.* Infinitives may function as adjectives, nouns, or adverbs:

adjective

The question to answer is why shoppers endure mall fatigue.

noun

The solution for mall fatigue is to leave.

adverb

Still, shoppers find it difficult to quit.

CULTURE LANGUAGE Infinitives and gerunds may follow some English verbs and not others and may differ in meaning after a verb: *The singer stopped to sing. The singer stopped singing.* (See pp. 288–90.)

▥ Verbal phrases

Participles, gerunds, and infinitives—like other verb forms—may take subjects, objects, or complements, and they may be modified by adverbs. The verbal and all the words immediately related to it make up a **verbal phrase.** With verbal phrases, we can create concise sentences packed with information.

Like participles, **participial phrases** always serve as adjectives, modifying nouns or pronouns:

Buying things, most shoppers feel themselves in control.

They make selections determined by personal taste.

Gerund phrases, like gerunds, always serve as nouns:

subject

Shopping for clothing and other items satisfies personal needs.

object of preposition

Malls are good at creating such needs.

Infinitive phrases may serve as nouns, adverbs, or adjectives:

┌ sentence subject ┐ ┌─────── subject complement ───────┐
To design a mall is to create an artificial environment.
    noun phrase   noun phrase

Malls are designed to make shoppers feel safe.
                  adverb phrase

The environment supports the impulse to shop for oneself.
                           adjective phrase

Note When an infinitive or infinitive phrase serves as a noun after verbs such as *hear, help, let, make, see,* and *watch,* the infinitive marker *to* is omitted: *We all heard her <u>tell</u>* [not *to tell*] *the story.*

Punctuating verbals and verbal phrases

Verbal phrases punctuated as complete sentences are sentence fragments (Chapter 17). A complete sentence must contain a subject and a finite verb (p. 248):

Fragment   <u>Treating</u> the patients kindly.
Revised   She <u>treats</u> the patients kindly.

A verbal or verbal phrase serving as a modifier is almost always set off with a comma when it introduces a sentence (see p. 433):

<u>To pay tuition,</u> some students work at two jobs.

A modifying verbal or verbal phrase that interrupts or concludes a sentence is *not* set off with punctuation when it is essential to the meaning of the word or words it modifies (see p. 435):

Jobs <u>paying well</u> are hard to find.

When an interrupting or concluding verbal modifier is *not* essential to meaning but merely adds information to the sentence, it *is* set off with punctuation, usually a comma or commas (see p. 435):

One good job, <u>paying twelve dollars an hour,</u> was filled in fifteen minutes.

The following sentences contain participles, gerunds, and infinitives as well as participial, gerund, and infinitive phrases. First identify each verbal or verbal phrase. Then indicate whether it is used as an adjective, an adverb, or a noun. (You can do this exercise online at *ablongman.com/littlebrown.*)

   Example:

     adjective   adverb
   <u>Laughing,</u> the talk-show host prodded her guest <u>to speak.</u>

Students might work independently on Exercise 12.11, then compare answers in small groups and work together on Exercise 12.12. Encourage each group to create more than one combination for each pair of sentences in Exercise 12.12.

ANSWERS: EXERCISE 12.11

               ADJ
1. <u>Written in 1850 by Nathaniel Hawthorne,</u> *The Scarlet Letter* tells the story of Hester Prynne.

          ADJ
2. <u>Shunned by the community,</u> Hester endures her loneliness.

                     ADV
3. Hester is humble enough <u>to withstand her Puritan neighbors' cutting remarks.</u>

                            ADJ
4. Despite the cruel treatment, the <u>determined</u>
                    N
   young woman refuses to <u>leave her home.</u>

                    N
5. By <u>living a life of patience and unselfishness,</u> Hester eventually becomes the community's angel.

1. Written in 1850 by Nathaniel Hawthorne, *The Scarlet Letter* tells the story of Hester Prynne.
2. Shunned by the community, Hester endures her loneliness.
3. Hester is humble enough to withstand her Puritan neighbors' cutting remarks.
4. Despite the cruel treatment, the determined young woman refuses to leave her home.
5. By living a life of patience and unselfishness, Hester eventually becomes the community's angel.

EXERCISE 12.12   Sentence combining: Verbals and verbal phrases

To practice writing sentences with verbals and verbal phrases, combine each of the following pairs of sentences into one sentence. You will have to add, delete, change, and rearrange words. Each item has more than one possible answer. (You can do this exercise online at *ablongman.com/littlebrown*.)

Example:

My father took pleasure in mean pranks. For instance, he hid the neighbor's cat.

My father took pleasure in mean pranks such as <u>hiding the neighbor's cat.</u>

1. Air pollution is a health problem. It affects millions of Americans.
2. The air has been polluted mainly by industries and automobiles. It contains toxic chemicals.
3. Environmentalists pressure politicians. They think politicians should pass stricter laws.
4. Many politicians waver. They are not necessarily against environmentalism.
5. The problems are too complex. They cannot be solved easily.

3 Using absolute phrases

Absolute phrases consist of a noun or pronoun and a participle, plus any modifiers:

┌────── absolute phrase ──────┐
Many ethnic groups, their own place established, are making way for new arrivals.

┌──── absolute phrase ────┐ ┌──── absolute phrase ────┐
Their native lands left behind, an uncertain future looming, immigrants face many obstacles.

These phrases are called *absolute* (from a Latin word meaning "free") because they have no specific grammatical connection to a noun, verb, or any other word in the rest of the sentence. Instead, they modify the entire rest of the sentence, adding information.

Notice that absolute phrases, unlike participial phrases, always contain a subject. Compare the following sentences:

ANSWERS: EXERCISE 12.12

Possible answers

1. Air pollution is a health problem <u>affecting millions of Americans.</u>
2. <u>Polluted mainly by industries and automobiles,</u> the air contains toxic chemicals.
3. Environmentalists pressure politicians <u>to pass stricter laws.</u>
4. <u>Wavering</u> politicians are not necessarily against environmentalism.
5. The problems are too complex <u>to be solved easily.</u>

EXPECTING PROBLEMS

As students begin practicing use of absolute phrases, you may find more comma splices and fragments in their essays. Warn students to expect these errors, so that they can proofread for such problems more carefully. Be understanding as you evaluate student papers in which the students are practicing these strategies for the first time. If you focus on grammar faults, they may lose the incentive to take further stylistic risks.

Students can work productively in pairs or small groups to combine the sentences in Exercise 12.13. The collaborative effort and consequent discussion can be useful for students who are having difficulty with absolute phrases.

ANSWERS: EXERCISE 12.13

Possible answers

1. Her face beaming, Geraldine Ferraro enjoyed the crowd's cheers after her nomination for Vice President.
2. A vacancy having occurred, Sandra Day O'Connor was appointed the first female Supreme Court justice.
3. Her appointment confirmed, Condoleezza Rice became the first female national security advisor.
4. The midterm elections over, Nancy Pelosi was elected the first female minority leader of the House of Representatives.
5. The election won, Elizabeth Dole was a US senator from North Carolina.

CREATE YOUR OWN

Divide the class into groups. Ask each group to create its own set of sentence-combining exercises following the pattern of the exercises in the handbook. Then ask the groups to trade exercises, work on them, and return them to the authors with both answers and constructive feedback.

┌──participial phrase──┐
For many immigrants learning English, the language introduces American culture.

┌───────── absolute phrase ─────────┐
The immigrants having learned English, their opportunities widen.

We often omit the participle from an absolute phrase when it is some form of *be*, such as *being* or *having been:*

┌───────── absolute phrase ─────────┐
Two languages [being] at hand, bilingual citizens in fact have many cultural and occupational advantages.

Punctuating absolute phrases

Absolute phrases are always set off from the rest of the sentence with punctuation, usually a comma or commas (see also pp. 440–41):

Their future more secure, these citizens will make room for new arrivals.

These citizens, their future more secure, will make room for new arrivals.

EXERCISE 12.13   Sentence combining: Absolute phrases

To practice writing sentences with absolute phrases, combine each pair of sentences below into one sentence that contains an absolute phrase. You will have to add, delete, change, and rearrange words. (You can do this exercise online at *ablongman.com/littlebrown*.)

> *Example:*
> The flower's petals wilted. It looked pathetic.
> Its petals wilted, the flower looked pathetic.

1. Geraldine Ferraro's face beamed. She enjoyed the crowd's cheers after her nomination for Vice President.
2. A vacancy had occurred. Sandra Day O'Connor was appointed the first female Supreme Court justice.
3. Her appointment was confirmed. Condoleezza Rice became the first female national security adviser.
4. The midterm elections were over. Nancy Pelosi was elected the first female minority leader of the House of Representatives.
5. The election was won. Elizabeth Dole was a US senator from North Carolina.

4   Using subordinate clauses

A **clause** is any group of words that contains both a subject and a predicate. There are two kinds of clauses, and the distinction between them is important:

- A *main* or *independent clause* makes a complete statement and can stand alone as a sentence: *The sky darkened.*

- **A *subordinate* or *dependent clause* is just like a main clause except that it begins with a subordinating word**: *when the sky darkened; because he wants it; whoever calls.* The subordinating word reduces the clause to a single part of speech—an adjective, an adverb, or a noun—that supports the idea in a main clause. Because it only modifies or names something, a subordinate clause cannot stand alone as a sentence (see the discussion of punctuation on p. 255). (The word *subordinate* means "secondary" or "controlled by another." It comes from the Latin *sub*, "under," and *ordo*, "order.")

The following examples show the differences between main and subordinate clauses:

┌──────── main clause ────────┐┌─main clause─┐
The school teaches parents. It is unusual.
┌──────── subordinate clause ────────┐ ┌─main clause─┐
Because the school teaches parents, it is unusual.

┌──────────── main clause ────────────┐┌──────── main clause ────────┐
Some parents avoid their children's schools. They are often illiterate.
┌───────────────────── main clause ─────────────────────┐
Parents who are illiterate often avoid their children's schools.
      └─subordinate clause─┘

Two kinds of subordinating words introduce subordinate clauses: subordinating conjunctions and relative pronouns.

- **Subordinating conjunctions**

Subordinating conjunctions, like prepositions, never change form in any way. In the following box they are arranged by the relationships they signal. (Some fit in more than one group.)

Common subordinating conjunctions

Cause or effect	Condition	Comparison or contrast	Space or time
as	even if	as	after
because	if	as if	as long as
in order that	if only	as though	before
since	provided	rather than	now that
so that	since	than	once
Concession	unless	whereas	since
although	when	whether	till
as if	whenever	while	until
even if	whether		when
even though		**Purpose**	whenever
though		in order that	where
		so that	wherever
		that	while

CULTURE LANGUAGE Subordinating conjunctions convey their meaning without help from other function words, such as the coordinating conjunctions *and, but, for,* and *so* (p. 259).

Faulty — Even though the parents are illiterate, but their children may read well. [*Even though* and *but* have the same meaning, so both are not needed.]

Revised — Even though the parents are illiterate, their children may read well.

■ **Relative pronouns**

Unlike subordinating conjunctions, **relative pronouns** usually act as subjects or objects in their own clauses, and two of them (*who* and *whoever*) change form accordingly (see pp. 271–73).

Relative pronouns

which	what	who (whose, whom)
that	whatever	whoever (whomever)

■ **Subordinate clauses**

Subordinate clauses function as adjectives, adverbs, or nouns.

Adjective clauses

Adjective clauses modify nouns and pronouns. They usually begin with the relative pronoun *who, whom, whose, which,* or *that,* although a few adjective clauses begin with *when* or *where* (standing for *in which, on which,* or *at which*). The pronoun is the subject or object of the clause it begins. The clause ordinarily falls immediately after the noun or pronoun it modifies:

Parents who are illiterate often have bad memories of school.

Schools that involve parents are more successful with children.

One school, which is open year-round, helps parents learn to read.

The school is in a city where the illiteracy rate is high.

Adverb clauses

Like adverbs, **adverb clauses** modify verbs, adjectives, other adverbs, and whole groups of words. They usually tell how, why, when, where, under what conditions, or with what result. They always begin with subordinating conjunctions.

The school began teaching parents when adult illiteracy gained national attention.

At first the program was not as successful as its founders had hoped.

Because it was directed at people who could not read, advertising had to be inventive.

Noun clauses

Noun clauses function as subjects, objects, and complements in sentences. They begin with *that, what, whatever, who, whom, whoever, whomever, when, where, whether, why,* or *how.* Unlike adjective and adverb clauses, noun clauses *replace* a word (a noun) within a clause; therefore, they can be difficult to identify.

———— sentence subject ————
Whether the program would succeed depended on door-to-door advertising.

———— object of verb ————
Teachers explained in person how the program would work.

———— object of preposition ————
A few parents were anxious about what their children would think.

Elliptical clauses

A subordinate clause that is grammatically incomplete but clear in meaning is an **elliptical clause** (*ellipsis* means "omission"). The meaning of the clause is clear because the missing element can be supplied from the context. Most often the elements omitted are the pronouns *that, which,* and *whom* or the predicate from the second part of a comparison.

Skepticism and fear were among the feelings [that] the parents voiced.

The parents knew their children could read better than they [could read].

Punctuating subordinate clauses

Subordinate clauses punctuated as complete sentences are sentence fragments (Chapter 17). Though a subordinate clause contains a subject and a predicate and thus resembles a complete sentence, it also begins with a subordinating word that makes it into an adjective, adverb, or noun. A single part of speech cannot stand alone as a complete sentence.

Fragment   Because a door was ajar.
Revised   A door was ajar.
Revised   The secret leaked because a door was ajar.

A subordinate clause serving as an adverb is almost always set off with a comma when it introduces a sentence (see p. 433):

Although the project was almost completed, it lost its funding.

CLAUSE CONNECTORS

ESL students may try unsuccessfully to use ellipsis in writing. Remind students that generally, in formal writing, clause connectors such as *that* and the relative pronouns *that, which,* and *whom* are not omitted. Students *will not* go wrong if they keep the clause connectors in their writing, but they *may* be wrong if they omit them.

A modifying subordinate clause that interrupts or concludes a main clause is *not* set off with punctuation when it is essential to the meaning of the word or words it modifies (see p. 435):

> The woman who directed the project lost her job.
> The project lost its funding because it was not completed on time.

When an interrupting or concluding subordinate clause is *not* essential to meaning, but merely adds information to the sentence, it *is* set off with punctuation, usually a comma or commas (see p. 435):

> The project lost its funding, although it was almost completed.
> The director, who holds a PhD, sought new funding.

EXERCISE 12.14   Identifying subordinate clauses

Identify the subordinate clauses in the following sentences. Then indicate whether each is used as an adjective, an adverb, or a noun. If the clause is a noun, indicate what function it performs in the sentence. (You can do this exercise online at *ablongman.com/littlebrown*.)

Example:

                               noun
The article explained how one could build an underground house. [Object of *explained*.]

1. Scientists who want to catch the slightest signals from space use extremely sensitive receivers.
2. Even though they have had to fight for funding, these scientists have persisted in their research.
3. The research is called SETI, which stands for Search for Extraterrestrial Intelligence.
4. The theory is that intelligent beings in space are trying to get in touch with us.
5. The challenge is to guess what frequency these beings would use to send signals.

EXERCISE 12.15   Sentence combining: Subordinate clauses

To practice writing sentences with subordinate clauses, combine each pair of main clauses into one sentence. Use either subordinating conjunctions or relative pronouns as appropriate, referring to the lists on pages 253 and 254 if necessary. You will have to add, delete, and rearrange words. Each item has more than one possible answer. (You can do this exercise online at *ablongman.com/littlebrown*.)

Example:

She did not have her tire irons with her. She could not change her bicycle tire.

Because she did not have her tire irons with her, she could not change her bicycle tire.

1. Moviegoers expect something. Movie sequels should be as exciting as the original films.

COLLABORATIVE LEARNING

Exercises 12.14 and 12.15 work well as collaborative projects. In particular, students with varying grammatical skills have the opportunity to discuss the parts of speech and their relative functions.

ANSWERS: EXERCISE 12.14

1.   ADJ
Scientists who want to catch the slightest signals from space use extremely sensitive receivers.
2.   ADV
Even though they have had to fight for funding, these scientists have persisted in their research.
3.   ADJ
The research is called SETI, which stands for Search for Extraterrestrial Intelligence.
4.   N (SUBJECT COMPLEMENT)
The theory is that intelligent beings in space are trying to get in touch with us.
5.   N (DIRECT OBJECT)
The challenge is to guess what frequency these beings would use to send signals.

ANSWERS: EXERCISE 12.15

Possible answers

1. Moviegoers expect that movie sequels should be as exciting as the original films.
2. Although a few sequels are good films, most are poor imitations of the originals.
3. Whenever a sequel to a blockbuster film arrives in the theater, crowds quickly line up to see it.
4. Viewers pay to see the same villains and heroes whom they remember fondly.
5. Afterward, viewers often grumble about filmmakers who rehash tired plots and characters.

2. A few sequels are good films. Most are poor imitations of the originals.
3. A sequel to a blockbuster film arrives in the theater. Crowds quickly line up to see it.
4. Viewers pay to see the same villains and heroes. They remember these characters fondly.
5. Afterward, viewers often grumble about filmmakers. The filmmakers rehash tired plots and characters.

5 Using appositives

An **appositive** is usually a noun that renames another noun nearby, most often the noun just before the appositive. (The word *appositive* derives from a Latin word that means "placed near to" or "applied to.") An appositive phrase includes modifiers as well.

Bizen ware, a dark stoneware, has been produced in Japan since the fourteenth century.

The name Bizen comes from the location of the kilns used to fire the pottery.

All appositives can replace the words they refer to: *A dark stoneware has been produced in Japan.*

Appositives are often introduced by words and phrases such as *or, that is, such as, for example,* and *in other words:*

Bizen ware is used in the Japanese tea ceremony, that is, the Zen Buddhist observance that links meditation and art.

Appositives are economical alternatives to adjective clauses containing a form of *be*, as shown in the next example.

Bizen ware, [which is] a dark stoneware, has been produced in Japan since the fourteenth century.

Although most appositives are nouns that rename other nouns, they may also be and rename other parts of speech, such as the verb *thrown* in the sentence below:

The pottery is thrown, or formed on a potter's wheel.

Punctuating appositives

Appositives punctuated as complete sentences are sentence fragments (see Chapter 17). To correct such fragments, you can usually connect the appositive to the main clause containing the word referred to:

Fragment   An exceedingly tall man with narrow shoulders.

Revised   He stood next to a basketball player, an exceedingly tall man with narrow shoulders.

EXPECTING PROBLEMS

As students begin using appositives, you may find more comma splices and fragments in their essays. Warn students to expect these errors, so that they will proofread more carefully. Be understanding as you evaluate student papers in which the students are practicing these strategies for the first time. If you focus on grammar faults, they may lose the incentive to take stylistic risks.

RESOURCES AND IDEAS

Sentence combining: Background and suggestions

Many of the exercises in this chapter can be used as the basis for a sequence of sentence-combining activities. The appropriate exercises are 8, 10, 12, 13, 15, 16, 17, 21.

Exercises in other chapters that can be part of a sentence-combining sequence are listed in the discussion "A Sequence for Sentence Combining" in the chapter "Using *The Little, Brown Handbook*," page IAE-7 of this instructor's edition.

Much has been written about sentence combining over the past two decades. The twenty-three essays in *Sentence Combining: A Rhetorical Perspective*, ed. Donald A. Daiker, Andrew Kerek, and Max Morenberg (Carbondale: Southern Illinois UP, 1985) provide excellent perspectives on the strengths and weaknesses of sentence combining as a way of improving the quality of writing and of developing an understanding of language and style.

The following articles are also useful resources:

Daiker, Donald, Andrew Kerek, and Max Morenberg. "Sentence-Combining and Syntactic Maturity in Freshman English." *College Composition and Communication* 29 (1978): 36–41. The authors discuss the results of an experiment demonstrating the effectiveness of sentence combining over fifteen weeks of intensive instruction.

Johnson, Karen E. "Cognitive Strategies and Second Language Writers: A Re-evaluation of Sentence Combining." *Journal of Second Language Writing* 1 (1992): 61–75. This essay reviews debates over the effectiveness of sentence combining in the context of ESL writers.

Larsen, Richard B. "Sentence Patterning." *College Composition and Communication* 37 (1986): 103–04. Larsen describes a sequence in which students are introduced to a variety of sentence patterns and then asked to use the patterns in their writing, including paragraph-length compositions.

Solomon, Martha. "Teaching the Nominative Absolute." *College Composition and Communication* 26 (1975): 356–61. Solomon offers advice on analyzing and teaching the absolute.

ANSWERS: EXERCISE 12.16

1. Some people, <u>geniuses from birth</u>, perform amazing feats when they are very young.
2. John Stuart Mill, <u>a British philosopher</u>, had written a history of Rome by age seven.
3. Paul Klee and Gustav Mahler, <u>two great artists</u>, began their work at age four.
4. <u>Mahler, a Bohemian composer of intensely emotional works</u>, was also the child of a brutal father.
5. As a child the Swiss painter <u>Paul Klee</u> was frightened by his own drawings of devils.

An appositive is *not* set off with punctuation when it is essential to the meaning of the word it refers to (see pp. 437–38):

> The verb <u>howl</u> comes from the Old English verb <u>houlen</u>.

When an appositive is *not* essential to the meaning of the word it refers to, it *is* set off with punctuation, usually a comma or commas (see pp. 437–38):

> <u>An aged elm</u>, the tree was struck by lightning.
> The tree, <u>an aged elm</u>, was struck by lightning.
> Lightning struck the tree, <u>an aged elm</u>.

A nonessential appositive is sometimes set off with a dash or dashes, especially when it contains commas (see p. 480):

> Three people—<u>Will, Erica, and Alex</u>—object to the new procedure.

A concluding appositive is sometimes set off with a colon (see p. 477):

> Two principles guide the judge's decisions: <u>justice and mercy</u>.

EXERCISE 12.16   Sentence combining: Appositives

To practice writing sentences with appositives, combine each pair of sentences into one sentence that contains an appositive. You will have to delete and rearrange words. Some items have more than one possible answer. (You can do this exercise online at *ablongman.com/littlebrown*.)

Example:

The largest land animal is the elephant. The elephant is also one of the most intelligent animals.

The largest land animal, <u>the elephant</u>, is also one of the most intelligent animals.

1. Some people perform amazing feats when they are very young. These people are geniuses from birth.
2. John Stuart Mill was a British philosopher. He had written a history of Rome by age seven.
3. Two great artists began their work at age four. They were Paul Klee and Gustav Mahler.
4. Mahler was a Bohemian composer of intensely emotional works. He was also the child of a brutal father.
5. Paul Klee was a Swiss painter. As a child he was frightened by his own drawings of devils.

12d   Compounding words, phrases, and clauses

A **compound construction** combines words that are closely related and equally important. It makes writing clearer and more economical because it pulls together linked information.

Headaches can be controlled by biofeedback. Heart rate can be controlled by biofeedback.

┌── compound subject ──┐
Headaches and heart rate can be controlled by biofeedback.

Without medication, biofeedback cures headaches. It steadies heart rate. It lowers blood pressure. It relaxes muscles.

┌──── compound predicate ────┐
Without medication, biofeedback cures headaches, steadies heart

rate, lowers blood pressure, and relaxes muscles.

1 Using coordinating conjunctions and correlative conjunctions

Two kinds of words create compound constructions: coordinating and correlative conjunctions. **Coordinating conjunctions** are few and do not change form. In the following box the relationship that each conjunction signals appears in parentheses.

Coordinating conjunctions

| and (*addition*) | nor (*alternative*) | for (*cause*) | yet (*contrast*) |
| but (*contrast*) | or (*alternative*) | so (*effect*) | |

To remember the coordinating conjunctions, use the word *fanboys*: <u>f</u>or, <u>a</u>nd, <u>n</u>or, <u>b</u>ut, <u>o</u>r, <u>y</u>et, <u>s</u>o.

The coordinating conjunctions *and, but, nor,* and *or* always connect words or word groups of the same kind—that is, two or more nouns, verbs, adjectives, adverbs, phrases, subordinate clauses, or main clauses:

Biofeedback or simple relaxation can relieve headaches.
Biofeedback is effective but costly.
Relaxation also works well, and it is inexpensive.

The conjunctions *for* and *so* connect only main clauses. *For* indicates cause; *so* indicates effect.

Biofeedback can be costly, for the training involves technical equipment and specialists.

Relaxation can be difficult to learn alone, so some people do seek help from specialists.

Some coordinating conjunctions pair up with other words to form **correlative conjunctions**. In the following box the relationship each conjunction signals appears in parentheses.

USING READINGS

Students can analyze passages from an essay in a reader (or some other source), looking for verbal phrases, passive sentences, compound and complex sentences, or any other features that you feel contribute to the effect of the essay and should be part of the students' prose style.

COLLABORATIVE LEARNING

REDO THE READINGS

Using the passages from the "Using readings" activity above (or other passages), ask students to work together to transform each occurrence of a structure—verbal phrases or compound sentences, and so on—into alternate structures of their choice without changing the meaning of the passage. Then have students comment on how the changes affect the passage, if at all. This activity is particularly well suited for collaborative work.

Common correlative conjunctions

both . . . and (*addition*)	neither . . . nor (*negation*)
not only . . . but also (*addition*)	whether . . . or (*alternative*)
not . . . but (*substitution*)	as . . . as (*comparison*)
either . . . or (*alternative*)	

Both biofeedback and relaxation can relieve headaches.

The techniques require neither psychotherapy nor medication.

The headache sufferer learns not only to recognize the causes of headaches but also to control those causes.

Punctuating compounded words, phrases, and clauses

Two words, phrases, or subordinate clauses that are connected by a coordinating conjunction are *not* separated by a comma (see p. 449):

The library needs renovation and rebuilding.

The work will begin after the spring term ends but before the fall term begins.

When two *main* clauses are joined into one sentence with a coordinating conjunction, a comma precedes the conjunction (see p. 432):

The project will be lengthy, and everyone will suffer some inconvenience.

When two main clauses are joined *without* a coordinating conjunction, they must be separated with a semicolon to avoid the error called a comma splice (see p. 342):

The work cannot be delayed; it's already overdue.

In a series of three or more items, commas separate the items, with *and* usually preceding the last item (see p. 441):

The renovated library will feature new study carrels, new shelving, and a larger reference section.

Semicolons sometimes separate the items in a series if they are long or contain commas (see p. 457).

A comma also separates two or more adjectives when they modify a noun equally and are not joined by a coordinating conjunction (see p. 442):

Cracked, crumbling walls will be repaired.

The comma does *not* separate adjectives when the one nearer the noun is more closely related to it in meaning (see p. 442):

New reading lounges will replace the old ones.

2 Using conjunctive adverbs

One other kind of connecting word, called a **conjunctive adverb**, relates only main clauses, not words, phrases, or subordinate clauses. In the following box the conjunctive adverbs are arranged by the relationships they signal.

Common conjunctive adverbs

Addition	Emphasis	Comparison or contrast	Cause or effect	Time
also	certainly	however	accordingly	finally
besides	indeed	in comparison	as a result	meanwhile
further	in fact	in contrast	consequently	next
furthermore	still	instead	hence	now
in addition	undoubtedly	likewise	similarly	then
incidentally		nevertheless	therefore	thereafter
moreover		nonetheless	thus	
		otherwise		

It's important to distinguish between conjunctive adverbs and conjunctions (coordinating and subordinating) because they demand different punctuation (see the next page). Conjunctive adverbs are *adverbs:* they describe the relation of ideas in two clauses, and, like most adverbs, they can move around in their clause:

Relaxation techniques have improved; however, few people know them.

Relaxation techniques have improved; few people know them, however.

In contrast, conjunctions bind two clauses into a single grammatical unit, and they cannot be moved:

Although few people know them, relaxation techniques have improved. [The subordinating conjunction can't be moved: *Few people know them although, relaxation techniques have improved.*]

Relaxation techniques have improved, but few people know them. [The coordinating conjunction can't be moved: *Relaxation techniques have improved, few people know them but.*]

Note Some connecting words have more than one use. *After, until,* and some other words may be either prepositions or subordi-

GRAMMAR TERMS

Terminology like *conjunctive adverb* is another reason that many students are convinced they can't "do" grammar, despite the fact that they construct sophisticated sentences every day. You may want to use a synonym like *movable adverb* or *floating adverb* to help students become more comfortable with this term.

nating conjunctions. Some prepositions, such as *behind* and *in,* can serve also as adverbs, as in *He trailed behind.* And some conjunctive adverbs, particularly *however,* may also serve simply as adverbs in sentences such as *However much the books cost, we must have them.* Again, the part of speech of a word depends on its function in a sentence.

Punctuating sentences containing conjunctive adverbs

Because the two main clauses related by a conjunctive adverb remain independent units, they must be separated by a semicolon (see p. 253). If they are separated by a comma, the result is a comma splice (Chapter 18):

| Comma splice | Interest rates rose, therefore, real estate prices declined. |
| Revised | Interest rates rose; therefore, real estate prices declined. |

A conjunctive adverb is almost always set off from its clause with a comma or commas (see p. 438):

The decline was small; however, some investors were badly hurt.
The decline was small; some investors, however, were badly hurt.

EXERCISE 12.17 Sentence combining: Compound constructions

To practice compounding words, phrases, and clauses, combine each of the following pairs of sentences into one sentence that is as short as possible without altering meaning. Use an appropriate connecting word of the type specified in parentheses, referring to the lists on pages 260–61 as necessary. You will have to add, delete, and rearrange words, and you may have to change or add punctuation. (You can do this exercise online at *ablongman.com/littlebrown.*)

Example:

The encyclopedia had some information. It was not detailed enough. (*Conjunctive adverb.*)

The encyclopedia had some information; however, it was not detailed enough.

1. All too often people assume that old age is not a productive time. Many people in their nineties have had great achievements. (*Conjunctive adverb.*)
2. In his nineties the philosopher Bertrand Russell spoke vigorously for international peace. He spoke for nuclear disarmament. (*Correlative conjunction.*)
3. Grandma Moses did not retire to an easy chair. She began painting at age seventy-six and was still going at one hundred. (*Conjunctive adverb.*)
4. The British general George Higginson published his memoirs after

ANSWERS: EXERCISE 12.17

Possible answers

1. All too often people assume that old age is not a productive time; however, many people in their nineties have had great achievements.
2. In his nineties the philosopher Bertrand Russell spoke vigorously for both international peace and nuclear disarmament.
3. Grandma Moses did not retire to an easy chair; instead, she began painting at age seventy-six and was still going at one hundred.
4. The British general George Higginson and the British archaeologist Margaret Murray published their memoirs after they were ninety.
5. The architect Frank Lloyd Wright designed his first building at age twenty and his last at age ninety.

he was ninety. The British archaeologist Margaret Murray published her memoirs after she was ninety. (*Coordinating conjunction.*)

5. The architect Frank Lloyd Wright designed his first building at age twenty. He designed his last building at age ninety. (*Coordinating conjunction.*)

12e Changing the usual word order

So far, all the examples of basic sentence grammar have been similar: the subject of the sentence comes first, naming the performer of the predicate's action, and the predicate comes second. This arrangement describes most English sentences, but four kinds of sentences change the order.

Questions

In most questions the verb or part of it precedes the subject:

verb   subject ⎯⎯ verb ⎯⎯
Have interest rates been rising?

verb subject verb
Did rates rise?

verb subject verb
Why did rates rise today?

subject verb
What is the answer? [Normal subject-verb order.]

Commands

In commands the subject *you* is omitted:

verb
Think of the options.

verb
Watch the news.

Passive sentences

Generally, the subject performs the action of a verb in the **active voice**. But sometimes the subject *receives* the action of a verb in the **passive voice**:

subject   verb
Active   **Kyong wrote the paper.**

subject ⎯⎯ verb ⎯⎯
Passive   **The paper was written by Kyong.**

See pages 302–03 for more on forming the passive voice, and see page 303 on overuse of the passive voice.

Sentences with postponed subjects

The subject follows the predicate in two sentence patterns. The normal order may be reversed for emphasis:

Henry comes here. [Normal order.]
Here comes Henry. [Reversed order.]

RESOURCES AND IDEAS

Gorrell, Donna. "Controlled Composition for Basic Writers." *College Composition and Communication* 32 (1981): 308–16. Gorrell suggests having students manipulate and alter previously written material to develop basic skills.

Or the word *there* or *it* may postpone the subject:

verb   subject
There will be eighteen people attending the meeting.

verb   subject
It was surprising that Marinetti was nominated.

There and *it* in such sentences are called **expletives.** Expletive sentences have their uses, but they can also be wordy and unemphatic (see p. 534).

 When you use an expletive construction, be careful to include *there* or *it.* Only commands and some questions can begin with verbs.

Faulty   No one predicted the nomination. Were no polls showing Marinetti ahead.

Revised   No one predicted the nomination. There were no polls showing Marinetti ahead.

EXERCISE 12.18   **Forming questions and commands**

Form a question and a command from the following noun and verb pairs. (You can do this exercise online at *ablongman.com/littlebrown.*)

Example:

wood, split
Did you split all this wood?
Split the wood for our fire.

1. water, boil
2. music, stop
3. table, set
4. dice, roll
5. telephone, use

EXERCISE 12.19   **Rewriting passives and expletives**

Rewrite each passive sentence below as active, and rewrite each expletive construction to restore normal subject-predicate order. (For additional exercises with the passive voice and with expletives, see pp. 303–04, 386, and 535–36.) (You can do this exercise online at *ablongman .com/littlebrown.*)

Example:

All the trees in the park were planted by the city.
The city planted all the trees in the park.

1. The screenplay for *Monster's Ball* was cowritten by Milo Addica and Will Rokos.
2. The film was directed by Marc Foster.
3. There was only one performance in the movie that received an Academy Award.
4. It was Halle Berry who won the award for best actress.
5. Berry was congratulated by the press for being the first African American to win the award.

EXPLETIVES

Remind students that because English is a subject-verb-object language, something must fill the subject position when the subject is delayed. *There* and *it* fulfill this requirement by acting as dummy subjects.

ANSWERS: EXERCISE 12.18

Possible answers

1. Will the water boil?
   Boil the water, please.
2. Did the music stop?
   Stop the music.
3. Have you set the table?
   Set the table.
4. Have you rolled the dice yet?
   Roll the dice.
5. Who can use the telephone?
   Use the telephone.

ANSWERS: EXERCISE 12.19

1. Milo Addica and Will Rokos cowrote the screenplay for *Monster's Ball.*
2. Marc Foster directed the film.
3. Only one performance in the movie received an Academy Award.
4. Halle Berry won the award for best actress.
5. The press congratulated Berry for being the first African American to win the award.

12f Classifying sentences

We describe and classify sentences in two different ways: by function (statement, question, command, exclamation, and so on) or by structure. Four basic sentence structures are possible: simple, compound, complex, and compound-complex. Each structure gives different emphasis to the sentence's main idea or ideas and to any supporting information.

1 Writing simple sentences

A **simple sentence** consists of a single main clause and no subordinate clause:

———— main clause ————
Last summer was unusually hot.

———————— main clause ————————
The summer made many farmers leave the area for good or reduced
them to bare existence.

2 Writing compound sentences

A **compound sentence** consists of two or more main clauses and no subordinate clause. The clauses may be joined by a coordinating conjunction and a comma, by a semicolon alone, or by a conjunctive adverb and a semicolon.

—— main clause ——   —— main clause ——
Last July was hot, but August was even hotter.

—— main clause ——   —— main clause ——
The hot sun scorched the earth; the lack of rain killed many crops.

3 Writing complex sentences

A **complex sentence** contains one main clause and one or more subordinate clauses:

—— main clause ——   ———— subordinate clause ————
Rain finally came, although many had left the area by then.

———— main clause ————   —— subordinate clause ——
Those who remained were able to start anew because the government
     subordinate clause
came to their aid.

Notice that length does not determine whether a sentence is complex or simple; both kinds can be short or long.

4 Writing compound-complex sentences

A **compound-complex sentence** has the characteristics of both the compound sentence (two or more main clauses) and the complex sentence (at least one subordinate clause):

COLLABORATIVE LEARNING

DECODING THE SENTENCE

Divide the class into small groups and have each group write a set of nonsense sentences that conform to English syntax and punctuation. Students should be sure to include nonsense prepositional phrases, verbals, appositives, absolutes, and subordinate and coordinate structures. Warn students to punctuate the sentences carefully. Students can use the nonsense sentence at the beginning of Chapter 12 as a model.

COLLABORATIVE LEARNING

PARTS OF SPEECH

Once the sentences are written, have groups exchange sentences or write them on the board and try to identify the part of speech for each nonsense word. If the creators of the sentences have made errors in punctuation, the puzzle-solvers should be prepared to correct them. This exercise should help students see how grammar and punctuation work together to define a word's role in a sentence and to create different kinds of sentences.

A WRITER'S PERSPECTIVE ——————

Prose is architecture, and the Baroque is over.
—ERNEST HEMINGWAY

RESOURCES AND IDEAS

Dawkins, John. "Teaching Punctuation as a Rhetorical Tool." *College Composition and Communication* 46 (1995): 533–48. Dawkins makes a case for teaching the rhetorical thinking processes that accompany decisions about punctuation marks.

Herrington, Anne J. "Grammar Recharted: Sentence Analysis for Writing." *Writing Exercises from "Exercise Exchange."* Vol. 2. Urbana: NCTE, 1984. 276–87. Herrington offers a number of useful classroom activities.

COLLABORATIVE LEARNING

Exercises 12.20 and 12.21 work well as group projects. Students might begin by working individually on Exercise 12.20, then compare responses in small groups and work together on Exercise 12.21.

ANSWERS: EXERCISE 12.20

1. *Simple:* ┌─────MAIN─────┐ Joseph Pulitzer endowed the Pulitzer Prizes.

2. *Simple:* ┌─────MAIN─────┐ Pulitzer, incidentally, was the publisher of the New York newspaper *The World.*

3. *Complex:* ┌────SUBORDINATE────┐ Although the first prizes were for journalism and letters only, ┌──MAIN──┐ Pulitzers are now awarded in music and other areas.

4. *Compound:* ┌────MAIN────┐ For example, Berke Breathed won for his *Bloom County* comic strip, and ┌────MAIN────┐ Roger Reynolds won for his musical composition *Whispers Out of Time.*

5. *Compound-complex:* ┌────SUBORDINATE────┐ Although only one prize is usually awarded in each category, in 1989 ┌────MAIN────┐ Taylor Branch's *Parting the Waters* won a history prize, and ┌────MAIN────┐ it shared the honor with James M. McPherson's *Battle Cry of Freedom.*

ANSWERS: EXERCISE 12.21

Possible answers

1. Recycling takes time, but it reduces garbage in landfills.
2. After people begin to recycle, they generate much less trash.
3. Although white tissues and paper towels biodegrade more easily than dyed ones, people still buy dyed papers.
4. Aluminum cans bring recyclers good money.
5. Environmentalists hope that more communities will recycle newspaper and glass, but many citizens refuse to participate.

┌──────── subordinate clause ────────┐┌──── main clause ────┐
Even though government aid finally came, many people had already
┌──────── main clause ────────┐
been reduced to poverty, and others had been forced to move.

EXERCISE 12.20   Identifying sentence structures

Mark the main clauses and subordinate clauses in the following sentences. Identify each sentence as simple, compound, complex, or compound-complex. (You can do this exercise online at *ablongman.com/littlebrown.*)

Example:

┌──────── main clause ────────┐┌──── subordinate clause ────┐
The police began patrolling more often when crime in the neighborhood increased. [Complex sentence.]

1. Joseph Pulitzer endowed the Pulitzer Prizes.
2. Pulitzer, incidentally, was the publisher of the New York newspaper *The World.*
3. Although the first prizes were for journalism and letters only, Pulitzers are now awarded in music and other areas.
4. For example, Berke Breathed won for his *Bloom County* comic strip, and Roger Reynolds won for his musical composition *Whispers Out of Time.*
5. Although only one prize is usually awarded in each category, in 1989 Taylor Branch's *Parting the Waters* won a history prize, and it shared the honor with James M. McPherson's *Battle Cry of Freedom.*

EXERCISE 12.21   Sentence combining: Sentence structures

Combine each set of simple sentences below to produce the kind of sentence specified in parentheses. You will have to add, delete, change, and rearrange words. (You can do this exercise online at *ablongman.com/littlebrown.*)

Example:

The traffic passed the house. It never stopped. (*Complex.*)
The traffic that passed the house never stopped.

1. Recycling takes time. It reduces garbage in landfills. (*Compound.*)
2. People begin to recycle. They generate much less trash. (*Complex.*)
3. White tissues and paper towels biodegrade more easily than dyed ones. People still buy dyed papers. (*Complex.*)
4. The cans are aluminum. They bring recyclers good money. (*Simple.*)
5. Environmentalists have hope. Perhaps more communities will recycle newspaper and glass. Many citizens refuse to participate. (*Compound-complex.*)

Guide to nouns

Summary and index of information in the student text (consult sections or pages in parentheses).

Description of nouns

Nouns as sentence subjects (12a-1, 12a-2)

Nouns as direct and indirect objects (12a-3), object complements (12a-3), objects of prepositions (12c-1), appositives (12c-5), modifiers (16f)

Classes of nouns: proper, common, collective, count, mass, concrete, abstract (12a-2)

Forms of nouns: subjective and objective case (13a, 13b), possessive case (30a), and plural (41b-6)

Other structures serving as nouns: gerunds and gerund phrases (12c-2), infinitives and infinitive phrases (12c-2), subordinate clauses (12c-4)

Conventions regarding nouns

Forms of nouns

Possessive forms: *boy's* vs. *boys'*; *Park's* vs. *Parks's* vs. *Parkses'* (30a)

Possessives before gerunds: *Nguyen's writing is clear.* (13h)

Plurals of nouns and compound nouns: *dish, dishes; child, children; mother-in-law, mothers-in-law* (41b-6)

Nouns and other sentence parts

Agreement of subjects and verbs: *The towel was wet. The towels were wet.* (15a)

Agreement of antecedents and pronouns: *The children surrounded their father.* (15b)

Grammatical fit between subjects and predicates (avoiding mixed grammar): *In the supervision of others is the best preparation for a management career.*→*The supervision of others is the best preparation for a management career.* (22a)

Fit in meaning of subjects and predicates (avoiding faulty predication): *The use of the airwaves is the ideal medium for campaigning.*→*The airwaves are the ideal medium for campaigning.* (22b)

Clarity and effectiveness

Nouns as modifiers (avoiding overuse): *adult education grants workshop*→*workshop on grants for adult education* (16f)

Consistency in subjects and the voice of verbs: *Tony woke suddenly, but his eyes were kept shut.*→*Tony woke suddenly, but he kept his eyes shut.* (20c)

SUMMARY GUIDES

The guides on this and the next five pages appear only in the *Instructor's Annotated Edition.* They are included here for use in conferences and labs. Each guide collects all the descriptions and conventions for a different element: nouns, pronouns, verbs and verbals, and modifiers. Thus the guides provide convenient indexes or texts for students having difficulty with, say, identifying and placing modifiers or distinguishing verbs and verbals. The listings under "Conventions" in each guide contain at least one example showing correct or preferred usage. For additional examples or detailed explanations, consult the sections or pages given in parentheses.

NOTE

This page does not appear in the students' edition.

Guide to pronouns

Summary and index of information in the student text (consult sections or pages in parentheses).

Description of pronouns

Pronouns as substitutes for nouns (12a-2; 15b)

Pronouns as subjects, objects, complements, appositives, modifiers (Chapter 13)

Case forms of pronouns: subjective, objective, possessive (Chapter 13)

Person, number, and gender of personal pronouns (12a-2; 15b)

Conventions regarding pronouns

Forms of pronouns

Subjective case for subjects and subject complements: *You and I can talk. It was she.* (13a)

Objective case for objects: *Ken gave me a dog. He gave her to me.* (13b)

We or *us* with nouns: *We drivers like highways. Many of us drivers like highways.* (13c)

Case in appositives: *Two drivers, she and Nell, won the award. The state rewarded two drivers, her and Nell.* (13d)

Case after *than* or *as*: *Nell likes Buddy more than [she likes] him. Nell likes Buddy more than he [likes Buddy].* (13e)

Objective case for subjects and objects of infinitives: *We invited him to meet her.* (13f)

Who vs. *whom*: *Who can predict whom he will ask?* (13g)

Possessives before gerunds: *his working* (13h)

Possessive forms of personal pronouns: *hers* (not *her's*); *theirs* (not *their's*) (30b)

Possessive pronouns vs. contractions: *its* vs. *it's; your* vs. *you're; their* vs. *they're* (30c)

Pronouns and other sentence parts

Agreement of pronoun subjects and verbs: *Neither he nor they are late. Everybody is finished.* (15a)

Agreement of pronouns and antecedents: *Everybody finished his or her paper. Lisa or Maria left her notebook.* (15b)

Reference of pronouns to antecedents (avoiding unclear or remote reference): *The first act of the play seemed weak, but then it improved.→The first act of the play started weakly but then improved.* Or: *Though the first act was weak, the play then improved.* (19a–19e)

Guide to verbs and verbals

Summary and index of information in the student text (consult sections or pages in parentheses).

Description of verbs and verbals

Verb as sentence predicate (12a-1, 12a-2, 12a-3)
Transitive, intransitive, and linking verbs (12a-3)
Forms of verbs: infinitive, past tense, past participle, present participle, -s form (pp. 275–92)
Regular vs. irregular verbs (14a)
Finite vs. nonfinite verbs (12c-2)
Helping (auxiliary) verbs (14d)
Tense of verbs: present, past, future, etc. (pp. 292–98)
Mood of verbs: indicative, imperative, subjunctive (pp. 299–301)
Voice of verbs: active and passive (pp. 302–03)
Verbals and verbal phrases: participles, gerunds, infinitives (12c-2)

Conventions regarding verbs and verbals

Forms and tenses of verbs

Principal parts of common irregular verbs: e.g., *begin, began, begun; run, ran, run* (14a)
Sit vs. *set, lie* vs. *lay,* and *rise* vs. *raise* (14b)
Needed -s and -ed endings: *He asks/asked too much.* (14c)
Needed helping verbs: *He is asking too much.* (14d)
Present tense (*runs*) and perfect tenses (*has/had/will have run*) (14g)
Sequence of tenses: e.g., *We would like to have gone* vs. *We would have liked to go.* (14h)
Subjunctive mood: *I wish I were there.* (14i)

Verbs and other sentence parts

Agreement of verbs and subjects: *The guests are here. Nobody is missing.* (15a)
Unseparated verb phrases and infinitives: *They had before long agreed to voluntarily surrender.→Before long they had agreed to surrender voluntarily.* (21e)
Grammatical fit between subjects and predicates (avoiding mixed grammar): *By saving is how they could buy a car.→By saving, they could buy a car.* (22a)
Fit in meaning of subjects and predicates (avoiding faulty predication): *The reason is because they were frugal.→The reason is that they were frugal.* (22b)

Problems with verbals

Verbs required in complete sentences (avoiding sentence fragments with verbals): *Rain falling silently.→Rain fell silently.* (17a, 17c)

NOTE

This page does not appear in the students' edition.

Clear and logical modifiers (avoiding dangling modifiers): *Flying home, her thoughts remained behind.→As she flew home, her thoughts remained behind.* (21h)

Punctuation with verbals

Commas after introductory verbal modifiers: *Struggling for air, the climbers reached the summit.* (28b)

Commas to set off nonessential verbal modifiers: *The climbers, struggling for air, reached the summit.* (28c)

Clarity and effectiveness

Active rather than passive voice: *Hands were raised by the students. →The students raised their hands.* (14j)

Consistency in voice: *Before you tighten the bolts, the car should be lowered to the ground.→Before you tighten the bolts, you should lower the car to the ground.* (20c)

Consistency in tense: *The hero escapes, but he was captured.→The hero escapes, but he is captured.* (20b)

Consistency in mood: *Unscrew the bolts, and then you remove the wheel.→Unscrew the bolts and then remove the wheel.* (20b)

Strong rather than weak verbs (avoiding wordiness): *The book is a depiction of family strife.→The book depicts family strife.* (23a, 39a)

Guide to modifiers

Summary and index of information in the student text (consult sections or pages in parentheses).

Description of modifiers

Functions of adjectives: modifying nouns and pronouns (p. 319–21)

Functions of adverbs: modifying verbs, adjectives, other adverbs, phrases, and clauses (pp. 319–21)

Forms of adjectives and adverbs: positive, comparative, superlative (16d)

Irregular adjectives and adverbs (16d-1)

Classes of adjectives: descriptive, limiting, proper, attributive, predicate (pp. 881–82)

Classes of adverbs: modifiers of verbs, adjectives, and other adverbs (pp. 319–21); transitional and parenthetical expressions (28b); conjunctive adverbs (12d-2)

Other structures serving as modifiers: nouns (16f); prepositional phrases (12c-1); participles and participial phrases (12c-2); infinitives and infinitive phrases (12c-2); subordinate clauses (12c-4)

Conventions regarding modifiers

Distinctions between adjectives and adverbs

Adverbs (not adjectives) to modify verbs, adjectives, adverbs: *Susan writes well* [not *good*]. (16a)

Adjectives after linking verbs, adverbs to modify other verbs: *I feel bad. She sings badly.* (16b)

Adjectives to modify objects, adverbs to modify verbs: *We believed him honest. We treated him honestly.* (16c)

Forms of adjectives and adverbs

Comparatives and superlatives: *steady, steadier/more steady, steadiest/ most steady; good/well, better, best* (16d-1); *most steadiest→ most steady* (16d-2); *the bigger of two and the biggest of three* (16d-3); *most unique→unique* (16d-4)

Modifiers and other sentence parts

Clear placement of modifiers: *We waited for the rain to stop in a doorway.→We waited in a doorway for the rain to stop.* (21a–21g)

Clear and logical modifiers (avoiding dangling modifiers): *Watching the rain, our hands and feet froze.→As we watched the rain, our hands and feet froze.* (21h)

NOTE

Punctuation and mechanics with modifiers

Commas after most introductory modifiers: *Happily, we have friends.* (28b)

Commas to set off nonessential modifiers: *Ellen, who is our best friend, checks in every day.* (28c)

Commas to set off absolute phrases: *Her workday finished, she calls us.* (28d)

Commas for coordinate adjectives: *She is a steady, reliable friend.* (28f-2)

Commas with conjunctive adverbs and transitional and parenthetical expressions: *Traffic was bad; we left, however, before it could get worse.* (28c-3, 29b)

Semicolons between clauses related by conjunctive adverbs: *We did not leave right away; instead, we waited for Ellen.* (18b, 29b)

Capital letters for proper adjectives: *Indian tea; Buddhist chant* (33d)

Figure vs. words for numbers: *327* vs. *twenty-three* (36a)

Hyphens in compound adjectives and numbers: *well-spoken words* vs. *words well spoken* (41d-1); *thirty-two minutes* (41d-2)

Clarity and effectiveness

Clear negation (avoiding double negatives): *They don't want no interruptions.→They don't want any interruptions.* Or: *They want no interruptions.* (16e)

Nouns as modifiers (avoiding overuse): *business managers spreadsheet analysis seminar→seminar in spreadsheet analysis for business managers* (16f)

Complete and logical comparisons: *The value of friendship is greater than money.→The value of friendship is greater than the value of* [or *that of*] *money.* (22d)

CHAPTER 13

Case of Nouns and Pronouns

Case is the form of a noun or pronoun that shows the reader how it functions in a sentence—that is, whether it functions as a subject, as an object, or in some other way. As shown in the box on the next page, only *I, we, he, she, they,* and *who* change form for each case. Thus these pronouns are the focus of this chapter.

The **subjective case** generally indicates that the word is a subject or a subject complement. (See pp. 233 and 239–40.)

[handwritten annotation: Subjective — word is a subject or S. complement]

> subject
> She and Novick discussed the proposal.

> subject
> The proposal ignores many who need help.

> subject complement
> The disgruntled planners were she and Novick.

The **objective case** generally indicates that the word is the object of a verb or preposition. (See pp. 238–41 and 245.)

> object of verb
> The proposal disappointed her and Novick.

> object   object
> of verb   of verb
> A colleague whom they respected let them down.

> object of
> preposition
> Their opinion of him suffered.

The **possessive case** generally indicates ownership or source:

> Her counterproposal is in preparation.
> Theirs is the more defensible position.
> The problem is not his.

Do not use an apostrophe to form the possessive of personal pronouns: *yours* (not *your's*); *theirs* (not *their's*). (See p. 465. See also p. 461 for the possessive forms of nouns, which do use apostrophes.)

---

mycomplab 2.0

Please visit MyCompLab at *www.mycomplab.com* for more on the writing process.

HIGHLIGHTS

The forms that nouns and pronouns take according to their role in a sentence are relatively few in English when compared with some other languages. Nonetheless, most students are likely to find compound subjects and objects or questions of *who* and *whom* occasionally troublesome. Others may need to review pronoun forms more extensively to gain control over this part of their writing.

This chapter opens with a review of the functions a pronoun can perform, functions that determine the form, or case, of the pronoun. In addition to the familiar list of forms of the personal pronouns, the chapter provides sentences illustrating the wide variety of uses for pronouns. Following this are brief discussions of the proper case for pronouns in contexts that usually cause difficulty for student writers, including compound subjects and objects, appositives, comparisons using *than* or *as*, possessive case with gerunds, and the different uses of *who* and *whom.*

The exercises ask students to select the appropriate forms of pronouns in the troublesome contexts treated in the discussion, to correct any case errors in a paragraph, and to combine sentences so as to use *who* or *whom* in relative clauses.

RESOURCES AND IDEAS

Redfern, Richard K. "Pronouns Are Highly Personal." *English Journal* 85 (1996): 80–81. Redfern presents further strategies for teaching pronoun usage.

COMPANION WEB SITE

See page IAE-53 for companion Web site content description.

---

http://www.ablongman.com/littlebrown ▶

Visit the companion Web site for more help and additional exercises on noun and pronoun case.

TRANSPARENCY MASTER 13.1

THE CHART

Students may be tempted to skip over this chart giving the case forms of nouns and pronouns. Get them to pay attention by asking them to fill out the whole chart in class—without looking at the text. The act of remembering the forms or figuring them out will be more valuable than listening to an explanation. Students who have trouble completing the chart probably need to spend time reviewing the chapter.

NOUN-NOUN POSSESSIVES

Students who are nonnative speakers of English learn that people and animals go in possessive case ("Phoebe's phone," "the ferret's fur") but that inanimate objects take "of" formations ("the end of the line"). Students may be confused by the exceptions to this rule ("table top," "car engine.") Have your students keep a list of exceptions to this rule and see how long the list grows by the end of your course.

Case forms of nouns and pronouns

	Subjective	Objective	Possessive
Nouns	boy	boy	boy's
	Jessie	Jessie	Jessie's
Personal pronouns			
Singular			
1st person	I	me	my, mine
2nd person	you	you	your, yours
3rd person	he	him	his
	she	her	her, hers
	it	it	its
Plural			
1st person	we	us	our, ours
2nd person	you	you	your, yours
3rd person	they	them	their, theirs
Relative and interrogative pronouns			
	who	whom	whose
	whoever	whomever	—
	which, that, what	which, that, what	—
Indefinite pronouns			
	everybody	everybody	everybody's

Note Grammar and style checkers may flag some problems with pronoun case, but they will also miss a lot. For instance, one checker spotted the error in *We asked whom would come* (should be *who would come*), but it overlooked *We dreaded them coming* (should be *their coming*).

CULTURE LANGUAGE In standard American English, *-self* pronouns do not change form to show function. Their only forms are *myself, yourself, himself, herself, itself, ourselves, yourselves, themselves*. Avoid nonstandard forms such as *hisself, ourself,* and *theirselves*.

13a Use the subjective case for compound subjects and for subject complements.

In compound subjects use the same pronoun form you would use if the pronoun stood alone as a subject:

subject
She and Novick will persist.

The others may lend their support when *she and Novick* [subject] get a hearing.

If you are in doubt about the correct form, try the test in the box below.

After a linking verb, such as a form of *be*, a pronoun renaming the subject (a subject complement) should be in the subjective case:

The ones who care most are *she and Novick*. [subject complement]

It was *they* [subject complement] whom the mayor appointed.

If this construction sounds stilted to you, use the more natural order: *She and Novick are the ones who care most. The mayor appointed them.*

A test for case forms in compound constructions

1. **Identify a compound construction** (one connected by *and, but, or, nor*).

   [He, Him] and [I, me] won the prize.
   The prize went to [he, him] and [I, me].

2. **Write a separate sentence for each part of the compound.**

   [He, Him] won the prize. [I, Me] won the prize.
   The prize went to [he, him]. The prize went to [I, me].

3. **Choose the pronouns that sound correct.**

   He won the prize. I won the prize. [Subjective.]
   The prize went to him. The prize went to me. [Objective.]

4. **Put the separate sentences back together.**

   He and I won the prize.
   The prize went to him and me.

13b **Use the objective case for compound objects.**

In compound objects use the same pronoun form you would use if the pronoun stood alone as an object:

The mayor nominated *Zhu and him*. [direct object]

The mayor gave *Zhu and him* awards. [indirect object]

Credit goes equally to *them and the mayor*. [object of preposition]

If you are in doubt about the correct form, try the test in the box above.

BACK TO NOUNS

Distribute copies of a paragraph taken from a magazine article, an essay in a reader, or a student paper. Ask students to rewrite it, substituting the appropriate noun for each pronoun. This exercise will help students to understand the role of pronouns and see the relationship between the case of a pronoun and the function of the noun it stands for.

ANSWERS: EXERCISE 13.1

1. I
2. she, I, we
3. She, I
4. her, me
5. her, me

US THE PEOPLE

If students try out pronoun forms in sentences, they can often "hear" the contrast between correct and incorrect forms by relying on their implicit understanding of the language or by using familiar phrases as touchstones:

Us the people.
Us are the world.
Are you going with *we*?
Take *we* to the movies.

This approach will not work with students for whom standard English is a second language or a second dialect.

ANSWERS: EXERCISE 13.2

1. us
2. we
3. him
4. us
5. we, I

EXERCISE 13.1 Choosing between subjective and objective pronouns

From the pairs in brackets, select the appropriate subjective or objective pronoun(s) for each of the following sentences. (You can do this exercise online at *ablongman.com/littlebrown*.)

> *Example:*
> "Between you and [I, me]," the seller said, "this deal is a steal."
> "Between you and me," the seller said, "this deal is a steal."

1. Lisa and [I, me] were competing for places on the relay team.
2. The fastest runners at our school were [she, her] and [I, me], so [we, us] expected to make the team.
3. [She, Her] and [I, me] were friends but also intense rivals.
4. The time trials went badly, excluding both [she, her] and [I, me] from the team.
5. Next season we are determined to earn at least one place between [she, her] and [I, me].

13c Use the appropriate case when the plural pronoun *we* or *us* occurs with a noun.

Whether to use *we* or *us* with a noun depends on the use of the noun:

Freezing weather is welcomed by us skaters. *[object of preposition]*

We skaters welcome freezing weather. *[subject]*

13d In appositives the case of a pronoun depends on the function of the word described or identified.

The class elected two representatives, DeShawn and me. *[object of verb; appositive identifies object]*

Two representatives, DeShawn and I, were elected. *[subject; appositive identifies subject]*

If you are in doubt about case in an appositive, try the sentence without the word the appositive identifies: *The class elected De-Shawn and me. DeShawn and I were elected.*

EXERCISE 13.2 Choosing between subjective and objective pronouns

From the pairs in brackets, select the appropriate subjective or objective pronoun for each of the following sentences. (You can do this exercise online at *ablongman.com/littlebrown*.)

Example:
Convincing [we, us] veterans to vote yes will be difficult.
Convincing us veterans to vote yes will be difficult.

1. Obtaining enough protein is important to [we, us] vegetarians.
2. Instead of obtaining protein from meat, [we, us] vegetarians get our protein from other sources.
3. Jeff claims to know only two vegetarians, Helena and [he, him], who avoid all animal products, including milk.
4. Some of [we, us] vegetarians eat fish, which is a good source of protein.
5. [We, Us] vegetarians in my family, my parents and [I, me], drink milk and eat fish.

13e The case of a pronoun after *than* or *as* in a comparison depends on the meaning.

When a pronoun follows *than* or *as* in a comparison, the case of the pronoun indicates what words may have been omitted. When the pronoun is subjective, it must serve as the subject of an omitted verb:

subject

Some critics like Glass more than he [does].

When the pronoun is objective, it must serve as the object of an omitted verb:

object

Some critics like Glass more than [they like] him.

13f Use the objective case for pronouns that are subjects or objects of infinitives.

subject of infinitive

The school asked him to speak.

object of infinitive

Students chose to invite him.

13g The case of the pronoun *who* depends on its function in its clause.

To choose between *who* and *whom, whoever* and *whomever,* you need to figure out whether the word serves as a subject or as an object. Use *who* where you would use *he* or *she*—all ending in vowels. Use *whom* where you would use *him* or *her*—all ending in consonants.

MAKE UP YOUR OWN TEST

Give students time in class to write out five to ten sentences in quiz form. The easiest way for students to do this is to pattern their questions after the exercises and sample sentences in the handbook:

Most of [we, us] college students realize that finding a good job isn't easy.
There is a five-hundred-dollar reward for [whomever, whoever] finds the missing stock certificates.

Students can use the handbook in preparing the questions, and as long as they know that one of the possible answers they have provided must be right, they need not be sure which one it is.

When the tests are completed, students should exchange them and fill them out. Correcting the tests is best done in small groups so that students can help one another or turn to the instructor for any information necessary to provide answers to the toughest questions.

I love you (example)

1 **At the beginning of questions use** *who* **for a subject and** *whom* **for an object.**

subject ⟶
Who wrote the policy?

object ⟵
Whom does it affect?

A test for *who* versus *whom* in questions

1. **Pose the question.**

   [Who, Whom] makes that decision?
   [Who, Whom] does one ask?

2. **Answer the question, using a personal pronoun.** Choose the pronoun that sounds correct, and note its case.

   [She, Her] makes that decision. She makes that decision. [Subjective.]
   One asks [she, her]. One asks her. [Objective.]

3. **Use the same case (*who* or *whom*) in the question.**

   Who makes that decision? [Subjective.]
   Whom does one ask? [Objective.]

Note In speech the subjective case *who* is commonly used whenever it is the first word of a question, regardless of whether it is a subject or an object. But formal writing requires a distinction between the forms:

Spoken   Who should we credit?

object ⟵
Written   Whom should we credit?

2 **In subordinate clauses use** *who* **and** *whoever* **for all subjects,** *whom* **and** *whomever* **for all objects.**

The case of a pronoun in a subordinate clause depends on its function in the clause, regardless of whether the clause itself functions as a subject, an object, or a modifier:

subject ⟶
Credit whoever wrote the policy.

object ⟵
Research should reveal whom to credit.

Note Don't let expressions such as *I think* and *she says* confuse you when they come between the subject *who* and its verb:

subject ⟶
He is the one who the polls say will win.

To choose between *who* and *whom* in such constructions, delete the interrupting phrase: *He is the one who will win.*

A test for *who* versus *whom* in subordinate clauses

1. **Locate the subordinate clause.**

   Few people know [who, whom] they should ask.
   They are unsure [who, whom] makes the decision.

2. **Rewrite the subordinate clause as a separate sentence, substituting a personal pronoun for *who, whom*.** Choose the pronoun that sounds correct, and note its case.

   They should ask [she, her]. They should ask her. [Objective.]
   [She, Her] makes the decision. She makes the decision. [Subjective.]

3. **Use the same case (*who* or *whom*) in the subordinate clause.**

   Few people know whom they should ask. [Objective.]
   They are unsure who makes the decision. [Subjective.]

EXERCISE 13.3 Choosing between *who* and *whom*

From the pairs in brackets, select the appropriate form of the pronoun in each of the following sentences. (You can do this exercise online at *ablongman.com/littlebrown*.)

Example:
My mother asked me [who, whom] I was going out with.
My mother asked me whom I was going out with.

1. The judges awarded first prize to Inez, [who, whom] they believed gave the best performance.
2. Inez beat the other contestants [who, whom] competed against her.
3. She is a consummate performer, singing to [whoever, whomever] would listen.
4. [Who, Whom] in the school has not heard Inez sing?
5. [Who, Whom] has she not performed for?

EXERCISE 13.4 Sentence combining: *Who* versus *whom*

Combine each pair of sentences below into one sentence that contains a clause beginning with *who* or *whom*. Be sure to use the appropriate case form. You will have to add, delete, and rearrange words. Each item may have more than one possible answer. (You can do this exercise online at *ablongman.com/littlebrown*.)

Example:
David is the candidate. We think David deserves to win.
David is the candidate who we think deserves to win.

1. Some children have undetected hearing problems. These children may do poorly in school.

COLLABORATIVE LEARNING

Students might complete Exercise 13.3 independently, then compare answers and work on Exercise 13.4 in pairs or in small groups. Ask each group to create several sentences of their own using *who* and *whom*, and based on the models provided in Exercise 13.4. Each group might present some of their most inventive responses to the class by writing them on the chalkboard, making transparencies, or posting them on the network.

ANSWERS: EXERCISE 13.3

1. whom
2. who
3. whoever
4. Who
5. Whom

ANSWERS: EXERCISE 13.4

Possible answers

1. Some children who have undetected hearing problems may do poorly in school.
2. They may not hear important instructions and information from teachers who speak softly.
3. Classmates whom the teacher calls on may not be audible.
4. Some hearing-impaired children who get a lot of encouragement at home may work harder to overcome their handicap.
5. Some hearing-impaired children may take refuge in fantasy friends whom they can rely on not to criticize or laugh.

2. They may not hear important instructions and information from teachers. Teachers may speak softly.
3. Classmates may not be audible. The teacher calls on those classmates.
4. Some hearing-impaired children may work harder to overcome their disability. These children get a lot of encouragement at home.
5. Some hearing-impaired children may take refuge in fantasy friends. They can rely on these friends not to criticize or laugh.

CREATE A STORY

On the board, write a sentence or two that introduces as many people's names as possible. For example, you might write,

Bob went to a party last night, and there he saw his first-grade teacher, Mrs. West; his neighbor George; his old girlfriend Sarah; and her children Susan and Jason. In the middle of the party, Bob's dog Bowser came racing into the living room.

Divide the class into small groups and ask each group to write a one-paragraph story that grows out of the sentences on the board. (In the example above, students would probably describe what happened after the dog's entrance.) In writing their story, students should try to use as many pronouns as possible without introducing any ambiguity into the tale.

Groups should then read their stories aloud or write them on the board so that other students can try to understand the stories and verify that all the pronoun cases are accurate.

13h Ordinarily, use a possessive pronoun or noun immediately before a gerund.

A **gerund** is the *-ing* form of a verb (*running, sleeping*) used as a noun (p. 248). Like nouns, gerunds are commonly preceded by possessive nouns and pronouns: *our vote* (noun), *our voting* (gerund).

The coach disapproved of their lifting weights.

The coach's disapproving was a surprise.

A noun or pronoun before an *-ing* verb form is not always possessive. Sometimes the *-ing* form will be a present participle modifying the preceding word:

Everyone had noticed him weightlifting. [Emphasis on *him*.]
     objective   participle
     pronoun

Everyone had noticed his weightlifting. [Emphasis on the activity.]
     possessive   gerund
     pronoun

Note that a gerund usually is not preceded by the possessive when the possessive would create an awkward construction:

Awkward	A rumor spread about everybody's on the team wanting to quit.
Less awkward	A rumor spread about everybody on the team wanting to quit.
Better	A rumor spread that everybody on the team wanted to quit.

ANSWERS: EXERCISE 13.5

Written four thousand years ago, *The Epic of Gilgamesh* tells of the friendship of Gilgamesh and Enkidu. Gilgamesh was a bored king who his people thought was too harsh. Then he met Enkidu, a wild man who had lived with the animals in the mountains. Immediately, he and

EXERCISE 13.5 Revising: Case

Revise all inappropriate case forms in the following paragraph, and explain the function of each case form. (You can do this exercise online at *ablongman.com/littlebrown*.)

Written four thousand years ago, *The Epic of Gilgamesh* tells of the friendship of Gilgamesh and Enkidu. Gilgamesh was a bored king who his people thought was too harsh. Then he met Enkidu, a wild man whom had lived with the animals in the mountains. Immediately, him and Gilgamesh wrestled to see whom was more powerful. After hours of struggle, Enkidu admitted that Gilgamesh was stronger than him. Now the friends needed adventures worthy of the two strongest men on earth. Gilgamesh said, "Between you and I, mighty deeds will be accomplished, and our fame will be everlasting." Among their acts, Enkidu and him defeated a giant bull, Humbaba, and cut down the bull's cedar forests. Them bringing back cedar logs to Gilgamesh's treeless land won great praise from the people. When Enkidu died, Gilgamesh mourned his death, realizing that no one had been a better friend than him. When Gilgamesh himself died many years later, his people raised a monument praising Enkidu and he for their friendship and their mighty deeds of courage.

Note See page 331 for an exercise involving case along with other aspects of grammar.

Gilgamesh wrestled to see who was more powerful. After hours of struggle, Enkidu admitted that Gilgamesh was stronger than he. Now the friends needed adventures worthy of the two strongest men on earth. Gilgamesh said, "Between you and me, mighty deeds will be accomplished, and our fame will be everlasting." Among their acts, Enkidu and he defeated a giant bull, Humbaba, and cut down the bull's cedar forests. Their bringing back cedar logs to Gilgamesh's treeless land won great praise from the people. When Enkidu died, Gilgamesh mourned his death, realizing that no one had been a better friend than he. When Gilgamesh himself died many years later, his people raised a monument praising Enkidu and him for their friendship and their mighty deeds of courage.

mycomplab²⁰

Please visit MyCompLab at *www.mycomplab.com* for more on the writing process.

CHAPTER **14**

Verbs

The verb is the most complicated part of speech in English, changing form to express a wide range of information.

Verb Forms

All verbs except *be* have five basic forms. The first three are the verb's **principal parts.**

- **The *plain form* is the dictionary form of the verb.** When the subject is a plural noun or the pronoun *I, we, you,* or *they,* the plain form indicates action that occurs in the present, occurs habitually, or is generally true.

A few artists live in town today.
They hold classes downtown.

http://www.ablongman.com/littlebrown ▶

Visit the companion Web site for more help and additional exercises on verb forms.

HIGHLIGHTS

Verbs can cause trouble for writers regardless of their level of skill. For some writers, choosing the correct tense or form of a verb can be a formidable challenge. In addition, certain regional and social dialects of English have different patterns for marking verb tenses and forms, which may add to the confusion. Even experienced writers may occasionally stumble over the choice between *sit* and *set* or struggle to maintain the correct sequence of tenses in a complex sentence.

For all these needs (and many others as well) this chapter can be useful, although it must be supplemented to provide the more sustained support and practice some students may require. Students whose first language is not English may benefit from the ESL coverage and the worksheets by Jocelyn Steer and Dawn Schmid. If your campus is fortunate enough to have a

COMPANION WEB SITE

See page IAE-54 for companion Web site content description.

writing center, your students may benefit from the extra support it can provide.

Students looking for help with verb *forms* will benefit from the chapter's thorough explanations, list of the principal parts of frequently used irregular verbs, discussion of the troublesome pairs *sit/set* and *lie/lay*, and treatment of two problems often associated with dialect interference: omitted *-s* and *-ed* endings and omitted helping verbs.

Students looking for help with verb *tense* can make use of the chapter's discussion of the major tenses and of appropriate sequences of tenses. Tense sequence becomes increasingly important as students begin to write ambitious narratives and expository or argumentative essays.

RESOURCES AND IDEAS

Yoder, Rhoda Byler. "Of Fake Verbs and Kid Words: Developing a Useful Grammar." *English Journal* 85 (1996): 82–7. Middle school teacher develops a simplified language for teaching students the functions of verbs and verbals.

Terms used to describe verbs

Tense

The time of the verb's action—for instance, present (*kick*), past (*kicked*), future (*will kick*). (See p. 292.)

Mood

The attitude of the verb's speaker or writer—the difference, for example, in *I kick the ball, Kick the ball,* and *I suggest that you kick the ball.* (See p. 299.)

Voice

The distinction between the **active**, in which the subject performs the verb's action (*I kick the ball*), and the **passive**, in which the subject is acted upon (*The ball is kicked by me*). (See p. 302.)

Person

The verb form that reflects whether the subject is speaking (*I/we kick the ball*), spoken to (*You kick the ball*), or spoken about (*She kicks the ball*). (See p. 306.)

Number

The verb form that reflects whether the subject is singular (*The girl kicks the ball*) or plural (*Girls kick the ball*). (See p. 308.)

- The *past-tense form* indicates that the action of the verb occurred before now. It usually adds *-d* or *-ed* to the plain form, although some irregular verbs form it in other ways (see p. 278).

  Many artists lived in town before this year.
  They held classes downtown. [Irregular verb.]

- The *past participle* is the same as the past-tense form, except in most irregular verbs. It combines with forms of *have* or *be* (*has climbed, was created*), or by itself it modifies nouns and pronouns (*the sliced apples*).

  Artists have lived in town for decades.
  They have held classes downtown. [Irregular verb.]

- The *present participle* adds *-ing* to the verb's plain form. It combines with forms of *be* (*is buying*), modifies nouns and pronouns (*the boiling water*), or functions as a noun (*Running exhausts me*).

  A few artists are living in town today.
  They are holding classes downtown.

- The *-s form* ends in *-s* or *-es*. When the subject is a singular noun, a pronoun such as *everyone,* or the personal pronoun *he, she,* or *it,* the *-s* form indicates action that occurs in the present, occurs habitually, or is generally true.

The artist <u>lives</u> in town today.
She <u>holds</u> classes downtown.

The verb *be* has eight forms rather than the five forms of most other verbs:

Plain form	be		
Present participle	being		
Past participle	been		
	I	*he, she, it*	*we, you, they*
Present tense	am	is	are
Past tense	was	was	were

🔹 **CULTURE LANGUAGE** 🔹 If standard American English is not your native language or dialect, you may have difficulty with verbs' *-s* forms (including those for *be: is, was*) or with the forms that indicate time (such as the past-tense form). See pages 282–83 and 295–96, respectively, for more on these forms.

■ **Helping verbs**

Helping verbs, also called **auxiliary verbs,** combine with some verb forms to indicate time and other kinds of meaning, as in *can run, was sleeping, <u>had been</u>* eaten. These combinations are **verb phrases.** Since the <u>plain form</u>, present participle, or past participle in any verb phrase always carries the principal meaning, it is sometimes called the **main verb.**

	Verb phrase	
Helping	*Main*	
Artists <u>can</u>	<u>train</u> others to draw.	
The techniques <u>have</u>	<u>changed</u> little.	

These are the most common helping verbs:

be able to	had better	must	used to
be supposed to	have to	ought to	will
can	may	shall	would
could	might	should	

Forms of *be:* be, am, is, are, was, were, been, being
Forms of *have:* have, has, had, having
Forms of *do:* do, does, did

🔹 **CULTURE LANGUAGE** 🔹 The helping verbs of standard American English may be problematic if you are used to speaking another language or dialect. See pages 283–87 for more on helping verbs.

THE ORIGIN OF IRREGULAR VERBS

Irregular verbs are antiques reflecting the history of English well before the Norman Conquest of England in 1066. In the first few centuries AD, speakers of the Germanic languages that evolved into English used changes in the internal vowel structure of words to show tense. Thus, verbs like *drink, throw,* and especially *be* preserve a little of the linguistic history of our ancestors. A very readable account of this period is found in Joseph Williams, *Origins of the English Language* (New York: Free Press, 1975).

HYPOTHETICAL VERBS

A good game to play to show students how well they intuitively understand how irregular verbs are formed is to invent some (e.g., *flink*) and ask students to decide what their other forms would be (*flink, flank, flunk* or *flink, flought, flought*). A variation is to take a more regular verb and pretend it's irregular: *My engine won't crank in cold weather; My engine hadn't crunk.*

14a Use the correct forms of regular and irregular verbs.

Most verbs are **regular;** that is, they form their past tense and past participle by adding *-d* or *-ed* to the plain form.

Plain form	Past tense	Past participle
live	lived	lived
act	acted	acted

Since the past tense and past participle are created in the same way, the forms of regular verbs do not often cause problems in speech and writing (but see p. 282).

About two hundred English verbs are **irregular;** that is, they form their past tense and past participle in some irregular way.

Plain form	Past tense	Past participle
begin	began	begun
break	broke	broken
sleep	slept	slept

You can see the difference between a regular and an irregular verb in these examples:

Plain form	Today the birds twitter.
	Today the birds sing.
Past tense	Yesterday the birds twittered.
	Yesterday the birds sang.
Past participle	In the past the birds have twittered.
	In the past the birds have sung.

Check a dictionary under the plain form if you have any doubt about a verb's principal parts. If no other forms are listed, the verb is regular: both the past tense and the past participle add *-d* or *-ed* to the plain form. If the verb is irregular, the dictionary will list the plain form, the past tense, and the past participle in that order (*go, went, gone*). If the dictionary gives only two forms (as in *think, thought*), then the past tense and the past participle are the same.

🔊 **CULTURE LANGUAGE** Some English dialects use distinctive verb forms that differ from those of standard American English: for instance, *drug* for *dragged, growed* for *grew, come* for *came,* or *went* for *gone.* In situations requiring standard American English, use the forms in the list opposite or in a dictionary.

Note A grammar and style checker may flag incorrect forms of irregular verbs, but it may also fail to do so. For example, a checker flagged *The runner stealed second base* (*stole* is correct) but not *The*

Principal parts of common irregular verbs

Plain form	Past tense	Past participle
arise	arose	arisen
become	became	become
begin	began	begun
bid	bid	bid
bite	bit	bitten, bit
blow	blew	blown
break	broke	broken
bring	brought	brought
burst	burst	burst
buy	bought	bought
catch	caught	caught
choose	chose	chosen
come	came	come
cut	cut	cut
dive	dived, dove	dived
do	did	done
draw	drew	drawn
dream	dreamed, dreamt	dreamed, dreamt
drink	drank	drunk
drive	drove	driven
eat	ate	eaten
fall	fell	fallen
find	found	found
flee	fled	fled
fly	flew	flown
forget	forgot	forgotten, forgot
freeze	froze	frozen
get	got	got, gotten
give	gave	given
go	went	gone
grow	grew	grown
hang (suspend)	hung	hung
hang (execute)	hanged	hanged
hear	heard	heard
hide	hid	hidden
hold	held	held
keep	kept	kept
know	knew	known
lay	laid	laid
lead	led	led
leave	left	left
lend	lent	lent
let	let	let
lie	lay	lain

(continued)

Principal parts of common irregular verbs
(continued)

Plain form	Past tense	Past participle
lose	lost	lost
pay	paid	paid
prove	proved	proved, proven
ride	rode	ridden
ring	rang	rung
rise	rose	risen
run	ran	run
say	said	said
see	saw	seen
set	set	set
shake	shook	shaken
shrink	shrank, shrunk	shrunk, shrunken
sing	sang, sung	sung
sink	sank, sunk	sunk
sit	sat	sat
sleep	slept	slept
slide	slid	slid
speak	spoke	spoken
spring	sprang, sprung	sprung
stand	stood	stood
steal	stole	stolen
swim	swam	swum
swing	swung	swung
take	took	taken
teach	taught	taught
tear	tore	torn
throw	threw	thrown
wear	wore	worn
write	wrote	written

runner had steal *second base* (*stolen* is correct). When in doubt about the forms of irregular verbs, refer to the preceding list, consult a dictionary, or consult the links at this book's companion Web site (*ablongman.com/littlebrown*).

ANSWERS: EXERCISE 14.1

1. The world population has grown by two-thirds of a billion people in less than a decade. (Past participle.)
2. In 2000 it broke the 6 billion mark. (Past tense.)
3. Experts have drawn pictures of a crowded future. (Past participle.)

EXERCISE 14.1 Using irregular verbs

For each irregular verb in brackets, give either the past tense or the past participle, as appropriate, and identify the form you used. (You can do this exercise online at *ablongman.com/littlebrown*.)

Example:
Though we had [hide] the cash box, it was [steal].

Though we had <u>hidden</u> the cash box, it was <u>stolen</u>. [Two past participles.]

1. The world population has [<u>grow</u>] by two-thirds of a billion people in less than a decade.
2. In 2000 it [<u>break</u>] the 6 billion mark.
3. Experts have [<u>draw</u>] pictures of a crowded future.
4. They predict that the world population may have [<u>slide</u>] up to as much as 10 billion by the year 2050.
5. Though the food supply [<u>rise</u>] in the last decade, the share to each person [<u>fall</u>].

4. They predict that the world population may have <u>slid</u> up to as much as 10 billion by the year 2050. (Past participle.)
5. Though the food supply <u>rose</u> in the last decade, the share to each person <u>fell</u>. (Both past tense.)

14b Distinguish between *sit* and *set*, *lie* and *lay*, and *rise* and *raise*.

The forms of *sit* and *set*, *lie* and *lay*, and *rise* and *raise* are easy to confuse:

Plain form	Past tense	Past participle
sit	sat	sat
set	set	set
lie	lay	lain
lay	laid	laid
rise	rose	risen
raise	raised	raised

In each of these confusing pairs, one verb is **intransitive** (it does not take an object) and one is **transitive** (it does take an object). (See pp. 238–41 for more on this distinction.)

Intransitive

The patients <u>lie</u> in their beds. [*Lie* means "recline" and takes no object.]

Visitors <u>sit</u> with them. [*Sit* means "be seated" or "be located" and takes no object.]

Patients' temperatures <u>rise</u>. [*Rise* means "increase" or "get up" and takes no object.]

Transitive

Orderlies <u>lay</u> the dinner trays on tables. [*Lay* means "place" and takes an object, here *trays*.]

Orderlies <u>set</u> the trays down. [*Set* means "place" and takes an object, here *trays*.]

Nursing aides <u>raise</u> the shades. [*Raise* means "lift" or "bring up" and takes an object, here *shades*.]

IRREGULAR VERBS AND THE DICTIONARY

The need to learn the uses of *sit* and *set*, *rise* and *raise*, and *lie* and *lay* makes a great excuse to introduce students to the wonders of the *Oxford English Dictionary*, in either its first or its second edition. The entries for these words, among the longest in the *OED*, will show students the number of meanings words can have and the reasons all writers find these particular words so difficult.

ANSWERS: EXERCISE 14.2

1. Yesterday afternoon the child <u>lay</u> down for a nap.
2. The child has been <u>raised</u> by her grandparents.
3. Most days her grandfather has <u>sat</u> with her, reading her stories.
4. She has <u>risen</u> at dawn most mornings.
5. Her toys were <u>laid</u> out on the floor.

CULTURE LANGUAGE

Speakers of Black English Vernacular may tend to use the verb forms of this dialect in their writing rather than those of standard written English, particularly by dropping *-s* and *-ed* endings. Becoming aware of the verb system of standard written English and the differences between it and the verb system of Black English Vernacular is an important step for students seeking control over their writing. But as Marcia Farr and Harvey Daniels point out in *Language Diversity and Writing Instruction* (New York: ERIC Clearing House on Urban Education and Urbana: NCTE, 1986), awareness of and practice in identifying and using the verb forms are useful only if they take place in a context that includes a wide range of reading and writing experiences; substantial practice in writing; collaborative activities; sentence combining or similar activities; and flexible, sensitive feedback from the instructor. Farr and Daniels also offer a detailed discussion of dialects and language variations, along with concrete suggestions for teaching.

EXERCISE 14.2 Distinguishing *sit/set, lie/lay, rise/raise*

Choose the correct verb from the pair given in brackets. Then supply the past tense or past participle, as appropriate. (You can do this exercise online at *ablongman.com/littlebrown*.)

Example:

After I washed all the windows, I [lie, lay] down the squeegee and then I [sit, set] the table.

After I washed all the windows, I <u>laid</u> down the squeegee and then I <u>set</u> the table.

1. Yesterday afternoon the child [lie, lay] down for a nap.
2. The child has been [rise, raise] by her grandparents.
3. Most days her grandfather has [sit, set] with her, reading her stories.
4. She has [rise, raise] at dawn most mornings.
5. Her toys were [lie, lay] out on the floor.

14c Use the *-s* and *-ed* forms of the verb when they are required. **CULTURE LANGUAGE**

Speakers of some English dialects and nonnative speakers of English sometimes omit the *-s* and *-ed* verb endings when they are required in standard American English.

Note A grammar and style checker will flag many omitted *-s* and *-ed* endings from verbs, such as in *he ask* and *was ask*. But it will miss many omissions, too.

■ **Required *-s* ending**

Use the *-s* form of a verb when *both* of these situations hold:

■ **The subject is a singular noun** (*boy*), **an indefinite pronoun** (*everyone*), or *he, she,* or *it*. These subjects are **third person,** used when someone or something is being spoken about.
■ **The verb's action occurs in the present.**

> The letter <u>asks</u> [not ask] for a quick response.
> Delay <u>costs</u> [not cost] money.

Be especially careful with the *-s* forms of *be* (*is*), *have* (*has*), and *do* (*does, doesn't*). These forms should always be used to indicate present time with third-person singular subjects.

> The company <u>is</u> [not be] late in responding.
> It <u>has</u> [not have] problems.
> It <u>doesn't</u> [not don't] have the needed data.
> The contract <u>does</u> [not do] depend on the response.

In addition, *be* has an *-s* form in the past tense with *I* and with third-person singular subjects:

The company <u>was</u> [not <u>were</u>] in trouble before.

I, you, and plural subjects do *not* take the *-s* form of verbs:

I <u>am</u> [not <u>is</u>] a student.
You <u>are</u> [not <u>is</u>] also a student.
They <u>are</u> [not <u>is</u>] students, too.

■ **Required *-ed* or *-d* ending**

The *-ed* or *-d* verb form is required in *any* of these situations:

■ **The verb's action occurred in the past:**

Yesterday the company <u>asked</u> [not <u>ask</u>] for more time.

■ **The verb form functions as a modifier:**

The data <u>concerned</u> [not <u>concern</u>] should be retrievable.

■ **The verb form combines with a form of *be* or *have*:**

The company is <u>supposed</u> [not <u>suppose</u>] to be the best.
It has <u>developed</u> [not <u>develop</u>] an excellent reputation.

Watch especially for a needed *-ed* or *-d* ending when it isn't pronounced clearly in speech, as in *asked, discussed, mixed, supposed, walked,* and *used.*

EXERCISE 14.3   Using *-s* and *-ed* verb endings

CULTURE LANGUAGE   Supply the correct form of each verb in brackets. Be careful to include *-s* and *-ed* (or *-d*) endings where they are needed for standard English. (You can do this exercise online at *ablongman.com/littlebrown.*)

A teacher sometimes [ask] too much of a student. In high school I was once [punish] for being sick. I had [miss] some school, and I [realize] that I would fail a test unless I had a chance to make up the classwork. I [discuss] the problem with the teacher, but he said I was [suppose] to make up the work while I was sick. At that I [walk] out of the class. I [receive] a failing grade then, but it did not change my attitude. Today I still balk when a teacher [make] unreasonable demands or [expect] miracles.

ANSWERS: EXERCISE 14.3

A teacher sometimes <u>asks</u> too much of a student. In high school I was once <u>punished</u> for being sick. I had <u>missed</u> some school, and I <u>realized</u> that I would fail a test unless I had a chance to make up the classwork. I <u>discussed</u> the problem with the teacher, but he said I was <u>supposed</u> to make up the work while I was sick. At that I <u>walked</u> out of the class. I <u>received</u> a failing grade then, but it did not change my attitude. Today I still balk when a teacher <u>makes</u> unreasonable demands or <u>expects</u> miracles.

14d   Use helping verbs with main verbs appropriately. **CULTURE LANGUAGE**

Helping verbs combine with main verbs to form verb phrases (see p. 277).

Note Grammar and style checkers often spot omitted helping verbs and incorrect main verbs with helping verbs, but sometimes they do not. A checker flagged *Many been fortunate* and *She working* but overlooked other examples on the following pages, such as *The conference will be occurred.*

1 **Use helping verbs when they are required.**

Standard American English requires helping verbs in certain situations:

- **The main verb ends in *-ing*:**

  Researchers <u>are</u> conducting fieldwork all over the world. [Not Re<u>searchers conducting</u>. . . .]

- **The main verb is *been* or *be*:**

  Many <u>have</u> been fortunate in their discoveries. [Not Many <u>been</u>. . . .]
  Some <u>could</u> be real-life Indiana Joneses. [Not Some <u>be</u>. . . .]

- **The main verb is a past participle, such as *talked, begun,* or *thrown.***

  Their discoveries <u>were</u> covered in newspapers and magazines. [Not Their <u>discoveries covered</u>. . . .]
  Often the researchers <u>have</u> done TV interviews. [Not the <u>researchers done</u>. . . .]

In every example above, omitting the helping verb would create an incomplete sentence, or **sentence fragment** (see Chapter 17). In a complete sentence, some part of the verb (helping or main) must be capable of changing form to show changes in time: *I <u>run</u>, I <u>ran</u>; you are <u>running</u>, you <u>were</u> running* (see p. 335). But a present participle (*conducting*), an irregular past participle (*been*), and the infinitive *be* cannot change form in this way. They need helping verbs to work as sentence verbs.

2 **Combine helping verbs and main verbs appropriately for your meaning.**

Helping verbs and main verbs combine into verb phrases in specific ways.

Note The main verb in a verb phrase (the one carrying the main meaning) does not change to show a change in subject or time: *she has <u>sung</u>, you had <u>sung</u>.* Only the helping verb may change.

- **Form of *be* + present participle**

The **progressive tenses** indicate action in progress (see p. 295). Create them with *be, am, is, are, was, were,* or *been* followed by the main verb's present participle:

She is working on a new book.

Be and *been* always require additional helping verbs to form the progressive tenses:

can	might	should		have		
could	must	will	} be working	has	}	been working
may	shall	would		had		

When forming the progressive tenses, be sure to use the *-ing* form of the main verb:

Faulty   Her ideas are grow more complex. She is developed a new approach to ethics.

Revised   Her ideas are growing more complex. She is developing a new approach to ethics.

■ Form of *be* + past participle

The **passive voice** of the verb indicates that the subject *receives* the action of the verb (see p. 302). Create the passive voice with *be, am, is, are, was, were, being,* or *been* followed by the main verb's past participle:

Her latest book was completed in four months.

Be, being, and *been* always require additional helping verbs to form the passive voice:

have			am	was		
has	}	been completed	is	were	}	being completed
had			are			

will be completed

Be sure to use the main verb's past participle for the passive voice:

Faulty   Her next book will be publish soon.

Revised   Her next book will be published soon.

Note Only transitive verbs may form the passive voice:

Faulty   A philosophy conference will be occurred in the same week. [*Occur* is not a transitive verb.]

Revised   A philosophy conference will occur in the same week.

See pages 302–03 for advice on when to use and when to avoid the passive voice.

■ Forms of *have*

Four forms of *have* serve as helping verbs: *have, has, had, having.* One of these forms plus the main verb's past participle creates one of the **perfect tenses,** those expressing action completed before another specific time or action (see p. 294):

> Some students <u>have complained</u> about the laboratory.
> Others <u>had complained</u> before.

Will and other helping verbs sometimes accompany forms of *have* in the perfect tenses:

> Several more students <u>will have complained</u> by the end of the week.

▪ Forms of do

Do, does, and *did* have three uses as helping verbs, always with the plain form of the main verb:

- **To pose a question:** *How <u>did</u> the trial <u>end</u>?*
- **To emphasize the main verb:** *It <u>did end</u> eventually.*
- **To negate the main verb, along with** *not* **or** *never: The judge <u>did not withdraw</u>.*

Be sure to use the main verb's plain form with any form of *do:*

Faulty   The judge did <u>remained</u> in court.
Revised   The judge did <u>remain</u> in court.

▪ Modals

The modal helping verbs include *can, could, may,* and *might,* along with several two- and three-word combinations, such as *have to* and *be able to.* (See p. 277 for a list of helping verbs.) Use the plain form of the main verb with a modal unless the modal combines with another helping verb (usually *have*):

Faulty   The equipment <u>can detects</u> small vibrations. It <u>should have detect</u> the change.
Revised   The equipment <u>can detect</u> small vibrations. It <u>should have detected</u> the change.

Modals convey various meanings, with these being most common:

- **Ability:** *can, could, be able to*

  The equipment <u>can detect</u> small vibrations. [Present.]
  The equipment <u>could detect</u> small vibrations. [Past.]
  The equipment <u>is able to detect</u> small vibrations. [Present. Past: <u>was able to.</u> Future: <u>will be able to.</u>]

- **Possibility:** *could, may, might, could/may/might have* + past participle

  The equipment <u>could fail.</u> [Present.]
  The equipment <u>may fail.</u> [Present or future.]

The equipment <u>might fail</u>. [Present or future.]
The equipment <u>may have failed</u>. [Past.]

- **Necessity or obligation:** *must, have to, be supposed to*

  The lab <u>must purchase</u> a backup. [Present or future.]
  The lab <u>has to purchase</u> a backup. [Present or future. Past: <u>had to</u>.]
  The lab <u>will have to purchase</u> a backup. [Future.]
  The lab is <u>supposed to purchase</u> a backup. [Present. Past: <u>was supposed to</u>.]

- **Permission:** *may, can, could*

  The lab <u>may spend</u> the money. [Present or future.]
  The lab <u>can spend</u> the money. [Present or future.]
  The lab <u>could spend</u> the money. [Present or future, more tentative.]
  With budget approval, the lab <u>could have spent</u> the money. [Past.]

- **Intention:** *will, shall, would*

  The lab <u>will spend</u> the money. [Future.]
  <u>Shall</u> we <u>offer</u> advice? [Future. Use *shall* for questions requesting opinion or consent.]
  We <u>would have offered</u> advice. [Past.]

- **Request:** *could, can, would*

  <u>Could</u> [or <u>can</u> or <u>would</u>] you please <u>obtain</u> a bid? [Present or future.]

- **Advisability:** *should, had better, ought to, should have* + past participle

  You <u>should obtain</u> three bids. [Present or future.]
  You <u>had better obtain</u> three bids. [Present or future.]
  You <u>ought to obtain</u> three bids. [Present or future.]
  You <u>should have obtained</u> three bids. [Past.]

- **Past habit:** *would, used to*

  In years past we <u>would obtain</u> five bids.
  We <u>used to obtain</u> five bids.

EXERCISE 14.4   Using helping verbs

CULTURE LANGUAGE Add helping verbs in the following sentences where they are needed for standard English. (You can do this exercise online at *ablongman.com/littlebrown*.)

Example:
The story been told for many years.
The story <u>has</u> been told for many years.

1. Each year thousands of new readers been discovering Agatha Christie's mysteries.

ANSWERS: EXERCISE 14.4

1. Each year thousands of new readers <u>have</u> been discovering Agatha Christie's mysteries.
2. The books <u>were</u> written by a prim woman who had worked as a nurse during World War I.
3. Christie never expected that her play *The Mousetrap* <u>would</u> be performed for decades.

4. During her life Christie <u>was</u> always complaining about movie versions of her stories.
5. Readers of her stories <u>have</u> been delighted to be baffled by her.

ANSWERS: EXERCISE 14.5

1. A report from the Bureau of the Census has <u>confirmed</u> a widening gap between rich and poor.
2. As suspected, the percentage of people below the poverty level did <u>increase</u> over the last decade.
3. More than 17 percent of the population is <u>making</u> 5 percent of all the income.
4. About 1 percent of the population will <u>be keeping</u> [*or* will <u>keep</u>] an average of $500,000 apiece after taxes.
5. Sentence correct.

CULTURE LANGUAGE

CHOOSING BETWEEN GERUNDS AND INFINITIVES

ESL students generally find gerunds more problematic than infinitives, perhaps because gerunds occur less frequently; as a result, students may use infinitives where gerunds are required. According to Marianne Celce-Murcia and Diane Larsen-Freeman in *The Grammar Book* (Boston: Heinle, 1983), gerunds tend to express "fulfilled action," whereas infinitives tend to express "unfulfilled action":

I *enjoyed meeting* your brother at the party. (The action, the meeting, was fulfilled.)

2. The books written by a prim woman who had worked as a nurse during World War I.
3. Christie never expected that her play *The Mousetrap* be performed for decades.
4. During her life Christie always complaining about movie versions of her stories.
5. Readers of her stories been delighted to be baffled by her.

EXERCISE 14.5 Revising: Helping verbs plus main verbs

CULTURE LANGUAGE Revise the following sentences so that helping verbs and main verbs are used correctly. Mark the number preceding any sentence that is already correct. (You can do this exercise online at *ablongman.com/littlebrown*.)

Example:

The college testing service has test as many as five hundred students at one time.

The college testing service has <u>tested</u> as many as five hundred students at one time.

1. A report from the Bureau of the Census has confirm a widening gap between rich and poor.
2. As suspected, the percentage of people below the poverty level did increased over the last decade.
3. More than 17 percent of the population is make 5 percent of all the income.
4. About 1 percent of the population will keeping an average of $500,000 apiece after taxes.
5. The other 99 percent all together may retain about $300,000.

14e Use a gerund or an infinitive after a verb as appropriate. <div>CULTURE LANGUAGE</div>

Nonnative speakers of English sometimes stumble over using a gerund or an infinitive after a verb. A **gerund** is the *-ing* form of a verb used as a noun (*opening*). An **infinitive** is the plain form of a verb preceded by *to* (*to open*). (See pp. 248–49 for more on these forms.)

Gerunds and infinitives may follow certain verbs but not others. And sometimes the use of a gerund or infinitive with the same verb changes the meaning.

Note A grammar and style checker will spot some but not all errors in matching gerunds or infinitives with verbs. For example, a checker failed to flag *I practice to swim* and *I promise helping out*. Use the lists given here and a dictionary of English as a second language to determine whether an infinitive or a gerund is appropriate. (See p. 537 for a list of ESL dictionaries.)

■ **Either gerund or infinitive**

A gerund or an infinitive may follow these verbs with no significant difference in meaning:

begin	hate	love
can't bear	hesitate	prefer
can't stand	intend	start
continue	like	

The pump began working.
The pump began to work.

■ **Meaning change with gerund or infinitive**

With four verbs, a gerund has quite a different meaning from an infinitive:

forget	stop
remember	try

The engineer stopped eating. [He no longer ate.]
The engineer stopped to eat. [He stopped in order to eat.]

■ **Gerund, not infinitive**

Do not use an infinitive after these verbs:

admit	discuss	mind	recollect
adore	dislike	miss	resent
appreciate	enjoy	postpone	resist
avoid	escape	practice	risk
consider	finish	put off	suggest
deny	imagine	quit	tolerate
detest	keep	recall	understand

Faulty   He finished to eat lunch.
Revised   He finished eating lunch.

■ **Infinitive, not gerund**

Do not use a gerund after these verbs:

agree	decide	mean	refuse
appear	expect	offer	say
ask	have	plan	wait
assent	hope	pretend	want
beg	manage	promise	wish
claim			

Faulty   He decided checking the pump.
Revised   He decided to check the pump.

I *hoped to meet* your brother at the party. (The action, the hoped-for meeting, was unfulfilled.)
I'll always *remember calling* my son when he was overseas. (The action, calling, was fulfilled before the remembering.)
I *remembered to call* my son on his birthday. (The action, calling, was unfulfilled until after the remembering.)

Refer students who need additional practice distinguishing gerunds and infinitives to Unit 8 of Carroll Washington Pollock, *Communicate What You Mean: Grammar for High-Level ESL Students* (Englewood Cliffs: Prentice-Hall, 1982), and Chapter 14 of Jocelyn Steer and Karen Carlisi, *The Advanced Grammar Book* (Boston: Heinle, 1991).

■ Noun or pronoun + infinitive

Some verbs may be followed by an infinitive alone or by a noun or pronoun and an infinitive. The presence of a noun or pronoun changes the meaning.

ask	dare	need	wish
beg	expect	promise	would like
choose	help	want	

He expected to watch.
He expected his workers to watch.

Some verbs *must* be followed by a noun or pronoun before an infinitive:

admonish	encourage	oblige	require
advise	forbid	order	teach
allow	force	permit	tell
cause	hire	persuade	train
challenge	instruct	remind	urge
command	invite	request	warn
convince			

He instructed his workers to watch.

Do not use *to* before the infinitive when it follows one of these verbs and a noun or pronoun:

feel	make ("force")
have	see
hear	watch
let	

He let his workers learn by observation.

ANSWERS: EXERCISE 14.6

1. A program called HELP Wanted tries to en-courage citizens to take action on behalf of American competitiveness.
2. Officials working on this program hope to improve education for work.
3. American businesses find that their workers need to learn to read.
4. In the next ten years the United States ex-pects to face a shortage of 350,000 scien-tists.
5. Sentence correct.

EXERCISE 14.6 Revising: Verbs plus gerunds or infinitives

CULTURE LANGUAGE Revise the following sentences so that gerunds or infini-tives are used correctly with verbs. Mark the number preceding any sentence that is already correct. (You can do this exercise online at *ablongman.com/littlebrown*.)

Example:
A politician cannot avoid to alienate some voters.
A politician cannot avoid alienating some voters.

1. A program called HELP Wanted tries to encourage citizens take action on behalf of American competitiveness.
2. Officials working on this program hope improving education for work.
3. American businesses find that their workers need learning to read.
4. In the next ten years the United States expects facing a shortage of 350,000 scientists.
5. HELP Wanted suggests creating a media campaign.

14f Use the appropriate particles with two-word verbs. CULTURE LANGUAGE

Standard American English includes some verbs that consist of two words: the verb itself and a **particle**, a preposition or adverb that affects the meaning of the verb. For example:

Look up the answer. [Research the answer.]
Look over the answer. [Examine the answer.]

The meanings of these two-word verbs are often quite different from the meanings of the individual words that make them up. (There are some three-word verbs, too, such as *put up with* and *run out of*.)

A dictionary of English as a second language will define two-word verbs and say whether the verb may be separated in a sentence, as explained below. (See p. 537 for a list of ESL dictionaries.) A grammar and style checker will recognize few if any misuses of two-word verbs.

Note Many two-word verbs are more common in speech than in more formal academic or business writing. For formal writing, consider using *research* instead of *look up, examine* or *inspect* instead of *look over*.

■ Inseparable two-word verbs

Verbs and particles that may not be separated by any other words include the following:

call on	go out with	run across	stay away
catch on	go over	run into	stay up
come across	grow up	run out of	take care of
get along	keep on	speak up	turn out
get up	look for	speak with	turn up at
give in	look into	stand up	work for
go on	play around		

Faulty   Children grow quickly up.
Revised   Children grow up quickly.

■ Separable two-word verbs

Most two-word verbs that take direct objects may be separated by the object:

Parents help out their children.
Parents help their children out.

If the direct object is a pronoun, the pronoun *must* separate the verb from the particle:

Faulty   Parents help out them.
Revised   Parents help them out.

The separable two-word verbs include the following:

bring up	give back	make up	throw out
call off	hand in	point out	try on
call up	hand out	put away	try out
drop off	help out	put back	turn down
fill out	leave out	put off	turn on
fill up	look over	take out	wrap up
give away	look up	take over	

ANSWERS: EXERCISE 14.7

1. American movies treat everything from going out with [correct] someone to making up [correct] an ethnic identity, but few people <u>look into</u> their significance.
2. While some viewers stay away from [correct] topical films, others <u>turn up at the theater</u> simply because a movie has sparked debate.
3. Some movies attracted rowdy spectators, and the theaters had to <u>throw them out</u>.
4. Filmmakers have always been eager to point their influence out [correct; *or* <u>point out their influence</u>] to the public.
5. Everyone agrees that filmmakers will <u>keep on creating controversy</u>, if only because it can fill up [correct] theaters.

EXERCISE 14.7 Revising: Verbs plus particles

CULTURE LANGUAGE The two- and three-word verbs in the sentences below are underlined. Some are correct as given, and some are not because they should or should not be separated by other words. Revise the verbs and other words that are incorrect. Consult the lists above and on the preceding page or an ESL dictionary if necessary to determine whether verbs are separable. (You can do this exercise online at *ablongman.com/littlebrown*.)

Example:

Hollywood producers never seem to <u>come up with</u> entirely new plots, but they also never <u>run</u> new ways <u>out of</u> to present old ones.

Hollywood producers never seem to come up with [correct] entirely new plots, but they also never <u>run out of new ways</u> to present old ones.

1. American movies treat everything from <u>going out with</u> someone to <u>making up</u> an ethnic identity, but few people <u>look</u> their significance <u>into</u>.
2. While some viewers <u>stay away from</u> topical films, others <u>turn</u> at the theater <u>up</u> simply because a movie has sparked debate.
3. Some movies attracted rowdy spectators, and the theaters had to <u>throw out</u> them.
4. Filmmakers have always been eager to <u>point</u> their influence <u>out</u> to the public.
5. Everyone agrees that filmmakers will <u>keep</u> creating controversy <u>on</u>, if only because it can <u>fill up</u> theaters.

Tense

Tense shows the time of a verb's action. The table on the facing page defines and illustrates the tense forms for a regular verb in the active voice. (See pp. 278 and 302 on regular verbs and voice.)

Note Grammar and style checkers can provide little help with incorrect verb tenses and tense sequences because correctness usu-

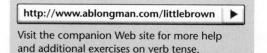

http://www.ablongman.com/littlebrown ▶

Visit the companion Web site for more help and additional exercises on verb tense.

Tenses of a regular verb (active voice)

Present Action that is occurring now, occurs habitually, or is generally true

Simple present Plain form or -s form

I walk.
You/we/they walk.
He/she/it walks.

Present progressive *Am, is,* or *are* plus -*ing* form

I am walking.
You/we/they are walking.
He/she/it is walking.

Past Action that occurred before now

Simple past Past-tense form (-*d* or -*ed*)

I/he/she/it walked.
You/we/they walked.

Past progressive *Was* or *were* plus -*ing* form

I/he/she/it was walking.
You/we/they were walking.

Future Action that will occur in the future

Simple future Plain form plus *will*

I/you/he/she/it/we/they will walk.

Future progressive *Will be* plus -*ing* form

I/you/he/she/it/we/they will be walking.

Present perfect Action that began in the past and is linked to the present

Present perfect *Have* or *has* plus past participle (-*d* or -*ed*)

I/you/we/they have walked.
He/she/it has walked.

Present perfect progressive *Have been* or *has been* plus -*ing* form

I/you/we/they have been walking.
He/she/it has been walking.

Past perfect Action that was completed before another past action

Past perfect *Had* plus past participle (-*d* or -*ed*)

I/you/he/she/it/we/they had walked.

Past perfect progressive *Had been* plus -*ing* form

I/you/he/she/it/we/they had been walking.

Future perfect Action that will be completed before another future action

Future perfect *Will have* plus past participle (-*d* or -*ed*)

I/you/he/she/it/we/they will have walked.

Future perfect progressive *Will have been* plus -*ing* form

I/you/he/she/it/we/they will have been walking.

t

ally depends on meaning. You'll have to proofread carefully yourself to catch errors in tense or tense sequence.

CULTURE LANGUAGE In standard American English, a verb conveys time and sequence through its form. In some other languages and English dialects, various markers besides verb form may indicate the time of a verb. For instance, in African American dialect *I be attending class on Friday* means that the speaker attends class every Friday. To a speaker of standard American English, however, the sentence may be unclear: last Friday? this Friday? every Friday? The intended meaning must be indicated by verb tense: *I attended class on Friday. I will attend class on Friday. I attend class on Friday.*

14g Use the appropriate tense to express your meaning.

Many errors in verb tense are actually errors in verb form like those discussed earlier. Still, the present tense, the perfect tenses, and the progressive tenses can cause problems.

1 Observe the special uses of the present tense.

Most academic and business writing uses the past tense (*the rebellion occurred*), but the present tense has several distinctive uses:

Action occurring now
She understands the problem.
We define the problem differently.

Habitual or recurring action
Banks regularly undergo audits.
The audits monitor the banks' activities.

A general truth
The mills of the gods grind slowly.
The earth is round.

Discussion of literature, film, and so on (see also p. 744)
Huckleberry Finn has adventures we all envy.
In that article, the author examines several causes of crime.

Future time
Next week we draft a new budget.
Funding ends in less than a year.

(In the last two examples, time is really indicated by *Next week* and *in less than a year*.)

2 Observe the uses of the perfect tenses.

The perfect tenses generally indicate action completed before another specific time or action. (The term *perfect* derives from the Latin perfectus, "completed.") The present perfect tense also indicates action begun in the past and continued into the present. The perfect tenses consist of a form of *have* plus the verb's past participle.

> present perfect
> The dancer has performed here only once. [The action is completed at the time of the statement.]

> present perfect
> Critics have written about the performance ever since. [The action began in the past and continues now.]

> past perfect
> The dancer had trained in Asia before his performance. [The action was completed before another past action.]

> future perfect
> He will have performed here again by next month. [The action begins now or in the future and will be completed by a specified time in the future.]

CULTURE LANGUAGE With the present perfect tense, the words *since* and *for* are followed by different information. After *since*, give a specific point in time: *The United States has been a member of the United Nations since 1945.* After *for*, give a span of time: *The United States has been a member of the United Nations for many decades.*

3 **Observe the uses of the progressive tenses.** **CULTURE LANGUAGE**

The progressive tenses indicate continuing (therefore progressive) action. In standard American English the progressive tenses consist of a form of *be* plus the verb's *-ing* form (present participle). (The words *be* and *been* must be combined with other helping verbs. See pp. 284–85.)

> present progressive
> The economy is improving.

> past progressive
> Last year the economy was stagnating.

> future progressive
> Economists will be watching for signs of growth.

> present perfect progressive
> The government has been expecting an upturn.

> past perfect progressive
> Various indicators had been suggesting improvement.

> future perfect progressive
> By the end of this month, investors will have been pushing the markets up for half a year.

Note Verbs that express unchanging states (especially mental states) rather than physical actions do not usually appear in the progressive tenses. These verbs include *adore, appear, believe, belong, care, doubt, hate, have, hear, imagine, know, like, love, mean, need, own, prefer, realize, remember, see, sound, taste, think, understand,* and *want.*

time lines helpful in distinguishing the present perfect from the simple past tense:

Past	Now	(Possible future
Event	Event 2	occurrence)

Past: The dancer performed here a year ago.

Present perfect: Critics have written about it ever since (and may continue to write about it).

In *The Advanced Grammar Book* (Boston: Heinle, 1991), Jocelyn Steer and Karen Carlisi include useful time lines for distinguishing tenses.

CULTURE LANGUAGE

THE USE OF PROGRESSIVE TENSES

Some languages (for example, Arabic) use progressive tenses to express habitual activities, whereas English uses simple tenses. Explain to students that in English, the progressive tenses emphasize the *duration* or *continuous nature* of an action. Perfect progressive tenses are also used for ongoing action that is intersected by another action.

EXCEPTIONS

As the text notes, verbs that express mental states or activities are generally not used in the progressive tenses. However, there are some exceptions:

> *see = date or consult: Marsha isn't seeing John any more. Gina is seeing a doctor about her allergies.*
> *think = consider: I'm thinking about taking a literature course next term.*
> *cumulative effects: I'm understanding English better and better as I go through this course.*

Faulty   She <u>is wanting</u> to study ethics.
Revised   She <u>wants</u> to study ethics.

14h Use the appropriate sequence of verb tenses.

The term **sequence of tenses** refers to the relation between the verb tense in a main clause and the verb tense in a subordinate clause or phrase. The tenses should change when necessary to reflect changes in actual or relative time. (For a discussion of tense shifts—changes *not* required by meaning—see pp. 359–60.)

1 Use the appropriate tense sequence with infinitives.

The **present infinitive** is the verb's plain form preceded by *to*. It indicates action *at the same time* as or *later* than that of the verb:

verb: infinitive:
present perfect   present

She <u>would have liked</u> <u>to see</u> [not <u>to have seen</u>] change before now.

The verb's **perfect infinitive** consists of *to have* followed by the past participle, as in *to have talked, to have won.* It indicates action *earlier* than that of the verb:

verb: infinitive:
present   perfect

Other researchers <u>would like</u> [not <u>would have liked</u>] <u>to have seen</u> change as well.

2 Use the appropriate tense sequence with participles.

The present participle shows action occurring *at the same time* as that of the verb:

participle: verb:
present   past perfect

<u>Testing</u> a large group, the researcher <u>had posed</u> multiple-choice questions.

The past participle and the present perfect participle show action occurring *earlier* than that of the verb:

participle: verb:
past   past

<u>Prepared</u> by earlier failures, she <u>knew</u> not to ask open questions.

participle: verb:
present perfect   past

<u>Having tested</u> many people, she <u>understood</u> the process.

3 Use the appropriate tense sequence with the past or past perfect tense.

When the verb in the main clause is in the past or past perfect tense, the verb in the subordinate clause must also be past or past perfect:

main clause: subordinate clause:
past   past

The researchers <u>discovered</u> that people <u>varied</u> widely in their knowledge of public events.

main clause: subordinate clause:
past   past perfect

The variation <u>occurred</u> because respondents <u>had been born</u> in different decades.

main clause: subordinate clause:
past perfect   past

None of them <u>had been born</u> when Warren G. Harding <u>was</u> President.

Exception Always use the present tense for a general truth, such as *The earth is round:*

main clause: subordinate clause:
past   present

Most <u>understood</u> that popular Presidents <u>are</u> not necessarily good Presidents.

4 **Use the appropriate tense sequence in conditional sentences.**

A **conditional sentence** states a factual relation between cause and effect, makes a prediction, or speculates about what might happen. Such a sentence usually contains a subordinate clause beginning with *if, when,* or *unless* along with a main clause stating the result. The three kinds of conditional sentences use distinctive verbs.

Factual relation

Statements linking factual causes and effects use matched tenses in the subordinate and main clauses:

subordinate clause: main clause:
present   present

When a voter <u>casts</u> a ballot, he or she <u>has</u> complete privacy.

subordinate clause: main clause:
past   past

When voters <u>registered</u> in some states, they <u>had</u> to pay a poll tax.

Prediction

Predictions generally use the present tense in the subordinate clause and the future tense in the main clause:

subordinate clause: main clause:
present   future

Unless citizens <u>regain</u> faith in politics, they <u>will not vote</u>.

Sometimes the verb in the main clause consists of *may, can, should,* or *might* plus the verb's plain form: *If citizens <u>regain</u> faith, they <u>may vote</u>.*

Speculation

The verbs in speculations depend on whether the linked events are possible or impossible. For possible events in the present, use the past tense in the subordinate clause and *would, could,* or *might* plus the verb's plain form in the main clause:

subordinate clause: main clause:
past   *would* + verb

If voters <u>had</u> more confidence, they <u>would vote</u> more often.

Always use *were* in the subordinate clause, even when the subject is *I, he, she, it* or a singular noun. (See p. 300 for more on this distinctive verb form.)

subordinate clause: main clause:
past   *would* + verb

If the voter <u>were</u> more confident, he or she <u>would vote</u> more often.

For impossible events in the present—events that are contrary to fact—use the same forms as above (including the distinctive *were* when applicable):

subordinate clause: main clause:
past   *might* + verb

If Lincoln <u>were</u> alive, he <u>might inspire</u> confidence.

For impossible events in the past, use the past perfect tense in the subordinate clause and *would, could,* or *might* plus the present perfect tense in the main clause:

subordinate clause: main clause:
past perfect   *might* + present perfect

If Lincoln <u>had lived</u> past the Civil War, he <u>might have helped</u> stabilize the country.

ANSWERS: EXERCISE 14.8

1. Diaries that Adolf Hitler <u>was supposed</u> to have written <u>had surfaced</u> in Germany.
2. Many people <u>believed</u> that the diaries <u>were</u> authentic because a well-known historian <u>had declared</u> them so.
3. However, the historian's evaluation <u>was questioned</u> by other authorities who <u>called</u> the diaries forgeries.
4. They <u>claimed</u>, among other things, that the paper <u>was</u> not old enough to have been used by Hitler.
5. Eventually, the doubters <u>won</u> the debate because they <u>had</u> the best evidence.

EXERCISE 14.8 Adjusting tense sequence: Past or past perfect tense

The tenses in each sentence below are in correct sequence. Change the tense of one verb as instructed. Then change the tense of infinitives, participles, and other verbs to restore correct sequence. Some items have more than one possible answer. (You can do this exercise online at *ablongman.com/littlebrown*.)

Example:

Delgado will call when he reaches his destination. (*Change will call to called.*)

Delgado <u>called</u> when he <u>reached</u> [or <u>had reached</u>] his destination.

1. Diaries that Adolf Hitler is supposed to have written have surfaced in Germany. (*Change have surfaced to had surfaced.*)
2. Many people believe that the diaries are authentic because a well-known historian has declared them so. (*Change believe to believed.*)
3. However, the historian's evaluation has been questioned by other authorities, who call the diaries forgeries. (*Change has been questioned to was questioned.*)
4. They claim, among other things, that the paper is not old enough to have been used by Hitler. (*Change claim to claimed.*)
5. Eventually, the doubters will win the debate because they have the best evidence. (*Change will win to won.*)

EXERCISE 14.9 Revising: Tense sequence with conditional sentences

Supply the appropriate tense for each verb in brackets below. (You can do this exercise online at *ablongman.com/littlebrown*.)

Example:

If Babe Ruth or Jim Thorpe [be] athletes today, they [remind] us that even sports heroes must contend with a harsh reality.

If Babe Ruth or Jim Thorpe <u>were</u> athletes today, they <u>might</u> [or <u>could</u> or <u>would</u>] remind us that even sports heroes must contend with a harsh reality.

1. When an athlete [turn] professional, he or she [commit] to a grueling regimen of mental and physical training.
2. If athletes [be] less committed, they [disappoint] teammates, fans, and themselves.
3. If professional athletes [be] very lucky, they [play] until age forty.
4. Unless an athlete [achieve] celebrity status, he or she [have] few employment choices after retirement.
5. If professional sports [be] less risky, athletes [have] longer careers and more choices after retirement.

Mood

Mood in grammar is a verb form that indicates the writer's or speaker's attitude toward what he or she is saying. The **indicative mood** states a fact or opinion or asks a question:

The theater <u>needs</u> help. [Opinion.]
The ceiling <u>is falling</u> in. [Fact.]
<u>Will</u> you <u>contribute</u> to the theater? [Question.]

The **imperative mood** expresses a command or gives a direction. It omits the subject of the sentence, *you:*

<u>Help</u> the theater. [Command.]
<u>Send</u> contributions to the theater. [Direction.]

The **subjunctive mood** expresses a suggestion, a requirement, or a desire, or it states a condition that is contrary to fact (that is, imaginary or hypothetical). The subjunctive mood uses distinctive verb forms.

- **Suggestion or requirement:** plain form with all subjects.

http://www.ablongman.com/littlebrown ▶

Visit the companion Web site for more help and additional exercises on verb mood.

The manager asked that he <u>donate</u> money. [Suggestion.]
Rules require that every donation <u>be</u> mailed. [Requirement.]

- **Desire or present condition contrary to fact:** past tense; for *be,* the past tense *were* for all subjects, singular as well as plural.

  We wish that the theater <u>had</u> more money. [Desire.]

  It would be in better shape if it <u>were</u> better funded. [Present condition contrary to fact.]

- **Past condition contrary to fact:** past perfect.

  The theater could have been better funded if it <u>had been</u> better managed.

Note that with conditions contrary to fact, the verb in the main clause also expresses the imaginary or hypothetical with the helping verb *could, would,* or *might.* (See also p. 298.)

For a discussion of keeping mood consistent within and among sentences, see page 360.

THE DISAPPEARING SUBJUNCTIVE

The blurring of the subjunctive mood is swiftly spreading; in another half-century it may be gone in all but the most formal writing. Linguistically this change is understandable; English has simplified its forms more than most other languages. The disappearance of the subjunctive is another example of this natural process. A very readable book on this subject is Jean Aitchison's *Language Change: Progress or Decay?* (Suffolk: Fontana, 1981).

14i **Use the subjunctive verb forms appropriately.**

Contemporary English uses distinctive subjunctive verb forms in only a few constructions and idioms. (For the sequence of tenses in many subjunctive sentences, see pp. 297–98.)

Note A grammar and style checker may spot some simple errors in the subjunctive mood, but it may miss others. For example, a checker flagged *I wish I <u>was</u> home* (should be *<u>were</u> home*) but not *If I had a hammer, I <u>will</u> hammer in the morning* (should be *<u>would</u> hammer*).

1 **Use the subjunctive in contrary-to-fact clauses beginning with *if* or expressing desire.**

If the theater <u>were</u> saved, the town would benefit.
We all wish the theater <u>were</u> not so decrepit.
I wish I <u>were</u> able to donate money.

Note The indicative form *was* (*We all wish the theater <u>was</u> not so decrepit*) is common in speech and in some informal writing, but the subjunctive *were* is usual in formal English.

Not all clauses beginning with *if* express conditions contrary to fact. In the sentence *If Joe <u>is</u> out of town, he hasn't heard the news,* the verb *is* is correct because the clause refers to a condition presumed to exist.

2   **Use *would, could,* or *might* only in the main clause of a conditional statement.**

The helping verb *would, could,* or *might* appears in the main clause of a sentence expressing a condition contrary to fact. The helping verb does not appear in the subordinate clause beginning with *if:*

Not   Many people would have helped if they <u>would have</u> known.
But   Many people would have helped if they <u>had</u> known.

3   **Use the subjunctive in *that* clauses following verbs that demand, request, or recommend.**

Verbs such as *ask, demand, insist, mandate, recommend, request, require, suggest,* and *urge* indicate demand or suggestion. They often precede subordinate clauses beginning with *that* and containing the substance of the demand or suggestion. The verb in such a *that* clause should be in the subjunctive mood:

The board urged that everyone <u>contribute</u>.
The members insisted that they themselves <u>be</u> donors.
They suggested that each <u>donate</u> both time and money.

Note These constructions have widely used alternative forms that do not require the subjunctive, such as *The board urged everyone to contribute* or *The members insisted on donating.*

EXERCISE 14.10   Revising: Subjunctive mood

Revise the following sentences with appropriate subjunctive verb forms. (You can do this exercise online at *ablongman.com/littlebrown.*)

Example:
I would help the old man if I was able to reach him.
I would help the old man if I <u>were</u> able to reach him.

1. If John Hawkins would have known of the dangerous side effects of smoking tobacco, would he have introduced the dried plant to England in 1565?
2. Hawkins noted that if a Florida Indian was to travel for several days, he would have smoked tobacco to satisfy his hunger and thirst.
3. Early tobacco growers feared that their product would not gain acceptance unless it was perceived as healthful.
4. To prevent fires, in 1646 the General Court of Massachusetts passed a law requiring that colonists smoked tobacco only if they were five miles from any town.
5. To prevent decadence, in 1647 Connecticut passed a law mandating that one's smoking of tobacco was limited to once a day in one's own home.

ANSWERS: EXERCISE 14.10

1. If John Hawkins <u>had known</u> of the dangerous side effects of smoking tobacco, would he have introduced the dried plant to England in 1565?
2. Hawkins noted that if a Florida Indian <u>were</u> to travel for several days, he <u>would smoke</u> tobacco to satisfy his hunger and thirst.
3. Early tobacco growers feared that their product would not gain acceptance unless it <u>were</u> perceived as healthful.
4. To prevent fires, in 1646 the General Court of Massachusetts passed a law requiring that colonists <u>smoke</u> tobacco only if they were five miles from any town.
5. To prevent decadence, in 1647 Connecticut passed a law mandating that one's smoking of tobacco <u>be</u> limited to once a day in one's own home.

PASSIVE SENTENCES—COUNT THE WORDS

Write on the board a number of sentences in the active voice, the sentences ranging from simple to relatively complex. Ask students to change the sentences into the passive voice and then to count the number of words in each version. Finally, ask students to read some of the passive sentences aloud and comment on their effectiveness. This exercise will allow you to check students' understanding of the passive voice and at the same time demonstrate its wordiness.

TRANSPARENCY MASTER 14.3

PROBLEMS WITH THE PAST PARTICIPLE

Not all languages include a passive voice. As a result, ESL students are not always certain about when passive voice is appropriate. Also, because ESL students do not always hear the past-participle *-ed* ending, particularly when *-ed* sounds like *t*, they may omit *-ed* in writing passive voice. Encourage students to listen for the use of the passive voice *-ed* ending in political speeches or in news programs or documentaries. Unit 5 of Carroll Washington Pollock, *Communicate What You Mean: Grammar for High-Level ESL Students* (Englewood Cliffs: Prentice-Hall, 1982), and Chapter 11 of Jocelyn Steer and Karen Carlisi, *The Advanced Grammar Book* (Boston: Heinle, 1991), include useful exercises both in writing and in determining when to use passive voice.

Voice

The **voice** of a verb tells whether the subject of the sentence performs the action (**active voice**) or is acted upon (**passive voice**). In the passive voice, the actual actor may be named in a prepositional phrase (such as *by the city*) or may be omitted.

CULTURE LANGUAGE A passive verb always consists of a form of *be* plus the past participle of the main verb: *rents are controlled*. Other helping verbs must also be used with *be, being,* and *been: rents have been controlled*. Only a transitive verb (one that takes an object) may be used in the passive voice. (See p. 285.)

Active and passive voice

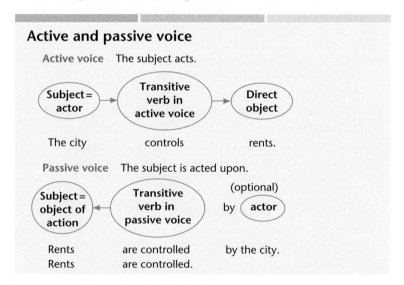

Active voice   The subject acts.

Subject = actor → Transitive verb in active voice → Direct object

The city   controls   rents.

Passive voice   The subject is acted upon.

Subject = object of action ← Transitive verb in passive voice   (optional) by actor

Rents   are controlled   by the city.
Rents   are controlled.

■ Converting active to passive

To change a transitive verb from active to passive voice, convert either an indirect object or a direct object into the subject of the sentence, and use the passive verb form:

	subject	transitive verb	indirect object	direct object
Active	The city	gives	tenants	leases.

	new subject	passive verb	direct object	
Passive	Tenants	are given	leases.	

	new subject	passive verb	indirect object	old subject
	Leases	are given	tenants	by the city.

http://www.ablongman.com/littlebrown ▶

Visit the companion Web site for more help and additional exercises on verb voice.

■ Converting passive to active

To change a passive verb to active, name the verb's actor as the subject, use an active verb form, and convert the old subject into an object:

	subject	passive verb	
Passive	Tenants	are protected	by leases.

	new subject	active verb	old subject = object
Active	Leases	protect	tenants.

14j Generally, prefer the active voice. Use the passive voice when the actor is unknown or unimportant.

Because the passive omits or de-emphasizes the actor (the performer of the verb's action), it can deprive writing of vigor and is often vague or confusing. The active voice is usually stronger, clearer, and more forthright.

Weak passive	The Internet is used for research by many scholars, and its expansion to the general public has been criticized by some.
Strong active	Many scholars use the Internet for research, and some have criticized its expansion to the general public.

The passive voice is useful in two situations: when the actor is unknown and when the actor is unimportant or less important than the object of the action.

The Internet was established in 1969 by the US Department of Defense. The network has now been extended internationally to governments, foundations, corporations, educational institutions, and private individuals. [In the first sentence the writer wishes to stress the Internet rather than the Department of Defense. In the second sentence the actor is unknown or too complicated to name.]

After the solution had been cooled to 10°C, the acid was added. [The person who cooled and added, perhaps the writer, is less important than the facts that the solution was cooled and acid was added. Passive sentences are common in scientific writing. See p. 809.]

Except in such situations, however, you should prefer the active voice in your writing.

Note Most grammar and style checkers can be set to spot the passive voice. (See p. 61.) But the checkers will flag appropriate passives as well, such as when the actor is unknown.

EXERCISE 14.11 Converting between active and passive voices

To practice using the two voices of the verb, convert the following sentences from active to passive or from passive to active. (In converting

PASSIVE SENTENCES—FINDING PASSAGES

Have students, working in groups, locate passive sentences in an essay from a reader or a similar source. Ask them to decide if the passive voice provides emphasis appropriate for the essay or if the active voice would be better. Tell them to be ready to defend their choice of the passive or to offer a revision of the sentence in the active voice. Have each group present its most hotly debated case to the class.

SCIENTIFIC STYLE

Many editors of scientific journals now recommend that authors use first person pronouns and active verbs where possible instead of relying on the passive. They recommend that authors use the passive when the performer of the action is unknown or unimportant or when emphasis should be placed on the recipient of the action. Students writing in science courses should check with their instructors to see what stylistic guide they should follow; see also Chapters 52 and 53.

ACTIVE/PASSIVE

Ask students to work on Exercise 14.11 in small groups; then ask each group to compose additional examples of active- and passive-voiced sentences.

ANSWERS: EXERCISE 14.11

Possible answers

1. When <u>engineers built</u> the Eiffel Tower in 1889, the <u>French thought</u> it was ugly.
2. At that time industrial <u>technology was</u> still resisted <u>by</u> many people.
3. This <u>technology was epitomized</u> by the tower's naked steel construction.
4. <u>People expected</u> beautiful ornament to grace fine buildings.
5. Further, <u>people could not even call</u> the tower a building because it had no solid walls.

ANSWERS: EXERCISE 14.12

For centuries the natives of Melanesia, a group of islands (lying) northeast of Australia, (have practiced) an unusual religion. It (began) in the eighteenth century when European explorers first (visited) the islands. The natives (were fascinated) by the rich goods or "cargo" (possessed) by the explorers. They (saw) the wealth as treasures of the gods, and cargo cults eventually (arose) among them. Over the centuries some Melanesians (turned) to Christianity in the belief that the white man's religion (would bring) them the white man's treasures. During World War II, US soldiers, (having arrived) by boat and airplane (to occupy) some of the islands, (introduced) new and even more wonderful cargo. Even today some leaders of the cargo cults (insist) that the airplane (be worshipped) as a vehicle of the Melanesians' future salvation.

COLLABORATIVE LEARNING

VERBS AND ADVERBS

Ask students to compare their responses to Exercise 14.12 and then to circle and revise the verbs and verbals in one paragraph from each student's work. This kind of application of the skills learned in an exercise to examples from students' own work can be extremely beneficial.

from passive to active, you may have to add a subject for the new sentence.) Which version of each sentence seems more effective, and why? (You can do this exercise online at *ablongman.com/littlebrown*.) For additional exercises with the passive voice, see pages 264 and 386.

Example:
The aspiring actor was discovered in a nightclub.
A <u>talent scout</u> <u>discovered</u> the aspiring actor in a nightclub.

1. When the Eiffel Tower was built in 1889, it was thought by the French to be ugly.
2. At that time many people still resisted industrial technology.
3. The tower's naked steel construction epitomized this technology.
4. Beautiful ornament was expected to grace fine buildings.
5. Further, the tower could not even be called a building because it had no solid walls.

EXERCISE 14.12 Revising: Verb forms, tense, mood

Mark all the verbs and verbals in the following paragraph and correct their form, tense, or mood if necessary. (You can do this exercise online at *ablongman.com/littlebrown*.)

For centuries the natives of Melanesia, a group of islands laying northeast of Australia, have practice an unusual religion. It began in the eighteenth century when European explorers first have visited the islands. The natives were fascinated by the rich goods or "cargo" possessed by the explorers. They saw the wealth as treasures of the gods, and cargo cults eventually had arised among them. Over the centuries some Melanesians turned to Christianity in the belief that the white man's religion will bring them the white man's treasures. During World War II, US soldiers, having arrived by boat and airplane to have occupied some of the islands, introduced new and even more wonderful cargo. Even today some leaders of the cargo cults insist that the airplane is worship as a vehicle of the Melanesians' future salvation.

Note See page 331 for an exercise involving verbs along with other aspects of grammar.

CHAPTER 15

Agreement

Agreement helps readers understand the relations between elements in a sentence. Subjects and verbs agree in number and person:

More Japanese Americans live in Hawaii and California than elsewhere.
subject   verb

Daniel Inouye was the first Japanese American in Congress.
subject   verb

Pronouns and their **antecedents**—the words they refer to—agree in person, number, and gender:

Inouye makes his home in Hawaii.
antecedent   pronoun

Hawaiians value his work for them.
antecedent   pronoun

15a Make subjects and verbs agree in number.

Most subject-verb agreement problems arise when endings are omitted from subjects or verbs or when the relation between sentence parts is uncertain.

Note A grammar and style checker will catch many simple errors in subject-verb agreement, such as *Addie and John is late*, and some more complicated errors, such as *Is Margaret and Tom going with us?* (should be *are* in both cases). But a checker failed to flag *The old group has gone their separate ways* (should be *have*) and offered a wrong correction for *The old group have gone their separate ways,* which is already correct.

1 The *-s* and *-es* endings work differently for nouns and verbs.

An *-s* or *-es* ending does opposite things to nouns and verbs: it usually makes a noun *plural,* but it always makes a present-tense

http://www.ablongman.com/littlebrown ▶

Visit the companion Web site for more help and additional exercises on subject-verb and pronoun-antecedent agreement.

---

mycomplab²·⁰

Please visit MyCompLab at *www.mycomplab.com* for more on the writing process.

Person and number in subject-verb agreement

Person	Singular	Plural
	Number	
First	I eat.	We eat.
Second	You eat.	You eat.
Third	He/she/it eats.	They eat.
	The bird eats.	Birds eat.

verb *singular.* Thus a singular noun as subject will not end in *-s,* but its verb will. A plural noun as subject will end in *-s,* but its verb will not. **Between them, subject and verb use only one *-s* ending.**

Singular	Plural
The boy plays.	The boys play.
The bird soars.	The birds soar.

The only exceptions to these rules involve the nouns that form irregular plurals, such as *child/children, woman/women.* The irregular plural still requires a plural verb: The *children play.*

CULTURE LANGUAGE If your first language or dialect is not standard American English, subject-verb agreement may be problematic, especially for these reasons:

- **Some English dialects follow different rules for subject-verb agreement,** such as omitting the *-s* ending for singular verbs or using the *-s* ending for plural verbs.

Nonstandard	The voter resist change.
Standard	The voter resists change.
Standard	The voters resist change.

The verb *be* changes spelling for singular and plural in both present and past tenses. (See also p. 276.)

Nonstandard	Taxes is high. They was raised just last year.
Standard	Taxes are high. They were raised just last year.

Have also has a distinctive *-s* form, *has:*

Nonstandard	The new tax have little chance of passing.
Standard	The new tax has little chance of passing.

- **Some other languages change all verb phrases to match their subjects,** but in English only the helping verbs *be, have,* and *do* change for different subjects. The modal helping verbs—*can, may, should, will,* and others—do not change:

CULTURE LANGUAGE

THE RULE OF ONE *-S*

Remind students that this is "the rule of one *-s*"—in the present tense, English sentences require one *-s* in the third person:

Singular noun + verb + *s*
Noun + *s* (plural noun) + verb

Refer students who need additional practice to Unit 3 of Len Fox, *Focus on Editing: A Grammar Workbook for Advanced Writers* (White Plains: Longman, 1992), and to Alan Meyers, *Writing with Confidence* (6th ed., New York: Longman, 2000).

Nonstandard	The tax <u>mays</u> pass next year.
Standard	The tax <u>may</u> pass next year.

The main verb in a verb phrase also does not change for different subjects:

Nonstandard	The tax may <u>passes</u> next year.
Standard	The tax may <u>pass</u> next year.

2 Subject and verb should agree even when other words come between them.

When the subject and verb are interrupted by other words, make sure the verb agrees with the subject:

A catalog of courses and requirements often <u>baffles</u> [not baffle] students.

The requirements stated in the catalog <u>are</u> [not is] unclear.

Note Phrases beginning with *as well as, together with, along with,* and *in addition to* do not change the number of the subject:

The president, as well as the deans, <u>has</u> [not have] agreed to revise the catalog.

If you really mean *and* in such a sentence, use it. Then the subject is compound, and the verb should be plural: *The president and the deans have agreed to revise the catalog.*

3 Subjects joined by *and* usually take plural verbs.

Two or more subjects joined by *and* usually take a plural verb, whether one or all of the subjects are singular:

Frost and Roethke <u>were</u> contemporaries.

Frost, Roethke, Stevens, and Pound <u>are</u> among the great American poets.

Exceptions When the parts of the subject form a single idea or refer to a single person or thing, they take a singular verb:

Avocado and bean sprouts <u>is</u> a California sandwich.

When a compound subject is preceded by the adjective *each* or *every,* the verb is usually singular:

Each man, woman, and child <u>has</u> a right to be heard.

WIDELY SEPARATED SUBJECTS AND VERBS

Ask students (working individually or in groups and using the handbook as a guide) to identify the sentence strategies that often result in widely separated subjects and verbs. Then ask them to write in their own words a description of these strategies (i.e., the grammatical rules governing them). Finally, ask students to write sentences using the strategies and containing proper subject-verb agreement. (This exercise can also be used with compound subjects, collective nouns, inverted word order, or other strategies that frequently lead to agreement problems.)

TRUE COMPLEXITY

Sometimes the sample sentences we offer to students by way of illustrating a point of grammar or style seem a bit artificial or a bit too simple. Writers such as Charles Dickens and Henry James offer sentences with considerable variety and flair in structure that can be used either as models themselves or as patterns for sentences with a more contemporary content and cast. The following sentence, from James's preface to *The Princess Casamassima*, illustrates tight control of subject-verb and pronoun-antecedent agreement:

> The troubled life mostly at the center of our subject—whatever our subject, for the artistic hour, happens to be—embraces them [fools] and deals with them for its amusement and its anguish: they are apt largely indeed, on a near view, to be all the cause of its trouble.

Although students often produce grammatically complex sentences, particularly in response to readings, it can be fun and enlightening for them to practice different kinds of complexity. Copy a sentence like this one on the board, on a transparency, or on the network, and ask students to compose sentences that mimic, even parody, its complex structure.

Summary of subject-verb agreement

- **Basic subject-verb agreement** (p. 305):

  Singular   Plural
  The kite flies.   The kites fly.

- **Words between subject and verb** (p. 307):

  The kite with two tails flies badly. The tails of the kite compete.

- **Subjects joined by *and*** (p. 307):

  The kite and the bird are almost indistinguishable.

- **Subjects joined by *or* or *nor*** (below):

  The kite or the bird dives. Kites or birds fill the sky.

- **Indefinite pronouns as subjects** (opposite):

  No one knows. All the spectators wonder.

- **Collective nouns as subjects** (p. 310):

  A flock appears. The flock disperse.

- **Inverted word order** (p. 310):

  Is the kite or the bird blue? Are the kite and the bird both blue?

- **Linking verbs** (p. 311):

  The kite is a flier and a dipper.

- ***Who, which, that* as subjects** (p. 311):

  The kite that flies longest wins. Kites that fall lose.

- **Subjects with plural form and singular meaning** (p. 312):

  Aeronautics plays a role in kite flying.

- **Titles and words named as words** (p. 312):

  Kite Dynamics is one title. *Vectors* is a key word.

But a compound subject *followed* by *each* takes a plural verb:

The man and the woman each have different problems.

4 When parts of a subject are joined by *or* or *nor*, the verb agrees with the nearer part.

When all parts of a subject joined by *or* or *nor* are singular, the verb is singular; when all parts are plural, the verb is plural.

Either the painter or the carpenter knows the cost.

The cabinets or the bookcases are too costly.

When one part of the subject is singular and the other plural, avoid awkwardness by placing the plural part closer to the verb so that the verb is plural:

Awkward   Neither the owners nor the contractor agrees.

Revised   Neither the contractor nor the owners agree.

When the subject consists of nouns and pronouns of different person requiring different verb forms, the verb agrees with the nearer part of the subject. Reword if this construction is awkward:

Awkward   Either Juarez or I am responsible.

Revised   Either Juarez is responsible, or I am.

5 With an indefinite pronoun, use a singular or plural verb as appropriate.

An **indefinite pronoun** is one that does not refer to a specific person or thing. Most indefinite pronouns take a singular verb, but some take a plural verb and some take a singular *or* a plural verb.

Common indefinite pronouns

Singular			Singular or plural	Plural
anybody	everyone	no one	all	both
anyone	everything	nothing	any	few
anything	much	one	more	many
each	neither	somebody	most	several
either	nobody	someone	some	
everybody	none	something		

The singular indefinite pronouns refer to a single unspecified person or thing, and they take a singular verb:

Something smells.   Neither is right.

The plural indefinite pronouns refer to more than one unspecified thing, and they take a plural verb:

Both are correct.   Several were invited.

The other indefinite pronouns take a singular or a plural verb depending on whether the word they refer to is singular or plural. The word may be stated in the sentence:

ARE EVERYONE READY?

Though many students will not, at first, hear anything wrong with sentences like *Everyone ought to pay attention to their own business* (a pattern that has wide acceptance in speech), almost all will find sentences like these unacceptable: *Are everyone ready for lunch? Do everybody have enough money to buy tickets for the rides?* Anyone who finds the latter sentences acceptable is probably having trouble recognizing the singular and plural forms of verbs. Sample sentences can, therefore, help you identify the real source of a student's problems with agreement.

All of the money is reserved for emergencies.

All of the funds are reserved for emergencies.

The word referred to by the pronoun may also be implied:

All are planning to attend. [*All* implies "all the people."]

All is lost. [*All* implies "everything."]

CULTURE LANGUAGE See page 330 for the distinction between *few* ("not many") and *a few* ("some").

6 **Collective nouns take singular or plural verbs depending on meaning.**

A **collective noun** has singular form but names a group of individuals or things—for example, *army, audience, committee, crowd, family, group, team.* As a subject, a collective noun may take a singular or plural verb, depending on the context. When the group acts as one unit, use a singular verb:

The group agrees that action is necessary.

But when considering the group's members as individuals who act separately, use the plural form of the verb:

The old group have gone their separate ways.

The collective noun *number* may be singular or plural. Preceded by *a*, it is plural; preceded by *the*, it is singular.

A number of people are in debt.

The number of people in debt is very large.

CULTURE LANGUAGE In English some noncount nouns (nouns that don't form plurals) are collective nouns because they name groups: for instance, *furniture, clothing, mail.* These noncount nouns usually take singular verbs: *Mail arrives daily.* But some of these nouns take plural verbs, including *clergy, military, people, police,* and any collective noun that comes from an adjective, such as *the poor, the rich, the young, the elderly.* If you mean one representative of the group, use a singular noun such as *police officer* or *poor person.*

7 **The verb agrees with the subject even when the normal word order is inverted.**

Inverted subject-verb order occurs mainly in questions and in constructions beginning with *there* or *it* and a form of *be:*

CULTURE LANGUAGE

SEPARATED BY A COMMON LANGUAGE?

In British usage, collective nouns are treated as plurals; students educated in British usage (such as those from former British dependencies) may use constructions like *The team were ready for the game.* Such constructions also appear in the works of British authors.

Is voting a right or a privilege?

Are a right and a privilege the same thing?

There are differences between them.

In constructions beginning with *there,* you may use *is* before a compound subject when the first element in the subject is singular:

There is much work to do and little time to do it.

Word order may sometimes be inverted for emphasis. The verb still agrees with its subject:

From the mountains comes an eerie, shimmering light.

8 A linking verb agrees with its subject, not the subject complement.

A linking verb such as *is* or *are* should agree with its subject, usually the first element in the sentence, not with the noun or pronoun serving as a subject complement (see p. 240):

The child's sole support is her court-appointed guardians.

Her court-appointed guardians are the child's sole support.

9 *Who, which,* and *that* take verbs that agree with their antecedents.

When used as subjects, *who, which,* and *that* refer to another word in the sentence, called the **antecedent.** The verb agrees with the antecedent:

Mayor Garber ought to listen to the people who work for her.

Bardini is the only aide who has her ear.

Agreement problems often occur with relative pronouns when the sentence includes *one of the* or *the only one of the:*

Bardini is one of the aides who work unpaid. [Of the aides who work unpaid, Bardini is one.]

Bardini is the only one of the aides who knows the community. [Of the aides, only one, Bardini, knows the community.]

CULTURE LANGUAGE In phrases like those above beginning with *one of the,* be sure the noun is plural: *Bardini is one of the aides* [not *aide*] *who work unpaid.*

A LITTLE INTERVENTION

Agreement problems with *who, which,* and *that* are often the result of a phrase's separating the subject from the relative clause. Give students a few examples of such phrases:

is one of those people who
is the only one of the workers that
are often believed to be creatures that
are generally considered to be people who
is representative of those executives who

Then ask them to write sample sentences of their own employing these or similar phrases and avoiding problems of agreement.

CULTURE LANGUAGE

REMINDER

Remind students that phrases like *one of* also require *the* before the noun: *Bardini is one of the aides* [not *one of aides*] *who work unpaid.*

RESOURCES AND IDEAS

Kolln, Martha. "Everyone's Right to Their Own Language." *College Composition and Communication* 37 (1986): 100–02. The frequency with which students treat indefinite pronouns as plural suggests that the widely accepted rules of usage discussed in this section may in some ways conflict with practice. Kolln takes a radical stance, arguing that "dicta that designate all indefinite pronouns as singular have no basis either in actual usage or in the rules of logic" (102).

Sklar, Elizabeth S. "The Tribunal of Use: Agreement in the Indefinite Constructions." *College Composition and Communication* 39 (1988): 410–22. Sklar reviews historical and textbook treatments of agreement with indefinites and offers some pragmatic strategies for teachers to use.

COLLABORATIVE LEARNING

Ask students to work together on Exercise 15.1 and then to look for agreement problems in each other's journal writing, drafts, or completed work.

ANSWERS: EXERCISE 15.1

1. Weinstein & Associates <u>is</u> a consulting firm that <u>tries</u> to make businesspeople laugh.
2. Statistics from recent research <u>suggest</u> that humor relieves stress.
3. Reduced stress in businesses in turn <u>reduces</u> illness and absenteeism.

---

10 **Nouns with plural form but singular meaning take singular verbs.**

Some nouns with plural form (that is, ending in -*s*) are usually regarded as singular in meaning. They include *athletics, economics, mathematics, measles, mumps, news, physics, politics,* and *statistics,* as well as place names such as *Athens, Wales,* and *United States.*

> After so long a wait, the news has to be good.

> Statistics is required of psychology majors.

A few of these words take plural verbs only when they describe individual items rather than whole bodies of activity or knowledge: *The statistics prove him wrong.*

Measurements and figures ending in -*s* may also be singular when the quantity they refer to is a unit:

> Three years is a long time to wait.

> Three-fourths of the library consists of reference books.

11 **Titles and words named as words take singular verbs.**

When your sentence subject is the name of a corporation, the title of a work (such as a book), or a word you are defining or describing, the verb should be singular even if the name, title, or word is plural:

> Hakada Associates is a new firm.

> *Dream Days* remains a favorite book.

> *Folks* is a down-home word for *people.*

EXERCISE 15.1   Revising: Subject-verb agreement

Revise the verbs in the following sentences as needed to make subjects and verbs agree in number. If the sentence is already correct as given, circle the number preceding it. (You can do this exercise online at *ablongman.com/littlebrown.*)

Example:
Each of the job applicants type sixty words per minute.
Each of the job applicants <u>types</u> sixty words per minute.

1. Weinstein & Associates are a consulting firm that try to make businesspeople laugh.
2. Statistics from recent research suggests that humor relieves stress.
3. Reduced stress in businesses in turn reduce illness and absenteeism.

4. Reduced stress can also reduce friction within an employee group, which then work more productively.
5. In special conferences held by one consultant, each of the partici- pants practice making the others laugh.
6. One consultant to many companies suggest cultivating office humor with practical jokes such as a rubber fish in the water cooler.
7. When employees or their manager regularly post cartoons on the bulletin board, office spirit usually picks up.
8. When someone who has seemed too easily distracted is entrusted with updating the cartoons, his or her concentration often im- proves.
9. In the face of levity, the former sourpuss becomes one of those who hides bad temper.
10. Every one of the consultants caution, however, that humor has no place in life-affecting corporate situations such as employee layoffs.

4. Reduced stress can also reduce friction within an employee group, which then <u>works</u> more productively.
5. In special conferences held by one consul- tant, each of the participants <u>practices</u> mak- ing the others laugh.
6. One consultant to many companies <u>sug- gests</u> cultivating office humor with practical jokes such as a rubber fish in the water cooler.
7. When the manager or employees regularly <u>post</u> cartoons on the bulletin board, office spirit usually picks up.
8. Sentence correct.
9. In the face of levity, the former sourpuss be- comes one of those who <u>hide</u> bad temper.
10. Every one of the consultants <u>cautions</u>, how- ever, that humor has no place in life-affect- ing corporate situations such as employee layoffs.

15b Make pronouns and their antecedents agree in person, number, and gender.

The **antecedent** of a pronoun is the noun or other pronoun to which the pronoun refers.

Homeowners fret over their tax bills.
    antecedent   pronoun

Its constant increases make the tax bill a dreaded document.
pronoun   antecedent

Since a pronoun derives its meaning from its antecedent, the two must agree in person, number, and gender.

Person, number, and gender in pronoun-antecedent agreement

Person	Number	
	Singular	Plural
First	*I*	*we*
Second	*you*	*you*
Third	*he, she, it,* indefinite pronouns, singular nouns	*they,* plural nouns
Gender		
Masculine	*he,* nouns naming males	
Feminine	*she,* nouns naming females	
Neuter	*it,* all other nouns	

Note Grammar and style checkers cannot help with agreement between pronoun and antecedent because they cannot recognize the intended relation between the two.

CULTURE LANGUAGE The gender of a pronoun should match its antecedent, not a noun that the pronoun may modify: *Sara Young invited her* [not *his*] *son to join the company's staff*. Also, nouns in English have only neuter gender unless they specifically refer to males or females. Thus nouns such as *book, table, sun,* and *earth* take the pronoun *it*.

Summary of pronoun-antecedent agreement

- **Basic pronoun-antecedent agreement:**

  Old Faithful spews its columns of water, each of them over 115 feet high.

- **Antecedents joined by *and* (below):**

  Old Faithful and Giant are geysers known for their height.

- **Antecedents joined by *or* or *nor* (opposite):**

  Either Giant or Giantess ejects its column the highest.

- **Indefinite words as antecedents (opposite):**

  Each of the geysers has its own personality. Each person who visits has his or her memories.

- **Collective nouns as antecedents (p. 316):**

  A crowd amuses itself watching Old Faithful. The crowd go their separate ways.

---

1 **Antecedents joined by *and* usually take plural pronouns.**

Two or more antecedents joined by *and* usually take a plural pronoun, whether one or all of the antecedents are singular:

Mr. Bartos and I cannot settle our dispute.

The dean and my adviser have offered their help.

Exceptions When the compound antecedent refers to a single idea, person, or thing, then the pronoun is singular:

My friend and adviser offered her help.

When the compound antecedent follows *each* or *every,* the pronoun is singular:

Every girl and woman took her seat.

2 When parts of an antecedent are joined by *or* or *nor,* the pronoun agrees with the nearer part.

When the parts of an antecedent are connected by *or* or *nor,* the pronoun should agree with the part closer to it:

Tenants or owners must present their grievances.

Either the tenant or the owner will have her way.

When one subject is plural and the other singular, the sentence will be awkward unless you put the plural one second:

Awkward   Neither the tenants nor the owner has yet made her case.

Revised   Neither the owner nor the tenants have yet made their case.

3 With an indefinite word as antecedent, use a singular or plural pronoun as appropriate.

Indefinite words do not refer to any specific person or thing. They include **indefinite pronouns** such as *anyone, everybody,* and *no one* (see p. 309 for a list). They also include **generic nouns,** or singular nouns that refer to typical members of a group, as in *The individual has rights* or *The job requires a person with computer skills.*

Most indefinite pronouns and all generic nouns are singular in meaning. When they serve as antecedents of pronouns, the pronouns should be singular.

Everyone on the women's team now has her own locker.
indefinite
pronoun

Every person on the women's team now has her own locker.
generic
noun

Five indefinite pronouns—*all, any, more, most, some*—may be singular or plural in meaning depending on what they refer to:

Few women athletes had changing spaces, so most had to change in their rooms.

Most of the changing space was dismal, its color a drab olive green.

CONFUSION OVER INDEFINITE PRONOUNS

ESL students may be confused by the indefinite pronouns *everyone, everybody,* and *everything* because they mean *all* of a group but are grammatically singular. Explain to students that the *endings* to these words—*one, body,* and *thing*—cause them to be singular rather than plural.

Four indefinite pronouns—*both, few, many, several*—are always plural in meaning:

Few realize how their athletic facilities have changed.

Most agreement problems arise with the singular indefinite words. We often use these words to mean something like "many" or "all" rather than "one" and then refer to them with plural pronouns, as in *Everyone has their own locker* or *A person can padlock their locker*. Often, too, we mean indefinite words to include both masculine and feminine genders and thus resort to *they* instead of the **generic he**—the masculine pronoun referring to both genders, as in *Everyone deserves his privacy*. (For more on the generic *he*, which many readers view as sexist, see p. 516.)

Although some experts accept *they, them,* and *their* with singular indefinite words, most do not, and many teachers and employers regard the plural as incorrect. To be safe, work for agreement between singular indefinite words and the pronouns that refer to them. You have several options:

Ways to correct agreement with indefinite words

- **Change the indefinite word to a plural, and use a plural pronoun to match:**

  Faulty   Every athlete deserves their privacy.
  Revised   Athletes deserve their privacy.

- **Rewrite the sentence to omit the pronoun:**

  Faulty   Everyone is entitled to their own locker.
  Revised   Everyone is entitled to a locker.

- **Use *he or she* (*him or her, his or her*) to refer to the indefinite word:**

  Faulty   Now everyone has their private space.
  Revised   Now everyone has his or her private space.

  However, used more than once in several sentences, *he or she* quickly becomes awkward. (Many readers do not accept the alternative *he/she*.) In most cases, using the plural or omitting the pronoun will not only correct agreement problems but also create more readable sentences.

4 **Collective noun antecedents take singular or plural pronouns depending on meaning.**

Collective nouns such as *army, committee, family, group,* and *team* have singular form but may be referred to by singular or plural pronouns, depending on the meaning intended. When the group acts as a unit, the pronoun is singular:

The committee voted to disband itself.

When the members of the group act separately, the pronoun is plural:

The old group have gone their separate ways.

In the last example, note that the verb and pronoun are consistent in number (see also pp. 358–59).

Inconsistent	The old group has gone their separate ways.
Consistent	The old group have gone their separate ways.

CULTURE LANGUAGE In standard American English, collective nouns that are noncount nouns (they don't form plurals) usually take singular pronouns: *The mail sits in its own basket.* A few noncount nouns take plural pronouns, including *clergy, military, people, police, the rich,* and *the poor: The police support their unions.* (See also p. 310.)

EXERCISE 15.2   Revising: Pronoun-antecedent agreement

Revise the following sentences so that pronouns and their antecedents agree in person and number. Some items have more than one possible answer. Try to avoid the generic *he* (see opposite). If you change the subject of a sentence, be sure to change verbs as necessary for agreement. If the sentence is already correct as given, mark the number preceding it. (You can do this exercise online at *ablongman.com/littlebrown.*)

Example:

Each of the Boudreaus' children brought their laundry home at Thanksgiving.

All of the Boudreaus' children brought their laundry home at Thanksgiving. *Or:* Each of the Boudreaus' children brought laundry home at Thanksgiving. *Or:* Each of the Boudreaus' children brought his or her laundry home at Thanksgiving.

1. Each girl raised in a Mexican American family in the Rio Grande Valley of Texas hopes that one day they will be given a *quinceañera* party for their fifteenth birthday.
2. Such celebrations are very expensive because it entails a religious service followed by a huge party.
3. A girl's immediate family, unless they are wealthy, cannot afford the party by themselves.
4. The parents will ask each close friend or relative if they can help with the preparations.
5. Surrounded by her family and attended by her friends and their escorts, the *quinceañera* is introduced as a young woman eligible for Mexican American society.

COLLABORATIVE LEARNING

Ask students to work on Exercises 15.2, 15.3, and 15.4 in groups and then to read examples from their own work looking for subject-verb and pronoun-antecedent problems.

ANSWERS: EXERCISE 15.2

1. Each girl raised in a Mexican American family in the Rio Grande Valley of Texas hopes that one day <u>she</u> will be given a *quinceañera* party for <u>her</u> fifteenth birthday.
2. Such <u>a celebration is</u> very expensive because it entails a religious service followed by a huge party. *Or:* Such celebrations are very expensive because <u>they entail</u> a religious service followed by a huge party.
3. A girl's immediate family, unless <u>it is</u> wealthy, cannot afford the party by <u>itself.</u>
4. The parents will ask each close friend or relative if <u>he or she</u> can help with the preparations. *Or:* The parents will ask <u>close friends or relatives</u> if they can help with the preparations.
5. Sentence correct.

ANSWERS: EXERCISE 15.3

1. <u>Biologists wish</u> to introduce captive red wolves into the Smoky Mountains in order to increase the wild population of this endangered species.
2. When freed, the <u>wolves</u> naturally <u>have</u> no fear of humans and thus <u>are</u> in danger of being shot.
3. The first <u>experiments</u> to release the wolves <u>were failures</u>.
4. Now researchers pen the wolf <u>puppies</u> in the wooded area that will eventually be <u>their</u> territory.
5. The <u>wolves have</u> little contact with people, even <u>their</u> own keeper, during the year of <u>their</u> captivity.

ANSWERS: EXERCISE 15.4

The writers Richard Rodriguez and Maxine Hong Kingston, despite their differences, <u>share</u> one characteristic: their parents <u>were</u> immigrants to California. A frequent theme of their writings <u>is</u> the difficulties of growing up with two languages and two cultures.

A child whose first language is not English is often ridiculed because <u>he or she</u> cannot communicate "properly." [*Or:* <u>Children</u> whose first language is not English <u>are</u> often ridiculed because they cannot communicate "properly."] Rodriguez learned Spanish at home, but at school <u>class-mates and teachers</u> expected him to use their language, English. He remembers his childish embarrassment because of his parents' poor English. College and graduate school, which usually <u>expand</u> one's knowledge, widened the gap between Rodriguez and his Latino culture. His essays <u>suggest</u> that he lost a part of himself, a loss that continues to bother him.

Kingston spoke Chinese at home and also learned her first English at school. She sometimes <u>writes</u> of these experiences, but more often she <u>writes</u> to recover and preserve her Chinese culture. *The Woman Warrior*, which <u>offers</u> a blend of autobiography, family history, and mythic tales, <u>describes</u> the struggle of Kingston's female relatives. *China Men* <u>focuses</u> on Kingston's male ancestors; each one traveled to Hawaii or California to make money for <u>his</u> wife back in China. Kingston's work, like Rodriguez's essays, <u>reflects</u> the tension and confusion that the child of immigrants often <u>feels</u> when <u>he or she tries</u> [*or:* that the <u>children</u> of immigrants often feel when <u>they try</u>] to blend two cultures.

EXERCISE 15.3 Adjusting for agreement

In the sentences below, subjects agree with verbs and pronouns agree with antecedents. Make the change specified in parentheses after each sentence, and then revise the sentence as necessary to maintain agreement. Some items have more than one possible answer. (You can do this exercise online at *ablongman.com/littlebrown*.)

Example:

The student attends weekly conferences with her teacher. (*Change The student to Students.*)

Students *attend* weekly conferences with their teacher.

1. A biologist wishes to introduce captive red wolves into the Smoky Mountains in order to increase the wild population of this endangered species. (*Change A biologist to Biologists.*)
2. When freed, the wolf naturally has no fear of humans and thus is in danger of being shot. (*Change wolf to wolves.*)
3. The first experiment to release the wolves was a failure. (*Change experiment to experiments.*)
4. Now researchers pen the wolf puppy in the wooded area that will eventually be its territory. (*Change puppy to puppies.*)
5. The wolf has little contact with people, even its own keeper, during the year of its captivity. (*Change wolf to wolves.*)

EXERCISE 15.4 Revising: Agreement

Revise the sentences in the following paragraphs to correct errors in agreement between subjects and verbs or between pronouns and their antecedents. Try to avoid the generic *he*. (You can do this exercise online at *ablongman.com/littlebrown*.)

The writers Richard Rodriguez and Maxine Hong Kingston, despite their differences, shares one characteristic: their parents was immigrants to California. A frequent theme of their writings are the difficulties of growing up with two languages and two cultures.

A child whose first language is not English is often ridiculed because they cannot communicate "properly." Rodriguez learned Spanish at home, but at school everyone expected him to use their language, English. He remembers his childish embarrassment because of his parents' poor English. College and graduate school, which usually expands one's knowledge, widened the gap between Rodriguez and his Latino culture. His essays suggests that he lost a part of himself, a loss that continue to bother him.

Kingston spoke Chinese at home and also learned her first English at school. She sometimes write of these experiences, but more often she write to recover and preserve her Chinese culture. *The Woman Warrior,* which offer a blend of autobiography, family history, and mythic tales, describe the struggle of Kingston's female relatives. *China Men* focus on Kingston's male ancestors; each one traveled to Hawaii or California to make money for their wife back in China. Kingston's work, like Rodriguez's essays, reflect the tension and confusion that the child of immigrants often feel when they try to blend two cultures.

Note See page 331 for an exercise involving agreement along with other aspects of grammar.

CHAPTER 16

Adjectives and Adverbs

Adjectives and adverbs are modifiers that describe, restrict, or otherwise qualify the words to which they relate.

Functions of adjectives and adverbs

Adjectives modify nouns:	serious student
pronouns:	ordinary one
Adverbs modify verbs:	warmly greet
adjectives:	only three people
adverbs:	quite seriously
phrases:	nearly to the edge of the cliff
clauses:	just when we arrived
sentences:	Fortunately, she is employed.

Many of the most common adjectives are familiar one-syllable words such as *bad, strange, large,* and *wrong.* Many others are formed by adding endings such as *-al, -able, -ful, -less, -ish, -ive,* and *-y* to nouns or verbs: *optional, fashionable, beautiful, fruitless, selfish, expressive, dreamy.*

Most adverbs are formed by adding *-ly* to adjectives: *badly, strangely, largely, beautifully.* But note that we cannot depend on *-ly* to identify adverbs, since some adjectives also end in *-ly* (*fatherly, lonely*) and since some common adverbs do not end in *-ly* (*always,*

http://www.ablongman.com/littlebrown ▶

Visit the companion Web site for more help and additional exercises on adjectives and adverbs.

Please visit MyCompLab at *www.mycomplab.com* for more on the writing process.

COMPANION WEB SITE

See page IAE-54 for companion Web site content description.

here, not, now, often, there). Thus the only sure way to distinguish between adjectives and adverbs is to determine what they modify.

Note Grammar and style checkers will spot some but not all problems with misused adjectives and adverbs. For instance, a checker flagged *Some children suffer bad* and *Chang was the most wisest person in town* and *Jenny did not feel nothing*. But it did not flag *Educating children good is everyone's focus.*

CULTURE LANGUAGE In standard American English an adjective does not change along with the noun it modifies to show plural number: *white* [not *whites*] *shoes*, *square* [not *squares*] *spaces*. Only nouns form plurals.

16a Use adjectives only to modify nouns and pronouns.

Adjectives modify only nouns and pronouns. Using adjectives instead of adverbs to modify verbs, adverbs, or other adjectives is non-standard:

Nonstandard   The groups view family values different.

Standard   The groups view family values differently.

The adjectives *good* and *bad* often appear where standard English requires the adverbs *well* and *badly*:

Nonstandard   Educating children good is everyone's focus.

Standard   Educating children well is everyone's focus.

Nonstandard   Some children suffer bad.

Standard   Some children suffer badly.

CULTURE LANGUAGE To negate a verb or an adjective, use the adverb *not:*

They are not learning. They are not stupid.

To negate a noun, use the adjective *no:*

No child should fail to read.

16b Use an adjective after a linking verb to modify the subject. Use an adverb to modify a verb.

A **linking verb** is one that links, or connects, a subject and its complement: *They are golfers. He is lucky.* (See also pp. 239–40.) Linking verbs are forms of *be*, the verbs associated with our five senses (*look, sound, smell, feel, taste*), and a few others (*appear, seem, become, grow, turn, prove, remain, stay*).

Some of these verbs may or may not be linking, depending on their meaning in the sentence. When the word after the verb modifies the subject, the verb is linking and the word should be an adjective: *He feels strong*. When the word modifies the verb, however, it should be an adverb: *He feels strongly about that*.

Two word pairs are especially troublesome in this context. One is *bad* and *badly:*

The weather grew bad.
      linking   adjective
      verb

She felt bad.
      linking   adjective
      verb

Flowers grow badly in such soil.
      verb   adverb

The other pair is *good* and *well. Good* serves only as an adjective. *Well* may serve as an adverb with a host of meanings or as an adjective meaning only "fit" or "healthy."

Decker trained well.
   verb   adverb

She felt well.
   linking   adjective
   verb

Her health was good.
      linking   adjective
      verb

16c   After a direct object, use an adjective to modify the object and an adverb to modify the verb.

After a direct object, an adjective modifies the object, whereas an adverb modifies the verb of the sentence. (See p. 238 for more on direct objects.)

Campus politics made Mungo angry.
                   adjective

Mungo repeated the words angrily.
                   adverb

You can test whether a modifier should be an adjective or an adverb by trying to separate it from the direct object. If you can separate it, it should be an adverb: *Mungo angrily repeated the words*. If you cannot separate it, it is probably an adjective.

The instructor considered the student's work thorough. [The adjective can be moved in front of *work* (*student's thorough work*), but it cannot be separated from *work*.]

The instructor considered the student's work thoroughly. [The adverb can be separated from *work*. Compare *The instructor thoroughly considered the student's work*.]

ANSWERS: EXERCISE 16.1

1. King George III of England declared Samuel Johnson <u>suitable</u> for a pension.
2. Johnson was taken <u>seriously</u> as a critic and dictionary maker.
3. Thinking about his meeting with the king, Johnson felt <u>proud</u>.
4. Sentence correct.
5. After living <u>cheaply</u> for over twenty years, Johnson finally had enough money from the pension to eat and dress <u>well</u>.

EXERCISE 16.1 Revising: Adjectives and adverbs

Revise the following sentences so that adjectives and adverbs are used appropriately. If any sentence is already correct as given, mark the number preceding it. (You can do this exercise online at *ablongman.com/littlebrown*.)

Example:
The announcer warned that traffic was moving very slow.
The announcer warned that traffic was moving very <u>slowly</u>.

1. King George III of England declared Samuel Johnson suitably for a pension.
2. Johnson was taken serious as a critic and dictionary maker.
3. Thinking about his meeting with the king, Johnson felt proudly.
4. Johnson was relieved that he had not behaved badly in the king's presence.
5. After living cheap for over twenty years, Johnson finally had enough money from the pension to eat and dress good.

16d Use the comparative and superlative forms of adjectives and adverbs appropriately.

Adjectives and adverbs can show degrees of quality or amount with the endings *-er* and *-est* or with the words *more* and *most* or *less* and *least*. Most modifiers have three forms:

Positive The basic form listed in the dictionary	Comparative A greater or lesser degree of the quality	Superlative The greatest or least degree of the quality
Adjectives		
red	redder	reddest
awful	more/less awful	most/least awful
Adverbs		
soon	sooner	soonest
quickly	more/less quickly	most/least quickly

If sound alone does not tell you whether to use *-er/-est* or *more/most*, consult a dictionary. If the endings can be used, the dictionary will list them. Otherwise, use *more* or *most*.

1 Use the correct forms of irregular adjectives and adverbs.

Certian adjectives and adverbs are irregular: they change the spelling of their positive form to show comparative and superlative degrees.

Degrees of irregular adjectives and adverbs

Positive	Comparative	Superlative
Adjectives		
good	better	best
bad	worse	worst
little	littler, less	littlest, least
many ⎤		
some ⎬	more	most
much ⎦		
Adverbs		
well	better	best
badly	worse	worst

2 **Use either *-er/-est* or *more/most*, not both.**

A double comparative or double superlative combines the *-er* or *-est* ending with the word *more* or *most*. It is redundant.

Chang was the wisest [not most wisest] person in town.
He was smarter [not more smarter] than anyone else.

3 **Use the comparative for comparing two things and the superlative for comparing three or more things.**

It is the shorter of her two books. [Comparative.]
The Yearling is the most popular of the six books. [Superlative.]

In conversation the superlative form is often used to compare only two things: *When two people argue, the angriest one is usually wrong.* But the distinction between the forms should be observed in writing.

4 **Use comparative or superlative forms only for modifiers that can logically be compared.**

Some adjectives and adverbs cannot logically be compared—for instance, *perfect, unique, dead, impossible, infinite.* These absolute words can be preceded by adverbs like *nearly* and *almost* that mean "approaching," but they cannot logically be modified by *more* or *most* (as in *most perfect*). This distinction is sometimes ignored in speech, but it should always be made in writing:

Not   He was the most unique teacher we had.
But   He was a unique teacher.

ANSWERS: EXERCISE 16.2

1. Charlotte was the <u>oldest</u> of the three Brontë sisters, all of whom were novelists.
2. Some readers think Emily Brontë's *Wuthering Heights* is the <u>saddest</u> novel they have ever read.
3. Sentence correct.
4. Critics still argue about whether Charlotte or Emily wrote <u>better</u>.
5. Certainly, this <u>family</u> of women novelists was <u>unique</u>.

EXERCISE 16.2 Revising: Comparatives and superlatives

Revise the sentences below so that the comparative and superlative forms of adjectives and adverbs are appropriate for formal usage. Mark the number preceding any sentence that is already correct. (You can do this exercise online at *ablongman.com/littlebrown*.)

Example:

Attending classes full time and working at two jobs was the most impossible thing I ever did.

Attending classes full time and working at two jobs was <u>impossible</u> [or <u>the hardest thing I ever did</u>].

1. Charlotte was the older of the three Brontë sisters, all of whom were novelists.
2. Some readers think Emily Brontë's *Wuthering Heights* is the most saddest novel they have ever read.
3. Of the other two sisters, Charlotte and Anne, Charlotte was probably the more talented.
4. Critics still argue about whether Charlotte or Emily wrote more better.
5. Certainly this family of women novelists was the most unique.

16e Watch for double negatives.

In a **double negative** two negative words such as *no, not, none, neither, barely, hardly,* or *scarcely* cancel each other out. Some double negatives are intentional: for instance, *She was <u>not unhappy</u>* indicates with understatement that she was indeed happy. But most double negatives say the opposite of what is intended: *Jenny did <u>not</u> feel <u>nothing</u>* asserts that Jenny felt other than nothing, or something. For the opposite meaning, one of the negatives must be eliminated or changed to a positive: *She felt <u>nothing</u>* or *She did not feel <u>anything</u>.*

Faulty	The IRS <u>cannot hardly</u> audit all tax returns. <u>None</u> of its audits <u>never</u> touch many cheaters.
Revised	The IRS <u>cannot</u> audit all tax returns. Its audits <u>never</u> touch many cheaters.

EXERCISE 16.3 Revising: Double negatives

Identify and revise the double negatives in the following paragraph. Each error may have more than one correct revision. (You can do this exercise online at *ablongman.com/littlebrown*.)

Interest in books about the founding of the United States seems to vary with the national mood. Americans show hardly no interest in books about the founders when things are going well in the United States. However, when Americans can't barely agree on major issues, sales of books about the Revolutionary War era increase. During such

ANSWERS: EXERCISE 16.3

Interest in books about the founding of the United States seems to vary with the national mood. Americans show <u>hardly any interest</u> [or <u>little interest</u>] in books about the founders when things are going well in the United States. However, when Americans <u>can barely</u> [or <u>cannot</u>] agree on major issues, sales of books about the Revolutionary War era increase. During such periods, one cannot go to <u>a</u> bookstore without seeing several new volumes about John Adams, Thomas Jefferson, and other founders. When Americans feel they <u>have nothing</u> [or <u>don't have anything</u>] in common, their increased interest in the early leaders may reflect a desire for unity.

periods, one cannot go to no bookstore without seeing several new volumes about John Adams, Thomas Jefferson, and other founders. When Americans feel they don't have nothing in common, their increased interest in the early leaders may reflect a desire for unity.

16f Use nouns sparingly as modifiers.

We often use one noun to modify another. For example:

child care   flood control   security guard

Such phrases can be both clear and concise, but overuse of noun modifiers can lead to flat, even senseless, writing. To avoid awkwardness or confusion, observe two principles. First, prefer possessives or adjectives as modifiers:

| Not | A student takes the state medical board exams to become a dentist technician. |
| But | A student takes the state medical board's exams to become a dental technician. |

Second, use only short nouns as modifiers and use them only in two- or three-word sequences:

| Confusing | Minimex maintains a plant employee relations improvement program. |
| Revised | Minimex maintains a program for improving relations among plant employees. |

16g Distinguish between present and past participles as adjectives. 🔊 CULTURE LANGUAGE

Both present participles and past participles may serve as adjectives: *a burning building, a burned building.* As in the examples, the two participles usually differ in the time they indicate.

But some present and past participles—those derived from verbs expressing feeling—can have altogether different meanings. The present participle modifies something that causes the feeling: *That was a frightening storm* (the storm frightens). The past participle modifies something that experiences the feeling: *They quieted the frightened horses* (the horses feel fright).

The following participles are among those likely to be confused:

amazing/amazed	confusing/confused
amusing/amused	depressing/depressed
annoying/annoyed	embarrassing/embarrassed
astonishing/astonished	exciting/excited
boring/bored	exhausting/exhausted

🔊 CULTURE LANGUAGE

Present participles generally describe inanimate or nonhuman nouns: *The storm was frightening.* Past participles generally describe animate nouns (since only animate beings experience feelings): *The horses were frightened.*

ANSWERS: EXERCISE 16.4

1. Several critics found Alice Walker's *The Color Purple* to be a <u>fascinating</u> book.
2. Sentence correct.
3. Another critic argued that although the book contained many <u>depressing</u> episodes, the overall impact was <u>exciting</u>.
4. Since other readers found the book <u>annoying</u>, this critic pointed out its many <u>surprising</u> qualities.
5. In the end most critics agreed that the book was a <u>satisfying</u> novel.

ARTICLE USE

As the text notes, because other languages use articles differently from English or not at all, even advanced ESL students may find articles difficult; some students may never completely master article use. Refer students who need additional practice with article use to Unit 2 of Len Fox, *Focus on Editing: A Grammar Workbook for Advanced Writers* (White Plains: Longman, 1992), and Chapter 10 of Jocelyn Steer and Karen Carlisi, *The Advanced Grammar Book* (Boston: Heinle, 1991).

fascinating/fascinated   satisfying/satisfied
frightening/frightened   shocking/shocked
frustrating/frustrated   surprising/surprised
interesting/interested   tiring/tired
pleasing/pleased   worrying/worried

EXERCISE 16.4   Revising: Present and past participles

CULTURE LANGUAGE Revise the adjectives in the following sentences as needed to distinguish between present and past participles. If the sentence is already correct as given, mark the number preceding it. (You can do this exercise online at *ablongman.com/littlebrown*.)

Example:
The subject was embarrassed to many people.
The subject was <u>embarrassing</u> to many people.

1. Several critics found Alice Walker's *The Color Purple* to be a fascinated book.
2. One confused critic wished that Walker had deleted the scenes set in Africa.
3. Another critic argued that although the book contained many depressed episodes, the overall impact was excited.
4. Since other readers found the book annoyed, this critic pointed out its many surprised qualities.
5. In the end most critics agreed that the book was a satisfied novel.

16h   Use *a, an, the,* and other determiners appropriately. **CULTURE LANGUAGE**

Determiners are special kinds of adjectives that mark nouns because they always precede nouns. Some common determiners are *a, an,* and *the* (called **articles**) and *my, their, whose, this, these, those, one, some,* and *any.* They convey information to readers—for instance, by specifying who owns what, which one of two is meant, or whether a subject is familiar or unfamiliar.

Native speakers of standard American English can rely on their intuition when using determiners, but speakers of other languages and dialects often have difficulty with them. In standard English the use of determiners depends on the context they appear in and the kind of noun they precede:

- A **proper noun** names a particular person, place, or thing and begins with a capital letter: *February, Joe Allen, Red River.* Most proper nouns are not preceded by determiners.
- A **count noun** names something that is countable in English and can form a plural: *girl/girls, apple/apples, child/children.* A singular count noun is always preceded by a determiner; a plural count noun sometimes is.

■ A **noncount noun** names something not usually considered countable in English, and so it does not form a plural. A noncount noun is sometimes preceded by a determiner. Here is a sample of noncount nouns, sorted into groups by meaning:

Abstractions: confidence, democracy, education, equality, evidence, health, information, intelligence, knowledge, luxury, peace, pollution, research, success, supervision, truth, wealth, work

Food and drink: bread, candy, cereal, flour, meat, milk, salt, water, wine

Emotions: anger, courage, happiness, hate, joy, love, respect, satisfaction

Natural events and substances: air, blood, dirt, gasoline, gold, hair, heat, ice, oil, oxygen, rain, silver, smoke, weather, wood

Groups: clergy, clothing, equipment, furniture, garbage, jewelry, junk, legislation, machinery, mail, military, money, police, vocabulary

Fields of study: architecture, accounting, biology, business, chemistry, engineering, literature, psychology, science

A dictionary of English as a second language will tell you whether a noun is a count noun, a noncount noun, or both. (See p. 537 for recommended dictionaries.)

Note Many nouns can be both count and noncount nouns:

The library has a room for readers. [*Room* is a count noun meaning "walled area."]

The library has room for reading. [*Room* is a noncount noun meaning "space."]

Partly because the same noun may fall into different groups, grammar and style checkers are unreliable guides to missing or misused articles and other determiners. For instance, a checker flagged the omitted *a* before *Scientist* in *Scientist developed new processes;* it did not flag the omitted *a* before *new* in *A scientist developed new process;* and it mistakenly flagged the correctly omitted article *the* before *Vegetation* in *Vegetation suffers from drought.*

1 Use *a, an,* and *the* where they are required.

■ **With singular count nouns**

A or *an* precedes a singular count noun when the reader does not already know its identity, usually because you have not mentioned it before:

A scientist in our chemistry department developed a process to strengthen metals. [*Scientist* and *process* are being introduced for the first time.]

The precedes a singular count noun that has a specific identity for the reader, for one of the following reasons:

CATEGORIES OF NONCOUNT NOUNS

Refer students who need additional practice with count and noncount nouns to Unit 2 of Len Fox, *Focus on Editing: A Grammar Workbook for Advanced Writers* (White Plains: Longman, 1992), and Chapter 1 of Jocelyn Steer and Karen Carlisi, *The Advanced Grammar Book* (Boston: Heinle, 1991).

■ You have mentioned the noun before:

A scientist in our chemistry department developed a process to strengthen metals. The scientist patented the process. [*Scientist* and *process* were identified in the preceding sentence.]

■ You identify the noun immediately before or after you state it:

The most productive laboratory is the research center in the chemistry department. [*Most productive* identifies *laboratory*. *In the chemistry department* identifies *research center*. And *chemistry department* is a shared facility.]

■ The noun names something unique—the only one in existence:

The sun rises in the east. [*Sun* and *east* are unique.]

■ The noun names an institution or facility that is shared by the community of readers:

Many men and women aspire to the presidency. [*Presidency* is a shared institution.]

The fax machine has changed business communication. [*Fax machine* is a shared facility.]

The is not used before a singular noun that names a general category:

Sherman said that war is hell. [*War* names a general category.]
The war in Croatia left many dead. [*War* names a specific war.]

With plural count nouns

A or *an* never precedes a plural noun. *The* does not precede a plural noun that names a general category. *The* does precede a plural noun that names specific representatives of a category.

Men and women are different. [*Men* and *women* name general categories.]

The women formed a team. [*Women* refers to specific people.]

With noncount nouns

A or *an* never precedes a noncount noun. *The* does precede a noncount noun when it names specific representatives of a general category:

Vegetation suffers from drought. [*Vegetation* names a general category.]

The vegetation in the park withered or died. [*Vegetation* refers to specific plants.]

With proper nouns

A or *an* never precedes a proper noun. *The* generally does not precede a proper noun:

Garcia lives in Boulder.

There are exceptions, however. For instance, we generally use *the* before plural proper nouns (*the Murphys, the Boston Celtics*) and the names of groups and organizations (*the Department of Justice, the Sierra Club*), ships (*the Lusitania*), oceans (*the Pacific*), mountain ranges (*the Alps*), regions (*the Middle East*), rivers (*the Mississippi*), and some countries (*the United States, the Sudan*).

2 Use other determiners appropriately.

The uses of English determiners besides articles also depend on context and kind of noun. The following determiners may be used as indicated with singular count nouns, plural count nouns, or non-count nouns.

■ **With any kind of noun (singular count, plural count, noncount)**

my, our, your, his, her, its, their
possessive nouns (*boy's, boys'*)
whose, which(ever), what(ever)
some, any, the other
no

Their account is overdrawn. [Singular count.]
Their funds are low. [Plural count.]
Their money is running out. [Noncount.]

■ **Only with singular nouns (count and noncount)**

this, that

This account has some money. [Count.]
That information may help. [Noncount.]

■ **Only with noncount nouns and plural count nouns**

most, enough, other, such, all, all of the, a lot of

Most money is needed elsewhere. [Noncount.]
Most funds are committed. [Plural count.]

■ **Only with singular count nouns**

one, every, each, either, neither, another

One car must be sold. [Singular count.]

■ **Only with plural count nouns**

these, those
both, many, few, a few, fewer, fewest, several
two, three, and so forth

Two cars are unnecessary. [Plural count.]

A LOT OF

ESL students tend to use *a lot of* in formal writing because they are unaware that it is an informal, conversational phrase. Give students formal substitutes for *a lot of,* such as *a large amount of* before noncount nouns and *many* before plural count nouns.

Note *Few* means "not many" or "not enough." *A few* means "some" or "a small but sufficient quantity."

<u>Few</u> committee members came to the meeting.
<u>A few</u> members can keep the committee going.

Do not use *much* with a plural count noun:

<u>Many</u> [not <u>Much</u>] members want to help.

■ **Only with noncount nouns**

much, more, little, a little, less, least, a large amount of

<u>Less</u> luxury is in order. [Noncount.]

Note *Little* means "not many" or "not enough." *A little* means "some" or "a small but sufficient quantity."

<u>Little</u> time remains before the conference.

The members need <u>a little</u> help from their colleagues.

Do not use *many* with a noncount noun:

<u>Much</u> [not <u>Many</u>] work remains.

EXERCISE 16.5 Revising: Articles

CULTURE LANGUAGE For each blank below, indicate whether *a, an, the,* or no article should be inserted. (You can do this exercise online at *ablongman .com/littlebrown*.)

From _____ native American Indians who migrated from _____ Asia 20,000 years ago to _____ new arrivals who now come by _____ planes, _____ United States is _____ nation of foreigners. It is _____ country of immigrants who are all living under _____ single flag.

Back in _____ seventeenth and eighteenth centuries, at least 75 percent of the population came from _____ England. However, between 1820 and 1975 more than 38 million immigrants came to this country from elsewhere in _____ Europe. Many children of _____ immigrants were self-conscious and denied their heritage; many even refused to learn _____ native language of their parents and grandparents. They tried to "Americanize" themselves. The so-called Melting Pot theory of _____ social change stressed _____ importance of blending everyone together into _____ kind of stew. Each nationality would contribute its own flavor, but _____ final stew would be something called "American."

This Melting Pot theory was never completely successful. In the last half of the twentieth century, _____ ethnic revival changed _____ metaphor. Many people now see _____ American society as _____ mosaic. Americans are once again proud of their heritage, and _____ ethnic differences make _____ mosaic colorful and interesting.

COLLABORATIVE LEARNING

Students can work in small groups to complete Exercises 16.5 and 16.6, then read each other's work to check article, adjective, and adverb usage.

ANSWERS: EXERCISE 16.5

From <u>the</u> native American Indians who migrated from <u>Asia</u> 20,000 years ago to <u>the</u> new arrivals who now come by <u>planes, the</u> United States is <u>a</u> nation of foreigners. It is <u>a</u> country of immigrants who are all living under <u>a</u> single flag.

Back in <u>the</u> seventeenth and eighteenth centuries, at least 75 percent of the population came from <u>England</u>. However, between 1820 and 1975 more than 38 million immigrants came to this country from elsewhere <u>in Europe</u>. Many children of <u>the</u> immigrants were self-conscious and denied <u>their</u> heritage; many even refused to learn <u>the</u> native language of their parents and grandparents. They tried to "Americanize" themselves. The so-called Melting Pot theory <u>of</u> social change stressed <u>the</u> importance of blending everyone together into <u>a</u> kind of stew. Each nationality would contribute <u>its</u> own flavor, but <u>the</u> final stew would be something called "American."

This Melting Pot theory was never completely successful. In the last half of the twentieth century, <u>an</u> ethnic revival changed <u>the</u> metaphor. Many people now see <u>American</u> society as a mosaic. Americans are <u>once</u> again proud of their heritage, and <u>ethnic</u> differences make <u>the</u> mosaic colorful and interesting.

EXERCISE 16.6   Revising: Adjectives and adverbs

Revise the following paragraph so that it conforms to formal usage of adjectives and adverbs. (You can do this exercise online at *ablongman.com/littlebrown.*)

Americans often argue about which professional sport is better: basketball, football, or baseball. Basketball fans contend that their sport offers more action because the players are constant running and shooting. Because it is played indoors in relative small arenas, basketball allows fans to be more closer to the action than the other sports do. Fans point to how graceful the players fly through the air to the hoop. Football fanatics say they don't hardly stop yelling once the game begins. They cheer when their team executes a real complicated play good. They roar more louder when the defense stops the opponents in a goal-line stand. They yell loudest when a fullback crashes in for a score. In contrast, the supporters of baseball believe that it might be the most perfect sport. It combines the one-on-one duel of pitcher and batter struggling valiant with the tight teamwork of double and triple plays. Because the game is played slow and careful, fans can analyze and discuss the manager's strategy. Besides, they don't never know when they might catch a foul ball as a souvenir. However, no matter what the sport, all fans feel happily only when their team wins!

EXERCISE ON CHAPTERS 13–16   Revising: Grammatical sentences

The paragraphs below contain errors in pronoun case, verb forms, subject-verb agreement, pronoun-antecedent agreement, and the forms of adjectives and adverbs. Revise the paragraphs to correct the errors. (You can do this exercise online at *ablongman.com/littlebrown.*)

Occasionally, musicians become "crossover artists" whom can perform good in more than one field of music. For example, Wynton and Branford Marsalis was train in jazz by their father, the great pianist Ellis Marsalis. Both of the sons has became successful classical artists. Branford's saxophone captures the richness of pieces by Ravel and Stravinsky. Wynton's albums of classical trumpet music from the Baroque period has brung him many awards. Still, if he was to choose which kind of music he likes best, Wynton would probable choose jazz. In contrast to the Marsalises, Yo-Yo Ma and Jean-Pierre Rampal growed up studying classical music. Then in the 1980s they was invited by Claude Bolling, a French pianist, to record Bolling's jazz compositions. In fact, Rampal's flute blended with Bolling's music so good that the two men have did three albums.

Such crossovers are often more harder for vocalists. Each type of music has their own style and feel that is hard to learn. For example, Luciano Pavarotti and Kiri te Kanawa, two great opera performers, have sang popular music and folk songs in concerts and on albums. On each occasion, their technique was the most perfect, yet each

ANSWERS: EXERCISE 16.6

Americans often argue about which professional sport is <u>best</u>: basketball, football, or baseball. Basketball fans contend that their sport offers more action because the players are <u>constantly</u> running and shooting. Because it is played indoors in <u>relatively</u> small arenas, basketball allows fans to be <u>closer</u> to the action than the other sports do. Fans point to how <u>gracefully</u> the players fly through the air to the hoop. Football fanatics say they <u>hardly</u> stop yelling once the game begins. They cheer when their team executes a <u>really</u> complicated play <u>well</u>. They roar more <u>loudly</u> when the defense stops the opponents in a goal-line stand. They yell <u>most loudly</u> when a fullback crashes in for a score. In contrast, the supporters of baseball believe that it might be the <u>perfect</u> sport. It combines the one-on-one duel of pitcher and batter struggling <u>valiantly</u> with the tight teamwork of double and triple plays. Because the game is played <u>slowly</u> and <u>carefully</u>, fans can analyze and discuss the manager's strategy. Besides, they <u>never</u> know when they might catch a foul ball as a souvenir. However, no matter what the sport, all fans feel <u>happy</u> only when their team wins!

ANSWERS: EXERCISE ON CHAPTERS 13–16

Occasionally, musicians become "crossover artists" <u>who</u> can perform <u>well</u> in more than one field of music. For example, Wynton and Branford Marsalis <u>were trained</u> in jazz by their father, the great pianist Ellis Marsalis. Both of the sons <u>have become</u> successful classical artists. Branford's saxophone captures the richness of pieces by Ravel and Stravinsky. Wynton's albums of classical trumpet music from the Baroque period <u>have brought</u> him many awards. Still, if he <u>were</u> to choose which kind of music he likes <u>better</u>, Wynton would <u>probably</u> choose jazz. In contrast to the Marsalises, Yo-Yo Ma and Jean-Pierre Rampal <u>grew</u> up studying classical music. Then in the 1980s <u>they were</u> invited by Claude Bolling, a French pianist, to record Bolling's jazz compositions. In fact, Rampal's flute blended with Bolling's music so <u>well</u> that the two men have <u>done</u> three albums.

Such crossovers are often <u>harder</u> for vocalists. Each type of music has <u>its</u> own style and feel that <u>are</u> hard to learn. For example, Luciano

Pavarotti and Kiri te Kanawa, two great opera performers, have <u>sung</u> popular music and folk songs in concerts and on albums. On each occasion, their technique was <u>nearly</u> perfect, yet each sounded as <u>if he or she were</u> simply trying to sing <u>properly</u>. It is even more <u>difficult</u> for pop or country vocalists to sing opera, as Linda Ronstadt and Gary Morris <u>found</u> when they <u>appeared</u> in *La Bohème*. Each of them <u>has</u> a clear, pure voice, but a few critics said that <u>he</u> and <u>she</u> lacked the vocal power necessary for opera. However, Bobby McFerrin <u>has</u> been successful singing both pop and classical pieces. He won a Grammy award for his song "Don't Worry, Be Happy." But he is <u>equally</u> able to sing classical pieces *a cappella* (without musical accompaniment). His voice's remarkable range and clarity <u>allow</u> him to imitate many musical instruments.

No matter how successful, all of these musicians <u>have</u> shown great courage by performing in a new field. They are willing to test and stretch their talents, and each of <u>us</u> music fans <u>benefits</u>.

sounded as if he was simply trying to sing proper. It is even more difficulter for pop or country vocalists to sing opera, as Linda Ronstadt and Gary Morris founded when they appear in *La Bohème*. Each of them have a clear, pure voice, but a few critics said that him and her lacked the vocal power necessary for opera. However, Bobby McFerrin been successful singing both pop and classical pieces. He won a Grammy award for his song "Don't Worry, Be Happy." But he is equal able to sing classical pieces *a cappella* (without musical accompaniment). His voice's remarkable range and clarity allows him to imitate many musical instruments.

No matter how successful, all of these musicians has shown great courage by performing in a new field. They are willing to test and stretch their talents, and each of we music fans benefit.

Clear Sentences

mycomplab 2.0

Please visit MyCompLab at *www.mycomplab.com* for more on the writing process.

HIGHLIGHTS

This chapter opens with a positive approach, showing students how to test sentences for completeness, revise any fragments, and punctuate revised fragments. Following the opening section are discussions of particular structures that are often mispunctuated as complete sentences: subordinate clauses; verbal and prepositional phrases; and other word groups such as appositives, parts of compound predicates, and nouns plus modifiers. The chapter concludes with a discussion of the acceptable uses of incomplete sentences.

TRANSPARENCY MASTER 17.1

RESOURCES AND IDEAS

Harris, Muriel. "Mending the Fragmented Free Modifier." *College Composition and Communication* 32 (1981): 175–82. Harris presents strategies for identifying kinds of fragments and correcting them.

Noguchi, Rei R. "Fragments and Beyond." Chapter 5 in *Grammar and the Teaching of Writing: Limits and Possibilities*. Urbana: NCTE, 1991. 84–112. Noguchi outlines a positive approach to teaching students how to recognize, revise, or make use of sentence fragments.

COMPANION WEB SITE

See page IAE-55 for companion Web site content description.

CHAPTER **17**

Sentence Fragments

A **sentence fragment** is part of a sentence that is set off as if it were a whole sentence by an initial capital letter and a final period or other end punctuation. Although writers occasionally use fragments deliberately and effectively (see p. 341), readers perceive most fragments as serious errors because, expecting complete sentences, they find partial sentences distracting or confusing. (Before reading further, you may find it helpful to review pp. 233–41 and 252–56 on sentences and clauses.)

Complete sentence versus sentence fragment

A **complete sentence** or **main clause**
- contains a subject and a verb (*The wind blows*)
- and is not a subordinate clause (beginning with a word such as *because* or *who*).

A **sentence fragment**
- lacks a verb (*The wind blowing*)
- or lacks a subject (*And blows*)
- or is a subordinate clause not attached to a complete sentence (*Because the wind blows*).

Note A grammar and style checker can spot many but not all sentence fragments, and it may flag sentences that are actually correct commands, such as *Continue reading*.

17a | **Test your sentences for completeness, and revise any fragments.**

The following three tests will help you determine whether a word group punctuated as a sentence is actually a complete sen-

http://www.ablongman.com/littlebrown ▶

Visit the companion Web site for more help and additional exercises on sentence fragments.

tence. If the word group does not pass *all three* tests, it is a fragment and needs to be revised.

Tests for complete sentences

Perform *all three* of the following tests to be sure your sentences are complete.
1. Find the verb.
2. Find the subject.
3. Make sure the clause is not subordinate.

▧ Test 1: Find the verb.

Look for a verb in the group of words. If you do not have one, the word group is a fragment:

Fragment	Uncountable numbers of sites on the World Wide Web.
Revised	Uncountable numbers of sites <u>make up</u> the World Wide Web.

Any verb form you find must be a **finite verb,** one that changes form as indicated below. A verbal does not change; it cannot serve as a sentence verb without the aid of a helping verb.

	Finite verbs in complete sentences	Verbals in sentence fragments
Singular	The network <u>grows</u>.	The network <u>growing</u>.
Plural	Networks <u>grow</u>.	Networks <u>growing</u>.
Present	The network <u>grows</u>.	
Past	The network <u>grew</u>.	The network <u>growing</u>.
Future	The network <u>will grow</u>.	

⟪ CULTURE LANGUAGE ⟫ Some languages allow forms of *be* to be omitted as helping or linking verbs. But English requires stating forms of *be:*

Fragments	The network growing. It already larger than its developers anticipated.
Revised	The network <u>is</u> growing. It <u>is</u> already larger than its developers anticipated.

▧ Test 2: Find the subject.

If you find a finite verb, look for its subject by asking *who* or *what* performs the action or makes the assertion of the verb. The subject of the sentence will usually come before the verb. If there is no subject, the word group is probably a fragment:

Fragment	And has great popular appeal.
Revised	And <u>the Web</u> has great popular appeal.

FRAGMENTS

Students have been bombarded with so many fragments in advertising and popular prose ("Less filling! Tastes great!") that they may in fact not realize that incomplete sentences are usually unacceptable. Your first job may be to convince them that what is acceptable in speech and informal writing is not always desirable in formal writing.

NEWSCASTERS

The breathless style of radio and television newscasters often includes fragments. Ask students to write down examples from the evening news. Newspapers, especially tabloids, can be a good source, too.

SUBORDINATING-WORD CLUES

Encourage students to look for subordinating words—that is, subordinating conjunctions or relative pronouns—as they read their papers. Remind students that a complete sentence with a subordinating word must include two subjects and verbs, one subject and verb in the subordinate clause and one subject and verb in the main clause. Reading papers backward, from last sentence to first, may help some students find sentence fragments.

In one kind of complete sentence, a command, the subject *you* is understood: [*You*] *Experiment with the Web.*

CULTURE LANGUAGE Some languages allow the omission of the sentence subject, especially when it is a pronoun. But in English, except in commands, the subject is always stated:

Fragments	Web commerce is expanding dramatically. Is threatening traditional stores.
Revised	Web commerce is expanding dramatically. It is threatening traditional stores.

■ Test 3: Make sure the clause is not subordinate.

A subordinate clause usually begins with a subordinating word:

Subordinating conjunctions			Relative pronouns	
after	once	until	that	who/whom
although	since	when	which	whoever/whomever
as	than	where		whose
because	that	whereas		
if	unless	while		

(See p. 253 for a longer list of subordinating conjunctions.)

Subordinate clauses serve as parts of sentences (nouns or modifiers), not as whole sentences:

Fragment	When the government devised the Internet.
Revised	The government devised the Internet.
Revised	When the government devised the Internet, no expansive computer network existed.

Fragment	The reason that the government devised the Internet.
Revised	The reason that the government devised the Internet was to provide secure links among departments and defense contractors.

Note Questions beginning with *how, what, when, where, which, who, whom, whose,* and *why* are not sentence fragments: *Who was responsible? When did it happen?*

■ Revising sentence fragments

Almost all sentence fragments can be corrected in one of two ways, the choice depending on the importance of the information in the fragment:

■ **Rewrite the fragment as a complete sentence,** giving the information in the fragment the same importance as that in other complete sentences:

Fragment	A major improvement of the Internet occurred with the World Wide Web. Which allows users to move easily between sites.

Revised   A major improvement of the Internet occurred with the World Wide Web. <u>It</u> allows users to move easily between sites.

Two main clauses may be separated by a semicolon instead of a period (see p. 453).

- **Combine the fragment with a main clause,** subordinating the information in the fragment to the information in the main clause:

Fragment   The Web is easy to use. <u>Loaded with links and graphics.</u>
Revised   The Web**,** loaded with links and graphics**,** is easy to use.

Punctuating corrected fragments

In the preceding example, commas separate the inserted phrase from the rest of the sentence because the phrase is not essential to the meaning of any word in the main clause but simply adds information (see p. 435). When a phrase or subordinate clause *is* essential to the meaning of a word in the main clause, a comma or commas do *not* separate the two elements:

Fragment   With the links, users can move to other Web sites. <u>That they want to consult.</u>
Revised   With the links, users can move to other Web sites that they want to consult.

Sometimes a fragment may be combined with the main clause using a colon or a dash (see pp. 477 and 480, respectively):

Fragment   The Web connects sites from all over the Internet. <u>Different databases, different software, different machines.</u>
Revised   The Web connects sites from all over the Internet**:** different databases, different software, different machines.

Fragment   The Web is a boon to researchers. <u>A vast and accessible library.</u>
Revised   The Web is a boon to researchers—a vast and accessible library.

EXERCISE 17.1   Identifying and revising sentence fragments

Apply the tests for completeness to each of the following word groups. If a word group is a complete sentence, mark the number preceding it. If it is a sentence fragment, revise it in two ways: by making it a complete sentence, and by combining it with a main clause written from the information given in other items. (You can do this exercise online at *ablongman.com/littlebrown.*)

Example:
And could not find his money. [The word group has a verb (*could . . . find*) but no subject.]

ANSWERS: EXERCISE 17.1

Possible answers

1. Lacks a subject and a verb.
    Complete: An <u>article</u> about vandalism against works of art <u>was</u> interesting.
    Combined: In an interesting article about vandalism against works of art, <u>the author says the vandals' motives vary widely.</u>
2. Lacks a verb.
    Complete: The motives of the vandals <u>vary</u> widely.
    Combined: The motives of the vandals varying widely, <u>researchers can make few generalizations.</u>
3. Complete sentence.
4. Lacks a subject and a verb.
    Complete: But <u>the vandal</u> is not necessarily <u>angry</u> at the artist or the owner.
    Combined: <u>Whoever harms artwork is usually angry,</u> but not necessarily at the artist or the owner.
5. Lacks a verb for the subject <u>man.</u>
    Complete: For instance, <u>a man hammered</u> at Michelangelo's Pietà.
    Combined: For instance, a man who hammered at Michelangelo's Pietà <u>was angry at the Roman Catholic Church.</u>
6. Lacks a subject.
    Complete: And <u>he</u> knocked off the Virgin Mary's nose.
    Combined: <u>A man hammered at Michelangelo's Pietà</u> and knocked off the Virgin Mary's nose.
7. Begins with a subordinating conjunction.
    Complete: He was angry at the Roman Catholic Church.
    Combined: <u>A man hammered at Michelangelo's Pietà</u> because he was angry at the Roman Catholic Church.

8. Begins with *which* but is not a question.
Complete: The Church knew nothing of his grievance.
Combined: He was angry at the Roman Catholic Church, which knew nothing of his grievance.
9. Begins with a subordinating conjunction.
Complete: Many damaged works can be repaired.
Combined: Although many damaged works can be repaired, even the most skillful repairs are forever visible.
10. Complete sentence.

COLLABORATIVE LEARNING

RECOGNIZING FRAGMENTS

After students have completed Exercise 17.1 independently, have them compare responses in small groups and then read each other's work for examples of sentence fragments. For students who are struggling with the concept of sentence structure and of the sentence fragment, the move to recognize errors in their own work can be extremely helpful.

ANALYZING PATTERNS

If students are keeping an error log in their journals, ask them to analyze the pattern(s) that lead them to commit fragments. Most students will commit fragments with only one or two of the problem sentence patterns discussed in 17b–17d.

Revised into a complete sentence: And he could not find his money.
Combined with a new main clause: He was lost and could not find his money.

1. In an interesting article about vandalism against works of art.
2. The motives of the vandals varying widely.
3. Those who harm artwork are usually angry.
4. But not necessarily at the artist or the owner.
5. For instance, a man who hammered at Michelangelo's *Pietà*.
6. And knocked off the Virgin Mary's nose.
7. Because he was angry at the Roman Catholic Church.
8. Which knew nothing of his grievance.
9. Although many damaged works can be repaired.
10. Usually even the most skillful repairs are forever visible.

17b A subordinate clause is not a complete sentence.

Subordinate clauses contain both subjects and verbs, but they always begin with a subordinating conjunction (*although, if,* and so on) or a relative pronoun (*who, which, that*). (See pp. 252–53.) Subordinate clauses serve as nouns or modifiers, but they cannot stand alone as complete sentences.

To correct a subordinate clause set off as a sentence, combine it with the main clause or remove or change the subordinating word to create a main clause.

Fragment	Many pine trees bear large cones. Which appear in August.
Revised	Many pine trees bear large cones, which appear in August.
Revised	Many pine trees bear large cones. They appear in August.

17c A verbal phrase or a prepositional phrase is not a complete sentence.

A **verbal phrase** consists of an infinitive (*to choose*), a past participle (*chosen*), or a present participle or gerund (*choosing*) together with any objects and modifiers it may have (see p. 249). A verbal phrase is a noun or modifier and cannot serve as the verb in a complete sentence:

Fragment	For many of the elderly, their house is their only asset. Offering some security but no income.
Revised	For many of the elderly, their house is their only asset, offering some security but no income.

Revised	For many of the elderly, their house is their only asset. <u>It offers</u> some security but no income.

A prepositional phrase is a modifier consisting of a preposition (such as *in, on, to,* and *with*) together with its object and any modifiers (see p. 245). A prepositional phrase cannot stand alone as a complete sentence:

Fragment	<u>In a squeeze between a valuable asset and little income.</u> Eventually many elderly people sell their homes.
Revised	In a squeeze between a valuable asset and little income, eventually many elderly people sell their homes.
Revised	<u>Many elderly people are</u> in a squeeze between a valuable asset and little income. Eventually they may sell their homes.

⬥ **CULTURE LANGUAGE** ⬥ Some English prepositions consist of two or three words: *as well as, along with, in addition to, on top of,* and others. Don't let prepositions of more than one word mislead you into writing sentence fragments.

Fragment	In today's retirement communities, the elderly may have health care, housekeeping, and new friends. <u>As well as financial security.</u>
Revised	In today's retirement communities, the elderly may have health care, housekeeping, and new friends, as well as financial security.

17d Any word group lacking a subject or a verb or both is not a complete sentence.

We often follow a noun with a modifier. No matter how long the noun and its modifier are, they cannot stand alone as a sentence:

Fragments	<u>People waving flags and cheering.</u> <u>Lined the streets for the parade.</u>
Revised	People waving flags and cheering lined the streets for the parade.
Fragment	<u>Veterans who fought in Vietnam.</u> They are finally being honored.
Revised	Veterans who fought in Vietnam are finally being honored.

Appositives are nouns, or nouns and their modifiers, that rename or describe other nouns (see p. 257). They cannot stand alone as sentences:

Fragment	When I was a child, my favorite adult was an old uncle. A retired sea captain who always told me long stories of wild adventures in faraway places.
Revised	When I was a child, my favorite adult was an old uncle, a retired sea captain who always told me long stories of wild adventures in faraway places.

Compound predicates are predicates made up of two or more verbs and their objects, if any (see p. 258). A verb or its object cannot stand alone as a sentence:

Fragment	Uncle Marlon drew out his tales. And embellished them.
Revised	Uncle Marlon drew out his tales and embellished them.
Fragment	He described characters he had met. And storms at sea.
Revised	He described characters he had met and storms at sea.

Note Beginning a sentence with a coordinating conjunction such as *and* or *but* can lead to a sentence fragment. Check every sentence you begin with a coordinating conjunction to be sure it is complete.

Students can work productively together on Exercises 17.2 and 17.3. Encourage each group to experiment with more than one response to each sentence.

ANSWERS: EXERCISE 17.2

Possible answers

1. Human beings who perfume themselves are not much different from other animals.
2. Animals as varied as insects and dogs release *pheromones,* chemicals that signal other animals.
3. Human beings have a diminished sense of smell and do not consciously detect most of their own species' pheromones.
4. The human substitute for pheromones may be perfumes, especially musk and other fragrances derived from animal oils.
5. Some sources say that humans began using perfume to cover up the smell of burning flesh during sacrifices to the gods.
6. No sentence fragment.
7. The earliest historical documents from the Middle East record the use of fragrances, not only in religious ceremonies but on the body.
8. In the nineteenth century chemists began synthesizing perfume oils, which previously could be made only from natural sources.

EXERCISE 17.2   Revising: Sentence fragments

Correct any sentence fragment below either by combining it with a main clause or by making it a main clause. If an item contains no sentence fragment, mark the number preceding it. (You can do this exercise online at *ablongman.com/littlebrown.*)

Example:

Jujitsu is good for self-protection. Because it enables one to overcome an opponent without the use of weapons.

Jujitsu is good for self-protection because it enables one to overcome an opponent without the use of weapons.

1. Human beings who perfume themselves. They are not much different from other animals.
2. Animals as varied as insects and dogs release *pheromones.* Chemicals that signal other animals.
3. Human beings have a diminished sense of smell. And do not consciously detect most of their own species' pheromones.
4. The human substitute for pheromones may be perfumes. Especially musk and other fragrances derived from animal oils.
5. Some sources say that humans began using perfume to cover up the smell of burning flesh. During sacrifices to the gods.
6. Perfumes became religious offerings in their own right. Being expensive to make, they were highly prized.
7. The earliest historical documents from the Middle East record the use of fragrances. Not only in religious ceremonies but on the body.

8. In the nineteenth century chemists began synthesizing perfume oils. Which previously could be made only from natural sources.
9. The most popular animal oil for perfume today is musk. Although some people dislike its heavy, sweet odor.
10. Synthetic musk oil would help conserve a certain species of deer. Whose gland is the source of musk.

9. The most popular animal oil for perfume today is musk, although some people dislike its heavy, sweet odor.
10. Synthetic musk oil would preserve a certain species of deer whose gland is the source of musk.

17e Be aware of the acceptable uses of incomplete sentences.

A few word groups lacking the usual subject-predicate combination are not sentence fragments because they conform to the expectations of most readers. They include exclamations (*Oh no!*); questions and answers (*Where next? To Kansas.*); and commands (*Move along. Shut the window.*). Another kind of incomplete sentence, occurring in special situations, is the transitional phrase (*So much for the causes, now for the results. One final point.*).

Experienced writers sometimes use sentence fragments when they want to achieve a special effect. Such fragments appear more in informal than in formal writing. Unless you are experienced and thoroughly secure in your own writing, you should avoid all fragments and concentrate on writing clear, well-formed sentences.

EXERCISE 17.3   Revising: Sentence fragments

Revise the following paragraph to eliminate sentence fragments by combining them with main clauses or rewriting them as main clauses. (You can do this exercise online at *ablongman.com/littlebrown*.)

Baby red-eared slider turtles are brightly colored. With bold patterns on their yellowish undershells. Which serve as a warning to predators. The bright colors of skunks and other animals. They signal that the animals will spray nasty chemicals. In contrast, the turtle's colors warn largemouth bass. That the baby turtle will actively defend itself. When a bass gulps down a turtle. The feisty baby claws and bites. Forcing the bass to spit it out. To avoid a similar painful experience. The bass will avoid other baby red-eared slider turtles. The turtle loses its bright colors as it grows too big. For a bass's afternoon snack.

Note See page 381 for an exercise involving sentence fragments along with comma splices, fused sentences, and other sentence errors.

CREATING PROBLEMS

If students have been assigned Chapter 18, "Comma Splices and Fused Sentences," along with this chapter, ask them to write sample sentences containing fused sentences, comma splices, and fragments. Then have them exchange papers and check to see if the errors have been executed properly. This exercise will help students recognize fused sentences, comma splices, and fragments. (It's much harder to create intentional errors, particularly sentence fragments, than most students will think.)

ANSWERS: EXERCISE 17.3

Possible revision

Baby red-eared slider turtles are brightly colored. Bold patterns on their yellowish undershells serve as a warning to predators. The bright colors of skunks and other animals signal that the animals will spray nasty chemicals. In contrast, the turtle's colors warn largemouth bass that the baby turtle will actively defend itself. When a bass gulps down a turtle, the feisty baby claws and bites, forcing the bass to spit it out. To avoid a similar painful experience, the bass will avoid other baby red-eared slider turtles. The turtle loses its bright colors as it grows too big for a bass's afternoon snack.

HIGHLIGHTS

This chapter begins with a summary of the accepted methods for punctuating consecutive main clauses and follows with advice for recognizing and correcting comma splices and fused sentences. Correction of comma splices and fused sentences may involve strategies that students should employ more frequently in their sentences, particularly subordination and use of the semicolon. To encourage variety in sentence structure along with the avoidance of error, exercises for the chapter ask students to combine sentences following different strategies as well as to recognize and revise comma splices and fused sentences.

It's important to remember that students will naturally commit more of these errors as they struggle to master more complex syntactic patterns. Although you want to point out their mistakes, be careful not to focus too tightly on punctuation errors that occur as they strive for stylistic growth.

RESOURCES AND IDEAS

Teachers and tutors who have little trouble punctuating sentences themselves may find it difficult to understand why some students have such difficulty with punctuation. In *The Practical Tutor* (New York: Oxford UP, 1987, 177–201), Emily Meyer and Louise Z. Smith offer detailed explanations of the causes of error and advice for diagnosing the roots of a student's punctuation difficulties. The teaching strategies they suggest include reading aloud, reading unpunctuated passages, asking probing questions (examples provided), and using simple diagrams. Rei R. Noguchi also offers innovative approaches to these errors in "Run-ons, Comma Splices, and Native-Speaker Abilities" in *Grammar and the Teaching of Writing: Limits and Possibilities* (Urbana: NCTE, 1991, 64–83).

COMPANION WEB SITE

See page IAE-55 for companion Web site content description.

CHAPTER **18**

Comma Splices and Fused Sentences

A sentence or main clause contains at least a subject and a predicate, which together express a complete thought (see p. 233). We can separate two consecutive main clauses in one of four ways:

- **With a period:**

  The ship was huge. Its mast stood eighty feet high.

- **With a semicolon:**

  The ship was huge; its mast stood eighty feet high.

- **With a comma preceding a coordinating conjunction** that joins the clauses and specifies the relation between them:

  The ship was huge, and its mast stood eighty feet high.

- **With a colon** when the second clause explains the first (see p. 477):

  The ship was huge: its mast stood eighty feet high.

The period, semicolon, or colon alone or the comma plus coordinating conjunction signals readers that one main clause (complete thought) is ending and another is beginning.

The comma splice and the fused sentence deprive readers of this signal and often force them to reread for sense. In a **comma splice** the two main clauses are joined (or spliced) *only* with a comma, not with a coordinating conjunction as well.

Comma splice
The ship was huge, its mast stood eighty feet high.

In a **fused sentence** no punctuation or coordinating conjunction appears between the main clauses.

Situations that may produce comma splices and fused sentences

- **The first clause is negative; the second, positive:**

  Splice Petric is not a nurse, she is a doctor.

  Revised Petric is not a nurse; she is a doctor.

- **The second clause amplifies or illustrates the first:**

  Fused She did well in college her average was 3.9.

  Revised She did well in college: her average was 3.9.

- **The second clause contains a conjunctive adverb or other transitional expression, such as *however* or *for example* (see p. 346):**

  Splice She had intended to become a biologist, however, medicine seemed more exciting.

  Revised She had intended to become a biologist; however, medicine seemed more exciting.

- **The subject of the second clause repeats or refers to the subject of the first clause:**

  Fused Petric is an internist she practices in Topeka.

  Revised Petric is an internist. She practices in Topeka.

- **Splicing or fusing is an attempt to link related ideas or to smooth choppy sentences:**

  Splice She is very committed to her work, she devotes almost all her time to patient care.

  Revised Because she is very committed to her work, she devotes almost all her time to patient care.

  Revised She is so committed to her work that she devotes almost all her time to patient care.

- **Words identifying the speaker divide a quotation between two complete sentences.** (See p. 444 for the punctuation to use in this case.)

  Splice "Medicine is a human frontier," Petric says, "The boundaries are unknown."

  Revised "Medicine is a human frontier," Petric says. "The boundaries are unknown."

Fused sentence

The ship was huge its mast stood eighty feet high.

Exception Experienced writers sometimes use a comma without a coordinating conjunction between very brief main clauses that are grammatically parallel:

He's not a person, he's a monster.

However, many readers view such punctuation as incorrect. Unless you are certain that your readers will not object to the comma in a sentence like this one, separate the clauses with periods or semicolons, as described in this chapter.

Note Grammar and style checkers can detect many comma splices, but they will miss most fused sentences. For example, a checker flagged *Money is tight, we need to spend carefully* but not *Money is tight we need to spend carefully*. A checker may also question sentences that are actually correct, such as *Money being tighter now than before, we need to spend carefully*. Verify that revision is actually needed on any flagged sentence.

CULTURE LANGUAGE An English sentence may not include more than one main clause unless the clauses are separated by a comma and a coordinating conjunction or by a semicolon or colon. If your native language does not have such a rule or has accustomed you to writing long sentences, you may need to edit your English writing especially for comma splices and fused sentences.

Comma Splices

18a Separate two main clauses with a comma *only* when they are joined by a coordinating conjunction.

A comma cannot separate main clauses unless they are linked by a coordinating conjunction (*and, but, or, nor, for, so, yet*). Readers expect the same main clause to continue after a comma alone. When they find themselves reading a second main clause before they realize they have finished the first, they may have to reread.

You have several options for revising comma splices.

▪ Making separate sentences

Revising a comma splice by making separate sentences from the main clauses will always be correct. The period is not only correct but preferable when the ideas expressed in the two main clauses are only loosely related:

Comma splice   Chemistry has contributed much to our understanding of foods, many foods such as wheat and beans can be produced in the laboratory.

Revised   Chemistry has contributed much to our understanding of foods. Many foods such as wheat and beans can be produced in the laboratory.

Revision of comma splices and fused sentences

1. **Underline the main clauses in your draft.**
2. **When two main clauses fall in the same sentence, check the connection between them.**
3. **If nothing falls between the clauses or only a comma does, revise in one of the following ways.** The revision depends on the relation you want to establish between the clauses. (See the text discussion for examples.)

   ■ Make the clauses into separate sentences.
   ■ Insert a comma followed by *and, but,* or another coordinating conjunction. Or, if the comma is already present, insert just the coordinating conjunction.
   ■ Insert a semicolon between clauses.
   ■ Subordinate one clause to the other.

CULTURE LANGUAGE Making separate sentences may be the best option if you are used to writing very long sentences in your native language and often write comma splices in English.

■ Inserting a coordinating conjunction

When the ideas in the main clauses are closely related and equally important, you may correct a comma splice by inserting the appropriate coordinating conjunction immediately after the comma to join the clauses:

Comma splice	Some laboratory-grown foods taste good, they are nutritious.
Revised	Some laboratory-grown foods taste good, and they are nutritious.

■ Using a semicolon

If the relation between the ideas expressed in the main clauses is very close and obvious without a conjunction, you can separate the clauses with a semicolon.

Comma splice	Good taste is rare in laboratory-grown vegetables, they are usually bland.
Revised	Good taste is rare in laboratory-grown vegetables; they are usually bland.

■ Subordinating one clause

When the idea in one clause is more important than that in the other, you can express the less important idea in a phrase or a sub-

IN CONTEXT

Identifying sentence problems in the context of an essay can be more challenging and rewarding than working with single-sentence examples. The content and flow of an essay can draw attention away from punctuation and sentence structure, making it hard to identify errors but also providing an experience similar to that of proofreading. To supplement the paragraph exercise at the end of this chapter (or at the end of Chapter 17), revise part of a professional essay to introduce errors (or find an error-filled student essay) and then distribute the essay to the class, asking students to locate and revise the errors.

ordinate clause. (See p. 253 for a list of subordinating conjunctions and pp. 398–402 for more on subordination.) Subordination is often more effective than forming separate sentences because it defines the relation between ideas more precisely:

Comma splice	The vitamins are adequate, the flavor is deficient.
Revised	The vitamins are adequate. The flavor is deficient. [Both ideas receive equal weight.]
Improved	Even though the vitamins are adequate, the flavor is deficient. [Emphasis on the second idea.]

18b Separate main clauses related by *however, for example,* and so on.

Two kinds of words that are not conjunctions describe how one main clause relates to another:

- **Conjunctive adverbs,** such as *consequently, finally, hence, however, indeed, therefore,* or *thus.* (See p. 261 for a longer list.)
- Other **transitional expressions,** such as *even so, for example, in fact, of course, to the right,* and *to this end.* (See pp. 86–87 for a longer list.)

When two main clauses are related by a conjunctive adverb or a transitional expression, they must be separated by a period or by a semicolon. The adverb or expression is also generally set off by a comma or commas (see p. 437):

Comma splice	Most Americans refuse to give up unhealthful habits, consequently our medical costs are higher than those of many other countries.
Revised	Most Americans refuse to give up unhealthful habits. Consequently, our medical costs are higher than those of many other countries.
Revised	Most Americans refuse to give up unhealthful habits; consequently, our medical costs are higher than those of many other countries.

Conjunctive adverbs and transitional expressions are different from coordinating conjunctions (*and, but,* and so on) and subordinating conjunctions (*although, because,* and so on):

- **Unlike conjunctions, conjunctive adverbs and transitional expressions do not join two clauses into a grammatical unit.** They merely describe the way two clauses relate in meaning.
- **Unlike conjunctions, conjunctive adverbs and transitional expressions can be moved within a clause** (see also p. 261). No

matter where in the clause an adverb or expression falls, though, the clause must be separated from another main clause by a period or semicolon.

Comma splice

The increased time devoted to watching television is not the only cause of the decline in reading ability, <u>however</u>, it is one of the important causes.

Period

The increased time devoted to watching television is not the only cause of the decline in reading ability. <u>However</u>, it is one of the important causes.

Semicolon

The increased time devoted to watching television is not the only cause of the decline in reading ability; <u>however</u>, it is one of the important causes.

The increased time devoted to watching television is not the only cause of the decline in reading ability; it is, <u>however</u>, one of the important causes.

EXERCISE 18.1   Identifying and revising comma splices

Correct each comma splice below in *two* of the ways described on pages 344–46. If an item contains no comma splice, mark the number preceding it. (You can do this exercise online at *ablongman.com/ littlebrown*.)

Example:
Carolyn still had a headache, she could not get the child-proof cap off the aspirin bottle.
Carolyn still had a headache <u>because</u> she could not get the child-proof cap off the aspirin bottle. [Subordination.]
Carolyn still had a headache, for she could not get the child-proof cap off the aspirin bottle. [Coordinating conjunction.]

1. Money has a long history, it goes back at least as far as the earliest records.
2. Many of the earliest records concern financial transactions, indeed, early history must often be inferred from commercial activity.
3. Every known society has had a system of money, though the objects serving as money have varied widely.
4. Sometimes the objects have had real value, in modern times, however, their value has been more abstract.
5. Cattle, fermented beverages, and rare shells have served as money, each one had actual value for the society.

ANSWERS: EXERCISE 18.1
Possible answers

1. Money has a long history. It goes back at least as far as the earliest records.
   Money has a long history that goes back at least as far as the earliest records.
2. Many of the earliest records concern financial transactions; indeed, early history must often be inferred from commercial activity.
   Many of the earliest records concern financial transactions. Indeed, early history must often be inferred from commercial activity.
3. No comma splice.
4. Sometimes the objects have had real value. In modern times, however, their value has been more abstract.
   Sometimes the objects have had real value; in modern times, however, their value has been more abstract.
5. Cattle, fermented beverages, and rare shells have served as money, and each one had actual value for the society.
   Cattle, fermented beverages, and rare shells have served as money. Each one had actual value for the society.

CREATING PROBLEMS

If students have been assigned Chapter 17, "Sentence Fragments," along with this chapter, ask them to write sample sentences containing comma splices, fused sentences, and fragments. Then have them exchange papers and check to see if the errors have been executed properly. This exercise will help students recognize comma splices, fused sentences, and fragments. (It's much harder to create intentional errors, particularly fused sentences and sentence fragments, than most students will think.)

ANSWERS: EXERCISE 18.2

Possible answers

1. Throughout history money and religion were closely linked <u>because</u> there was little distinction between government and religion.
   Throughout history money and religion were closely linked<u>, for</u> there was little distinction between government and religion.
2. The head of state and the religious leader were often the same person. <u>All</u> power rested in one ruler.
   The head of state and the religious leader were often the same person; all power rested in one ruler.
3. These powerful leaders decided what objects would serve as money<u>, and</u> their backing encouraged public faith in the money.
   These powerful leaders decided what objects would serve as money. <u>Their</u> backing encouraged public faith in the money.
4. <u>When</u> coins were minted of precious metals, the religious overtones of money were strengthened.
   Coins were minted of precious metals. <u>The</u> religious overtones of money were then strengthened.
5. People already believed the precious metals to be divine<u>, so</u> their use in money intensified its allure.
   People already believed the precious metals to be divine; their use in money intensified its allure.

Fused Sentences

18c **Combine two main clauses only with an appropriate conjunction or punctuation mark between them.**

When two main clauses are joined without a word to connect them or a punctuation mark to separate them, the result is a **fused sentence.** Fused sentences can rarely be understood on first reading, and they are never acceptable in standard written English.

> Fused   Our foreign policy is not well defined it confuses many countries.

Fused sentences may be corrected in the same ways as comma splices. See pages 344–46.

Separate sentences
Our foreign policy is not well defined<u>.</u> It confuses many countries.

Comma and coordinating conjunction
Our foreign policy is not well defined<u>, and</u> it confuses many countries.

Semicolon
Our foreign policy is not well defined<u>;</u> it confuses many countries.

Subordinating conjunction
<u>Because</u> our foreign policy is not well defined<u>,</u> it confuses many countries.

EXERCISE 18.2 Identifying and revising fused sentences

Revise each of the fused sentences below in *two* of the four ways shown above. (You can do this exercise online at *ablongman.com/littlebrown.*)

> *Example:*
> Tim was shy he usually refused invitations.
> Tim was shy<u>, so</u> he usually refused invitations.
> Tim was shy<u>;</u> he usually refused invitations.

1. Throughout history money and religion were closely linked there was little distinction between government and religion.
2. The head of state and the religious leader were often the same person all power rested in one ruler.
3. These powerful leaders decided what objects would serve as money their backing encouraged public faith in the money.
4. Coins were minted of precious metals the religious overtones of money were then strengthened.

5. People already believed the precious metals to be divine their use in money intensified its allure.

EXERCISE 18.3 Sentence combining: Comma splices and fused sentences

Combine each pair of sentences below into one sentence without creating a comma splice or fused sentence. Combine sentences by (1) supplying a comma and coordinating conjunction, (2) supplying a semicolon, or (3) subordinating one clause to the other. You will have to add, delete, or change words as well as punctuation. (You can do this exercise online at *ablongman.com/littlebrown*.)

Example:
The sun sank lower in the sky. The colors gradually faded.

As the sun sank lower in the sky, the colors gradually faded. [The first clause is subordinated to the second.]

1. The exact origin of paper money is unknown. It has not survived as coins, shells, and other durable objects have.
2. Perhaps goldsmiths were also bankers. Thus they held the gold of their wealthy customers.
3. The goldsmiths probably gave customers receipts for their gold. These receipts were then used in trade.
4. The goldsmiths were something like modern-day bankers. Their receipts were something like modern-day money.
5. The goldsmiths became even more like modern-day bankers. They began issuing receipts for more gold than they actually held in their vaults.

EXERCISE 18.4 Revising: Comma splices and fused sentences

Identify and revise the comma splices and fused sentences in the following paragraph. (You can do this exercise online at *ablongman.com/littlebrown*.)

All those parents who urged their children to eat broccoli were right, the vegetable really is healthful. Broccoli contains sulforaphane, moreover, this mustard oil can be found in kale and Brussels sprouts. Sulforaphane causes the body to make an enzyme that attacks carcinogens, these substances cause cancer. The enzyme speeds up the work of the kidneys then they can flush harmful chemicals out of the body. Other vegetables have similar benefits however, green, leafy vegetables like broccoli are the most efficient. Thus wise people will eat their broccoli it could save their lives.

Note See page 381 for an exercise involving comma splices and fused sentences along with other sentence errors.

ANSWERS: EXERCISE 18.3
Possible answers

1. The exact origin of paper money is unknown <u>because it</u> has not survived as coins, shells, and other durable objects have.
2. Perhaps goldsmiths were also bankers<u>;</u> thus they held the gold of their wealthy customers.
3. The goldsmiths probably gave customers receipts for their gold, <u>and</u> these receipts were then used in trade.
4. The goldsmiths were something like modern-day bankers<u>;</u> their receipts were something like modern-day money.
5. The goldsmiths became even more like modern-day bankers <u>when</u> they began issuing receipts for more gold than they actually held in their vaults.

TRANSPARENCY MASTER 18.2

ANSWERS: EXERCISE 18.4

All those parents who urged their children to eat broccoli were right<u>;</u> the vegetable really is healthful. Broccoli contains sulforaphane<u>;</u> moreover, this mustard oil can be found in kale and Brussels sprouts. Sulforaphane causes the body to make an enzyme that attacks carcinogens, <u>substances that</u> cause cancer. The enzyme speeds up the work of the kidneys <u>so that</u> they can flush harmful chemicals out of the body. Other vegetables have similar benefits<u>;</u> however, green, leafy vegetables like broccoli are the most efficient. Thus, wise people will eat their broccoli<u>;</u> it could save their lives.

mycomplab 2.0

Please visit MyCompLab at *www.mycomplab.com* for more on the writing process.

HIGHLIGHTS

Writers at all levels—advanced or struggling—will be likely to consult this chapter often, for problems with pronoun reference can arise in short, uncomplicated sentences as well as in papers that are ambitious in style and content. The discussion covers a number of particularly troublesome problems: unclear or ambiguous antecedents; broad reference with *this, that, which,* and *it;* indefinite use of *it* and *they;* and inappropriate use of *who, which,* and *that.* In each case, the discussion stresses the need for precision in reference as a way of ensuring that readers can follow the meaning of a passage. The examples and exercises mostly show reference problems within sentences as a way of keeping the discussion as simple and accessible as possible; however, the text points out that reference problems are just as likely to occur between sentences, and the paragraph exercise at the end of the chapter stresses this fact.

Because strings of pronouns are an important device for creating coherence over long stretches of discourse, reference problems between or among sentences can cause considerable misunderstanding. In this sense, pronoun reference errors can point to students' larger conceptual difficulties (such as defining or elaborating on key terms or thinking through a transition). This means that when students learn to recognize their pronoun reference errors, that recognition can provide the occasion for substantive revision and paragraph development.

COMPANION WEB SITE

See page IAE-55 for companion Web site content description.

CHAPTER 19

Pronoun Reference

A **pronoun** such as *it* or *they* derives its meaning from its **antecedent,** the noun it substitutes for. Therefore, a pronoun must refer clearly and unmistakably to its antecedent in order for the meaning to be clear. A sentence such as *Jim told Mark he was not invited* is not clear because the reader does not know whether *he* refers to Jim or to Mark.

One way to make pronoun reference clear is to ensure that the pronoun and antecedent agree in person, number, and gender (see p. 313). The other way is to ensure that the pronoun refers unambiguously to a single, close, specific antecedent.

Note Grammar and style checkers cannot recognize unclear pronoun reference. For instance, a checker did not spot any of the problems in Exercise 19.2 on page 356.

CULTURE LANGUAGE An English pronoun does need a clear antecedent nearby, but don't use both a pronoun and its antecedent as the subject of the same sentence or clause: *Jim* [not *Jim he*] *told Mark to go alone.* (See also pp. 375–76.)

19a Make a pronoun refer clearly to one antecedent.

When either of two nouns can be a pronoun's antecedent, the reference will not be clear:

Confusing Emily Dickinson is sometimes compared with Jane Austen, but she was quite different.

Revise such a sentence in one of two ways:

■ **Replace the pronoun with the appropriate noun:**

Clear Emily Dickinson is sometimes compared with Jane Austen, but Dickinson [or Austen] was quite different.

http://www.ablongman.com/littlebrown ▶

Visit the companion Web site for more help and additional exercises on pronoun reference.

Principal causes of unclear pronoun reference

■ **More than one possible antecedent** (facing page and below):

Confusing	To keep birds from eating seeds, soak <u>them</u> in blue food coloring.
Clear	To keep birds from eating seeds, soak <u>the seeds</u> in blue food coloring.

■ **Antecedent too far away** (p. 352):

Confusing	Employees should consult with their supervisor <u>who</u> require personal time.
Clear	Employees <u>who</u> require personal time should consult with their supervisor.

■ **Antecedent only implied** (p. 353):

Confusing	Many children begin reading on their own by watching television, but <u>this</u> should probably be discounted in government policy.
Clear	Many children begin reading on their own by watching television, but <u>such self-instruction</u> should probably be discounted in government policy.

See also pages 354–56.

■ **Avoid repetition by rewriting the sentence.** If you use the pronoun, make sure it has only one possible antecedent:

Clear	Despite occasional comparison, Emily Dickinson and Jane Austen were quite different.
Clear	Though sometimes compared with <u>her</u>, Emily Dickinson was quite different from Jane Austen.

Sentences that report what someone said, using verbs such as *said* or *told*, often require direct rather than indirect quotation:

Confusing	Juliet Noble told Ann Torre that <u>she</u> was next in line for the job.
Clear	Juliet Noble told Ann Torre, "I am next in line for the job."
Clear	Juliet Noble told Ann Torre, "You are next in line for the job."

Note Avoid the awkward device of using a pronoun followed by the appropriate noun in parentheses, as in the following example:

RETRIEVING SENTENCES

Reverse the process of sentence combining by asking students to reconstruct (or retrieve) the shorter (kernel) sentences that lie behind a long sentence containing a reference error. You may wish to use sentences from the text as a basis for the exercise. This activity will help students spot ambiguity or vague reference in the long sentence. After they have found the shorter sentences, ask students to recombine, this time avoiding the reference problem.

Original sentence: After the van hit John's car, its engine stopped running and its radiator started leaking.

Kernels: The van hit John's car. The van's engine stopped running. The van's radiator started leaking.

Recombined sentence: After the van hit John's car, the van's engine stopped running and its radiator started leaking.

OMITTED RELATIVE CLAUSE PRONOUNS

Sentences in which the relative clause pronoun is omitted often give ESL students difficulty, and they may make the mistake of adding an extra redundant pronoun. Give them a model sentence to help them remember the rule, such as the following:

We are going to the flea market that we read about in the newspaper.

This can be especially helpful when they are doing sentence-combining exercises, and they may want to keep a few of their own models in a computer file for handy reference. (See also 22a-2 for more on repeated sentence parts.)

| Weak | Noble and Torre had both hoped for the job, so <u>she</u> (Noble) was disappointed. |
| Improved | Noble was disappointed because she and Torre had both hoped for the job. |

19b Place a pronoun close enough to its antecedent to ensure clarity.

A clause beginning *who, which,* or *that* generally should fall immediately after the word to which it refers:

| Confusing | Jody found a lamp in the attic that her aunt had used. |
| Clear | In the attic Jody found a lamp that her aunt had used. |

Even when only one word could possibly serve as the antecedent of a pronoun, the relationship between the two may still be unclear if they are widely separated:

| Confusing | Jane Austen had little formal education but was well educated at home. Far from living an isolated life in the English countryside, the Austens were a large family with a wide circle of friends who provided entertainment and cultural enrichment. They also provided material for <u>her</u> stories. |
| Clear | Jane Austen had little formal education but was well educated at home. Far from living an isolated life in the English countryside, the Austens were a large family with a wide circle of friends who provided entertainment and cultural enrichment. They also provided material for <u>Jane Austen's</u> stories. |

EXERCISE 19.1 Revising: Ambiguous and remote pronoun reference

Rewrite the following sentences to eliminate unclear pronoun reference. If you use a pronoun in your revision, be sure that it refers to only one antecedent and that it falls close enough to its antecedent to ensure clarity. (You can do this exercise online at *ablongman.com/ littlebrown.*)

Example:
Saul found an old gun in the rotting shed that was just as his grandfather had left it.

In the rotting shed Saul found an old <u>gun that</u> was just as his grandfather had left it.

1. There is a difference between the heroes of the twentieth century and the heroes of earlier times: they have flaws in their characters.

2. Sports fans still admire Pete Rose, Babe Ruth, and Joe Namath even though they could not be perfect.
3. Fans liked Rose for having his young son serve as batboy when he was in Cincinnati.
4. The reputation Rose earned as a gambler and tax evader may overshadow his reputation as a ballplayer, but it will survive.
5. Rose amassed an unequaled record as a hitter, using his bat to do things no one else has ever done. It stands even though Rose was banned from baseball.

19c Make a pronoun refer to a specific antecedent, not an implied one.

A pronoun should refer to a specific noun or other pronoun. The reader can only guess at the meaning of a pronoun when its antecedent is implied by the context, not stated outright.

1 Use *this, that, which,* and *it* cautiously.

The most common kind of implied reference occurs when the pronoun *this, that, which,* or *it* refers to a whole idea or situation described in the preceding clause, sentence, or even paragraph. Such reference, often called **broad reference,** is acceptable only when the pronoun refers clearly to the entire preceding clause. In the following sentence, *which* could not possibly refer to anything but the whole preceding clause:

I can be kind and civil to people, which is more than you can.
—George Bernard Shaw

But if a pronoun might confuse a reader, you should avoid using it or provide an appropriate noun:

Confusing   The British knew little of the American countryside, and they had no experience with the colonists' guerilla tactics. This gave the colonists an advantage.

Clear   The British knew little of the American countryside, and they had no experience with the colonists' guerrilla tactics. This ignorance and inexperience gave the colonists an advantage.

2 Implied nouns are not clear antecedents.

A noun may be implied in some other word or phrase, as *happiness* is implied in *happy, driver* is implied in *drive,* and *mother*

RESOURCES AND IDEAS

Moskovit, Leonard. "When Is Broad Reference Clear?" *College Composition and Communication* 34 (1983): 454–69. The question of the acceptability of broad reference is a complicated one, as Moskovit points out, and anyone interested in looking at how broad reference operates in sophisticated prose will enjoy his essay.

CORRECTING A NARRATIVE

Find or write a brief narrative containing several events and more than one character. Introduce enough reference problems so that readers have difficulty unraveling the events. If you wish, include dialogue in the narrative in such a way that the reference problems make it hard to identify the speakers. (Using *He said* as a tag when there are two men in the narrative is one possibility.) Ask students to work in groups to untangle the problems in the narrative and to rewrite it, removing vague and ambiguous references.

is implied in *mother's*. But a pronoun cannot refer clearly to an implied noun, only to a specific, stated one:

Confusing	Cohen's report brought her a lawsuit.
Clear	Cohen was sued over her report.
Confusing	Her reports on psychological development generally go unnoticed outside it.
Clear	Her reports on psychological development generally go unnoticed outside the field.

3 Titles of papers are not clear antecedents.

The title of a paper is entirely separate from the paper itself, so a pronoun should not be used in the opening sentence of a paper to refer to the title:

Title	How to Row a Boat
Not	This is not as easy as it looks.
But	Rowing a boat is not as easy as it looks.

IT, WHICH, AND THEY

Distribute copies of a student paper that uses *it, which, they,* and other pronouns in sentences without supplying clear antecedents in preceding sentences. Ask students to work in groups to revise the reference problems. In each case ask the group to consider whether the revision simply involves correcting the error or whether it calls for the writer to clarify and develop his or her transition between sentences or paragraphs.

19d Use *it* and *they* to refer only to definite antecedents.

Although common in speech, using *it* and *they* to refer to indefinite antecedents is inappropriate in writing.

Confusing	In Chapter 4 of this book, it describes the early flights of the Wright brothers.
Clear	Chapter 4 of this book describes the early flights of the Wright brothers.
Confusing	Even in reality TV shows, they present a false picture of life.
Clear	Even reality TV shows present a false picture of life.

19e Use *you* only to mean "you, the reader."

You should clearly mean "you, the reader." The context must be appropriate for such a meaning:

| Inappropriate | In the fourteenth century you had to struggle simply to survive. |
| Revised | In the fourteenth century one [or a person] had to struggle simply to survive. |

Writers sometimes drift into *you* because *one, a person, the individual,* or a similar indefinite word can be difficult to sustain. Sentence after sentence, the indefinite word may sound stuffy, and it requires the sexist *he* or the awkward *he or she* for pronoun-antecedent agreement (see pp. 315–16). To avoid these difficulties, try using plural nouns and pronouns:

Original   In the fourteenth century one had to struggle simply to survive.

Revised   In the fourteenth century people had to struggle simply to survive.

19f   Use the pronoun *it* only one way in a sentence.

We use *it* idiomatically in expressions such as *It is raining.* We use *it* to postpone the subject in sentences such as *It is true that more jobs are available to women today.* And we use *it* as a personal pronoun in sentences such as *Nicole wanted the book, but she couldn't find it.* All these uses are standard, but two of them in the same passage can confuse the reader:

Confusing   It is true that the Constitution sets limits, but it is also flexible.

Clear   The Constitution does set limits, but it is also flexible.

19g   Use *who, which,* and *that* for appropriate antecedents.

The relative pronouns *who, which,* and *that* commonly refer to persons, animals, or things. *Who* refers most often to persons but may also refer to animals that have names:

Dorothy is the girl who visits Oz.
Her dog, Toto, who accompanies her, gives her courage.

Which refers to animals and things:

The Orinoco River, which is 1600 miles long, flows through Venezuela into the Atlantic Ocean.

That refers to animals and things and occasionally to persons when they are collective or anonymous:

The rocket that failed cost millions.
Infants that walk need constant tending.

(See also p. 437 for the use of *which* and *that* in nonessential and essential clauses.)

USE OF *THAT* OR *WHICH*

Students are often confused about whether to use *which, who,* or *that* because they misunderstand essential and nonessential elements. Students who suffer from this confusion should also consult Chapter 28 and *that/which* in the Glossary of Usage.

COLLABORATIVE LEARNING

Students can work productively together on Exercises 19.2 and 19.3. After they have completed both exercises, ask them to look for and revise instances of unclear pronoun references in other examples from each other's work. Each group might present one example of an unclear pronoun reference discovered in a student paper to the class.

ANSWERS: EXERCISE 19.2

Possible answers

1. "Life begins at forty" is a cliché many people live by, and this <u>saying</u> may well be true.
2. When <u>Pearl Buck</u> was forty, her novel *The Good Earth* won the Pulitzer Prize.
3. Buck was a novelist <u>who</u> wrote primarily about China.
4. In *The Good Earth* <u>the characters</u> have to struggle, but fortitude is rewarded.
5. Buck received much critical praise and earned over $7 million, but she was very modest about <u>her success</u> [*or* <u>the praise</u> *or* <u>the money</u>].
6. Kenneth Kaunda was elected to the <u>presidency of Zambia</u> in 1964, at age forty.
7. When Catherine I became empress of Russia at age forty, <u>the Russians</u> feared more than loved her.
8. At forty, Paul Revere made his famous ride to warn American revolutionary leaders that the British were going to arrest them. <u>His warning</u> gave the colonists time to prepare for battle.
9. <u>The members of the British House of Commons</u> did not welcome forty-year-old Nancy Astor as the first female member when she entered in 1919.
10. In 610 CE, Muhammad, age forty, began to have a series of visions that became the foundation of the Muslim faith. Since then, millions of people have become <u>Muslims</u>.

ANSWERS: EXERCISE 19.3

Possible revision

In Charlotte Brontë's *Jane Eyre*, <u>Jane</u> is a shy young woman <u>who</u> takes a job as governess. Her employer is a rude, brooding man named Rochester. He lives in a mysterious mansion on the English moors, <u>and both the mansion and the moors</u> contribute an eerie quality to Jane's expe-

The possessive *whose* generally refers to people but may refer to animals and things to avoid awkward and wordy *of which* constructions:

The book <u>whose</u> binding broke was rare. [Compare *The book <u>of which</u> the binding broke was rare.*]

EXERCISE 19.2 Revising: Indefinite and inappropriate pronoun reference

Many of the pronouns in the following sentences do not refer to specific, appropriate antecedents. Revise the sentences as necessary to make them clear. (You can do this exercise online at *ablongman.com/littlebrown.*)

Example:
In Glacier National Park, they have moose, elk, and wolves.
<u>Moose, elk, and wolves live</u> in Glacier National Park.

1. "Life begins at forty" is a cliché many people live by, and this may well be true.
2. When she was forty, Pearl Buck's novel *The Good Earth* won the Pulitzer Prize.
3. Buck was a novelist which wrote primarily about China.
4. In *The Good Earth* you have to struggle, but fortitude is rewarded.
5. Buck received much critical praise and earned over $7 million, but she was very modest about it.
6. Kenneth Kaunda, past president of Zambia, was elected to it in 1964, at age forty.
7. When Catherine I became empress of Russia at age forty, they feared more than loved her.
8. At forty, Paul Revere made his famous ride to warn American revolutionary leaders that the British were going to arrest them. This gave the colonists time to prepare for battle.
9. In the British House of Commons they did not welcome forty-year-old Nancy Astor as the first female member when she entered in 1919.
10. In 610 CE, Muhammad, age forty, began to have a series of visions that became the foundation of the Muslim faith. Since then, millions of people have become one.

EXERCISE 19.3 Revising: Pronoun reference

Revise the following paragraph so that each pronoun refers clearly to a single specific and appropriate antecedent. (You can do this exercise online at *ablongman.com/littlebrown.*)

In Charlotte Brontë's *Jane Eyre*, she is a shy young woman that takes a job as governess. Her employer is a rude, brooding man named Rochester. He lives in a mysterious mansion on the English moors, which contributes an eerie quality to Jane's experience. Eerier still are the fires, strange noises, and other unexplained happenings in the house; but Rochester refuses to discuss this. Eventually, they fall in love. On the day they are to be married, however, she learns that he has a wife hidden in the house. She is hopelessly insane and violent and must be guarded at all times, which explains his strange behavior. Heartbroken, Jane leaves the moors, and many years pass before they are reunited.

Note See page 381 for an exercise involving unclear pronoun reference along with sentence fragments, comma splices, and other sentence errors.

rience. Eerier still are the fires, strange noises, and other unexplained happenings in the house; but Rochester refuses to discuss <u>them</u>. Eventually, <u>Jane and Rochester</u> fall in love. On the day they are to be married, however, <u>Jane</u> learns that <u>Rochester</u> has a wife hidden in the house. <u>The wife</u> is hopelessly insane and violent and must be guarded at all times, <u>circumstances that explain Rochester's</u> strange behavior. Heartbroken, Jane leaves the moors, and many years pass before <u>she and Rochester</u> are reunited.

CHAPTER 20

Shifts

Inconsistencies in grammatical elements will confuse your readers and distort your meaning. In the following passage from a first draft, the underlining indicates confusing inconsistencies in verbs, nouns, and pronouns:

First draft

A bank commonly <u>owes</u> more to its customers than <u>is held</u> in reserve. <u>They kept</u> enough <u>assets</u> to meet reasonable withdrawals, but panicked <u>customers</u> may demand all their deposits. Then demands <u>will exceed</u> supplies, and <u>banks failed</u>. These days, <u>a person's</u> losses are not likely to be great because the government insures <u>your</u> deposits.

Revised

A bank commonly owes more to its customers than |it holds| in reserve. |It keeps| enough assets to meet reasonable withdrawals, but panicked customers may demand all their deposits. Then demands will exceed supplies, and |the bank| |will fail.| These days, the losses of |customers| are not likely to be great because the government insures |their| deposits.

Match *bank . . . owes*

Matches *bank*
Matches *will fail*
Matches *customers*
Matches *customers*

http://www.ablongman.com/littlebrown ▶

Visit the companion Web site for more help and additional exercises on shifts.

mycomplab 2.0

Please visit MyCompLab at *www.mycomplab.com* for more on the writing process.

HIGHLIGHTS

Shifts in person and number, in tense and mood, in subject and voice, or between direct and indirect quotation can be irritating to readers and occasionally make it hard to follow the meaning of a passage. Often, however, students are not fully aware of the shifts or their effect on a reader. This chapter describes in detail and illustrates the various shifts so that students can learn to identify the problems in their own writing. The exercises ask students to revise sentences and a longer passage, much as they will need to do in revising their own work.

COMPANION WEB SITE

See page IAE-55 for companion Web site content description.

Shifts like those in the first draft are likely to occur while you are trying to piece together meaning during drafting. But during editing you should make your sentences consistent in grammatical elements.

Note Grammar and style checkers cannot recognize most shifts in sentences. Proofread your work on your own, looking carefully for inconsistencies.

20a Keep a sentence or related sentences consistent in person and number.

Person in grammar refers to the distinction among the person talking (first person), the person spoken to (second person), and the person, object, or concept being talked about (third person). **Number** refers to the distinction between one (singular) and more than one (plural).

■ Shifts in person

Most shifts in person occur because we can refer to people in general, including our readers, either in the third person (*a person, one; people, they*) or in the second person (*you*):

People should not drive when they have been drinking.
One should not drive when he or she has been drinking.
You should not drive when you have been drinking.

Although any one of these possibilities is acceptable in an appropriate context, a mixture of them is inconsistent:

Inconsistent	If a person works hard, you can gain satisfaction.
Revised	If you work hard, you can gain satisfaction.
Revised	If a person works hard, he or she can gain satisfaction.
Better	If people work hard, they can gain satisfaction.

■ Shifts in number

Inconsistency in number occurs most often between a pronoun and its antecedent (see p. 313):

Inconsistent	If a student does not understand a problem, they should consult the instructor.
Revised	If a student does not understand a problem, he or she should consult the instructor.
Better	If students do not understand a problem, they should consult the instructor.
Or	A student who does not understand a problem should consult the instructor.

Note Generic nouns and most indefinite pronouns take singular pronouns with a definite gender: *he, she,* or *it.* When we use a generic noun like *student* or *person* or an indefinite pronoun like *everyone* or *each,* we often mean to include both males and females. To indicate this meaning, use *he or she* rather than *he* (as in the first of the preceding revisions) or, better still, rewrite in the plural or rewrite to avoid the pronoun (as in the second and third of the revisions). See page 316 for more discussion and examples.

Inconsistency in number can also occur between other words (usually nouns) that relate to each other in meaning.

Inconsistent	All the <u>boys</u> have a good <u>reputation</u>.
Revised	All the <u>boys</u> have good <u>reputations</u>.

The consistency in the revised sentence is called **logical agreement** because the nouns are consistent (the *boys* have *reputations,* not a single *reputation*).

EXERCISE 20.1   Revising: Shifts in person and number

Revise the following sentences to make them consistent in person and number. (You can do this exercise online at *ablongman.com/littlebrown.*)

Example:
A plumber will fix burst pipes, but they won't repair waterlogged appliances.
<u>Plumbers</u> will fix burst pipes, but they won't repair waterlogged appliances.

1. When a taxpayer is waiting to receive a tax refund from the Internal Revenue Service, you begin to notice what time the mail carrier arrives.
2. If the taxpayer does not receive a refund check within six weeks of filing a return, they may not have followed the rules of the IRS.
3. If a taxpayer does not include a Social Security number on a return, you will have to wait for a refund.
4. When taxpayers do not file their return early, they will not get a refund quickly.
5. If one makes errors on the tax form, they might even be audited, thereby delaying a refund even longer.

20b   Keep a sentence or related sentences consistent in tense and mood.

■ Shifts in tense

Within a sentence or from one sentence to another, certain changes in tense may be required to indicate changes in actual or relative time (see p. 296). The following changes are necessary:

ANSWERS: EXERCISE 20.1

1. When a taxpayer is waiting to receive a tax refund from the Internal Revenue Service, <u>he or she begins</u> to notice what time the mail carrier arrives. *Or:* When <u>taxpayers are</u> waiting to receive <u>tax refunds</u> . . . , <u>they</u> begin to notice what time the mail carrier arrives.
2. If the taxpayer does not receive a refund check within six weeks of filing a return, <u>he or she</u> may not have followed the rules of the IRS. *Or:* If <u>taxpayers do</u> not receive <u>refund checks</u> within six weeks of filing a return, they may not have followed the rules of the IRS.
3. If <u>taxpayers do</u> not include their Social Security <u>numbers</u> on <u>returns, they</u> will have to wait for <u>refunds.</u> *Or:* A taxpayer <u>who</u> does not include a Social Security number on a return will have to wait for a refund.
4. When taxpayers do not file their <u>returns</u> early, they will not get <u>refunds</u> quickly.
5. If <u>taxpayers make</u> errors on the tax <u>forms,</u> <u>they</u> might even be audited, thereby delaying <u>refunds</u> even longer. *Or:* If one has made errors on the tax form, <u>he or she</u> might even be audited, thereby delaying a refund even longer.

CULTURE LANGUAGE

TENSE SEQUENCING AND SHIFTS

ESL students may be particularly confused about how to tell the difference between correct tense sequencing and incorrect tense shifting. You might need to include a review of section 14h when you are teaching this topic.

Ramon <u>will graduate</u> from college thirty-one years after his father <u>arrived</u> in the United States.

But changes that are not required by meaning distract readers. Unnecessary shifts between past and present in passages narrating a series of events are particularly confusing:

| Inconsistent | Immediately after Booth <u>shot</u> Lincoln, Major Rathbone <u>threw</u> himself upon the <u>assassin</u>. But Booth <u>pulls</u> a knife and <u>plunges</u> it into the major's arm. |
| Revised | Immediately after Booth <u>shot</u> Lincoln, Major Rathbone <u>threw</u> himself upon the <u>assassin</u>. But Booth <u>pulled</u> a knife and <u>plunged</u> it into the major's arm. |

Use the present tense consistently to describe what an author has written, including the action in literature or a film:

| Inconsistent | The main character in the novel <u>suffers</u> psychologically because he <u>has</u> a clubfoot, but he eventually <u>triumphed</u> over his disability. |
| Revised | The main character in the novel <u>suffers</u> psychologically because he <u>has</u> a clubfoot, but he eventually <u>triumphs</u> over his disability. |

■ **Shifts in mood**

Shifts in the mood of verbs occur most frequently in directions when the writer moves between the imperative mood (*Unplug the appliance*) and the indicative mood (*You should unplug the appliance*). (See p. 299.) Directions are usually clearer and more concise in the imperative, as long as its use is consistent:

| Inconsistent | <u>Cook</u> the mixture slowly, and <u>you should stir</u> it until the sugar is dissolved. |
| Revised | <u>Cook</u> the mixture slowly, and <u>stir</u> it until the sugar is dissolved. |

EXERCISE 20.2   Revising: Shifts in tense and mood

Revise the following sentences to make them consistent in tense and mood. (You can do this exercise online at *ablongman.com/littlebrown*.)

Example:

Lynn ran to first, rounded the base, and keeps running until she slides into second.

Lynn ran to first, rounded the base, and <u>kept</u> running until she <u>slid</u> into second.

1. When your cholesterol count is too high, adjusting your diet and exercise level reduced it.

2. After you lowered your cholesterol rate, you decrease the chances of heart attack and stroke.
3. First eliminate saturated fats from your diet; then you should consume more whole grains and raw vegetables.
4. To avoid saturated fats, substitute turkey and chicken for beef, and you should use cholesterol-free salad dressing and cooking oil.
5. A regular program of aerobic exercise, such as walking or swimming, improves your cholesterol rate and made you feel much healthier.

20c Keep a sentence or related sentences consistent in subject and voice.

When a verb is in the **active voice**, the subject names the actor: *Linda passed the peas.* When a verb is in the **passive voice**, the subject names the receiver of the action: *The peas were passed [by Linda].* (See pp. 302–03.)

A shift in voice may sometimes help focus the reader's attention on a single subject, as in *The candidate campaigned vigorously and was nominated on the first ballot.* However, most shifts in voice also involve shifts in subject. They are unnecessary and confusing.

Inconsistent — Internet newsgroups cover an enormous range of topics for discussion. Forums for meeting people with like interests are provided in these groups.

Revised — Internet newsgroups cover an enormous range of topics for discussion and provide forums for meeting people with like interests.

EXERCISE 20.3 Revising: Shifts in subject and voice

Make the following sentences consistent in subject and voice. (You can do this exercise online at *ablongman.com/littlebrown*.)

Example:
At the reunion they ate hot dogs and volleyball was played.
At the reunion they ate hot dogs and played volleyball.

1. If students learn how to study efficiently, much better grades will be made on tests.
2. Conscientious students begin to prepare for tests immediately after the first class is attended.
3. Before each class all reading assignments are completed, and the students outline the material and answer any study questions.
4. In class they listen carefully and good notes are taken.
5. Questions are asked by the students when they do not understand the professor.

CLASS READING

Use the passage below, or find or write another that contains several kinds of shifts. Distribute copies to the class and read through the passage with students, asking them to identify the problems. This exercise will help make students aware of the different kinds of shifts as they appear in the context of an essay.

As soon as the avalanche was over, Jim pulls himself out of the snowbank and yells, "Where's everybody?" and were we still alive. As each of us in turn started digging out, you could see the damage the huge wall of snow had caused. The snow had destroyed the lodge and cars were swept away.

ANSWERS: EXERCISE 20.3

1. If students learn how to study efficiently, they will make much better grades on tests.
2. Conscientious students begin to prepare for tests immediately after they attend the first class.
3. Before each class the students complete all reading assignments, outline the material, and answer any study questions.
4. In class they listen carefully and take good notes.
5. The students ask questions when they do not understand the professor.

20d Keep a quotation or a question consistently direct or indirect.

Direct quotations or questions report the exact words of a quotation or question:

"I am the greatest," bragged Muhammad Ali.
In his day few people asked, "Is he right?"

Indirect quotations or questions report that someone said or asked something, but not in the exact words:

Muhammad Ali bragged that he was the greatest.
In his day few people asked whether he was right.

Shifts between direct and indirect quotations or questions are difficult to follow.

Shift in quotation	Kapek reported that the rats avoided the maze and "as of this writing, none responds to conditioning."
Revised (indirect)	Kapek reported that the rats avoided the maze and that as of his writing none responded to conditioning.
Revised (direct)	Kapek reported, "The rats avoid the maze. As of this writing, none responds to conditioning."
Shift in question	The reader wonders whether the experiment failed or did it perhaps succeed?
Revised (indirect)	The reader wonders whether the experiment failed or whether it perhaps succeeded.
Revised (direct)	Did the experiment fail? Or did it perhaps succeed?

For more on quotations, see pages 444–46 (commas with signal phrases such as *she said*), 469–75 (quotation marks), and 623–28 (integrating quotations into your writing). For more on questions, see pages 427–28.

EXERCISE 20.4 Revising: Shifts in direct and indirect quotations and questions

Revise each of the following sentences twice, once to make it consistently direct, once to make it consistently indirect. You will have to guess at the exact wording of direct quotations and questions that are now stated indirectly. (You can do this exercise online at *ablongman.com/littlebrown*.)

Example:

We all wonder what the next decade will bring and will we thrive or not?

COLLABORATIVE LEARNING

Students can create their own examples of direct and indirect quotations and questions, using the models provided in Exercise 20.4. Ask students to work through Exercise 20.4 in small groups and then to create two or three additional examples.

Alternatively, you might ask students to compare their independent responses to Exercises 20.1–20.4, then work in small groups to revise the paragraph in Exercise 20.5. This gives students the opportunity to help each other recognize shifts and to discuss the effects of unnecessary shifts. You might have each group present their responses to one or two sentences of the paragraph in Exercise 20.5 and encourage the presenters to foreground the group's questions and comments.

ANSWERS: EXERCISE 20.4

1. *Direct:* One anthropologist says, "The functions of marriage have changed, nowhere more dramatically than in industrialized cultures."
Indirect: One anthropologist says that the functions of marriage have changed, most dramatically in industrialized cultures.

Direct: What will the next decade bring? Will we thrive or not?

Indirect: We all wonder what the next decade will bring and whether we will thrive or not.

1. One anthropologist says that the functions of marriage have changed and "nowhere more dramatically than in industrialized cultures."
2. The question even arises of whether siblings may marry and would the union be immoral?
3. The author points out, "Sibling marriage is still illegal everywhere in the United States" and that people are still prosecuted under the law.
4. She says that incest could be considered a universal taboo and "the questions asked about the taboo vary widely."
5. Some ask is the taboo a way of protecting the family or whether it may be instinctive.

EXERCISE 20.5   Revising: Shifts

Revise the following paragraph to eliminate unnecessary shifts in person, number, tense, mood, and voice. (You can do this exercise online at *ablongman.com/littlebrown*.)

    Driving in snow need not be dangerous if you practice a few rules. First, one should avoid fast starts, which prevent the wheels from gaining traction and may result in the car's getting stuck. Second, drive more slowly than usual, and you should pay attention to the feel of the car: if the steering seemed unusually loose or the wheels did not seem to be grabbing the road, slow down. Third, avoid fast stops, which lead to skids. One should be alert for other cars and intersections that may necessitate that the brakes be applied suddenly. If you need to slow down, the car's momentum can be reduced by downshifting as well as by applying the brakes. When braking, press the pedal to the floor only if you have antilock brakes; otherwise, the pedal should be pumped in short bursts. If you feel the car skidding, the brakes should be released and the wheel should be turned into the direction of the skid, and then the brakes should be pressed or pumped again. If one repeated these motions, the skid would be stopped and the speed of the car would be reduced.

Note See page 381 for an exercise involving shifts along with sentence fragments, comma splices, and other sentence errors.

2. *Direct:* May siblings marry? Would the union be immoral?
   Indirect: The question even arises of whether siblings may marry and whether the union would be immoral.
3. *Direct:* The author points out, "Sibling marriage is still illegal everywhere in the United States, and people are still prosecuted under the law."
   Indirect: The author points out that sibling marriage is still illegal everywhere in the United States and that people are still prosecuted under the law.
4. *Direct:* She says, "Incest could be considered a universal taboo. The questions asked about the taboo vary widely."
   Indirect: She says that incest could be considered a universal taboo and that the questions asked about the taboo vary widely.
5. *Direct:* Is the taboo a way of protecting the family? Might it be instinctive?
   Indirect: Some ask whether the taboo is a way of protecting the family or whether it may be instinctive.

ANSWERS: EXERCISE 20.5

Possible revision

    Driving in snow need not be dangerous if you practice a few simple rules. First, <u>avoid</u> fast starts, which prevent the wheels from gaining traction and may result in the car's getting stuck. Second, drive more slowly than usual, and <u>pay</u> attention to the feel of the car: if the steering <u>seems</u> unusually loose or the wheels <u>do not seem</u> to be grabbing the road, slow down. Third, avoid fast stops, which lead to skids. <u>Be alert</u> for other cars and intersections that may necessitate <u>applying the brakes</u> suddenly. If you need to slow down, <u>reduce the car's momentum</u> by downshifting as well as by applying the brakes. When braking, press the pedal to the floor only if you have antilock brakes; otherwise, <u>pump the pedal</u> in short bursts. If you feel the car skidding, <u>release the brakes, turn the wheel</u> into the direction of the skid, and then <u>press or pump the brakes</u> again. <u>Repeating these motions <u>will stop the skid</u> and <u>reduce the speed</u> of the car.

mycomplab
Please visit MyCompLab at *www.mycomplab.com* for more on the writing process.

HIGHLIGHTS

Misplaced and dangling modifiers often interest students because the faulty constructions can be amusing. To tie together all the different problems discussed in the chapter, however, you may want to point out that they all illustrate the importance of position and arrangement in sentences. Split constructions (21d and 21e) conveniently emphasize the need to keep the parts of related syntactic groups clearly unified. Yet both standard speech and formal writing provide frequent examples of freely placed limiting modifiers and of split infinitives. Part of our difficulty in teaching composition is in giving students effective advice about when freedom is constructive and when it is confusing. As in all such matters, the advice of the handbook is largely conservative; you may therefore want to modify it somewhat.

COMPANION WEB SITE

See page IAE-55 for companion Web site content description.

CHAPTER 21

Misplaced and Dangling Modifiers

In reading a sentence in English, we depend principally on the arrangement of the words to tell us how they are related. In writing, we may create confusion if we fail to connect modifiers to the words they modify.

Note Grammar and style checkers cannot recognize most problems with modifiers. For instance, a checker failed to flag the misplaced modifiers in *Gasoline high prices affect usually car sales* or the dangling modifier in *The vandalism was visible passing the building.*

Misplaced Modifiers

A modifier is **misplaced** if readers can't easily relate it to the word it modifies. Misplaced modifiers may be awkward, confusing, or even unintentionally funny.

21a Place modifiers where they will clearly modify the words intended.

Readers tend to link a modifying word, phrase, or clause to the nearest word it could modify: *I saw a man in a green hat.* Thus the writer must place the phrase so that it clearly modifies the intended word and not some other.

Confusing	He served steak to the men on paper plates.
Revised	He served the men steak on paper plates.
Confusing	Many dogs are killed by automobiles and trucks roaming unleashed.

http://www.ablongman.com/littlebrown ▶

Visit the companion Web site for more help and additional exercises on misplaced and dangling modifiers.

Revised   Many dogs roaming unleashed are killed by automobiles and trucks.

Confusing   This is the only chocolate chip cookie in a bag that tastes like Mom's. [Actual advertisement.]

Revised   This is the only bagged [or packaged] chocolate chip cookie that tastes like Mom's.

EXERCISE 21.1   Revising: Misplaced phrases and clauses

Revise the following sentences so that phrases and clauses clearly modify the appropriate words. (You can do this exercise online at *ablongman.com/littlebrown*.)

Example:
I came to enjoy flying over time.
Over time I came to enjoy flying.

1. Women have contributed much to knowledge and culture of great value.
2. Emma Willard founded the Troy Female Seminary, the first institution to provide a college-level education for women in 1821.
3. Sixteen years later Mary Lyon founded Mount Holyoke Female Seminary, the first true women's college with directors and a campus who would sustain the college even after Lyon's death.
4. *Una* was the first US newspaper, which was founded by Pauline Wright Davis in 1853, that was dedicated to gaining women's rights.
5. Mitchell's Comet was discovered in 1847, which was named for Maria Mitchell.

21b   Place limiting modifiers carefully.

Limiting modifiers include *almost, even, exactly, hardly, just, merely, nearly, only, scarcely,* and *simply.* In speech these modifiers often occur before the verb, regardless of the words they are intended to modify. In writing, however, these modifiers should fall immediately before the word or word group they modify to avoid any ambiguity:

Unclear   She only found that fossil on her last dig.

Revised   She found only that fossil on her last dig.

Revised   She found that fossil only on her last dig.

ANSWERS: EXERCISE 21.1

1. Women have contributed much of great value to knowledge and culture.
2. In 1821 Emma Willard founded the Troy Female Seminary, the first institution to provide a college-level education for women.
3. Sixteen years later Mary Lyon founded Mount Holyoke Female Seminary, the first true women's college with a campus and directors who would sustain the college even after Lyon's death.
4. *Una*, which was founded by Pauline Wright Davis in 1853, was the first US newspaper that was dedicated to gaining women's rights.
5. Mitchell's Comet, which was named for Maria Mitchell, was discovered in 1847.

MOVING ONLY

Ask students to create sentences whose meaning changes as a modifier like *only* moves from place to place:

Only students were asked to bring gym shorts and running shoes.
Students were *only* asked to bring gym shorts and running shoes.
Students were asked *only* to bring gym shorts and running shoes.
Students were asked to bring *only* gym shorts and running shoes.

COLLABORATIVE LEARNING

LIMITING AND SQUINTING MODIFIERS

Students can work productively together (in pairs or small groups) on Exercises 21.2 and 21.3. This collaborative effort can be particularly useful when students are asked to create more than one possible revision.

ANSWERS: EXERCISE 21.2

Possible answers

1. <u>Almost</u> everybody hates him.
   Everybody <u>almost</u> hates him.
2. <u>Even</u> now <u>I</u> remember the details of the event.
   Now I remember <u>even</u> the details of the event.
3. We <u>hardly</u> heard him call our names.
   We heard him <u>hardly</u> call our names.
4. Write <u>simply</u>.
   <u>Simply</u> write.
5. I <u>nearly</u> missed the performance that was booed off the stage.
   I missed the performance that was <u>nearly</u> booed off the stage.

ANSWERS: EXERCISE 21.3

1. People who <u>often</u> sunbathe can damage their skin. *Or:* People who sunbathe can <u>often</u> damage their skin.
2. Sunbathers who <u>frequently</u> apply a sunscreen block some of the sun's harmful rays. *Or:* <u>Frequently</u>, sunbathers who apply a sunscreen block some of the sun's harmful rays.
3. Men and women who <u>often</u> lie out in the sun have leathery, dry <u>skin</u>. *Or:* <u>Often</u> men and women who lie out in the sun have leathery, dry skin.
4. Doctors tell sunbathers they risk skin cancer <u>when they are older</u>. *Or:* Doctors tell <u>older</u> sunbathers they risk skin cancer.
5. People who <u>usually</u> stay out of the sun will have better <u>skin</u> and fewer chances of skin cancer. *Or:* People who stay out of the sun will <u>usually</u> have better skin and fewer chances of skin cancer.

Use each of the following limiting modifiers in two versions of the same sentence. (You can do this exercise online at *ablongman.com/littlebrown.*)

> *Example:*
> only
> He is the <u>only</u> one I like. He is the one <u>only</u> I like.

1. almost   3. hardly   5. nearly
2. even   4. simply

21c | Make each modifier refer to only one grammatical element.

A modifier can modify only *one* element in a sentence—the subject, the verb, or some other element. A **squinting modifier** seems confusingly to refer to either of two words:

Squinting   Snipers who fired on the soldiers often escaped capture.

Clear   Snipers who often fired on the soldiers escaped capture.

Clear   Snipers who fired on the soldiers escaped capture often.

When an adverb modifies an entire main clause, as in the last example, it can usually be moved to the beginning of the sentence: *Often, snipers who fired on the soldiers escaped capture.*

Revise each sentence twice so that the squinting modifier applies clearly first to one element and then to the other. (You can do this exercise online at *ablongman.com/littlebrown.*)

> *Example:*
> The work that he hoped would satisfy him completely frustrated him.
>
> The work that he hoped would <u>completely</u> satisfy him frustrated him.
>
> The work that he hoped would satisfy him frustrated him <u>completely</u>.

1. People who sunbathe often can damage their skin.
2. Sunbathers who apply a sunscreen frequently block some of the sun's harmful ultraviolet rays.
3. Men and women who lie out in the sun often have leathery, dry skin.
4. Doctors tell sunbathers when they are older they risk skin cancer.
5. People who stay out of the sun usually will have better skin and fewer chances of skin cancer.

21d Keep subjects, verbs, and objects together.

English sentences tend to move from subject to verb to object. The movement is so familiar that modifiers between these elements can be awkward.

A subject and verb may be separated by an adjective that modifies the subject: *Kuwait, which has a population of 1.3 million, is a rich nation.* But an adverb of more than a word usually stops the flow of the sentence:

Awkward
subject ⌐————— adverb —————⌐ verb
Kuwait, after the first Gulf War ended in 1991, began returning to normal.

Revised
⌐————— adverb —————⌐ subject verb
After the first Gulf War ended in 1991, Kuwait began returning to normal.

Even a one-word adverb will be awkward between a verb and its object:

Awkward
⌐ verb ⌐ adverb object
The war had damaged badly many of Kuwait's oil fields.

Revised
⌐ verb ⌐ object
The war had badly damaged many of Kuwait's oil fields.
adverb

21e Keep parts of infinitives or verb phrases together.

An **infinitive** consists of the marker *to* plus the plain form of a verb: *to produce, to enjoy.* The two parts of the infinitive are widely regarded as a grammatical unit that should not be split:

Awkward
infinitive
The weather service expected temperatures to not rise.

Revised
infinitive
The weather service expected temperatures not to rise.

A split infinitive may sometimes be natural and preferable, though it may still bother some readers:

infinitive
Several US industries expect to more than triple their use of robots.

Here the split infinitive is more economical than the alternatives, such as *Several US industries expect to increase their use of robots by more than three times.*

A **verb phrase** consists of a helping verb plus a main verb, as in *will call, was going, had been writing* (see p. 277). A single-word adverb may be inserted after the helping verb in a verb phrase (or the first helping verb if more than one): *Scientists have lately been using spacecraft to study the sun.* But when longer adverbs interrupt verb phrases, the result is almost always awkward:

THE MEDIA

Radio and television newscasts are rich sources of dangling and misplaced modifiers, perhaps because reporters have little time to pay attention to the structure of their sentences. Have students listen to newscasts and record errors: doing so will help them to understand the perspective of a reader who comes across similar errors in an essay. Newspaper headlines and public announcements are also rich sources; from time to time, magazine articles and paperback books appear with collections of particularly humorous errors. But students will be able to find many on their own by looking at the newspaper for headlines like *Young man slain with flowers.*

COLLABORATIVE LEARNING

HOME-GROWN STAR REPORTERS

Ask students to form groups in order to write their own newscasts filled with the kinds of errors they might spot through the activity above. The newscasts (and the errors) should be plausible in style and content, though the content will probably have to be the product of students' imaginations. Having heard many newscasts, however, students will probably have little trouble parodying them in form and matter.

helping
verb ┌─────────── adverb ───────────┐
Awkward   The spacecraft *Ulysses* will after traveling close to the sun
main verb
report on the sun's energy fields.

┌────────────── adverb ──────────────┐
Revised   After traveling close to the sun, the spacecraft *Ulysses*
verb phrase
will report on the sun's energy fields.

CULTURE LANGUAGE In an English question, place a one-word adverb after the first helping verb and the subject:

helping   rest of
verb   subject   adverb   verb phrase
Will spacecraft ever be able to leave the solar system?

EXERCISE 21.4   Revising: Separated sentence parts

Revise the following sentences to connect separated parts (subject-predicate, verb-object, verb phrase, infinitive). (You can do this exercise online at *ablongman.com/littlebrown*.)

Example:
Most children have by the time they are seven lost a tooth.
By the time they are seven, most children have lost a tooth.

1. Myra Bradwell founded in 1868 the *Chicago Legal News*.
2. Bradwell was later denied, although she had qualified, admission to the Illinois Bar Association.
3. In an attempt to finally gain admission to the bar, she carried the case to the Supreme Court, but the justices decided against her.
4. Bradwell was determined that no other woman would, if she were qualified, be denied entrance to a profession.
5. The Illinois legislature finally passed, in response to Bradwell's persuasion, a bill ensuring that no one on the basis of gender would be restricted from a profession.

21f   Position adverbs with care. **CULTURE LANGUAGE**

A few adverbs are subject to conventions that can trouble non-native speakers of English.

■ Adverbs of frequency

Adverbs of frequency include *always, never, often, rarely, seldom, sometimes,* and *usually.* They appear at the beginning of a sentence, before a one-word verb, or after the helping verb in a verb phrase:

verb phrase   adverb
Awkward   Robots have put sometimes humans out of work.

ANSWERS: EXERCISE 21.4

1. In 1868 Myra Bradwell founded the *Chicago Legal News.*
2. Although she had qualified, Bradwell was later denied admission to the Illinois Bar Association.
3. In an attempt finally *to* gain admission to the bar, she carried the case to the Supreme Court, but the justices decided against her.
4. Bradwell was determined that no other woman would be denied entrance to a profession if she were qualified.
5. In response to Bradwell's persuasion, the Illinois legislature finally passed a bill ensuring that no one would be restricted from a profession on the basis of gender.

| | helping verb | adverb | main verb |
| Revised | Robots have <u>sometimes</u> put humans out of work. | | |

| | adverb | verb phrase |
| Revised | <u>Sometimes</u> robots have put humans out of work. | |

Adverbs of frequency always follow the verb *be:*

| | adverb verb |
| Awkward | Robots <u>often</u> are helpful to workers. |

| | verb adverb |
| Revised | Robots are <u>often</u> helpful to workers. |

■ Adverbs of degree

Adverbs of degree include *absolutely, almost, certainly, completely, especially, extremely, hardly,* and *only.* They fall just before the word modified (an adjective, another adverb, sometimes a verb).

| | adjective adverb |
| Awkward | Robots have been useful <u>especially</u> in making cars. |

| | adverb adjective |
| Revised | Robots have been <u>especially</u> useful in making cars. |

■ Adverbs of manner

Adverbs of manner include *badly, beautifully, openly, sweetly, tightly, well,* and others that describe how something is done. They usually fall after the verb:

| | adverb verb |
| Awkward | Robots <u>smoothly</u> work on assembly lines. |

| | verb adverb |
| Revised | Robots work <u>smoothly</u> on assembly lines. |

■ The adverb *not*

When the adverb *not* modifies a verb, place it after the helping verb (or the first helping verb if more than one):

| | helping main verb verb |
| Awkward | Robots do think <u>not</u>. |

| | helping main verb verb |
| Revised | Robots do <u>not</u> think. |

Place *not* after a form of *be: Robots are <u>not</u> thinkers.*

When *not* modifies another adverb or an adjective, place it before the other modifier: *Robots are <u>not</u> sleek machines.*

21g   Arrange adjectives appropriately. CULTURE LANGUAGE

English follows distinctive rules for arranging two or three adjectives before a noun. (A string of more than three adjectives be-

MODIFICATIONS OF MODIFICATION RULES

ESL students may make errors with modifiers because of insufficient knowledge of adjective order and agreement. For instance, in many languages (Spanish, Korean, Vietnamese, Armenian, and others) adjectives follow the nouns they modify ("the sky blue" instead of "the blue sky"). Spanish speakers may make adjectives agree in number with the nouns they modify ("the greys clouds" instead of "the grey clouds"). To help your ESL students remember the English rules and to give your native English-speaking students some exposure to other languages' rules, have your ESL students teach the rest of the class how modifier word order and agreement works in their native language.

fore a noun is rare.) The order depends on the meaning of the adjectives, as indicated in the following table:

Determiner	Opinion	Size or shape	Color	Origin	Material	Noun used as adjective	Noun
many						state	**laws**
	striking		green	Thai			**birds**
a	fine			German			**camera**
this		square			wooden		**table**
all						business	**reports**
the			blue		litmus		**paper**

See page 442 for guidelines on punctuating two or more adjectives before a noun.

EXERCISE 21.5   Revising: Placement of adverbs and adjectives

CULTURE LANGUAGE Revise the sentences below to correct the positions of adverbs or adjectives. If a sentence is already correct as given, circle the number preceding it. (You can do this exercise online at *ablongman .com/littlebrown*.)

Example:
Gasoline high prices affect usually car sales.
High gasoline prices usually affect car sales.

1. Some years ago Detroit cars often were praised.
2. Luxury large cars especially were prized.
3. Then a serious oil shortage led drivers to value small foreign cars that got good mileage.
4. When gasoline ample supplies returned, consumers bought again American large cars.
5. However, the large cars not were luxury sedans but vans and sport-utility vehicles.

Dangling Modifiers

21h   Relate dangling modifiers to their sentences.

A **dangling modifier** does not sensibly modify anything in its sentence:

Dangling   Passing the building, the vandalism became visible. ⟶ ⑦

Dangling modifiers usually introduce sentences, contain a verb form, and imply but do not name a subject: in the preceding

---

ANSWERS: EXERCISE 21.5

1. Some years ago Detroit cars <u>were often</u> praised.
2. <u>Large luxury</u> cars <u>were especially</u> prized.
3. Sentence correct.
4. When <u>ample gasoline</u> supplies returned, consumers <u>again bought</u> <u>large American</u> cars.
5. However, the large cars <u>were not</u> luxury sedans but vans and sport-utility vehicles.

COLLABORATIVE LEARNING

COLLECTING HOWLERS

An amusing exercise is to have students collect examples of misplaced and dangling modifiers to share; reward the team that collects the most examples with a prize like a day's extension on the next assignment. The "finds" may include some particularly funny ones like this: *Stitched on 14-count canvas, your daughter will enjoy learning to cross-stitch.*

example, the implied subject is the someone or something passing the building. Readers assume that this implied subject is the same as the subject of the sentence (*vandalism* in the example). When it is not, the modifier "dangles" unconnected to the rest of the sentence.

Certain modifiers are the most likely to dangle:

- **Participial phrases:**

  Dangling | Passing the building, the vandalism became visible.
  Revised | <u>As we passed</u> the building, the vandalism became visible.

- **Infinitive phrases:**

  Dangling | To understand the causes, vandalism has been extensively investigated.
  Revised | To understand the causes, <u>researchers have</u> extensively <u>investigated</u> vandalism.

- **Prepositional phrases in which the object of the preposition is a gerund:**

  Dangling | After studying the problem, vandals are now thought to share certain characteristics.
  Revised | After studying the problem, <u>researchers think that</u> vandals share certain characteristics.

- **Elliptical clauses in which the subject and perhaps the verb are omitted:**

  Dangling | When destructive, researchers have learned that vandals are more likely to be in groups.
  Revised | When <u>vandals are</u> destructive, researchers have learned, <u>they</u> are more likely to be in groups.

Dangling modifiers are especially likely when the verb in the main clause is in the **passive voice** instead of the **active voice,** as in *vandalism has been investigated* and *vandals are thought.* (See pp. 302–03 for more on the passive voice.)

Note A modifier may be dangling even when the sentence elsewhere contains a word the modifier might seem to describe, such as *vandals* below:

  Dangling | When destructive, researchers have learned that vandals are more likely to be in groups.

In addition, a dangling modifier may fall at the end of a sentence:

  Dangling | The vandalism was visible passing the building.

RESOURCES AND IDEAS

Chaika, Elaine. "Grammars and Teaching." *College English* 39 (1978): 770–83. Chaika offers fresh explanations from a linguistic perspective for a number of standard errors, including dangling modifiers.

Pixton, William H. "The Dangling Gerund: A Working Definition." *College Composition and Communication* 24 (1973): 193–99. Pixton reviews discussions of dangling modifiers and, using a variety of sample sentences, formulates a definition of the dangling gerund.

Have students work in small groups to discuss their responses to Exercises 21.6 and 21.7. Then ask each group to complete Exercise 21.8 together and present part of the revised paragraph to the class. As each group gives its presentation, encourage other groups to contribute their differing revisions of the same sentences. This helps students to become more aware of the numerous possibilities for revision.

ANSWERS: EXERCISE 21.6

Possible answers

1. After Andrew Jackson had accomplished many deeds of valor, his fame led to his election to the presidency in 1828 and 1832.
2. By the time Jackson was fourteen, both of his parents had died.
3. To aid the American Revolution, Jackson chose service as a mounted courier.

Identifying and revising dangling modifiers

- **Identify the modifier's subject.** If the modifier lacks a stated subject (as *when in diapers* does), identify what the modifier describes.
- **Compare the subject of the modifier and the subject of the sentence.** Verify that what the modifier describes is in fact the subject of the main clause. If it is not, the modifier probably dangles.
- **Revise as needed.** Either (*a*) recast the dangling modifier with a stated subject of its own, or (*b*) change the subject of the main clause to be what the modifier describes.

Dangling   When in diapers, my mother remarried.

Revision *a*   When I was in diapers, my mother remarried.

Revision *b*   When in diapers, I attended my mother's second wedding.

■ **Revising dangling modifiers**

Revise most dangling modifiers in one of two ways, depending on what you want to emphasize in the sentence.

- **Change the subject of the main clause to a word the modifier properly describes:**

Dangling   To express themselves, graffiti decorate walls.

Revised   To express themselves, some youths decorate walls with graffiti.

- **Rewrite the dangling modifier as a complete clause with its own stated subject and verb:**

Revised   Because some youths need to express themselves, graffiti decorate walls.

EXERCISE 21.6   Revising: Dangling modifiers

Revise the following sentences to eliminate any dangling modifiers. Each item has more than one possible answer. (You can do this exercise online at *ablongman.com/littlebrown*.)

Example:

Driving north, the vegetation became increasingly sparse.

Driving north, we noticed that the vegetation became increasingly sparse.

As we drove north, the vegetation became increasingly sparse.

1. After accomplishing many deeds of valor, Andrew Jackson's fame led to his election to the presidency in 1828 and 1832.

2. By the age of fourteen, both of Jackson's parents had died.
3. To aid the American Revolution, service as a mounted courier was chosen by Jackson.
4. Though not well educated, a successful career as a lawyer and judge proved Jackson's ability.
5. Winning many military battles, the American public believed in Jackson's leadership.

EXERCISE 21.7 Sentence combining: Placing modifiers

Combine each pair of sentences below into a single sentence by rewriting one as a modifier. Make sure the modifier applies clearly to the appropriate word. You will have to add, delete, and rearrange words, and you may find that more than one answer is possible in each case. (You can do this exercise online at *ablongman.com/littlebrown.*)

Example:

Bob demanded a hearing from the faculty. Bob wanted to appeal the decision.

Wanting to appeal the decision, Bob demanded a hearing from the faculty.

1. Evening falls in the Central American rain forests. The tungara frogs begin their croaking chorus.
2. Male tungara frogs croak loudly at night. The "songs" they sing are designed to attract female frogs.
3. But predators also hear the croaking. They gather to feast on the frogs.
4. The predators are lured by their croaking dinners. The predators include bullfrogs, snakes, bats, and opossums.
5. The frogs hope to mate. Their nightly chorus can result in death instead.

EXERCISE 21.8 Revising: Misplaced and dangling modifiers

Revise the following paragraph to eliminate any misplaced or dangling modifiers. (You can do this exercise online at *ablongman.com/littlebrown.*)

Central American tungara frogs silence several nights a week their mating croaks. When not croaking, the chance that the frogs will be eaten by predators is reduced. The frogs seem to fully believe in "safety in numbers." They more than likely will croak along with a large group rather than by themselves. By forgoing croaking on some nights, the frogs' behavior prevents the species from "croaking."

Note See page 381 for an exercise involving misplaced and dangling modifiers along with other sentence errors.

SENTENCE COMBINING

Exercise 21.7 requires students to combine pairs of sentences whose content and structure make them likely causes of misplaced or dangling modifiers. Extend this activity by having students create their own sentences that would be easy to miscombine. Choose the best pairs, copy them, and have the class do them for an exercise. This activity leads to considerable discussion and some imaginative and amusing results when the students work in groups.

ANSWERS: EXERCISE 21.7

Possible answers

1. As evening falls in the Central American rain forests, the tungara frogs begin their croaking chorus.
2. Croaking loudly at night, male tungara frogs sing "songs" designed to attract female frogs.
3. But predators, also hearing the croaking, gather to feast on the frogs.
4. Lured by their croaking dinners, the predators include bullfrogs, snakes, bats, and opossums.
5. Although the frogs hope to mate, their nightly chorus can result in death instead.

ANSWERS: EXERCISE 21.8

Possible revision

Several nights a week, Central American tungara frogs silence their mating croaks. When not croaking, they reduce the chance that they will be eaten by predators. The frogs seem to believe fully in "safety in numbers." More than likely, they will croak along with a large group rather than by themselves. By forgoing croaking on some nights, the frogs prevent the species from "croaking."

Also shown above in the answer column (items 4 and 5):

4. Though not well educated, Jackson proved his ability in a successful career as a lawyer and judge.
5. Because Jackson won many military battles, the American public believed in his leadership.

HIGHLIGHTS

The first two sections of Chapter 22 treat sentences whose subjects and predicates are incompatible. The tangled sentences in some student writing have more complex causes than this brief discussion of mixed sentences can address. But the two most common problems do seem to be subjects and predicates that are incompatible in grammar and in meaning.

The third section deals with compound constructions that are grammatically or idiomatically incomplete. Ill-prepared students seem to encounter this problem less often than better-prepared students do, perhaps because only the latter use such constructions. On the other hand, incomplete comparisons (22d) are common, and you may wish to call particular attention to them.

The final section, covering omission of needed words, is designed primarily as an aid to grading papers. Instructors who notice words missing in a student essay can call attention to the problem by using the number-and-letter code to refer students to this section.

USING STUDENT WRITING

Because the mixed and incomplete sentences in student writing have complicated causes and because the problems in one student's essay are likely to differ widely from those in another student's paper, most instructors choose simply to discuss the chapter and use some of the exercises rather than to elaborate with classroom activities and assignments. In working with individual students, however, most instructors are able to devise activities that suit individual needs. Instructors who wish to alert students to the problem of incomplete compound constructions, incomplete comparisons, and omission of needed words can draw from a student paper or write a passage containing these problems and then ask students

COMPANION WEB SITE

See page IAE-56 for companion Web site content description.

CHAPTER 22

Mixed and Incomplete Sentences

Mixed Sentences

A **mixed sentence** contains two or more parts that are incompatible—that is, the parts do not fit together. The misfit may be in grammar or in meaning.

Note Grammar and style checkers may recognize a simple mixed construction such as *reason is because,* but they will fail to flag most mixed sentences.

22a　Untangle sentences that are mixed in grammar.

Sentences mixed in grammar combine two or more incompatible grammatical structures.

1　Make sure subject and verb fit together grammatically.

A mixed sentence may occur when you start a sentence with one plan and end it with another:

Mixed	┌── modifier (prepositional phrase) ──┐ verb By paying more attention to impressions than facts leads us to misjudge others.
Revised	┌── modifier (prepositional phrase) ──┐ subject + By paying more attention to impressions than facts, we mis- verb judge others.
Revised	┌── subject (gerund phrase) ──┐ verb Paying more attention to impressions than facts leads us to misjudge others.

Mixed subject ┌──────── modifier (adjective clause)────────┐
The fact that someone may be considered guilty just for associating with someone guilty.

Revised subject verb
The fact is that someone may be considered guilty just for
associating with someone guilty.

Revised subject ┌───── verb ─────┐
Someone may be considered guilty just for associating with
someone guilty.

In some mixed sentences the grammar is so jumbled that the writer has little choice but to start over:

Mixed My long-range goal is through law school and government work I hope to help people deal with those problems we all deal with more effectively.

Possible My long-range goal is to go to law school and then work in government so that I can help people deal more effectively with problems we all face.

Mixed sentences are especially likely on a computer when you connect parts of two sentences or rewrite half a sentence but not the other half. Mixed sentences may also occur when you don't focus your sentences on the subject and verb so that these elements carry the principal meaning. (See pp. 384–86.) If you need help identifying the subject and verb, see pages 233–36.

2 State parts of sentences, such as subjects, only once. ❧ CULTURE LANGUAGE ❧

In some languages other than English, certain parts of sentences may be repeated. These include the subject in any kind of clause or an object or adverb in an adjective clause. In English, however, these parts are stated only once in a clause.

■ **Repetition of subject**

You may be tempted to restate a subject as a pronoun before the verb. But the subject needs stating only once in its clause.

Faulty The liquid it reached a temperature of 180°F.
Revised The liquid reached a temperature of 180°F.

Faulty Gases in the liquid they escaped.
Revised Gases in the liquid escaped.

■ **Repetition in an adjective clause**

Adjective clauses begin with *who, whom, whose, which, that, where,* and *when* (see p. 254). The beginning word replaces another word: the subject (*He is the person who called*), an object of a verb or

to work with the passage, perhaps in small groups, proofreading it and correcting the errors. Students' journals and error logs are excellent sources of material as well as good places to practice revision strategies. Encourage students to keep a log of the patterns of error that tend to recur in their work, along with corrected examples. That log can provide a good resource for future revision and editing sessions.

RESOURCES AND IDEAS

Krishna, Valerie. "The Syntax of Error." *Journal of Basic Writing* 1 (1975): 43–9. The author views problems like mixed constructions and shifts as the result of a weak sentence core, and she encourages teachers to pay attention to this underlying problem in helping students avoid such errors.

Shuman, R. Baird. "Grammar for Writers: How Much Is Enough?" *The Place of Grammar in Writing Instruction: Past, Present, Future.* Ed. Susan Hunter and Ray Wallace. Portsmouth, NH: Boynton, 1995. 114–28. Shuman offers simplified strategies for presenting sentence structure as a meaningful concept in an effort to prevent some student errors.

preposition (*He is the person* whom *I mentioned*), or a preposition and pronoun (*He knows the office* where [*in which*] *the conference will occur*).

Do not state the word that *who, whom,* and so on replace in an adjective clause:

> Faulty   The technician whom the test depended on her was burned. [*Whom* should replace *her*.]
>
> Revised   The technician whom the test depended on was burned.

Adjective clauses beginning with *where* or *when* do not need an adverb such as *there* or *then:*

> Faulty   Gases escaped at a moment when the technician was unprepared then.
>
> Revised   Gases escaped at a moment when the technician was unprepared.

22b   Match subjects and predicates in meaning.

In a sentence with mixed meaning, the subject is said to be or do something it cannot logically be or do. Such a mixture is sometimes called **faulty predication** because the predicate conflicts with the subject.

■ Illogical equation with *be*

When a form of *be* connects a subject and a word that describes the subject (a complement), the subject and complement must be logically related:

> Mixed   A compromise between the city and the country would be the ideal place to live.
>
> Revised   A community that offered the best qualities of both city and country would be the ideal place to live.

■ *Is when, is where*

Definitions require nouns on both sides of *be.* Definition clauses beginning with *when* or *where* are common in speech but should be avoided in writing:

> Mixed   An examination is when you are tested on what you know.
>
> Revised   An examination is a test of what you know.

■ *Reason is because*

The commonly heard construction *reason is because* is redundant since *because* means "for the reason that":

Mixed	The <u>reason</u> the temple requests donations <u>is because</u> the school needs expansion.
Revised	The <u>reason</u> the temple requests donations <u>is that</u> the school needs expansion.
Revised	The temple requests donations <u>because</u> the school needs expansion.

▪ Other mixed meanings

Mismatched subjects and predicates are not confined to sentences with *be:*

| Mixed | The <u>use</u> of emission controls <u>was created</u> to reduce air pollution. |
| Revised | Emission <u>controls</u> <u>were created</u> to reduce air pollution. |

EXERCISE 22.1 Revising: Sentences mixed in grammar or meaning

Revise the following sentences so that their parts fit together both in grammar and in meaning. Each item has more than one possible answer. (You can do this exercise online at *ablongman.com/littlebrown.*)

Example:

When they found out how expensive pianos are is why they were discouraged.

They were discouraged <u>because</u> they found out how expensive pianos are.

When they found out how expensive pianos are, <u>they</u> were discouraged.

1. A hurricane is when the winds in a tropical depression rotate counterclockwise at more than seventy-four miles per hour.
2. Because hurricanes can destroy so many lives and so much property is why people fear them.
3. Through high winds, storm surge, floods, and tornadoes is how a hurricane can kill thousands of people.
4. Many scientists observe that hurricanes in recent years they have become more ferocious and destructive.
5. However, in the last half-century, with improved communications systems and weather satellites have made hurricanes less deadly.

EXERCISE 22.2 Revising: Repeated sentence parts

⚑ **CULTURE LANGUAGE** ⚐ Revise the following sentences to eliminate any unnecessary repetition of sentence parts. (You can do this exercise online at *ablongman.com/littlebrown.*)

Example:

Over 79 percent of Americans they have heard of global warming.
Over 79 percent of <u>Americans have</u> heard of global warming.

COLLABORATIVE LEARNING

Students can work together to create or to compare their responses to Exercise 22.1. Encourage each group to explore various possible answers.

ANSWERS: EXERCISE 22.1

Possible answers

1. A hurricane <u>occurs</u> when the winds in a tropical depression rotate counterclockwise at more than seventy-four miles per hour.
2. Because hurricanes can destroy so many lives and much propert<u>y, pe</u>ople fear them.
3. Through high winds, storm surge, floods, and tornadoes<u>, a</u> hurricane can kill thousands of people.
4. Many scientists observe that hurricanes in recent <u>years have</u> become more ferocious and destructive.
5. However, in the last <u>half-century, improved</u> communications systems and weather satellites have made hurricanes less deadly.

ANSWERS: EXERCISE 22.2

1. <u>Global warming</u> is caused by the gradual erosion of the ozone layer that protects the earth from the sun.
2. Scientists who study this <u>problem say</u> that the primary causes of erosion are the use of fossil fuels and the reduction of forests.
3. Many <u>nonscientists mistakenly</u> believe that aerosol spray cans are the primary cause of erosion.
4. One scientist whom others <u>respect argues</u> that Americans have effectively reduced their use of aerosol sprays.
5. He argues that we will stop global warming only when the public learns the real causes.

1. Global warming it is caused by the gradual erosion of the ozone layer that protects the earth from the sun.
2. Scientists who study this problem they say that the primary causes of erosion are the use of fossil fuels and the reduction of forests.
3. Many nonscientists they mistakenly believe that aerosol spray cans are the primary cause of erosion.
4. One scientist whom others respect him argues that Americans have effectively reduced their use of aerosol sprays.
5. He argues that we will stop global warming only when the public learns the real causes then.

Incomplete Sentences

The most serious kind of incomplete sentence is the fragment (see Chapter 17). But sentences are also incomplete when they omit one or more words needed for clarity.

Note Grammar and style checkers will not flag most kinds of incomplete sentences discussed in this section.

22c Omissions from compound constructions should be consistent with grammar or idiom.

In both speech and writing, we commonly omit words not necessary for meaning, such as those in brackets in the following examples. Notice that all the sentences contain compound constructions (see p. 258):

> By 2010 automobile-emission standards will be tougher, and by 2015 [automobile-emission standards will be] tougher still.

> Some cars will run on electricity and some [will run] on methane or another alternative fuel.

> Environmentalists have hopes for alternative fuels and [for] public transportation.

Such omissions are possible only when you omit words that are common to all the parts of a compound construction. When the parts differ in either grammar or idiom, all words must be included in all parts:

> One new car <u>gets</u> eighty miles per gallon of gasoline; some old cars <u>get</u> as little as five miles per gallon. [One verb is singular, the other plural.]

> Environmentalists <u>were</u> invited to submit proposals and <u>were</u> eager to do so. [Each *were* has a different grammatical function: the first is a helping verb; the second is a linking verb.]

> They believe <u>in</u> and work <u>for</u> fuel conservation. [Idiom requires different prepositions with *believe* and *work*.]

In the sentence *My brother and friend moved to Dallas,* the omission of *my* before *friend* indicates that *brother* and *friend* are the same person. If two different persons are meant, the modifier or article must be repeated: *My brother and my friend moved to Dallas.*

(See pp. 523–25 for a list of English idioms with prepositions and pp. 405–08 for a discussion of grammatical parallelism.)

22d All comparisons should be complete and logical.

Comparisons make statements about the relation between two or more things, as in *Dogs are more intelligent than cats.*

1 State a comparison fully enough to ensure clarity.

Unclear	Automakers worry about their industry more than environmentalists.
Clear	Automakers worry about their industry more than environmentalists do.
Clear	Automakers worry about their industry more than they worry about environmentalists.

2 The items being compared should in fact be comparable.

Illogical	The cost of an electric car is greater than a gasoline-powered car. [Illogically compares a cost and a car.]
Revised	The cost of an electric car is greater than the cost of [or that of] a gasoline-powered car.

3 Use *any* or *any other* appropriately in comparisons.

Comparing a person or thing with all others in the same group creates two units: (1) the individual person or thing and (2) all *other* persons or things in the group. The two units need to be distinguished:

Illogical	Los Angeles is larger than any city in California. [Since Los Angeles is itself a city in California, the sentence seems to say that Los Angeles is larger than itself.]
Logical	Los Angeles is larger than any other city in California.

Comparing a person or thing with the members of a *different* group assumes separate units to begin with. The two units do not need to be distinguished with *other:*

Illogical	Los Angeles is larger than any other city in Canada. [The cities in Canada constitute a group to which Los Angeles does not belong.]
Logical	Los Angeles is larger than any city in Canada.

4 Comparisons should state what is being compared.

Brand X gets clothes whiter. [Whiter than what?]
Brand Y is so much better. [Better than what?]

22e Include all needed prepositions, articles, and other words.

In haste or carelessness we sometimes omit small words such as articles and prepositions that are needed for clarity:

Incomplete   Regular payroll deductions are a type painless savings. You hardly notice missing amounts, and after period of years the contributions can add a large total.

Revised   Regular payroll deductions are a type of painless savings. You hardly notice the missing amounts, and after a period of years the contributions can add up to a large total.

Be careful not to omit *that* when the omission is confusing:

Incomplete   The personnel director expects many employees will benefit from the plan. [*Many employees* seems to be the object of *expects*.]

Revised   The personnel director expects that many employees will benefit from the plan.

Attentive proofreading is the best insurance against the kinds of omissions described in this section. *Proofread all your papers carefully.* See page 63 for tips.

CULTURE LANGUAGE If your native language or dialect is not standard American English, you may have difficulty knowing when to use the English articles *a, an,* and *the.* For guidelines on using articles, see pages 326–30.

EXERCISE 22.3 Revising: Incomplete sentences

Revise the following sentences so that they are complete, logical, and clear. Some items have more than one possible answer. (You can do this exercise online at *ablongman.com/littlebrown.*)

Example:
Our house is closer to the bank than the subway stop.
Our house is closer to the bank than it is to the subway stop.
Our house is closer to the bank than the subway stop is.

1. The first ice cream, eaten in China in about 2000 BC, was more lumpy than the modern era.
2. The Chinese made their ice cream of milk, spices, and overcooked rice and packed in snow to solidify.

Exercises 22.3 and 22.4 work well as an extended group project. Encourage groups to experiment with alternate responses, and ask each group to present any problem points they encountered as well as their successful responses to one or more sections.

ANSWERS: EXERCISE 22.3

Possible answers

1. The first ice cream, eaten in China in about 2000 BC, was more lumpy than ice cream in [*or* that in] the modern era.
2. The Chinese made their ice cream of milk, spices, and overcooked rice and packed it in snow to solidify.
3. In the fourteenth century ice milk and fruit ices appeared in Italy and on the tables of the wealthy.
4. At her wedding in 1533 to the King of France, Catherine de Médicis offered more flavors of fruit ices than any other hostess offered.
5. Modern sherbets resemble her ices; modern ice cream resembles her soft dessert of thick, sweetened cream.

3. In the fourteenth century ice milk and fruit ices appeared in Italy and the tables of the wealthy.
4. At her wedding in 1533 to the king of France, Catherine de Médicis offered more flavors of fruit ices than any hostess offered.
5. Modern sherbets resemble her ices; modern ice cream her soft dessert of thick, sweetened cream.

EXERCISE 22.4   Revising: Mixed and incomplete sentences

Revise the following paragraph to eliminate mixed or incomplete constructions. (You can do this exercise online at *ablongman.com/littlebrown*.)

The Hancock Tower in Boston is thin mirror-glass slab that rises almost eight hundred feet. When it was being constructed was when its windows began cracking, and some fell crashing to the ground. In order to minimize risks is why the architects and owners replaced over a third the huge windows with plywood until the problem could be found and solved. With its plywood sheath, the building was homelier than any skyscraper, the butt of many jokes. Eventually, however, it was discovered that the reason the windows cracked was because joint between the double panes of glass was too rigid. The solution of thicker single-pane windows was installed, and the silly plywood building crystallized into reflective jewel.

EXERCISE ON CHAPTERS 17–22   Revising: Clear sentences

Clarify meaning in the following paragraphs by revising sentence fragments, comma splices, fused sentences, problems with pronoun reference, awkward shifts, misplaced and dangling modifiers, and mixed and incomplete sentences. Most errors can be corrected in more than one way. (You can do this exercise online at *ablongman.com/littlebrown*.)

Many people who are physically challenged. They have accomplished much. Which proves that they are not "handicapped." Confined to wheelchairs, successful careers have been forged by Bob Sampson and Stephen Hawking. Despite Sampson's muscular dystrophy, he has earned a law degree he has also worked for United Airlines for more than thirty years. Stephen Hawking most famous for his book *A Brief History of Time*. Unable to speak, Hawking's voice synthesizer allows him to dictate his books and conduct public lectures. And teach mathematics classes at Cambridge University.

Franklin D. Roosevelt, Ann Adams, and Itzhak Perlman all refused let polio destroy their lives. Indeed, Roosevelt led the United States during two of the worst periods of its history as President. The Great Depression and World War II. Reassured by his strong, firm voice, Roosevelt inspired hope and determination in the American people. Ann Adams, who was talented in art before polio paralyzed her, knew she had to continue to be one. Having retrained herself to draw with a pencil grasped in her teeth. She produces sketches of children and pets. That were turned into greeting cards. The profits from the cards

ANSWERS: EXERCISE 22.4
Possible answers

The Hancock Tower in Boston is a thin mirror-glass slab that rises almost eight hundred feet. When it was being constructed, its windows began cracking, and some fell crashing to the ground. In order to minimize risks, the architects and owners replaced over a third of the huge windows with plywood until the problem could be found and solved. With its plywood sheath, the building was homelier than any other skyscraper, the butt of many jokes. Eventually, however, it was discovered that the windows cracked because the joint between the double panes of glass was too rigid. Thicker single-pane windows were installed, and the silly plywood building crystallized into a reflective jewel.

ANSWERS: EXERCISE ON CHAPTERS 17–22
Possible answers

Many people who are physically challenged have accomplished much, which proves that they are not "handicapped." Confined to wheelchairs, Bob Sampson and Stephen Hawking have forged successful careers. Despite his muscular dystrophy, Sampson has earned a law degree. He has also worked for United Airlines for more than thirty years. Stephen Hawking is most famous for his book *A Brief History of Time*. Hawking is unable to speak, but his voice synthesizer allows him to dictate his books, conduct public lectures, and teach mathematics classes at Cambridge University.

Franklin D. Roosevelt, Ann Adams, and Itzhak Perlman all refused to let polio destroy their lives. Indeed, as President, Roosevelt led the United States during two of the worst periods of its history: the Great Depression and World War II. Roosevelt inspired hope and determination in the American people, reassuring them with his strong, clear voice. Ann Adams, who was talented in art before polio paralyzed her, knew she had to continue to be an artist. Having retrained herself to draw with a pencil grasped in her teeth, she produced sketches of children and pets. These drawings were turned into greeting cards whose profits sustained her. Roosevelt and Adams were stricken with polio when they were adults; Itzhak Perlman was stricken when he was a child. He was unable to play sports; instead, he studied the violin. Now many think he is greater than any other violinist in the world.

Like Perlman, many physically challenged individuals turn to the arts. Perhaps they do so because [*or:* the reason is that] the joy of artistic achievement compensates for other pleasures they cannot experience. Stevie Wonder, José Feliciano, and Andrea Bocelli all express their souls through their music. Although they are unable to see physically, their music reveals how well they truly see. Hearing impairment struck Ludwig van Beethoven and Marlee Matlin, but it did not stop them from developing their talents. Already a successful composer, Beethoven wrote many of his most powerful pieces after he became deaf. Similarly, Matlin has had excellent acting roles in movies, plays, and television programs; indeed, she won an Oscar for *Children of a Lesser God*. She encourages others to develop their abilities, and she has inspired many hearing-impaired actors.

sustained her. Roosevelt and Adams were stricken with polio when they were adults; Itzhak Perlman when a child. He was unable to play sports, instead he studied the violin, now many think he is greater than any violinist in the world.

Like Perlman, many physically challenged individuals turn to the arts. Perhaps the reason is because the joy of artistic achievement compensates for other pleasures they cannot experience. Stevie Wonder, José Feliciano, and Andrea Bocelli all express, through their music, their souls. Although unable to see physically, their music reveals truly how well they see. Hearing impairment struck Ludwig van Beethoven and Marlee Matlin it did not stop them from developing their talents. Already a successful composer, many of Beethoven's most powerful pieces were written after he became deaf. Similarly, Matlin has had excellent acting roles in movies, plays, and television programs, indeed she won an Oscar for *Children of a Lesser God*. She encourages others to develop their ability, and many hearing-impaired actors have been inspired by her.

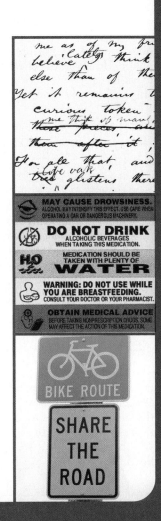

mycomplab²·⁰

Please visit MyCompLab at *www.mycomplab.com* for more on the writing process.

HIGHLIGHTS

This chapter looks at two ways to achieve emphasis within sentences: by the distribution of information and by the choice of strategies to create specific effects. The opening sections consider subjects and verbs as the heart of sentences and the importance of beginnings and endings. Additional special features of the chapter include its treatment of cumulative and periodic sentences and discussions that stress the rhetorical effect of each sentence pattern. The exercises are designed to help students feel comfortable using these patterns in their writing. Most students benefit from some work with these basic ways of controlling emphasis as well as from discussion of conciseness (23f). Students who have problems with sentence structure, however, may have more difficulty with the effective uses of repetition (23d) and separation (23e) for emphasis.

TRANSPARENCY MASTER 23.1

COMPANION WEB SITE

See page IAE-56 for companion Web site content description.

CHAPTER **23**

Emphasizing Ideas

When you emphasize the main ideas in your sentences, you hold and channel readers' attention.

Note Many grammar and style checkers can spot some problems with emphasis, such as nouns made from verbs, passive voice, wordy phrases, and long sentences that may also be flabby and unemphatic. However, the checkers cannot help you identify the important ideas in your sentences or whether those ideas receive appropriate emphasis.

Ways to emphasize ideas

- Use the subjects and verbs of sentences to state key actors and actions (below).
- Use the beginnings and endings of sentences to pace and stress information (p. 386).
- Arrange series items in order of increasing importance (p. 387).
- Use an occasional balanced sentence (p. 389).
- Carefully repeat key words and phrases (p. 390).
- Set off important ideas with punctuation (p. 391).
- Write concisely (p. 392).

23a Using subjects and verbs effectively

The heart of every sentence is its subject, which usually names the actor, and its verb, which usually specifies the subject's action: *Children* [subject] *grow* [verb]. When these elements do not identify the sentence's key actor and action, readers must find that information elsewhere and the sentence may be wordy and unemphatic.

In the following sentences, the subjects and verbs are underlined.

http://www.ablongman.com/littlebrown ▶

Visit the companion Web site for more help and additional exercises on emphasis.

| Unemphatic | The <u>intention</u> of the company <u>was</u> to expand its workforce. A <u>proposal</u> <u>was</u> also <u>made</u> to diversify the backgrounds and abilities of employees. |

These sentences are unemphatic because their key ideas do not appear in their subjects and verbs. Revised, the sentences are not only clearer but more concise:

| Revised | The <u>company</u> <u>intended</u> to expand its workforce. <u>It</u> also <u>proposed</u> to diversify the backgrounds and abilities of employees. |

The constructions below usually drain meaning from a sentence's subject and verb.

▣ Nouns made from verbs

Nouns made from verbs can obscure the key actions of sentences and add words. These nouns include *intention* (from *intend*), *proposal* (from *propose*), *decision* (from *decide*), *expectation* (from *expect*), *persistence* (from *persist*), *argument* (from *argue*), and *inclusion* (from *include*).

| Unemphatic | After the company made a <u>decision</u> to hire more disabled workers, its next step <u>was</u> the <u>construction</u> of wheelchair ramps and other facilities. |
| Revised | After the company <u>decided</u> to hire more disabled workers, it next <u>constructed</u> wheelchair ramps and other facilities. |

▣ Weak verbs

Weak verbs, such as *made* and *was* in the unemphatic sentence above, tend to stall sentences just where they should be moving and often bury key actions:

| Unemphatic | The company <u>is</u> now the leader among businesses in complying with the 1990 Americans with Disabilities Act. Its officers <u>make</u> speeches on the act to business groups. |
| Revised | The company now <u>leads</u> other businesses in complying with the 1990 Americans with Disabilities Act. Its officers <u>speak</u> on the act to business groups. |

▣ Passive voice

Verbs in the passive voice state actions received by, not performed by, their subjects. Thus the passive de-emphasizes the true actor of the sentence, sometimes omitting it entirely. Generally, prefer the active voice, in which the subject performs the verb's action. (See also pp. 302–03.)

RESOURCES AND IDEAS

An understanding of the roles of topics and comments and of the possible relationships of old and new information can be very useful for writers seeking greater clarity and more effective emphasis in their writing. To supplement the discussion in this section of the handbook you may wish to turn to three excellent texts:

Lanham, Richard. *Analyzing Prose.* New York: Scribner, 1983. Lanham offers extensive advice on revising for stylistic effect.

Vande Koppel, William J. *Clear and Coherent Prose.* Glenview: Scott Foresman, 1989.

Williams, Joseph M. *Style: Ten Lessons in Clarity and Grace.* 6th ed. New York: Longman, 1999.

Unemphatic	The 1990 <u>law</u> <u>is seen</u> by most businesses as fair, but the costs of complying <u>have</u> sometimes <u>been exaggerated</u>.
Revised	Most <u>businesses</u> <u>see</u> the 1990 law as fair, but some <u>opponents</u> <u>have exaggerated</u> the costs of complying.

ANSWERS: EXERCISE 23.1

Possible answers

1. <u>Many heroes helped</u> to emancipate the slaves.
2. <u>Harriet Tubman</u>, an escaped slave herself, <u>guided</u> hundreds of other slaves to freedom on the Underground Railroad.
3. <u>Tubman risked</u> a return to slavery or possible death.
4. During the Civil War <u>she</u> also <u>carried</u> information from the South to the North.
5. After the war <u>Tubman helped</u> needy former slaves by raising money for refugees.

EXERCISE 23.1 Revising: Emphasis of subjects and verbs

Rewrite the following sentences so that their subjects and verbs identify their key actors and actions. (You can do this exercise online at *ablongman.com/littlebrown*.)

> *Example:*
>
> The issue of students making a competition over grades is a reason why their focus on learning may be lost.
>
> <u>Students</u> who compete over grades <u>may lose</u> their focus on learning.

1. The work of many heroes was crucial in helping to emancipate the slaves.
2. The contribution of Harriet Tubman, an escaped slave herself, included the guidance of hundreds of other slaves to freedom on the Underground Railroad.
3. A return to slavery was risked by Tubman or possibly death.
4. During the Civil War she was also a carrier of information from the South to the North.
5. After the war needy former slaves were helped by Tubman's raising of money for refugees.

23b Using sentence beginnings and endings

Readers automatically seek a writer's principal meaning in the main clause of a sentence—essentially, in the subject that names the actor and the verb that usually specifies the action (see the preceding pages). Thus you can help readers understand your intended meaning by controlling the information in your subjects and the relation of the main clause to any modifiers attached to it.

■ Old and new information

Generally, readers expect the beginning of a sentence to contain information that they already know or that you have already introduced. They then look to the sentence ending for new information. In the unemphatic passage below, the second and third sentences both begin with new topics, while the old topics appear at the ends of the sentences. The pattern of the passage is A→B. C→B. D→A.

	A B
Unemphatic	<u>Education</u> almost means <u>controversy</u> these days, with rising costs and constant complaints about its inade-

quacies. But the value^C of schooling should not be obscured by the controversy^B. The single best means^D of economic advancement, despite its shortcomings, remains education^A.

In the more emphatic revision, old information begins each sentence and new information ends the sentence. The passage follows the pattern A→B. B→C. A→D.

Revised Education^A almost means controversy^B these days, with rising costs and constant complaints about its inadequacies. But the controversy^B should not obscure the value^C of schooling. Education^A remains, despite its shortcomings, the single best means of economic advancement^D.

■ Cumulative and periodic sentences

You can call attention to information by placing it first or last in a sentence, reserving the middle for incidentals:

Unemphatic Education remains the single best means of economic advancement, despite its shortcomings. [Emphasizes shortcomings.]

Revised Despite its shortcomings, education remains the single best means of economic advancement. [Emphasizes advancement more than shortcomings.]

Revised Education remains, despite its shortcomings, the single best means of economic advancement. [De-emphasizes shortcomings.]

Many sentences begin with the main clause and then add more modifiers to explain, amplify, or illustrate it. Such sentences are called **cumulative** (because they accumulate information as they proceed) or **loose** (because they are not tightly structured). They parallel the way we naturally think.

Cumulative Education has no equal in opening minds, instilling values, and creating opportunities.

Cumulative Most of the Great American Desert is made up of bare rock, rugged cliffs, mesas, canyons, mountains, separated from one another by broad flat basins covered with sunbaked mud and alkali, supporting a sparse and measured growth of sagebrush or creosote or saltbush, depending on location and elevation.
—Edward Abbey

RESOURCES AND IDEAS

Christensen, Francis. "A Generative Rhetoric of the Sentence." In *Notes Toward a New Rhetoric: Nine Essays for Teachers*. Ed. Francis Christensen and Bonniejean Christensen. 2nd ed. New York: HarperCollins, 1978. 23–44. Christensen demonstrates how to analyze the levels of generality in sentences and discusses and illustrates the structure of the cumulative sentence.

COLLABORATIVE LEARNING

Ask students to complete Exercise 23.2 individually and then to compare and revise their responses in groups. Have each group present one of their responses to the class, and encourage the other groups to call attention to places where they created an alternative response.

ANSWERS: EXERCISE 23.2

Possible answers

1. Pat Taylor strode into the packed room, greeting students called "Taylor's Kids" and nodding to their parents and teachers.
2. This wealthy Louisiana oilman had promised his "Kids" free college educations because he was determined to make higher education available to all qualified but disadvantaged students.
3. The students welcomed Taylor, their voices singing "You Are the Wind Beneath My Wings," their faces flashing with self-confidence.
4. They had thought a college education was beyond their dreams, seeming too costly and too demanding.
5. To help ease the costs and demands of getting to college, Taylor created a bold plan of scholarships, tutoring, and counseling.

The opposite kind of sentence, called **periodic,** saves the main clause until just before the end (the period) of the sentence. Everything before the main clause points toward it.

Periodic In opening minds, instilling values, and creating opportunities, education has no equal.

Periodic With people from all over the world—Korean grocers, Jamaican cricket players, Vietnamese fishers, Haitian cabdrivers, Chinese doctors—the American mosaic is continually changing.

The periodic sentence creates suspense for readers by reserving important information for the end. But readers should already have an idea of the sentence's subject—because it was discussed or introduced in the preceding sentence—so that they know what the opening modifiers describe. A variation of the periodic sentence names the subject at the beginning, follows it with a modifier, and then completes the main clause:

> Dick Hayne, who works in jeans and loafers and likes to let a question cure in the air for a while before answering it, bears all the markings of what his generation used to call a laid-back kind of guy.
>
> —George Rush

EXERCISE 23.2 Sentence combining: Beginnings and endings

Locate the main idea in each group of sentences below. Then combine each group into a single sentence that emphasizes that idea by placing it at the beginning or the end. For sentences 2–5, determine the position of the main idea by considering its relation to the previous sentences: if the main idea picks up a topic that's already been introduced, place it at the beginning; if it adds new information, place it at the end. (You can do this exercise online at *ablongman.com/littlebrown*.)

Example:
The storm blew roofs off buildings. It caused extensive damage. It knocked down many trees. It severed power lines.

Main idea at beginning: The storm caused extensive damage, blowing roofs off buildings, knocking down many trees, and severing power lines.

Main idea at end: Blowing roofs off buildings, knocking down many trees, and severing power lines, the storm caused extensive damage.

1. Pat Taylor strode into the room. The room was packed. He greeted students called "Taylor's Kids." He nodded to their parents and teachers.
2. This was a wealthy Louisiana oilman. He had promised his "Kids" free college educations. He was determined to make higher education available to all qualified but disadvantaged students.

3. The students welcomed Taylor. Their voices joined in singing. They sang "You Are the Wind Beneath My Wings." Their faces beamed with hope. Their eyes flashed with self-confidence.
4. The students had thought a college education was beyond their dreams. It seemed too costly. It seemed too demanding.
5. Taylor had to ease the costs and the demands of getting to college. He created a bold plan. The plan consisted of scholarships, tutoring, and counseling.

23c Arranging parallel elements effectively

■ Series

With parallelism, you use similar grammatical structures for ideas linked by *and, but,* and similar words: *Blustery winds and upturned leaves often signal thunderstorms.* (See Chapter 25.) In addition, you should arrange the parallel ideas in order of their importance:

| Unemphatic | The storm ripped the roofs off several buildings, killed ten people, and knocked down many trees in town. [Buries the most serious damage—deaths—in the middle.] |
| Emphatic | The storm knocked down many trees in town, ripped the roofs off several buildings, and killed ten people. [Arranges items in order of increasing importance.] |

You may want to use an unexpected item at the end of a series for humor or for another special effect:

Early to bed and early to rise makes a man healthy, wealthy, and dead.
—James Thurber

But be careful not to use such a series carelessly. The following series seems thoughtlessly random rather than intentionally humorous:

| Unemphatic | The painting has subdued tone, intense feeling, and a length of about three feet. |
| Emphatic | The painting, about three feet long, has subdued tone and intense feeling. |

■ Balanced sentences

A sentence is **balanced** when its clauses are parallel—that is, matched in grammatical structure (Chapter 25). When used carefully, balanced sentences can be especially effective in alerting readers to a strong comparison between two ideas. Read the following examples aloud to hear their rhythm.

The fickleness of the women I love is equalled only by the infernal constancy of the women who love me. —George Bernard Shaw

emph

In a pure balanced sentence two main clauses are exactly parallel: they match item for item.

> Scratch a lover, and find a foe.
>
> —Dorothy Parker

But the term is commonly applied to sentences that are only approximately parallel or that have only some parallel parts:

> If thought corrupts language, language can also corrupt thought.
>
> —George Orwell

> As the traveler who has once been from home is wiser than he who has never left his own doorstep, so a knowledge of one other culture should sharpen our ability to scrutinize more steadily, to appreciate more lovingly, our own.
>
> —Margaret Mead

COLLABORATIVE LEARNING

Ask students to work in pairs or small groups on Exercise 23.3 and present their responses to the class. You might also ask each group to create two additional sentences, one with elements in a series and one with balanced elements.

ANSWERS: EXERCISE 23.3

Possible answers

1. Remembering her days as a "conductor" on the Underground Railroad made Harriet Tubman proud, but <u>remembering her years as a slave made her angry.</u>
2. Tubman wanted freedom regardless of personal danger, whereas <u>her husband, John, wanted personal safety regardless of freedom.</u>
3. Tubman proved her fearlessness in many ways: <u>she disobeyed John's order not to run away,</u> she was a spy for the North during the Civil War, <u>and she led hundreds of other slaves to freedom.</u>
4. To conduct slaves north to freedom, Tubman risked <u>being caught by Southern patrollers, being returned to slavery, and being hanged for a huge reward.</u>
5. After the war Tubman worked tirelessly for civil rights and women's suffrage; <u>she also raised money for homes for needy former slaves.</u>

EXERCISE 23.3 Revising: Series and balanced elements

Revise the following sentences so that elements in a series or balanced elements are arranged to give maximum emphasis to main ideas. (You can do this exercise online at *ablongman.com/littlebrown*.)

Example:

The campers were stranded without matches, without food or water, and without a tent.

The campers were stranded without matches, without a tent, and without food or water.

1. Remembering her days as a "conductor" on the Underground Railroad made Harriet Tubman proud, but she got angry when she remembered her years as a slave.
2. Tubman wanted freedom regardless of personal danger, whereas for her husband, John, personal safety was more important than freedom.
3. Tubman proved her fearlessness in many ways: she led hundreds of other slaves to freedom, she was a spy for the North during the Civil War, and she disobeyed John's order not to run away.
4. To conduct slaves north to freedom, Tubman risked being returned to slavery, being hanged for a huge reward, and being caught by Southern patrollers.
5. After the war Tubman worked tirelessly for civil rights and women's suffrage; raising money for homes for needy former slaves was something else she did.

23d Repeating ideas

Repetition of words and phrases often clutters and weakens sentences, as discussed on pages 532–33. But carefully planned repetition can be an effective means of emphasis. Such repetition often combines with parallelism. It may occur in a series of sentences (see p. 83) or in a series of words, phrases, or clauses within a sentence, as in the following examples:

> There is something uneasy in the Los Angeles air this afternoon, some unnatural stillness, some tension.   —Joan Didion

> We have the tools, all the tools—we are suffocating in tools—but we cannot find the actual wood to work or even the actual hand to work it.
> —Archibald MacLeish

23e Separating ideas

When you save important information for the end of a sentence, you can emphasize it even more by setting it off from the rest of the sentence, as in the second example below:

> Mothers and housewives are the only workers who do not have regular time off, so they are the great vacationless class.

> Mothers and housewives are the only workers who do not have regular time off. They are the great vacationless class.
> —Anne Morrow Lindbergh

You can vary the degree of emphasis by varying the extent to which you separate one idea from the others. A semicolon provides more separation than a comma, and a period provides still more separation. Compare the following sentences:

> Most of the reading which is praised for itself is neither literary nor intellectual, but narcotic.

> Most of the reading which is praised for itself is neither literary nor intellectual; it is narcotic.

> Most of the reading which is praised for itself is neither literary nor intellectual. It is narcotic.   —Donald Hall

Sometimes a dash or a pair of dashes will isolate and thus emphasize a part of a statement (see also pp. 480–81):

> His schemes were always elaborate, ingenious, and exciting—and wholly impractical.

> Athletics—that is, winning athletics—has become a profitable university operation.

EXERCISE 23.4 Emphasizing with repetition or separation

Emphasize the main idea in each of the following sentences or groups of sentences by following the instructions in parentheses: either combine sentences so that parallelism and repetition stress the main idea, or place the main idea in a separate sentence. Each item has more than one possible answer. (You can do this exercise online at *ablongman.com/littlebrown*.)

ANSWERS: EXERCISE 23.4

1. One of the few worthwhile habits is daily reading: <u>reading for</u> information, <u>reading for</u> entertainment, <u>reading for</u> a broader view of the world.
2. Reading introduces new words and <u>new styles of expression.</u>
3. Students who read a great deal will more likely write vividly, coherently, and grammatically. <u>They will have learned from other authors.</u>
4. Reading gives <u>knowledge about</u> other cultures, <u>knowledge about</u> history and current events, and <u>knowledge about</u> human nature.
5. As a result of reading, writers have more resources and more flexibility. <u>Thus reading creates better writers.</u>

Example:

I try to listen to other people's opinions. When my mind is closed, I find that other opinions open it. And they can change my mind when it is wrong. (*Parallelism and repetition.*)

I try to listen to other people's opinions, for they can open my mind when it is closed and they can change my mind when it is wrong.

1. One of the few worthwhile habits is daily reading. One can read for information. One can read for entertainment. Reading can give one a broader view of the world. (*Parallelism and repetition.*)
2. Reading introduces new words. One encounters unfamiliar styles of expression through reading. (*Parallelism and repetition.*)
3. Students who read a great deal will more likely write vividly, coherently, and grammatically, for they will have learned from other authors. (*Separation.*)
4. Reading gives knowledge. One gets knowledge about other cultures. One will know about history and current events. One gains information about human nature. (*Parallelism and repetition.*)
5. As a result of reading, writers have more resources and more flexibility, and thus reading creates better writers. (*Separation.*)

23f   Being concise

Conciseness—brevity of expression—aids emphasis no matter what the sentence structure. Unnecessary words detract from necessary words. They clutter sentences and obscure ideas.

Weak   In my opinion the competition in the area of grades is distracting. It distracts many students from their goal, which is to obtain an education that is good. There seems to be a belief among a few students that grades are more important than what is measured by them.

Emphatic   The competition for grades distracts many students from their goal of obtaining a good education. A few students seem to believe that grades are more important than what they measure.

Techniques for tightening sentences are listed in the box opposite. Some of these techniques appear earlier in this chapter. All of them are covered in Chapter 39 on writing concisely.

EXERCISE 23.5   Revising: Conciseness

Revise the following sentences to make them more emphatic by eliminating wordiness. (You can do this exercise online at *ablongman.com/ littlebrown.*)

Ways to achieve conciseness

- **Make the subject and verb of each sentence identify its actor and action** (pp. 384, 529):

  Avoid nouns made from verbs.
  Use strong verbs.
  Rewrite the passive voice as active.

- **Cut or shorten empty words or phrases** (p. 531):

  Shorten filler phrases, such as *by virtue of the fact that.*
  Cut all-purpose words, such as *area, factor.*
  Cut unneeded qualifiers, such as *in my opinion, for the most part.*

- **Cut unnecessary repetition** (p. 532).
- **Reduce clauses to phrases and phrases to single words** (p. 534).
- **Avoid constructions beginning with *there is* or *it is*** (p. 534).
- **Combine sentences** (p. 535).
- **Cut or rewrite jargon** (p. 535).

Example:
  The problem in this particular situation is that we owe more money than we can afford under present circumstances.

  The problem is that we owe more money than we can afford.

1. As far as I am concerned, customers who are dining out in restaurants in our country must be wary of suggestive selling, so to speak.
2. In suggestive selling, diners are asked by the waiter to buy additional menu selections in addition to what was ordered by them.
3. For each item on the menu, there is another food that will naturally complement it.
4. For example, customers will be presented with the question of whether they want to order french fries along with a sandwich or whether they want to order a salad along with a steak dinner.
5. Due to the fact that customers often give in to suggestive selling, they often find that their restaurant meals are more costly than they had intended to pay.

EXERCISE 23.6   Revising: Emphasizing ideas

Drawing on the advice in this chapter, rewrite the following paragraph to emphasize main ideas and to de-emphasize less important information. (You can do this exercise online at *ablongman.com/littlebrown.*)

In preparing pasta, there is a requirement for common sense and imagination rather than for complicated recipes. The key to success in this area is fresh ingredients for the sauce and perfectly cooked pasta.

ANSWERS: EXERCISE 23.5

Possible answers

1. <u>Customers in restaurants</u> must be wary of suggestive selling.
2. In suggestive selling, <u>the waiter asks diners</u> to <u>buy menu</u> selections <u>besides</u> what <u>they ordered.</u>
3. For each item on the menu, <u>another food will</u> naturally complement it.
4. For example, customers will <u>be asked</u> whether they <u>want french fries with</u> a sandwich <u>or a salad with</u> a steak dinner.
5. <u>Customers who</u> give in to suggestive <u>selling often</u> find that their restaurant meals <u>cost more</u> than they had intended to pay.

COLLABORATIVE LEARNING

Have students work in groups to revise the paragraph in Exercise 23.6. Encourage each group to discuss various possible responses and to make a case for the effectiveness of their revision. Then have each group present their revised paragraph to the class either by writing on the blackboard or by photocopying it for a subsequent class meeting. This exercise works well in a networked classroom where each group's response can be posted for general discussion.

ANSWERS: EXERCISE 23.6

Possible revision

<u>Preparing pasta requires</u> common sense and imagination rather <u>than complicated</u> recipes. The key to <u>success is</u> fresh ingredients for the

sauce and perfectly cooked pasta. The sauce <u>may contain</u> just about any fresh fish, meat, cheese, herb, or vegetable. <u>The pasta itself may</u> be dried or fresh, although <u>many experienced cooks find fresh pasta</u> more delicate and flavorful. Dried pasta is fine with zesty sauces; <u>fresh pasta is best with light oil and cream sauces.</u> <u>Dried pasta takes longer to cook than fresh pasta does.</u> <u>The cook should follow</u> the package directions <u>and should test</u> the pasta before the cooking time is up. <u>According to the Italians, who ought to know,</u> the pasta is done when the texture is neither tough nor mushy but *al dente*, or "firm to the bite."

The sauce may be made with just about any fresh fish, meat, cheese, herb, or vegetable. As for the pasta itself, it may be dried or fresh, although fresh pasta is usually more delicate and flavorful, as many experienced cooks find. Dried pasta is fine with zesty sauces; with light oil and cream sauces fresh pasta is the best choice. There is a difference in the cooking time for dried and fresh pasta, with dried pasta taking longer. It is important that the cook follow the package directions and that the pasta be tested before the cooking time is up. The pasta is done when the texture is neither tough nor mushy but *al dente*, or "firm to the bite," according to the Italians, who ought to know.

Note See page 420 for an exercise involving emphasis along with parallelism and other techniques for effective sentences.

mycomplab 2.0

Please visit MyCompLab at *www.mycomplab.com* for more on the writing process.

HIGHLIGHTS

The material in this chapter emphasizes how writers can use coordination and subordination to relate ideas and distinguish central ideas from less important material. The opening section illustrates how coordination relates facts and ideas and then goes on to address the problems of excessive and faulty coordination. The second section follows a parallel pattern in discussing subordination, focusing on subordinate clauses. But since effective writing depends on a writer's ability to work with the whole range of subordinate structures, the uses of single words, appositives, and prepositional, verbal, and absolute phrases are also illustrated. The final section cautions briefly against the often unclear and misused connectors *like, while,* and *as.*

Included in this chapter are subsections on punctuating coordinated and subordinated elements, designed to help students not only punctuate correctly but also see punctuation as an instrument and extension of effective sentence structure. Coordination and subordination are strategies that can be enhanced by practicing

CHAPTER **24**

Using Coordination and Subordination

When clearly written, your sentences show the relations between ideas and stress the more important ideas over the lesser ones. Two techniques can help you achieve such clarity:

■ *Coordination* shows that two or more elements in a sentence are **equally important in meaning.** You signal coordination with words such as *and, but,* and *or.*

—— equally important ——
Car insurance is costly, but health insurance seems a luxury.

■ *Subordination* shows that some elements in a sentence are **less important than other elements** for your meaning. Usually, the main idea appears in the main clause, and supporting information appears in single words, phrases, and subordinate clauses.

COMPANION WEB SITE

See page IAE-56 for companion Web site content description.

http://www.ablongman.com/littlebrown ▶

Visit the companion Web site for more help and additional exercises on coordination and subordination.

```
            less important                          more important
       ┌─── (subordinate clause) ───┐         ┌─── (main clause) ───┐
Because accidents and thefts occur frequently, car insurance is costly.
```

Note Grammar and style checkers may spot some errors in punctuating coordinated and subordinated elements, and they can flag long sentences that may contain excessive coordination or subordination. But otherwise they provide little help because they cannot recognize the relations among ideas in sentences.

24a Coordinating to relate equal ideas

By linking equally important information, you can emphasize the relations for readers. Compare the passages below:

String of simple sentences

We should not rely so heavily on oil. Coal and uranium are also overused. We have a substantial energy resource in the moving waters of our rivers. Smaller streams add to the total volume of water. The resource renews itself. Oil and coal are irreplaceable. Uranium is also irreplaceable. The cost of water does not increase much over time. The costs of coal, oil, and uranium rise dramatically.

Ideas coordinated

We should not rely so heavily on oil, coal, and uranium, for we have a substantial energy resource in the moving waters of our rivers and streams. Oil, coal, and uranium are irreplaceable and thus subject to dramatic cost increases; water, however, is self-renewing and more stable in cost.

Ways to coordinate information in sentences

- **Link main clauses with a comma and a coordinating conjunction:** *and, but, or, nor, for, so, yet* (p. 432).

  Independence Hall in Philadelphia is now restored, but fifty years ago it was in bad shape.

- **Relate main clauses with a semicolon alone or a semicolon and a conjunctive adverb:** *however, indeed, thus,* etc. (pp. 453, 455).

  The building was standing; however, it suffered from neglect.

- **Within clauses, link words and phrases with a coordinating conjunction:** *and, but, or, nor* (p. 259).

  The people and officials of the nation were indifferent to Independence Hall or took it for granted.

- **Link main clauses, words, or phrases with a correlative conjunction:** *both . . . and, not only . . . but also,* etc. (p. 260).

  People not only took the building for granted but also neglected it.

sentence-combining techniques. Such practices work best if students are encouraged to work on them over the course of a semester, as this handbook recommends, rather than just in one unit or lesson. The exercises in this chapter ask students to revise sentences and longer passages and to combine sentences in ways that implement the range of strategies introduced in the chapter.

COLLABORATIVE LEARNING

COORDINATING FOR FUN

Have each small group write a paragraph or two made up of short declarative sentences. (Students often enjoy the opportunity to create humorously short sentences on a topic of their choice.) Groups then trade exercises and revise them using the sentence-combining techniques they have learned in this section.

COMPUTER ACTIVITY

I'VE GOT A LITTLE LIST

You may wish to remind students that section 12d of the handbook contains a detailed discussion of coordinating conjunctions. If students make a simple list of the conjunctions and keep it on their computer where it is handy, they may find themselves becoming more aware of the words and their functions as they read and write:

and	or	for	yet
but	nor	so	

TRANSPARENCY MASTER 24.1

ANOTHER LITTLE LIST

Section 12d of the handbook also contains a detailed discussion of conjunctive adverbs. You can help create awareness of conjunctive adverbs by asking students to make a list of the words and keep it in a convenient place on their computer. As they read and write later, students may pay greater attention to the conjunctive adverbs and their functions:

also	namely	anyway
next	besides	now
certainly	otherwise	finally
similarly	further	still
however	then	indeed
therefore	likewise	thus
meanwhile	undoubtedly	

The information in both passages is essentially the same, but the second is shorter and considerably easier to read and understand because it links coordinate ideas with the underlined words.

Punctuating coordinated words, phrases, and clauses

Most coordinated words, phrases, and subordinate clauses are not punctuated with commas (see p. 448). The exceptions are items in a series and coordinate adjectives:

> We rely heavily on <u>coal, oil, and uranium</u>. [A series; see p. 441.]
> <u>Dirty, unhealthy</u> air is one result. [Coordinate adjectives; see p. 442.]

In a sentence consisting of two main clauses, punctuation depends on whether a coordinating conjunction, a conjunctive adverb, or no connecting word links the clauses:

> Oil is irreplaceable, <u>but</u> water is self-renewing. [See p. 432.]
> Oil is irreplaceable; <u>however</u>, water is self-renewing. [See p. 455.]
> Oil is irreplaceable; water is self-renewing. [See p. 453.]

1 Using coordination effectively

A string of coordinated elements—especially main clauses—creates the same effect as a string of simple sentences: it obscures the relative importance of ideas and details.

Excessive coordination	The weeks leading up to the resignation of President Richard Nixon were eventful, and the Supreme Court and the Congress closed in on him, and the Senate Judiciary Committee voted to begin impeachment proceedings, and finally the President resigned on August 9, 1974.

Such a passage needs editing to stress the important points (underlined below) and to de-emphasize the less important information:

Revised	The weeks leading up to the resignation of President <u>Richard Nixon were eventful</u>, as the Supreme Court and the Congress closed in on him and the Senate Judiciary Committee voted to begin impeachment proceedings. Finally, <u>the President resigned</u> on August 9, 1974.

2 Coordinating logically

Coordinated sentence elements should be logically equal and related, and the relation between them should be the one expressed by the connecting word. If either principle is violated, the result is **faulty coordination**.

Faulty	John Stuart Mill was a nineteenth-century utilitarian, and he believed that actions should be judged by their usefulness or by the happiness they cause. [The two clauses are not separate and equal: the second expands on the first by explaining what a utilitarian such as Mill believed.]
Revised	John Stuart Mill, a nineteenth-century utilitarian, believed that actions should be judged by their usefulness or by the happiness they cause.
Faulty	Mill is recognized as a utilitarian, and he did not found the utilitarian school of philosophy. [The two clauses seem to contrast, requiring *but* or *yet* between them.]
Revised	Mill is recognized as a utilitarian, but he did not found the utilitarian school of philosophy.

EXERCISE 24.1   Sentence combining: Coordination

Combine sentences in the following passages to coordinate related ideas in the ways that seem most effective to you. You will have to supply coordinating conjunctions or conjunctive adverbs and the appropriate punctuation. (You can do this exercise online at *ablongman.com/littlebrown*.)

1. Many chronic misspellers do not have the time to master spelling rules. They may not have the motivation. They may rely on dictionaries to catch misspellings. Most dictionaries list words under their correct spellings. One kind of dictionary is designed for chronic misspellers. It lists each word under its common *mis*spellings. It then provides the correct spelling. It also provides the definition.
2. Henry Hudson was an English explorer. He captained ships for the Dutch East India Company. On a voyage in 1610 he passed by Greenland. He sailed into a great bay in today's northern Canada. He thought he and his sailors could winter there. The cold was terrible. Food ran out. The sailors mutinied. The sailors cast Hudson adrift in a small boat. Eight others were also in the boat. Hudson and his companions perished.

EXERCISE 24.2   Revising: Excessive or faulty coordination

Revise the following sentences to eliminate excessive or faulty coordination. Relate ideas effectively by adding or subordinating information or by forming more than one sentence. Each item has more than one possible answer. (You can do this exercise online at *ablongman.com/littlebrown*.)

Example:

My dog barks, and I have to move out of my apartment.

Because my dog's barking disturbs my neighbors, I have to move out of my apartment.

Ask students to complete Exercises 24.1 and 24.2 individually and then to compare and revise their responses in small groups. You might ask each group to present a successful combination to the class and to discuss why it seems more effective.

ANSWERS: EXERCISE 24.1

Possible revisions

1. Many chronic misspellers do not have the time or motivation to master spelling rules. They may rely on dictionaries to catch misspellings, but most dictionaries list words under their correct spellings. One kind of dictionary is designed for chronic misspellers. It lists each word under its common *mis*spellings and then provides the correct spelling and definition.
2. Henry Hudson was an English explorer, but he captained ships for the Dutch East India Company. On a voyage in 1610 he passed Greenland and sailed into a great bay in today's northern Canada. He thought he and his sailors could winter there, but the cold was terrible and food ran out. The sailors mutinied and cast Hudson and eight others adrift in a small boat. Hudson and his companions perished.

USING STUDENT WRITING

Ask students to share a paragraph or two from their drafts with the other members of their group. Group members should comment on the use of coordination and subordination and suggest places where more or less of either might aid the writer in achieving her or his purpose.

AVOIDING EXCESSIVE SUBORDINATION

Choose paragraphs from student essays that demonstrate overuse or faulty use of subordination, and distribute them to the class. Have students rewrite the paragraphs and then compare their versions in small groups to determine which are the most clear and effective revisions.

ANSWERS: EXERCISE 24.2

Possible answers

1. <u>Because</u> soldiers admired their commanding officers, <u>they often</u> gave them nicknames <u>containing</u> the word "old," <u>even though</u> not all of the commanders were old.
2. General Thomas "Stonewall" Jackson was also called "Old Jack," <u>although</u> he was not yet forty years old.
3. Another Southern general, <u>whose full name was James Longstreet</u>, was called "Old Pete."
4. The Union General Henry W. Halleck had a reputation as a good military strategist, and he was an expert on the work of a French military authority, Henri Jomini. <u>Therefore</u>, Halleck was called "Old Brains."
5. <u>After</u> General William Henry Harrison won a victory at the Battle of Tippecanoe, <u>he</u> received the nickname "Old Tippecanoe." He used the name in his presidential campaign slogan "Tippecanoe and Tyler, Too." <u>Although</u> he won the election in 1840, <u>he</u> died of pneumonia a month after taking office.

COMPUTER ACTIVITY

SCAVENGER HUNT

Ask students to hunt around on the Web for one example of each kind of subordinating structure (space or time, cause or effect, condition, concession, purpose, and identification.) If your classroom is networked, you can do this exercise as a race during a class period, and have students post their examples (and the links to where they found them) to the rest of the class.

---

1. Often soldiers admired their commanding officers, and they gave them nicknames, and these names frequently contained the word "old," but not all of the commanders were old.
2. General Thomas "Stonewall" Jackson was also called "Old Jack," and he was not yet forty years old.
3. Another Southern general in the Civil War was called "Old Pete," and his full name was James Longstreet.
4. The Union general Henry W. Halleck had a reputation as a good military strategist, and he was an expert on the work of a French military authority, Henri Jomini, and Halleck was called "Old Brains."
5. General William Henry Harrison won the Battle of Tippecanoe, and he received the nickname "Old Tippecanoe," and he used the name in his presidential campaign slogan "Tippecanoe and Tyler, Too," and he won the election in 1840, but he died of pneumonia a month after taking office.

24b   Subordinating to distinguish main ideas

With **subordination** you use words or word groups to indicate that some ideas in a sentence are less important than the idea in the main clause. In the following sentence, it is difficult to tell what is most important:

| Excessive coordination | Computer prices have dropped, and production costs have dropped more slowly, and computer manufacturers have had to contend with shrinking profits. |

The following revision places the point of the sentence (shrinking profits) in the main clause and reduces the rest of the information to a modifier (underlined):

| Revised | <u>Because production costs have dropped more slowly than prices</u>, computer manufacturers have had to contend with shrinking profits. |

No rules can specify what information in a sentence you should make primary and what you should subordinate; the decision will depend on your meaning. But, in general, you should consider using subordinate structures for details of time, cause, condition, concession, purpose, and identification (size, location, and the like). You can subordinate information with the structures listed in the box opposite.

In general, the shorter a subordinate structure is, the less emphasis it has. The following examples show how subordinate structures may convey various meanings with various weights. (Some appropriate subordinating words for each meaning appear in parentheses.)

Ways to subordinate information in sentences

- **Use a subordinate clause beginning with a subordinating conjunction:** *although, because, if, whereas,* etc. (p. 253).

  Although some citizens had tried to rescue Independence Hall, they had not gained substantial public support.

- **Use a subordinate clause beginning with a relative pronoun:** *who, whoever, which, that* (p. 254).

  The first strong step was taken by the federal government, which made the building a national monument.

- **Use a phrase** (p. 244).

  Like most national monuments, Independence Hall is protected by the National Park Service. [Prepositional phrase.]

  Protecting many popular tourist sites, the service is a highly visible government agency. [Verbal phrase.]

- **Use an appositive** (p. 257).

  The National Park Service, a branch of the Department of Interior, also runs Yosemite and other wilderness parks.

- **Use a modifying word.**

  At the red brick Independence Hall, park rangers give guided tours and protect the irreplaceable building from vandalism.

Space or time (*after, before, since, until, when, while; at, in, on, until*)

The mine explosion killed six workers. The owners adopted safety measures.

After the mine explosion killed six workers, the owners adopted safety measures. [Subordinate clause.]

After six deaths in a mine explosion, the owners adopted safety measures. [Prepositional phrases.]

Cause or effect (*as, because, since, so that; because of, due to*)

Jones had been without work for six months. He was having trouble paying his bills.

Because Jones had been without work for six months, he was having trouble paying his bills. [Subordinate clause.]

Having been jobless for six months, Jones could not pay his bills. [Verbal phrase.]

Condition (*if, provided, since, unless, whenever; with, without*)

Forecasters predict a mild winter. Farmers hope for an early spring.

Whenever forecasters predict a mild winter, farmers hope for an early spring. [Subordinate clause.]

TRANSPARENCY MASTER 24.2

GETTING A FRESH LOOK

Give students a fresh look at their own writing by asking them to revise a portion of a graded essay following specific directions, such as "Add subordination" or "Use more imaginative subordinating words." To maximize the freshness of the viewing process, tell students who have been composing on the computer screen to perform this revision on a printout copy of their draft; students who have been working on printouts can try performing the revision onscreen.

DISTINCTIONS BETWEEN SUBORDINATING WORDS

Some ESL students may understand the conceptual differences among words that subordinate according to space or time, cause or effect, condition, concession, purpose, and identification (see the list on pp. 399–400). However, within each category, they may have a harder time knowing which word to use; so, for instance, they may use *although, as if, even though, though, despite, except for,* and *in spite of* interchangeably. Ask them to collect examples of proper use of each of these terms from their reading, and then discuss why each one works in its particular context.

RESOURCES AND IDEAS

On sentence combining

Crowhurst, Marion. "Sentence Combining: Maintaining Realistic Expectations." *College Composition and Communication* 34 (1983): 62–72. Crowhurst offers pragmatic suggestions about what teachers should and should not expect when introducing sentence combining into their classrooms.

Daiker, Donald, Andrew Kerek, and Max Morenberg. *Sentence Combining: A Rhetorical Perspective.* Carbondale: Southern Illinois UP, 1985.

Melamed, Evelyn B., and Harvey Minkoff. "Transitions: A Key to Mature Reading and Writing." In *Teaching the Basics—Really!* Ed.

With forecasts for a mild winter, farmers hope for an early spring. [Prepositional phrase.]

Concession (although, as if, even though, though; despite, except for, in spite of)

The horse looked gentle. It proved hard to manage.

Although the horse looked gentle, it proved hard to manage. [Subordinate clause.]

The horse, a gentle-looking animal, proved hard to manage. [Appositive.]

The gentle-looking horse proved hard to manage. [Single word.]

Purpose (in order that, so that, that; for, toward)

Congress passed new immigration laws. Many Vietnamese refugees could enter the United States.

Congress passed new immigration laws so that many Vietnamese refugees could enter the United States. [Subordinate clause.]

Congress passed new immigration laws, permitting many Vietnamese refugees to enter the United States. [Verbal phrase.]

Identification (that, when, where, which, who; by, from, of)

Old barns are common in New England. They are often painted red.

Old barns, which are often painted red, are common in New England. [Subordinate clause.]

Old barns, often painted red, are common in New England. [Verbal phrase.]

Old red barns are common in New England. [Single word.]

Punctuating subordinate constructions

A modifying word, phrase, or clause that introduces a sentence is usually set off from the rest of the sentence with a comma (see p. 433):

Unfortunately, the bank failed.
In a little over six months, the bank became insolvent.
When the bank failed, many reporters investigated.

A modifier that interrupts or concludes a main clause is *not* set off with punctuation when it is essential to the meaning of a word or words in the clause (see p. 435):

One article about the bank failure won a prize.
The article that won the prize appeared in the local newspaper.
The reporter wrote the article because the bank failure affected many residents of the town.

When an interrupting or concluding modifier is *not* essential to meaning, but simply adds information to the sentence, it *is* set off with punctuation, usually a comma or commas (see p. 435):

> The bank, over forty years old, never reopened after its doors were closed.
> The bank managers, who were cleared of any wrongdoing, all found new jobs.
> Some customers of the bank never recovered all their money, though most of them tried to do so.

Like a modifier, an appositive is set off with punctuation (usually a comma or commas) only when it is *not* essential to the meaning of the word it refers to (see p. 437):

> The bank, First City, was the oldest in town.
> Our newspaper, the *Chronicle*, was one of several reporting the story.

A dash or dashes may also be used to set off a nonessential appositive, particularly when it contains commas (see p. 480). A concluding appositive is sometimes set off with a colon (see p. 477).

1   Subordinating logically

Use subordination only for the less important information in a sentence. **Faulty subordination** reverses the dependent relation the reader expects:

Faulty	Ms. Angelo was in her first year of teaching, although she was a better instructor than others with many years of experience. [The sentence suggests that Angelo's inexperience is the main idea, whereas the writer meant to stress her skill *despite* her inexperience.]
Revised	Although Ms. Angelo was in her first year of teaching, she was a better instructor than others with many years of experience.

2   Using subordination effectively

Subordination can do much to organize and emphasize information. But it loses that power when you try to cram too much loosely related detail into one long sentence:

Overloaded	The boats that were moored at the dock when the hurricane, which was one of the worst in three decades, struck were ripped from their moorings, because the owners had not been adequately prepared, since the weather service had predicted that the storm would blow out to sea, which storms do at this time of year.

Ouida Clapp. Urbana: NCTE, 1977, 17–21. The authors describe exercises to help students make logical links between sentences and parts of sentences with transitions.

O'Hare, Frank. *Sentence-Combining: Improving Student Writing without Formal Grammar Instruction*. Urbana: NCTE, 1973. O'Hare demonstrates the improvements that can be effected when students practice sentence combining.

Strong, William. "Creative Approaches to Sentence Combining." ERIC, 1986. ED 274 985. Strong offers a number of examples and classroom activities to help teach sentence-combining techniques.

Williams, James D. *Preparing to Teach Writing*. Mahwah, NJ: Lawrence Erlbaum Associates, 1996. See the section on "Style and Sentence Combining," which explores the connections between syntactic and developmental maturity in teaching sentence combining (124–130).

On improving sentence style

Angell, David, and Brent Heslop. *The Elements of E-Mail Style*. Boston: Addison, 1994. This account of the particular conventions of e-mail style makes clear how the context and medium shape writers' stylistic choices and effects.

Lanham, Richard. *Analyzing Prose*. New York: Scribner, 1983. Lanham offers extensive advice on revising for stylistic effect.

Soles, Derek. "An Analysis of the Style of Exemplary Freshman Writing." *Teaching English in the Two-Year College* 33 (September 2005): 38–49. Using Corbett's prose style matrix, Soles analyzes the style of exemplary freshman essays and concludes that there is an identifiable, hence teachable style valued by freshman writing instructors.

Williams, Joseph. *Style: Ten Lessons in Clarity and Grace*. 6th ed. New York: Longman, 1999. Williams's how-to manual for improving style at the sentence and word level is especially strong in discussing coordination and subordination.

Such sentences usually have more than one idea that deserves a main clause, so they are best revised by sorting their details into more than one sentence:

> Revised   Struck by one of the worst hurricanes in three decades, <u>the boats at the dock were ripped from their moorings</u>. <u>The owners were unprepared</u> because the weather service had said that storms at this time of year blow out to sea.

A common form of excessive subordination occurs with a string of adjective clauses, each beginning with *which, who,* or *that:*

> Stringy   The company opened a new plant outside Louisville, which is in Kentucky and which is on the Ohio River, which forms the border between Kentucky and Ohio.

To revise such sentences, recast some of the subordinate clauses as other kinds of modifying structures:

> Revised   The company opened a new plant outside Louisville, <u>Kentucky</u>, <u>a city across the Ohio River from Ohio</u>.

EXERCISE 24.3   Sentence combining: Subordination

Combine each of the following pairs of sentences twice, each time using one of the subordinate structures in parentheses to make a single sentence. You will have to add, delete, change, and rearrange words. (You can do this exercise online at *ablongman.com/littlebrown*.)

> *Example:*
> During the late eighteenth century, workers carried beverages in brightly colored bottles. The bottles had cork stoppers. (*Clause beginning that. Phrase beginning with.*)
>
> During the late eighteenth century, workers carried beverages in brightly colored bottles <u>that had cork stoppers</u>.
>
> During the late eighteenth century, workers carried beverages in brightly colored bottles <u>with cork stoppers</u>.

1. The bombardier beetle sees an enemy. It shoots out a jet of chemicals to protect itself. (*Clause beginning <u>when</u>. Phrase beginning <u>seeing</u>.*)
2. The beetle's spray is very potent. It consists of hot and irritating chemicals. (*Phrase beginning <u>consisting</u>. Phrase beginning <u>of</u>.*)
3. The spray's two chemicals are stored separately in the beetle's body and mixed in the spraying gland. The chemicals resemble a nerve-gas weapon. (*Phrase beginning <u>stored</u>. Clause beginning <u>which</u>.*)
4. The tip of the beetle's abdomen sprays the chemicals. The tip revolves like a turret on a World War II bomber. (*Phrase beginning <u>revolving</u>. Phrase beginning <u>spraying</u>.*)
5. The beetle defeats most of its enemies. It is still eaten by spiders and birds. (*Clause beginning <u>although</u>. Phrase beginning <u>except</u>.*)

ANSWERS: EXERCISE 24.3

Possible answers

1. <u>When the bombardier beetle sees an enemy,</u> it shoots out a jet of chemicals to protect itself.

   <u>Seeing an enemy,</u> the bombardier beetle shoots out a jet of chemicals to protect itself.

2. <u>Consisting of hot and irritating chemicals,</u> the beetle's spray is very potent.

   The beetle's spray <u>of hot and irritating chemicals</u> is very potent.

3. <u>Stored separately in the beetle's body and mixed in the spraying gland</u>, the spray's two chemicals resemble a nerve-gas weapon.

   The spray's two chemicals, <u>which are stored separately in the beetle's body and mixed in the spraying gland</u>, resemble a nerve-gas weapon.

4. <u>Revolving like a turret on a World War II bomber,</u> the tip of the beetle's abdomen sprays the chemicals.

   <u>Spraying the chemicals,</u> the tip of the beetle's abdomen revolves like a turret on a World War II bomber.

5. <u>Although the beetle defeats most of its enemies,</u> it is still eaten by spiders and birds.

   The beetle defeats most of its enemies <u>except spiders and birds</u>.

EXERCISE 24.4   Revising: Subordination

Rewrite the following paragraph in the way you think most effective to subordinate the less important ideas to the more important ones. Use subordinate clauses, phrases, and single words as you think appropriate. (You can do this exercise online at *ablongman.com/littlebrown*.)

    Fewer students today are majoring in the liberal arts. I mean by "liberal arts" such subjects as history, English, and the social sciences. Students think a liberal arts degree will not help them get jobs. They are wrong. They may not get practical, job-related experience from the liberal arts, but they will get a broad education, and it will never again be available to them. Many employers look for more than a technical, professional education. They think such an education can make an employee's views too narrow. The employers want open-minded employees. They want employees to think about problems from many angles. The liberal arts curriculum instills such flexibility. The flexibility is vital to the health of our society.

EXERCISE 24.5   Revising: Faulty or excessive subordination

Revise the following sentences to eliminate faulty or excessive subordination. Correct faulty subordination by reversing main and subordinate structures. Correct excessive subordination by coordinating equal ideas or by making separate sentences. (You can do this exercise online at *ablongman.com/littlebrown*.)

Example:

Terrified to return home, he had driven his mother's car into a cornfield.

<u>Having driven his mother's car into a cornfield</u>, he was terrified to return home.

1. Genaro González is blessed with great writing talent, which means that his novel *Rainbow's End* and his story collection *Only Sons* have been published.
2. He loves to write, although he has also earned a doctorate in psychology.
3. His first story, which reflects his consciousness of his Aztec heritage and place in the world, is titled "Un Hijo del Sol."
4. González, who writes equally well in English and Spanish, received a large fellowship that enabled him to take a leave of absence from the University of Texas–Pan American, where he teaches psychology, so that he could write without worrying about an income.
5. González wrote the first version of "Un Hijo del Sol" while he was a sophomore at Pan American, which is in the Rio Grande valley of southern Texas, which González calls "el Valle" in the story.

24c   Choosing clear connectors

    Most connecting words signal specific and unambiguous relations; for instance, *but* clearly indicates contrast, and *because*

ANSWERS: EXERCISE 24.4
Possible revision

    Fewer students today are majoring in the liberal arts—that is, in such subjects as history, English, and the social sciences. Although students think a liberal arts degree will not help them get jobs, they are wrong. They may not get practical, job-related experience from the liberal arts, but they will get a broad education <u>that will</u> never again be available to them. Many employers look for more than a technical, professional education <u>because</u> they think such an education can make an employee's views too narrow. <u>Instead, they</u> want open-minded employees <u>who can think</u> about problems from many angles. <u>Such flexibility</u>—vital to the health of our society—is just what the liberal arts curriculum instills.

ANSWERS: EXERCISE 24.5
Possible answers

1. Because Genaro González is blessed with great writing talent, his novel *Rainbow's End* and his story collection *Only Sons* have been published.
2. Although he loves to write, he has also earned a doctorate in psychology.
3. His first story, which is entitled "Un Hijo del Sol," reflects his consciousness of his Aztec heritage and place in the world.
4. González writes equally well in English and Spanish. He received a large fellowship enabling him to take a leave of absence from the University of Texas–Pan American, where he teaches psychology. He could write without worrying about an income.
5. González wrote the first version of "Un Hijo del Sol" while he was a sophomore at Pan American. The university is in the Rio Grande valley of southern Texas, which González calls "el Valle" in the story.

REWRITING AN ESSAY

    Give students a passage from a student or professional essay (posted to your class Web site or sent as an e-mail attachment) and ask them to rewrite it following a specified strategy: adding subordination, using different subordinators, or adding coordination. They can use one color script for subordination revisions, and another color script for coordination revisions. This exercise can be extended by having students rewrite the passage to change its emphasis.

clearly indicates cause. A few connectors, however, require careful use, either because they are ambiguous in many contexts or because they are often misused.

1 Using *as* and *while* clearly

The subordinating conjunction *as* can indicate several relations, including comparison and time:

| Comparison | The technicians work quickly, as they are required to do. |
| Time | One shift starts as the other stops. |

Avoid using *as* to indicate cause. It is unclear.

Unclear	As the experiment was occurring, the laboratory was sealed. [Time or cause intended?]
Revised	When the experiment was occurring, the laboratory was sealed. [Time.]
Revised	Because the experiment was occurring, the laboratory was sealed. [Cause.]

The subordinating conjunction *while* can indicate either time or concession. Unless the context makes the meaning of *while* unmistakably clear, choose a more exact connector:

Unclear	While technicians work in the next room, they cannot hear the noise. [Time or concession intended?]
Revised	When technicians work in the next room, they cannot hear the noise. [Time.]
Revised	Although technicians work in the next room, they cannot hear the noise. [Concession.]

2 Using *as* and *like* correctly

The use of *as* as a substitute for *whether* or *that* is considered nonstandard (it does not conform to spoken and written standard English):

| Nonstandard | They are not sure as the study succeeded. |
| Revised | They are not sure whether [or that] the study succeeded. |

Although the preposition *like* is often used as a conjunction in informal speech and in advertising (*Dirt-Away works like a soap should*), writing generally requires the conjunction *as*, *as if*, *as though*, or *that*:

| Speech | It seemed like it did succeed. |
| Writing | It seemed as if [or as though or that] it did succeed. |

EXERCISE 24.6 Revising: Coordination and subordination

The following paragraph consists entirely of simple sentences. Use co-ordination and subordination to combine sentences in the ways you think most effective to emphasize main ideas. (You can do this exercise online at *ablongman.com/littlebrown*.)

Sir Walter Raleigh personified the Elizabethan Age. That was the period of Elizabeth I's rule of England. The period occurred in the last half of the sixteenth century. Raleigh was a courtier and poet. He was also an explorer and entrepreneur. Supposedly, he gained Queen Elizabeth's favor. He did this by throwing his cloak beneath her feet at the right moment. She was just about to step over a puddle. There is no evidence for this story. It does illustrate Raleigh's dramatic and dy-namic personality. His energy drew others to him. He was one of Elizabeth's favorites. She supported him. She also dispensed favors to him. However, he lost his queen's goodwill. Without her permission he seduced one of her maids of honor. He eventually married the maid of honor. Elizabeth died. Then her successor imprisoned Raleigh in the Tower of London. Her successor was James I. The king falsely charged Raleigh with treason. Raleigh was released after thirteen years. He was arrested again two years later on the old treason charges. At the age of sixty-six he was beheaded.

Note See page 420 for an exercise involving coordination and subordination along with parallelism and other techniques for effec-tive sentences.

CHAPTER 25

Using Parallelism

Parallelism is a similarity of grammatical form between two or more elements.

The air is dirtied by	‖	factories belching smoke
and	‖	cars spewing exhaust.

Parallel structure reinforces and highlights a close relation between compound sentence elements, whether words, phrases, or clauses.

> http://www.ablongman.com/littlebrown ▶
>
> Visit the companion Web site for more help and additional exercises on parallelism.

TRANSPARENCY MASTER 24.3

ANSWERS: EXERCISE 24.6

Possible revision

Sir Walter Raleigh personified the Elizabethan <u>Age, the</u> period of Elizabeth I's rule of <u>England, in</u> the last half of the sixteenth century. Raleigh was a courtier, a poet, an explorer, and an entrepre-neur. Supposedly, he gained Queen Elizabeth's <u>fa-vor by</u> throwing his cloak beneath her feet at the right moment, <u>just as she was</u> about to step over a puddle. <u>Although</u> there is no evidence for this <u>story, it</u> illustrates Raleigh's dramatic and dy-namic personality. His energy drew others to <u>him, and</u> he was one of Elizabeth's favorites. She sup-ported <u>him and</u> dispensed favors to him. However, he lost <u>his queen's goodwill when without</u> her per-mission he <u>seduced and eventually married</u> one of her maids of honor. <u>After Elizabeth died,</u> her suc-cessor, <u>James I,</u> imprisoned Raleigh in the Tower of London <u>on false charges of treason.</u> Raleigh was released after thirteen <u>years but</u> arrested again two years later on the old treason charges. At the age of sixty-six he was beheaded.

mycomplab

Please visit MyCompLab at *www.mycomplab.com* for more on the writing process.

HIGHLIGHTS

This discussion of parallelism is divided into two sections, and it moves from correctness to ef-fective style. The opening section addresses the obligatory use of parallelism in coordinate con-structions—those linked by coordinating con-junctions and correlative conjunctions; those in comparisons and contrasts; and those in lists, outlines, and the like. The second section exam-ines how parallelism can be used within and among sentences to increase coherence, empha-size meaning, and heighten the effect. For some students you may wish to emphasize the items in the opening section. But students who have no

COMPANION WEB SITE

See page IAE-56 for companion Web site content description.

trouble maintaining obligatory parallelism can often profit by working more creatively with parallelism to tighten and clarify their writing. Exercise 25.3, a sentence-combining exercise, is designed to give students a chance to explore the options for expression that parallelism provides. The exercise is likely to be most effective when students are given a chance to (1) discuss with one another the impact of various combinations or (2) work collaboratively in exploring various sentence-combining options.

RESOURCES AND IDEAS

Brooks, Phyllis. "Mimesis: Grammar and the Echoing Voice." *College English* 35 (1973): 161–68. Brooks suggests the writing of paragraphs that imitate the style of a writer but use different content. She indicates that the practice helps students learn to use a variety of structures, including parenthetical expressions, appositives and modifiers, and parallelism plus reference.

Graves, Richard L. "Symmetrical Form and the Rhetoric of the Sentence." *Rhetoric and Composition: A Sourcebook for Teachers.* Upper Montclair: Boynton/Cook, 1984. 119–27. Graves argues that since comparison is a natural way for humans to organize information, parallelism is an effective way of helping readers acquire and interpret information.

Walker, Robert L. "The Common Writer: A Case for Parallel Structure." *College Composition and Communication* 21 (1970): 373–79. Walker believes that students should be encouraged to use a variety of sentence structures and parallelism, which he considers important features of mature sentences.

Williams, Joseph M. "The Phenomenology of Error." *College Composition and Communication* 32 (1981): 152–68. Williams describes parallelism problems from the point of view of a writer's stylistic choices.

The principle underlying parallelism is that form should reflect meaning: since the parts of compound constructions have the same function and importance, they should have the same grammatical form.

Note A grammar and style checker cannot recognize problems with parallelism because it cannot recognize the relations among ideas.

25a Using parallelism for coordinate elements

Use parallelism in all the situations illustrated in the box on the facing page.

Note Parallel elements match each other in structure, but they do not always match word for word:

The pioneers passed ‖ through the town
　　　　　　　and ‖ into the vast, unpopulated desert.

1 Using parallelism for elements linked by coordinating conjunctions

The coordinating conjunctions *and, but, or, nor,* and *yet* always signal a need for parallelism:

The industrial base was shifting and shrinking.

Politicians rarely acknowledged the problem or proposed alternatives.

Industrial workers were understandably disturbed that they were losing their jobs and that no one seemed to care.

If sentence elements linked by coordinating conjunctions are not parallel in structure, the resulting sentence will be awkward and distracting:

Nonparallel	Three reasons why steel companies kept losing money were that their plants were inefficient, high labor costs, and foreign competition was increasing.
Revised	Three reasons why steel companies kept losing money were inefficient plants, high labor costs, and increasing foreign competition.

All the words required by idiom or grammar must be stated in compound constructions (see also p. 258).

Nonparallel	Given training, workers can acquire the skills and interest in other jobs. [*Skills* and *interest* require different prepositions, so both must be stated.]
Revised	Given training, workers can acquire the skills for and interest in other jobs.

Patterns of parallelism

- **Use parallel structures for elements connected by coordinating conjunctions** (*and, but, or,* etc.) **or correlative conjunctions** (*both . . . and, neither . . . nor,* etc.):

In 1988 a Greek cyclist, backed up by ‖ engineers,
 physiologists,
 and ‖ athletes,
broke the world's record for human flight
with neither ‖ a boost
 nor ‖ a motor.

- **Use parallel structures for elements being compared or contrasted:**

 ‖ Pedal power
rather than ‖ horse power
propelled the plane.

- **Use parallel structures for lists, outlines, or headings:**

The four-hour flight was successful because
 ‖ (1) the cyclist was very fit,
 ‖ (2) he flew a straight course over water,
and ‖ (3) he kept the aircraft near the water's surface.

Often, the same word must be repeated to avoid confusion:

Confusing | Thoreau stood up for his principles by not paying his taxes and spending a night in jail. [Did he spend a night in jail or not?]

Revised | Thoreau stood up for his principles by not paying his taxes and by spending a night in jail.

Be sure that clauses beginning *who* or *which* are coordinated only with other *who* or *which* clauses, even when the pronoun is not repeated:

Nonparallel | Thoreau is the nineteenth-century essayist who retired to the woods and he wrote about nature.

Revised | Thoreau is the nineteenth-century essayist who retired to the woods and [who] wrote about nature.

2 Using parallelism for elements linked by correlative conjunctions

Correlative conjunctions are pairs of connectors. For example:

both . . . and neither . . . nor not only . . . but also
either . . . or not . . . but whether . . . or

SAMPLE ESSAYS

Journal entries and student drafts, along with essays from a reader or a similar source, provide a gold mine of material on which to practice. Ask students to look for parallelism in essays from a reader or a similar source. If the students are working in groups, ask them not only to reach consensus on which elements are parallel but also to decide what functions the parallelism performs.

ADDING PARALLELISM

Take a loose-jointed student essay or a professional essay and distribute it to students (working individually or in groups), asking them to make the sentences denser by adding parallelism wherever possible. Ask them also to decide when the parallelism adds to the essay and when it detracts.

Correlative conjunctions stress equality and balance and thus emphasize the relation between elements, even long phrases and clauses. The elements should be parallel to confirm their relation:

> It is not a tax bill but a tax relief bill, providing relief not for the needy but for the greedy. —Franklin Delano Roosevelt

> At the end of the novel, Huck Finn both rejects society's values by turning down money and a home and affirms his own values by setting out for "the territory."

Most errors in parallelism with correlative conjunctions occur when the element after the second connector does not match the element after the first connector.

Nonparallel	Mark Twain refused either to ignore the moral blindness of his society or spare the reader's sensibilities. [*To* follows *either*, so it must also follow *or*.]
Revised	Mark Twain refused either to ignore the moral blindness of his society or to spare the reader's sensibilities.
Nonparallel	Huck Finn learns not only that human beings have an enormous capacity for folly but also enormous dignity. [The first element includes *that human beings have;* the second element does not.]
Revised	Huck Finn learns that human beings have not only an enormous capacity for folly but also enormous dignity.

3 Using parallelism for elements being compared or contrasted

Elements being compared or contrasted should ordinarily be cast in the same grammatical form.

> It is better to live rich than to die rich. —Samuel Johnson

Weak	The study found that most welfare recipients wanted to work rather than handouts.
Revised	The study found that most welfare recipients wanted work rather than handouts.
Revised	The study found that most welfare recipients wanted to work rather than to accept handouts.

4 Using parallelism for lists, outlines, or headings

The elements of a list or outline that divides a larger subject are coordinate and should be parallel in structure. Parallelism is essential in the headings that divide a paper into sections (see p. 119) and in a formal topic outline (see p. 37).

Faulty	Improved
Changes in Renaissance England	Changes in Renaissance England
1. Extension of trade routes	1. Extension of trade routes
2. <u>Merchant class became</u> more powerful	2. <u>Increased power</u> of the merchant class
3. <u>The death</u> of feudalism	3. <u>Death</u> of feudalism
4. <u>Upsurging</u> of the arts	4. <u>Upsurge</u> of the arts
5. <u>The sciences were encouraged</u>	5. <u>Encouragement</u> of the sciences
6. <u>Religious quarrels began</u>	6. <u>Rise</u> of religious quarrels

EXERCISE 25.1   Identifying parallel elements

Identify the parallel elements in the following sentences. How does parallelism contribute to the effectiveness of each sentence? (You can do this exercise online at *ablongman.com/littlebrown*.)

1. Eating an animal has not always been an automatic or an everyday affair; it has tended to be done on solemn occasions and for a special treat.   —Margaret Visser
2. They [pioneer women] rolled out dough on the wagon seats, cooked with fires made out of buffalo chips, tended the sick, and marked the graves of their children, their husbands and each other.   —Ellen Goodman
3. The mornings are the pleasantest times in the apartment, exhaustion having set in, the sated mosquitoes at rest on ceiling and walls, sleeping it off, the room a swirl of tortured bedclothes and abandoned garments, the vines in their full leafiness filtering the hard light of day, the air conditioner silent at last, like the mosquitoes.   —E. B. White
4. Aging paints every action gray, lies heavy on every movement, imprisons every thought.   —Sharon Curtin

EXERCISE 25.2   Revising: Parallelism

Revise the following sentences to make coordinate, compared, or listed elements parallel in structure. Add or delete words or rephrase as necessary. (You can do this exercise online at *ablongman.com/littlebrown*.)

Example:
After emptying her bag, searching the apartment, and she called the library, Jennifer realized she had lost the book.
After emptying her bag, searching the apartment, and <u>calling</u> the library, Jennifer realized she had lost the book.

ANSWERS: EXERCISE 25.2

Possible answers

1. The ancient Greeks celebrated four athletic contests: the Olympic Games at Olympia, the Isthmian Games near Corinth, the Pythian Games at Delphi, and the Nemean Games at Cleonae.
2. Each day of the games consisted of either athletic events or ceremonies and sacrifices to the gods.
3. In the years between the games, competitors were taught wrestling, javelin throwing, and boxing.
4. Competitors ran sprints, participated in spectacular chariot and horse races, and ran long distances while wearing full armor.
5. The purpose of such events was developing physical strength, demonstrating skill and endurance, and sharpening the skills needed for war.
6. Events were held both for men and for boys.
7. At the Olympic Games the spectators cheered their favorites to victory, attended sacrifices to the gods, and feasted on the meat not burned in offerings.
8. The athletes competed less to achieve great wealth than to gain honor for both themselves and their cities.
9. Of course, exceptional athletes received financial support from patrons, poems and statues by admiring artists, and even lavish living quarters from their sponsoring cities.
10. With the medal counts and flag ceremonies, today's Olympians sometimes seem to be proving their countries' superiority more than demonstrating individual talent.

1. The ancient Greeks celebrated four athletic contests: the Olympic Games at Olympia, the Isthmian Games were held near Corinth, at Delphi the Pythian Games, and the Nemean Games were sponsored by the people of Cleonae.
2. Each day of the games consisted of either athletic events or holding ceremonies and sacrifices to the gods.
3. In the years between the games, competitors were taught wrestling, javelin throwing, and how to box.
4. Competitors participated in running sprints, spectacular chariot and horse races, and running long distances while wearing full armor.
5. The purpose of such events was developing physical strength, demonstrating skill and endurance, and to sharpen the skills needed for war.
6. Events were held for both men and for boys.
7. At the Olympic Games the spectators cheered their favorites to victory, attended sacrifices to the gods, and they feasted on the meat not burned in offerings.
8. The athletes competed less to achieve great wealth than for gaining honor both for themselves and their cities.
9. Of course, exceptional athletes received financial support from patrons, poems and statues by admiring artists, and they even got lavish living quarters from their sponsoring cities.
10. With the medal counts and flag ceremonies, today's Olympians sometimes seem to be proving their countries' superiority more than to demonstrate individual talent.

25b   Using parallelism to increase coherence

Effective parallelism will enable you to combine in a single, well-ordered sentence related ideas that you might have expressed in separate sentences. Compare the following three sentences with the original single sentence written by H. L. Mencken:

> Slang originates in the effort of ingenious individuals to make the language more pungent and picturesque. They increase the store of terse and striking words or widen the boundaries of metaphor. Thus a vocabulary for new shades and differences in meaning is provided by slang.

> Slang originates in the effort of ingenious individuals to make the language more pungent and picturesque—to increase the store of terse and striking words, to widen the boundaries of metaphor, and to provide a vocabulary for new shades and differences in meaning.
>
> —H. L. Mencken

Parallel structure works as well to emphasize the connections among related sentences in a paragraph:

> Lewis Mumford stands high in the company of this century's sages. A scholar of cosmic cultural reach and conspicuous public conscience,

a distinguished critic of life, arts, and letters, <u>an unequaled observer of cities and civilizations,</u> *he is* secure in the modern pantheon of great men. *He is* also an enigma and an anachronism. <u>A legend of epic proportions in intellectual and academic circles,</u> *he is* surprisingly little known to the public. —Ada Louise Huxtable

Here, Huxtable tightly binds her sentences with two layers of parallelism: the subject-verb patterns of all four sentences (italic and underlined) and the appositives of the second and fourth sentences (underlined). (See pp. 83–84 for another illustration of parallelism among sentences.)

EXERCISE 25.3 Sentence combining: Parallelism

Combine each group of sentences below into one concise sentence in which parallel elements appear in parallel structures. You will have to add, delete, change, and rearrange words. Each item has more than one possible answer. (You can do this exercise online at *ablongman .com/littlebrown*.)

Example:
The new process works smoothly. It is efficient, too.
The new process works smoothly <u>and efficiently</u>.

1. People can develop post-traumatic stress disorder (PTSD). They develop it after experiencing a dangerous situation. They will also have felt fear for their survival.
2. The disorder can be triggered by a wide variety of events. Combat is a typical cause. Similarly, natural disasters can result in PTSD. Some people experience PTSD after a hostage situation.
3. PTSD can occur immediately after the stressful incident. Or it may not appear until many years later.
4. Sometimes people with PTSD will act irrationally. Moreover, they often become angry.
5. Other symptoms include dreaming that one is reliving the experience. They include hallucinating that one is back in the terrifying place. In another symptom one imagines that strangers are actually one's former torturers.

EXERCISE 25.4 Revising: Parallelism

Revise the following paragraph to create parallelism wherever it is required for grammar or for coherence. (You can do this exercise online at *ablongman.com/littlebrown*.)

The great white shark has an undeserved bad reputation. Many people consider the great white not only swift and powerful but also to be a cunning and cruel predator on humans. However, scientists claim that the great white attacks humans not by choice but as a result of chance. To a shark, our behavior in the water is similar to that of porpoises, seals, and sea lions—the shark's favorite foods. These sea mammals are both agile enough and can move fast enough to evade fast enough to evade the shark. Thus the shark must attack swiftly and noiselessly to surprise the prey and give it little chance to escape. Humans become the shark's victims not because the shark has any preference for or hatred of humans but because humans can neither outswim nor outmaneuver the shark. If the fish were truly a cruel human-eater, it would prolong the terror of its attacks, perhaps by circling or bumping into its intended victims before attacking them.

the shark. Thus the shark must attack with swiftness and noiselessly to surprise the prey and giving it little chance to escape. Humans become the shark's victims not because the shark has any preference or hatred of humans but because humans can neither outswim nor can they outmaneuver the shark. If the fish were truly a cruel human-eater, it would prolong the terror of its attacks, perhaps by circling or bumping into its intended victims before they were attacked.

Note See page 420 for an exercise involving parallelism along with other techniques for effective sentences.

mycomplab2.0

Please visit MyCompLab at *www.mycomplab.com* for more on the writing process.

HIGHLIGHTS

This chapter asks students to think of sentences not as single units but as a sequence of ideas working together. Emphasis, coordination, subordination, and parallelism—topics covered in the preceding chapters—all come into play in the examples in this chapter. You will probably want to direct attention to the introduction to this chapter and to the first two sections, covering strategies for varying the length and structure of sentences and for varying sentence beginnings. You may have to decide, though, how much time to devote to the last two sections, which cover the occasional uses of inverted sentence order and of minor sentence types such as questions and commands.

TRANSPARENCY MASTER 26.1

COMPANION WEB SITE

See page IAE-56 for companion Web site content description.

CHAPTER 26

Achieving Variety

In a paragraph or an essay, each sentence stands in relation to those before and after it. To make sentences work together effectively, you need to vary their length, structure, and word order to reflect the importance and complexity of ideas. Variety sometimes takes care of itself, but you can practice established techniques for achieving varied sentences:

Ways to achieve variety among sentences

- Vary the length and structure of sentences so that important ideas stand out (opposite).
- Vary the beginnings of sentences with modifiers, transitional words and expressions, and occasional expletive constructions (p. 415).
- Occasionally, invert the normal order of subject, verb, and object or complement (p. 418).
- Occasionally, use a command, question, or exclamation (p. 418).

A series of similar sentences will prove monotonous and ineffective, as the following passage illustrates.

http://www.ablongman.com/littlebrown ▶

Visit the companion Web site for more help and an additional exercise on sentence variety.

Ulysses S. Grant and Robert E. Lee met on April 9, 1865. Their meeting place was the parlor of a modest house at Appomattox Court House, Virginia. They met to work out the terms for the surrender of Lee's Army of Northern Virginia. One great chapter of American life ended with their meeting, and another began. Grant and Lee were bringing the Civil War to its virtual finish. Other armies still had to surrender, and the fugitive Confederate government would struggle desperately and vainly. It would try to find some way to go on living with its chief support gone. Grant and Lee had signed the papers, however, and it was all over in effect.

These eight sentences are all between twelve and sixteen words long (counting initials and dates), they are about equally detailed, and they all begin with the subject. We get a sense of names, dates, and events but no immediate sense of how they relate or what is most important.

Now compare the preceding passage with the actual passage written by Bruce Catton. Here the four sentences range from eleven to fifty-five words, and only one sentence begins with its subject:

When Ulysses S. Grant and Robert E. Lee met in the parlor of a modest house at Appomattox Court House, Virginia, on April 9, 1865, to work out the terms for the surrender of Lee's Army of Northern Virginia, a great chapter in American life came to a close, and a great new chapter began.
> Suspenseful periodic sentence (p. 388) focuses attention on meeting; details of place, time, and cause are in opening subordinate clause

These men were bringing the Civil War to its virtual finish.
> Short sentence sums up

To be sure, other armies had yet to surrender, and for a few days the fugitive Confederate government would struggle desperately and vainly, trying to find some way to go on living now that its chief support was gone.
> Cumulative sentence (p. 387) reflects lingering obstacles to peace

But in effect it was all over when Grant and Lee signed the papers.
> Short final sentence indicates futility of further struggle

—Bruce Catton, "Grant and Lee"

The rest of this chapter suggests how you can vary your sentences for the kind of interest and clarity achieved by Catton.

Note Some grammar and style checkers will flag long sentences, and you can check for appropriate variety in a series of such sentences. But generally these programs cannot help you see where variety may be needed because they cannot recognize the relative importance and complexity of your ideas.

26a   Varying sentence length and structure

The sentences of a stylistically effective essay will vary most obviously in their length and the arrangement of main clauses and

RESOURCES AND IDEAS

Barrett, Edward. "Collaboration in the Electronic Classroom." *Technology Review* (February/March 1993): 51–55. This article suggests strategies for structuring group work using computers.

Lanham, Richard. *Analyzing Prose.* New York: Scribner, 1983. Lanham offers extensive advice on revising for stylistic effect.

Rubin, Donald, and Kathryn Greene. "Gender-Typical Style in Written Language." *Research in the Teaching of English* 26 (1992): 7–40. The authors catalog stylistic and syntactic variations that fall along gender lines.

ADDITIONAL ACTIVITIES

Many of the student activities described for Chapters 23 and 24 can be easily adapted for this chapter.

COMPUTER ACTIVITY

USING STYLE CHECKERS

Computerized style checkers are now widely available; however, the quality of the advice they offer varies considerably. These programs are based on standardized readability tests and are not particularly sensitive to writers' purposes or the levels of sophistication of their audiences. (Try feeding the *Gettysburg Address* or *A Letter from Birmingham Jail* into such a program; the advice the style checkers provide for "improving" these essays will shock and amuse you and your students.)

SIMPLE SENTENCES

Take a professional or student essay, reduce it to simple sentences, and ask students to rewrite it, adding variety. Then ask them to work in groups to compare their versions with the original, analyze the differences, and decide as a group which versions are more effective and why.

VISUAL ANALYSIS

Students may wish to make bar charts showing sentence lengths to see the average lengths of sentences they use and to target the variations in length they might want to consider.

RESOURCES AND IDEAS

Walpole, Jane R. "The Vigorous Pursuit of Grace and Style." *The Writing Instructor* 1 (1982): 163–69. Walpole offers a number of exercises for developing students' "ear" for style, with particular emphasis on simple sentences.

Williams, Joseph. *Style: Ten Lessons in Clarity and Grace.* 7th ed. New York: Longman, 2003. Williams provides an excellent how-to manual for improving style at the sentence and word level.

modifiers. The variation in length and structure makes writing both readable and clear.

1 Varying length

In most contemporary writing, sentences vary from about ten to about forty words. When sentences are all at one extreme or the other, readers may have difficulty focusing on main ideas and seeing the relations among them:

- **Long sentences.** If most of your sentences contain thirty-five words or more, your main ideas may not stand out from the details that support them. Break some of the long sentences into shorter, simpler ones.
- **Short sentences.** If most of your sentences contain fewer than ten or fifteen words, all your ideas may seem equally important and the links between them may not be clear. Try combining them with coordination (p. 395) and subordination (p. 398) to show relationships and to stress main ideas over supporting information.

2 Rewriting strings of brief and simple sentences

A series of brief and simple sentences is both monotonous and hard to understand because it forces the reader to sort out relations among ideas. If you find that you depend on brief, simple sentences, work to increase variety by combining some of them into longer units that emphasize and link important ideas while de-emphasizing incidental information. (See Chapter 24.)

The following examples show how a string of simple sentences can be revised into an effective piece of writing:

Monotonous The moon is now drifting away from the earth. It moves away at the rate of about one inch a year. This movement is lengthening our days. They increase a thousandth of a second every century. Forty-seven of our present days will someday make up a month. We might eventually lose the moon altogether. Such great planetary movement rightly concerns astronomers, but it need not worry us. It will take 50 million years.

Revised The moon is now drifting away from the earth about one inch a year. At a thousandth of a second every century, this movement is lengthening our days. Forty-seven of our present days will someday make up a month, if we don't eventually lose the moon altogether. Such great planetary movement rightly concerns astronomers, but it need not worry us. It will take 50 million years.

In the revision, underlining indicates subordinate structures that were simple sentences in the original. With five sentences instead of the original eight, the revision emphasizes the moon's movement, our lengthening days, and the enormous span of time involved.

3 Rewriting strings of compound sentences

Compound sentences are usually just simple sentences linked with conjunctions. Thus a series of them will be as weak as a series of brief, simple sentences, especially if the clauses of the compound sentences are all about the same length:

Monotonous | Physical illness may involve more than the body, for the mind may also be affected. Disorientation is common among sick people, but they are often unaware of it. They may reason abnormally, or they may behave immaturely.

Revised | Physical illness may involve the mind <u>as well as the body. Though often unaware of it,</u> sick people are commonly disoriented. They may reason abnormally <u>or behave immaturely.</u>

The first passage creates a seesaw effect. The revision, with some main clauses shortened or changed into modifiers (underlined), is both clearer and more emphatic. (See p. 396 for more on avoiding excessive coordination.)

EXERCISE 26.1 Revising: Varied sentence structures

Rewrite the following paragraph to increase variety so that important ideas receive greater emphasis than supporting information does. You will have to change some main clauses into modifiers and then combine and reposition the modifiers and the remaining main clauses. (You can do this exercise online at *ablongman.com/littlebrown*.)

Charlotte Perkins Gilman was a leading intellectual in the women's movement during the first decades of the twentieth century. She wrote *Women and Economics*. This book challenged Victorian assumptions about differences between the sexes, and it explored the economic roots of women's oppression. Gilman wrote little about gaining the vote for women, but many feminists were then preoccupied with this issue, and historians have since focused their analyses on this issue. As a result, Gilman's contribution to today's women's movement has often been overlooked.

26b Varying sentence beginnings

An English sentence often begins with its subject, which generally captures old information from a preceding sentence (see pp. 386–87):

ANSWERS: EXERCISE 26.1

Possible revision

Charlotte Perkins Gilman was a leading intellectual in the women's movement during the first decades of the twentieth century. <u>Her book</u> *Women and Economics* <u>challenged</u> Victorian assumptions about the differences between the sexes <u>and</u> explored the economic roots of women's oppression. Gilman wrote little about gaining the vote for women, <u>the issue that then preoccupied feminists and that</u> historians have since focused their analyses on. As a result, Gilman's contribution to today's women's movement has often been overlooked.

SENTENCE LENGTH AND VARIETY

ESL students may replicate the sentence length and sentence variety conventions of their first language when creating sentences in English. It may require considerable practice before they develop an ear for the rhythm and variety of sentences according to English conventions. The same may hold true for native English speakers if they are unfamiliar with the conventions of a particular genre of English writing. The first two paragraphs of Jane Austen's *Pride and Prejudice* are a good example of long sentences used effectively:

> It is a truth universally acknowledged, that a single man in possession of a good fortune, must be in want of a wife.
>
> However little known the feelings or views of such a man may be on his first entering a neighbourhood, this truth is so well fixed in the minds of the surrounding families, that he is considered as the rightful property of some one or other of their daughters.

Contrast these paragraphs with an excerpt from Ralph Ellison's *Invisible Man*, in which Ellison uses both short and long sentences to accentuate the content of the story he is telling:

> Once I saw a prizefighter boxing a yokel. The fighter was swift and amazingly scientific. His body was one violent flow of rapid rhythmic action. He hit the yokel a hundred times while the yokel held up his arms in stunned surprise. But suddenly the yokel, rolling about in the gale of boxing gloves, struck one blow and knocked science, speed and footwork as cold as a well-digger's posterior. The smart money hit the canvas. The long shot got the nod.

Invite your students to become attuned to sentence variety in their reading. Reading assignments for your course or their other courses can be plumbed for examples, and your class can make a collection of examples from various genres and forms of writing. This exercise may be especially helpful to students who are just beginning to develop an ear for rhythm and variety in sentence patterns.

> The defendant's <u>lawyer</u> was determined to break the prosecution's witness. <u>She</u> relentlessly cross-examined the stubborn witness for a week.

However, an unbroken sequence of sentences beginning with the subject quickly becomes monotonous, as shown by the unvaried passage on Grant and Lee that opened this chapter (p. 413). You can vary this subject-first pattern by adding modifiers or other elements before the subject.

Note The final arrangement of sentence elements should always depend on two concerns: the relation of a sentence to those preceding and following it and the emphasis required by your meaning.

■ **Adverb modifiers**

Adverbs modify verbs, adjectives, other adverbs, and whole clauses. They can often fall in a variety of spots in a sentence. Consider these different emphases:

> <u>For a week</u>, the defendant's lawyer <u>relentlessly</u> cross-examined the stubborn witness.
>
> <u>Relentlessly</u>, the defendant's lawyer cross-examined the stubborn wit<u>ness for a week</u>.
>
> <u>Relentlessly</u>, <u>for a week</u>, the defendant's lawyer cross-examined the stubborn witness.

Notice that the last sentence, with both modifiers at the beginning, is periodic and thus highly emphatic (see p. 388).

CULTURE LANGUAGE In standard American English, placing certain adverb modifiers at the beginning of a sentence requires you to change the normal subject-verb order as well. The most common of these modifiers are negatives, including *seldom, rarely, in no case, not since,* and *not until.*

	adverb	subject	verb phrase
Faulty	Seldom <u>a witness</u> <u>has held</u> the stand for so long.		

		helping adverb verb	subject	main verb
Revised	Seldom <u>has</u> <u>a witness</u> <u>held</u> the stand for so long.			

■ **Adjective modifiers**

Adjectives, modifying nouns and pronouns, may include participles and participial phrases, as in *flying geese* or *money well spent* (see pp. 247–50). These modifiers may sometimes fall at the beginning of a sentence to postpone the subject:

> The witness was exhausted from his testimony, and he did not cooperate.
>
> <u>Exhausted from his testimony</u>, the witness did not cooperate.

■ **Coordinating conjunctions and transitional expressions**

When the relation between two successive sentences demands, you may begin the second with a coordinating conjunction such as *and* or *but* (p. 259) or with a transitional expression such as *first, for instance, however,* or *therefore* (pp. 86–87).

> The witness had expected to be dismissed after his first long day of cross-examination. But he was not.
>
> The price of clothes has risen astronomically in recent years. For example, a cheap cotton shirt that once cost $6 now costs $25.

■ **Occasional expletive constructions**

An expletive construction—*it* or *there* plus a form of *be*—may occasionally be useful to delay and thus emphasize the subject of the sentence:

> His judgment seems questionable, not his desire.
> It is his judgment that seems questionable, not his desire.

However, expletive constructions are more likely to flatten writing by adding extra words. You should use them rarely, only when you can justify doing so. (See also p. 534.)

EXERCISE 26.2   Revising: Varied sentence beginnings

Follow the instructions in parentheses to revise each group of sentences below: either create a single sentence that begins with an adverb or adjective modifier, or make one sentence begin with an appropriate connector. (You can do this exercise online at *ablongman.com/ littlebrown*.)

> *Example:*
> The *Seabird* took first place. It moved quickly in the wind. (*One sentence with adjective modifier beginning moving.*)
> Moving quickly in the wind, the *Seabird* took first place.

1. Some people are champion procrastinators. They seldom complete their work on time. (*Two sentences with transitional expression.*)
2. Procrastinators may fear criticism. They may fear rejection. They will delay completing an assignment. (*One sentence with adverb modifier beginning if.*)
3. Procrastinators often desire to please a boss or a teacher. They fear failure so much that they cannot do the work. (*Two sentences with coordinating conjunction.*)
4. Procrastination seems a hopeless habit. It is conquerable. (*One sentence with adverb modifier beginning although.*)
5. Teachers or employers can be helpful. They can encourage procrastinators. They can give procrastinators the confidence to do good work on time. (*One sentence with adjective modifier beginning helpfully encouraging.*)

ANSWERS: EXERCISE 26.2

Possible answers

1. Some people are champion procrastinators. Consequently, they seldom complete their work on time.
2. If procrastinators fear criticism or rejection, they will delay completing an assignment.
3. Procrastinators often desire to please a boss or a teacher. Yet they fear failure so much that they cannot do the work.
4. Although procrastination seems a hopeless habit, it is conquerable.
5. Helpfully encouraging procrastinators, teachers or employers can give them the confidence to do good work on time.

COLLABORATIVE LEARNING

Have students work in pairs or in small groups to create responses to Exercise 26.3. This exercise works well in a networked classroom where groups can post their responses for general discussion.

ANSWERS: EXERCISE 26.3

Possible revision

When scientists in Egypt dug up 40-million-year-old fossil bones, they had evidence of primitive whales. Called mesonychids, the whale ancestors were small, furry land mammals with four legs. These limbs were complete with kneecaps, ankles, and little toes. In contrast, gigantic modern whales have tiny hind legs inside their bodies and flippers instead of front legs. But scientists are certain that these two very different creatures share the same family tree.

USING FORMS

Tell students to write a paragraph making use of the strategies suggested in this chapter. Leave the content of the paragraph up to them; they will discover how form can help suggest content. Then have them work in groups to compare paragraphs written with these strategies in mind to paragraphs taken from previous papers. This kind of comparison can encourage students to become more aware of their stylistic strengths and weaknesses.

EXERCISE 26.3 Revising: Varied sentence beginnings

Revise the following paragraph to vary sentence beginnings by using each of the following at least once: an adverb modifier, an adjective modifier, a coordinating conjunction, and a transitional expression. (You can do this exercise online at *ablongman.com/littlebrown*.)

Scientists in Egypt dug up 40-million-year-old fossil bones. They had evidence of primitive whales. The whale ancestors are called mesonychids. They were small, furry land mammals with four legs. These limbs were complete with kneecaps, ankles, and little toes. Gigantic modern whales have tiny hind legs inside their bodies and flippers instead of front legs. Scientists are certain that these two very different creatures share the same family tree.

26c   Inverting the normal word order

The word order of subject, verb, and object or complement is strongly fixed in English (see pp. 238–41). Thus an inverted sentence can be emphatic:

Voters once had some faith in politicians, and they were fond of incumbents. But now all politicians, especially incumbents, voters seem to detest. [The object *all politicians* precedes the verb *detests*.]

Inverting the normal order of subject, verb, and complement can be useful in two successive sentences when the second expands on the first:

Critics have not been kind to Presidents who have tried to apply the ways of private business to public affairs. Particularly explicit was the curt verdict of one critic of President Hoover: Mr. Hoover was never President of the United States; he was four years chairman of the board.
— Adapted from Emmet John Hughes,
"The Presidency vs. Jimmy Carter"

Inverted sentences used without need are artificial. Avoid descriptive sentences such as *Up came Ben and down went Katie's spirits.*

26d   Mixing types of sentences

Most written sentences make statements. Occasionally, however, questions, commands, or exclamations may enhance variety.

Questions may set the direction of a paragraph, as in *What does a detective do?* or *How is the percentage of unemployed workers calculated?* More often, though, the questions used in exposition or argument do not require answers but simply emphasize ideas that readers can be expected to agree with. Such **rhetorical questions** are illustrated in the following passage:

> Another word that has ceased to have meaning due to overuse is *attractive. Attractive* has become verbal chaff. Who, by some stretch of language and imagination, cannot be described as attractive? And just what is it that attractive individuals are attracting?   —Diane White

Commands occur frequently in an explanation of a process, particularly in directions, as this passage on freewriting illustrates:

> The idea is simply to write for ten minutes (later on, perhaps fifteen or twenty). Don't stop for anything. Go quickly, without rushing. Never stop to look back, to cross something out, to wonder how to spell something, to wonder what word or thought to use, or to think about what you are doing.   —Peter Elbow

Notice that the authors of these examples use questions and commands to achieve some special purpose. Variety occurs because a particular sentence type is effective for the context, not because the writer set out to achieve variety for its own sake.

EXERCISE 26.4   Writing varied sentences

Imagine that you are writing an essay on a transportation problem at your school. Practice varying sentences by composing a sentence or passage to serve each purpose listed below. (You can do this exercise online at *ablongman.com/littlebrown*.)

1. Write a question that could open the essay.
2. Write a command that could open the essay.
3. Write an exclamation that could open the essay.
4. For the body of the essay, write an appropriately varied paragraph of at least five sentences, including at least one short and one long sentence beginning with the subject; at least one sentence beginning with an adverb modifier; at least one sentence beginning with a coordinating conjunction or transitional expression; and one rhetorical question or command.

EXERCISE 26.5   Analyzing variety

Examine the following paragraph for sentence variety. By analyzing your own response to each sentence, try to explain why the author wrote each short or long sentence, each cumulative or periodic sentence, each sentence beginning with its subject or beginning some other way, and each question. (You can do this exercise online at *ablongman.com/littlebrown*.)

> That night in my rented room, while letting the hot water run over my can of pork and beans in the sink, I opened [H. L. Mencken's] *A Book of Prefaces* and began to read. I was jarred and shocked by the style, the clear, clean, sweeping sentences. Why did he write like that?

Have students create individual responses to Exercise 26.4, then ask them to discuss their responses in small groups and create revisions. In a computer classroom, students might trade seats in order to read and comment on each other's work (in each case the commentator can add revision suggestions using a different font). Students can print out and share responses, or post them—in a networked classroom.

ANSWERS: EXERCISE 26.4

Possible answers

1. How many cars are registered on this campus?
2. Try to find a parking space on this campus any weekday morning after nine o'clock.
3. What an unexpected pleasure to find a parking space within two blocks of the library!
4. Can the frustration caused by the parking problem be healthy for students? They drive round and round the campus, the minutes of lost study or class time ticking away. Tension builds. As they pass filled row upon filled row in one lot after another, drivers begin to tremble, sweat, and swear. And the anger and panic, instead of abating when finally the car is safely stowed, stays with the students throughout the day.

Have students complete Exercise 26.5 individually and then discuss their responses in small groups. Encourage students to debate the effects of sentence variety in the passage and to use detailed evidence from the passage to support their claims. You might follow up this group activity by leading a general discussion in which you invite groups to report back on the debates they have generated.

ANSWERS: EXERCISE 26.5

Possible answers

The shortest sentence is one word: *No.* The longest is sentence 5, *I pictured the man as.* . . . The opening periodic sentence sets the scene before coming to the point. The longest sentence gains its length and power from the six modifying verbal phrases that convey Wright's first impression of Mencken. Wright relies on questions interspersed with tentative answers to show his own incremental awakening on discovering Mencken. Repetition—*fighting, fighting; using . . . using; maybe, perhaps*—also shows Wright wrestling with what he has found. The last question leads to the conclusion of the final three sentences, which gradually increase in length and complexity.

COLLABORATIVE LEARNING

Ask students to complete Exercise 26.6 individually and then discuss their responses in groups in preparation for revising them. You might choose several of the revised responses to photocopy and hand out in order to generate discussion of the effects of variety. In a networked classroom, you might ask several student volunteers to post their revised responses in order to provide the basis for discussion.

ANSWERS: EXERCISE 26.6

Possible revision

After being dormant for many years, the Italian volcano Vesuvius exploded on August 24 in the year AD 79. The ash, pumice, and mud from the volcano buried two towns—Herculaneum and the more famous Pompeii—which lay undiscovered until 1709 and 1748, respectively. The excavation of Pompeii was the more systematic, the occasion for initiating modern methods of conservation and restoration. Whereas Herculaneum was simply looted of its most valuable finds and then left to disintegrate, Pompeii appears much as it did during the eruption. A luxurious house opens onto a lush central garden. An election poster decorates a wall. And a dining table is set for breakfast.

And how did one write like that? I pictured the man as a raging demon, slashing with his pen, consumed with hate, denouncing everything American, extolling everything European or German, laughing at the weaknesses of people, mocking God, authority. What was this? I stood up, trying to realize what reality lay behind the meaning of the words. Yes, this man was fighting, fighting with words. He was using words as a weapon, using them as one would use a club. Could words be weapons? Well, yes, for here they were. Then, maybe, perhaps, I could use them as a weapon? No. It frightened me. I read on and what amazed me was not what he said, but how on earth anybody had the courage to say it.
—Richard Wright, *Black Boy*

EXERCISE 26.6 Revising: Variety

The following paragraph consists entirely of simple sentences that begin with their subjects. As appropriate, use the techniques discussed in this chapter to vary sentences. Your goal is to make the paragraph more readable and make its important ideas stand out clearly. You will have to delete, add, change, and rearrange words. (You can do this exercise online at *ablongman.com/littlebrown*.)

The Italian volcano Vesuvius had been dormant for many years. It then exploded on August 24 in the year AD 79. The ash, pumice, and mud from the volcano buried two busy towns. Herculaneum is one. The more famous is Pompeii. Both towns lay undiscovered for many centuries. Herculaneum and Pompeii were discovered in 1709 and 1748, respectively. The excavation of Pompeii was the more systematic. It was the occasion for initiating modern methods of conservation and restoration. Herculaneum was simply looted of its most valuable finds. It was then left to disintegrate. Pompeii appears much as it did before the eruption. A luxurious house opens onto a lush central garden. An election poster decorates a wall. A dining table is set for breakfast.

EXERCISE ON CHAPTERS 23–26 Revising: Effective sentences

Revise the paragraphs below to emphasize main ideas, de-emphasize supporting information, and achieve a pleasing, clear variety in sentences. As appropriate, employ the techniques discussed in Chapters 23–26, such as using subjects and verbs effectively, subordinating and coordinating, creating parallelism, and varying sentence beginnings. Edit the finished product for punctuation. (You can do this exercise online at *ablongman.com/littlebrown*.)

Modern Americans owe many debts to Native Americans. Several pleasures are among the debts. Native Americans originated two fine junk foods. They discovered popcorn. Potato chips were also one of their contributions.

The introduction of popcorn to the European settlers came from Native Americans. Massasoit provided popcorn at the first Thanksgiving feast. The Aztecs offered popcorn to the Spanish explorer Hernando Cortés. The Aztecs wore popcorn necklaces. So did the natives of the West Indies. There were three ways that the Native Americans popped the corn. First, they roasted an ear over fire. The ear was skewered on a stick. They ate only some of the popcorn. They ate the corn that fell outside the flames. Second, they scraped the corn off the cob. The kernels would be thrown into the fire. Of course, the fire had to be low. Then the popped kernels that did not fall into the fire were eaten. The third method was the most sophisticated. It involved a shallow pottery vessel. It contained sand. The vessel was heated. The sand soon got hot. Corn kernels were stirred in. They popped to the surface of the sand and were eaten.

A Native American chef was responsible for devising the crunchy potato chip. His name was George Crum. In 1853 Crum was cooking at Moon Lake Lodge. The lodge was in Saratoga Springs, New York. Complaints were sent in by a customer. The man thought Crum's french-fried potatoes were too thick. Crum tried a thinner batch. These were also unsuitable. Crum became frustrated. He deliberately made the potatoes thin and crisp. They could not be cut with a knife and fork. Crum's joke backfired. The customer raved about the potato chips. The chips were named Saratoga Chips. Soon they appeared on the lodge's menu. They also appeared throughout New England. Crum later opened his own restaurant. Of course, he offered potato chips.

Now all Americans munch popcorn in movies. They crunch potato chips at parties. They gorge on both when alone and bored. They can be grateful to Native Americans for these guilty pleasures.

ANSWERS: EXERCISE ON CHAPTERS 23–26

Possible revision

Modern Americans owe many debts to Native Americans, including several pleasures. Native Americans originated two fine junk foods: popcorn and potato chips.

Native Americans introduced popcorn to the European settlers, Massasoit providing popcorn at the first Thanksgiving feast and the Aztecs offering popcorn to the Spanish explorer Hernando Cortés. The Aztecs and natives of the West Indies wore popcorn necklaces. Native Americans popped the corn in three ways. First, they roasted an ear skewered on a stick over fire and ate the corn that fell outside the flames. Second, they scraped the corn off the cob, threw the kernels into a low fire, and ate the popped kernels that did not fall into the fire. Third and most sophisticated, they heated a shallow pottery vessel containing sand, stirred corn kernels into the hot sand, and ate what popped up to the surface.

A Native American chef named George Crum devised the crunchy potato chip. In 1853 Crum was cooking at Moon Lake Lodge in Saratoga Springs, New York. A customer complained that Crum's french-fried potatoes were too thick. Crum tried a thinner batch, but these were also unsuitable. Frustrated, Crum deliberately made the potatoes so thin and crisp that they could not be cut with a knife and fork. Crum's joke backfired, for the customer raved about the potato chips. Soon these Saratoga Chips appeared on the lodge's menu and throughout New England. Crum later opened his own restaurant, of course offering potato chips.

Now all Americans munch popcorn in movies, crunch potato chips at parties, and gorge on both when alone and bored. They can be grateful to Native Americans for these guilty pleasures.

Punctuation

t based on love but on the understan
ght thing to do. Illych finds that his
an he wants and life becomes unplea
ven after the birth of their child Illyc
f his self-involvement. He blames his
omings and disappointments, believ
d social success can make him happy

Commas, semicolons, colons, dashes, parentheses
(For explanations, consult the pages in parentheses.)

■ Sentences with two main clauses

The bus stopped, but no one got off. (p. 432)
The bus stopped; no one got off. (p. 453)
The bus stopped; however, no one got off. (p. 455)
The mechanic replaced the battery, the distributor cap, and the starter; but still the car would not start. (p. 457)
Her duty was clear: she had to locate the problem. (p. 477)

■ Introductory elements

Modifiers (p. 433)

After the argument was over, we laughed at ourselves.
Racing over the plain, the gazelle escaped the lion.
To dance in the contest, he had to tape his knee.
Suddenly, the door flew open.
With 125 passengers aboard, the plane was half full.
In 1983 he won the Nobel Prize.

Absolute phrases (p. 440)

Its wing broken, the bird hopped around on the ground.

■ Interrupting and concluding elements

Nonessential modifiers (p. 435)

Jim's car, which barely runs, has been impounded.
We consulted the dean, who had promised to help us.
The boy, like his sister, wants to be a pilot.
They moved across the desert, shielding their eyes from the sun.
The men do not speak to each other, although they share a car.

Nonessential appositives

Bergen's only daughter, Candice, became an actress. (p. 437)
The residents of three counties—Suffolk, Springfield, and Morrison—were urged to evacuate. (p. 480)
Father demanded one promise: that we not lie to him. (p. 477)

Essential modifiers (p. 436)

The car that hit mine was uninsured.
We consulted a teacher who had promised to help us.
The boy in the black hat is my cousin.
They were surprised to find the desert teeming with life.
The men do not speak to each other because they are feuding.

Essential appositives (p. 438)

Shaw's play *Saint Joan* was performed last year.

Their sons Tony, William, and Steve all chose military careers, leaving only Matthew to run the family business.

Transitional or parenthetical expressions

We suspect, however, that he will not come. (p. 438)

Jessica is respected by many people—including me. (p. 480)

George Balanchine (1904–83) was a brilliant choreographer of classical ballet. (p. 482)

Absolute phrases (p. 440)

The bird, its wing broken, hopped about on the ground.

The bird hopped about on the ground, its wing broken.

Phrases expressing contrast (p. 441)

The humidity, not just the heat, gives me headaches.

My headaches are caused by the humidity, not just the heat.

Concluding summaries and explanations

The movie opened to bad notices: the characters were judged shallow and unrealistic. (p. 477)

We dined on gumbo and jambalaya—a Cajun feast. (p. 480)

■ Items in a series

Three or more items

Chimpanzees, gorillas, orangutans, and gibbons are all apes. (p. 441)

The cities singled out for praise were Birmingham, Alabama; Lincoln, Nebraska; Austin, Texas; and Troy, New York. (p. 457)

Two or more adjectives before a noun (p. 442)

Dingy, smelly clothes decorated their room.

Dessert consisted of one tiny scoop of ice cream.

Introductory series (p. 480)

Appropriateness, accuracy, and necessity—these criteria should govern your selection of words.

Concluding series

Every word should be appropriate, accurate, and necessary. (p. 448)

Every word should meet three criteria: appropriateness, accuracy, and necessity. (p. 477)

Pay attention to your words—to their appropriateness, their accuracy, and their necessity. (p. 480)

mycomplab 2.0

Please visit MyCompLab at *www.mycomplab.com* for more on the writing process.

HIGHLIGHTS

This chapter discusses the three marks of punctuation used to end sentences: periods, question marks, and exclamation points. Encourage students to see that these are not just physical boundaries but important parts of the meaning of sentences—and that they therefore deserve careful consideration.

RESOURCES AND IDEAS

Dawkins, John. "Teaching Punctuation as a Rhetorical Tool." *College Composition and Communication* 46 (1995): 533–48. Dawkins makes a case for teaching the rhetorical thinking processes that accompany decisions about punctuation marks.

COMPANION WEB SITE

See page IAE-57 for companion Web site content description.

CHAPTER **27**

End Punctuation

End punctuation marks—the period, the question mark, and the exclamation point—signal the ends of sentences.

Note A grammar checker may flag missing question marks after direct questions or incorrect combinations of marks (such as a question mark and a period at the end of a sentence), but it cannot do much else.

27a Use periods after most sentences and with some abbreviations.

1 Use a period to end a statement, mild command, or indirect question.

Statements
These are exciting and trying times.
The airline went bankrupt.

Mild commands
Please do not smoke.
Think of the possibilities.

If you are unsure whether to use an exclamation point or a period after a command, use a period. The exclamation point should be used only rarely (see p. 429).

An **indirect question** reports what someone has asked but not in the form or exact words of the original:

Indirect questions
Students sometimes wonder whether their teachers read the papers they write.
Abused children eventually stop asking why they are being punished.

http://www.ablongman.com/littlebrown ▶

Visit the companion Web site for more help and an additional exercise on end punctuation.

CULTURE LANGUAGE In standard American English, an indirect question uses the wording and subject-verb order of a statement: *The reporter asked why the negotiations failed*, not *why did the negotiations fail*.

2 Use periods with some abbreviations.

Use periods with abbreviations that consist of or end in small letters. Otherwise, omit periods from abbreviations.

Dr.	Mr., Mrs.	e.g.	Feb.	ft.
St.	Ms.	i.e.	p.	a.m., p.m.
PhD	BC, BCE	USA	IBM	AM, PM
BA	AD, CE	US	USMC	AIDS

Note When a sentence ends in an abbreviation with a period, don't add a second period: *My first class is at 8 a.m.*

See also pages 500–03 on uses of abbreviations in writing.

EXERCISE 27.1 Revising: Periods

Revise the following sentences so that periods are used correctly. (You can do this exercise online at *ablongman.com/littlebrown*.)

Example:
Several times I wrote to ask when my subscription ended?
Several times I wrote to ask when my subscription ended.

1. The instructor asked when Plato wrote *The Republic*?
2. Give the date within one century
3. The exact date is not known, but it is estimated at 370 BCE
4. Dr Arn will lecture on Plato at 7:30 p.m..
5. The area of the lecture hall is only 1600 sq ft

27b Use question marks after direct questions and sometimes to indicate doubt.

1 Use a question mark with a direct question.

What is the difference between these two people**?**
Will economists ever really understand the economy**?**

After an indirect question, use a period: *The senator asked why the bill had passed.* (See opposite.)

Questions in a series are each followed by a question mark:

The officer asked how many times the suspect had been arrested. Three times**?** Four times**?** More than that**?**

The use of capital letters for questions in a series is optional (see p. 491).

Note Question marks are never combined with other question marks, exclamation points, periods, or commas:

Faulty   "What is the point?," readers ask.
Revised "What is the point?" readers ask.

2 Use a question mark within parentheses to indicate doubt about a number or date.

The Greek philosopher Socrates was born in 470 (**?**) BC and died in 399 BC from drinking poison after having been condemned to death.

Note Don't use a question mark within parentheses to express sarcasm or irony. Express these attitudes through sentence structure and word choice. (See Chapters 23 and 38.)

Faulty   Stern's friendliness (?) bothered Crane.
Revised Stern's insincerity bothered Crane.

EXERCISE 27.2 Revising: Question marks

Revise the following sentences so that question marks (along with other punctuation marks) are used correctly. (You can do this exercise online at *ablongman.com/littlebrown*.)

Example:
"When will it end?," cried the man dressed in rags.
"When will it end?" cried the man dressed in rags.

1. In Homer's *Odyssey*, Odysseus took seven years to travel from Troy to Ithaca. Or was it eight years. Or more?
2. Odysseus must have wondered whether he would ever make it home?
3. "What man are you and whence?," asks Odysseus's wife, Penelope.
4. Why does Penelope ask, "Where is your city? Your family?"?
5. Penelope does not recognize Odysseus and asks who this stranger is?

ANSWERS: EXERCISE 27.2

1. In Homer's *Odyssey*, Odysseus took seven years to travel from Troy to Ithaca. Or was it eight years? Or more?
2. Odysseus must have wondered whether he would ever make it home.
3. "What man are you and whence?" asks Odysseus's wife, Penelope.
4. Why does Penelope ask, "Where is your city? Your family?"
5. Penelope does not recognize Odysseus and asks who this stranger is.

27c Use an exclamation point after an emphatic statement, interjection, or command.

No**!** We must not lose this election**!**
Come here immediately**!**

Follow mild interjections and commands with commas or periods, as appropriate:

No**,** the response was not terrific**.**
To prolong your car's life, change its oil regularly**.**

Use exclamation points sparingly, not to express sarcasm, irony, or amazement. Rely on sentence structure and word choice to express these attitudes. (See Chapters 23 and 38.)

Faulty   After traveling 4.4 billion miles through space, *Voyager 2* was off-target by 21 miles (!).

Revised After traveling 4.4 billion miles through space, *Voyager 2* was off-target by a mere 21 miles.

Relying on the exclamation point for emphasis is like crying wolf: the mark loses its power to impress the reader. Frequent exclamation points can also make writing sound overemotional:

Overused exclamation points

Our city government is a mess! After just six months in office, the mayor has had to fire four city officials! In the same period the city councilors have done nothing but argue! And city services decline with each passing day!

Note Exclamation points are never combined with other exclamation points, question marks, periods, or commas:

Faulty   "This will not be endured!," he roared.

Revised "This will not be endured!" he roared.

EXERCISE 27.3 Revising: Exclamation points

Revise the following sentences so that exclamation points (along with other punctuation marks) are used correctly. If a sentence is punctuated correctly as given, mark the number preceding it. (You can do this exercise online at *ablongman.com/littlebrown*.)

Example:
"Well, now!," he said loudly.
"Well, now!" he said loudly.

1. As the firefighters moved their equipment into place, the police shouted, "Move back!".
2. A child's cries could be heard from above: "Help me. Help."
3. When the child was rescued, the crowd called "Hooray."
4. The rescue was the most exciting event of the day!
5. Let me tell you about it.

EXERCISE 27.4 Revising: End punctuation

Insert appropriate punctuation (periods, question marks, or exclamation points) where needed in the following paragraph. (You can do this exercise online at *ablongman.com/littlebrown*.)

When visitors first arrive in Hawaii, they often encounter an unexpected language barrier Standard English is the language of business and government, but many of the people speak Pidgin English Instead of an excited "Aloha" the visitors may be greeted with an excited

---

"Howzit!" or asked if they know "how fo' find one good hotel." Many Hawaiians question whether Pidgin will hold children back because it prevents communication with the *haoles,* or Caucasians, who run businesses. Yet many others feel that Pidgin is a last defense of ethnic diversity on the islands. To those who want to make standard English the official language of the state, these Hawaiians may respond, "Just 'cause I speak Pidgin no mean I dumb." They may ask, "Why you no listen?" or, in standard English, "Why don't you listen?"

mycomplab

Please visit MyCompLab at *www.mycomplab.com* for more on the writing process.

HIGHLIGHTS

The comma probably causes more anguish for apprentice writers than any other punctuation mark. There's no magic formula for accurate use of the comma. Most uses are conventional, but a few require judgment calls—and writers can develop the necessary judgment only through lots of reading and writing. For example, the problem of whether to use commas with essential and nonessential modifiers is probably not a punctuation problem but a matter of understanding what these modifiers do. Commas, or their absence, are just a graphic way of reinforcing the meaning of the modifier. The text's discussion of how context determines a modifier's role in a sentence can help students see this point.

Forcing students to memorize these rules may not make them more accurate writers. Students need to learn how to take the generalizations conveyed by these rules and apply them to specific situations; that means helping them understand the rules, not just getting them to memorize.

COMPANION WEB SITE

See page IAE-57 for companion Web site content description.

Pidgin "Howzit" or asked if they know "how fo' find one good hotel" Many Hawaiians question whether Pidgin will hold children back because it prevents communication with the *haoles,* or Caucasians, who run businesses Yet many others feel that Pidgin is a last defense of ethnic diversity on the islands To those who want to make standard English the official language of the state, these Hawaiians may respond, "Just 'cause I speak Pidgin no mean I dumb" They may ask, "Why you no listen" or, in standard English, "Why don't you listen"

Note See page 488 for a punctuation exercise combining periods with other marks of punctuation.

CHAPTER **28**

The Comma

Commas usually function within sentences to separate elements (see the box on the next page). Omitting needed commas or inserting needless ones can confuse the reader:

Comma needed	Though very tall Abraham Lincoln was not an overbearing man.
Revised	Though very tall, Abraham Lincoln was not an overbearing man.
Unneeded commas	The hectic pace of Beirut, broke suddenly into frightening chaos when the city became, the focus of civil war.
Revised	The hectic pace of Beirut broke suddenly into frightening chaos when the city became the focus of civil war.

Note Grammar and style checkers will ignore many comma errors. For example, a checker failed to catch the missing commas in *The boat ran aground_and we were stranded* and in *We cooked lasagna_spinach_and apple pie.* At the same time the checker overlooked the misused commas in *The trip was short but, the weather was perfect* and *The travelers were tempted by, the many shops, and varied restaurants.*

http://www.ablongman.com/littlebrown ▶

Visit the companion Web site for more help and additional exercises on the comma.

Principal uses of the comma

- **Separate main clauses linked by a coordinating conjunction** (next page):

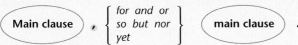

The building is finished, but it has no tenants.

- **Set off most introductory elements** (p. 433):

Unfortunately, the only tenant pulled out.

- **Set off nonessential elements** (p. 435):

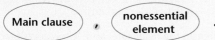

The empty building symbolizes a weak local economy, which affects everyone.

Beginning of main clause , nonessential element , end of main clause .

The primary cause, the decline of local industry, is not news.

- **Separate items in a series** (p. 441):

. . . item 1 , item 2 , { and / or } item 3 . . .

The city needs healthier businesses, new schools, and improved housing.

- **Separate coordinate adjectives** (p. 442):

. . . first adjective , second adjective word modified . . .

A tall, sleek skyscraper is not needed.

Other uses of the comma:

Set off absolute phrases (p. 440).
Set off phrases expressing contrast (p. 441).
Separate parts of dates, addresses, long numbers (p. 443).
Separate quotations and signal phrases (p. 444).
Prevent misreading (p. 447).

See also page 448 for when *not* to use the comma.

TRANSPARENCY MASTER 28.1

A WRITER'S PERSPECTIVE

It is highly important to put [commas] in place as you go along. If you try to come back after doing a paragraph and stick them in the various spots that tempt you you will discover that they tend to swarm like minnows into all sorts of crevices whose existence you hadn't realized and before you know it the whole long sentence becomes immobilized and lashed up squirming in commas. Better to use them sparingly, and with affection, precisely when the need for one arises, nicely, by itself.

—Lewis Thomas, "Notes on Punctuation"

RESOURCES AND IDEAS

Punctuation

Dawkins, John. "Teaching Punctuation as a Rhetorical Tool." *College Composition and Communication* 46 (1995): 533–48. Dawkins makes a case for teaching the rhetorical thinking processes that accompany decisions about punctuation marks.

Meyer, Emily, and Louise Z. Smith, "Punctuation." In *The Practical Tutor.* New York: Oxford UP, 1989. The authors offer detailed advice for the often frustrating task of helping students develop effective punctuation skills.

Commas

Meyer, Charles F. "Teaching Punctuation to Advanced Writers." *Journal of Advanced Composition* 6 (1985–86): 117–29. Meyer offers a number of strategies that can be used in any classroom.

Shaughnessy, Mina P. *Errors and Expectations: A Guide for the Teacher of Basic Writing.* New York: Oxford UP, 1977. 14–43. Shaughnessy explains teaching punctuation in the context of understanding students' hypotheses about their texts.

Thomas, Lewis. "Notes on Punctuation." *New England Journal of Medicine* 296 (1977): 1103–05. Reprinted in *The Medusa and the Snail: More Notes of a Biology Watcher.* New York: Viking, 1979. An experienced scientist and writer explores how punctuation use can affect the meaning of texts.

COMMA POWER

Though writing instructors often treat commas and other marks of punctuation as if they were primarily cues to grammatical structures, these marks also function legitimately as stylistic cues, as indicators of the writer's voice—or so argues Wallace Chafe in "What Good Is Punctuation?" (*The Quarterly of the National Writing Project and the Center for the Study of Writing* 10 [1988]: 8–11). Chafe supports his argument with examples from the work of Herman Melville and James Agee and concludes with some useful advice for teaching:

> Students, in addition to being sensitized to their inner voices, will benefit from knowing the range of punctuating options that are available, and from being shown, through examples, what is most appropriate to one style and another. They can learn from practice in writing advertising copy as well as the more academic kinds of exposition, and from experimenting with fiction that mimics the very different punctuation styles of, say, Melville and Agee. At the same time, developing writers need to know that there are certain specific rules for punctuating that violate the prosody of their inner voices and that simply have to be learned. These arbitrary rules are few in number and well defined, and to learn them need be no burden . . . The bottom line is that punctuation contributes substantially to the effectiveness of a piece of writing, and that its successful use calls for an awareness of something that is, for this and other reasons, essential to good writing; a sensitivity to the sound of written language.

"In Praise of the Humble Comma," a short and amusing paean to the power of punctuation to affect meaning, might also be handed out to students as a useful reminder of the connections between grammar and content. (Pico Iyer, *Time*, June 13, 1988: 348).

ANSWERS: EXERCISE 28.1

1. Parents once automatically gave their children the father's surname, but some no longer do.
2. Instead, they bestow the mother's name, for they believe that the mother's importance should be recognized.
3. The child's surname may be just the mother's, or it may link the mother's and the father's with a hyphen.

28a　**Use a comma before *and, but,* or another coordinating conjunction linking main clauses.**

The coordinating conjunctions are *and, but, or, nor, for, so,* and *yet.* When these link words or phrases, do not use a comma: *Dugain plays and sings Irish and English folk songs.* However, *do* use a comma when a coordinating conjunction joins main clauses. A **main clause** has a subject and a predicate (but no subordinating word at the beginning) and makes a complete statement (see p. 252).

> Caffeine can keep coffee drinkers alert, and it may elevate their mood.
>
> Caffeine was once thought to be safe, but now researchers warn of harmful effects.
>
> Coffee drinkers may suffer sleeplessness, for the drug acts as a stimulant to the nervous system.

Note Do not add a comma *after* a coordinating conjunction between main clauses (see also pp. 448–49):

Not	Caffeine increases the heart rate, and, it constricts blood vessels.
But	Caffeine increases the heart rate, and it constricts blood vessels.

Exceptions When the main clauses in a sentence are very long or grammatically complicated, or when they contain internal punctuation, a semicolon before the coordinating conjunction will clarify the division between clauses (see p. 457):

> Caffeine may increase alertness, elevate mood, and provide energy; but it may also cause irritability, anxiety, stomach pains, and other ills.

When main clauses are very short and closely related in meaning, you may omit the comma between them as long as the resulting sentence is clear:

> Caffeine helps but it also hurts.

If you are in doubt about whether to use a comma in such a sentence, use it. It will always be correct.

EXERCISE 28.1　Punctuating linked main clauses

Insert a comma before each coordinating conjunction that links main clauses in the following sentences. (You can do this exercise online at *ablongman.com/littlebrown*.)

Example:

I would have attended the concert and the reception but I had to baby-sit for my niece.

I would have attended the concert and the reception, but I had to baby-sit for my niece.

1. Parents once automatically gave their children the father's surname but some no longer do.
2. Instead, they bestow the mother's name for they believe that the mother's importance should be recognized.
3. The child's surname may be just the mother's or it may link the mother's and the father's with a hyphen.
4. Sometimes the first and third children will have the mother's surname and the second child will have the father's.
5. Occasionally the mother and father combine parts of their names and a new hybrid surname is born.

EXERCISE 28.2   Sentence combining: Linked main clauses

Combine each group of sentences below into one sentence that contains only two main clauses connected by the coordinating conjunction in parentheses. Separate the main clauses with a comma. You will have to add, delete, and rearrange words. (You can do this exercise online at *ablongman.com/littlebrown*.)

Example:
The circus had come to town. The children wanted to see it. Their parents wanted to see it. (*and*)

The circus had come to town, and the children and their parents wanted to see it.

1. Parents were once legally required to bestow the father's surname on their children. These laws have been contested in court. They have been found invalid. (*but*)
2. Parents may now give their children any surname they choose. The arguments for bestowing the mother's surname are often strong. They are often convincing. (*and*)
3. Critics sometimes question the effects of unusual surnames on children. They wonder how confusing the new surnames will be. They wonder how fleeting the surnames will be. (*or*)
4. Children with surnames different from their parents' may suffer embarrassment. They may suffer identity problems. Giving children their father's surname is still very much the norm. (*for*)
5. Hyphenated names are awkward. They are also difficult to pass on. Some observers think they will die out in the next generation. Or they may die out before. (*so*)

28b   Use a comma to set off most introductory elements.

An introductory element modifies a word or words in the main clause that follows. These elements are usually set off from the rest of the sentence with a comma:

Subordinate clause (p. 252)

Even when identical twins are raised apart, they grow up very like each other.

Because they are similar, such twins interest scientists.

---

4. Sometimes the first and third children will have the mother's surname, and the second child will have the father's.
5. Occasionally the mother and father combine parts of their names, and a new hybrid surname is born.

COLLABORATIVE LEARNING

Ask students to complete Exercise 28.2 individually and then discuss their responses in small groups. Have each group discuss the effect of alternative answers and then present one or two of the most successful responses.

ANSWERS: EXERCISE 28.2
Possible answers

1. Parents were once legally required to bestow the father's surname on their children, but these laws have been contested in court and found invalid.
2. Parents may now give their children any surname they choose, and the arguments for bestowing the mother's surname are often strong and convincing.
3. Critics sometimes question the effects of unusual surnames on children, or they wonder how confusing or fleeting the new surnames will be.
4. Children with surnames different from their parents' may suffer embarrassment or identity problems, for giving children their father's surname is still very much the norm.
5. Hyphenated names are awkward and difficult to pass on, so some observers think they will die out in the next generation or before.

COURT REPORTER

To help students understand how commas affect understanding, have them play "court reporter." Ask one or two students to read a passage from their papers or some reading for the class while the other students try to write what they say. Then have the reporters prepare a transcript of what they heard, inserting punctuation where they think it is needed. Each group should compare the reporters' versions with the originals and solve any disputes over comma use by referring to the appropriate sections of this chapter.

Have students complete Exercise 28.3 individually and then compare their responses in small groups. This allows students to debate different kinds of comma usage in a nonintimidating setting.

ANSWERS: EXERCISE 28.3

1. Sentence correct.
2. Because it is sudden and apparently well coordinated, the movement of flocks and schools has seemed to be directed by a leader.
3. However, new studies have discovered that flocks and schools are leaderless.
4. When each bird or fish senses a predator, it follows individual rules for fleeing.
5. Multiplied over hundreds of individuals, these responses look as if they have been choreographed.

Verbal or verbal phrase (p. 247)

Explaining the similarity, some researchers claim that one's genes are one's destiny.

Concerned, other researchers deny the claim.

Prepositional phrase (p. 245)

In a debate that has lasted centuries, scientists use identical twins to argue for or against genetic destiny.

Transitional or parenthetical expression (pp. 85–86)

Of course, scientists can now look directly at the genes themselves.

The comma may be omitted after short introductory elements if its omission does not create confusion. (If you are in doubt, however, the comma is always correct.)

Clear	In a hundred years genetics may no longer be a mystery.
Confusing	Despite intensive research scientists still have more questions than answers.
Clear	Despite intensive research, scientists still have more questions than answers.

Note Take care to distinguish *-ing* words used as modifiers from *-ing* words used as subjects, as shown in the following examples. The former almost always take a comma; the latter never do.

┌────── modifier ──────┐ subject   verb
Studying identical twins, geneticists learn about inheritance.

┌────── subject ──────┐ verb
Studying identical twins helps geneticists learn about inheritance.

EXERCISE 28.3   Punctuating introductory elements

Insert commas where needed after introductory elements in the following sentences. If a sentence is punctuated correctly as given, mark the number preceding it. (You can do this exercise online at *ablongman.com/ littlebrown*.)

Example:
After the new library opened the old one became a student union.
After the new library opened, the old one became a student union.

1. Moving in a fluid mass is typical of flocks of birds and schools of fish.
2. Because it is sudden and apparently well coordinated the movement of flocks and schools has seemed to be directed by a leader.
3. However new studies have discovered that flocks and schools are leaderless.
4. When each bird or fish senses a predator it follows individual rules for fleeing.
5. Multiplied over hundreds of individuals these responses look as if they have been choreographed.

EXERCISE 28.4   Sentence combining: Introductory elements

Combine each pair of sentences below into one sentence that begins with an introductory phrase or clause as specified in parentheses. Follow the introductory element with a comma. You will have to add, delete, change, and rearrange words. (You can do this exercise online at *ablongman.com/littlebrown*.)

Example:
The girl was humming to herself. She walked upstairs. (*Phrase beginning Humming.*)
Humming to herself, the girl walked upstairs.

1. Scientists have made an effort to explain the mysteries of flocks and schools. They have proposed bizarre magnetic fields and telepathy. (*Phrase beginning In.*)
2. Scientists developed computer models. They have abandoned earlier explanations. (*Clause beginning Since.*)
3. The movement of a flock or school starts with each individual. It is rapidly and perhaps automatically coordinated among individuals. (*Phrase beginning Starting.*)
4. One zoologist observes that human beings seek coherent patterns. He suggests that investigators saw purpose in the movement of flocks and schools where none existed. (*Phrase beginning Observing.*)
5. One may want to study the movement of flocks or schools. Then one must abandon a search for purpose or design. (*Phrase beginning To.*)

28c   Use a comma or commas to set off nonessential elements.

Commas around part of a sentence often signal that the element is not essential to the meaning of the sentence:

Nonessential element
The company, which is located in Oklahoma, has a good reputation.

This **nonessential element** may modify or rename the word it refers to (*company* in the example), but it does not limit the word to a particular individual or group. (Because it does not restrict meaning, a nonessential element is also called a **nonrestrictive element**.) Nonessential elements are *not* essential, but punctuation *is*.

In contrast, an **essential** (or **restrictive**) element *does* limit the word it refers to:

Essential element
The company rewards employees who work hard.

In this example the underlined essential element cannot be omitted without leaving the meaning of *employees* too general. Because it is

Ask students to complete Exercise 28.4 individually and then compare responses in small groups. You might then have each group create one or two sentences of their own involving introductory clauses set off by commas.

ANSWERS: EXERCISE 28.4
Possible answers

1. In an effort to explain the mysteries of flocks and schools, scientists have proposed bizarre magnetic fields and telepathy.
2. Since scientists developed computer models, they have abandoned earlier explanations.
3. Starting with each individual, the movement of a flock or school is rapidly and perhaps automatically coordinated among individuals.
4. Observing that human beings seek coherent patterns, one zoologist suggests that investigators saw purpose in the movement of flocks and schools where none existed.
5. To study the movement of flocks or schools, one must abandon a search for purpose or design.

ESSENTIAL VS. NONESSENTIAL MODIFIERS

The difference between essential and nonessential elements is one of the most difficult concepts for students to grasp. Try using these two examples as a way of illustrating the difference:

Bring me the books that are on the desk.
Bring me the books, which are on the desk.

In the first example, the essential modifier *that are on the desk* selects a specific group of books: only those that are on the desk, as opposed to others in the room. In the second sentence, the nonessential modifier *which are on the desk* tells us that the location of the books is not a restricting factor; the requester wants *all* the books, and they just happen to be on the desk. Ask students to make up other pairs of examples to show the difference between essential and nonessential modifiers, and stress that only the nonessential (nonselecting) modifier is set off by a comma.

RECOGNIZING NONESSENTIAL ELEMENTS

For students who are still uncertain about whether elements are nonessential or essential, emphasize that nonessential elements *require* punctuation and *follow* these types of items:

1. One of a kind (including proper nouns):
   Secretariat, a beautiful chestnut colt, won the Triple Crown in 1973.
2. All of a kind:
   United States senators, who serve six-year terms, face constant pressure to raise campaign funds.
3. Previously mentioned:
   Animal rights activists have been known to stage outrageous demonstrations. The activists, who seek media attention, are prepared to risk criticism to promote their cause.

TRANSPARENCY MASTER 28.2

essential, such an element is *not* set off with commas. The element *is* essential, but punctuation is *not*.

◼ Meaning and context

The same element in the same sentence may be essential or nonessential depending on your intended meaning and the context in which the sentence appears. For example, look at the second sentence in each of the following passages:

Essential

Not all the bands were equally well received, however. The band playing old music held the audience's attention. The other groups created much less excitement. [*Playing old music* identifies a particular band.]

Nonessential

A new band called Fats made its debut on Saturday night. The band, playing old music, held the audience's attention. If this performance is typical, the group has a bright future. [*Playing old music* adds information about a band already named.]

◼ Punctuation of interrupting nonessential elements

When a nonessential element falls in the middle of a sentence, be sure to set it off with a pair of commas, one *before* and one *after* the element. Dashes or parentheses may also set off nonessential elements (see pp. 480 and 482).

A test for essential and nonessential elements

1. **Identify the element.**

   Hai Nguyen who emigrated from Vietnam lives in Denver.
   Those who emigrated with him live elsewhere.

2. **Remove the element. Does the fundamental meaning of the sentence change?**

   Hai Nguyen lives in Denver. *No.*
   Those live elsewhere. *Yes.* [Who are *Those?*]

3. **If *no,* the element is *nonessential* and should be set off with punctuation.**

   Hai Nguyen, who emigrated from Vietnam, lives in Denver.

   If *yes,* the element is *essential* and should *not* be set off with punctuation.

   Those who emigrated with him live elsewhere.

1 Use a comma or commas to set off nonessential clauses and phrases.

Clauses and phrases serving as adjectives and adverbs may be either nonessential or essential. In the following examples the underlined clauses and phrases are nonessential: they could be omitted without changing the meaning of the words they modify.

Nonessential

Elizabeth Blackwell was the first woman to graduate from an American medical school, in 1849.

She was a medical pioneer, helping to found the first medical college for women.

She taught at the school, which was affiliated with the New York Infirmary.

Blackwell, who published books and papers on medicine, practiced pediatrics and gynecology.

She moved to England in 1869, when she was forty-eight.

Note Most adverb clauses are essential because they describe conditions necessary to the main clause. They are set off by a comma only when they introduce sentences (see p. 433) and when they are truly nonessential, adding incidental information (as in the last example above) or expressing a contrast beginning *although, even though, though, whereas,* and the like.

In the following sentences, the underlined elements limit the meaning of the words they modify. Removing the elements would leave the meaning too general.

Essential

The history of aspirin began with the ancient Greeks.

Physicians who sought to relieve their patients' pains recommended chewing willow bark.

Willow bark contains a chemical that is similar to aspirin.

Note Whereas both nonessential and essential clauses may begin with *which,* only essential clauses begin with *that.* Some writers prefer *that* exclusively for essential clauses and *which* exclusively for nonessential clauses. See the Glossary of Usage, page 879, for advice on the use of *that* and *which.*

2 Use a comma or commas to set off nonessential appositives.

An **appositive** is a noun or noun substitute that renames another noun just before it. (See p. 257.) Many appositives are nonessential; thus they are set off, usually with commas.

WORD PUZZLES

Divide the class into small groups and give them word puzzles like the following. Each of these puzzles can be solved only if the reader knows how essential and nonessential phrases are punctuated.

1. You are a CIA agent whose job is to keep track of all the Russian spies in Melopolia. One day you receive this telegram from Washington: "All the Russian spies, formerly residing in the Russian embassy, have been sent home."

Is there anyone left for you to watch?

2. After a long and successful season the university basketball team played its cross-state rival for the conference championship. Pandemonium broke out when a long shot dropped in at the buzzer to give the university the victory. Parties were held all over campus.

When Professor Kean arrived at class the next morning, the students, who had celebrated long into the night, were fast asleep at their desks.

Can you tell what portion of the class was asleep?

3. A severe electrical storm swept through town just after noon. Lightning struck several buildings, including the computer center. Technicians repairing damage there found that the microcomputers which were not equipped with electrical surge protectors needed to have their circuit boards replaced.

Are any of the microcomputers still usable?

COMMAS AND PARENTHESES

Students who know math will appreciate that the commas around parenthetical expressions are like the parentheses in a mathematical equation; if you use one to open the expression, you must have one to close it, or it can't be "solved" properly.

RESOURCES AND IDEAS

Christensen, Francis. "Restrictive and Nonrestrictive Modifiers Again." In *Notes Toward a New Rhetoric: Nine Essays for Teachers.* 2nd ed. Ed. Francis Christensen and Bonniejean Christensen. New York: HarperCollins, 1978. 117–32. Christensen discusses and illustrates uses of the comma with a variety of modifying elements.

Nonessential

Toni Morrison's fifth novel, *Beloved,* won the Pulitzer Prize in 1988. Morrison, a native of Ohio, won the Nobel Prize in 1993.

Take care *not* to set off essential appositives; like other essential elements, they limit or define the word to which they refer.

Essential

Morrison's novel *The Bluest Eye* is about an African American girl who longs for blue eyes.

The critic Michiko Kakutani says that Morrison's work "stands radiantly on its own as an American epic."

3 **Use a comma or commas to set off transitional or parenthetical expressions.**

■ **Transitional expressions**

Transitional expressions form links between ideas. They include conjunctive adverbs such as *however* and *moreover* as well as other words or phrases such as *for example* and *of course.* (See pp. 85–86 for a list of transitional words and phrases.) Transitional expressions are nonessential, so set them off with a comma or commas:

American workers, for example, receive fewer holidays than European workers do.

When a transitional expression links main clauses, precede it with a semicolon and follow it with a comma. (See p. 455.)

European workers often have long paid vacations; indeed, they may receive a full month.

Note The conjunctions *and, but,* and *yet* are sometimes used as transitional expressions but are not followed by commas (see p. 448). Nor are commas required after some transitional expressions that we read without pauses, such as *also, hence, next, now,* and *thus.* A few transitional expressions, notably *therefore* and *instead,* do not need commas when they fall inside or at the ends of clauses.

American workers thus put in more work days. But the days themselves may be shorter.

■ **Parenthetical expressions**

Parenthetical expressions provide comments, explanations, digressions, or other supplementary information not essential to meaning—for example, *fortunately, unfortunately, all things considered, to be frank, in other words.* Set parenthetical expressions off with commas:

Few people would know, or even guess, the most celebrated holiday on earth.

That holiday is, surprisingly, New Year's Day.

(Dashes and parentheses may also set off parenthetical expressions. See pp. 480 and 482, respectively.)

4   Use a comma or commas to set off *yes* and *no,* tag questions, words of direct address, and mild interjections.

Yes and *no*

Yes, the editorial did have a point.
No, that can never be.

Tag questions

Jones should be allowed to vote, should he not?
They don't stop to consider others, do they?

Direct address

Cody, please bring me the newspaper.
With all due respect, sir, I will not do that.

Mild interjections

Well, you will never know who did it.
Oh, they forgot all about the baby.

(You may want to use an exclamation point to set off a forceful interjection. See p. 428.)

EXERCISE 28.5   Punctuating essential and nonessential elements

Insert commas in the following sentences to set off nonessential elements, and delete any commas that incorrectly set off essential elements. If a sentence is correct as given, mark the number preceding it. (You can do this exercise online at *ablongman.com/littlebrown*.)

Example:
Our language has adopted the words, *garage* and *fanfare*, from the French.

Our language has adopted the words *garage* and *fanfare* from the French.

1. Italians insist that Marco Polo the thirteenth-century explorer did not import pasta from China.
2. Pasta which consists of flour and water and often egg existed in Italy long before Marco Polo left for his travels.
3. A historian who studied pasta says that it originated in the Middle East in the fifth century.
4. Most Italians dispute this account although their evidence is shaky.

COLLABORATIVE LEARNING

Have students complete Exercise 28.5 individually and then compare their responses in small groups. This allows students the opportunity to discuss the differences between essential and nonessential elements in a supportive setting. You might then ask each group to present one or two of their corrected responses on the blackboard or on transparencies while explaining how they reached their conclusions.

ANSWERS: EXERCISE 28.5

1. Italians insist that Marco Polo, the thirteenth-century explorer, did not import pasta from China.
2. Pasta, which consists of flour and water and often egg, existed in Italy long before Marco Polo left for his travels.
3. Sentence correct.
4. Most Italians dispute this account, although their evidence is shaky.
5. Wherever it originated, the Italians are now the undisputed masters in making and cooking pasta.
6. Sentence correct.
7. Most cooks must buy dried pasta, lacking the time to make their own.
8. Sentence correct.
9. Pasta manufacturers choose hard durum wheat because it makes firmer cooked pasta than common wheat does.
10. Pasta made from common wheat tends to get soggy in boiling water.

COLLABORATIVE LEARNING

Ask students to complete Exercise 28.6 individually and then compare their responses in small groups. Encourage the groups to focus on the places where individuals reached alternative conclusions and to discuss the effects of those differences on the meaning of the sentence.

ANSWERS: EXERCISE 28.6

Possible answers

1. American colonists first imported pasta from the English, who discovered it as tourists in Italy.
2. The English returning from their grand tours of Italy were called macaronis because of their fancy airs.
3. A hair style with elaborate curls was also called *macaroni*.
4. The song "Yankee Doodle" refers to this hairdo when it reports that Yankee Doodle "stuck a feather in his cap and called it macaroni."
5. The song, a creation of the English, was actually intended to poke fun at unrefined American colonists.

5. Wherever pasta originated, the Italians are now the undisputed masters, in making and cooking it.
6. Marcella Hazan, who has written several books on Italian cooking, insists that homemade and hand-rolled pasta is the best.
7. Most cooks must buy dried pasta lacking the time to make their own.
8. The finest pasta is made from semolina, a flour from hard durum wheat.
9. Pasta manufacturers choose hard durum wheat, because it makes firmer cooked pasta than common wheat does.
10. Pasta, made from common wheat, tends to get soggy in boiling water.

EXERCISE 28.6 Sentence combining: Essential and nonessential elements

Combine each pair of sentences below into one sentence that uses the element described in parentheses. Insert commas as appropriate. You will have to add, delete, change, and rearrange words. Some items have more than one possible answer. (You can do this exercise online at *ablongman.com/littlebrown*.)

Example:

Mr. Ward's oldest sister helped keep him alive. She was a nurse in the hospital. (*Nonessential clause beginning who.*)

Mr. Ward's oldest sister, who was a nurse in the hospital, helped keep him alive.

1. American colonists first imported pasta from the English. The English had discovered it as tourists in Italy. (*Nonessential clause beginning who.*)
2. The English returned from their grand tours of Italy. They were called macaronis because of their fancy airs. (*Essential phrase beginning returning.*)
3. A hair style was also called macaroni. It had elaborate curls. (*Essential phrase beginning with.*)
4. The song "Yankee Doodle" refers to this hairdo. It reports that Yankee Doodle "stuck a feather in his cap and called it macaroni." (*Essential clause beginning when.*)
5. The song was actually intended to poke fun at unrefined American colonists. It was a creation of the English. (*Nonessential appositive beginning a creation.*)

28d Use a comma or commas to set off absolute phrases.

An **absolute phrase** modifies a whole main clause rather than any word in the clause, and it usually consists of at least a participle (such as *done* or *having torn*) and its subject (a noun or pronoun). (See p. 251.) Absolute phrases can occur at almost any point in the sentence, and they are always set off by a comma or commas:

Household recycling having succeeded, the city now wants to extend the program to businesses.

Many businesses, their profits already squeezed, resist recycling.

28e Use a comma or commas to set off phrases expressing contrast.

The essay needs less wit, more pith.
The substance, not the style, is important.
Substance, unlike style, cannot be faked.

Note Writers often omit commas around contrasting phrases beginning with *but: A full but hazy moon shone down.*

EXERCISE 28.7   Punctuating absolute phrases and phrases of contrast

Insert commas in the following sentences to set off absolute phrases and phrases of contrast. (You can do this exercise online at *ablongman .com/littlebrown*.)

Example:
The recording contract was canceled the band having broken up.
The recording contract was canceled, the band having broken up.

1. Prices having risen rapidly the government debated a price freeze.
2. A price freeze unlike a rise in interest rates seemed a sure solution.
3. The President would have to persuade businesses to accept a price freeze his methods depending on their resistance.
4. No doubt the President his advisers having urged it would first try a patriotic appeal.
5. The President not his advisers insisted on negotiations with businesses.

28f Use commas between items in a series and between coordinate adjectives.

1 Use commas between words, phrases, or clauses forming a series.

Place commas between all elements of a **series**—that is, three or more items of equal importance:

Anna Spingle married at the age of seventeen, had three children by twenty-one, and divorced at twenty-two.
She worked as a cook, a baby-sitter, and a crossing guard.

Some writers omit the comma before the coordinating conjunction in a series (*Breakfast consisted of coffee, eggs and kippers*). But the

COLLABORATIVE LEARNING

WHEN HANDBOOKS DISAGREE

Often, the advice on using commas in a series varies from handbook to handbook and style guide to style guide. Ask students as teams to compare the comma rules given in this handbook with the advice in a newspaper usage manual (for instance, *The Associated Press Stylebook* or *The New York Times Manual of Style and Usage*). These and other newspaper guides are available in the writing reference section of the library or bookstore. They can then report back to the class on where these guides agree and disagree. Although it is widely if not universally used in academic and business writing, the serial comma is expressly omitted in journalism.

final comma is never wrong, and it always helps the reader see the last two items as separate:

Confusing   Spingle's new job involves typing, filing and answering correspondence.

Clear   Spingle's new job involves typing, filing, and answering correspondence.

Exception When items in a series are long and grammatically complicated, they may be separated by semicolons. When the items contain commas, they must be separated by semicolons. (See p. 257.)

2 Use commas between two or more adjectives that equally modify the same word.

When two or more adjectives modify the same word equally, they are said to be **coordinate**. The adjectives may be separated either by *and* or by a comma, as in the following examples.

Spingle's scratched and dented car is old, but it gets her to work.

She has dreams of a sleek, shiny car.

Adjectives are not coordinate—and should *not* be separated by commas—when the one nearer the noun is more closely related to the

Punctuating two or more adjectives

1. **Identify the adjectives.**

   She was a faithful sincere friend.
   They are dedicated medical students.

2. **Can the adjectives be reversed without changing meaning?**

   She was a sincere faithful friend. *Yes.*
   They are medical dedicated students. *No.*

3. **Can the word *and* be inserted between the adjectives without changing meaning?**

   She was a faithful and sincere friend. *Yes.*
   They are dedicated and medical students. *No.*

4. **If *yes* to both questions, the adjectives *are* coordinate and *should* be separated by a comma.**

   She was a faithful, sincere friend.

   If *no* to both questions, the adjectives are *not* coordinate and should *not* be separated by a comma.

   They are dedicated medical students.

noun in meaning. In each of the next examples, the second adjective and the noun form a unit that is modified by the first adjective:

> Spingle's children work at various part-time jobs.
> They all expect to go to a nearby community college.

See the box above for a test to use in punctuating adjectives.
   Note   Numbers are not coordinate with other adjectives:

> Faulty   Spingle has three, teenaged children.
> Revised   Spingle has three teenaged children.

Do not use a comma between the final adjective and the noun:

> Faulty   The children hope to achieve good, well-paying, jobs.
> Revised   The children hope to achieve good, well-paying jobs.

EXERCISE 28.8   Punctuating series and coordinate adjectives

Insert commas in the following sentences to separate coordinate adjectives or elements in series. Mark the number preceding each sentence whose punctuation is already correct. (You can do this exercise online at *ablongman.com/littlebrown*.)

> *Example:*
> Quiet by day, the club became a noisy smoky dive at night.
> Quiet by day, the club became a noisy, smoky dive at night.

1. Shoes with high heels originated to protect feet from the mud garbage and animal waste in the streets.
2. The first known high heels worn strictly for fashion appeared in the sixteenth century.
3. The heels were worn by men and made of colorful silk brocades soft suedes or smooth leathers.
4. High-heeled shoes received a boost when the short powerful King Louis XIV of France began wearing them.
5. Eventually only wealthy fashionable French women wore high heels.

28g   Use commas according to convention in dates, addresses, place names, and long numbers.

     Use commas to separate most parts of dates, addresses, and place names: *June 20, 1950; 24 Fifth Avenue, Suite 601; Cairo, Illinois.* Within a sentence, any element preceded by a comma should be followed by a comma as well, as in the examples below:

Dates

July 4, 1776, is the date the Declaration of Independence was signed.
The bombing of Pearl Harbor on Sunday, December 7, 1941, prompted American entry into World War II.

ANSWERS: EXERCISE 28.8

1. Shoes with high heels originated to protect feet from the mud, garbage, and animal waste in the streets.
2. Sentence correct.
3. The heels were worn by men and made of colorful silk brocades, soft suedes, or smooth leathers.
4. High-heeled shoes received a boost when the short, powerful King Louis XIV of France began wearing them.
5. Eventually only wealthy, fashionable French women wore high heels.

COMPUTER ACTIVITY

US POSTAL REGULATIONS

     In addresses on envelopes, the United States Postal Service now asks that the city name be written in block capitals with no comma, followed by the state abbreviation, one space, and the zip code, as in the following example: BERKELEY CA 94720. This format enables their automatic sorting devices to process mail more effectively. See the sample envelope on p. 843.

     Students using word-processing or mail-merge programs may find that the computer automatically puts addresses into this format. However, writers still use the format shown in these examples when writing town and state names in the body of their texts. (See 55a for a sample envelope that illustrates the format recommended by the Postal Service.)

Do not use commas between the parts of a date in inverted order: *Their anniversary on 15 December 2005 was their fiftieth.* You need not use commas in dates consisting of a month or season and a year: *For the United States the war ended in August 1945.*

Addresses and place names

Columbus, Ohio, is the state capital and the location of Ohio State University.

The population of Garden City, Long Island, New York, is 30,000.

Use the address 220 Cornell Road, Woodside, California 94062, for all correspondence.

Do not use a comma between a state and a zip code.

Long numbers

Use the comma to separate the figures in long numbers into groups of three, counting from the right. With numbers of four digits, the comma is optional.

A kilometer is 3,281 feet [or 3281 feet].
The new assembly plant cost $7,535,000 to design and build.

CULTURE LANGUAGE Usage in American English differs from that in some other languages and dialects, which use a period, not a comma, to separate the figures in long numbers.

EXERCISE 28.9   **Punctuating dates, addresses, place names, numbers**

Insert commas as needed in the following sentences.

Example:
The house cost $27000 fifteen years ago.
The house cost $27,000 fifteen years ago.

1. The festival will hold a benefit dinner and performance on March 10 2006 in Asheville.
2. The organizers hope to raise more than $100000 from donations and ticket sales.
3. Performers are expected from as far away as Milan Italy and Kyoto Japan.
4. All inquiries sent to Mozart Festival PO Box 725 Asheville North Carolina 28803 will receive a quick response.
5. The deadline for ordering tickets by mail is Monday December 3 2005.

28h   Use commas with quotations according to standard practice.

The words *he said, she writes,* and so on identify the source of a quotation. These **signal phrases** may come before, after, or in the

---

middle of the quotation. A signal phrase must always be separated from the quotation by punctuation, usually a comma or commas.

Note Additional issues with quotations are discussed elsewhere in this book:

- Using quotation marks conventionally, pages 468–75.
- Choosing and transcribing quotations from sources, pages 620–21.
- Integrating source material into your text, pages 623–28.
- Acknowledging the sources of quotations to avoid plagiarism, pages 633–34 and 637–38.
- Formatting long prose quotations and poetry quotations in MLA style, pages 688–89; Chicago style, page 776; and APA style, pages 802–03.

1 Ordinarily, use a comma with a signal phrase before or after a quotation.

Eleanor Roosevelt said, "You must do the thing you think you cannot do."

"Knowledge is power," writes Francis Bacon.

Exceptions Do not use a comma when a signal phrase follows a quotation ending in an exclamation point or a question mark:

"Claude!" Mrs. Harrison called.
"Why must I come home?" he asked.

Do not use commas with a quotation introduced by *that* or with a quotation that is integrated into your sentence structure:

James Baldwin insists that "one must never, in one's life, accept . . . injustices as commonplace."

Baldwin thought that the violence of a riot "had been devised as a corrective" to his own violence.

Use a colon instead of a comma between a signal phrase and a quotation when the signal phrase is actually a complete sentence and the quotation is very formal or longer than a sentence.

The Bill of Rights is unambiguous: "Congress shall make no law respecting an establishment of religion, or prohibiting the free exercise thereof."

2 With an interrupted quotation, precede the signal phrase with a comma and follow it with the punctuation required by the quotation.

Quotation
"The shore has a dual nature, changing with the swing of the tides."

Signal phrase

"The shore has a dual nature," observes Rachel Carson, "changing with the swing of the tides." [The signal phrase interrupts the quotation at a comma and thus ends with a comma.]

Quotation

"However mean your life is, meet it and live it; do not shun it and call it hard names."

Signal phrase

"However mean your life is, meet it and live it," Thoreau advises in *Walden*; "do not shun it and call it hard names." [The signal phrase interrupts the quotation at a semicolon and thus ends with a semicolon.]

Quotation

"This is the faith with which I return to the South. With this new faith we will be able to hew out of the mountain of despair a stone of hope."

Signal phrase

"This is the faith with which I return to the South," Martin Luther King, Jr., proclaimed. "With this new faith we will be able to hew out of the mountain of despair a stone of hope." [The signal phrase interrupts the quotation at the end of a sentence and thus ends with a period.]

Note Using a comma instead of a semicolon or a period after the Thoreau and King signal phrases would result in the error called a comma splice: two main clauses separated only by a comma. (See pp. 342–47.)

3 **Place commas that follow quotations within quotation marks.**

"Death is not the greatest loss in life," claims Norman Cousins.

"The greatest loss," Cousins says, "is what dies inside us while we live."

ANSWERS: EXERCISE 28.10

1. Sentence correct.
2. "I think of the open-ended writing process as a voyage in two stages," Elbow says.
3. "The sea voyage is a process of divergence, branching, proliferation, and confusion," Elbow continues; "the coming to land is a process of convergence, pruning, centralizing, and clarifying."

EXERCISE 28.10   Punctuating quotations

Insert commas or semicolons in the following sentences to correct punctuation with quotations. Mark the number preceding any sentence whose punctuation is already correct. (You can do this exercise online at *ablongman.com/littlebrown*.)

Example:
The shoplifter declared "I didn't steal anything."
The shoplifter declared, "I didn't steal anything."

1. The writer and writing teacher Peter Elbow proposes an "open-ended writing process" that "can change you, not just your words."
2. "I think of the open-ended writing process as a voyage in two stages" Elbow says.
3. "The sea voyage is a process of divergence, branching, proliferation, and confusion" Elbow continues "the coming to land is a process of convergence, pruning, centralizing, and clarifying."
4. "Keep up one session of writing long enough to get loosened up and tired" advises Elbow "long enough in fact to make a bit of a voyage."
5. "In coming to new land" Elbow says "you develop a new conception of what you are writing about."

4. "Keep up one session of writing long enough to get loosened up and tired," advises Elbow, "long enough in fact to make a bit of a voyage."
5. "In coming to new land," Elbow says, "you develop a new conception of what you are writing about."

28i Use commas to prevent misreading.

In some sentences words may run together in unintended and confusing ways unless a comma separates them:

Confusing   Soon after the business closed its doors.
Clear   Soon after, the business closed its doors.

Always check whether a comma added to prevent misreading might cause some other confusion or error. In the first example below, the comma prevents *pasta* and *places* from running into each other as *pasta places*, but it separates the subject (*historian*) and the verb (*places*). The revision solves both problems.

Faulty   A historian who studied pasta, places its origin in the Middle East.
Revised   A historian who studied pasta says that it originated in the Middle East.

EXERCISE 28.11 Punctuating to prevent misreading

Insert commas in the following sentences to prevent misreading. (You can do this exercise online at *ablongman.com/littlebrown*.)

Example:
To Laura Ann symbolized decadence.
To Laura, Ann symbolized decadence.

1. Though happy people still have moments of self-doubt.
2. In research subjects have reported themselves to be generally happy people.
3. Among those who have life has included sufferings as well as joys.
4. Of fifty eight subjects reported bouts of serious depression.
5. For half the preceding year had included at least one personal crisis.

Ask students to complete Exercise 28.11 individually and then have them compare their responses in small groups. Encourage the groups to consider the effect of varied comma placement on the meaning of each sentence. As a follow-up exercise you might ask each student to bring in a sentence taken from a magazine or newspaper in which the removal or addition of a comma creates a noticeable change in meaning.

ANSWERS: EXERCISE 28.11

1. Though happy, people still have moments of self-doubt.
2. In research, subjects have reported themselves to be generally happy people.
3. Among those who have, life has included sufferings as well as joys.
4. Of fifty, eight subjects reported bouts of serious depression.
5. For half, the preceding year had included at least one personal crisis.

28j **Use commas only where required.**

Commas can make sentences choppy and even confusing if they are used more often than needed. The main misuses of commas are summarized in the box opposite.

1 **Delete any comma after a subject or a verb.**

Commas interrupt the movement from subject to verb to object or complement, as in the following faulty examples.

> Faulty   The returning soldiers, received a warmer welcome than they expected. [Separation of subject and verb.]
>
> Revised   The returning soldiers received a warmer welcome than they expected.
>
> Faulty   They had chosen, to fight for their country. [Separation of verb *chosen* and object *to fight*.]
>
> Revised   They had chosen to fight for their country.

Exception Use commas between subject, verb, and object or complement only when other words between these elements require punctuation:

> Americans, who are preoccupied with other sports, have only recently developed an interest in professional soccer. [Commas set off a nonessential clause.]

2 **Delete any comma that separates a pair of words, phrases, or subordinate clauses joined by a coordinating conjunction.**

When linking elements with *and*, *or*, or another coordinating conjunction, do not use a comma unless the elements are main clauses (see p. 432):

> Faulty   Banks could, and should help older people manage their money. [Compound helping verb.]
>
> Revised   Banks could and should help older people manage their money.
>
> Faulty   Older people need special assistance because they live on fixed incomes, and because they are not familiar with new accounts, and rates. [Compound subordinate clauses *because . . . because* and compound object of preposition *with.*]
>
> Revised   Older people need special assistance because they live on fixed incomes and because they are not familiar with new accounts and rates.

Principal misuses of the comma

- **Don't use a comma after a subject or verb:**

  Faulty   <u>Anyone</u> with breathing problems, <u>should not exercise</u> during smog alerts.

  Revised   Anyone with breathing problems should not exercise during smog alerts.

- **Don't separate a pair of words, phrases, or subordinate clauses joined by *and, or,* or *nor*:**

  Faulty   Asthmatics are affected by <u>ozone, and sulfur oxides.</u>

  Revised   Asthmatics are affected by ozone and sulfur oxides.

- **Don't use a comma after *and, but, although, because,* or another conjunction:**

  Faulty   Smog is dangerous <u>and,</u> sometimes even fatal.

  Revised   Smog is dangerous and sometimes even fatal.

- **Don't set off essential elements:**

  Faulty   Even people, <u>who are healthy,</u> should be careful.

  Revised   Even people who are healthy should be careful.

  Faulty   Bruce Springsteen's song, <u>"Born in the USA,"</u> became an anthem.

  Revised   Bruce Springsteen's song "Born in the USA" became an anthem.

- **Don't set off a series:**

  Faulty   <u>Cars, factories, and even bakeries,</u> contribute to smog.

  Revised   Cars, factories, and even bakeries contribute to smog.

- **Don't set off an indirect quotation:**

  Faulty   Experts <u>say, that</u> the pollutant ozone is especially damaging.

  Revised   Experts say that the pollutant ozone is especially damaging.

  Faulty   <u>Banks, and community groups</u> can assist the elderly, <u>and eliminate</u> the confusion they often feel. [Compound subject and compound predicate.]

  Revised   Banks and community groups can assist the elderly and eliminate the confusion they often feel.

3 Delete any comma after a conjunction.

The coordinating conjunctions (*and, but,* and so on) and the subordinating conjunctions (*although, because,* and so on) are not followed by commas:

COLLABORATIVE LEARNING

REPUNCTUATING

Take an essay from a reader or a similar source, remove the punctuation you wish to emphasize, make copies of the essay, and ask students to work in groups in order to reach consensus about how it should be punctuated. Tell them not to look at the handbook but to decide on their own the best way to serve the reader's needs through punctuation. When the students have finished, they can compare their work with the original and, using the handbook as a reference, decide which punctuation they think best serves the needs of the essay and the reader. If they decide to disagree with the advice given in the handbook, ask them to write out their own punctuation rules.

Have students practice proofreading, first on articles taken from local newspapers or papers written by members of other classes, and then on their own papers. Discuss why it is more difficult to find mistakes in their own papers than in the writings of others. For many, the difficulty arises because they are looking for what they wanted to write, or thought they wrote, not what they actually put on the page. Advise students to wait several hours between writing and proofreading so that their short-term memories clear and they can see what they've actually written instead of what they wanted to write.

Faulty	Parents of adolescents notice increased conflict at puberty, and, they complain of bickering.
Revised	Parents of adolescents notice increased conflict at puberty, and they complain of bickering.
Faulty	Although, other primates leave the family at adolescence, humans do not.
Revised	Although other primates leave the family at adolescence, humans do not.

4 Delete any commas that set off essential elements.

Commas do not set off an essential element, which limits the meaning of the word to which it refers (see p. 435):

Faulty	Hawthorne's work, *The Scarlet Letter,* was the first major American novel. [The title is essential to distinguish the novel from the rest of Hawthorne's work.]
Revised	Hawthorne's work *The Scarlet Letter* was the first major American novel.
Faulty	The symbols, that Hawthorne uses, have influenced other novelists. [The clause identifies which symbols have been influential.]
Revised	The symbols that Hawthorne uses have influenced other novelists.

Quoted or italicized words are essential appositives when they limit the word they refer to (see p. 437). Do not use commas around an essential appositive:

Faulty	James Joyce's short story, "The Dead," was made into an affecting film. [The commas imply wrongly that Joyce wrote only one story.]
Revised	James Joyce's short story "The Dead" was made into an affecting film.
Faulty	The word, *open,* can be either a verb or an adjective.
Revised	The word *open* can be either a verb or an adjective.

The following sentence requires commas because the quoted title is a nonessential appositive:

> Her only poem about death, "Mourning," was printed in *The New Yorker.*

5 Delete any comma before or after a series unless a rule requires it.

Commas separate the items *within* a series (p. 441) but do not separate the series from the rest of the sentence:

Faulty   The skills of, <u>hunting, herding, and agriculture,</u> sustained the Native Americans.

Revised   The skills of hunting, herding, and agriculture sustained the Native Americans.

In the sentence below, the commas around the series are appropriate because the series is a nonessential appositive (p. 437):

The four major television networks, ABC, CBS, Fox, and NBC, face fierce competition from the cable networks.

However, many writers prefer to use dashes rather than commas to set off series functioning as appositives (see p. 480).

6 Delete any comma setting off an indirect quotation.

Faulty   The report <u>concluded, that</u> dieting could be more dangerous than overeating.

Revised   The report concluded that dieting could be more dangerous than overeating.

EXERCISE 28.12   Revising: Needless or misused commas

Revise the following sentences to eliminate needless or misused commas. Mark the number preceding each sentence that is already punctuated correctly. (You can do this exercise online at *ablongman.com/ littlebrown.*)

Example:
The portrait of the founder, that hung in the dining hall, was stolen by pranksters.
The portrait of the founder that hung in the dining hall was stolen by pranksters.

1. Nearly 32 million US residents, speak a first language other than English.
2. After English the languages most commonly spoken in the United States are, Spanish, French, and German.
3. Almost 75 percent of the people, who speak foreign languages, used the words, "good" or "very good," when judging their proficiency in English.
4. Recent immigrants, especially those speaking Spanish, Chinese, and Korean, tended to judge their English more harshly.
5. The states with the highest proportion of foreign language speakers, are New Mexico, and California.

EXERCISE 28.13   Revising: Commas

Insert commas in the following paragraphs wherever they are needed, and eliminate any misused or needless commas. (You can do this exercise online at *ablongman.com/littlebrown.*)

RESOURCES AND IDEAS

Benson, S. Kenneth. "Profitable Proofreading." In *Teaching the Basics—Really!* Ed. Ouida Clapp. Urbana: NCTE, 1977. 80–81. Benson describes exercises in proofreading and in getting students to pay attention to correction symbols.

COLLABORATIVE LEARNING

Ask students to complete Exercise 28.12 individually and to compare their responses in small groups. Then have each group complete Exercise 28.13 as a collaborative project, encouraging each group to debate the placement and elimination of commas.

TRANSPARENCY MASTER 28.5

ANSWERS: EXERCISE 28.12

1. Nearly 32 million US residents speak a first language other than English.
2. After English the languages most commonly spoken in the United States are Spanish, French, and German.
3. Almost 75 percent of the people who speak foreign languages used the words "good" or "very good" when judging their proficiency in English.
4. Sentence correct.
5. The states with the highest proportion of foreign language speakers are New Mexico and California.

ANSWERS: EXERCISE 28.13

Ellis Island, New York, reopened for business in 1990, but now the customers are tourists, not immigrants. This spot, which lies in New York Harbor, was the first American soil seen or touched by many of the nation's immigrants. Though other places also served as ports of entry for foreigners, none has the symbolic power of Ellis Island. Between its opening in 1892 and its closing in 1954, over 20 million people, about two-thirds of all immigrants, were detained there before taking up their new lives in the United States. Ellis Island processed over 2000 [*or* 2,000] newcomers a day when immigration was at its peak between 1900 and 1920.

As the end of a long voyage and the introduction to the New World, Ellis Island must have left something to be desired. The "huddled masses," as the Statue of Liberty calls them, indeed were huddled. New arrivals were herded about, kept standing in lines for hours or days, yelled at, and abused. Assigned numbers, they submitted their bodies to the pokings and proddings of the silent nurses and doctors who were charged with ferreting out the slightest sign of sickness, disability, or insanity. That test having been passed, the immigrants faced interrogation by an official through an interpreter. Those with names deemed inconveniently long or difficult to pronounce often found themselves permanently labeled with abbreviations of their names or with the names of their hometowns. But millions survived the examination, humiliation, and confusion to take the last short boat ride to New York City. For many of them and especially for their descendants, Ellis Island eventually became, not a nightmare, but the place where life began.

Ellis Island New York reopened for business in 1990 but now the customers are tourists not immigrants. This spot which lies in New York Harbor was the first American soil seen, or touched by many of the nation's immigrants. Though other places also served as ports of entry for foreigners none has the symbolic power of, Ellis Island. Between its opening in 1892 and its closing in 1954, over 20 million people about two-thirds of all immigrants were detained there before taking up their new lives in the United States. Ellis Island processed over 2000 newcomers a day when immigration was at its peak between 1900 and 1920.

As the end of a long voyage and the introduction to the New World Ellis Island must have left something to be desired. The "huddled masses" as the Statue of Liberty calls them indeed were huddled. New arrivals were herded about kept standing in lines for hours or days yelled at and abused. Assigned numbers they submitted their bodies to the pokings and proddings of the silent nurses and doctors, who were charged with ferreting out the slightest sign of sickness, disability or insanity. That test having been passed the immigrants faced interrogation by an official through an interpreter. Those, with names deemed inconveniently long or difficult to pronounce, often found themselves permanently labeled with abbreviations, of their names, or with the names, of their hometowns. But, millions survived the examination humiliation and confusion, to take the last short boat ride to New York City. For many of them and especially for their descendants Ellis Island eventually became not a nightmare but the place where life began.

Note See page 488 for a punctuation exercise combining commas with other marks of punctuation.

mycomplab 2.0

Please visit MyCompLab at *www.mycomplab.com* for more on the writing process.

HIGHLIGHTS

Many inexperienced writers are hesitant to use the semicolon. They may be unfamiliar with the purposes of the mark and therefore reluctant to use it. This chapter should help students understand the four main uses of the semicolon: to separate main clauses not joined by a coordinating conjunction; to separate main clauses joined

COMPANION WEB SITE

See page IAE-57 for companion Web site content description.

CHAPTER **29**

The Semicolon

The semicolon separates equal and balanced sentence elements, usually main clauses (opposite through p. 456), sometimes items in series (p. 457).

http://www.ablongman.com/littlebrown ▶

Visit the companion Web site for more help and additional exercises on the semicolon.

Note A grammar and style checker can spot a few errors in the use of semicolons. For example, a checker suggested using a semicolon after *perfect* in *The set was perfect, the director had planned every detail*, thus correcting a comma splice. But it missed the incorrect semicolon in *The set was perfect; deserted streets, dark houses, and gloomy mist* (a colon would be correct; see p. 477).

29a Use a semicolon between main clauses not joined by *and, but,* or another coordinating conjunction.

Main clauses contain a subject and a predicate and do not begin with a subordinating word (see p. 252). When you join two main clauses in a sentence, you have two primary options for separating them:

- **Insert a comma and a coordinating conjunction:** *and, but, or, nor, for, so, yet*. (See p. 432.)

  The drug does little to relieve symptoms, and it can have side effects.

- **Insert a semicolon:**

  The side effects are not minor; some leave the patient quite ill.

Note If you do not link main clauses with a coordinating conjunction and you separate them only with a comma or with no punctuation at all, you will produce a comma splice or a fused sentence. (See Chapter 18.)

EXERCISE 29.1 Punctuating between main clauses

Insert semicolons to separate main clauses in the following sentences. (You can do this exercise online at *ablongman.com/littlebrown*.)

Example:
One man at the auction bid prudently another spent his bank account.

One man at the auction bid prudently; another spent his bank account.

1. More and more musicians are playing computerized instruments more and more listeners are worrying about the future of acoustic instruments.
2. The computer is not the first new technology in music the pipe organ and saxophone were also technological breakthroughs in their day.
3. Musicians have always experimented with new technology audiences have always resisted the experiments.

by a conjunctive adverb; to separate main clauses if they are very long and complex, even when they are joined by a coordinating conjunction; and to separate items in a series if they are long or contain commas. The chapter also covers the places where the semicolon can be misused. When students take risks in using the semicolon, positive reinforcement from you will help encourage them to add this useful punctuation mark to their repertoire.

ANSWERS: EXERCISE 29.1

1. More and more musicians are playing computerized instruments; more and more listeners are worrying about the future of acoustic instruments.
2. The computer is not the first new technology in music; the pipe organ and saxophone were also technological breakthroughs in their day.
3. Musicians have always experimented with new technology; audiences have always resisted the experiments.
4. Most computer musicians are not merely following the latest fad; they are discovering new sounds and new ways to manipulate sound.
5. Few musicians have abandoned acoustic instruments; most value acoustic sounds as much as electronic sounds.

Distinguishing the comma, the semicolon, and the colon

The *comma* chiefly separates both equal and unequal sentence elements.

- It separates main clauses when they are linked by a coordinating conjunction (p. 432):

  An airline once tried to boost sales by advertising the tense alertness of its crews, but nervous fliers did not want to hear about pilots' sweaty palms.

- It separates subordinate information that is part of or attached to a main clause, such as an introductory element or a nonessential modifier (pp. 433, 435):

  Although the airline campaign failed, many advertising agencies, including some clever ones, copied its underlying message.

The *semicolon* chiefly separates equal and balanced sentence elements. Often the first clause creates an expectation, and the second clause fulfills the expectation.

- It separates complementary main clauses that are *not* linked by a coordinating conjunction (previous page):

  The airline campaign had highlighted only half the story; the other half was buried in the copy.

- It separates complementary main clauses that are related by a conjunctive adverb or other transitional expression (opposite):

  The campaign should not have stressed the pilots' insecurity; instead, the campaign should have stressed the improved performance resulting from that insecurity.

The *colon* chiefly separates unequal sentence elements.

- It separates a main clause from a following explanation or summary, which may or may not be a main clause (pp. 477–78):

  Many successful advertising campaigns have used this message: the anxious seller is harder working and smarter than the competitor.

4. Most computer musicians are not merely following the latest fad they are discovering new sounds and new ways to manipulate sound.
5. Few musicians have abandoned acoustic instruments most value acoustic sounds as much as electronic sounds.

EXERCISE 29.2   Sentence combining: Related main clauses

Combine each set of three sentences below into one sentence containing only two main clauses, and insert a semicolon between the

Ask students to complete Exercise 29.2 individually and then to compare their responses in small groups. Encourage group members to discuss their varying responses and to consider the effects of those differences on the meaning of each sentence. Then have each group present one of their responses to the class and explain the reasons for their sentence-combining choices.

clauses. You will have to add, delete, change, and rearrange words. Most items have more than one possible answer. (You can do this exercise online at *ablongman.com/littlebrown*.)

Example:

The painter Andrew Wyeth is widely admired. He is not universally admired. Some critics view his work as sentimental.

The painter Andrew Wyeth is widely but not universally admired; some critics view his work as sentimental.

1. Electronic instruments are prevalent in jazz. They are also prevalent in rock music. They are less common in classical music.
2. Jazz and rock change rapidly. They nourish experimentation. They nourish improvisation.
3. Traditional classical music does not change. Its notes and instrumentation were established by a composer. The composer was writing decades or centuries ago.
4. Contemporary classical music not only can draw on tradition. It also can respond to innovations. These are innovations such as jazz rhythms and electronic sounds.
5. Much contemporary electronic music is more than just one type of music. It is more than just jazz, rock, or classical. It is a fusion of all three.

29b Use a semicolon between main clauses related by *however, for example,* and so on.

Two kinds of words can relate main clauses: **conjunctive adverbs,** such as *consequently, hence, however, indeed,* and *thus* (see p. 261), and other **transitional expressions,** such as *even so, for example,* and *of course* (see pp. 85–86). When either of these connects two main clauses, the clauses should be separated by a semicolon:

An American immigrant, Levi Strauss, invented blue jeans in the 1860s; eventually, his product clothed working men throughout the West.

The position of the semicolon between main clauses never changes, but the conjunctive adverb or transitional expression may move around within a clause. The adverb or expression is usually set off with a comma or commas (see p. 436):

Blue jeans have become fashionable all over the world; however, the American originators still wear more jeans than anyone else.

Blue jeans have become fashionable all over the world; the American originators, however, still wear more jeans than anyone else.

Its mobility distinguishes a conjunctive adverb or transitional expression from other connecting words, such as coordinating and subordinating conjunctions. See pages 261–62 on this distinction.

ANSWERS: EXERCISE 29.2

Possible answers

1. Electronic instruments are prevalent in jazz and rock music; they are less common in classical music.
2. Jazz and rock change rapidly; they nourish experimentation and improvisation.
3. Traditional classical music does not change; its notes and instrumentation were established by a composer writing decades or centuries ago.
4. Contemporary classical music not only can draw on tradition; it also can respond to innovations such as jazz rhythms and electronic sounds.
5. Much contemporary electronic music is more than just jazz, rock, or classical; it is a fusion of all three.

RESOURCES AND IDEAS

Petit, Angela. "Stylish Semicolon: Teaching Punctuation as Rhetorical Choice." *English Journal* 92 (January 2003): 66–72. Using the semicolon as her example, Petit argues that punctuation is best taught in the context of lessons on style.

COLLABORATIVE LEARNING

Ask students to complete Exercise 29.3 individually and then to compare their responses in small groups. Have each group complete Exercise 4 as a collaborative project, and encourage group members to debate various possible answers to each question. Then have each group present one of their responses to the class and explain the reasons for their choices.

ANSWERS: EXERCISE 29.3

1. Music is a form of communication like language; the basic elements, however, are not letters but notes.
2. Computers can process any information that can be represented numerically; as a result, they can process musical information.
3. A computer's ability to process music depends on what software it can run; it must, moreover, be connected to a system that converts electrical vibration into sound.
4. Computers and their sound systems can produce many different sounds; indeed, the number of possible sounds is infinite.
5. The powerful music computers are very expensive; therefore, they are used only by professional musicians.

ANSWERS: EXERCISE 29.4

Possible answers

1. Most music computers are too expensive for the average consumer; however, digital keyboard instruments can be inexpensive and are widely available.
2. Inside the keyboard is a small computer that controls a sound synthesizer; consequently, the instrument can both process and produce music.
3. The person playing the keyboard presses keys or other controls; immediately, the computer and synthesizer convert these signals into vibrations and sounds.
4. The inexpensive keyboards can perform only a few functions; still, to the novice computer musician the range of drum rhythms and simulated instruments is exciting.
5. Would-be musicians can orchestrate whole songs from just the melody lines; thus [or thus,] they need never again play "Chopsticks."

Note If you use a comma or no punctuation at all between main clauses connected by a conjunctive adverb or transitional expression, you will produce a comma splice or a fused sentence. (See Chapter 18.)

EXERCISE 29.3 Punctuating main clauses related by conjunctive adverbs or transitional expressions

Insert a semicolon in each of the following sentences to separate main clauses related by a conjunctive adverb or transitional expression. Also insert a comma or commas where needed to set off the adverb or expression. (You can do this exercise online at *ablongman.com/littlebrown*.)

Example:

He knew that tickets for the concert would be scarce therefore he arrived at the box office hours before it opened.

He knew that tickets for the concert would be scarce; therefore, he arrived at the box office hours before it opened.

1. Music is a form of communication like language the basic elements however are not letters but notes.
2. Computers can process any information that can be represented numerically as a result they can process musical information.
3. A computer's ability to process music depends on what software it can run it must moreover be connected to a system that converts electrical vibration into sound.
4. Computers and their sound systems can produce many different sounds indeed the number of possible sounds is infinite.
5. The powerful music computers are very expensive therefore they are used only by professional musicians.

EXERCISE 29.4 Sentence combining: Main clauses related by conjunctive adverbs or transitional expressions

Combine each set of three sentences below into one sentence containing only two main clauses. Connect the clauses with the conjunctive adverb or transitional expression in parentheses, and separate them with a semicolon. Be sure the adverbs and expressions are punctuated appropriately. You will have to add, delete, change, and rearrange words. Each item has more than one possible answer. (You can do this exercise online at *ablongman.com/littlebrown*.)

Example:

The Albanians censored their news. We got little news from them. And what we got was unreliable. (*therefore*)

The Albanians censored their news; therefore, the little news we got from them was unreliable.

1. Most music computers are too expensive for the average consumer. Digital keyboard instruments can be inexpensive. They are widely available. (*however*)

2. Inside the keyboard is a small computer. The computer controls a sound synthesizer. The instrument can both process and produce music. (*consequently*)
3. The person playing the keyboard presses keys or manipulates other controls. The computer and synthesizer convert these signals. The signals are converted into vibrations and sounds. (*immediately*)
4. The inexpensive keyboards can perform only a few functions. To the novice computer musician, the range is exciting. The range includes drum rhythms and simulated instruments. (*still*)
5. Would-be musicians can orchestrate whole songs. They start from just the melody lines. They need never again play "Chopsticks." (*thus*)

29c Use a semicolon to separate main clauses if they are complicated or contain commas, even with a coordinating conjunction.

We normally use a comma with a coordinating conjunction such as *and* or *but* between main clauses (see p. 432). But a semicolon makes a sentence easier to read when the main clauses contain commas or are grammatically complicated:

> By a conscious effort of the mind, we can stand aloof from actions and their consequences; and all things, good and bad, go by us like a torrent.
> —Henry David Thoreau

> I doubt if the texture of Southern life is any more grotesque than that of the rest of the nation, but it does seem evident that the Southern writer is particularly adept at recognizing the grotesque; and to recognize the grotesque, you have to have some notion of what is not grotesque and why.
> —Flannery O'Connor

29d Use semicolons to separate items in a series if they are long or contain commas.

We normally use commas to separate items in a series (see p. 441). But when the items are long or internally punctuated, semicolons help readers identify the items:

> The custody case involved Amy Dalton, the child; Ellen and Mark Dalton, the parents; and Ruth and Hal Blum, the grandparents.

> One may even reasonably advance the claim that the sort of communication that really counts, and is therefore embodied into permanent records, is primarily written; that "words fly away, but written messages endure," as the Latin saying put it two thousand years ago; and that there is no basic significance to at least fifty percent of the oral interchange that goes on among all sorts of persons, high and low.
> —Mario Pei

COMPUTER ACTIVITY

STYLE CHECKERS

Often, style checkers may reject uses of semicolons like the ones shown here, since they are apparent exceptions to semicolon rules. When such conflicts arise, have students check to see that their sentences are well constructed and that the semicolons are needed. As a case in point, you might have students run a passage from a published writer (such as Thoreau or O'Connor) through their grammar checkers and present the results to the class. Encourage students to discuss the effects of semicolon placement on the meaning of each passage.

ANSWERS: EXERCISE 29.5

1. The Indian subcontinent is separated from the rest of the world by clear barriers: the Bay of Bengal and the Arabian Sea to the east and west, respectively; the Indian Ocean to the south; and 1600 miles of mountain ranges to the north.
2. In the north of India are the world's highest mountains, the Himalayas; and farther south are fertile farmlands, unpopulated deserts, and rain forests.
3. India is a nation of ethnic and linguistic diversity, with numerous religions, including Hinduism, Islam, and Christianity; with distinct castes and ethnic groups; and with sixteen languages, including the official Hindi and the "associate official" English.
4. Between the seventeenth and nineteenth centuries, the British colonized most of India, taking control of government, the bureaucracy, and industry; and they assumed a social position above all Indians.
5. During British rule the Indians' own unresolved differences and their frustrations with the British erupted in violent incidents such as the Sepoy Mutiny, which began on February 26, 1857, and lasted two years; the Amritsar Massacre on April 13, 1919; and violence between Hindus and Muslims during World War II that resulted in the separation of Pakistan from India.

MEMORY AID

Introduce students to this brief list of ways *not* to use the semicolon.

Do not use a semicolon to separate a subordinate clause from a main clause.
Do not use a semicolon to introduce a series.
Do not overuse a semicolon.

EXERCISE 29.5 Punctuating long main clauses and series items

Substitute semicolons for commas in the following sentences to separate main clauses or series items that are long or contain commas. (You can do this exercise online at *ablongman.com/littlebrown*.)

Example:

After graduation he debated whether to settle in San Francisco, which was temperate but far from his parents, New York City, which was exciting but expensive, or Atlanta, which was close to home but already familiar.

After graduation he debated whether to settle in San Francisco, which was temperate but far from his parents; New York City, which was exciting but expensive; or Atlanta, which was close to home but already familiar.

1. The Indian subcontinent is separated from the rest of the world by clear barriers: the Bay of Bengal and the Arabian Sea to the east and west, respectively, the Indian Ocean to the south, and 1600 miles of mountain ranges to the north.
2. In the north of India are the world's highest mountains, the Himalayas, and farther south are fertile farmlands, unpopulated deserts, and rain forests.
3. India is a nation of ethnic and linguistic diversity, with numerous religions, including Hinduism, Islam, and Christianity, with distinct castes and ethnic groups, and with sixteen languages, including the official Hindi and the "associate official" English.
4. Between the seventeenth and nineteenth centuries, the British colonized most of India, taking control of government, the bureaucracy, and industry, and they assumed a social position above all Indians.
5. During British rule the Indians' own unresolved differences and their frustrations with the British erupted in violent incidents such as the Sepoy Mutiny, which began on February 26, 1857, and lasted two years, the Amritsar Massacre on April 13, 1919, and violence between Hindus and Muslims during World War II that resulted in the separation of Pakistan from India.

29e Use the semicolon only where required.

Semicolons do not separate unequal sentence elements and should not be overused.

1 Delete or replace any semicolon that separates a subordinate clause or a phrase from a main clause.

The semicolon does not separate subordinate clauses from main clauses or phrases from main clauses:

Faulty Pygmies are in danger of extinction; because of encroaching development.

Revised	Pygmies are in danger of extinction because of encroaching development.
Faulty	According to African authorities; only about 35,000 Pygmies exist today.
Revised	According to African authorities, only about 35,000 Pygmies exist today.

Note Many readers regard a phrase or subordinate clause set off with a semicolon as a kind of sentence fragment. (See Chapter 17.)

2 Delete or replace any semicolon that introduces a series or explanation.

Colons and dashes, not semicolons, introduce series, explanations, and so forth. (See p. 477.)

Faulty	Teachers have heard all sorts of reasons why students do poorly; psychological problems, family illness, too much work, too little time.
Revised	Teachers have heard all sorts of reasons why students do poorly: psychological problems, family illness, too much work, too little time.
Revised	Teachers have heard all sorts of reasons why students do poorly—psychological problems, family illness, too much work, too little time.

3 Use the semicolon sparingly.

Use the semicolon only occasionally. Many semicolons in a passage, even when they are required by rule, often indicate repetitive sentence structure. To revise a passage with too many semicolons, you'll need to restructure your sentences, not just remove the semicolons. (See Chapter 26 for tips on varying sentences.)

Semicolon overused

The Make-a-Wish Foundation helps sick children; it grants the wishes of children who are terminally ill. The foundation learns of a child's wish; the information usually comes from parents, friends, or hospital staff; the wish may be for a special toy, a trip to the circus, or a visit to Disneyland. The foundation grants some wishes with its own funds; for other wishes it appeals to those who have what the child desires.

Revised

The Make-a-Wish Foundation grants the wishes of children who are terminally ill. From parents, friends, or hospital staff, the foundation learns of a child's wish for a special toy, a trip to the circus, or a visit to Disneyland. It grants some wishes with its own funds; for other wishes it appeals to those who have what the child desires.

COLLABORATIVE LEARNING

Ask students to complete Exercise 29.6 individually and to compare their responses in small groups. Then ask each group to work collaboratively on Exercise 29.7, encouraging them to debate the effectiveness of each change in punctuation.

ANSWERS: EXERCISE 29.6

1. The main religion in India is Hinduism, a way of life as well as a theology and philosophy.
2. Unlike Christianity and Judaism, Hinduism is a polytheistic religion, with deities numbering in the hundreds.
3. *Possible revision:* Unlike many other religions, Hinduism allows its creeds and practices to vary widely from place to place and person to person. Whereas other religions have churches and principal prophets and holy books, Hinduism does not. And whereas other religions center on specially trained priests or other leaders, Hinduism promotes the individual as his or her own priest.
4. In Hindu belief there are four types of people: reflective, emotional, active, and experimental.
5. Each type of person has a different technique for realizing the true, immortal self, which has infinite existence, infinite knowledge, and infinite joy.

ANSWERS: EXERCISE 29.7

The set, sounds, and actors in the movie captured the essence of horror films. The set was ideal: dark, deserted streets; trees dipping their branches over the sidewalks; mist hugging the ground and creeping up to meet the trees; looming shadows of unlighted, turreted houses. The sounds, too, were appropriate; especially terrifying was the hard, hollow sound of footsteps echoing throughout the film. But the best feature of the movie was its actors, all of them tall, pale, and thin to the point of emaciation. With one exception, they were dressed uniformly in gray and had gray hair. The exception was an actress who dressed only in black, as if to set off her pale yellow, nearly white, long hair, the only color in the film. The glinting black eyes of another actor stole almost every scene; indeed, they were the source of all the film's mischief.

EXERCISE 29.6   Revising: Misused or overused semicolons

Revise the following sentences to eliminate misused or overused semicolons, substituting other punctuation as appropriate. (You can do this exercise online at *ablongman.com/littlebrown.*)

> *Example:*
> The doctor gave everyone the same advice; get exercise.
> The doctor gave everyone the same advice: get exercise.

1. The main religion in India is Hinduism; a way of life as well as a theology and philosophy.
2. Unlike Christianity and Judaism; Hinduism is a polytheistic religion; with deities numbering in the hundreds.
3. Hinduism is unlike many other religions; it allows its creeds and practices to vary widely from place to place and person to person. Other religions have churches; Hinduism does not. Other religions have principal prophets and holy books; Hinduism does not. Other religions center on specially trained priests or other leaders; Hinduism promotes the individual as his or her own priest.
4. In Hindu belief there are four types of people; reflective, emotional, active, and experimental.
5. Each type of person has a different technique for realizing the true, immortal self; which has infinite existence, infinite knowledge, and infinite joy.

EXERCISE 29.7   Revising: Semicolons

Insert semicolons in the following paragraph wherever they are needed. Eliminate any misused or needless semicolons, substituting other punctuation as appropriate. (You can do this exercise online at *ablongman.com/littlebrown.*)

The set, sounds, and actors in the movie captured the essence of horror films. The set was ideal; dark, deserted streets, trees dipping their branches over the sidewalks, mist hugging the ground and creeping up to meet the trees, looming shadows of unlighted, turreted houses. The sounds, too, were appropriate, especially terrifying was the hard, hollow sound of footsteps echoing throughout the film. But the best feature of the movie was its actors; all of them tall, pale, and thin to the point of emaciation. With one exception, they were dressed uniformly in gray and had gray hair. The exception was an actress who dressed only in black; as if to set off her pale yellow, nearly white, long hair; the only color in the film. The glinting black eyes of another actor stole almost every scene, indeed, they were the source of all the film's mischief.

Note See page 488 for a punctuation exercise combining semicolons with other marks of punctuation.

CHAPTER 30

The Apostrophe

Unlike other punctuation marks, which separate words, the apostrophe (') appears as *part* of a word to indicate possession or the omission of one or more letters.

Note Grammar and style checkers have mixed results in recognizing apostrophe errors. For instance, most flag missing apostrophes in contractions (as in *isnt*), but many cannot distinguish between *its* and *it's*, *their* and *they're*, *your* and *you're*, *whose* and *who's*. The checkers can identify some apostrophe errors in possessives but will overlook others and may flag correct plurals. Instead of relying on your checker, try using your computer's Search or Find function to hunt for all words you have ended in *-s*. Then check each one to ensure that you have used apostrophes correctly.

30a Use the apostrophe to indicate the possessive case for nouns and indefinite pronouns.

In English the **possessive case** shows ownership or possession of one person or thing by another. Possession may be shown with an *of* phrase (*the hair of the dog*); or it may be shown with the addition of an apostrophe and, usually, an *-s* (*the dog's hair*).

Note Apostrophes are easy to misuse. Always check your drafts to ensure the following:

- Every word ending in *-s* neither omits a needed apostrophe nor adds an unneeded one.
- The apostrophe or apostrophe-plus-*s* is an *addition*. Before this addition, always spell the name of the owner or owners without dropping or adding letters: *girls* becomes *girls'*, not *girl's*.

1 Add -'s to singular nouns and indefinite pronouns.

Bill Boughton**'s** skillful card tricks amaze children.
Anyone**'s** eyes would widen. [Indefinite pronoun.]
Most tricks will pique an adult**'s** curiosity, too.

http://www.ablongman.com/littlebrown ▶

Visit the companion Web site for more help and additional exercises on the apostrophe.

mycomplab²·⁰

Please visit MyCompLab at *www.mycomplab.com* for more on the writing process.

HIGHLIGHTS

This chapter deals with the three reasons to use an apostrophe: to show possession; to indicate a contraction; or to form the plural of letters, numbers, and words named as words. It also explains when the apostrophe should not be used. The chapter focuses on the trouble spots writers are most likely to face and on the strategies they can use to avoid such problems.

COMPUTER ACTIVITY

SPELLING CHECKERS

Spelling checkers vary; some require both an apostrophe and an *s* after words ending in *s*, while others don't.

COMPANION WEB SITE

See page IAE-57 for companion Web site content description.

RESOURCES AND IDEAS

Hashimoto, Irvin. "Pain and Suffering: Apostrophes and Academic Life." *Journal of Basic Writing* 7(2) (1988): 91–98. Hashimoto reviews, in often humorous fashion, some of the problems students have with apostrophe use.

Wiener, Harvey S. *The Writing Room: A Resource Book for Teachers of English.* New York: Oxford UP, 1981. 175–80. Wiener offers advice on explaining possession to students and describes several exercises designed to help them master the possessive forms of words.

Add -'s as well to singular nouns that end in -s:

Henry James's novels reward the patient reader.
Los Angeles's weather is mostly warm.
The business's customers filed suit.

Exception   We often do not pronounce the possessive -s of a few singular nouns ending in an s or z sound: names with more than one s sound (*Moses*), names that sound like plurals (*Rivers, Bridges*), and nouns followed by a word beginning in s. In these cases, many writers add only the apostrophe to show possession.

Moses' mother concealed him in the bulrushes.
Joan Rivers' jokes offend many people.
For conscience' sake she confessed her lie.

However, usage varies widely, and the final -s is not wrong with words like these (*Moses's, Rivers's, conscience's*).

2   Add -'s to plural nouns not ending in -s.

The bill establishes children's rights.
Publicity grabbed the media's attention.

3   Add only an apostrophe to plural nouns ending in -s.

Workers' incomes have not risen much over the past decade.
Many students benefit from several years' work after high school.
The Jameses' talents are extraordinary.

Note the difference in the possessives of singular and plural words ending in -s. The singular form usually takes -s: *James's.* The plural takes only the apostrophe: *Jameses'.*

4   Add -'s only to the last word of compound words or word groups.

The council president's address was a bore.
The brother-in-law's business failed.
Taxes are always somebody else's fault.

5   With two or more words, add -'s to one or both depending on meaning.

Individual possession

Zimbale's and Mason's comedy techniques are similar. [Each comedian has his own technique.]

Joint possession

The child recovered despite her mother and father's neglect. [The mother and father were jointly neglectful.]

Uses and misuses of the apostrophe

Uses of the apostrophe

- **Use an apostrophe to form the possessives of nouns and indefinite pronouns** (p. 461 and opposite).

Singular	Plural
Ms. Park's	the Parks'
lawyer's	lawyers'
everyone's	two weeks'

- **Use an apostrophe to form contractions** (p. 465).

it's a girl	shouldn't
you're	won't

- **The apostrophe is optional for plurals of abbreviations, dates, and words or characters named as words** (p. 467).

MAs or MA's	Cs or C's
1960s or 1960's	ifs or if's

Misuses of the apostrophe

- **Do not use an apostrophe plus -s to form the possessives of plural nouns ending in -s** (opposite). Instead, use an apostrophe alone after the -s that forms the plural.

Not	But
the Kim's car	the Kims' car
boy's fathers	boys' fathers
babie's care	babies' care

- **Do not use an apostrophe to form plurals of nouns** (p. 464).

Not	But
book's are	books are
the Freed's	the Freeds

- **Do not use an apostrophe with verbs ending in -s** (p. 464).

Not	But
swim's	swims

- **Do not use an apostrophe to form the possessives of personal pronouns** (p. 465).

Not	But
it's toes	its toes
your's	yours

EXERCISE 30.1   Forming possessives

Form the possessive case of each word or word group in brackets. (You can do this exercise online at *ablongman.com/littlebrown*.)

ANSWERS: EXERCISE 30.1

1. In the myths of the ancient Greeks, the god-desses' roles vary widely.
2. Demeter's responsibility is the fruitfulness of the earth.
3. Athena's role is to guard the city of Athens.
4. Artemis's function is to care for wild animals and small children.
5. Athena and Artemis's father, Zeus, is the king of the gods.
6. Even a single goddess's responsibilities are often varied.
7. Over several centuries' time, Athena changes from a mariner's goddess to the patron of crafts.
8. Athena is also concerned with fertility and with children's well-being, since Athena's strength depended on a large and healthy population.
9. Athena often changes into birds' forms.
10. In Homer's *Odyssey* she assumes a sea eagle's form.
11. In ancient Athens the myths of Athena were part of everyone's knowledge and life.
12. A cherished myth tells how Athena fights to retain possession of her people's land when the god Poseidon wants it.
13. Athena's and Poseidon's skills are different, and each promises a special gift to the Athenians.
14. At the contest's conclusion, Poseidon has given water and Athena has given an olive tree, for sustenance.
15. The other gods decide that the Athenians' lives depend more on Athena than on Poseidon.

Example:

The [men] blood pressures were higher than the [women].
The men**'s** blood pressures were higher than the women**'s**.

1. In the myths of the ancient Greeks, the [goddesses] roles vary widely.
2. [Demeter] responsibility is the fruitfulness of the earth.
3. [Athena] role is to guard the city of Athens.
4. [Artemis] function is to care for wild animals and small children.
5. [Athena and Artemis] father, Zeus, is the king of the gods.
6. Even a single [goddess] responsibilities are often varied.
7. Over several [centuries] time, Athena changes from a [mariner] goddess to the patron of crafts.
8. Athena is also concerned with fertility and with [children] well-being, since [Athens] strength depended on a large and healthy population.
9. Athena often changes into [birds] forms.
10. In [Homer] *Odyssey* she assumes a [sea eagle] form.
11. In ancient Athens the myths of Athena were part of [everyone] knowledge and life.
12. A cherished myth tells how Athena fights to retain possession of her [people] land when the god Poseidon wants it.
13. [Athena and Poseidon] skills are different, and each promises a special gift to the Athenians.
14. At the [contest] conclusion, Poseidon has given water and Athena has given an olive tree, for sustenance.
15. The other gods decide that the [Athenians] lives depend more on Athena than on Poseidon.

30b Delete or replace any apostrophe in a plural noun, a singular verb, or a possessive personal pronoun.

Not all words ending in -*s* take an apostrophe. Three kinds of words are especially likely to attract unneeded apostrophes.

■ Plural nouns

Form most plural nouns by adding -*s* or -*es* (*boys, Smiths, families, Joneses*). Never add an apostrophe to form the plural:

| Faulty | The unleashed dog's began traveling in a pack. |
| Revised | The unleashed dogs began traveling in a pack. |

| Faulty | The Jones' and Bass' were feuding. |
| Revised | The Jones**es** and Bass**es** were feuding. |

■ Singular verbs

Do not add an apostrophe to present-tense verbs used with *he, she, it,* and other third-person singular subjects. These verbs always end in -*s* but *never* with an apostrophe:

Faulty	The subway <u>break's</u> down less often now.
Revised	The subway <u>breaks</u> down less often now.

Faulty	It <u>run's</u> more reliably.
Revised	It <u>runs</u> more reliably.

■ **Possessive personal pronouns**

His, hers, its, ours, yours, theirs, and *whose* are possessive forms of the pronouns *he, she, it, we, you, they,* and *who.* They do not take apostrophes:

Faulty	The credit is <u>her's</u> not <u>their's.</u>
Revised	The credit is <u>hers,</u> not <u>theirs.</u>

The personal pronouns are often confused with contractions, such as *it's, you're,* and *who's.* See below.

EXERCISE 30.2   Distinguishing between plurals and possessives

Supply the appropriate form—possessive or plural—of each word given in brackets. Some answers require apostrophes, and some do not. (You can do this exercise online at *ablongman.com/littlebrown.*)

Example:
A dozen Hawaiian [shirt], each with [it] own loud design, hung in the window.
A dozen Hawaiian <u>shirts</u>, each with <u>its</u> own loud design, hung in the window.

1. Demeter may be the oldest of the Greek [god], older than Zeus.
2. Many prehistoric [culture] had earth [goddess] like Demeter.
3. In myth she is the earth mother, which means that the responsibility for the fertility of both [animal] and [plant] is [she].
4. The [goddess] festival came at harvest time, with [it] celebration of bounty.
5. The [people] [prayer] to Demeter thanked her for grain and other [gift].

30c   **Use an apostrophe to indicate the omission in a standard contraction.**

it is, it has	it's	let us	let's
he is	he's	does not	doesn't
she is	she's	were not	weren't
they are	they're	class of 2009	class of '09
you are	you're	of the clock	o'clock
who is, who has	who's	madam	ma'am

Contractions are common in speech and in informal writing. They may also be used to relax style in more formal kinds of writing, as they are in this handbook. But be aware that many people disapprove of contractions in any kind of formal writing.

Note Contractions are easily confused with the possessive personal pronouns:

Contraction	Possessive pronoun
it's	its
they're	their
you're	your
who's	whose

Faulty   Legislators know their going to have to cut the budget to eliminate it's deficit.

Revised   Legislators know they're going to have to cut the budget to eliminate its deficit.

If you tend to confuse these forms, search for both spellings throughout your drafts. Then test for correctness:

- **Use an apostrophe when you intend the word to contain the sentence verb *is*, *are*, or *has*,** as in *It is* [*It's*] *a shame, It has* [*It's*] *happened, They are* [*They're*] *to blame, You are* [*You're*] *right, Who is* [*Who's*] *coming? Who has* [*Who's*] *responded?*
- **Don't use an apostrophe when you intend the word to indicate possession,** as in *Its tail was wagging, Their car broke down, Your eyes are blue, Whose book is that?*

ANSWERS: EXERCISE 30.3

Possible answers

1. She'd rather be dancing.
2. He couldn't see her in the crowd.
3. They're at the front door now.
4. He's my brother.
5. We don't like the beach.
6. She'll speak her mind.
7. The recent storm was nearly as bad as the hurricane of '62.
8. Isn't that your cousin?
9. It's a fact.
10. The door won't budge.

ANSWERS: EXERCISE 30.4

1. In Greek myth the goddess Demeter has a special fondness for Eleusis, near Athens, and its people.
2. Sentence correct.

EXERCISE 30.3   Forming contractions

Form contractions from each set of words below. Use each contraction in a complete sentence. (You can do this exercise online at *ablongman.com/littlebrown*.)

Example:
we are: we're
We're open to ideas.

1. she would
2. could not
3. they are
4. he is
5. do not
6. she will
7. hurricane of 1962
8. is not
9. it is
10. will not

EXERCISE 30.4   Revising: Contractions and personal pronouns

Revise the following sentences to correct mistakes in the use of contractions and personal pronouns. Mark the number preceding any sentence that is already correct. (You can do this exercise online at *ablongman.com/littlebrown*.)

Example:
The agencies give they're employees their birthdays off.
The agencies give th**eir** employees their birthdays off.

1. In Greek myth the goddess Demeter has a special fondness for Eleusis, near Athens, and it's people.
2. She finds rest among the people and is touched by their kindness.
3. Demeter rewards the Eleusians with the secret for making they're land fruitful.
4. The Eleusians begin a cult in honor of Demeter, whose worshiped in secret ceremonies.
5. Its unknown what happened in the ceremonies, for no participant ever revealed their rituals.

3. Demeter rewards the Eleusians with the se-cret for making <u>their</u> land fruitful.
4. The Eleusians <u>begin</u> a cult in honor of Demeter, <u>who's</u> worshipped in secret cere-monies.
5. <u>It's</u> unknown what happened in the cere-monies, for no participant ever revealed their [correct] rituals.

30d Increasingly, the apostrophe does not mark plural abbreviations, dates, and words or characters named as words.

You'll sometimes see apostrophes used to form the plurals of abbreviations (*BA's*), dates (*1900's*), and words or characters named as words (*but's*). However, most current style guides do not recom-mend the apostrophe in these cases.

BAs	PhDs
1990s	2000s

The sentence has too many <u>buts</u> [or *buts*].
Two <u>3s</u> [or *3s*] end the zip code.

Note Underline or italicize a word or character named as a word (see p. 498), but not the added *-s*.

EXERCISE 30.5 Revising: Apostrophes

In the following paragraph correct any mistakes in the use of the apos-trophe or any confusion between contractions and possessive personal pronouns. (You can do this exercise online at *ablongman.com/littlebrown.*)

Landlocked Chad is among the worlds most troubled countries. The people's of Chad are poor: they're average per capita income equals just over $1000 a year. Less than half of Chads population is lit-erate, and every five hundred people must share only two teacher's. The natural resources of the nation have never been plentiful, and now, as it's slowly being absorbed into the growing Sahara Desert, even water is scarce. Chads political conflicts go back to the nine-teenth century, when the French colonized the land by brutally subdu-ing it's people. The rule of the French—who's inept government of the colony did nothing to ease tensions among racial, tribal, and religious

Have students complete Exercise 30.5 indi-vidually and then compare their responses in groups. Then ask the groups to review para-graphs from each student's work in order to check apostrophe usage. It's important that stu-dents make the connection between the hand-book exercises and correct apostrophe usage in their own work.

ANSWERS: EXERCISE 30.5

Landlocked Chad is among the <u>world's</u> most troubled countries. The <u>peoples</u> of Chad are poor: <u>their</u> average per capita income equals just over $1000 a year. Less than half of <u>Chad's</u> popu-lation is literate, and every five hundred people must share only two <u>teachers</u>. The natural re-sources of the nation have never been plentiful, and now, as it's [correct] slowly being absorbed into the growing Sahara Desert, even water is scarce. <u>Chad's</u> political conflicts go back to the nineteenth century, when the French colonized the land by brutally subduing <u>its</u> people. The rule of the French—<u>whose</u> inept government of the colony did nothing to ease tensions among racial, tribal, and religious <u>groups</u>—ended with inde-pendence in 1960. But since then the <u>Chadians'</u> experience has been one of civil war and oppres-sion, and now <u>they're</u> also threatened with inva-sions from <u>their</u> neighbors.

group's—ended with independence in 1960. But since then the Chadians experience has been one of civil war and oppression, and their also threatened with invasions from they're neighbors.

Note See page 488 for a punctuation exercise involving apostrophes along with other marks of punctuation.

mycomplab

Please visit MyCompLab at *www.mycomplab.com* for more on the writing process.

HIGHLIGHTS

The two most common problems students have with quotation marks are failing to close the quotation (see the special cautionary note in the chapter's introduction) and misplacing other punctuation marks inside or outside quotation marks. Take time to review these rules and encourage students to double-check their use of quotation marks. Both practices may save you a great deal of time in marking papers, especially when the students are preparing papers that require the use of cited material.

CHAPTER **31**

Quotation Marks

Quotation marks—either double (" ") or single (' ')—mainly enclose direct quotations from speech and from writing. The chart on the next two pages summarizes this use and the combination of quotation marks with commas, ellipsis marks, and other punctuation. Additional information on using quotations appears elsewhere in this book:

- **Using commas with signal phrases introducing quotations,** pages 444–46.
- **Using brackets and the ellipsis mark to indicate changes in quotations,** pages 483–86.
- **Quoting sources versus paraphrasing or summarizing them,** pages 617–22.
- **Integrating quotations into your text,** pages 623–28.
- **Acknowledging the sources of quotations to avoid plagiarism,** pages 633–34 and 637–38.
- **Formatting long prose quotations and poetry quotations** in MLA style, pages 688–89; Chicago style, page 776; and APA style, pages 802–03.

Note Always use quotation marks in pairs, one at the beginning of a quotation and one at the end. Most grammar and style checkers will help you use quotation marks in pairs by flagging a lone mark. Most checkers can also be set to ignore other marks of

Handling quotations from speech or writing

■ Direct and indirect quotation

Direct quotation

According to Lewis Thomas, "We are, perhaps uniquely among the earth's creatures, the worrying animal. We worry away our lives."

Do not use quotation marks with a direct quotation that is set off from your text. See pages 688–89 (MLA style), 776 (Chicago style), and 802–03 (APA style).

Quotation within quotation

Quoting a phrase by Lewis Thomas, the author adds, "We are 'the worrying animal.'"

Indirect quotation

Lewis Thomas says that human beings are unique among animals in their worrying.

■ Quotation marks with other punctuation marks

Commas and periods

Human beings are the "worrying animal," says Thomas.
Thomas calls human beings "the worrying animal."

Semicolons and colons

Machiavelli says that "the majority of men live content"; in contrast, Thomas calls us "the worrying animal."

Thomas believes that we are "the worrying animal": we spend our lives afraid and restless.

Question marks, exclamation points, dashes

When part of your own sentence:

Who said that human beings are "the worrying animal"?
Imagine saying that we human beings "worry away our lives"!
Thomas's phrase—"the worrying animal"—seems too narrow.

When part of the original quotation:

"Will you discuss this with me?" she asked.
"I demand that you discuss this with me!" she yelled.
"Please, won't you—" She paused.

■ Altering quotations

Brackets for additions

"We [human beings] worry away our lives," says Thomas.

Brackets for altered capitalization

"[T]he worrying animal" is what Thomas calls us. He says that "[w]e worry away our lives."

(continued)

INDENTED QUOTATIONS AND POETRY

MLA style for double-spacing indented quotations of poetry or prose is new to some students, who may have been taught to single-space such quotations in high school and who see them single spaced in published works. If you are conducting draft-review workshops, ask students to check the spacing of such quotations in their drafts. If they are preparing papers on word processors, they may be able to take advantage of automatic indentation and spacing features to format such quotations.

Handling quotations from speech or writing
(continued)

Ellipsis marks for omissions

"We are . . . the worrying animal," says Thomas.

Worrying places us "uniquely among the earth's creatures. . . . We worry away our lives."

■ **Punctuating signal phrases with quotations**

Introductory signal phrase

He says, "We worry away our lives."

An answer is in these words by Lewis Thomas: "We are, perhaps uniquely among the earth's creatures, the worrying animal."

Thomas says that "the worrying animal" is afraid and restless.

Concluding signal phrase

We are "the worrying animal," says Thomas.
"Who says?" she demanded.
"I do!" he shouted.

Interrupting signal phrase

"We are," says Thomas, "perhaps uniquely among the earth's creatures, the worrying animal."

"I do not like the idea," she said; "however, I agree with it."

Human beings are "the worrying animal," says Thomas. "We worry away our lives."

punctuation with quotations or to look for punctuation inside or outside quotation marks. (see p. 61), but they may still fail to detect some errors.

(see p. 61)

31a Use double quotation marks to enclose direct quotations.

Direct quotations report what someone has said or written in the exact words of the original. Always enclose direct quotations in quotation marks:

> "Fortunately," said the psychoanalyst Karen Horney, "analysis is not the only way to resolve inner conflicts. Life itself still remains a very effective therapist."

Indirect quotations report what has been said or written, but not in the exact words of the person being quoted. Indirect quotations are *not* enclosed in quotation marks:

The psychoanalyst Karen Horney remarked that analysis is but one solution to personal problems, for life is a good therapist.

(See also p. 618 on paraphrasing quotations.)

31b Use single quotation marks to enclose a quotation within a quotation.

When you quote a writer or speaker, use double quotation marks. When the material you quote contains yet another quotation, distinguish the two by enclosing the second one in single quotation marks:

> "In formulating any philosophy," Woody Allen writes, "the first consideration must always be: What can we know? Descartes hinted at the problem when he wrote, 'My mind can never know my body, although it has become quite friendly with my leg.'"

Notice that two different quotation marks appear at the end of the sentence—one single (to finish the interior quotation) and one double (to finish the main quotation).

EXERCISE 31.1 Using double and single quotation marks

Insert double and single quotation marks as needed in the following sentences. Mark the number preceding any sentence that is already correct. (You can do this exercise online at *ablongman.com/littlebrown*.)

> *Example:*
> The purpose of this book, explains the preface, is to examine the meaning of the expression Dance is poetry.
> "The purpose of this book," explains the preface, "is to examine the meaning of the expression 'Dance is poetry.'"

1. Why, the lecturer asked, do we say Bless you! or something else when people sneeze but not acknowledge coughs, hiccups, and other eruptions?
2. She said that sneezes have always been regarded differently.
3. Sneezes feel more uncontrollable than some other eruptions, she said.
4. Unlike coughs and hiccups, she explained, sneezes feel as if they come from inside the head.
5. She concluded, People thus wish to recognize a sneeze, if only with a Gosh.

31c Set off quotations of dialog according to standard practice.

When quoting conversations, begin a new paragraph for each speaker:

ANSWERS: EXERCISE 31.1

1. "Why," the lecturer asked, "do we say 'Bless you!' or something else when people sneeze but not acknowledge coughs, hiccups, and other eruptions?"
2. Sentence correct.
3. "Sneezes feel more uncontrollable than some other eruptions," she said.
4. "Unlike coughs and hiccups," she explained, "sneezes feel as if they come from inside the head."
5. She concluded, "People thus wish to recognize a sneeze, if only with a 'Gosh.'"

"What shall I call you? Your name?" Andrews whispered rapidly, as with a high squeak the latch of the door rose.

"Elizabeth," she said. "Elizabeth."

—Graham Greene, *The Man Within*

Note When you quote a single speaker for more than one paragraph, put quotation marks at the beginning of each paragraph but at the end of only the last paragraph. The absence of quotation marks at the end of each paragraph but the last tells readers that the speech is continuing.

31d Put quotation marks around the titles of works that are parts of other works.

Use quotation marks to enclose the titles of works that are published or released within larger works: see the box below. As in the second article title in the box, use single quotation marks for a quotation within a quoted title, and enclose all punctuation in the title within the quotation marks. Use underlining or italics for all other titles, such as books, plays, periodicals, and movies. (See p. 497.)

Titles to be enclosed in quotation marks
Other titles should be underlined or italicized. (See p. 497.)

Songs
"Lucy in the Sky with Diamonds"
"America the Beautiful"

Short poems
"Stopping by Woods on a Snowy Evening"
"Sunday Morning"

Articles in periodicals
"Comedy and Tragedy Transposed"
"Does 'Scaring' Work?"

Essays
"Politics and the English Language"
"Joey: A 'Mechanical Boy'"

Short stories
"The Battler"
"The Gift of the Magi"

Page or document on a Web site
"Readers' Page" (on site *Friends of Prufrock*)

Episodes of television and radio programs
"The Mexican Connection" (on *60 Minutes*)
"Cooking with Clams" (on *Eating In*)

Subdivisions of books
"Voyage to the Houyhnhnms" (Part IV of *Gulliver's Travels*)
"The Mast Head" (Chapter 35 of *Moby-Dick*)

Note Some academic disciplines do not require quotation marks for titles within source citations. See pages 788–800 (APA style) and 814–19 (CSE style).

EXERCISE 31.2   Quoting titles

Insert quotation marks as needed for titles in the following sentences. If quotation marks should be used instead of underlining, insert them. (You can do this exercise online at *ablongman.com/littlebrown*.)

Example:
She published an article titled Marriage in Grace Paley's An Interest in Life.
She published an article titled "Marriage in Grace Paley's 'An Interest in Life.'"

1. In Chapter 8, titled How to Be Interesting, the author explains the art of conversation.
2. The Beatles' song Let It Be reminds Martin of his uncle.
3. The article that appeared in Mental Health was titled Children of Divorce Ask, "Why?"
4. In the encyclopedia the discussion under Modern Art fills less than a column.
5. One prizewinning essay, Cowgirls on Wall Street, first appeared in Entrepreneur magazine.

31e   Quotation marks may be used to enclose words used in a special sense.

On movie sets movable "wild walls" make a one-walled room seem four-walled on film.

Writers often put quotation marks around a word they are using with irony—that is, with a different or even opposite meaning than usual:

With all the "compassion" it could muster, the agency turned away two-thirds of those seeking help.   —Joan Simonson

Readers quickly tire of such irony, though, so use it sparingly. Prefer language that expresses your meaning exactly. (See Chapter 38.)
Note For words you are defining, use underlining or italics. (See p. 498.)

31f   Use quotation marks only where they are required.

Don't use quotation marks in the titles of your papers unless they contain or are themselves direct quotations:

ANSWERS: EXERCISE 31.2

1. In Chapter 8, titled "How to Be Interesting," the author explains the art of conversation.
2. The Beatles' song "Let It Be" reminds Martin of his uncle.
3. The article that appeared in Mental Health [correct] was titled "Children of Divorce Ask, 'Why?'"
4. In the encyclopedia the discussion under "Modern Art" fills less than a column.
5. One prizewinning essay, "Cowgirls on Wall Street," first appeared in Entrepreneur [correct] magazine.

Not	"The Death Wish in One Poem by Robert Frost"
But	"The Death Wish in One Poem by Robert Frost"
Or	The Death Wish in "Stopping by Woods on a Snowy Evening"

Don't use quotation marks to enclose common nicknames or technical terms that are not being defined:

Not	As President, "Jimmy" Carter preferred to use his nickname.
But	As President, Jimmy Carter preferred to use his nickname.

Not	"Mitosis" in a cell is fascinating to watch.
But	Mitosis in a cell is fascinating to watch.

Don't use quotation marks in an attempt to justify or apologize for slang and trite expressions that are inappropriate to your writing. If slang is appropriate, use it without quotation marks.

Not	We should support the President in his "hour of need" rather than "wimp out" on him.
But	We should give the President the support he needs rather than turn away like cowards.

(See pp. 512 and 527 for more on slang and trite expressions.)

31g Place other punctuation marks inside or outside quotation marks according to standard practice.

The position of another punctuation mark inside or outside a closing quotation mark depends on what the other mark is, whether it appears in the quotation, and whether a source citation immediately follows the quotation.

1 Place commas and periods inside quotation marks.

Commas or periods fall *inside* closing quotation marks, even when (as in the third example) single and double quotation marks are combined:

> Swift uses irony in his essay "A Modest Proposal."
>
> Many first-time readers are shocked to see infants described as "delicious."
>
> "'A Modest Proposal,'" writes one critic, "is so outrageous that it cannot be believed."

(See pp. 444–48 for the use of commas, as in the preceding example, to separate a quotation from a signal phrase such as *writes one critic*.)

Exception When a parenthetical source citation immediately follows a quotation, place any period or comma *after* the citation:

One critic calls the essay "outrageous" (Olms 26).

Partly because of "the cool calculation of its delivery" (Olms 27), Swift's satire still chills a modern reader.

See page 654 for more on placing parenthetical citations.

2 **Place colons and semicolons outside quotation marks.**

Some years ago the slogan in elementary education was "learning by playing"; now educators are concerned with basic skills.

We all know what is meant by "inflation": more money buys less.

3 **Place dashes, question marks, and exclamation points inside quotation marks only if they belong to the quotation.**

When a dash, question mark, or exclamation point is part of the quotation, put it *inside* quotation marks. Don't use any other punctuation such as a period or comma:

"But must you—" Marcia hesitated, afraid of the answer.

"Go away!" I yelled.

Did you say, "Who is she?" [When both your sentence and the quotation would end in a question mark or exclamation point, use only the mark in the quotation.]

When a dash, question mark, or exclamation point applies only to the larger sentence, not to the quotation, place it *outside* quotation marks—again, with no other punctuation:

One evocative line in English poetry—"After many a summer dies the swan"—comes from Alfred, Lord Tennyson.

Who said, "Now cracks a noble heart"?

The woman called me "stupid"!

EXERCISE 31.3 Revising: Quotation marks

The underlined words in the following sentences are titles or direct quotations. Remove incorrect underlining, and insert quotation marks. Be sure that other marks of punctuation are correctly placed inside or outside the quotation marks. (You can do this exercise online at *ablongman.com/littlebrown*.)

Example:

The award-winning essay is <u>Science and Values</u>.

The award-winning essay is "Science and Values."

1. In the title essay of her book <u>The Death of the Moth and Other Essays</u>, Virginia Woolf describes the last moments of a <u>frail and diminutive body</u>.

COLLABORATIVE LEARNING

Ask students to complete Exercise 31.3 individually and to compare their responses in small groups. Then have the groups work through Exercise 31.4 as a collaborative project and present their conclusions to the class.

TRANSPARENCY MASTER 31.3

ANSWERS: EXERCISE 31.3

1. In the title essay of her book <u>"The Death of the Moth" and Other Essays</u>, Virginia Woolf describes the last moments of a "frail and diminutive body." [Underlining correct for book title, but essay title within it is quoted.]

2. An insect's death may seem insignificant, but the moth is, in Woolf's words, "life, a pure bead."
3. The moth's struggle against death, "indifferent, impersonal," is heroic.
4. Where else but in such a bit of life could one see a protest so "superb"?
5. At the end Woolf sees the moth lying "most decently and uncomplainingly composed"; in death it finds dignity.

ANSWERS: EXERCISE 31.4

In one class we talked about a passage from "I Have a Dream," the speech delivered by Martin Luther King, Jr., on the steps of the Lincoln Memorial on August 28, 1963:

> When the architects of our republic wrote the magnificent words of the Constitution and the Declaration of Independence, they were signing a promissory note to which every American was to fall heir. This note was a promise that all men would be guaranteed the unalienable rights of life, liberty, and the pursuit of happiness.

"What did Dr. King mean by this statement?" the teacher asked. "Perhaps we should define 'promissory note' first." Then she explained that a person who signs such a note agrees to pay a specific sum of money on a particular date or on demand by the holder of the note. One student suggested, "Maybe Dr. King meant that the writers of the Constitution and Declaration promised that all people in America should be equal." "He and over 200,000 people had gathered in Washington, DC," added another student. "Maybe their purpose was to demand payment, to demand those rights for African Americans." The whole discussion was an eye opener for those of us (including me) who had never considered that those documents make promises that we should expect our country to fulfill.

2. An insect's death may seem insignificant, but the moth is, in Woolf's words, <u>life, a pure bead</u>.
3. The moth's struggle against death, <u>indifferent, impersonal</u>, is heroic.
4. Where else but in such a bit of life could one see a protest so <u>superb</u>?
5. At the end Woolf sees the moth lying <u>most decently and uncomplainingly composed</u>; in death it finds dignity.

EXERCISE 31.4   Revising: Quotation marks

Insert quotation marks as needed in the following paragraph. (You can do this exercise online at *ablongman.com/littlebrown*.)

In one class we talked about a passage from I Have a Dream, the speech delivered by Martin Luther King, Jr., on the steps of the Lincoln Memorial on August 28, 1963:

> When the architects of our republic wrote the magnificent words of the Constitution and the Declaration of Independence, they were signing a promissory note to which every American was to fall heir. This note was a promise that all men would be guaranteed the unalienable rights of life, liberty, and the pursuit of happiness.

What did Dr. King mean by this statement? the teacher asked. Perhaps we should define promissory note first. Then she explained that a person who signs such a note agrees to pay a specific sum of money on a particular date or on demand by the holder of the note. One student suggested, Maybe Dr. King meant that the writers of the Constitution and Declaration promised that all people in America should be equal. He and over 200,000 people had gathered in Washington, DC, added another student. Maybe their purpose was to demand payment, to demand those rights for African Americans. The whole discussion was an eye opener for those of us (including me) who had never considered that those documents make promises that we should expect our country to fulfill.

Note See page 488 for a punctuation exercise involving quotation marks along with other marks of punctuation.

CHAPTER 32

Other Punctuation Marks

This chapter covers the colon (below), the dash (p. 480), parentheses (p. 482), brackets (p. 483), the ellipsis mark (p. 484), and the slash (p. 487).

Note Many grammar and style checkers will flag a lone parenthesis or bracket so that you can match it with another parenthesis or bracket. But most checkers cannot recognize other misuses of the marks covered here and instead simply ignore the marks.

32a Use the colon to introduce and to separate.

The colon is mainly a mark of introduction: it signals that the words following will explain or amplify. The colon also has several conventional uses, such as in expressions of time.

In its main use as an introducer, a colon is *always* preceded by a complete **main clause**—one containing a subject and a predicate and not starting with a subordinating word (see p. 252 for more on main clauses). A colon may or may not be followed by a main clause. This is one way the colon differs from the semicolon (see the box on the next page). The colon is interchangeable with the dash, though the dash is more informal and more abrupt (see p. 480).

Note Don't use a colon more than once in a sentence. The sentence should end with the element introduced by the colon.

1 Use a colon to introduce a concluding explanation, series, appositive, or long or formal quotation.

Depending on your preference, a complete sentence *after* the colon may begin with a capital letter or a small letter. Just be consistent throughout an essay.

> http://www.ablongman.com/littlebrown ▶
>
> Visit the companion Web site for more help and additional exercises on the colon, the dash, parentheses, brackets, the ellipsis mark, and the slash.

mycomplab²·⁰

Please visit MyCompLab at *www.mycomplab.com* for more on the writing process.

HIGHLIGHTS

Chapter 32 covers the marks of punctuation not treated in the preceding chapters (27–31): the colon, the dash, parentheses, brackets, the ellipsis mark, and the slash. In addition to exercises for these marks of punctuation, an exercise at the end of the part (p. 488) asks students to practice using all the punctuation marks covered in Chapters 27–32.

A WRITER'S PERSPECTIVE _____

Q. What is the purpose of the colon?

A. The colon forms a barrier alerting the reader not to go any farther in the sentence.
—DAVE BARRY

COLONS WITH LISTS

In business and professional writing, colons often end phrases or subordinate clauses that precede lists formatted vertically:

The software requires:
  Pentium 60 MHz or higher
  64 MB RAM
  SVGA video
  Microsoft Windows XP

COMPANION WEB SITE

See page IAE-58 for companion Web site content description.

Distinguishing the colon and the semicolon

■ **The *colon* is a mark of introduction that separates elements of *unequal* importance,** such as statements and explanations or introductions and quotations. The first element must be a complete main clause; the second element need not be. (See below.)

The business school caters to working students: it offers special evening courses in business writing, finance, and management.

The school has one goal: to train students to be responsible, competent businesspeople.

■ **The *semicolon* separates elements of *equal* importance,** almost always complete main clauses. (See p. 452.)

Few enrolling students know exactly what they want from the school; most hope generally for a managerial career.

Explanation

Soul food is a varied cuisine: it includes spicy gumbos, black-eyed peas, and collard greens.

Soul food has a deceptively simple definition: African American ethnic cooking.

Sometimes a concluding explanation is preceded by *the following* or *as follows* and a colon:

A more precise definition might be the following: ingredients, cooking methods, and dishes originating in Africa, brought to the New World by black slaves, and modified or supplemented in the Caribbean and the American South.

Series (p. 441)

At least three soul food dishes are familiar to most Americans: fried chicken, barbecued spareribs, and sweet potato pie.

Appositive (p. 257)

Soul food has one disadvantage: fat.

Certain expressions commonly introduce appositives, such as *namely* and *that is.* These expressions should *follow* the colon: *Soul food has one disadvantage: namely, fat.*

Long or formal quotation

The comma generally separates a signal phrase from a quotation (see p. 444). But when you introduce a long or formal quotation with a complete sentence, use a colon instead:

One soul food chef has a solution: "Soul food doesn't have to be greasy to taste good. Instead of using ham hocks to flavor beans, I use smoked turkey wings. The soulful, smoky taste remains, but without all the fat of pork."

2 **Use a colon to separate titles and subtitles and the subdivisions of time.**

Titles and subtitles

Charles Dickens: *An Introduction to His Novels*
Eros and Civilization: *An Inquiry into Freud*

Time

1:30 AM
12:26 PM

3 **Use the colon only where required.**

Use the colon only at the *end* of a main clause. Do not use it directly after a verb or preposition.

Not   Two critically acclaimed movies directed by Steven Spielberg are: *Schindler's List* and *Saving Private Ryan*.

But   Two critically acclaimed movies directed by Steven Spielberg are *Schindler's List* and *Saving Private Ryan*.

Not   Shakespeare had the qualities of a Renaissance thinker, such as: humanism and an interest in Greek and Roman literature.

But   Shakespeare had the qualities of a Renaissance thinker, such as humanism and an interest in Greek and Roman literature.

EXERCISE 32.1   Revising: Colons

Insert colons as needed in the following sentences, or delete colons that are misused. (You can do this exercise online at *ablongman.com/littlebrown*.)

   Example:
   Mix the ingredients as follows sift the flour and salt together, add the milk, and slowly beat in the egg yolk.
   Mix the ingredients as follows: sift the flour and salt together, add the milk, and slowly beat in the egg yolk.

1. In remote areas of many developing countries, simple signs mark human habitation a dirt path, a few huts, smoke from a campfire.
2. In the built-up sections of industrialized countries, nature is all but obliterated by signs of human life, such as: houses, factories, skyscrapers, and highways.
3. The spectacle makes many question the words of Ecclesiastes 1.4 "One generation passeth away, and another cometh; but the earth abideth forever."
4. Yet many scientists see the future differently they hold that human beings have all the technology necessary to clean up the earth and restore the cycles of nature.
5. All that is needed is: a change in the attitudes of those who use technology.

ANSWERS: EXERCISE 32.1

1. In remote areas of many developing countries, simple signs mark human habitation: a dirt path, a few huts, smoke from a campfire.
2. In the built-up sections of industrialized countries, nature is all but obliterated by signs of human life, such as houses, factories, skyscrapers, and highways.
3. The spectacle makes many question the words of Ecclesiastes 1.4: "One generation passeth away, and another generation cometh; but the earth abideth forever."
4. Yet many scientists see the future differently: they hold that human beings have all the technology necessary to clean up the earth and restore the cycles of nature.
5. All that is needed is a change in the attitudes of those who use technology.

ADDING THE DASH

For many students, using dashes is a way of avoiding a decision about which punctuation mark to use. Dashes can be used this way in informal writing, but in more formal situations, students should use dashes only in the accepted ways discussed in the text.

32b Use a dash to indicate shifts in tone or thought and to set off some sentence elements.

The dash is mainly a mark of interruption: it signals an insertion or break.

Note In your papers, form a dash with two hyphens (--), or use the character called an em dash on your word processor. Do not add extra space around or between the hyphens or around the em dash.

1 Use a dash or dashes to indicate shifts and hesitations.

Shift in tone

The novel—if one can call it that—appeared in 2004.

Unfinished thought

If the book had a plot—but a plot would be conventional.

Hesitation in dialog

"I was worried you might think I had stayed away because I was influenced by—" He stopped and lowered his eyes.
Astonished, Howe said, "Influenced by what?"
"Well, by—" Blackburn hesitated and for an answer pointed to the table.
                                                                    —Lionel Trilling

2 Use a dash or dashes to emphasize nonessential elements.

Dashes may be used in place of commas or parentheses to set off and emphasize nonessential elements. (See the box on the facing page.) Dashes are especially useful when these elements are internally punctuated. Be sure to use a pair of dashes when the element interrupts a main clause.

Appositive (p. 257)

The qualities Monet painted—bright sunlight, rich shadows, deep colors—abounded near the rivers and gardens he used as subjects.

Modifier

Though they are close together—separated by only a few blocks—the two neighborhoods could be in different countries.

Parenthetical expression (p. 482)

At any given time there exists an inventory of undiscovered embezzlement in—or more precisely not in—the country's businesses and banks.
                                                                    —John Kenneth Galbraith

3 Use a dash to set off introductory series and concluding series and explanations.

Introductory series

Shortness of breath, skin discoloration or the sudden appearance of moles, persistent indigestion, the presence of small lumps—all these may signify cancer.

Distinguishing dashes, commas, and parentheses

Dashes, commas, and parentheses may all set off nonessential elements.

- *Dashes* **give the information the greatest emphasis** (facing page):

  Many students—including some employed by the college—disapprove of the new work rules.

- *Commas* **are less emphatic** (p. 435):

  Many students, including some employed by the college, disapprove of the new work rules.

- *Parentheses* **are the least emphatic,** signaling that the information is just worth a mention (next page):

  Many students (including some employed by the college) disapprove of the new work rules.

A dash sets off concluding series and explanations more informally and more abruptly than a colon does (see p. 478):

Concluding series

The patient undergoes a battery of tests—CAT scan, bronchoscopy, perhaps even biopsy.

Concluding explanation

Many patients are disturbed by the CAT scan—by the need to keep still for long periods in an exceedingly small space.

4 Use the dash only where needed.

Don't use the dash when commas, semicolons, and periods are more appropriate. And don't use too many dashes. They can create a jumpy or breathy quality in writing.

Not In all his life—eighty-seven years—my great-grandfather never allowed his picture to be taken—not even once. He claimed the "black box"—the camera—would steal his soul.

But In all his eighty-seven years my great-grandfather did not allow his picture to be taken even once. He claimed the "black box"—the camera—would steal his soul.

EXERCISE 32.2 Revising: Dashes

Insert dashes as needed in the following sentences. (You can do this exercise online at *ablongman.com/littlebrown*.)

> Example:
> What would we do if someone like Adolf Hitler that monster appeared among us?
> What would we do if someone like Adolf Hitler—that monster—appeared among us?

1. The movie-theater business is undergoing dramatic changes—changes that may affect what movies are made and shown.
2. The closing of independent theaters, the control of theaters by fewer and fewer owners, and the increasing ownership of theaters by movie studios and distributors—these changes may reduce the availability of noncommercial films.
3. Yet at the same time the number of movie screens is increasing—primarily in multiscreen complexes—so that smaller films may find more outlets.
4. The number of active movie screens—that is, screens showing films or booked to do so—is higher now than at any time since World War II.
5. The biggest theater complexes seem to be something else as well—art galleries, amusement arcades, restaurants, spectacles.

ALTERNATIVE EXAMPLE

When you are enclosing a complete sentence within another complete sentence, you need not start the sentence in parentheses with a capital letter nor end it with a punctuation mark. For example:

I spent the weekend buried in books (this is my usual practice) and emerged on Monday in time to go to the library.

RESOURCES AND IDEAS

Arthur L. Palacas in "Parenthetics and Personal Voice" (*Written Communication* 6 [1989]: 506–28) argues that the use of parenthetical expressions (including those punctuated by parentheses, commas, and dashes) is an important factor in developing a personal style.

1. The movie-theater business is undergoing dramatic changes changes that may affect what movies are made and shown.
2. The closing of independent theaters, the control of theaters by fewer and fewer owners, and the increasing ownership of theaters by movie studios and distributors these changes may reduce the availability of noncommercial films.
3. Yet at the same time the number of movie screens is increasing primarily in multiscreen complexes so that smaller films may find more outlets.
4. The number of active movie screens that is, screens showing films or booked to do so is higher now than at any time since World War II.
5. The biggest theater complexes seem to be something else as well art galleries, amusement arcades, restaurants, spectacles.

32c Use parentheses to enclose parenthetical expressions and labels for lists within sentences.

Parentheses *always* come in pairs: one before and one after the punctuated material.

1 Use parentheses to enclose parenthetical expressions.

Parenthetical expressions include explanations, digressions, and examples that may be helpful or interesting but are not essential to meaning. They are emphasized least when set off with a pair of parentheses instead of commas or dashes. (See the box on p. 481.)

> The population of Philadelphia (now about 1.5 million) has declined since 1950.
> *Ariel* (published in 1965) contains Sylvia Plath's last poems.

Note Don't put a comma before a parenthetical expression enclosed in parentheses:

Not Philadelphia's population compares with Houston's, (just over 1.6 million).

But Philadelphia's population compares with Houston's (just over 1.6 million).

A comma, semicolon, or period falling after a parenthetical expression should be placed *outside* the closing parenthesis:

> Philadelphia has a larger African American population (nearly 40 percent), while Houston has a larger Latino population (nearly 28 percent).

When it falls between other complete sentences, a complete sentence enclosed in parentheses has a capital letter and end punctuation:

> In general, coaches will tell you that scouts are just guys who can't coach. (But then, so are brain surgeons.)
> —Roy Blount

2 **Use parentheses to enclose labels for lists within sentences.**

Outside the Middle East, the countries with the largest oil reserves are (1) Venezuela (63 billion barrels), (2) Russia (57 billion barrels), and (3) Mexico (51 billion barrels).

When you set a list off from your text, do not enclose such labels in parentheses.

EXERCISE 32.3   Revising: Parentheses

Insert parentheses as needed in the following sentences. (You can do this exercise online at *ablongman.com/littlebrown*.)

Example:
Students can find good-quality, inexpensive furniture for example, desks, tables, chairs, sofas, even beds in junk stores.
Students can find good-quality, inexpensive furniture (for example, desks, tables, chairs, sofas, even beds) in junk stores.

1. Many of those involved in the movie business agree that multiscreen complexes are good for two reasons: 1 they cut the costs of exhibitors, and 2 they offer more choices to audiences.
2. Those who produce and distribute films and not just the big studios argue that the multiscreen theaters give exhibitors too much power.
3. The major studios are buying movie theaters to gain control over important parts of the distribution process what gets shown and for how much money.
4. For twelve years 1938–50 the federal government forced the studios to sell all their movie theaters.
5. But because they now have more competition television and DVD players, for instance, the studios are permitted to own theaters.

32d **Use brackets within quotations to indicate your own comments or changes.**

Brackets have specialized uses in mathematical equations, but their main use for all kinds of writing is to indicate that you have altered a quotation. If you need to explain, clarify, or correct the words of the writer you quote, place your additions in a pair of brackets:

"That Texaco station [just outside Chicago] is one of the busiest in the nation," said a company spokesperson.

Use brackets if you need to alter the capitalization of a quotation so that it will fit into your sentence. (See also p. 491.)

"[O]ne of the busiest in the nation" is how a company spokesperson described the station.

You may also use a bracketed word or words to substitute for parts of a quotation that would otherwise be unclear. In the following sentence, the bracketed word substitutes for *they* in the original:

ANSWERS: EXERCISE 32.3

1. Many of those involved in the movie business agree that multiscreen complexes are good for two reasons: (1) they cut the costs of exhibitors, and (2) they offer more choices to audiences.
2. Those who produce and distribute films (and not just the big studios) argue that the multiscreen theaters give exhibitors too much power.
3. The major studios are buying movie theaters to gain control over important parts of the distribution process (what gets shown and for how much money).
4. For twelve years (1938–50) the federal government forced the studios to sell all their movie theaters.
5. But because they now have more competition (television and DVD players, for instance), the studios are permitted to own theaters.

ADDITIONAL USES OF BRACKETS

Brackets may also be used to supply missing letters to complete names that are given partly in initials in a quotation: E[lwyn] B[rooks] White.

"Despite considerable achievements in other areas, [humans] still cannot control the weather and probably will never be able to do so."

See pages 624–25 for additional examples of using brackets with quotations.

The word *sic* (Latin for "in this manner") in brackets indicates that an error in the quotation appeared in the original and was not made by you. When following MLA style, do not underline or italicize *sic* in brackets. Most other styles—including Chicago, APA, and CSE—do italicize *sic*.

According to the newspaper report, "The car slammed thru [sic] the railing and into oncoming traffic."

Don't use *sic* to make fun of a writer or to note errors in a passage that is clearly nonstandard or illiterate.

Note Always acknowledge the sources of quotations in order to avoid plagiarism. (See pp. 633–34 and 637–38.)

RESOURCES AND IDEAS

See Keith Grant-Davie's "Functional Redundancy and Ellipsis as Strategies in Reading and Writing" (*Journal of Advanced Composition* 15:3 [1995]: 455–69). Grant-Davie looks at the differences between functional and needless redundancy in relation to the use of ellipses, particularly in the field of technical writing.

32e   Use the ellipsis mark to indicate omissions from quotations and pauses in speech.

The **ellipsis mark** consists of three spaced periods (. . .). It usually indicates an omission from a quotation, although it may also show an interruption in dialog.

Note Additional issues with quotations are discussed elsewhere in this book:

- **Integrating source material into your text,** pages 623–28.
- **Acknowledging the sources of quotations to avoid plagiarism,** pages 633–34 and 637–38. See also example 3 on the facing page.

1   The ellipsis mark substitutes for omissions from quotations.

When you omit a part of a quotation, show the omission with an ellipsis mark. All the following examples quote from the passage below about environmentalism.

Original quotation

"At the heart of the environmentalist world view is the conviction that human physical and spiritual health depends on sustaining the planet in a relatively unaltered state. Earth is our home in the full, genetic sense, where humanity and its ancestors existed for all the millions of years of their evolution. Natural ecosystems—forests, coral reefs, marine blue waters—maintain the world exactly as we would wish it to be maintained. When we debase the global environment and extinguish the variety of life, we are dismantling a support system that is too complex to understand, let alone replace, in the foreseeable future."   —Edward O. Wilson, "Is Humanity Suicidal?"

1. Omission of the middle of a sentence

"Natural ecosystems . . . maintain the world exactly as we would wish it to be maintained."

2. Omission of the end of a sentence, without source citation

"Earth is our home. . . ." [The sentence period, closed up to the last word, precedes the ellipsis mark.]

3. Omission of the end of a sentence, with source citation

"Earth is our home . . ." (Wilson 27). [The sentence period follows the source citation.]

4. Omission of parts of two or more sentences

Wilson writes, "At the heart of the environmentalist world view is the conviction that human physical and spiritual health depends on sustaining the planet . . . where humanity and its ancestors existed for all the millions of years of their evolution."

5. Omission of one or more sentences

As Wilson puts it, "At the heart of the environmentalist world view is the conviction that human physical and spiritual health depends on sustaining the planet in a relatively unaltered state. . . . When we debase the global environment and extinguish the variety of life, we are dismantling a support system that is too complex to understand, let alone replace, in the foreseeable future."

6. Omission from the middle of a sentence through the end of another sentence

"Earth is our home. . . . When we debase the global environment and extinguish the variety of life, we are dismantling a support system that is too complex to understand, let alone replace, in the foreseeable future."

7. Omission of the beginning of a sentence, leaving a complete sentence

a. Bracketed capital letter

"[H]uman physical and spiritual health," Wilson writes, "depends on sustaining the planet in a relatively unaltered state." [No ellipsis mark is needed because the brackets around the *H* indicate that the letter was not capitalized originally and thus that the beginning of the sentence has been omitted.]

b. Small letter

According to Wilson, "human physical and spiritual health depends on sustaining the planet in a relatively unaltered state." [No ellipsis mark is needed because the small *h* indicates that the beginning of the sentence has been omitted.]

c. Capital letter from the original

Hami comments, ". . . Wilson argues eloquently for the environmentalist world view." [An ellipsis mark is needed because the quoted part of the sentence begins with a capital letter and it is not clear that the beginning of the original sentence has been omitted.]

8. Use of a word or phrase
Wilson describes the earth as "our home." [No ellipsis mark needed.]

Note the following features of the examples:

- **Use an ellipsis mark when it is not otherwise clear that you have left out material from the source,** as when you omit one or more sentences (examples 5 and 6) or when the words you quote form a complete sentence that is different in the original (examples 1–4 and 7c).
- **You don't need an ellipsis mark when it is obvious that you have omitted something,** such as when capitalization indicates omission (examples 7a and 7b) or when a phrase clearly comes from a larger sentence (example 8).
- **Place as ellipsis mark after a sentence period** *except* **when a parenthetical source citation follows the quotation,** as in example 3. Then the sentence period falls after the citation.

If you omit one or more lines of poetry or paragraphs of prose from a quotation, use a separate line of ellipsis marks across the full width of the quotation to show the omission:

In "Song: Love Armed" from 1676, Aphra Behn contrasts two lovers' experiences of a romance:

> Love in fantastic triumph sate,
> Whilst bleeding hearts around him flowed,
> . . . .
> But my poor heart alone is harmed,
> Whilst thine the victor is, and free. (lines 1-2, 15-16)

(See pp. 688–89 for the format of displayed quotations like this one. And see p. 653 on the source-citation form illustrated here.)

2 The ellipsis mark indicates pauses or unfinished statements.

When writing dialog or when writing informally (not in academic writing), you can show hesitation or interruption with an ellipsis mark instead of a dash (p. 480).

"I wish **. . .**" His voice trailed off.

EXERCISE 32.4 Using ellipsis marks

Use ellipsis marks and any other needed punctuation to follow the numbered instructions for quoting from the following paragraph. (You can do this exercise online at *ablongman.com/littlebrown.*)

Women in the sixteenth and seventeenth centuries were educated in the home and, in some cases, in boarding schools. Men were educated at home, in grammar schools, and at the universities. The

ANSWERS: EXERCISE 32.4

1. "To be able to read the Bible in the vernacular was a liberating experience. . . ."
2. "To be able to read the Bible in the vernacular . . . freed the reader from hearing only the set passages read in the church and interpreted by the church."

universities were closed to female students. For women, "learning the Bible," as Elizabeth Joceline puts it, was an impetus to learning to read. To be able to read the Bible in the vernacular was a liberating experience that freed the reader from hearing only the set passages read in the church and interpreted by the church. A Protestant woman was expected to read the scriptures daily, to meditate on them, and to memorize portions of them. In addition, a woman was expected to instruct her entire household in "learning the Bible" by holding instructional and devotional times each day for all household members, including the servants.

— Charlotte F. Otten, *English Women's Voices, 1540–1700*

1. Quote the fifth sentence, but omit everything from *that freed the reader* to the end.
2. Quote the fifth sentence, but omit the words *was a liberating experience that.*
3. Quote the first and sixth sentences.

32f Use the slash between options, between lines of poetry, and in electronic addresses.

Option

I don't know why some teachers oppose pass**/**fail courses.

Between options, the slash is not surrounded by extra space.
Note The options *and/or* and *he/she* should be avoided. (See the Glossary of Usage, pp. 865 and 872.)

Poetry

Many readers have sensed a reluctant turn away from death in Frost's lines "The woods are lovely, dark and deep, **/** But I have promises to keep" (13–14).

When you run lines of poetry into your text, separate them with a slash surrounded by space. (See pp. 688–89 for more on quoting poetry.)

Electronic address

http://www.stanford.edu/depts/spc/spc.html

EXERCISE 32.5 Revising: Colons, dashes, parentheses, brackets, ellipsis marks, slashes

Insert colons, dashes, parentheses, brackets, ellipsis marks, or slashes as needed in the following paragraph. When different marks would be appropriate in the same place, be able to defend the choice you make. (You can do this exercise online at *ablongman.com/littlebrown.*)

"Let all the learned say what they can, 'Tis ready money makes the man." These two lines of poetry by the Englishman William Somerville 1645–1742 may apply to a current American economic

---

3. "Women in the sixteenth and seventeenth centuries were educated in the home and, in some cases, in boarding schools. . . . A Protestant woman was expected to read the scriptures daily, to meditate on them, and to memorize portions of them."

SLASHING

The rules governing when to put spaces around the slash confuse many students; it's worth a moment's time to review them. In addition, warn students that many word-processing programs that justify (align) the right margins of text may add or remove spaces around slashes.

COLLABORATIVE LEARNING

Ask students to work individually or in pairs to complete Exercise 32.5, then have them work in small groups to compare and discuss their responses. In asking the groups to report on their findings, encourage students to debate the effect of each punctuation mark.

ANSWERS: EXERCISE 32.5

"Let all the learned say what they can, / 'Tis ready money makes the man." These two lines of poetry by the Englishman William Somerville (1645–1742) may apply to a current American economic problem. Non-American investors with "ready money" pour some of it—as much as $1.3 trillion in recent years—into the United States. The investments of foreigners are varied: stocks and bonds, savings deposits, service companies, factories, art works, even the campaigns of political candidates. Proponents of foreign investment argue that it revives industry, strengthens the economy, creates jobs (more than 3 million, they say), and encourages free trade among nations. Opponents discuss the risks of heavy foreign investment: it makes the American economy vulnerable to outsiders, sucks profits from the country, and gives foreigners an influence in governmental decision making. On both sides, it seems, "the learned say . . . / 'Tis ready money makes the man [or country]." The question is, whose money?

REVISING PUNCTUATION

Have students work in small groups to complete the following punctuation exercise. Encourage group members to debate the effect of each punctuation mark, and ask them to present some portion of the passage for class discussion.

ANSWERS: EXERCISE ON CHAPTERS 27–32

Brewed coffee is the most widely consumed beverage in the world. The trade in coffee beans alone amounts to well over $6,000,000,000 a year, and the total volume of beans traded exceeds 4,250,000 tons a year. It's believed that the beverage was introduced into Arabia in the fifteenth century AD [correct; or A.D.], probably by Ethiopians. By the middle or late sixteenth century, the Arabs had introduced the beverage to the Europeans, who at first resisted it because of its strong flavor and effect as a mild stimulant. The French, Italians, and other Europeans incorporated coffee into their diets by the seventeenth century; the English, however, preferred tea, which they were then importing from India. Since America was colonized primarily by the English, Americans also preferred tea. Only after the Boston Tea Party (1773) did Americans begin drinking coffee in large quantities. Now, though, the US [correct; or U.S.] is one of the top coffee-consuming countries, consumption having been spurred on by familiar advertising claims: "Good till the last drop"; "Rich, hearty aroma"; "Always rich, never bitter."

Produced from the fruit of an evergreen tree, coffee is grown primarily in Latin America, southern Asia, and Africa. Coffee trees require a hot climate, high humidity, rich soil with good drainage, and partial shade; consequently, they thrive on the east or west slopes of tropical volcanic mountains, where the soil is laced with potash and drains easily. The coffee beans—actually seeds—grow inside bright red berries. The berries are picked by hand, and the beans are extracted by machine, leaving a pulpy fruit residue that can be used for fertilizer. The beans are usually roasted in ovens, a chemical process that releases the beans' essential oil (caffeol), which gives coffee its distinctive aroma. Over a hundred different varieties of beans are produced in the world, each with a different flavor attributable to three factors: the species of plant (*Coffea arabica* and *Coffea robusta* are the most common) and the soil and climate where the variety was grown.

problem. Non-American investors with "ready money" pour some of it as much as $1.3 trillion in recent years into the United States. The investments of foreigners are varied stocks and bonds, savings deposits, service companies, factories, art works, even the campaigns of political candidates. Proponents of foreign investment argue that it revives industry, strengthens the economy, creates jobs more than 3 million, they say, and encourages free trade among nations. Opponents discuss the risks of heavy foreign investment it makes the American economy vulnerable to outsiders, sucks profits from the country, and gives foreigners an influence in governmental decision making. On both sides, it seems, "the learned say 'Tis ready money makes the man or country." The question is, whose money?

EXERCISE ON CHAPTERS 27–32   Revising: Punctuation

The following paragraphs are unpunctuated except for end-of-sentence periods. Insert periods, commas, semicolons, apostrophes, quotation marks, colons, dashes, or parentheses where they are required. When different marks would be appropriate in the same place, be able to defend the choice you make. (You can do this exercise online at *ablongman.com/littlebrown*.)

Brewed coffee is the most widely consumed beverage in the world. The trade in coffee beans alone amounts to well over $6000000000 a year and the total volume of beans traded exceeds 4250000 tons a year. Its believed that the beverage was introduced into Arabia in the fifteenth century AD probably by Ethiopians. By the middle or late sixteenth century the Arabs had introduced the beverage to the Europeans who at first resisted it because of its strong flavor and effect as a mild stimulant. The French Italians and other Europeans incorporated coffee into their diets by the seventeenth century the English however preferred tea which they were then importing from India. Since America was colonized primarily by the English Americans also preferred tea. Only after the Boston Tea Party 1773 did Americans begin drinking coffee in large quantities. Now though the US is one of the top coffee-consuming countries consumption having been spurred on by familiar advertising claims Good till the last drop Rich hearty aroma Always rich never bitter.

Produced from the fruit of an evergreen tree coffee is grown primarily in Latin America southern Asia and Africa. Coffee trees require a hot climate high humidity rich soil with good drainage and partial shade consequently they thrive on the east or west slopes of tropical volcanic mountains where the soil is laced with potash and drains easily. The coffee beans actually seeds grow inside bright red berries. The berries are picked by hand and the beans are extracted by machine leaving a pulpy fruit residue that can be used for fertilizer. The beans are usually roasted in ovens a chemical process that releases the beans essential oil caffeol which gives coffee its distinctive aroma. Over a hundred different varieties of beans are produced in the world each with a different flavor attributable to three factors the species of plant *Coffea arabica* and *Coffea robusta* are the most common and the soil and climate where the variety was grown.

PART 7

Mechanics

mycomplab 2.0

Please visit MyCompLab at *www.mycomplab.com* for more on the writing process.

HIGHLIGHTS

Capitalization at the beginning of sentences will probably not trouble most native speakers of English; however, capitalization within sentences, and in acronyms, can be a challenge for all writers. If your campus has a writing center, check to see if it has special instructional modules that students who have problems with capitalization can use for review.

RESOURCES AND IDEAS

Relatively little has been written about the teaching of capitalization, and most teachers probably assume that rules and drills are the only available instructional strategies. In *The Writing Room: A Resource Book for Teachers of English* (New York: Oxford UP, 1981, 172–74), however, Harvey S. Wiener looks at the sources of capitalization problems for many basic writers—particularly problems of misunderstanding the rules governing sentence boundaries, of confusion over the capitalization of *I* and other personal pronouns, and of difficulty with the sometimes inexact categories of words that are to be treated as proper nouns. Wiener suggests looking for patterns of error in a student's writing, creating groups of words illustrating a particular rule, and asking a student to prepare sentences that demonstrate his or her grasp of a particular convention. These strategies can be used for more skilled writers as well.

COMPANION WEB SITE

See page IAE-58 for companion Web site content description.

CHAPTER 33

Capitals

Generally, capitalize a word only when a dictionary or conventional use says you must. Consult one of the style guides listed on pages 784 and 812 for special uses of capitals in the social, natural, and applied sciences.

Note A grammar and style checker will flag overused capital letters and missing capitals at the beginnings of sentences. It will also spot missing capitals at the beginnings of proper nouns and adjectives—*if* the nouns and adjectives are in the checker's dictionary. For example, a checker caught *christianity* and *europe* but not *china* (for the country) or *Stephen king*.

CULTURE LANGUAGE Conventions of capitalization vary from language to language. English, for instance, is the only language to capitalize the first-person singular pronoun (*I*), and its practice of capitalizing proper nouns but not most common nouns also distinguishes it from some other languages.

33a Capitalize the first word of every sentence.

Every writer should own a good dictionary.
Will inflation be curbed?
Watch out!

When quoting other writers, you must either reproduce the capital letters beginning their sentences or indicate with brackets that you have altered the source. Whenever possible, integrate the quotation into your own sentence so that its capital letters coincide with your own:

"Psychotherapists often overlook the benefits of self-deception," the author argues.

The author argues that "the benefits of self-deception" are not always recognized by psychotherapists.

http://www.ablongman.com/littlebrown ▶

Visit the companion Web site for more help and an additional exercise on capital letters.

If you need to alter the capitalization in the source, indicate the change with brackets (see p. 483):

> "[T]he benefits of self-deception" are not always recognized by psychotherapists, the author argues.
>
> The author argues that "[p]sychotherapists often overlook the benefits of self-deception."

Note Capitalization of questions in a series is optional. Both examples below are correct:

> Is the population a hundred? Two hundred? More?
> Is the population a hundred? two hundred? more?

Also optional is capitalization of the first word in a complete sentence after a colon (see p. 477).

33b Capitalize most words in titles and subtitles of works.

Within your text, capitalize all the words in a title *except* the following: articles (*a, an, the*), *to* in infinitives, and connecting words (prepositions and coordinating and subordinating conjunctions) of fewer than five letters. Capitalize even these short words when they are the first or last word in a title or when they fall after a colon or semicolon.

The Sound and the Fury	*Management: A New Theory*
"Courtship Through the Ages"	"Once More to the Lake"
A Diamond Is Forever	*An End to Live For*
"Knowing Whom to Ask"	"Power: How to Get It"
Learning from Las Vegas	*File Under Architecture*
"The Truth About AIDS"	*Only when I Laugh*

Always capitalize the prefix or first word in a hyphenated word within a title. Capitalize the second word only if it is a noun or an adjective or is as important as the first word.

"Applying Stage Make-up"	*Through the Looking-Glass*
The Pre-Raphaelites	

Note The style guides of the academic disciplines have their own rules for capitals in titles. For instance, MLA style for English and some other humanities capitalizes all subordinating conjunctions but no prepositions. In addition, APA style for the social sciences and CSE style for the sciences capitalize only the first word and proper names in book and article titles within source citations. See pages 788–800 (APA) and 814–19 (CSE).

CULTURE LANGUAGE

PROPER NOUNS IN OTHER LANGUAGES

Not all languages capitalize proper adjectives and proper nouns used as adjectives. Remind students that in English such words are always capitalized: *Swahili culture*, not *swahili culture*.

33c **Always capitalize the pronoun *I* and the interjection *O*. Capitalize *oh* only when it begins a sentence.**

I love to stay up at night, but, oh, I hate to get up in the morning.
He who thinks himself wise, O heavens, is a great fool.

—Voltaire

33d **Capitalize proper nouns, proper adjectives, and words used as essential parts of proper nouns.**

Proper nouns name specific persons, places, and things: *Shakespeare, California, World War I*. **Proper adjectives** are formed from some proper nouns: *Shakespearean, Californian*.

1 Capitalize proper nouns and proper adjectives.

Capitalize all proper nouns and proper adjectives but not the articles (*a, an, the*) that precede them.

Proper nouns and adjectives to be capitalized

Specific persons and things

Stephen King	the Leaning Tower of Pisa
Napoleon Bonaparte	Boulder Dam
Doris Lessing	the Empire State Building

Specific places and geographical regions

New York City	the Mediterranean Sea
China	Lake Victoria
Europe	the Northeast, the South
North America	the Rocky Mountains

But: northeast of the city, going south

Days of the week, months, holidays

Monday	Yom Kippur
May	Christmas
Thanksgiving	Columbus Day

Historical events, documents, periods, movements

World War II	the Middle Ages
the Vietnam War	the Age of Reason
the Boston Tea Party	the Renaissance
the Treaty of Ghent	the Great Depression
the Constitution	the Romantic Movement
the Bill of Rights	the Cultural Revolution

Government offices or departments and institutions

House of Representatives	Polk Municipal Court
Department of Defense	Warren County Hospital
Appropriations Committee	Northeast High School

Political, social, athletic, and other organizations and associations and their members

Democratic Party, Democrats	Rotary Club, Rotarians
Sierra Club	League of Women Voters
Girl Scouts of America, Scout	Boston Celtics
B'nai B'rith	Chicago Symphony Orchestra

Races, nationalities, and their languages

Native American	Germans
African American	Swahili
Caucasian	Italian

But: blacks, whites

Religions and their followers

Christianity, Christians	Judaism, Orthodox Jews
Protestantism, Protestants	Hinduism, Hindus
Catholicism, Catholics	Islam, Muslims

Religious terms for the sacred

God	Buddha
Allah	the Bible [*but* biblical]
Christ	the Koran, the Qur'an

Note Follow your own preference in capitalizing *he, his,* or *him* when referring to God or Allah.

2 Capitalize common nouns used as essential parts of proper nouns.

Common nouns name general classes of persons, places, or things, and they generally are not capitalized. However, capitalize the common nouns *street, avenue, park, river, ocean, lake, company, college, county,* and *memorial* when they are part of proper nouns naming specific places or institutions:

Main Street	Lake Superior
Central Park	Ford Motor Company
Mississippi River	Madison College
Pacific Ocean	George Washington Memorial

3 Capitalize trade names.

Trade names identify individual brands of certain products. When a trade name loses its association with a brand and comes to refer to a product in general, it is not capitalized. Refer to a dictionary for current usage when you are in doubt about a name.

Scotch tape	Xerox
Chevrolet	Bunsen burner

But: nylon, thermos

33e Capitalize most titles of persons only when they precede proper names.

Professor Otto Osborne	Otto Osborne, a professor of English
Doctor Jane Covington	Jane Covington, a medical doctor
Governor Ella Moore	Ella Moore, the governor

Not   The Senator supported the bill.
But   The senator supported the bill.
Or   Senator Carmine supported the bill.

Exception Many writers capitalize a title denoting very high rank even when it follows a proper name or is used alone:

Ronald Reagan, past President of the United States
the Chief Justice of the United States Supreme Court

33f Avoid common misuses of capital letters.

1 Use small letters for common nouns replacing proper nouns.

Not   I am determined to take an Economics course before I graduate from College.
But   I am determined to take an economics course before I graduate from college.
Or   I am determined to take Economics 101 before I graduate from Madison College.

2 Capitalize compass directions only when they refer to specific geographical areas.

The storm blew in from the northeast and then veered south along the coast. [Here *northeast* and *south* refer to general directions.]

Students from the South have trouble adjusting to the Northeast's bitter winters. [Here *South* and *Northeast* refer to specific regions.]

3 Use small letters for the names of seasons or the names of academic years or terms.

spring	autumn	senior year
summer	fall quarter	winter term

NOTE

You may wish to remind students not to capitalize *doctor, madame, sir,* or similar forms of address unless they occur directly before a name.

WHEN STYLES CONFLICT

Students may notice that newspapers and some magazines sometimes capitalize more words than the handbook advises them to capitalize. The trend is toward less rather than more capitalization, but popular periodicals often have their own style guides and use capitals to reflect local interests, punch up their copy, or call attention to important distinctions (like Federal and State governments).

4 Capitalize the names of relationships only when they form part of or substitute for proper names.

my mother   the father of my friend
my uncle Brad   Brad's brother

I remember how Dad scolded us.
Aunt Annie and Uncle Jake died within two months of each other.

5 Use capitals according to convention in online communication.

Online messages written in all-capital letters or with no capital letters are difficult to read. Further, messages in all-capital letters may be considered rude. Use capital letters according to rules 33a–33f in all your online communication.

EXERCISE 33.1 Revising: Capitals

Capitalize words as necessary in the following sentences, or substitute small letters for unnecessary capitals. Consult a dictionary if you are in doubt. If the capitalization in a sentence is already correct, mark the number preceding the sentence. (You can do this exercise online at *ablongman.com/littlebrown.*)

Example:
The first book on the reading list is mark twain's *a connecticut yankee in king arthur's court.*

The first book on the reading list is Mark Twain's *A Connecticut Yankee in King Arthur's Court.*

1. San Antonio, texas, is a thriving city in the southwest.
2. The city has always offered much to tourists interested in the roots of spanish settlement of the new world.
3. The alamo is one of five Catholic Missions built by Priests to convert native americans and to maintain spain's claims in the area.
4. But the alamo is more famous for being the site of an 1836 battle that helped to create the republic of Texas.
5. Many of the nearby Streets, such as Crockett street, are named for men who gave their lives in that Battle.
6. The Hemisfair plaza and the San Antonio river link new tourist and convention facilities developed during mayor Cisneros's terms.
7. Restaurants, Hotels, and shops line the River. the haunting melodies of "Una paloma blanca" and "malagueña" lure passing tourists into Casa rio and other excellent mexican restaurants.
8. The university of Texas at San Antonio has expanded, and a Medical Center has been developed in the Northwest part of the city.
9. Sea World, on the west side of San Antonio, entertains grandparents, fathers and mothers, and children with the antics of dolphins and seals.

ANSWERS: EXERCISE 33.1

1. San Antonio, Texas, is a thriving city in the Southwest.
2. The city has always offered much to tourists interested in the roots of Spanish settlement of the New World.
3. The Alamo is one of five Catholic missions built by priests to convert Native Americans and to maintain Spain's claims in the area.
4. But the Alamo is more famous for being the site of an 1836 battle that helped to create the Republic of Texas.
5. Many of the nearby streets, such as Crockett Street, are named for men who gave their lives in that battle.
6. The Hemisfair Plaza and the San Antonio River link new tourist and convention facilities developed during Mayor Cisneros's terms.
7. Restaurants, hotels, and shops line the river. The haunting melodies of "Una Paloma Blanca" and "Malagueña" lure passing tourists into Casa Rio and other excellent Mexican restaurants.
8. The University of Texas at San Antonio has expanded, and a medical center has been developed in the northwest part of the city.
9. Sentence correct.

10. The city has attracted high-tech industry, creating a corridor of economic growth between San Antonio and Austin and contributing to the Texas economy.

mycomplab 2.0

Please visit MyCompLab at *www.mycomplab.com* for more on the writing process.

HIGHLIGHTS

Of all the chapters on mechanics, this chapter, on the uses of underlining or italics, most frequently needs to be reviewed, particularly by students writing essays or research papers that require incorporating material from outside the classroom. The chapter includes the rules for underlining or italicizing titles; the names of various craft; foreign words and phrases that have not yet become part of the English language; and words or characters named as words. It also gives the rules for underlining or italicizing for emphasis.

A WRITER'S PERSPECTIVE

Her letters to Kitty, though rather longer, were much too full of lines under the words to be made public.

—JANE AUSTEN, *Pride and Prejudice*

COMPANION WEB SITE

See page IAE-58 for companion Web site content description.

10. The City has attracted high-tech industry, creating a corridor of economic growth between san antonio and austin and contributing to the texas economy.

Note See page 507 for an exercise involving capitals along with underlining or italics and other mechanics.

CHAPTER 34

Underlining or Italics

Underlining and *italic type* indicate the same thing: the word or words are being distinguished or emphasized. If you underline two or more words in a row, underline the space between the words, too: Criminal Statistics: Misuses of Numbers.

Note A grammar and style checker cannot recognize problems with underlining or italics. Use the guidelines in this chapter to edit your work.

34a **Use underlining or italics consistently and appropriately for your writing situation.**

Italic type is now used almost universally in business and academic writing. Still, some academic style guides, notably the *MLA Handbook,* continue to prefer underlining, especially in source citations. Ask your instructor for his or her own preference. (We use underlining for the examples in this chapter because it is easier to see than italics.)

Use either italics or underlining consistently throughout a document. For instance, if you are writing an English paper and following MLA style for underlining in source citations, use underlining in the body of your paper as well.

http://www.ablongman.com/littlebrown ▶

Visit the companion Web site for more help and an additional exercise on underlining or italics.

34b　Underline or italicize the titles of works that appear independently.

Within your text, underline or italicize the titles of works that are published, released, or produced separately from other works (see the box below). Use quotation marks for all other titles (see p. 472).

Titles to be underlined or italicized

Other titles should be placed in quotation marks. (See p. 472.)

Books
War and Peace
Psychology: An Introduction

Plays
Hamlet
The Phantom of the Opera

Computer software
Microsoft Internet Explorer
Acrobat Reader

Web sites
Google
Friends of Prufrock

Pamphlets
The Truth About Alcoholism
Plants of the Desert

Long musical works
Tchaikovsky's Swan Lake
The Beatles' Revolver
But: Symphony in C

Television and radio programs
All Things Considered
NBC Sports Hour

Long poems
Beowulf
Paradise Lost

Periodicals
Time
Boston Globe
Yale Law Review

Published speeches
Lincoln's Gettysburg Address
Pericles's Funeral Oration

Movies, DVDs, and videos
Schindler's List
How to Relax

Works of visual art
Michelangelo's David
Picasso's Guernica

Note Underline or italicize marks of punctuation only when they are part of the title: *Did you read Catch-22?* (not *Catch-22?*). In titles of newspapers underline or italicize the name of the city only when it is part of the title:

New York Times　　　　　　Manchester Guardian

When giving the title of a periodical in your text, you need not capitalize, underline, or italicize the article *the*, even if it is part of the title: *She has the New York Times delivered to her in Japan.*

Exceptions Legal documents, the Bible, the Koran, and their parts are generally not underlined or italicized:

Not　They registered their deed.
But　They registered their deed.

| Not | We studied the <u>Book of Revelation</u> in the <u>Bible</u>. |
| But | We studied the Book of Revelation in the Bible. |

Many sciences do not use underlining or italics for some or all titles within source citations. (See pp. 814–19 on CSE style.)

34c Underline or italicize the names of ships, aircraft, spacecraft, and trains.

| <u>Queen Elizabeth 2</u> | <u>Orient Express</u> | <u>Apollo XI</u> |
| <u>Challenger</u> | <u>Spirit of St. Louis</u> | <u>Montrealer</u> |

34d Underline or italicize foreign words and phrases that have not been absorbed into English.

English has adopted many foreign words and phrases—such as the French "bon voyage"—and these need not be underlined or italicized. Do underline or italicize words considered foreign, consulting a dictionary if needed.

The scientific name for the brown trout is <u>Salmo trutta</u>. [The Latin scientific names for plants and animals are always underlined or italicized.]

What a life he led! He was a true <u>bon vivant</u>.

The Latin <u>De gustibus non est disputandum</u> translates roughly as "There's no accounting for taste."

34e Underline or italicize words or characters named as words.

Use underlining or italics to indicate that you are citing a character or word as a word rather than using it for its meaning. Words you are defining fall under this convention:

The word <u>syzygy</u> refers to a straight line formed by three celestial bodies, as in the alignment of the earth, sun, and moon.

Some people say <u>th</u>, as in <u>thought</u>, with a faint <u>s</u> or <u>f</u> sound.

Carved into the column, twenty feet up, was a mysterious <u>7</u>.

34f Occasionally, underlining or italics may be used for emphasis.

Underlining or italics can stress an important word or phrase, especially in reporting how someone said something:

NOTE

You may wish to remind students that when sounds (e.g., *kerplunk, oof*) are represented in writing, they are usually underlined or italicized.

ADD THE MECHANICS

If you have assigned one or more of Chapters 33–36, this activity may be useful and interesting. Take an essay, either student or professional; remove capitals, italics, and the like; and ask students to work in groups reaching consensus on how to correct the mechanics in the "new" essay. Tell them not to look at the handbook but to decide on their own the best way to serve the readers' needs through mechanics. When the students have finished, they can compare their work with the original and, using the handbook as a reference, decide which choices in mechanics they think best serve the needs of the essay and the readers. If they decide to disagree with the advice given in the handbook, ask them to write out their own rules.

"Why on earth would <u>you</u> do that?" she cried.

But use such emphasis very rarely. Excessive underlining or italics will make your writing sound immature or hysterical:

> The settlers had <u>no</u> firewood and <u>no</u> food. Many of them <u>starved</u> or <u>froze</u> to death that first winter.

34g In online communication, use alternatives for underlining or italics.

Electronic mail and other forms of online communication sometimes do not allow underlining or italics for the purposes described in this chapter. On Web sites, for instance, underlining often indicates a link to another site.

To distinguish elements that usually require underlining or italics, type an underscore before and after the element: *Measurements coincide with those in _Joule's Handbook_.* You can also emphasize words with asterisks: *I *will not* be able to attend.*

Avoid using all-capital letters for emphasis. (See also p. 495.)

EXERCISE 34.1 Revising: Underlining or italics

Underline or italicize words and phrases as needed in the following sentences, or circle any words or phrases that are underlined unnecessarily. Note that some highlighting is correct as given. (You can do this exercise online at *ablongman.com/littlebrown*.)

Example:
Of Hitchcock's movies, Psycho is the scariest.
Of Hitchcock's movies, <u>Psycho</u> is the scariest.

1. Of the many Vietnam veterans who are writers, Oliver Stone is perhaps the most famous for writing and directing the films Platoon and Born on the Fourth of July.
2. Tim O'Brien has written short stories for Esquire, GQ, and Massachusetts Review.
3. Going After Cacciato is O'Brien's dreamlike novel about the horrors of combat.
4. The word Vietnam is technically two words (<u>Viet</u> and <u>Nam</u>), but most American writers spell it as <u>one</u> word.
5. American writers use words or phrases borrowed from Vietnamese, such as di di mau ("go quickly") or dinky dau ("crazy").
6. Philip Caputo's <u>gripping</u> account of his service in Vietnam appears in the book A Rumor of War.
7. Caputo's book was made into a television movie, also titled <u>A Rumor of War</u>.
8. <u>David Rabe's</u> plays—including The Basic Training of Pavlo Hummel, Streamers, and Sticks and Bones—depict the effects of the war <u>not only</u> on the soldiers <u>but</u> on their families.

ANSWERS: EXERCISE 34.1

1. Of the many Vietnam veterans who are writers, Oliver Stone is perhaps the most famous for writing and directing the films <u>Platoon</u> and <u>Born on the Fourth of July</u>.
2. Tim O'Brien has written short stories for <u>Esquire</u>, <u>GQ</u>, and <u>Massachusetts Review</u>.
3. <u>Going After Cacciato</u> is O'Brien's dreamlike novel about the horrors of combat.
4. The word <u>Vietnam</u> is technically two words (<u>Viet</u> and <u>Nam</u>), but most American writers spell it as ⃝one word. [Viet and Nam were correctly underlined.]
5. American writers use words or phrases borrowed from Vietnamese, such as <u>di di mau</u> ("go quickly") or <u>dinky dau</u> ("crazy").
6. Philip Caputo's ⃝gripping account of his service in Vietnam appears in the book <u>A Rumor of War</u>.
7. Sentence correct.
8. David Rabe's plays—including <u>The Basic Training of Pavlo Hummel</u>, <u>Streamers</u>, and <u>Sticks and Bones</u>—depict the effects of the war ⃝(not only) on the soldiers ⃝but on their families.

9. Called ("the poet laureate of the Vietnam war,") Steve Mason has published two collections of poems: Johnny's Song and Warrior for Peace.
10. The Washington Post published (rave) reviews of Veteran's Day, an autobiography by Rod Kane.

9. Called the poet laureate of the Vietnam war, Steve Mason has published two collections of poems: Johnny's Song and Warrior for Peace.
10. The Washington Post published rave reviews of Veteran's Day, an autobiography by Rod Kane.

Note See page 507 for an exercise involving underlining or italics along with capitals and other mechanics.

mycomplab 2.0

Please visit MyCompLab at *www.mycomplab.com* for more on the writing process.

HIGHLIGHTS

The discussion in this chapter covers the rules for using abbreviations in general writing. The first four sections cover the use of standard abbreviations for titles, the appropriate use of familiar abbreviations and acronyms, the abbreviations that accompany dates and numbers to show time and amount, and the use of common Latin abbreviations. The last two sections deal with the misuse of abbreviations.

ADDITIONAL RULES

Civil and military titles are abbreviated only when used before a full name, not before the last name only.

Scholarly degrees are abbreviated when the degree follows a name. When a name is followed by an abbreviated title, no other title goes before the name.

COMPANION WEB SITE

See page IAE-58 for companion Web site content description.

CHAPTER 35

Abbreviations

The following guidelines on abbreviations pertain to the text of a nontechnical document. All academic disciplines use abbreviations in source citations, and much technical writing, such as in the sciences and engineering, uses many abbreviations in the document text. For the requirements of the discipline you are writing in, consult one of the style guides listed on pages 764 (humanities), 784 (social sciences), and 812 (natural and applied sciences).

Usage varies, but writers increasingly omit periods from abbreviations that consist of or end in capital letters: *US, BA, USMC, PhD.* See page 427 on punctuating abbreviations.

Note A grammar and style checker may flag some abbreviations, such as *ft.* (for *foot*) and *st.* (for *street*). A spelling checker will flag abbreviations it does not recognize. But neither checker can tell you whether an abbreviation is appropriate for your writing situation or will be clear to your readers.

35a **Use standard abbreviations for titles immediately before and after proper names.**

Before the name	After the name
Dr. James Hsu	James Hsu, MD
Mr., Mrs., Ms., Hon., St.,	DDS, DVM, PhD, EdD,
Rev., Msgr., Gen.	OSB, SJ, Sr., Jr.

http://www.ablongman.com/littlebrown ▶

Visit the companion Web site for more help and an additional exercise on abbreviations.

Abbreviations for nontechnical writing

- Titles before or after proper names: *Dr. Jorge Rodriguez; Jorge Rodriguez, PhD.*
- Familiar abbreviations and acronyms: *USA, AIDS.*
- *BC, BCE, AD, CE, AM, PM, no.,* and *$* with dates and numbers.
- *I.e., e.g.,* and other Latin abbreviations within parentheses and in source citations.
- *Inc., Bros., Co.,* and *&* with names of business firms.

Use abbreviations such as *Rev., Hon., Prof., Rep., Sen., Dr.,* and *St.* (for *Saint*) only if they appear with a proper name. Spell them out in the absence of a proper name:

Not   We learned to trust the <u>Dr.</u>
But   We learned to trust the <u>doctor.</u>
Or   We learned to trust Dr. <u>Kaplan.</u>

The abbreviations for academic degrees—*PhD, MA, BA,* and the like—may be used without a proper name: *My brother took seven years to get his <u>PhD</u>. It will probably take me just as long to earn my <u>BA</u>.*

35b Familiar abbreviations and acronyms are acceptable in most writing.

An **acronym** is an abbreviation that spells a pronounceable word, such as WHO, NATO, and AIDS. These and other abbreviations that use initials are acceptable in most writing as long as they are familiar to readers. Abbreviations of two or more words written in all capital letters may be written without periods (see p. 427):

Institutions	LSU, UCLA, TCU
Organizations	CIA, FBI, YMCA, AFL-CIO
Corporations	IBM, CBS, ITT
People	JFK, LBJ, FDR
Countries	US, USA

Note If a name or term (such as *operating room*) appears often in a piece of writing, then its abbreviation (*OR*) can cut down on extra words. Spell out the full term at its first appearance, give its abbreviation in parentheses, and use the abbreviation from then on.

ABBREVIATIONS AND ARTICLES

Abbreviations can be particularly challenging for nonnative writers; for instance, when do we use words like *a, an,* or *the* (*the FBI* but *NATO*)? Encourage ESL students to build a word list of abbreviations and acronyms and sort them by the use (or nonuse) of such markers.

IBID.* AND *OP. CIT.

Many students are unsure about how to use scholarly abbreviations like *ibid.* ("in the same place") or *op. cit.* ("in the work cited"). These Latin abbreviations are no longer used in the citation styles of the Modern Language Association, American Psychological Association, or Council of Science Editors. *The Chicago Manual of Style* still sanctions the use of *ibid.* in some circumstances; see Chapter 51.

35c Use *BC, BCE, AD, CE, AM, PM, no.,* and *$* only with specific dates and numbers.

44 BC	44 BCE	8:05 PM (*or* p.m.)	no. 36 (*or* No. 36)
AD 1492	1492 CE	11:26 AM (*or* a.m.)	$7.41

Not   Hospital routine is easier to follow in the AM than in the PM.

But   Hospital routine is easier to follow in the morning than in the afternoon or evening.

Note The abbreviation BC ("before Christ") always follows a date, whereas AD (*anno Domini*, Latin for "in the year of the Lord") precedes a date. Increasingly, these abbreviations are being replaced by BCE ("before the common era") and CE ("common era"), respectively. Both follow the date.

35d Generally, reserve Latin abbreviations for source citations and comments in parentheses.

The following common Latin abbreviations are generally not italicized or underlined.

i.e.	*id est:* that is
cf.	*confer:* compare
e.g.	*exempli gratia:* for example
et al.	*et alii:* and others
etc.	*et cetera:* and so forth
NB	*nota bene:* note well

He said he would be gone a fortnight (i.e., two weeks).
Trees, too, are susceptible to disease (e.g., Dutch elm disease).
Bloom et al., editors, *Anthology of Light Verse*

Some writers avoid these abbreviations in formal writing, even within parentheses.

35e Use *Inc., Bros., Co.,* or *&* (for *and*) only in official names of business firms.

Not   The Santini bros. operate a large moving firm in New York City.

But   The Santini brothers operate a large moving firm in New York City.

Or   Santini Bros. is a large moving firm in New York City.

Not   We read about the Hardy Boys & Nancy Drew.

But   We read about the Hardy Boys and Nancy Drew.

35f Spell out most units of measurement and names of places, calendar designations, people, and courses.

In most academic, general, and business writing, certain words should always be spelled out. (In source citations and technical writing, however, these words are more often abbreviated.)

Units of measurement

The dog is thirty inches [not in.] high.
The building is 150 feet [not ft.] tall.

Exception Long phrases such as *miles per hour* (*m.p.h.*) or *cycles per second* (*c.p.s.*) are usually abbreviated, with or without periods: *The speed limit on that road was once 75 m.p.h.* [or *mph*].

Geographical names

The publisher is in Massachusetts [not Mass. or MA].
He came from Auckland, New Zealand [not NZ].
She lived on Morrissey Boulevard [not Blvd.].

Exceptions The United States is often referred to as the USA or the US. In writing of the US capital, use the abbreviation DC for District of Columbia when it follows the city's name: Washington, DC.

Names of days, months, and holidays

The truce was signed on Tuesday [not Tues.], April [not Apr.] 16.
The Christmas [not Xmas] holidays are uneventful.

Names of people

Virginia [not Va.] Woolf was British.
Robert [not Robt.] Frost wrote accessible poems.

Courses of instruction

I'm majoring in political science [not poli. sci.].
Economics [not Econ.] is a difficult course.

EXERCISE 35.1 Revising: Abbreviations

Revise the following sentences as needed to correct inappropriate use of abbreviations for nontechnical writing. Mark the number preceding any sentence in which abbreviations are appropriate as written. (You can do this exercise online at *ablongman.com/littlebrown*.)

Example:
One prof. lectured for five hrs.
One professor lectured for five hours.

1. In the Sept. 17, 2003, issue of *Science* magazine, Virgil L. Sharpton discusses a theory that could help explain the extinction of dinosaurs.

WHEN TO ABBREVIATE

Many writers use abbreviations like *in.* or *yr.* in their drafts. However, in all but informal or technical writing situations, the audience expects such abbreviations to be spelled out. Writers who don't want to confuse their readers will make sure that their final drafts meet these expectations.

TRANSPARENCY MASTER 35.2

ANSWERS: EXERCISE 35.1

1. In the September 17, 2003, issue of *Science* magazine, Virgil L. Sharpton discusses a theory that could help explain the extinction of dinosaurs.

2. About 65 <u>million years</u> ago, a comet or asteroid crashed into the earth.
3. The result was a huge crater about 10 <u>kilometers</u> (6.2 <u>miles</u>) deep in the Gulf of <u>Mexico</u>.
4. Sharpton's new measurements suggest that the crater is 50 <u>percent</u> larger than scientists previously believed.
5. Indeed, 20-year-old drilling cores reveal that the crater is about 186 <u>miles</u> wide, roughly the size of <u>Connecticut</u>.
6. Sentence correct.
7. On impact, 200,000 cubic <u>kilometers</u> of rock and soil were vaporized or thrown into the air.
8. That's the equivalent of 2.34 <u>billion</u> cubic <u>feet</u> of matter.
9. <u>The</u> impact would have created 400-<u>foot</u> tidal waves across the <u>Atlantic Ocean</u>, <u>temperatures</u> higher than 20,000 <u>degrees</u>, and powerful earthquakes.
10. Sharpton theorizes that the dust, vapor, and smoke from this impact blocked the sun's rays for <u>months</u>, cooled the earth, and thus resulted in the death of the dinosaurs.

---

2. About 65 mill. yrs. ago, a comet or asteroid crashed into the earth.
3. The result was a huge crater about 10 km. (6.2 mi.) deep in the Gulf of Mex.
4. Sharpton's new measurements suggest that the crater is 50 pct. larger than scientists previously believed.
5. Indeed, 20-yr.-old drilling cores reveal that the crater is about 186 mi. wide, roughly the size of Conn.
6. The space object was traveling more than 100,000 m.p.h. and hit earth with the impact of 100 to 300 million megatons of TNT.
7. On impact, 200,000 cubic km. of rock and soil were vaporized or thrown into the air.
8. That's the equivalent of 2.34 bill. cubic ft. of matter.
9. The impact would have created 400-ft. tidal waves across the Atl. Ocean, temps. higher than 20,000 degs., and powerful earthquakes.
10. Sharpton theorizes that the dust, vapor, and smoke from this impact blocked the sun's rays for mos., cooled the earth, and thus resulted in the death of the dinosaurs.

Note See page 507 for an exercise involving abbreviations along with capitals and other mechanics.

mycomplab

Please visit MyCompLab at *www.mycomplab.com* for more on the writing process.

CHAPTER 36

Numbers

This chapter addresses the use of numbers (numerals versus words) in the text of a document. All disciplines use many more numerals in source citations.

Note Grammar and style checkers will flag numerals beginning sentences and can be customized to ignore or to look for numerals (see p. 61). But they can't tell you whether numerals or spelled-out numbers are appropriate for your writing situation.

http://www.ablongman.com/littlebrown ▶

Visit the companion Web site for more help and an additional exercise on numbers.

36a Use numerals according to standard practice in the field you are writing in.

Always use numerals for numbers that require more than two words to spell out:

The leap year has 366 days.
The population of Minot, North Dakota, is about 32,800.

In nontechnical academic writing, spell out numbers of one or two words:

Twelve nations signed the treaty.
The ball game drew forty-two thousand people. [A hyphenated number may be considered one word.]

In much business writing, use numerals for all numbers over ten (*five reasons, 11 participants*). In technical academic and business writing, such as in science and engineering, use numerals for all numbers over ten, and use numerals for zero through nine when they refer to exact measurements (*2 liters, 1 hour*). (Consult one of the style guides listed on pp. 784 and 812 for more details.)

Note Use a combination of numerals and words for round numbers over a million: *26 million, 2.45 billion*. And use either all numerals or all words when several numbers appear together in a passage, even if convention would require a mixture:

Inconsistent   The satellite Galatea is about twenty-six thousand miles from Neptune. It is 110 miles in diameter and orbits Neptune in just over ten hours.

Revised   The satellite Galatea is about 26,000 miles from Neptune. It is 110 miles in diameter and orbits Neptune in just over 10 hours.

CULTURE LANGUAGE In American English a comma separates the numerals in long numbers (*26,000*), and a period functions as a decimal point (*2.06*).

36b Use numerals according to convention for dates, addresses, and other information.

Even when a number requires one or two words to spell out, we conventionally use numerals in the following situations:

Days and years
June 18, 2000   AD 12   456 BCE   1999

Exception The day of a month may be expressed in words when it is not followed by a year (*June fifth; October first*).

Pages, chapters, volumes, acts, scenes, lines	Decimals, percentages, and fractions
Chapter 9, page 123	22.5
Hamlet, act 5, scene 3, lines 35–40	48% (*or* 48 percent) 3½

Addresses	Scores and statistics
RD 2	21 to 7
419 Stonewall Street	a mean of 26
Washington, DC 20036	a ratio of 8 to 1

Exact amounts of money	The time of day
$4.50	9:00 AM
$3.5 million (*or* $3,500,000)	2:30 PM

Exceptions Round dollar or cent amounts of only a few words may be expressed in words: *seventeen dollars; fifteen hundred dollars; sixty cents.* When the word *o'clock* is used for the time of day, also express the number in words: *two o'clock* (not *2 o'clock*).

36c Always spell out numbers that begin sentences.

For clarity, spell out any number that begins a sentence. If the number requires more than two words, reword the sentence so that the number falls later and can be expressed as a numeral:

Not 3.7 billion people live in Asia.

But The population of Asia is 3.7 billion.

EXERCISE 36.1 Revising: Numbers

Revise the following sentences so that numbers are used appropriately for nontechnical writing. Mark the number preceding any sentence in which numbers are already used appropriately. (You can do this exercise online at *ablongman.com/littlebrown.*)

Example:
Carol paid two hundred five dollars for used scuba gear.
Carol paid $205 for used scuba gear.

1. The planet Saturn is nine hundred million miles, or nearly one billion five hundred million kilometers, from the sun.
2. A year on Saturn equals almost thirty of our years.
3. Thus, Saturn orbits the sun only two and four-tenths times during the average human life span.
4. It travels in its orbit at about twenty-one thousand six hundred miles per hour.
5. 15 to 20 times denser than Earth's core, Saturn's core measures 17,000 miles across.

ANSWERS: EXERCISE 36.1

1. The planet Saturn is 900 million miles, or nearly 1.5 billion kilometers, from the sun.
2. Sentence correct.
3. Thus, Saturn orbits the sun only 2.4 times during the average human life span.
4. It travels in its orbit at about 21,600 miles per hour.
5. Fifteen to twenty times denser than Earth's core, Saturn's core measures seventeen thousand miles across.

6. The temperature at Saturn's cloud tops is minus one hundred seventy degrees Fahrenheit.
7. In nineteen hundred thirty-three, astronomers found on Saturn's surface a huge white spot 2 times the size of Earth and 7 times the size of Mercury.
8. Saturn's famous rings reflect almost seventy percent of the sunlight that approaches the planet.
9. The ring system is almost forty thousand miles wide, beginning 8800 miles from the planet's visible surface and ending forty-seven thousand miles from that surface.
10. Saturn generates about one hundred thirty trillion kilowatts of electricity.

EXERCISE ON CHAPTERS 33–36   Revising: Mechanics

Revise the paragraphs below to correct any errors in the use of capital letters, underlining or italics, abbreviations, and numbers. (For abbreviations and numbers follow standard practice for nontechnical writing.) Consult a dictionary as needed. (You can do this exercise online at *ablongman.com/littlebrown*.)

According to many sources—e.g., the Cambridge Ancient History and Gardiner's Egypt of the Pharaohs—the ancient egyptians devoted much attention to making Life more convenient and pleasurable for themselves.

Our word pharaoh for the ancient egyptian rulers comes from the egyptian word pr'o, meaning "great house." Indeed, the egyptians placed great emphasis on family residences, adding small bedrms. as early as 3500 yrs. bce. By 3000 bce, the egyptians made ice through evaporation of water at night and then used it to cool their homes. About the same time they used fans made of palm fronds or papyrus to cool themselves in the day. To light their homes, the egyptians abandoned the animal-fat lamps Humans had used for 50 thousand yrs. Instead, around 1300 bce the people of Egt. devised the 1st oil lamps.

egyptians found great pleasure in playing games. Four thousand three hundred yrs. ago or so they created one of the oldest board games known. the game involved racing ivory or stone pieces across a papyrus playing board. By three thousand bce, egyptian children played marbles with semi-precious stones, some of which have been found in gravesites at nagada, EG. Around one thousand three hundred sixty bce, small children played with clay rattles covered in silk and shaped like animals.

To play the game of love, egyptian men and women experimented with cosmetics applied to skin and eyelids. kohl, history's first eyeliner, was used by both sexes to ward off evil. 5000 yrs. ago egyptians wore wigs made of vegetable fibers or human hair. In 9 hundred bce, queen Isimkheb wore a wig so heavy that she needed assistance in walking. To adjust their make-up and wigs, egyptians adapted the simple metal

6. The temperature at Saturn's cloud tops is –170 degrees Fahrenheit.
7. In <u>1933</u>, astronomers found on Saturn's surface a huge white spot <u>two</u> times the size of Earth and <u>seven</u> times the size of Mercury.
8. Saturn's famous rings reflect almost <u>70</u> percent of the sunlight that approaches the planet.
9. The ring system is almost <u>40,000</u> miles wide, beginning 8800 miles from the planet's visible surface and ending <u>47,000</u> miles from that surface.
10. Saturn generates about <u>130</u> trillion kilowatts of electricity.

ANSWERS: EXERCISE ON CHAPTERS 33–37

According to many sources—for example, the <u>Cambridge Ancient History</u> and Gardiner's <u>Egypt of the Pharaohs</u>—the ancient <u>E</u>gyptians devoted much attention to making <u>life</u> more convenient and pleasurable for themselves.

Our word <u>pharaoh</u> for the ancient Egyptian rulers comes from the <u>E</u>gyptian word <u>pr'o</u>, meaning "great house." Indeed, the <u>E</u>gyptians placed great emphasis on family residences, adding small <u>bedrooms</u> as early as <u>3500 BCE</u>. By 3000 <u>BCE</u>, the <u>E</u>gyptians made ice through evaporation of water at night and then used it to cool their homes. About the same time they used fans made of palm fronds or papyrus to cool themselves in the day. To light their homes, the <u>E</u>gyptians abandoned the animal-fat lamps <u>h</u>umans had used for <u>fifty</u> thousand <u>years</u>. Instead, around 1300 <u>BCE</u> the people of <u>Egypt</u> devised the <u>first</u> oil lamps.

<u>E</u>gyptians found great pleasure in playing games. <u>Around 4300 years</u> ago they created one of the oldest board games known. <u>T</u>he game involved racing ivory or stone pieces across a papyrus playing board. By <u>3000 BCE</u>, <u>E</u>gyptian children played marbles with <u>semiprecious</u> stones, some of which have been found in gravesites at <u>N</u>agada, <u>E</u>gypt. Around <u>1360 BCE</u>, small children played with clay rattles covered in silk and shaped like animals.

To play the game of love, <u>E</u>gyptian men and women experimented with cosmetics applied to skin and eyelids. <u>K</u>ohl, history's first eyeliner, was used by both sexes to ward off evil. <u>Five thousand years</u> ago Egyptians wore wigs made of vegetable fibers or human hair. In <u>900 BCE</u>,

Queen Isimkheb wore a wig so heavy that she needed assistance in walking. To adjust their make-up and wigs, Egyptians adapted the simple metal mirrors devised by the Sumerians in the Bronze Age, ornamenting them with carved handles of ivory, gold, or wood. Feeling that only those who smelled sweet could be attractive, the Egyptians made deodorants from perfumed oils, for example, cinnamon and citrus.

mirrors devised by the sumerians in the bronze age, ornamenting them with carved handles of ivory, gold, or wood. Feeling that only those who smelled sweet could be attractive, the egyptians made deodorants from perfumed oils, e.g., cinnamon and citrus.

mycomplab 2.0

Please visit MyCompLab at *www.mycomplab.com* for more on the writing process.

HIGHLIGHTS

There's no substitute for experience when it comes to choosing the right words, and students with limited experience in reading and writing, or whose first language is not English, may find learning to use proper diction a formidable hurdle. Time, encouragement, and careful explanations can help them gain confidence. If your campus has a writing center, check to see if it offers drills or instructional materials to help students improve their resources in language.

This chapter covers types of diction to be avoided or used with care in formal standard American English: dialect, regionalisms, slang, colloquialisms, archaic terms, neologisms, technical language, pretentious language, sexist or biased language, and labels. The chart on "Eliminating sexist language" (pp. 515–16) should be particularly helpful for students who have had little or spotty exposure to standards of inclusive, nonsexist language.

A WRITER'S PERSPECTIVE

Proper words in proper places make the true definition of a style.
—JONATHAN SWIFT, "Letter to a Young Clergyman"

RESOURCES AND IDEAS

On vocabulary building

Harklau, Linda. "From the 'Good Kids' to the 'Worst': Representation of English Language Learners across Educational Settings." *TESOL Quarterly* 34 (Spring 2000): 35–67. Harklau shows how the institutional image of language minority students changes in negative ways as these students transition from nurturing high school to indifferent college.

COMPANION WEB SITE

See page IAE-58 for companion Web site content description.

CHAPTER **37**

Using Appropriate Language

Appropriate language suits your writing situation—your subject, purpose, and audience. Like everyone, you vary your words depending on the context in which you are speaking and writing. Look, for example, at the underlined words in these two sentences:

> Some patients decide to <u>bag</u> counseling because their <u>shrinks</u> seem <u>strung out</u>.
>
> Some patients decide to <u>abandon</u> counseling because their <u>therapists</u> seem <u>disturbed</u>.

The first sentence might be addressed to friends in casual conversation. The second is more suitable for an academic audience.

The more formal language of the second example is typical of **standard American English.** This is the dialect of English normally expected and used in school, business, government, the professions, and the communications media. (For more on its role in academic writing, see pp. 132–33.)

The vocabulary of standard American English is huge, allowing expression of an infinite range of ideas and feelings; but it does exclude words that only some groups of people use, understand, or find inoffensive. Some of those more limited vocabularies should be avoided altogether; others should be used cautiously and in special situations, as when aiming for a special effect with an audience you know will appreciate it. Whenever you doubt a word's status, consult a dictionary (see p. 536).

Note Many grammar and style checkers can be set to flag potentially inappropriate words (see p. 61), such as nonstandard dialect, slang, colloquialisms, and gender-specific terms (*manmade, mailman*). However, the checker can flag only words listed in its dictionary of questionable words. For example, a checker flagged *businessman* as potentially sexist in *A successful businessman puts clients*

http://www.ablongman.com/littlebrown ▶

Visit the companion Web site for more help and additional exercises on appropriate language.

Language in academic and public writing

Always appropriate
Standard American English

Sometimes appropriate

Regional words and expressions   Neologisms
Slang   Technical language
Colloquial language   Euphemisms

Rarely or never appropriate

Nonstandard dialect
Double talk   Biased language: sexist, racist,
Pretentious writing   ethnocentric, etc.

first, but the checker did not flag *his* in *A successful businessperson listens to his clients*. If you use a checker to review your language, you'll need to determine whether a flagged word is or is not appropriate for your writing situation.

37a   Revising nonstandard dialect ⟨CULTURE LANGUAGE⟩

Like many countries, the United States consists of scores of regional, social, and ethnic groups with their own distinct dialects, or versions of English. Standard American English is one of these dialects, and so are Black English, Appalachian English, Creole, and the English of coastal Maine. All the dialects of English share many features, but each also has its own vocabulary, pronunciation, and grammar.

If you speak a dialect of English besides standard American English, be careful about using your dialect in situations where standard English is the norm, such as in academic or public writing. Dialects are not wrong in themselves, but forms imported from one dialect into another may still be perceived as unclear or incorrect. When you know standard English is expected in your writing, edit to eliminate expressions in your dialect that you know (or have been told) differ from standard English. These expressions may include *theirselves, hisn, them books*, and others labeled "nonstandard" by a dictionary. They may also include verb forms, as discussed on pages 278–92. For help identifying and editing nonstandard language, see "⟨CULTURE LANGUAGE⟩ Guide" inside the back cover of this book.

Your participation in the community of standard English does not require you to abandon your own dialect. You may want to use it in writing you do for yourself, such as journals, notes, and drafts, which should be composed as freely as possible. You may want to

HUCK FINN

You may wish to make the following examples the subject of class discussion. Students usually find them quite interesting.

In his explanatory note at the beginning of *The Adventures of Huckleberry Finn,* Mark Twain explains one of the difficulties with using non-standard language:

> In this book a number of dialects are used, to wit: the Missouri negro dialect; the extremist form of the backwoods Southwestern dialect; the ordinary "Pike County" dialect; and four modified varieties of this last. The shadings have not been done in a haphazard fashion, or by guesswork; but painstakingly, and with the trustworthy guidance and support of personal familiarity with these several forms of speech. I make this explanation for the reason that without it many readers would suppose that all these characters were trying to talk alike and not succeeding.
> —THE AUTHOR

From the opening lines of *The Adventures of Huckleberry Finn:*

> You don't know about me without you have read a book by the name of *The Adventures of Tom Sawyer;* but that ain't no matter. That book was made by Mr. Mark Twain, and he told the truth, mainly. There was things which he stretched; but mainly he told the truth. That is nothing. I never seen anybody but lied one time or another, without it was Aunt Polly, or the widow, or maybe Mary. Aunt Polly—Tom's Aunt Polly, she is—and Mary, and the widow Douglas is all told about in that book, which is mostly a true book, with some stretchers, as I said before.

COLLABORATIVE LEARNING

FIELD RESEARCH

Have students work in teams as "anthropologists" to collect examples of college slang on your campus. They can compare their research with the collections published in *College Slang 101* by Connie Eble (Georgetown: Spectacle Lane, 1989) or *Slang U* by Pamela Munro (New York: Harmony, 1989). Other topics for research reports might be the languages of rap or rock music, of some activity (skateboarding or football), or of some social group (fraternities, volunteer firefighters).

quote it in an academic paper, as when analyzing or reporting conversation in dialect. And, of course, you will want to use it with others who speak it.

37b Using regionalisms only when appropriate

Regionalisms are expressions or pronunciations peculiar to a particular area. Southerners may say they *reckon,* meaning "think" or "suppose." People in Maine invite their Boston friends to come *down* rather than *up* (north) to visit. New Yorkers stand *on* rather than *in* line for a movie.

Regional expressions are appropriate in writing addressed to local readers and may lend realism to regional description, but they should be avoided in writing intended for a general audience.

37c Using slang only when appropriate

All groups of people—from musicians and computer scientists to vegetarians and golfers—create novel and colorful expressions called **slang.** The following quotation, for instance, is from an essay on the slang of "skaters" (skateboarders):

> Curtis slashed ultra-punk crunchers on his longboard, while the Rubeman flailed his usual Gumbyness on tweaked frontsides and lofty fakie ollies.   —Miles Orkin, "Mucho Slingage by the Pool"

Among those who understand it, slang may be vivid and forceful. It often occurs in dialog, and an occasional slang expression can enliven an informal essay. Some slang, such as *dropout* (*She was a high school dropout*), has proved so useful that it has passed into the general vocabulary.

But most slang is too flippant and imprecise for effective communication, and it is generally inappropriate for college or business writing. Notice the gain in seriousness and precision achieved in the following revision:

Slang   Many students start out <u>pretty together</u> but then <u>get weird</u>.
Revised   Many students start out <u>with clear goals</u> but then <u>lose their direction</u>.

37d Using colloquial language only when appropriate

Colloquial language designates the words and expressions appropriate to everyday spoken language. Regardless of our backgrounds and how we live, we all try to *get along with* each other. We play with *kids, go crazy* for something, and in our worst moments try to *get back at* someone who has made us do the *dirty work.*

When you write informally, colloquial language may be appropriate to achieve the casual, relaxed effect of conversation. An occasional colloquial word dropped into otherwise more formal writing can also help you achieve a desired emphasis. But colloquial language does not provide the exactness needed in more formal college, public, and professional writing. In such writing you should generally avoid any words and expressions labeled "informal" or "colloquial" in your dictionary. Take special care to avoid **mixed diction,** a combination of standard and colloquial words:

Mixed diction	According to a Native American myth, the Great Creator <u>had a dog hanging around with him</u> when he created the earth.
Revised	According to a Native American myth, the Great Creator <u>was accompanied by a dog</u> when he created the earth.

37e Revising neologisms

Neologisms are words created (or coined) so recently that they have not come into established use. An example is *prequel* (made up of *pre-*, meaning "before," and the ending of *sequel*), a movie or book that takes the story of an existing movie or book back in time. Some neologisms do become accepted as part of our general vocabulary—*motel,* coined from *motor* and *hotel,* is an example. But most neologisms pass quickly from the language. Unless such words serve a special purpose in your writing and are sure to be understood by your readers, you should avoid them.

37f Using technical words with care

All disciplines and professions rely on special words or give common words special meanings. Chemists speak of *esters* and *phosphatides,* geographers and mapmakers refer to *isobars* and *isotherms,* and literary critics write about *motifs* and *subtexts.* Such technical language allows specialists to communicate precisely and economically with other specialists who share their vocabulary. But without explanation these words are meaningless to nonspecialists. When you are writing for nonspecialists, avoid unnecessary technical terms and carefully define terms you must use.

37g Revising indirect or pretentious writing

In most writing, small, plain, and direct words are preferable to big, showy, or evasive words. Avoid euphemisms, double talk, and pretentious writing.

A **euphemism** is a presumably inoffensive word that a writer or speaker substitutes for a word deemed potentially offensive or too

CULTURE LANGUAGE

THEORETICAL PERSPECTIVE ON DIALECT

If your students are interested in the matter of what ought to be done about language variation, you could share a theoretical perspective from linguistics. Linguists have identified three different philosophies about how to resolve the problem of language variation. One philosophy is that of *eradication,* which holds that language variations should be completely eliminated. A second philosophy is that of *appreciation,* which holds that dialects ought to be celebrated as reflections of our diverse cultural traditions. A third philosophy is that of *biloquialism* or *bidialectalism,* which holds that people should learn more than one language variety so that they can express themselves in multiple situations without giving up their ways of relating in the multiple communities to which they belong. A class discussion on the relative merits of these three approaches might be a lively one.

TECHNICAL JARGON

Using technical language is appropriate when both writers and readers understand the specialized body of knowledge to which the technical language refers. Have students practice translating between technical and nontechnical language to gain experience in deciding what level of language might be appropriate for particular situations. For a study of the sources of academic and newspaper jargon see Walter Nash's *Jargon: Its Uses and Abuses* (Oxford: Blackwell, 1993).

COLLABORATIVE LEARNING

EUPHEMISTICALLY SPEAKING

Have small groups of students find examples of pretentious or euphemistic language in political or other public speeches. Groups can compare notes in class and decide which examples are the most silly and which are the most duplicitous.

blunt, such as *passed away* for "died." Euphemisms appear whenever a writer or speaker wants to bury the truth, as when a governor mentions the *negative growth* (meaning "decline") in her state. Use euphemisms only when you know that blunt, truthful words would needlessly hurt or offend members of your audience.

A kind of euphemism that deliberately evades the truth is **double talk** (also called **doublespeak** or **weasel words**): language intended to confuse or to be misunderstood. Today double talk is unfortunately common in politics and advertising—the *revenue enhancement* that is really a tax, the *biodegradable* bags that last decades. Double talk has no place in honest writing.

Euphemism and sometimes double talk seem to keep company with fancy writing. Any writing that is more elaborate than its subject requires will sound **pretentious**—that is, excessively showy. Choose your words for their exactness and economy. The big, ornate word may be tempting, but pass it up. Your readers will be grateful.

| Pretentious | To perpetuate our endeavor of providing funds for our elderly citizens as we do at the present moment, we will face the exigency of enhanced contributions from all our citizens. |
| Revised | We cannot continue to fund Social Security and Medicare for the elderly unless we raise taxes. |

37h Revising sexist and other biased language

Even when we do not mean it to, our language can reflect and perpetuate hurtful prejudices toward groups of people, especially racial, ethnic, religious, age, and sexual groups. Such biased language can be obvious—words such as *nigger, whitey, mick, kike, fag, dyke,* and *broad.* But it can also be subtle, generalizing about groups in ways that may be familiar but that are also inaccurate or unfair. For instance, people with physical disabilities are as varied a group as any other: the only thing they have in common is some form of impairment. To assume that people with disabilities share certain attitudes (shyness, helplessness, victimization, whatever) is to disregard the uniqueness of each person.

Biased language reflects poorly on the user, not on the person or persons whom it mischaracterizes or insults. Unbiased language does not submit to false generalizations. It treats people as individuals and labels groups as they wish to be labeled.

1 Avoiding stereotypes of race, ethnicity, religion, age, and other characteristics

A **stereotype** is a generalization based on poor evidence, a kind of formula for understanding and judging people simply because of their membership in a group:

Men are uncommunicative.
Women are emotional.
Liberals want to raise taxes.
Conservatives are affluent.

At best, stereotypes betray an uncritical writer, one who is not thinking beyond notions received from others. Worse, they betray a writer who does not mind hurting others or even *wants* to hurt others.

In your writing, be alert for any general statements about people based on only one or a few characteristics. Be especially cautious about substituting such statements for the evidence you should be providing instead.

Stereotype	Elderly drivers should have their licenses limited to daytime driving. [Implies that all elderly people are poor night drivers.]
Revised	Drivers with impaired night vision should have their licenses limited to daytime driving.

Some stereotypes have become part of the language, but they are still potentially offensive.

Stereotype	The administrators are too blind to see the need for a new gymnasium.
Revised	The administrators do not understand the need for a new gymnasium.

2 Avoiding sexist language

Among the most subtle and persistent biased language is that expressing narrow ideas about men's and women's roles, position, and value in society. This **sexist language** distinguishes needlessly between men and women in such matters as occupation, ability, behavior, temperament, and maturity. Like other stereotypes, it can wound or irritate readers, and it indicates the writer's thoughtlessness or unfairness. The following box suggests some ways of eliminating sexist language.

Eliminating sexist language

- **Avoid demeaning and patronizing language**—for instance, identifying women and men differently or trivializing either gender:

Sexist	<u>Dr. Keith Kim</u> and Lydia Hawkins wrote the article.
Revised	Dr. Keith Kim and <u>Dr.</u> Lydia Hawkins wrote the article.
Revised	<u>Keith Kim</u> and Lydia Hawkins wrote the article.
Sexist	<u>Ladies</u> are entering formerly male occupations.
Revised	<u>Women</u> are entering formerly male occupations.

(continued)

---

where biased language can be found. Tell your students to explore some such sites. Their explorations can prompt a class discussion about why bias seems to flourish in such discussion groups—whether, for instance, the anonymity the Web provides encourages participants to use stronger or more biased language than they otherwise would.

TRANSPARENCY MASTER 37.2

Eliminating sexist language

(continued)

- **Avoid occupational or social stereotypes,** assuming that a role or profession is exclusively male or female:

  Sexist   The considerate doctor commends a nurse when <u>she</u> provides <u>his</u> patients with good care.

  Revised   The considerate doctor commends a nurse <u>who provides good care for patients</u>.

- **Avoid referring needlessly to gender:**

  Sexist   Marie Curie, <u>a woman chemist</u>, discovered radium.

  Revised   Marie Curie, <u>a chemist</u>, discovered radium.

  Sexist   The patients were tended by <u>a male nurse</u>.

  Revised   The patients were tended by <u>a nurse</u>.

- **Avoid using *man* or words containing *man* to refer to all human beings.** Here are a few alternatives:

businessman	businessperson
chairman	chair, chairperson
congressman	representative in Congress, legislator
craftsman	craftsperson, artisan
layman	layperson
mankind	humankind, humanity, human beings, people
policeman	police officer
salesman	salesperson, sales representative

  Sexist   <u>Man</u> has not reached the limits of social justice.

  Revised   <u>Humankind</u> [or <u>Humanity</u>] has not reached the limits of social justice.

  Sexist   The furniture consists of <u>manmade</u> materials.

  Revised   The furniture consists of <u>synthetic</u> materials.

- **Avoid the generic *he*,** the male pronoun used to refer to both genders. (See also pp. 315–16.)

  Sexist   The newborn child explores <u>his</u> world.

  Revised   Newborn <u>children</u> explore <u>their</u> world. [Use the plural for the pronoun and the word it refers to.]

  Revised   The newborn child explores <u>the</u> world. [Avoid the pronoun altogether.]

  Revised   The newborn child explores <u>his or her</u> world. [Substitute male and female pronouns.]

Use the last option sparingly—only once in a group of sentences and only to stress the singular individual.

CULTURE LANGUAGE Forms of address vary widely from culture to culture. In some cultures, for instance, one shows respect by referring to all older women as if they were married, using the equivalent of the title *Mrs.* Usage in the United States is changing toward making no assumptions about marital status, rank, or other characteristics—for instance, using the title *Ms.* for a woman unless she is known to prefer *Mrs.* or *Miss.*

3 Using appropriate labels

We often need to label groups: *swimmers, politicians, mothers, Christians, westerners, students.* But labels can be shorthand stereotypes that slight the person labeled and ignore the preferences of the group members themselves. Showing sensitivity when applying labels reveals you to be alert to readers' needs and concerns. Although sometimes dismissed as "political correctness," such sensitivity hurts no one and helps gain your readers' trust and respect.

- **Avoid labels that (intentionally or not) disparage the person or group you refer to.** A person with emotional problems is not a *mental patient.* A person with cancer is not a *cancer victim.* A person using a wheelchair is not *wheelchair-bound.*
- **Use names for racial, ethnic, and other groups that reflect the preferences of each group's members,** or at least many of them. Examples of current preferences include *African American* or *black, latino/latina* (for Americans and American immigrants of Spanish-speaking descent), and *people with disabilities* (rather than *the handicapped*). But labels change often. To learn how a group's members wish to be labeled, ask them directly, attend to usage in reputable periodicals, or check a recent dictionary.

A helpful reference for appropriate labels is *Guidelines for Bias-Free Writing,* by Marilyn Schwartz and the Task Force on Bias-Free Language of the Association of American University Presses.

EXERCISE 37.1   Revising: Appropriate words

Rewrite the following sentences as needed for standard American English. Consult a dictionary to determine whether particular words are appropriate and to find suitable substitutes. (You can do this exercise online at *ablongman.com/littlebrown.*)

Example:
If negotiators get hyper during contract discussions, they may mess up chances for a settlement.
If negotiators become excited or upset during contract discussions, they may harm chances for a settlement.

3. Those who think the disease is limited to <u>ho-mosexuals</u>, <u>drug users</u>, and foreigners are quite mistaken.
4. <u>Statistics</u> suggest that in the United States one in every five hundred college <u>students</u> carries the virus.
5. <u>People</u> with AIDS do not deserve others' <u>exclusion</u> or callousness. Instead, <u>they need</u> all the compassion, medical care, and financial assistance due the seriously ill.
6. A <u>person with AIDS</u> often sees a team of doctors or a single doctor with a specialized practice.
7. The doctor may <u>help patients</u> by obtaining social services for them as well as providing medical care.
8. The <u>person with AIDS</u> who loses <u>his or her</u> job may need public assistance.
9. For someone who is very ill, a full-time nurse may be necessary. <u>The nurse</u> can administer medications and <u>make</u> the sick person as comfortable as possible.
10. Some people with AIDS have insurance, but others lack the <u>money</u> for premiums.

1. Acquired immune deficiency syndrome (AIDS) is a major deal all over the world.
2. The disease gets around primarily by sexual intercourse, exchange of bodily fluids, shared needles, and blood transfusions.
3. Those who think the disease is limited to homos, druggies, and foreigners are quite mistaken.
4. Stats suggest that in the United States one in every five hundred college kids carries the virus.
5. A person with AIDS does not deserve to be subjected to exclusionary behavior or callousness on the part of his fellow citizens. Instead, he has the necessity for all the compassion, medical care, and financial assistance due those who are in the extremity of illness.
6. An AIDS victim often sees a team of doctors or a single doctor with a specialized practice.
7. The doctor may help his patients by obtaining social services for them as well as by providing medical care.
8. The AIDS sufferer who loses his job may need public assistance.
9. For someone who is very ill, a full-time nurse may be necessary. She can administer medications and make the sick person as comfortable as possible.
10. Some people with AIDS have insurance, but others lack the bread for premiums.

mycomplab™⁰

Please visit MyCompLab at *www.mycomplab.com* for more on the writing process.

HIGHLIGHTS

Chapter 38 helps students understand the value of precision in word choice. It begins with a discussion of the difference between denotative and connotative meanings and the necessity of knowing both kinds of meanings when choosing a word. The second section explains why maintaining balance between abstract and concrete terms, and between general and specific terms, is an important element of good writing. Next, the chapter treats idiomatic language. This section contains a useful chart listing idioms and the prepositions they take, which will be helpful for ESL students and native speakers alike. The

COMPANION WEB SITE

See page IAE-59 for companion Web site content description.

CHAPTER 38

Using Exact Language

To write clearly and effectively, you will want to find the words that fit your meaning exactly and convey your attitude precisely. Don't worry too much about choosing exact words while you are drafting an essay. If the right word doesn't come to you, leave a blank. Revision (p. 48) or editing (p. 58) is the stage to consider tone, specificity, and precision.

Note A grammar and style checker can provide some help with inexact language. For instance, you can set it to flag commonly confused words (such as *continuous/continual*), misused preposi-

http://www.ablongman.com/littlebrown ▶

Visit the companion Web site for more help and additional exercises on exact language.

tions in idioms (such as *accuse for* instead of *accuse of*), and clichés. (See p. 61 on setting a checker.) But the checker can flag only words stored in its dictionary. It can't help you at all with inappropriate connotation, excessive abstraction, or other problems discussed in this chapter.

38a   Using the right word for your meaning

Precisely expressing your meaning requires understanding both the denotations and the connotations of words. A word's **denotation** is the thing or idea it refers to, the meaning listed in the dictionary without reference to the emotional associations it may arouse in a reader. Using words according to their established denotations is essential if readers are to grasp your meaning. Here are a few guidelines:

- **Become acquainted with a dictionary.** Consult it whenever you are unsure of a word's meaning.
- **Distinguish between similar-sounding words that have widely different denotations:**

  Inexact   Older people often suffer <u>infirmaries</u> [places for the sick].
  Exact   Older people often suffer <u>infirmities</u> [disabilities].

  Some words, called **homonyms** (from the Greek meaning "same name"), sound exactly alike but differ in meaning: for example, *principal/principle* or *rain/reign/rein*. (See pp. 543–44 for a list of commonly confused homonyms.)

- **Distinguish between words with related but distinct denotations:**

  Inexact   Television commercials <u>continuously</u> [unceasingly] interrupt programming.
  Exact   Television commercials <u>continually</u> [regularly] interrupt programming.

In addition to their emotion-free denotations, many words also carry associations with specific feelings. These **connotations** can shape readers' responses and are thus a powerful tool for writers. (At the same time they are a potential snare for readers. See p. 189.) Some connotations are personal: the word *dog*, for instance, may have negative connotations for the letter carrier who has been bitten three times. Usually, though, people agree about connotations. The following word pairs are just a few of many that have related denotations but very different connotations:

pride: sense of self-worth
vanity: excessive regard for oneself

chapter closes with sections on figurative language and clichés. The exercises in this chapter will be easier to complete if students use a dictionary.

A WRITER'S PERSPECTIVE

Whenever we come upon one of those intensely right words [. . .] the resulting effect is physical as well as spiritual, and electrically prompt.
—MARK TWAIN, "William Dean Howells"

RESOURCES AND IDEAS

Ammirati, Theresa, and Ellen Strenski. "Using Astrology to Teach Connotation and Bias." *Exercise Exchange* 25 (1980): 9–11. The authors tell how to use the language in astrology books as a source of examples of connotation and bias.

Nilsen, Don L. F. "Clichés, Trite Sayings, Dead Metaphors, and Stale Figures of Speech in Composition Instruction." *College Composition and Communication* 27 (1976): 278–82. Nilsen points out that reviving dead metaphors and clichés in class discussion can create an awareness of figurative language.

Sossaman, Stephen. "Detroit Designers: A Game to Teach Metaphors." *Exercise Exchange* 21 (1976): 2–3. Sossaman points out that car names provide good examples of metaphoric language.

Williams, Joseph M. *Style: Ten Lessons in Clarity and Grace*, 7th ed. Boston: Longman, 2002. Williams' book is full of practical and relevant advice students can heed to improve their writing style.

COLLABORATIVE LEARNING

SYNONYMY

To help students develop their sensitivity to denotation and connotation, give them a group of words and phrases like *overweight*, *out of money*, and *failing the class* and ask them to come up with as many different ways of expressing the term as possible. Then, either alone or in groups, have them decide what connotations each synonym has, and for what audiences and situations each might be appropriate. (Some synonyms for *overweight*, for instance, might be *plump* [neutral], *tubby* [probably negative], *porky* [negative], and so on.)

COLLABORATIVE LEARNING

When students have completed Exercises 38.1 and 38.2 individually, have them compare their answers in small groups. Encourage group members to discuss the connotation and denotation of each of the choices, and to consider the effect on the sentence when an inappropriate word is used.

ANSWERS: EXERCISE 38.1

1. Maxine Hong Kingston was <u>awarded</u> many prizes for her first two books, *The Woman Warrior* and *China Men*.
2. Kingston <u>cites</u> her mother's tales about ancestors and ancient Chinese customs as the sources of these memoirs.
3. In her childhood Kingston was greatly <u>affected</u> by her mother's tale about a pregnant aunt who was ostracized by villagers. [<u>Ostracized</u> correct.]
4. The aunt gained <u>vengeance</u> by drowning herself in the village's water supply.
5. Kingston decided to make her nameless relative <u>famous</u> by giving her immortality in *The Woman Warrior*. [<u>Immortality</u> correct.]

---

firm: steady, unchanging, unyielding
stubborn: unreasonable, bullheaded

enthusiasm: excitement
mania: excessive interest or desire

Understanding connotation is especially important in choosing among **synonyms,** words with approximately, but often not exactly, the same meanings. For instance, *cry* and *weep* both denote the shedding of tears, but *cry* more than *weep* connotes a sobbing sound accompanying the tears. *Sob* itself connotes broken, gasping crying, with tears, whereas *wail* connotes sustained sound, perhaps without tears.

Several resources can help you track down words with the exact connotations you want:

- **A standard dictionary distinguishes among synonyms.** See page 539 for an example.
- **A dictionary of synonyms lists and defines synonyms in groups.** See page 538 for a title.
- **A thesaurus lists synonyms but does not distinguish among them.** See page 538 for a title.

Note Because a thesaurus lacks definitions, it can only suggest possibilities. You will still need a dictionary to discover words' exact denotations and connotations.

EXERCISE 38.1   Revising: Denotation

Revise any underlined word below that is not used according to its established denotation. Circle any word used correctly. Consult a dictionary if you are uncertain of a word's precise meaning. (You can do this exercise online at *ablongman.com/littlebrown*.)

Example:

Sam and Dave are going to Bermuda and Hauppauge, <u>respectfully</u>, for spring vacation.

Sam and Dave are going to Bermuda and Hauppauge, <u>respectively</u>, for spring vacation.

1. Maxine Hong Kingston was <u>rewarded</u> many prizes for her first two books, *The Woman Warrior* and *China Men*.
2. Kingston <u>sites</u> her mother's tales about ancestors and ancient Chinese customs as the sources of these memoirs.
3. In her childhood Kingston was greatly <u>effected</u> by her mother's tale about a pregnant aunt who was <u>ostracized</u> by villagers.
4. The aunt gained <u>avengeance</u> by drowning herself in the village's water supply.
5. Kingston decided to make her nameless relative <u>infamous</u> by giving her <u>immortality</u> in *The Woman Warrior*.

EXERCISE 38.2 Considering the connotations of words

Fill the blank in each sentence below with the most appropriate word from the list in parentheses. Consult a dictionary to be sure of your choice. (You can do this exercise online at *ablongman.com/littlebrown*.)

> *Example:*
> Channel 5 _____ Oshu the winner before the polls closed. (*advertised, declared, broadcast, promulgated*)
>
> Channel 5 declared Oshu the winner before the polls closed.

1. AIDS is a serious health _____. (*problem, worry, difficulty, plight*)
2. Once the virus has entered the blood system, it _____ T-cells. (*murders, destroys, slaughters, executes*)
3. The _____ of T-cells is to combat infections. (*ambition, function, aim, goal*)
4. Without enough T-cells, the body is nearly _____ against infections. (*defenseless, hopeless, desperate*)
5. To prevent exposure to the disease, one should be especially _____ in sexual relationships. (*chary, circumspect, cautious, calculating*)

38b Balancing the abstract and concrete, the general and specific

To understand a subject as you understand it, your readers need ample guidance from your words. When you describe a building as *beautiful* and nothing more, you force readers to provide their own ideas of what makes a building beautiful. If readers bother (and they may not), they surely will not conjure up the image you had in mind. Use words to tell readers what you want them to know, that the beautiful building is *a sleek, silver skyscraper with blue-tinted windows,* for instance, or *a Victorian brick courthouse with tall, arched windows.*

Clear, exact writing balances abstract and general words, which outline ideas and objects, with concrete and specific words, which sharpen and solidify.

- **Abstract words** name qualities and ideas: *beauty, inflation, management, culture, liberal.* **Concrete words** name things we can know by our five senses of sight, hearing, touch, taste, and smell: *sleek, humming, brick, bitter, musty.*
- **General words** name classes or groups of things, such as *buildings, weather,* or *birds,* and include all the varieties of the class. **Specific words** limit a general class, such as *buildings,* by naming a variety, such as *skyscraper, Victorian courthouse,* or *hut.*

ANSWERS: EXERCISE 38.2

1. AIDS is a serious health <u>problem</u>.
2. Once the virus has entered the blood system, it <u>destroys</u> T-cells.
3. The <u>function</u> of T-cells is to combat infections.
4. Without enough T-cells, the body is nearly <u>defenseless</u> against infections.
5. To prevent exposure to the disease, one should be especially <u>cautious</u> in sexual relationships.

COLLABORATIVE LEARNING

FILLER WORDS

Asking students to come up with more descriptive synonyms for adjectives like *nice* or *good* in a draft is an easy way to begin class (or small group) discussion of the distinctions between abstract and concrete or general and specific words.

ANSWERS: EXERCISE 38.3

Possible revision

I remember as if it were last week how <u>frightened</u> I felt the first time I <u>neared</u> Mrs. Murphy's second-grade class. <u>Just three days before</u>, I had moved from a rural one-street town in Missouri to a suburb of Chicago <u>where the houses and the people were jammed together</u>. My new school looked <u>monstrous</u> from the outside and seemed <u>forbiddingly dim</u> inside as I <u>walked haltingly</u> down the <u>endless</u> corridor toward the classroom. The class was <u>clamorous</u> as I neared the door; but when I <u>slipped inside</u>, <u>twenty faces</u> became

---

Note that *general* and *specific* are relative terms: the same word may be more general than some words but more specific than others.

Abstract and general words are useful in the broad statements that set the course for your writing:

> The wild horse in America has a <u>romantic</u> history.
>
> We must be <u>free</u> from <u>government interference</u> in our <u>affairs</u>.
>
> <u>Relations</u> between the sexes today are only a <u>little</u> more <u>relaxed</u> than they were in the past.

But the sentences following these would have to develop the ideas with concrete and specific details. When your meaning calls for an abstract or general word, make sure you define it, explain it, and narrow it. Look at how concrete and specific information turns vague sentences into exact ones in the examples below:

Vague   The size of his hands made his smallness real. [How big were his hands? How small was he?]

Exact   Not until I saw his delicate, doll-like hands did I realize that he stood a full head shorter than most other men.

Vague   The long flood caused a lot of awful destruction in the town. [How long did the flood last? What destruction did it cause? Why was the destruction awful?]

Exact   The flood waters, which rose swiftly and then stayed stubbornly high for days, killed at least six townspeople and made life a misery for the hundreds who had to evacuate their ruined homes and stores.

Note You can use your computer's Find function to help you find and revise abstract and general words that you tend to overuse. Examples of such words might include *nice, interesting, things, very, good, a lot, a little,* and *some.*

> **EXERCISE 38.3   Revising: Concrete and specific words**
>
> Make the following paragraph vivid by expanding the sentences with appropriate details of your own choosing. Substitute concrete and specific words for the abstract and general ones that are underlined. (You can do this exercise online at *ablongman.com/littlebrown.*)
>
> I remember <u>clearly</u> how <u>awful</u> I felt the first time I <u>attended</u> Mrs. Murphy's second-grade class. I had <u>recently</u> moved from a <u>small</u> town in Missouri to a <u>crowded</u> suburb of Chicago. My new school looked

big from the outside and seemed dark inside as I walked down the long corridor toward the classroom. The class was noisy as I neared the door; but when I entered, everyone became quiet and looked at me. I felt uncomfortable and wanted a place to hide. However, in a loud voice Mrs. Murphy directed me to the front of the room to introduce myself.

EXERCISE 38.4   Using concrete and specific words

For each abstract or general word below, give at least two other words or phrases that illustrate increasing specificity or concreteness. Consult a dictionary as needed. Use the most specific or concrete word from each group in a sentence of your own. (You can do this exercise online at ablongman.com/littlebrown.)

Example:

awake, watchful, vigilant
Vigilant guards patrol the buildings.

1. fabric
2. delicious
3. car
4. narrow-minded
5. reach (*verb*)
6. green
7. walk (*verb*)
8. flower
9. serious
10. pretty
11. teacher
12. nice
13. virtue
14. angry
15. crime

38c   Using idioms

Idioms are expressions in any language whose meanings cannot be determined simply from the words in them or whose component words cannot be predicted by any rule of grammar; often, they violate conventional grammar. Examples of English idioms include *put up with*, *plug away at*, and *make off with*.

Idiomatic combinations of verbs or adjectives and prepositions can be confusing for both native and nonnative speakers of English. A number of these pairings are listed in the box below.

Idioms with prepositions

abide by a rule	agree on a plan as a group
abide in a place or state	agree to someone else's plan
accords with	agree with a person
according to	angry with
accuse of a crime	aware of
adapt from a source	based on
adapt to a situation	capable of
afraid of	certain of

(continued)

still and gawked at me. I felt terrified and longed for a place to hide. However, in a booming voice Mrs. Murphy ordered me to the front of the room to introduce myself.

ANSWERS: EXERCISE 38.4

Possible answers

1. fabric, upholstery fabric, velvet
   She chose a wine-colored velvet for backing the pillow.
2. delicious, tart, lemony
   He made a meringue pie, lemony and delicately brown.
3. car, foreign car, Volvo station wagon
   He bought a 1973 Volvo station wagon.
4. narrow-minded, prejudiced, sexist
   My uncle's sexist attitudes cause many arguments in our family.
5. reach, stretch, lunge
   Each child lunged for the prize thrown by the clown.
6. green, dark green, bilious green
   The algae covered the surface with a bilious green scum.
7. walk, march, goose-step
   The soldiers goose-stepped menacingly.
8. flower, daisy, ox-eyed daisy
   Some people call the ox-eyed daisy a "brown-eyed Susan."
9. serious, solemn, grim
   His grim expression frightened us.
10. pretty; with small, regular features; with a button nose and a tiny, smiling mouth
    The infant, with a button nose and a tiny, smiling mouth, was a perfect model for baby products.
11. teacher, history teacher, American history teacher
    My American history teacher requires three research papers.

TRANSPARENCY MASTER 38.1

12. nice, considerate, sympathetic
    I need a sympathetic friend.
13. virtue, honesty, frankness
    His frankness was refreshing after I had heard so much flattery.
14. angry, furious, raging
    Raging uncontrollably, Andy insulted everyone around him.
15. crime, theft, armed robbery
    Drug addicts sometimes commit armed robbery to pay for their habits.

RARE SPECIMENS

Establish a "gallery" of interesting idioms on your class shareware/Web site. As students come across interesting or unusual examples of idioms they can post them to the site. They should check a dictionary of idioms and report on what they find about their specimen.

IDIOMS

Idioms are particularly challenging for non-native speakers of English, and even native speakers may find some idioms impenetrable. Asking students to add to the lists in this chapter, or to examine dictionaries of idioms, may yield interesting discussions and paper topics.

PREPOSITIONS

As the text notes, prepositions follow few specific rules, and, because of idiomatic usage, they often cannot be translated directly into students' first languages. As a result, even advanced ESL students find prepositions difficult. In addition to consulting an ESL dictionary, as recommended in the text, students who need additional help with prepositions might refer to Unit 6 of Len

Idioms with prepositions
(continued)

charge <u>for</u> a purchase
charge <u>with</u> a crime
concur <u>in</u> an opinion
concur <u>with</u> a person
contend <u>for</u> a principle
contend <u>with</u> a person
dependent <u>on</u>
differ <u>about</u> or <u>over</u> a question
differ <u>from</u> in some quality
differ <u>with</u> a person
disappointed <u>by</u> or <u>in</u> a person
disappointed <u>in</u> or <u>with</u> a thing
familiar <u>with</u>
identical <u>with</u> or <u>to</u>
impatient <u>for</u> a raise
impatient <u>with</u> a person
independent <u>of</u>
infer <u>from</u>
inferior <u>to</u>
involved <u>in</u> a task
involved <u>with</u> a person

oblivious <u>of</u> or <u>to</u> one's surroundings
oblivious <u>of</u> something forgotten
occupied <u>by</u> a person
occupied <u>in</u> study
occupied <u>with</u> a thing
opposed <u>to</u>
part <u>from</u> a person
part <u>with</u> a possession
prior <u>to</u>
proud <u>of</u>
related <u>to</u>
rewarded <u>by</u> the judge
rewarded <u>for</u> something done
rewarded <u>with</u> a gift
similar <u>to</u>
superior <u>to</u>
wait <u>at</u> a place
wait <u>for</u> a train, a person
wait <u>on</u> a customer

CULTURE & LANGUAGE If you are learning standard American English, you are justified in stumbling over its prepositions: their meanings can shift depending on context, and they have many idiomatic uses. In mastering the prepositions of standard English, you probably can't avoid memorization. But you can help yourself by memorizing related groups, such as the following.

At, in, **or** *on* **in expressions of time**

- Use *at* before actual clock time: *at 8:30.*
- Use *in* before a month, year, century, or period: *in April, in 2007, in the twenty-first century, in the next month.*
- Use *on* before a day or date: *on Tuesday, on August 3, on Labor Day.*

At, in, **or** *on* **in expressions of place**

- Use *at* before a specific place or address: *at the school, at 511 Iris Street.*
- Use *in* before a place with limits or before a city, state, country, or continent: *in the house, in a box, in Oklahoma City, in China, in Asia.*

■ Use *on* to mean "supported by" or "touching the surface of": *on the table, on Iris Street, on page 150.*

For or *since* in expressions of time

■ Use *for* before a period of time: *for an hour, for two years.*

■ Use *since* before a specific point in time: *since 1999, since Friday.*

A dictionary of English as a second language is the best source for the meanings of prepositions; see the recommendations on page 537. In addition, some references focus on prepositions. See, for instance, volume 1 (*Verbs with Prepositions and Particles*) of the *Oxford Dictionary of Current Idiomatic English.*

Fox, *Focus on Editing: A Grammar Workbook for Advanced Writers* (White Plains: Longman, 1992), and Appendix C of Alan Meyers, *Writing with Confidence,* 8th ed. (New York: Longman, 2006).

EXERCISE 38.5   Using prepositions in idioms

Insert the preposition that correctly completes each idiom in the following sentences. Consult the box on the previous page or a dictionary as needed. (You can do this exercise online at *ablongman.com/littlebrown.*)

Example:

I disagree _____ many feminists who say women should not be homemakers.

I disagree with many feminists who say women should not be homemakers.

1. As Mark and Lana waited _____ the justice of the peace, they seemed oblivious _____ the other people in the lobby.
2. But Mark inferred _____ Lana's glance at a handsome man that she was no longer occupied _____ him alone.
3. Angry _____ Lana, Mark charged her _____ not loving him enough to get married.
4. Impatient _____ Mark's childish behavior, Lana disagreed _____ his interpretation of her glance.
5. They decided that if they could differ so violently _____ a minor incident, they should part _____ each other.

ANSWERS: EXERCISE 38.5

1. As Mark and Lana waited for the justice of the peace, they seemed oblivious to [or of] the other people in the lobby.
2. But Mark inferred from Lana's glance at a handsome man that she was no longer occupied by him alone.
3. Angry with Lana, Mark charged her with not loving him enough to get married.
4. Impatient at Mark's childish behavior, Lana disagreed with his interpretation of her glance.
5. They decided that if they could differ so violently over a minor incident, they should part from each other.

38d   Using figurative language

Figurative language (or a **figure of speech**) departs from the literal meanings (the denotations) of words, usually by comparing very different ideas or objects:

Literal	As I try to write, I can think of nothing to say.
Figurative	As I try to write, my mind is a slab of black slate.

Imaginatively and carefully used, figurative language can capture meaning more precisely and feelingly than literal language.

COLLABORATIVE LEARNING

FIGURATIVE CLICHES

Have students brainstorm commonplace figures of speech like those listed in the text (others might include "I was sick as a dog," "you lie like a rug," "he eats like a horse") and list them on the board. Ask students to work in small groups to identify the figurative connection implied in each saying, and then to substitute a fresher or more accurate image to convey a similar idea.

Figurative language is commonplace in speech. Having *slept like a log*, you may get up to find it *raining cats and dogs*. But the rapid exchange of speech leaves little time for inventiveness, and most figures of daily conversation, like those above, are worn and hackneyed. Writing gives you time to reject the tired figure and to search out fresh, concrete words and phrases.

The two most common figures of speech are the simile and the metaphor. Both compare two things of different classes, often one abstract and the other concrete. A **simile** makes the comparison explicit and usually begins with *like* or *as:*

> Whenever we grow, we tend to feel it, as a young seed must feel the weight and inertia of the earth when it seeks to break out of its shell on its way to becoming a plant. —Alice Walker

> To hold America in one's thoughts is like holding a love letter in one's hand—it has so special a meaning. —E. B. White

Instead of stating a comparison, a **metaphor** implies it, omitting such words as *like* or *as:*

> I cannot and will not cut my conscience to fit this year's fashions. —Lillian Hellman

> A school is a hopper into which children are heaved while they are young and tender; therein they are pressed into certain standard shapes and covered from head to heels with official rubber stamps. —H. L. Mencken

Two other figures of speech are personification and hyperbole. **Personification** treats ideas and objects as if they were human:

> The economy consumes my money and gives me little in return.

> I could hear the whisper of snowflakes, nudging each other as they fell.

Hyperbole deliberately exaggerates:

> She appeared in a mile of billowing chiffon, flashing a rhinestone as big as an ostrich egg.

> He yelled so loud that his voice carried to the next county.

To be successful, figurative language must be fresh and unstrained, calling attention not to itself but to the writer's meaning. One kind of figurative language gone wrong is the **mixed metaphor,** in which the writer combines two or more incompatible figures. Since metaphors often generate visual images in the reader's mind, a mixed metaphor can be laughable:

> Mixed   Various thorny problems that we try to sweep under the rug continue to bob up all the same.

To revise a mixed metaphor, follow through consistently with just one image:

Improved   Various thorny problems that we try to weed out continue to thrive all the same.

EXERCISE 38.6   Analyzing figurative language

Identify each figure of speech in the following sentences as a simile or a metaphor, and analyze how it adds to the writer's meaning. (You can do this exercise online at *ablongman.com/littlebrown*.)

1. A distant airplane, a delta wing out of nightmare, made a gliding shadow on the creek's bottom that looked like a stingray crossing upstream.   —Annie Dillard
2. Her roots ran deep into the earth, and from those roots she drew strength enough to hold still against all the forces of chance and disorder.   —N. Scott Momaday
3. As a member of the winning team (the graduating class of 1940) I had outdistanced unpleasant sensations by miles. I was headed for the freedom of open fields.   —Maya Angelou
4. All artists quiver under the lash of adverse criticism.
                                                          —Catherine Drinker Bowen
5. Every writer, in a roomful of writers, wants to be the best, and the judge, or umpire, or referee is soon overwhelmed and shouted down like a chickadee trying to take charge of a caucus of crows.
                                                                    —James Thurber

EXERCISE 38.7   Using figurative language

Invent appropriate figurative language of your own (simile, metaphor, hyperbole, or personification) to describe each scene or quality below, and use the figure in a sentence. (You can do this exercise online at *ablongman.com/littlebrown*.)

> *Example:*
> The attraction of a lake on a hot day
> The small waves <u>like fingers beckoned</u> us irresistibly.

1. The sound of a kindergarten classroom
2. People waiting in line to buy tickets to a rock concert
3. The politeness of strangers meeting for the first time
4. A streetlight seen through dense fog
5. The effect of watching television for ten hours straight

38e   Using fresh, not trite, expressions

Trite expressions, or **clichés,** are phrases so old and so often repeated that they have become stale. They include the following:

acid test	beyond the shadow of a doubt
add insult to injury	brought back to reality
better late than never	cold, hard facts

ANSWERS: EXERCISE 38.6

1. *A delta wing out of nightmare* is a metaphor. *Like a stingray crossing upstream* is a simile. Both convey the menace of an airplane and its shadow.
2. *Her roots ran deep into the earth* and *from those roots she drew strength* are both metaphors establishing the person's indomitability.
3. *Outdistanced unpleasant sensations* and *headed for the freedom of open fields* are both metaphors equating Angelou's sense of release with the runner's freedom.
4. *Lash of adverse criticism* is a metaphor that makes clear the words' power to hurt.
5. The judge is like a *chickadee* and the roomful of writers is like a *caucus of crows*—two similes that convey the judge's powerlessness in the face of the writers' bombast.

ANSWERS: EXERCISE 38.7

Individual response.

cool as a cucumber	point with pride
crushing blow	ripe old age
easier said than done	shoulder the burden
face the music	smart as a whip
flat as a pancake	sneaking suspicion
green with envy	sober as a judge
hard as a rock	stand in awe
heavy as lead	strong as an ox
hit the nail on the head	thin as a rail
hour of need	tired but happy
ladder of success	tried and true
moving experience	untimely death
needle in a haystack	wise as an owl

Besides these old phrases, stale writing may also depend on fashionable words that are losing their effect: for instance, *lifestyle, enhance, excellent, fantastic,* and *caring.*

Many of these expressions were once fresh and forceful, but constant use has dulled them. They, in turn, will dull your writing by suggesting that you have not thought about what you are saying and have resorted to the easiest phrase.

Clichés may slide into your drafts while you are trying to express your meaning. In editing, then, be wary of any expression you have heard or used before. Substitute fresh words of your own or restate the idea in plain language.

Trite	A healthful lifestyle enhances your ability to go for the gold, allows you to enjoy life to the fullest, and helps you live to a ripe old age.
Revised	Living healthfully helps you perform well, enjoy life thoroughly, and live long.

EXERCISE 38.8   Revising: Trite expressions

Revise the following sentences to eliminate trite expressions. (You can do this exercise online at *ablongman.com/littlebrown*.)

Example:

The basketball team had almost seized victory, but it faced the test of truth in the last quarter of the game.

The basketball team seemed about to win, but the real test came in the last quarter of the game.

1. The disastrous consequences of the war have shaken the small nation to its roots.
2. Prices for food have shot sky high, and citizens have sneaking suspicions that others are making a killing on the black market.
3. Medical supplies are so few and far between that even civilians who are as sick as dogs cannot get treatment.

COLLABORATIVE LEARNING

CLICHÉ HUNTING

Have students work in small groups to scan each other's drafts for trite expressions or clichés. (For this exercise, students might work in groups of three or four to scan each paper, circle possible clichés, and then hand the paper to the next person in the group.) Each group should then consider the circled expressions and decide if they are appropriate to the context or could be replaced by fresher or more accurate expressions.

COLLABORATIVE LEARNING

Have students complete Exercise 38.8 individually and then discuss their responses in small groups. Encourage groups to discuss the effects of the substitutions on the meaning of each sentence, and have them report their findings to the class. You might have each group follow up on this exercise by scanning samples of their own work for trite expressions in preparation for revision.

TRANSPARENCY MASTER 38.3

ANSWERS: EXERCISE 38.8

Possible answers

1. These disasters of the war have shaken the small nation severely.
2. Prices for food have risen markedly, and citizens suspect that others are profiting on the black market.
3. Medical supplies are so scarce that even very sick civilians cannot get treatment.

4. With most men fighting or injured or killed, women have had to
bite the bullet and bear the men's burden in farming and manufacturing.
5. Last but not least, the war's heavy drain on the nation's pocket-
book has left the economy in a shambles.

4. With most men fighting or injured or killed, women have had to <u>take the men's places</u> in farming and manufacturing.
5. <u>Finally</u>, the war's <u>high cost</u> has <u>destroyed the nation's economy</u>.

CHAPTER 39

Writing Concisely

Concise writing makes every word count. Conciseness is not the same as mere brevity: detail and originality should not be cut along with needless words. Rather, the length of an expression should be appropriate to the thought.

You may find yourself writing wordily when you are unsure of your subject or when your thoughts are tangled. It's fine, even necessary, to stumble and grope while drafting. But you should straighten out your ideas and eliminate wordiness during revision and editing.

Note Any grammar and style checker will identify at least some wordy structures, such as repeated words, weak verbs, passive voice, and *there is* and *it is* constructions. But a checker can't identify all potentially wordy structures, nor can it tell you whether a structure is appropriate for your ideas.

CULTURE LANGUAGE As you'll see in the examples that follow, wordiness is not a problem of incorrect grammar. A sentence may be perfectly grammatical but still contain unneeded words that interfere with your idea.

39a Focusing on the subject and verb

Using the subjects and verbs of your sentences for the key actors and actions will reduce words and emphasize important ideas. (See pp. 384–86 for more on this topic.)

http://www.ablongman.com/littlebrown ▶

Visit the companion Web site for more help and additional exercises on writing concisely.

mycomplab 2.0

Please visit MyCompLab at *www.mycomplab.com* for more on the writing process.

HIGHLIGHTS

Eliminating unnecessary words is a task almost as difficult as choosing the right word. Students often revert to very simple sentence structures when they begin to cut flab from their sentences. You'll have to help them see that lean sentences can still be complex sentences. This chapter can help show your students techniques to achieve conciseness: strengthening subjects and verbs; cutting empty words; cutting excess repetition; reducing or combining sentences, clauses, and phrases; eliminating expletives; and rewriting jargon.

A WRITER'S PERSPECTIVE

A good word is like a good tree whose roots are firmly fixed and whose top is in the sky.
—THE KORAN 14.24

RESOURCES AND IDEAS

Connors, Robert J. "The Erasure of the Sentence." *College Composition and Communication* 52:1 (2001): 96–128. Argues for the efficacy of pedagogy that uses sentence-based rhetorics.

COMPANION WEB SITE

See page IAE-59 for companion Web site content description.

COLLABORATIVE LEARNING

CUTTING WORDS

Before your students hand in their essays, ask them to cut a specific number of words (ten to fifteen for a start) without harming the meaning. This approach can work with paragraphs as well and makes a good small-group activity.

COMPUTER ACTIVITY

THE LARD FACTOR

Richard Lanham in *Revising Prose* (4th ed., New York: Longman, 1999) uses this equation to calculate the "lard factor" of unnecessary words in any piece of writing:

# of words cut from original ÷
# of words in original =
% of lard in original

Lanham argues that as much as 40 percent of any piece of writing may be lard; this estimate emphasizes the need to revise for unnecessary words. Ask students to revise sample passages of published writing or one another's work and calculate the lard factor to test this argument. Students working on computers can use the Word Count function of their word processor to estimate the "lard factor" in a longer piece.

Ways to achieve conciseness

Wordy (87 words)

The highly pressured nature of critical-care nursing is due to the fact that the patients have life-threatening illnesses. Critical-care nurses must have possession of steady nerves to care for patients who are critically ill and very sick. The nurses must also have possession of interpersonal skills. They must also have medical skills. It is considered by most health-care professionals that these nurses are essential if there is to be improvement of patients who are now in critical care from that status to the status of intermediate care.

Focus on subject and verb, and cut or shorten empty words and phrases.
Avoid nouns made from verbs.
Cut unneeded repetition.
Combine sentences.
Change passive voice to active voice.
Eliminate *there is* constructions.
Cut unneeded repetition, and reduce clauses and phrases.

Concise (37 words)

Critical-care nursing is highly pressured because the patients have life-threatening illnesses. Critical-care nurses must possess steady nerves and interpersonal and medical skills. Most health-care professionals consider these nurses essential if patients are to improve to intermediate care.

Wordy   The reason why most of the country shifts to daylight savings time is that winter days are much shorter than summer days.

Concise   Most of the country shifts to daylight savings time because winter days are much shorter than summer days.

Focusing on subjects and verbs will also help you avoid several other causes of wordiness (also discussed further on pp. 384–86):

Nouns made from verbs

Wordy   The occurrence of the winter solstice, the shortest day of the year, is an event occurring about December 22.

Concise   The winter solstice, the shortest day of the year, occurs about December 22.

Weak verbs

Wordy   The earth's axis has a tilt as the planet is in orbit around the sun so that the northern and southern hemispheres are alternately in alignment toward the sun.

Concise   The earth's axis tilts as the planet orbits the sun so that the northern and southern hemispheres alternately align toward the sun.

Passive voice

Wordy   During its winter the northern hemisphere <u>is tilted</u> farthest away from the sun, so the nights <u>are made</u> longer and the days <u>are made</u> shorter.

Concise   During its winter the northern hemisphere <u>tilts</u> away from the sun, <u>making</u> the nights longer and the days shorter.

See also pages 302–03 on changing the passive voice to the active voice, as in the example above.

39b Cutting or shortening empty words and phrases

Empty words and phrases walk in place, gaining little or nothing in meaning. When you cut or shorten them, your writing will move faster and work harder.

Many empty phrases can be cut entirely:

all things considered	in a manner of speaking
as far as I'm concerned	in my opinion
for all intents and purposes	last but not least
for the most part	more or less

Wordy   <u>As far as I am concerned</u>, discrimination against women still exists in medicine <u>for all intents and purposes</u>.

Revised   Discrimination against women still exists in medicine.

Other empty words can be cut along with some words around them:

angle	character	kind	situation
area	element	manner	thing
aspect	factor	nature	type
case	field		

Wordy   The <u>type</u> of large expenditures on advertising that manufacturers must make is a very important <u>aspect</u> of the cost of detergents.

Concise   Manufacturers' large advertising expenditures increase the cost of detergents.

Still other empty phrases can be reduced from several words to a single word:

For	Substitute
at all times	always
at the present time	now
at this point in time	now
in today's society	now
in the nature of	like
for the purpose of	for
in order to	to
until such time as	until

Have students complete Exercise 39.1 individually and then work in small groups to compare their responses. As a follow-up exercise, ask each group to create an overly wordy paragraph. Have groups exchange paragraphs and revise them.

ANSWERS: EXERCISE 39.1

Possible answers

1. *Gerrymandering* means redrawing the lines of a voting district to benefit a particular party or ethnic group.
2. The name refers to Elbridge Gerry, who as governor of Massachusetts in 1812 redrew voting districts in Essex County.
3. On the map one new district looked like a salamander.
4. Upon seeing the map, a critic of Governor Gerry's administration cried out, "Gerrymander!"
5. Now a political group may try to change a district's voting pattern by gerrymandering to exclude rival groups' supporters.

For	Substitute
for the reason that	because
due to the fact that	because
because of the fact that	because
by virtue of the fact that	because
despite the fact that	although
in the event that	if
by means of	by
in the final analysis	finally

Wordy   At this point in time, the software is expensive due to the fact that it has no competition.

Revised   The software is expensive now because it has no competition.

EXERCISE 39.1   **Revising: Subjects and verbs; empty words and phrases**

Revise the following sentences to achieve conciseness by focusing on subjects and verbs and by cutting or reducing empty words and phrases. (You can do this exercise online at *ablongman.com/littlebrown*.) See also page 386 for an additional exercise in focusing on subjects and verbs.

    Example:

    I made college my destination because of many factors, but most of all because of the fact that I want a career in medicine.

    I came to college mainly because I want a career in medicine.

1. *Gerrymandering* refers to a situation in which the lines of a voting district are redrawn so that a particular party or ethnic group has benefits.
2. The name is a reference to the fact that Elbridge Gerry, the governor of Massachusetts in 1812, redrew voting districts in Essex County.
3. On the map one new district was seen to resemble something in the nature of a salamander.
4. Upon seeing the map, a man who was for all intents and purposes a critic of Governor Gerry's administration cried out, "Gerrymander!"
5. At the present time, changes may be made in the character of a district's voting pattern by a political group by gerrymandering to achieve the exclusion of rival groups' supporters.

39c   Cutting unnecessary repetition

Planned repetition and restatement can make writing more coherent (p. 83) or emphatic (pp. 390–91). But unnecessary repetition weakens sentences:

Wordy	Many unskilled workers <u>without training in a particular job</u> are unemployed <u>and do not have any work</u>.
Concise	Many unskilled workers are unemployed.

The use of one word two different ways within a sentence is confusing:

Confusing	Preschool instructors play a <u>role</u> in the child's understanding of male and female <u>roles</u>.
Clear	Preschool instructors contribute to the child's understanding of male and female roles.

The simplest kind of useless repetition is the phrase that says the same thing twice. In the following examples, the unneeded words are underlined:

biography <u>of his life</u>	<u>habitual</u> custom
circle <u>around</u>	important [basic] essentials
consensus <u>of opinion</u>	large <u>in size</u>
continue <u>on</u>	puzzling <u>in nature</u>
cooperate <u>together</u>	repeat <u>again</u>
few <u>in number</u>	return <u>again</u>
final <u>completion</u>	revert <u>back</u>
frank and honest <u>exchange</u>	square [round] <u>in shape</u>
the future <u>to come</u>	<u>surrounding</u> circumstances

CULTURE LANGUAGE Phrases like those above are redundant because the main word already implies the underlined word or words. The repetition is not emphatic but tedious. A dictionary will tell you what meanings a word implies. *Assassinate,* for instance, means "murder someone well known," so the following sentence is redundant: *Julius Caesar was <u>assassinated and killed</u>.*

EXERCISE 39.2 Revising: Unnecessary repetition

Revise the following sentences to achieve conciseness. Concentrate on eliminating repetition and redundancy. (You can do this exercise online at *ablongman.com/littlebrown.*)

Example:

Because the circumstances surrounding the cancellation of classes were murky and unclear, the editor of the student newspaper assigned a staff reporter to investigate and file a report on the circumstances.

Because the circumstances <u>leading to</u> the cancellation of classes were <u>unclear</u>, the editor of the student newspaper assigned a <u>staffer</u> to investigate and <u>report the story</u>.

1. Some Vietnam veterans coming back to the United States after their tours of duty in Vietnam had problems readjusting again to life in America.

LEGAL BILINGUALISM

Sometimes, particularly in legal language, phrases contain paired synonyms like *last will and testament.* These go back to the time immediately after the Norman Conquest of England in 1066, when English law proceedings were conducted in both French and English, and the words had to be clear to speakers of either language.

CULTURE LANGUAGE

DISCURSIVE VERSUS CONCISE STYLES

ESL students may have difficulty being concise if their native language is more discursive, or if repetition is encouraged in their native language. Reinforce with these students that English is an extremely compact language compared to many. Remind them as well that as their English vocabulary increases, they will have more words at their disposal to use in place of longer, more descriptive phrases.

COLLABORATIVE LEARNING

When students have completed Exercise 39.2 individually, have them compare their responses in small groups and discuss the effects of their varying strategies.

ANSWERS: EXERCISE 39.2

Possible answers

1. <u>After their tours of duty,</u> some Vietnam veterans had problems <u>readjusting to</u> life in America.

2. Afflicted with post-traumatic stress disorder, <u>some veterans had</u> trouble holding jobs
and maintaining relationships.
3. Some who <u>used drugs</u> in Vietnam could not
break their <u>habits</u> after they <u>returned to the</u>
United States.
4. The few veterans who committed crimes
and violent acts gained so much <u>notoriety</u>
<u>that</u> many Americans thought all veterans
were <u>crazy</u>.
5. As a <u>result</u> of such <u>stereotyping</u>, Vietnam-
era <u>veterans are protected by</u> antidiscrimination laws.

2. Afflicted with post-traumatic stress disorder, a psychological disor-
der that sometimes arises after a trauma, some veterans had psychological problems that caused them to have trouble holding
jobs and maintaining relationships.
3. Some who used to use drugs in Vietnam could not break their
drug habits after they returned back to the United States.
4. The few veterans who committed crimes and violent acts gained
so much notoriety and fame that many Americans thought all veterans were crazy, insane maniacs.
5. As a result of such stereotyping of Vietnam-era veterans, veterans
are included in the same antidiscrimination laws that protect
other victims of discrimination.

39d Reducing clauses to phrases, phrases to single words

Modifiers—subordinate clauses, phrases, and single words—
can be expanded or contracted depending on the emphasis you
want to achieve. (See pp. 254–58 on phrases and clauses and 398–401
on working with modifiers.) When editing your sentences, consider
whether any modifiers can be reduced without loss of emphasis or
clarity:

Wordy   The Channel Tunnel, <u>which runs between Britain and</u>
<u>France,</u> bores through <u>a bed of solid chalk that is twenty-</u>
<u>three miles across.</u>

Concise   The Channel Tunnel <u>between Britain and France</u> bores
through <u>twenty-three miles of solid chalk.</u>

39e Eliminating *there is* and *it is* constructions

You can postpone the sentence subject with the words *there is*
(*there are, there was, there were*) and *it is* (*it was*). (See p. 264.) These
constructions can be useful to emphasize the subject (as when introducing it for the first time) or to indicate a change in direction.
But often they just add words and create limp substitutes for more
vigorous sentences:

Wordy   <u>There were</u> delays and cost overruns that plagued construction of the Channel Tunnel. <u>It is the expectation of investors</u>
to earn profits at last, now that <u>there are trains passing</u> daily
through the tunnel.

Concise   Delays and cost overruns plagued construction of the Channel Tunnel. <u>Investors expect</u> to earn profits at last, now that
<u>trains pass</u> daily through the tunnel.

39f Combining sentences

Often the information in two or more sentences can be combined into one tight sentence:

Wordy   An unexpected problem with the Channel Tunnel is stowaways. The stowaways are mostly illegal immigrants. They are trying to smuggle themselves into England. They cling to train roofs and undercarriages.

Concise   An unexpected problem with the Channel Tunnel is stowaways, mostly illegal immigrants who are trying to smuggle themselves into England by clinging to train roofs and undercarriages.

A number of exercises in this handbook give you practice in sentence combining. For a list, see "Sentence combining" in the Index.

39g Rewriting jargon

Jargon can refer to the special vocabulary of any discipline or profession (see p. 513). But it has also come to describe vague, inflated language that is overcomplicated, even incomprehensible. When it comes from government or business, we call it *bureaucratese*.

Jargon   The weekly social gatherings stimulate networking by members of management from various divisions, with the aim of developing contacts and maximizing the flow of creative information.

Translation   The weekly parties give managers from different divisions a chance to meet and to share ideas.

EXERCISE 39.3   Revising: Conciseness

Rewrite each passage below into a single concise sentence, using the techniques described in this chapter. (You can do this exercise online at *ablongman.com/littlebrown*.)

Example:
He was taking some exercise in the park. Then several thugs were suddenly ahead of him in his path.

He was exercising [or jogging or strolling] in the park when several thugs suddenly loomed in his path.

1. Chewing gum was originally introduced to the United States by Antonio López de Santa Anna. He was the Mexican general.
2. After he had been defeated by the Texans in 1845, the general, who was exiled, made the choice to settle in New York.
3. A piece of chicle had been stashed by the general in his baggage. Chicle is the dried milky sap of the Mexican sapodilla tree.

REVISING STUDENT PARAGRAPHS

As a revision exercise, ask students to work in groups to identify paragraphs from their own work that seem jargon laden or that simply "don't sound right." You might display several of these sample paragraphs (using an overhead projector or networked computers and screen-sharing applications) to provide the basis for a class discussion on effective condensing strategies. Some teachers ask for paragraphs from student volunteers or only use examples from other classes because they fear that in-class attention to weaker paragraphs may discourage the students whose work is selected. However, if such discussions of student work are presented constructively, and if all students take a turn, students seem to benefit most from working on their own texts.

COLLABORATIVE LEARNING

When students have completed Exercise 39.4 individually, have them discuss their responses in pairs, noting places where they used different strategies to achieve conciseness. As a follow-up to this exercise you might use several student revisions as the basis for a general discussion of the point at which a productive revision for conciseness might become reductive of the meaning of the passage.

ANSWERS: EXERCISE 39.3
Possible answers

1. The Mexican general Antonio López de Santa Anna introduced chewing gum to the United States.
2. After defeat by the Texans in 1845, the exiled general chose to settle in New York.
3. In his baggage the general had stashed a piece of chicle, the dried milky sap of the Mexican sapodilla tree.
4. Santa Anna's friend Thomas Adams brought more of this resin into the country, planning to make rubber.
5. When the plan failed, Adams got a much more successful idea from the way General Santa Anna used the resin, as a gum for chewing.

4. There was more of this resin brought into the country by Santa Anna's friend Thomas Adams. Adams had a plan to make rubber.
5. The plan failed. Then the occasion arose for Adams to get a much more successful idea on the basis of the use to which the resin was put by General Santa Anna. That is, Adams decided to make a gum that could be chewed.

EXERCISE 39.4   Revising: Conciseness

Make the following passage as concise as possible. Be merciless. (You can do this exercise online at *ablongman.com/littlebrown*.)

At the end of a lengthy line of reasoning, he came to the conclusion that the situation with carcinogens [cancer-causing substances] should be regarded as similar to the situation with the automobile. Instead of giving in to an irrational fear of cancer, we should consider all aspects of the problem in a balanced and dispassionate frame of mind, making a total of the benefits received from potential carcinogens (plastics, pesticides, and other similar products) and measuring said total against the damage done by such products. This is the nature of most discussions about the automobile. Instead of responding irrationally to the visual, aural, and air pollution caused by automobiles, we have decided to live with them (while simultaneously working to improve on them) for the benefits brought to society as a whole.

TRANSPARENCY MASTER 39.2

ANSWERS: EXERCISE 39.4

Possible answers

After <u>much thought</u>, he <u>concluded</u> that carcinogens <u>could be treated like automobiles</u>. Instead of giving in to <u>a fear</u> of cancer, we should <u>balance</u> the benefits we receive from potential carcinogens (<u>such as</u> plastic <u>and pesticides</u>) against the damage <u>they do. Similarly</u>, instead of responding irrationally to <u>the pollution</u> caused by automobiles, we have decided to live with them <u>and enjoy their benefits</u> while simultaneously working to improve them.

mycomplab 2.0

Please visit MyCompLab at *www.mycomplab.com* for more on the writing process.

HIGHLIGHTS

Chapter 40 describes the information provided in a good dictionary, summarizes briefly the characteristics of several widely used desk dictionaries (in print and electronic form) and some unabridged and specialized dictionaries, and explains a typical entry from an abridged dictionary to help students find information. Although the unavoidable accumulation of detail in such a brief chapter makes dense reading in places, the chapter is organized for easy reference so that you and your students can single out the most useful sections. Throughout the handbook, students are urged to consult a dictionary for answers to particular questions—the right prepo-

COMPANION WEB SITE

See page IAE-59 for companion Web site content description.

CHAPTER 40

Using Dictionaries

A dictionary can answer most questions about words. This chapter shows you how to choose a dictionary that suits your purpose and how to read a dictionary without difficulty.

40a   Choosing a dictionary

1   Abridged dictionaries

Abridged dictionaries are the most practical for everyday use. Often called desk dictionaries because of their convenient size, they

http://www.ablongman.com/littlebrown ▶

Visit the companion Web site for links to online dictionaries and other language resources.

usually list 150,000 to 200,000 words and concentrate on fairly common words and meanings.

The American Heritage College Dictionary
Merriam-Webster's Collegiate Dictionary
The Random House Webster's College Dictionary
Webster's New World College Dictionary

Most of these dictionaries are available both in print and on CD-ROM, and some are available online (visit *ablongman.com/ littlebrown* for links). Your computer may include a dictionary that you can customize with words or meanings it does not cover. With an electronic dictionary, as with a print dictionary, you can look up words as you write, checking spellings, meanings, synonyms, and other information.

CULTURE LANGUAGE If English is not your first language, you probably should have a dictionary prepared especially for ESL students in addition to one of the dictionaries listed above. The dictionaries listed below give much more information on such matters as count versus noncount nouns, prepositions with verbs and adjectives, and other concerns of ESL students.

COBUILD English Language Dictionary
Longman Dictionary of Contemporary English. Longman Dictionary of American English is the American version.
Oxford Advanced Learner's Dictionary. Oxford Dictionary of American English is the American version.

2 Unabridged dictionaries

Unabridged dictionaries are the most scholarly and comprehensive of all dictionaries, sometimes consisting of many volumes. They emphasize the history of words and the variety of their uses. An unabridged dictionary is useful when you are studying a word in depth, reading or writing about the literature of another century, or looking for a quotation containing a particular word. The following unabridged dictionaries are available at most libraries.

The Oxford English Dictionary, 20 volumes
The Random House Webster's Unabridged Dictionary
Webster's Third New International Dictionary of the English Language

3 Special dictionaries

Special dictionaries limit their attention to a single class of word (for example, slang, engineering terms, abbreviations), to a single kind of information (synonyms, usage, word origins), or to a specific subject (African American culture, biography, history). (See Chapters 50–53 for lists of subject dictionaries in various academic disciplines.)

sition to use in an idiom, the usage status of a word, the forms of an irregular verb, and the like. No other supplementary reference will serve students as well as a good desk dictionary, as long as they know how to use it and do so. Students should be required, whenever practicable, to purchase one of the standard desk dictionaries.

CULTURE LANGUAGE

For ESL students, the most difficult part of learning English is learning idiomatic usage. In addition to the dictionaries cited here, the following sourcebooks may be particularly helpful to these students:

Cowie, A. P., and R. Mackin. *The Oxford Dictionary of Current Idiomatic English.* 2 vols. London: Oxford UP, 1975.

Freeman, William. *A Concise Dictionary of English Idioms.* Boston: Writer, 1976.

Whitford, Harold C., and Robert J. Dixson. *Handbook of American Idioms and Idiomatic Usage.* New York: Regents, 1973.

A WRITER'S PERSPECTIVE

"When I use a word," Humpty Dumpty said, "it means just what I choose it to mean—neither more nor less."

"The question is," said Alice, "whether you can make words mean so many different things."

"The question is," said Humpty Dumpty, "which is to be master—that's all."

—LEWIS CARROLL, *Through the Looking-Glass*

A BRIEF HISTORY OF DICTIONARIES

1721—Nathaniel Bailey's *Universal Etymological Dictionary of the English Language,* the first dictionary to resemble the dictionaries we have at present.

1755—Samuel Johnson's two-volume *Dictionary.*

1828—Noah Webster's *American Dictionary of the English Language.*

1857–1928—The compilation of the most comprehensive dictionary, the twelve-volume (now sixteen-volume) *Oxford English Dictionary.*

DICTIONARY VARIATION

Dictionaries come in many varieties, and students should be encouraged to examine the different kinds. For instance, the inexpensive dictionaries found in grocery store racks are probably less comprehensive than collegiate work demands. Dictionaries published more than a decade ago may lack up-to-date words or usage information.

CHOOSING A DICTIONARY

To unify the answers that students give to the exercises in this chapter, select a dictionary suitable to your class's needs and make it a required text for your course. Some teachers allow students to bring in any one from a selected list of dictionaries, and then make their varied answers to exercises part of the ongoing class discussion.

USAGE EXPERTS

Some dictionary publishers ask panels of usage experts about the acceptability of certain terms. Though the recommendations are usually helpful, students should understand that these are still opinions, and they may not apply to the situations in the student's own writing. Some dictionaries also censor the terms they include, omitting vulgar words or other offensive terms.

JUDGING STYLE

Some good references on usage judgments are found in Harvey A. Daniels, *Famous Last Words: The American Language Crisis Reconsidered* (Urbana: NCTE, 1983) and Dennis Baron, *Grammar and Good Taste* (New Haven: Yale UP, 1982). See also Walter Nash's *An Uncommon Tongue: The Uses and Resources of English* (New

■ For guidance on English usage

Usage guides provide help with commonly confused and misused words, phrases, idioms, and other matters:

R. W. Burchfield, *The New Fowler's Modern English Usage*
Bryan A. Garner, *A Dictionary of Modern American Usage*

CULTURE LANGUAGE *Practical English Usage,* by Michael Swan, is a usage guide prepared especially for nonnative speakers of English.

■ For the origins of words

Dictionaries of etymology, or word history, explain how words have evolved:

Charles T. Onions et al., eds., *Oxford Dictionary of English Etymology*
Eric Partridge, *Origins: A Short Etymological Dictionary of Modern English*

■ For information on slang

Dictionaries of slang explain the histories and meanings of conversational expressions. They can make entertaining reading.

J. E. Lighter, ed., *Historical Dictionary of American Slang*
Harold Wentworth and Stuart Berg Flexner, *Dictionary of American Slang*

■ For information about synonyms

A thesaurus like *Roget's* provides extensive lists of words with related meanings. A dictionary of synonyms like *Webster's* contains discussions and illustrations of shades of meaning.

Robert L. Chapman, ed., *Roget's International Thesaurus*
Webster's New Dictionary of Synonyms

Many electronic dictionaries include a thesaurus as well, and some thesauruses are available independently on CD-ROM or online. (Visit *ablongman.com/littlebrown* for links.) With an online thesaurus, you can easily find synonyms and insert them into your documents. Take care with any thesaurus, ensuring that you know the meaning of a synonym before you use it.

40b Working with a dictionary's contents

Dictionaries use abbreviations and symbols to squeeze a lot of information into a relatively small book. This system of condensed information may at first seem difficult to read. But all dictionaries include in their opening pages detailed information on the arrangement of entries, pronunciation symbols, and abbreviations.

Here is a fairly typical entry, from *Merriam-Webster's Collegiate Dictionary.* The labeled parts are discussed on the pages that follow.

Dictionary entry for *reckon*

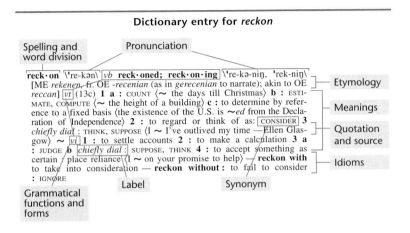

Spelling and word division
Pronunciation
Etymology
Meanings
Quotation and source
Idioms
Grammatical functions and forms
Label
Synonym

■ Spelling and word division

The small initial letters for *reckon* indicate that it is not normally capitalized. (In contrast, *Franklin stove* is capitalized in *Merriam-Webster's* because *Franklin* is a proper noun.)

The centered period in **reck·on** shows the division into syllables. If you are breaking a word at the end of a line, follow the dictionary's division of the word into syllables. For a hyphenated compound word, such as *cross-question*, a dictionary shows the hyphen as part of the spelling: **cross-ques·tion.**

Dictionaries provide any acceptable variant spellings of a word at the beginning of an entry. For the word *dexterous, Merriam-Webster's* has "**dex·ter·ous** *or* **dex·trous.**"

■ Pronunciation

In *Merriam-Webster's* the pronunciation appears between reversed slashes (\\). The stressed syllable is preceded by an accent mark ('re-kən).

Dictionaries use symbols to indicate how to pronounce a word because the alphabet itself does not record all the sounds in the language. (Listen, for example, to the different sounds of *a* in only three words: *far, make,* and *answer.*) Most dictionaries provide a key to the pronunciation symbols at least every other page.

■ Grammatical functions and forms

Dictionaries give helpful information about a word's functions and forms. The *Merriam-Webster's* entry for *reckon* shows the word to be a verb (*vb*), with the past tense and past participle *reckoned* and the present participle *reckoning,* and with both transitive (*vt*) and intransitive (*vi*) meanings. (For the definitions of these terms, see p. 238.)

York: Routledge, 1992) for a broader study of usage, including dictionaries, punctuation, paraphrase, and parody.

MISSPELLER'S DICTIONARY

Frequently, students complain that they cannot spell words correctly because they do not know how to find them in the dictionary without being able to spell them. Using a thesaurus is one solution to this problem. A second solution is to have students create a misspeller's dictionary based on the words incorrectly spelled in their papers. This dictionary would include all the variant spellings as well as the correct spellings for the misspelled words. The activity will use the efforts of both the good and the fair spellers and can be "published" for future use in classes that involve writing. The misspeller's dictionary can also be placed online so that students can add material to it each semester.

ELECTRONIC SPELLING AIDS

Some students use electronic spelling aids to check their spelling. Because such machines have limited memories, they may not include all the words students use in their writing. Students need to understand the limits of such machines. Since more and more students rely on spell-checking computer software, you might also remind students that spelling checkers are not context sensitive and are not usually case sensitive. However, students can add words to customize and enlarge their electronic dictionaries.

READING THE WHOLE ENTRY

Remind students to read the entire entry, not just the spelling, when they look up a word. Many dictionaries include the word *alot,* for instance, defining it as "a common misspelling for *a lot.*" Students who see *alot* in the list of entries may assume it's correct if they don't actually read the definition. In addition, careful reading of all the meanings of a word often reveals symbolism and intentions frequently missed by an assumed understanding of a word's usage.

ANALOGOUS FORMS

Students often invent new forms for words by analogy; thus, from *drink, drank, drunk* they create *think, thank, thunk.* Such irregular forms exist in a few verbs surviving from Anglo-Saxon times. However, since the time of the Norman

Conquest of England in 1066, every new verb that has entered the English language has followed the regular verb pattern of *-d* or *-ed* ending for the past tense and the past participle.

A DICTIONARY WITH PLENTY OF SYNONYMS

Of the many dictionaries that include synonyms with their definitions of words, the *Funk & Wagnall's New Standard College Dictionary* gives more extensive coverage than most. The *Funk & Wagnall's* includes paragraphs on synonyms that define the various shades of meaning.

ADDITIONAL SAMPLE ENTRY

From Webster's *New Universal Unabridged Dictionary*, 1983.

reck'ŏn, v.t.; reckoned, pt., pp.; reckoning, ppr. (ME. *rekenen, reknen,* from AS, *gerecenian,* to explain. A derivative verb allied to AS, *gereccan,* to rule, direct, order, explain, tell; D. *rekenen:* Ice. *reikna,* to reckon.)

1. to count; to figure up; to compute; to calculate. I *reckoned* above two hundred and fifty on the outside of the church. —ADDISON
2. to consider as; to regard as being. He was *reckoned* among the transgressors. —LUKE XXII. 37
3. to make account or reckoning of. (Obs.) Faith was *reckoned* to Abraham for righteousness. —ROM. IV. 9
4. to judge; to consider; to estimate.
5. to suppose, think, or believe; as, *I reckon* it will rain. (Colloq. or Dial.)

reck'ŏn, v.i.,

1. to count up; to figure
2. to depend; to rely (with *on*)
3. to settle an account
4. to pay a penalty; to be answerable (Obs.) If they fail in their bounden duty, they shall reckon for it one day. —SANDERSON

Most dictionaries provide not only the principal forms of regular and irregular verbs but also the plural forms of irregular nouns and the *-er* and *-est* forms of adjectives and adverbs. An adjective or adverb without *-er* and *-est* forms in the dictionary requires the addition of *more* and *most* to show comparison (see pp. 322–23).

■ Etymology

Dictionaries provide the **etymology** of a word (its history) to indicate its origin and the evolution of its meanings and forms. The dictionary can compress much information about a word into a small space through symbols, abbreviations, and different type fonts. An explanation of these systems appears in the dictionary's opening pages. *Merriam-Webster's* traces *reckon* back most recently to Middle English (ME) and then further back to Old English (OE). The notation "(13c)" before the first definition indicates that the first recorded use of *reckon* to mean "count" occurred in the thirteenth century. When seeking the etymology of a word, be sure to read the entire history, not just the most recent event.

■ Meanings

Dictionaries divide the general meaning of a word into particular meanings on the basis of how the word is or has been actually used. They arrange a word's meanings differently, either in order of their appearance in the language, earliest first, or in order of their frequency of use, most common first. (*Merriam-Webster's* follows the former practice.) To learn your dictionary's arrangement, consult its opening pages. Then read through a word's entire entry before settling on the meaning that fits the context of what you're reading or writing.

The *Merriam-Webster's* entry for *reckon* ends with two uses of the word in idiomatic expressions (*reckon with* and *reckon without*). These phrases are defined because, as with all idioms, their meanings cannot be inferred simply from the words they consist of (see p. 523).

■ Labels

Dictionaries apply labels to words or to particular meanings that have a special status or use.

Style labels restrict a word or one of its meanings to a particular level of usage:

- *Slang:* words or meanings inappropriate in writing except for a special effect, such as *crumb* for "a worthless or despicable person."
- *Informal* or *colloquial:* words or meanings appropriate for informal writing but not formal writing, such as *great* to mean "very good," as in *a great movie.*

- *Nonstandard* or *substandard:* words or meanings inappropriate for standard American English, such as *ain't.*
- *Vulgar* or *vulgar slang:* words or meanings considered offensive in speech and writing, such as profanity.
- *Poetic* or *literary:* words or meanings used only in poetry or the most formal writing, such as *eve* for *evening* and *o'er* for *over.*

Subject labels tell us that a word or one of its meanings has a special use in a discipline or profession. In its entry for *relaxation,* for instance, *American Heritage* presents specialized meanings with the subject labels *physiology, physics,* and *mathematics.*

Region labels indicate that a particular spelling, pronunciation, or meaning of a word is not national but limited to an area. A regional difference may be indicated by the label *dialect. Merriam-Webster's* labels as dialect (*dial*) the uses of *reckon* to mean "suppose" or "think" (as in *I reckon I'll do that*). More specific region labels may designate areas of the United States or other countries.

Time labels indicate words or their meanings that the language, in evolving, has discarded. *Obsolete* designates words or meanings that are no longer used; *archaic* designates words or meanings that are out of date but are used occasionally.

See pages 510–17 for further discussion of levels of usage and their appropriateness in your writing.

Synonyms

Synonyms are words whose meanings are approximately the same, such as *small* and *little. Merriam-Webster's* defines *reckon* with some words in small capital letters (COUNT, ESTIMATE, CONSIDER, and so on). These are both synonyms and cross-references, in that each word may be looked up in its alphabetical place. Some dictionaries devote separate paragraphs to words with many synonyms.

Illustrative quotations

Dictionaries are made by collecting quotations showing actual uses of words in all kinds of speech and writing. Some of these quotations, or others that the dictionary makers invent, may appear in the dictionary's entries as illustrations of how a word may be used. Five such quotations illustrate uses of *reckon* in the *Merriam-Webster's* entry (in these quotations, ~ stands for the word being illustrated).

EXERCISE 40.1   Using a dictionary

Consult your dictionary on five of the following words. First find out whether your dictionary lists the oldest or the most common meanings first in its entries. Then, for each word, write down (*a*) the division into syllables, (*b*) the pronunciation, (*c*) the grammatical functions and forms, (*d*) the etymology, (*e*) each meaning, and (*f*) any special uses

---

to reckon for: to be answerable or responsible for.

to reckon with: (a) to balance accounts and make a settlement with; (b) to take into consideration.

ADDITIONAL EXAMPLES OF DICTIONARY LABELS

Slang—novel and colorful expressions that reflect a group's special experiences and set it off from others. Examples: *cool, into, funky, awesome.*

Colloquial—words and expressions appropriate to everyday spoken language and to informal writing. Example: Housework often takes a *bite* out of my weekend.

Regional—words and expressions used only in some geographical locations. For example, one kind of sandwich may be called a *hero,* a *hoagie,* a *submarine,* a *torpedo,* or a *grinder,* depending upon which region you are in.

Nonstandard—words and grammatical forms frequently used in speech but never acceptable in standard written English. Examples: *nowheres, hisself, throwed, could of,* and *hadn't ought.*

Obsolete or archaic—words or meanings of words that we never or rarely use but that appear in older documents and literature still read today. Examples: *enwheel* ("to encircle") and *belike* ("perhaps").

RESOURCES AND IDEAS

For more synonyms and antonyms, students can consult Norman Lewis, *The New Roget's Thesaurus of the English Language in Dictionary Form* (New York: Putnam, 1978).

ANSWERS: EXERCISE 40.1

The answers to the exercise in Chapter 40 will depend on the dictionary being consulted. Each one uses a different notation system, and in some cases they disagree over syllable divisions. Thus, no answers are provided.

indicated by labels. Finally, use the word in at least two sentences of your own. (You can do this exercise online at *ablongman.com/littlebrown*.)

1. depreciation	4. manifest	7. potlatch	10. toxic
2. secretary	5. assassin	8. plain (*adj.*)	11. steal
3. grammar	6. astrology	9. ceremony	12. obelisk

mycomplab 2.0

Please visit MyCompLab at *www.mycomplab.com* for more on the writing process.

HIGHLIGHTS

No quick formula exists for turning poor spellers into good ones. Students with serious spelling problems may need systematic instruction in spelling, which, like systematic instruction in vocabulary, is rarely allowed by course time. You may want to refer such students to a skills center on campus or, if there are no such services, to a good spelling workbook. There are, however, activities and assignments that can help. Most students can improve their spelling markedly by learning and actually applying the limited number of standard rules, by maintaining a record of words that repeatedly cause them trouble, and by faithfully practicing brief groups of words from a spelling list. Such advice, though uninspired and unoriginal, does produce real improvement if a student can be persuaded to follow it, perhaps with the added reminder that lack of confidence in spelling distracts the student from more important matters in writing.

A WRITER'S PERSPECTIVE

Everyone misspells occasionally, usually because of carelessness or simple failure to observe closely. Good spelling requires an eye for detail.
—WILLIAM F. IRMSCHER

It's a poor imagination that can only think of one way to spell a word.
—ATTRIBUTED TO MARK TWAIN

COMPANION WEB SITE

See page IAE-59 for companion Web site content description.

CHAPTER **41**

Spelling and the Hyphen

English spelling is difficult, even for some very experienced and competent writers. You can train yourself to spell better, and this chapter will help you. But you can also improve instantly by acquiring three habits:

- **Carefully proofread all of your writing.**
- **Be suspicious of your spellings.**
- **Check a dictionary *every time* you doubt a spelling.**

Note A spelling checker can help you find and track spelling errors in your papers. But its usefulness is limited, mainly because it can't spot the common error of confusing words with similar spellings, such as *now/not*, *to/too*, *their/they're/there*, and *principal/ principle*. See pages 60–61 for more on spelling checkers.

41a Recognizing typical spelling problems

Spelling well involves recognizing situations that commonly lead to misspelling: pronunciation can mislead you in several ways; different forms of the same word may have different spellings; and some words have more than one acceptable spelling.

http://www.ablongman.com/littlebrown ▶

Visit the companion Web site for more help and an additional exercise on spelling and the hyphen.

1 Being wary of pronunciation

In English, unlike some other languages, pronunciation of words is an unreliable guide to their spelling. The same letter or combination of letters may have different sounds in different words. (Say aloud these different ways of pronouncing the letters *ough: tough, dough, cough, through, bough.*) In addition, some words contain letters that are not pronounced clearly or at all, such as the *ed* in *asked*, the silent *e* in *swipe*, or the unpronounced *gh* in *tight*.

Pronunciation is a particularly unreliable guide in spelling **homonyms,** words pronounced the same though they have different spellings and meanings: *great/grate, to/too/two.* Some commonly confused homonyms and near-homonyms, such as *accept/except*, are listed below. (See p. 551 for tips on how to use spelling lists.)

Words commonly confused

accept (to receive)
except (other than)

affect (to have an influence on)
effect (result)

all ready (prepared)
already (by this time)

allude (to refer to indirectly)
elude (to avoid)

allusion (indirect reference)
illusion (erroneous belief or
   perception)

ascent (a movement up)
assent (agreement)

bare (unclothed)
bear (to carry, or an animal)

board (a plane of wood)
bored (uninterested)

born (brought into life)
borne (carried)

brake (stop)
break (smash)

buy (purchase)
by (next to)

capital (the seat of a government)
capitol (the building where a
   legislature meets)

cite (to quote an authority)
sight (the ability to see)
site (a place)

desert (to abandon)
dessert (after-dinner course)

discreet (reserved, respectful)
discrete (individual or distinct)

elicit (to bring out)
illicit (illegal)

eminent (well known)
imminent (soon to happen)

fair (average, or lovely)
fare (a fee for transportation)

forth (forward)
fourth (after *third*)

gorilla (a large primate)
guerrilla (a kind of soldier)

hear (to perceive by ear)
here (in this place)

heard (past tense of *hear*)
herd (a group of animals)

hole (an opening)
whole (complete)

its (possessive of *it*)
it's (contraction of *it is* or *it has*)

lead (heavy metal)
led (past tense of *lead*)

lessen (to make less)
lesson (something learned)

meat (flesh)
meet (encounter)

(continued)

A WRITER'S PERSPECTIVE _____

The French don't care what they do, actually, so long as they pronounce it properly.
   —ALAN JAY LERNER, *My Fair Lady*

TRANSPARENCY MASTER 41.1

COLLABORATIVE LEARNING

HOMONYM HOMEWORK

Sometimes the quickest way to learn distinctions in spelling between words that sound the same is to memorize the words and their definitions. The context in which the word is encountered can also become a kind of mnemonic (in addition to deliberately constructed mnemonics such as "the principal is a pal"). Divide the text's list of homonyms among the class and have students work in groups to create exercise questions by posing one-sentence contexts for several of the words on this list, as for example: "I [*accept/except*] the package from the UPS driver." The compiled exercise questions might be assigned as a quiz either in a subsequent class or on the network.

A WRITER'S PERSPECTIVE _____

The educated Southerner has no use for an r, except at the beginning of a word.
   —MARK TWAIN, *Life on the Mississippi*

RESOURCES AND IDEAS

Some good references on teaching spelling are:

Brown, Alan S. "Encountering Misspellings and Spelling Performance: Why Wrong Isn't Right." *Journal of Educational Psychology* 80 (1988): 488–94. Brown analyzes the psychology of student misspellings.

Chomsky, Carol. "Reading, Writing, and Phonology." *Harvard Educational Review* 40 (1970): 287–309. Chomsky ties problems with spelling and word recognition to problems with hearing and distinguishing certain morphemes.

Clapp, Ouida, ed. *Teaching the Basics—Really!* Urbana: NCTE, 1977. The book includes several chapters on teaching spelling.

Clark, Roger, and I. Y. Hashimoto. "A Spelling Program for College Students." *Teaching English in the Two-Year College* 11 (1984): 34–38. The authors describe activities to help students improve spelling over the course of a semester.

Dobie, Ann R. "Orthographical Theory and Practice; or, How to Teach Spelling." *Journal of Basic Writing* 5 (1986): 41–48. Responses to this article appear in both the 1987 and 1988 volumes of this journal.

Irmscher, William F. *The Holt Guide to English.* 3rd ed. New York: Holt, 1981. Ch. 12. Irmscher offers concrete diagnostics and remedies for common spelling problems.

Sensenbaugh, Roger. "Spelling Instruction and the Use of Word Lists." *Composition Chronicle* 6.3 (April 1993): 8–9. The author describes techniques for helping students become better spellers.

Taylor, Karl, and Ede Kidder. "The Development of Spelling Skills from First Grade through Eighth Grade." *Written Communication* 5 (April 1988): 222–44. The authors tie spelling development to cognitive development and show instructors how to diagnose and help correct spelling problems.

EXTRA EXAMPLES

In addition to the words listed in the text, words that can be expressed by different forms, depending on the intended meaning, might also give students trouble. For example, *a while* is

Words commonly confused

(continued)

no (the opposite of *yes*)
know (to be certain)

passed (past tense of *pass*)
past (after, or a time gone by)

patience (forbearance)
patients (persons under medical care)

peace (the absence of war)
piece (a portion of something)

persecute (to oppress, to harass)
prosecute (to pursue, to take legal action against)

plain (clear)
plane (a carpenter's tool, or an airborne vehicle)

presence (the state of being at hand)
presents (gifts)

principal (most important, or the head of a school)
principle (a basic truth or law)

rain (precipitation)
reign (to rule)
rein (a strap for controlling an animal)

raise (to build up)
raze (to tear down)

right (correct)
rite (a religious ceremony)
write (to make letters)

road (a surface for driving)
rode (past tense of *ride*)

scene (where an action occurs)
seen (past participle of *see*)

seam (a junction)
seem (appear)

stationary (unmoving)
stationery (writing paper)

straight (unbending)
strait (a water passageway)

their (possessive of *they*)
there (opposite of *here*)
they're (contraction of *they are*)

to (toward)
too (also)
two (following *one*)

waist (the middle of the body)
waste (discarded material)

weak (not strong)
week (Sunday through Saturday)

weather (climate)
whether (*if*, or introducing a choice)

which (one of a group)
witch (a sorcerer)

who's (contraction of *who is* or *who has*)
whose (possessive of *who*)

your (possessive of *you*)
you're (contraction of *you are*)

2 Distinguishing between different forms of the same word

Spelling problems may occur when forms of the same word have different spellings, as in the following examples.

Verbs and nouns

Verb	Noun	Verb	Noun
advise	advice	enter	entrance
describe	description	marry	marriage
speak	speech	omit	omission

Nouns and adjectives

Noun	Adjective	Noun	Adjective
comedy	comic	height	high
courtesy	courteous	Britain	British
generosity	generous		

Irregular verbs

begin, began, begun   know, knew, known

break, broke, broken   ring, rang, rung

Irregular nouns

child, children   shelf, shelves

goose, geese   tooth, teeth

mouse, mice   woman, women

Other differences

four, forty   thief, theft

3 Using preferred spellings   CULTURE LANGUAGE

Many words have variant spellings as well as preferred spellings. Often the variant spellings listed in an American dictionary are British spellings.

American	British
color, humor	colour, humour
theater, center	theatre, centre
canceled, traveled	cancelled, travelled
judgment	judgement
realize	realise

41b   Following spelling rules

Misspelling is often a matter of misspelling a syllable rather than the whole word. The following general rules focus on troublesome syllables, with notes for the occasional exceptions.

1 Distinguishing between *ie* and *ei*

Words like *believe* and *receive* sound alike in the second syllable, but the syllable is spelled differently. Use the familiar jingle to distinguish between *ie* and *ei*:

I before *e*, except after *c*, or when pronounced "ay" as in *neighbor* and *weigh*.

i before *e*	believe	bier	hygiene
	grief	thief	friend

often written *awhile*. The two most frequently miswritten expressions, however, are *a lot* (commonly written "*alot*") and *all right* (commonly written "*alright*").

SPELLING PATRIOTICALLY

The confusion between British and American spellings can be blamed on American patriots at the time of the Revolutionary War. Led by Noah Webster, a group of linguistic patriots set out to make America linguistically independent of Britain and invented the American spellings of these common words.

LEARNING THE RULES

Most spelling rules have only a few exceptions, so it's often easier for students to memorize the short list of exceptions and assume that any other word follows the normal pattern. An excellent list of these deviations appears in the *National Labor Relations Board Style Manual* (Washington, DC: Government Printing Office, 1984).

ANSWERS: EXERCISE 41.1

1.	brief	9.	leisurely
2.	deceive	10.	achieve
3.	receipt	11.	patience
4.	seize	12.	pierce
5.	foreign	13.	height
6.	priest	14.	freight
7.	grievance	15.	feint
8.	fiend	16.	sieve

ei after *c*	ceiling	conceive	perceive
	receive	deceit	conceit
ei sounded as "ay"	neighbor	weight	eight
	sleigh	freight	vein

Exceptions In some words an *ei* combination neither follows *c* nor is pronounced "ay." These words include *either, neither, foreign, forfeit, height, leisure, weird, seize,* and *seizure.* This sentence might help you remember some of them: *The weird foreigner neither seizes leisure nor forfeits height.*

EXERCISE 41.1 **Distinguishing between *ie* and *ei***

Insert *ie* or *ei* in the words below. Check doubtful spellings in a dictionary. (You can do this exercise online at *ablongman.com/littlebrown.*)

1. br__f	5. for__gn	9. l__surely	13. h__ght
2. dec__ve	6. pr__st	10. ach__ve	14. fr__ght
3. rec__pt	7. gr__vance	11. pat__nce	15. f__nt
4. s__ze	8. f__nd	12. p__rce	16. s__ve

2 Keeping or dropping a final *e*

Many words end with an unpronounced or silent *e: move, brave, late, rinse.* Drop the final *e* when adding an ending that begins with a vowel:

advise + able = advisable	surprise + ing = surprising
force + ible = forcible	guide + ance = guidance

Keep the final, silent *e* when adding an ending that begins with a consonant:

battle + ment = battlement	care + ful = careful
accurate + ly = accurately	like + ness = likeness

Exceptions The silent *e* is sometimes retained before an ending beginning with a vowel. It is kept when *dye* becomes *dyeing,* to avoid confusion with *dying.* It is kept to prevent mispronunciation of words like *shoeing* (not *shoing*) and *mileage* (not *milage*). And the final *e* is often retained after a soft *c* or *g,* to keep the sound of the consonant soft rather than hard:

courageous	changeable	noticeable
outrageous	manageable	embraceable

The silent *e* is also sometimes *dropped* before an ending beginning with a consonant, when the *e* is preceded by another vowel:

argue + ment = argument
due + ly = duly
true + ly = truly

EXERCISE 41.2 Keeping or dropping a final *e*

Combine the following words and endings, keeping or dropping a final *e* as necessary to make correctly spelled words. Check doubtful spellings in a dictionary. (You can do this exercise online at *ablongman.com/littlebrown*.)

1. malice + ious
2. love + able
3. service + able
4. retire + ment
5. sue + ing
6. virtue + ous
7. note + able
8. battle + ing
9. suspense + ion

ANSWERS: EXERCISE 41.2

1. malicious
2. lovable *or* loveable
3. serviceable
4. retirement
5. suing
6. virtuous
7. notable
8. battling
9. suspension

3 Keeping or dropping a final *y*

Words ending in *y* often change their spelling when an ending is added to them. Change the final *y* to an *i* when it follows a consonant:

beauty, beauties
folly, follies

worry, worried
merry, merrier

supply, supplies
deputy, deputize

But keep the *y* when it follows a vowel, when the ending is *-ing*, or when it ends a proper name:

day, days
obey, obeyed

cry, crying
study, studying

May, Mays
Minsky, Minskys

EXERCISE 41.3 Keeping or dropping a final *y*

Combine the following words and endings, changing or keeping a final *y* as necessary to make correctly spelled words. Check doubtful spellings in a dictionary. (You can do this exercise online at *ablongman.com/littlebrown*.)

1. imply + s
2. messy + er
3. apply + ing
4. delay + ing
5. defy + ance
6. say + s
7. solidify + s
8. Murphy + s
9. supply + ed

ANSWERS: EXERCISE 41.3

1. implies
2. messier
3. applying
4. delaying
5. defiance
6. says
7. solidifies
8. Murphys
9. supplied

4 Doubling consonants

Whether to double a word's final consonant depends first on the number of syllables in the word. In one-syllable words, double the final consonant when a single vowel precedes the final consonant. Otherwise, don't double the consonant.

slap, slapping
tip, tipping

pair, paired
park, parking

In words of more than one syllable, double the final consonant when a single vowel precedes the final consonant *and* the consonant ends a stressed syllable once the ending is added. Otherwise, don't double the consonant.

refer, referring
begin, beginning
occur, occurrence

refer, reference
relent, relented
despair, despairing

ANSWERS: EXERCISE 41.4

1. repairing
2. admittance
3. benefited
4. shopped
5. concealed

6. allotted
7. dripping
8. declaimed
9. paralleling

IRREGULAR PLURALS

There are a few irregular plurals in English; most survive from Anglo-Saxon (for example, *child/children*) or are borrowed from other languages (*alumnus/alumni*). All native English nouns added since the Norman Conquest of England in 1066 have been regular, using the *-s* or *-es* suffixes to form the plural.

EXERCISE 41.4 Doubling consonants

Combine the following words and endings, doubling final consonants as necessary to make correctly spelled words. Check doubtful spellings in a dictionary. (You can do this exercise online at *ablongman.com/littlebrown.*)

1. repair + ing
2. admit + ance
3. benefit + ed
4. shop + ed
5. conceal + ed
6. allot + ed
7. drip + ing
8. declaim + ed
9. parallel + ing

5 Attaching prefixes

Adding a prefix such as *dis*, *mis*, and *un* does not change the spelling of a word. When adding a prefix, do not drop a letter from or add a letter to the original word:

uneasy	anti-intellectual	defuse	misstate
unnecessary	disappoint	de-emphasize	misspell
antifreeze	dissatisfied	misinform	

(See also p. 555 for when to use hyphens with prefixes: *prehistory* versus *ex-student*.)

6 Forming plurals

■ **Nouns**

Most nouns form plurals by adding *s* to the singular form:

boy, boys	table, tables
carnival, carnivals	Murphy, Murphys

Some nouns ending in *f* or *fe* form the plural by changing the ending to *ve* before adding *s:*

leaf, leaves	wife, wives
life, lives	yourself, yourselves

Singular nouns ending in *s*, *sh*, *ch*, or *x* form the plural by adding *es:*

kiss, kisses	church, churches
wish, wishes	Jones, Joneses

(Notice that verbs ending in *s*, *sh*, *ch*, or *x* form the third-person singular in the same way. *Taxes* and *lurches* are examples.)

Nouns ending in *o* preceded by a vowel usually form the plural by adding *s:*

ratio, ratios	zoo, zoos

Nouns ending in *o* preceded by a consonant usually form the plural by adding *es:*

hero, heroes	tomato, tomatoes

Exceptions Some very common nouns form irregular plurals:

child, children   man, men
mouse, mice   woman, women

Some English nouns that were originally Italian, Greek, Latin, or French form the plural according to their original language:

analysis, analyses   datum, data
basis, bases   medium, media
beau, beaux   phenomenon, phenomena
crisis, crises   piano, pianos
criterion, criteria   thesis, theses

A few such nouns may form irregular or regular plurals: for instance, *index, indices, indexes*; *curriculum, curricula, curriculums*. The regular plural is more contemporary.

CULTURE LANGUAGE Noncount nouns do not form plurals, either regularly (with an added *s*) or irregularly. Examples of noncount nouns include *equipment, courage,* and *wealth.* (See p. 327.)

▓ Compound nouns

Form plurals of compound nouns in one of two ways. Add *s* to the last word when the component words are roughly equal in importance, whether or not they are hyphenated:

city-states   breakthroughs
painter-sculptors   bucket seats

Add *s* to a noun combined with other parts of speech:

fathers-in-law   passersby

Note, however, that most modern dictionaries give the plural of *spoonful* as *spoonfuls.*

EXERCISE 41.5 Forming plurals

Make the correct plural of each of the following singular words. Check doubtful spellings in a dictionary. (You can do this exercise online at *ablongman.com/littlebrown.*)

1. pile   5. mile per hour   9. Bales   13. thief
2. donkey   6. box   10. cupful   14. goose
3. beach   7. switch   11. libretto   15. hiss
4. summary   8. sister-in-law 12. video   16. appendix

ANSWERS: EXERCISE 41.5

1. piles   9. Baleses
2. donkeys   10. cupfuls
3. beaches   11. librettos *or* libretti
4. summaries   12. videos
5. miles per hour 13. thieves
6. boxes   14. geese
7. switches   15. hisses
8. sisters-in-law 16. appendices *or* appendixes

41c Developing spelling skills

The following techniques can help you improve your spelling. In addition, do not overrely on your computer's spelling checker (see pp. 60–61).

CAREFUL PROOFREADING

Many of the errors made with spelling can be avoided through careful proofreading. Two proofreading techniques that force the writer to read more slowly and carefully are (1) reading the essay aloud and (2) reading the essay backward, from the last sentence to the first.

1 Editing and proofreading carefully

If spelling is a problem for you, give it high priority while editing your writing (p. 48) and again while proofreading, your last chance to catch misspelled words (p. 58). Reading a draft backward, word by word, can help you spot mistakes such as switched or omitted letters in words you know. Because the procedure forces you to consider each word in isolation, it can also highlight spellings you may be less sure of. A sense of uncertainty is crucial in spotting and correcting spelling errors, even for good spellers who make relatively few errors. Listen to your own uncertainty, and let it lead you to the dictionary.

2 Using a dictionary

How can you look up a word you can't spell? Start by guessing at the spelling and looking up your guess. If that doesn't work, pronounce the word aloud to come up with other possible spellings, and look them up. Unless the word is too specialized to be included in your dictionary, trial and error will eventually pay off.

If you're using a spelling checker, it may do the guessing for you by providing several choices for misspelled words. But you may still need to check a dictionary to verify your choice.

3 Pronouncing carefully

Careful pronunciation is not always a reliable guide to spelling (see p. 543), but it can keep you from misspelling words that are often mispronounced. For example:

athletics (*not* atheletics)	laboratory (*not* labratory)
disastrous (*not* disasterous)	library (*not* libary)
environment (*not* envirnment)	lightning (*not* lightening)
frustrate (*not* fustrate)	mischievous (*not* mischievious)
government (*not* goverment)	nuclear (*not* nucular)
height (*not* heighth)	recognize (*not* reconize)
history (*not* histry)	representative (*not* representive)
irrelevant (*not* irrevelant)	strictly (*not* stricly)

MAKING WORDS YOUR OWN

One way to help students remember words they look up in a dictionary is to have them highlight the word, jot it down on an ongoing list, and then use it in a sentence of their own. At a later date, students should go back to their "dictionary list" and try to use each word in a one-sentence context. If students keep up this practice throughout a semester they will have added those words to their working vocabularies.

4 Tracking and analyzing your errors

Keep a list of the words marked "misspelled" or "spelling" or "sp" in your papers. This list will contain hints about your particular spelling problems, such as confusing *affect* and *effect* or forming plurals incorrectly. (If you need help analyzing the list, consult your writing instructor.) The list will also provide a personalized study guide, a focus for your efforts to spell better.

5 Using mnemonics

Mnemonics (pronounced with an initial *n* sound) are techniques for assisting your memory. The *er* in *letter* and *paper* can remind you that *stationery* (meaning "writing paper") has an *er* near the end; *stationary* with an *a* means "standing in place." Or the word *dome* with its long *o* sound can remind you that the building in which the legislature meets is spelled *capitol*, with an *o*. The *capital* city is spelled with *al* like *Albany*, the capital of New York. If you identify the words you have trouble spelling, you can think of your own mnemonics, which may work better for you than someone else's.

6 Studying spelling lists

Learning to spell commonly misspelled words will reduce your spelling errors. For general improvement, work with the following list of commonly misspelled words. Study only six or seven words at a time. If you are unsure of the meaning of a word, look it up in a dictionary and try using it in a sentence. Pronounce the word out loud, syllable by syllable, and write the word out. (The list of similar-sounding words on pp. 543–44 should be considered an extension of the one below.)

absence	amateur	beginning
abundance	among	belief
acceptable	amount	believe
accessible	analysis	beneficial
accidentally	analyze	benefited
accommodate	angel	boundary
accomplish	annual	breath
accumulate	answer	Britain
accuracy	apology	bureaucracy
accustomed	apparent	business
achieve	appearance	
acknowledge	appetite	calculator
acquire	appreciate	calendar
across	appropriate	caricature
actually	approximately	carrying
address	argument	cede
admission	arrest	ceiling
adolescent	ascend	cello
advice	assassinate	cemetery
advising	assimilation	certain
against	assistance	changeable
aggravate	associate	changing
aggressive	atheist	characteristic
all right	athlete	chief
all together	attendance	chocolate
allegiance	audience	choose
almost	average	chose
a lot		climbed
already	bargain	coarse
although	basically	column
altogether	because	coming

commercial
commitment
committed
committee
competent
competition
complement
compliment
conceive
concentrate
concert
condemn
conquer
conscience
conscious
consistency
consistent
continuous
controlled
controversial
convenience
convenient
coolly
course
courteous
criticism
criticize
crowd
cruelty
curiosity
curious
curriculum

deceive
deception
decide
decision
deductible
definitely
degree
dependent
descend
descendant
describe
description
desirable
despair
desperate
destroy
determine
develop

device
devise
dictionary
difference
dining
disagree
disappear
disappoint
disapprove
disastrous
discipline
discriminate
discussion
disease
disgusted
dissatisfied
distinction
divide
divine
division
doctor
drawer

easily
ecstasy
efficiency
efficient
eighth
either
eligible
embarrass
emphasize
empty
enemy
entirely
entrepreneur
environment
equipped
especially
essential
every
exaggerate
exceed
excellent
exercise
exhaust
exhilarate
existence
expense
experience
experiment

explanation
extremely

familiar
fascinate
favorite
February
fiery
finally
forcibly
foreign
foresee
forty
forward
friend
frightening
fulfill

gauge
generally
ghost
government
grammar
grief
guarantee
guard
guidance

happily
harass
height
heroes
hideous
humorous
hungry
hurriedly
hurrying
hypocrisy
hypocrite

ideally
illogical
imaginary
imagine
imitation
immediately
immigrant
incidentally
incredible
independence
independent

individually
inevitably
influential
initiate
innocuous
inoculate
insistent
integrate
intelligence
interest
interference
interpret
irrelevant
irresistible
irritable
island

jealousy
judgment

kindergarten
knowledge

laboratory
leisure
length
library
license
lieutenant
lightning
likelihood
literally
livelihood
loneliness
loose
lose
luxury
lying

magazine
maintenance
manageable
marriage
mathematics
meant
medicine
miniature
minor
minutes
mirror
mischievous

missile
misspelled
morale
morals
mortgage
mournful
muscle
mysterious

naturally
necessary
neighbor
neither
nickel
niece
ninety
ninth
noticeable
nuclear
nuisance
numerous

obstacle
occasion
occasionally
occur
occurrence
official
omission
omit
omitted
opinion
opponent
opportunity
opposite
ordinary
originally

paid
panicky
paralleled
parliament
particularly
peaceable
peculiar
pedal
perceive
perception
performance
permanent
permissible

persistence
personnel
perspiration
persuade
persuasion
physical
physiology
physique
pitiful
planning
playwright
pleasant
poison
politician
pollute
possession
possibly
practically
practice
prairie
precede
preference
preferred
prejudice
preparation
prevalent
primitive
privilege
probably
procedure
proceed
process
professor
prominent
pronunciation
psychology
purpose
pursue
pursuit

quandary
quantity
quarter
questionnaire
quiet
quizzes

realistically
realize
really
rebel

RESOURCES AND IDEAS

Gere, Anne Ruggles. "Alternatives to Tradition in Teaching Spelling." In *Teaching the Basics— Really!* Ed. Ouida H. Clapp. Urbana: NCTE, 1977. 100–03. Gere proposes the use of individualized word lists and classroom games and also the teaching of phoneme-grapheme correspondences and word division.

Harris, Muriel. "The Big Five: Individualizing Improvement in Spelling." In *Teaching the Basics—Really!* Ed. Ouida H. Clapp. Urbana: NCTE, 1977. 104–07. Harris suggests making students aware of their habitual problems deriving from homophones, pronunciation, doubled consonants, word roots, and the schwa.

McClellan, Jane. "A Clinic for Misspellers." *College English* 40 (1978): 324–29. McClellan suggests using several kinds of word lists and frequent drills to bring about improvement.

rebelled
recede
receipt
receive
recognize
recommend
reference
referred
relief
relieve
religious
remembrance
reminisce
renown
repetition
representative
resemblance
resistance
restaurant
rhyme
rhythm
ridiculous
roommate

sacrifice
sacrilegious
safety
satellite
scarcity
schedule
science
secretary
seize
separate
sergeant
several
sheriff
shining

shoulder
siege
significance
similar
sincerely
sophomore
source
speak
specimen
speech
sponsor
strategy
strength
strenuous
stretch
strict
strictly
studying
succeed
successful
sufficient
summary
superintendent
supersede
suppress
surely
surprise
suspicious

teammate
technical
technique
temperature
tendency
than
then
thorough
though

throughout
together
tomatoes
tomorrow
tragedy
transferred
truly
twelfth
tyranny

unanimous
unconscious
undoubtedly
unnecessary
until
usable
usually

vacuum
vegetable
vengeance
vicious
villain
visible

weather
Wednesday
weird
wherever
whether
wholly
woman
women
writing

yacht

THE *A-B-C* RULE

A useful rule for determining whether an adjective before a noun is compound and should be hyphenated is the *a-b-c* rule. For example, in the phrase *record-setting pace*, the first word, *record*, is term *a*. The second word, *setting*, is term *b*, and the noun being modified, *pace*, is term *c*. According to the *a-b-c* rule, if the writer can make the statement "The *c* was *a* and *b*," no hyphen is needed. If that statement is impossi-

41d Using the hyphen to form or divide words

The hyphen (-) is a mark of punctuation used either to form words or to divide them at the ends of lines.

1 Forming compound adjectives

When two or more words serve together as a single modifier before a noun, a hyphen or hyphens form the modifying words clearly into a unit:

She is a well-known actor.
The conclusions are based on out-of-date statistics.
Some Spanish-speaking students work as translators.

When the same compound adjectives follow the noun, hyphens are unnecessary and are usually left out.

The actor is well known.
The statistics were out of date.
Many students are Spanish speaking.

Hyphens are also unnecessary in compound modifiers containing an *-ly* adverb, even when these fall before the noun: *clearly defined terms; swiftly moving train.*

When part of a compound adjective appears only once in two or more parallel compound adjectives, hyphens indicate which words the reader should mentally join with the missing part:

School-aged children should have eight- or nine-o'clock bedtimes.

2 Writing fractions and compound numbers

Hyphens join the numerator and denominator of fractions and the parts of the whole numbers twenty-one to ninety-nine:

three-fourths	twenty-four
one-half	eighty-seven

3 Forming coined compounds

Writers sometimes create (coin) temporary compounds and join the words with hyphens:

Muhammad Ali gave his opponent a come-and-get-me look.

4 Attaching some prefixes and suffixes

Do not use hyphens with prefixes except as follows:

- With the prefixes *self-*, *all-*, and *ex-*: *self-control, all-inclusive, ex-student.*
- With a prefix before a capitalized word: *un-American.*
- With a capital letter before a word: *T-shirt.*
- To prevent misreading: *de-emphasize, anti-intellectual.*

The only suffix that regularly requires a hyphen is *-elect,* as in *president-elect.*

5 Eliminating confusion

If you wrote the sentence *Doonesbury is a comic strip character,* the reader might stumble briefly over your meaning. Is Doonesbury

ble, *a* and *b* must be hyphenated. Since the writer can't say "The pace was record and set-ting," *record-setting pace* needs to be hyphen-ated. The test here is similar to the one for coor-dinate adjectives in 28f-2.

a character in a comic strip or a comic (funny) character who strips? A hyphen would prevent any possible confusion: *Doonesbury is a comic-strip character.*

Adding prefixes to words can sometimes create ambiguity. *Recreation* (*creation* with the prefix *re-*) could mean either "a new creation" or "diverting, pleasurable activity." The use of a hyphen, *re-creation*, limits the word to the first meaning. Without a hyphen the word suggests the second meaning.

6 Dividing words at the ends of lines

You can avoid occasional short lines in your documents by dividing some words between the end of one line and the beginning of the next. On a word processor, you can set the program to divide words automatically at appropriate breaks (in the Tools menu, select Language and then Hyphenation). To divide words manually, follow these guidelines:

- **Divide words only between syllables**—for instance, *win-dows*, not *wi-ndows*. Check a dictionary for correct syllable breaks.
- **Never divide a one-syllable word.**
- **Leave at least two letters on the first line and three on the second line.** If a word cannot be divided to follow this rule (for instance, *a-bus-er*), don't divide it.
- **Break an electronic address only after a slash.** Do not hyphenate, because readers may preceive any added hyphens as part of the address.

ANSWERS: EXERCISE 41.6

1. Correct
2. de-escalate
3. forty-odd soldiers
4. little-known bar
5. seven-eighths
6. seventy-eight
7. happy-go-lucky
8. pre-existing
9. senator-elect
10. Correct
11. two- and six-person cars
12. ex-songwriter
13. V-shaped
14. re-educate

EXERCISE 41.6 Using hyphens in compound words

Insert hyphens as needed in the following compounds. Mark all compounds that are correct as given. Consult a dictionary as needed. (You can do this exercise online at *ablongman.com/littlebrown*.)

1. reimburse
2. deescalate
3. forty odd soldiers
4. little known bar
5. seven eighths
6. seventy eight
7. happy go lucky
8. preexisting
9. senator elect
10. postwar
11. two and six person cars
12. ex songwriter
13. V shaped
14. reeducate

PART 9

Research Writing

mycomplab

Please visit MyCompLab at *www.mycomplab.com* for more on the writing process.

HIGHLIGHTS

Many students actively dislike or fear writing research papers—either because of misconceptions about the purpose of such assignments or because of previous unpleasant or purely mechanistic experiences with research writing. As a result, you may find that some students resist this type of writing. The chapters in Part 9 show students not only how valuable and interesting research writing can be, but that it is an extension of the critical thinking, reading, and writing skills stressed in the handbook.

Part 9 offers a detailed overview of research writing, from finding information (using both electronic and print resources) to shaping it, documenting it, and presenting it according to a consistent set of standards. It includes a discussion of computer-aided research and standard reference sources and a chapter-length treatment of plagiarism.

A special feature of Part 9 is its use of the research and writing process of two students (Edward Begay and Vanessa Haley) as examples. Following Begay's and Haley's progress from beginning to end of their research process will give your students a better sense of how the strategies discussed in the handbook might be applied in actual first-year college writing projects.

Chapter 42 presents research gathering as a strategic task and offers a series of descriptions and suggestions to help students move through a research project effectively. This edition includes a new section (42d3) on annotating a working bibliography.

A WRITER'S PERSPECTIVE

Not the least part of discovery is asking the right questions.

—St. Augustine

COMPANION WEB SITE

See page IAE-59 for companion Web site content description.

CHAPTER 42

Planning a Research Project

If you've ever watched a TV or movie detective pursue a culprit, you know that research can be exciting. When an investigator has a goal in sight, the seemingly mundane work of digging through files, interviewing witnesses, and piecing together clues becomes a concentrated and enthusiastic search.

This same excitement can be yours as you conduct research in school. Honest and inquisitive research writing does demand close attention to details, but the work will not be tedious if you see the details as steadily contributing to discoveries about yourself and the world around you. As you consider what others have to say about your subject and build on that to create new knowledge, you will become an expert in your own right. You will have a significant, in-depth understanding of a subject you care about, and you will communicate that understanding to others.

Through research writing, you will also learn skills that will help you in school, in work, and in life:

- **Using the library and the Internet for research,** carefully recording information on where you find sources.
- **Analyzing and evaluating others' work.**
- **Drawing on others' work** to form, support, and extend your own opinions.
- **Practicing intellectual integrity** by presenting others' work accurately and acknowledging your sources fully.

Your investigation will be influenced by whether you are expected mainly to report, to interpret, or to analyze sources.

- In **reporting,** you survey, organize, and objectively present the available evidence about a topic.
- In **interpreting,** you examine a range of views on a topic in order to answer a question with your own conclusions.

---

http://www.ablongman.com/littlebrown ▶

Visit the companion Web site for more help and an additional exercise on planning a research project.

■ In **analyzing,** you attempt to solve a problem or answer a question through critical thinking about texts such as scholarly or literary works. (In this context, *analysis* stands for the entire process of critical reading and writing. See pp. 150–63.)

Throughout Chapters 42–46, we will follow the development of research papers by two students, Edward Begay and Vanessa Haley. Begay's work, emphasizing interpretation, receives somewhat more attention; Haley's work, emphasizing analysis, enters the discussion whenever her process differed significantly from Begay's. Both students' final papers appear in Chapter 48.

42a Starting out

With its diverse and overlapping activities, research writing demands more planning than other kinds of writing. A thoughtful plan and systematic procedures will help you anticipate your needs, schedule your time, and complete the work successfully.

1 Preparing a schedule

As soon as you receive an assignment for a research project, you can begin developing a strategy for completing it. The first step should be making a schedule that apportions the available time to the necessary work. A possible schedule appears on the next page. In it the research-writing process corresponds to the general writing process discussed in Chapters 1–3: planning or developing (steps 1–9), drafting (step 10), and revising and editing (step 11), plus the additional important stage of documenting the sources you use (steps 12–13).

2 Keeping a research journal

To keep track of your activities and ideas during research, maintain a research journal throughout the process. (See pp. 17 and 154 on journal keeping.) Make your journal portable so that you can carry it with you conveniently. Many researchers use paper notebooks or handheld or notebook computers. Some schools offer students Web log space for recording research and other learning activities.

In the research journal's dated entries, you can keep a record of sources you consult, the leads you want to pursue, any dead ends you reach, and, most important, your thoughts about sources, leads, dead ends, new directions, relationships, and anything else that strikes you. You will probably find that the very act of writing in your journal opens your mind and clarifies your thinking, making your research increasingly productive and rewarding.

RESOURCES AND IDEAS

Ford, James E., ed. *Teaching the Research Paper: From Theory to Practice, From Research to Writing.* Metuchen: Scarecrow Press, 1995. These essays address the value of teaching research papers in composition classes; models of research units and practical suggestions are included.

Lutzker, Marilyn. *Research Projects for College Students: What to Write Across the Curriculum.* Westport: Greenwood, 1988. Lutzker provides a librarian's guide to intellectually challenging projects from all disciplines.

Moulton, Margaret and Vicki Homes. "The Research Paper: A Historical Perspective." *Teaching English in the Two-Year College* 35 (May 2003): 365–373. The authors present a fascinating historical account, from the 1870s to the present, of the value and relevance of the research paper assignment.

Nelson, Jennie. "The Research Paper: A 'Rhetoric of Doing' or a 'Rhetoric of the Finished Word'?" *Composition Studies* 22 (Fall 1994): 65–75. Nelson argues that the research paper does not serve any useful educational purpose unless students understand it as a learning process.

Pelham, Fran O'Byrne. "The Research Journal: Integrating Reading, Writing, and Research." *Composition Chronicle* 6.3 (April 1993): 4–5. O'Byrne recommends using a journal to supplement typical research activities and to allow students to "research, reflect, write, and then attend recursively to these events."

Quantic, Diane. "Insights into the Research Process from Student Logs." *Journal of Teaching Writing* 6 (1986): 211–25. Quantic analyzes aspects of research projects that may cause writing anxiety or blocks and suggests ways to overcome these problems.

Strickland, James. "The Research Sequence: What to Do Before the Term Paper." *College Composition and Communication* 37 (1986): 233–36. Strickland presents a sequence moving students from opinion papers to documented research projects.

Wilson, Matthew. "Research, Expressivism and Silence." *Journal of Advanced Composition* 15 (1995): 241–60. A thought-provoking analysis of the challenges that teachers face in defining research papers, and that students face in writing them.

COLLABORATIVE LEARNING

SUPPORT FOR THE RESEARCH-PHOBIC

Some students, especially those who have never done a research project before, may have significant anxiety about their ability to undertake a research project, manage all the phases, and end up with a decent final product. It may be helpful for students to share anxieties in small groups as a way of overcoming them. Such discussions work only if there is mutual trust among members of the group, so this activity would work best with a group that has been working together regularly for a while and has had a chance to build trust.

SMART SCHEDULING

Beginning college students need help in establishing a realistic schedule. Emphasize strongly that each of the four segments in the "Scheduling steps" chart on this page truly will take about a quarter of the time. Share with them the schedule for a writing project you've recently completed, and point out the kinds of places where delays are likely to occur.

COMPUTER ACTIVITY

PUT IT ON THE CALENDAR

If students have calendar or scheduling software, they can put their research schedule in calendar format and keep it handy for easy reference. Revising the schedule becomes a matter of a few keystrokes.

NOTEKEEPING

Note cards or notebooks are fairly easy tools for inexperienced writers to use. However, some students just aren't comfortable with cards, and their research actually may suffer if they are forced to use them. If students have great trouble keeping cards, suggest that they keep their notes in their journal; the greater space may give them more freedom to compose effectively.

Scheduling steps in research writing

(See the pages in parentheses for discussion of the steps.)

Complete
by:

_____ 1. Setting a schedule and beginning a research journal (previous page)
_____ 2. Finding a researchable subject and question (below)
_____ 3. Developing a research strategy (p. 564)
_____ 4. Finding sources, both print and electronic (p. 571), and making a working bibliography (p. 567)

_____ 5. Evaluating and synthesizing sources (pp. 599, 610)
_____ 6. Mining and interacting with sources (p. 613), often using summary, paraphrase, and direct quotation (p. 617)
_____ 7. Taking steps to avoid plagiarism (p. 629)
_____ 8. Developing a thesis statement (p. 639)

_____ 9. Creating a structure (p. 640)
_____ 10. Drafting the paper (p. 643), integrating summaries, paraphrases, and direct quotations into your ideas (p. 623)

_____ 11. Revising and editing the paper (p. 645)
_____ 12. Citing sources in your text (p. 637)
_____ 13. Preparing the list of works cited (p. 637)
_____ 14. Preparing and proofreading the final manuscript (p. 646)

_____ Final paper due

Each segment marked off by a horizontal line will occupy *roughly* one-fourth of the total time. The most unpredictable segments are the first two, so get started early enough to accommodate the unexpected.

You can download this schedule from *ablongman.com/littlebrown*. Use a duplicate to plan and time the specific steps of each research project you work on.

Note The research journal is the place to track and develop your own ideas. To avoid mixing up your thoughts and those of others, keep separate notes on what your sources actually say, using one of the methods discussed on pages 615–17.

42b Finding a researchable subject and question

Before reading this section, review the suggestions given on pages 6–9 for finding and limiting an essay subject. Generally, the same procedure applies to writing any kind of research paper: begin with an assigned subject or one that interests you (perhaps one you've already written about without benefit of research), and then narrow the subject to manageable size by asking questions about it. However, selecting and limiting a subject for a research paper can present special opportunities and problems.

1 Choosing an appropriate subject

A subject for a research paper has four primary requirements, each with corresponding pitfalls:

1. **Ample sources of information are available on the subject.** Other researchers should have had a chance to produce evidence on the subject, weigh the evidence, and publish their conclusions. And the sources should be accessible.

   Avoid very recent subjects, such as a new medical discovery or a breaking story in today's newspaper.

2. **The subject encourages research in the kinds and number of sources required by the assignment.**

   Avoid (*a*) subjects that depend entirely on personal opinion and experience, such as the virtues of your hobby; and (*b*) subjects that require research in only one source, such as a straight factual biography or a how-to like "Making Lenses for Eyeglasses." (An exception to *b* is a paper in which you analyze a single work such as a novel or painting.)

3. **The subject will lead you to an assessment of sources and to defensible conclusions.** Even when a research paper is intended to persuade, the success of the argument will depend on the balanced presentation of all significant points of view.

   Avoid controversial subjects that rest entirely on belief or prejudice, such as when human life begins or why women (or men) are superior. Though these subjects may certainly be disputed, your own preconceptions could slant your research or conclusions. Further, your readers are unlikely to be swayed from their own beliefs.

Checklist for a good research subject

1. **Published sources are ample:** the subject is not so recent that other researchers will still be discovering it.
2. **Sources are diverse:** the subject is neither wholly personal nor wholly factual.
3. **Sources can be assessed objectively:** the subject is not solely a matter of belief or prejudice.
4. **Sources can be examined thoroughly** in the assigned time and length: the subject is not too broad.

TRADING SCHEDULES

After students have drafted schedules for their research projects individually, have them show their schedule to a partner, who can help to evaluate the feasibility of the project and consider how to adjust the schedule if necessary.

LIBRARIANS AS ALLIES

It's useful to work with the research librarians at your school throughout the process of planning and implementing a research course. In particular, you might consult with the librarians before students begin to generate subjects for their research papers. The librarians can tell you which subjects may have limited resources available or describe new materials they've recently acquired. This will help you guide your students in selecting workable subjects.

COMPUTER ACTIVITY

COMPUTER JOURNAL

The advantage to keeping a hard copy journal is that the student can write in it anywhere at any time. However, some students may find it easier to keep an electronic journal, particularly if they are doing a lot of their searching and source consultation on computers. Students can carry a floppy disk with their journal file and load the file whenever they want to make a journal entry.

COMPUTER ACTIVITY

SCOPE ASSESSMENT

Beginning researchers often have difficulty assessing the scope of the subject they have chosen. Ask all students to post their subject ideas to the class Web site. Then, have an online class discussion in which everyone helps to evaluate the scope of each student's subject.

TRANSPARENCY MASTER 42.2

DOUBLING UP

If students have been assigned research projects in other courses, and the instructors of those other courses don't object, permit students to work on those papers in your class or to write a separate paper for you based on the same research materials. Such dual assignments help students transfer writing skills from your classroom to other courses, and your colleagues may appreciate your helping students to write better papers in their disciplines.

COLLABORATIVE LEARNING

RESEARCH ABOUT RESEARCH

Assign teams of students to interview researchers—professors in other departments, employees of local businesses, salespeople looking for new leads, and so on. Have them ask how these researchers go about looking for and limiting subjects, what kinds of "tricks" or strategies they use, why they value research, and what rewards they get from it. In this way, students will see that research is a valued activity outside the writing classroom as well as in it. Each team should report its findings to the entire class.

COMPUTER ACTIVITY

E-MAIL BUDDIES

E-mail can be an extremely productive forum, particularly in freeing students from the anxiety of formal writing. You can promote ongoing e-mail conversations by asking students to designate one or two e-mail partners in the class and encouraging them to write to each other once a week about their progress with the research project. You might occasionally assign an exercise that the e-mail partners should also copy to you, such as "Tell your e-mail partners exactly what you want to argue in your paper," or "Describe one of the sources you've found to your e-mail partners in a way that makes them understand how interesting and important the source is to your project." You can also have students prepare for their revision groups by e-mailing and reading drafts before the class meeting.

4. **The subject suits the length of paper assigned and the time given for research and writing.**

Avoid broad subjects that have too many sources to survey adequately, such as a major event in history or the collected works of a poet.

2 Posing a research question

Asking a question about your subject can give direction to your research by focusing your thinking on a particular approach. You can even begin asking questions before you find your specific subject, as a way of opening avenues you may not have considered.

The students Edward Begay and Vanessa Haley arrived at their research questions by slightly different paths. For a composition course, Begay's instructor assigned an interpretation with a persuasive purpose but left the selection of subject to the student. Begay

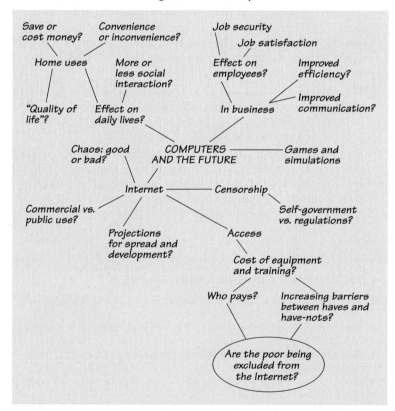

Clustering for a research question

had recently read several newspaper articles on a subject that intrigued him: how computers will alter the future. Taking this broad subject as his starting point, he used clustering (see p. 22) to pursue some ideas. While generating the cluster diagram on the facing page, Begay found himself giving the most thought to the Internet. He posed questions until a cluster about access to the Internet led him to a question that seemed interesting and significant: *Will the poor be excluded from the Internet?*

In developing a topic and question for an analysis paper assigned in a composition course, Vanessa Haley followed a somewhat different procedure. Instead of starting with a general subject, as Begay did, Haley began by looking for an unresolved question, an interesting problem, or a disagreement among the experts in some field of study. She had recently been reading an anthology of writings on the environment, and she had been disturbed by how many naturalists and environmentalists view human beings not as part of "nature" but as something separate from it, usually as its destroyer. In her journal, Haley wrote this entry:

> Many writers see nature as a place for humans to retreat to, or a wonderful thing that humans are ruining. Humans aren't considered natural themselves— human civilization isn't considered natural. Human civ. is "anti-natural." Isn't such a separation unrealistic and damaging? We *are* natural. We're here to stay, and we're not going back to the Stone Age, so we'd better focus on the connections between "us" and "it" (nature) rather than just the differences. Dillard seems to do this—seems to connect human and natural worlds. People are neither better nor worse than nature but just bound up in it. "Nature is as careless as it is bountiful, and . . . with that extravagance goes a crushing waste that will one day include our own cheap lives" ("Fecundity").

At the end of this entry, Haley refers to and quotes the writer Annie Dillard, one of the authors represented in the anthology. Haley decided to explore Dillard's views further by reading and analyzing more of her work. Haley's opening question for investigation, then, was *How does Annie Dillard see the place of humanity in nature?*

EXERCISE 42.1 Finding a topic and question

Choose three of the following subjects (or three subjects of your own), and narrow each one to at least one subject and question suitable for beginning work on a research paper. (This exercise can be the first step in a research-writing project that continues through Chapters 42–46.)

1. Bilingual education
2. National security and civil rights
3. Distribution of music by conventional versus electronic means
4. Dance in America
5. The history of women's suffrage
6. Genetically modified foods
7. Immigrants in the United States
8. Space exploration
9. Business espionage

COLLABORATIVE LEARNING

CREATING QUESTION LISTS

If students have trouble formulating questions on the basis of discovery techniques, you can have them work in groups to come up with question lists for each group member's subject.

COLLABORATIVE LEARNING

In Exercise 42.1 (as with all the exercises in this chapter) students should complete the assigned task individually in order to focus their research interests and develop their own projects. However, you can greatly enhance this process of individual learning by creating ongoing collaborative workshops in which students share their findings from each exercise and keep up on the progress of each other's research projects. When students have completed Exercise 42.1, for example, you might divide them into groups according to the subjects they have chosen so that they have the opportunity to learn how other students narrowed particular subjects in different directions. You might also invite students to propose other areas of interest that could be added to the list in Exercise 42.1 and then narrowed.

ANSWERS: EXERCISE 42.1

Individual response.

RESOURCES AND IDEAS

Brent, Doug. *Reading as Rhetorical Invention: Knowledge, Persuasion, and the Teaching of Research-Based Writing.* Urbana: NCTE, 1992. Brent shows how students can use sources to generate researched essays and includes directed reading projects that help students to develop individualized subjects.

Capossela, Toni-Lee. "Students as Sociolinguists: Getting Real Research from Freshman Writers." *College Composition and Communication* 42 (1991): 75–79. Capossela uses students' command of their own language to engage in real-world issues and write research papers.

Davis, Robert and Mark Shadle. "'Building a Mystery': Alternative Research Writing and the Academic Act of Seeking." *College Composition and Communication* 52 (February 2000): 417–466. The authors urge us to expand our definition of the research paper and allow students to write personal research papers and compose multi-genre/media/disciplinary/cultural research papers.

Dellinger, Dixie G. "Alternatives to Clip-and-Stitch: Real Research and Writing in the Classroom." *English Journal* 78 (1989): 31–38. Dellinger claims that engaging students in primary research helps them generate material and enthusiasm for writing.

Nelson, Jennie. "The Library Revisited: Exploring Students' Research Processes." In *Hearing Ourselves Think: Cognitive Research in the College Writing Classroom.* Ed. Ann M. Penrose and Barbara M. Sitko. New York: Oxford UP, 1993. 102–24. Includes case studies of students' composing processes throughout the research paper project, including assembling sources and developing subjects.

10. The effect of television on professional sports
11. Child abuse
12. African Americans and civil rights
13. Successes in cancer research
14. Computer piracy
15. The European exploration of North America before Columbus
16. Hazardous substances in the workplace
17. Television evangelism
18. Science fiction
19. Treatment or prevention of AIDS in the United States or Africa
20. Water pollution
21. Women writers
22. Campaign financing
23. Comic film actors
24. An unsolved crime
25. Alternative fuels
26. Male and female heroes in modern fiction
27. Computers and the privacy of the individual
28. Gothic or romance novels in the nineteenth and twenty-first centuries
29. The social responsibility of business
30. Stem-cell research

42c Developing a research strategy

Before you start looking for sources, consider what you already know about your subject and where you are likely to find information on it.

1 Tapping into your own knowledge

Discovering what you already know about your subject will guide you in discovering what you don't know. Take some time to spell out facts you have learned, opinions you have heard or read elsewhere, and of course your own opinions. Use one of the discovery techniques discussed in Chapter 2 to explore and develop your ideas: keeping a journal, observing your surroundings, freewriting, list making, clustering, asking the journalist's questions, using the patterns of development, or thinking critically.

When you've explored your thoughts, make a list of questions for which you don't have answers, whether factual (*What is the distribution of computers among affluent and poor schools?*) or more open-ended (*Are computers a positive force in education?*). These questions will give you clues about the sources you need to look for first.

2 Setting goals for sources

For many research projects, you'll want to consult a mix of sources, as described on the following pages. You may start by seeking the outlines of your topic—the range and depth of opinions about it—in reference works and articles in popular periodicals or through a Web search. Then, as you refine your views and your research question, you'll move on to more specialized sources, such as scholarly books and periodicals and your own interviews or surveys. (See pp. 575–97 for more on each kind of source.)

▧ Library and Internet sources

The print and electronic sources available through your library—mainly reference works, periodicals, and books—have two big advantages over most of what you'll find on the Internet: they are cataloged and indexed for easy retrieval; and they are generally reliable, having been screened first by their publishers and then by the library's staff. In contrast, the Internet's retrieval systems are more difficult to use effectively, and Internet sources tend to be less reliable because most do not pass through any screening before being posted. (There are many exceptions, such as online scholarly journals and reference works. But these sources are generally available through your library's Web site as well.)

Most instructors expect research writers to consult sources found in and through the library, including print sources. But most will accept Internet sources, too, if you have used them judiciously. Even with its disadvantages, the Internet can be a valuable resource for primary sources, current information, and a diversity of views. For guidelines on evaluating both library and Internet sources, see pages 599–609.

▧ Primary and secondary sources

As much as possible, you should rely on **primary sources,** or firsthand accounts: historical documents (letters, speeches, and so on), eyewitness reports, works of literature, reports on experiments or surveys conducted by the writer, or your own interviews, experiments, observations, or correspondence.

In contrast, **secondary sources** report and analyze information drawn from other sources (often primary ones): a reporter's summary of a controversial issue, a historian's account of a battle, a critic's reading of a poem, a physicist's evaluation of several studies. Secondary sources may contain helpful summaries and interpretations that direct, support, and extend your own thinking. However, most research-writing assignments expect your ideas to go beyond those in such sources.

▧ Scholarly and popular sources

The scholarship of acknowledged experts is essential for depth, authority, and specificity. Most instructors expect you to emphasize scholarly sources in your research. But the general-interest views and information of popular sources can help you apply more scholarly approaches to daily life.

As a follow-up exercise, you might have students present one of their sources verbally, identify it as primary or secondary, scholarly or popular, old or new, impartial or biased, describe useful features such as bibliographies and indexes, and suggest how its content might function in their research paper.

It is important for students to understand that this process of evaluating and synthesizing their sources will help them to generate a critical argument as well as the information for their paper. Discussing the different purposes and audiences for college writing will also help students who may have written successful research papers in high school using only an entry or two from a general encyclopedia.

COMPUTER ACTIVITY

LET YOUR FINGERS DO THE WALKING

Students who are inexperienced in Web navigation and searching may avoid doing any searching online. On the other hand, some students are so comfortable Web surfing that they would just as soon research their papers without ever setting foot in the library to look at a print source. In both cases, students may end up with bibliographies that are limited. To make sure that they explore all the avenues of research available to them, you may want to require that your students use both print and some online sources in their papers.

COMPUTER ACTIVITY

SCHOLARLY VERSUS POPULAR SOURCES

Post some examples of sources on your class Web site or courseware, and ask students to evaluate whether they are scholarly or popular sources. Students should cite the evidence upon which they base their judgments.

- **Check the title.** Is it technical, or does it use a general vocabulary?
- **Check the publisher.** Is it a scholarly journal (such as *Education Forum*) or a publisher of scholarly books (such as Harvard University Press), or is it a popular magazine (such as *Time* or *Newsweek*) or a publisher of popular books (such as Random House)?
- **Check the length of periodical articles.** Scholarly articles are generally much longer than magazine and newspaper articles.
- **Check the author.** Have you seen the name elsewhere, which might suggest that the author is an expert?
- **Check the electronic address.** Addresses, or URLs, for Internet sources often include an abbreviation that tells you something about the origin of the source: *edu* means the source comes from an educational institution, *gov* from a government body, *org* from a nonprofit organization, *com* from a commercial organization such as a corporation. The abbreviation is not a firm guide to the kind of source—*edu* sites, for instance, may include student papers and Web logs as well as works by scholars—but it can indicate the context. (See pp. 592–93 for more on types of online sources.)

Older and newer sources

- **Check the publication date.** For most subjects a combination of older, established sources (such as books) and current sources (such as newspaper articles, interviews, or Web sites) will provide both background and up-to-date information. Only historical subjects or very current subjects like Edward Begay's (the Internet) require an emphasis on one extreme or another.

Impartial and biased sources

Seek a range of viewpoints. Sources that attempt to be impartial can offer trustworthy facts and an overview of your subject. Sources with clear biases can offer a diversity of opinion. Of course, to discover bias, you may have to read the source carefully (see p. 601); but even a bibliographical listing can be informative.

- **Check the title.** It may reveal something about point of view. (Consider these contrasting titles uncovered by Edward Begay: "Computer Literacy and Ideology" versus "The Process of Introducing Internet-Based Classroom Projects and the Role of School Librarians.")
- **Check the author.** You may have heard of the author before as a respected researcher (thus more likely to be objective) or as a leading proponent of a certain view (less likely to be objective).

Note Internet sources must be approached with particular care. See pages 602–09.

■ Sources with helpful features

Depending on your topic and how far along your research is, you may want to look for sources with features such as illustrations (which can clarify important concepts), bibliographies (which can direct you to other sources), and indexes (which can help you develop keywords for electronic searches; see pp. 573–75).

EXERCISE 42.2 Developing a research strategy

Following the suggestions on page 564, write what you already know about the topic you selected in Exercise 42.1 (pp. 563–64), and then frame some questions for which you'll need to find answers. Also in writing, consider the kinds of sources you'll probably need to consult, using the categories given on the preceding pages.

42d   Making a working, annotated bibliography

When you begin searching for sources, it may be tempting to pursue each possibility as you come across it. But that approach would prove inefficient and probably ineffective. Instead, you'll want to find out the *full range* of sources available—from scholarly and popular articles to books and Web sites—and then decide on a good number to consult. For a paper of 1800 to 2500 words, try for ten to thirty promising titles as a start.

To keep track of where sources are, compile a **working bibliography,** as you uncover possibilities. Record the information for a source as soon as you think you may want to use it, following the guidelines on pages 568–69. Then you'll be able to find the source when you're ready to consult it, and you'll have the information needed to cite the source in your paper.

Many instructors ask student to prepare an annotated bibliography that records not only *where* sources are but also *what* they are. Suggestions for compiling an annotated bibliography appear on pages 570 and 600.

1   Tracking source information

You have several options for making a working bibliography:

■ **Copy source information by hand on note cards** (usually 3" × 5"), one source to a card. With this system, you can record source information no matter where you are, as long as you have a pen or pencil, and you can easily add, delete, and rearrange sources.

ANSWERS: EXERCISE 42.2

Individual response.

HOW MANY SOURCES?

Students always ask, "How many sources do I need in my working bibliography?" A good rule of thumb is two sources per anticipated page of paper: if students are writing a five-page paper, they should try to find at least ten sources. This rule of thumb should give them ample material from which to choose while preventing them from becoming obsessed with finding sources at the expense of getting on with their writing.

Some instructors require that a working bibliography be submitted on note cards.

- **Create the working bibliography on your word processor or handheld computer,** either typing the information yourself or downloading it from online indexes, catalogs, and other sources. You'll be able to sort sources by subject or by author and to copy bibliographic data into your paper when you prepare final source citations.
- **Combine the two systems:** print and cut up computer-generated source listings, and then paste or tape each source on a note card.

Whatever system you use, be sure to record all the information you will need. A downloaded listing, for instance, may look complete but lack the name of the database and other crucial information.

The two records below come from Edward Begay's working bibliography. The first, for a book, Begay handwrote on a note card. The second, for a magazine article, Begay downloaded from a subscription service, printed out, and then annotated with information he knew he would need.

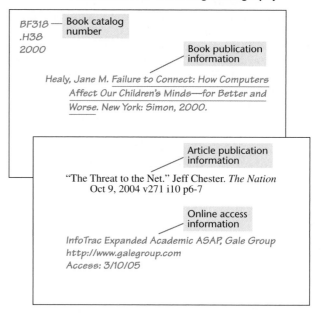

Basic entries for a working bibliography

BF318
.H38
2000 — Book catalog number

Book publication information

Healy, Jane M. *Failure to Connect: How Computers Affect Our Children's Minds—for Better and Worse.* New York: Simon, 2000.

Article publication information

"The Threat to the Net." Jeff Chester. *The Nation* Oct 9, 2004 v271 i10 p6-7

Online access information

InfoTrac Expanded Academic ASAP, Gale Group
http://www.galegroup.com
Access: 3/10/05

2 Recording source information

When you turn in your paper, you will be expected to attach a list of the sources you have used. So that readers can check or follow up on your sources, your list must include all the information needed to find the sources, in a format readers can understand. The box below shows the information you should record for each type of source so that you will not have to retrace your steps later. See later pages for illustrations of how to locate this information for books (660), journal articles (667), newspaper articles (669), Web sites (675), and sources you find through subscription databases (672).

Information for a working bibliography

For books

Library call number
Name(s) of author(s), editor(s),
    translator(s), or others listed
Title and subtitle
Publication data:
    Place of publication
    Publisher's name
    Date of publication
Other important data, such as
    edition or volume number

For periodical articles

Name(s) of author(s)
Title and subtitle of article
Title of periodical
Publication data:
    Volume number and issue
        number (if any) in which
        article appears
    Date of issue
    Page numbers on which
        article appears

For electronic sources

Name(s) of author(s)
Title and subtitle
Publication data for books and
    articles (see above)
Date of release, online posting,
    or latest revision

Medium (online, CD-ROM, etc.)
Format of online source (Web site,
    Web page, e-mail, etc.)
Date you consulted the source
Complete URL (unless source was
    obtained through a subscrip-
    tion service and has no
    usable address)
For source obtained through a
    subscription service:
    Name of database
    Name of service
    Electronic address of the service
        home page *or* search terms
        used to reach the source

For other sources

Name(s) of author(s), creator(s), or
    others listed, such as a gov-
    ernment department, record-
    ing artist, or photographer
Title of work
Format, such as unpublished letter,
    live performance, or photo-
    graph
Publication or production data:
    Publication title
    Publisher's or producer's name
    Date of publication, release, or
        production
    Identifying numbers (if any)

You can download these lists from *ablongman.com/littlebrown.* Copy the appropriate list for each source you're using, and fill in the required information.

Note Whenever possible, record source information in the correct format for the documentation style you will be using. Then you will be less likely to omit needed information or to confuse dates,

RESOURCES AND IDEAS

Chappell, Virginia A., Randall Hensley, and Elizabeth Simmons-O'Neill. "Beyond Information Retrieval: Transforming Research Assignments into Genuine Inquiry." *Journal of Teaching Writing* 13:2 (1994): 209–24. Describes techniques for teaching students to evaluate sources, develop research questions, and analyze data within a range of disciplinary contexts.

Horning, Alice. "Advising Undecided Students Through Research Writing." *College Composition and Communication* 42 (1991): 80–84. Horning provides a sequence of assignments encouraging students to explore various career options, incorporating a number of research strategies.

Macrorie, Ken. *Searching Writing.* Upper Montclair: Boynton/Cook, 1986. Macrorie teaches students to conduct "I-search," personally motivated and inspired research using primary sources as well as library work.

Randall, Sally N. "Information Charts: A Strategy for Organizing Student Research." *Journal of Adolescent and Adult Literacy* 39 (April 1996): 536–43. Randall suggests methods for helping students to organize information and plan further research strategies.

Schwegler, Robert A., and Linda K. Shamoon. "The Aims and Processes of the Research Paper." *College English* 44 (1982): 812–24. The authors contend that all academic research begins with a review of the literature, followed by either examination of a theory, clarification or amplification of previous research, or contesting a hypothesis.

COLLABORATIVE LEARNING

COMPUTER ACTIVITY

COLLECTIVE ANNOTATIONS

As a class, create an online annotated bibliography on a subject of interest to students on campus. Each student can be responsible for finding and annotating a certain number of sources.

numbers, and other data when it's time to write your citations. This book describes four styles: MLA (p. 647), Chicago (p. 764), APA (p. 784), and CSE (p. 812). For others, consult one of the guides listed on pages 784 and 812. (Begay's first card on p. 568 follows MLA style.) See also page 638 for tips on using bibliography software to format source information.

3 Annotating your bibliography

Annotating a working bibliography converts a simple list into a tool for assessing sources. When you discover a possible source, record not only its publication information but also the following:

- **What you know about the source's content.** Periodical databases and book catalogs generally include abstracts or summaries of sources that can help you with this part of the annotation.
- **How you think the source may be helpful in your research.** Does it offer expert opinion, statistics, an important example, or a range of views? Does it place your subject in a historical, social, or economic context?

Taking time to prepare thorough annotations can help you discover gaps that may remain in your sources and will later help you decide which sources to pursue in depth. Edward Begay annotated a bibliography entry on his computer with a summary and a note on the source features he thought would be most useful to him:

Entry for an annotated working bibliography

Publication and access information for source	United States. Dept. of Education. National Center for Education Statistics. <u>Internet Access in US Public Schools and Classrooms.</u> 24 Feb. 2005. 12 Mar. 2005 <http://nces.ed.gov/pubsearch/pubsinfo.asp?pubid=2005015>.
Summary of source Ideas on use of source	Report on the annual NCES survey of the quantity and quality of technology used in K-12 classrooms. Includes important statistics on trends—student-to-computer ratios, teacher training, computer availability to students in different socioeconomic brackets.

As you become more familiar with your sources, you can use your initial annotated bibliography to record your evaluation of them and more detailed thoughts on how they fit into your research. See page 600 on this later stage.

EXERCISE 42.3 Compiling an annotated working bibliography

Prepare an annotated working bibliography of at least ten sources for a research paper on one of the following people or on someone of your own choosing. Begin by limiting the subject to a manageable size, posing a question about a particular characteristic or achievement of the person. Then consult reference works, periodical indexes, the library's book catalog, and the Web. (See pp. 575–91 for more on these resources.) For each source, record complete publication information as well as a summary and a note on the source's potential use.

1. Steven Jobs (a founder of Apple Computer), or another business entrepreneur
2. Ruth Bader Ginsburg, or another Supreme Court justice
3. Emily Dickinson, or another writer
4. Shaquille O'Neal, or another sports figure
5. Isamu Noguchi, or another artist

CHAPTER 43

Finding Sources

Once you have discovered a research subject and question, have developed a research strategy, and know how to make an annotated working bibliography, you're ready to find sources. This chapter discusses electronic searches and the kinds of sources, both print and electronic, that are available to you.

Note If you require sources that are not available from your own library, you may be able to obtain them from another library by mail, fax, or computer. Ask your librarian for help, and plan ahead: interlibrary loans can take a week or longer.

43a Searching electronically

1 Beginning with your library's Web site

As you conduct research, the World Wide Web will be your gateway to ideas and information. Always start with the Web site of your

http://www.ablongman.com/littlebrown ▶

Visit the companion Web site for more help and additional exercises on finding sources, including searching electronically.

synchronous communication. Students are told how to use a search engine effectively, and a sample search is provided for them to follow. A list of the most popular search engines is also provided.

The final sections of this chapter cover images, government publications, and how to conduct original research through interviewing. Woven throughout the chapter are examples drawn from Edward Begay's search for sources.

A WRITER'S PERSPECTIVE _____

Magazines all too frequently lead to books.
—FRAN LEBOWITZ

_____

COMPUTER ACTIVITIES

GETTING THE BEST SOURCES

If your students are going to have a library instruction session covering online searching, you might reconnoiter with the reference librarian before your class meets. Give the librarian a list of your students' research questions, so that when class meets, the librarian can help point your students to the most useful sources and search tools.

COMPARING SEARCHES

Ask students to enter the same search phrase into Google and one or more other search engines. Then ask them to compare the source links each search yields.

THE LIBRARY AS OFFICE

If space and library regulations permit, consider holding office hours in the library while students are conducting their research there. Your presence will encourage more consultation between you and your students. This practice is especially useful in conjunction with whatever library orientation programs your school offers first-year students.

MAKING THE LIBRARY ACCESSIBLE

Students are often confused when the library provides both an electronic catalog of its own books and access to online subscription services. They may think that every source they find on a subscription service is in the library, or that

_____

A tip for researchers

Take advantage of two valuable resources offered by your library:

- **An orientation,** which introduces the library's resources and explains how to reach and use the Web site and the print holdings.
- **Reference librarians,** whose job it is to help you and others navigate the library's resources. Even very experienced researchers often consult reference librarians.

_____

library, not with a public search engine such as *Google*. (*Google Scholar,* a new tool that searches for scholarly articles, is discussed on p. 583.) The library's site will lead you to vast resources, including books, periodical articles, and reference works. More important, every source you find on the library's site will have passed through filters to ensure its value. A scholarly journal article, for instance, undergoes at least three successive reviews: first, subject-matter experts deem it worth publishing in the journal; next, a database vendor deems the journal worth including in the database; and finally, your school's librarians deem the database worth subscribing to.

Google and other search engines may seem more user-friendly than the library's Web site and may seem to return plenty of sources for you to work with. Many of the sources may indeed be reliable and relevant to your research, but many more will not be. In the end, a library Web search will be more efficient and more effective than a direct Web search. (For help with evaluating sources from any resource, see pp. 599–609.)

Note Start with your library's Web site, but don't stop there. Many books, periodicals, and other excellent sources are available only on library shelves, not online, and most instructors expect research papers to be built to some extent on these resources. When you spot promising print sources while browsing a library's online databases, make records of them and then look them up at the library. You can also browse the bookshelves to discover sources (see p. 580).

2 Anticipating the kinds of electronic sources

Your school's library and the Web offer several kinds of electronic resources that are suitable for academic research. For more on searching these resources, see pages 575–92.

- **The library's catalog of holdings** is a database that lists all the resources that the library owns or subscribes to: books, journals, magazines, newspapers, reference works, and more. The catalog may also include the holdings of other school libraries nearby or in your state.

- **Online databases** include indexes, bibliographies, and other reference works. They are your main route to articles in periodicals, providing publication information, summaries, and often full text (see below). Your library subscribes to the databases and makes them available through its Web site. (You may also discover databases directly on the Web, but, again, the library is the more productive starting place.)
- **Databases on CD-ROM** include the same information as online databases, but they must be read at a library computer terminal. Increasingly, libraries are providing CD-ROM databases through their Web sites or are moving away from CD-ROMs in favor of online databases.
- **Full-text resources** contain the entire contents of articles, book chapters, even whole books. The library's databases provide access to the full text of many listed sources. In addition, many Web sites, such as those for government agencies, offer the full text of articles, reports, and other publications.

3 Using keywords

Once you determine what resources are available, you should plan your search. Careful planning is essential: a too-casual search can miss helpful sources while returning hundreds, even thousands, of irrelevant sources.

Probably the most important element in planning a search is to develop **keywords,** or **descriptors,** that name your subject for databases and Web search engines.

▪ Databases vs. the Web

To develop keywords it helps to understand an important difference in how library databases and the open Web work:

- **A database indexes sources by authors, titles, publication years, and its own subject headings.** The subject headings reflect the database's directory of terms and are assigned by people who have read the sources. You can find these subject headings by using your own keywords until you locate a promising source. The information for the source will list the headings under which the database indexes it and other sources like it. (See p. 585 for an illustration.) You can then use those headings for further searches.
- **A Web search engine seeks your keywords in the titles and texts of sites.** The process is entirely electronic, so the results

searching the library catalog is the same as searching the other databases. Make sure that students understand what kind of information is available from each source.

Also keep in mind that learning to use a new cataloging system (electronic or print) can be frustrating and slow and may involve a series of baffling dead ends. To help students through this process, you might implement a combination of the following:

Plan frequent trips to the library (or allow for ongoing work with research databases in your own electronic classroom).

Assign students to ongoing research teams, partnering students who are more skilled with computers in mentoring relationships with those who are tackling the electronic medium for the first time.

Demonstrate (or ask your research librarian to demonstrate) common dead ends, such as keyword searches that generate plentiful sources in one database and no sources in another.

Frequently direct the students to bring their research journals to class and to report their progress and their setbacks, so that they understand that they are sharing a learning process.

Remind students to vary electronic information with material found in print sources (for example, the bibliography of one good article can often yield several more productive sources and start the student off on a new set of electronic searches).

COLLABORATIVE LEARNING

KEYWORD BRAINSTORMING

Have students work together to brainstorm keywords that might work for each student's subject.

COLLABORATIVE LEARNING

HANDS-ON LEARNING

The barrage of information about various types of sources available through the library can be overwhelming to your students, and they may not retain it unless they have a chance to use the databases, search engines, and catalogs themselves. If you have time, consider an experiential approach rather than a long lecture about sources and how to use them. Create a worksheet of questions for students to answer, working in groups. The students will be the detectives, and will have to discover sources and figure out how to use them in order to complete the worksheet. You can give strategic hints along the way, and at the end of the exercise ask them to report on what they have discovered.

COMPUTER ACTIVITY

TO WORKS CITED

If your students have bibliographic software, they may be able to e-mail source citations to themselves in a compatible format, so that they can get the information into their bibliographies without retyping.

COMPUTER ACTIVITY

KEYWORD LISTS

Have students meet you in the library or the electronic classroom with individual lists of keywords in their areas of interest. Have students try their keywords in several databases, noting subheadings of interest and revising the keywords in places where a database or search engine works from a different system of subject headings. The goal of the exercise is not only for students to generate the variations on keywords that may be needed for different databases but also to narrow and define their topics further.

TRANSPARENCY MASTER 43.1

RESOURCES AND IDEAS

Anderson, Daniel, Bret Benjamin, Christopher Busiel, and Bill Paredes-Holt. *Teaching Online: Internet Research, Conversation, and Composition.* New York: Longman, 1998. A useful and practical guide to electronic research; in particular, see Chapter 5, "The Electronic Library."

from a search engine depend on how well your keywords describe your subject and anticipate the words used in sources. If you describe your subject too broadly or describe it specifically but don't match the vocabulary in relevant sources, your search will turn up few relevant sources and probably many that aren't relevant.

■ **Keyword refinement**

Every database and search engine provides a system that you can use to refine your keywords for a productive search. The basic operations appear in the box below, but resources do differ. For instance, some assume that *AND* should link two or more keywords, while others provide options specifying "Must contain all the words," "May contain any of the words," and other equivalents for the operations in the box. You can learn a search engine's system by consulting its Advanced Search page.

Ways to refine keywords

Most databases and many search engines work with **Boolean operators,** terms or symbols that allow you to expand or limit your keywords and thus your search.

■ **Use *AND* or + to narrow the search** by including only sources that use all the given words. The keywords *Internet AND access* request only the sources in the shaded area:

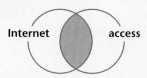

■ **Use *NOT* or – ("minus") to narrow the search** by excluding irrelevant words. *Internet AND access NOT provider* excludes sources that use the word *provider:*

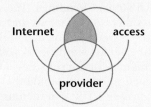

■ **Use *OR* to broaden the search** by giving alternate keywords. *Internet AND access OR use* allows for sources that use a synonym for *access:*

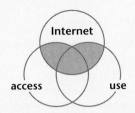

- **Use parentheses or quotation marks to form search phrases.** For instance, *(Internet access)* requests the exact phrase, not the separate words. Only sources using *Internet access* would turn up.
- **Use *NEAR* to narrow the search** by requiring the keywords to be close to each other—for instance, *Internet NEAR education.* Depending on the resource you're using, the words could be directly next to each other or many words apart. Some resources use *WITHIN ___* so that you can specify the exact number of words apart—for instance, *Internet WITHIN 10 education.*
- **Use wild cards to permit different versions of the same word.** In *child**, for instance, the wild card * indicates that sources may include *child, children, childcare, childhood, childish, childlike,* and *childproof.* The example suggests that you have to consider all the variations allowed by a wild card and whether it opens up your search too much. If you seek only two or three from many variations, you may be better off using *OR: child OR children.* (Note that some systems use ?, :, or + for a wild card instead of *.)
- **Be sure to spell your keywords correctly.** Some search tools will look for close matches or approximations, but correct spelling gives you the best chance of finding relevant sources.

▪ Trial and error

You will probably have to use trial and error in developing your keywords. Because different databases have different directories and many search tools have no directory at all, you should count on occasionally running dry (turning up few or no sources) or hitting uncontrollable gushers (turning up hundreds or thousands of mostly irrelevant sources). But the process is not busywork—far from it. Besides leading you eventually to worthwhile sources, it can also teach you a great deal about your subject: how you can or should narrow it, how it is and is not described by others, what others consider interesting or debatable about it, and what the major arguments are.

43b Finding reference works

Reference works, often available online or on CD-ROM, include encyclopedias, dictionaries, digests, bibliographies, indexes, atlases, and handbooks. Your research *must* go beyond reference

Gavin, Christy. "Guiding Students Along the Information Highway: Librarians Collaborating with Composition Instructors." *Journal of Teaching Writing* 13:2 (1994): 225–35. Gavin explores the possibilities of cooperative instruction between reference librarians and writing teachers. Given the rapidly transforming nature of bibliographic instruction, this kind of collaborative work seems crucial.

Mark, Beth L., and Trudi E. Jacobson. "Teaching Anxious Students Skills for the Electronic Library." *College Teaching* 43.1 (Fall 1995): 28–31. Suggests do's and don't's when introducing students to electronic library databases.

Selfe, Cynthia L., and Richard J. Selfe, Jr. "The Politics of the Interface: Power and Its Exercise in Electronic Contact Zones." *College Composition and Communication* 45:4 (1994): 480–504. The authors probe some of the larger cultural issues surrounding technological innovations such as the World Wide Web, including their political and ideological ramifications for education.

COLLABORATIVE LEARNING

REFERENCE REVIEWS

Assign a small group of students to each category of reference works. Have the group find which of these sources their library holds and what kind(s) of information these works contain. Ask them to report to the class either orally or in writing. If students have begun to work on topics, have them shape their reports around the usefulness of the resource for those particular topics.

TRANSPARENCY MASTER 43.2

Guide to research sources

Reference works: helpful for summaries of topics and information for further research

General books: literary works, nonfiction surveys, in-depth studies, and other materials, available for circulation

Periodicals: magazines, journals, and newspapers, containing detailed and current information

The Web: a network of computers providing access to libraries, publications, organizations, governments, and individuals

Other online sources:

works; indeed, many instructors discourage students from relying on such sources for ideas and information in final papers. But reference works can help you get started:

- **They can help you decide whether your subject interests you and meets the requirements for a research paper (p. 561).**

- They can direct you to more detailed sources on your subject.
- They can help you refine keywords for electronic searches, giving you the terminology of the field you're researching.
- They can identify the main debates in a field and the proponents of each side.

Edward Begay's use of reference works illustrates how helpful such sources can be as a starting point, even for a topic as current as the Internet. Begay first consulted *Bibliographic Guide to the History of Computing, Computers, and the Information Processing Industry* (to get some background on computers and the Internet) and *Encyclopedia of Sociology* (to explore the concept of equality in education).

The following lists give the types of reference works. Ask a reference librarian if you're unsure of where to start. The librarian can also advise you which sources are available through the library's Web site, in print or on CD-ROM at the library, or directly via the Web.

General encyclopedias

General encyclopedias give brief overviews and bibliographies. Covering all fields, they are convenient but very limited.

Academic American Encyclopedia
Collier's Encyclopedia
The Columbia Encyclopedia
Encyclopedia Americana
Encyclopaedia Britannica
Encyclopedia International
Random House Encyclopedia

Specialized encyclopedias, dictionaries, bibliographies

A specialized encyclopedia, dictionary, or bibliography generally covers a single field or subject. These works will give you more detailed and more technical information than a general reference work will, and many of them (especially bibliographies) will direct you to particular books and articles on your subject. For information on specialized reference works in various disciplines, consult lists elsewhere in this book:

- **Literature** (p. 744)
- **Other humanities,** including history, the arts, philosophy, and religion (p. 761)
- **Social sciences,** such as business and economics, criminal justice, education, and psychology (p. 781)
- **Natural and applied sciences,** such as biology, engineering, mathematics, and physics (p. 810)

Two general references provide a wide range of information in many fields:

Essay and General Literature Index. Lists tens of thousands of articles and essays that appear in books (rather than periodicals) and that might not be listed elsewhere.

Oxford Reference Online. A compilation of general and specialized dictionaries, encyclopedias, and other sources.

◼ Unabridged dictionaries and special dictionaries on language

Unabridged dictionaries are more comprehensive than college or abridged dictionaries. Special dictionaries give authoritative information on aspects of language. (See Chapter 40 for more on the kinds of dictionaries and how to use them.)

Unabridged dictionaries

A Dictionary of American English on Historical Principles
The Oxford English Dictionary
Webster's Third New International Dictionary of the English Language

Special dictionaries

R. W. Burchfield, ed., *The New Fowler's Modern English Usage*
Frederic G. Cassidy et al., eds., *Dictionary of American Regional English*
Robert L. Chapman, ed., *Roget's International Thesaurus*
Bryan A. Garner, *A Dictionary of Modern American Usage*
J. E. Lighter, ed., *Historical Dictionary of American Slang*
Charles T. Onions et al., eds., *The Oxford Dictionary of English Etymology*

◼ Biographical reference works

If you want to learn about someone's life, achievements, credentials, or position, or if you want to learn the significance of a name you've come across, consult one of the reference works below.

American Men and Women of Science
Contemporary Authors
Current Biography
Dictionary of American Biography
Dictionary of American Negro Biography
Dictionary of Literary Biography
Dictionary of National Biography (British)
Dictionary of Scientific Biography
Marquis Who's Who (nearly twenty publications organized by geography, profession, and other categories)
Notable American Women
Webster's New Biographical Dictionary
World Authors

◼ Atlases and gazetteers

Atlases are bound collections of maps; gazetteers are geographical dictionaries.

Britannica Atlas
Cosmopolitan World Atlas

National Atlas of the United States of America
National Geographic Atlas of the World
Times Atlas of the World
Times Atlas of World History
Webster's New Geographical Dictionary

◾ Almanacs and yearbooks

Both almanacs and yearbooks are annual compilations of facts. Yearbooks record information about the previous year in a country, field, or other subject. Almanacs give facts about a variety of fields.

Americana Annual
Britannica Book of the Year
Facts on File Yearbook
Information Please Almanac
US Bureau of the Census, *Statistical Abstract of the United States*
World Almanac and Book of Facts

43c Finding books

Books can provide background information, subject surveys, popular views of culture, statements of scholarly theory, research results—in short, a broad range of secondary and primary sources (see p. 565).

1 Using the library catalog

Your library's catalog is searchable at terminals in the library and via the library's Web site. With *WorldCat*, available through most libraries, you can also search for specific books in the catalogs of tens of thousands of libraries worldwide. You may be able to borrow books from another library in your area. Ask a librarian for assistance with remote searches and loans. And allow time for a book to be sent after your request.

All book catalogs contain similar information, though it may be organized differently from one library to the next. By far the most widely used format derives from the Library of Congress cataloging system and includes author, title, publisher, date of publication, description (number of pages, size, and other data), subject headings the book is listed under, and the library's call number (which directs you to the book's location in the stacks). See page 581 for a complete book record showing all this information.

2 Using a search strategy

Unless you seek a specific author or title, you'll want to find books with a subject or keyword search of the library's catalog. In a subject search, you start with headings found in *Library of Congress*

COMPUTER ACTIVITY

BROWSING NEARBY BOOKS

Once your students have located a book relevant to their topics, they might try browsing the nearby shelves for additional titles. Some library e-catalogs will allow you to do this onscreen.

Subject Headings (*LCSH*), the massive directory under which the Library of Congress catalogs books. In a keyword search, you start with your own description of your subject as a way of locating appropriate *LCSH* headings.

The keyword approach is illustrated by part of Edward Begay's catalog search, shown below and on the next page. In his initial keyword search (screen 1), Begay used *Internet and access*. The search returned several books (screen 2), including a promising one titled *Social Consequences of Internet Use*. The complete record for this book (screen 3) showed that it was indexed under three *LCSH* subject headings: *Internet—Social aspects—United States; Digital divide —United States;* and *Telecommunication—Social aspects—United States.* Begay then used these headings to search the catalog further.

Note In addition to searching the book catalog, you can also browse the library shelves. The first part of the call number for a promising title (*HM851* in the full record opposite) will lead you to other books on the same subject that a catalog search might miss.

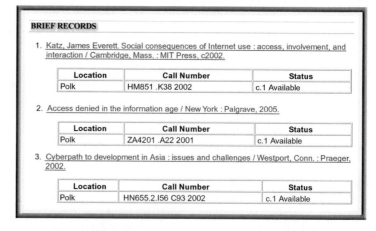

1. Initial keyword search of book catalog

CATALOG LINKS	**BASIC CATALOG SEARCH**
BASIC SEARCH	
ADVANCED SEARCH	**Enter Search Terms and Select Search Type:**
SEARCH RESERVES	
BORROWER SERVICES	Internet and access Keyword
ASK A LIBRARIAN	
HELP	Keywords Search Clear Search
TELNET	

2. Book catalog search results

BRIEF RECORDS

1. Katz, James Everett. Social consequences of Internet use : access, involvement, and interaction / Cambridge, Mass. : MIT Press, c2002.

Location	Call Number	Status
Polk	HM851 .K38 2002	c.1 Available

2. Access denied in the information age / New York : Palgrave, 2005.

Location	Call Number	Status
Polk	ZA4201 .A22 2001	c.1 Available

3. Cyberpath to development in Asia : issues and challenges / Westport, Conn. : Praeger, 2002.

Location	Call Number	Status
Polk	HN655.2.I56 C93 2002	c.1 Available

3. Book catalog full record

```
FULL RECORD
  Record #1                                          ●——— Title and subtitle
  Title:      Social consequences of Internet use : access, involvement, and interaction / James
              E. Katz and Ronald E. Rice.
  Author:     Katz, James Everett. ●————————————————— Author
  Publisher:  Cambridge, Mass. : MIT Press, c2002. ●—— Publisher and date
  Subject:    Internet--Social aspects--United States.
              Digital divide--United States.          Subject headings
              Telecommunication--Social aspects--United States.   for book
  Description: xxiv, 460 p. : ill. ; 24 cm.
  Notes:      Includes bibliographical references (p. [411]-438) and index.
  Other Entry: Rice, Ronald E. ●——————————————— Coauthor
  ISBN:       0262112698 (hc : alk. paper)
  OCLC No:    49260842                    Library call number
```

Location	Call Number	Status
Polk	HM851 .K38 2002 ●	c.1 Available

3 Using references to books

Two types of references can help you identify general books that have information about your topic:

- **Publishing bibliographies** tell whether a book is still in print, whether a paperback edition is available, what books were published on a certain topic in a certain year, and so on:

  Books in Print. Books indexed by author, title, and subject.
  Cumulative Book Index

  You might, for example, want to know if the author of an encyclopedia article has published any relevant books since the date of the encyclopedia. You could look up the author's name in the latest *Books in Print* to find out.

- **Review indexes** list published reviews of books and can help you evaluate whether a book is relevant to your subject:

  Book Review Digest. Summarizes and indexes reviews of books.
  Book Review Index
  Current Book Review Citations

  For specialized review indexes, see pages 783 (social sciences) and 811 (natural and applied sciences).

43d Finding periodicals

Periodicals include newspapers, journals, and magazines. Newspapers, the easiest to recognize, are useful for detailed accounts of

PERIODICAL JUNGLE

Students will sometimes rely on books rather than periodical articles in an attempt to avoid the complications of periodical indexes. You can help them get started by planning a library visit in which students work in pairs to find and photocopy or download periodical articles on their topics.

past and current events. Journals and magazines can be harder to distinguish, but their differences are important. Most college instructors expect students' research to rely more on journals than on magazines.

Journals	Magazines
Examples: *American Anthropologist, Journal of Black Studies, Journal of Chemical Education*	Examples: *The New Yorker, Time, Rolling Stone, People*
Available mainly through college and university libraries.	Available in public libraries, on newsstands, and in bookstores.
Articles are intended to advance knowledge in a particular field.	Articles are intended to express opinion, inform, or entertain.
Writers and readers are specialists in the field.	Writers may or may not be specialists in their subjects. Readers are members of the general public or a subgroup with a particular interest.
Articles always include source citations.	Articles rarely include source citations.
Articles are usually long, ten pages or more	Articles are usually short, fewer than ten pages
Appearance is bland, with black-only type, little or no decoration, and only illustrations that directly amplify the text, such as graphs.	Appearance varies but is generally lively, with color, decoration (headings, sidebars, and other elements), and illustrations (drawings, photographs).
Issues may appear quarterly or less often.	Issues may appear weekly, bi-weekly, or monthly.
Issues may be paged separately (like a magazine) or may be paged sequentially throughout an annual volume, so that issue number 3 (the third issue of the year) could open on page 327. (The method of pagination affects source citations. See p. 666.)	Issues are paged separately, each beginning on page 1.

1   Using periodical databases

Periodical databases index the articles in journals, magazines, and newspapers. Often, these databases include abstracts, or summaries, of the articles, and they may offer the full texts of the articles as well. Your library subscribes to many periodical databases and to services that offer multiple databases. (See p. 586 for a list.) Most databases and services will be searchable through the library's Web site.

Note The search engine *Google* is developing *Google Scholar*, an engine at *scholar.google.com* that seeks out scholarly articles. Although it could eventually prove a valuable research tool, at this point *Google Scholar* produces results that are far from complete and include more from science and engineering than from the humanities and social sciences. Your library probably subscribes to most of the periodicals searched by *Google Scholar*, so begin there.

▣ Selection of databases

To decide which databases to consult, you'll need to consider what you're looking for:

- **How broadly and deeply should you search?** Periodical databases vary widely in what they index. Some, such as *ProQuest Research Library*, cover many subjects but don't index the full range of periodicals in each subject. Others, such as *Historical Abstracts*, cover a single subject but then include most of the available periodicals and other resources as well. If your subject ranges across disciplines, as Edward Begay's Internet subject does, then start with a broad database. If your subject focuses on a particular discipline, then start with a narrower database.

- **Which databases most likely include the kinds of resources you need?** The Web sites of most libraries allow you to narrow a database search to a particular kind of periodical (such as newspapers or journals) or to a particular discipline. You can then discover each database's focus by checking the description of the database (sometimes labeled "Help" or "Guide") or the list of indexed resources (sometimes labeled "Publications" or "Index"). The description will also tell you the time period the database covers, so you'll know whether you also need to consult older print indexes at the library.

▣ Database searches

When you first search a database, use your own keywords to locate sources. The general procedure is discussed on page 573. Your goal is to find at least one source that seems just right for your subject, so that you can then see what subject headings the database itself uses for such sources. Using one or more of those headings will focus and speed your search.

Edward Begay first searched *EBSCOhost Academic Search Elite*, a broad database covering nearly 3500 periodicals. His keywords *Internet AND access* returned more than 2000 articles, and none on the first page dealt with his subject. He then tried *Internet AND access AND education*, getting fewer returns but still nothing usable on the first page. He stopped there to brainstorm other terms that might work better, some of them synonyms and some narrower:

Internet	access	education
World Wide Web	use	schools
Web	equality	public schools
computers	poverty	
technology		

The three screen shots here show Begay's use of one combination of these terms, *Internet AND equality AND education*. The returns (screen 2) included one source clearly related to Begay's subject. The full record for the source (screen 3) provided an abstract of

1. Initial keyword search of periodical database

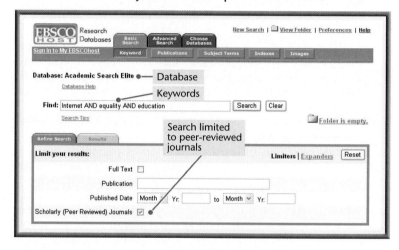

2. Partial keyword search results

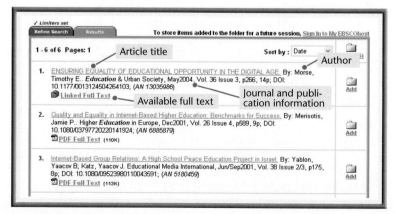

3. Full article record with abstract

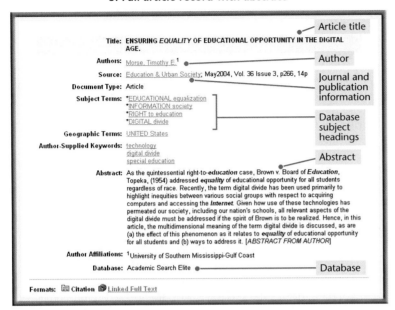

Title: ENSURING *EQUALITY* OF EDUCATIONAL OPPORTUNITY IN THE DIGITAL AGE. ——— Article title

Authors: Morse, Timothy E.[1] ——— Author

Source: Education & Urban Society; May2004, Vol. 36 Issue 3, p266, 14p

Document Type: Article ——— Journal and publication information

Subject Terms: *EDUCATIONAL equalization
*INFORMATION society
*RIGHT to education
*DIGITAL divide ——— Database subject headings

Geographic Terms: UNITED States

Author-Supplied Keywords: technology
digital divide
special education ——— Abstract

Abstract: As the quintessential right-to-*education* case, Brown v. Board of *Education*, Topeka, (1954) addressed *equality* of educational opportunity for all students regardless of race. Recently, the term digital divide has been used primarily to highlight inequities between various social groups with respect to acquiring computers and accessing the *Internet*. Given how use of these technologies has permeated our society, including our nation's schools, all relevant aspects of the digital divide must be addressed if the spirit of Brown is to be realized. Hence, in this article, the multidimensional meaning of the term digital divide is discussed, as are (a) the effect of this phenomenon as it relates to *equality* of educational opportunity for all students and (b) ways to address it. [ABSTRACT FROM AUTHOR]

Author Affiliations: [1]University of Southern Mississippi-Gulf Coast

Database: Academic Search Elite ——— Database

Formats: Citation   Linked Full Text

the source along with the database's headings for the article. Begay had seen one of these headings, *DIGITAL divide*, in his background research, but he had thought the term might be too current to produce good results. Now he tried it on *Academic Search Elite* and found dozens of additional source possibilities. To broaden his search, he also tried some of the subject headings for these other sources, such as *Educational technology* and *Technology—sociological aspects*. When he thought he had found a good range of possible sources, including government publications as well as scholarly and popular articles, he moved on to other databases.

Many databases allow you to limit your search to so-called peer-reviewed or refereed journals—that is, scholarly journals whose articles have been reviewed before publication by experts in the field and then revised by the author. (Begay's initial search of *EBSCOhost Academic Search Elite* included this limitation, as shown in screen 1.) Limiting your search to peer-reviewed journals can help you navigate huge databases that might otherwise return scores of unusable articles from other kinds of periodicals.

Note As you follow leads in online indexes, it's easy to lose track of what database you're using. You'll need this information for any article you obtain online, so make sure you have it. If you print search records or e-mail them to yourself, the database information will appear on the record along with other bibliographic information (see screen 3 above).

■ The use of abstracts

The full article record on the previous page shows a key feature of many databases' periodical listings: an abstract that summarizes the article. Describing research methods, conclusions, and other information, an abstract can tell you whether you want to pursue an article and thus save you time. However, the abstract cannot replace the actual article. If you want to use the work as a source, you must consult the full text, as described on the facing page.

■ Helpful databases

The list below includes databases to which academic libraries commonly subscribe. Some of these databases—for instance, *ProQuest Research Library* and *EBSCOhost Academic Search*—cover much the same material, so your library may subscribe to several of them but not all.

Note More specific lists of indexes for academic disciplines appear later in this book: see pages 745 (literature), 762 (other humanities), 782–83 (social sciences), and 810 (natural and applied sciences).

EBSCOhost Academic Search. A periodical index covering magazines and journals in the social sciences, sciences, arts, and humanities. Many articles are available full-text.

FirstSearch. A Web interface to more than sixty databases, including *WorldCat, Books in Print, Dissertation Abstracts, Wilson Select, ArticleFirst, Biography Index, Book Review Index, Education Abstracts, ERIC, Medline, PAIS,* and many more.

InfoTrac Expanded Academic. The Gale Group's general periodical index covering the social sciences, sciences, arts, and humanities as well as national news periodicals. It includes full-text articles.

JSTOR. Full-text articles from older volumes of several hundred journals in the sciences, social sciences, arts, humanities, and business.

LexisNexis Academic. An index of news and business, legal, and reference information, with full-text articles. *LexisNexis* includes international, national, and regional newspapers, newsmagazines, legal and business publications, and court cases.

Nineteenth-Century Masterfile. Perhaps the only electronic database for materials from the nineteenth century, including *Poole's Index to Periodical Literature* (1802–1906), W. T. Stead's *Index to Periodicals* (1890–1902), and indexes to books and journals.

ProQuest Research Library. A periodical index covering the sciences, social sciences, arts, and humanities, including many full-text articles.

Wilson Databases. A collection of indexes, often provided in a package, including *Business Periodicals Index, Education Index, General Science Index, Humanities Index, Readers' Guide to Periodical Literature,* and *Social Sciences Index.*

While using databases like those above, you may want to consult a **citation index** to see what has been written *about* an article or book, as when one scholar comments on the work of another. The three main citation indexes are *Arts and Humanities Citation Index,* *Social Science Citation Index,* and *Science Citation Index.* All three are available on the database *ISI Web of Science,* which many libraries subscribe to.

2 Locating the articles in periodicals

Many article listings you find will include or link directly to the full text of the article, which you'll be able to read online and print or e-mail to yourself. If the full text is not available online, you'll need to consult the periodical itself. Usually the article listing will also say whether the periodical is available in your library. If you don't see this information, then consult the library's list of periodicals (often called *serials*) either in the main catalog or in a separate catalog.

Your library probably holds recent issues of periodicals in the periodicals room. Back issues are usually stored elsewhere, in one of three forms:

- **In bound volumes**
- **On** *microfilm,* a filmstrip showing pages side by side
- **On** *microfiche,* a sheet of film with pages arranged in rows and columns.

Consulting periodicals stored on microfilm or microfiche requires using a special machine, or "reader," with which you locate the page and project it on a screen. (Some readers are also attached to scanners or photocopiers.) Any member of the library's staff will show you how to operate the reader.

If the periodical you seek is not available in your library, you may be able to obtain the article by interlibrary loan. The article may arrive online, by mail, or by fax, and there may be a fee for the service. Even electronic loans can sometimes take a week or more, so place your order early.

Note Many periodicals are available both online and in print, and most documentation styles require you to specify which version you consulted. For scholarly journals, the two versions are likely to be identical in content though not in format: for instance, the online version may not include the print version's page breaks and numbers. (However, a full-text version in PDF format reproduces the actual pages of the print journal. To open PDF files, you may need to download a program called *Acrobat Reader.*) For newspapers and magazines, the two versions often differ more: for instance, the online version may be shorter or longer than the print version, may contain fewer illustrations, or may include links to other resources.

WEB SOURCE EVALUATION

Since sources found on the Web are sometimes difficult to evaluate, you might devote class time to helping students analyze sample sources. Begin by reviewing a sample item in class: What clues are there about whether the material is primary or secondary, scholarly or popular? Is it dated? Did the material come from an individual's home page, an institutional archive? Is the author named? Has that author published additional work found in print? Is the material referenced in a scholarly bibliography? Does the author cite other sources; does the piece include a bibliography of its own sources? Then have each student bring in a printout of material gleaned from the Web along with a record of the search procedures he or she used to find it (in an electronic classroom you might have students work directly from the screen). Ask students to work in small groups to evaluate their sources and to report their findings on one source to the class.

REVVING THE SEARCH ENGINE

Pick one subject for all your students to search. Have students use different search engines to conduct their searches and then report their findings to the class.

ALL ROADS LEAD TO ROME

Hold a contest to see which of your students can find the greatest number of different paths to

43e Finding sources on the Web

As an academic researcher, you enter the World Wide Web in two ways: through your library's Web site, and through public search engines such as *Yahoo!* and *Google*. The library entrance, covered in the preceding sections, is your main path to the books and periodicals that, for most subjects, should make up most of your sources. The public entrance, discussed here, can lead to a wealth of information and ideas, but it also has a number of disadvantages:

- **The Web is a wide-open network.** Anyone with the right hardware and software can place information on the Internet, and even a carefully conceived search can turn up sources with widely varying reliability: journal articles, government documents, scholarly data, term papers written by high school students, sales pitches masked as objective reports, wild theories. You must be especially diligent about evaluating Internet sources (see pp. 602–09).
- **The Web changes constantly.** No search engine can keep up with the Web's daily additions and deletions, and a source you find today may be different or gone tomorrow. You should not put off consulting an online source that you think you may want to use. If it seems appropriate for your needs, take notes from it or (if the source allows) download it to your own computer. Be sure to record complete source information at the same time (see p. 569 for a list of what to record).
- **The Web provides limited information on the past.** Sources dating from before the 1980s or even more recently probably will not appear on the Web.
- **The Web is not all-inclusive.** Most books and many periodicals are available only via the library, not directly via the Web.

Clearly, the Web warrants cautious use. It should not be the only resource you work with.

1 Using a search engine

To find sources on the Web, you use a **search engine** that catalogs Web sites in a series of directories and conducts keyword searches. Generally, use a directory when you haven't yet refined your topic or you want a general overview. Use keywords when you have refined your topic and you seek specific information.

■ Current search engines

Dozens of search engines are available. The box opposite lists the currently most popular engines. (To reach any of them, enter its URL in the Address or Location field of your Web browser.)

Web search engines

The features of search engines change often, and new ones appear constantly. For the latest on search engines, see the links collected by *Search Engine Watch* at *searchenginewatch.com/links*.

Directories that review sites

BUBL Link (*bubl.ac.uk*)
Internet Public Library (*ipl.org/div/subject*)
Internet Scout Project (*scout.wisc.edu/archives*)
Librarians' Index to the Internet (*lii.org*)

The most advanced and efficient engines

AlltheWeb (*alltheweb.com*)
One of the fastest and most comprehensive engines, *AlltheWeb* updates its database frequently so that it returns more of the Web's most recent sites. It allows searches for news, pictures, and audio and video files.

Google (*google.com*)
Also fast and comprehensive, *Google* ranks a site based not only on its content but also on the other sites that are linked to it, thus providing a measure of a site's usefulness. *Google* also allows searches for news, discussion groups, and images.

Other engines

AltaVista (*altavista.com*)
Ask Jeeves (*ask.com*)
Dogpile (*dogpile.com*)
Excite (*excite.com*)
Lycos (*lycos.com*)
MetaCrawler (*metacrawler.com*)
Yahoo! (*yahoo.com*)

Note For a good range of reliable sources, try out more than a single search engine, perhaps as many as four or five. No search engine can catalog the entire Web—indeed, even the most powerful engine may not include half the sites available at any given time, and most engines include only a fifth or less. In addition, most search engines accept paid placements, giving higher billing to sites that pay a fee. These so-called sponsored links are usually marked as such, but they can compromise a search engine's method for arranging sites in response to your keywords.

▦ A sample search engine

The screen shot on the following page from *Google* shows the features common to most search engines. Any search engine's Advanced Search option allows you to customize your search (for instance, by selecting a date range, a language, or a number of results

Google home page

to see) and to limit or expand your keywords (for instance, by using *AND, NOT,* and other operators). It may also tell you how the search engine determines the order in which it presents results. (Criteria include the number of times your keywords appear on a site, whether the terms appear in the site's title or address, and, in *Google*'s case, which other sites link to the site.)

■ Search records

Your Web browser includes functions that allow you to keep track of Web sources and your search:

- *Favorites* or *Bookmarks* **save site addresses as links.** Click one of these terms near the top of the browser screen to add a site you want to return to. A favorite or bookmark remains on file until you delete it.

- *History* **records the sites you visited over a certain period,** such as a day, a week, or a month. (You can set the period from the browser's Tools menu.) After the period elapses, the history is deleted. If you forgot to bookmark a site, click History or Go to recover the site from the search history.

Note If you do Web research on a public computer, such as in a lab at school, your favorites and history probably will not be saved from one day to the next. To track sources that you may want to return to, copy the site URLs and e-mail them to yourself.

2　Following a sample Web search

For his initial search of the Web, Edward Begay started with the keywords *digital divide* on *Google*. But the search returned more than 6.6 *million* items, as shown on screen 1 opposite. Although some sources on the first page looked promising, Begay realized he had to alter his strategy to get more focused results. Following the same procedure he used with a periodical database, Begay experimented with combinations of synonyms and narrower terms. The keywords *"digital divide" "public education" US* did refine the search but still produced 31,000 results.

From *Google*'s Advanced Search help, Begay learned that he could specify what he wanted to see in the URLs of sources. Adding *site:.gov* limited the results to government publications, whose URLs end in *gov*. With *"digital divide" "public education" US site:.gov*, Begay received 547 results (see screen 2). Although the number was

1. First *Google* search results

2. *Google* results with refined keywords

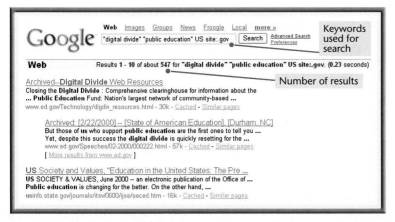

RESOURCES AND IDEAS

Crump, Eric, and Nick Carbone. *The English Student's Guide to the Internet.* New York: Houghton, 1996. A useful guide for narrowing the Web's vast search capabilities toward directed areas.

Davis, Chris. "The I-Search Paper Goes Global: Using the Internet as a Research Tool." *English Journal* 84:6 (1995): 27–33. Davis shows how the Internet enhances students' abilities to develop and follow through on their own research interests.

COLLABORATIVE LEARNING

LEVELS OF DISCOURSE

To help students learn to differentiate between the more scholarly discussions found on discussion lists and the less scholarly ones found on Web logs and newsgroups, assign pairs of students to explore one example of each kind of conversation on a single topic. For instance, a discussion list about World War II will probably have historians as participants, discussing approaches to interpretation, primary and secondary data, or historiography. In contrast, a Web forum about World War II would be more likely to attract war buffs and veterans as participants, discussing their own experiences and opinions. Each kind of conversation has its usefulness for research, but they should not be granted equal authority.

COMPUTER ACTIVITY

ONLINE LURKING

Ask your students to join one discussion list, Web log, or newsgroup relevant to their topic and read postings for one week. Then ask them to write a brief evaluation of the list, forum, or newsgroup and e-mail it to the other members of the class.

still large, the government origin combined with *Google*'s criteria for ranking sources gave Begay confidence that the first fifty or so would serve his needs. He continued to limit the search by replacing *site:.gov* with *site:.edu* (educational institutions), *site:.org* (nonprofit organizations), and *site:.com* (commercial organizations).

Knowing that no search engine catalogs every Web site, Begay also tried his successful keywords at two other engines, *AlltheWeb* and *Dogpile*. The *AlltheWeb* search turned up an additional promising site among the first thirty. The *Dogpile* search, which worked through multiple search engines, returned more than a thousand items, including many irrelevant ones but also (among the first thirty) one more possible source.

Begay's Web search illustrates the trial-and-error approach required to refine keywords so that they locate worthwhile sources. Almost any successful Web search will require similar persistence and patience.

43f Finding other online sources

Several online sources can put you directly in touch with experts and others whose ideas and information may inform your research. Because these sources, like Web sites, are unfiltered, you must always evaluate them carefully. (See pp. 607–09.)

1 Using electronic mail

As a research tool, e-mail allows you to communicate with others who are interested in your topic. You may, for instance, carry on an e-mail conversation with a teacher at your school or interview an expert in another state to follow up on a scholarly article he or she published. (See pp. 826–29 on using e-mail.)

2 Using discussion lists

A **discussion list** (sometimes called a **listserv** or just a **list**) uses e-mail to connect individuals who are interested in a common subject, often with a scholarly or technical focus. By sending a question to an appropriate list, you may be able to reach scores of people who know something about your topic. For an index of discussion lists, see *tile.net/lists*.

When conducting research on a discussion list, follow the guidelines for e-mail etiquette on pages 828–29 as well as these:

- *Lurk* for a while—reading without posting messages. Make sure the discussion is relevant to your topic, and get a sense of how the group interacts.

- **Don't ask for information you can find elsewhere.** Most list members are glad to help with legitimate questions but resent messages that rehash familiar debates or that ask them to do someone else's work.
- **Evaluate messages carefully.** Many list subscribers are passionate experts with fair-minded approaches to their topics, but almost anyone with an Internet connection can post a message to a list. See pages 607–09 on evaluating online sources.

3 Using Web forums and newsgroups

Web forums and newsgroups are more open and less scholarly than discussion lists, so their messages require even more diligent evaluation. **Web forums** allow participants to join a conversation simply by selecting a link on a Web page. For a directory of forums, see *delphiforums.com*. **Newsgroups** are organized under subject headings such as *soc* for social issues and *biz* for business. For a directory of newsgroups, see *groups.google.com*.

4 Using Web logs

Web logs, or **blogs,** are personal sites on which an author posts time-stamped comments, generally centering on a common theme, in a format that allows readers to respond to the author and to one another. You can find directories of blogs at *bloglines.com* and *blogwise.com*. See also pages 830–32 for a discussion and example of communicating via blogs.

Like all other online media discussed in this section, Web logs consulted as potential sources must be evaluated carefully. Some are reliable sources of opinion, news, or evolving scholarship, and many refer to worthy books, articles, Web sites, and other resources. But lots of blogs are little more than outlets for their authors' gripes and prejudices. See pages 607–09 for tips on telling the good from the bad.

5 Using synchronous communication

Synchronous (or simultaneous) **communication** allows conversations in real time, the way we talk on the phone. Synchronous programs include instant-messaging applications, Web courseware, Internet relay chat (IRC), and virtual environments called **MOOs**.

Synchronous communication can be used to conduct interviews or hold debates. Your instructor may ask you to use it for your coursework or research and will provide the software and instructions to get started. You can also find out more about synchronous communication at *du.org/cybercomp.html* or *internet101.org/chat.html*.

43g　Finding government publications

Government publications provide a vast array of data compilations, reports, policy statements, public records, and other historical and contemporary information. For US government publications, by far the most numerous, consult the Government Printing Office's *GPO Access* at *gpoaccess.gov/index.html.* Many federal, state, and local government agencies post important publications—legislation, reports, press releases—on their own Web sites. You can find lists of sites for various federal agencies by using the keywords *United States federal government* with any search engine. Edward Begay took this approach to find statistics from the Department of Commerce on computer use by people of various incomes and races (see the screen shot below).

Chart from a government publication

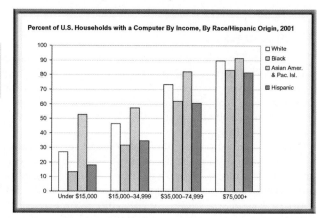

Besides what's available online, your library will have a large collection of printed government publications only if it is a depository library (that is, designated to receive such documents). If yours is a depository library, ask a librarian to help you locate the documents you seek.

43h　Finding images

Pages 225–29 discuss the use of images to support an argument. To find images, you have a number of options. (The Web links in the following lists are available online at *ablongman.com/ littlebrown.*)

- **Scout for images while reading print or online sources.** Your sources may include charts, graphs, photographs, and other images that can support your ideas. When you find an image you may want to use, photocopy or download it so you'll have it available later.
- **Create your own images,** such as photographs or charts. See pages 120–21 for suggestions on graphics software programs.
- **Use an image search engine.** *Google, Yahoo!, AlltheWeb,* and some other search engines conduct specialized image searches. They can find scores of images, but the results may be inaccurate or incomplete because the sources surveyed often do not include descriptions of the images. (The engines search file names and any text accompanying the images.)
- **Use a public image database.** The following sites generally conduct accurate searches because their images are filed with information such as a description of the image, the artist's name, and the image's date:

  Adflip (adflip.com). Historical and contemporary print advertisements.
  Duke University, *Ad*Access (scriptorium.lib.duke.edu/adaccess).* Print advertisements spanning 1911–55.
  Library of Congress, *American Memory (memory.loc.gov/ammem).* Maps, photographs, and prints documenting the American experience.
  Library of Congress, *Prints and Photographs Online Catalog (loc.gov/rr/ print/catalog.html).* Images from the library's collection, including those available through *American Memory.*
  New York Public Library Digital Gallery (digitalgallery.nypl.org/nypldigital). Maps, drawings, photographs, and paintings from the library's collection.
  Political Cartoons (politicalcartoons.com). Cartoons on contemporary issues and events.

- **Use a public image directory.** The following sites collect links to image sources:

  Art Source (ilpi.com/artsource/general.html). Sources on art and architecture.
  ARTstor (artstor.org). Museum collections and a database of images typically used in art history courses.
  Museum Computer Network (mcn.edu/resources/sitesonline.htm). Museum collections.
  Washington State University, *Popular Culture. Resources for Critical Analysis (wsu.edu/%7Eamerstu/pop/tvrguide.html).* Sources on advertising, fashion, magazines, toys, and other artifacts of popular culture.
  Yale University Arts Library, *Image Resources (www.library.yale.edu/art/ imageresources.html).* Sources on the visual and performing arts.

- **Use a subscription database.** Your library may subscribe to the following resources:

Associated Press, *AccuNet/AP Multimedia Archives.* Historical and contemporary news images.

Grove Art Online. Art images and links to museum sites.

Many images you find will be available at no charge for copying or downloading, but some sources do charge a fee for use. Before paying for an image, check with a librarian to see if it is available elsewhere for free.

Note You must cite every image source fully in your paper, just as you cite text sources, with author, title, and publication information. In addition, some sources will require that you seek permission from the copyright holder, either the source itself or a third party such as a photographer. Permission is especially likely to be required if you are submitting your paper on the public Web. See pages 635–37 for more about online publication.

43i Generating your own sources

Many of the sources you consult for a research project—and most of the resources of the library—are likely to be secondary sources whose authors draw their information from other authors. However, academic writing will also require you to consult primary sources and to conduct primary research for information of your own. In many papers this primary research will be the sole basis for your writing, as when you analyze a poem or report on an experiment you conducted. In other papers you will be expected to use your research to support, extend, or refute the ideas of others.

Chapters 49–53 discuss the textual analyses, surveys, experiments, and other primary sources you may use in writing for various academic disciplines. One primary source not covered there is the personal interview with an expert in the topic you are researching. Because of the give-and-take of an interview, you can obtain answers to questions precisely geared to your topic, and you can follow up on points of confusion and unexpected leads. In addition, quotations and paraphrases from an interview can give your paper immediacy and authority. Edward Begay used just such an interview in his paper about the Internet (see p. 704).

You can conduct an interview in person, over the telephone, or online using electronic mail or a form of synchronous communication. A personal interview is preferable if you can arrange it because you can see the person's expressions and gestures as well as hear his or her tone and words. But telephone and online interviews allow you to consult someone who resists a personal interview or who lives far away from you, while still retaining most advantages of interaction.

ETHNOGRAPHY AND RESEARCH

Many instructors require students to begin their research projects with an interview so that they get a human perspective on their topic before they begin locating secondary sources. You can have students practice by interviewing a partner in class.

SYNCHRONOUS INTERVIEWING

To help students understand the value of in-person interviews, have them conduct a brief practice interview with a classmate using e-mail or synchronous communication and then compare the results with a practice in-person interview (using the same questions but a different subject). Ask them to record their impressions of the interviewee's tone, gestures, and expressions and then report back to you about how those factors influenced the content of what the interviewee said.

A few precautions will help you get the maximum information from an interview with the minimum disruption to the person you are interviewing:

- **Choose your interviewee carefully.** If you do not already know whom to consult for an interview, ask a teacher in the field or do some telephone or library research. Likely sources, depending on your topic, are those who have written about your topic or something closely related, officials in government, businesspeople, even a relative, if he or she is an expert in your topic because of experience, scholarship, or both.
- **Call or write for an appointment.** Tell the person exactly why you are calling, what you want to discuss, and how long you expect the interview to take. Be true to your word on all points.
- **Prepare a list of open-ended questions to ask**—perhaps ten or twelve for a one-hour interview. Plan on doing some research for these questions to discover background on the issues and your subject's published views on the issues.
- **Give your subject time to consider your questions.** Don't rush into silences with more questions.
- **Pay attention to your subject's answers** so that you can ask appropriate follow-up questions and pick up on unexpected but worthwhile points.
- **Take care in interpreting answers,** especially if you are online and thus can't depend on facial expressions, gestures, and tone of voice to convey the subject's attitudes. Ask for clarification when you need it.
- **Keep thorough notes.** Take notes during an in-person or telephone interview, or tape-record the interview, if you have the equipment and your subject agrees. For online interviews, save the discussion in a file of its own.
- **Verify quotations.** Before you quote your subject in your paper, check with him or her to ensure that the quotations are accurate.
- **Send a thank-you note immediately after the interview.** Promise your subject a copy of your finished paper, and send the paper promptly.

EXERCISE 43.1 Using the library

To become familiar with the research sources available through your library, visit both the library and its Web site for answers to the following questions. Ask a librarian for help whenever necessary. (You can do this exercise online at *ablongman.com/littlebrown*.)

1. Which resources does the library include on its Web site? Which resources require a visit to the library?

RESOURCES AND IDEAS

Heath, Shirley Brice. *Ways with Words: Language, Life, and Work in Communities.* New York: Cambridge UP, 1983. Heath provides a thorough and accessible demonstration of how to conduct ethnographic research, illustrated by her study of the communities of Roadville and Trackton.

Tryzna, Thomas N. "Research Outside the Library: Learning a Field." *College Composition and Communication* 37 (1986): 217–23. Tryzna shows how to begin a research project outside the library and find valuable primary sources.

COLLABORATIVE LEARNING

Have students complete Exercise 43.1 in teams. Hold a contest to see which team can find answers to all five sets of questions in the shortest amount of time.

Have students complete Exercises 43.2 and 43.3 individually and bring three of the sources to class. Then ask students to work in small groups to write a very brief summary of each source. Students can use the summaries as annotations in their working bibliographies.

ANSWERS: EXERCISE 43.1

Individual response.

2. Where are reference books stored in the library? How are they cataloged and arranged? Which ones are available through the Web site or on CD-ROM? Where and in what format(s) are (*a*) *Contemporary Authors,* (*b*) *Encyclopaedia Britannica,* and (*c*) *MLA International Bibliography of Books and Articles on the Modern Languages and Literatures*?

3. Where is the catalog of the library's periodicals? Where and in what format(s) does the library have current and back issues of the following periodicals: (*a*) the *New York Times,* (*b*) *Harper's* magazine, and (*c*) *Journal of Social Psychology*?

4. What tools does the library's Web site offer for finding periodical databases that are appropriate for a particular research subject?

5. Research the focus and indexed publications of two periodical databases, such as *InfoTrac, JSTOR, LexisNexis, PAIS,* or *ProQuest Research Library.* What disciplines does each database seem most suited for?

6. Does the book catalog cover all of the library's book holdings? If not, which books are not included, and where are they cataloged?

7. What are the library call numbers of the following books: (*a*) *The Power Broker,* by Robert Caro; (*b*) *Heart of Darkness,* by Joseph Conrad; and (*c*) *The Hero with a Thousand Faces,* by Joseph Campbell?

ANSWERS: EXERCISE 43.2

Individual response.

EXERCISE 43.2 Finding library sources

Locate at least six promising articles and books for the subject you began working on in the previous chapter (Exercise 42.1, p. 563, and Exercise 42.2, p. 567). Consider the sources "promising" if they seem directly to address your central research question. Following the guidelines on pages 567–70, make an annotated working bibliography of the sources. Be sure to include all the information you will need to acknowledge the sources in your final paper.

ANSWERS: EXERCISE 43.3

Individual response.

EXERCISE 43.3 Finding Web sources

Use at least two Web search engines to locate six or seven promising sources for your research project. Begin by developing a list of keywords that can be used to query one of the search engines (see pp. 574–75). Check the Advanced Search option of the engine if you need to narrow your search. Then try your refined keywords on the other search engine as well. How do the results differ? What keyword strategies worked best for finding relevant information? Add promising sources to your annotated working bibliography.

CHAPTER **44**

Working with Sources

The previous chapters helped you lay the groundwork for a research project. This chapter takes you into the most personal, most intensive, and most rewarding part of research writing: using the sources you've found to extend and support your own ideas, to make your subject your own. As before, the work of Edward Begay (on access to the Internet) and Vanessa Haley (on the work of Annie Dillard) will illustrate the activity and thought that go into research writing.

CULTURE LANGUAGE Making a subject your own requires thinking critically about sources and developing independent ideas. These goals may at first be uncomfortable if your native culture emphasizes understanding and respecting established authority more than questioning and enlarging it. This chapter offers guidance in working with sources so that you can become an expert in your own right and convincingly convey your expertise to others.

44a Evaluating sources

1 Gaining an overview

Once you have a satisfactory working bibliography, you want to get a sense of your sources' usefulness and value.

■ **Look first at sources that seem most likely to define your subject.** Edward Begay initially consulted a government report on computer use by different segments of society. Vanessa Haley turned first to a book by Annie Dillard, Haley's subject. (For a paper like Haley's that analyzes a writer's work, that work is always the starting point.)

■ **Scan sources to gauge the kind and extent of their ideas and information.** Don't get bogged down collecting information at this point. Instead, ensure that your sources are appropriately

---

http://www.ablongman.com/littlebrown ▶

Visit the companion Web site for more help and an additional exercise on working with sources.

---

mycomplab 2.0

Please visit MyCompLab at *www.mycomplab.com* for more on the writing process.

HIGHLIGHTS

This chapter tackles one of the most difficult aspects of research writing. Students unskilled in research or with comparatively undeveloped critical thinking skills may not know what to do with the sources they find. Students will follow Edward Begay's and Vanessa Haley's research in progress and observe how these students work with sources. New to this edition of the handbook is an expanded discussion (44a) of how to evaluate Web sites and online discussions, including a new section on Web logs.

Subsequent sections focus on how students may respond to and interact with the sources they find, including detailed coverage of methods of gathering and organizing information. Section 44d, which covers summary, paraphrase, and quotation, includes new detailed examples of summary and paraphrase that students should find helpful. The final section covers methods of introducing source material into the text of a research paper. The chapter's exercises provide practice in all aspects of handling sources.

COLLABORATIVE LEARNING

GETTING A CLUE

Because students are often unfamiliar with the clues provided by the publication context, bibliographic and indexing apparatus, and tone of a source, they may find the task of scanning sources difficult and confusing. Pose a sample paper topic that is related to the material found in a source you distribute, and ask students to work in small groups to evaluate the source for relevance and reliability. Then lead a discussion in which you help students to identify the kinds of clues they used to help them decide whether the source was appropriate to the topic, whether it was too specialized or too simplistic, too out-of-date, or too biased.

COMPANION WEB SITE

See page IAE-60 for companion Web site content description.

GROUP EVALUATION

As a follow-up to the "Getting a Clue" exercise on the previous page, ask students to bring to class one or two sources they are considering using in their own research papers. Have them work with their groups to evaluate the sources and then present their findings to the rest of the class.

ANNOTATION ASSIGNMENT

Ask students to submit an annotated bibliography of sources as a mini-assignment. This assignment can be one phase of a larger research assignment; by breaking the assignment into mini-assignments, you can help ensure that students pay adequate attention to all parts of the research process.

detailed and cover the full range of your subject—that together they promise to help you answer your research question.

- **Update your annotated bibliography with assessments of sources.** As you take the measure of sources, add your evaluations to your working bibliography. The writing will help you differentiate sources and start you on building connections among them. In each annotation, summarize the purpose, main argument, and any apparent bias of the source. Also note any questions you have about it. Here is an example from Edward Begay's evolving bibliography, adding to the entry on page 570.

Annotated bibliography entry with assessment

Publication and access information for source

United States. Dept. of Education. National Center for Education Statistics. Internet Access in US Public Schools and Classrooms. 24 Feb. 2005. 12 Mar. 2005 <http://nces.ed.gov/pubsearch/pubsinfo.asp?pubid=2005015>.

Summary of source (from working bibliography)

Report on the annual NCES survey of the quantity and quality of technology used in K-12 classrooms. Includes important statistics on trends—student-to-computer ratios, teacher training, computer availability to students in different socioeconomic brackets.

Assessment of source

Current and reliable statistics compiled to track "progress" made in availability of computers and the Internet in public education. Cautious, qualified results find widespread Internet connectivity among all socioeconomic levels but significant differences in quality of connection, support, and especially student-to-computer ratios. Statistics confirmed in other studies?

Question

2 Judging relevance and reliability

Not all the sources you find will prove worthwhile: some may be irrelevant to your subject, and others may be unreliable. Gauging the relevance and reliability of sources is the essential task of evaluating them. If you haven't already done so, read this book's Chapters 8 and 9 on critical reading. They provide a foundation for answering the questions in the box opposite.

Note In evaluating sources, you need to consider how they came to you. The sources you find through the library, both print and online, have been previewed for you by their publishers and by the library's staff. They still require your critical reading, but you can have some confidence in the information they contain. With online sources you reach directly, however, you cannot assume

Questions for evaluating sources

For online sources, supplement these questions with those on pages 602 and 608.

Relevance

- **Does the source devote some attention to your subject?** Check whether the source focuses on your subject or covers it marginally, and compare the source's coverage to that in other sources.
- **Is the source appropriately specialized for your needs?** Check the source's treatment of a topic you know something about, to ensure that it is neither too superficial nor too technical.
- **Is the source up to date enough for your subject?** Check the publication date. If your subject is current, your sources should be, too.

Reliability

- **Where does the source come from?** It matters whether you found the source through your library or directly on the Internet. (If the latter, see the following pages.) Check whether a library source is popular or scholarly. Scholarly sources, such as refereed journals and university press books, are generally deeper and more reliable.
- **Is the author an expert in the field?** The authors of scholarly publications tend to be experts. To verify expertise, check an author's credentials in a biography (if the source includes one), in a biographical reference (see p. 578), or by a keyword search of the Web. Look for the author's other publications and for his or her job and any affiliation, such as teacher at a university, researcher with a nonprofit organization, author of general-interest books, or writer for popular magazines.
- **What is the author's bias?** Every author has a point of view that influences the selection and interpretation of evidence. You may be able to learn about an author's bias from biographies, citation indexes (pp. 586–87), and review indexes (p. 581). But also look at the source itself. How do the author's ideas relate to those in other sources? What areas does the author emphasize, ignore, or dismiss? When you're aware of sources' biases, you can attempt to balance them.
- **Is the source fair and reasonable?** Even a strongly biased work should present sound reasoning, adequate evidence, and a fair picture of opposing views—all in an objective, calm tone. The absence of any of these qualities should raise a warning flag.
- **Is the source well written?** A logical organization and clear, error-free sentences indicate a careful author.

You can download these questions from *ablongman.com/littlebrown*. Use a copy of the file for each source you are evaluating, providing written answers between the questions.

similar previewing, so your critical reading must be especially rigorous. Special tips for evaluating Web sites and other online sources appear on the following pages.

WEB CLUES

Since electronic sources pose special problems, particularly for determining reliability, it will be helpful to conduct additional in-class evaluations of such sources. In a networked classroom, you might run through a short Web search and then ask students to help you evaluate the reliability of the sources you find, using the criteria provided by the handbook. Then ask students to work in pairs to evaluate one or two of their Web site sources and to report their findings to the class. In each case, encourage students to recount (and to keep journal records of) the methods they used to determine a source's reliability and relevance.

DISINGENUOUS SITES

Some Web sites, particularly those sponsored by some kinds of activist organizations, attempt to appear nonbiased when in fact they have a very strong bias. They may post pseudo-scholarship on their sites in an attempt to look research-based and academic. If you come across such sites, they can be excellent teaching tools. Students will be eager to develop the savvy to uncover the true bias underlying a Web site, and you can point out to them that intelligent readers use the same methods of analysis to evaluate all texts, including student research papers.

3 Evaluating a Web site

To a great extent, the same critical reading that helps you evaluate library sources will help you evaluate Web sites. But most Web sites have not undergone prior screening by editors and librarians. On your own, you must distinguish scholarship from corporate promotion, valid data from invented statistics, well-founded opinion from clever propaganda.

The following strategy, summarized in the box below, can help you make such distinctions. We'll apply the strategy to the Web site shown on the next several pages, *Global Warming Information Center*, which turned up in a search for views and data on global warming.

Questions for evaluating Web sites

Supplement these questions with those on the previous page.

- **What type of site are you viewing?** What does the type lead you to expect about the site's purpose and content?
- **Who is the author or sponsor?** How credible is the person or group responsible for the site?
- **What is the purpose of the site?** What does the site's author or sponsor intend to achieve?
- **What does context tell you?** What do you already know about the site's subject that can inform your evaluation? What kinds of support or other information do the site's links provide?
- **What does presentation tell you?** Is the site's design well thought out and effective? Is the writing clear and error-free?
- **How worthwhile is the content?** Are the site's claims well supported by evidence? Is the evidence from reliable sources?

You can download these questions from *ablongman.com/littlebrown*. Use a copy of the file for each source you are evaluating, providing written answers between the questions.

Note To evaluate a Web document, you'll often need to travel to the site's home page to discover the author or sponsoring organization, date of publication, and other relevant information. The page you're reading may include a link to the home page. If it doesn't, you can find it by editing the URL in the Address or Location field of your browser. Working backward, delete the end of the URL up to the last slash and hit Enter. Repeat this step until you reach the home page. There you may also find a menu option, often labeled "About," that will lead you to a description of the site's author or sponsor.

■ Determine the type of site.

When you search the Web, you're likely to encounter various types of sites. Although they overlap—a primarily informational site may include scholarship as well—the types can usually be identified by their content and purposes. Here are the main types:

- **Sites focusing on scholarship:** These sites have a knowledge-building interest and include research reports with supporting data and extensive documentation of scholarly sources. The URLs of the sites generally end in *edu* (originating from an educational institution), *org* (a nonprofit organization), or *gov* (a government department or agency). Such sites are more likely to be reliable than the others described below.

- **Sites with an informational purpose:** Individuals, nonprofit organizations, schools, corporations, and government bodies all produce sites intended to centralize information on subjects as diverse as astronomy, hip-hop music, computer architecture, and zoo design. The sites' URLs may end in *edu, org, gov,* or *com* (originating from a commercial organization). Such sites generally do not have the knowledge-building focus of scholarly sites and may omit supporting data and documentation, but they can provide useful information and often include links to scholarly and other sources.

- **Sites focusing on advocacy:** Many sites present the views of individuals or organizations that advocate certain policies or actions. Their URLs usually end in *org*, but they may end in *edu* or *com*. Some advocacy sites include serious, well-documented research to support their positions, but others select or distort evidence.

- **Sites with a commercial purpose:** Corporations and other businesses maintain Web sites to explain themselves, promote themselves, or sell goods and services. The URLs of commercial sites end in *com*. Although the information on such a site furthers the sponsor's profit-making purpose, it can include reliable data.

- **Personal sites:** The sites maintained by individuals range from diaries of a family's travels to opinions on political issues to reports on evolving scholarship. The sites' URLs usually end in *com* or *edu*. Personal sites are only as reliable as their authors, but some do provide valuable eyewitness accounts, links to worthy sources, and other usable information. A particular kind of personal site, the Web log, is discussed on pages 607–09.

The following home page of the *Global Warming Information Center* gives some information that can be used to tell what type of site it is:

TRYING OUT SITES

Ask students to provide you with an example of these five types of sites (scholarly, informational, advocacy, commercial, and personal) on their research topic. Then ask them to outline a research paragraph based on each site to get a better understanding of how useful (or useless) each kind of site is for their purposes.

1. Home page of the *Global Warming Information Center*

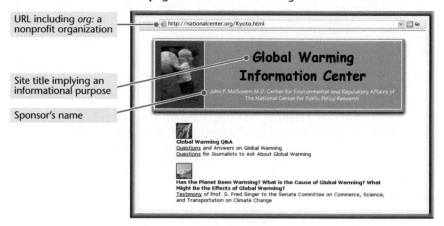

URL including *org:* a nonprofit organization

Site title implying an informational purpose

Sponsor's name

▣ Identify the author or sponsor.

A reputable site will list the author or group responsible for the site and will provide information or a link for contacting the author or group. If none of this information is provided, you should not use the source. If you have only the author or group name, you may be able to discover more in a biographical dictionary, through a keyword search, or in your other sources.

As screen 1 shows, the *Global Warming* site names its sponsor right up front: the John P. McGovern M.D. Center for Environmental and Regulatory Affairs. The bottom of this home page gives links to information about the McGovern Center and its parent organization, the National Center for Public Policy Research. Their names imply that both groups are involved in research, so the site does indeed seem to be informational or possibly even scholarly.

▣ Gauge purpose.

A Web site's purpose determines what ideas and information it offers. Inferring that purpose tells you how to interpret what you see on the site. If a site is intended to sell a product or an opinion, it will likely emphasize favorable ideas and information while ignoring or even distorting what is unfavorable. In contrast, if a site is intended to build knowledge—for instance, a scholarly project or journal—it will likely acknowledge diverse views and evidence.

Determining the purpose of a site often requires looking beyond the first page and beneath the surface of words and images. The elements of the *Global Warming* site—the title, the green color, the photo of a child carrying a globe through a field of grass—suggest an environmentalist purpose of informing readers about the theory and consequences of rising earth temperatures caused by pollution. The site's purpose is actually different, though. The home-page links lead to statements about the aims of the McGovern Center and its parent, the National Center. Screen 2 shows the McGovern Center statement.

---

2. Information about the sponsoring organization

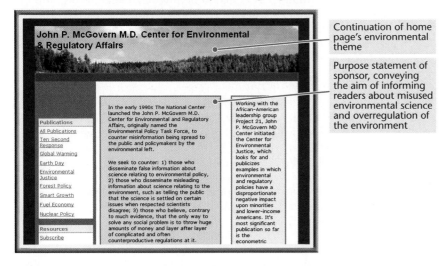

Continuation of home page's environmental theme

Purpose statement of sponsor, conveying the aim of informing readers about misused environmental science and overregulation of the environment

The National Center's purpose statement expands the McGovern Center's:

> The National Center for Public Policy Research is a communications and research foundation supportive of a strong national defense and dedicated to providing free market solutions to today's public policy problems. We believe that the principles of a free market, individual liberty and personal responsibility provide the greatest hope for meeting the challenges facing America in the 21st century.

These two statements imply that the purpose of the McGovern Center's *Global Warming* site is to inform readers about the evidence against global warming in the interest of reducing or overturning environmental regulations.

▓ Consider context.

Your evaluation of a Web site should be informed by considerations outside the site itself. Chief among these is your own knowledge: What do you already know about the site's subject and the prevailing views of it? Where does this site seem to fit into that picture? What can you learn from this site that you don't already know?

In addition, you can follow some of the site's links to see how they support, or don't support, the site's credibility. For instance, links to scholarly sources lend authority to a site—but *only if* the scholarly sources actually relate to and back up the site's claims.

The *Global Warming* site has a clear anti-regulatory bias, but this view is a significant one in the debates over global warming, that is, the bias does not necessarily disqualify the site as a source on global warming. The question is how reliable its information is: does it come from trustworthy, less biased sources? All the site's links lead to publications of the McGovern Center or the National Center, so the question can be answered only by looking more deeply at these publications.

■ Look at presentation.

Considering both the look of a site and the way it's written can illuminate its intentions and reliability. Are the site's elements all functional and well integrated, or is the site cluttered with irrelevant material and graphics? Does the site seem carefully constructed and well maintained, or is it sloppy and outdated? Does the design reflect the apparent purpose of the site, or does it undercut or conceal that purpose in some way? Is the text clearly written, or is it difficult to understand? Is it error-free, or does it contain typos and grammatical errors?

At first glance, as noted earlier, the *Global Warming* site casts a pro-environmentalist image that turns out not to coincide with its purpose. Otherwise, the site is cleanly designed, with minimal elements laid out clearly. The text on other pages is straightforward and readable. Together, design and readability indicate that the sponsor takes its purpose seriously and has thought out its presentation.

■ Analyze content.

With information about a site's author, purpose, and context, you're in a position to evaluate its content. Are the ideas and information slanted and, if so, in what direction? Are the views and data authoritative, or do you need to balance them—or even reject them? These questions require close reading of both the text and its sources.

The *Global Warming* site links to a wealth of reports and prominently features "Questions and Answers on Global Warming." The screen shots opposite show two of the items from this page and the footnotes citing sources for the answers. The source mix in the footnotes is similar in the other publications found through the *Global Warming* site. Scholars do disagree over whether the earth's temperatures are rising significantly, whether human-made pollution is an important cause, how serious the consequences may be, and how to

3. Content and documentation from the site

Questions and Answers on Global Warming

1. Is global warming occurring? Have the forecasts of global warming been confirmed by actual measurements?

There is no serious evidence that man-made global warming is taking place. The computer models used in U.N. studies say the first area to heat under the "greenhouse gas effect" should be the lower atmosphere - known as the troposphere.1 Highly accurate, carefully checked satellite data have shown absolutely no such tropospheric warming. There has been surface warming of about half a degree Celsius, but this is far below the customary natural swings in surface temperatures.2

2. Are carbon dioxide emissions from burning fossil fuels the primary cause of climate change? Can the Earth's temperature be expected to rise between 2.5 and 10.4 degrees Fahrenheit in this century as has been reported?

There are many indications that carbon dioxide does not play a significant role in global warming. Richard Lindzen, Ph.D., professor at the Massachusetts Institute of Technology and one of the 11 scientists who prepared a 2001 National Academy of Sciences (NAS) report on climate change, estimates that a doubling of carbon dioxide in the atmosphere would produce a temperature increase of only one degree Celsius.3 In fact, clouds and water vapor appear to be far more important factors related to global temperature. According to Dr. Lindzen and NASA scientists, clouds and water vapor may play a significant role in regulating the Earth's temperature to keep it more constant.4

> Assertions about the validity and causes of global warming, citing data and expert opinion as evidence

Footnotes

1 James K. Glassman and Sallie Baliunas, *The Weekly Standard*, June 25, 2001.
2 *Ibid.*
3 Richard Lindzen, professor of meteorology, Massachusetts Institute of Technology and member of the National Academy of Sciences, "Scientists' Report Doesn't Support The Kyoto Treaty," *The Wall Street Journal*, June 11, 2001.
4 Glassman and Baliunas.

> Footnotes citing an article in the conservative magazine *The Weekly Standard* and a newspaper report, not scholarly publications that explain methods of gathering and interpreting the data used as evidence

solve the problem. However, the *Global Warming* site does not offer or refer to the scholarly research. As a result, the claims and evidence must be viewed suspiciously and probably rejected for use in a research paper. A usable source need not be less biased, but it must be more substantial.

4 Evaluating other online sources

Web logs and the postings to online discussions require the same critical scrutiny as Web sites do. Web logs can be sources of in-depth information and informed opinion, but they can also be virtually useless. Web forums and newsgroups are similarly suspect. Even if a reliable blog or discussion-group message provides very current information or eyewitness testimony, it will not have the authority of a scholarly publication. An e-mail discussion list may be more trustworthy if its subscribers are professionals in the field, but you will still find wrong or misleading data and skewed opinions.

BLOG HALL OF FAME

As a class, compile a collection of memorable blogs. Give awards for the most boring, the most redundant, the most entertaining, the most self-indulgent, the one with the most grammatical errors, the most heartfelt, or ask students to make up their own award categories.

Use the following strategy for evaluating blogs and messages in online discussions.

Questions for evaluating Web logs and online discussions

Supplement these questions with those on page 601.

- **Who is the author?** How credible is the person writing?
- **What is the author's purpose?** What can you tell about why the author is writing?
- **What does the context reveal?** What do others' responses on a blog or the other messages in a discussion thread indicate about the source's balance and reliability?
- **How worthwhile is the content?** Are the author's claims supported by evidence? Is the evidence from reliable sources?
- **How does the blog or message compare with other sources?** Do the author's claims seem accurate and fair given what you've seen in sources you know to be reliable?

You can download these questions from *ablongman.com/littlebrown*. Use a copy of the file for each source you are evaluating, providing written answers between the questions.

Identify the author.

Checking out the author of a blog or online posting can help you judge the reliability of the message. If the author uses a screen name, write directly to him or her requesting full name and credentials. Do not use the message as a source if the author fails to respond. Once you know an author's name, you may be able to obtain background information from a keyword search of the Web or a biographical dictionary.

You can also get a sense of the interests and biases of an author by tracking down his or her other writing. For a blog, check whether the author cites or links to other publications. For a newsgroup message, look for a feature that allows you to find other messages by the author of any posting. For a discussion list or Web forum, use the group's archive to locate other messages by a particular author.

Analyze the author's purpose.

As with Web sites, you can use cues in the author's writing to figure out *why* he or she is writing and thus how to position the blog or message among your other sources. The claims, use (or not) of evidence, and treatment of opposing views all convey the author's stand on the subject and general fairness.

▣ Consider the context.

Web logs and discussion-group postings are often difficult to evaluate in isolation. Looking outside a particular contribution to the responses of others will give you a sense of how the author's view is regarded. On a blog, look at the comments others have posted. Do the same with discussion-group messages, going back to the initial posting in the discussion thread and reading forward.

▣ Analyze content.

A reliable source will offer evidence for claims and sources for evidence. If you don't see such supporting information, ask the author for it. (If he or she fails to respond, don't use the source.) Then verify the sources with your own research: are they reputable?

The tone of the writing can also be a clue to its purpose and reliability. Blogs and online discussions tend to be more informal and often more heated than other kinds of dialog, but look askance at writing that's contemptuous, dismissive, or shrill.

▣ Compare with other sources.

Always consider blogs and discussion-group messages in comparison to other sources so that you can distinguish singular, untested views from more mainstream views that have been subject to verification. Don't assume that a blog author's information and opinions are mainstream just because you see them on other blogs. The technology allows content to be picked up instantly on other blogs, so widespread distribution indicates only popularity, not reliability.

Be wary of blogs or messages that reproduce periodical articles, reports, or other publications. Try to locate the original version of the publication to be sure it has been reproduced fully and accurately, not quoted selectively or distorted. If you can't locate the original version, then don't use the publication as a source.

EXERCISE 44.1 Evaluating a source

Imagine that you are researching a paper on the advertising techniques that are designed to persuade consumers to buy products. You have listed the following book in your working bibliography:

> Vance Packard, *The Hidden Persuaders*, revised edition, 1981.

On your own or with your classmates (as your instructor wishes), obtain this book from a library and evaluate it as a source for your paper. Use the guidelines on page 601. (You can do this exercise online at *ablongman.com/littlebrown*.)

EXERCISE 44.2 Evaluating Web sites

Find and evaluate three Web sites: a commercial site, such as Microsoft's or Apple's; a site for a nonprofit organization, such as the American

---

In a networked classroom, you could do Exercises 44.3 and 44.4 as a class. Look at the postings together and discuss them, using the chart for evaluating online discussions and blogs on page 608. Or have students e-mail their evaluation paragraphs to the rest of the class or post them on your class Web site. As a class, you can develop your own annotated list of newsgroups, Web forums, and blogs.

ANSWERS: EXERCISE 44.3

Individual response.

ANSWERS: EXERCISE 44.4

Individual response.

RESOURCES AND IDEAS

Higgens, Lorraine. "Reading to Argue: Helping Students Transform Source Texts." In *Hearing Ourselves Think: Cognitive Research in the College Writing Classroom*. Ed. Ann M. Penrose and Barbara M. Sitko. New York, Oxford: Oxford UP, 1993. 70–101. Higgens explores strategies through which students learn to use their sources, and debates between their sources, as the basis for developing their own arguments.

Spivey, Nancy Nelson. "The Shaping of Meaning: Options in Writing the Comparison." *Research in the Teaching of English* 25 (1991): 390–418. Spivey shows that the use of sources can affect students' processes of invention, arrangement, and style.

UNDERSTANDING THE DEBATES

Students often experience some difficulty in identifying connections among their sources. To help them develop a better sense of the debates surrounding their topic and the major authors involved in these debates, ask your students to look through the bibliographies and footnotes (or endnotes) of their principal sources for additional sources to read. Likely prospects include titles or authors that are more frequently cited than others. As a follow-up exercise, you might have stu-

Medical Association or Greenpeace; and the personal site of an individual. What do you know or can you infer about each site's sponsor or author? What seems to be the site's purpose or purposes? What do the site's links contribute? How effective is the site's design? How reliable do you judge the site's information to be? How do the three types of sites differ in these respects?

EXERCISE 44.3 Evaluating a Web log

Visit *bloglines.com* or *blogwise.com* to find a Web log on a controversial subject such as stem-cell research or online sharing of music files. Who is responsible for the blog? What can you tell about its purpose? How reliable do you judge its ideas and information to be?

EXERCISE 44.4 Evaluating an online discussion

Using *groups.google.com,* locate a newsgroup on a subject that interests you. (If you already participate in an online discussion group, you can use it instead.) Pick one series of at least ten related messages on a single topic. Write a brief summary of each message (see pp. 140–42 on summarizing). Then analyze and synthesize the messages to develop a one- or two-paragraph evaluation of the discussion. Which messages seem reliable? Which don't? Why?

44b   Synthesizing sources

When you begin to locate the differences and similarities among sources, you move into the most significant part of research writing: forging relationships for your own purpose. This **synthesis**, an essential step in critical reading (pp. 161–62), continues through the drafting and revision of a research paper. As you infer connections—say, between one writer's ideas and another's or between two works by the same author—you create new knowledge.

All kinds of connections may occur to you as you work with sources. Edward Begay, researching the potential accessibility of the Internet to both the affluent and the poor, found data in one source to support another source's assertions about a technological gap between private and public schools. He also uncovered a central disagreement among sources over whether the Internet would prove a boon or an obstruction to education. Vanessa Haley, writing about Annie Dillard, sought and found similarities in Dillard's ideas about the place of humanity in nature, ideas expressed in varying contexts throughout Dillard's best-known book. Haley also discovered that her view of Dillard was partly supported by some of the critics she consulted but not supported by others. She knew she would have to take account of these divergent views in her paper.

Your synthesis of sources will grow more detailed and sophisticated as you proceed through the research-writing process. Unless, like Vanessa Haley, you are analyzing primary sources such as the works of a writer, at first read your sources quickly and selectively to obtain an overview of your subject and a sense of how the sources approach it. Instead of taking detailed notes about what sources say, record your own ideas about the sources in your research journal (p. 559) or your annotated bibliography (p. 600).

■ Respond to sources.

Write down what your sources make you think. Do you agree or disagree with the author? Do you find his or her views narrow, or do they open up new approaches for you? Is there anything in the source that you need to research further before you can understand it? Does the source prompt questions that you should keep in mind while reading other sources?

■ Connect sources.

When you notice a link between sources, jot it down. Do two sources differ in their theories or their interpretations of facts? Does one source illuminate another—perhaps commenting or clarifying or supplying additional data? Do two or more sources report studies that support a theory you've read about or an idea of your own?

■ Heed your own insights.

Apart from ideas prompted by your sources, you are sure to come up with independent thoughts: a conviction, a point of confusion that suddenly becomes clear, a question you haven't seen anyone else ask. These insights may occur at unexpected times, so it's good practice to keep a notebook or computer handy to record them.

■ Use sources to support your own ideas.

As your research proceeds, the responses, connections, and insights you form through synthesis will lead you to answer your starting research question with a statement of your thesis (see p. 639). They will also lead you to the main ideas supporting your thesis—conclusions you have drawn from your synthesis of sources, forming the main divisions of your paper. When drafting the paper, make sure each paragraph focuses on an idea of your own, with the support for the idea coming from your sources. In this way, your paper will synthesize others' work into something wholly your own.

EXERCISE 44.5 Synthesizing sources

The following three passages address the same issue, the legalization of drugs. What similarities do you see in the authors' ideas? What differ-

---

dents work in groups to give oral presentations about the connections and debates as developed among three of their sources. You might also have students turn in a one-page analysis of the crucial connections among those three sources.

COLLABORATIVE LEARNING

As a preliminary activity to Exercise 44.5, have students work in groups to debate the similarities and differences among the three authors and their approaches. Encourage students to support their views with evidence from the three passages. Then have each student create the paragraph specified by Exercise 4 and share it with his or her group. The collaborative approach will enrich students' interpretive responses to the passages, and will help make them aware that their own views on the topic are not self-evident but must be argued on the basis of evidence.

ANSWERS: EXERCISE 44.5

The key similarities and differences are these:

Similarities: Nadelmann and Posey agree that crackdowns or penalties do not stop the drug trade. Nadelmann and Runkle agree that the drug trade affects the young, who are most impressionable.

Differences: Nadelmann maintains that the illegal drug trade does more to entice youths to drugs than do the drugs themselves, whereas Runkle maintains that the illegality discourages youths from using prohibited drugs. Posey, in contrast to Runkle, claims that penalties do nothing to discourage drug abusers.

Students' paragraphs will depend on their views, but here is a sample response:

Posey seems to invalidate the whole debate over drug legalization: nothing, he says from experience, will stop drug abuse. But such a futile view, whatever its truth, cannot stop the search for a solution. We have tried the prohibition favored by Runkle. Even if, as she claims, students are using fewer illegal drugs, prohibition has not worked. It may be time to try the admittedly risky approach proposed by Nadelmann, legalizing drugs to "drive the drug-dealing business off the streets."

COMPUTER ACTIVITY

SOUNDING BOARDS

If you are teaching a distance education course, your students may miss out on the opportunity to have a sounding board for their impressions of a source. Let pairs or small groups read the same source and then have an open-ended discussion about the source online, using e-mail, your courseware, or synchronous communication.

ences? Write a paragraph of your own in which you use these authors' views as a point of departure for your own view about drug legalization. (You can do this exercise online at *ablongman.com/littlebrown*.)

Perhaps the most unfortunate victims of drug prohibition laws have been the residents of America's ghettos. These laws have proved largely futile in deterring ghetto-dwellers from becoming drug abusers, but they do account for much of what ghetto residents identify as the drug problem. Aggressive, gun-toting drug dealers often upset law-abiding residents far more than do addicts nodding out in doorways. Meanwhile other residents perceive the drug dealers as heroes and successful role models. They're symbols of success to children who see no other options. At the same time the increasingly harsh criminal penalties imposed on adult drug dealers have led drug traffickers to recruit juveniles. Where once children started dealing drugs only after they had been using them for a few years, today the sequence is often reversed. Many children start using drugs only after working for older drug dealers for a while. Legalization of drugs, like legalization of alcohol in the early 1930s, would drive the drug-dealing business off the streets and out of apartment buildings and into government-regulated, tax-paying stores. It also would force many of the gun-toting dealers out of the business and convert others into legitimate businessmen.
—Ethan A. Nadelmann, "Shooting Up"

Statistics argue against legalization. The University of Michigan conducts an annual survey of twelfth graders, asking the students about their drug consumption. In 1980, 56.4 percent of those polled said they had used marijuana in the past twelve months, whereas in 2004 only 45.7 percent had done so. Cocaine use was also reduced in the same period (22.6 percent to 15.4 percent). At the same time, twelve-month use of legally available drugs—alcohol and nicotine-containing cigarettes—remained fairly steady around 75 percent and 55 percent, respectively. The numbers of illegal drug users haven't declined nearly enough: those teenaged marijuana and cocaine users are still vulnerable to addiction and even death, and they threaten to infect their impressionable peers. But clearly the prohibition of illegal drugs has helped, while the legal status of alcohol and cigarettes has not made them less popular.
—Sylvia Runkle, "The Case Against Legalization"

I have to laugh at the debate over what to do about the drug problem. Everyone is running around offering solutions—from making drug use a more serious criminal offense to legalizing it. But there isn't a real solution. I know that. I used and abused drugs, and people, and society, for two decades. Nothing worked to get me to stop all that behavior except just plain being sick and tired. Nothing. Not threats, not ten-plus years in prison, not anything that was said to me. I used until I got through. Period. And that's when you'll win the war. When all the dope fiends are done. Not a minute before.
—Michael W. Posey, "I Did Drugs Until They Wore Me Out. Then I Stopped."

EXERCISE 44.6   Evaluating and synthesizing sources

Look up the sources in the working bibliography you made in Exercises 43.2 and 43.3 (p. 598). Evaluate the sources for their relevance and reliability. If the sources seem unreliable or don't seem to give you what you need, expand your working bibliography and evaluate the new sources. In your research journal or annotated bibliography, write down your responses to sources, the connections you perceive among sources, and other original ideas that occur to you.

44c   Mining and interacting with sources

When you have decided which sources to pursue, you may be ready to gather information, or you may want to step back and get your bearings. Your choice will depend mainly on how familiar you are with the main issues of your subject and whether you have formed a central idea about it.

- **When you know what you're looking for, proceed with information gathering.** If you've formed a good idea of your thesis and a sense of the subjects you will cover, you'll have a framework in which to use sources.
- **When you're uncertain of your direction, stop to draft a thesis statement and create an outline.** These steps (discussed on pp. 639–43) can help when you're attracted to several different theses or when you don't see how the various areas of your subject relate.

The following sections discuss a way of reading sources and methods of gathering and organizing information from sources.

1 Skimming and then reading

The most efficient method of reading secondary sources during research is **skimming,** reading quickly to look for pertinent information. (Primary sources usually need to be read more carefully, especially when they are the focus of your paper.) Follow these guidelines for skimming:

- **Read with a specific question in mind,** not randomly in hopes of hitting something worthwhile.
- **Consult reference aids**—tables of contents, menus, indexes, or headings—to find what you want.
- **Concentrate on headings and main ideas,** skipping material unrelated to the specific question you are researching.

When you find something relevant, read slowly and carefully to achieve a clear understanding of what the author is saying and to

ANSWERS: EXERCISE 44.6

Individual response.

RESOURCES AND IDEAS

Kantz, Margaret. "Helping Students Use Textual Sources Persuasively." *College English* 52 (1990): 74–91. Kantz suggests using analysis of the rhetorical situation and lists of questions to help students meet the demands of research essays.

Pelham, Fran O'Byrne. "The Research Journal: Integrating Reading, Writing, and Research." *Composition Chronicle* 6.3 (April 1993): 4–5. O'Byrne advocates using a journal to supplement typical research activities and to allow students to "research, reflect, write, and then attend recursively to these events."

COLLABORATIVE LEARNING

SKIMMING TOGETHER

Give your students a medium-length article and tell them to skim it with a pertinent research question (of your choosing) in mind. Give them a time limit for skimming, plus a few more minutes to reread key passages. Then, working in small groups, they can discuss what they gleaned from the article in relation to the research question.

COLLABORATIVE LEARNING

PARTNERS FOR GATHERING

Students can show a partner the results of their efforts to gather and organize information. The partner should evaluate the researcher's material, checking for accuracy in the recording of source information and advising the researcher on efficient methods of information gathering.

COMPUTER ACTIVITY

SOURCE ACCESSIBILITY

Students working on popular topics or on topics for which little information is available may find that they do better accessing sources online than in the library stacks. Popular books and articles in the library sometimes have a way of disappearing from the shelves, and students often aren't able to consult them again if they need to. Encourage students working on such topics to use full-text databases and download where possible.

READING AND THINKING WHILE GATHERING

To combat the problem of indiscriminate downloading or printing of information that interferes with the researcher's interaction with sources, encourage your students to skim and summarize sources they find online as they print them out or download them. This will help them make sure that the information they are gathering is truly relevant to their subject and may give them ideas for next steps in their research.

interpret and evaluate the material in the context of your own and others' opinions.

2 Gathering and organizing information

Before you begin mining your sources, decide on categories into which your subject can be divided. (If you have previously outlined your preliminary ideas, use outline headings for these categories.) Edward Begay, for instance, divided his general subject of Internet access into these categories:

> History of the Internet
> Traditional vs. innovative models of education
> Differences between rich and poor schools
> Training of Internet users
> Costs of hooking up to the Internet
> Internet and economic inequality
> Role of librarians and teachers in Internet use
> Role of businesses in Internet use
> Role of government in Internet use

Headings for your categories will go at the top of each note to cue you about its content.

Researchers vary in their methods for working with sources, but all methods share the same goals:

- **Keep accurate records of what sources say.** Accuracy helps prevent misrepresentation and plagiarism.
- **Keep accurate records of how to find sources.** These records are essential for retracing steps and for citing sources in the final paper. (See pp. 567–70 on recording information in a working bibliography.)
- **Interact with sources.** Information gathering is not mechanical but critical, leading to an understanding of sources, the relationships among them, and their support for one's own ideas.

You can accomplish these goals by taking handwritten notes, typing notes into a computer, annotating photocopies or printouts of sources, or annotating downloaded documents. On any given project, you may use all the methods. Each has advantages and disadvantages.

Note Whichever method you use, take two steps with every note, photocopy, printout, or downloaded document:

- **Key the material to your outline** so that you know where it belongs.
- **Record the source's complete publication information,** or use the author's name as a shorthand reference to a list where you keep complete publication information.

■ Handwritten notes

The traditional method of writing notes on 4″ × 6″ cards will prove useful when you come across a source with no computer or photocopier handy or when you need to record something brief. Handwritten notes can be risky, though. It's easy to introduce errors as you work from source to note card. And it's possible to copy source language and then later mistake and use it as your own, thus plagiarizing the source. Always take care to make accurate notes and to place big quotation marks around any passage you quote. Some researchers reduce the risk of plagiarism by summarizing or paraphrasing sources on notes instead of quoting them, as described on pages 617–20. Other researchers delay this step until drafting because it increases the risk of error.

■ Notes on computer

Taking notes on a computer can streamline the path of source to note to paper because you can import the notes into your draft as you write. Using word-processor files, you can label and sort notes much as you would on note cards. (The examples on pages 618–22 illustrate one way of labeling computer notes.)

Computer notes have the same disadvantages as handwritten notes: the risk of introducing errors and the risk of plagiarizing. As with handwritten notes, strive for accuracy, and use quotation marks for quotations.

■ Photocopies and printouts

Photocopying from print sources or printing out online sources each has distinct advantages for researchers:

- **Both methods are convenient,** particularly when sources must remain in the library (for instance, bound periodicals and reference works) or when you find sources online (for instance, full-text articles or trustworthy Web pages).
- **Both methods may be safer than handwritten or computer notes.** Many researchers and teachers believe that photocopying or printing out sources reduces the risks of error and plagiarism. Each method requires manipulating source material only once, not twice, to use it in your paper. And with each method you see exactly what's quoted as you work the source material into your draft.

But photocopies and printouts have disadvantages, too:

- **They can discourage interaction with sources** by substituting busywork for thinking. You must read photocopies and printouts as critically as you would any other sources. Highlight or annotate the relevant passages with underlining, circles, and marginal notes about their significance for your subject. (See the example below.)

- **Source records can get lost.** You must take special care to note the publication information for sources directly on a printout or photocopy. If you don't have this information for your final paper, you can't use the source.

- **Photocopies and printouts can encourage unselective quotation.** When drafting from a complete source rather than notes on the source, you may be tempted to import whole blocks rather than the bits that advance and support your ideas. See page 620 for guidelines on judicious use of quotations.

Downloaded source with annotations

Internet and income inequality
Commerce Dept., <u>Falling</u> . . . *http://www.ntia.gov/ntiahome/*
fttn00/Falling.htm#2.1

Figure I-9 presents some evidence that <u>both income and education are in-</u><u>dependently associated with Internet access</u>. Although the average Internet access rate for incomes of $75,000 and greater is 77.7%, it ranges from <u>82% for those with a college degree</u> or more down to 51% for those with less than a high school education. Likewise, households with incomes be-tween $15,000 and $34,999 had an average access rate of 28%, ranging from 46% for college or more down to 11% for less than high school. The same wide disparities occur within education categories. For example, among households in which the householder had some schooling beyond high school but not a college degree, home Internet access reached 76% in the over $75,000 income group but only 26% in the under $15,000 income group. Among households with incomes below $15,000 and <u>less than a</u> <u>high school education</u>, only 4% had Internet access at home.

Marginal annotations:
greatest access = high educ. high income

least access = low educ. low income

■ Downloads

Researching online, you can usually download full-text articles, Web pages, discussion-group messages, and other materials onto your computer. If you also take notes on your computer, you can use it to organize much or all of your research and then, while drafting, import source information from one file into another.

These advantages of downloading are offset by clear disadvantages:

- **Directly importing source material creates a high risk of plagiarism.** You must keep clear boundaries between your own ideas and words and those of others—perhaps by using distinctive type fonts or colors. And make sure to record publication information as part of every downloaded document.

- **Downloading can discourage interaction with sources.** Even more than with photocopies and printouts, you must make an effort with downloads to analyze and synthesize sources. Many researchers print out downloaded sources and mark up paper copies. Alternatively, you can use your word processor's Comment and Highlight functions to annotate the electronic file or simply type your own comments into the source. (But use a different color or font!)

44d   Using summary, paraphrase, and quotation

As you take notes from sources or work source material into your draft, you can summarize, paraphrase, quote, or combine methods. The choice should depend on why you are using a source.

Note Summaries, paraphrases, and quotations all require source citations. A summary or paraphrase without a source citation or a quotation without quotation marks and a source citation is plagiarism. (See pp. 629–37 for more on plagiarism.)

1   Summarizing

When you **summarize,** you condense an extended idea or argument into a sentence or more in your own words. A full discussion of summary appears on pages 140–42, and you should read that section if you have not already done so.

Summary is most useful when you want to record the gist of an author's idea without the background or supporting evidence. Edward Begay summarized the following quotation from one of his sources—Larry Irving, "The Still-Yawning Divide," *Newsweek*, page 64:

> Internet access is affecting our everyday lives in important ways, from how we shop to how we define the notion of community. Yet the digital divide between the information haves and have-nots is still very wide, especially between households of high and low income and between whites and minorities. Although competition will continue to drive down the cost of technology, and corporations and educational institutions will continue to bring people online, the market, private enterprise, and local governments cannot seal the divide by themselves. The federal government must assume leadership in ensuring that all Americans have the access and skills they need to participate fully in the digital age.

In the following one-sentence summary, Begay picks out the kernel of Irving's passage and expresses it in his own words.

RESOURCES AND IDEAS

Kennedy, Mary Lynch. "The Composing Process of College Students Writing from Sources." *Written Communication* 2 (1985): 434–56. Kennedy's research shows that "fluent" readers and writers take more notes, do more planning, and reread more frequently than do less effective readers.

McGinley, William. "The Role of Reading and Writing while Composing from Sources." *Reading Research Quarterly* 27 (1992): 227–48. McGinley demonstrates that students writing from sources use highly recursive nonlinear as well as linear reading, writing, and reasoning processes.

COLLABORATIVE LEARNING

SKILLS DRILL

Pick an essay or article to use in class, and practice taking notes from it with your students. If they all summarize, paraphrase, and quote from the same article and discuss their results in groups, they may gain confidence when moving on to their own research materials.

SUMMARIES AND ADD

Students who have attention deficit disorder (ADD or ADHD) often have difficulty summarizing texts. They may benefit from working on summarizing assignments with their learning specialist.

BEGAY'S EXAMPLE

The trickiest aspect of paraphrasing is changing the language without changing the meaning. Note for your students that Begay's paraphrase uses very few words from the orginal (you might want to have your students count them). Note that he does not merely replace words with synonyms, but changes sentence structure as well.

A MNEMONIC FOR PARAPHRASING

A useful mnemonic that helps students remember how to paraphrase effectively is "New words and new word order." The emphasis on syntactic change in the mnemonic helps prevent mere synonym substitution.

Summary of source

> Role of government in Internet use
>
> Irving 64
>
> The US government must take the leading role in closing the technology gap between income levels and races/ethnic groups.

2 Paraphrasing

When you **paraphrase,** you follow much more closely the author's original presentation, but you still restate it in your own words. Paraphrase is most useful when you want to present or examine an author's line of reasoning but don't feel the original words merit direct quotation.

The note below shows how Begay might have paraphrased the passage by Irving given on the preceding page.

Complete paraphrase of source

> Role of government in Internet use
>
> Irving 64
>
> Significant areas of daily life are changing because of online communication, but many people, particularly the poor and nonwhite, are being left behind by this change. Market forces, businesses, and schools will help to narrow the gap, but they can't close it unless the US government takes the lead to see that everyone benefits.

Notice how the paraphrase differs from the Irving passage in sentence structures and wording, except in the case of terms that lack synonyms such as *government* and *market:*

Irving's words	Begay's paraphrase
Internet access is affecting our everyday lives in important ways, from how we shop to how we define the notion of community.	Significant areas of daily life are changing because of online communication,
Yet the digital divide between the information haves and have-nots is still very wide, especially between households of high and low income and between whites and minorities.	but many people, particularly the poor and nonwhite, are being left behind by this change.

Irving's words	Begay's paraphrase
Although competition will continue to drive down the cost of technology, and corporations and educational institutions will continue to bring people online,	Market forces, businesses, and schools will help to narrow the gap,
the market, private enterprise, and local governments cannot seal the divide by themselves.	but they can't close it
The federal government must assume leadership in ensuring that all Americans have the access and skills they need to participate fully in the digital age.	unless the US government takes the lead to see that everyone benefits.

Follow these guidelines when paraphrasing:

- **Read the material several times to be sure you understand it.**
- **Restate the main ideas in your own words and sentence structures.** You need not put down in new words the whole passage or all the details. Select what is pertinent and restate only that. If complete sentences seem too detailed or cumbersome, use phrases. Edward Begay might have written the following more telegraphic paraphrase of the quotation by Irving.

Abbreviated paraphrase of source

> Role of government in Internet use
>
> Irving 64
>
> Many Americans—partic. poor and nonwhite—are being left behind. Market forces, businesses, and schools can't close gap—US govt. must lead the way.

- **Be careful not to distort meaning.** Don't change the source's emphasis or omit connecting words, qualifiers, and other material whose absence will confuse you later or cause you to misrepresent the source. (See also p. 622.)

See page 634 for examples of unacceptable (plagiarized) paraphrases.

 If English is not your native language and you have difficulty paraphrasing the ideas in sources, try this: Before attempting a paraphrase, read the original passage several times. Then, instead of "translating" line by line, try to state the gist of the passage without looking at it. Check your effort against the original to be sure you have captured the source author's meaning and

CULTURE LANGUAGE

PARAPHRASE AND SENTENCE STRUCTURE

While ESL students may be comfortable using synonyms to express the content of a source, they may feel insecure about using other sentence structures. Emphasize to students that they must change the sentence structure as well as the vocabulary of the original in writing paraphrases. Collaborative work on paraphrasing helps students develop their vocabularies and find alternative ways to express ideas. In addition, more advanced ESL students (and native speakers) can reinforce their own writing skills by helping less advanced students.

KEY QUOTATIONS

Students often have trouble identifying the key passages or parts of passages that will become effective quotations. Remind students that the quotation should represent the author's position fairly and that quoting provides an occasion for the student to speak directly back to that author. It can also help to conduct workshops in which students practice choosing key quotations from a shared text and write one-paragraph responses to one of their chosen quotations.

COLLABORATIVE LEARNING

QUOTATION EVALUATION

Have students work in small groups to review every quotation in one another's drafts-in-progress. Is each quotation necessary and appropriate? Is the writer integrating the quotation smoothly into the paper? Is the writer making effective use of the quotation, supplying an interpretation of it, and making it work toward some larger purpose in his or her own argument? This discussion can often help student writers rethink their uses of quotation and elaborate on their interpretive responses, thus helping them to create effective revisions of their drafts.

TRANSPARENCY MASTER 44.4

emphasis without using his or her words and sentence structures. If you need a synonym for a word, look it up in a dictionary.

3 Quoting

■ Deciding when to quote

Your notes from sources may include many quotations, especially if you rely on photocopies, printouts, or downloads. Whether to use a quotation in your draft, instead of a summary or paraphrase, depends on whether the source is primary or secondary and on how important the exact words are:

- **Quote extensively when you are analyzing primary sources,** such as literary works and historical documents. The quotations will often be both the target of your analysis and the chief support for your ideas. You may need to quote many brief passages, integrated into your sentences, and then comment on the quotations to clarify your analysis and win readers' agreement with it. For examples, see Vanessa Haley's analysis of Annie Dillard's writing (p. 725) and the three literary analyses in Chapter 50 (pp. 750, 752, and 756).
- **Quote selectively when you are drawing on secondary sources.** Favor summaries and paraphrases over quotations, and put every quotation to each test in the box below. Most papers of ten or so pages should not need more than two or three quotations that are longer than a few lines each.

Tests for direct quotations from secondary sources

The author's original satisfies one of these requirements:

- The language is unusually vivid, bold, or inventive.
- The quotation cannot be paraphrased without distortion or loss of meaning.
- The words themselves are at issue in your interpretation.
- The quotation represents and emphasizes a body of opinion or the view of an important expert.
- The quotation emphatically reinforces your own idea.
- The quotation is an illustration, such as a graph, diagram, or table.

The quotation is as short as possible:

- It includes only material relevant to your point.
- It is edited to eliminate examples and other unneeded material. (For editing quotations, see the bulleted list on the facing page.)

■ **Transcribing and using quotations**

When you quote a source, either in your notes or in your draft, take precautions to avoid plagiarism or misrepresentaton of the source:

- **Copy the material carefully.** Take down the author's exact wording, spelling, capitalization, and punctuation.
- **Proofread every direct quotation at least twice.**
- **Use quotation marks around the quotation** so that later you won't confuse it with a paraphrase or summary. Be sure to transfer the quotation marks into your draft as well, unless the quotation is long. See later pages for handling long quotations in MLA style (688–89), Chicago style (776), and APA style (802–03).
- **Use brackets** to add words for clarity or to change the capitalization of letters (see pp. 483, 491).
- **Use ellipsis marks** to omit irrelevant words or sentences (see p. 484).
- **Cite the source of the quotation in your draft.** See pages 637–38 on documenting sources.

For a summary of conventions regarding quotations, see the chart on pages 469–70.

The note below shows how Edward Begay might have quoted part of the passage by Larry Irving on page 617, using ellipsis marks and brackets to make the quotation more concise.

Quotation of source

Role of government in Internet use

Irving 64

"Internet access is affecting our lives in important ways. . . . Yet the digital divide . . . is still very wide, especially between households of high and low income and between whites and minorities. . . . [T]he market, private enterprise, and local governments cannot seal the divide by themselves. The federal government must assume leadership in ensuring that all Americans have the access and skills they need to participate fully in the digital age."

---

4 Combining quotation, summary, and paraphrase

Using quotation in combination with summary or paraphrase can help you shape the material to suit your purposes (although you must be careful not to distort the author's meaning). The note

RESPONSIBLE USE

Students can learn a great deal about the ethics of responsible summary, paraphrase, and quotation by practicing on each other. Have each student e-mail an abstract of his or her paper-in-progress to a partner in the class. Ask the partner to quote directly from the abstract, to paraphrase part of the abstract, and then to summarize the other person's project. Have each student check the accuracy of his or her partner's quotation, paraphrase, and summary.

IRRESPONSIBLE USE

As a follow-up to the previous exercise you might ask each student's partner to misquote deliberately or to paraphrase or summarize in a way that misrepresents the project. Then ask the student authors to identify the particular ways in which their work has been misrepresented.

COLLABORATIVE LEARNING

Have students complete Exercise 44.7 individually and then discuss and revise their responses in small groups. Students will learn a great deal by seeing the alternative strategies that other group members employed in completing the exercise. Encourage the groups to discuss the effectiveness of various strategies and to consider how fairly Eisinger's views have been represented in each student's response.

Have students complete Exercise 44.8 individually and then discuss and revise their responses in small groups. Ask each group to report any strategies for condensing and organizing material that they discover in the process.

ANSWERS: EXERCISE 44.7

Possible summary

Eisinger et al. 44
Federalism, unlike a unitary system, allows the states autonomy. Its strength and its weakness—which are in balance—lie in the regional differences it permits.

below shows how Edward Begay might have used a combination of quotation and paraphrase to record the statement by Irving.

Combined paraphrase and quotation of source

Role of government in Internet use

Irving 64

Many people—particularly the poor and nonwhite—are being left behind by Internet communication. Market forces, businesses, and schools can't close the gap unless the US government takes the lead "in ensuring that all Americans have the access and skills they need to participate fully in the digital age."

---

5 **Using sources accurately and fairly**

In borrowing from sources, you must represent the author's meaning exactly, without distorting it. In the following inaccurate summary, the writer has stated a meaning exactly opposite that of the original. The original quotation, from the artist Henri Matisse, appears in Jack D. Flam, *Matisse on Art*, page 148.

Original	For the artist creation begins with vision. To see is itself a creative operation, requiring an effort. Everything that we see in our daily life is more or less distorted by acquired habits, and this is perhaps more evident in an age like ours when cinema posters and magazines present us every day with a flood of ready-made images which are to the eye what prejudices are to the mind.
Inaccurate summary	Matisse said that the artist can learn how to see creatively by looking at posters and magazines (qtd. in Flam 148).

The revision below combines summary and quotation to represent the author's meaning exactly:

Accurate summary	Matisse said that the artist must overcome visual "habits" and "prejudices," particularly those developed in response to images of popular culture (qtd. in Flam 148).

EXERCISE 44.7 Summarizing and paraphrasing

Prepare two source notes, one summarizing the entire following paragraph and the other paraphrasing the first four sentences (ending with the word *autonomy*). Use the note format illustrated in the preceding section, omitting only the subject heading. (You can do this exercise online at *ablongman.com/littlebrown*.)

Federal organization [of the United States] has made it possible for the different states to deal with the same problems in many different ways. One consequence of federalism, then, has been that people are treated differently, by law, from state to state. The great strength of this system is that differences from state to state in cultural preferences, moral standards, and levels of wealth can be accommodated. In contrast to a unitary system in which the central government makes all important decisions (as in France), federalism is a powerful arrangement for maximizing regional freedom and autonomy. The great weakness of our federal system, however, is that people in some states receive less than the best or the most advanced or the least expensive services and policies that government can offer. The federal dilemma does not invite easy solutions, for the costs and benefits of the arrangement have tended to balance out.

—Peter K. Eisinger et al., *American Politics,* page 44

EXERCISE 44.8   Combining summary, paraphrase, and direct quotation

Prepare a source note that combines paraphrase or summary and direct quotation to state the main idea of the passage below. Use the note format illustrated in the preceding section, omitting only the heading. (You can do this exercise online at *ablongman.com/littlebrown.*)

Most speakers unconsciously duel even during seemingly casual conversations, as can often be observed at social gatherings where they show less concern for exchanging information with other guests than for asserting their own dominance. Their verbal dueling often employs very subtle weapons like mumbling, a hostile act which defeats the listener's desire to understand what the speaker claims he is trying to say (but is really not saying because he is mumbling!). Or the verbal dueler may keep talking after someone has passed out of hearing range—which is often an aggressive challenge to the listener to return and acknowledge the dominance of the speaker.

—Peter K. Farb, *Word Play,* page 107

EXERCISE 44.9   Gathering information from sources

Continuing from Exercise 44.6 (p. 613), as the next step in preparing a research paper, gather and organize the information from your sources. Mark every note, photocopy, printout, and download with the source's publication information and a heading related to your paper. Annotate relevant passages of photocopies, printouts, and downloads. For handwritten or computer notes, use direct quotation, summary, or paraphrase as seems appropriate, being careful to avoid inaccuracy and plagiarism. (If you need help recognizing plagiarism, see Chapter 45.)

44e   Integrating sources into your text

The evidence of others' information and opinions should *back up* your conclusions. You don't want to let your evidence overwhelm your own point of view and voice. The point of research

Possible paraphrase

Eisinger et al. 44

Under federalism, each state can devise its own ways of handling problems and its own laws. The system's advantage is that a state can operate according to its people's culture, morals, and wealth. A unitary system like that in France does not permit such diversity.

ANSWERS: EXERCISE 44.8

Possible answer

Farb 107

Speakers at parties often "unconsciously duel" in conversations in order to assert "dominance" over others. A speaker may mumble, thus preventing a listener from understanding what is said. Or he or she may continue talking after the listener has moved away, a "challenge to the listener to return and acknowledge the dominance of the speaker."

ANSWERS: EXERCISE 44.9

Individual response.

RESOURCES AND IDEAS

Sherrard, Carol. "Summary Writing: A Topographical Study." *Written Communication* 3 (1986): 324–43. Sherrard discusses both common and effective summary-writing techniques of college students.

writing is to investigate and go beyond sources, to interpret them and use them to support your own independent ideas.

Note Integrating borrowed material into your sentences involves several conventions discussed elsewhere in this book:

- **Using commas to punctuate signal phrases,** pages 444–46.
- **Placing other punctuation marks with quotation marks,** pages 474–75.
- **Using brackets for changes in quotations,** pages 483–84 and below.
- **Using ellipsis marks for omissions from quotations,** pages 484–86.
- **Punctuating and placing parenthetical citations,** pages 654–56.
- **Setting off long quotations from your text without quotation marks,** pages 688–89 (MLA style), 776 (Chicago style), and 802–03 (APA style).

1 Introducing borrowed material

When using a summary, paraphrase, or quotation, smooth the transition between your ideas and words and those of the source.

Note The examples in this and the next section use the MLA style of source documentation and also present-tense verbs (such as *disagrees*). For specific variations in documentation and verb tense within the academic disciplines, see pages 627–28.

■ Links between borrowed material and your own sentences

Readers will be distracted from your point if borrowed material does not fit into your sentence. In the passage below, the writer has not meshed the structures of her own and her source's sentences:

> Awkward   One editor disagrees with this view and "a good reporter does not fail to separate opinions from facts" (Lyman 52).

In the following revision the writer adds words to integrate the quotation into her sentence:

> Revised   One editor disagrees with this view, <u>maintaining that</u> "a good reporter does not fail to separate opinions from facts" (Lyman 52).

■ Alterations of quotations

To mesh your own and your source's words, you may sometimes need to make a substitution or addition to the quotation, signaling your change with brackets:

> Words added
> "The tabloids [of England] are a journalistic case study in bad reporting," claims Lyman (52).

Verb form changed

A bad reporter, Lyman implies, is one who "[fails] to separate opinions from facts" (52). [The bracketed verb replaces *fail* in the original.]

Capitalization changed

"[T]o separate opinions from facts" is a goal of good reporting (Lyman 52). [In the original, *to* is not capitalized.]

Noun supplied for pronoun

The reliability of a news organization "depends on [reporters'] trust-worthiness," says Lyman (52). [The bracketed noun replaces *their* in the original.]

2 Interpreting borrowed material

Even when it does not conflict with your own sentence structure, borrowed material will be ineffective if you merely dump it in readers' laps without explaining how you intend it to be understood. Reading the following passage, we must figure out for ourselves that the writer's sentence and the quotation state opposite points of view.

Dumped   Many news editors and reporters maintain that it is impossible to keep personal opinions from influencing the selection and presentation of facts. "True, news reporters, like everyone else, form impressions of what they see and hear. However, a good reporter does not fail to separate opinions from facts" (Lyman 52).

In the revision the underlined additions tell us how to interpret the quotation:

Revised   Many news editors and reporters maintain that it is impossible to keep personal opinions from influencing the selection and presentation of facts. <u>Yet not all authorities agree with this view. One editor grants that</u> "news reporters, like everyone else, form impressions of what they see and hear." <u>But, he insists,</u> "a good reporter does not fail to separate opinions from facts" (Lyman 52).

▪ Signal phrases

In the revised passage above, the words *One editor grants* and *he insists* are **signal phrases:** they tell readers who the source is and what to expect in the quotations that follow. Signal phrases usually contain (1) the source author's name (or a substitute for it, such as *One editor* and *he*) and (2) a verb that indicates the source author's attitude or approach to what he or she says. In the preceding example, *grants* implies concession and *insists* implies argument. The box on the next page includes a list of verbs for signal phrases.

COLLABORATIVE LEARNING

SIGNAL PHRASES

Assign students to work as partners to practice using signal phrases. Students can trade drafts of their papers, and each reader can write a short summary of the writer's paper, using signal phrases as appropriate.

COMPUTER ACTIVITY

TENSE EXAMPLES

Students unfamiliar with the humanities convention of using present tense in signal phrases may have difficulty applying this principle to their own writing. Ask them to collect examples of present-tense signal phrases in published works and post them to the class Web site.

Verbs for signal phrases

Use verbs that convey information about source authors' attitudes or approaches. In the sentence *Smith* _____ *that the flood might have been disastrous,* filling the blank with *observes, finds,* or *insists* would create different meanings.

Note Disciplines vary in the tenses of verbs within signal phrases. The verbs listed below are in the present tense, typical of writing in the humanities. But in the social and natural sciences, the past tense or present perfect tense is more common. See page 625.

Author is neutral	Author infers or suggests	Author argues	Author is uneasy or disparaging
comments	analyzes	claims	belittles
describes	asks	contends	bemoans
explains	assesses	defends	complains
illustrates	concludes	disagrees	condemns
notes	finds	holds	deplores
observes	predicts	insists	deprecates
points out	proposes	maintains	derides
records	reveals		laments
relates	shows	**Author agrees**	warns
reports	speculates	admits	
says	suggests	agrees	
sees	supposes	concedes	
thinks		concurs	
writes		grants	

Vary your signal phrases to suit your interpretation of borrowed material and also to keep readers' interest. A signal phrase may precede, interrupt, or follow the borrowed material:

Signal phrase precedes

Lyman insists that "a good reporter does not fail to separate opinions from facts" (52).

Signal phrase interrupts

"However," Lyman insists, "a good reporter does not fail to separate opinions from facts" (52).

Signal phrase follows

"[A] good reporter does not fail to separate opinions from facts," Lyman insists (52).

■ **Background information**

You can add information to a signal phrase to inform readers why you are using a source. In most cases, provide the author's name in the text, especially if the author is an expert or if readers will recognize the name:

Author named

Harold Lyman grants that "news reporters, like everyone else, form impressions of what they see and hear." But, Lyman insists, "a good reporter does not fail to separate opinions from facts" (52).

If the source title contributes information about the author or the context of the quotation, you can provide it in the text:

Title given

Harold Lyman, in his book *The Conscience of the Journalist,* grants that "news reporters, like everyone else, form impressions of what they see and hear." But, Lyman insists, "a good reporter does not fail to separate opinions from facts" (52).

Finally, if the quoted author's background and experience reinforce or clarify the quotation, you can provide these credentials in the text:

Credentials given

Harold Lyman, a newspaper editor for more than forty years, grants that "news reporters, like everyone else, form impressions of what they see and hear." But, Lyman insists, "a good reporter does not fail to separate opinions from facts" (52).

You need not always name the author, source, or credentials in your text. In fact, such introductions may get in the way when you are simply establishing facts or weaving together facts and opinions from varied sources. In the following passage, the information is more important than the source, so the name of the source is confined to a parenthetical acknowledgment:

To end the abuses of the British, many colonists were urging three actions: forming a united front, seceding from Britain, and taking control of their own international relations (Wills 325–36).

3 Following discipline styles for integrating sources

The preceding guidelines for introducing and interpreting borrowed material apply generally across academic disciplines, but there are differences in verb tenses and documentation style.

■ English and some other humanities

Writers in English, foreign languages, and related disciplines use MLA style for documenting sources (see Chapter 47) and generally use the present tense of verbs in signal phrases. In discussing sources other than works of literature, the present perfect tense is also sometimes appropriate:

Lyman insists . . . [present].
Lyman has insisted . . . [present perfect].

In discussing works of literature, use only the present tense to describe both the work of the author and the action in the work:

Kate Chopin <u>builds</u> irony into every turn of "The Story of an Hour." For example, Mrs. Mallard, the central character, <u>finds</u> joy in the death of her husband, whom she <u>loves</u>, because she <u>anticipates</u> "the long procession of years that would belong to her absolutely" (23).

Avoid shifting tenses in writing about literature. You can, for instance, shorten quotations to avoid their past-tense verbs:

Shift   Her freedom <u>elevates</u> her, so that "she <u>carried</u> herself unwittingly like a goddess of victory" (24).

No shift   Her freedom <u>elevates</u> her, so that she <u>walks</u> "unwittingly like a goddess of victory" (24).

■ History and other humanities

Writers in history, art history, philosophy, and related disciplines generally use the present tense or present perfect tense of verbs in signal phrases:

Lincoln persisted, as Haworth <u>has noted</u>, in "feeling that events controlled him."[3]

What Miller <u>calls</u> Lincoln's "severe self-doubt"[6] undermined his effectiveness on at least two occasions.

The raised numbers after the quotations are part of the Chicago documentation style, used in history and other disciplines and discussed on pages 764–65.

■ Social and natural sciences

Writers in the sciences generally use a verb's present tense just for reporting the results of a study (*The data suggest* . . .). Otherwise, they use a verb's past tense or present perfect tense in a signal phrase, as when introducing an explanation, interpretation, or other commentary. (Thus when you are writing for the sciences, generally convert the list of signal-phrase verbs on p. 626 from the present to the past or present perfect tense.)

Lin (1999) <u>has suggested</u> that preschooling may significantly affect children's academic performance through high school (pp. 22–23).

In an exhaustive survey of the literature published between 1990 and 2000, Walker (2001) <u>found</u> "no proof, merely a weak correlation, linking place of residence and rate of illness" (p. 121).

These passages conform to APA documentation style, discussed on pages 784–800. APA style, or one quite similar to it, is also used in sociology, education, nursing, biology, and many other sciences.

COMPUTER ACTIVITY

Have students circulate their responses to Exercise 44.10 to the rest of the class via e-mail or Web posting. Students will see that there are multiple ways of using the source material and integrating it into a paragraph of one's own.

EXERCISE 44.10   Introducing and interpreting borrowed material

Drawing on the ideas in the following paragraph and using examples from your own observations and experiences, write a paragraph about anxiety. Integrate at least one direct quotation and one paraphrase from the following paragraph into your own sentences. In your paragraph identify the author by name and give his credentials: he is a professor of psychiatry and a practicing psychoanalyst. (You can do this exercise online at *ablongman.com/littlebrown*.)

There are so many ways in which man is different from all the lower forms of animals, and almost all of them make us uniquely susceptible to feelings of anxiousness. Our imagination and reasoning powers facilitate anxiety; the anxious feeling is precipitated not by an absolute impending threat—such as the worry about an examination, a speech, travel—but rather by the symbolic and often unconscious representations. We do not have to be experiencing a potential danger. We can experience something related to it. We can recall, through our incredible memories, the original symbolic sense of vulnerability in childhood and suffer the feeling attached to that. We can even forget the original memory and still be stuck with the emotion—which is then compounded by its seemingly irrational quality at this time. It is not just the fear of death which pains us, but the anticipation of it; or the anniversary of a specific death; or a street, a hospital, a time of day, a color, a flower, a symbol associated with death.

—Willard Gaylin, "Feeling Anxious," page 23

CHAPTER 45

Avoiding Plagiarism and Documenting Sources

The knowledge building that is the focus of academic writing rests on participants' integrity in using sources. This standard of integrity derives from the idea that the work of an author is his or her intellectual property: if you use that work, you must acknowledge the author's ownership. At the same time, source acknowledgments tell readers what your own writing is based on, creating the trust that knowledge building requires.

http://www.ablongman.com/littlebrown ▶

Visit the companion Web site for more help and an additional exercise on avoiding plagiarism and documenting sources.

ANSWERS: EXERCISE 44.10

Sample paragraph

Why does a woman who is otherwise happy regularly suffer anxiety attacks at the first sign of spring? Why does a man who is otherwise a competent, relaxed driver feel panic whenever he approaches a traffic rotary? According to Willard Gaylin, a professor of psychiatry and a practicing psychoanalyst, such feelings of anxiety are attributable to the uniquely human capacities for remembering, imagining, and forming "symbolic and often unconscious representations" of experiences (23). The feeling of anxiety, Gaylin says, "is . . . compounded by its seemingly irrational quality": it may appear despite the absence of an immediate source of worry or pain (23). The anxious woman is not aware of it, but her father's death twenty years before in April has caused her to equate spring with death. Similarly, the man has forgotten that a terrible accident he witnessed as a child occurred at a rotary. For both people, the anxious feelings are not reduced but heightened because they seem to be unfounded.

mycomplab²·⁰

Please visit MyCompLab at *www.mycomplab.com* for more on the writing process.

HIGHLIGHTS

Chapter 45 focuses exclusively on plagiarism and documentation. As students increasingly conduct research online, they have more opportunities for both accidental and deliberate plagiarism. Inculcating good habits of documentation in your students is an essential task of the writing and research educator. Section 45a introduces the subject of plagiarism on the Internet. Students may want to keep a copy of the checklist at the beginning of this chapter handy in their research journals. Sections 45b and 45c discuss how students

COMPANION WEB SITE

See page IAE-60 for companion Web site content description.

can determine what they do and do not need to acknowledge, section 45d focuses on acknowledgment of online sources, and section 45e explains and points students to documentation formats in the various disciplines.

COMPUTER ACTIVITY

THWARTING PLAGIARISM

To impress upon your students how easy it is for you to catch deliberate plagiarism, have the whole class visit a site that sells term papers and see how easy it is to find papers and key passages on the site. You can also guard against plagiarism by requiring drafts and research reports and holding workshops to show work in progress.

COLLABORATIVE LEARNING

LEARN BY DOING

One way to teach students how not to plagiarize is to require deliberate plagiarism. Have students practice deliberately plagiarizing from an online source. Then have them exchange their plagiarized passages with fellow group members, who must locate and correct the plagiarism.

A WRITER'S PERSPECTIVE

If you copy from one author, it's plagiarism; if you copy from two, it's research.

—WILSON MIZNER

Plagiarism (from a Latin word for "kidnapper") is the presentation of someone else's ideas or words as your own. Whether deliberate or accidental, plagiarism is a serious offense.

- *Deliberate* plagiarism:

  Copying or downloading a phrase, a sentence, or a longer passage from a source and passing it off as your own by omitting quotation marks and a source citation.

  Summarizing or paraphrasing someone else's ideas without acknowledging your debt in a source citation.

  Handing in as your own work a paper you have bought, copied off the Web, had a friend write, or accepted from another student.

Checklist for avoiding plagiarism

Type of source

Are you using

- your own independent material,
- common knowledge, or
- someone else's independent material?

You must acknowledge someone else's material.

Quotations

- Do all quotations exactly match their sources? Check them.
- Have you inserted quotation marks around quotations that are run into your text?
- Have you shown omissions with ellipsis marks and additions with brackets?
- Does every quotation have a source citation?

Paraphrases and summaries

- Have you used your own words and sentence structures for every paraphrase and summary? If not, use quotation marks around the original author's words.
- Does every paraphrase and summary have a source citation?

The Web

- Have you obtained any necessary permission to use someone else's material on the Web?

Source citations

- Have you acknowledged every use of someone else's material in the place where you use it?
- Does your list of works cited include all the sources you have used?

You can download this checklist from *ablongman.com/littlebrown*. Working with a copy of the list, question every use you make of someone else's material.

- *Accidental* plagiarism:
  Forgetting to place quotation marks around another writer's words.
  Carelessly omitting a source citation for a paraphrase.
  Omitting a source citation for another's idea because you are unaware of the need to acknowledge the idea.

In most schools a code of academic honesty calls for severe consequences for deliberate or accidental plagiarism: a failing grade, suspension from school, or even expulsion.

The way to avoid plagiarism is to acknowledge your sources by documenting them. This chapter discusses plagiarism and the Internet (below), shows how to distinguish what doesn't require acknowledgment from what does (pp. 632–34), covers issues particular to online sources (pp. 635–37), and provides an overview of source documentation (pp. 637–38).

CULTURE LANGUAGE The concept of intellectual property and thus the rules governing plagiarism are not universal. In some other cultures, for instance, students may be encouraged to copy the words of scholars without acknowledgment, in order to demonstrate their mastery of or respect for the scholars' work. In the United States, however, using an author's work without a source citation is considered theft. When in doubt about the guidelines in this chapter, ask your instructor for advice.

45a Committing and detecting plagiarism on the Internet

The Internet has made it easier to plagiarize than ever before, but it has also made plagiarism easier to catch.

Even honest students risk accidental plagiarism by downloading sources and importing portions into their drafts. Dishonest students may take advantage of the downloading process to steal others' work. They may also use the term-paper businesses on the Web, which offer both ready-made research and complete papers, usually for a fee. **Paying for research or a paper does not make it the buyer's work.** Anyone who submits someone else's work as his or her own is a plagiarist.

Students who plagiarize from the Internet deprive themselves of an education in honest research, and they also expose themselves to detection. Teachers can use search engines to find specific phrases or sentences anywhere on the Web, including among scholarly publications, all kinds of Web sites, and term-paper collections. They can search term-paper sites as easily as students can, looking for similarities with papers they've received. They can also use special detection software that compares students' work with other

RESOURCES AND IDEAS

Fulkerson, Richard. "Oh, What a Cite! A Teaching Tip to Help Students Document Researched Papers Accurately." *The Writing Instructor* 7 (1988): 167–72. Fulkerson suggests giving students a sample research paper with documentation removed to help them determine where and what kind(s) of citation must be used.

Kroll, Barry M. "How College Freshmen View Plagiarism." *Written Communication* 5 (1988): 203–21. A survey of 150 students shows the five most popular reasons they think plagiarism is wrong and discusses effective means to teach students the seriousness and possible consequences of plagiarism.

Whitaker, Elaine E. "A Pedagogy to Address Plagiarism." *College Composition and Communication* 44 (1993): 509–14. Whitaker describes classroom activities designed to help students understand and avoid plagiarism.

CULTURE LANGUAGE

INTELLECTUAL PROPERTY AND CULTURE

Ideas about ownership of intellectual property vary among cultures. In some cultures scholarly research consists of finding expert sources and copying information without attribution. ESL students who copy without attribution or too closely paraphrase sources may be following the procedures they have been taught. In their countries plagiarism may be considered less objectionable than in the United States, or perhaps in their culture students are encouraged to use classic works in their own writing. See "Teaching Writing to ESL Students" (p. IAE-65 of this manual) for further discussion of ESL students' attitudes toward plagiarism. Discuss the issue of intellectual ownership with your students, emphasizing that in the United States research and writing are valued for their originality.

work anywhere on the Internet, seeking matches as short as a few words.

Some instructors suggest that their students use plagiarism-detection programs to verify that their own work does not include accidental plagiarism, at least not from the Internet. Links to such programs appear on this book's Web site at *ablongman.com/ littlebrown*.

45b Knowing what you need not acknowledge

Two kinds of information do not have to be acknowledged in source citations: your own independent material and common knowledge.

1 Using your independent material

Your own independent material includes your thoughts, observations from experience, compilations of facts, or experimental results, expressed in your words or format. For example, you might offer a conclusion about crowd behavior based on watching crowds at concerts or draw a diagram from information you gathered yourself. Though you generally should describe the basis for your conclusions so that readers can evaluate your thinking, you need not cite sources for them.

Note that someone else's ideas and facts are not yours, even when you express them entirely in your own words and sentence structures. The ideas and facts require acknowledgment.

2 Using common knowledge

Common knowledge consists of the standard information of a field of study as well as folk literature and commonsense observations.

- **Standard information** includes the major facts of history, such as the dates during which Charlemagne ruled as emperor of Rome (800–14). It does *not* include interpretations of facts, such as a historian's opinion that Charlemagne was sometimes needlessly cruel in extending his power.
- **Folk literature,** such as the fairy tale "Snow White," is popularly known and cannot be traced to a particular writer. Literature traceable to a writer is *not* folk literature, even if it is very familiar.
- **Commonsense observations** are things most people know, such as that inflation is most troublesome for people with low and fixed incomes. A particular economist's idea about the effects of inflation on Chinese immigrants is *not* a commonsense observation.

As long as you express it in your own words and sentence structures, you may use common knowledge as your own.

The first time you come across an idea or a piece of information that you may want to use, record the publication information for the source. If in wider reading you repeatedly encounter the same idea or information without cited sources, then you may assume it's common knowledge. Don't take unnecessary risks, however: a source citation for common knowledge is not wrong.

45c Knowing what you *must* acknowledge

You must always acknowledge other people's independent material—that is, any facts or ideas that are not common knowledge or your own. The source may be anything, including a book, an article, a movie, an interview, a microfilmed document, a Web page, a newsgroup posting, or an opinion expressed on the radio. You must acknowledge summaries or paraphrases of ideas or facts as well as quotations of the language and format in which ideas or facts appear: wording, sentence structures, arrangement, and special graphics (such as a diagram).

You need to acknowledge another's material no matter how you use it, how much of it you use, or how often you use it. Whether you are quoting a single important word, paraphrasing a single sentence, or summarizing three paragraphs, and whether you are using the source only once or a dozen times, you must acknowledge the original author every time. See pages 637–38 for how to acknowledge sources and pages 654–55 for where to place source citations in relation to cited material.

1 Using copied language: Quotation marks and a source citation

■ Copied words and sentence structure

The following example baldly plagiarizes the original quotation from Jessica Mitford's *Kind and Usual Punishment*, page 9. Without quotation marks or a source citation, the example matches Mitford's wording (underlined) and closely parallels her sentence structure:

Original   "The character and mentality of the keepers may be of more importance in understanding prisons than the character and mentality of the kept."

Plagiarism   But the character of prison officials (the keepers) is more important in understanding prisons than the character of prisoners (the kept).

To avoid plagiarism, the writer can paraphrase and cite the source (see the next page) or use Mitford's actual words *in quotation marks and with a source citation* (here, in MLA style):

COLLABORATIVE LEARNING

CITED MATERIAL AND ORIGINALITY

Students who are new to research writing may fail to document their sources properly out of the fear that their papers will look insufficiently original if they are full of in-text citations. Reassure students that research papers are meant to be full of documented material and that the originality in their papers resides in their approach to the subject, their thesis, the choice of sources and the way they present them, and the conclusions they draw. Students who have been successful in writing good research papers for other courses can volunteer to bring those papers in and pass them around, so that their classmates can see how much of the material in their papers is from outside sources.

COMPUTER ACTIVITY

HIGHLIGHTING NONORIGINAL MATERIAL

To help students avoid plagiarism, have each one use the Highlight function on a word processor to mark all passages in his or her paper that are not original. Then you or a classmate can review the draft to ensure that the writer quoted, paraphrased, and cited properly and to ensure that the writer did not neglect to highlight a borrowed passage.

Revision (quotation)	According to one critic of the penal system, *"*The character and mentality of the keepers may be of more importance in understanding prisons than the character and mentality of the kept*"* (Mitford 9).

▪ Changed sentence structure but copied words

Even with a source citation and with a different sentence structure, the next example is still plagiarism because it uses some of Mitford's words (underlined) without quotation marks:

Plagiarism	According to one critic of the penal system, the psychology of the kept may say less about prisons than the psychology of the keepers (Mitford 9).
Revision (quotation)	According to one critic of the penal system, the psychology of *"*the kept*"* may say less about prisons than the psychology of *"*the keepers*"* (Mitford 9).

2 Using a paraphrase or summary: Your own words and sentence structure and a source citation

▪ Changed sentence structure but copied words

The following example changes the sentence structure of the original Mitford quotation above, but it still uses Mitford's words (underlined) without quotation marks and without a source citation:

Plagiarism	In understanding prisons, we might focus less on the character and mentality of the kept than on those of the keepers.

To avoid plagiarism, the writer can use quotation marks and cite the source or *use his or her own words* and still *cite the source* (because the idea is Mitford's, not the writer's):

Revision (paraphrase)	Mitford holds that we may be able to learn less about prisons from the psychology of prisoners than from the psychology of prison officials (9).
Revision (paraphrase)	We may understand prisons better if we focus on the personalities and attitudes of the prison workers rather than those of the inmates (Mitford 9).

▪ Changed words but copied sentence structure

In the next example, the writer cites Mitford and does not use her words but still plagiarizes her sentence structure:

Plagiarism	One critic of the penal system maintains that the psychology of prison officials may be more informative about prisons than the psychology of prisoners (Mitford 9).
Revision (paraphrase)	One critic of the penal system maintains that we may be able to learn less from the psychology of prisoners than from the psychology of prison officials (Mitford 9).

EXERCISE 45.1 Recognizing plagiarism

The numbered items below show various attempts to quote or paraphrase the following passage. Carefully compare each attempt with the original passage. Which attempts are plagiarized, inaccurate, or both, and which are acceptable? Why? (You can do this exercise online at *ablongman.com/littlebrown*.)

I would agree with the sociologists that psychiatric labeling is dangerous. Society can inflict terrible wounds by discrimination, and by confusing health with disease and disease with badness.
—George E. Vaillant, *Adaptation to Life*, p. 361

1. According to George Vaillant, society often inflicts wounds by using psychiatric labeling, confusing health, disease, and badness (361).
2. According to George Vaillant, "psychiatric labeling [such as 'homosexual' or 'schizophrenic'] is dangerous. Society can inflict terrible wounds by . . . confusing health with disease and disease with badness" (361).
3. According to George Vaillant, when psychiatric labeling discriminates between health and disease or between disease and badness, it can inflict wounds on those labeled (361).
4. Psychiatric labels can badly hurt those labeled, says George Vaillant, because they fail to distinguish among health, illness, and immorality (361).
5. Labels such as "homosexual" and "schizophrenic" can be hurtful when they fail to distinguish among health, illness, and immorality.
6. "I would agree with the sociologists that society can inflict terrible wounds by discrimination, and by confusing health with disease and disease with badness" (Vaillant 361).

45d Acknowledging online sources

Online sources are so accessible and so easy to download into your own documents that it may seem they are freely available, exempting you from the obligation to acknowledge them. They are not. Acknowledging online sources is somewhat trickier than acknowledging print sources, but no less essential. Further, if you are publishing your work on the Web, you need to take account of sources' copyright restrictions as well.

Note Ask your instructor for advice whenever you are unsure about citing an online source or seeking permission to use copyrighted material.

1 Acknowledging online sources in an unpublished project

When you use material from an online source in a print or online document to be distributed just to your class, your obligation to cite sources does not change: you must acknowledge someone else's

ANSWERS: EXERCISE 45.1

1. Plagiarized: takes phrases directly from the original without quotation marks.
2. Acceptable.
3. Inaccurate and plagiarized: the passage uses phrases from the original without quotation marks and distorts its meaning.
4. Acceptable: puts the original into the author's own words and correctly conveys its meaning.
5. Inaccurate and plagiarized: fails to acknowledge the source and fails to convey accurately the concepts of "discrimination" and "confusing" outlined in the original.
6. Inaccurate: ellipses are needed to indicate that material was omitted, and brackets must be placed around lowercase *s* to indicate revision.

independent material in whatever form you find it. With online sources, that obligation can present additional challenges:

- **Record complete publication information each time you consult an online source.** Online sources may change from one day to the next or even disappear entirely. See page 569 for the information to record, such as the electronic address and the publication date. Without the proper information, you *may not* use the source.
- **Acknowledge linked sites.** If you use not only a Web site but also one or more of its linked sites, you must acknowledge the linked sites as well. The fact that one person has used a second person's work does not release you from the responsibility to cite the second work.
- **Seek the author's permission before using an e-mail message, discussion-group posting, or Web log contribution.** Obtaining permission advises the author that his or her ideas are about to be distributed more widely and lets the author verify that you have not misrepresented the ideas. (See p. 608 for advice on tracing authors.)

2 **Acknowledging print and online sources in a Web composition**

When you use material from print or online sources in a composition for the Web, you must not only acknowledge your sources, as discussed above, but take the additional precaution of observing copyright restrictions.

A Web site is a medium of publication just as a book or magazine is and so involves the same responsibility to obtain reprint permission from copyright holders. The exception is a password-protected site (such as a course site), which many copyright holders regard as private. You can find information about copyright holders and permissions on the copyright page of a print publication (following the title page) and on a page labeled something like "Terms of Use" on a Web site. If you don't see an explicit release for student use or publication on private Web sites, assume you must seek permission.

The legal convention of **fair use** allows an author to reprint a small portion of copyrighted material without obtaining the copyright holder's permission, as long as the author acknowledges the source. The online standards of fair use differ for print and online sources and are not fixed in either case. The guidelines below are conservative:

- **Print sources:** Quote without permission fewer than fifty words from an article or fewer than three hundred words from a book. You'll need permission to use any longer quotation from an article or book; any quotation at all from a play, poem, or song; and any use of an entire work—such as a photograph, chart, or other illustration.

- **Online sources:** Quote without permission text that represents just a small portion of the whole—say, forty words out of three hundred. Follow the preceding print guidelines for plays, poems, songs, and illustrations, adding multimedia elements (audio or video clips) to the list of works that require reprint permission for any use.

- **Links:** You may need to seek permission to link your site to another one—for instance, if you rely on the linked site to provide substantial evidence for your claims or if you incorporate a linked site's multimedia element (an image or a sound or video clip) into your site.

Note Although most online sources are copyrighted, much valuable material is not: either the creator does not claim copyright, or the copyright has lapsed so that the work is in the public domain. The first category includes most government documents; the second includes most works by authors who have been dead at least fifty years. You do not need permission to reprint from such a source, but *you still must cite the source.*

45e Documenting sources

Every time you borrow the words, facts, or ideas of others, you must **document** the source—that is, supply a reference (or document) telling readers that you borrowed the material and where you borrowed it from.

Editors and teachers in most academic disciplines require special documentation formats (or styles) in their scholarly journals and in students' papers. All the styles use a citation in the text that serves two purposes: it signals that material is borrowed, and it refers readers to detailed information about the source so that they can locate both the source and the place in the source where the borrowed material appears. The detailed source information appears either in footnotes or at the end of the paper.

Aside from these essential similarities, the disciplines' documentation styles differ markedly in citation form, arrangement of source information, and other particulars. Each discipline's style reflects the needs of its practitioners for certain kinds of information presented in certain ways. For instance, the currency of a source is important in the social and natural sciences, where studies build on and correct each other; thus in-text citations in these disciplines usually include a source's date of publication. In the humanities, however, currency is less important, so in-text citations do not include date of publication.

The disciplines' documentation formats are described in style guides listed elsewhere in this book for the humanities (p. 764), the social sciences (p. 784), and the natural and applied sciences (p. 812). This book discusses and illustrates four common documentation styles:

- **MLA style,** used in English, foreign languages, and some other humanities (p. 647).
- **Chicago style,** used in history, art history, philosophy, religion, and some other humanities (p. 764).
- **APA style,** used in psychology and some other social sciences (p. 784).
- **CSE style,** used in the biological and some other sciences (p. 812).

Ask your instructor which style you should use. If no style is required, use the guide that's most appropriate for the discipline in which you're writing. Do follow one system for citing sources—and one system only—so that you provide all the necessary information in a consistent format.

Note Bibliography software—*Biblio, Refworks, Endnote, Pro-Cite,* and others—can help you format your source citations in the style of your choice. Always ask your instructors if you may use such software for your papers. The programs prompt you for needed information (author's name, book title, and so on) and then arrange, capitalize, underline, and punctuate the information as required by the style. But no program can anticipate all the varieties of source information, nor can it substitute for your own care and attention in giving your sources complete acknowledgment using the required form.

mycomplab 2.0

Please visit MyCompLab at *www.mycomplab.com* for more on the writing process.

HIGHLIGHTS

Some students can read and conduct research indefinitely but have trouble getting down to writing the paper. Chapter 46 helps students move from the preliminary stages of research to the paper-writing stage. It begins with the tenta-

COMPANION WEB SITE

See page IAE-60 for companion Web site content description.

CHAPTER **46**

Writing the Paper

Writing a research paper begins when you seek a topic and continues as you evaluate and gather information from your sources.

http://www.ablongman.com/littlebrown ▶

Visit the companion Web site for more help on writing and revising a research paper.

During research, you might even pause to draft paragraphs or sections that pull your sources together to support your ideas. At some point, though, you'll need to turn your attention to the whole paper—ensuring that it has a clear thesis (below), creating a structure (next page), writing the complete draft (p. 643), revising and editing the paper (p. 645), and preparing the final draft (p. 646). To illustrate these stages, we continue to draw on Edward Begay's and Vanessa Haley's work.

Note This chapter complements and extends the detailed discussion of the writing situation and the writing process in Chapters 1–3, which also include many tips for using a word processor. If you haven't already done so, read Chapters 1–3 before this one.

46a Developing a thesis statement

Perhaps earlier in the research-writing process, but certainly once you have gathered information from your sources, you will want to express your central idea and perspective in a thesis statement of one or two sentences. (See pp. 27–31 if you need guidance on developing a thesis statement.) Drafting a thesis statement will help you see the overall picture and organize your notes.

Edward Begay's and Vanessa Haley's work on their research papers illustrates how a thesis statement evolves to become complete and specific. Before finishing his reading on access to the Internet, Begay wrote the following draft of a thesis statement:

Tentative thesis statement
Because of the cost of hooking up to the Internet and training people to use it, the nation faces the possibility of a widening gap between rich and poor in information, skills, and income.

This statement captured Begay's preliminary idea that the Internet poses a threat to equality. But with further reading, Begay rethought this idea: many of his sources mentioned Internet access through public schools and libraries, and he began to focus on these institutions as a solution to the problem. The solution opened up new questions: How would schools and libraries have to change, what would the change cost, and who should pay for it? With more reading, Begay revised his thesis statement:

Revised thesis statement
Governments and businesses must ensure that libraries and schools have the hardware, connections, and training capabilities needed for computer technology to make Americans more rather than less equal.

For Vanessa Haley, framing a thesis statement for her paper on Annie Dillard required drawing together (synthesizing) Dillard's

tive thesis statements of student writers Edward Begay and Vanessa Haley and shows how each student revised the thesis in a later phase of research. Next come discussions of how to use formal and informal outlines to create a structure for the paper. The second half of the chapter covers drafting, revising, and proofreading, with special attention given to the necessity of tracking and completing source citations. The exercises ask students to apply the strategies discussed in the chapter to their own research essays.

STATED INTENTIONS

Have students complete this sentence in their journals or on a stick-on note they can post at their workplaces: "In this paper I intend to [statement of purpose], so that my audience, [describe intended readers], will [desired result]." This sentence reminds students to consider purpose, audience, and desired results as they write, and it should lead to clearer thesis statements.

COLLABORATIVE LEARNING

THESIS STATEMENT

Have students write their thesis statements on large sheets of paper. Exchange thesis lists among groups, and have each group analyze and suggest revisions for the theses on their lists. The revising group should be prepared to explain its suggestions to the original writers.

In the later stages of their projects have students repeat this exercise as they read one another's drafts. In this case, groups should check to make sure that each student's thesis accurately represents the crucial project of his or her paper.

THE EVOLVING THESIS

Remind students that the thesis of a research paper can change. As they conduct their research and write their papers, they may find that their purpose, opinion, or conception of their audience has shifted. In such circumstances, revising the thesis is not only desirable but necessary to compose an effective paper.

ideas about humanity and nature into a single statement of Haley's own. The first draft merely conveyed Haley's interest in Dillard:

> Tentative thesis statement
> Unlike many other nature writers, Dillard does not reinforce the separation between humanity and nature.

Haley's revision stated her synthesis of Dillard's ideas:

> Revised thesis statement
> In her encounters with nature, Dillard probes a spiritual as well as a physical identity between human beings and nature that could help to heal the rift between them.

EXERCISE 46.1   Developing a thesis statement

Draft and revise a thesis statement for your developing research paper. Make sure the revised version specifically asserts your main idea.

46b   Creating a structure

Before starting to draft your research paper, organize your ideas and information so that you know the main divisions of your paper, the order you'll cover them in, and the important supporting ideas for each division. The goal is to create a structure that presents your ideas in a sensible and persuasive sequence and that supports ideas at each level with enough explanation and evidence. Consult the discussion of organization on pages 32–42 if you need help distinguishing general and specific information, arranging groups of information, or using a computer effectively for developing a structure.

1   Arranging ideas and support

Creating a structure for a research paper involves almost constant synthesis, the forging of relationships among ideas (see p. 610). As you arrange and rearrange source information and your own thoughts, you find connections among ideas and determine which are most important, which are merely supportive, and which are not relevant at all.

To build a structure, follow these guidelines:

- **Arrange your source information in categories** according to the subject headings you attached to each note, photocopy, or printout. Each category should correspond to a main section of your paper: a key idea of your own that supports the thesis along with the evidence for that idea.

- **Review your research journal and annotated bibliography.** Hunt for connections between sources, opinions of sources, and other thoughts that can help you organize your paper.
- **Look objectively at your categories.** If some are skimpy, with little information, consider whether you should drop the categories or conduct more research to fill them out. If most of your information falls into one or two categories, consider whether the categories are too broad and should be divided. (Does any of this rethinking affect your thesis statement? If so, revise it accordingly.)
- **Within each category, distinguish between the main idea and the supporting ideas and evidence.** Only the support should come from your sources. The main idea should be your own.

2 Using an outline

An outline can help you shape your research and also discover potential problems, such as inadequate support and overlapping or irrelevant ideas.

Informal outline

For some research projects, you may find an **informal outline** sufficient: you list main points and supporting information in the order you expect to discuss them. Because of its informality, such an outline can help you try out different arrangements of material, even fairly early in the research process.

Edward Begay experimented with an informal outline while examining his sources, in order to see how his developing ideas might fit together:

History of the Internet

    Packet-switching networks—UK, France
    ARPANET—linked US Defense Dept., contractors, universities
    Network of networks—UNIX, NSFNET, and onward

Commercial vs. public use

    1st users universities, libraries, govts.
    Business sees commercial uses
    PCs, modems increase home use

Access to Internet

    Tech. skills needed
    Problems for equality, democracy
    Expense of going online
    Imp. of Internet to democratic society
    Libraries & schools: sites for widespread access
    Libraries & schools need to adapt, find money to go online

This informal outline helped Begay decide not to continue researching the history of the Internet or the conflicts between commercial and public use (the first two sections) because they seemed likely to overwhelm his central concern, equal access to the Internet (last section).

▪ Formal outline

Unlike an informal outline, a **formal outline** arranges ideas tightly and in considerable detail, with close attention to hierarchy and phrasing. The example below shows the formal outline's format and schematic content:

I. First main idea
    A. First subordinate idea
        1. First evidence for subordinate idea
           a. First detail of evidence
           b. Second detail of evidence
        2. Second evidence for subordinate idea
    B. Second subordinate idea
II. Second main idea

In this model, levels of headings correspond to levels of importance or detail in the paper:

- **Main ideas (Roman numerals) are the major divisions of the paper.** Each division covers a part of your thesis statement and will probably take a number of paragraphs to develop.
- **Subordinate ideas (capital letters) are the building blocks.** These ideas are your own and will probably take a paragraph or two to develop. They may serve as the topic sentences of paragraphs.
- **Evidence (Arabic numerals) and its details (small letters) support each idea.** The evidence from one or more sources will occupy much of each body paragraph. (A fourth sublevel, if needed, is labeled with Arabic numerals enclosed in parentheses.)

Each level of the outline is indented farther than the level it supports. (Your word processor may be able to help you with labels and indentions.)

A formal outline can help you decide not only what your main ideas are and how you will arrange them but also how you will support them. Some of this information may not emerge until you are drafting, however, so remain open to revising the outline as you proceed. And consider using a formal outline as a revision tool as well, creating a map of your completed first draft to check and improve the structure (see p. 49).

To be an effective organizer for your thoughts or an effective revision tool, a formal outline should be detailed and should adhere to several principles of logical arrangement, clarity, balance, and completeness. (See pp. 35–38 for examples and more details.)

- **The outline should indicate which ideas are primary and which are subordinate.** A long, undivided list of parallel items probably needs to be subdivided.
- **Parallel headings should represent ideas of equal importance and generality.** They should not overlap one another.
- **Single sublevels should be avoided.** They illogically imply that something is divided into only one part.

A formal outline is usually written either in phrases (a **topic outline**) or in sentences (a **sentence outline**). A complete topic outline is illustrated on page 36. A complete sentence outline accompanies Edward Begay's research paper on pages 692–93. Either is suitable for a research paper, though a sentence outline, because it requires complete statements, conveys more information.

EXERCISE 46.2   Creating a structure

Continuing from Exercise 46.1 (p. 640), arrange your notes into a structure. As specified by your instructor, make an informal outline or a formal sentence or topic outline to guide the drafting of your paper.

46c   Drafting the paper

Beginning a draft of what will be a relatively long and complicated paper can be difficult, so it may help to remember that you do not have to proceed methodically from beginning to end.

Tips for drafting a research paper

- **Reread the assignment to review your instructor's criteria.** Make sure you have all the materials you'll need to meet the criteria.
- **Write a quick two- or three-paragraph summary of what the paper will be about.** This writing will get your juices flowing and give you a sense of direction. (Pretend you're writing to a friend if that will help loosen you up.) A version of the material you generate in this way may eventually prove useful for your paper's introduction or conclusion.
- **Start with the section of the paper you feel most confident about.** At first, skip any parts that scare you or give you undue trouble, even the introduction.
- **Work in chunks, one unit or principal idea at a time.** Fit the sections together only after you begin to see the draft take shape.
- **Center each section on an idea of your own.** Use source material to back up the idea.
- **Take great care in working with source material.** Integrate sources into your own ideas (p. 623), and do not plagiarize (p. 629).
- **Insert source citations into the draft as you quote, paraphrase, or summarize.** Use authors' names and page numbers.

THE FIVE-MINUTE OVERVIEW

A variation on the short summary suggested in the text is the five-minute overview. Students (perhaps in their journals) try, in five minutes, to give readers as full an overview of the paper they intend to write as they can. This five-minute overview might then serve as a road map for creating a draft of the paper itself.

To avoid the initial anxiety of beginning a draft, have students bring in their notes and outlines and write for a full class period. Then ask students to go home and rework this initial piece of writing into a typed rough draft that they can share with their revision groups.

1　Working section by section

In writing a first draft, remember that a primary reason for doing a research paper is learning how to interpret and evaluate the evidence in sources, draw your own conclusions from the evidence, and weave the two together in a way that establishes your expertise in your subject. The weaving will be easier if you view each principal idea of your paper (each Roman numeral of your outline) as a unit. Usually these principal ideas require a block of paragraphs to develop.

Compose the units of your paper as if each will stand alone (though of course you will pull the units together before your draft is complete).

- **Begin each unit by stating the idea,** which should be a conclusion you have drawn from reading and responding to your sources.
- **Follow the statement with specific support from your sources:** facts and examples; summaries, paraphrases, or quotations of secondary sources; quotations of passages from primary sources with your analysis.
- **Present fairly any disagreements among experts.** Give the evidence that leads you to side with one expert or another.
- **Try to remain open to new interpretations or new arrangements of ideas that occur to you.**

Note Proceeding in this way will help you avoid a common trap of research writing: allowing your sources to control you, rather than vice versa. Make sure each unit of your paper centers on an idea of your own, not someone else's, and that your paragraphs are pointed toward demonstrating that idea, not merely presenting sources.

2　Tracking source citations

As you draft your paper, insert the source of each summary, paraphrase, and quotation in parentheses in the text—for instance, "(Irving 64)," referring to page 64 in a work by Irving. If you are conscientious about inserting these notes and carrying them through successive drafts, you will be less likely to plagiarize accidentally and you will have little difficulty documenting your sources in the final paper.

EXERCISE 46.3　Drafting your paper

Draft the research paper you have been developing in Chapters 42–45. Before beginning the draft, study your research journal and your source information. While drafting, follow your thesis statement and outline as closely as you need to, but stay open to new ideas, associations, and arrangements.

46d Revising and editing the paper

When you have written a first draft, take a break for at least a day so that you can gain some objectivity about your work and can read the draft critically when you begin to revise.

1 Revising

Always revise your draft first, satisfying yourself with the content and shape of the whole before trying to edit sentences and words. For revision, begin with the advice and checklist on pages 48–54, and supplement with the checklist below.

Checklist for revising a research paper

Assignment
How does the draft satisfy all of the criteria stated in your instructor's assignment?

Thesis statement
How well does your thesis statement describe your subject and your perspective as they emerged during drafting?

Structure
(Outlining your draft as suggested on p. 642 can help you see structure at a glance.)
How consistently does borrowed material illuminate and support—not lead and dominate—your own ideas? How well is the importance of ideas reflected in the emphasis they receive? Will the arrangement of ideas be clear to readers?

Evidence
Where might readers need more evidence in order to accept your ideas? Where might the evidence seem weak or irrelevant?

Reasonableness and clarity
How reasonable will readers find your arguments? (See pp. 202–06.) Where do you need to define terms or concepts that readers may not know or may dispute?

You can download this checklist from *ablongman.com/littlebrown*. Copy the checklist for each research paper, answering the questions in writing.

2 Editing

When you complete your revision—and only then—you are ready to edit. If you do not compose on a computer, copy or retype the new draft if possible so that you have a clean copy to work on. If you do compose on a computer, you can edit directly on screen or

TRANSPARENCY MASTER 46.2

COLLABORATIVE LEARNING

REVISION OUTLINES

Some students will profit by using outlining as a revision strategy. Once students have written one or two drafts of their research papers, have them work in pairs or small groups to outline their drafts, paying particular attention to connections between paragraphs and the presentation of major points.

ELEVENTH-HOUR THESES

Students can panic when it becomes clear in the final revision stages that the paper still lacks a crucial source or a strong thesis. You can prepare students for these moments by helping them to understand that papers often develop beyond the scope or direction of writers' original research, outlines, and planned theses. Taking advantage of these developments by finding an additional source or writing a new thesis statement is often the key to a successful revision.

print a clean copy. (Some writers find it easier to spot errors on paper than on screen.)

For editing, consult the advice and checklist on pages 58–62. Try to read the paper from the point of view of someone who has not spent hours planning and researching but instead has come fresh to the paper. Look for lapses in sense, awkward passages, wordiness, poor transitions between ideas and evidence, unnecessary repetition, wrong or misspelled words, errors in grammar, punctuation, or mechanics—in short, anything that is likely to interfere with a reader's understanding of your meaning.

3 Completing source citations

Before you prepare your final draft (next section), you must insert final source citations into your text and prepare the list of sources for the end of the paper. See pages 635–37 on documenting sources in various disciplines' styles.

EXERCISE 46.4 Revising and editing your paper

Using the revision and editing checklists on pages 51 and 58–59 and the checklist and pointers here, revise and edit your research paper. Work to improve not only the presentation of ideas but also, if necessary, the ideas themselves. Make sure you have provided an in-text citation for every summary, paraphrase, and direct quotation of a source and that your list of sources is complete.

46e Preparing and proofreading the final draft

Prepare the final draft of your paper when you have edited the text, added the source citations, and written the list of works cited. Most instructors expect research papers to be neatly typed with clear titling, double spacing, standard margins, and minimal handwritten corrections. Your instructor may have additional requirements, suggested by the discipline in which you are writing. This book explains four such document formats:

- **MLA format,** used in English, foreign languages, and some other humanities, pages 656 and 687–89. See also Chapter 48 for the sample research papers of Edward Begay and Vanessa Haley.
- **Chicago format,** used in history, art history, religion, philosophy, and some other humanities, pages 765–66 and 775–77.
- **APA format,** used in psychology and other social sciences, pages 788–90 and 800–03.
- **CSE format,** used in the natural and applied sciences, pages 813–15 and 820.

In any discipline, you can use a word processor to present your ideas effectively and attractively with readable type fonts, headings, illustrations, and other elements. See Chapter 5 for ideas and examples.

Before you submit your paper, proofread it carefully for typographical errors, misspellings, and other errors. (See p. 63 for proofreading tips.) Unless the errors are very numerous (more than several on a page), you can correct them by whiting out or crossing out (neatly) and inserting the correction (neatly) in ink. Don't let the pressure of a deadline prevent you from proofreading, for even minor errors can impair clarity or annoy readers and thus negate some of the hard work you have put into your project.

EXERCISE 46.5 Preparing and proofreading your final draft

Prepare the final draft of your research paper, following your instructor's requirements for document format. If your instructor does not specify a format, follow the MLA guidelines on pages 687–89. Proofread and correct the paper before submitting it.

CHAPTER 47

Using MLA Documentation and Format

English, foreign languages, and some other humanities use the documentation style and document format of the Modern Language Association, detailed in the *MLA Handbook for Writers of Research Papers*, 6th ed. (2003).

MLA documentation style employs brief parenthetical citations within the text that direct readers to a list of works cited at the end of the text. A parenthetical citation might look like this:

Only one article mentions this discrepancy (Wolfe 62).

---

http://www.ablongman.com/littlebrown ▶

Visit the companion Web site for more help and an additional exercise on MLA documentation and format.

RESOURCES AND IDEAS

Gallagher, Chris W. *Radical Departures: Composition and Progressive Pedagogy*. Urbana: NCTE, 2002. Gallagher advocates a composition pedagogy based upon shared knowledge building, collective action, and reflexive inquiry, a pedagogy that includes community outreach.

Walvoord, B. E., V. J. Anderson, J. R. Breihan, L. P. McCarthy, S. M. Robinson, and A. K. Sherman. "Functions of Outlining Among College Students in Four Disciplines." *Research in the Teaching of English* 29 (1995): 390–421. This statistical study of the functions of outlining shows that students who produce successful papers tend to outline at several points in the drafting process.

mycomplab[2.0]

Please visit MyCompLab at *www.mycomplab.com* for more on the writing process.

HIGHLIGHTS

This chapter explains the procedure for documenting sources as stipulated by the Modern Language Association (MLA), conforming to the latest guidelines as specified by the *MLA Handbook for Writers of Research Papers*, 6th ed. (2003). Students are shown both how to document sources within the text using parenthetical citations and how to prepare a Works Cited list for the end of the paper; indexes on pages 649 and 658–59 provide quick reference to the models.

New graphic representations of book and article title and copyright pages, along with screenshots of online sources, show students exactly where to look for the information they need for citations. New models have been added for citing

COMPANION WEB SITE

See page IAE-60 for companion Web site content description.

a variety of images as well as Web log and Web forum entries.

Two sample student research papers are included in their entirety, with annotations showing correct application of MLA citation rules.

BASKETBALL ANALOGY

Students frequently ask why there are so many different styles for them to learn. Use the analogy of basketball: while some rules are the same in all games (regular field goals count as two points, free throws one), others differ depending on the court and players. For instance, the three-point line is farther from the basket in professional basketball than it is in college. These different rules are designed to suit the abilities and expectations of players at each level. Likewise, different documentation systems are designed for the needs of each audience. The social sciences value the timeliness of information, so the date of publication is included in in-text citations and emphasized in references. The humanities value titles and authors' names, so humanities citations emphasize those elements.

The name Wolfe directs readers to the article by Wolfe in the list of works cited, and the page number 62 specifies the page in the article on which the cited material appears.

This chapter describes MLA style: what to include in a parenthetical citation (below), where to place citations (p. 654), when to use footnotes or endnotes in addition to parenthetical citations (p. 656), how to create the list of works cited (p. 656), and how to format the entire paper (p. 687).

47a Using MLA in-text citations

1 Writing parenthetical text citations

In-text citations of sources must include just enough information for the reader to locate the following:

- The *source* in your list of works cited.
- The *place* in the source where the borrowed material appears.

For any kind of source, you can usually meet both these requirements by providing the author's last name and (if the source uses them) the page numbers where the material appears. The reader can find the source in your list of works cited and find the borrowed material in the source itself.

Note For most sources, you will provide the author's or authors' last names and a page reference. Do not include the title unless you are citing more than one work by exactly the same author(s) or the source has no listed author (models 8 and 9, p. 651). The examples below cite a book to which neither of these exceptions applies:

Not	One textbook discusses the "ethical dilemmas in public relations practice" (Wilcox, Ault, and Agee, Public Relations 125).
Not	One textbook discusses the "ethical dilemmas in public relations practice" (Public Relations 125).
But	One textbook discusses the "ethical dilemmas in public relations practice" (Wilcox, Ault, and Agee 125).

1. Author not named in your text

When you have not already named the author in your sentence, provide the author's last name and the page number(s), with no punctuation between them, in parentheses.

One researcher concludes that "women impose a distinctive construction on moral problems, seeing moral dilemmas in terms of conflicting responsibilities" (Gilligan 105-06).

See models 5 and 6 for the forms to use when the source does not provide page numbers.

MLA parenthetical text citations

1. Author not named in your text *648*
2. Author named in your text *649*
3. A work with two or three authors *649*
4. A work with more than three authors *649*
5. A work with numbered paragraphs or screens instead of pages *650*
6. An entire work or a work with no page or other reference numbers *650*
7. A multivolume work *650*
8. A work by an author of two or more cited works *651*
9. An anonymous work *651*
10. A government publication or a work with a corporate author *652*
11. An indirect source *652*
12. A literary work *652*
13. The Bible *653*
14. An electronic source *653*
15. Two or more works in the same citation *653*

2. Author named in your text

If the author's name is already given with the material you're citing, you need not repeat it in the parenthetical citation. The citation gives just the page number(s).

> Carol Gilligan concludes that "women impose a distinctive construction on moral problems, seeing moral dilemmas in terms of conflicting responsibilities" (105-06).

3. A work with two or three authors

If the source has two or three authors, give all their last names in the text or in the citation. Separate two authors' names with and:

> As Frieden and Sagalyn observe, "The poor and the minorities were the leading victims of highway and renewal programs" (29).

> According to one study, "The poor and the minorities were the leading victims of highway and renewal programs" (Frieden and Sagalyn 29).

With three authors, add commas and also and before the final name:

> The textbook by Wilcox, Ault, and Agee discusses the "ethical dilemmas in public relations practice" (125).

> One textbook discusses the "ethical dilemmas in public relations practice" (Wilcox, Ault, and Agee 125).

4. A work with more than three authors

If the source has more than three authors, you may list all their last names or use only the first author's name followed by et al. (the abbreviation for the Latin *et alii*, "and others"). The choice depends on what you do in your list of works cited (see p. 659).

> It took the combined forces of the Americans, Europeans, and Japanese to break the rebel siege of Beijing in 1900 (Lopez et al. 362).

> It took the combined forces of the Americans, Europeans, and Japanese to break the rebel siege of Beijing in 1900 (Lopez, Blum, Cameron, and Barnes 362).

5. A work with numbered paragraphs or screens instead of pages

Some electronic sources number each paragraph or screen instead of each page. In citing passages in these sources, give the paragraph or screen number(s) and distinguish them from page numbers: after the author's name, put a comma, a space, and par. (one paragraph), pars. (more than one paragraph), screen, or screens.

> Twins reared apart report similar feelings (Palfrey, pars. 6-7).

6. An entire work or a work with no page or other reference numbers

When you cite an entire work rather than a part of it, you may omit any page or paragraph number. Try to work the author's name into your text, in which case you will not need a parenthetical citation. But remember that the source must appear in the list of works cited.

> Boyd deals with the need to acknowledge and come to terms with our fear of nuclear technology.

Use the same format when you cite a specific passage from a work with no page, paragraph, or other reference numbers, such as an online source.

If the author's name does not appear in your text, put it in a parenthetical citation.

> Almost 20 percent of commercial banks have been audited for the practice (Friis).

7. A multivolume work

If you consulted only one volume of a multivolume work, your list of works cited will say so (see model 14 on p. 653), and you can treat the volume as any book.

If you consulted more than one volume of a multivolume work, give the appropriate volume in your text citation.

> After issuing the Emancipation Proclamation, Lincoln said, "What I did, I did
> after very full deliberations, and under a very heavy and solemn sense of re-
> sponsibility" (5: 438).

The number 5 indicates the volume from which the quotation was taken; the number 438 indicates the page number in that volume. When the author's name appears in such a citation, place it before the volume number with no punctuation: (Lincoln 5: 438).

If you are referring generally to an entire volume of a multi-volume work and are not citing specific page numbers, add the abbreviation vol. before the volume number as in (vol. 5) or (Lincoln, vol. 5) (note the comma after the author's name). Then readers will not misinterpret the volume number as a page number.

8. A work by an author of two or more cited works

If your list of works cited includes two or more works by the same author, then your citation must tell the reader which of the author's works you are referring to. Give the title either in the text or in a parenthetical citation. In a parenthetical citation, give the full title only if it is brief; otherwise, shorten the title to the first one, two, or three main words (excluding *A, An,* or *The*).

> At about age seven, children begin to use appropriate gestures with their sto-
> ries (Gardner, Arts 144-45).

The full title of Gardner's book is *The Arts and Human Development* (see the works-cited entry on p. 661). This shortened title is underlined because the source is a book.

9. An anonymous work

For a work with no named author or editor (whether an individual or an organization), use a full or shortened version of the title, as explained above. In your list of works cited, you alphabetize an anonymous work by the first main word of the title (see p. 662), so the first word of a shortened title should be the same. The following citation refers to an unsigned source titled "The Right to Die." This shortened title is placed in quotation marks because the source is a periodical article.

> One article notes that a death-row inmate may demand his own execution to
> achieve a fleeting notoriety ("Right").

(A page number may be omitted for this source because the article is only one page. See the entry for the article on p. 668.)

If two or more anonymous works have the same title, distinguish them with additional information in the text citation, such as the publication date.

10. A government publication or a work with a corporate author

Some works list as author a government body, association, committee, company, or other group. Cite such a work by the organization's name. If the name is long, work it into the text to avoid an intrusive parenthetical citation.

> A 2005 report by the Hawaii Department of Education predicts an increase in enrollments (6).

11. An indirect source

When you want to use a quotation that is already in quotation marks—indicating that the author you are reading is quoting someone else—try to find the original source and quote directly from it. If you can't find the original source, then your citation must indicate that your quotation of it is indirect. In the following citation, qtd. in ("quoted in") says that Davino was quoted by Boyd:

> George Davino maintains that "even small children have vivid ideas about nuclear energy" (qtd. in Boyd 22).

The list of works cited then includes only Boyd (the work consulted), not Davino.

12. A literary work

Novels, plays, and poems are often available in many editions, so your instructor may ask you to provide information that will help readers find the passage you cite no matter what edition they consult.

- **Novels:** The page number comes first, followed by a semicolon and then information on the appropriate part or chapter of the work.

  > Toward the end of James's novel, Maggie suddenly feels "the thick breath of the definite—which was the intimate, the immediate, the familiar, as she hadn't had them for so long" (535; pt. 6, ch. 41).

- **Poems that are not divided into parts:** You may omit the page number and supply the line number(s) for the quotation. To prevent confusion with page numbers, precede the numbers with line or lines in the first citation; then use just the numbers.

  > In Shakespeare's Sonnet 73 the speaker identifies with the trees of late autumn, "Bare ruined choirs, where late the sweet birds sang" (line 4). "In me," Shakespeare writes, "thou seest the glowing of such fire / That on the ashes of his youth doth lie . . ." (9-10).

(See pp. 752–54 for a sample paper on a poem.)

- **Verse plays and poems that are divided into parts:** Omit a page number and cite the appropriate part—act (and scene, if any), canto, book, and so on—plus the line number(s). Use Arabic numerals for parts, including acts and scenes (3.4), unless your instructor specifies Roman numerals (III.iv).

  Later in King Lear the disguised Edgar says, "The prince of darkness is a gentleman" (3.4.147).

  (See pp. 756–59 for a sample paper on a verse play.)

- **Prose plays:** Provide the page number followed by the act and scene, if any. See the reference to *Death of a Salesman* on page 655.

13. The Bible

When you cite passages of the Bible in parentheses, abbreviate the title of any book longer than four letters—for instance, Gen. (Genesis), 1 Sam. (1 Samuel), Ps. (Psalms), Prov. (Proverbs), Matt. (Matthew), Rom. (Romans). Then give the chapter and verse(s) in Arabic numerals.

According to the Bible, at Babel God "did . . . confound the language of all the earth" (Gen. 11.9).

14. An electronic source

Cite an electronic source as you would any other source: usually by author's name or, if there is no author, by title.

Business forecasts for the fourth quarter tended to be optimistic (White 4).

This example cites a source with page numbers. For a source with paragraph or screen numbers or no numbering, see models 5 and 6 (p. 650).

15. Two or more works in the same citation

If you use a single parenthetical citation to refer to more than one work, separate the references with a semicolon.

Two recent articles point out that a computer badly used can be less efficient than no computer at all (Gough and Hall 201; Richards 162).

Since long citations in the text can distract the reader, you may choose to cite several or more works in an endnote or footnote rather than in the text. See page 656.

PUNCTUATION PRACTICE

Give students the following sentences, but omit the citation punctuation. Ask them to work in small groups to punctuate them properly.

In his biography of his father, Aram Saroyan notes that William Saroyan turned down a Pulitzer Prize, which "created far more publicity than the award itself had" (44).

"The realization dawns simultaneously on the hero and the reader of the story alike", comments Aram Saroyan, "that the young man . . . is on the verge of a fatal swing, that he is working without a net" (31).

Saroyan's outlook on life may have been shaped by his experience as a member of an ethnic minority:

Saroyan had known prejudice against Armenians at first hand in his childhood: "For Sale" signs posted in front of houses with "No Armenians" written beneath in smaller letters; a grammar school teacher who complained to the class of the odor of spicy food on the Armenian children's breath. (72)

HIGHLIGHT THE CITATIONS

It is always a good practice to keep citation information together with cited content, but occasionally your students may find as they write that they want to use a quotation for which they have forgotten to find a page reference or are unsure of the spelling of the author's name. To avoid derailing their drafting process, they can put in a parenthetical in-text citation with as much information as they do have, highlight it in their word processor, and then go on drafting their paper. They can go back and find the missing information later.

2 Positioning and punctuating parenthetical citations

The following guidelines will help you place and punctuate text citations to distinguish between your and your sources' ideas and to make your own text readable. See also pages 623–28 on editing quotations and using signal phrases to integrate source material into your sentences.

■ Where to place citations

Position text citations to accomplish two goals:

- **Make it clear exactly where your borrowing begins and ends.**
- **Keep the citation as unobtrusive as possible.**

You can accomplish both goals by placing the parenthetical citation at the end of the sentence element containing the borrowed material. This sentence element may be a phrase or a clause, and it may begin, interrupt, or conclude the sentence. Usually, as in the following examples, the element ends with a punctuation mark.

The inflation rate might climb as high as 30 percent (Kim 164), an increase that could threaten the small nation's stability.

The inflation rate, which might climb as high as 30 percent (Kim 164), could threaten the small nation's stability.

The small nation's stability could be threatened by its inflation rate, which, one source predicts, might climb as high as 30 percent (Kim 164).

In the last example the addition of one source predicts clarifies that Kim is responsible only for the inflation-rate prediction, not for the statement about stability.

When your paraphrase or summary of a source runs longer than a sentence, clarify the boundaries by using the author's name in the first sentence and placing the parenthetical citation at the end of the last sentence.

Juliette Kim studied the effects of acutely high inflation in several South American and African countries since World War II. She discovered that a major change in government accompanied or followed the inflationary period in 56 percent of cases (22-23).

When you cite two or more sources in the same paragraph, position authors' names and parenthetical citations so that readers can see who said what. In the following example, the beginnings and ends of sentences clearly mark the different sources:

For some time, schools have been using computers extensively for drill-and-practice exercises, in which students repeat specific skills such as spelling words, using the multiplication facts, or, at a higher level, doing chemistry problems. But many education experts criticize such exercises for boring students and failing to engage their critical thinking and creativity. Jane M. Healy, a noted educational psychologist and teacher, takes issue with "interactive" software for children as well as drill-and-practice software, arguing that "some of the most popular 'educational' software . . . may be damaging to independent thinking, attention, and motivation" (20). Another education expert, Harold Wenglinsky of the Educational Testing Service, found in a well-regarded 1998 study that fourth and eighth graders who used computers frequently, including for drill and practice, actually did worse on tests than their peers who used computers less often (Does It Compute? 21). In a later article, Wenglinsky concludes that "the quantity of use matters far less than the quality of use." In schools, he says, high-quality computer work, involving critical thinking, is still rare ("In Search" 17).

■ How to punctuate citations

Generally place a parenthetical citation *before* any punctuation required by your sentence. If the borrowed material is a quotation, place the citation *between* the closing quotation mark and the punctuation:

> Spelling argues that during the 1970s American automobile manufacturers met consumer needs "as well as could be expected" (26), but not everyone agrees with him.

The exception is a quotation ending in a question mark or exclamation point. Then use the appropriate punctuation inside the closing quotation mark, and follow the quotation with the text citation and a period:

> "Of what use is genius," Emerson asks, "if the organ . . . cannot find a focal distance within the actual horizon of human life?" ("Experience" 60). Mad genius is no genius.

When a citation appears at the end of a quotation set off from the text, place it one space *after* the punctuation ending the quotation. Do not use additional punctuation with the citation or quotation marks around the quotation:

> In Arthur Miller's Death of a Salesman, the most poignant defense of Willie Loman comes from his wife, Linda:
>
>> He's not the finest character that ever lived. But he's a human being, and a terrible thing is happening to him. So attention must be paid. He's not to be allowed to fall into his grave like an old dog. Attention, attention must finally be paid to such a person. (56; act 1)

(This citation of a play includes the act number as well as the page number. See p. 653.)

See the two sample research papers starting on pages 690 and 725 for further examples of placing parenthetical references in relation to summaries, paraphrases, and quotations.

3 Using footnotes or endnotes in special circumstances

Occasionally, you may want to use footnotes or endnotes in place of parenthetical citations. If you need to refer to several sources at once, listing them in a long parenthetical citation could be intrusive. In that case, signal the citation with a numeral raised above the appropriate line of text and write a note with the same numeral to cite the sources:

Text   At least five studies have confirmed these results.[1]

Note   [1] Abbott and Winger 266-68; Casner 27; Hoyenga 78-79; Marino 36; Tripp, Tripp, and Walk 179-83.

You may also use a footnote or endnote to comment on a source or provide information that does not fit easily in the text:

Text   So far, no one has confirmed these results.[2]

Note   [2] Manter reports spending a year trying to replicate the experiment, but he was never able to produce the high temperatures (616).

In a note, the raised numeral is indented five spaces or one-half inch and is followed by a space. If the note appears as a footnote, place it at the bottom of the page on which the citation appears, set it off from the text with quadruple spacing, and single-space the note itself. If the note appears as an endnote, place it in numerical order with the other endnotes on a page between the text and the list of works cited. Double-space all the endnotes. (See pp. 718–19 for examples of endnotes and the format to use in typing a page of endnotes.)

47b Preparing the MLA list of works cited

In the documentation style of the *MLA Handbook*, your in-text parenthetical citations (discussed in 47a) refer the reader to complete information on your sources in a list you title Works Cited and place at the end of your paper. The list should include all the sources you quoted, paraphrased, or summarized in your paper. (If your instructor asks you to include sources you examined but did not cite, title the list Works Consulted.)

MLA works-cited page

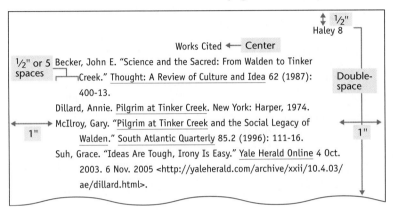

Follow this format for the list of works cited:

- **Arrange your sources in alphabetical order** by the last name of the author. If an author is not given in the source, alphabetize the source by the first main word of the title (excluding *A*, *An*, or *The*).
- **Type the entire list double-spaced,** both within and between entries.
- **Indent the second and subsequent lines of each entry one-half inch or five spaces from the left.** Your word processor can format this so-called hanging indent automatically. First highlight the material to be indented. Then, on the Format menu, click Paragraph and then either Hanging Indent (in *Word-Perfect*) or Special: Hanging (in *Microsoft Word*).

For complete lists of works cited, see the papers by Edward Begay (p. 720) and Vanessa Haley (p. 730).

The box on the next two pages directs you to the MLA formats for works-cited entries. Use your best judgment in adapting the models to your particular sources. If you can't find a model that exactly matches a source you used, locate and follow the closest possible match. You will certainly need to combine formats—for instance, drawing on model 2 ("A book with two or three authors") and model 26 ("An article in a daily newspaper") for a newspaper article with two authors.

MLA works-cited models

TRANSPARENCY MASTER 47.2

1 Listing books

The next page shows the basic format for a book and the location of the required information in a book. When other information is required, it usually falls either between the author's name and the title or between the title and the publication information, as in the following models.

1. A book with one author

Gilligan, Carol. In a Different Voice: Psychological Theory and Women's Development. Cambridge: Harvard UP, 1982.

2. A book with two or three authors

Lifton, Robert Jay, and Greg Mitchell. Who Owns Death: Capital Punishment, the American Conscience, and the End of Executions. New York: Morrow, 2000.

Wilcox, Dennis L., Phillip H. Ault, and Warren K. Agee. Public Relations: Strategies and Tactics. 6th ed. New York: Irwin, 2005.

Give the authors' names in the order provided on the title page. Reverse the first and last names of the first author *only*, not of any other authors. Separate two authors' names with a comma and and; separate three authors' names with commas and with and before the third name.

3. A book with more than three authors

Lopez, Geraldo, Judith P. Salt, Anne Ming, and Henry Reisen. China and the West. Boston: Little, 2004.

Lopez, Geraldo, et al. China and the West. Boston: Little, 2004.

Information for a book

Gilligan, Carol. In a Different Voice: Psychological Theory and Women's Development.
Cambridge: Harvard UP, 1982.

①②③④⑤

Title page

② **Title,** underlined. Give the full title and any sub-title, separating them with a colon. End the title with a period.

In a Different Voice

Psychological Theory and Women's Development

① **Author.** Give the full name —last name first, a comma, first name, and any middle name or initial. Omit *Dr., PhD,* or any other title. End the name with a period.

Carol Gilligan

④ **Publisher's name.** Shorten most publishers' names ("UP" for University Press, "Little" for Little, Brown). Give both imprint and publisher's names when they appear on the title page: e.g., "Vintage-Random" for Vintage Books and Random House.

③ **City of publication.** Precede the publisher's name with its city, followed by a colon. Use only the first city if the title page lists more than one.

Harvard University Press
Cambridge, Massachusetts, and London, England

Copyright page

⑤ **Date of publication.** If the date doesn't appear on the title page, look for it on the next page. End the date with a period.

Copyright © 1982 by Carol Gilligan
All rights reserved
Printed in the United States of America

You may, but need not, give all authors' names if the work has more than three authors. If you choose not to give all names, provide the name of the first author only, and follow the name with a comma and the abbreviation et al. (for the Latin *et alii,* meaning "and others").

4. Two or more works by the same author(s)

Gardner, Howard. The Arts and Human Development. New York: Wiley, 1973.

---. The Quest for Mind: Piaget, Lévi-Strauss, and the Structuralist Movement.
New York: Knopf, 1973.

Give the author's name only in the first entry. For the second and any subsequent works by the same author, substitute three hyphens for the author's name, followed by a period. (If you are citing two or more works by the same editor, editors, or translator, follow the hyphens with a comma and ed., eds., or trans. as appropriate. See models 5, 6, and 7.) Note that the three hyphens stand for *exactly* the same name or names. If the second Gardner source were by Gardner and somebody else, both names would have to be given in full.

Place an entry or entries using three hyphens immediately after the entry that names the author. Within the set of entries by the same author, arrange the sources alphabetically by the first main word of the title, as in the Gardner examples (Arts, then Quest).

5. A book with an editor

Holland, Merlin, and Rupert Hart-Davis, eds. The Complete Letters of Oscar
Wilde. New York: Holt, 2000.

Handle editors' names like authors' names (models 1–3), but add a comma and the abbreviation ed. (one editor) or eds. (two or more editors) after the last editor's name.

6. A book with an author and an editor

Mumford, Lewis. The City in History. Ed. Donald L. Miller. New York: Pantheon,
1986.

When citing the work of the author, give his or her name first, and give the editor's name after the title, preceded by Ed. (singular only, meaning "Edited by"). When citing the work of the editor, use model 5 for a book with an editor, adding By and the author's name after the title: Miller, Donald L., ed. The City in History. By Lewis Mumford.

7. A translation

Alighieri, Dante. The Inferno. Trans. John Ciardi. New York: NAL, 1971.

When citing the work of the author, give his or her name first, and give the translator's name after the title, preceded by Trans. ("Translated by"). When citing the work of the translator, give his or her name first, followed by a comma and trans.; then follow the title with By and the author's name: Ciardi, John, trans. The Inferno. By Dante Alighieri.

When a book you cite by author has a translator *and* an editor, give the translator's and editor's names in the order used on the book's title page.

8. A book with a corporate author

Lorenz Research, Inc. Research in Social Studies Teaching. Baltimore: Arrow, 2000.

Corporate authors include associations, committees, institutions, government bodies, companies, and other groups. List the name of the group as author when a source gives only that name and not an individual's.

9. An anonymous book

The Dorling Kindersley World Reference Atlas. London: Dorling, 2005.

List a book that names no author—neither an individual nor a group—by its full title. Alphabetize the book by the title's first main word (here Dorling), excluding *A*, *An*, or *The*.

10. The Bible

The Bible. King James Version.

The New English Bible. London: Oxford UP and Cambridge UP, 1970.

When citing a standard version of the Bible (first example), do not underline the title or the name of the version, and you need not provide publication information. For an edition of the Bible (second example), underline the title and give full publication information.

11. A later edition

Bolinger, Dwight L. Aspects of Language. 3rd ed. New York: Harcourt, 1981.

For any edition after the first, place the edition number after the title. (If an editor's name follows the title, place the edition number after the name. See model 18.) Use the appropriate designation for editions that are named or dated rather than numbered—for instance, Rev. ed. for "Revised edition."

12. A republished book

James, Henry. The Golden Bowl. 1904. London: Penguin, 1966.

Republished books include paperbound editions of books originally released in hard bindings and books reissued under new titles. Place the original date of publication (but not the place of publication or the publisher's name) after the title, and then provide the full publication information for the source you are using. If the book was originally published under a different title, add this title after Rpt. of ("Reprint of") at the end of the entry and move the original publication date to follow the title—for example, Rpt. of Thomas Hardy: A Life. 1941.

13. A book with a title in its title

Eco, Umberto. Postscript to The Name of the Rose. Trans. William Weaver. New
York: Harcourt, 1983.

When a book's title contains another book title (as here: *The Name of the Rose*), do not underline the second title. When a book's title contains a quotation or the title of a work normally placed in quotation marks, keep the quotation marks and underline both titles: Critical Response to Henry James's "The Beast in the Jungle." (Note that the underlining extends under the closing quotation mark.)

14. A work in more than one volume

Lincoln, Abraham. The Collected Works of Abraham Lincoln. Ed. Roy P. Basler.
8 vols. New Brunswick: Rutgers UP, 1953.

Lincoln, Abraham. The Collected Works of Abraham Lincoln. Ed. Roy P. Basler.
Vol. 5. New Brunswick: Rutgers UP, 1953. 8 vols.

If you use two or more volumes of a multivolume work, give the work's total number of volumes before the publication information (8 vols. in the first example). Your text citation will indicate which volume you are citing (see pp. 650–51). If you use only one volume, give that volume number before the publication information (Vol. 5 in the second example). You may add the total number of volumes to the end of the entry (8 vols. in the second example).

If you cite a multivolume work published over a period of years, give the inclusive years as the publication date: for instance, Cambridge: Harvard UP, 1978-90.

15. A work in a series

Bergman, Ingmar. The Seventh Seal. Mod. Film Scripts Ser. 12. New York:
Simon, 1995.

Place the name of the series (not quoted or underlined) just before the publication information. Abbreviate common words such as *modern* and *series*. Add any series number after the series title.

16. Published proceedings of a conference

Watching Our Language: A Conference Sponsored by the Program in Architecture and Design Criticism. 6-8 May 2005. New York: Parsons School of Design, 2005.

Whether in or after the title of the conference, supply information about who sponsored the conference, when it was held, and who published the proceedings. Treat a particular presentation at the conference like a selection from an anthology (model 18).

17. An anthology

Kennedy, X. J., and Dana Gioia, eds. Literature: An Introduction to Fiction, Poetry, and Drama. 9th ed. New York: Longman, 2005.

Cite an entire anthology only when citing the work of the editor or editors or when your instructor permits cross-referencing like that shown in model 19. Give the name of the editor or editors (followed by ed. or eds.) and then the title of the anthology.

18. A selection from an anthology

Mason, Bobbie Ann. "Shiloh." Literature: An Introduction to Fiction, Poetry, and Drama. Ed. X. J. Kennedy and Dana Gioia. 9th ed. New York: Longman, 2005. 643-54.

The essentials of this listing are these: author of selection; title of selection (in quotation marks); title of anthology (underlined); editors' names preceded by Ed. (meaning "Edited by"); publication information for the anthology; and inclusive page numbers for the selection (without the abbreviation "pp."). In addition, this source requires an edition number for the anthology. If you wish, you may also supply the original date of publication for the work you are citing, after its title. See model 12 on page 662.

If the work you cite comes from a collection of works by one author and with no editor, use the following form:

Auden, W. H. "Family Ghosts." The Collected Poetry of W. H. Auden. New York: Random, 1945. 132-33.

If the work you cite is a scholarly article that was previously printed elsewhere, provide the complete information for the earlier publication of the piece, followed by Rpt. in ("Reprinted in") and the information for the source in which you found the piece:

Molloy, Francis C. "The Suburban Vision in John O'Hara's Short Stories." Critique: Studies in Modern Fiction 25.2 (1984): 101-13. Rpt. in Short Story Criticism: Excerpts from Criticism of the Works of Short Fiction Writers. Ed. David Segal. Vol. 15. Detroit: Gale, 1989. 287-92.

San Juan, E. "Theme Versus Imitation: D. H. Lawrence's 'The Rocking-Horse
    Winner.'" <u>D. H. Lawrence Review</u> 3 (1970): 136-40. Rpt. in <u>From Fiction</u>
    <u>to Film: D. H. Lawrence's "The Rocking-Horse Winner."</u> Ed. Gerald R.
    Barrett and Thomas L. Erskine. Dickenson Literature and Film Ser.
    Encino: Dickenson, 1974. 70-74.

19. Two or more selections from the same anthology

Chopin, Kate. "The Storm." Kennedy and Gioia 127-31.

Kennedy, X. J., and Dana Gioia, eds. <u>Literature: An Introduction to Fiction,</u>
    <u>Poetry, and Drama.</u> 9th ed. New York: Longman, 2005.

O'Connor, Flannery. "Revelation." Kennedy and Gioia 443-58.

When you are citing more than one selection from the same source, your instructor may allow you to avoid repetition by giving the source in full (as in the Kennedy and Gioia entry) and then simply cross-referencing it in entries for the works you used. Thus, instead of full information for the Chopin and O'Connor works, give Kennedy and Gioia and the appropriate pages in that book. Note that each entry appears in its proper alphabetical place among other works cited.

20. An introduction, preface, foreword, or afterword

Donaldson, Norman. Introduction. <u>The Claverings</u>. By Anthony Trollope. New
    York: Dover, 1977. vii-xv.

An introduction, foreword, or afterword is often written by someone other than the book's author. When citing such a piece, give its name without quotation marks or underlining. (If the piece has a title of its own, provide it, in quotation marks, between the name of the author and the name of the piece.) Follow the title of the book with its author's name preceded by By. Give the inclusive page numbers of the part you cite. (In the preceding example, the small Roman numerals refer to the front matter of the book, before page 1.)

When the author of a preface or introduction is the same as the author of the book, give only the last name after the title:

Gould, Stephen Jay. Prologue. <u>The Flamingo's Smile: Reflections in Natural</u>
    <u>History</u>. By Gould. New York: Norton, 1985. 13-20.

21. An article in a reference work

Mark, Herman F. "Polymers." <u>The New Encyclopaedia Britannica: Macropaedia</u>.
    15th ed. 1991.

"Reckon." <u>Merriam-Webster's Collegiate Dictionary</u>. 11th ed. 2003.

List an article in a reference work by its title (second example) unless the article is signed (first example). For works with entries arranged alphabetically, you need not include volume or page numbers. For well-known works like those listed on the previous page, you may also omit the editors' names and all publication information except any edition number and the year of publication. For works that are not well known, give full publication information:

> "Hungarians in America." The Ethnic Almanac. Ed. Stephanie Bernardo. New
>   York: Doubleday, 2001. 109-11.

See also pages 677 and 681, respectively, for encyclopedias appearing online or on a CD-ROM.

2 Listing periodicals: Journals, magazines, and newspapers

The facing page shows the basic format for an article in a periodical (a journal) and the location of the required information in a journal. See page 669 for parallel information on a newspaper article.

Note The treatment of volume and issue numbers and publication dates varies depending on the kind of periodical being cited, as the models indicate. For the distinction between journals and magazines, see page 582.

22. An article in a journal with continuous pagination throughout the annual volume

> Lever, Janet. "Sex Differences in the Games Children Play." Social Problems 23
>   (1996): 478-87.

Some journals number the pages of issues consecutively throughout a year, so that each issue after the first in a year begins numbering where the previous issue left off—say, at page 132 or 416. For this kind of journal, give the volume number after the title (23 in the example above) and place the year of publication in parentheses. The page numbers will be enough to guide readers to the issue you used.

23. An article in a journal that pages issues separately or that numbers only issues, not volumes

> Selwyn, Neil. "The Social Processes of Learning to Use Computers." Social
>   Science Computer Review 23.1 (2005): 122-35.

Some journals page each issue separately (starting each issue at page 1). For these journals, give the volume number, a period, and the issue number (23.1 in the Selwyn entry above and opposite). When citing an article in a journal that numbers only issues, not annual volumes, treat the issue number as if it were a volume number, as in model 22.

Information for a journal article

①
Selwyn, Neil. ②"The Social Processes of Learning to Use Computers." ③Social Science
Computer Review ④23.1 ⑤(2005): ⑥122-35.

Journal cover

SPRING 2005   VOLUME 23   NUMBER 1

SOCIAL SCIENCE COMPUTER REVIEW

First page of article

The Social Processes of Learning to Use Computers

NEIL SELWYN
Cardiff School of Social Sciences

The ability to use a computer is assumed to be a cornerstone of effective citi[zenship in the information]
Age, with a range of initiatives and educational provisions being introduc[ed to ensure that all citizens]
become competent with information technology (IT). Despite such provision, levels of computer use
and competence have been found to vary widely throughout the general population, and we know little
of how different ways of learning to use computers contribute to people's eventual use of IT. Based on
data from in-depth interviews with 100 adults in the United Kingdom, this article examines the range
and social stratification of formal and informal learning about computers that is taking place, suggesting that formal computer instruction orientated toward the general public may inadvertently widen the
digital knowledge gap. In particular, the data highlight the importance of informal learning about IT
and of encouraging such learning, especially in the home.

AUTHOR'S NOTE: This article is based on a project funded by the Economic and Social Research Council
(R000239518). I would like to thank the other members of the Adults Learning@Home project (Stephen Gorard and
John Furlong) as well as the individuals who took part in the in-depth interviews. Correspondence concerning this
article may be addressed to Neil Selwyn, School of Social Sciences, Cardiff University, Glamorgan Building, King
Edward VII Avenue, Cardiff CF10 3WT, UK; e-mail: selwynnc@cardiff.ac.uk.

122

④ **Volume and/or issue number,** in Arabic numerals.

⑤ **Year of publication,** in parentheses and followed by a colon.

③ **Title of periodical,** under-lined. Omit any *A, An,* or *The* from the beginning of the title. Do not end with a period.

② **Title of article,** in quota-tion marks. Give the full title and any subtitle, separating them with a colon. End the title with a period inside the final quotation mark.

① **Author.** Give the full name—last name first, a comma, first name, and any middle name or initial. Omit *Dr., PhD,* or any other title. End the name with a period.

⑥ **Inclusive page numbers of article,** without "pp." Go to the end of the article for the last page number. Pro-vide only as many digits in the last number as needed for clarity, usually two.

24. An article in a monthly or bimonthly magazine

Garber, Marjorie. "Our Genius Problem." <u>Atlantic Monthly</u> Sept. 2002: 46-53.

Follow the magazine title with the month and the year of publication. (Abbreviate all months except May, June, and July.) Don't place the date in parentheses, and don't provide a volume or issue number.

25. An article in a weekly or biweekly magazine

Talbot, Margaret. "The Bad Mother." <u>New Yorker</u> 5 Aug. 2004: 40-46.

Follow the magazine title with the day, the month, and the year of publication. (Abbreviate all months except May, June, and July.) Don't place the date in parentheses, and don't provide a volume or issue number.

26. An article in a daily newspaper

Zeller, Tom, Jr. "To Go Global, Do You Ignore Censorship?" <u>New York Times</u>
     24 Oct. 2005, natl. ed.: C3+.

See the facing page for an analysis of this entry and the location of the required information in the newspaper.

27. An anonymous article

"The Right to Die." <u>Time</u> 11 Oct. 1996: 101.

For an article with no named author, begin the entry with the title of the article. In the list of works cited, alphabetize an anonymous source by the first main word of the title (Right in this model).

28. An editorial or letter to the editor

"Dualing Power Centers." Editorial. <u>New York Times</u> 14 Jan. 2005, natl. ed.:
     A16.

Add the word Editorial or Letter after the title if there is one or after the author's name, as follows:

Dowding, Michael. Letter. <u>Economist</u> 5-11 Jan. 2005: 4.

(The numbers 5-11 in this entry are the publication days of the periodical: the issue spans January 5 through 11.)

29. A review

Nelson, Cary. "Between Anonymity and Celebrity." Rev. of <u>Anxious Intellects:</u>
     <u>Academic Professionals, Public Intellectuals, and Enlightenment Values,</u>
     by John Michael. <u>College English</u> 64 (2002): 710-19.

Information for a newspaper article

①　　　　　②　　　　　　　　　③　　　④
Zeller, Tom, Jr. "To Go Global, Do You Ignore Censorship?" New York Times 24 Oct.

　　⑤　　⑥
2005, natl. ed.: C3+.

⑥ Page number of article, without "pp." Include a section designation before the number when the newspaper does the same, as here. Otherwise, give the section between the edition and the colon. Add a plus sign to the page number when the article continues on a later page.

① Author. Give the full name—last name first, a comma, first name, and any middle name or initial. Omit *Dr., PhD,* or any other title. End with a period.

First page of article

THE NEW YORK TIMES, MONDAY, OCTOBER 24, 2005　　　　YT　　● C3

LINK BY LINK
● Tom Zeller Jr.

To Go Global, Do You Ignore Censorship?

IT'S bad enough when newspaper editorials, Western human rights groups and ordinary American customers condemn your company for bowing to the Chinese dictatorship and contributing to oppression. But when the outrage begins rising, at great personal risk, from dissident voices trapped inside that dictatorship, well, that has to hurt.

Or not.

Yahoo has suffered a good deal of opprobrium after it was revealed last month that, when government officials came calling, the company's Hong Kong division simply surrendered information on a Chinese citizen who had presumably sought refuge, anonymity and a bit of freedom in the bosom of a Yahoo e-mail address: huoyan1989@yahoo.com.cn.

② Title of article, in quotation marks. Give the full title and any subtitle, separating them with a colon. Unless the title has its own end punctuation (as this one does), end it with a period inside the final quotation mark.

③ Name of newspaper, underlined. Give the title as it appears on the first page, omitting *A, An,* or *The.*

First page of newspaper

"All the News That's Fit to Print"　**The New York Times**　National Edition

VOL. CLV .... No. 53,377　Copyright © 2005 The New York Times　● MONDAY, OCTOBER 24, 2005　ONE DOLLAR

④ Date of publication. Give the day of the month first, then month, then year. Abbreviate all months except May, June, and July. End the date with a comma if listing the newspaper edition and/or the section designation. Otherwise, end with a colon.

⑤ Edition. If the newspaper lists an edition at the top of the first page, include it after the date. End with a comma if listing the section designation. Otherwise, end with a colon.

Rev. is an abbreviation for "Review." The name of the author of the work being reviewed follows the title of the work, a comma, and by. If the review has no title of its own, then Rev. of and the title of the reviewed work immediately follow the name of the reviewer.

30. An abstract of a dissertation or article

Steciw, Steven K. "Alterations to the Pessac Project of Le Corbusier." Diss. U of

Cambridge, England, 1986. DAI 46 (1986): 565C.

For an abstract appearing in *Dissertation Abstracts* (*DA*) or *Dissertation Abstracts International* (*DAI*), give the author's name and the title, Diss. (for "Dissertation"), the institution granting the author's degree, the date of the dissertation, and the publication information. See page 683 for listing an entire dissertation rather than an abstract.

For an abstract of an article, first provide the publication information for the article itself, followed by the information for the abstract. If the abstract publisher lists abstracts by item rather than page number, add item before the number.

> Lever, Janet. "Sex Differences in the Games Children Play." Social Problems 23 (1996): 478-87. Psychological Abstracts 63 (1996): item 1431.

Note Most instructors expect you to consult and cite full articles, not abstracts. See page 586.

3 Listing electronic sources

Electronic sources include those you find online (either through the library Web site or directly over the Internet) and those you find on CD-ROM (see p. 681). The following list, adapted from the *MLA Handbook*, itemizes the possible elements of an online source, in order of their appearance in a works-cited entry. *No source will include all the elements.*

1. **Name of author, editor, compiler, or translator,** arranged and punctuated as in models 1–3, page 659. Use ed., comp., or trans. after the name as appropriate, as shown in models 5 and 7, page 661.
2. **Title of a short work,** in quotation marks. Short works include poems, articles, documents or pages on a Web site, Web log entries, and postings to discussion groups. (Follow the last with Online posting.)
3. **Title of a book,** underlined.
4. **Name of editor, compiler, or translator of the source,** if not cited before, preceded by Ed., Comp., or Trans. as appropriate. See models 6 and 7, page 661.
5. **Publication information for any print version of the source,** following earlier models for books and periodical articles. For a periodical article, the publication information includes the periodical title.
6. **Title of the online site,** underlined. The title might be that of a periodical (if not already given), a scholarly project, a database, a Web log, and so on. For a site with no title, add Home page, Course home page, or another description.

7. **Name of site editor,** if any, preceded by Ed.
8. **Version number,** if any, or volume/issue numbers for an online journal. See models 22 and 23, page 666, for journals.
9. **Date of electronic publication,** latest revision, or posting.
10. **Title of a subscription database,** name of the subscription service, and name and location of the subscriber.
11. **Title of a discussion group.**
12. **Inclusive page numbers,** number of paragraphs, or other identifying numbers, if any.
13. **Name of site sponsor,** such as an institution or organization, if not cited before.
14. **Date you consulted the source.**
15. **URL of the source.** To ensure the accuracy of URLs, use Copy and Paste to duplicate them in a file or an e-mail to yourself. In the list of works cited, break URLs *only* after slashes—do not hyphenate. Unless you are submitting your paper online, use the Tools menu of your word processor to eliminate hyperlinks in works-cited entries (click on AutoCorrect in *Microsoft Word*, Settings in *WordPerfect*).

Note A URL does not always provide a usable route to a source, especially with subscription services. See models 31 and 32 below and on the next page.

31. A work from an online service to which your library subscribes

Gorski, Paul C. "Privilege and Repression in the Digital Era: Rethinking the
     Sociopolitics of the Digital Divide." Race, Gender and Class 10.4 (2003):
     145-76. Ethnic NewsWatch. ProQuest. U of Minnesota, Twin Cities,
     Wilson Lib. 24 July 2005 <http://proquest.umi.com>.

See the next page for an analysis of the preceding entry and the location of the required information on the subscription-service screen.

Note Many subscription services provide source URLs that are temporary, specific to the library, or too long to copy with certain accuracy. If any of these applies to the URL of the source you're consulting, you can use the service's home page URL instead or omit a URL. Some services provide a "Permanent link" or "Document URL" on each source record: a URL for finding the source from within the library's system (not from the open Web). You can see such a link on the database screen on the next page. Like the one in the example, permanent links are often unmanageably long and complex. In that case, use the service's home-page URL, which runs through *com* in the permanent link.

Information for an article from a subscription service

Gorski, Paul C. "Privilege and Repression in the Digital Era: Rethinking the Sociopolitics of the Digital Divide." Race, Gender and Class 10.4 (2003): 145-76. Ethnic NewsWatch. ProQuest. U of Minnesota, Twin Cities, Wilson Lib. 24 July 2005 <http://www.proquest.umi.com>.

⑤ **Name of the service,** not underlined, ending with a period.

④ **Name of the database,** underlined, ending with a period.

⑥ **Names of the subscribing institution and library,** separated by a comma and ending with a period.

② **Title of the article,** in quotation marks. End the title with a period inside the final quotation mark.

③ **Publication information for any print version.** If the site gives information for a print version of the source, give it after the source title, following an appropriate model on pp. 659–70.

① **Author.** Give the full name—last name first, a comma, first name, and any middle name or initial. Omit *Dr., PhD,* or any other title. End with a period.

⑧ **URL,** enclosed in angle brackets. But if the source URL is temporary, unique to your search, or too long (as in the example), use the URL of the site's home page. See the note on the preceding page.

⑦ **Date of your access.** Give the day first, then month, then year. Abbreviate all months except May, June, and July. Do not end the date with a period. (Since this date does not appear on the site, record it separately.)

32. A work from an online service to which you subscribe

"China—Dragon Kings." The Encyclopedia Mythica. America Online. 6 Jan. 2005. Path: Research and Learn; Encyclopedia; More Encyclopedias; Encyclopedia Mythica.

If you find a source through America Online, MSN, or another personal online service, you may not see a usable URL or any URL for the source. In that case, provide the path you used to get to the source, as in the preceding example: ① Title of source, in quotation marks, and title of larger work, underlined. ② Name of the service, neither underlined nor quoted. ③ Date of your access, followed by a period. ④ Path: and the sequence of topics required to reach the source, with the topics separated by semicolons.

If you used a keyword instead of a path to reach the source, give that information instead: Keyword: Chinese dragon kings.

33. An entire online site (scholarly project, professional site, personal site, etc.)

A scholarly project or professional site:

① American Verse Project. ② 16 May 2001. ③ U of Michigan Humanities Text Initiative. ④ 21 July 2005 ⑤ <http://www.hti.umich.edu/a/amverse>.

When citing a scholarly project or professional site, include the following: ① Title of the site, underlined. ② Date of publication or most recent update. ③ Name of any organization or institution that sponsors the site. ④ Date of your access. ⑤ URL. If the project or site has an editor, add the name, preceded by Ed., between the site title and the publication date. See the Conrad entry on the next page.

A personal site:

① Lederman, Leon. ② Topics in Modern Physics—Lederman. ③ 28 Aug. 2005. ④ 12 Dec. 2005 ⑤ <http://www-ed.fnal.gov/samplers/hsphys/people/ ⑤ lederman.html>.

Cite a personal site with this information: ① Author's name, if any. ② Title, if any, underlined. If the site has no title, describe it with a label such as Home page, without quotation marks or underlining. ③ Date of last revision. ④ Date of your access. ⑤ URL.

A business site:

① ② ③ ④ ⑤ Prius. 2006. Toyota Motor Corp. 2 Feb. 2006 <http://www.toyota.com/prius>.

For the site of a corporation or other business, give the following: ① Site title, underlined. ② Date of site. ③ Name of sponsoring business. ④ Date of your access. ⑤ URL.

34. A poem, essay, or other short work from an online site

Wheatley, Phillis. "On Virtue." Poems on Various Subjects, Religious and Moral. London: A. Bell, 1773. American Verse Project. 16 May 2001. U of Michigan Humanities Text Initiative. 21 July 2005 <http:// name.umdl.umich.edu/BAP5379>.

See the facing page for an analysis of the preceding entry and the location of the required information on the Web site.

35. An online book

An entire book:

Austen, Jane. Emma. 1816. Ed. R. W. Chapman. Oxford: Clarendon, 1926. Oxford Text Archive. 1994. Oxford U. 15 Dec. 2005 <http://ota.ahds.ac.uk/ Austen/Emma.1519>.

For a book published online, give the following information: ① Author and title. ② Date of original publication of the book, if not given in item 4. ③ Name of any editor or translator. ④ Any publication information for the original print version of the book, following one of models 1–17. ⑤ Title of the site, underlined. ⑥ Date of electronic publication. ⑦ Name of any sponsoring organization or institution. ⑧ Date of your access. ⑨ URL for the book. If the site has an editor, add the name after the site's title, as below.

A part of a book:

Conrad, Joseph. "A Familiar Preface." Modern Essays. Ed. Christopher Morley. New York: Harcourt, 1921. Bartleby.com: Great Books Online. Ed. Steven van Leeuwan. Nov. 2000. 16 Feb. 2006 <http://www.bartleby.com/237/ 8.html>.

For a part of a book published online, provide this information: ① Author of the part. ② Title of the part, in quotation marks. (Do not use quotation marks for Introduction, Foreword, or another standard part.) ③ Title of the book (underlined), editor of the book (if any), and publication information for the print version of the book. ④ Title of the site (underlined) and editor of the site (if any). ⑤ Date of electronic publication. ⑥ Date of your access. ⑦ URL for the part of the book. If the site as a whole has a sponsoring organization, give the name between items 5 and 6, as in the Austen model above.

36. An article in an online journal

Palfrey, Andrew. "Choice of Mates in Identical Twins." Modern Psychology 4.1 (2003): 26-40. 25 Feb. 2006 <http://www.liasu.edu/modpsy/ palfrey4(1).htm>.

Give the following information for an online scholarly article that you reach directly: ① Author, article title, journal title, volume and

Information for a short work from an online site

Wheatley, Phillis. "On Virtue." Poems on Various Subjects, Religious and Moral. Lon-

don: A. Bell, 1773. American Verse Project. 16 May 2001. U of Michigan Human-

ities Text Initiative. 21 July 2005 <http://name.umdl.umich.edu/BAP5379>.

Home page of site

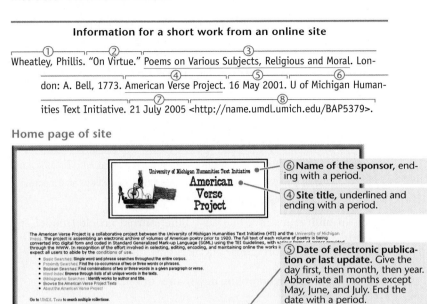

⑥ **Name of the sponsor,** ending with a period.

④ **Site title,** underlined and ending with a period.

⑤ **Date of electronic publication or last update.** Give the day first, then month, then year. Abbreviate all months except May, June, and July. End the date with a period.

Source record for poem

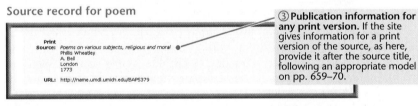

③ **Publication information for any print version.** If the site gives information for a print version of the source, as here, provide it after the source title, following an appropriate model on pp. 659–70.

Poem

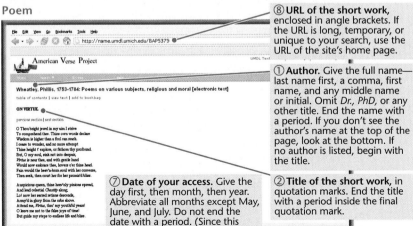

⑧ **URL of the short work,** enclosed in angle brackets. If the URL is long, temporary, or unique to your search, use the URL of the site's home page.

① **Author.** Give the full name—last name first, a comma, first name, and any middle name or initial. Omit *Dr., PhD,* or any other title. End the name with a period. If you don't see the author's name at the top of the page, look at the bottom. If no author is listed, begin with the title.

⑦ **Date of your access.** Give the day first, then month, then year. Abbreviate all months except May, June, and July. Do not end the date with a period. (Since this date does not appear on the site, record it separately.)

② **Title of the short work,** in quotation marks. End the title with a period inside the final quotation mark.

any issue numbers, and publication date, as in model 22 or 23 on page 666. ② Page numbers in the journal or total number of pages, paragraphs, or sections, if any of these are given. Omit reference numbers if the source does not use them. ③ Date of your access. ④ URL for the article.

For a journal article reached through a subscription service, see model 31 (pp. 671–72).

37. An online abstract

Palfrey, Andrew. "Choice of Mates in Identical Twins." Modern Psychology 4.1

    (2003): 26-40. Abstract. 25 Feb. 2006 <http://www.liasu.edu/modpsy/

    abstractpalfrey4(1).htm>.

Treat an online abstract like an online journal article (model 36), but add "Abstract" (without quotation marks or underlining) between the publication information and the date of your access.

38. An article in an online newspaper or on a newswire

Still, Lucia. "On the Battlefields of Business, Millions of Casualties." New York

    Times on the Web 3 Mar. 2005. 17 Aug. 2005 <http://www.nytimes.com/

    specials/downsize/05down1.html>.

Provide the following information for an online newspaper article that you reach directly: ① Author, article title, newspaper title, and publication date as in model 26 (p. 668). Give section, page, or paragraph numbers if the newspaper does. ② Date of your access. ③ URL for the article.

Treat a newswire article similarly, substituting the title of the online wire service for the newspaper title (this article has no named author):

"Film, Fashion Asked to Stop Glamorizing Smoking." Reuters 18 Feb.

    2003. 28 Feb. 2003 <http://www.reuters.com/

    newsArticle.jhtml?type=industryNewsID2246811>.

See model 31 (pp. 671–72) when citing a newspaper or newswire article that you reached through a subscription service.

39. An article in an online magazine

Lewis, Ricki. "The Return of Thalidomide." Scientist 22 Jan. 2001: 5. 24 Jan.

    2006 <http://www.the-scientist.com/yr2001/jan/lewis_pl_010122.html>.

Provide the following information for an online magazine article that you reach directly: ① Author's name, article title, magazine title, and publication date, as in model 24 or 25 on page 668. ② Any page, paragraph, or other reference numbers. ③ Date of your access. ④ URL for the article.

See model 31 (pp. 671–72) when citing a magazine article that you reached through a subscription service.

40. An online review

Detwiler, Donald S., and Chu Shao-Kang. Rev. of Important Documents of the
Republic of China, ed. Tan Quon Chin. Journal of Military History 56.4
(1992): 669-84. 16 Sept. 2005 <http://www.jstor.org/fcgi-bin/jstor/
viewitem.fcg/08993718/96p0008x>.

Cite an online review as follows: ① Author, any review title, Rev. of and the title of the reviewed book, author or editor of the reviewed book, and publication information—all as in model 29 (p. 668). ② Date of your access. ③ URL for the review.

See model 31 (pp. 671–72) when citing a review that you reached through a subscription service.

41. An online government publication

United States. Dept. of Commerce. National Telecommunications and Information Admin. A Nation Online: Entering the Broadband Age. Feb. 2005.
1 Mar. 2005 <http://www.ntia.doc.gov/reports/anol/index.html>.

See page 682 for models of government publications in print. Provide the same information for online publications, and add facts of electronic publication. The model above includes the following: ① Names of government, department, and agency. ② Title of publication, underlined. ③ Date of publication. ④ Date of your access. ⑤ URL for the publication.

42. An article in an online encyclopedia or other information database

Dull, Jack L. "Wu-ti." Encyclopaedia Britannica Online. 2004. Encyclopaedia
Britannica. 23 Dec. 2005 <http://www.britannica.com/eb/
article?tocid:9077599>.

For an article in an online encyclopedia or other information database, provide the following: ① Author's name, if any is given. ② Title of the article, in quotation marks. ③ Title of the database, underlined. ④ Date of electronic publication. ⑤ Name of sponsoring organization or publisher. ⑥ Date of your access. ⑦ URL for the article.

See models 31 and 32 (pp. 671–72) when citing an information database that you reached through a library or personal subscription service. For encyclopedias and other reference works that you find in print or on CD-ROM, see pages 665 and 681, respectively.

43. An online image (artwork, advertisement, graph, etc.)

In general, you can base citations of online images on the examples in model 59 (pp. 683–84), adding information for the online source, particularly site title, date of your access, and URL. The following examples show a range of possibilities:

A work of art:

> Pollock, Jackson. Shimmering Substance. 1946. Museum of Modern Art, New
> York. WebMuseum. 12 Mar. 2006 <http://www.ibiblio.org/wm/paint/
> auth/Pollock/pollock.shimmering.jpg>.

A photograph:

> Curtis, Edward S. Canyon de Chelly—Navaho. 1904. Lib. of Congress. American
> Memory. 21 July 2005 <http://hdl.loc.gov/loc.award/
> iencurt.cp01028>.

An advertisement:

> Absolut Vodka. Advertisement. Vanity Fair Jan. 2003. Adflip. 18 Nov. 2005
> <http://adflip.com/php?adID=14714>.

A cartoon or comic strip:

> Keefe, Mike. "Suspicious Package." Cartoon. Denver Post 21 July 2005.
> PoliticalCartoons.com. 6 Jan. 2006 <http://www.politicalcartoons.com>.

A map, chart, graph, or diagram:

> Hamilton, Calvin J. "Components of Comets." Diagram. Space Art. 2003.
> 20 Dec. 2005 <http://solarviews.com/eng/comet.htm>.

44. An online television or radio program

Base citations of online television and radio programs on model 60, page 684, adding your access date and the URL.

> Gross, Terry, host. Fresh Air. National Public Radio. 11 Feb. 2006. 12 Feb. 2006
> <http://discover.npr.org/freshair/day_fa.html?display=February/11/2006>.

45. An online sound recording or clip

Base citations of online sound recordings or clips on model 61, page 684, adding your access date and the URL.

Reagan, Ronald W. State of the Union Address. 26 Jan. 1982. <u>Vincent Voice</u>
<u>Library</u>. Digital and Multimedia Center, U of Michigan. 6 May 2005
<http://www.lib.msu.edu/vincent/presidents/reagan.htm>.

46. An online film or film clip

Base citations of online films or film clips on model 62, pages
684–85, adding your access date and the URL.

Stewart, Leslie J. <u>96 Ranch Rodeo and Barbecue</u>. 1951. Lib. of Congress.
<u>American Memory</u>. 7 Jan. 2006 <http://lcweb2.loc.gov/ammem/
afc96ran_v034>.

47. The home page for a course or department

Anderson, Daniel. Business Communication. Course home page. Jan.-June
2003. Dept. of English, U of North Carolina. 16 Feb. 2003 <http://
sites.unc.edu/daniel/eng32/index.html>.

For the home page of a course, provide this information: ① Instructor's name. ② Course title, without quotation marks or underlining.
③ The description Course home page. ④ Inclusive dates of the course.
⑤ Names of the department and the school, separated by a comma.
⑥ Date of your access. ⑦ URL for the home page.

For a department home page, give the department name first,
followed by Dept. home page, the name of the school, your access date,
and the URL:

Computer Engineering. Dept. home page. Santa Clara U School of Engineering.
12 Oct. 2005 <http://www.cse.scu.edu>.

48. An entry on a Web log

Daswani, Susheel. "Hollywood vs. Silicon Valley." Berkeley Intellectual Property Weblog. 16 Mar. 2005. 22 Aug. 2005 <http://www.biplog.com/
archive/cat_hollywood.html>.

To cite an entry on a Web log, give the following: ① Author's name.
(See p. 608 for tips on finding the full names of authors who use
only screen names.) ② Title of the entry, in quotation marks. ③ Title of the Web log, underlined. ④ Date of the entry. ⑤ Date of your
access. ⑥ URL for the entry.

49. Electronic mail

Millon, Michele. "Re: Grief Therapy." E-mail to the author. 4 May 2005.

For e-mail, give the following: ① Writer's name. ② Title, if any, from the e-mail's subject heading, in quotation marks. ③ Description of the transmission, including to whom it was sent. ④ Date of posting.

50. A posting to an e-mail discussion list

Tourville, Michael. "European Currency Reform." Online posting. 6 Jan. 2006.
  International Finance Discussion List. 12 Jan. 2006 <http://
  www.weg.isu.edu/finance-dl/archive/46732>.

Whenever possible, cite an archived version of a posting to an e-mail discussion list so that readers can find it without difficulty. Give this information for the posting: ① Author's name. (See p. 608 for tips on finding the full names of authors who use only screen names.) ② Title, if any, from the e-mail's subject heading, in quotation marks. ③ Online posting. ④ Date of posting. ⑤ Name of the discussion list, without quotation marks or underlining. ⑥ Date of your access. ⑦ URL, if known, or e-mail address for the list's moderator or supervisor.

51. A posting to a newsgroup or Web forum

A newsgroup:

Cramer, Sherry. "Recent Investment Practices in US Business." Online posting.
  26 Mar. 2005. Young Entrepreneurs. 3 Apr. 2005 <http://
  finance.groups.yahoo.com/group/youngentrepreneurs3>.

For a posting to a newsgroup, give the following: ① Author's name. (See p. 608 for tips on finding the full names of authors who use only screen names.) ② Title from the subject heading, in quotation marks. ③ Online posting. ④ Date of posting. ⑤ Name of the newsgroup, without quotation marks or underlining. ⑥ Date of your access. ⑦ URL for the group. If you read the posting on a news server instead of on the Web, omit the group name before your access date and give the group name in the URL, preceded by news: <news:biz.startups.youngentrepreneurs.2700>.

A Web forum:

Razi, N. M. "Hypothyroidism." Online posting. 6 July 2005. Homeopathy
  Forum. 28 Jan. 2006 <http://www.hpathy.com/homeopathy/forums/
  forum_topics.asp?FID=328>.

For a posting to a Web forum, provide this information: ① Author's name. (See p. 608 for tips on finding the full names of authors who use only screen names.) ② Title, if any, in quotation marks. ③ Online posting. ④ Date of posting. ⑤ Name of the forum, without quotation marks or underlining. ⑥ Date of your access. ⑦ URL for the forum.

52. A synchronous communication

Bruckman, Amy. MediaMOO Symposium: Virtual Worlds for Business? 20 Jan. 2006. MediaMOO. 26 Feb. 2006 <http://www.co.gatech.edu/fac/ Amy.Bruckman/MediaMOO/cscw-symposium-06.html>.

Whenever possible, cite an archived version of a synchronous communication so that readers can find it without difficulty. Provide this information: ① Speaker's name. ② Description of the event, without quotation marks or underlining. ③ Date of the event. ④ Forum, without quotation marks or underlining. ⑤ Date of your access. ⑥ URL for the archive.

53. A source on a periodical CD-ROM database

Hakim, Danny. "Iacocca, Away from the Grind, Still Has a Lot to Say." New York Times 19 July 2005, natl. ed.: C1+. New York Times Ondisc. CD-ROM. UMI-ProQuest. Sept. 2005.

Databases on CD-ROM are issued periodically—for instance, every six months or every year. The journals, newspapers, and other publications included in such a database are generally available in print as well, so your works-cited entry should give the information for both formats: ① Information for the print version, following models on pages 666–70. ② Title of the CD-ROM, underlined. ③ Medium, CD-ROM. ④ Name of the vendor (or distributor) of the CD-ROM. ⑤ Date of electronic publication.

54. A source on a nonperiodical CD-ROM

Nunberg, Geoffrey. "Usage in the Dictionary." The American Heritage Dictionary of the English Language. 4th ed. CD-ROM. Boston: Houghton, 2005.

Single-issue CD-ROMs may be encyclopedias, dictionaries, books, and other resources that are published just once, like printed books. Use this format: ① Author's name, if any. ② Title of the source. Use quotation marks for short works, such as an article.

Underline the title if it is a book. ③ Title of the entire CD-ROM, underlined. This CD-ROM also includes an edition number. ④ Medium, CD-ROM. ⑤ CD-ROM's place of publication, publisher, and date of publication.

See also pages 665 and 677, respectively, for models of print and online reference works.

55. Computer software

Project Scheduler 9000. Vers. 5.1. Orlando: Scitor, 2006.

For software, provide the following: ① Title, underlined. ② Version number. ③ Publication information, including place of publication, publisher, and date. If the software has a listed author, give his or her name first in the entry. If you consulted or obtained the software online, replace the publication information with the date of your access and the URL, as in earlier examples.

1 Listing other print and nonprint sources

56. A government publication

Board of Governors. US Federal Reserve System. Federal Reserve Bulletin Aug.
    2005: 20-21.

Hawaii. Dept. of Education. Kauai District Schools, Profile 2004-05. Honolulu:
    Hawaii Dept. of Education, 2005.

Stiller, Ann. Historic Preservation and Tax Incentives. US Dept. of Interior.
    Washington: GPO, 2002.

United States. Cong. House. Committee on Ways and Means. Medicare Payment
    for Outpatient Occupational Therapy Services. 108th Cong., 1st sess.
    Washington: GPO, 2003.

If an author is not listed for a government publication, give the appropriate agency as author, as in the first, second, and last examples. Provide information in the order illustrated, separating elements with a period: the name of the government, the name of the agency (which may be abbreviated), and the title and publication information. For a congressional publication (last example), give the house and committee involved before the title, and give the number and session of Congress after the title. In the last two examples, GPO stands for the US Government Printing Office.

57. A pamphlet

Medical Answers About AIDS. New York: Gay Men's Health Crisis, 2006.

Most pamphlets can be treated as books. In the example above, the pamphlet has no listed author, so the title comes first. If the pamphlet has an author, list his or her name first, followed by the title and publication information as given here.

58. An unpublished dissertation or thesis

Wilson, Stuart M. "John Stuart Mill as a Literary Critic." Diss. U of Michigan,
    1990.

The title is quoted rather than underlined. Diss. stands for "Dissertation." U of Michigan is the institution that granted the author's degree.

59. An image (artwork, advertisement, graph, etc.)

A work of art:

Hockney, David. Place Furstenberg, Paris. 1985. College Art Gallery, New Paltz,
    New York. David Hockney: A Retrospective. Ed. Maurice Tuchman and
    Stephanie Barron. Los Angeles: Los Angeles County Museum of Art,
    1988. 247.

For a work of art, name the artist and give the title (underlined), the date of creation, and the name and location of the owner. For a work you see only in a reproduction, provide the complete publication information, too, as in the Hockney model. Omit such information only if you examined the actual work.

A photograph:

Heinz, Thomas A. Fallingwater: Exterior Detail. Frank Lloyd Wright: Architect.
    Ed. Terence Riley. New York: Museum of Modern Art, 2000. 236.

Treat a photograph you find in a collection or book like a work of art, with photographer's name (if known), photograph title (underlined), and date. Add the owner's name (as in the Hockney entry above) if the photograph is an artwork and not an illustration. Give the publication information unless you examined an actual print of the photograph.

For a personal photograph by you or someone else, describe the subject (without quotation marks or underlining), say who took the photograph, and add the date:

Children in Central Park. Personal photograph by the author. 16 Mar. 2006.

An advertisement:

Jetta by Volkswagen. Advertisement. New Yorker 25 July 2005: 31.

Cite an advertisement with the name of the product or company advertised, the description Advertisement, and the publication information.

A cartoon or comic strip:

> Trudeau, Garry. "Doonesbury." Comic strip. <u>San Francisco Chronicle</u> 28 Aug.
> 2005: E6.

Cite a cartoon or comic strip with the artist's name, the title (in quotation marks), the description Cartoon or Comic strip, and the publication information.

A map, chart, graph, or diagram:

> <u>Women in the Armed Forces</u>. Map. <u>Women in the World: An International Atlas</u>.
> By Joni Seager and Ann Olson. New York: Touchstone, 2006. 44-45.

List the image by its title (underlined) unless its creator is credited on the source. Provide a description (Map, Chart, and so on) and then the publication information.

60. A television or radio program

> "I'm Sorry, I'm Lost." By Alan Ball. Dir. Jill Soloway. <u>Six Feet Under</u>. HBO.
> 2 July 2005.

Start with the title unless you are citing the work of a person or persons. The example here includes an episode title (in quotation marks), the writer's and director's names, the program title (underlined), the name of the network, and the date. If the program aired on a local TV station, identify the station between the network and the date—for example, WGBH, Boston.

61. A sound recording

> Brahms, Johannes. Piano Concerto no. 2 in B-flat, op. 83. Perf. Artur Rubinstein. Cond. Eugene Ormandy. Philadelphia Orch. LP. RCA, 1972.
> Springsteen, Bruce. "Empty Sky." <u>The Rising</u>. Columbia, 2002.

Begin with the name of the individual whose work you are citing. If you're citing a song or song lyrics, give the title in quotation marks. Then provide the title of the recording, not underlined if it identifies a composition by form, number, and key (first example). After the title, provide the names of any other artists it seems appropriate to mention, the manufacturer of the recording, and the date of release. If the medium is other than compact disk, provide it immediately before the manufacturer's name—for instance, LP (as in the first example) or Audiocassette.

62. A film, DVD, or video recording

> <u>The Lord of the Rings: The Return of the King</u>. Dir. Peter Jackson. New Line, 2003.

Start with the title of the work you are citing, unless you are citing the contribution of a particular individual (see the next model). Give additional information (director, writer, lead performers, and so on) as you judge appropriate. For a film, end with the distributor and date.

For a DVD or videocassette, include the original release date (if any) and the medium (DVD, Videocassette) before the distributor's name:

> George Balanchine, chor. <u>Serenade</u>. Perf. San Francisco Ballet. Dir. Hilary Bean.
>> 1991. Videocassette. PBS Video, 1997.

63. A musical composition

> Fauré, Gabriel. Sonata for Violin and Piano no. 1 in A Major, op. 15.

Don't underline musical compositions, such as the one above, that are identified only by form, number, and key. Do underline titled operas, ballets, and compositions (<u>Carmen</u>, <u>Sleeping Beauty</u>, <u>The 1812 Overture</u>). Use quotation marks for songs.

64. A performance

> Barenboim, Daniel, cond. Chicago Symphony Orch. Symphony Center, Chicago.
>> 22 Jan. 2006.
>
> <u>The English Only Restaurant</u>. By Silvio Martinez Palau. Dir. Susana Tubert.
>> Puerto Rican Traveling Theater, New York. 27 July 2005.

As with films and television programs, place the title first unless you are citing the work of an individual (first example). Provide additional information about participants after the title, as well as the theater, city, and date. Note that the orchestra name in the first example is neither quoted nor underlined.

65. A letter

> Buttolph, Mrs. Laura E. Letter to Rev. and Mrs. C. C. Jones. 20 June 1857. In
>> <u>The Children of Pride: A True Story of Georgia and the Civil War</u>. Ed.
>> Robert Manson Myers. New Haven: Yale UP, 1972. 334-35.

List a published letter under the writer's name. Specify that the source is a letter and to whom it was addressed, and give the date on which it was written. Treat the remaining information like that for a selection from an anthology (model 18, p. 664). (See also p. 668 for the format of a letter to the editor of a periodical.)

For a letter in the collection of a library or archive, specify the writer, recipient, and date, as above, and give the name and location of the archive as well:

James, Jonathan E. Letter to his sister. 16 Apr. 1970. Jonathan E. James Papers. South Dakota State Archive, Pierre.

For a letter you receive, give the name of the writer, note the fact that the letter was sent to you, and provide the date of the letter:

Packer, Ann E. Letter to the author. 15 June 2005.

Use the form above for personal e-mail as well, substituting E-mail for Letter: E-mail to the author (see p. 679).

66. A lecture or address

Carlone, Dennis. "Architecture for the City of the Twenty-First Century." Symposium on the City. Urban Issues Group. Cambridge City Hall, Cambridge. 22 May 2005.

Give the speaker's name, the title (in quotation marks), the title of the meeting, the name of the sponsoring organization, the location of the lecture, and the date. If the lecture has no title, use Lecture, Address, or another description instead.

Although the *MLA Handbook* does not provide a specific style for classroom lectures in your courses, you can adapt the preceding format for this purpose:

Chang, Julia. Class lecture on the realist novel. Homans College. 20 Jan. 2006.

67. An interview

Graaf, Vera. Personal interview. 19 Dec. 2005.

Rumsfeld, Donald. Interview. Frontline. PBS. WGBH, Boston. 10 Oct. 2005.

Begin with the name of the person interviewed. For an interview you conducted, specify Personal interview or the medium (such as Telephone interview or E-mail interview), and then give the date. For an interview you read, heard, or saw, provide the title if any or Interview if there is no title, along with other bibliographic information and the date.

EXERCISE 47.1 Writing works-cited entries

Prepare works-cited entries from the following information. Follow the models of the *MLA Handbook* given in this chapter unless your instructor specifies a different style. For titles, use underlining (as here) unless your instructor requests italics. Arrange the finished entries in alphabetical order, not numbered. (You can do this exercise online at *ablongman.com/littlebrown*.)

1. An article titled "Use of Third Parties to Collect State and Local Taxes on Internet Sales," appearing in The Pacific Business Journal, volume 5, issue 2, in 2004. The authors are Malai Zimmerman and Kent Hoover. The article appears on pages 45 through 48 of the journal.

2. A government publication you consulted on November 12, 2005, over the Internet. The author is the Advisory Commission on Electronic Commerce. The commission is an agency of the United States government. The title of the publication is Report to Congress. It was published in April 2005 and can be reached at http://www.ecommercecommission.org/report.htm.

3. A Web site with no listed author. The title is The Internet Tax Freedom Act Home Page, and the site is dated June 3, 2005. The address is http://cox.house.gov/nettax/frmain.htm. You consulted the site on November 2, 2005.

4. An article in the magazine Forbes, published December 17, 2003, on pages 56 through 58. The author is Anne Granfield. The title is "Taxing the Internet."

5. A book titled All's Fair in Internet Commerce, or Is It? by Sally G. Osborne. The book was published in 2004 by Random House in New York, New York.

6. An e-mail interview you conducted with Nora James on November 1, 2005.

7. An article titled "State and Local Sales/Use Tax Simplification," appearing on pages 67 through 80 of an anthology, The Sales Tax in the Twenty-First Century. The anthology is edited by Matthew N. Murray and William F. Fox. The article is by Wayne G. Eggert. The anthology was published in 2004 by Praeger in Westport, Connecticut.

47c Using MLA document format

The document format recommended by the *MLA Handbook* is fairly simple, with just a few elements. See also pages 112–26 for guidelines on type fonts, headings, lists, illustrations, and other features that are not specified in MLA style.

The samples below and on the next page show the formats for the first page and a later page of a paper. For the format of the list of works cited, see page 657.

First page of MLA paper

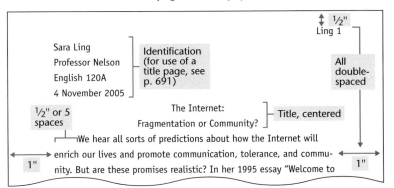

James, Nora. E-mail interview. 1 Nov. 2005.

Osborne, Sally G. All's Fair in Internet Commerce, or Is It? New York: Random, 2004.

United States. Advisory Commission on Electronic Commerce. Report to Congress. Apr. 2005. 12 Nov. 2005 <http://www.ecommercecommission.org/report.htm>.

Zimmerman, Malai, and Kent Hoover. "Use of Third Parties to Collect State and Local Taxes on Internet Sales." Pacific Business Journal 5.2 (2004): 45-48.

Later page of MLA paper

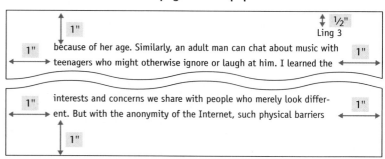

Margins Use minimum one-inch margins on all sides of every page.

Spacing and indentions Double-space throughout. Indent paragraphs one-half inch or five spaces. (See below for indention of poetry and long prose quotations.)

Paging Begin numbering on the first page, and number consecutively through the end (including the list of works cited). Type Arabic numerals (1, 2, 3) in the upper right about one-half inch from the top. Place your last name before the page number in case the pages later become separated.

Identification and title The *MLA Handbook* does not require a title page for a paper. If your instructor asks you to supply a title page, see pages 690–91. Otherwise, follow the sample on the previous page, providing your name, the date, and other information requested by your instructor. Place this identification an inch from the top of the page, aligned with the left margin and double-spaced.

Double-space again, and center the title. Do not highlight the title with underlining, boldface, larger type, or quotation marks. Capitalize the words in the title according to guidelines on page 491. Double-space the lines of the title and between the title and the text.

Poetry and long prose quotations Treat a single line of poetry like any other quotation, running it into your text and enclosing it in quotation marks. You may run in two or three lines of poetry as well, separating the lines with a slash surrounded by space.

> An example of Robert Frost's incisiveness is in two lines from "Death of the Hired Man": "Home is the place where, when you have to go there / They have to take you in" (119-20).

Always set off from your text a poetry quotation of more than three lines. Use double spacing above and below the quotation and for the quotation itself. Indent the quotation one inch or ten spaces from the left margin. *Do not add quotation marks.*

Emily Dickinson stripped ideas to their essence, as in this description of "A narrow Fellow in the Grass," a snake:

> I more than once at Noon
>
> Have passed, I thought, a Whip lash
>
> Unbraiding in the Sun
>
> When stopping to secure it
>
> It wrinkled, and was gone – (12-16)

Also set off a prose quotation of more than four typed lines. (See p. 620 on when to use such long quotations.) Double-space and indent as with the poetry example above. *Do not add quotation marks*.

> In the influential Talley's Corner from 1967, Elliot Liebow observes that "unskilled" construction work requires more skill than is generally assumed:
>
> > A healthy, sturdy, active man of good intelligence requires from two to four weeks to break in on a construction job. . . . It frequently happens that his foreman or the craftsman he services is not willing to wait that long for him to get into condition or to learn at a glance the difference in size between a rough 2 x 8 and a finished 2 x 10. (62)

Do not use a paragraph indention for a quotation of a single complete paragraph or a part of a paragraph. Use paragraph indentions of one-quarter inch or three spaces only for a quotation of two or more complete paragraphs.

RESOURCES AND IDEAS

National Council of Writing Program Administrators. "Defining and Avoiding Plagiarism: The WPA Statement on Best Practices." (*http://www.wpacouncil.org*) A clear statement from an authoritative professional body on what plagiarism is and is not.

Price, Margaret. "Beyond 'Gotcha!': Situating Plagiarism in Policy and Pedagogy." *College Composition and Communication* 54 (September 2002): 85–115. Price reviews current scholarship on plagiarism and offers practical advice on helping students understand and hence forestall the growing tendency to plagiarize.

mycomplab[2.0]

Please visit MyCompLab at *www.mycomplab.com* for more on the writing process.

CHAPTER 48

Two Research Papers in MLA Style

The following pages show the research papers of Edward Begay and Vanessa Haley, whose work we followed in Chapters 42–46. (Begay's paper begins on the next page, Haley's on p. 725.) Both students followed the style of the *MLA Handbook* for documenting sources and formatting their papers. Accompanying both students' papers are comments on format, source citations, and other matters.

HIGHLIGHTS

This chapter contains annotated versions of Edward Begay's and Vanessa Haley's final research papers for students to examine and discuss. Even if your students are not yet able to produce papers as strong as the ones in this chapter, they may find it helpful to have concrete examples to emulate. Both papers are presented as papers-in-progress throughout the chapters in Part 9; if your students have read Chapters 42–47, they will be able to trace the processes by which Begay and Haley arrived at their final papers. You can also discuss the papers in terms of the rhetorical features and mechanical requirements of good research writing.

You might want to begin by asking your students to respond to either or both of the papers in their journals and to discuss their responses in small groups. Students may have strong opinions about these final drafts. Both papers are effective, but neither is perfect, so you can ask your students to reflect upon any aspect of the final drafts that surprised them, how they themselves would have written the paper differently, or what, as readers, they would like to see added, omitted, or changed.

MODELS OF STUDENT WRITING

Edward Begay's paper is an example of a successful student effort at research writing. One of its best features, and one which you may want to discuss at some length with your students, is the balance between argument and presentation of evidence. Students who are new to research may have trouble determining how much of the research paper is meant to be reportage. Some may get so caught up in reporting evidence that they lose track of their argument; others may produce an argument paper based upon insufficient research. You can emphasize for your students that Begay's outline sketches the argument, not the evidence, and that using an outline is one of the best ways to make sure that a research paper is more than a mere report. You can also point out that Begay's argument arose and evolved out of his research and that he worked hard to shape his paper and make it argument-driven.

Another strength of this paper is the deftness of its transitions. Begay connects chunks of his research logically and astutely. The first major pivot occurs on page 3 of his paper (see comment 13), where he begins to make his argument for improved Internet access in public libraries. The second pivot occurs on page 4 of his paper (see comment 20). Here, Begay turns his attention to schools, arguing that they need not only improved Internet access but also improved quality of use from a pedagogical perspective. The third pivot, occurring on page 9 of his paper (see comment 39) begins the final section of the paper, in which Begay discusses the role of government and business in bridging the digital divide.

You can also use this paper to discuss the mechanical issues associated with research writing, from the introduction of quoted material to cita-

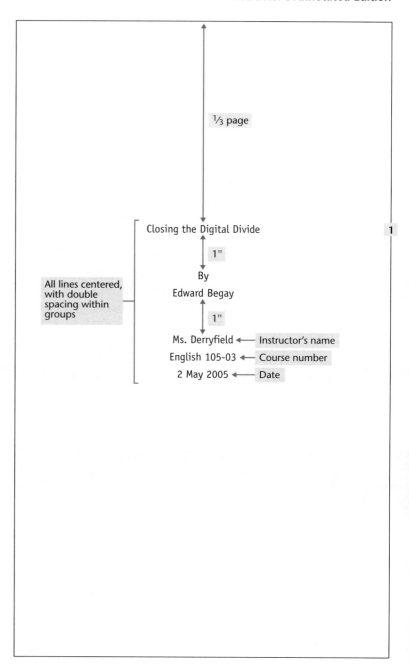

1 **Title page format.** A title page is not required by MLA style but may be required by your instructor. If so, or if you are required to submit an outline with your paper, prepare a title page as shown opposite.

If your instructor does not require a title page for your paper, follow MLA style: place your name, the identifying information, and the date on the first page of the paper. See Vanessa Haley's paper, page 725, for this format.

Next two pages

2 **Outline format.** If your instructor asks you to include your final outline, place it between the title page and the text and number the pages with small Roman numerals (i, ii). Follow the formatting annotations on the next two pages.

3 **Outline content.** Begay includes his final thesis statement as part of his outline so that his instructor can see how the parts relate to the whole. Notice that each main division (numbered with Roman numerals) relates to the thesis statement and that all the subdivisions relate to their main division.

Begay casts his final outline in full sentences. Some instructors request topic outlines, in which ideas appear in phrases instead of in sentences and do not end with periods. (See pp. 35–36 for this format.)

tion style to page layout. The annotations provide detailed comments on all these features, and a variety of electronic sources for the paper gives students examples of proper citation of such sources.

COLLABORATIVE LEARNING

USING THE COMMENTARY TECHNIQUE

The commentary on Begay's paper is very comprehensive and addresses content, structure, and mechanics. Your students may benefit from practicing this holistic method. Give them a short research-based article of your choice and have them work as partners or in small groups to evaluate the essay using the commentary method demonstrated in this chapter. In earlier chapters of the handbook, commentary focuses on discrete elements of writing one at a time. But as student writers become more experienced, it will be helpful for them to be able to expand their focus. Try having them make one pass for content, one for structure, one for grammar and mechanics, and one for citations.

Author's name and page number →Begay i

1"   ½"

Center ——→ Outline

2 | 3

Double-space

Thesis statement: Government and business must ensure that libraries and schools have the hardware, connections, and training capabilities for computer technology to make Americans more rather than less equal.

I. The digital divide is wide.

   A. Poor people have much less access to computer technology than middle-class and affluent people do.

   B. People who aren't online are at risk for missing important information.

II. Public libraries can provide Internet access to those who do not own computers, but they face several challenges.

   A. Those who have no access to computers at work or school take advantage of library computers for Internet access.

   B. Providing Internet access creates significant funding challenges for libraries.

   C. The FCC's E-Rate program is the most reliable funding source for library technology, but it is modest.

III. Schools offer many children their main exposure to computers, but computers raise educational as well as funding issues.

   A. Some experts question the value of technology in the classroom, but evidence suggests that Internet access can enhance learning.

      1. Some critics say technology undermines education.

      2. Some teachers say that technology fits in well with recent theories of education.

      3. Students in many schools are using the Internet effectively.

   B. Low-income students have far less access to technology than high-income students do.

Begay ii

    1. Low-income students use the Internet half as often.

    2. When low-income students have access to computers, they spend more of the time using instructional software.

IV. Governments and businesses must play a more active role in financing Internet access for libraries and schools.

    A. The federal government must reverse the recent cuts in funding of technology-assistance programs.

    B. Businesses must recognize their long-term interest in bringing potential employees online.

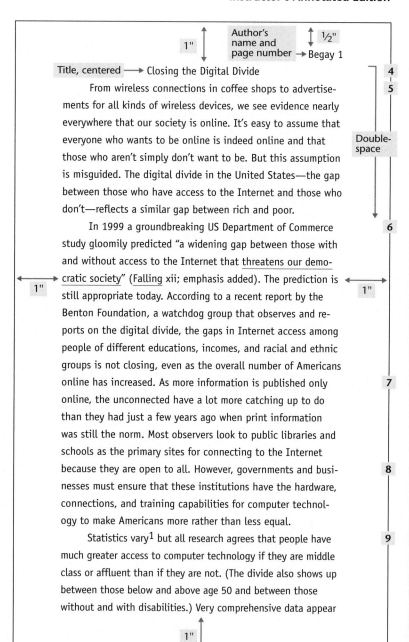

Author's name and page number → Begay 1   ½"

1"

Title, centered ⟶ Closing the Digital Divide

From wireless connections in coffee shops to advertisements for all kinds of wireless devices, we see evidence nearly everywhere that our society is online. It's easy to assume that everyone who wants to be online is indeed online and that those who aren't simply don't want to be. But this assumption is misguided. The digital divide in the United States—the gap between those who have access to the Internet and those who don't—reflects a similar gap between rich and poor.

Double-space

In 1999 a groundbreaking US Department of Commerce study gloomily predicted "a widening gap between those with and without access to the Internet that threatens our democratic society" (Falling xii; emphasis added). The prediction is still appropriate today. According to a recent report by the Benton Foundation, a watchdog group that observes and reports on the digital divide, the gaps in Internet access among people of different educations, incomes, and racial and ethnic groups is not closing, even as the overall number of Americans online has increased. As more information is published only online, the unconnected have a lot more catching up to do than they had just a few years ago when print information was still the norm. Most observers look to public libraries and schools as the primary sites for connecting to the Internet because they are open to all. However, governments and businesses must ensure that these institutions have the hardware, connections, and training capabilities for computer technology to make Americans more rather than less equal.

Statistics vary[1] but all research agrees that people have much greater access to computer technology if they are middle class or affluent than if they are not. (The divide also shows up between those below and above age 50 and between those without and with disabilities.) Very comprehensive data appear

1"   1"

4
5
6
7
8
9

4 **a** **Title.** Begay's title captures the image of a wide gap between two places. A more descriptive title, such as "Equality on the Internet," would also have been appropriate. **b** **Paper format.** Because he provides a title page as requested by his instructor, Begay does not repeat his full name on the first page of text. For MLA style, which omits a title page, the following would appear in the upper left of this first page:

Edward Begay

Ms. Derryfield

English 105-03

2 May 2005

(See Vanessa Haley's paper, p. 725, for an example of a research paper without a title page.) Follow the formatting annotations on the facing page for margins and spacing.

5 **Introduction.** Begay defines *digital divide*, a term he uses to discuss the problem of Internet access. He delays presenting his thesis in order to establish some background about the persistence of unequal access.

6 **a** **Citation of two works with corporate authors.** The sources Begay cites here do not name individual authors, so he lists the sponsor organizations as authors. **b** **Citation when the author is named in your text.** Because Begay names the US Department of Commerce in his text, he does not repeat the name in the parenthetical citation. **c** **Citation of a work by the author of two or more works.** To distinguish this Department Commerce study from another one he also cites, Begay gives a shortened form of the title in the parenthetical citation. **d** **Adding emphasis to a quotation.** Begay underlines important words in the quotation. He acknowledges this change in the parenthetical citation with emphasis added, separated from the page number by a semicolon.

7 **Omission of a parenthetical citation.** The Benton Foundation report comes from the Internet and lacks page or other identifying numbers. Since Begay names the author in his text, he doesn't include a parenthetical citation.

8 **Thesis statement.** Begay's introduction has led up to this statement, which asserts the claim that he will support in the paper.

9 **a** **Relation to outline.** This paragraph begins part I of Begay's outline (see p. 692). **b** **Using an endnote for supplementary information.** Here Begay inserts a reference to a note at the end of the paper in which he explains the difficulty of interpreting statistics about Internet use. He signals the note with the raised numeral 1.

Begay 2

in the most recent Department of Commerce study, which paints the unsettling picture shown in Table 1. The bottom three groups total 41.2 percent of all US households, yet many fewer than half of them use the Internet.

Table 1

Internet Use by Household Income, 2003

Annual Household Income	Percentage of All US Households	Percentage Using the Internet
Less than $15,000	16.1	31.2
$15,000-$24,999	13.2	38.0
$25,000-$34,999	11.9	48.9
$35,000-$49,999	15.1	62.1
More than $75,000	26.3	82.9

Source: Data from United States, Dept. of Commerce, Natl. Telecommunications and Information Admin., A Nation Online: Entering the Broadband Age, Feb. 2005, 1 Mar. 2005 <http://www.ntia.gov/reports/anol/index.html> 9, 47.

People who aren't online are at risk for missing important information and may not even know they are missing it. For example, in early 2005 the US Department of Agriculture unveiled a new, interactive version of the Food Pyramid, the familiar triangle that provides guidelines for healthy eating. Previous versions of the pyramid had been published in print and distributed through schools, local health departments, local libraries, and so on. The new version, however, is available primarily on the Web, and its interactive features can be accessed only online. According to the journalist Andy Carvin,

10

11

10 **a** **Use of a table.** Begay uses a table to present statistics from the Department of Commerce study so that the data are easy to compare and the differences are emphatic. **b** **Table format.** Following MLA style, Begay double-spaces the entire table. **c** **Citation of a source for a table.** Also following MLA style, Begay provides a source note indicating where he obtained the data in the table. The note includes complete information on the source even though Begay also cites the work fully in his list of works cited. The numbers following the URL are the pages where Begay found the table's data.

11 **Selecting supporting evidence.** Begay paraphrases and quotes two sources in this paragraph to support his point that low-income people who aren't online may miss important information. The uses of the authors' names in the text clarify who said what.

Begay 3

the pyramid provides more specific information about nutrition, but being online it can't reach many low-income people who, like everyone else, would benefit from its guidelines. The sociologists Susan Dykstra and William L. Brown observe that "as US government agencies expand e-government . . . , a pressing question remains what will happen to underserved populations, particularly as traditionally offline government services are replaced entirely by online services." The answer, for now, is that those populations will be more underserved than before.

For people without home or work Internet access, an important link is public libraries. Nearly all public libraries in the United States do have some level of Internet access to serve their patrons: 97 percent, according to recent numbers (Bertot, McClure, and Jaeger 4). The access specifically benefits those who need it most. The American Library Association states the role of libraries and librarians this way:

> People from households making less than $15,000 annually are three times more likely to rely on library computers than those earning more than $75,000. . . . [P]ublic access to the Internet through public libraries is a major step toward closing the digital divide. But access is not enough: librarians and their interactions with patrons make the biggest difference. Librarians help patrons develop vital information-literacy skills by providing one-to-one tutoring in how to access relevant, well-organized sources. (par. 2)

However, providing not only up-to-date computers and Internet connections but also intensive training creates significant funding challenges for libraries. Almost 75 percent of public libraries have three or fewer computer terminals through which they can offer Internet access, and fewer than 30

12 **Editing a quotation with an ellipsis mark.** Begay uses an ellipsis mark (three spaced periods) to show that he has omitted some words from the quotation.

13 **Relation to outline.** This paragraph begins part II of Begay's outline. See page 692.

14 **a** **Citation when the author is not named in your text.** Because Begay does not give the three authors' names in his text, he provides the names in the parenthetical citation along with a page number. **b** **Citation of a work with three authors.** Begay gives all three authors' last names, separating them with commas and *and* before final name.

15 **a** **Format of a long quotation.** This quotation exceeds four typed lines, so Begay sets it off from his text without quotation marks, with double spacing throughout, and with an extra indention of ten spaces or one inch. **b** **Editing a quotation with brackets.** By using brackets around the capital *P*, Begay indicates that he has omitted the beginning of the original sentence and changed the capitalization.

16 **a** **Citation with displayed quotation.** The parenthetical citation after the quotation falls *outside* the sentence period. **b** **Citation of a source using a paragraph number.** Begay uses par. ("paragraph") to indicate that the source numbers paragraphs rather than pages. He cites paragraph 2.

17 **Revision of a draft.** In his first draft Begay sometimes strung his source information together without interpreting it. In revising he added comments of his own (in blue) to introduce the information in the context of his ideas:

However, providing not only up-to-date computers and Internet connections but also intensive training creates significant funding challenges for libraries. But a~~Almost 75 percent of public libraries have three or fewer computer terminals through which they can offer Internet access, and fewer than 30 percent of librarians believe they have the staff needed to train users (Bertot and McClure 35). Clearly, with the length of time Internet searches can take, three terminals and an overstretched staff cannot serve many library patrons. Yet terminals and staff are costly.

Begay 4

percent of librarians believe they have the staff needed to train users (Bertot and McClure 35). Clearly, with the length of time Internet searches can take, three terminals and an over-stretched staff cannot serve many library patrons. Yet terminals and staff are costly.

Many librarians worry that these costs will cause libraries themselves to fall into the digital divide. Library funding is often cut and rarely increased by state and local governments trying to trim their budgets. Among nongovernment groups, according to the American Library Association, only the Bill and Melinda Gates Foundation (established by the Microsoft founder and his wife) has provided significant help for libraries. Since 1997 the foundation has given grants of more than $250 million to provide libraries with public-access computers and software. The grants have especially benefited poor, rural library systems, many of which otherwise could not have afforded the equipment (par. 7).

The most reliable source of government funding for library technology is the Universal Service Program, established by the US Federal Communications Commission. Telecommunications providers and individuals who subscribe to their services pay a fee commonly called the E-Rate. From the Universal Service Program, the FCC allocates up to $2.25 billion annually to help both libraries and primary and secondary schools purchase telecommunications services. However, the fund is modest and does not cover training of staff or purchase of computers. Given the transformation of our economy and culture caused by the Internet, $2.25 billion barely amounts to a token gesture. More must be done to connect libraries and help them train Internet users.

Whereas mostly adults benefit from library funding, many children receive their exposure to computers in the

18

19

20

18 **a** **Common knowledge.** In his reading, Begay saw many references to government cuts in library funding, so he treats this information as common knowledge and does not cite a source for it. (See pp. 632–33 for more on common knowledge.) **b** **Clarifying boundaries of source material.** The rest of this paragraph summarizes information from a report by the American Library Association. Begay makes the extent of the summary clear by giving the ALA's name at the beginning and a parenthetical citation at the end.

19 **Omission of a parenthetical citation.** Begay does not provide a parenthetical citation for the Federal Communications Commission report because he names the author in his text and the online source has no page or other reference numbers.

20 **a** **Relation to outline.** With this paragraph, Begay begins part III of his outline (see p. 692). **b** **Transitional paragraph.** Begay devotes a paragraph to the shift in focus from libraries to schools.

Begay 5

public schools. In fact, nearly all schools in the United States now provide some computers for student use (Conte 924). But the digital divide in schools has as much to do with how students use computers as it does with whether they have access to them.

For some time, schools have been using computers extensively for drill-and-practice exercises, in which students repeat specific skills such as spelling words, using the multiplication facts, or, at a higher level, doing chemistry problems. But many education experts criticize such exercises for boring students and failing to engage their critical thinking and creativity. Jane M. Healy, a noted educational psychologist and teacher, takes issue with "interactive" software for children as well as drill-and-practice software, arguing that "some of the most popular 'educational' software . . . may be damaging to independent thinking, attention, and motivation" (20). Another education expert, Harold Wenglinsky of the Educational Testing Service, found in a well-regarded 1998 study that fourth and eighth graders who used computers frequently, including for drill and practice, actually did worse on tests than their peers who used computers less often (Does It Compute? 21). In a later article, Wenglinsky concludes that "the quantity of use matters far less than the quality of use." In schools, he says, high-quality computer work, involving critical thinking, is still rare ("In Search" 17).[2]

Drill-and-practice exercises reinforce the "transmission" model of education, in which teachers transmit knowledge to passive students (Conte 925). Some experts argue that this type of teaching does not prepare students to work in the information age (Conte 923-24). Instead, these experts favor a model closer to cognitive psychology and constructivism, emphasizing active learning and "dealing with complex,

21 a Integrating source material. Here and elsewhere, Begay establishes his source's credentials in a signal phrase and effectively integrates paraphrases and quotations into his own sentences. **b Omission of ellipsis mark.** Begay does not use an ellipsis mark at the beginning of the Healy quotation beginning "some" because the small *s* makes it clear that he omitted the opening of Healy's sentence.

22 Punctuation with a parenthetical citation. The period that ends a sentence containing a quotation comes after the citation.

23 a Citation of two works by the same author. Begay gives brief versions of Wenglinsky's two titles in the parenthetical citations here and below in order to distinguish the sources. **b Clarifying boundaries of source material.** By mentioning Wenglinsky's name at the beginning of the paragraph's last two sentences and giving the rest of the citation at the end, Begay indicates that everything in between comes from Wenglinsky. **c Mixing quotation and paraphrase.** Begay quotes and paraphrases from Wenglinsky's article to give readers a good sense of the issue Wenglinsky raises. **d Punctuation with a quotation.** The period falls inside the closing quotation mark because the quotation is not immediately followed by a parenthetical citation.

24 a Introducing borrowed material. Begay here begins paraphrasing and quoting Conte as an expert, so he should have named Conte in the text and identified him with his credentials. **b Paraphrasing.** Begay paraphrases Conte's words. His note for the second paraphrase transcribed a quotation from Conte:

Traditional vs. innovative models of education

Conte 923-24

"[T]he traditional classroom, with its strong central authority and its emphasis on training students to take orders and perform narrow tasks, may have prepared students for work in 20th-century factories. But it can't impart the skills they need in the workplace of the 21st century, where there's a premium on workers who are flexible, creative, self-directed and able to solve problems collaboratively."

c Citation of paraphrases. Because he does not use Conte's name in the text, Begay correctly gives it in the citations.

25 Defining terms. Begay uses two terms here, *cognitive psychology* and *constructivism*, that he picked up from Conte and other sources. He should have defined the terms to avoid confusing readers.

Begay 6

real-world problems"—a model well served by Internet-connected computers (Conte 935-36).

Many teachers see the Internet as a powerful resource for just this kind of teaching. Mary E. McArthur, a veteran teacher in Massachusetts, told me in an online interview that the Internet presents new possibilities for student learning:

> My students have a much better sense of the relevance of their education how now that they're online. When we were studying ecology, for example, some students e-mailed a representative of the EPA [Environmental Protection Agency] in Washington, asking questions and offering suggestions about a proposed local landfill, and received an immediate response. They took that response to the town's planning board when the landfill was discussed.

The Internet, according to McArthur, has made her students not only better learners but better citizens as well. And contrary to Healy's vision of uncreative, unmotivated students, McArthur told me that since her students began using technology, "conversation is constant. Students are talking online, to each other, and to me—questioning, criticizing, analyzing what they're learning."

McArthur's and her students' experiences are not unique: success stories about online education are common in popular and scholarly sources.[3] But many teachers and students are not discovering what they might accomplish with the Internet because their schools cannot afford enough terminals and training to give everyone ample hands-on experience.

In general, student access to online computers is improving considerably. A 2004 study conducted by Market Data Retrieval and quoted in Students and Internet Access by the

26

27

28

29

30

31

26 **Primary source: personal interview.** Begay tested his ideas by conducting an e-mail interview with a teacher in a public school. He uses both paraphrase and quotation from the interview, with the subject's permission.

27 **Adding to a quotation with brackets.** Begay spells out the full name of the EPA for readers who may not recognize the abbreviation, and he encloses the addition with brackets.

28 **Omission of parenthetical citation.** Begay does not use a parenthetical citation at the end of the quotation because the source (an interview) has no page or other reference numbers and the necessary information (McArthur's name) appears in the text before the quotation.

29 **a Summary of sources.** Rather than belabor the Internet success stories, Begay wraps up with a summary. **b Using an endnote for citation of several sources.** Begay avoids a lengthy and obtrusive parenthetical citation by referring readers to endnote 3, which lists several sources (see p. 718). **c Transitional paragraph.** This paragraph within the section on schools shifts the emphasis from the educational value of technology to its cost.

30 **Synthesis of sources.** In this and the next several paragraphs, Begay integrates information from sources with his own conclusions about the significance of the data.

31 **a Citation of a long source named in the text.** A parenthetical citation here would have read (qtd. in United States, Dept. of Education, Students). Begay chose to avoid the awkwardly long citation by naming both the indirect and the direct source in his text. The Department of Education site had no page or other reference numbers for Begay to cite. **b Indirect sources.** Indirect sources are appropriate only when the quoted material is not available to consult. Begay's use of the indirect source is appropriate here because he could not find the original Market Data Retrieval report.

Begay 7

US Department of Education shows that the ratio of students to computers decreased from 12 to 1 in 1998 to 4 to 1 in 2004. However, those are averages across all public schools. Another Department of Education source shows that in schools with students of low income, the ratio remains higher than the 1998 average, at 13 to 1, and only 34 percent of those students use the Internet at all in school, compared with 68 percent of their high-income peers. At the same time, the difference in overall computer use between low- and high-income students is not nearly as pronounced: 80 percent for those of low income, 88 percent for those of high income (Internet 29-30). (See fig. 1.)

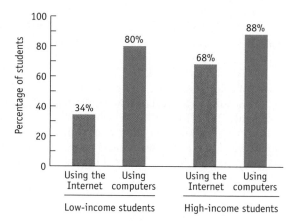

Fig. 1. Computer use in public schools, showing the disparity in Internet and overall computer use between low-income and high-income students. Data from United States, Dept. of Education, National Center for Educational Statistics, Internet Access in US Public Schools and Classrooms, 24 Feb. 2005, 12 Mar. 2005 <http://nces.ed.gov/pubsearch/pubsinfo.sap?pubid=2005025>.

32

33

32 **Use of a figure.** Begay created a bar chart to show the differences between low-income and high-income students. He refers to the figure in his text.

33 **a** **Figure caption.** Begay captions the figure so that readers know how to interpret it. **b** **Citation of a source for data.** Following MLA style, Begay provides a source note indicating where he obtained the data in the chart. The note includes complete information for the source even though Begay also cites the work fully in his list of works cited.

Begay 8

The increase in both kinds of schools is due to the use of instructional software programs, primarily drill and practice. Clearly, poorer schools rely much more on such use than wealthier schools do.

Real stories back up the data shown in fig. 1. An example is La Entrada High School in a poor section of Oakland, California (Richards). La Entrada's ratio of students to computers is 15 to 1, and the computers are used machines that are slow to load Web sites. With limited equipment, students at La Entrada cannot match their more affluent peers in using the Web or communicating online with experts. In fact, they are often so frustrated by waiting in line for computers and then by the machines' slowness that they simply give up, using the computers only when scheduled for drill in reading and math. In the words of Delia Neuman of the University of Maryland, they "learn to do what the computer tells them" (qtd. in Conte 931).

Students who do not learn to use the Internet may find themselves left out of a society in which computer skills will earn a high school graduate 39 percent more than another graduate without such skills (Twist 6). And the nation's economy will suffer as well. The risk is described by Larry Irving, a former assistant secretary of the Department of Commerce and the author of its first report on the digital divide, Falling through the Net:

> Almost 60 percent of jobs created today . . . require an understanding of information technology. Yet too many of our students are graduating from schools that don't give them the training required for the jobs they seek. Already, the nation's businesses are having trouble filling the skilled jobs they're creating, and in another five years the situation is likely to reach a crisis.

34

35

36

37

34 **Citation of an online article without page numbers.** The Richards article, which Begay found online, does not have any page or other reference numbers, so the citation includes only the author's name.

35 **Editing quotations.** Begay had a long quotation by Neuman, but he selected from it only the words that supported the point he was making. The entire quotation appears in his note:

Difference between rich & poor schools

Conte 931

From Delia Neuman, prof., U Maryland Coll. of Library & Information Services: "Economically disadvantaged students, who often use the computer for remediation and basic skills, learn to do what the computer tells them, while more affluent students, who use it to learn programming and tool application, learn to tell the computer what to do."

---

36 **a** **Citation of an indirect source.** With the use of qtd. in, Begay indicates correctly that he found the quotation by Neuman (an indirect source) in the article by Conte (a direct source). **b** **Indirect sources.** Indirect sources are appropriate only when the quoted material is not available to consult. Begay's source, Conte, gave full bibliographic information on Neuman's article, and Begay should have gone directly to it.

37 **Omission of a parenthetical citation.** Begay took this quotation from an online source lacking page or other reference numbers. Since the author is named in the text, he does not provide a parenthetical citation.

Begay 9

The results, then, are unavailable jobs for the graduating students who need them and a shortage of just the kind of workers the country needs.

The problem for schools like La Entrada is, of course, money. Leaders in poor school districts are aware of the importance of technology, but they are also worried about leaking roofs, aging furniture, and overcrowded classrooms. The money to buy the equipment, make the connections, and train teachers and staff to use and maintain the networks is not easily found even in middle-class school districts, much less in poorer districts.

38

If libraries and schools are to provide widespread access to the Internet, they must find ways not only to integrate technology into their programs but also to pay the bills associated with going and staying online. Adapting the work of libraries and schools to the technological age is the responsibility of the experts within those systems. But finding the money to finance technological advances should involve more elements of society, specifically governments and businesses. These two groups must play a more active role in wiring libraries and schools, providing hardware, and training librarians, teachers, and students to work with the technology.

39

Governments are already encouraging cooperation between businesses and schools. For instance, many states organize annual NetDay campaigns designed to bring educators, community volunteers, and corporations together to keep schools online and up to date (Jordahl and Orwig 25; NetDay). However, to close the digital divide, government support must be direct. The E-Rate program of the Federal Communications Commission is a start, but just a start, because it covers only connection fees, not hardware or training. Furthermore, divided as it is among nearly 17,000 public libraries and 114,000

40

38 Drawing conclusions. Rather than leave it to his readers to figure out the significance of the preceding paragraphs, Begay here wraps up the discussion of schools with his own conclusions about the costs and thus the limits of technological change in education.

39 a Relation to outline. With this paragraph, Begay begins part IV of his outline (see p. 693). **b Summary statement.** Begay introduces this final section with a statement that pulls together libraries and schools and clearly distinguishes their role from the financial responsibilities for broadening Internet access.

40 Parenthetical citation of more than one work. Begay discovered information about NetDay campaigns in two sources, so he cites both in parentheses, separating them with a semicolon. The second source lacks page or other reference numbers, so its citation does not include a number.

Begay 10

primary and secondary schools (<u>World Almanac</u> 251, 253), the

41

program's $2.25 billion comes to less than $20,000 per institu-

tion per year. According to the Benton Foundation, the federal

42

government once made closing the divide a priority, funding

programs to bring the disadvantaged online and train them in

using Internet resources. But the foundation reports that since

2001 the federal government has actually slashed funding of

three significant programs: Preparing Tomorrow's Teachers to

Use Technology, providing grants to help teachers gain more

competence teaching with computers; Technology Opportunity

Program, providing hardware grants to the public and nonprofit

sectors; and Community Technology Centers, providing grants to

expand access of the rural and urban poor to technology. Fig. 2

shows the funding of these programs from 2001 to 2005.

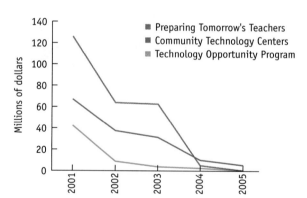

43

Fig. 2. Funding levels 2001-05 for three federal government

44

programs intended to help close the digital divide. Chart from

Benton Foundation, <u>National Strategy to Bridge the Digital</u>

<u>Divide Abandoned</u>, Jan. 2005, 3 Apr. 2005 <http://

www.benton.org/press/2005/pro211.html>.

41 a Use of an almanac. Begay consulted an almanac for the number of public libraries and primary and secondary schools so that he could calculate the average amount of aid under the E-Rate program. **b Placement of a parenthetical citation.** Because Begay used the almanac only for the number of libraries and schools, not for the calculation, he places the parenthetical citation directly after the almanac data.

42 Omission of a parenthetical citation. Since Begay names the Benton Foundation in his text and the online source has no page or other reference number, he does not add a parenthetical citation.

43 Use of a figure. Begay uses a graph to show the dramatic funding decrease in the programs he mentions. He refers to the figure in his text.

44 a Figure caption. Begay captions the figure so that readers know how to interpret it. **b Citation of a source for a figure.** Following MLA style, Begay provides a source note indicating where he obtained the figure. The note includes complete information for the source even though Begay also cites the work fully in his list of works cited.

Begay 11

Cuts like these propel government efforts backward rather **45** than forward. If the digital divide is to close, as it must, the federal government needs to reverse direction, taking the lead to ensure that its citizens have equal access to information technology.

Businesses must join in as well. Commercial enterprises have long recognized their responsibility to the larger community—for instance, supporting youth athletics and contributing to charities through the Chamber of Commerce. Some businesses also work with schools and libraries to increase Internet access. For many years, computer manufacturers such **46** as IBM and Apple have donated new and used computers to schools. Recently, the 3COM Corporation has provided grants and consultants to help train public school teachers and students in the use of technology (Jordahl and Orwig 25).

For computer companies, cooperation with schools and libraries seems good business, paying off in free advertising, enhanced image, and potential sales. In some locations, other kinds of companies are also stepping in to improve Internet access for the disadvantaged. For example, three Seattle banks assign employee mentors to low-income public schools to help the students use the Internet effectively for schoolwork (Jordahl and Orwig 24). And insurance companies and law firms in Boston have joined technology companies to provide computer training and equipment in the public libraries and schools, making Boston one of the most Internet-connected cities in the nation (Pace 36). But these efforts and a few **47** others like them are unusual in the literature on the digital divide. Most businesses, no doubt focusing on the short term and receiving little incentive from government to do otherwise, may train their own employees but contribute nothing to bring the larger community online. As Larry Irving notes in

45 Drawing conclusions. Begay ends his discussion of government funding with his own conclusion about what has happened and what must be done.

46 Common knowledge. Begay already knew of manufacturers' programs to place computers in schools; in fact, he had used a donated computer in high school. Thus he treats this information as common knowledge.

47 Drawing conclusions. Begay ends his discussion of business with his own conclusions about the causes and results of low funding.

the quotation cited earlier, businesses are already suffering from such shortsightedness. They must recognize their interest in fostering widespread access to technology.

The Internet is now "the central nervous system of our democracy," says Jeff Chester of the Center for Digital Democracy (6). Providing Internet access through libraries and schools seems the only way to ensure equal access for poor and rich alike. The schools and libraries cannot close the digital divide on their own, however. They need strong financial support from government and business to make Chester's neural pathway truly open to all.

48

48 **Conclusion.** In his final paragraph Begay summarizes the main points of his paper to remind readers of both the need for universal Internet access and the ways it can be funded.

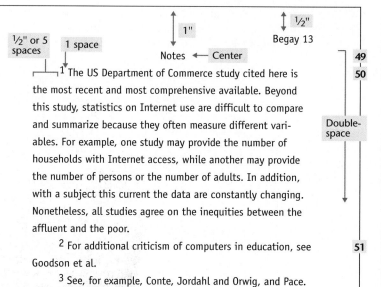

½" or 5 spaces 1 space 1" Notes ← Center ½" Begay 13 49 50

¹ The US Department of Commerce study cited here is the most recent and most comprehensive available. Beyond this study, statistics on Internet use are difficult to compare and summarize because they often measure different variables. For example, one study may provide the number of households with Internet access, while another may provide the number of persons or the number of adults. In addition, with a subject this current the data are constantly changing. Nonetheless, all studies agree on the inequities between the affluent and the poor.

² For additional criticism of computers in education, see Goodson et al.

³ See, for example, Conte, Jordahl and Orwig, and Pace.

Double-space

51

49 **Format of notes.** The heading Notes is centered one inch from the top of the page. (The heading would be singular—Note—if Begay had only one note.) Follow the annotations on the facing page for formatting.

50 **Endnotes for additional relevant information.** Begay uses endnotes for sources and information that are somewhat relevant to his thesis but not essential and that don't fit easily into the text. Note 1 provides information on Begay's difficulties interpreting statistics. Note 2 highlights a notable critique of computers in education. And note 3 cites several sources that would be obtrusive in a parenthetical citation. (See p. 656 for more on supplementary notes.)

51 **Citation of a source with more than three authors.** The Goodson citation indicates with et al. ("and others") that Goodson was a coauthor with at least three others. See the works-cited entry for this source on the next page.

½"

1"

Begay 14

Works Cited ← Center

½" or 5 spaces

American Library Assn. "Digital Divide Talking Points." ALA.
Sept. 2003; 12 pars. 2 Apr. 2005 <http://ala.org/ala/
issues/keymessages/divide.htm>.

Benton Foundation. National Strategy to Bridge the Digital
Divide Abandoned. Jan. 2005. 3 Apr. 2005.
<http://www.benton.org/press/2005/pro211.html>.

Bertot, John Carlos, Charles R. McClure, and Paul T. Jaeger.
Public Libraries and the Internet: Survey Results and
Findings. 2005. Information Use Management and Policy
Institute. Dir. Charles R. McClure. Florida State U. 26
Mar. 2005 <http://iumpi.fsu.edu/internet_report.cfm>.

Carvin, Andy. "My.Pyramid.gov: Achieving E-Health for All?"
Digital Divide Network. 22 Feb. 2005. 23 Mar. 2005
<http://www.digitaldivide.net/articles/ArticleID=401>.

Chester, Jeff. "The Threat to the Net." Nation 9 Oct. 2004: 6-7.
Expanded Academic ASAP. InfoTrac. Southeast State U,
Polk Lib. 10 Mar. 2005 <http://www.galegroup.com>.

Conte, Christopher. "Networking the Classroom." CQ Researcher
5 (2004): 923-43.

Dykstra, Susan, and William L. Brown. "E-Government and
Underserved Populations." Digital Divide Network. May
2004. 23 Mar. 2005 <http://www.digitaldivide.net/
articles/ArticleID=261>.

Goodson, Ivor F., et al. "Computer Literacy as Ideology."
British Journal of Sociology of Education 17 (2001):
65-80.

Healy, Jane M. Failure to Connect: How Computers Affect
Our Children's Minds—for Better and Worse. New York:
Simon, 2000.

Irving, Larry. "The Still-Yawning Divide." Newsweek 12 Mar.
2005: 64.

Double-space

52
53
54
55
56
57
58
59
60

52 **Format of a list of works cited.** The heading Works Cited is centered at the top of the page. The entries are alphabetized by the last name of the first author or (for sources without authors) by the first main word of the title. Each entry has a hanging indention (see p. 657 on creating this indention). For additional formatting, see the annotations on the facing page.

53 **a** **An online source,** including Begay's access date and the URL in angle brackets. **b** **A corporate author.** Since the source does not list an individual as author, Begay names the organization as author. **c** **Paragraphs instead of pages.** This source does not number pages but does number paragraphs, so Begay lists the total paragraphs.

54 **a** **Source with three authors.** The first name is reversed, and the other two are given in normal order, separated by and. **b** **Scholarly project.** The entry includes the title of the project, the name of the director, and the name of the sponsoring university.

55 **Article from an online service to which the library subscribes** (see pp. 671–72). Because the service does not provide usable URLs for articles—that is, URLs that readers can use to reach the articles directly—Begay instead gives the names of the database and service, the names of his school and library, and the URL for the home page of the service.

56 **Article in a journal with continuous pagination throughout an annual volume** (see p. 666).

57 **Source with two authors.** The first name is reversed. After and the second name is given in normal order.

58 **Source with more than three authors.** A source with more than three authors may be listed with all authors' names or just with the first author's name followed by et al. ("and others"). (See p. 659.) Begay had all the names in his working bibliography, but he opted not to use them. His parenthetical citation is consistent with this decision (p. 718).

59 **Book with one author.**

60 **Article in a weekly magazine.**

Begay 15

Jordahl, Gregory, and Ann Orwig. "Getting Equipped and Stay-
    ing Equipped, Part 6: Finding the Funds." Technology
    and Learning Apr. 2004: 20-26.   **61**

McArthur, Mary E. E-mail interview. 20 Mar. 2005.   **62**

NetDay. "About Us." NetDay. Jan. 2003. 21 Mar. 2003 <http://   **63**
    www.netday.org/about.html>.

Pace, Don. "Building the Digital Bridge in Boston." Converge
    Dec. 2004: 35-37.

Richards, Greg. "Digital Divide on Site." San Jose Mercury   **64**
    News 22 Nov. 2004, morning final ed. NewsBank.
    Southeast State U, Polk Lib. 17 Mar. 2005 <http://
    www.newsbank.com>.

Twist, Kade. "Disparities along the Information Age Career
    Path." Digital Divide Network. 2003. 3 Mar. 2005
    <http://www.digitaldivide.net/articles/ArticleID=292>.

United States. Dept. of Commerce. National Telecommunica-   **65**
    tions and Information Admin. Falling through the Net:
    Defining the Digital Divide. Nov 1999. 1 Mar. 2005
    <http://www.ntia.doc.gov/ntiahome/fttn99/
    contents.html>

---. ---. ---. A Nation Online: Entering the Broadband Age.   **66**
    Feb. 2005. 1 Mar. 2005 <http://www.ntia.doc.gov/
    reports/anol/index.html>.

---. Dept. of Education. Advisory Commission on Student Fi-   **67**
    nancial Assistance. Students and Internet Access. Apr.
    2004. 16 Mar. 2005 <http://www.ed.gov/about/acsfa/
    students_internet.html>.

---. ---. Natl. Center for Education Statistics. Internet Access
    in Public Schools and Classrooms. 24 Feb. 2005. 12
    Mar. 2005 <http://nces.ed.gov/pubsearch/
    pubsinfo.asp?pubid=2005025>.

61 Article in a monthly magazine.

62 Personal interview by e-mail.

63 A page on an organization's Web site. MLA does not specifically cover an online site for this type of organization, so Begay adapted the format for a short work from an online site (p. 673). He provided all the information a reader would need to find the source—including the page title, site title, date of publication, and URL of the page—along with the date of his access.

64 Article from an online service to which the library subscribes. See annotation 55 on page 721.

65 Online government publications. This and the next four entries all cite government publications that Begay found online. Since none of the sources had a named author, Begay lists as author the government body responsible for the source: the government (United States), the department, and (in the first two and fourth sources) the group within the department.

66 Additional source by the same author. Since the author of the previous entry is also United States, Department of Commerce, National Telecommunications and Information Administration, in this entry Begay replaces each of those names with three hyphens followed by a period.

67 Additional source by the same government. Since the previous entry also lists United States as the government, in this entry Begay replaces the name with three hyphens followed by a period. Note that he does not replace author information that is unique to this source, but in the next entry he does replace the repeated department name.

Next page

68 Anonymous source. *The World Almanac* has no named author and so is listed and alphabetized by its title. It appears last in the list of works cited because World appears last alphabetically.

Begay 16

---. Federal Communications Commission. <u>Universal Service
Program</u>. 28 Sept. 2002. 6 Mar. 2005 <http://
www.fcc.gov/Bureaus/Common_Carrier/Public_Notices/
1998/da971374.html>.

Wenglinsky, Harold. <u>Does It Compute? The Relationship
Between Educational Technology and Student Achieve-
ment</u>. Princeton: Educational Testing Service, 1998.

---. "In Search of the Workable." <u>Converge</u> Oct. 2004: 16-17.

<u>The World Almanac and Book of Facts 2005</u>. New York: World
Almanac, 2005.

68

Haley 1

Vanessa Haley

Professor Moisan

English 101

6 Feb. 2006

Annie Dillard's Healing Vision

It is almost a commonplace these days that human arrogance is destroying the environment. Environmentalists, naturalists, and now the man or woman on the street seem to agree: the long-held belief that human beings are separate from nature, destined to rise above its laws and conquer it, has been ruinous.

Unfortunately, the defenders of nature tend to respond to this ruinous belief with harmful myths of their own: nature is pure and harmonious; humanity is corrupt and dangerous. Much writing about nature lacks a recognition that human beings and their civilization are as much a part of nature as trees and whales are, neither better nor worse. Yet without such a recognition, how can humans overcome the damaging sense of separation between themselves and the earth? How can humans develop realistic solutions to environmental problems that will work for humanity <u>and</u> the rest of nature?

One nature writer who seems to recognize the naturalness of humanity is Annie Dillard. In her best-known work, the Pulitzer Prize-winning <u>Pilgrim at Tinker Creek</u>, she is a solitary person encountering the natural world, and some critics fault her for turning her back on society. But in those encounters with nature, Dillard probes a spiritual as well as a physical identity between human beings and nature that could help to heal the rift between them.

Dillard is not renowned for her sense of involvement with human society. Like Henry David Thoreau, with whom she is often compared, she retreats from rather than confronts human society. The critic Gary McIlroy points out that although

Format of heading and title when no title page is required (see also p. 687)

Introduction of environmental theme

Focus on issue to be resolved

Introduction of Dillard to resolve issue

Thesis statement

Acknowledgment of opposing critical view

MODELS OF STUDENT WRITING

Vanessa Haley's paper is a good example of a short essay with limited outside research. Students who are new to critical writing often have difficulty establishing their own position in contradistinction to those of other critics. In her paper, Haley has accomplished the delicate task of drawing upon the perspectives of critics while articulating her own unique perspective, and you may want to spend some time discussing this with your students. You could even ask them to read the same outside sources Haley read and then to evaluate how successful she was in distinguishing her own point of view from those of the other critics.

This paper also features a sophisticated introduction, in which Haley identifies two reductive and mutually opposed points of view about nature and rejects them both in favor of a third alternative. You can use this paragraph as an example of writing that goes beyond binary thinking. You may also find that your students want to talk about Haley's contention that human civilization is a part of nature—it's an interesting, debatable claim, one that Haley wields well but that may be controversial in your classroom.

Haley 2

Thoreau discusses society a great deal in Walden, he makes no attempt "to find a middle ground between it and his experiment in the woods" (113). Dillard has been similarly criticized. For instance, the writer Eudora Welty comments that

> Annie Dillard is the only person in her book, substantially the only one in her world; I recall no outside human speech coming to break the long soliloquy of the author. Speaking of the universe very often, she is yet self-surrounded and, beyond that, book-surrounded. Her own book might have taken in more of human life without losing a bit of the wonder she was after. (37)

First response to opposing view

It is true, as Welty says, that in Pilgrim Dillard seems detached from human society. However, she actually was always close to it at Tinker Creek. In a later book, Teaching a Stone to Talk, she says of the neighborhood, "This is, mind you, suburbia. It is a five-minute walk in three directions to rows of houses. . . . There's a 55 mph highway at one end of the pond, and a nesting pair of wood ducks at the other" (qtd. in Suh).

Second response to opposing view

Rather than hiding from humanity, Dillard seems to be trying to understand it through nature. In Pilgrim she reports buying a goldfish, which she names Ellery Channing. She recalls once seeing through a microscope "red blood cells whip, one by one, through the capillaries" of yet another goldfish (124). Now watching Ellery Channing, she sees the blood in his body as a bond between fish and human being: "Those red blood cells are coursing in Ellery's tail now, too, in just that way, and through his mouth and eyes as well, and through mine" (125). Gary McIlroy observes that this blood, "a symbol of the sanctity of life, is a common bond between Dillard and the fish, between animal and human life in general, and between Dillard and other people" (115).

Secondary source's analysis of Dillard

Haley 3

For Dillard, the terror and unpredictability of death unify all life. The most sinister image in Pilgrim—one that haunts Dillard—is that of the frog and the water bug. Dillard reports walking along an embankment scaring frogs into the water when one frog refused to budge. As Dillard leaned over to investigate, the frog "slowly crumpled and began to sag. The spirit vanished from his eyes as if snuffed. His skin emptied and dropped; his very skull seemed to collapse and settle like a kicked tent" (6). The frog was the victim of a water bug that injects poisons to "dissolve the victim's muscles and bones and organs" (6). Such events lead Dillard to wonder about a creator who would make all life "power and beauty, grace tangled in a rapture with violence" (8). Human beings no less than frogs and water bugs are implicated in this tangle.

Dillard is equally as disturbed by birth as by death. In a chapter of Pilgrim called "Fecundity," she focuses on the undeniable reproductive urge of entire species. Her attitude is far from sentimental:

> I don't know what it is about fecundity that so
> appalls. I suppose it is the teeming evidence that
> birth and growth, which we value, are ubiquitous
> and blind, that life itself is so astonishingly cheap,
> that nature is as careless as it is bountiful, and
> that with extravagance goes a crushing waste that
> will one day include our own cheap lives. (160)

The cheapness and brutality of life are problems Dillard wrestles with, wondering which is "amiss": the world, a "monster," or human beings, with their "excessive emotions" (177-78). No matter how hard she tries to leave human society, Dillard has no choice but to "bring human values to the creek" (179). The violent, seemingly pointless birth and death of all life are, spiritually,

[Annotations:]

Combination of quotation and Haley's own analysis (next four paragraphs) interprets and synthesizes Dillard's ideas

Mixture of summary and quotation provides context and keeps quotations trim

Discussion of physical identity of all creatures: death and birth

Comment on quotation advises reader what to look for

Quotations, including some long ones set off from the text, convey Dillard's voice as well as her ideas

Discussion of spiritual identity of all creatures

Haley 4

two branches of the same creek, the creek that

waters the world. . . . We could have planned

things more mercifully, perhaps, but our plan

would never get off the drawing board until we

agreed to the very compromising terms that are

the only ones that being offers. (180)

Haley's interpretation of Dillard's ideas

Resolution of Dillard's concerns

For Dillard, accepting the monstrousness as well as the beauty of "being" is the price all living things pay for freedom.

In "The Waters of Separation," the final chapter of Pilgrim, Dillard writes about a winged maple key, or seed. At this point in the book, the critic Sandra Humble Johnson notes, Dillard "has been humbled and emptied; she can no longer apply effort to her search for meaning in a parasitic world" (4). It is the winter solstice—the shortest day of the year. And then Dillard spies the maple key descending to earth and germination. "It rose, just before it would have touched a thistle, and hovered pirouetting in one spot, then twirled on and finally came to rest" (267). The key moved, says Dillard, "like a creature muscled and vigorous, or a creature spread thin to that other wind, the wind of the spirit . . . , a generous, unending breath" (268). Dillard vows to see the maple key in all of the earth and in herself. "If I am a maple key falling, at least I can twirl" (268).

Conclusion: ties together divergent critical views, environmental theme, and Dillard's work

According to the critic John Becker, "Annie Dillard does not walk out on ordinary life in order to bear witness against it"; instead, she uses the distance from other people "to make meaning out of the grotesque disjointedness of man and nature" (408). Gary McIlroy says, nonetheless, that Dillard "does not succeed in encompassing within her vision any but the most fragmentary consequences for society at large" (116). Possibly both are correct. In Pilgrim at Tinker Creek, Annie Dillard suggests a vision of identity among all living things

Haley 6

Works Cited

Becker, John E. "Science and the Sacred: From Walden to
Tinker Creek." Thought: A Review of Culture and Idea
62 (1989): 400-13.

Dillard, Annie. Pilgrim at Tinker Creek. New York: Harper,
1974.

Johnson, Sandra Humble. The Space Between: Literary
Epiphany in the Work of Annie Dillard. Kent: Kent State
UP, 1992.

McIlroy, Gary. "Pilgrim at Tinker Creek and the Social Legacy of
Walden." South Atlantic Quarterly 85.2 (1996): 111-16.

Suh, Grace. "Ideas Are Tough, Irony Is Easy." Yale Herald
Online 4 Oct. 2005. 22 Jan. 2006 <http://
yaleherald.com/archive/xxii/10.4.05/ae/dillard.html>.

Welty, Eudora. Rev. of Pilgrim at Tinker Creek, by Annie Dil-
lard. New York Times Book Review 24 Mar. 1974: 36-37.
ProQuest Historical Newspapers. ProQuest. Santa Clara U,
Orradre Lib. 20 Jan. 2006 <http://proquest.umi.com>.

COLLABORATIVE LEARNING

ANALYZING THE PAPERS

Break students into four groups and have each group compare one of the following aspects of Begay's and Haley's papers: rhetorical strategy, structure, appropriateness of sources, and introduction of borrowed material.

COMPUTER ACTIVITY

HYPERTEXT COMMENTARY

The numbered comments that go with Begay's paper and the marginal comments on Haley's paper can provide your students with a model of how readers (including you) evaluate papers. They can practice this sort of holistic critique and commentary on one another's papers. Have them trade computer files of their papers with a partner. Have each partner provide commentary on the other's paper, using the commentary in this chapter as a model. They can either insert comments (highlighted or in a different color) directly into the text, or they can use the Comment function of their word processor.

RESOURCES AND IDEAS

Soles, Derek. "Grading as a Teaching Strategy." *Teaching English in the Two-Year College* 29 (December 2001): 122–134. Grading supports process instruction when teachers grade drafts, grade with colleagues, comment in a positive and encouraging voice, and share with students their evaluative criteria.

Haley 5

that could inform modern humanity's efforts to thrive in harmony with its environment, but she does not make the leap to practicalities. Life, she says, "is a faint tracing on the surface of a mystery. . . . We must somehow take a wider view, look at the whole landscape, really see it, and describe what's going on here" (9). The description, and acting on it, may take generations. As we proceed, however, we may be guided by Dillard's efforts to mend the disjointedness, to see that human beings and maple keys alike twirl equally.

PART 10

Writing in the Academic Disciplines

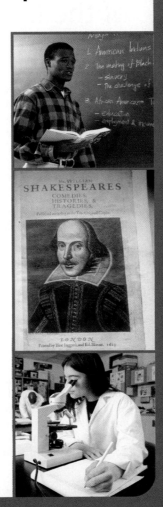

mycomplab

Please visit MyCompLab at *www.mycomplab.com* for more on the writing process.

HIGHLIGHTS

Students in their first semester of college are already learning that they will have to write in most of their classes, not just in their English classes. This new pressure can be overwhelming because students most likely will be required to use writing to show their professors what they know. Chapter 49 introduces Part 10 by reminding students that writing can be a powerful tool for learning in all disciplines. While each discipline has its own conventions and expectations, students should see that the foundations of each lie in critical thinking, reading, and writing and in the process of communicating what has been learned. Chapters 50–53 discuss conventions for writing and documentation in specific disciplines and present sample student papers as illustrations.

A WRITER'S PERSPECTIVE

If no one knows what you have done, then you have done nothing.
—ATTRIBUTED TO MICHEL DE MONTAIGNE

RESOURCES AND IDEAS

Bartholomae, David. "Inventing the University." *When a Writer Can't Write*. Ed. Mike Rose. New York: Guilford, 1985. 134–65. For Bartholomae, mastering the various specialized discourses of the academic community is an essential part of being a college student but is also a gradual process that is likely to pass through several stages, each more closely approximating the work of thinking and writing that characterizes a discipline.

Fulwiler, Toby, and Art Young, eds. *Programs That Work: Models and Methods for Writing Across the Curriculum*. Upper Montclair: Boynton/ Cook, 1990. Teachers describe how writing has

COMPANION WEB SITE

See page IAE-61 for companion Web site content description.

CHAPTER 49

Working with the Goals and Requirements of the Disciplines

Chapter 6 outlines the general concerns of subject, purpose, and audience that figure in most academic writing situations. The disciplines have more in common as well: methods of gathering evidence, kinds of assignments, scholarly tools, language conventions, and styles for source citations and document formats. This chapter introduces these common goals and requirements. The following chapters then distinguish the disciplines along the same lines, focusing on literature (Chapter 50), other humanities (51), the social sciences (52), and the natural and applied sciences (53).

49a Using methods and evidence

The **methodology** of a discipline is the way its practitioners study their subjects—that is, how they proceed when investigating the answers to questions. Methodology relates to the way practitioners analyze evidence and ideas. For instance, a literary critic and a social historian would probably approach Shakespeare's *Hamlet* quite differently: the literary critic might study the play for a theme among its poetic images; the historian might examine the play's relation to Shakespeare's context—England at the turn of the seventeenth century.

Whatever their approach, academic writers do not compose entirely out of their personal experience. Rather, they combine the evidence of their experience with that appropriate to the discipline, drawing well-supported conclusions about their subjects. The evidence of the discipline comes from research like that described in Chapters 42–44—from primary or secondary sources.

http://www.ablongman.com/littlebrown ▶

Visit the companion Web site for more help with writing in the academic disciplines.

Guidelines for academic writers

- Become familiar with the methodology and the kinds of evidence for the discipline in which you are writing.
- Analyze the special demands of each assignment. The questions you set out to answer, the assertions you wish to support, will govern how you choose your sources and evidence.
- Become familiar with the discipline's specialized tools and language.
- Use the discipline's style for source citations and document format.

- **Primary sources** are firsthand or original accounts, such as historical documents, works of art, and reports on experiments that the writer has conducted. When you use primary sources, you conduct original research, generating your own evidence. You might use your analysis of a painting as evidence for an interpretation of the painting. Or you might use data from your own survey of students to support your conclusions about students' attitudes.
- **Secondary sources** are books and articles written *about* primary sources. Much academic writing requires that you use such sources to spark, extend, or support your own ideas, as when you review the published opinions on your subject before contributing conclusions from your original research.

49b Understanding writing assignments

For most academic writing, your primary purpose will be either to explain something to your readers or to persuade them to accept your conclusions. To achieve your purpose, you will adapt your writing process to the writing situation, particularly to your readers' likely expectations for evidence and how you use it. Most assignments will contain key words that imply some of these expectations—words such as *compare, define, analyze,* and *illustrate* that express customary ways of thinking about and organizing a vast range of subjects. Pages 91–100 and 145 explore these so-called patterns of development. You should be aware of them and alert to the wording in assignments that directs you to use them.

49c Using tools and language

When you write in an academic discipline, you use the scholarly tools of that discipline, particularly its periodical indexes. In

TRANSPARENCY MASTER 49.1

been incorporated throughout the disciplines at their fourteen institutions nationwide.

Herrington, Anne, and Charles Moran, eds. *Writing, Teaching, and Learning in the Disciplines.* New York: MLA, 1992. The essays in this collection examine the "history, theory, practice, and prospects" of writing across the curriculum.

Kerr, Nancy H., and Madeleine Picciotto. "Linked Composition Courses: Effects on Student Performance." *Journal of Teaching Writing* 11.1 (1992): 105–28. The authors use a case study at Oglethorpe University to show the pros and cons of linking writing courses to introductory courses in the disciplines—a currently popular WAC approach.

Walvoord, Barbara E. "The Future of WAC." *College English* 58.1 (1996): 58–79. Walvoord, a long-time WAC program administrator, examines the challenges facing this "movement," including its relationship to other programs and institutions and its role in assessment.

Wiley, Mark. "The Popularity of Formulaic Writing (and Why We Need to Resist)." *English Journal* 62 (September 2000): 61–67. Wiley argues that some instruction in formulaic writing is appropriate because many standardized tests require the extemporaneous writing of an essay.

COLLABORATIVE LEARNING

CLARIFYING ASSIGNMENTS

Many students have trouble identifying the primary expectations of some assignments. It is important for students to learn to read assignments carefully and to learn to ask teachers for more information when the assignment is unclear. Have students bring in paper assignments from previous and current courses. Choose a selection of assignments from various disciplines and photocopy them for the class. Then ask students to work in small groups to highlight the primary expectations of each assignment, consider the goal implied by the assignment, and make lists of additional questions that might help clarify each assignment further. As groups present their findings, you might also generate a discussion of the similarities and differences in expectations across the disciplines.

A WRITER'S PERSPECTIVE

Has not every one of us struggled for words, although the connection between "things" was already clear?

—ALBERT EINSTEIN

DISCIPLINE STYLES

Divide students into groups according to their intended majors (humanities majors, business majors, and so on). Send them to the library to survey professional journals in their intended fields and discover what style(s) of documentation these journals require. (The style is often found in an "Instructions to Authors" section, usually located somewhere near the table of contents.) Ask groups to report their discoveries to the class.

RESOURCES AND IDEAS

Anderson, Worth, et al. "Cross-Curricular Underlife: A Collaborative Report on Ways with Academic Words." *College Composition and Communication* 41 (1990): 11–36. A research project by faculty and students revealed that the content of a typical first-year composition course had little in common with the type of writing expected in introductory courses within the disciplines.

Astin, Alexander. *What Matters in College?* San Francisco: Jossey-Bass, 1993. Astin argues that both the number of writing courses students take and the number of courses that require writing strongly affect students' general knowledge, skills, and success in college.

McCleod, Susan and Elaine Maimon. "Clearing the Air: WAC Myths and Realities." *College English* 62 (May 2000):573–583. The authors provide an excellent summary of why WAC programs fail and discuss model programs.

Palmquist, Mike. "A Brief History of Computer Support for Writing Centers and Writing-Across-the Curriculum Programs." *Computers and Composition* 20.4 (2003): 395–413. Palmquist reviews the literature on the efficacy or lack thereof of the use of computers in writing centers and WAC programs.

addition, you may use the aids developed by practitioners of the discipline for efficiently and effectively approaching research, conducting it, and recording the findings. Many of these aids, such as a system for recording evidence from sources, are discussed in Chapters 42–44 and can be adapted to any discipline. Other aids are discussed in the following chapters.

Pay close attention to the texts assigned in a course and any materials given out in class, for these items may introduce you to valuable references and other research aids, and they will use the specialized language of the discipline. This specialized language allows practitioners to write to each other both efficiently and precisely. It also furthers certain concerns of the discipline, such as accuracy and objectivity. Scientists, for example, try to interpret their data objectively, so they avoid *undoubtedly, obviously,* and other words that slant conclusions. Some of the language conventions like this one are discussed in the following chapters. As you gain experience in a particular discipline, keep alert for such conventions and train yourself to follow them.

49d Following styles for source citations and document format

Most disciplines publish journals that require authors to use a certain style for source citations and a certain format for documents. In turn, most instructors in a discipline require the same of students writing papers for their courses.

When you cite your sources, you tell readers which ideas and information you borrowed and where they can find your sources. Thus source citations indicate how much knowledge you have and how broad and deep your research was. They also help you avoid **plagiarism,** the serious offense of presenting the words, ideas, and data of others as if they were your own. (See Chapter 45 on avoiding plagiarism.)

Document format includes such features as margins and the placement of the title. But it also extends to special elements of the manuscript, such as tables or an abstract, that may be required by the discipline.

Chapters 51–53 direct you to the style guides published by different disciplines and outline the requirements of the ones used most often. If your instructor does not require a particular style, use that of the Modern Language Association, which is described and illustrated at length in Chapter 47.

CHAPTER 50

Reading and Writing About Literature

By Sylvan Barnet

Why read literature? Let's approach this question indirectly by asking why people *write* literature. A thousand years ago a Japanese writer, Lady Murasaki, offered an answer. Here is one of her characters talking about what motivates a writer:

> Again and again something in one's own life or in the life around one will seem so important that one cannot bear to let it pass into oblivion. There must never come a time, the writer feels, when people do not know about this.

When we read certain works—Murasaki's *The Tale of Genji* is one of them—we share this feeling; we are caught up in the writer's world, whether it is the Denmark of Shakespeare's *Hamlet* or the America of Toni Morrison's *Beloved*. We read literature because it gives us an experience that seems important, usually an experience that is both new and familiar. A common way of putting this is to say that reading broadens us and helps us understand our own experience.

50a Using the methods and evidence of literary analysis

When we read nonliterary writings, it may be enough to get the gist of the argument; in fact, we may have to peer through a good deal of wordiness to find the heart of the matter—say, three claims on behalf of capital punishment. But when we read a story, a poem, or a play, we must pay extremely close attention to what might be called the feel of the words. For instance, the word *woods* in Robert Frost's "Stopping by Woods on a Snowy Evening" has a rural, folksy quality that *forest* doesn't have, and many such small distinctions contribute to the poem's effect.

http://www.ablongman.com/littlebrown ▶

Visit the companion Web site for more help with reading and writing about literature.

mycomplab 2.0

Please visit MyCompLab at *www.mycomplab.com* for more on the writing process.

HIGHLIGHTS

In classes where literature is studied, there's a temptation to spend more time talking about literature and less time writing about it, which can be counterproductive to the goals of a writing class. To keep students developing positively, this chapter stresses using the processes of critical reading, thinking, and writing skills as a way of analyzing imaginative writing. It also focuses on helping students to transfer the skills they have worked on throughout their writing course to other courses and purposes. The chapter covers different kinds of writing assignments about literature and points students to a wide variety of library and online resources for research. It also takes students through the process of researching and drafting essays about literature and includes sample student essays on works of fiction, poetry, and drama.

RESOURCES AND IDEAS

Bawarshi, Anis. "The Genre Function." *College English* 62 (2000): 335–60. Bawarshi explores genre as constitutive of texts, authors, readers, and social identity and argues against the privileging of literary texts by teachers.

Gould, Christopher. "Literature in the Basic Writing Course: A Bibliographic Survey." *College English* 49 (1987): 558–74. Gould provides a survey of "easily accessible materials that relate to the use of literature" in introductory courses.

(*continued on p. 736*)

COMPANION WEB SITE

See page IAE-61 for companion Web site content description.

Hayes, John R., Jill A. Hatch, and Christine M. Silk. "Does Holistic Assessment Predict Writing Performance? Estimating the Consistency of Student Performance on Holistically Scored Writing Assignments." *Written Communication* 17 (January 2000): 3–26. The authors report on their study that indicates considerable divergence in the grades of some 800 student essays, holistically graded by experts.

Lindemann, Erika. "Freshman Composition: No Place for Literature." *College English* 55 (1993): 311–16. Lindemann warns that using literature in composition classes may lead to a de-emphasis on student writing; she includes useful advice for class design.

Lynn, Steven. *Texts and Contexts: Writing About Literature with Critical Theory.* New York: HarperCollins, 1994. Lynn introduces a number of critical approaches from New Criticism through deconstruction to feminist studies, and he brings all methods to bear on a selected group of texts to demonstrate how they might "open up" texts for students.

Reilly, Jill M., et al. "The Effects of Prewriting on Literary Interpretation." ERIC, 1986. ED 276 058. Reilly shows how focused prewriting exercises can lead students to write more effectively about literature.

Tate, Gary. "A Place for Literature in Freshman Composition." *College English* 55 (1993): 317–21. Tate argues that using literature makes student writers more aware of the resources implicit in language.

NO "RIGHT" OR "WRONG"

Students tend to have tunnel vision about literary interpretation, believing there's only one "right way" to read a work. In guiding their reading and response, encourage them to see the multiple possibilities implicit in literary works. You might ask them to compose point-counterpoint readings of texts or to use a text like Steven Lynn's *Texts and Contexts* (reference above) to construct a spectrum of responses to the literature they are reading. A consistent use of group workshops in which students discuss their varying responses to a literary text can also help students to recognize the multiplicity of possible responses.

Literary authors are concerned with presenting human experience concretely, with *showing* rather than *telling*. Consider the following proverb and an unmemorable paraphrase of it:

> A rolling stone gathers no moss.
>
> If a rock is always moving around, vegetation won't have a chance to grow on it.

The familiar original offers a small but complete world: hard (stone) and soft (moss), inorganic and organic, at rest and in motion. The original is also shapely: each noun (*stone, moss*) has one syllable, and each word of motion (*rolling, gathers*) has two syllables, with the accent on the first of the two. Such relationships unify the proverb into a pleasing whole that stays in our minds.

1 Reading a work of literature

Reading literature critically involves interacting with a text. The techniques complement those for critically reading any text, so if you haven't read Chapter 8 on such reading, you should do so. Responding critically is a matter not of making negative judgments but of analyzing the parts, interpreting their meanings, seeing how the parts relate, and evaluating significance or quality.

■ Previewing and responding

You can preview a literary text somewhat as you can preview any other text. You may gauge the length of the text to determine whether you can read it in one sitting, and you may read a biographical note to learn about the author. In a literary text, however, you won't find aids such as section headings or summaries that can make previewing other texts especially informative. You have to dive into the words themselves.

Do write while reading. If you own the book you are reading, don't hesitate to underline or highlight passages that especially interest you for one reason or another. Don't hesitate to annotate the margins, indicating your pleasures, displeasures, and uncertainties with remarks such as *Nice detail* or *Do we need this long description?* or *Not believable.* If you don't own the book, make these notes on separate sheets or on your computer.

An effective way to interact with a text is to keep a **reading journal**. A journal is not a diary in which you record your doings; instead, it is a place to develop and store your reflections on what you read, such as an answer to a question you may have posed in the margin of the text. You could make an entry in the form of a letter to the author or from one character to another. In many literature courses, students collaborate to develop their understanding of a literary work. In such a case, you may want to use your journal to reflect on what other students have said—for instance, why your opinion differs so much from someone else's.

You can keep a reading journal in a notebook or on your computer. Some readers prefer a two-column format like that illustrated on page 154, with summaries, paraphrases, and quotations from the text on the left and with their own responses to these passages on the right. Or you may prefer a less structured format like that illustrated on page 740.

■ Reading a sample story

Here is a very short story by Kate Chopin (1851–1904). (The last name is pronounced in the French way, something like "show pan.") Following the story are a student's annotations and journal entry on the story.

Kate Chopin

The Story of an Hour

Knowing that Mrs. Mallard was afflicted with a heart trouble, great care was taken to break to her as gently as possible the news of her husband's death.

It was her sister Josephine who told her, in broken sentences, veiled hints that revealed in half concealing. Her husband's friend Richards was there, too, near her. It was he who had been in the newspaper office when intelligence of the railroad disaster was received, with Brently Mallard's name leading the list of "killed." He had only taken the time to assure himself of its truth by a second telegram, and had hastened to forestall any less careful, less tender friend in bearing the sad message.

She did not hear the story as many women have heard the same, with a paralyzed inability to accept its significance. She wept at once with sudden, wild abandonment, in her sister's arms. When the storm of grief had spent itself she went away to her room alone. She would have no one follow her.

There stood, facing the open window, a comfortable, roomy armchair. Into this she sank, pressed down by a physical exhaustion that haunted her body and seemed to reach into her soul.

She could see in the open square before her house the tops of trees that were all aquiver with the new spring life. The delicious breath of rain was in the air. In the street below a peddler was crying his wares. The notes of a distant song which some one was singing reached her faintly, and countless sparrows were twittering in the eaves.

There were patches of blue sky showing here and there through the clouds that had met and piled one above the other in the west facing her window.

She sat with her head thrown back upon the cushion of the chair quite motionless, except when a sob came up into her throat and shook her, as a child who has cried itself to sleep continues to sob in its dreams.

She was young, with a fair, calm face, whose lines bespoke repression and even a certain strength. But now there was a dull stare in her eyes, whose gaze was fixed away off yonder on one of those patches of blue sky. It was not a glance of reflection, but rather indicated a suspension of intelligent thought.

There was something coming to her and she was waiting for it, fearfully. What was it? She did not know; it was too subtle and elusive to name. But she felt it creeping out of the sky, reaching toward her through the sounds, the scents, the color that filled the air.

Now her bosom rose and fell tumultuously. She was beginning to recognize this thing that was approaching to possess her, and she was striving to beat it back with her will—as powerless as her two white slender hands would have been.

When she abandoned herself a little whispered word escaped her slightly parted lips. She said it over and over under her breath: "Free, free, free!" The vacant stare and the look of terror that had followed it went from her eyes. They stayed keen and bright. Her pulses beat fast, and the coursing blood warmed and relaxed every inch of her body.

She did not stop to ask if it were not a monstrous joy that held her. A clear and exalted perception enabled her to dismiss the suggestion as trivial.

She knew that she would weep again when she saw the kind, tender hands folded in death; the face that had never looked save with love upon her, fixed and gray and dead. But she saw beyond that bitter moment a long procession of years to come that would belong to her absolutely. And she opened and spread her arms out to them in welcome.

There would be no one to live for her during those coming years; she would live for herself. There would be no powerful will bending her in the blind persistence with which men and women believe they have a right to impose a private will upon a fellow creature. A kind intention or a cruel intention made the act seem no less a crime as she looked upon it in that brief moment of illumination.

And yet she had loved him—sometimes. Often she had not. What did it matter! What could love, the unsolved mystery, count for in face of this possession of self-assertion which she suddenly recognized as the strongest impulse of her being.

"Free! Body and soul free!" she kept whispering.

Josephine was kneeling before the closed door with her lips to the keyhole, imploring for admission. "Louise, open the door! I beg; open the door—you will make yourself ill. What are you doing, Louise? For heaven's sake open the door."

"Go away. I am not making myself ill." No; she was drinking in the very elixir of life through that open window.

Her fancy was running riot along those days ahead of her. Spring days, and summer days, and all sorts of days that would be her own. She breathed a quick prayer that life might be long. It was only yesterday she had thought with a shudder that life might be long.

She arose at length and opened the door to her sister's importunities. There was a feverish triumph in her eyes, and she carried herself unwittingly like a goddess of Victory. She clasped her sister's waist and together they descended the stairs. Richards stood waiting for them at the bottom.

Some one was opening the front door with a latchkey. It was Brently Mallard who entered, a little travel-stained, composedly carrying his grip-sack and umbrella. He had been far from the scene of accident, and did not even know there had been one. He stood amazed at Josephine's piercing cry; at Richards' quick motion to screen him from the view of his wife.

But Richards was too late.

When the doctors came they said she had died of heart disease—of joy that kills.

◼ Following a student's work

In this chapter we'll follow the analysis and writing of a student, Janet Vong, to see one approach to Chopin's story. Vong first annotated the story while reading it. The opening five paragraphs, with her notes, appear below:

Knowing that Mrs. Mallard was afflicted with a heart trouble, great care was taken to break to her as gently as possible the news of her husband's death.

> *"heart disease" at end of story*

It was her sister Josephine who told her, in broken sentences, veiled hints that revealed in half concealing. Her husband's friend Richards was there, too, near her. It was he who had been in the newspaper office when intelligence of the railroad disaster was received, with Brently Mallard's name leading the list of "killed." He had only taken the time to assure himself of its truth by a second telegram, and had hastened to forestall any less careful, less tender friend in bearing the sad message.

> *Too hasty, it turns out*

She did not hear the story as many women have heard the same, with a paralyzed inability to accept its significance. She wept at once with sudden, wild abandonment, in her sister's arms. When the storm of grief had spent itself she went away to her room alone. She would have no one follow her.

> *Would men have heard differently? Is au. sexist?*

> *←old-fashioned style*

There stood, facing the open window, a comfortable, roomy armchair. Into this she sank, pressed down by a physical exhaustion that haunted her body and seemed to reach into her soul.

She could see in the open square before her house the tops of trees that were all aquiver with the new spring life. The delicious breath of rain was in the air. In the street below a peddler was crying his wares. The notes of a distant song which some one was singing reached her faintly, and countless sparrows were twittering in the eaves.

> *Notices spring: odd in a story of death*

Writing in her journal, Vong posed questions about the story—critical points, curiosities about characters, possible implications:

LOOKING BACK

Remind students of the reasons they have been keeping journals throughout your course. You may want to encourage them to review 2a-1 as they begin keeping a reading journal.

Title nothing special. What might be a better title?
Could a woman who loved her husband be so heartless? <u>Is</u> she heartless? <u>Did</u> she love him?
What are (were) Louise's feelings about her husband?
Did she want too much? <u>What</u> did she want?
Could this story happen <u>today</u>? Feminist interpretation?
Sister (Josephine)—a busybody?
Tricky ending—but maybe it could be true.
"And yet she had loved him—sometimes. Often she had not." Why does one love someone "sometimes"?
Irony: plot has reversal. Are characters ironic too?

Vong's journal entry illustrates brainstorming—the discovery technique of listing ideas (or questions) however they occur, without editing (see pp. 21–22). Another productive journal technique is focused freewriting—concentrating on a single issue (such as one of Vong's questions) and writing nonstop for a set amount of time, again without editing (p. 20).

2 Analyzing a work of literature

Like any discipline, the study of literature involves particular frameworks of analysis—particular ways of seeing literary works that help determine what parts the critical reader identifies and how he or she interprets them. For instance, some critics look at a literary work mainly as an artifact of the particular time and culture in which it was created, while other critics emphasize the work's effect on its readers.

This chapter emphasizes so-called formalist criticism, which focuses on a literary work primarily as something to be understood in itself. This critical framework engages the reader immediately in the work of literature, without requiring extensive historical or cultural background, and introduces the conventional elements of literature that all critical approaches discuss, even though they view the elements differently. The box on the next two pages lists these elements—plot, characters, setting, and so on—and offers questions about each one that can help you think constructively and imaginatively about what you read.

One significant attribute of a literary work is its *meaning,* or what we can interpret to be its meaning. Readers may well disagree over the persuasiveness of someone's argument, but they will rarely disagree over its meaning. With literature, however, disagreements over meaning occur all the time because (as we have seen) literature *shows* rather than *tells:* it gives us concrete images of imagined human experiences, but it usually does not say how we ought to understand the images.

Further, readers bring to their reading not only different critical views, as noted earlier, but also different personal experiences. A woman who has recently lost her husband may interpret "The Story

---

ANALYZING PASSAGES

Have students work in small groups to analyze a key passage from Kate Chopin's "The Story of an Hour." Ask each group to consider the appropriate questions provided by the handbook: Does the passage reveal a significant move in the plot? Does it explore a key development for one of the characters? What evidence of point of view and tone are available in the passage? Does it contain imagery or symbolism? Then have each group give their analysis of the passage. Where student readings differ markedly, encourage those groups to find additional evidence for their readings.

FINDING THEMES

Divide the class into several groups and have each group brainstorm about the many themes that occur in a particular work. Choose Kate Chopin's "The Story of an Hour" or another short work from an anthology. Have each group explain its three favorite themes to the rest of the class, supplying evidence for each theme with one or two explicated passages from the piece.

Questions for a literary analysis

See later boxes for specific questions on fiction (pp. 751–52), poetry (p. 753), and drama (pp. 755–56).

Plot

The relationships and patterns of events. Even a poem has a plot, such as a change in mood from bitterness to resignation.

What actions happen?
What conflicts occur?
How do the events connect to each other and to the whole?

Characters

The people the author creates, including the narrator of a story or the speaker of a poem.

Who are the principal people in the work?
How do they interact?
What do their actions, words, and thoughts reveal about their personalities and the personalities of others?
Do the characters stay the same, or do they change? Why?

Point of view

The perspective or attitude of the speaker in a poem or the voice who tells a story. The point of view may be **first person** (a participant, using *I*) or **third person** (an outsider, using *he, she, it, they*). A first-person narrator may be a major or a minor character in the narrative and may be **reliable** or **unreliable** (unable to report events wholly or accurately). A third-person narrator may be **omniscient** (knows what goes on in all characters' minds), **limited** (knows what goes on in the mind of only one or two characters), or **objective** (knows only what is external to the characters).

Who is the narrator (or the speaker of a poem)?
How does the narrator's point of view affect the narrative?

Tone

The narrator's or speaker's attitude, perceived through the words (for instance, joyful, bitter, or confident).

What tone (or tones) do you hear? If there is a change, how do you account for it?
Is there an ironic contrast between the narrator's tone (for instance, confidence) and what you take to be the author's attitude (for instance, pity for human overconfidence)?

Imagery

Word pictures or details involving the senses: sight, sound, touch, smell, taste.

What images does the writer use? What senses do they draw on?
What patterns are evident in the images (for instance, religious or commercial images)?
What is the significance of the imagery?

(continued)

RESOURCES AND IDEAS

Biddle, Arthur W., and Toby Fulwiler, eds. *Reading, Writing, and the Study of Literature.* New York: McGraw, 1989. This collection of essays details many ways of introducing students to various methods of literary interpretation; the authors provide extensive bibliographies.

Lentricchia, Frank, and Thomas McLaughlin. *Critical Terms for Literary Study.* Chicago: U of Chicago P, 1989. The authors have compiled twenty-two cogent essays defining key terms in light of contemporary theory.

Rockas, Leo. *Ways In: Analyzing and Responding to Literature.* Upper Montclair: Boynton/Cook, 1984. Rockas offers students a number of ways of beginning the work of literary analysis, providing numerous examples and exercises.

COMPUTER ACTIVITY

CONTINUATIONS

Post the opening paragraph of a published short story on the class network and ask students to continue the story, keeping in mind the expectations about plot, character, setting, and tone that have been set up by that opening paragraph. Have students "publish" the resulting stories on the network, and lead a discussion about the different choices that various students made in their continuations, the elements in the original paragraph that they picked up on or discarded, and the extent to which the tone of the original was maintained or parodied. Encourage students to talk about the elements that they noticed in the original paragraph as they created their continuations.

Questions for a literary analysis

(continued)

Symbolism

Concrete things standing for larger and more abstract ideas. For instance, the American flag may symbolize freedom, a tweeting bird may symbolize happiness, or a dead flower may symbolize mortality.

What symbols does the author use? What do they seem to signify?
How does the symbolism relate to the other elements of the work, such as character or theme?

Setting

The place where the action happens.

What does the locale contribute to the work?
Are scene shifts significant?

Form

The shape or structure of the work.

What *is* the form? (For example, a story might divide sharply in the middle, moving from happiness to sorrow.)
What parts of the work does the form emphasize, and why?

Theme

The central idea, a conception of human experience suggested by the work as a whole. Theme is neither plot (what happens) nor subject (such as mourning or marriage). Rather it is what the author says with that plot about that subject.

Can you state the theme in a sentence? For instance, you might state the following about Kate Chopin's "The Story of an Hour": *Happiness depends partly on freedom.*
Do certain words, passages of dialog or description, or situations seem to represent the theme most clearly?
How do the work's elements combine to develop the theme?

Appeal

The degree to which the work pleases you.

What do you especially like or dislike about the work?
Do you think your responses are unique, or would they be common to most readers? Why?

You can download these questions from *ablongman.com/littlebrown*. Copy the questions for each work you read, and answer the questions in writing.

of an Hour" differently from most other readers. Or a story that bores a reader at age fifteen may deeply move him at twenty-five. The words on the page remain the same, but their meaning changes.

In writing about literature, then, we can offer only our *interpretation* of meaning rather than *the* meaning. Still, most people agree that there are limits to interpretation: it must be supported by evidence that a reasonable reader finds at least plausible if not totally convincing. For instance, the student who says that in "The Story of an Hour" Mrs. Mallard does not die but merely falls into a deathlike trance goes beyond the permissible limits because the story offers no evidence for such an interpretation.

3 Using evidence in writing about literature

The evidence for a literary analysis always comes from at least one primary source (the work or works being discussed) and may come from secondary sources (critical and historical works). (See p. 733 for more on primary and secondary sources.) For example, if you were writing about Chopin's "The Story of an Hour," the primary material would be the story itself, and the secondary material (if you used it) might be critical studies of Chopin.

The bulk of your evidence in writing about literature will usually be quotations from the work, although you will occasionally summarize or paraphrase as well (see pp. 617–20). When using quotations, keep in mind the criteria in the box on page 747.

Your instructor will probably tell you if you are expected to consult secondary sources for an assignment. They can help you understand a writer's work, but your primary concern should always be the work itself, not what critics A, B, and C say about it. In general, then, quote or summarize secondary material sparingly. And always cite your sources.

50b Understanding writing assignments in literature

A literature instructor may ask you to write one or more of the following types of papers. The first two are the most common.

- **A literary analysis paper:** Give your ideas about a work of literature—your interpretation of its meaning, context, or representations based on specific words, characters, and events.
- **A literary research paper:** Combine analysis of a literary work with research about the work and perhaps its author. A literary research paper draws on both primary and secondary sources. For example, you might respond to what scholars have written about the symbolism in a play by Tennessee Williams, or you might research medieval England as a way to understand the context of Chaucer's *Canterbury Tales*.
- **A personal response or reaction paper:** Give your thoughts and feelings about a work of literature. For example, you might

compare a novel's description of a city with your experience of the same city.

- **A book review:** Give a summary of a book and a judgment about the book's value. In a review of a novel, for example, you might discuss whether the plot is interesting, the characters are believable, and the writing style is enjoyable. You might also compare the work to other works by the author.
- **A theater review:** Give your reactions to and opinions about a theatrical performance. You might summarize the plot of the play, describe the characters, identify the prominent themes, evaluate the other elements (writing, performances, direction, stage setting), and make a recommendation to potential viewers.

50c Using the tools and language of literary analysis

1 Writing tools

The fundamental tool for writing about literature is reading critically. Asking analytical questions such as those on pages 741–42 can help you focus your ideas. In addition, keeping a reading journal can help you develop your thoughts. Keep careful, well-organized notes on any research materials. Finally, discuss the work with others who have read it. They may offer reactions and insights that will help you shape your own ideas.

2 Language considerations

Use the present tense of verbs to describe both the action in a literary work (*Brently Mallard suddenly appears*) and the writing of an author (*Chopin briefly describes the view* or *In his essay he comments that . . .*). Use the past tense to describe events that actually occurred in the past (*Chopin was born in 1851*).

Some instructors discourage students from using the first-person *I* (as in *I felt sorry for the character*) in writing about literature. At least use *I* sparingly to avoid sounding egotistical. Rephrase sentences to avoid using *I* unnecessarily—for instance, *The character evokes the reader's sympathy.*

3 Research sources

In addition to these resources on literature, you may also want to consult some on other humanities (pp. 761–64).

- **Specialized encyclopedias, dictionaries, and bibliographies**
  Bibliographical Guide to the Study of the Literature of the USA
  Cambridge Bibliography of English Literature
  Cambridge Encyclopedia of Language
  Cambridge Guide to Literature in English

THE MYSTIQUE OF LITERATURE

Most students will need to be convinced that critical thinking, reading, and writing skills can be transferred to literature. Students sometimes acquire the attitude that literature is somehow "untouchable," that it is "special," different from other works they read. Work through Janet Vong's critical strategies (pp. 739–40) with your students to help them understand how the skills they've developed will enable them to read and write about literature.

COLLABORATIVE LEARNING

TENSES

Students sometimes have trouble making their prose conform to the conventions of tense usage in critical writing about literature. To get them used to these conventions, have students review each other's drafts and make suggestions for revision of tense usage.

COLLABORATIVE LEARNING

SOURCES

To help students become familiar with the literary research sources listed in the text (pp. 744–45), have each student look up one source (either a library source or a Web source) and make a brief presentation on it in class.

Dictionary of Literary Biography
Handbook to Literature
Literary Criticism Index
McGraw-Hill Encyclopedia of World Drama
MLA International Bibliography of Books and Articles on the Modern Languages and Literatures
New Princeton Encyclopedia of Poetry and Poetics
Oxford Companion to American Literature
Oxford Companion to the Theatre
Schomburg Center Guide to Black Literature from the Eighteenth Century to the Present

▪ Indexes

Abstracts of Folklore Studies
Dissertation Abstracts International (doctoral dissertations)
Humanities Index
Literary Criticism Index
MLA International Bibliography of Books and Articles on the Modern Languages and Literatures

▪ Book reviews

Book Review Digest
Book Review Index
Index to Book Reviews in the Humanities

▪ Web sources

For updates of these sources and URLs, visit *ablongman.com/ littlebrown*.

Alex Catalog of Electronic Texts (*infomotions.com/alex*)
EServer (*eserver.org*)
Internet Public Library: Online Literary Criticism (*ipl.org/div/litcrit*)
Key Sites on American Literature (*usinfo.state.gov/products/pubs/oal/ amlitweb.htm*)
Literary Index (*www.galenet.com/servlet/LitIndex*)
Literary Resources on the Net (*andromeda.rutgers.edu/~jlynch/Lit*)
Online Books Page (*online books.library.upenn.edu*)
Voice of the Shuttle: Drama, Theater, and Performance Art Studies (*vos.ucsb.edu/browse.asp?id=782*)
Voice of the Shuttle: Literature (*in English*) (*vos.ucsb.edu/ browse.asp?id=3*)
Voice of the Shuttle: Literatures (*Other than English*) (*vos.ucsb.edu/ browse.asp?id=2719*)

50d Citing sources and formatting documents in writing about literature

Unless your instructor specifies otherwise, use the style of the Modern Language Association (MLA), detailed in Chapter 47. In this style, parenthetical citations in the text of the paper refer to a list of works cited at the end. Sample papers illustrating this style appear in Chapter 48 as well as in this chapter.

Use MLA format for headings, margins, and other elements, as detailed on pages 687–89.

50e Drafting and revising a literary analysis

The process for writing a literary analysis is similar to that for any other kind of essay: once you've done the reading and thought about it, you need to focus your ideas, gather evidence, draft, and revise.

1 Conceiving a thesis

After reading, rereading, and making notes, you probably will be able to formulate a tentative thesis statement—an assertion of your main point, your argument. (For more on thesis statements, see pp. 27–31.) Clear the air by glancing over your notes and by jotting down a few especially promising ideas—brief statements of what you think your key points may be and their main support. One approach is to seek patterns in the work, such as recurring words, phrases, images, events, symbols, or other elements. (Go back to the work, if necessary, to expand the patterns your notes reveal.) Such patterns can help you see themes both in the work itself and in your ideas about it.

Considering Kate Chopin's "The Story of an Hour," Janet Vong at first explored the idea that Mrs. Mallard, the main character, was unrealistic and thus unconvincing. (See Vong's journal entry on p. 740.) But the more Vong examined the story and her notes, the more she was impressed by a pattern of ironies, or reversals, that actually helped to make Mrs. Mallard believable. In her journal Vong explored the idea that the many small reversals paved the way for Mrs. Mallard's own reversal from grief to joy:

> title? "Ironies in an Hour" (?) "An Hour of Irony" (?) "Kate Chopin's Irony" (?)
> thesis: irony at end is prepared for
> chief irony: Mrs. M. dies just as she is beginning to enjoy life
> smaller ironies:
>   1. "sad message" brings her joy
>   2. Richards is "too late" at end
>   3. Richards is too early at start
>   4. "joy that kills"
>   5. death brings joy and life

From these notes Vong developed her thesis statement:

> The irony of the ending is believable partly because it is consistent with earlier ironies in the story.

This thesis statement asserts a specific idea that can be developed and convincingly argued with evidence from Chopin's story. A good thesis statement will neither assert a fact (*Mrs. Mallard dies soon after hearing that her husband has died*) nor overgeneralize (*The story is an insult to women*).

2 Gathering evidence

In writing about literature, you use mainly evidence gathered from the work itself: quotations and sometimes paraphrases that support your ideas about the work. You can see examples of such quoting and paraphrasing in Janet Vong's final draft on pages 750–51. The box below offers guidelines for using quotations in literary analysis.

COLLABORATIVE LEARNING

PLOT SUMMARIES

Give your students a short story to read, and ask them to work in small groups to write a brief plot summary. See which group can come up with the most economical summary.

Guidelines for using quotations in literary analysis

- **Use quotations to support your assertions, not to pad the paper.** Quote at length only when necessary to your argument.
- **Specify how each quotation relates to your idea.** Introduce the quotation—for example, *At the outset Chopin conveys the sort of person Richards is:* ". . ." Sometimes, comment after the quotation. (See pages 623–28 for more on integrating quotations into your writing.)
- **Reproduce spelling, punctuation, capitalization, and all other features exactly as they appear in the source.** See page 483 for the use of brackets when you need to add something to a quotation, and see page 484 for the use of an ellipsis mark when you need to omit something from a quotation.
- **Document your sources.** See page 637.

You may wonder how much you should summarize the plot of the work. A brief plot summary can be helpful to readers who are unfamiliar with the work. Sometimes plot elements place your ideas in the context of the work or remind readers where your quotations come from. Plot elements may even be used as evidence, as Vong uses the ironic ending of the Chopin story. But plot summary is not literary analysis, and summary alone is not sufficient evidence to support a thesis. Keep any plot summaries brief and to the point.

For a literary research paper, evidence will come from the work itself and from secondary sources such as scholarly works and critical appraisals. The thesis and principal ideas of the paper must still be your own, but you may supplement your reading of the work with the views of respected scholars or critics. Sometimes you may choose to build your own argument in part by disputing others' views. However you draw on secondary sources, remember that they must be clearly identified and documented, even when you use your own words.

Note You can find student essays on the Web that may lead you to other sources or may suggest ideas you hadn't considered. If you want to use another student's paper as a secondary source, you must evaluate it with special care because it will not have passed through a reviewing process, as an article in a scholarly journal does. (See pp. 602–09 on evaluating online sources.) You must also, of course, clearly identify and document the source: borrowing other students' ideas or words without credit is plagiarism. (See pp. 629–37.)

3 Writing a draft

Drafting your essay is your opportunity to develop your thesis or to discover it if you haven't already. The draft below was actually Janet Vong's second: she deleted some digressions from her first draft and added more evidence for her points. The numbers in parentheses refer to the pages from which she drew the quotations. (See pp. 648–56 on this form of documentation.) Ask your instructor whether you should always give such citations, especially for a short poem or story like Chopin's.

Ironies in an Hour

After we know how the story turns out, if we reread it we find irony at the very start, as is true of many other stories. Mrs. Mallard's friends assume, mistakenly, that Mrs. Mallard was deeply in love with her husband, Brently Mallard. They take great care to tell her gently of his death. The friends mean well, and in fact they do well. They bring her an hour of life, an hour of freedom. They think their news is sad. Mrs. Mallard at first expresses grief when she hears the news, but soon she finds joy in it. So Richards's "sad message" (23), though sad in Richards's eyes, is in fact a happy message.

Among the ironic details is the statement that when Mallard entered the house, Richards tried to conceal him from Mrs. Mallard, but "Richards was too late" (24). This is ironic because earlier Richards "hastened" (23) to bring his sad message; if he had been too late at the start, Brently Mallard would have arrived at home first, and Mrs. Mallard's life would not have ended an hour later but would simply have gone on as it had been. Yet another irony at the end of the story is the diagnosis of the doctors. The doctors say she died of "heart disease—of joy that kills" (24). In one sense the doctors are right: Mrs. Mallard has experienced a great joy. But of course the doctors totally misunderstand the joy that kills her.

The central irony resides not in the well-intentioned but ironic actions of Richards, or in the unconsciously ironic words of the doctors, but in her own life.

She "sometimes" (24) loved her husband, but in a way she has been dead. Now, his apparent death brings her new life. This new life comes to her at the season of the year when "the tops of trees . . . were all aquiver with the new spring life" (23). But, ironically, her new life will last only an hour. She looks forward to "summer days" (24), but she will not see even the end of this spring day. Her years of marriage were ironic. They brought her a sort of living death instead of joy. Her new life is ironic, too. It grows out of her moment of grief for her supposedly dead husband, and her vision of a new life is cut short.

4 Revising and editing

As in other writing, use at least two drafts to revise and edit, so that you can attend separately to the big structural issues and the smaller surface problems. See pages 51 and 58–59 for general revision and editing checklists. The additional checklist below can help you with a literary analysis.

Checklist for revising a literary analysis

- **Title:** Does the title of your essay give the title and author of the work you discuss and also an idea of your approach to the work?
- **Introduction:** Does the introductory paragraph name the author and the title so that readers know exactly what work you are discussing? (Avoid opening sentences such as "In this story. . . .") Does the introduction state and develop your thesis a bit so that readers know where they will be going?
- **Organization:** How effective is the organization? The essay should not dwindle or become anticlimactic; rather, it should build up.
- **Quotations:** What evidence does each quotation provide? Do quotations let readers hear the author's voice?
- **Analysis vs. summary:** Is the essay chiefly devoted to analysis, not to summary? Summarize the plot only briefly and only to further your own ideas. A summary is not an essay.
- **Verb tenses:** Have you used the present tense of verbs to describe both the author's work and the action in the work (for example, *Chopin shows* or *Mrs. Mallard dies*)?
- **Evaluation:** How well will readers understand your evaluation of the work and what it is based on? Your evaluation may be implied (as in Janet Vong's essay on "The Story of an Hour"), or it may be explicit. In either case, give the reasons for judging the work to be effective or not, worth reading or not. It is not enough to express your likes or dislikes; readers need the support of specific evidence from the work.
- **Are all your sources documented in MLA style?**

You can download the checklist from *ablongman.com/littlebrown*. Using a duplicate, write out answers for each paper you revise.

COLLABORATIVE LEARNING

MODELS OF STUDENT WRITING

This final draft of Janet Vong's paper on Kate Chopin's "The Story of an Hour" is a fine model of the short literary analysis, and you may wish to spend some time discussing it with students. It features a creative thesis and a tightly organized, economical development. Students who have little experience writing about literature sometimes organize their papers to match the progression of the text they are analyzing instead of around the development of their thesis statements. If your students have this difficulty, they may find it particularly helpful to see that Vong's paper moves from the least important to the most important of her arguments and that in presenting evidence she moves back and forth from the beginning to the end of Chopin's story.

You might also want to use Chopin's story to talk about irony, a literary device students sometimes have difficulty identifying. Vong does a particularly nice job of discussing how readers may come to a deeper understanding of Chopin's story as its ironic implications sink in.

Janet Vong's final draft appears below with annotations that highlight some of its features.

■ An essay on fiction (no secondary sources)

Janet Vong

Mr. Romano

English 102

20 February 2006

Ironies of Life in Kate Chopin's
"The Story of an Hour"

Kate Chopin's "The Story of an Hour"—which takes only a few minutes to read—has an ironic ending: Mrs. Mallard dies just when she is beginning to live. On first reading, the ending seems almost too ironic for belief. On rereading the story, however, one sees that the ending is believable partly because it is consistent with other ironies in the story.

Irony appears at the very start of the story. Because Mrs. Mallard's friends and her sister assume, mistakenly, that she was deeply in love with her husband, Brently Mallard, they take great care to tell her gently of his death. They mean well, and in fact they <u>do</u> well, bringing her an hour of life, an hour of joyous freedom, but it is ironic that they think their news is sad. True, Mrs. Mallard at first expresses grief when she hears the news, but soon (unknown to the others) she finds joy. So Richards's "sad message" (23), though sad in Richards's eyes, is in fact a happy message.

Among the small but significant ironic details is the statement near the end of the story that when Mallard entered the house, Richards tried to conceal him from Mrs. Mallard, but "Richards was too late" (24). Almost at the start of the story, in the second paragraph, Richards "hastened" (23) to bring his sad news. But if Richards had arrived too late at the start, Brently Mallard would have arrived at home first, and Mrs. Mallard's life would not have ended an hour later but would simply have gone on as it had been. Yet another irony at the end of the story is the diagnosis of the doctors. They say she died of "heart disease—of joy that kills" (24). In one sense they are right: Mrs. Mallard has for the last hour experienced a great joy. But of course the doctors totally misunderstand the joy that kills her. It is not joy at seeing her husband alive, but her realization that the great joy she experienced during the last hour is over.

All of these ironic details add richness to the story, but the central irony resides not in the well-intentioned but ironic actions of Richards, or in the unconsciously ironic words of the doctors, but in Mrs. Mallard's own life. She "sometimes" (24) loved her husband, but in a way

Annotations (left margin):

Author's name and identification in MLA format (p. 687)

Paper title incorporating author and title of analyzed work

Introduction naming author/title and stating thesis

Detailing of story's ironies, using quotations and some summary to emphasize the reversals

Parenthetical citations in MLA style referring to the work cited at the end of the paper (see p. 648)

she has been dead, a body subjected to her husband's will. Now, his apparent death brings her new life. Appropriately, this new life comes to her at the season of the year when "the tops of trees . . . were all aquiver with the new spring life" (23). But, ironically, her new life will last only an hour. She is "Free, free, free" (24)—but only until her husband walks through the doorway. She looks forward to "summer days" (24), but she will not see even the end of this spring day. If her years of marriage were ironic, bringing her a sort of living death instead of joy, her new life is ironic, too, not only because it grows out of her moment of grief for her supposedly dead husband, but also because her vision of "a long procession of years" (24) is cut short within an hour on a spring day.

[New page.]

Work Cited

New page for work cited in MLA style (p. 656)

Chopin, Kate. "The Story of an Hour." An Introduction to Literature: Fiction, Poetry, and Drama. Ed. Sylvan Barnet, William Burto, and William E. Cain. 13th ed. New York: Longman, 2004. 23-24.

50f Writing about fiction, poetry, and drama

A work of literature falls into a category, or **genre**—fiction, poetry, or drama—depending on how it is structured. The different genres of literature require different approaches in writing.

1 Writing about fiction

The "Questions for a literary analysis" on pages 741–42 will help you think about any work of literature, including a story or novel, and find a topic to write on. The following questions provide additional prompts for thinking about fiction. For an example of writing about fiction, see Janet Vong's essay opposite and above.

Questions for analyzing fiction

- **What happens in the story?** For yourself, summarize the plot (the gist of the happenings). Think about what your summary *leaves out*.
- **Is the story told in chronological order, or are there flashbacks or flashforwards?** On rereading, what foreshadowing (hints of what is to come) do you detect?
- **What conflicts does the work include?**
- **How does the writer develop characters?** Is character revealed by explicit comment or through action? With which character(s) do you

(continued)

OPENING PARAGRAPH

Students can learn a great deal about the choices a writer makes in creating a piece of fiction by writing fiction of their own. Ask each student to create a one-paragraph opening for a short story; then have students work in small groups to analyze their fictional paragraphs. What does each opening paragraph reveal about the kind of story being told—will it be comic, tragic, realistic, supernatural? What expectations does the opening set up about the characters and events that will follow? What questions does it raise?

As a follow-up to this exercise, ask each group to turn back to the Kate Chopin story and analyze its one-sentence opening with some of the same questions in mind. Having read the story, students may be surprised to find how much they can deduce from that seemingly simple statement.

RESOURCES AND IDEAS

Barnet, Sylvan, and William Cain. *A Short Guide to Writing About Literature.* 10th ed. New York: Longman, 2006.

Rockas, Leo. *Ways In: Analyzing and Responding to Literature.* Upper Montclair: Boynton/Cook, 1984. Chapter 4 offers examples of and exercises for writing about fiction.

Questions for analyzing fiction
(continued)

sympathize? Are the characters plausible? What motivates them? What do minor characters contribute to the work?

- **Who tells the story?** Is the narrator a character, or does the narrator stand entirely outside the characters' world? What does the narrator's point of view contribute to the story's theme? (On narrative points of view, see p. 741.)
- **What is the setting?** What do the time and place of the action contribute to the work?
- **Are certain characters, settings, or actions symbolic?** Do they stand for something in addition to themselves?
- **What is the theme?** That is, what does the work add up to? Does the theme reinforce your values, or does it challenge them?
- **Is the title informative?** Did its meaning change for you after you read the work?

You can download these questions from *ablongman.com/littlebrown* and answer them for each work you read.

A WRITER'S PERSPECTIVE

A poem is a perhaps.

—IVOR WILLIAMS

You can tear a poem apart to see what makes it technically tick, . . . but you come back to the mystery of having been moved by words.

—DYLAN THOMAS

RESOURCES AND IDEAS

Bizzaro, Patrick. *Responding to Student Poems: Applications of Critical Theory.* Urbana: NCTE, 1993. See Chapter 7 in particular for a discussion of having students read and produce poetry as complementary activities (159–91).

Hollander, John. *Rhyme's Reason: A Guide to English Verse.* 3rd ed. New Haven: Yale UP, 2001. Hollander offers a brief guide to poetry analysis, with amusing examples and some innovative analysis strategies.

Rockas, Leo. *Ways In: Analyzing and Responding to Literature.* Upper Montclair: Boynton/Cook, 1984. Chapter 5 contains examples of and exercises for writing about drama. Chapter 6 offers examples of and exercises for writing about poetry.

2 Writing about poetry

Two types of essays on poetry are especially common. One is an analysis of some aspect of the poem in relation to the whole—for instance, the changes in the speaker's tone or the functions of meter and rhyme. The second is an **explication,** a line-by-line (sometimes almost word-by-word) reading that seeks to make explicit everything that is implicit in the poem. Thus an explication of the first line of Robert Frost's "Stopping by Woods on a Snowy Evening" (the line goes "Whose woods these are I think I know") might call attention to the tentativeness of the line ("I think I know") and to the fact that the words are not in the normal order ("I think I know whose woods these are"). These features might support the explanation that the poet is introducing—very quietly—a note of the *un*usual, in preparation for the experience that follows. Although one might conceivably explicate a long poem, the method is so detailed that in practice writers usually confine it to short poems or to short passages from long poems.

The "Questions for a literary analysis" on pages 741–42 will help you think about any work of literature, including a poem, and find a topic to write on. The questions on the facing page provide additional ways to think about poetry.

■ An essay on poetry with secondary sources

The following sample paper on a short poem by Gwendolyn Brooks illustrates a literary analysis that draws not only on the poem itself but also on secondary sources—that is, critical works

Questions for analyzing poetry

- **What parts of the poem interest or puzzle you?** What words seem especially striking or unusual?
- **How can you describe the poem's *speaker* (sometimes called the *persona* or the *voice*)?** The speaker may be very different from the author.
- **What tone or emotion do you detect**—for instance, anger, affection, sarcasm? Does the tone change during the poem?
- **What is the structure of the poem?** Are there stanzas (groups of lines separated by space)? If so, how is the thought related to the stanzas?
- **What is the theme of the poem?** What is it about? Is the theme stated or implied?
- **What images do you find?** Look for evocations of sight, sound, taste, touch, or smell. Is there a surprising pattern of images—say, images of business in a poem about love? What does the poem suggest symbolically as well as literally? (Trust your responses. If you don't sense a symbolic overtone, move on. Don't hunt for symbols.)

You can download these questions from *ablongman.com/littlebrown* and answer them for each poem you read.

about the poem. In the opening paragraph, for instance, the writer uses brief quotations from two secondary sources to establish the problem, the topic that he will address. These quotations, like the two later quotations from secondary material, are used to make points, not to pad the essay.

Note In the paper, the parenthetical citations for Brooks's poem give line numbers of the poem, whereas the citations for the secondary sources give page numbers of the sources. See pages 648 and 652, respectively, for these two forms of citation.

Gwendolyn Brooks

The Bean Eaters

They eat beans mostly, this old yellow pair.
Dinner is a casual affair.
Plain chipware on a plain and creaking wood,
Tin flatware.

Two who are Mostly Good.   5
Two who have lived their day,
But keep on putting on their clothes
And putting things away.

And remembering . . .
Remembering, with twinklings and twinges,   10
As they lean over the beans in their rented back room that
    is full of beads and receipts and dolls and cloths,
    tobacco crumbs, vases and fringes.

TRANSPARENCY MASTER 50.2

Suchet, David. "Caliban in *The Tempest*." In *Players of Shakespeare*. Ed. Philip Brockbank. Cambridge: Cambridge UP, 1985. 167–79. Suchet, an experienced Shakespearean actor, shows how he reads and rereads a drama to find the clues that lead him to create a character.

MODELS OF STUDENT WRITING

Gwendolyn Brooks's "The Bean Eaters" may strike students as being so quotidian in its language and subject as to defy interpretation. Particularly if they are new to literary interpretation, students may not be sensitive to the nuances a single word or phrase can carry and may think that critics like Kenneth Scheff and those he quotes read too much into poetry. If your students feel this way, try having several of them read the poem aloud in class to see if their readings come across in different ways. Ask them to try to see how much they can affect the meaning of the poem by reading it aloud in as many different ways as possible.

You can also use Scheff's paper to talk about how to incorporate the perspectives of other critics in one's own interpretations. Scheff's paper is strong overall, but you might ask your students if they think he has differentiated his own perspective sufficiently from those of his critics or whether his interpretation is too derivative of those he cites. Ask them to suggest ways Scheff could strengthen his argument.

Kenneth Scheff

Professor MacGregor

English 101A

7 February 2006

Marking Time Versus Enduring in

Gwendolyn Brooks's "The Bean Eaters"

Gwendolyn Brooks's poem "The Bean Eaters" runs only eleven lines. It is written in plain language about very plain people. Yet its meaning is ambiguous. One critic, George E. Kent, says the old couple who eat beans "have had their day and exist now as time-markers" (141). However, another reader, D. H. Melhem, perceives not so much time marking as "endurance" in the old couple (123). Is this poem a despairing picture of old age or a more positive portrait?

"The Bean Eaters" describes an "old yellow pair" who "eat beans mostly" (line 1) off "Plain chipware" (3) with "Tin flatware" (4) in "their rented back room" (11). Clearly, they are poor. Their existence is accompanied not by friends or relatives—children or grandchildren are not mentioned—but by memories and a few possessions (9-11). They are "Mostly Good" (5), words Brooks capitalizes at the end of a line, perhaps to stress the old people's adherence to traditional values as well as their lack of saintliness. They are unexceptional, whatever message they have for readers.

The isolated routine of the couple's life is something Brooks draws attention to with a separate stanza:

> Two who are Mostly Good.
> Two who have lived their day,
> But keep on putting on their clothes
> And putting things away. (5-8)

Brooks emphasizes how isolated the couple is by repeating "Two who." Then she emphasizes how routine their life is by repeating "putting."

A pessimistic reading of this poem seems justified. The critic Harry B. Shaw reads the lines just quoted as perhaps despairing: "they are putting things away as if winding down an operation and readying for withdrawal from activity" (80). However, Shaw observes, the word "But" also indicates that the couple resist slipping away, that they intend to hold on (80). This dual meaning is at the heart of Brooks's poem: the old people live a meager existence, yes, but their will, their self-control, and their connection with another person—their essential humanity— are unharmed.

The truly positive nature of the poem is revealed in the last stanza. In Brooks's words, the old couple remember with some "twinges" perhaps, but also with "twinklings" (10), a cheerful image. As Melhem says, these people are "strong in mutual affection and shared memories" (123). And the final line, which is much longer than all the rest and which catalogs the evidence of the couple's long life together, is almost musically affirmative: "As they lean over the beans in their rented back room that is full of beads and receipts and dolls and cloths, tobacco crumbs, vases and fringes" (11).

What these people have is not much, but it is something.

[New page.]

Works Cited

Brooks, Gwendolyn. "The Bean Eaters." An Introduction to Literature: Fiction, Poetry, and Drama. Ed. Sylvan Barnet, William Burto, and William E. Cain. 13th ed. New York: Longman, 2004. 807.

Kent, George E. A Life of Gwendolyn Brooks. Lexington: UP of Kentucky, 1990.

Melhem, D. H. Gwendolyn Brooks: Poetry and the Heroic Voice. Lexington: UP of Kentucky, 1987.

Shaw, Harry B. Gwendolyn Brooks. Twayne's United States Authors Ser. 395. Boston: Twayne, 1980.

3 Writing about drama

Because plays—even some one-act plays—are relatively long, analytic essays on drama usually focus on only one aspect of the play, such as the structure of the play, the function of a single scene, or a character's responsibility for his or her fate. The essay's introduction indicates what the topic is and why it is of some importance, and the introduction may also state the thesis. The conclusion often extends the analysis, showing how a study of the apparently small topic helps to illuminate the play as a whole.

The "Questions for a literary analysis" on pages 741–42 will help you think about any work of literature, including a play, and find a topic to write on. The questions below provide additional prompts for thinking about drama.

Questions for analyzing drama

- **How does the plot (the sequence of happenings) unfold?** Does it seem plausible? If not, is the implausibility a fault? If there is more than one plot, are the plots parallel, or are they related by way of contrast?
- **Are certain happenings recurrent?** If so, how are they significant?
- **What kinds of conflict are in the play**—for instance, between two groups, two individuals, or two aspects of a single individual? How are the conflicts resolved? Is the resolution satisfying to you?

(continued)

DRAMA ONSTAGE

Many students have only read dramas in literature classes and have never seen them acted. If your campus or local library has videotapes of the dramas you are studying, arrange to show scenes (or even the entire work) to the class. Many students are genuinely shocked to see and hear how performers interpret (i.e., analyze) dramatic works, and their resulting papers often benefit from the insights they gain by watching performances.

TRANSPARENCY MASTER 50.3

Questions for analyzing drama
(continued)

- **How does the author develop the characters?** How trustworthy are the characters when they describe themselves or others? Do some characters serve as **foils**, or contrasts, for other characters, thus helping to define the other characters? Do the characters change as the play proceeds? Are the characters' motivations convincing?
- **What do the author's stage directions add to your understanding and appreciation of the play?** If there are few stage directions, what do the speeches imply about the characters' manner, tone, and gestures?
- **What do you make of the setting, or location?** Does it help to reveal character or theme?
- **Do certain costumes** (dark suits, flowery shawls, stiff collars) or **properties** (books, pictures, candlesticks) **strike you as symbolic?**

You can download these questions from *ablongman.com/littlebrown* and answer them for each play you read.

■ An essay on drama (no secondary sources)

The following essay on William Shakespeare's *Macbeth* focuses on the title character, examining the extent to which he is and is not a tragic hero. Although the writer bases the essay on his personal response to the play, he does not simply state a preference, as if saying he likes vanilla more than chocolate; instead, he argues a case and offers evidence from the play to support his claims.

The writer delays stating his thesis fully until the final paragraph: Macbeth is a hero even though he is a villain. But this thesis is nonetheless evident throughout the essay, from the title through the opening three paragraphs (which establish a context and the case the writer will oppose) through each of the five body paragraphs (which offer five kinds of evidence for the thesis).

Note The parenthetical citations in this essay include act, scene, and line numbers—MLA style for citations of verse plays (see p. 653).

Michael Spinter
Professor Nelson
English 211, sec. 4
6 May 2005

Macbeth as Hero

When we think of a tragic hero, we probably think of a fundamentally sympathetic person who is entangled in terrifying circumstances and who ultimately dies, leaving us with a sense that the world has suffered a loss. For instance, Hamlet must

---

COLLABORATIVE LEARNING

PERFORMING A SCENE

Break the class into small groups and ask each group to perform a scene from a play for their classmates. You can allow students to bring in props or encourage them to make their interpretations through voice and gesture. Then ask the rest of the class to analyze the group's interpretation. What aspects did the group emphasize, and why?

MODELS OF STUDENT WRITING

Michael Spinter's paper on *Macbeth* is strong in both argumentation and organization. Spinter makes an excellent case for his claim that Macbeth is heroic. Your students may wish to discuss this claim, and you can ask them whether they find Spinter's arguments persuasive. If they don't think Spinter is persuasive, ask them what he could have done to make his case stronger, or how they would suggest he modify his thesis.

avenge his father's murder, and in doing so he performs certain actions that verge on the wrongful, such as behaving cruelly to his beloved Ophelia and his mother and killing Rosencrantz and Guildenstern; but we believe that Hamlet is fundamentally a decent man and that Denmark is the poorer for his death.

Macbeth, however, is different. He kills King Duncan and Duncan's grooms, kills Banquo, attempts to kill Banquo's son, and finally kills Lady Macduff and her children and her servants. True, the only people whom he kills with his own hands are Duncan and the grooms—the other victims are destroyed by hired murderers—but clearly Macbeth is responsible for all of the deaths. He could seem an utterly unscrupulous, sneaking crook rather than a tragic hero for whom a reader can feel sympathy.

Certainly most of the other characters in the play feel no sympathy for Macbeth. Macduff calls him a "hell-kite," or a hellish bird of prey (4.3.217), a "tyrant" (5.7.14), a "hell-hound" (5.8.3), and a "coward" (5.8.23). To Malcolm he is a "tyrant" (4.3.12), "devilish Macbeth" (4.3.117), and a "butcher" (5.8.69). Readers and spectators can hardly deny the truth of these characterizations. And yet Macbeth does not seem merely villainous. It would be going too far to say that we always sympathize with him, but we are deeply interested in him and do not dismiss him in disgust as an out-and-out monster. How can we account for his hold on our feelings? At least five factors play their parts.

First, Macbeth is an impressive military figure. In the first extended description of Macbeth, the Captain speaks of "brave Macbeth—well he deserves that name" (1.2.16). The Captain tells how Macbeth valiantly fought on behalf of his king, and King Duncan exclaims, "O valiant cousin! Worthy gentleman!" (1.2.2). True, Macbeth sometimes cringes, such as when he denies responsibility for Banquo's death: "Thou canst not say I did it" (3.4.51). But throughout most of the play, we see him as a bold and courageous soldier.

Of course, Macbeth's ability as a soldier is not enough by itself to explain his hold on us. A second reason is that he is in some degree a victim—a victim of his wife's ambition and a victim of the witches. Yes, he ought to see through his wife's schemes, and he ought to resist the witches, just as Banquo resists them, but surely Macbeth is partly tricked into crime. He is responsible, but we can imagine ourselves falling as he does, and his status as a victim arouses our sympathy.

A third source of his hold on us is that although Macbeth engages in terrible deeds, he almost always retains his conscience. For instance, after he murders Duncan he cannot sleep at night. When he tells Lady Macbeth that he has heard a voice saying, "Macbeth does murder sleep" (2.2.35), she ridicules him, but the voice is prophetic: he is doomed to sleepless nights. We in the audience are glad that Macbeth is tormented by his deed, since it shows that he knows he has done wrong and that he still has some decent human feelings.

You may also want to use this paper to talk about matters of structure. It takes a skillful writer to make a paper work with a thesis positioned at the end. Ask your students whether they think it works in Michael Spinter's paper or whether he would have been better off putting the thesis at the beginning, and ask them to justify their opinions.

Finally, you might ask students to reflect upon all three sample papers in this chapter (Janet Vong's, Kenneth Scheff's, and Michael Spinter's) and to compare and contrast their respective strengths and weaknesses.

A fourth reason why we retain some sympathy for Macbeth is that he eventually loses all of his allies, even his wife, and he stands before us a lonely, guilt-haunted figure. On this point, scene 2 of act 3 is especially significant. When Lady Macbeth asks Macbeth why he keeps to himself (line 8), he confides something of the mental stress that he is undergoing. But when she asks, "What's to be done?" (44), he cannot bring himself to tell her that he is plotting the deaths of Banquo and Fleance. Instead of further involving his wife, the only person with whom he might still have a human connection, Macbeth says, "Be innocent of the knowledge, dearest chuck . . ." (45). The word <u>chuck</u>, an affectionate form of <u>chick</u>, shows warmth and intimacy that are touching, but his refusal or his inability to confide in his wife and former partner in crime shows how fully isolated he is from all human contact. We cannot help feeling some sympathy for him.

Finally, Macbeth holds our interest, instead of disgusting us, because he speaks so wonderfully. The greatness of his language compels us to listen to him with rapt attention. Some speeches are very familiar, such as "My way of life / Is fall'n into the sear, the yellow leaf . . ." (5.3.23-24) and "Tomorrow and tomorrow and tomorrow / Creeps in this petty pace from day to day . . ." (5.5.19-20). But almost every speech Macbeth utters is equally memorable, from his first, "So foul and fair a day I have not seen" (1.3.38), to his last:

> Before my body
> I throw my warlike shield. Lay on, Macduff:
> And damned be him that first cries, "Hold, enough!" (5.8.32-34)

If we stand back and judge Macbeth only by what he does, we of course say that he is a foul murderer. But if we read the play attentively, or witness a performance, and give due weight to Macbeth's bravery, his role as a victim, his tormented conscience, his isolation, and especially his moving language, we do not simply judge him. Rather, we see that, villain though he is, he is not merely awful but also awesome.

[New page.]

Work Cited

Shakespeare, William. <u>The Tragedy of Macbeth</u>. Ed. Sylvan Barnet. Rev. ed. New York: NAL, 1987.

CHAPTER 51

Writing in Other Humanities

The humanities include literature, the visual arts, music, film, dance, history, philosophy, and religion. The preceding chapter discusses the particular requirements of reading and writing about literature. This chapter concentrates on history. Although the arts, religion, and other humanities have their own concerns, they share many important goals and methods with literature and history.

51a Using the methods and evidence of the humanities

Writers in the humanities record and speculate about the growth, ideas, and emotions of human beings. Based on the evidence of written words, artworks, and other human traces and creations, humanities writers explain, interpret, analyze, and reconstruct the human experience.

The discipline of history focuses particularly on reconstructing the past. In Greek the word for history means "to inquire": historians inquire into the past to understand the events of the past. Then they report, explain, analyze, and evaluate those events in their context, asking such questions as what happened before or after the events or how the events were related to then existing political and social structures.

Historians' reconstructions of the past—their conclusions about what happened and why—are always supported with reference to the written record. The evidence of history is mainly primary sources, such as eyewitness accounts and contemporary documents, letters, commercial records, and the like. For history papers, you might also be asked to support your conclusions with those in secondary sources.

http://www.ablongman.com/littlebrown ▶

Visit the companion Web site for more help with writing in history, the visual arts, and other humanities.

mycomplab

Please visit MyCompLab at *www.mycomplab.com* for more on the writing process.

HIGHLIGHTS

Chapter 51 gives students some of the essentials they need to know about writing in history and the other humanities. The opening discussions define the operations of explanation, analysis, interpretation, synthesis, and evaluation and explain writing tools and language conventions. Next, students are told about a wide variety of library and online resources for research. The chapter also includes sections on how to cite sources and format documents in the humanities according to *The Chicago Manual of Style*.

NOT JUST THE FACTS

Students may need to be persuaded that writing history is an interpretive endeavor and not merely a matter of recording facts. To help students understand that historians construct the past as they write about it, bring to class two brief accounts of a single historical incident written by two different writers. Let your students evaluate how the inclusion or exclusion of data, the organization, and the narrative style used by the writer influence the reader's understanding of the "facts."

RESOURCES AND IDEAS

Anson, Chris, M. "Response and the Social Construction of Error." *Assessing Writing* 7 (2000): 5-21. Anson suggests teachers reflect upon the significance of their response to errors students make in their writing, because the rules that govern language use change as social contexts evolve.

Bawarshi, Anis. "The Genre Function." *College English* 62.3 (2000): 335–60. Bawarshi shows how the genre in which a text is written influences the composing process and shapes ways readers respond to the text.

COMPANION WEB SITE

See page IAE-61 for companion Web site content description.

Beyer, Barry K. "Using Writing to Learn in History." *The History Teacher* 13 (1980): 167–78. Beyer suggests using writing not only to seek and report information but to help students understand the ways of thinking characteristic of historians.

MacNealy, Mary Sue. *Strategies for Empirical Research in Writing.* Needham Heights, MA: Allyn & Bacon, 1999. An introduction to research methods in the humanities, geared for students but useful to teachers as well.

Thelin, William H. "Understanding Problems in Critical Classrooms." *College Composition and Communication* 57 (September 2005): 114–141. The author offers a defense of critical pedagogy in the face of mounting criticism against it.

Tuchman, Barbara. *Practicing History: Selected Essays.* New York: Knopf, 1981. Tuchman demonstrates and gives practical recommendations for analytic writing in history.

Weisser, Christian. *Moving Beyond Academic Discourse: Composition Studies and the Public Sphere.* Carbondale: Southern Illinois UP, 2002. Weisser argues that student writing will improve if students do more non-academic writing for specific audiences.

ADDITIONAL RESOURCES FOR STUDENTS

If your students need more help in writing for the humanities, you might refer them to the following:

Barnet, Sylvan. *A Short Guide to Writing About Art.* 6th ed. New York: Longman, 1999.

Bellman, Jonathan. *A Short Guide to Writing About Music.* New York, Longman, 2000.

Corrigan, Timothy. *A Short Guide to Writing About Film.* 5th ed. New York: Longman, 2004.

Marius, Richard. *A Short Guide to Writing About History.* 5th ed. New York: Longman, 2005.

Steffens, Henry, Mary Jane Dickerson, and Toby Fulweiler. *Writer's Guide: History.* Boston: Heath, 1987.

COLLABORATIVE LEARNING

WRITING ASSIGNMENTS

Ask students to bring in examples of writing assignments from their other humanities courses and to classify them according to the list on this

In reading historical sources, you need to weigh and evaluate their evidence. If, for example, you find conflicting accounts of the same event, you need to consider the possible biases of the authors. In general, the more a historian's conclusions are supported by public records such as deeds, marriage licenses, and newspaper accounts, the more reliable the conclusions are likely to be.

51b Understanding writing assignments in the humanities

Papers in the humanities generally perform one or more of the following operations:

- **Explanation:** for instance, showing how a painter developed a particular technique or clarifying a general's role in a historical battle.
- **Analysis:** examining the elements of a philosophical argument or breaking down the causes of a historical event.
- **Interpretation:** inferring the meaning of a film from its images or the significance of a historical event from contemporary accounts of it.
- **Synthesis:** finding a pattern in a historical period or in a composer's works.
- **Evaluation:** judging the quality of an architect's design or a historian's conclusions.

Most likely, you will use these operations in combination—say, interpreting and explaining the meaning of a painting and then evaluating it. (These operations are discussed in more detail in Chapter 8.)

51c Using the tools and language of the humanities

The tools and language of the humanities vary according to the discipline. Major reference works in each field, such as those listed on the next four pages, can clarify specific tools you need and language you should use.

1 Writing tools

A useful tool for the arts is to ask a series of questions to analyze and evaluate a work. (A list of such questions for reading literature appears on pp. 741–42.) In any humanities discipline, a journal—a log of questions, reactions, and insights—can help you discover and record your thoughts. (See pp. 152–53 and 559–60.)

In history the tools are those of any thorough and efficient researcher, as discussed in Chapters 42–44: a system for finding and tracking sources; a methodical examination of sources, including evaluating and synthesizing them; a system for gathering source information; and a separate system, such as a research journal, for tracking one's own evolving thoughts.

2 Language considerations

Historians strive for precision and logic. They do not guess about what happened or speculate about "what if." They avoid trying to influence readers' opinions with words having strongly negative or positive connotations, such as *stupid* or *brilliant*. Instead, historians show the evidence and draw conclusions from that. Generally, they avoid using *I* because it tends to draw attention away from the evidence and toward the writer.

Writing about history demands some attention to the tenses of verbs to maintain consistency. Generally, historians use the past tense to refer to events that occurred in the past. They reserve the present tense only for statements about the present or statements of general truths. For example:

> Franklin Delano Roosevelt died in 1945. Many of Roosevelt's economic reforms persist in programs such as Social Security, unemployment compensation, and farm subsidies.

3 Research sources

The following lists give resources in the humanities. (Resources for literature appear on pp. 744–45.)

■ Specialized encyclopedias, dictionaries, and bibliographies

The arts
Architecture: From Prehistory to Post-Modernism
Dance Encyclopedia
Dictionary of Art
Encyclopedia of Pop, Rock, and Soul
Encyclopedia of World Art
Film Research: A Critical Bibliography
Film Review Annual
Guide to the Literature of Art History
International Cyclopedia of Music and Musicians
International Encyclopedia of Communications
International Television and Video Almanac
MLA International Bibliography of Books and Articles on the Modern Languages and Literatures
New Grove Dictionary of Music and Musicians
New Grove Dictionary of Opera
New Harvard Dictionary of Music

page. Which are most and least frequently used? Students might also interview professors from their other courses, individually or in teams, to learn which writing strategies are most important for success in those courses.

COLLABORATIVE LEARNING

TENSES

Students sometimes have trouble making judgments about which tense to use in historical writing. To get them used to conventions of tense usage, have students review each other's drafts and suggest revisions.

SOURCES

To help students become familiar with the humanities research sources listed in the text (pp. 761–64), have each student look up one source (either a library source or a Web source) and make a brief presentation on it in class.

Oxford Companion to Twentieth-Century Art
Variety's Film Reviews

History

Afro-American Reference
American Heritage Encyclopedia of American History
American Indian Studies: A Bibliographic Guide
Cambridge Ancient History
Cambridge History of China
Dictionary of American History
Dictionary of American Immigration History
Dictionary of the Middle Ages
Encyclopedia of American History
Encyclopedia of Asian History
Encyclopedia of Latin-American History
Encyclopedia of World History
Guide to American Foreign Relations Since 1700
Harvard Guide to American History
History: Illustrated Search Strategy and Sources
Middle East Bibliography
Modern Encyclopedia of Russian and Soviet History
New Cambridge Modern History
Oxford Classical Dictionary
The Study of the Middle East: Research and Scholarship in the Humanities and Social Sciences

Philosophy and religion

Catholic Encyclopedia
Concise Encyclopedia of Islam
Dictionary of the History of Ideas
Encyclopedia Judaica
Encyclopedia of Asian Philosophy
Encyclopedia of Ethics
Encyclopedia of Philosophy
Encyclopedia of Religion
Interpreter's Dictionary of the Bible
Library Research Guide to Religion and Theology
New Standard Jewish Encyclopedia
Oxford Dictionary of the Christian Church
Research Guide to Philosophy

■ Indexes

America: History and Life
Art Index
Arts and Humanities Citation Index
Avery Index to Architectural Periodicals
Dissertation Abstracts International (doctoral dissertations)
Film Literature Index
Historical Abstracts
Humanities Index

Musical Literature International
Music Index
Philosopher's Index
Religion Index

▣ Book reviews

Book Review Digest
Book Review Index

▣ Web sources

For updates of these sources and URLs, visit *ablongman.com/ littlebrown.*

General
Arts and Humanities Data Service (ahds.ac.uk)
BUBL Information Service (bubl.ac.uk)
EDSITEment (edsitement.neh.gov)
Humbul Humanities Hub (humbul.ac.uk)
Internet Public Library (ipl.org/div/subject/browse/hum00.00.00)
Librarians' Index to the Internet: Arts and Humanities (lii.org/search/file/ artscraftshum)
Voice of the Shuttle Humanities (vos.ucsb.edu)

Art
Artnet (artnet.com)
BUBL Link: The Arts (bubl.ac.uk/link/linkbrowse.cfm?menuid=9847)
World Wide Arts Resources (wwar.com/browse.html)

Dance
BUBL Link: Dance (bubl.ac.uk/link/d/dance.htm)
Google Directory: Dance (directory.google.com/Top/Arts/Performing_Arts/ Dance)

Film
CinemaSpot (cinemaspot.com)
Film Studies on the Internet (www.ualberta.ca/~slis/guides/films/film.htm)
Internet Movie Database (imdb.com)

History
British History Resources on the Internet (libraries.rutgers.edu/rul/rr_gateway/ research_guides/history.shtml)
Best of History Web Sites (besthistorysites.net)
Librarians' Index to the Internet: History (lii.org/search/file/history)
National Women's History Project (nwhp.org)

Music
American Music Resource (amrhome.net)
MusicMoz (musicmoz.org)
Music Theory Online (societymusictheory.org/mto)
Web Resources for Research in Music (www.music.ucc.ie/wrrm)

Philosophy
Guide to Philosophy on the Internet (*www.earlham.edu/~peters/gpi*)
Philosophy Documentation Center (*pdcnet.org*)
Philosophy Pages (*philosophypages.com*)
Social Science Information Gateway: Philosophy (*sosig.ac.uk/philosophy*)

Religion
Academic Info: Religion Gateway (*academicinfo.net/religindex.html*)
Pluralism Project (*pluralism.org/directory/index.php*)
Religious Studies Web Guide (*www.acs.ucalgary.ca/~lipton*)
Virtual Religion Index (*religion.rutgers.edu/vri*)

Theater
McCoy's Brief Guide to Internet Resources in Theater and Performance Studies (*stetson.edu/departments/csata/thr_guid.html*)
Theater Connections (*uncc.edu/jvanoate/theater*)
TheatreHistory.com (*theatrehistory.com*)

51d Citing sources in Chicago style

Writers in the humanities generally rely on one of the following guides for source-citation style:

The Chicago Manual of Style, 15th ed., 2003
Joseph Gibaldi, *MLA Handbook for Writers of Research Papers,* 6th ed., 2003
Kate L. Turabian, *A Manual for Writers of Term Papers, Theses, and Dissertations,* 6th ed., rev. John Grossman and Alice Bennett, 1996

The recommendations of the *MLA Handbook* are discussed and illustrated in Chapter 47. Unless your instructor specifies otherwise, use these recommendations for papers in English and foreign languages. In history, art history, and many other disciplines, however, writers rely on *The Chicago Manual of Style* or the student reference adapted from it, *A Manual for Writers.*

Both books detail two documentation styles. One, used mainly by scientists and social scientists, closely resembles the style of the American Psychological Association, covered in Chapter 52. The other style, used more in the humanities, calls for footnotes or endnotes and an optional bibliography. This style is described below.

1 Using Chicago notes and a list of works cited

In the Chicago note style, a raised numeral in the text refers the reader to source information in endnotes or footnotes. In these notes, the first citation of each source contains all the information readers need to find the source. Thus your instructor may consider

---

a list of works cited optional because it provides much the same information. Ask your instructor whether you should use footnotes or endnotes and whether you should include a list of works cited.

Whether providing footnotes or endnotes, use single spacing for each note and double spacing between notes, as shown in the samples below. Separate footnotes from the text with a short line. Place endnotes directly after the text, beginning on a new page. For the list of sources at the end of the paper, use the format on the following page. Arrange the sources alphabetically by the authors' last names.

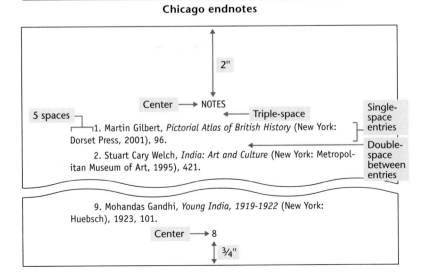

Chicago footnotes

In 1901, Madras, Bengal, and Punjab were a few of the huge Indian provinces governed by the British viceroy.[6] British rule, observes Stuart Cary Welch, "seemed as permanent as Mount Everest."[7]

1" — 1"

5 spaces — Double-space — Line

6. Martin Gilbert, *Pictorial Atlas of British History* (New York: Dorset Press, 2001), 96. — Single-space

7. Stuart Cary Welch, *India: Art and Culture* (New York: Metropolitan Museum of Art, 1995), 421. — Single-space

1"

Chicago endnotes

2"

Center → NOTES — Triple-space

5 spaces

1. Martin Gilbert, *Pictorial Atlas of British History* (New York: Dorset Press, 2001), 96. — Single-space entries

2. Stuart Cary Welch, *India: Art and Culture* (New York: Metropolitan Museum of Art, 1995), 421. — Double-space between entries

9. Mohandas Gandhi, *Young India, 1919-1922* (New York: Huebsch), 1923, 101.

Center → 8

¾"

Chicago list of works cited

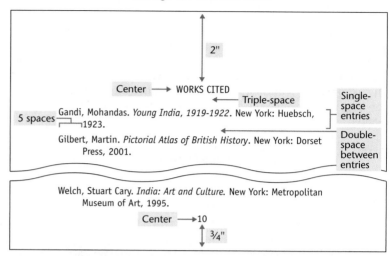

The examples below illustrate the essentials of a note and a works-cited entry.

Note

6. Martin Gilbert, *Pictorial Atlas of British History* (New York: Dorset Press, 2001), 96.

Works-cited entry

Gilbert, Martin. *Pictorial Atlas of British History*. New York: Dorset Press, 2001.

Notes and works-cited entries share certain features:

- Single-space each note or entry, and double-space between them.
- Italicize or underline the titles of books and periodicals. Ask your instructor for his or her preference.
- Enclose in quotation marks the titles of parts of books or articles in periodicals.
- Do not abbreviate publishers' names, but omit "Inc.," "Co.," and similar abbreviations.
- Do not use "p." or "pp." before page numbers.

Notes and works-cited entries also differ in important ways:

Note	Works-cited entry
Start with a number that corresponds to the note number in the text.	Do not begin with a number.

Note	Works-cited entry
Indent the first line five spaces.	Indent the second and subsequent lines five spaces.
Give the author's name in normal order.	Begin with the author's last name.
Use commas between elements such as author's name and title.	Use periods between elements.
Enclose publication information in parentheses, with no preceding punctuation	Precede the publication information with a period, and don't use parentheses.
Include the specific page number(s) you borrowed from, omitting "p." or "pp."	Omit page numbers except for parts of books or articles in periodicals.

You can instruct your computer to position footnotes at the bottoms of appropriate pages. It will also automatically number notes and renumber them if you add or delete one or more.

2 Following Chicago models

The Chicago models for common sources are indexed on the next page. The models show notes and works-cited entries together for easy reference. Be sure to use the numbered note form for notes and the unnumbered works-cited form for works-cited entries.

■ Books

1. A book with one, two, or three authors

1. Carol Gilligan, *In a Different Voice: Psychological Theory and Women's Development* (Cambridge: Harvard University Press, 1982), 27.

Gilligan, Carol. *In a Different Voice: Psychological Theory and Women's Development*. Cambridge: Harvard University Press, 1982.

1. Dennis L. Wilcox, Phillip H. Ault, and Warren K. Agee, *Public Relations: Strategies and Tactics,* 6th ed. (New York: Irwin, 2005), 182.

Wilcox, Dennis L., Phillip H. Ault, and Warren K. Agee. *Public Relations: Strategies and Tactics*. 6th ed. New York: Irwin, 2005.

2. A book with more than three authors

2. Geraldo Lopez and others, *China and the West* (Boston: Little, Brown, 2004), 461.

Lopez, Geraldo, Judith P. Salt, Anne Ming, and Henry Reisen. *China and the West*. Boston: Little, Brown, 2004.

3. A book with an editor

3. Hendrick Ruitenbeek, ed., *Freud as We Knew Him* (Detroit: Wayne State University Press, 1973), 64.

Chicago note and works-cited models

Books

1. A book with one, two, or three authors *767*
2. A book with more than three authors *767*
3. A book with an editor *767*
4. A book with an author and an editor *768*
5. A translation *768*
6. An anonymous work *769*
7. A later edition *769*
8. A work in more than one volume *769*
9. A selection from an anthology *769*
10. A work in a series *769*
11. An article in a reference work *769*

Periodicals

12. An article in a journal *770*
13. An article in a magazine *770*
14. An article in a newspaper *770*
15. A review *770*

Electronic sources

16. A work on CD-ROM or DVD-ROM *771*
17. A work from an online database *771*

18. An online book *771*
19. An article in an online journal *771*
20. An article in an online magazine *772*
21. An article in an online newspaper *772*
22. An article in an online reference work *772*
23. An online audio or visual source *772*
24. An entry on a Web log or a posting to a discussion group *773*
25. Electronic mail *773*

Other sources

26. A government publication *773*
27. A published letter *774*
28. A published or broadcast interview *774*
29. A personal letter or interview *774*
30. A work of art *774*
31. A film, DVD, or video recording *774*
32. A sound recording *774*

Shortened notes *774*

Ruitenbeek, Hendrick, ed. *Freud as We Knew Him*. Detroit: Wayne State University Press, 1973.

4. A book with an author and an editor

4. Lewis Mumford, *The City in History,* ed. Donald L. Miller (New York: Pantheon, 1986), 216-17.

Mumford, Lewis. *The City in History*. Edited by Donald L. Miller. New York: Pantheon, 1986.

5. A translation

5. Dante Alighieri, *The Inferno,* trans. John Ciardi (New York: New American Library, 1971), 51.

Alighieri, Dante. *The Inferno*. Translated by John Ciardi. New York: New American Library, 1971.

6. An anonymous work

6. *The Dorling Kindersley World Reference Atlas* (London: Dorling Kindersley, 2005), 150-51.

The Dorling Kindersley World Reference Atlas. London: Dorling Kindersley, 2005.

7. A later edition

7. Dwight L. Bolinger, *Aspects of Language,* 3rd ed. (New York: Harcourt Brace Jovanovich, 1981), 20.

Bolinger, Dwight L. *Aspects of Language*. 3rd ed. New York: Harcourt Brace Jovanovich, 1981.

8. A work in more than one volume

Citation of one volume without a title:

8. Abraham Lincoln, *The Collected Works of Abraham Lincoln,* ed. Roy P. Basler (New Brunswick: Rutgers University Press, 1953), 5:426-28.

Lincoln, Abraham. *The Collected Works of Abraham Lincoln*. Edited by Roy P. Basler. Vol. 5. New Brunswick: Rutgers University Press, 1953.

Citation of one volume with a title:

8. Linda B. Welkin, *The Age of Balanchine,* vol. 3 of *The History of Ballet* (New York: Columbia University Press, 1999), 56.

Welkin, Linda B. *The Age of Balanchine*. Vol. 3 of *The History of Ballet*. New York: Columbia University Press, 1999.

9. A selection from an anthology

9. Rosetta Brooks, "Streetwise," in *The New Urban Landscape,* ed. Richard Martin (New York: Rizzoli, 2005), 38-39.

Brooks, Rosetta. "Streetwise." In *The New Urban Landscape,* ed. Richard Martin, 37-60. New York: Rizzoli, 2005.

10. A work in a series

10. Ingmar Bergman, *The Seventh Seal,* Modern Film Scripts, no. 12 (New York: Simon and Schuster, 1995), 27.

Bergman, Ingmar. *The Seventh Seal*. Modern Film Scripts, no. 12. New York: Simon and Schuster, 1995.

11. An article in a reference work

11. *Merriam-Webster's Collegiate Dictionary,* 11th ed., s.v. "reckon."

Merriam-Webster's Collegiate Dictionary, 11th ed. S.v. "reckon."

As in the example, use the abbreviation s.v. (Latin *sub verbo,* "under the word") for reference works that are alphabetically arranged. Well-known works like the one listed here do not need publication information except for edition number. Chicago style generally recommends notes only, not works-cited entries, for reference works; a works-cited model is given here in case your instructor requires such entries.

■ Periodicals: Journals, magazines, newspapers

12. An article in a journal

> 12. Janet Lever, "Sex Differences in the Games Children Play," *Social Problems* 23 (1996): 482.

> Lever, Janet. "Sex Differences in the Games Children Play." *Social Problems* 23 (1996): 478-87.

Provide the issue number if the journal numbers issues. The issue number is required for any journal that pages each issue separately or that numbers only issues, not volumes:

> 12. June Dacey, "Management Participation in Corporate Buy-Outs," *Management Perspectives* 7, no. 4 (1998): 22.

> Dacey, June. "Management Participation in Corporate Buy-Outs." *Management Perspectives* 7, no. 4 (1998): 20-31.

13. An article in a magazine

> 13. Mark Stevens, "Low and Behold," *New Republic,* December 24, 2005, 28.

> Stevens, Mark. "Low and Behold." *New Republic,* December 24, 2005, 27-33.

Chicago works-cited style does not require inclusive page numbers for magazine articles, so 27-33 could be omitted from the preceding example.

14. An article in a newspaper

> 14. Gina Kolata, "Kill All the Bacteria!" *New York Times,* January 7, 2006, national edition, B1.

> Kolata, Gina. "Kill All the Bacteria!" *New York Times,* January 7, 2006, national edition, B1, B6.

Chicago style does not require page numbers for newspaper citations, whether in notes or in works-cited entries. Thus B1 and B1, B6 could be omitted from the above examples.

15. A review

> 15. John Gregory Dunne, "The Secret of Danny Santiago," review of *Famous All over Town,* by Danny Santiago, *New York Review of Books,* August 16, 1994, 25.

> Dunne, John Gregory. "The Secret of Danny Santiago." Review of *Famous All over Town,* by Danny Santiago. *New York Review of Books,* August 16, 1994, 17-27.

▪ Electronic sources

The Chicago Manual's models for documenting electronic sources derive mainly from those for print sources, with the addition of an electronic address (URL) or other indication of the medium along with any other information that may help readers locate the source. Chicago requires the date of your access to an online source only if the source could change significantly (for instance, a report on medical research). However, your instructor may require access dates for a broader range of online sources, so they are included in the following models (in parentheses at the end).

Note Chicago style allows many ways to break URLs between the end of one line and the beginning of the next: after slashes, before most punctuation marks (periods, commas, question marks, and so on), and before or after equal signs and ampersands (&). *Do not* break after a hyphen or add any hyphens.

16. A work on CD-ROM or DVD-ROM

16. *The American Heritage Dictionary of the English Language,* 4th ed., CD-ROM (Boston: Houghton Mifflin, 2000).

The American Heritage Dictionary of the English Language. 4th ed. CD-ROM. Boston: Houghton Mifflin, 2000.

17. A work from an online database

17. Irina Netchaeva, "E-Government and E-Democracy," *International Journal for Communication Studies* 64 (2002): 470-71, http://www.epnet.com (accessed December 20, 2005).

Netchaeva, Irina. "E-Government and E-Democracy." *International Journal for Communication Studies* 64 (2002): 467-78. http://www.epnet.com (accessed December 20, 2005).

For news and journal databases, including those to which your library subscribes, you may omit the name of the database. Give its main URL (as in the examples) unless the work has a usable URL of its own. (See p. 671 for more on database URLs.)

18. An online book

18. Jane Austen, *Emma*, ed. R. W. Chapman (1816; Oxford: Clarendon, 1926; Oxford Text Archive, 2004), chap. 1, http://ota.ahds.ac.uk/Austen/Emma.1519 (accessed December 15, 2005).

Austen, Jane. *Emma*. Edited by R. W. Chapman. 1816. Oxford: Clarendon, 1926. Oxford Text Archive, 2004. http://ota.ahds.ac.uk/Austen/Emma.1519 (accessed December 15, 2005).

19. An article in an online journal

19. Andrew Palfrey, "Choice of Mates in Identical Twins," *Modern Psychology* 4, no. 1 (2003): 28, http://www.liasu/edu/modpsy/palfrey4(1).htm (accessed February 25, 2006).

Palfrey, Andrew. "Choice of Mates in Identical Twins." *Modern Psychology* 4, no. 1 (2003): 26-40. http://www.liasu/edu/modpsy/palfrey4(1).htm (accessed February 25, 2006).

20. An article in an online magazine

20. Ricki Lewis, "The Return of Thalidomide," *Scientist,* January 22, 2001, http://www.the-scientist.com/yr2001/jan/lewis_pl_010122.html (accessed January 24, 2006).

Lewis, Ricki. "The Return of Thalidomide." *Scientist,* January 22, 2001. http://www.the-scientist.com/yr2001/jan/lewis_pl_010122.html (accessed January 24, 2006).

21. An article in an online newspaper

21. Lucia Still, "On the Battlefields of Business, Millions of Casualties," *New York Times on the Web,* March 3, 2005, http://www.nytimes.com/specials/ downsize/03down1.html (accessed August 17, 2005).

Still, Lucia. "On the Battlefields of Business, Millions of Casualties." *New York Times on the Web,* March 3, 2005. http://www.nytimes.com/specials/ downsize/03down1.html (accessed August 17, 2005).

22. An article in an online reference work

22. *Encyclopaedia Britannica Online,* s.v. "Wu-ti," http://www.eb.com:80 (accessed December 23, 2005).

Encyclopaedia Britannica Online. S.v. "Wu-ti." http://www.eb.com:80 (accessed December 23, 2005).

23. An online audio or visual source

A work of art:

23. Jackson Pollock, *Shimmering Substance,* oil on canvas, 1946, Museum of Modern Art, New York, WebMuseum, http://www.ibiblio.org/ wm/paint/auth/Pollock/pollock.shimmering.jpg (accessed March 12, 2006).

Pollock, Jackson. *Shimmering Substance.* Oil on canvas, 1946. Museum of Modern Art, New York. WebMuseum. http://www.ibiblio.org/wm/paint/ auth/Pollock/pollock.shimmering.jpg (accessed March 12, 2006).

A sound recording:

23. Ronald W. Reagan, State of the Union Address, January 26, 1982, Vincent Voice Library, Digital and Multimedia Center, University of Michigan, http://www.lib.msu.edu/vincent/presidents/reagan.html (accessed May 6, 2005).

Reagan, Ronald W. State of the Union Address. January 26, 1982. Vincent Voice Library. Digital and Multimedia Center, University of Michigan. http://www.lib.msu.edu/vincent/presidents/reagan.html (accessed May 6, 2005).

A film or film clip:

> 23. Leslie J. Stewart, *96 Ranch Rodeo and Barbecue* (1951), 16mm, from Library of Congress, *Buckaroos in Paradise: Ranching Culture in Northern Nevada, 1945-1982,* MPEG, http://lcweb2.loc.gov/ammem/afc96ran_v034 (accessed January 7, 2006).

Stewart, Leslie J. *96 Ranch Rodeo and Barbecue*. 1951, 16 mm. From Library of Congress, *Buckaroos in Paradise: Ranching Culture in Northern Nevada, 1945-1982*. MPEG. http://lcweb2.loc.gov/ammem/afc96ran_v034 (accessed January 7, 2006).

24. An entry on a Web log or posting to a discussion group

> 24. Susheel Daswani, "Hollywood vs. Silicon Valley," Berkeley Intellectual Property Weblog, March 16, 2005, http://www.biplog.com/archive/cat_hollywood.html (accessed August 22, 2005).

Daswani, Susheel. "Hollywood vs. Silicon Valley." Berkeley Intellectual Property Weblog. March 16, 2005. http://www.biplog.com/archive/cat_hollywood.html (accessed August 22, 2005).

> 24. Michael Tourville, "European Currency Reform," e-mail to International Finance Discussion List, January 6, 2006, http://www.weg.isu.edu/finance-dl/archive/46732 (accessed January 12, 2006).

Tourville, Michael. "European Currency Reform." E-mail to International Finance Discussion List. January 6, 2006. http://www.weg.isu.edu/finance-dl/archive/46732 (accessed January 12, 2006).

25. Electronic mail

> 25. Michele Millon, "Re: Grief Therapy," e-mail message to author, May 4, 2005.

Millon, Michele. "Re: Grief Therapy." E-mail message to author. May 4, 2005.

■ Other sources

26. A government publication

> 26. House Committee on Ways and Means, *Medicare Payment for Outpatient Physical and Occupational Therapy Services,* 108th Cong., 1st sess., 2003, H. Doc. 409, 12-13.

U.S. Congress. House. Committee on Ways and Means. *Medicare Payment for Outpatient Physical and Occupational Therapy Services*. 108th Cong., 1st sess., 2003. H. Doc. 409.

> 26. Hawaii Department of Education, *Kauai District Schools, Profile 2004-05* (Honolulu, 2005), 27.

Hawaii. Department of Education. *Kauai District Schools, Profile 2004-05*. Honolulu, 2005.

27. A published letter

27. Mrs. Laura E. Buttolph to Rev. and Mrs. C. C. Jones, June 20, 1857, in *The Children of Pride: A True Story of Georgia and the Civil War,* ed. Robert Manson Myers (New Haven, CT: Yale University Press, 1972), 334.

Buttolph, Laura E. Mrs. Laura E. Buttolph to Rev. and Mrs. C. C. Jones, June 20, 1857. In *The Children of Pride: A True Story of Georgia and the Civil War,* edited by Robert Manson Myers. New Haven, CT: Yale University Press, 1972.

28. A published or broadcast interview

28. Donald Rumsfeld, interview by William Lindon, *Frontline,* PBS, October 13, 2005.

Rumsfeld, Donald. Interview by William Lindon. *Frontline*. PBS, October 13, 2005.

29. A personal letter or interview

29. Ann E. Packer, letter to author, June 15, 2005.

Packer, Ann E. Letter to author. June 15, 2005.

29. Vera Graaf, interview by author, December 19, 2005.

Graaf, Vera. Interview by author. December 19, 2005.

30. A work of art

30. John Singer Sargent, *In Switzerland,* watercolor, 1908, Metropolitan Museum of Art, New York.

Sargent, John Singer. *In Switzerland*. Watercolor, 1908. Metropolitan Museum of Art, New York.

31. A film, DVD, or video recording

31. George Balanchine, *Serenade,* DVD, San Francisco Ballet (New York: PBS Video, 2003).

Balanchine, George. *Serenade*. DVD. San Francisco Ballet. New York: PBS Video, 2003.

32. A sound recording

32. Johannes Brahms, Piano Concerto no. 2 in B-flat, Artur Rubinstein, Philadelphia Orchestra, Eugene Ormandy, compact disc, RCA BRC4-6731.

Brahms, Johannes. Piano Concerto no. 2 in B-flat. Artur Rubinstein. Philadelphia Orchestra. Eugene Ormandy. Compact disc. RCA BRC4-6731.

■ Shortened notes

To streamline documentation, Chicago style recommends short-ened notes for sources that are fully cited elsewhere, either in a complete list of works cited or in previous notes. Ask your instructor whether your paper should include a list of works cited and, if so, whether you may use shortened notes for first references to sources as well as for subsequent references.

A shortened note contains the author's last name, the work's title (minus any initial *A*, *An*, or *The*), and the page number. Reduce long titles to four or fewer key words.

Complete note

> 8. Janet Lever, "Sex Differences in the Games Children Play," *Social Problems* 23 (1996): 482.

Complete works-cited entry

> Lever, Janet. "Sex Differences in the Games Children Play." *Social Problems* 23 (1996): 478-87.

Shortened note

> 12. Lever, "Sex Differences," 483.

You may use the Latin abbreviation ibid. (meaning "in the same place") to refer to the same source cited in the preceding note. Give a page number if it differs from that in the preceding note.

> 12. Lever, "Sex Differences," 483.
>
> 13. Gilligan, *In a Different Voice,* 92.
>
> 14. Ibid., 93.
>
> 15. Lever, "Sex Differences," 483.

Chicago style allows for in-text parenthetical citations when you cite one or more works repeatedly. In the following example, the raised number 2 refers to the source information in a note; the number in parentheses is a page number in the same source.

> British rule, observes Stuart Cary Welch, "seemed as permanent as Mount Everest."[2] Most Indians submitted, willingly or not, to British influence in every facet of life (42).

51e Formatting documents in Chicago style

The following guidelines for document format come mainly from Turabian's *Manual for Writers*, which offers more specific advice than *The Chicago Manual* on the format of students' papers. See pages 765–66 for the format of footnotes, endnotes, and a list of works cited. And see pages 116–26 for advice on type fonts, lists, illustrations, and other elements of document design.

Margins and spacing Use minimum one-inch margins on all pages of the body. (The first page of endnotes or works cited begins two inches from the top; see pp. 765–66.) Double-space your own text and between notes and works-cited entries; single-space displayed quotations (see below) and each note and works-cited entry.

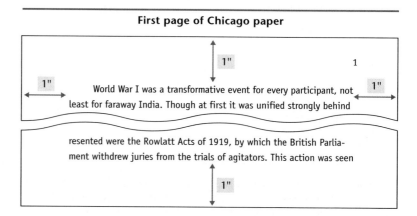

First page of Chicago paper

1"
1
1"
World War I was a transformative event for every participant, not least for faraway India. Though at first it was unified strongly behind

resented were the Rowlatt Acts of 1919, by which the British Parliament withdrew juries from the trials of agitators. This action was seen
1"

Paging Number pages consecutively from the first text page through the end (endnotes or works cited). Use Arabic numerals (1, 2, 3) in the upper right corner of all pages except the first page of endnotes and first page of works cited. On those pages, the number falls at the foot of the page (see pp. 765–66).

Title page On an unnumbered title page provide the title of the paper, your name, the course title, your instructor's name, and the date. Use all capital letters, and center everything horizontally. Double-space between adjacent lines, and add extra space as shown opposite.

Poetry and long prose quotations Display certain quotations separately from your text: three or more lines of poetry and two or more sentences of prose. Indent a displayed quotation four spaces from the left, single-space the quotation, and double-space both above it and below it. *Do not add quotation marks.*

Gandhi articulated the principles of his movement in 1922:

> I discovered that pursuit of truth did not permit violence being inflicted on one's opponent, but that he must be weaned from error by patience and sympathy. For what appears to be truth to one may appear to be error to the other. And patience means self-suffering.[9]

Chicago title page

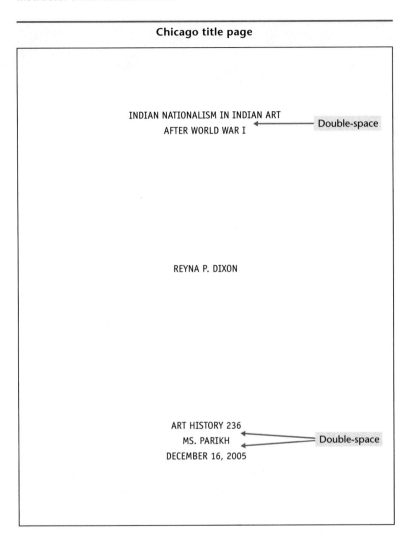

HIGHLIGHTS

Chapter 52 begins by introducing students to research methods in the social sciences, including observation, interviewing, survey conducting, and experimentation. It also covers the distinction between quantitative and qualitative data, types of social science assignments, writing tools, and language conventions. Updated resources for research in the various disciplines, including both print and online resources, are listed in 52c. Section 52d explains to students how to cite sources in the social sciences according to American Psychological Association (APA) standards. This section includes expanded coverage of how to document online and media sources. Section 52e shows students how to format documents using APA style. The chapter concludes with excerpts from a sample student paper for a sociology course.

RESOURCES AND IDEAS

Bazerman, Charles. *The Informed Writer: Using Sources in the Disciplines.* 5th ed. Boston: Houghton, 1995. Bazerman offers a number of examples and exercises to help students learn the discourse conventions of various academic disciplines.

College Composition and Communication 36 (1985). All four numbers of this volume are devoted to the role(s) writing plays in professional and academic disciplines; numbers 2 and 4 are particularly rich.

Daemmrich, Ingrid. "A Bridge to Academic Discourse: Social Science Research Strategies in the Freshman Composition Course." *College Composition and Communication* 40 (1989): 343–48. Daemmrich argues for use of social-science writing as a way to help students move from personal to academic writing.

COMPANION WEB SITE

See page IAE-61 for companion Web site content description.

CHAPTER 52

Writing in the Social Sciences

The social sciences—including anthropology, economics, education, management, political science, psychology, and sociology—focus on the study of human behavior. As the name implies, the social sciences examine the way human beings relate to themselves, to their environment, and to one another.

52a Using the methods and evidence of the social sciences

Researchers in the social sciences systematically pose a question, formulate a **hypothesis** (a generalization that can be tested), collect data, analyze those data, and draw conclusions to support, refine, or disprove their hypothesis. This is the scientific method developed in the natural sciences (see p. 807).

Social scientists gather data in several ways:

- **They make firsthand observations of human behavior,** recording the observations in writing or on audio- or videotape.
- **They interview subjects about their attitudes and behavior,** recording responses in writing or on tape. (See pp. 596–97 for guidelines on conducting an interview.)
- **They conduct broader surveys using questionnaires,** asking people about their attitudes and behavior. (See the box on the facing page.)
- **They conduct controlled experiments,** structuring an environment in which to encourage and measure a specific behavior.

In their writing, social scientists explain their own research or analyze and evaluate others' research.

http://www.ablongman.com/littlebrown ▶

Visit the companion Web site for more help with writing in the social sciences.

Conducting a survey

- **Decide what you want to find out—what your hypothesis is.** The questions you ask should be dictated by your purpose.
- **Define your population.** Think about the kinds of people your hypothesis is about—for instance, college men, or five-year-old children. Plan to sample this population so that your findings will be representative.
- **Write your questions.** Surveys may contain closed questions that direct the respondent's answers (checklists and multiple-choice, true/false, or yes/no questions) or open-ended questions allowing brief, descriptive answers. Avoid loaded questions that reveal your own biases or make assumptions about subjects' answers, such as "Do you want the United States to support democracy in China?" or "How much more money does your father make than your mother?"
- **Test your questions.** Use a few respondents with whom you can discuss the answers. Eliminate or recast questions that respondents find unclear, discomforting, or unanswerable.
- **Tally the results.** Count the actual numbers of answers, including any nonanswers.
- **Seek patterns in the raw data.** Such patterns may confirm or contradict your hypothesis. Revise the hypothesis or conduct additional research if necessary.

Social science research methods generate two kinds of data:

- *Quantitative data* **are numerical,** such as statistical evidence based on surveys, polls, tests, and experiments. When public-opinion pollsters announce that 47 percent of US citizens polled approve of the President's leadership, they are offering quantitative data gained from a survey. Social science writers present quantitative data in graphs, charts, and other illustrations that accompany their text.
- *Qualitative data* **are not numerical but more subjective:** they are based on interviews, firsthand observations, and inferences, taking into account the subjective nature of human experience. Examples include an anthropologist's description of the initiation rites in a culture she is studying or a psychologist's interpretation of interviews he conducted with a group of adolescents.

52b Understanding writing assignments in the social sciences

Depending on what social science courses you take, you may be asked to complete a variety of assignments:

Hemmeter, Thomas, and David Conners. "Research Papers in Economics: A Collaborative Approach." *Journal of Advanced Composition* 7 (1987): 81–91. The authors describe a course taught collaboratively by an economist and a writing specialist, focusing on activities leading to the term-ending research paper.

Shamoon, Linda K., and Robert A. Schwegler. "Sociologists Reading Student Texts: Expectations and Perceptions." *The Writing Instructor* 7 (1988): 71–81. The authors argue that the way sociologists perceive the features of a student paper differ considerably from the way composition instructors often perceive the features. Sociologists look first of all for a line of sociological reasoning carried throughout a paper, supported by evidence acceptable to sociologists and made clear by indicators such as topic sentences.

QUALITATIVE AND QUANTITATIVE DATA

To help your students become more familiar with the two kinds of data, have them conduct a brief study of a topical conversation while lurking on an online discussion (but not a synchronous one). Ask them to choose a collection of postings from the discussion (a day's worth, perhaps) and to gather some statistical data about the conversation (for instance, the number of participants, the number of times a word or phrase is mentioned, or the number of participants adhering to each opinion stated). After amassing the data, they can graph it and post the graph to your class Web site. Then ask them to go back over the same collection of postings and write a qualitative description of them in the style of one of the social science disciplines.

LINKS TO EXAMPLES

Go online to locate good published examples of each of the kinds of papers listed in 50b: a research summary, a case analysis, a problem-solving analysis, a research paper, and a research report. Download them or post links on your class Web site so that students can have models easily available to them.

Further reading for students

If your students need more help in writing for the social sciences, you might refer them to some of the following:

Becker, Howard S., et al. *Writing for Social Scientists: How to Start and Finish Your Thesis, Book, or Article.* Chicago: U of Chicago P, 1986.

Cuba, Lee. *A Short Guide to Writing About Social Science.* 4th ed. New York: Longman, 2002.

Dunn, Dana. *A Short Guide to Writing About Psychology.* New York: Longman, 2004.

Holland, Kenneth, and Arthur W. Biddle. *Writer's Guide: Political Science.* Lexington: Heath, 1987.

McCloskey, Donald. *The Writing of Economics.* New York: Macmillan, 1987.

Richlin-Klonsky, Judith, and Ellen Strenski, eds. *A Guide to Writing Sociology Papers.* 4th ed. New York: Worth, 1997.

SMART QUESTIONS

Framing questions is one of the most important aspects of good social-science research, and students will need to apply their skills in critical thinking and in writing to the task of composing research questions and survey questions. Have your students practice question writing by conceiving a research question and then carrying out a small survey among the members of the class. Then have them work in small groups to look at survey results and evaluate each student's research and survey questions.

- **A summary or review of research** reports on the available research literature on a subject, such as infants' perception of color.
- **A case analysis** explains the components of a phenomenon, such as a factory closing.
- **A problem-solving analysis** explains the components of a problem, such as unreported child abuse, and suggests ways to solve it.
- **A research paper** interprets and sometimes analyzes and evaluates the writings of other social scientists about a subject, such as the effect of national appeals in advertising. An example appears in Chapter 48, pages 690–724.
- **A research report** explains the author's own original research or the author's attempt to replicate someone else's research. A research report begins on page 803.

Many social science disciplines have special requirements for the content and organization of each kind of paper. The requirements appear in the style guides of the disciplines, listed on page 784. For instance, the American Psychological Association specifies the outline for research reports that is illustrated on pages 803–06. Because of the differences among disciplines and even among different kinds of papers in the same discipline, you should always ask your instructor what he or she requires for an assignment.

52c Using the tools and language of the social sciences

The following guidelines for tools and language apply to most social sciences. However, the particular discipline you are writing in, or an instructor in a particular course, may have additional requirements. Many of the research sources listed on the next several pages can tell you more about your discipline's conventions.

1 Writing tools

Many social scientists rely on a **research journal** or **log**, in which they record their ideas throughout the research-writing process. Even if a research journal is not required in your courses, you may want to use one. As you begin formulating a hypothesis, you can record preliminary questions. Then when you are in the field conducting research, you can use the journal to react to the evidence you are collecting, to record changes in your perceptions and ideas, and to assess your progress. (See pp. 152–53 and 559–60 for more on journals.)

To avoid confusing your reflections on the evidence with the evidence itself, keep records of actual data—notes from interviews, observations, surveys, and experiments—separately from the journal.

2 Language considerations

Each social science discipline has specialized terminology for concepts basic to the discipline. In sociology, for example, the words *mechanism, identity,* and *deviance* have specific meanings different from those of everyday usage. And *identity* means something different in sociology, where it applies to groups of people, than in psychology, where it applies to the individual. Social scientists also use precise terms to describe or interpret research. For instance, they say *The subject expressed a feeling of* rather than *The subject felt* because human feelings are not knowable for certain; or they say *These studies indicate* rather than *These studies prove* because conclusions are only tentative.

Just as social scientists strive for objectivity in their research, so they strive to demonstrate their objectivity through language in their writing. They avoid expressions such as *I think* in order to focus attention on what the evidence shows, not the researcher's opinions. (However, many social scientists prefer *I* to *the researcher* when they refer to their own actions, as in *I then interviewed the subjects.* Ask your instructor for his or her preferences.) Social scientists also avoid direct or indirect expression of their personal biases or emotions, either in discussions of other researchers' work or in descriptions of research subjects. Thus one social scientist does not call another's work *sloppy* or *immaculate* and does not refer to his or her own subjects as *drunks* or *innocent victims.* Instead, the writer uses neutral language and ties conclusions strictly to the data.

3 Research sources

■ Specialized encyclopedias, dictionaries, and bibliographies

General
International Bibliography of the Social Sciences
International Encyclopedia of the Social and Behavioral Sciences
The Social Science Encyclopedia

Business and economics
Accountant's Handbook
Dictionary of Business and Economics
Encyclopedia of Advertising
Encyclopedia of Banking and Finance
Encyclopedia of Business Information Sources
Encyclopedia of Management
Handbook of Modern Marketing

RESEARCH LOGS

Encourage any student considering a career in research to keep a research log. Almost every company that employs researchers will require those workers to document each day's activities in a log in order to record and protect potentially patent-worthy research.

COLLABORATIVE LEARNING

CLASSIFYING SAMPLES

Ask students to bring in examples of writing assignments from their social-science courses and to classify them according to the list on page 780. They might also work in teams to interview professors from their other courses about which writing strategies are most important for success in those courses.

COLLABORATIVE LEARNING

LANGUAGE CHECK

Have students work in small groups to check each other's drafts for biased language and make suggestions for revision.

COLLABORATIVE LEARNING

SOURCES

To help students become familiar with the social-science research sources listed on pages 781–84, have each student look up one source and make a brief presentation on it in class.

McGraw-Hill Encyclopedia of Economics
The MIT Dictionary of Modern Economics
The New Palgrave Dictionary of Economics and the Law

Education
Bibliographic Guide to Education
Encyclopedia of American Education
Encyclopedia of Education
Encyclopedia of Educational Research
The Philosophy of Education: An Encyclopedia

Political science and law
Black's Law Dictionary
Guide to American Law
Index to Legal Periodicals and Books
Information Sources of Political Sciences
Political Science: A Guide to Reference and Information Sources

Psychology, sociology, and anthropology
African American Encyclopedia
Afro-American Reference
Asian American Studies
Bibliographic Guide to Psychology
Encyclopedia of Anthropology
Encyclopedia of Crime and Justice
Encyclopedia of Psychology
Encyclopedia of Sociology
Guide to Research on North American Indians
Library Use: A Handbook for Psychology
Macmillan Dictionary of Anthropology
A Native American Encyclopedia: History, Culture, and Peoples
Race and Ethnic Relations: A Bibliography
Sociology: A Guide to Reference and Information Sources
Sourcebook of Hispanic Culture in the United States

■ Indexes

ABC: Pol Sci
ABI/INFORM (business)
Abstracts in Anthropology
Business Periodicals Index
Business Publications Index and Abstracts
Business Source Premier
Criminal Justice Periodicals Index
Dissertation Abstracts International (doctoral dissertations)
EconLit
Education Index
ERIC, Current Index to Journals in Education
Human Resources Abstracts
Index to Legal Periodicals
International Political Science Abstracts

Journal of Economic Literature
PAIS International in Print (government publications and political science journals)
PsychInfo
PsychLIT
Psychological Abstracts
Social Sciences Index
Sociofile
Sociological Abstracts
Urban Affairs Abstracts
Wilson Business Abstracts

▓ Book reviews

Index to Book Reviews in the Social Sciences

▓ Web sources

For updates of these sources and URLs, visit *ablongman.com/ littlebrown.*

General

Data on the Net (*odwin.ucsd.edu/idata*)
Social Science Information Gateway (*sosig.ac.uk*)
WWW Virtual Library: Social and Behavorial Sciences (*vlib.org/ SocialSciences*)

Anthropology

American Anthropological Association (*aaanet.org*)
American Folklife Center (*loc.gov/folklife*)
Anthro.Net (*anthro.net*)
Anthropology Resources on the Internet (*anthropologie.net*)

Business and economics

Biz/ed (*bized.ac.uk*)
Academic Info: Business Administration (*academicinfo.net/bus.html*)
Resources for Economists on the Internet (*rfe.org*)
Virtual International Business and Economic Sources (*library.uncc.edu/ display/?dept=reference&format=open&page=68*)

Education

Education Reference Desk (*eduref.org*)
Gateway to Educational Materials (*thegateway.org*)
Learner.org (*learner.org*)
Social Science Information Gateway: Education (*sosig.ac.uk/roads/ subject-listing/World/educ.html*)
US Department of Education (*ed.gov*)

Ethnic and gender studies

Diversity and Ethnic Studies (*public.iastate.edu/~savega/divweb2.htm*)
Diversity Database (*inform.umd.edu/EdRes/Topic/Diversity*)
Voice of the Shuttle: Gender Studies (*vos.ucsb.edu/browse.asp?id=2711*)
Gender Inn (*www.uni-koeln.de/phil-fak/englisch/datenbank/e_index.htm*)

Political science and law
Legal Information Institute (*www.law.cornell.edu*)
Librarians' Index to the Internet: Law (*lii.org/search/file/law*)
Oyez: US Supreme Court Multimedia (*www.oyez.org*)
Political Science Resources (*psr.keele.ac.uk*)
Thomas Legislative Information on the Internet (*thomas.loc.gov*)
Ultimate Political Science Links (*www.rvc.cc.il.us/faclink/pruckman/*
PSLinks.htm)

Psychology
Encyclopedia of Psychology (*www.psychology.org*)
PsychCrawler (*www.psychcrawler.com*)
Psychology: Online Resource Central (*psych-central.com*)
Psych Web (*psywww.com*)

Sociology
Social Science Information Gateway: Sociology (*sosig.ac.uk/roads/*
subject-listing/World/sociol.html)
SocioSite (*www2.fmg.uva.nl/sociosite*)
SocioWeb (*socioweb.com*)
WWW Virtual Library: Sociology (*socserv2.socsci.mcmaster.ca/*
w3virtsoclib)

52d   Citing sources in APA style

Some of the social sciences publish style guides that advise practitioners how to organize, document, and type papers. The following is a partial list:

American Anthropological Association, *AAA Style Guide*, 2002, *http://*
www.aaanet.org/pubs/style_guide.htm
American Political Science Association, *Style Manual for Political Science*, 2001
American Psychological Association, *Publication Manual of the American Psychological Association*, 5th ed., 2001
American Sociological Association, *ASA Style Guide*, 2nd ed., 1997
Linguistic Society of America, "LSA Style Sheet," published every December in *LSA Bulletin*
A Uniform System of Citation (law), 17th ed., 2001

By far the most widely used style is that of the American Psychological Association (APA), so we detail it here. Always ask your instructor in any discipline what style you should use.

Note If you use APA style frequently and write on a computer, you may want to obtain *APA-Style Helper*, a student's companion to the *Publication Manual of the American Psychological Association* that formats source citations in APA style. It can be downloaded (for a fee) from the APA Web site at *apa.org/software*. Other bibliography programs can also help with APA style. See page 638.

APA parenthetical text citations

1. Author not named in your text *785*
2. Author named in your text *785*
3. A work with two authors *786*
4. A work with three to five authors *786*
5. A work with six or more authors *786*
6. A work with a group author *787*
7. A work with no author or an anonymous work *787*
8. One of two or more works by the same author(s) *787*
9. Two or more works by different authors *787*
10. An indirect source *787*
11. An electronic source *788*

1 Using APA parenthetical text citations

In the APA documentation style, parenthetical citations within the text refer the reader to a list of sources at the end of the text. A parenthetical citation contains the author's last name, the date of publication, and sometimes the page number from which material is borrowed.

1. Author not named in your text

One critic of Milgram's experiments insisted that the subjects "should have been fully informed of the possible effects on them" (Baumrind, 1988, p. 34).

When you do not name the author in your text, place in parentheses the author's last name and the date of the source. Separate the elements with commas. Position the reference so that it is clear what material is being documented *and* so that the reference fits as smoothly as possible into your sentence structure. (See pp. 654–56 for guidelines.) The following would also be correct:

In the view of one critic of Milgram's experiments (Baumrind, 1988), the subjects "should have been fully informed of the possible effects on them" (p. 34).

Unless none is available, the APA requires a page or other identifying number for a direct quotation (as in the preceding examples) and recommends an identifying number for a paraphrase. Use an appropriate abbreviation or symbol before the number—for instance, p. for *page* and ¶ for *paragraph* (or para. if you do not have the symbol). The identifying number may fall with the author and date (first example) or by itself in a separate pair of parentheses (second example). See also model 11, page 788.

2. Author named in your text

Baumrind (1988) insisted that the subjects in Milgram's study "should have been fully informed of the possible effects on them" (p. 34).

When you use the author's name in the text, do not repeat it in the reference. Place the source date in parentheses after the author's name. Place any page or paragraph reference either after the borrowed material (as in the example) or with the date: (1988, p. 34). If you cite the same source again in the paragraph, you need not repeat the reference as long as it is clear that you are using the same source and the page number (if any) is the same. Here is a later sentence from the paragraph containing the preceding example:

> Baumrind also criticized the experimenters' rationale.

3. A work with two authors

> Pepinsky and DeStefano (1997) demonstrated that a teacher's language often reveals hidden biases.

> One study (Pepinsky & DeStefano, 1997) demonstrated the hidden biases often revealed in a teacher's language.

When given in the text, two authors' names are connected by and. In a parenthetical citation, they are connected by an ampersand, &.

4. A work with three to five authors

> Pepinsky, Dunn, Rentl, and Corson (1999) further demonstrated the biases evident in gestures.

In the first citation of a work with three to five authors, name all the authors, as in the example above.

In the second and subsequent references to a work with three to five authors, generally give only the first author's name, followed by et al. (Latin abbreviation for "and others"):

> In the work of Pepinsky et al. (1999), the loaded gestures included head shakes and eye contact.

However, two or more sources published in the same year could shorten to the same form—for instance, two references shortening to Pepinsky et al., 1999. In that case, cite the last names of as many authors as you need to distinguish the sources, and then give et al.: for instance, (Pepinsky, Dunn, et al., 1999) and (Pepinsky, Bradley, et al., 1999).

5. A work with six or more authors

> One study (Rutter et al., 2003) attempted to explain these geographical differences in adolescent experience.

For six or more authors, even in the first citation of the work, give only the first author's name, followed by et al. If two or more sources published in the same year shorten to the same form, give additional names as explained with model 4.

6. A work with a group author

An earlier prediction was even more somber (Lorenz Research, 2003).

For a work that lists an institution, agency, corporation, or other group as author, treat the name of the group as if it were an individual's name. If the name is long and has a familiar abbreviation, you may use the abbreviation in the second and subsequent citations. For example, you might abbreviate American Psychological Association as APA.

7. A work with no author or an anonymous work

One article ("Right to Die," 1996) noted that a death-row inmate may crave notoriety.

For a work with no named author, use the first two or three words of the title in place of an author's name, excluding an initial *The, A,* or *An.* Italicize book and journal titles, place quotation marks around article titles, and capitalize the significant words in all titles cited in the text. (In the reference list, however, do not use quotation marks for article titles, and capitalize only the first word in all but periodical titles. See pp. 788 and 789.)

For a work that lists "Anonymous" as the author, use this word in the citation: (Anonymous, 1999).

8. One of two or more works by the same author(s)

At about age seven, most children begin to use appropriate gestures to reinforce their stories (Gardner, 1973a).

When you cite one of two or more works by the same author(s), the date will tell readers which source you mean—as long as your reference list includes only one source published by the author(s) in that year. If your reference list includes two or more works published by the same author(s) *in the same year,* the works should be lettered in the reference list (see p. 792). Then your parenthetical citation should include the appropriate letter: 1973a in the preceding example.

9. Two or more works by different authors

Two studies (Herskowitz, 1994; Marconi & Hamblen, 1999) found that periodic safety instruction can dramatically reduce employees' accidents.

List the sources in alphabetical order by their authors' names. Insert a semicolon between sources.

10. An indirect source

Supporting data appeared in a study by Wong (cited in Marconi, 2004).

The phrase cited in indicates that the reference to Wong's study was found in Marconi. Only Marconi then appears in the list of references.

11. An electronic source

Ferguson and Hawkins (2002) did not anticipate the "evident hostility" of participants (¶ 6).

Electronic sources can be cited like printed sources, usually with the author's last name and the publication date. When quoting or paraphrasing electronic sources that number paragraphs instead of pages, provide the paragraph number preceded by the symbol ¶ if you have it, or by para. Even if the source does not number its paragraphs, you can still direct readers to a specific location by listing the heading under which the quotation appears and then (counting paragraphs yourself) the number of the paragraph in which the quotation appears—for example, (Morrison & Lee, 2004, Method section, ¶ 4). When the source does not number pages or paragraphs or provide frequent headings, omit any reference number.

2 Using an APA reference list

In APA style, the in-text parenthetical citations refer to the list of sources at the end of the text. This list, titled References, includes full publication information on every source cited in the paper. The list falls at the end of the paper, numbered in sequence with the preceding pages.

The following sample shows the format of the first page of the APA reference list:

APA reference list

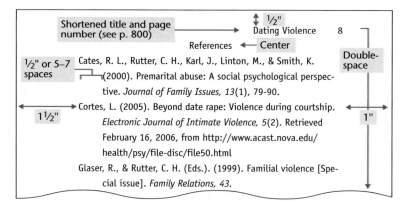

Arrangement Arrange sources alphabetically by the author's last name. If there is no author, alphabetize by the first main word of the title.

Spacing Double-space everything in the references, as shown in the sample, unless your instructor requests single spacing. (If you do single-space the entries themselves, always double-space *between* them.)

Indention As illustrated in the sample, begin each entry at the left margin, and indent the second and subsequent lines five to seven spaces or one-half inch. See page 657 for instructions on creating this so-called hanging indent on your word processor.

Punctuation Separate the parts of the reference (author, date, title, and publication information) with a period and one space. Do not use a final period in references to electronic sources, which conclude with an electronic address (see pp. 795–97).

Authors For works with up to six authors, list all authors with last name first, separating names and parts of names with commas. Use initials for first and middle names even when names are listed fully on the source itself. Use an ampersand (&) before the last author's name. See model 3, page 791, for the treatment of seven or more authors.

Publication date Place the publication date in parentheses after the author's or authors' names, followed by a period. Generally, this date is the year only, though for some sources (such as magazine and newspaper articles) it includes month and sometimes day as well.

Titles In titles of books and articles, capitalize only the first word of the title, the first word of the subtitle, and proper nouns; all other words begin with small letters. In titles of journals, capitalize all significant words (see p. 491 for guidelines). Italicize the titles of books and journals. Do not italicize or use quotation marks around the titles of articles.

City of publication For sources that are not periodicals (such as books or government publications), give the city of publication. The following US cities do not require state names as well: Baltimore, Boston, Chicago, Los Angeles, New York, Philadelphia, and San Francisco. Follow their names with a colon. For most other cities, add a comma after the city name, give the two-letter postal abbreviation of the state, and then add a colon. (You may omit the state if the publisher is a university whose name includes the state name, such as University of Arizona.)

Publisher's name Also for nonperiodical sources, give the publisher's name after the place of publication and a colon. Use shortened names for many publishers (such as Morrow for William Morrow), and omit *Co., Inc.,* and *Publishers.* However, give full names for associations, corporations, and university presses (such as Harvard University Press), and do not omit *Books* or *Press* from a publisher's name.

THE IMPORTANCE OF RESEARCH DATES

Remind students that since the social sciences prize the timeliness of research as much as the author's name, APA text citations combine name and date while references place the date just after the author's name. If students understand why a documentation system looks the way it does, they are more likely to learn how to use it correctly.

Page numbers Use the abbreviation p. or pp. before page numbers in books and in newspapers. Do *not* use the abbreviation for journals and magazines. For inclusive page numbers, include all figures: 667–668.

If the following pages don't provide a model for a kind of source you used, try to find one that comes close, and provide ample information so that readers can trace the source. Often, you will have to combine models to cite a source accurately—for instance, combining

APA reference-list models

Books

1. A book with one author *791*
2. A book with two to six authors *791*
3. A book with seven or more authors *791*
4. A book with an editor *791*
5. A book with a translator *791*
6. A book with a group author *791*
7. A book with no author or an anonymous book *792*
8. Two or more works by the same author(s) published in the same year *792*
9. A later edition *792*
10. A work in more than one volume *792*
11. An article or chapter in an edited book *793*

Periodicals

12. An article in a journal with continuous pagination throughout the annual volume *793*
13. An article in a journal that pages issues separately *793*
14. An abstract of a journal article *793*
15. An article in a magazine *794*
16. An article in a newspaper *794*
17. An unsigned article *794*
18. A review *794*

Electronic sources

19. A journal article that is published online and in print *795*
20. An article in an online journal *795*
21. A journal article retrieved from an electronic database *795*
22. An abstract retrieved from an electronic database *796*
23. An article in an online newspaper *796*
24. An entire Web site *796*
25. An independent document on the Web *796*
26. A document from the Web site of a university or government agency *796*
27. An online government report *796*
28. A multipage online document *796*
29. A part of an online document *797*
30. An entry on a Web log *797*
31. A retrievable online posting *797*
32. Electronic mail or a nonretrievable online posting *797*
33. Software *797*

Other sources

34. A report *798*
35. A government publication *798*
36. A doctoral dissertation *798*
37. An interview *799*
38. A motion picture *799*
39. A musical recording *799*
40. A television series or episode *799*

"A book with two to six authors" (model 2) and "An article in a journal" (model 12) for a journal article with two or more authors.

■ Books

1. A book with one author

Rodriguez, R. (1982). *A hunger of memory: The education of Richard Rodriguez.* Boston: Godine.

The initial R appears instead of the author's first name, even though the author's full first name appears on the source. In the title, only the first words of title and subtitle and the proper name are capitalized.

2. A book with two to six authors

Nesselroade, J. R., & Baltes, P. B. (1999). *Longitudinal research in behavioral studies.* New York: Academic Press.

An ampersand (&) precedes the last author's name.

3. A book with seven or more authors

Wimple, P. B., Van Eijk, M., Potts, C. A., Hayes, J., Obergau, W. R., Zimmer, S., et al. (2001). *Case studies in moral decision making among adolescents.* San Francisco: Jossey-Bass.

Substitute et al. (Latin abbreviation for "and others") for all authors' names after the first six.

4. A book with an editor

Dohrenwend, B. S., & Dohrenwend, B. P. (Eds.). (1999). *Stressful life events: Their nature and effects.* New York: Wiley.

List the editors' names as if they were authors, but follow the last name with (Eds.).—or (Ed.). with only one editor. Note the periods inside and outside the final parenthesis.

5. A book with a translator

Trajan, P. D. (1927). *Psychology of animals* (H. Simone, Trans.). Washington, DC: Halperin.

The name of the translator appears in parentheses after the title, followed by a comma, Trans. and a closing parenthesis, and a final period. Note also the absence of periods in DC.

6. A book with a group author

Lorenz Research. (2003). *Research in social studies teaching.* Baltimore: Arrow Books.

For a work with a group author—such as a research group, government agency, or corporation—begin the entry with the group name. In the references list, alphabetize the work as if the first main word (excluding *The, A,* and *An*) were an author's last name.

7. A book with no author or an anonymous book

Merriam-Webster's collegiate dictionary (11th ed.). (2003). Springfield, MA: Merriam-Webster.

When no author is named, list the work under its title, and alphabetize it by the first main word (excluding *The, A, An*).

For a work whose author is actually given as "Anonymous," use this word in place of the author's name and alphabetize it as if it were a name:

Anonymous. (2006). *Teaching research, researching teaching.* New York: Alpine Press.

8. Two or more works by the same author(s) published in the same year

Gardner, H. (1973a). *The arts and human development.* New York: Wiley.

Gardner, H. (1973b). *The quest for mind: Piaget, Lévi-Strauss, and the structuralist movement.* New York: Knopf.

When citing two or more works by exactly the same author(s), published in the same year—as in the examples above—arrange them alphabetically by the first main word of the title and distinguish the sources by adding a letter to the date. Both the date *and* the letter are used in citing the source in your text (see p. 787).

When citing two or more works by exactly the same author(s) but *not* published in the same year, arrange the sources in order of their publication dates, earliest first.

9. A later edition

Bolinger, D. L. (1981). *Aspects of language* (3rd ed.). New York: Harcourt Brace Jovanovich.

The edition number in parentheses follows the title and is followed by a period.

10. A work in more than one volume

Lincoln, A. (1953). *The collected works of Abraham Lincoln* (R. P. Basler, Ed.). (Vol. 5). New Brunswick, NJ: Rutgers University Press.

Lincoln, A. (1953). *The collected works of Abraham Lincoln* (R. P. Basler, Ed.). (Vols. 1–8). New Brunswick, NJ: Rutgers University Press.

The first entry cites a single volume (5) in the eight-volume set. The second cites all eight volumes. Use the abbreviation Vol. or Vols. in parentheses, and follow the closing parenthesis with a period. In the absence of an editor's name, the description of volumes would follow the title directly: *The collected works of Abraham Lincoln* (Vol. 5).

11. An article or chapter in an edited book

Paykel, E. S. (1999). Life stress and psychiatric disorder: Applications of the
   clinical approach. In B. S. Dohrenwend & B. P. Dohrenwend (Eds.),
   Stressful life events: Their nature and effects (pp. 239-264). New York:
   Wiley.

Give the publication date of the collection (1999 above) as the publication date of the article or chapter. After the article or chapter title and a period, say In and then provide the editors' names (in normal order), (Eds.) and a comma, the title of the collection, and the page numbers of the article in parentheses.

■ Periodicals: Journals, magazines, newspapers

12. An article in a journal with continuous pagination throughout the annual volume

Emery, R. E. (2005). Marital turmoil: Interpersonal conflict and the children of
   discord and divorce. *Psychological Bulletin, 92,* 310-330.

See page 666 for an explanation of journal pagination. Note that you do not place the article title in quotation marks and that you capitalize only the first words of the title and subtitle. In contrast, you italicize the journal title and capitalize all significant words. Separate the volume number from the title with a comma, and italicize the number. Do not add "pp." before the page numbers.

13. An article in a journal that pages issues separately

Dacey, J. (1998). Management participation in corporate buy-outs.
   Management Perspectives, 7(4), 20-31.

Consult page 666 for an explanation of journal pagination. In this case, place the issue number in parentheses after the volume number without intervening space. Do *not* italicize the issue number.

14. An abstract of a journal article

Emery, R. E. (2005). Marital turmoil: Interpersonal conflict and the children of
   discord and divorce. *Psychological Bulletin, 92,* 310-330. Abstract
   obtained from *Psychological Abstracts,* 2005, *69,* Item 1320.

When you cite the abstract of an article, rather than the article itself, give full publication information for the article, followed by

Abstract obtained from and the information for the collection of abstracts, including title, date, volume number, and either page number or other reference number (Item 1320 in the example).

15. An article in a magazine

Williams, N. (2005, October 24). Beethoven's late quartets. *The New York Review of Books*, 16-18.

If a magazine has volume and issue numbers, give them as in models 12 and 13. Also give the full date of the issue: year, followed by a comma, month, and day (if any). Give all page numbers even when the article appears on discontinuous pages, without "pp."

16. An article in a newspaper

Kolata, G. (2006, January 7). Kill all the bacteria! *The New York Times*, pp. B1, B6.

Give month *and* day along with year of publication. Use *The* in the newspaper name if the paper itself does. Precede the page number(s) with p. or pp.

17. An unsigned article

The right to die. (1996, October 11). *Time, 121*, 101.

List and alphabetize the article under its title, as you would a book with no author (model 7, p. 792).

18. A review

Dinnage, R. (1987, November 29). Against the master and his men [Review of the book *A mind of her own: The life of Karen Horney*]. *The New York Times Book Review*, 10-11.

If the review is not titled, use the bracketed information as the title, keeping the brackets.

■ Electronic sources

In general, the APA's electronic-source references begin as those for print references do: author(s), date, title. Then you add information on when and where you retrieved the source—for example, an online source might end Retrieved January 8, 2006, from http://www.isu.edu/finance-dl/46732 (in APA style, no period follows a URL at the end of the reference).

Using the following models for electronic sources, you may have to improvise to match your source to a model. Try to locate all the information required by a model, referring to the sample sources on pages 567–70 for help. However, if you search for and still cannot find some information, then give what you can find. If a source has no publication date, use n.d. (for *no date*) in place of a publication date (see model 28, p. 796).

Note When you need to divide a URL from one line to the next, APA style calls for breaking *only* after a slash or before a period. Do not hyphenate a URL.

19. A journal article that is published online and in print

Palfrey, A. (2003). Choice of mates in identical twins [Electronic version].
Modern Psychology, 4(1), 26-40.

If you consulted the online version of a journal article that appears the same way both online and in print, follow model 12 or 13 (p. 793) for a print journal article, and insert [Electronic version] between the article title and the following period.

If you believe that the online version you consulted differs in some way from the print version, omit the bracketed insert and provide a retrieval statement with the date of your access and the complete URL for the article:

Grady, G. F. (2003). The here and now of hepatitis B immunization. *Today's*
Medicine, 13, 145-151. Retrieved December 27, 2005, from
http://www.fmrt.org/todaysmedicine/Grady050203.html

20. An article in an online journal

Wissink, J. A. (2004). Techniques of smoking cessation among teens and
adults. *Adolescent Medicine, 2.* Retrieved August 16, 2005, from
http://www.easu.edu/AdolescentMedicine/2-Wissink.html

If the article has an identifying number, give it after the volume number and a comma.

21. A journal article retrieved from an electronic database

Wilkins, J. M. (1999). The myths of the only child. *Psychology Update, 11*(1),
16-23. Retrieved December 20, 2005, from ProQuest Direct database.

Many reference works and periodicals are available full-text from electronic databases to which your library subscribes, such as ProQuest Direct or LexisNexis. Your reference need not specify how you reached the database—for instance, through a Web site or on a CD-ROM. However, it should provide the appropriate information for the source itself—in the example here, for a journal article—and it should conclude with a retrieval statement giving the date of your access and the name of the database.

22. An abstract retrieved from an electronic database

Wilkins, J. M. (1999). The myths of the only child. *Psychology Update, 11*(1), 16-23. Abstract retrieved December 20, 2005, from ProQuest Direct database.

23. An article in an online newspaper

Pear, R. (2006, January 23). Gains reported for children of welfare to work families. *The New York Times on the Web.* Retrieved January 23, 2006, from http://www.nytimes.com/2006/01/23/national/23/WELF.html

24. An entire Web site (text citation)

The APA's Web site provides answers to frequently asked questions about style (http://www.apa.org).

Cite an entire Web site (rather than a specific page or document) by giving the URL in your text.

25. An independent document on the Web

Anderson, D. (2005, May 1). *Social constructionism and MOOs.* Retrieved August 6, 2005, from http://sites.unc.edu/~daniel/social_constructionism

Treat the title of an independent Web document like the title of a book. If the document has no named author, begin with the title and place the publication date after the title.

26. A document from the Web site of a university or government agency

McConnell, L. M., Koenig, B. A., Greeley, H. T., & Raffin, T. A. (2004, August 17). *Genetic testing and Alzheimer's disease: Has the time come?* Retrieved September 1, 2005, from Stanford University, Project in Genomics, Ethics, and Society Web site: http://scbe.stanford.edu/pges

Provide the name of the host organization and any sponsoring program as part of the retrieval statement.

27. An online government report

U.S. Department of Commerce, National Telecommunications and Information Administration. (2005, February). *A nation online: Entering the broadband age.* Retrieved January 22, 2006, from http://www.ntia.doc.gov/reports/anol/index.html

28. A multipage online document

Elston, C. (n.d.). *Multiple intelligences.* Retrieved June 6, 2005, from http://education.com/teachspace/intelligences

For an Internet document with multiple pages, each with its own URL, give the URL of the document's home page. Note the use of n.d. after the author's name to indicate that the document provides no publication date.

29. A part of an online document

Elston, C. (n.d.). Logical/math intelligence. In *Multiple intelligences*. Retrieved
June 6, 2005, from http://education.com/teachspace/intelligences/
logical.jsp

If the part of a document you cite has a label (such as "chapter 6" or "section 4"), provide that in parentheses after the document title: *Multiple intelligences* (chap. 6).

30. An entry on a Web log

Daswani, S. (2005, March 16). Hollywood vs. Silicon Valley. *Berkeley intellectual property Weblog.* Retrieved August 22, 2005, from http://www
.biplog.com/archive/cat_hollywood.html

31. A retrievable online posting

Tourville, M. (2006, January 6). European currency reform. Message posted to
International Finance electronic mailing list, archived at http://www.isu
.edu/finance-dl/46732

Include postings to discussion lists and newsgroups in your list of references *only* if they are retrievable by others. The source above is archived (as the reference makes plain) and is thus retrievable at the address given.

32. Electronic mail or a nonretrievable online posting (text citation)

At least one member of the research team has expressed reservations about the
design of the study (L. Kogod, personal communication, February 6, 2006).

Personal electronic mail and other online postings that are not retrievable by others should be cited only in your text, as in the preceding example.

33. Software

Project scheduler 9000 [Computer software]. (2006). Orlando, FL: Scitor.

Provide an author's name for the software if an individual has the rights to the program. If you obtain the software online, you can generally replace the producer's city and name with a retrieval statement that includes the URL.

■ **Other sources**

34. A report

> Gerald, K. (2003). *Medico-moral problems in obstetric care* (Report No. NP-71).
> St. Louis, MO: Catholic Hospital Association.

Treat the report like a book, but provide any report number in parentheses immediately after the title, with no punctuation between them.

For a report from the Educational Resources Information Center (ERIC), provide the ERIC document number in parentheses at the end of the entry:

> Jolson, M. K. (2001). *Music education for preschoolers* (Report No. TC-622).
> New York: Teachers College, Columbia University. (ERIC Document Reproduction Service No. ED 264488)

35. A government publication

> Hawaii. Department of Education. (2005). *Kauai district schools, profile 2004-05*. Honolulu, HI: Author.
>
> Stiller, A. (2002). *Historic preservation and tax incentives*. Washington, DC: U.S. Department of the Interior.
>
> U.S. House. Committee on Ways and Means. (2003). *Medicare payment for outpatient physical and occupational therapy services*. 108th Cong., 1st Sess. Washington, DC: U.S. Government Printing Office.

If no individual is given as the author, list the publication under the name of the sponsoring agency. When the agency is both the author and the publisher, use Author in place of the publisher's name, as in the first example.

36. A doctoral dissertation

A dissertation abstracted in DAI *and obtained from UMI:*

> Steciw, S. K. (1986). Alterations to the Pessac project of Le Corbusier. *Dissertation Abstracts International, 46,* 565C. (UMI No. 6216202)

A dissertation abstracted in DAI *and obtained from the university:*

> Chang, J. K. (2003). Therapeutic intervention in treatment of injuries to the hand and wrist (Doctoral dissertation, University of Michigan, 2003). *Dissertation Abstracts International, 50,* 162.

An unpublished dissertation:

> Delaune, M. L. (2005). *Child care in single-mother and single-father families: Differences in time, activity, and stress*. Unpublished doctoral dissertation, University of California, Davis.

37. An interview

Brisick, W. C. (2005, July 1). [Interview with Ishmael Reed]. *Publishers Weekly*,
41-42.

List a published interview under the interviewer's name. Provide
the publication information for the kind of source the interview appears in (here, a magazine). Immediately after the date, in brackets,
specify that the piece is an interview and give the subject's name if
necessary. For an interview with a title, add the title (with an initial
capital letter, no quotation marks, and no closing period) before the
bracketed information.

An interview you conduct yourself should not be included in
the list of references. Instead, use an in-text parenthetical citation,
as shown in model 32 (p. 797) for a nonretrievable online posting.

38. A motion picture

American Psychological Association (Producer). (2001). *Ethnocultural psychotherapy* [Motion picture]. (Available from the American Psychological
Association, 750 First Street, NE, Washington, DC 20002-4242, or online
from http://www.apa.org/videos/4310240.html)

Spielberg, S. (Director). (1993). *Schindler's list* [Motion picture]. United
States: Viacom.

A motion picture may be a film, DVD, or video. Depending on whose
work you are citing, begin with the name or names of the creator, director, producer, or primary contributor, followed by the function in
parentheses. (The second model above would begin with the producer's name if you were citing the motion picture as a whole, not
specifically the work of the director.) Add [Motion picture] after the title.
For a motion picture in wide circulation (second example), give the
country of origin and the name of the organization that released the
picture. For a motion picture that is not widely circulated (first example), give the distributor's name and address in parentheses.

39. A musical recording

Springsteen, B. (2002). Empty sky. *The rising* [CD]. New York: Columbia.

Begin with the name of the writer or composer. (If you cite another
artist's recording of the work, provide this information after the title
of the work—for example, [Recorded by E. Davila].) Give the medium in
brackets ([CD], [Cassette recording], and so on). Finish with the city and
name of the recording label.

40. A television series or episode

Cleveland, R., Andries, L., & Taylor, C. (Producers). (2005). *Six feet under*
[Television series]. New York: HBO.

Cleveland, R. (Writer), & Engler, M. (Director). (2005). Dillon Michael Cooper [Television series episode]. In R. Cleveland, L. Andries, & C. Taylor (Producers), *Six feet under*. New York: HBO.

For a television series, begin with the producers' names and identify their function in parentheses. Add [Television series] after the series title, and give the city and name of the network. For an episode, begin with the writer and then the director, identifying the function of each in parentheses, and add [Television series episode] after the episode title. Then provide the series information, beginning with In and the producers' names and function, giving the series title, and ending with the city and name of the network.

52e Formatting documents in APA style

The APA *Publication Manual* distinguishes between documents intended for publication (which will be set in type) and those submitted by students (which are the final copy). The guidelines below apply to most undergraduate papers. Check with your instructor for any modifications to this format.

Note See pages 788–90 for the APA format of a reference list. And see pages 116–26 for guidelines on type fonts, lists, tables and figures, and other elements of document design.

Margins Use one-inch margins on the top, bottom, and right side. Add another half-inch on the left to accommodate a binder.

Spacing and indentions Double-space your text and references. (See pp. 802–03 for spacing of displayed quotations.) Indent paragraphs and displayed quotations one-half inch or five to seven spaces.

Paging Begin numbering on the title page, and number consecutively through the end (including the reference list). Type Arabic numerals (1, 2, 3) in the upper right, about half an inch from the top.

Place a shortened version of your title five spaces to the left of the page number.

Title page Include the full title, your name, the course title, the instructor's name, and the date. Type the title on the top half of the page, followed by the identifying information, all centered horizontally and double-spaced. Include a shortened form of the title along with the page number at the top of this and all other pages.

Abstract Summarize (in a maximum of 120 words) your subject, research method, findings, and conclusions. Put the abstract on a page by itself.

APA title page

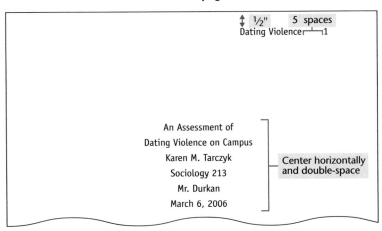

APA abstract

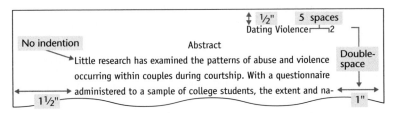

First page of APA body

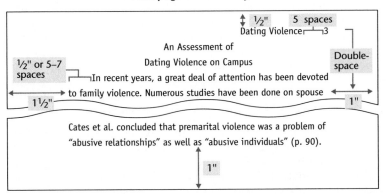

Body Begin with a restatement of the paper's title and then an introduction (not labeled). The introduction concisely presents the problem you researched, your research method, the relevant background (such as related studies), and the purpose of your research.

The next section, labeled Method, provides a detailed discussion of how you conducted your research, including a description of the research subjects, any materials or tools you used (such as questionnaires), and the procedure you followed. In the illustration below, the label Method is a first-level heading and the label *Sample* is a second-level heading.

Later page of APA body

Dating Violence   4

All the studies indicate a problem that is being neglected. My objective was to gather data on the extent and nature of pre-marital violence and to discuss possible interpretations.

Method ← Double-

Sample ← space

I conducted a survey of 200 students (134 females, 66 males) at a large state university in the northeastern United States. The sample consisted of students enrolled in an introductory sociology

---

Format headings (including a third level, if needed) as follows:

First-Level Heading

Second-Level Heading

Third-level heading. Run this heading into the text paragraph with a standard paragraph indention.

The Results section (labeled with a first-level heading) summarizes the data you collected, explains how you analyzed them, and presents them in detail, often in tables, graphs, or charts.

The Discussion section (labeled with a first-level heading) interprets the data and presents your conclusions. (When the discussion is brief, you may combine it with the previous section under the heading Results and Discussion.)

The References section, beginning a new page, includes all your sources. See pages 788–90 for an explanation and sample.

Long quotations Run into your text all quotations of forty words or less, and enclose them in quotation marks. For quotations of more than forty words, set them off from your text by indenting all lines one-half inch or five spaces, double-spacing above and below. For student papers, the APA allows single-spacing of displayed quotations:

Echoing the opinions of other Europeans at the time, Freud (1961) had a poor view of Americans:

> The Americans are really too bad. . . . Competition is much more pungent with them, not succeeding means civil death to every one, and they have no private resources apart from their profession, no hobby, games, love or other interests of a cultured person. And success means money. (p. 86)

Do not use quotation marks around a quotation displayed in this way.

Illustrations Present data in tables, graphs, or charts, as appropriate. (See the sample on p. 805 for a clear table format to follow.) Begin each illustration on a separate page. Number each kind of illustration consecutively and separately from the other (Table 1, Table 2, etc., and Figure 1, Figure 2, etc.). Refer to all illustrations in your text—for instance, (see Figure 3). Generally, place illustrations immediately after the text references to them. (See pp. 121–25 for more on illustrations.)

52f Examining a sample social science paper

On the following pages are excerpts from a sociology paper. The student followed the organization described on the preceding pages both in establishing the background for her study and in explaining her own research. She also followed the APA style of source citation and document format, although page borders and running heads are omitted here and only the required page breaks are indicated.

■ Excerpts from a research report

[Title page. See also pp. 801–02]

An Assessment of

Dating Violence on Campus

Karen M. Tarczyk

Sociology 213

Mr. Durkan

March 6, 2006

[New page.]

Abstract

Little research has examined the patterns of abuse and violence occurring within couples during courtship. With a questionnaire administered to a sample of college students, the extent and nature of such abuse and violence were investigated. The results, some interpretations, and implications for further research are discussed.

MODELS OF STUDENT WRITING

Karen Tarczyk's paper may give your students a better idea of what their social-science professors will expect from their writing. Her report is well organized, and she uses unbiased language throughout. You may want to discuss the conciseness and clarity of her abstract, the way she sets up the central problem and reviews the relevant research, her presentation of methodology and results, and the cogency of her discussion and interpretation of results.

COLLABORATIVE LEARNING

APPROACHING THE TOPIC

The topic of Karen Tarczyk's paper and its findings about dating violence may be interesting to your students. They may have a lot to say about James Makepeace's contention that violence in dating relationships potentially leads to violence in later domestic relationships. If you have received other papers on the subject, you might bring them in to give students a sense of approaches to the topic. Then, have them work in groups to brainstorm ideas and questions for further research.

[New page.]

An Assessment of Dating
Violence on Campus

In recent years, a great deal of attention has been devoted to family violence. Numerous studies have been done on spouse and child abuse. However, violent behavior occurs in dating relationships as well, yet the problem of dating violence has been relatively ignored by sociological research. It should be examined further since the premarital relationship is one context in which individuals learn and adopt behaviors that surface later in marriage.

The sociologist James Makepeace (1989) contended that courtship violence is a "potential mediating link" between violence in one's family of orientation and violence in one's later family of procreation (p. 103). Studying dating behaviors at Bemidji State University in Minnesota, Makepeace reported that one-fifth of the respondents had had at least one encounter with dating violence. He then extended these percentages to students nationwide, suggesting the existence of a major hidden social problem.

More recent research supports Makepeace's. Cates, Rutter, Karl, Linton, and Smith (2000) found that 22.3% of respondents at Oregon State University had been either the victim or the perpetrator of premarital violence. Another study (Cortes, 2005) found that so-called date rape, while much more publicized and discussed, was reported by many fewer woman respondents (2%) than was other violence during courtship (21%).

[The introduction continues.]

All these studies indicate a problem that is being neglected. My objective was to gather data on the extent and nature of premarital violence and to discuss possible interpretations.

Method

Sample

I conducted a survey of 200 students (134 females, 66 males) at a large state university in the northeastern United States. The sample consisted of students enrolled in an introductory sociology course.

[The explanation of method continues.]

The Questionnaire

A questionnaire exploring the personal dynamics of relationships was distributed during regularly scheduled class. Questions were answered anonymously in a 30-minute time period. The survey consisted of three sections.

[The explanation of method continues.]

Section 3 required participants to provide information about their current dating relationships. Levels of stress and frustration, communication between partners, and patterns of decision making were examined. These variables were expected to influence the amount of violence in a relationship. The next part of the survey was adopted from Murray Strauss's Conflict Tactics Scales (1992). These scales contain 19 items designed to measure conflict and the means of conflict resolution, including reasoning, verbal aggression, and actual violence.

Results

The questionnaire revealed significant levels of verbal aggression and threatened and actual violence among dating couples. A high number of students, 50% (62 of 123 subjects), reported that they had been the victim of verbal abuse. In addition, almost 14% (17 of 123) of respondents admitted being threatened with some type of violence, and more than 14% (18 of 123) reported being pushed, grabbed, or shoved. (See Table 1.)

[The explanation of results continues.]

[Table on a page by itself.]

Table 1

Incidence of Courtship Violence

Type of violence	Number of students reporting	Percentage of sample
Insulted or swore	62	50.4
Threatened to hit or throw something	17	13.8
Threw something	8	6.5
Pushed, grabbed, or shoved	18	14.6
Slapped	8	6.5
Kicked, bit, or hit with fist	7	5.7
Hit or tried to hit with something	2	1.6
Threatened with a knife or gun	1	0.8
Used a knife or gun	1	0.8

Discussion

Violence within premarital relationships has been relatively ignored. The results of the present study indicate that abuse and force do occur in dating relationships. Although the percentages are small, so was the sample. Extending them to the entire campus population would mean significant numbers. For example, if the nearly 6% incidence of being kicked, bitten, or hit with a fist is typical, then 300 students of a 5,000-member student body might have experienced this type of violence.

[The discussion continues.]

If the courtship period is characterized by abuse and violence, what accounts for it? The other sections of the survey examined some variables that appear to influence the relationship. Level of stress and frustration, both within the relationship and in the respondent's life, was one such variable. The communication level between partners, both the frequency of discussion and the frequency of agreement, was another.

[The discussion continues.]

The method of analyzing the data in this study, utilizing frequency distributions, provided a clear overview. However, more tests of significance and correlation and a closer look at the social and individual variables affecting the relationship are warranted. The courtship period may set the stage for patterns of married life. It merits more attention.

[New page.]

References

Cates, R. L., Rutter, C. H., Karl, J., Linton, M., & Smith, K. (2000). Premarital abuse: A social psychological perspective. *Journal of Family Issues, 13*(1), 79-90.

Cortes, L. (2005). Beyond date rape: Violence during courtship. *Electronic Journal of Intimate Violence, 5*(2). Retrieved February 16, 2006, from http://www.acast .nova.edu/health/psy/file-disc/file50.html

Glaser, R., & Rutter, C. H. (Eds.). (1999). Familial violence [Special issue]. *Family Relations, 43.*

Makepeace, J. M. (1989). Courtship violence among college students. *Family Relations, 28,* 97-103.

Strauss, M. L. (1992). *Conflict Tactics Scales.* New York: Sociological Tests.

CHAPTER 53

Writing in the Natural and Applied Sciences

The natural and applied sciences include biology, chemistry, physics, mathematics, engineering, computer science, and their branches. Their purpose is to understand natural and technological phenomena. (A *phenomenon* is a fact or event that can be known by the senses.) Scientists conduct experiments and write to explain the step-by-step processes in their methods of inquiry and discovery.

53a Using the methods and evidence of the sciences

Scientists investigate phenomena by the **scientific method,** a process of continual testing and refinement.

The scientific method

- **Observe carefully.** Accurately note all details of the phenomenon being researched.
- **Ask questions about the observations.**
- **Formulate a** *hypothesis,* or preliminary generalization, that explains the observed facts.
- **Test the hypothesis** with additional observation or controlled experiments.
- **If the hypothesis proves accurate, formulate a** *theory,* or unified model, that explains *why.*
- **If the hypothesis is disproved, revise it or start anew.**

Scientific evidence is almost always quantitative—that is, it consists of numerical data obtained from the measurement of phenomena. These data are called **empirical** (from a Greek word for

| http://www.ablongman.com/littlebrown ▶ |

Visit the companion Web site for more help with writing in the natural and applied sciences.

mycomplab 2.0

Please visit MyCompLab at *www.mycomplab.com* for more on the writing process.

HIGHLIGHTS

Chapter 53 introduces students to the essentials of writing in the natural and applied sciences. A brief discussion of the scientific method and empirical evidence begins the chapter, followed by discussions of types of science assignments (summaries, critiques, lab reports, research reports, and research proposals), writing tools, and language conventions. Library and online resources for research are listed, and there are sections on how to cite sources and format documents in the natural and applied sciences according to the style of the Council of Science Editors (CSE). The chapter concludes with excerpts from a sample student lab report for a biology course.

RESOURCES AND IDEAS

Greenway, William. "Imaginary Gardens with Real Toads: Nature Writing in the Curriculum." *Teaching English in the Two-Year College* 17 (1990): 189–92. Greenway demonstrates that nature writing, such as Annie Dillard's personal essays and Wordsworth's poetry, can help prepare students to write scientific research papers.

Hamilton, David. "Writing Science." *College English* 40 (1978): 32–40. Hamilton argues that instruction in science writing should emphasize writing not simply as a tool for scientists but as an essential and creative part of the scientific act.

Vargas, Marjorie Fink. "Writing Skills for Science Labs." *The Science Teacher* 53.8 (1986): 29–33. The author describes a fifty-minute class activity that helps students understand choices of person and voice dictated by the stylistic conventions of lab reports.

Winsor, Dorothy A. "Engineering Writing/Writing Engineering." *College Composition and Com-*

COMPANION WEB SITE

See page IAE-61 for companion Web site content description.

munication 41 (1990): 58–70. Winsor uses "contemporary views about the textual shaping of knowledge" to examine engineers' writing and their "domain-specific" knowledge.

FURTHER READING FOR STUDENTS

If your students need more help in writing about the sciences, you might refer them to these student texts:

Beall, Herbert, and John Trimbur. *A Short Guide to Writing About Chemistry.* 2nd ed. New York: Longman 2001.

Day, Robert. *How to Write and Publish a Scientific Paper.* 5th ed. Phoenix: Oryx, 1995.

Pechenik, Jan. *A Short Guide to Writing About Biology.* 5th ed. New York: Longman, 2004.

Porush, David. *A Short Guide to Writing About Science.* New York: Longman, 1994.

SCIENTISTS AS WRITERS

Students might think that good writing is not all that important in science. You can dispel this myth by pointing out that scientists need to be good critical thinkers and to wield language with power and accuracy in order to articulate their ideas and present their research.

COLLABORATIVE LEARNING

Ask students to bring in examples of writing assignments from their science courses and to classify them according to the list on this page. Which assignments are most and least frequently used? They might also interview professors from their science courses, individually or in teams, to learn which writing strategies are most important for success in those courses.

"experience"); they result from observation and experience, generally in a controlled laboratory setting but also (as sometimes in astronomy or biology) in the natural world. Often the empirical evidence for scientific writing comes from library research into other people's reports of their investigations. Surveys of known data or existing literature are common in scientific writing.

53b Understanding writing assignments in the sciences

No matter what your assignment, you will be expected to document and explain your evidence carefully so that anyone reading can check your sources and replicate your research. It is important for your reader to know the context of your research—both the previous experimentation and research on your particular subject (acknowledged in the survey of the literature) and the physical conditions and other variables surrounding your own work.

Assignments in the natural and applied sciences include the following:

- **A summary** distills a research article to its essence in brief, concise form. (Summary is discussed in detail on pp. 140–42.)
- **A critique** summarizes and critically evaluates a scientific report.
- **A laboratory report** explains the procedure and results of an experiment conducted by the writer. (See p. 820 for an example.)
- **A research report** explains the experimental research of other scientists and the writer's own methods, findings, and conclusions.
- **A research proposal** reviews the relevant literature and explains a plan for further research.

A laboratory report has four or five major sections:

1. **"Abstract"**: a summary of the report.
2. **"Introduction"** or **"Objective"**: a review of why the study was undertaken, a summary of the background of the study, and a statement of the problem being studied.
3. **"Method"** or **"Procedure"**: a detailed explanation of how the study was conducted, including any statistical analysis.
4. **"Results"**: an explanation of the major findings (including unexpected results) and a summary of the data presented in graphs and tables.
5. **"Discussion"**: an interpretation of the results and an explanation of how they relate to the goals of the experiment. This section also describes new hypotheses that might be tested as a result of the experiment. If the section is brief, it may be combined with the previous section in a single section labeled "Conclusions."

In addition, laboratory or research reports may include a list of references (if other sources were consulted). They almost always include tables and figures (graphs and charts) containing the data from the research (see p. 822).

53c Using the tools and language of the sciences

Tools and language concerns vary from discipline to discipline in the sciences. Consult your instructor for specifics about the field in which you are writing. You can also discover much about a discipline's tools and language from the research sources listed on the next three pages.

1 Writing tools

In the sciences a **lab notebook** or **scientific journal** is almost indispensable for accurately recording the empirical data from observations and experiments. Use such a notebook or journal for these purposes:

- **Record observations** from reading, from class, or from the lab.
- **Ask questions and refine hypotheses.**
- **Record procedures.**
- **Record results.**
- **Keep an ongoing record of ideas and findings** and how they change as data accumulate.
- **Sequence and organize your material** as you compile your findings and write your report.

Make sure that your records of data are clearly separate from your reflections on the data so that you don't mistakenly confuse the two in drawing your conclusions.

2 Language considerations

Science writers prefer to use objective language that removes the writer as a character in the situation and events being explained, except as the impersonal agent of change, the experimenter. Although usage is changing, scientists still rarely use *I* in their reports and evaluations, and they often resort to the passive voice of verbs, as in *The mixture was then subjected to centrifugal force.* This conscious objectivity focuses attention (including the writer's) on the empirical data and what they show. It discourages the writer from, say, ascribing motives and will to animals and plants. For instance, instead of asserting that the sea tortoise *evolved* its hard shell *to protect* its body, a scientist would write only what could be observed: that the hard shell *covers and thus protects* the tortoise's body.

Science writers typically change verb tenses to distinguish between established information and their own research. For established information, such as that found in journals and other reliable sources, use the present tense: *Baroreceptors monitor blood pressure.* For your own and others' research, use the past tense: *The bacteria died within three hours. Marti reported some success.*

Each discipline in the natural and applied sciences has a specialized vocabulary that permits precise, accurate, and efficient communication. Some of these terms, such as *pressure* in physics, have different meanings in the common language and must be handled carefully in science writing. Others, such as *enthalpy* in chemistry, have no meanings in the common language and must simply be learned and used correctly.

3   Research sources

The following lists give resources in the sciences.

■ Specialized encyclopedias, dictionaries, and bibliographies

American Medical Association Encyclopedia of Medicine
Bibliographic Guide to the History of Computing, Computers, and the Information Processing Industry
Concise Oxford Dictionary of Mathematics
Dorland's Illustrated Medical Dictionary
Encyclopedia of Bioethics
Encyclopedia of Chemistry
Encyclopedia of Computer Science and Technology
Encyclopedia of Ecology
Encyclopedia of Electronics
Encyclopedia of Oceanography
Encyclopedia of Physics
Encyclopedic Dictionary of Mathematics
Grzimek's Animal Life Encyclopedia
Information Sources in the Life Sciences
Introduction to Reference Sources in Health Sciences
McGraw-Hill Encyclopedia of Engineering
McGraw-Hill Encyclopedia of the Geological Sciences
McGraw-Hill Encyclopedia of Science and Technology
Science and Technology in World History
Space Almanac
Van Nostrand's Scientific Encyclopedia
World Resources (environment)

■ Indexes

ACM Guide to Computing Literature
Applied Science and Technology Index
Bibliography and Index of Geology
Biological Abstracts
Biological and Agricultural Index

Chemical Abstracts
Compendex Engineering Index
Computer Abstracts
Computer Literature Index
Cumulative Index to Nursing and Allied Health Literature
Dissertation Abstracts International
Ecology Abstracts
Engineering Index
Environment Abstracts
General Science Index
Index Medicus
MathSciNet: Mathematical Reviews
Physics Abstracts
Science Citation Index

■ Book reviews

Technical Book Review Index

■ Web sources

For updates of these sources and URLs, visit *ablongman.com/littlebrown*.

General

BUBL Link: Natural Sciences and Mathematics (*bubl.ac.uk/link/linkbrowse .cfm?menuid=6402*)
Google Directory: Science (*directory.google.com/Top/Science*)
Librarians' Index to the Internet: Science (*lii.org/search/file/scitech*)
The National Academies: Science, Engineering, and Medicine (*nas.edu*)
WWW Virtual Library: Natural Sciences and Mathematics (*vlib.org/Science .html*)

Biology

BioMedNet (*bmn.com*)
Biology Online (*biology-online.org*)
Biology.Arizona.Edu (*biology.arizona.edu*)
National Biological Information Infrastructure (*www.nbii.gov*)

Chemistry

Chemistry.org (*chemistry.org/portal/a/c/s/1/home.html*)
WWW Virtual Library: Links for Chemists (*liv.ac.uk/Chemistry/Links/links .html*)

Computer science

IEEE Computer Society (*computer.org*)
University of Texas Virtual Computer Library (*utexas.edu/computer/vcl*)
WWW Virtual Library: Computing and Computer Science (*vlib.org/ Computing*)

Engineering

American Society of Civil Engineers (*pubs.asce.org*)
Internet Guide to Engineering, Mathematics, and Computing (*eevl.ac.uk*)
National Academy of Engineering (*nae.edu*)

involving peer group interaction." The method requires "students to carry out an independent investigation of the synthesis of one or more aliphatic esters and to present their research in the form of professional papers."

Johnstone, Anne C., et al. *Uses for Journal-Keeping: An Ethnography of Writing in a University Science Class*. Norwood: Ablex, 1994. Johnstone offers an ethnographic study of the uses of different writing activities in learning science.

Killingsworth, M. Jimmie, and Michael K. Gilbertson. *Signs, Genres, and Communities in Technical Communication*. Amityville: Baywood, 1992. An examination of reports, manuals, and proposals characterizes them as "crystals of social action" within particular discourse communities.

Olmsted, John III. "Teaching Varied Technical Writing Styles in the Upper Division Laboratory." *Journal of Chemical Education* 61 (1984): 798–800. Olmsted describes a course that asks students to prepare reports in a variety of styles on experiments they have conducted. He describes in detail the twelve different kinds of reports students must submit during the course.

Wilkinson, A. M. "Jargon and the Passive Voice: Prescriptions and Proscriptions for Scientific Writing." *Journal of Technical Writing and Communication* 22 (1992): 319–25. The author reviews circumstances under which scientific writers should use the passive and warns against sweeping prohibitions of this strategy.

Young, Art, and Toby Fulwiler. *Writing Across the Disciplines: Research into Practice*. Upper Montclair: Boynton/Cook, 1986. This collection contains a number of essays demonstrating writing assignments in the sciences.

Environmental science
Center for International Earth Science Information Network (ciesin.org)
EE-Link: Environmental Education on the Internet (eelink.net)
EnviroLink (envirolink.org)
Environment Directory (webdirectory.com)

Geology
American Geological Institute (www.agiweb.org)
Digital Library for Earth System Education (dlese.org)
Geosource (www.library.uu.nl/geosource)
US Geological Survey Library (library.usgs.gov)

Health sciences
American Medical Association (ama-assn.org)
Centers for Disease Control and Prevention (www.cdc.gov)
Hardin MD (www.lib.uiowa.edu/hardin/md)
World Health Organization (who.int/en)

Mathematics
Math on the Web (www.ams.org/mathweb)
Internet Mathematics Library (mathforum.org/library)
Mathematical Atlas (math-atlas.org)

Physics and astronomy
American Institute of Physics (aip.org)
Astronomy Links (astronomylinks.com)
PhysicsWeb (physicsweb.org)
Science@NASA (science.hq.nasa.gov/index.html)

53d   Citing sources in CSE style

Within the natural and applied sciences, practitioners use one of two styles of documentation, varying slightly from discipline to discipline. Following are some of the style guides most often consulted:

American Chemical Society, *ACS Style Guide: A Manual for Authors and Editors,* 2nd ed., 1997
American Institute of Physics, *Style Manual for Guidance in the Preparation of Papers,* 4th ed., 1997
American Medical Association Manual of Style, 9th ed., 1998
Council of Biology Editors, *Scientific Style and Format: The CBE Manual for Authors, Editors, and Publishers,* 6th ed., 1994

The most thorough and widely used of these guides is the last one, *Scientific Style and Format.* Its sponsoring organization, the Council of Science Editors, was until 2000 called the Council of Biology Editors, so the style is abbreviated either CSE (as in this book) or CBE.

Scientific Style and Format details both styles of scientific documentation: one using author and date and one using numbers. Both types of text citation refer to a list of references at the end of the paper (see the next page). Ask your instructor which style you should use.

1 Using CSE name-year text citations

In the CSE name-year style, parenthetical text citations provide the last name of the author being cited and the source's year of publication. At the end of the paper, a list of references, arranged alphabetically by authors' last names, provides complete information on each source.

The CSE name-year style closely resembles the APA name-year style detailed on pages 785–88. You can follow the APA examples for in-text citations, making several notable changes for CSE:

- **Do not use a comma to separate the author's name and the date:** (Baumrind 1968, p. 34).
- **Separate two authors' names with and (not "&"):** (Pepinsky and DeStefano 1997).
- **Use and others (not "et al.") for three or more authors:** (Rutter and others 1996).
- **List unnamed or anonymous authors as Anonymous,** both in the citation and in the list of references: (Anonymous 1976).

2 Using CSE numbered text citations

In the CSE number style, raised numbers in the text refer to a numbered list of references at the end of the paper.

Two standard references[1,2] use this term.

These forms of immunity have been extensively researched.[3]

Hepburn and Tatin[2] do not discuss this project.

Assignment of numbers The number for each source is based on the order in which you cite the source in the text: the first cited source is 1, the second is 2, and so on.

Reuse of numbers When you cite a source you have already cited and numbered, use the original number again (see the last example above, which reuses the number 2 from the first example).

This reuse is the key difference between the CSE numbered citations and numbered references to footnotes or endnotes. In the CSE style, each source has only one number, determined by the order in which the source is cited. With notes, in contrast, the numbering proceeds in sequence, so that each source has as many numbers as it has citations in the text.

Citation of two or more sources When you cite two or more sources at once, arrange their numbers in sequence and separate them with a comma and no space, as in the first example on the previous page.

3 Using a CSE reference list

For both the name-year and the number styles of in-text citation, provide a list, titled References, of all sources you have cited. Format the page as shown for APA references on page 788, except that CSE entries are single-spaced.

The following examples show the differences and similarities between the name-year and number styles:

Name-year style

Hepburn PX, Tatin JM. 2005. Human physiology. New York: Columbia Univ Pr. 1026 p.

Number style

2. Hepburn PX, Tatin JM. Human physiology. New York: Columbia Univ Pr; 2005. 1026 p.

Spacing In both styles, single-space each entry and double-space between entries.

Arrangement In the name-year style, arrange entries alphabetically by authors' last names. In the number style, arrange entries in numerical order—that is, in order of their citation in the text.

Format In both styles, begin the first line of each entry at the left margin and indent subsequent lines.

Authors In both styles, list each author's name with the last name first, followed by initials for first and middle names. Do not use a comma between an author's last name and initials, and do not use periods or spaces with the initials. Do use a comma to separate authors' names.

Placement of dates In the name-year style, the date follows the author's or authors' names. In the number style, the date follows the publication information (for a book) or the periodical title (for a journal, magazine, or newspaper).

Journal titles In both styles, do not underline or italicize journal titles. For titles of two or more words, abbreviate words of six or more letters (without periods) and omit most prepositions, articles, and conjunctions. Capitalize each word. For example, *Journal of Chemical and Biochemical Studies* becomes J Chem Biochem Stud.

Book and article titles In both styles, do not underline, italicize, or use quotation marks around a book or an article title. Capitalize only the first word and any proper nouns.

Publication information for journal articles The name-year and number styles differ in the placement of the publication date (see opposite). However, both styles end with the journal's volume number, any issue number in parentheses, a colon, and the inclusive page numbers of the article, run together without space: 28:329-30 or 62(2):26-40.

The following box indexes the CSE models. The examples include both a name-year reference and a number reference for each type of source.

CSE reference-list models

Books

1. A book with one author *815*
2. A book with two to ten authors *815*
3. A book with more than ten authors *816*
4. A book with an editor *816*
5. A selection from a book *816*
6. An anonymous work *816*
7. Two or more cited works by the same author published in the same year *816*

Periodicals

8. An article in a journal with continuous pagination throughout the annual volume *816*
9. An article in a journal that pages issues separately *817*
10. An article in a newspaper *817*
11. An article in a magazine *817*

Electronic sources

12. A source on CD-ROM *817*
13. An online journal article *817*
14. An online book *818*
15. A source retrieved from an online database *818*
16. A Web site *818*
17. Electronic mail *818*
18. A posting to a discussion list *819*
19. Computer software *819*

Other sources

20. A government publication *819*
21. A nongovernment report *819*
22. A sound recording, video recording, DVD, or film *819*

■ Books

1. A book with one author

Gould SJ. 1987. Time's arrow, time's cycle. Cambridge: Harvard Univ Pr. 222 p.

1. Gould SJ. Time's arrow, time's cycle. Cambridge: Harvard Univ Pr; 1987. 222 p.

2. A book with two to ten authors

Hepburn PX, Tatin JM. 2005. Human physiology. New York: Columbia Univ Pr. 1026 p.

2. Hepburn PX, Tatin JM. Human physiology. New York: Columbia Univ Pr; 2005. 1026 p.

3. A book with more than ten authors

Evans RW, Bowditch L, Dana KL, Drummond A, Wildovitch WP, Young SL, Mills P, Mills RR, Livak SR, Lisi OL, and others. 2004. Organ transplants: ethical issues. Ann Arbor: Univ of Michigan Pr. 498 p.

3. Evans RW, Bowditch L, Dana KL, Drummond A, Wildovitch WP, Young SL, Mills P, Mills RR, Livak SR, Lisi OL, and others. Organ transplants: ethical issues. Ann Arbor: Univ of Michigan Pr; 2004. 498 p.

4. A book with an editor

Jonson P, editor. 2006. Anatomy yearbook 2005. Los Angeles: Anatco. 628 p.

4. Jonson P, editor. Anatomy yearbook 2005. Los Angeles: Anatco; 2006. 628 p.

5. A selection from a book

Krigel R, Laubenstein L, Muggia F. 2005. Kaposi's sarcoma. In: Ebbeson P, Biggar RS, Melbye M, editors. AIDS: a basic guide for clinicians. 2nd ed. Philadelphia: WB Saunders. p 100-26.

5. Krigel R, Laubenstein L, Muggia F. Kaposi's sarcoma. In: Ebbeson P, Biggar RS, Melbye M, editors. AIDS: a basic guide for clinicians. 2nd ed. Philadelphia: WB Saunders; 2005. p 100-26.

6. An anonymous work

[Anonymous]. 2006. Health care for multiple sclerosis. New York: US Health Care. 86 p.

6. [Anonymous]. Health care for multiple sclerosis. New York: US Health Care; 2006. 86 p.

7. Two or more cited works by the same author published in the same year

Gardner H. 1973a. The arts and human development. New York: J Wiley. 406 p.

Gardner H. 1973b. The quest for mind: Piaget, Lévi-Strauss, and the structuralist movement. New York: AA Knopf. 492 p.

(The number style does not require such forms.)

■ Periodicals: Journals, magazines, newspapers

8. An article in a journal with continuous pagination throughout the annual volume

Ancino R, Carter KV, Elwin DJ. 2004. Factors contributing to viral immunity: a review of the research. Dev Biol 30:156-9.

8. Ancino R, Carter KV, Elwin DJ. Factors contributing to viral immunity: a review of the research. Dev Biol 2004;30:156-9.

9. An article in a journal that pages issues separately

Kim P. 2001 Feb. Medical decision making for the dying. Milbank Quar
       64(2):26-40.

9. Kim P. Medical decision making for the dying. Milbank Quar 2001
       Feb;64(2):26-40.

10. An article in a newspaper

Kolata G. 2006 Jan 7. Kill all the bacteria! New York Times;Sect B:1(col 3).

10. Kolata G. Kill all the bacteria! New York Times 2006 Jan 7;Sect B:1(col 3).

11. An article in a magazine

Scheiber N. 2004 June 24. Finger tip: why fingerprinting won't work. New
       Republic:15-6.

11. Scheiber N. Finger tip: why fingerprinting won't work. New Republic 2004
       June 24:15-6.

■ Electronic sources

Scientific Style and Format includes a few formats for citing
electronic sources, derived from *National Library of Medicine Recommended Formats for Bibliographic Citation*. For additional formats, the CSE Web site recommends the NLM 2001 supplement for
Internet sources. The following models adapt these NLM formats to
CSE name-year and number styles.

Note Since neither the CSE nor the NLM specifies how to break
URLs at the ends of lines, follow APA style: break only after slashes
or before periods, and do not hyphenate.

12. A source on CD-ROM

Reich WT, editor. 2005. Encyclopedia of bioethics [CD-ROM]. New York:
       Co-Health.

12. Reich WT, editor. Encyclopedia of bioethics [CD-ROM]. New York:
       Co-Health; 2005.

13. An online journal article

Grady GF. 2005. The here and now of hepatitis B immunization. Today's Med
       [Internet] [cited 2005 Dec 7];6(2):39-41. Available from: http://
       www.fmrt.org/todaysmedicine/Grady050293.pdf6

13. Grady GF. The here and now of hepatitis B immunization. Today's Med
       [Internet] 2005 [cited 2005 Dec 7];6(2):39-41. Available from:
       http://www.fmrt.org/todaysmedicine/Grady050293.pdf6

Give the date of your access, preceded by "cited," in brackets: [cited
2005 Dec 7] in the models above. If the article has no reference

numbers (pages, paragraphs, and so on), estimate the length in brackets—for instance, [about 15 p.] or [about 6 screens].

14. An online book

Ruch BJ, Ruch DB. 2004. Homeopathy and medicine: resolving the conflict [Internet]. New York: Albert Einstein Coll of Medicine [cited 2006 Jan 28]. [about 50 p.]. Available from: http://www.einstein.edu/ medicine/books/ruch.html

14. Ruch BJ, Ruch DB. Homeopathy and medicine: resolving the conflict [Internet]. New York: Albert Einstein Coll of Medicine; 2004 [cited 2006 Jan 28]. [about 50 p.]. Available from: http://www.einstein.edu/ medicine/books/ruch.html

As with an online journal article, give the date of your access, preceded by cited, in brackets. If the source uses page or other reference numbers, provide the total as in model 1 on page 815. If no reference numbers are provided, you may estimate them in brackets, as in the examples above.

15. A source retrieved from an online database

McAskill MR, Anderson TJ, Jones RD. 2005. Saccadic adaptation in neurological disorders. Prog Brain Res 140:417-31. In: PubMed [Internet]. Bethesda (MD): National Library of Medicine; [cited 2005 Mar 6]. Available from: http://www.ncbi.nlm.nih.gov/PubMed; PMID: 12508606.

15. McAskill MR, Anderson TJ, Jones RD. Saccadic adaptation in neurological disorders. Prog Brain Res 2005;140:417-31. In: PubMed [Internet]. Bethesda (MD): National Library of Medicine; [cited 2005 Mar 6]. Available from: http://www.ncbi.nlm.nih.gov/PubMed; PMID: 12508606.

After In: provide information on the database: title, place of publication, and publisher. (If the database author is different from the publisher, give the author's name before the title.) If you see a date of publication or copyright date for the database, give it after the publisher's name. Add the date of your access, preceded by cited, in brackets. After the availability statement, add any identifying number the database uses for the source.

16. A Web site

American Medical Association [Internet]. 2006. Chicago: American Medical Association; [cited 2006 Jan 26]. Available from: http://ama-assn.org

16. American Medical Association [Internet]. Chicago: American Medical Association; 2006 [cited 2006 Jan 26]. Available from: http://ama-assn.org

17. Electronic mail

Millon M. 2005 May 4. Grief therapy [Internet]. Message to: Naomi Sakai. 3:16 pm [cited 2005 May 4]. [about 2 screens].

17. Millon M. Grief therapy [Internet]. Message to: Naomi Sakai. 2005 May 4, 3:16 pm [cited 2005 May 4]. [about 2 screens].

18. A posting to a discussion list

Stalinsky Q. 2005 Aug 16. The hormone-replacement study. In: Women Physicians Congress [Internet]. [Chicago: American Medical Association]; 9:26 am [cited 2005 Aug 17]. [about 8 paragraphs]. Available from: ama-wpc@ama-assn.org

18. Stalinsky Q. The hormone-replacement study. In: Women Physicians Congress [Internet]. [Chicago: American Medical Association]; 2005 Aug 16, 9:26 am [cited 2005 Aug 17]. [about 8 paragraphs]. Available from: ama-wpc@ama-assn.org

19. Computer software

Project scheduler 9000 [computer program]. 2006. Version 5.1. Orlando (FL): Scitor. CD-ROM. System requirements: IBM PC or compatible; Windows 98 or higher; 32 MB RAM; minimum 50 MB free disk space.

19. Project scheduler 9000 [computer program]. Version 5.1. Orlando (FL): Scitor; 2006. CD-ROM. System requirements: IBM PC or compatible; Windows 98 or higher; 32 MB RAM; minimum 50 MB free disk space.

◼ Other sources

20. A government publication

Committee on Science and Technology, House (US). 2003. Hearing on procurement and allocation of human organs for transplantation. 108th Cong., 1st Sess. House Doc. nr 409.

20. Committee on Science and Technology, House (US). Hearing on procurement and allocation of human organs for transplantation. 108th Cong., 1st Sess. House Doc. nr 409; 2003.

21. A nongovernment report

Warnock M. 2004. Report of the Committee on Fertilization and Embryology. Baylor University, Department of Embryology. Waco (TX): Baylor Univ. Report nr BU/DE.4261.

21. Warnock M. Report of the Committee on Fertilization and Embryology. Baylor University, Department of Embryology. Waco (TX): Baylor Univ; 2004. Report nr BU/DE.4261.

22. A sound recording, video recording, DVD, or film

Teaching Media. 2005. Cell mitosis [DVD]. White Plains (NY): Teaching Media. 40 min, sound, color.

22. Cell mitosis [DVD]. White Plains (NY): Teaching Media; 2005. 40 min, sound, color.

MODELS OF STUDENT WRITING

Liz Garson's paper on the effects of exercise on blood pressure is a properly documented and clearly written lab report, appropriately organized into sections (abstract, introduction, method, results, discussion, and references). Garson correctly uses the present tense when talking about established facts and the past tense when talking about her own research. She uses objective language and specialized vocabulary, properly conforming to the conventions of writing in biology. Students who have to write lab reports for their science courses may find Garson's paper helpful as a model of how to structure, write, and document their own reports.

53e   Formatting documents in CSE style

Scientific Style and Format is not specific about margins, spacing for headings, and other elements of document format. Unless your instructor specifies otherwise, you can use the format of the APA (pp. 800–03). The CSE exception to this style is the list of references, which is described on pages 814–15.

The most troublesome aspects of manuscript preparation in the sciences are equations or formulas, tables, and figures. When typing equations or formulas, be careful to reproduce alignments, indentions, underlining, and characters accurately. If your word processor lacks special characters, leave space for them and write them in by hand.

Because you will be expected to share your data with your readers, most of your writing for the sciences is likely to require illustrations to present the data in concise, readable form. Tables usually summarize raw data (see p. 822 for an example), whereas figures (mainly charts and graphs) recast the data to show noteworthy comparisons or changes. Follow the guidelines on pages 121–25 for preparing tables and figures.

53f   Examining a sample science paper

The following biology paper illustrates the CSE number style for documenting sources. On page 823 passages from the paper and a reformatted list of references show the name-year style. Except for the citations and the references, the paper is formatted in APA style because CSE does not specify a format.

■ A laboratory report: CSE number style

[Title page.]

Exercise and Blood Pressure

Liz Garson

Biology 161

Ms. Traversa

December 13, 2005

[New page.]

Abstract

The transient elevation of blood pressure following exercise was demonstrated by pressure measurements of twenty human subjects before and after exercise.

[New page.]

Exercise and Blood Pressure

Introduction

The purpose of this experiment was to verify the changes in blood pressure that accompany exercise, as commonly reported.[1,2] A certain blood pressure is necessary for the blood to supply nutrients to the body tissues. Baroreceptors near the heart monitor pressure by determining the degree to which blood stretches the wall of the blood vessel.

[The introduction continues.]

During exercise, the metabolic needs of the muscles override the influence of the baroreceptors and result in an increase in blood pressure. This increase in blood pressure is observed uniformly (irrespective of sex or race), although men demonstrate a higher absolute systolic pressure than do women.[3] During strenuous exercise, blood pressure can rise to 40 percent above baseline.[1]

Method

The subjects for this experiment were twenty volunteers from laboratory classes, ten men and ten women. All pressure measurements were performed using a standard sphygmomanometer, which was tested for accuracy. To ensure consistency, the same sphygmomanometer was used to take all readings. In addition, all measurements were taken by the same person to avoid discrepancies in method or interpretation.

The first pressure reading was taken prior to exercise as the subject sat in a chair. This pressure was considered the baseline for each subject. All subsequent readings were interpreted relative to this baseline.

In the experiment, the subjects ran up and down stairs for fifteen minutes. Immediately after exercising, the subjects returned to the laboratory to have their pressure measured. Thirty minutes later, the pressure was measured for the final time.

Results

Table 1 contains the blood pressure measurements for the male and female subjects. With the exception of subjects 3 and 14, all subjects demonstrated the expected post-exercise increase in blood pressure, with a decline to baseline or near baseline thirty minutes after exercise. The data for subjects 3 and 14 were invalid because the subjects did not perform the experiment as directed.

Discussion

As expected, most of the subjects demonstrated an increase in blood pressure immediately after exercise and a decline to near baseline levels thirty minutes after exercise. The usual pressure increase was 20-40 mmHg for the systolic pressure and 5-10 mmHg for the diastolic pressure.

[Table on a page by itself.]

Table 1. Blood pressure measurements for all subjects (mmHg)

Subject	Baseline[a]	Post-exercise	30-minute reading
Male			
1	110/75	135/80	115/75
2	125/80	140/90	135/85
3	125/70	125/70	125/70
4	130/85	170/100	140/90
5	120/80	125/95	120/80
6	115/70	135/80	125/75
7	125/70	150/80	130/70
8	130/80	145/85	130/80
9	140/75	180/85	155/80
10	110/85	135/95	115/80
Female			
11	110/60	140/85	115/60
12	130/75	180/85	130/75
13	125/80	140/90	130/80
14	90/60	90/60	90/60
15	115/65	145/70	125/65
16	100/50	130/65	110/50
17	120/80	140/80	130/80
18	110/70	135/80	120/75
19	120/80	140/90	130/80
20	110/80	145/90	120/80

[a]Normal blood pressure at rest: males, 110-130/60-90; females, 110-120/50-80.

In the two cases in which blood pressure did not elevate with exercise (subjects 3 and 14), the subjects simply left the laboratory and returned fifteen minutes later without having exercised. The experimental design was flawed in not assigning someone to observe the subjects as they exercised.

[New page.]

References

1. Guyton AC. Textbook of medical physiology. Philadelphia: WB Saunders; 2004. 998 p.

2. Rowell LB. Blood pressure regulation during exercise. Ann Med 1999;28:329-33.

3. Gleim GW, Stachenfeld NS. Gender differences in the systolic blood pressure response to exercise. Am Heart J 2001;121:524-30.

■ A laboratory report: CSE name-year style

These excerpts from the preceding paper show documentation in CSE name-year style:

The purpose of this experiment was to verify the changes in blood pressure that accompany exercise, as commonly reported (Guyton 2004; Rowell 1999).

This increase in blood pressure is observed uniformly (irrespective of sex or race), although men demonstrate a higher absolute systolic pressure than do women (Gleim and Stachenfeld 2001). During strenuous exercise, blood pressure can rise to 40 percent above baseline (Guyton 2004).

References

Gleim GW, Stachenfeld NS. 2001. Gender differences in the systolic blood pressure response to exercise. Am Heart J 121:524-30.

Guyton AC. 2004. Textbook of medical physiology. Philadelphia: WB Saunders. 998 p.

Rowell LB. 1999. Blood pressure regulation during exercise. Ann Med 28:329-33.

PART 11

Special Writing Situations

mycomplab

Please visit MyCompLab at *www.mycomplab.com* for more on the writing process.

HIGHLIGHTS

Chapter 54 provides up-to-date information about online writing from e-mail and online discussion to composing documents and Web sites. The degree of familiarity with online writing technology is likely to vary widely amongst your students. Some students may already have their own personal Web pages or blogs, while to others the process of creating Web pages may seem arcane and mysterious. For all students, this chapter covers essential skills needed to utilize online writing and collaboration tools and to participate appropriately online.

Students are first introduced to e-mail composition, netiquette, and methods of handling file attachments. Next, they are taught about two methods of online collaboration they are likely to use in their courses: online discussions and peer review of document drafts.

The second half of the chapter discusses how to create an original Web site. Topics covered include structure and content development, how to achieve good flow and ease of navigation, and the use of images, video, and sound on Web sites.

RESOURCES AND IDEAS

Hawisher, Gail E., and Paul LeBlanc, eds. *Reimagining Computers and Composition: Teaching and Research in the Virtual Age.* Portsmouth: Boynton/Cook, 1992. This collection of essays explores the implications of using computers in the classroom, from electronic conferencing to hypermedia. Teachers who are new to computer technology might benefit from Chapter 12, "What Are They Talking About? Computer Terms That English Teachers May Need to Know," by Richard J. Selfe (207–18).

COMPANION WEB SITE

See page IAE-61 for companion Web site content description.

CHAPTER 54

Writing Online

Both in and out of college, you will write extensively online. Many forms of online writing expand your options as a writer, but they also present distinctive challenges, both conceptual and technical. This chapter discusses some of the options and challenges of e-mail (below), online collaboration (p. 829), and Web composition (p. 832).

54a Writing effective electronic mail

You may be using e-mail every day to converse quickly and casually with friends and family. In college you'll also use e-mail for a host of academic reasons, from collaborating with classmates to conducting research, and you'll want to communicate both purposefully and efficiently. This section covers composing and responding to messages and observing Internet etiquette. For more on using e-mail to interact with the other students in a course, see pages 829–32. For more on using e-mail as a research tool, see page 592.

1 Composing messages

To use e-mail productively, pause to weigh each element of the message. Consider especially your audience and purpose and how your tone will come across to readers. In the message shown opposite, the writer knows the recipients well and yet has serious information to convey to them, so he writes informally but states his points and concerns carefully. Writing to the corporation mentioned in the message, the writer would be more formal in both tone and approach. Although e-mail is typically more casual than printed correspondence, in academic settings a crafted message is more likely to achieve the intended purpose. Proofread all but the most informal messages for errors in grammar, punctuation, and spelling.

| http://www.ablongman.com/littlebrown | ▶ |

Visit the companion Web site for more help with electronic mail, online collaboration, and Web composition.

E-mail message

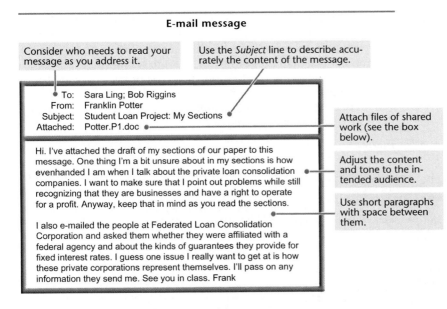

Consider who needs to read your message as you address it.

Use the *Subject* line to describe accurately the content of the message.

> To: Sara Ling; Bob Riggins
> From: Franklin Potter
> Subject: Student Loan Project: My Sections
> Attached: Potter.P1.doc
>
> Hi. I've attached the draft of my sections of our paper to this message. One thing I'm a bit unsure about in my sections is how evenhanded I am when I talk about the private loan consolidation companies. I want to make sure that I point out problems while still recognizing that they are businesses and have a right to operate for a profit. Anyway, keep that in mind as you read the sections.
>
> I also e-mailed the people at Federated Loan Consolidation Corporation and asked them whether they were affiliated with a federal agency and about the kinds of guarantees they provide for fixed interest rates. I guess one issue I really want to get at is how these private corporations represent themselves. I'll pass on any information they send me. See you in class. Frank

Attach files of shared work (see the box below).

Adjust the content and tone to the intended audience.

Use short paragraphs with space between them.

2 Responding to messages

When you respond to a message, consider whom you're addressing and what your readers will see. The Reply function will automatically address the person who wrote you, whereas the Reply All function will address others who may have been sent copies of

Incompatible or encoded attachments

E-mail attachments are not always readable because of incompatible file formats or because of compression or encoding that requires special software at the recipient's end. If you have trouble sending or receiving attachments, try these strategies:

- **Send your documents in rich text format (RTF) or in text-only format,** both of which can be read by most word processors. RTF preserves most formatting, whereas text-only format does not. With either option, save a *copy* of your document (not the original) in the new format. In your word processor's File menu, first choose Save to preserve the original document. Then choose Save As, give the document a new name, go to the Save As Type option, and choose Rich Text Format or Text Only.
- **Copy the document into the body of an e-mail message.** You will lose most, if not all, of your document's formatting.
- **Use special software to read encoded or compressed files.** Your school's technology advisers can help you obtain and use such programs, which are usually free and available over the Internet.

Hawisher, Gail E., and Charles Moran. "Electronic Mail and the Writing Instructor." *College English* 55 (1993): 627–43. The authors discuss the use of e-mail in teaching, with extensive bibliography.

Monroe, Rick. *Writing and Thinking with Computers: A Practical and Progressive Approach.* Urbana: NCTE, 1993. Monroe models hands-on practice in the computer classroom, including assignments and exercises such as "Electronic Read-Arounds" and "the business letter."

Reiss, Donna, et al., eds. *Electronic Communication Across the Curriculum.* Urbana, IL: NCTE, 1998. Written from a range of disciplinary perspectives, these essays discuss how teachers have used electronic communication to create communities within and across disciplines.

Tornow, Joan. *Link/Age: Composing in the Online Classroom.* Logan: Utah State UP, 1997. An ethnographical study of how students use language online and the implications for teaching composition.

COMPUTER ACTIVITIES

STRATEGIES FOR NOVICES

Students new to e-mail and/or the Web may find it difficult to master the technology, focus on a project, and fine-tune their etiquette all at once. You might want to give them a purely social topic the first time they send e-mail or chat messages, so that they can focus on getting comfortable with the software. Then they can begin working on group dynamics and writing collaborations.

FILING MAIL

Most e-mail programs allow you to make folders or mailboxes in which to store messages. Students might want to set up e-mail folders in which to keep incoming and outgoing mail on different topics or regarding different class projects.

E-MAIL AND COMMUNITY

Some teachers find that e-mail is an excellent tool for developing a sense of community and fostering dialogue among the members of their classes. Each small group can function as a study group and can stay in touch by e-mail. Larger conversations might include all the members of one class, or even members of different class sections.

COMPOSED MESSAGES

If your students are using e-mail to request access to information from outside sources (institutions, archives, individuals, etc.) you may want to have them draft a polite e-mail request and circulate it to the class for comment before sending it out.

DISCRETION AND THE GROUP ADDRESS

It can be helpful to create a nickname the group members can all use to send mail to one another, with the complete list of e-mail addresses linked to the nickname in each students electronic address book. But if groups use this shortcut method, they should be reminded to keep their electronic address books up to date: if a student drops out of the group, all other members should delete that student's address from the nickname list. New members of the group must be added to each other member's electronic address book to ensure they receive all group mailings.

E-MAIL AND COURTESY

It might be interesting for your students to think about why people incline to discourtesy online, either in their e-mail or when posting to electronic discussion groups. This topic might be especially helpful when you teach audience, tone, or rhetorical stance. Ask students to bring in examples of discourteous discussion postings and suggest revisions that would change the tone of those postings.

the original message. The *Subject* line will automatically contain the original subject heading preceded by *Re:* (from Latin, meaning "In reference to"), so change the heading if you change or expand the subject. Many e-mail programs can be set to reprint the entire original message, allowing you to insert your responses where appropriate or to respond to part of the message and delete the rest. If you add more recipients to your response, make sure not to pass on previous private messages by mistake.

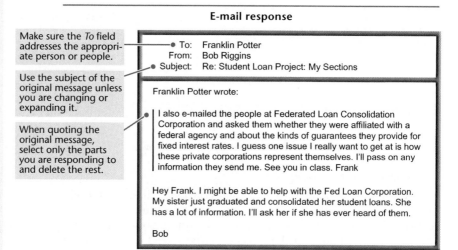

E-mail response

Make sure the *To* field addresses the appropriate person or people.

Use the subject of the original message unless you are changing or expanding it.

When quoting the original message, select only the parts you are responding to and delete the rest.

> To: Franklin Potter
> From: Bob Riggins
> Subject: Re: Student Loan Project: My Sections
>
> Franklin Potter wrote:
>
> I also e-mailed the people at Federated Loan Consolidation Corporation and asked them whether they were affiliated with a federal agency and about the kinds of guarantees they provide for fixed interest rates. I guess one issue I really want to get at is how these private corporations represent themselves. I'll pass on any information they send me. See you in class. Frank
>
> Hey Frank. I might be able to help with the Fed Loan Corporation. My sister just graduated and consolidated her student loans. She has a lot of information. I'll ask her if she has ever heard of them.
>
> Bob

3 Observing netiquette

To communicate effectively online, you'll need to abide by some rules of behavior and simple courtesies. You won't always see others observing this **netiquette,** or Internet etiquette, but you will see that those who do observe it receive the more thoughtful and considerate replies.

■ Addressing messages

- **Avoid spamming.** With a few keystrokes, you can broadcast a message to many recipients at once—all the students in a course, say, or all the participants in a discussion group. Occasionally, you may indeed have a worthwhile idea or important information that everyone on the list will want to know. But flooding whole lists with irrelevant messages—called **spamming**—is rude and irritating.
- **Avoid sending frivolous messages to all the members of a group.** Instead of dashing off "I agree" and distributing the two-word message widely, put some time into composing a thoughtful response and send it only to those who will be interested.

■ **Composing messages**

■ **Remember that the messages you receive represent individuals.** Don't say or do anything that you wouldn't say or do face to face.

■ **Use names.** In the body of your message, address your reader(s) by name if possible and sign off with your own name and information on how to contact you. Your own name is especially important if your e-mail address does not spell it out.

■ **Pay careful attention to tone.** Refrain from **flaming,** or attacking, correspondents. Don't use all capital letters, which SHOUT. And use irony or sarcasm only cautiously: in the absence of facial expressions, they can lead to misunderstandings. To indicate irony and emotions, you can use **emoticons,** such as the smiley :-). These sideways faces can easily be overused, though, and should not substitute for thoughtfully worded opinions.

■ **Avoid saying anything in e-mail that you would not say in a printed document such as a letter or memo.** E-mail can usually be retrieved from the server, and in business and academic settings it may well be retrieved in disputes over contracts, grades, and other matters.

■ **Reading and responding to messages**

■ **Be a forgiving reader.** Avoid nitpicking over spelling or other surface errors. And because attitudes are sometimes difficult to convey, give authors an initial benefit of the doubt: a writer who at first seems hostile may simply have tried too hard to be concise; a writer who at first seems unserious may simply have failed at injecting humor into a worthwhile message.

■ **Forward messages only with permission.** You may want to send a message you've received to someone else, but do so only if you know that the author of the message won't mind.

■ **Avoid participating in flame "wars,"** overheated dialogs that contribute little or no information or understanding. If a war breaks out in a discussion, ignore it: don't rush to defend someone who is being attacked, and don't respond even if you are under attack yourself.

54b Collaborating online

Writing often involves collaborating with others as much as it does working in solitude. Indeed, many businesses and teachers expect writers to collaborate on generating ideas and producing and revising drafts. Computers have vastly expanded the options for collaboration, ranging from simple e-mail exchanges to video conferencing and virtual environments.

In this section we look at strategies for online collaboration in your courses. Your instructors or your school's technology advisers

COLLABORATIVE LEARNING

KEEP IT SMALL

Students can experience shyness online just as they do in person, and you may find some voices dominating while others are always silent. Working in very small groups can help reticent students feel more comfortable about adding their voices to the conversation.

COMPUTER ACTIVITY

COLLABORATIVE LEARNING

BACKUP CLASS PLAN

If you have to cancel a class, you can still hold class discussion if you have Blackboard or WebCT software for your course. Create a discussion topic and start several discussion threads. If you wish to have a live chat, you can set it up for the time your class would normally meet. Alternatively, you can have a delayed discussion and ask students to contribute to at least one thread before class meets again.

will introduce you to the system and help set you up. Here we focus on nontechnical matters of participating in discussions and working on drafts.

1 Participating in discussions

Many instructors use online conversations for discussing class readings and other topics and to help students generate ideas for writing. There are two basic types of online conversation: delayed conversation, such as that occurring by e-mail or on a Web forum or blog; and real-time **chat** (also called **synchronous communication**), which occurs immediately, like a telephone conversation.

■ Delayed conversation

E-mail, Web discussion groups, and Web logs allow detailed, thoughtful messages and responses, so they are good places to try out ideas, explore assignments, and respond to others' work. When writing in such media, observe the netiquette guidelines on pages 828–29.

Discussion on *Blackboard*

Author: Sara Ling
Subject: Internet Identity

Hi everyone. I'm hoping you can give me some advice about my topic and maybe share some of your experiences. I disagree with Kadi's argument that the Internet will lead to more fragmentation, not community. On the snowboarding forum that I sometimes participate in, I received a lot of hostile responses when I logged on as a woman. But another member of the group wrote to tell me that when she logged on as a man, she was welcomed into the group. It made me realize that the anonymity of the Internet could be used to bring people together, not split them apart.

Have any of you had similar experiences when you've been online? Do you think that anonymity can bring people together?

Sara

Author: Franklin Potter
Subject: Re: Internet Identity

I think you have a point about the names used on the Internet having a lot to do with how people relate. But I'm not sure that your experience totally challenges what Kadi is saying. When I've been online, I've found that people who are a lot alike tend to hang out and encourage each other. Even if the other woman on the snowboarding forum was able to change her identity, she still ended up confiding in you. I guess I would just be careful about claiming that anonymity will automatically bring different kinds of people together. Hope this helps.

Frank

The screen shots on these pages show part of a discussion thread on *Blackboard* courseware and a query and responses on a course blog. The writing is casual but also thoughtful and specific. In the *Blackboard* examples, notice that the second writer actually challenges the first writer's assumption but frames the challenge productively in the context of the issue being discussed. Disagreements are bound to occur in online conversation, but they need not be unpleasant.

▪ Online chat

You may be familiar with chat conversations from using instant messaging with friends and family. In academic settings, chat will likely occur with courseware such as *WebCT* or *Blackboard*.

Collaborating via chat discussions will be more productive if you take a few tips:

- **Use the chat space for brainstorming topics and exchanging impressions.** The pace of online chat rarely allows lengthy consideration and articulation of messages.
- **Focus on a thread or common topic.** Online chat can be the electronic equivalent of a party, with different conversations

---

Discussion on a course Web log

English 1201
Writing in the World

Tuesday, 9/13/05

Service-learning projects

Some of you have asked for names of groups needing help from students, especially groups that will really *use* students. I've got some ideas, but maybe other students do, too. Suggestions? 9:24 AM

Comments

Try the Neighborhood Hunger Program (326-1135). I'm going to be working with them on a project to increase food and furniture donations from the community. It'll involve a lot of writing, I think. The group also needs help organizing the warehouse and reaching out to needy families in the community.
Posted by Jessica C 9/13/05 11:03 AM

I'm talking to ReadingWorks at the Springfield VA Hospital. They teach reading and writing to veterans. They always need volunteer tutors, but I don't think I'm ready for that yet, so I hope to do some publicity for them. The director is open to my involvement, but she's very busy and worried about supervising such work. Maybe if three or four of us presented a team proposal and proved we could work independently, she'd be encouraged. Anyone want to join in?
Posted by AlexRamirez 9/13/05 5:46 PM

COMPUTER ACTIVITY

NAMING CONVENTIONS

As a class, come up with a set of conventions for naming shared files that will work well for class assignments throughout the semester.

COMPUTER ACTIVITY

COLLABORATIVE LEARNING

COMMENT REQUESTS

In peer review, requests from the author about what the group should pay attention to in review are often helpful. Tell your students to use the comment function of their word processor to insert questions they would like their peer group to respond to on their draft. This can help focus the critique so that it is as helpful as possible.

COMPUTER ACTIVITY

SAVING ALL THE VERSIONS

Tell students to keep each draft of their paper, including those that include the comments of their peer groups, in a separate file so that they can have a record of the progression of their writing process. Later, they can look back over the drafts and discuss their writing process with you.

RESOURCES AND IDEAS

Bass, Randy. "Story and Archive in the Twenty-First Century." *College English* 61 (1999): 659–70. Bass discusses the impact of hypertext and electronic media on English Studies.

Myers, Jamie, et al. "Opportunities for Critical Literacy and Pedagogy in Student-Authored Hypermedia." *Handbook of Literacy and Technology: Transformations in a Post-Typographic World.* Eds. David Reinking, et al. 63–78. An exploration of how students may develop their powers of critical literacy as they construct hypermedia texts.

occurring in the same space. If you have trouble tracking all the messages, concentrate on the ones that relate to your interest.

- **Write as quickly and fluidly as possible.** Don't worry about producing perfect prose.

2 Working on drafts

In writing and other courses, you and your fellow students may be invited to exchange and respond to one another's projects by e-mail or over the Web. To guide your reading of others' work, use the revision checklist on page 51 and the collaboration tips on pages 66–69. Focus on the deep issues in others' drafts, especially early drafts: thesis, purpose, audience, organization, and support for the thesis. Hold comments on style, grammar, punctuation, and other surface matters until you're reviewing late drafts, if indeed you are expected to comment on them at all.

Exchanging drafts online generally requires a file-naming system that identifies each project's writer, title, and version. Your instructor may establish such a system, or you and your classmates can develop one. See pages 53–54 for tips.

54c   Creating effective Web compositions

Creating a Web page or site is sometimes as simple as saving a document in a different format, but more often it means thinking in a new way.

The diagrams on the facing page show a key difference between traditional printed documents and Web sites. Most traditional documents are meant to be read in sequence from start to finish. In contrast, most Web sites are so-called hypertexts: they are intended to be examined in whatever order readers choose as they follow links to pages within the site and to other sites.

When you create a composition for the Web, it will likely fall into one of two categories discussed in this section: pages such as class papers that resemble printed documents in being linear and text-heavy and that call for familiar ways of writing and reading; or "native" hypertext documents that you build from scratch, which call for screen-oriented writing and reading.

These general guidelines will help you create effective Web sites:

- **Plan the site carefully.** A hypertext can disorient readers as they scroll up and down and pursue various links. Page length, links, menus, and other cues should work to keep readers oriented.
- **Anticipate what readers may see on their screens.** Each reader's screen frames and organizes the experience of a Web

Traditional print document

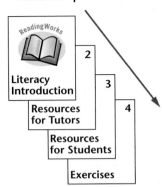

Web site

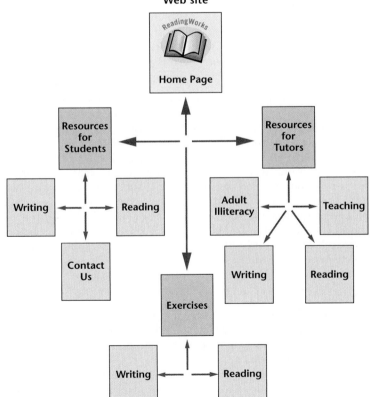

Your students are probably already familiar with hypertext documents. You can point out to them that a hard copy of a paper-in-progress becomes a hypertext document when it includes any of the following: peer review comments, instructor's comments, the author's notes for revision, or the next draft of the paper.

COMPUTER ACTIVITY

ONLINE COMMUNITY III

Ask your students to collect clippings from the Web forum they explored in the "Online community II" exercise on page 831. Have them share their clipping files with the rest of their small group, and have group members respond with comments.

SPATIAL LEARNERS

Some students will excel at creating architectural diagrams of their Web sites like the one shown on this page. For students with comparatively weak writing skills, the knowledge that they have strengths in visual skills may boost their confidence and suggest how they can best approach prewriting.

CITE THE SITE

Students should be reminded that borrowing text from the Web sites of others is a form of plagiarism unless they give attribution. They should use proper quotation, paraphrase, and summary technique, and they may want to include links to the original sites from which they have borrowed material.

composition. Screen space is limited, and it varies from one computer to another. Text and visual elements should be managed for maximum clarity and effectiveness on a variety of screens.

- **Integrate visual and sound elements into the text.** Web compositions can include not only tables, charts, and photographs (which printed documents may also have) but also video (such as animation or film clips) and audio (such as music or excerpts from speeches). However, any visual or sound elements should not merely embellish the text but contribute substantially to it. In addition, you should find out whether your readers' equipment will likely be able to handle multimedia elements and whether readers themselves may have disabilities that prevent their seeing or hearing such elements (see the note below).

- **Acknowledge your sources.** It's easy to incorporate material from other sources into a Web site, but you have the same obligation to cite your sources as you do in a printed document (see pp. 629–34). Further, your Web site is a form of publication, like a magazine or a book. Unless the material you are using explicitly allows copying without permission, you may need to seek the copyright holder's permission, just as print publishers do. (See pp. 635–37 for more on copyright.)

Note If you anticipate that some of your readers may have visual, hearing, or reading disabilities, you'll need to consider their needs while designing Web sites. Some of these considerations are covered under document design on pages 125–26, and others are fundamental to any effective Web design, as discussed in this section. In addition, avoid any content that relies exclusively on images or sound, instead supplementing such elements with text descriptions. At the same time, try to provide key concepts both as text and as images and sound. For more on Web design for readers with disabilities, visit the World Wide Web Consortium at *w3.org/tr/wai-webcontent* or the American Council for the Blind at *acb.org/accessible-formats.html*.

1 Using HTML

Most Web pages are created using hypertext markup language, or HTML, and an HTML editor. The HTML editing program inserts command codes into your document that achieve the effects you want when the material appears on the Web.

From the user's point of view, most HTML editors work much as word processors do, with similar options for sizing, formatting, and highlighting copy and with a display that shows what you will see in the final version. Indeed, you can compose a Web page without bothering at all about the behind-the-scenes HTML coding. As you gain experience with Web building, however, you may want to create more sophisticated pages by editing the codes themselves.

There are many HTML editors on the market. The Web site for this book (*ablongman.com/littlebrown*) provides links to free or low-cost editors.

2 Creating online papers

If an instructor asks you to post a paper to a Web site, you can compose it on your word processor and then use the Save As HTML function available on most programs to translate it into a Web page. After translating the paper, your word processor should allow you to modify some of the elements on the page, or you can open the translated document in an HTML editor. The illustration below shows the opening screen of a student's project for a composition course.

Paper submitted on the Web

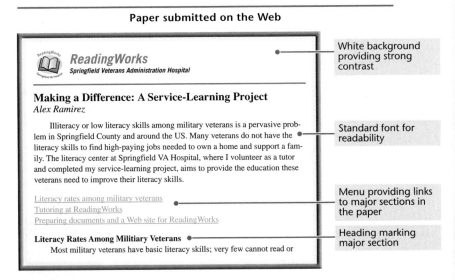

3 Creating original sites

When you create an original Web site, you need to be aware that Web readers generally alternate between skimming pages for highlights and focusing intently on sections of text. To facilitate this kind of reading, you'll want to consider the guidelines on pages 833–34 for handling text and also your site's structure and content, flow, ease of navigation, and use of images, video, and sound.

■ **Structure and content**

Organize your site so that it efficiently arranges your content and also orients readers:

- **Sketch possible site plans before getting started.** (See p. 833 for an example.) Your aim is to develop a sense of the major components of your project and to create a logical space for each component.
- **Consider how menus on the site's pages can provide overviews of the organization as well as direct access to the pages.** The Web page below includes a menu on the left side of the page.
- **Treat the first few sentences of any page as a get-acquainted space for you and your readers.** On the page below, the text hooks readers with questions and orients them with general information.
- **Distill your text so that it includes only essential information.** Concise prose is essential in any writing situation, of course. But Web readers expect to scan text quickly and, in any event, have difficulty following long text passages on a computer screen.

Original Web site

Banner identifying sponsoring organization

Introductory text appealing to readers' interests

Menu providing overview of the site's organization and content

Invitation to use the site menu

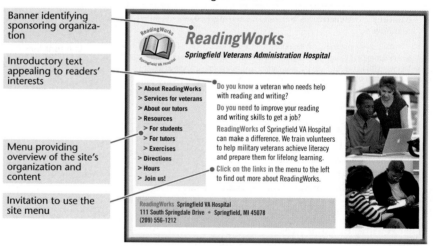

■ **Flow**

Beginning Web authors sometimes start at the top of the page and then add element upon element until information proceeds down the screen much as it would in a printed document. However, by thinking about how information will flow on a page, you can take better advantage of the Web's visual nature:

- **Standardize elements of your design to create expectations in readers and to fulfill those expectations.** For instance, develop a uniform style for the main headings of pages, for headings within pages, and for menus.
- **Make scanning easy for readers.** Focus readers on crucial text by adding space around it. Add headings to break up text and to highlight content. Use lists to reinforce the parallel importance of items. (See pp. 116–20 for more on all these design elements.)

■ Easy navigation

A Web site of more than a few pages requires a menu on every page so that readers can navigate the site. Like the table of contents in a book, a menu lists the features of the site, giving its plan at a glance. By clicking on any item in the list, readers can go directly to a page that interests them.

You can embed a menu at the top, side, or bottom of a page. Menus at the top or side are best on short pages because they will not scroll off the screen as readers move down the page. On longer pages, menus at the bottom prevent readers from dead-ending—that is, reaching a point where they can't easily move forward or backward. You can also use a combination of menus.

In designing a menu, keep it simple: many different type fonts and colors will overwhelm readers instead of orienting them. And make the menus look the same from one page to the next so that readers recognize them easily.

■ Images, video, and sound

Exploring the Web, you'll see that site designers have taken advantage of the Web's ability to handle multimedia elements—images, video, and sound. Most Web readers expect at least some enhancement of text.

Note See pages 636–37 on observing copyright restrictions with images, video, and sound.

Images

Several guidelines can help you use images effectively in your Web compositions:

- **Use visual elements for a purpose.** They should supplement or replace text, highlight important features, and direct the flow of information. Don't use them for their own sake, as mere decoration.
- **Make the size of your files a central concern** so that readers don't have to wait forever for your site to download. If you are using lines or other icons, choose a limited number. If you are using photographs or other images, try to keep the file size below thirty kilobytes (30k).

VIRTUAL GALLERY

To give students practice in the technical side of putting images on their Web sites, establish a gallery page on your class Web site. Ask each student to select or create a photo or drawing on a theme of your choice, scan it, and post it to your class Web site.

VIRTUAL CINEMA

To give students practice in the technical side of putting video clips on their Web sites, have a film festival on your class Web site. Each student can find or create a 1 minute video on a topic of your choice. If you choose a humorous topic, you can have a lot of fun with this activity.

VIRTUAL CONCERT HALL

To give students practice in the technical side of putting sound recordings on their Web sites, establish a concert hall on your class Web site. Students can post sound recordings. You might want to establish a topical theme, such as "songs about peace," or see how many versions of a single song (John Lennon's "Imagine," for instance) your students can locate.

- **Compose descriptions of images that relate them to your text.** Don't ask the elements to convey your meaning by themselves.
- **Provide alternative descriptions of images** to give a sense of them to readers with disabilities or readers whose Web browsers can't display them.

Video and sound

Video and sound files can provide information that is simply unavailable in printed documents. For instance, as part of a film review you might place a short clip from the film on your Web page and then provide a close reading of the clip. Or as part of a project on a controversial issue you might provide links to sound files containing political speeches.

However, the advantages of video and sound in Web compositions are offset by at least two complications: the files are generally large and difficult to work with, and readers need a fast connection and special software to download and open the files. Before you incorporate such elements into your Web compositions, make certain that they have a legitimate purpose. They should add essential information that can't be provided in any other medium, and they should be well integrated with the rest of your composition.

Sources

For the multimedia elements in a Web composition, you can use your own or obtain them from other sources:

- **Create your own graphs, diagrams, and other illustrations using a graphics program.** See pages 120–25 for tips on creating effective images.
- **Incorporate your own artwork, photographs, video clips, and sound recordings.** You may be able to find the needed equipment and software at your campus computer lab.
- **Obtain icons, photographs, video, and other multimedia elements from other electronic sources.** Be sure that you have enough space on your hard drive or a disk to hold the file. Also be sure to acknowledge your sources and to obtain reprint permission if neeeded (see pp. 635–37).

CHAPTER 55

Public Writing

Writing outside of school, such as for business or for community work, resembles academic writing in many ways. It usually involves the same basic writing process, discussed in Part 1: assessing the writing situation, developing what you want to say, freely working out your meaning in a draft, and editing and revising so that your writing will achieve your purpose with readers. It often involves research, as discussed in Part 9. And it involves the standards of conciseness, appropriate and exact language, and correct grammar and usage discussed in Parts 3–8.

But public writing has its own conventions, too. They vary widely depending on what you're writing and why, whether a proposal for your job or a flyer announcing a dinner for a community group. This chapter covers several types of public writing: business letters and memos (next page); job applications (p. 845); business reports and proposals (p. 848); and flyers, newsletters, and brochures for community work (p. 851).

Note Chapter 5 discusses type fonts, headings, illustrations, and other elements of document design. In addition, a word processor's wizards or templates can help you format documents such as letters, résumés, and brochures. Before using such a tool, be sure the format is appropriate for your writing situation. And remember that a formatting tool can do nothing to help you express your ideas effectively.

CULTURE LANGUAGE Public writing in the United States, especially in business, favors efficiency. If you are accustomed to public writing in another culture, the US style may seem abrupt or impolite. A business letter elsewhere may be expected to begin with polite questions about the addressee or with compliments for the addressee's company, whereas US business letters are expected to get right to the point. (See the sample letters in this chapter for examples.)

http://www.ablongman.com/littlebrown ▶

Visit the companion Web site for more help with job applications, business reports, and other kinds of public writing.

mycomplab 2.0

Please visit MyCompLab at *www.mycomplab.com* for more on the writing process.

HIGHLIGHTS

This chapter focuses on multiple forms of public writing, including business letters and memos, job applications, reports and proposals, and a new section on writing for community work. The proliferation of service learning curricula in colleges and universities means that students may find themselves needing to write on behalf of a community organization. They may also need to write about their experience for their service learning course. Section 55d, "Writing for community work," includes samples of a flyer, a newsletter, and a brochure for a nonprofit organization.

Public writing should be a subject of considerable interest to your students, for almost all of them can imagine a future in which it plays an important role. Although people in business and nonprofit organizations generally write under strict time constraints, they use the same critical thinking, reading, and writing skills presented throughout the handbook to analyze their audiences, plan their strategies, and compose their work. Professionals who write documents that represent their company or organization need to put a high value on correctness and clarity. Job applicants and laypeople writing business correspondence have similar needs for clarity and accuracy. This chapter emphasizes those virtues in all public writing situations.

COMPANION WEB SITE

See page IAE-61 for companion Web site content description.

RESOURCES AND IDEAS

Drenk, Dean. "Teaching Finance Through Writing." *Teaching Writing in All Disciplines.* Ed. C. Williams Griffith. San Francisco: Jossey-Bass, 1982. 53–58. Drenk discusses the use of writing exercises to improve student handling of business discourse.

Hafer, Gary R. "Computer-Assisted Illustration and Instructional Documents in Technical Writing Classes." *Computers and Composition* 13 (1996): 49–56. Hafer argues for the advantages of teaching technical writing in the electronic classroom and offers practical advice on how to create instructional teams and design assignments.

Keene, Michael L. "Technical Information in the Information Economy." *Perspectives on Research and Scholarship in Composition.* Ed. Ben W. McClelland and Timothy R. Donovan. New York: MLA, 1985. Keene reviews research in technical and business communication.

Lanham, Richard. *Revising Business Prose.* 4th ed. New York: Macmillan, 1999. Lanham offers strategies for recognizing and eliminating "businessese" from professional writing.

MODELS OF STUDENT WRITING

Janet Marley's letter of complaint is at once direct, concise, firm, and unemotional, and students may want to discuss exactly how Marley achieves this balance in the tone of her letter. Be prepared for your students to differ in their assessments of Marley's letter: some may think it quite daring while others may think it insufficiently forceful. They probably have their own ideas about how to write a letter of complaint, so you might want to let them revise the letter according to their own predilections. Then pass the revisions around the room and let the class assess the effectiveness of each student's revisions. If students pretend that they are Ann Herzog when they read one another's versions of the letter, they may find it easier to imagine how a circulation supervisor of a magazine would be likely to respond.

Students may find it helpful to use this letter as a model when formatting their own letters.

55a Writing business letters and memos

When you write in business, you are addressing busy people who want to see quickly why you are writing and how they should respond to you. A wordy letter or a memo with grammatical errors may prevent you from getting what you want, either because the reader cannot understand your wish or because you present yourself poorly.

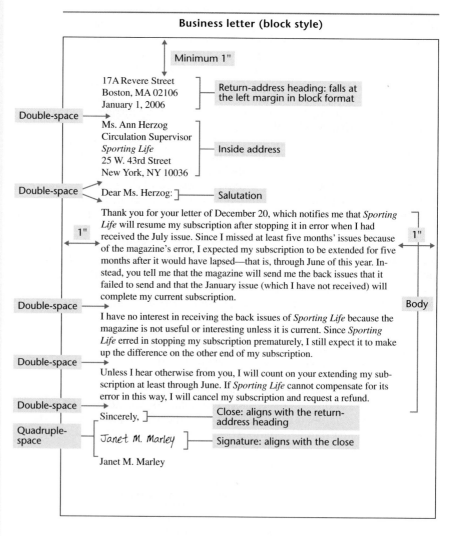

Business letter (block style)

Minimum 1"

17A Revere Street
Boston, MA 02106
January 1, 2006 — **Return-address heading: falls at the left margin in block format**

Double-space

Ms. Ann Herzog
Circulation Supervisor
Sporting Life
25 W. 43rd Street
New York, NY 10036 — **Inside address**

Double-space

Dear Ms. Herzog: — **Salutation**

Thank you for your letter of December 20, which notifies me that *Sporting Life* will resume my subscription after stopping it in error when I had received the July issue. Since I missed at least five months' issues because of the magazine's error, I expected my subscription to be extended for five months after it would have lapsed—that is, through June of this year. Instead, you tell me that the magazine will send me the back issues that it failed to send and that the January issue (which I have not received) will complete my current subscription.

Double-space

I have no interest in receiving the back issues of *Sporting Life* because the magazine is not useful or interesting unless it is current. Since *Sporting Life* erred in stopping my subscription prematurely, I still expect it to make up the difference on the other end of my subscription.

Double-space

Unless I hear otherwise from you, I will count on your extending my subscription at least through June. If *Sporting Life* cannot compensate for its error in this way, I will cancel my subscription and request a refund.

1"   1"   **Body**

Double-space

Sincerely, — **Close: aligns with the return-address heading**

Quadruple-space

Janet M. Marley — **Signature: aligns with the close**

Janet M. Marley

In all business writing, follow these general guidelines:

- **State your purpose right at the start.**
- **Be straightforward, clear, concise, objective, and courteous.**
- **Observe conventions of grammar and usage,** which make your writing clear and impress your reader with your care.

The formats of business letters and memos are fairly standardized and are thus expected by your correspondents.

1 Using a standard format for letters

Use either unlined white paper measuring 8½" × 11" or what is called letterhead stationery with your address printed at the top of the sheet. Type the letter single-spaced, with double space between elements, on only one side of a sheet.

The two most common forms for business letters—the full block and the modified block—are illustrated opposite and on page 846, respectively. Annotations on the samples indicate spacing, margins, and other aspects of format.

The letter

Return-address heading Unless you're using letterhead stationery, the return-address heading of the letter gives your address (but not your name) and the date. If you are using letterhead, you need add only the date.

Inside address The inside address shows the name, title, and complete address of the person you are writing to. (See p. 842 for abbreviations of state names.)

Salutation The salutation greets the addressee. Whenever possible, address your letter to a specific person. (Call the company or department to ask whom to address.) If you can't find a person's name, then use a job title (*Dear Human Resources Manager, Dear Customer Service Manager*) or use a general salutation (*Dear Smythe Shoes*). Use *Ms.* as the title for a woman when she has no other title, when you don't know how she prefers to be addressed, or when you know that she prefers to be addressed as *Ms.* If you know a woman prefers to be addressed as *Mrs.* or *Miss,* use the appropriate title.

Body The body of the letter, containing its substance, begins at the left margin in both letter styles. Instead of indenting the first line of each paragraph, place an extra line of space between paragraphs so that they are readily visible.

Close The letter's close should reflect the level of formality in the salutation. For formal letters, *Cordially, Yours truly,* and

Mehaffy, Robert, and Constance Warloe. "Corporate Communications: Next Step for the Community Colleges?" *The Technical Writing Teacher* 16 (1989): 1–11. Mehaffy and Warloe show the curriculum design for a professional writing course taking into account adult learning styles, computer-assisted composition, reader-centered writing, interviewing for information, project management, and team design.

Mendelson, Michael. "Business Prose and the Nature of the Plain Style." *Journal of Business Communication* 24.2 (1987): 3–18. Mendelson demonstrates how various stylistic possibilities afford students different persuasive strategies.

Odell, Lee, and Dixie Goswami, eds. *Writing in Nonacademic Settings.* New York: Guilford, 1985. This essay collection encompasses the theory and practice of writing in the workplace, with heavy emphasis on ethnographic studies of "real" writers at work.

Rogers, Priscilla S. and Jone Rymer. "Analytical Tools to Facilitate Translations Into New Writing Contexts: A Communicative Perspective." Journal of Business Communication 38.2 (2001): 112–50. The authors studied the writing of business students and developed a matrix for assessing and overcoming deficiencies.

COLLABORATIVE LEARNING

FROM THE MAILBOX TO THE CLASSROOM

Encourage students to bring in copies of professional correspondence they have received (on the job, from the college or university, as junk mail) and discuss the different kinds of formats and rhetorical strategies they find. What similarities and differences do they discover? Can they relate these to the purpose and audience of each communication? Making students aware of such factors helps them realize that business communication employs the same writing strategies as other kinds of writing.

Sincerely are common closes. For less formal letters, you may choose to use *Regards, Best wishes,* or the like. Only the first word of the close is capitalized, and the close is followed by a comma.

Signature The signature of a business letter falls below the close and has two parts. One is your name typed on the fourth line below the close. The other is your handwritten signature, which fills the space between the close and your typed name. The signature should consist only of your name, as you sign checks and other documents.

Other information Below the signature at the left margin, you may want to include additional information such as *Enc. 3* (indicating that there are three enclosures with the letter) or *cc: Margaret Newton* (indicating that a copy is being sent to the person named).

■ The envelope

The envelope should accommodate the letter once it is folded horizontally in thirds. The following are the common Postal Service abbreviations for addresses:

Street names

Avenue	AVE	Expressway	EXPY	Road	RD
Boulevard	BLVD	Freeway	FWY	Square	SQ
Circle	CIR	Lane	LN	Street	ST
Court	CT	Parkway	PKY	Turnpike	TPKE

Compass points

North	N	West	W	Southwest	SW
East	E	Northeast	NE	Northwest	NW

State names

Alabama	AL	Kentucky	KY	North Dakota	ND
Alaska	AK	Louisiana	LA	Ohio	OH
Arizona	AZ	Maine	ME	Oklahoma	OK
Arkansas	AR	Maryland	MD	Oregon	OR
California	CA	Massachusetts	MA	Pennsylvania	PA
Colorado	CO	Michigan	MI	Puerto Rico	PR
Connecticut	CT	Minnesota	MN	Rhode Island	RI
Delaware	DE	Mississippi	MS	South Carolina	SC
District of		Missouri	MO	South Dakota	SD
Columbia	DC	Montana	MT	Tennessee	TN
Florida	FL	Nebraska	NE	Texas	TX
Georgia	GA	Nevada	NV	Utah	UT
Hawaii	HI	New		Vermont	VT
Idaho	ID	Hampshire	NH	Virginia	VA
Illinois	IL	New Jersey	NJ	Washington	WA
Indiana	IN	New Mexico	NM	West Virginia	WV
Iowa	IA	New York	NY	Wisconsin	WI
Kansas	KS	North Carolina	NC	Wyoming	WY

Envelope for a business letter

JANET M MARLEY
17A REVERE ST — Sender's name and address
BOSTON MA 02106

MS ANN HERZOG
CIRCULATION SUPERVISOR — Addressee's name, title, and
SPORTING LIFE address
25 W 43RD ST
NEW YORK NY 10036

US Postal Service preference:
all capitals and no punctuation

2 Writing requests and complaints

Letters requesting something—for instance, a pamphlet, information about a product, a T-shirt advertised in a magazine—must be specific and accurate about the item you are requesting. The letter should describe the item completely and, if applicable, include a copy or description of the advertisement or other source that prompted your request.

Letters complaining about a product or a service (such as a wrong billing from the telephone company) should be written in a reasonable but firm tone. (See the sample letter on p. 840.) Assume that the addressee is willing to resolve the problem when he or she has the relevant information. In the first sentence of the letter, say what you are writing about. Then provide as much background as needed, including any relevant details from past correspondence (as in the sample letter). Describe exactly what you see as the problem, sticking to facts and avoiding discourse on the company's social responsibility or your low opinion of its management. In the clearest and fewest possible words and sentences, proceed directly from one point to the next without repeating yourself. Always include your opinion of how the problem can be solved. Many companies are required by law to establish a specific procedure for complaints about products and services. If you know of such a procedure, be sure to follow it.

3 Writing business memos

Unlike business letters, which address people in other organizations, business memorandums (memos, for short) address people within the same organization. A memo can be quite long, but more often it deals briefly with a specific topic, such as an answer to a question, a progress report, or an evaluation. Both the content and the format of a memo aim to get to the point and dispose of it quickly.

- **Content**
- **State your reason for writing in the first sentence.** You might outline a problem, make a request, refer to a request that prompted the memo, or briefly summarize new findings. Do not, however, waste words with expressions like *The purpose of this memo is. . . .*

MODELS OF STUDENT WRITING

Patricia Phillips's memo is a fine example, one that might prompt a class discussion on how purpose for writing and audience can vary widely in business writing. Each of the other models of writing in this chapter (the letter of complaint on p. 840, the application letter on p. 846, and the résumés on pp. 848 and 849) asks for something significant and is addressed to readers who may be disinclined to do what the writer asks. Those situations demand that the writer pay extra attention to tone. Memo writers, on the other hand, usually want to write as quickly and efficiently as possible, and unless they are writing about a very sensitive matter, they do not need to fine-tune their tone or presentation. Ask your students to evaluate Phillips's purpose and audience in order to see why directness is appropriate in her memo.

Business memo

Heading: company's name, addressee's name, writer's name and initials, date, and subject description

Bigelow Wax Company

TO: Aileen Rosen, Director of Sales
FROM: Patricia Phillips, Territory 12 *PP*
DATE: March 17, 2006
SUBJECT: 2005 sales of Quick Wax in Territory 12

Body: single-spaced with double spacing between paragraphs; paragraphs not indented

Since it was introduced in January 2005, Quick Wax has been unsuccessful in Territory 12 and has not affected the sales of our Easy Shine. Discussions with customers and my own analysis of Quick Wax suggest three reasons for its failure to compete with our product.

1. Quick Wax has not received the promotion necessary for a new product. Advertising—primarily on radio—has been sporadic and has not developed a clear, consistent image for the product. In addition, the Quick Wax sales representative in Territory 12 is new and inexperienced; he is not known to customers, and his sales pitch (which I once overheard) is weak. As far as I can tell, his efforts are not supported by phone calls or mailings from his home office.

2. When Quick Wax does make it to the store shelves, buyers do not choose it over our product. Though priced competitively with our product, Quick Wax is poorly packaged. The container seems smaller than ours, though in fact it holds the same eight ounces. The lettering on the Quick Wax package (red on blue) is difficult to read, in contrast to the white-on-green lettering on the Easy Shine package.

3. Our special purchase offers and my increased efforts to serve existing customers have had the intended effect of keeping customers satisfied with our product and reducing their inclination to stock something new.

People receiving copies

Copies: L. Mendes, Director of Marketing
          J. MacGregor, Customer Service Manager

- **Devote the first paragraph to a succinct presentation of your solution, recommendation, answer, or evaluation.** The first paragraph should be short, and by its end your reader should know precisely what to expect from the rest of the memo: the details and reasoning that support your conclusion.
- **Deliver the support in the body of the memo.** The paragraphs may be numbered or bulleted so that the main divisions of your message are easy to see. In a long memo, you may need headings (see pp. 119–20).
- **Suit your style and tone to your audience.** For instance, you'll want to address your boss or a large group of readers more formally than you would a coworker who is also a friend.
- **Write concisely.** Keep your sentences short and your language simple, using technical terms only when your readers will understand them. Say only what readers need to know.

4 Communicating electronically

Electronic communication—mainly e-mail and faxes—adds a few twists to business writing. E-mail plays such a prominent role in communication of all sorts that we discuss it extensively as part of writing online (see pp. 826–29). Generally, the standards for business e-mail are the same as for other business correspondence.

Faxes follow closely the formats of print documents, but there are some unique concerns:

- **Consider legibility.** Small type, photographs, horizontal lines, and other elements that look fine on your copy may not be legible to the addressee.
- **Include a cover sheet.** Most faxes require a cover sheet with the addressee's name, company, and fax number; the date, time, and subject; your own name and fax and telephone numbers; and the total number of pages (including the cover sheet) in the fax.
- **Advise your addressee to expect a fax.** The advice is essential if the fax is confidential because the machine is often shared.
- **Consider urgency.** Transmission by fax can imply that the correspondence is urgent. If yours isn't, you may want to use the mail instead.

55b Writing a job application

In applying for a job or requesting a job interview, send both a résumé and a cover letter. If you need to submit your application electronically, see pages 847 and 849.

COMPUTER ACTIVITY

MEMO TEMPLATES

Your students' word-processing software probably has one or more memo templates that can streamline the process of creating a memo. Your students may wish to use one of these templates or modify one of them to suit their purposes more exactly. Alternatively, your students can create a template entirely of their own devising and store it on their computers. They might want to refer to the content guidelines listed in 55a3 as they write.

COLLABORATIVE LEARNING

EVALUATING THE URGENCY

Give your students a set of memos and have them work in small groups to discuss which memos are urgent enough to be sent by fax and which ought to go by e-mail.

COMPUTER ACTIVITY

ELECTRONIC WIZARDS

Most word-processing programs have wizards, tools that can help students create memos and faxes and then help them send their documents electronically, either as faxes or as e-mail.

MODELS OF STUDENT WRITING

Students (and job applicants in general) often have a hard time writing reader-based letters of application. Some have difficulty selling their skills strongly enough; some focus on why they need or want the job more than on what they have to offer. Ian Irvine presents his qualifications succinctly and organizes his information well. Your students may disagree, however, about the effectiveness of his letter: some may think it lacks pizzazz; others may like the formality and professionalism of its tone.

Irvine's letter (and the two versions of Irvine's résumé on pp. 848 and 849) may make for a good class discussion. Begin by asking your students to imagine they are Raymond Chipault at the *Dallas News*. Have them read Irvine's letter and decide whether it makes them want to read his résumé. Have them give justifications for their decisions and make any suggestions for revision they deem appropriate. Finally, ask them to read one of the résumés and decide whether they would want to interview Irvine. Again, they should justify their decisions and make suggestions for revision.

1 Writing the cover letter

The cover letter should be formatted in block style (p. 840) or modified block style (below). Use the sample below and these guidelines in composing the letter:

- **Interpret your résumé for the particular job.** Don't detail your entire résumé, reciting your job history. Instead, highlight and reshape only the relevant parts.

Job-application letter (modified block style)

> Return-address heading: falls to the right of center in modified block format
>
> 3712 Swiss Avenue
> Dallas, TX 75204
> March 2, 2006

Raymond Chipault
Human Resources Manager
Dallas News
Communications Center
Dallas, TX 75222

Dear Mr. Chipault:

In response to your posting in the English Department of Southern Methodist University, I am applying for the summer job of part-time editorial assistant for the *Dallas News*.

I am now enrolled at Southern Methodist University as a sophomore, with a dual major in English literature and journalism. My courses so far have included news reporting, copy editing, and electronic publishing. I worked a summer as a copy aide for my hometown newspaper, and for two years I have edited and written sports stories and features for the university newspaper. My feature articles cover subjects as diverse as campus elections, parking regulations, visiting professors, and speech codes.

As the enclosed résumé and writing samples indicate, my education and knowledge of newspaper work prepare me for the opening you have.

I am available for an interview at your convenience and would be happy to show more samples of my writing. Please e-mail me at ianirv@mail.smu.edu or call me at 214-744-3816.

> Close and signature: align with the return-address heading
>
> Sincerely,
>
> *Ian M. Irvine*
>
> Ian M. Irvine

Enc.

- **Announce at the outset what job you seek and how you heard about it.**
- **Include any special reason you have for applying,** such as a specific career goal.
- **Summarize your qualifications for this particular job,** including relevant facts about education and employment and emphasizing notable accomplishments. Mention that additional information appears in an accompanying résumé.
- **Describe your availability.** At the end of the letter, mention that you are free for an interview at the convenience of the addressee, or specify when you will be available (for instance, when your current job or classes leave you free).

2 Writing and formatting the résumé

The résumé that accompanies your letter of application should provide information in table format that allows a potential employer to evaluate your qualifications. The résumé should include your name and address, a career objective, your education and employment history, special skills or awards, and information about how to obtain your references. All the information should fit on one uncrowded page, unless your education and experience are extensive. See the sample on the next page for writing and formatting guidelines for a résumé that you submit in print.

Some employers may ask for an electronic version of your résumé so that they can add it to a computerized database of applicants. The employers may scan your printed résumé to convert it to an electronic file, which they can then store in an appropriate database. Or they may ask you to provide the résumé electronically, either attaching it to or embedding it in an e-mail message. If an employer requests a scannable or electronic résumé, follow the guidelines below and consult the sample on page 849.

- **Keep the design simple for accurate scanning or electronic transmittal.** Avoid images, unusual type, more than one column, vertical or horizontal lines, italics, or underlining.
- **Use concise, specific words to describe your skills and experience.** The employer's computer may use keywords (often nouns) to identify the résumés of suitable job candidates, and you want to ensure that your résumé includes the appropriate keywords. Name your specific skills—for example, the computer programs you can operate—and write concretely with words like *manager* (not *person with responsibility for*) and *reporter* (not *staff member who reports*). Look for likely keywords in the employer's description of the job you seek.

MODELS OF STUDENT WRITING

These two résumés present the same content in different design formats. In both versions, the content is well arranged and the use of parallelism is precise. You can have your students read these résumés in conjunction with Irvine's application letter on page 846. Ask students to react to the two different designs—traditional and contemporary—and to discuss what kinds of jobs each design might be best suited for.

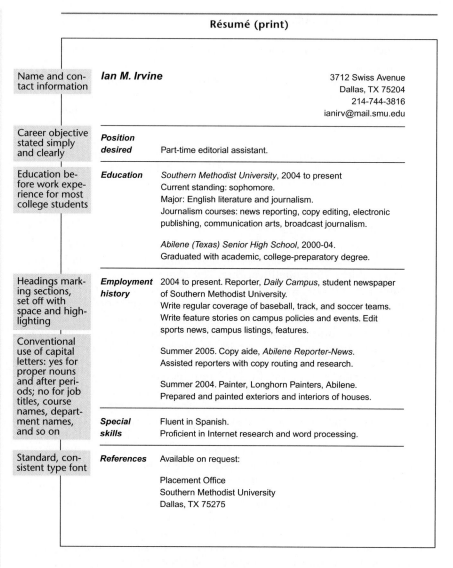

Résumé (print)

Name and contact information

Ian M. Irvine
                                          3712 Swiss Avenue
                                          Dallas, TX 75204
                                          214-744-3816
                                          ianirv@mail.smu.edu

Career objective stated simply and clearly

Position desired   Part-time editorial assistant.

Education before work experience for most college students

Education   *Southern Methodist University*, 2004 to present
                 Current standing: sophomore.
                 Major: English literature and journalism.
                 Journalism courses: news reporting, copy editing, electronic publishing, communication arts, broadcast journalism.

                 Abilene (Texas) Senior High School, 2000-04.
                 Graduated with academic, college-preparatory degree.

Headings marking sections, set off with space and highlighting

Employment history   2004 to present. Reporter, *Daily Campus*, student newspaper of Southern Methodist University.
                          Write regular coverage of baseball, track, and soccer teams. Write feature stories on campus policies and events. Edit sports news, campus listings, features.

Conventional use of capital letters: yes for proper nouns and after periods; no for job titles, course names, department names, and so on

                          Summer 2005. Copy aide, *Abilene Reporter-News*. Assisted reporters with copy routing and research.

                          Summer 2004. Painter, Longhorn Painters, Abilene. Prepared and painted exteriors and interiors of houses.

Special skills   Fluent in Spanish.
                      Proficient in Internet research and word processing.

Standard, consistent type font

References   Available on request:

                  Placement Office
                  Southern Methodist University
                  Dallas, TX 75275

OTHER COURSE ASSIGNMENTS

If your students are taking other courses in which they have report-writing assignments, you could allow them to work on one of those in your course. Contact the instructor of the other course first to discuss whether such an arrangement is feasible and desirable.

55c   Writing business reports and proposals

Reports and proposals are text-heavy documents, sometimes lengthy, that convey information such as the results of research, a plan for action, or a recommendation for change. As with other business correspondence, you will prepare a report or proposal for a specific purpose, and you will be addressing interested but busy readers.

Résumé (scannable or electronic)

Ian M. Irvine
3712 Swiss Avenue
Dallas, TX 75204
214-744-3816

KEYWORDS: Editor, editorial assistant, publishing, electronic publishing.

OBJECTIVE
Part-time editorial assistant.

EDUCATION
Southern Methodist University, 2004 to present.
Major: English literature and journalism.
Journalism courses: news reporting, copy editing, electronic publishing, communication arts, broadcast journalism.

Abilene (Texas) Senior High School, 2000-04.
Academic, college preparatory degree.

EMPLOYMENT HISTORY
Reporter, Daily Campus, Southern Methodist University, 2004 to present.
Writer of articles for student newspaper on sports teams, campus policies, and local events. Editor of sports news, campus listings, and features.

Copy aide, Abilene Reporter-News, Abilene, summer 2005.
Assistant to reporters, routing copy and doing research.

Painter, Longhorn Painters, Abilene, summer 2004.
Preparation and painting of exteriors and interiors of houses.

SPECIAL SKILLS
Fluent in Spanish.
Proficient in Internet research and word processing.

REFERENCES
Available upon request:
Placement Office
Southern Methodist University
Dallas, TX 75275

Accurate keywords, allowing the employer to place the résumé into an appropriate database

Simple design, avoiding unusual type, italics, multiple columns, decorative lines, and images

Standard font easily read by scanners

Every line aligning at left margin

Reports and proposals usually divide into sections. The sections vary depending on the purpose of the document, but usually they include an overview or summary, which tells the reader what the document is about; a statement of the problem or need, which justifies the report or proposal; a statement of the plan or solution, which responds to the need or problem; and a recommendation or evaluation. Consider the following guidelines as you prepare a report or proposal:

- **Do your research.** The standard formats of reports and proposals require you to be well informed, so be alert to where you have enough information or where you don't.
- **Focus on the purpose of each section.** Stick to the point of each section, saying only what you need to say, even if you have additional information. Each section should accomplish its purpose and contribute to the whole.
- **Follow an appropriate format.** In many businesses, reports and proposals have specific formatting requirements. If you are unsure about the requirements, ask your supervisor.

Report

Descriptive title conveying report's contents

Standard format: summary, statement of the problem, solutions, and (not shown) recommendations

Major sections delineated by headings

Formal tone, appropriate to a business-writing situation

Single spacing with double spacing between paragraphs and around the list

Bulleted list emphasizing alternative solutions

Canada Geese at ABC Institute: An Environmental Problem

Summary

The flock of Canada geese on and around ABC Institute's grounds has grown dramatically in recent years to become a nuisance and an environmental problem. This report reviews the problem, considers possible solutions, and proposes that ABC Institute and the US Fish and Wildlife Service cooperate to reduce the flock by humane means.

The Problem

Canada geese began living at Taylor Lake next to ABC Institute when they were relocated there in 1985 by the state game department. As a nonmigratory flock, the geese are present year-round, with the highest population each year occurring in early spring. In recent years the flock has grown dramatically. The Audubon Society's annual Christmas bird census shows a thirty-fold increase from the 37 geese counted in 1986 to the 1125 counted in 2005.

The principal environmental problem caused by the geese is pollution of grass and water by defecation. Geese droppings cover the ABC Institute's grounds as well as the park's picnicking areas. The runoff from these droppings into Taylor Lake has substantially affected the quality of the lake's water, so that local authorities have twice (2004 and 2005) issued warnings against swimming.

Possible Solutions

The goose overpopulation and resulting environmental problems have several possible solutions:

- Harass the geese with dogs and audiovisual effects (light and noise) so that the geese choose to leave. This solution is inhumane to the geese and unpleasant for human neighbors.
- Feed the geese a chemical that will weaken the shells of their eggs and thus reduce growth of the flock. This solution is inhumane to the geese and also impractical, because geese are long-lived.
- Kill adult geese. This solution is, obviously, inhumane to the geese.
- Thin the goose population by trapping and removing many geese (perhaps 600) to areas less populated by humans, such as wildlife preserves.

Though costly (see figures below), the last solution is the most humane. It would be harmless to the geese, provided that sizable netted enclosures are used for traps. [Discussion of solution and "Recommendations" follow.]

Internal proposal

Springfield Veterans Administration Hospital

To: Jefferson Green, Director, Finance and Operations
From: Kate Goodman, Director, ReadingWorks *KG*
Date: October 17, 2005
Subject: Budget proposal for ReadingWorks Awards Dinner

OVERVIEW

ReadingWorks requests funding for an awards dinner.

NEED

ReadingWorks, the literacy center operated by Springfield VA Hospital, has for 6 years served between 50 and 70 patients/students a year with a small paid staff and a corps of dedicated volunteers. In the past year the center's paid staff and 20 volunteers provided more than 1260 hours of literacy tutoring to 67 students, an increase of 14 students over last year. I want to recognize the efforts and accomplishments of our students and tutors by holding an awards dinner for them and their families.

PLAN

I propose the following event for Friday, May 25, 7:30 to 10:30 PM: dinner and nonalcoholic beverages for approximately 135 students, tutors, and their guests; entertainment; and certificates for approximately 20 students and tutors. I request the use of Suite 42 because it can accommodate as many as 200 people as well as caterers and a DJ. Hospital staff will need to have the room ready by 6:00 PM on May 25.

BUDGET

Dinner and beverages for about 135 attendees	$2700
Music for two hours	200
Certificates	50
TOTAL	$2950

Bids from local businesses are attached.

PERSONNEL

Five hospital employees will be needed to set up, take down, and clean Suite 42 before and after the dinner.

Annotations (right margin):
- Memo format for internal proposal (p. 844)
- "Overview": statement of proposal
- "Need": justification for the request
- Formal tone appropriate for a proposal
- "Plan": explanation of request
- "Budget" and "Personnel": details on the proposal's requirements
- Single spacing with double spacing between sections

COLLABORATIVE LEARNING

As an in-class exercise, have students draft a proposal that ice cream should be served in all campus classes daily. Then have them trade papers with a partner and evaluate each other's proposals.

55d   Writing for community work

At some point in your life, you're likely to volunteer for a community organization such as a soup kitchen, a daycare center, a literacy program, or a tutoring center for immigrants learning English. Many college courses involve service learning, in which you do such volunteer work, write about the experience for your course, and write *for* the organization you're helping.

PRESENTING DOCUMENTS

Ask students to bring in a written document from an organization for which they volunteer or would like to volunteer. Each student can pass the document around and explain what its purpose is, whether they think it is a good example of its kind, and what they might do to improve it.

The writing you do for a community group may range from flyers to newsletters to grant proposals. Two guidelines in particular will help you prepare effective projects:

- **Craft each document for its purpose and audience.** You are trying to achieve a specific aim with your readers, and the approach and tone you use will influence their responses. If, for example, you are writing letters to local businesses to raise funds for a homeless shelter, bring to mind the person or people who will read your letter. How can you best persuade those readers to donate money?

Flyer

Large type and color focusing a distant reader's attention on important information: what's happening, when, where, and who is invited

White space drawing viewers' eyes to main message and creating flow among elements

Color highlighting only key information

Less important information set in smaller type

FIRST ANNUAL AWARDS DINNER

WHEN
Friday night
May 25
7:30 to 10:30

**For information
contact ReadingWorks
209-556-1212**

WHERE
Suite 42
Springfield VA Hospital

WHO
Students, tutors, and their families are invited to join us for an evening of food and music as we celebrate their efforts and accomplishments.

ReadingWorks of Springfield Veterans Administration Hospital
111 South Springdale Drive
Springfield, MI 45078

■ **Expect to work with others.** Much public writing is the work of more than one person. Even if you draft the document on your own, others will review the content, tone, and design. Such collaboration is rewarding, but it sometimes requires patience and goodwill. See pages 66–69 and 829–32 for advice on collaborating.

The illustrations here and on the next page show a flyer, a newsletter, and a brochure prepared for ReadingWorks, a literacy program. See also pages 840–45 and 848–51 on business letters, memos, and proposals, as well as pages 861–62 on *PowerPoint* presentations.

Newsletter

ReadingWorks

Springfield Veterans Administration Hospital   **SUMMER 2005**

From the director

Can you help? With more and more learners in the ReadingWorks program, we need more and more tutors. You may know people who would be interested in participating in the program, if only they knew about it.

Those of you who have been tutoring VA patients in reading and writing know both the great need you fulfill and the great benefits you bring to the students. New tutors need no special skills—we'll provide the training—only patience and an interest in helping others.

We've scheduled an orientation meeting for Friday, September 12, at 6:30 PM. Please come and bring a friend who is willing to contribute a couple of hours a week to our work.

Thanks,
Kate Goodman

IN THIS ISSUE

First Annual Awards Dinner	1
New Guidelines on PTSD	1
Textbooks	2
Lesson Planning	2
Dyslexia Workshop	2
Support for Tutors	3
Writing by Students	3
Calendar of Events	4

FIRST ANNUAL AWARDS DINNER

A festive night for students and tutors

The first annual Reading-Works Awards Dinner on May 25th was a great success. Springfield's own Golden Fork provided tasty food and Amber Allen supplied lively music. The students decorated Suite 42 on the theme of books and reading. In all, 127 people attended.

The highlight of the night was the awards ceremony. Nine students, recommended by their tutors, received certificates recognizing their efforts and special accomplishments in learning to read and write:

Ramon Berva
Edward Byar
David Dunbar
Tony Garnier
Chris Guigni
Akili Haynes
Josh Livingston
Alex Obeld
B. J. Resnansky

In addition, nine tutors received certificates commemorating five years of service to ReadingWorks:

Anita Crumpton
Felix Cruz-Rivera
Bette Elgen

Kayleah Bortoluzzi
Harriotte Henderson
Ben Obiso
Meggie Puente
Max Smith
Sara Villante

Congratulations to all!

PTSD: New Guidelines

Most of us are working with veterans who have been diagnosed with post-traumatic stress disorder. Because this disorder is often complicated by alcoholism, depression, anxiety, and other problems, the National Center for PTSD has issued some guidelines for helping PTSD patients in ways that reduce their stress.

• The hospital must know your tutoring schedule, and you need to sign in and out before and after each tutoring session.

• To protect patients' privacy, meet them only in designated visiting and tutoring areas, never in their rooms.

• Treat patients with dignity and respect, even when (as sometimes happens) they grow frustrated and angry. Seek help from a nurse or orderly if you need it.

Multicolumn format allowing room for headings, articles, and other elements on a single page

Two-column heading emphasizing the main article

Elements helping readers skim for highlights: spacing, varied font sizes, lines, and a bulleted list

Color focusing readers' attention on banner, headlines, and table of contents

Lively but uncluttered overall appearance

Box in the first column highlighting table of contents

Brochure

Do you know a veteran who needs help with reading and writing?

Do you need to improve your reading and writing skills to get a job?

ReadingWorks can make a difference. We organize volunteers to help military veterans achieve literacy and to prepare them for life-long learning.

For more information about our services, call Kate Goodman at 209-556-1212 or visit www.readingworks.org.

ReadingWorks
Springfield VA Hospital
111 South Springdale Drive
Springfield, MI 45078

ReadingWorks
Springfield VA Hospital

Helping
military
veterans
achieve
literacy

Panel 2: The right page when the cover is opened, the first one readers see, containing key information

Panel 6: The back, usually including the return address and space for a mailing label and postage

Panel 1: The cover, drawing readers' attention to the group's name, purpose, and affiliation

---

ReadingWorks
Springfield VA Hospital

OUR MISSION
- We provide workshops and formal lessons for veterans wishing to develop their reading and writing skills
- We train volunteers to tutor veterans one on one.
- We maintain outreach programs to provide access to literacy training for all veterans.
- We create literacy resources and share them with others who promote literacy for veterans.

OUR SERVICES

One-on-one tutoring
One to three hours a week with a trained volunteer tutor.

Workshops and classes
Small-group meetings centered on reading and writing, computer skills, and English as a second language.

Library
Books and other resources for students at various literacy levels.

Computer lab
Five computers with high-speed Internet access and a full range of software.

OUR TUTORS
The goodwill and generosity of our volunteer tutors allows us to reach out to those who have served our country.

If you or someone you know can join our team, contact Kate Goodman at 209-556-1212.

Hours
12:00 to 8:00, Mon., Wed.
9:00 to 5:00, Tues., Thurs., Fri.

Eligibility
Any veteran of the US military is eligible for our services.

How to reach us
Springfield VA Hospital
Room 172, first floor
111 South Springdale Drive
Springfield, MI 45078
209-556-1212
www.readingworks.org

Panel 3: The left page when the cover is opened, reinforcing the message of panel 2

Varied type, color, and photographs, adding visual interest and focusing readers' attention

Panels 4 and 5: The inside panels, containing contact information and other details

CHAPTER 56

Oral Presentations

At some point during your education or your work, you will probably be called on to speak to a group. Oral presentation can be anxiety producing, even for those who are experienced at it. This chapter shows you how you can apply your experiences as a writer to public speaking, and it offers some techniques that are uniquely appropriate for effective oral presentations.

56a Writing and speaking

Writing and speechmaking have much in common: both require careful consideration of your subject, purpose, and audience. Thus the mental and physical activities that go into the writing process can also help you prepare and deliver a successful oral presentation.

Despite many similarities, however, writing for readers is not the same as speaking to listeners. Whereas a reader can go back and reread a written message, a listener cannot stop a speech to rehear a section. Several studies have reported that immediately after hearing a short talk, most listeners cannot recall half of what was said.

Effective speakers adapt to their audience's listening ability by reinforcing their ideas through repetition and restatement. They use simple words, short sentences, personal pronouns, contractions, and colloquial expressions. In formal writing, these strategies might seem redundant and too informal; but in speaking, they improve listeners' comprehension.

56b Considering purpose and audience

The most important step in developing an oral presentation is to identify your purpose: what do you want your audience to know or do as a result of your speech? Topic and purpose are *not* the same thing. Asking *What am I talking about?* is not the same as asking *Why am I speaking?*

http://www.ablongman.com/littlebrown ▶

Visit the companion Web site for more help with oral presentations and *PowerPoint.*

mycomplab

Please visit MyCompLab at *www.mycomplab.com* for more on the writing process.

HIGHLIGHTS

Many educators, businesses, and institutions consider the ability to articulate ideas thoughtfully and effectively within a group or in larger public settings to be the most significant and most underemphasized of educational goals. While writing classes often include an informal speech component, planned oral presentations can help students to develop their critical reading, writing, and *speaking* skills as part of a cohesive process.

Chapter 56 suggests ways to integrate a speechmaking component into the writing curriculum. In particular, it identifies ways in which the handbook's emphasis on critical thinking can be expanded to help students prepare and deliver oral presentations, including identifying the topic, purpose, and audience for the speech; organizing and presenting the material in a way that effectively foregrounds the motivational or informational qualities of the speech; and becoming aware of various strategies for vocal and physical delivery and of ways to cope with presentation anxiety. The chapter also includes a "Checklist for an oral presentation" (p. 856) that students can use in preparing for their speeches and in critiquing each other's presentations. Finally, this edition of the handbook includes a new discussion of how to use PowerPoint effectively in oral presentations.

COMPUTER ACTIVITY

GLOBAL WARMING PRESENTATION I

Have your students do a Web search to gather the most current information on the topic of global warming and write up a brief statement of purpose for a presentation they could make on this topic. (Note: This is the first of a series of

COMPANION WEB SITE

See page IAE-62 for companion Web site content description.

activities suggested for this chapter. You can do them either individually or as a linked series. You can stick with the topic of global warming or use another topic of your own choosing. If you focus on global warming, you may want to direct students to the case study on evaluating a Web site on pages 604–08.)

COLLABORATIVE LEARNING

CHECKLIST INTERVIEWS

Have students break into pairs and work through the checklist for oral presentation. Each partner can take turns asking the checklist questions about the other partner's oral presentation. The "interviewer" can take notes about what the "interviewee" says and then give feedback.

COLLABORATIVE LEARNING

MODEL SPEECHES

Watching or listening to speechmakers is a good way to get some experience in how they work. Invite students to gather with classmates outside of class to tune in to speeches on C-Span or network television. They can hold informal discussions about the speeches they hear and then share their findings with the rest of the class.

Checklist for an oral presentation

- **Purpose:** What do you want your audience to know or do as a result of your presentation? How can you achieve your purpose in the time and setting you've been given? (See the previous page and below.)
- **Audience:** What do you know about the characteristics and opinions of your audience? How can this information help you adapt your presentation to your audience's interests, needs, and opinions? (See below.)
- **Organization and content:** How are your ideas arranged? Where might listeners have difficulty following you? What functions do your introduction and conclusion perform? How relevant and interesting is your supporting material for your topic and your audience? (See opposite.)
- **Method of delivery:** What method of delivery do you plan: extemporaneous? reading from a text? memorized? a mixture? How does your method suit the purpose, setting, and occasion of your presentation? (See pp. 855–57.)
- **Vocal and physical delivery:** In rehearsing your presentation, what do you perceive as your strengths and weaknesses? Is your voice suitably loud for the setting? Are you speaking clearly? Are you able to move your eyes around the room so that you'll be making eye contact during the presentation? Is your posture straight but not stiff? Do your gestures reinforce your ideas? Do you use visual aids appropriately? (See pp. 861–62.)
- **Confidence and credibility:** What techniques will you use to overcome the inevitable anxiety about speaking? How will you project your confidence and competence? (See pp. 862–63.)

In school and work settings, oral presentations may include anything from a five-minute report before a few peers to an hour-long address before a hundred people. Whatever the situation, you're likely to be speaking for the same reasons that you write in school or at work: to explain something to listeners or to persuade listeners to accept your opinion or take an action. See pages 14–15 for more on these purposes.

Adapting to your audience is a critical task in public speaking as well as in writing. You'll want to consider the questions about audience on page 11. But a listening audience requires additional considerations as well:

- **Why is your audience assembled?** Listeners who attend because they want to hear you and your ideas may be easier to interest and motivate then listeners who are required to attend.
- **How large is your audience?** With a small group you can be informal. If you are speaking to a hundred or more people, you

may need a public address system, a lectern, special lighting, and audiovisual equipment.

- **Where will you speak?** Your approach should match the setting—more casual for a small classroom, more formal for an auditorium.
- **How long are you scheduled to speak?** Whatever the time limit, stick to it. Audiences lose patience with someone who speaks longer than expected.

When speaking, unlike when writing, you can see and hear your audience's responses during your presentation. If you sense that an audience is bored, try to spice up your presentation. If an audience is restless, consult your watch to make sure you have not gone over your time. If you sense resistance, try to make midspeech adjustments to respond to that resistance.

56c Organizing the presentation

An effective oral presentation, like an effective essay, has a recognizable shape. The advice in Chapter 2 for organizing and outlining an essay serves the speechmaker as well as the writer (see pp. 32–43). Here are additional considerations for the introduction, conclusion, and supporting material.

1 The Introduction

First impressions count. A strong beginning establishes an important relationship among three elements in an oral presentation: you, your topic, and your audience. More specifically, the beginning of an oral presentation should try to accomplish three goals:

- **Gain the audience's attention and interest.** Begin with a question, an unusual example or statistic, or a short, relevant story.
- **Put yourself in the speech.** If you demonstrate your expertise, experience, or concern, your audience will be more interested in what you say and more trusting of you.
- **Introduce and preview your topic and purpose.** By the time your introduction is over, listeners should know what your topic is and the direction in which you wish to take them as you develop your ideas.

In addition to these guidelines for beginning a speech, there are some important pitfalls to avoid:

- **Don't try to cram too much into your introduction.** Focus on engaging the audience and quickly previewing your talk.

- **Don't begin with an apology.** A statement such as *I wish I'd been given more time to get ready for this presentation* will only undermine your listeners' confidence in you.
- **Don't begin with *My speech is about.* . . .** The statement is dull, and it does little to clarify purpose.

2 Supporting material

Just as you do when writing, you can and should use facts, statistics, examples, and expert opinions to support spoken arguments (see pp. 184–85). In addition, as a speaker you can draw on other kinds of supporting material:

- **Use vivid description.** Paint a mental image of a scene, a concept, an event, or a person.
- **Use well-chosen quotations.** They can add an emotional or humorous moment to your speech.
- **Use true or fictional stories.** A memorable narrative can rivet the audience's attention and illustrate your point.
- **Use analogies.** Comparisons between essentially unlike things, such as a politician and a tightrope walker, link concepts memorably. (For more on analogy, see pp. 97–98.)

Use a variety of supporting material in your speech. A presentation that is nothing but statistics can bore an audience. Nonstop storytelling may interest listeners but fail to achieve your purpose.

3 The conclusion

Last impressions count as much as first impressions. You may hope that listeners will remember every detail of your speech, but they are more likely to leave with a general impression and a few ideas about you and your message. You want your conclusion to be clear, of course, but you also want it to be memorable. Remind listeners of how your topic and main idea connect to their needs and interests.

56d Delivering the presentation

Writing and speaking differ most obviously in the form of delivery: the writer is represented in print; the speaker is represented in person. This section describes the methods and techniques of oral presentation as well as some ways of coping with stage fright.

1 Methods of delivery

An oral presentation may be delivered impromptu, extemporaneously, from a text, or from memory. No one technique is best for all speeches; indeed, a single speech may include two or more forms or even all four—perhaps a memorized introduction, an extemporaneous body in which quotations are read from a text, and impromptu responses to audience questions during or after the speech.

■ Speaking impromptu

Impromptu means "without preparation": an impromptu presentation is one you deliver off-the-cuff, with no planning or practice. You may be called on in a class to express your opinion or to summarize something you've written. You may speak up at a neighborhood meeting. An audience member may ask you a question at the end of an oral presentation. The only way to prepare for such incidents is to be well prepared in general—to be caught up on course reading, for instance, or to know the facts in a debate.

■ Speaking extemporaneously

Extemporaneous speaking—that done with some preparation, but without reading from a text—is the most common form of presentation, typical of class lectures and business briefings. With extemporaneous speaking, you have time to prepare and practice in advance. Then, instead of following a script of every word, you speak from notes that guide you through the presentation.

■ Speaking from a text

Delivering a presentation from a text involves writing the text out in advance and then reading aloud from it. With a text in front of you, you're unlikely to lose your way. However, a reading speaker can be dull for an audience. Try to avoid this form of delivery for an entire presentation.

If you do use a text, write it so that it sounds spoken (less formal) rather than written (more formal): for instance, the sentence *Although costs rose, profits remained steady* would sound fine in writing but stiff and awkward in speech because in conversation we rarely use such a structure. In addition, rehearse thoroughly so that you can read with expression and can look up frequently to make eye contact with listeners (see the next page).

■ Speaking from memory

A memorized presentation has a distinct advantage: complete freedom from notes or a text. That means you can look at your audience every minute and can move away from a lectern and even into the audience. However, you may be like most speakers in seeming less relaxed, not more relaxed, when presenting from memory: your mind is too busy retrieving the next words to attend to the responses of the audience. Further, you risk forgetting your place or a whole passage.

For these reasons, many experts discourage memorization. At least reserve the method for the introduction, perhaps, or some other part with which you want to make a strong impression. Rehearse not only to memorize the words but, beyond that, to deliver the words fresh, as if for the first time.

2 Vocal delivery

The sound of your voice will influence how your listeners receive you. When rehearsing, consider volume, speed, and articulation.

- **Speak loudly.** In a meeting with five other people, you can speak in a normal volume. As your audience grows in size, so should your volume. Most speakers can project to as many as a hundred people, but a larger audience may require a microphone.
- **Speak slowly enough to be understandable.**
- **Speak clearly and correctly.** To avoid mumbling or slurring words, practice articulating. Sometimes it helps to open your mouth a little wider than usual.

3 Physical delivery

You are more than your spoken words when you make an oral presentation. Your face and body also play a role in how your speech is received.

- **Make eye contact with listeners.** Move your gaze around the entire room, settle on someone, and establish direct eye contact; then move on to someone else.
- **Stand up.** Always stand for a presentation, unless it takes place in a small room where standing would be inappropriate. You can see more audience members when you stand, and they in turn can hear your voice and see your gestures more clearly.
- **Stand straight, and move around.** Turn your body toward one side of the room and then the other, step out from behind any lectern or desk, and gesture appropriately, as you would in conversation.

4 Visual aids

You can supplement an oral presentation with visual aids such as posters, models, slides, videos, or presentation software such as *PowerPoint*. Visual aids can emphasize key points, organize related concepts, and illustrate complex procedures. They can gain the attention of listeners and improve their understanding and memory.

The following guidelines can help you create effective and appropriate visual aids:

- **Use visual aids to underscore your points.** Short lists of key ideas, illustrations such as graphs or photographs, or objects such as models can make your presentation more interesting and memorable. But use visual aids judiciously: a constant flow of illustrations or objects will bury your message.
- **Match visual aids and setting.** An audience of five people may be able to see a photograph and share a chart; an audience of a hundred will need projected images.
- **Coordinate visual aids with your message.** Time each visual aid to reinforce a point you're making. Tell listeners what they're looking at—what they should be getting from the aid. Give them enough viewing time so they don't mind turning their attention back to you.
- **Show visual aids only while they're needed.** To regain your audience's attention, remove or turn off any aid as soon as you have finished with it.

Many speakers use *PowerPoint* or other software to project visual aids. (See the sample slides on the next page.) Screens of brief points supported by data, images, or video can help listeners follow your main points. To use *PowerPoint* or other software effectively, follow the guidelines above and also the following:

- **Don't put your whole presentation on screen.** Select key points, and distill them to as few words as possible. Think of the slides as quick, easy-to-remember summaries.
- **Use a simple design.** Avoid turning your presentation into a show about the software's many capabilities.
- **Use a consistent design.** For optimal flow through the presentation, each slide should be formatted similarly.
- **Add only relevant illustrations.** Avoid loading the presentation with mere decoration.

5 Practice

Practicing an oral presentation is the speechmaker's equivalent of editing and proofreading a written text. You won't gain much by practicing silently in your head; instead, you need to rehearse out loud, with the notes you will be using. For your initial rehearsals, you can gauge your performance by making an audio- or videotape of yourself or by practicing in front of a mirror. A recording will let you hear mumbling, too-rapid delivery, grammatical errors, mispronounced words, and unclear concepts. A mirror or video will reveal your stance, your gestures, and your eye contact. Any of these practice techniques will tell you if your presentation is running too long or too short.

COLLABORATIVE LEARNING

POWERPOINT TRYOUT

Students can try out different feature options (such as backgrounds, colors, and fonts) in drafts of their presentation. Peer groups can provide quick assessments of the effectiveness of various feature choices to help each writer know what revisions to make.

RESOURCES AND IDEAS

Beason, Larry. "Ethos and Error: How Business People React to Errors." *College Composition and Communication* 53 (September 2001): 33–64. Beason's study suggests that business leaders see errors in business communication as a sign of carelessness and faulty thinking and would be reluctant to hire applicants who commit such errors.

Felske, Claudia Klein. "Beyond the Page: Students as Actor-Readers." *English Journal* 95 (September 2005): 58–63. The author explains a method she uses to help students understand Shakespeare and develop their oral language skills.

George, Don. "Peer Support in Speech Preparation." *Speech Communication Teacher* 7.3 (1993): 4–5. A brief piece describing exercises for cultivating a team approach to public speaking using debating club strategies.

Hallmark, James R. and Arnie Madson. "Using Your Computer to Evaluate Speeches." "Computer-Assisted Comments for Research Papers and Speeches." Both in *Speech Communication Teacher* 9.3 (Spring 1995): 14–15. These two short pieces on CNEs (computerized narrative evaluations) identify the uses and limitations of programs that supply generic evaluations that can be tailored to individual student presentations.

Henry, Jim. *Writing Workplace Cultures: An Archaeology of Professional Writing.* Carbondale: Southern Illinois University Press, 2000. Henry describes a fascinating study of workplace cultures and of how such cultures shape discourse.

Lucas, Stephen E. *The Art of Public Speaking.* 9th ed. New York: McGraw Hill, 2007. This is a standard speech communication textbook that can be used to integrate a speechmaking component onto the writing classroom. See also Lucas's videotaped collection, *Speeches for Analysis and Discussion* (New York: Random, 1989).

Menzel, Kent E., and Lori J. Carrell. "The Relationship Between Preparation and Performance in Public Speaking." *Communication Education* 43 (1994): 17–26. Explores the effects of factors like anxiety level, preparation time, and scholastic ability on the quality of oral presentations. The authors show, for ex-

PowerPoint slides

First slide, introducing the project and presentation

Simple, consistent slide design focusing viewers' attention on information, not *PowerPoint* features

Later slide, using brief, bulleted points to be explained by the speaker

Photographs reinforcing the project's activities

If you plan to use visual aids, you'll need to practice with them, too, preferably in the room where you'll make the presentation and certainly with the help of anyone who will be assisting you. Your goal is to eliminate hitches (upside-down slides, missing charts) and to weave the visuals seamlessly into your presentation.

6   Stage fright

Many people report that speaking in front of an audience is their number-one fear. Even many experienced and polished speakers have some anxiety about delivering an oral presentation, but they use this nervous energy to their advantage, letting it propel them into working hard on each presentation, and rehearsing until they're satisfied with their delivery. They know that the symptoms of anxiety are usually imperceptible to listeners, who cannot see or hear a racing heart, upset stomach, cold hands, and worried thoughts. Several techniques can help you reduce your level of anxiety:

- **Use simple relaxation exercises.** Deep breathing or tensing and relaxing your stomach muscles can ease some of the physical symptoms of speech anxiety.
- **Think positively.** Instead of worrying about the mistakes you might make, concentrate on how well you've prepared and practiced your presentation and how significant your ideas are.
- **Don't avoid opportunities to speak in public.** Practice and experience build speaking skills and offer the best insurance for success.

ample, that time spent on preparing visual aids adds to an effective delivery, partly because of the motivational and anxiety-reducing effects.

Rowan, Katherine E. "A New Pedagogy for Explanatory Public Speaking: Why Arrangement Should Not Substitute for Invention." *Communication Education* 44.3 (1995): 236–50. Rowan makes the case against current speech communication textbooks that focus on the organization of definitions, examples, and visual aids without recognizing the process of critical thinking through which students develop the content of the speech in relation to effective modes of presentation.

Shachtman, Thomas. *The Inarticulate Society: Eloquence and Culture in America.* New York : Free Press, 1995. Shachtman uses an historical overview of the changing value put on eloquence in American society to argue that there is a marked decline in public articulateness, a decline that is rapidly undermining the democratic system.

Sullivan, Gwendolyn F. "Improving Delivery Skills: The Practice Impromptu." *Speech Communication Teacher* 11.2 (1997): 5–6. This short piece describes group activities and preparatory exercises (such as inviting a guest speaker) that help students learn to deliver impromptu speeches.

Whitworth, Randolph H., and Claudia Cochran. "Evaluation of Integrated Versus Unitary Treatment for Reducing Public Speaking Anxiety." *Communication Education* 45 (1996): 306–21. A highly technical case study of the relative merits of using or combining skills training, visualization therapy, and "communication orientation motivation therapy" in overcoming presentation anxiety. The results show the importance of combining skills training with other anxiety-reducing approaches.

Glossary of Usage

This glossary provides notes on words or phrases that often cause problems for writers. The recommendations for standard American English are based on current dictionaries and usage guides such as the ones listed on pp. 536–38. Items labeled **nonstandard** should be avoided in academic and business settings. Those labeled **colloquial** and **slang** occur in speech and in some informal writing but are best avoided in formal college and business writing. (Words and phrases labeled *colloquial* include those labeled by many dictionaries with the equivalent term *informal.*) See Chapters 37 and 38 for further discussion of word choice and for exercises in usage. See pp. 538–41 for a description of dictionary labels. Also see pp. 543–44 for a list of commonly confused words that are pronounced the same or similarly. The words and definitions provided there supplement this glossary.

The glossary is necessarily brief. Keep a dictionary handy for all your writing, and make a habit of referring to it whenever you doubt the appropriateness of a word or phrase.

a, an   Use *a* before words beginning with consonant sounds, including those spelled with an initial pronounced *h* and those spelled with vowels that are sounded as consonants: *a historian, a one-o'clock class, a university.* Use *an* before words that begin with vowel sounds, including those spelled with an initial silent *h: an orgy, an L, an honor.*

The article before an abbreviation depends on how the abbreviation is read: *She was once an AEC undersecretary* (*AEC* is read as three separate letters); *Many Americans opposed a SALT treaty* (*SALT* is read as one word, *salt*).

For the use of *a/an* versus *the,* see pp. 326–29.

accept, except   *Accept* is a verb meaning "receive." *Except* is usually a preposition or conjunction meaning "but for" or "other than"; when it is used as a verb, it means "leave out." *I can accept all your suggestions except the last one. I'm sorry you excepted my last suggestion from your list.*

adverse, averse   *Adverse* and *averse* both mean "opposed" or "hostile." But *averse* describes the subject's opposition to something, whereas *adverse* describes something opposed to the subject: *The President was averse to adverse criticism.*

advice, advise   *Advice* is a noun, and *advise* is a verb: *Take my advice; do as I advise you.*

affect, effect   Usually *affect* is a verb, meaning "to influence," and *effect* is a noun, meaning "result": *The drug did not affect his driving; in fact, it seemed to have no effect at all.* But *effect* occasionally is used as a verb meaning "to bring about": *Her efforts effected a change.* And *affect* is used in psychology as a noun meaning "feeling or emotion": *One can infer much about affect from behavior.*

aggravate *Aggravate* should not be used in its colloquial meaning of "irritate" or "exasperate" (for example, *We were aggravated by her constant arguing*). *Aggravate* means "make worse": *The President was irritated by the Senate's indecision because he feared any delay might aggravate the unrest in the Middle East.*

agree to, agree with *Agree to* means "consent to," and *agree with* means "be in accord with": *How can they agree to a treaty when they don't agree with each other about the terms?*

ain't Nonstandard for *am not, isn't,* or *aren't.*

all, all of Usually *all* is sufficient to modify a noun: *all my loving, all the things you are.* Before a pronoun or proper noun, *all of* is usually appropriate: *all of me, in all of France.*

all ready, already *All ready* means "completely prepared," and *already* means "by now" or "before now": *We were all ready to go to the movie, but it had already started.*

all right *All right* is always two words. *Alright* is a common misspelling.

all together, altogether *All together* means "in unison" or "gathered in one place." *Altogether* means "entirely." *It's not altogether true that our family never spends vacations all together.*

allusion, illusion An *allusion* is an indirect reference, and an *illusion* is a deceptive appearance: *Paul's constant allusions to Shakespeare created the illusion that he was an intellectual.*

almost, most *Almost* means "nearly"; *most* means "the greater number (or part) of." In formal writing, *most* should not be used as a substitute for *almost: We see each other almost* [not *most*] *every day.*

a lot *A lot* is always two words, used informally to mean "many." *Alot* is a common misspelling.

among, between Use *among* for relationships involving more than two people or things. Use *between* for relationships involving only two or for comparing one thing to a group to which it belongs. *The four of them agreed among themselves that the choice was between New York and Los Angeles.*

amongst Although common in British English, in American English *amongst* is an overrefined substitute for *among.*

amount, number Use *amount* with a singular noun that names something not countable (a noncount noun): *The amount of food varies.* Use *number* with a plural noun that names more than one of something countable (a plural count noun): *The number of calories must stay the same.*

an, and *An* is an article (see *a, an*). *And* is a coordinating conjunction.

and etc. *Et cetera* (*etc.*) means "and the rest"; *and etc.* therefore is redundant. See also *et al., etc.*

and/or *And/or* indicates three options: one or the other or both (*The decision is made by the mayor and/or the council*). If you mean all three options, *and/or* is appropriate. Otherwise, use *and* if you mean both, *or* if you mean either.

and which, and who   *And which* or *and who* is correct only when used to introduce a second clause beginning with the same relative pronoun: *Jill is my cousin who goes to school here and who calls me constantly.* Otherwise, *and* is not needed: *WCAS is my favorite AM radio station, which* [not *and which*] *I listen to every morning.*

ante-, anti-   The prefix *ante-* means "before" (*antedate, antebellum*); *anti-* means "against" (*antiwar, antinuclear*). Before a capital letter or *i*, *anti-* takes a hyphen: *anti-Freudian, anti-isolationist.*

anxious, eager   *Anxious* means "nervous" or "worried" and is usually followed by *about. Eager* means "looking forward" and is usually followed by *to. I've been anxious about getting blisters. I'm eager* [not *anxious*] *to get new running shoes.*

anybody, any body; anyone, any one   *Anybody* and *anyone* are indefinite pronouns; *any body* is a noun modified by *any; any one* is a pronoun or adjective modified by *any. How can anybody communicate with any body of government? Can anyone help Amy? She has more work than any one person can handle.*

any more, anymore   *Any more* means "no more"; *anymore* means "now." Both are used in negative constructions: *He doesn't want any more. She doesn't live here anymore.*

anyplace   Colloquial for *anywhere.*

anyways, anywheres   Nonstandard for *anyway* and *anywhere.*

apt, liable, likely   *Apt* and *likely* are interchangeable. Strictly speaking, though, *apt* means "having a tendency to": *Horace is apt to forget his lunch in the morning. Likely* means "probably going to": *Horace is leaving so early today that he's likely to catch the first bus.*
    Liable normally means "in danger of" and should be confined to situations with undesirable consequences: *Horace is liable to trip over that hose.* Strictly, *liable* means "responsible" or "exposed to": *The owner will be liable for Horace's injuries.*

are, is   Use *are* with a plural subject (*books are*), *is* with a singular subject (*book is*).

as   Substituting for *because, since,* or *while, as* may be vague or ambiguous: *As the researchers asked more questions, their money ran out.* (Does *as* mean "while" or "because"?) *As* should never be used as a substitute for *whether* or *who. I'm not sure whether* [not *as*] *we can make it. That's the man who* [not *as*] *gave me directions.*

as, like   See *like, as.*

as, than   In comparisons, *as* and *than* precede a subjective-case pronoun when the pronoun is a subject: *I love you more than he* [*loves you*]. *As* and *than* precede an objective-case pronoun when the pronoun is an object: *I love you as much as* [*I love*] *him.* (See also p. 271.)

assure, ensure, insure   *Assure* means "to promise": *He assured us that we would miss the traffic. Ensure* and *insure* often are used interchangeably to mean "make certain," but some reserve *insure* for matters of legal and financial protection and use *ensure* for more general meanings: *We left early to ensure that we would miss the traffic. It's expensive to insure yourself against floods.*

as to A stuffy substitute for *about: The suspect was questioned about* [not *as to*] *her actions.*

at The use of *at* after *where* is wordy and should be avoided: *Where are you meeting him?* is preferable to *Where are you meeting him at?*

at this point in time Wordy for *now, at this point,* or *at this time.*

averse, adverse See *adverse, averse.*

awful, awfully Strictly speaking, *awful* means "awe-inspiring." As intensifiers meaning "very" or "extremely" (*He tried awfully hard*), *awful* and *awfully* should be avoided in formal speech or writing.

a while, awhile *Awhile* is an adverb; *a while* is an article and a noun. Thus *awhile* can modify a verb but cannot serve as the object of a preposition, and *a while* is just the opposite: *I will be gone awhile* [not *a while*]. *I will be gone for a while* [not *awhile*].

bad, badly In formal speech and writing, *bad* should be used only as an adjective; the adverb is *badly. He felt bad because his tooth ached badly.* In *He felt bad,* the verb *felt* is a linking verb and the adjective *bad* is a subject complement. (See also pp. 322–23.)

being as, being that Colloquial for *because,* the preferable word in formal speech or writing: *Because* [not *Being as*] *the world is round, Columbus never did fall off the edge.*

beside, besides *Beside* is a preposition meaning "next to." *Besides* is a preposition meaning "except" or "in addition to" as well as an adverb meaning "in addition." *Besides, several other people besides you want to sit beside Dr. Christensen.*

better, had better *Had better* (meaning "ought to") is a verb modified by an adverb. The verb is necessary and should not be omitted: *You had better* [not just *better*] *go.*

between, among See *among, between.*

bring, take Use *bring* only for movement from a farther place to a nearer one and *take* for any other movement. *First, take these books to the library for renewal, then take them to Mr. Daniels. Bring them back to me when he's finished.*

bunch In formal speech and writing, *bunch* (as a noun) should be used only to refer to clusters of things growing or fastened together, such as bananas and grapes. Its use to mean a group of items or people is colloquial; *crowd* or *group* is preferable.

burst, bursted; bust, busted *Burst* is a standard verb form meaning "to fly apart suddenly." Its main forms are *burst, burst, burst;* the form *bursted* is nonstandard. The verb *bust* (*busted*) is slang.

but, hardly, scarcely These words are negative in their own right; using *not* with any of them produces a double negative (see p. 324). *We have but* [not *haven't got but*] *an hour before our plane leaves. I could hardly* [not *couldn't hardly*] *make out her face.*

but, however, yet Each of these words is adequate to express contrast. Don't combine them. *He said he had finished, yet* [not *but yet*] *he continued.*

but that, but what These wordy substitutes for *that* and *what* should be avoided: *I don't doubt that* [not *but that*] *you are right.*

calculate, figure, reckon As substitutes for *expect* or *imagine* (*I figure I'll go*), these words are colloquial.

can, may Strictly, *can* indicates capacity or ability, and *may* indicates permission: *If I may talk with you a moment, I believe I can solve your problem. May* also indicates possibility: *You may like what you hear.*

can't help but This idiom is common but redundant. Either *I can't help wishing* or the more formal *I cannot but wish* is preferable to *I can't help but wish.*

case, instance, line Expressions such as *in the case of, in the instance of,* and *along the lines of* are usually unnecessary padding and should be avoided.

censor, censure To *censor* is to edit or remove from public view on moral or some other grounds; to *censure* is to give a formal scolding. *The lieutenant was censured by Major Taylor for censoring the letters her soldiers wrote home from boot camp.*

center around *Center on* is more logical than, and preferable to, *center around.*

climatic, climactic *Climatic* comes from *climate* and refers to weather: *Last winter's temperatures may indicate a climatic change. Climactic* comes from *climax* and refers to a dramatic high point: *During the climactic duel between Hamlet and Laertes, Gertrude drinks poisoned wine.*

complement, compliment To *complement* something is to add to, complete, or reinforce it: *Her yellow blouse complemented her black hair.* To *compliment* something is to make a flattering remark about it: *He complimented her on her hair. Compliment* also functions as a noun: *She thanked him for the compliment.* The adjective *complimentary* can also mean "free": *complimentary tickets.*

compose, comprise *Compose* means "to make up": *The parts compose the whole. Comprise* means "to consist of": *The whole comprises the parts.* Thus, *The band comprises* [not *is comprised of*] *twelve musicians. Twelve musicians compose* [not *comprise*] *the band.*

conscience, conscious *Conscience* is a noun meaning "a sense of right and wrong"; *conscious* is an adjective meaning "aware" or "awake." *Though I was barely conscious, my conscience nagged me.*

contact Often used imprecisely as a verb instead of a more exact word such as *consult, talk with, telephone,* or *write to.*

continual, continuous *Continual* means "constantly recurring": *Most movies on television are continually interrupted by commercials. Continuous* means "unceasing": *Some cable channels present movies continuously without commercials.*

convince, persuade   In the strictest sense, to *convince* someone means to change his or her opinion; to *persuade* someone means to move him or her to action. *Convince* is thus properly followed by *of* or *that*, whereas *persuade* is followed by *to: Once he convinced Othello of Desdemona's infidelity, Iago easily persuaded him to kill her.*

could care less   The expression is *could not* [*couldn't*] *care less. Could care less* indicates some care, the opposite of what is intended.

could of   See *have, of.*

couple of   Used colloquially to mean "a few" or "several."

credible, creditable, credulous   *Credible* means "believable": *It's a strange story, but it seems credible to me. Creditable* means "deserving of credit" or "worthy": *Steve gave a creditable performance. Credulous* means "gullible": *The credulous Claire believed Tim's lies.* See also *incredible, incredulous.*

criteria   The plural of *criterion* (meaning "standard for judgment"): *Our criteria are strict. The most important criterion is a sense of humor.*

data   The plural of *datum* (meaning "fact"): *Out of all the data generated by these experiments, not one datum supports our hypothesis.* Usually, a more common term such as *fact, result,* or *figure* is preferred to *datum.* Though *data* is often used with a singular verb, many readers prefer the plural verb and it is always correct: *The data fail* [not *fails*] *to support the hypothesis.*

device, devise   *Device* is the noun, and *devise* is the verb: *Can you devise some device for getting his attention?*

different from, different than   *Different from* is preferred: *His purpose is different from mine.* But *different than* is widely accepted when a construction using *from* would be wordy: *I'm a different person now than I used to be* is preferable to *I'm a different person now from the person I used to be.*

differ from, differ with   To *differ from* is to be unlike: *The twins differ from each other only in their hairstyles.* To *differ with* is to disagree with: *I have to differ with you on that point.*

discreet, discrete   *Discreet* (noun form *discretion*) means "tactful": *What's a discreet way of telling Maud to be quiet? Discrete* (noun form *discreteness*) means "separate and distinct": *Within a computer's memory are millions of discrete bits of information.*

disinterested, uninterested   *Disinterested* means "impartial": *We chose Pete, as a disinterested third party, to decide who was right. Uninterested* means "bored" or "lacking interest": *Unfortunately, Pete was completely uninterested in the question.*

don't   *Don't* is the contraction for *do not,* not for *does not: I don't care, you don't care,* and *he doesn't* [not *don't*] *care.*

due to   *Due* is an adjective or noun; thus *due to* is always acceptable as a subject complement: *His gray hairs were due to age.* Many object to *due to* as a preposition meaning "because of" (*Due to the holiday, class was canceled*). A rule of thumb is that *due to* is always correct after a form of the verb *be* but questionable otherwise.

due to the fact that   Wordy for *because.*

each and every   Wordy for *each* or *every.* Write *each one of us* or *every one of us,* not *each and every one of us.*

eager, anxious   See *anxious, eager.*

effect   See *affect, effect.*

elicit, illicit   *Elicit* is a verb meaning "bring out" or "call forth." *Illicit* is an adjective meaning "unlawful." *The crime elicited an outcry against illicit drugs.*

emigrate, immigrate   *Emigrate* means "to leave one place and move to another" (the Latin prefix *e-* means "out of": "migrate out of"): *The Chus emigrated from Korea. Immigrate* means "to move into a place where one was not born" (the Latin prefix *im-* means "into": "migrate into"): *They immigrated to the United States.*

ensure   See *assure, ensure, insure.*

enthused   Used colloquially as an adjective meaning "showing enthusiasm." The preferred adjective is *enthusiastic: The coach was enthusiastic* [not *enthused*] *about the team's victory.*

especially, specially   *Especially* means "particularly" or "more than other things"; *specially* means "for a specific reason." *I especially treasure my boots. They were made specially for me.*

et al., etc.   Use *et al.,* the Latin abbreviation for "and other people," only in source citations: *Jones et al.* Avoid *etc.,* the Latin abbreviation for "and other things," in formal writing, and do not use it to refer to people or to substitute for precision, as in *The government provides health care, etc.* See also *and etc.*

everybody, every body; everyone, every one   *Everybody* and *everyone* are indefinite pronouns: *Everybody* [or *Everyone*] *knows Tom steals. Every one* is a pronoun modified by *every,* and *every body* is a noun modified by *every.* Both refer to each thing or person of a specific group and are typically followed by *of: The game commissioner has stocked every body of fresh water in the state with fish, and now every one of our rivers is a potential trout stream.*

everyday, every day   *Everyday* is an adjective meaning "used daily" or "common"; *every day* is a noun modified by *every: Everyday problems tend to arise every day.*

everywheres   Nonstandard for *everywhere.*

except   See *accept, except.*

except for the fact that   Wordy for *except that.*

explicit, implicit   *Explicit* means "stated outright": *I left explicit instructions. The movie contains explicit sex. Implicit* means "implied, unstated": *We had an implicit understanding. I trust Marcia implicitly.*

farther, further   *Farther* refers to additional distance (*How much farther is it to the beach?*), and *further* refers to additional time, amount, or other abstract matters (*I don't want to discuss this any further*).

feel   Avoid this word in place of *think* or *believe: She thinks* [not *feels*] *that the law should be changed.*

fewer, less   *Fewer* refers to individual countable items (a plural count noun), *less* to general amounts (a noncount noun, always singular): *Skim milk has fewer calories than whole milk. We have less milk left than I thought.*

field   The phrase *the field of* is wordy and generally unnecessary: *Margaret plans to specialize in* [not *in the field of*] *family medicine.*

figure   See *calculate, figure, reckon.*

fixing to   Avoid this colloquial substitute for "intend to": *The school intends* [not *is fixing*] *to build a new library.*

flaunt, flout   *Flaunt* means "show off": *If you have style, flaunt it. Flout* means "scorn" or "defy": *Hester Prynne flouted convention and paid the price.*

flunk   A colloquial substitute for *fail.*

former, latter   *Former* refers to the first-named of two things, *latter* to the second-named: *I like both skiing and swimming, the former in the winter and the latter all year round.* To refer to the first- or last-named of three or more things, say *first* or *last: I like jogging, swimming, and hang gliding, but the last is inconvenient in the city.*

fun   As an adjective, *fun* is colloquial and should be avoided in most writing: *It was a pleasurable* [not *fun*] *evening.*

further   See *farther, further.*

get   This common verb is used in many slang and colloquial expressions: *get lost, that really gets me, getting on. Get* is easy to overuse; watch out for it in expressions such as *it's getting better* (substitute *improving*) and *we got done* (substitute *finished*).

go   As a substitute for *say* or *reply, go* is colloquial: *He says* [not *goes*], *"How do you do, madam?"*

good, well   *Good* is an adjective, and *well* is nearly always an adverb: *Larry's a good dancer. He and Linda dance well together. Well* is properly used as an adjective only to refer to health: *You look well.* (*You look good,* in contrast, means "Your appearance is pleasing.")

good and   Colloquial for "very": *I was very* [not *good and*] *tired.*

had better   See *better, had better.*

had ought   The *had* is unnecessary and should be omitted: *He ought* [not *had ought*] *to listen to his mother.*

half   Either *half a* or *a half* is appropriate usage, but *a half a* is redundant: *Half a loaf* [not *A half a loaf*] *is better than none. I'd like a half-gallon* [not *a half a gallon*] *of mineral water, please.*

hanged, hung   Though both are past-tense forms of *hang, hanged* is used to refer to executions and *hung* is used for all other meanings: *Tom Dooley was hanged* [not *hung*] *from a white oak tree. I hung* [not *hanged*] *the picture you gave me.*

hardly   See *but, hardly, scarcely.*

have, of   Use *have,* not *of,* after helping verbs such as *could, should, would, may,* and *might: You should have* [not *should of*] *told me.*

he, she; he/she   Convention has allowed the use of *he* to mean "he or she": *After the infant learns to creep, he progresses to crawling.* However, many writers today consider this usage inaccurate and unfair because it seems to exclude females. The construction *he/she*, one substitute for *he*, is awkward and objectionable to most readers. The better choice is to make the pronoun plural, to rephrase, or, sparingly, to use *he or she.* For instance: *After infants learn to creep, they progress to crawling. After learning to creep, the infant progresses to crawling. After the infant learns to creep, he or she progresses to crawling.* (See also pp. 315–17 and 516.)

herself, himself   See *myself, herself, himself, yourself.*

hisself   Nonstandard for *himself.*

hopefully   *Hopefully* means "with hope": *Freddy waited hopefully for a glimpse of Eliza.* The use of *hopefully* to mean "it is to be hoped," "I hope," or "let's hope" is now very common; but since many readers continue to object strongly to the usage, you should avoid it. *I hope* [not *Hopefully*] *the law will pass.*

idea, ideal   An *idea* is a thought or conception. An *ideal* (noun) is a model of perfection or a goal. *Ideal* should not be used in place of *idea*: *The idea* [not *ideal*] *of the play is that our ideals often sustain us.*

if, whether   For clarity, use *whether* rather than *if* when you are expressing an alternative: *If I laugh hard, people can't tell whether I'm crying.*

illicit   See *elicit, illicit.*

illusion   See *allusion, illusion.*

immigrate, emigrate   See *emigrate, immigrate.*

impact   Both the noun and the verb *impact* connote forceful or even violent collision. Avoid the increasingly common diluted meanings of *impact*: "an effect" (noun) or "to have an effect on" (verb). The diluted verb (*The budget cuts impacted social science research*) is bureaucratic jargon.

implicit   See *explicit, implicit.*

imply, infer   Writers or speakers *imply*, meaning "suggest": *Jim's letter implies he's having a good time.* Readers or listeners *infer*, meaning "conclude": *From Jim's letter I infer he's having a good time.*

in, into   *In* indicates location or condition: *He was in the garage. She was in a coma. Into* indicates movement or a change in condition: *He went into the garage. She fell into a coma.* Generally avoid the slang sense of *into* meaning "interested in" or "involved in": *I am into Zen.*

in . . .   A number of phrases beginning with *in* are needlessly wordy and should be avoided: *in the event that* (for *if*); *in the neighborhood of* (for *approximately* or *about*); *in this day and age* (for *now* or *nowadays*); *in spite of the fact that* (for *although* or *even though*); and *in view of the fact that* (for *because* or *considering that*). Certain other *in* phrases are nothing but padding and can be omitted entirely: *in nature, in number, in reality,* and *in a very real sense.* (See also pp. 531–32.)

incredible, incredulous   *Incredible* means "unbelievable"; *incredulous* means "unbelieving": *When Nancy heard Dennis's incredible story, she was frankly incredulous.* See also *credible, creditable, credulous.*

individual, person, party   *Individual* should refer to a single human being in contrast to a group or should stress uniqueness: *The US Constitution places strong emphasis on the rights of the individual.* For other meanings *person* is preferable: *What person* [not *individual*] *wouldn't want the security promised in that advertisement? Party* means "group" (*Can you seat a party of four for dinner?*) and should not be used to refer to an individual except in legal documents. See also *people, persons.*

infer   See *imply, infer.*

in regards to   Nonstandard for *in regard to, as regards,* or *regarding.* See also *regarding.*

inside of, outside of   The *of* is unnecessary when *inside* and *outside* are used as prepositions: *Stay inside* [not *inside of*] *the house. The decision is outside* [not *outside of*] *my authority. Inside of* may refer colloquially to time, though in formal English *within* is preferred: *The law was passed within* [not *inside of*] *a year.*

instance   See *case, instance, line.*

insure   See *assure, ensure, insure.*

irregardless   Nonstandard for *regardless.*

is, are   See *are, is.*

is because   See *reason is because.*

is when, is where   These are faulty constructions in sentences that define: *Adolescence is a stage* [not *is when a person is*] *between childhood and adulthood. Socialism is a system in which* [not *is where*] *government owns the means of production.* (See also p. 376.)

its, it's   *Its* is the pronoun *it* in the possessive case: *That plant is losing its leaves. It's* is a contraction for *it is* or *it has: It's* [*It is*] *likely to die. It's* [*It has*] *got a fungus.* Many people confuse *it's* and *its* because possessives are most often formed with *-'s;* but the possessive *its,* like *his* and *hers,* never takes an apostrophe.

-ize, -wise   The suffix *-ize* changes a noun or adjective into a verb: *revolutionize, immunize.* The suffix *-wise* changes a noun or adjective into an adverb: *clockwise, otherwise, likewise.* Avoid the two suffixes except in established words: *The two nations are ready to settle on* [not *finalize*] *an agreement. I'm highly sensitive* [not *sensitized*] *to that kind of criticism. Financially* [not *Moneywise*], *it's a good time to invest in real estate.*

kind of, sort of, type of   In formal speech and writing, avoid using *kind of* or *sort of* to mean "somewhat": *He was rather* [not *kind of*] *tall.*

   Kind, sort, and *type* are singular and take singular modifiers and verbs: *This kind of dog is easily trained.* Agreement errors often occur when these singular nouns are combined with the plural adjectives *these* and *those: These kinds* [not *kind*] *of dogs are easily trained. Kind, sort*, and *type* should be followed by *of* but not by *a*: *I don't know what type of* [not *type* or *type of a*] *dog that is.*

Use *kind of*, *sort of*, or *type of* only when the word *kind*, *sort*, or *type* is important: *That was a strange* [not *strange sort of*] *statement.*

later, latter   *Later* refers to time; *latter* refers to the second-named of two items. See also *former, latter*.

lay, lie   *Lay* means "put" or "place" and takes a direct object: *We could lay the tablecloth in the sun*. Its main forms are *lay, laid, laid. Lie* means "recline" or "be situated" and does not take an object: *I lie awake at night. The town lies east of the river*. Its main forms are *lie, lay, lain*. (See also p. 218.)

leave, let   *Leave* and *let* are interchangeable only when followed by *alone*; *leave me alone* is the same as *let me alone*. Otherwise, *leave* means "depart" and *let* means "allow": *Julia would not let Susan leave*.

less   See *fewer, less*.

let   See *leave, let*.

liable   See *apt, liable, likely*.

lie, lay   See *lay, lie*.

like, as   In formal speech and writing, *like* should not introduce a full clause (with a subject and a verb) because it is a preposition. The preferred choice is *as* or *as if*: *The plan succeeded as* [not *like*] *we hoped. It seemed as if* [not *like*] *it might fail. Other plans like it have failed.*

When *as* serves as a preposition, the distinction between *as* and *like* depends on meaning. *As* suggests that the subject is equivalent or identical to the description: *She was hired as an engineer. Like* suggests resemblance but not identity: *People like her do well in such jobs*. See also *like, such as*.

like, such as   Strictly, *such as* precedes an example that represents a larger subject, whereas *like* indicates that two subjects are comparable. *Steve has recordings of many great saxophonists such as Ben Webster and Lee Konitz. Steve wants to be a great jazz saxophonist like Ben Webster and Lee Konitz.*

Many writers prefer to keep *such* and *as* together: *Steve admires saxophonists such as . . .* rather than *Steve admires such saxophonists as. . . .*

likely   See *apt, liable, likely*.

line   See *case, instance, line*.

literally   This word means "actually" or "just as the words say," and it should not be used to qualify or intensify expressions whose words are not to be taken at face value. The sentence *He was literally climbing the walls* describes a person behaving like an insect, not a person who is restless or anxious. For the latter meaning, *literally* should be omitted.

lose, loose   *Lose* means "mislay": *Did you lose a brown glove? Loose* means "unrestrained" or "not tight": *Ann's canary got loose. Loose* also can function as a verb meaning "let loose": *They loose the dogs as soon as they spot the bear.*

lots, lots of   Colloquial substitutes for *very many, a great many*, or *much*. Avoid *lots* and *lots of* in college or business writing. When you use either one informally, be careful to maintain subject-verb agreement: *There are* [not *is*] *lots of fish in the pond.*

may, can   See *can, may.*

may be, maybe   *May be* is a verb, and *maybe* is an adverb meaning "perhaps": *Tuesday may be a legal holiday. Maybe we won't have classes.*

may of   See *have, of.*

media   *Media* is the plural of *medium* and takes a plural verb: *All the news media are increasingly visual.* The singular verb is common, even in the media, but many readers prefer the plural verb and it is always correct.

might of   See *have, of.*

moral, morale   As a noun, *moral* means "ethical conclusion" or "lesson": *The moral of the story escapes me. Morale* means "spirit" or "state of mind": *Victory improved the team's morale.*

most, almost   See *almost, most.*

must of   See *have, of.*

myself, herself, himself, yourself   The *-self* pronouns refer to or intensify another word or words: *Paul helped himself; Jill herself said so.* The *-self* pronouns are often used colloquially in place of personal pronouns, but that use should be avoided in formal speech and writing: *No one except me* [not *myself*] *saw the accident. Our delegates will be Susan and you* [not *yourself*]. See also p. 268 on the unchanging forms of the *-self* pronouns in standard American English.

nohow   Nonstandard for *in no way* or *in any way.*

nothing like, nowhere near   These colloquial substitutes for *not nearly* are best avoided in formal speech and writing: *That program is not nearly* [not *nowhere near*] *as expensive.*

nowheres   Nonstandard for *nowhere.*

number   See *amount, number.*

of, have   See *have, of.*

off of   *Of* is unnecessary. Use *off* or *from* rather than *off of: He jumped off* [or *from,* not *off of*] *the roof.*

OK, O.K., okay   All three spellings are acceptable, but avoid this colloquial term in formal speech and writing.

on, upon   In modern English, *upon* is usually just a stuffy way of saying *on.* Unless you need a formal effect, use *on: We decided on* [not *upon*] *a location for our next meeting.*

on account of   Wordy for *because of.*

on the other hand   This transitional expression of contrast should be preceded by its mate, *on the one hand: On the one hand, we hoped for snow. On the other hand, we feared that it would harm the animals.* However, the two combined can be unwieldy, and a simple *but, however, yet,* or *in contrast* often suffices: *We hoped for snow. Yet we feared that it would harm the animals.*

outside of   See *inside of, outside of.*

owing to the fact that   Wordy for *because.*

party See *individual, person, party.*

people, persons In formal usage, *people* refers to a general group: *We the people of the United States. . . . Persons* refers to a collection of individuals: *Will the person or persons who saw the accident please notify. . . .* Except when emphasizing individuals, prefer *people* to *persons.* See also *individual, person, party.*

per Except in technical writing, an English equivalent is usually preferable to the Latin *per: $10 an* [not *per*] *hour; sent by* [not *per*] *parcel post; requested in* [not *per* or *as per*] *your letter.*

percent (per cent), percentage Both these terms refer to fractions of one hundred. *Percent* always follows a numeral (*40 percent of the voters*), and the word should be used instead of the symbol (%) in general writing. *Percentage* stands alone (*the percentage of votes*) or follows an adjective (*a high percentage*).

person See *individual, person, party.*

persons See *people, persons.*

persuade See *convince, persuade.*

phenomena The plural of *phenomenon* (meaning "perceivable fact" or "unusual occurrence"): *Many phenomena are not recorded. One phenomenon is attracting attention.*

plenty A colloquial substitute for *very: The reaction occurred very* [not *plenty*] *fast.*

plus *Plus* is standard as a preposition meaning *in addition to: His income plus mine is sufficient.* But *plus* is colloquial as a conjunctive adverb: *Our organization is larger than theirs; moreover* [not *plus*], *we have more money.*

practicable, practical *Practicable* means "capable of being put into practice"; *practical* means "useful" or "sensible": *We figured out a practical new design for our kitchen, but it was too expensive to be practicable.*

precede, proceed The verb *precede* means "come before": *My name precedes yours in the alphabet.* The verb *proceed* means "move on": *We were told to proceed to the waiting room.*

prejudice, prejudiced *Prejudice* is a noun; *prejudiced* is an adjective. Do not drop the *-d* from *prejudiced: I knew that my parents were prejudiced* [not *prejudice*].

pretty Overworked as an adverb meaning "rather" or "somewhat": *He was somewhat* [not *pretty*] *irked at the suggestion.*

previous to, prior to Wordy for *before.*

principal, principle *Principal* is an adjective meaning "foremost" or "major," a noun meaning "chief official," or, in finance, a noun meaning "capital sum." *Principle* is a noun only, meaning "rule" or "axiom." *Her principal reasons for confessing were her principles of right and wrong.*

proceed, precede See *precede, proceed.*

provided, providing *Provided* may serve as a subordinating conjunction meaning "on the condition (that)"; *providing* may not. *The grocer* *will begin providing food for the soup kitchen provided* [not *providing*] *we find a suitable space.*

question of whether, question as to whether   Wordy substitutes for *whether.*

raise, rise   *Raise* means "lift" or "bring up" and takes a direct object: *The Kirks raise cattle.* Its main forms are *raise, raised, raised. Rise* means "get up" and does not take an object: *They must rise at dawn.* Its main forms are *rise, rose, risen.* (See also p. 281.)

real, really   In formal speech and writing, *real* should not be used as an adverb; *really* is the adverb and *real* an adjective. *Popular reaction to the announcement was really* [not *real*] *enthusiastic.*

reason is because   Although colloquially common, this expression should be avoided in formal speech and writing. Use a *that* clause after *reason is: The reason he is absent is that* [not *is because*] *he is sick.* Or: *He is absent because he is sick.*

reckon   See *calculate, figure, reckon.*

regarding, in regard to, with regard to, relating to, relative to, with respect to, respecting   Stuffy substitutes for *on, about,* or *concerning: Mr. McGee spoke about* [not *with regard to*] *the plans for the merger.*

respectful, respective   *Respectful* means "full of (or showing) respect": *Be respectful of other people. Respective* means "separate": *The French and the Germans occupied their respective trenches.*

rise, raise   See *raise, rise.*

scarcely   See *but, hardly, scarcely.*

sensual, sensuous   *Sensual* suggests sexuality; *sensuous* means "pleasing to the senses." *Stirred by the sensuous scent of meadow grass and flowers, Cheryl and Paul found their thoughts growing increasingly sensual.*

set, sit   *Set* means "put" or "place" and takes a direct object: *He sets the pitcher down.* Its main forms are *set, set, set. Sit* means "be seated" and does not take an object: *She sits on the sofa.* Its main forms are *sit, sat, sat.* (See also p. 281.)

shall, will   *Will* is the future-tense helping verb for all persons: *I will go, you will go, they will go.* The main use of *shall* is for first-person questions requesting an opinion or consent: *Shall I order a pizza? Shall we dance?* (Questions that merely inquire about the future use *will: When will I see you again?*) *Shall* can also be used for the first person when a formal effect is desired (*I shall expect you around three*), and it is occasionally used with the second or third person to express the speaker's determination (*You shall do as I say*).

should, would   *Should* expresses obligation: *I should fix dinner. You should set the table. Jack should wash the dishes. Would* expresses a wish or hypothetical condition: *I would do it. Wouldn't you?* When the context is formal, however, *should* is sometimes used instead of *would* in the first person: *We should be delighted to accept.*

should of   See *have, of.*

since   *Since* mainly relates to time: *I've been waiting since noon.* But *since* is also often used to mean "because": *Since you ask, I'll tell you.*

Revise sentences in which the word could have either meaning, such as *Since you left, my life is empty*.

sit, set   See *set, sit*.

situation   Often unnecessary, as in *The situation is that we have to get some help* (revise to *We have to get some help*) or *The team was faced with a punting situation* (revise to *The team was faced with punting* or *The team had to punt*).

so   Avoid using *so* alone as a vague intensifier: *He was so late*. So needs to be followed by *that* and a clause that states a result: *He was so late that I left without him*.

some   *Some* is colloquial as an adverb meaning "somewhat" or "to some extent" and as an adjective meaning "remarkable": *We'll have to hurry somewhat* [not *some*] *to get there in time. Those are remarkable* [not *some*] *photographs*.

somebody, some body; someone, some one   *Somebody* and *someone* are indefinite pronouns; *some body* is a noun modified by *some*; and *some one* is a pronoun or an adjective modified by *some*. *Somebody ought to invent a shampoo that will give hair some body. Someone told Janine she should choose some one plan and stick with it*.

someplace   Informal for *somewhere*.

sometime, sometimes, some time   *Sometime* means "at an indefinite time in the future": *Why don't you come up and see me sometime? Sometimes* means "now and then": *I still see my old friend Joe sometimes. Some time* means "a span of time": *I need some time to make the payments*.

somewheres   Nonstandard for *somewhere*.

sort of, sort of a   See *kind of, sort of, type of*.

specially   See *especially, specially*.

such   Avoid using *such* as a vague intensifier: *It was such a cold winter. Such* should be followed by *that* and a clause that states a result: *It was such a cold winter that Napoleon's troops had to turn back*.

such as   See *like, such as*.

supposed to, used to   In both these expressions, the *-d* is essential: *I used to* [not *use to*] *think so. He's supposed to* [not *suppose to*] *meet us*.

sure   Colloquial when used as an adverb meaning *surely: James Madison sure was right about the need for the Bill of Rights*. If you merely want to be emphatic, use *certainly: Madison certainly was right*. If your goal is to convince a possibly reluctant reader, use *surely: Madison surely was right. Surely Madison was right*.

sure and, sure to; try and, try to   *Sure to* and *try to* are the correct forms: *Be sure to* [not *sure and*] *vote. Try to* [not *Try and*] *vote early to avoid a line*.

take, bring   See *bring, take*.

than, as   See *as, than*.

than, then   *Than* is a conjunction used in comparisons, *then* an adverb indicating time: *Holmes knew then that Moriarty was wilier than he had thought*.

that, which   *That* always introduces an essential clause: *We should use the lettuce that Susan bought* (*that Susan bought* limits *lettuce* to a particular lettuce). *Which* can introduce both essential and nonessential clauses, but many writers reserve *which* only for nonessential clauses: *The leftover lettuce, which is in the refrigerator, would make a good salad* (*which is in the refrigerator* simply provides more information about the lettuce we already know of). Essential clauses (with *that* or *which*) are not set off by commas; nonessential clauses (with *which*) are. (See also pp. 435–38.)

that, who, which   Use *that* to refer to most animals and to things: *The animals that escaped included a zebra. The rocket that failed cost millions.* Use *who* to refer to people and to animals with names: *Dorothy is the girl who visits Oz. Her dog, Toto, who accompanies her, gives her courage.* Use *which* only to refer to animals and things: *The river, which runs more than a thousand miles, empties into the Indian Ocean.* (See also pp. 355–56.)

their, there, they're   *Their* is the possessive form of *they: Give them their money. There* indicates place (*I saw her standing there*) or functions to postpone the sentence subject (*There is a hole behind you*). *They're* is a contraction for *they are: They're going fast.*

theirselves   Nonstandard for *themselves.*

them   In standard American English, *them* does not serve as an adjective: *Those* [not *Them*] *people want to know.*

then, than   See *than, then.*

these kind, these sort, these type, those kind   See *kind of, sort of, type of.*

this, these   *This* is singular: *this car* or *This is the reason I left. These* is plural: *these cars* or *These are not valid reasons.*

this here, these here, that there, them there   Nonstandard for *this, these, that,* or *those.*

thru   A colloquial spelling of *through* that should be avoided in all academic and business writing.

thusly   A mistaken form of *thus.*

till, until, 'til   *Till* and *until* have the same meaning; either is acceptable. *'Til,* a contraction of *until,* is an old form that has been replaced by *till.*

time period   Since a *period* is an interval of time, this expression is redundant: *They did not see each other for a long time* [not *time period*]. *Six accidents occurred in a three-week period* [not *time period*].

to, too, two   *To* is a preposition; *too* is an adverb meaning "also" or "excessively"; and *two* is a number. *I too have been to Europe two times.*

too   Avoid using *too* as a vague intensifier: *Monkeys are too mean.* When you do use *too,* explain the consequences of the excessive quality: *Monkeys are too mean to make good pets.*

toward, towards   Both are acceptable, though *toward* is preferred. Use one or the other consistently.

try and, try to   See *sure and, sure to; try and, try to.*

type of   See *kind of, sort of, type of.* Don't use *type* without *of: It was a family type of* [not *type*] *restaurant.* Or, better: *It was a family restaurant.*

uninterested   See *disinterested, uninterested.*

unique   *Unique* means "the only one of its kind" and so cannot sensibly be modified with words such as *very* or *most*: *That was a unique* [not *a very unique* or *the most unique*] *movie.*

until   See *till, until, 'til.*

upon, on   See *on, upon.*

usage, use   *Usage* refers to conventions, most often those of a language: *Is "hadn't ought" proper usage? Usage* is often misused in place of the noun *use: Wise use* [not *usage*] *of insulation can save fuel.*

use, utilize   *Utilize* can be used to mean "make good use of": *Many teachers utilize computers for instruction.* But for all other senses of "place in service" or "employ," prefer *use.*

used to   See *supposed to, used to.*

wait for, wait on   In formal speech and writing, *wait for* means "await" (*I'm waiting for Paul*), and *wait on* means "serve" (*The owner of the store herself waited on us*).

ways   Colloquial as a substitute for *way: We have only a little way* [not *ways*] *to go.*

well   See *good, well.*

whether, if   See *if, whether.*

which, that   See *that, which.*

which, who, that   See *that, who, which.*

who, whom   *Who* is the subject of a sentence or clause (*We don't know who will come*). *Whom* is the object of a verb or preposition (*We do not know whom we invited*). (See also pp. 271–73.)

who's, whose   *Who's* is the contraction of *who is* or *who has: Who's* [*Who is*] *at the door? Jim is the only one who's* [*who has*] *passed. Whose* is the possessive form of *who: Whose book is that?*

will, shall   See *shall, will.*

wise   See *-ize, -wise.*

with regard to, with respect to   See *regarding.*

would   See *should, would.*

would have   Avoid this construction in place of *had* in clauses that begin *if* and state a condition contrary to fact: *If the tree had* [not *would have*] *withstood the fire, it would have been the oldest in the state.* (See also p. 301.)

would of   See *have, of.*

you   In all but very formal writing, *you* is generally appropriate as long as it means "you, the reader." In all writing, avoid indefinite uses of *you,* such as *In one ancient tribe your first loyalty was to your parents.* (See also pp. 354–55)

your, you're   *Your* is the possessive form of *you: Your dinner is ready. You're* is the contraction of *you are: You're bound to be late.*

yourself   See *myself, herself, himself, yourself.*

Glossary of Terms

This glossary defines terms of grammar, rhetoric, literature, and Internet research. Page numbers in parentheses refer you to sections of the text where the term is explained more fully.

absolute phrase A phrase consisting of a noun or pronoun plus the *-ing* or *-ed* form of a verb (a participle): *Our accommodations arranged, we set out on our journey. They will hire a local person, other things being equal.* An absolute phrase modifies a whole clause or sentence (rather than a single word), and it is not joined to the rest of the sentence by a connector. (See pp. 251–52.)

abstract and concrete Two kinds of language. **Abstract** words refer to ideas, qualities, attitudes, and conditions that can't be perceived with the senses: *beauty, guilty, victory*. **Concrete** words refer to objects, persons, places, or conditions that can be perceived with the senses: *Abilene, scratchy, toolbox*. See also *general and specific*. (See pp. 521–22.)

acronym A pronounceable word formed from the initial letter or letters of each word in an organization's title: NATO (North Atlantic Treaty Organization).

active voice See *voice*.

adjectival A term sometimes used to describe any word or word group, other than an adjective, that is used to modify a noun. Common adjectivals include nouns (*wagon train, railroad ties*), phrases (*fool on the hill*), and clauses (*the man that I used to be*).

adjective A word used to modify a noun (*beautiful morning*) or a pronoun (*ordinary one*). (See Chapter 16.) Nouns, some verb forms, phrases, and clauses may also serve as adjectives: *book sale; a used book; sale of old books; the sale, which occurs annually.* (See *clauses, prepositional phrases,* and *verbals and verbal phrases.*)

Adjectives come in several classes:

- A **descriptive adjective** names some quality of the noun: *beautiful morning, dark horse*.
- A **limiting adjective** narrows the scope of a noun. It may be a **possessive** (*my, their*); a **demonstrative adjective** (*this train, these days*); an **interrogative adjective** (*what time? whose body?*); or a number (*two boys*).
- A **proper adjective** is derived from a proper noun: *French language, Machiavellian scheme*.

Adjectives also can be classified according to position:

- An **attributive adjective** appears next to the noun it modifies: *full moon*.
- A **predicate adjective** is connected to its noun by a linking verb: *The moon is full*. See also *complement*.

adjective clause See *adjective*.

adjective phrase See *adjective*.

adverb A word used to modify a verb (*warmly greet*), an adjective (*only three people*), another adverb (*quite seriously*), or a whole sentence (*Fortunately, she is employed*). (See Chapter 16.) Some verb forms, phrases, and clauses may also serve as adverbs: *easy to stop, drove by a farm, plowed the fields when the earth thawed*. (See *clause*, *prepositional phrase*, and *verbals and verbal phrases*.)

adverb clause See *adverb*.

adverbial A term sometimes used to describe any word or word group, other than an adverb, that is used to modify a verb, an adjective, another adverb, or a whole sentence. Common adverbials include nouns (*This little piggy stayed home*), phrases (*This little piggy went to market*), and clauses (*This little piggy went wherever he wanted*).

adverbial conjunction See *conjunctive adverb*.

adverb phrase See *adverb*.

agreement The correspondence of one word to another in person, number, or gender. A verb must agree with its subject (*The chef orders egg sandwiches*), a pronoun must agree with its antecedent (*The chef surveys her breakfast*), and a demonstrative adjective must agree with its noun (*She likes these kinds of sandwiches*). (See Chapter 15.)
   Logical agreement requires consistency in number between other related words, usually nouns: *The students brought their books* [not *book*]. (See pp. 358–59.)

analogy A comparison between members of different classes, such as a nursery school and a barnyard or a molecule and a pair of dancers. Usually, the purpose is to explain something unfamiliar to readers through something familiar. (See pp. 97–98.)

analysis The separation of a subject into its elements. Sometimes called **division,** analysis is fundamental to critical thinking, reading, and writing (pp. 158–59, 167–69) and is a useful tool for developing essays (p. 25) and paragraphs (pp. 94–95).

antecedent The word to which a pronoun refers: *Jonah, who is not yet ten, has already chosen the college he will attend* (*Jonah* is the antecedent of the pronouns *who* and *he*). (See pp. 313–17.)

APA style The style of documentation recommended by the American Psychological Association and used in many of the social sciences. (For discussion and examples, see pp. 784–800.)

appeals Attempts to engage and persuade readers. An **emotional appeal** touches readers' feelings, beliefs, and values. An **ethical appeal** presents the writer as competent, sincere, and fair. A **rational appeal** engages readers' powers of reasoning. (See pp. 208–10.)

appositive A word or phrase appearing next to a noun or pronoun that renames or identifies it and is equivalent to it: *My brother Michael, the best horn player in town, won the state competition* (*Michael* identifies which brother is being referred to; *the best horn player in town* renames *Michael*). (See pp. 257–58.)

argument   Writing whose primary purpose is to convince readers of an idea or persuade them to act. (See Chapters 9–11.)

article   The word *a, an,* or *the.* Articles are sometimes called **determiners** because they always signal that a noun follows. (See pp. 326–29 for when to use *a/an* versus *the.* See p. 864 for when to use *a* versus *an.*)

assertion   See *claim.*

assumption   A stated or unstated belief or opinion. Uncovering assumptions is part of critical thinking, reading, and writing (see pp. 159–61, 170–71). In argument, assumptions connect claims and evidence (see pp. 187–88).

audience   The intended readers of a piece of writing. Knowledge of the audience's needs and expectations helps a writer shape writing so that it is clear, interesting, and convincing. (See pp. 9–13, 129–30.)

auxiliary verb   See *helping verb.*

balanced sentence   A sentence consisting of two clauses with parallel constructions: *Do as I say, not as I do. Befriend all animals; exploit none.* Their balance makes such sentences highly emphatic. (See p. 389.)

belief   A conviction based on morality, values, or faith. Statements of belief often serve as assumptions and sometimes as evidence, but they are not arguable and so cannot serve as the thesis in an argument. (See p. 185.)

body   In a piece of writing, the large central part where ideas supporting the thesis are presented and developed. See also *conclusion* and *introduction.*

bookmark   In Internet use, an electronic address you save for later reference. (See p. 590.)

brainstorming   A technique for generating ideas about a subject: concentrating on the subject for a fixed time (say, fifteen minutes), you list every idea and detail that comes to mind. (See pp. 21–22.)

browser   A computer program that makes it possible to search the World Wide Web.

cardinal number   The type of number that shows amount: *two, sixty, ninety-seven.* Contrast *ordinal number* (such as *second, ninety-seventh*).

case   The form of a noun or pronoun that indicates its function in the sentence. Most pronouns have three cases:

- The **subjective case** (*I, she*) for the subject of a verb or for a subject complement.
- The **objective case** (*me, her*) for the object of a verb, verbal, or preposition.
- The **possessive case** to indicate ownership, used either as an adjective (*my, her*) or as a noun (*mine, hers*).

(See p. 268 for a list of the forms of personal and relative pronouns.)

Nouns use the subjective form (*dog, America*) for all cases except the possessive (*dog's, America's*).

cause-and-effect analysis   The determination of why something happened or what its consequences were or will be. (See pp. 25 and 98–99.)

characters The people in a literary work, including the narrator of a story or the speaker of a poem. (See p. 741.)

Chicago style A style of documentation recommended by *The Chicago Manual of Style* and used in history, art, and other humanities. (For discussion and examples, see pp. 764–75.)

chronological organization The arrangement of events as they occurred in time, usually from first to last. (See pp. 39–40, 80.)

citation In research writing, the way of acknowledging material borrowed from sources. Most systems of citation are basically similar: a number or brief parenthetical reference in the text indicates that particular material is borrowed and directs the reader to information on the source at the end of the work. The systems do differ, however. (See pp. 647–87 for MLA style, pp. 764–75 for Chicago style, pp. 784–800 for APA style, and pp. 812–19 for CSE style.)

claim A positive statement or assertion that requires support. Claims are the backbone of any argument. (See pp. 180–83.)

classification The sorting of many elements into groups based on their similarities. (See pp. 25 and 95–96.)

clause A group of related words containing a subject and predicate. A **main (independent) clause** can stand by itself as a sentence. A **subordinate (dependent) clause** serves as a single part of speech and so cannot stand by itself as a sentence.

| Main clause | We can go to the movies. |
| Subordinate clause | We can go if Julie gets back on time. |

A subordinate clause may function as an adjective (*The car that hit Fred was speeding*), an adverb (*The car hit Fred when it ran a red light*), or a noun (*Whoever was driving should be arrested*). (See pp. 254–55.)

clichés See *trite expressions.*

climactic organization The arrangement of material in order of increasing drama or interest, leading to a climax. (See pp. 41, 82.)

clip art Drawings and icons available on word processors, CD-ROMs, and the Web, generally used to embellish documents. (See pp. 124–25.)

clustering A technique for generating ideas about a subject: drawing and writing, you branch outward from a center point (the subject) to pursue the implications of ideas. (See pp. 22–23.)

coherence The quality of an effective essay or paragraph that helps readers see relations among ideas and move easily from one idea to the next. (See pp. 41–42, 77–88.)

collaborative learning In a writing course, students working together in groups to help each other become better writers and readers. (See pp. 66–69, 829–32.)

collective noun See *noun.*

colloquial language The words and expressions of everyday speech. Colloquial language can enliven informal writing but is generally inappropriate in formal academic or business writing. See also *formal and informal.* (See pp. 512–13.)

comma splice   A sentence error in which two main clauses are separated by a comma with no coordinating conjunction. (See Chapter 18.)

Comma splice	The book was long, it contained useful data.
Revised	The book was long; it contained useful data.
Revised	The book was long, and it contained useful data.

common noun   See *noun*.

comparative   See *comparison*.

comparison   The form of an adverb or adjective that shows its degree of quality or amount.

- The **positive degree** is the simple, uncompared form: *gross, shyly*.
- The **comparative degree** compares the thing modified to at least one other thing: *grosser, more shyly*.
- The **superlative degree** indicates that the thing modified exceeds all other things to which it is being compared: *grossest, most shyly*.

The comparative and superlative degrees are formed either with the endings *-er* and *-est* or with the words *more* and *most, less* and *least*. (See pp. 322–23.)

comparison and contrast   The identification of similarities (comparison) and differences (contrast) between two or more subjects. (See pp. 25, 96–97.)

complement   A word or word group that completes the sense of a subject, an object, or a verb. (See pp. 238–41.)

- A **subject complement** follows a linking verb and renames or describes the subject. It may be an adjective, noun, or pronoun. *I am a lion tamer, but I am not yet experienced* (the noun *lion tamer* and the adjective *experienced* complement the subject *I*). Adjective complements are also called **predicate adjectives.** Noun complements are also called **predicate nouns** or **predicate nominatives.**
- An **object complement** follows and modifies or refers to a direct object. The complement may be an adjective or a noun. *If you elect me president, I'll keep the students satisfied* (the noun *president* complements the direct object *me*, and the adjective *satisfied* complements the direct object *students*).
- A **verb complement** is a direct or indirect object of a verb. It may be a noun or pronoun. *Don't give the chimp that peanut* (*chimp* is the indirect object and *peanut* is the direct object of the verb *give;* both objects are verb complements).

complete predicate   See *predicate*.

complete subject   See *subject*.

complex sentence   See *sentence*.

compound construction   Two or more words or word groups serving the same function, such as a **compound subject** (*Harriet and Peter poled their barge down the river*), **compound predicate** (*The scout watched and waited*) or parts of a predicate (*She grew tired and hungry*), and **compound sentence** (*He smiled, and I laughed*). (See p. 258.) **Compound words** include nouns (*featherbrain, strip-mining*) and adjectives (*two-year-old, downtrodden*).

compound-complex sentence   See *sentence.*

compound predicate   See *compound construction.*

compound sentence   See *sentence.*

compound subject   See *compound construction.*

conciseness   Use of the fewest and freshest words to express meaning clearly and achieve the desired effect with readers. (See Chapter 39.)

conclusion   The closing of an essay, tying off the writer's thoughts and leaving readers with a sense of completion. (See pp. 106–08 for suggestions.)

A *conclusion* is also the result of deductive reasoning. See *deductive reasoning* and *syllogism.*

concrete   See *abstract and concrete.*

conditional statement   A statement expressing a condition contrary to fact and using the subjunctive mood of the verb: *If she were mayor, the unions would cooperate.* See also *mood.*

conjugation   A list of the forms of a verb showing tense, voice, mood, person, and number. The conjugation of the verb *know* in present tense, active voice, indicative mood is *I know, you know, he/she/it knows, we know, you know, they know.* (See p. 293 for a fuller conjugation.)

conjunction   A word that links and relates parts of a sentence.

- **Coordinating conjunctions** (*and, but, or, nor, for, so, yet*) connect words or word groups of equal grammatical rank: *The lights went out, but the doctors and nurses kept caring for patients.* (See p. 259.)
- **Correlative conjunctions** or correlatives (such as *either . . . or, not only . . . but also*) are two or more connecting words that work together: *He was certain that either his parents or his brother would help him.* (See p. 260.)
- **Subordinating conjunctions** (*after, although, as if, because, if, when,* and so on) begin subordinate clauses and link them to main clauses: *The seven dwarfs whistle while they work.* (See p. 253.)

conjunctive adverb (adverbial conjunction)   An adverb (such as *besides, consequently, however, indeed,* or *therefore*) that relates two main clauses in a sentence: *We had hoped to own a house by now; however, housing costs have risen too fast.* (See pp. 261–62.) The error known as a comma splice results when two main clauses related by a conjunctive adverb are separated only by a comma. (See pp. 346–47.)

connector (connective)   Any word or phrase that links words, phrases, clauses, or sentences. Common connectors include coordinating, correlative, and subordinating conjunctions; conjunctive adverbs; and prepositions.

connotation   An association called up by a word, beyond its dictionary definition. Contrast *denotation.* (See pp. 519–20.)

construction   Any group of grammatically related words, such as a phrase, a clause, or a sentence.

contraction   A condensation of an expression, with an apostrophe replacing the missing letters: for example, *doesn't* (for *does not*), *we'll* (for *we will*). (See pp. 465–66.)

contrast   See *comparison and contrast.*

coordinate adjectives   Two or more adjectives that equally modify the same noun or pronoun: *The camera panned the vast, empty desert.* (See pp. 441–43.)

coordinating conjunction   See *conjunction.*

coordination   The linking of words, phrases, or clauses that are of equal importance, usually with a coordinating conjunction: *He and I laughed, but she was not amused.* Contrast *subordination.* (See pp. 395–97.)

correlative conjunction (correlative)   See *conjunction.*

count noun   See *noun.*

courseware   A program for online communication and collaboration among the teacher and students in a course. (See pp. 830–32.)

critical thinking, reading, and writing   Looking beneath the surface of words and images to discern meaning and relationships and to build knowledge. (See Chapter 8.)

CSE style   Either of two styles of documenting sources recommended by the Council of Science Editors (formerly the Council of Biology Editors) and frequently used in the natural and applied sciences and in mathematics. (For discussion and examples, see pp. 812–19.)

cumulative (loose) sentence   A sentence in which modifiers follow the subject and verb: *Ducks waddled by, their tails swaying and their quacks rising to heaven.* Contrast *periodic sentence.* (See pp. 387–88.)

dangling modifier   A modifier that does not sensibly describe anything in its sentence. (See pp. 370–72.)

Dangling	<u>Having arrived late</u>, the concert had already begun.
Revised	Having arrived late, <u>we found that</u> the concert had already begun.

data   In argument, a term used for *evidence.* See *evidence.*

database   A collection and organization of information (data). A database may be printed, but the term is most often used for electronic sources.

declension   A list of the forms of a noun or pronoun, showing inflections for person (for pronouns), number, and case. See p. 268 for a declension of the personal and relative pronouns.

deductive reasoning   Applying a generalization to specific circumstances in order to reach a conclusion. See also *syllogism.* Contrast *inductive reasoning.* (See pp. 203–06.)

definition   Specifying the characteristics of something to establish what it is and is not. (See pp. 24, 93–94, 183.)

degree   See *comparison.*

demonstrative adjective   See *adjective.*

demonstrative pronoun   See *pronoun.*

denotation   The main or dictionary definition of a word. Contrast *connotation.* (See pp. 519–20.)

dependent clause   See *clause.*

derivational suffix   See *suffix.*

description   Detailing the sensory qualities of a thing, person, place, or feeling. (See pp. 24 and 92.)

descriptive adjective   See *adjective.*

descriptor   See *keyword(s).*

determiner   A word that marks and precedes a noun: for example, *a, an, the, my, your.* See also *article.* (See pp. 326–30 for the uses of determiners before nouns.)

developing (planning)   The stage of the writing process when one finds a subject, explores ideas, gathers information, focuses on a central theme, and organizes material. Compare *drafting* and *revising.* (See Chapters 1–2.)

dialect   A variety of a language used by a specific group or in a specific region. A dialect may be distinguished by its pronunciation, vocabulary, and grammar. (See pp. 132–34 and 511–12.)

diction   The choice and use of words. (See Chapters 37–39.)

dictionary form   See *plain form.*

direct address   A construction in which a word or phrase indicates the person or group spoken to: *Have you finished, John? Farmers, unite.*

direct object   See *object.*

direct question   A sentence asking a question and concluding with a question mark: *Do they know we are watching?* Contrast *indirect question.*

direct quotation (direct discourse)   See *quotation.*

discussion list   A mailing list of subscribers who use e-mail to converse on a particular subject.

division   See *analysis.*

documentation   In research writing, supplying citations that legitimate the use of borrowed material and support claims about its origins. Contrast *plagiarism.* (See pp. 637–38.)

document design   The control of a document's elements to achieve the flow, spacing, grouping, emphasis, and standardization that are appropriate for the writing situation. (See Chapter 5.)

domain   The part of a Web address (or URL) that gives the organization sponsoring the site.

double negative   A generally nonstandard form consisting of two negative words used in the same construction so that they effectively cancel each other: *I don't have no money.* Rephrase as *I have no money* or *I don't have any money.* (See p. 324.)

double possessive   A possessive using both the ending *-'s* and the preposition *of: That is a favorite expression of Mark's.*

double talk (doublespeak)   Language intended to confuse or to be misunderstood. (See p. 514.)

download   To transfer data from another computer.

drafting   The stage of the writing process when ideas are expressed in connected sentences and paragraphs. Compare *developing (planning)* and *revising*. (See pp. 45–47.)

editing   A distinct step in revising a written work, focusing on clarity, tone, and correctness. Compare *revising*. (See pp. 58–62.)

ellipsis   The omission of a word or words from a quotation, indicated by the three spaced periods of an **ellipsis mark:** *"that all . . . are created equal."*

elliptical clause   A clause omitting a word or words whose meaning is understood from the rest of the clause: *David likes Minneapolis better than* [*he likes*] *Chicago*. (See p. 255.)

emoticon   Sideways faces made up of punctuation, used to convey emotion or irony in electronic communication. (See p. 829.)

emotional appeal   See *appeals*.

emphasis   The manipulation of words, sentences, and paragraphs to stress important ideas. (See Chapter 23.)

essay   A nonfiction composition of multiple paragraphs, focused on a single subject and with a central idea or thesis.

essential element   A word or word group that is necessary to the meaning of a sentence because it limits the thing it refers to: removing it would leave the meaning unclear or too general. Also called a **restrictive element,** an essential element is not set off by punctuation: *The keys to the car are on the table. That man who called about the apartment said he'd try again tonight.* Contrast *nonessential element*. (See pp. 435–38, 450.)

ethical appeal   See *appeals*.

etymology   The history of a word's meanings and forms.

euphemism   A presumably inoffensive word that a writer or speaker substitutes for a word deemed possibly offensive or too blunt—for example, *passed away* for "died." (See pp. 514–15.)

evaluation   A judgment of the quality, value, currency, bias, or other aspects of a work. (See pp. 162–63, 172, 599–609.)

evidence   The facts, examples, expert opinions, and other information that support the claims in an argument. (See pp. 183–87, 207–08.)

expletive   A sentence that postpones the subject by beginning with *there* or *it* and a form of the verb *be: It is impossible to get a ticket. There should be more seats available.* (See p. 264.)

exposition   Writing whose primary purpose is to explain something about a subject.

fallacies   Errors in reasoning. Some evade the issue of the argument; others oversimplify the argument. (See pp. 192–98.)

faulty predication   A sentence error in which the meanings of subject and predicate conflict, so that the subject is said to be or do something illogical: *The installation of air bags takes up space in a car's steering wheel and dashboard.* (See pp. 376–77.)

figurative language (figures of speech)   Expressions that suggest meanings different from their literal meanings in order to achieve special effects. (See pp. 525–27.) Some common figures:

- **Hyperbole,** deliberate exaggeration: *The bag weighed a ton.*
- **Metaphor,** an implied comparison between two unlike things: *The wind stabbed through our clothes.*
- **Personification,** the attribution of human qualities to a thing or idea: *The water beckoned seductively.*
- **Simile,** an explicit comparison, using *like* or *as,* between two unlike things: *The sky glowered like an angry parent.*

A **mixed metaphor** is a confusing or ludicrous combination of incompatible figures: *The wind stabbed through our clothes and shook our bones.*

finite verb   Any verb that makes an assertion or expresses a state of being and can stand as the main verb of a sentence or clause: *The moose eats the leaves.* (See p. 248.) Contrast *verbal,* which is formed from a finite verb but is unable to stand alone as the main verb of a sentence: *I saw the moose eating the leaves.*

first person   See *person.*

flame   To attack an online correspondent personally, as in a discussion list or newsgroup. (See p. 829.)

foil   A character in a literary work who contrasts with another character and thus helps to define that other character. (See p. 756.)

formal and informal   Levels of usage achieved through word choice and sentence structure. More informal writing, as in a letter to an acquaintance or a personal essay, resembles some speech in its colloquial language, contractions, and short, fairly simple sentences. More formal writing, as in academic papers and business reports, avoids these attributes of speech and tends to rely on longer and more complicated sentences.

format   In a document such as an academic paper or a business letter, the arrangement and spacing of elements on the page. See also *document design.*

fragment   See *sentence fragment.*

frame   A window on a computer screen. With two or more frames on the same screen, a Web designer can show two or more documents at once.

freewriting   A technique for generating ideas: in a fixed amount of time (say, fifteen minutes), you write continuously without stopping to reread. (See pp. 20–21.)

function word   A word, such as an article, conjunction, or preposition, that serves primarily to clarify the roles of and relations between other words in a sentence: *We chased the goat for an hour but finally caught it.* Contrast *lexical word.*

fused sentence (run-on sentence)   A sentence error in which two main clauses are joined with no punctuation or connecting word between them. (See p. 342.)

Fused	I heard his lecture it was dull.
Revised	I heard his lecture; it was dull.

future perfect tense   See *tense*.

future tense   See *tense*.

gender   The classification of nouns or pronouns as masculine (*he, boy, handyman*), feminine (*she, woman, actress*), or neuter (*it, typewriter, dog*).

general and specific   Terms designating the relative number of instances or objects included in a group signified by a word. The following list moves from most **general** (including the most objects) to most **specific** (including the fewest objects): *vehicle, four-wheeled vehicle, automobile, sedan, Ford Taurus, blue Ford Taurus, my sister's blue Ford Taurus named Hank*. See also *abstract and concrete*. (See pp. 521–22)

generalization   A claim inferred from evidence. See also *inductive reasoning*.

generic he   *He* used to mean *he or she*. For ways to avoid *he* when you intend either or both genders, see pp. 315–17 and 516.

generic noun   A noun that refers to a typical member of a group rather than to a specific person or thing: *Any person may come. A student needs good work habits. A school with financial problems may short-change its students.* A singular generic noun takes a singular pronoun (*he, she,* or *it*). (See pp. 315–16.)

genitive case   Another term for possessive case. See *case*.

gerund   A verbal that ends in *-ing* and functions as a noun: *Working is all right for killing time* (*working* is the subject of the verb *is; killing* is the object of the preposition *for*). See also *verbals and verbal phrases*. (See p. 248.)

gerund phrase   A word group consisting of a gerund plus any modifiers or objects. See also *verbals and verbal phrases*.

grammar   A description of how a language works.

grounds   A term used for *evidence* in argument. See *evidence*.

helping verb (auxiliary verb)   A verb used with another verb to convey time, obligation, and other meanings: *You should write a letter. You have written other letters.* The **modals** include *can, could, may, might, must, ought, shall, should, will, would*. The other helping verbs are forms of *be, have,* and *do*. (See pp. 277, 283–87.)

homonyms   Words that are pronounced the same but have different spellings and meanings, such as *heard/herd* and *to/too/two*. (See pp. 543–44 for a list.)

HTML (hypertext markup language)   A computer language used for creating Web pages. An **HTML editor** is a program for coding documents in HTML. (See pp. 834–35.)

hyperbole   See *figurative language*.

hypertext   Text such as that on the Web that provides links allowing users to move easily and variously within and among documents. Contrast *linear text*.

idiom   An expression that is peculiar to a language and that may not make sense if taken literally: for example, *bide your time,* and *by and large.* See pp. 523–24 for a list of idioms involving prepositions, such as *agree with them* and *agree to the contract.*

illustration or support   Supplying examples or reasons to develop an idea. (See pp. 24–25 and 92–93.)

imagery   Pictures created by words that appeal to the sense of sight, hearing, touch, taste, or smell.

imperative   See *mood.*

indefinite pronoun   See *pronoun.*

independent clause   See *clause.*

indicative   See *mood.*

indirect object   See *object.*

indirect question   A sentence reporting a question, usually in a subordinate clause, and ending with a period: *Writers wonder whether their work must be lonely.* Contrast *direct question.*

indirect quotation (indirect discourse)   See *quotation.*

inductive reasoning   Inferring a generalization from specific evidence. Contrast *deductive reasoning.* (See pp. 202–03.)

infinitive   A verbal formed from the plain form of the verb plus the **infinitive marker** *to: to swim, to write.* Infinitives and infinitive phrases may function as nouns, adjectives, or adverbs. See also *verbals and verbal phrases.* (See p. 249.)

infinitive marker   See *infinitive.*

infinitive phrase   A word group consisting of an infinitive plus any subject, objects, or modifiers. See also *verbals and verbal phrases.*

inflection   The variation in the form of a word that indicates its function in a particular context. See *declension,* the inflection of nouns and pronouns; *conjugation,* the inflection of verbs; and *comparison,* the inflection of adjectives and adverbs.

inflectional suffix   See *suffix.*

informal   See *formal and informal.*

intensifier   A modifier that adds emphasis to the word(s) it modifies: for example, *very slow, so angry.*

intensive pronoun   See *pronoun.*

interjection   A word standing by itself or inserted in a construction to exclaim or command attention: *Hey! Ouch! What the heck did you do that for?*

interpretation   The determination of meaning or significance—for instance, in a work such as a poem or photograph or in the literature on some issue such as job discrimination. (See pp. 159–61, 170–71.)

interrogative   Functioning as or involving a question.

interrogative adjective   See *adjective.*

interrogative pronoun   See *pronoun.*

intransitive verb   A verb that does not take a direct object: *The woman laughed.* (See p. 238.)

introduction   The opening of an essay, a transition for readers between their world and the writer's. The introduction often contains a statement of the writer's thesis. (See pp. 102–06 for suggestions.)

invention   The discovery and exploration of ideas, usually occurring most intensively in the early stages of the writing process. (See pp. 16–26 for invention techniques.)

inversion   A reversal of usual word order in a sentence, as when a verb precedes its subject or an object precedes its verb: *Down swooped the hawk. Our aims we stated clearly.*

IRC   See *synchronous communication.*

irony   The use of words to suggest a meaning different from what the words say literally: *What a happy face!* (said to someone scowling miserably); *With that kind of planning, prices are sure to go down* (written with the expectation that prices will rise).

irregular verb   A verb that forms its past tense and past participle in some other way than by the addition of *-d* or *-ed* to the plain form: for example, *go, went, gone; give, gave, given.* Contrast *regular verb.* (See pp. 279–80 for a list of irregular verbs.)

jargon   In one sense, jargon is the specialized language of any group, such as doctors or baseball players. In another sense, jargon is vague, pretentious, wordy, and ultimately unclear writing such as that found in some academic, business, and government publications. (See p. 535.)

journal   A personal record of observations, reactions, ideas, and other thoughts. Besides providing a private place to think in writing, a journal is useful for making notes about reading (pp. 152–53, 154–55, 166–67, 736–37), discovering ideas for essays (pp. 17–19), and keeping track of research (pp. 559–60, 736–37, 780–81, 809).

journalist's questions   A set of questions useful for probing a subject to discover ideas about it. (See pp. 23–24.)

keyword(s)   A word or words that define a subject, used for searching databases such as library catalogs and periodical indexes and for searching the Web. (See pp. 573–75.)

lexical word   A word, such as a noun, verb, or modifier, that carries part of the meaning of language. Contrast *function word.*

linear text   Text such as a conventional printed document that is intended to be read in sequence. Contrast *hypertext.* (See pp. 832–33.)

linking verb   A verb that relates a subject to its complement: *Julie is a Democrat. He looks harmless. The boy became a man.* Common linking verbs are the forms of *be;* the verbs relating to the senses, such as *look* and *smell;* and the verbs *become, appear,* and *seem.* (See p. 240.)

listserv   See *discussion list.*

logical agreement   See *agreement.*

logical fallacies   See *fallacies.*

894   Terms   Glossary of terms

894   Terms   Glossary of terms
Instructor's Annotated Edition

lurking   Reading but not participating in an Internet discussion list, newsgroup, or Web forum. (See p. 592.)

main clause   See *clause.*

main verb   The part of a verb phrase that carries the principal meaning: *had been walking, could happen, was chilled.* See also *verb phrase.*

mass noun   Another term for noncount noun. See *noun.*

mechanics   The use of capital letters, underlining or italics, abbreviations, numbers, and divided words. (See Chapters 33–36.)

metaphor   See *figurative language.*

misplaced modifier   A modifier so far from the term it modifies or so close to another term it could modify that its relation to the rest of the sentence is unclear. (See Chapter 21.)

Misplaced	The boys played with firecrackers that they bought illegally in the field.
Revised	The boys played in the field with firecrackers that they bought illegally.

A squinting modifier could modify the words on either side of it: *The plan we considered seriously worries me.*

mixed construction   A sentence containing two or more parts that do not fit together in grammar or in meaning. (See pp. 374–77.)

mixed metaphor   See *figurative language.*

MLA style   The style of documenting sources recommended by the Modern Language Association and used in many of the humanities, including English. (For explanation and examples, see Chapter 47.)

modal   See *helping verb.*

modifier   Any word or word group that limits or qualifies the meaning of another word or word group. Modifiers include adjectives and adverbs as well as words, phrases, and clauses that act as adjectives and adverbs.

MOO   See *synchronous communication.*

mood   The form of a verb that shows how the speaker or writer views the action. (See pp. 299–301.)

- The **indicative mood,** the most common, is used to make statements or ask questions: *The play will be performed Saturday. Did you get the tickets?*
- The **imperative mood** gives a command: *Please get good seats.*
- The **subjunctive mood** expresses a wish, a condition contrary to fact, a recommendation, or a request: *I wish George were coming with us. Did you suggest that he join us?*

narration   Recounting a sequence of events, usually in the order of their occurrence. (See pp. 24 and 91–92.) Literary narration tells a story. (See Chapter 50.)

narrator   The speaker in a poem or the voice who tells a story. (See pp. 741, 752, 753.)

neologism   A word coined recently and not in established use. (See p. 513.)

netiquette   Conventions and courtesies for Internet communication. (See pp. 828–29.)

newsgroup   An Internet discussion group with a common site where all postings are recorded. (See p. 593.)

nominal   A noun, a pronoun, or a word or word group used as a noun: *Joan and I talked. The rich owe a debt to the poor* (adjectives acting as subject and object). *Baby-sitting can be exhausting* (gerund acting as subject). *I like to play with children* (infinitive phrase acting as object).

nominative   Another term for subjective case. See *case.*

noncount noun   See *noun.*

nonessential element   A word or word group that does not limit the term or construction it refers to and thus is not essential to the meaning of the sentence. Also called a **nonrestrictive element,** a nonessential element is set off by punctuation, usually commas: *The new apartment building, in shades of tan and gray, will house fifty people* (nonessential adjective phrase). *Sleep, which we all need, occupies a third of our lives* (nonessential adjective clause). *His wife, Patricia, is a chemist* (nonessential appositive). Contrast *essential element.* (See pp. 435–38.)

nonfinite verb   See *verbals and verbal phrases.*

nonrestrictive element   See *nonessential element.*

nonstandard   Words and grammatical forms not conforming to standard American English. (See pp. 511–12.)

noun   A word that names a person, place, thing, quality, or idea: *Maggie, Alabama, clarinet, satisfaction, socialism.* Nouns normally form the possessive case by adding -'s (*Maggie's*) and the plural by adding -s or -es (*clarinets, messes*), although there are exceptions (*men, women, children*). The forms of nouns depend partly on where they fit in certain overlapping groups:

- **Common nouns** name general classes and are not capitalized: *book, government, music.*
- **Proper nouns** name specific people, places, and things and are capitalized: *Susan, Athens, Fenway Park.*
- **Count nouns** name things considered countable in English (they form plurals): *ounce/ounces, camera/cameras, person/people.*
- **Noncount nouns** name things not considered countable in English (they don't form plurals): *chaos, fortitude, silver, earth, information.*
- **Collective nouns** are singular in form but name groups: *team, class, family.*

noun clause   A word group containing a subject and a verb and functioning as a subject, object, or complement: *Everyone wondered how the door opened. Whoever opened it had left.*

number   The form of a noun, pronoun, demonstrative adjective, or verb that indicates whether it is singular or plural: *woman, women; I, we; this, these; runs, run.*

object   A noun, pronoun, or word group that receives the action of or is influenced by a transitive verb, a verbal, or a preposition.

- A **direct object** receives the action of a verb or verbal and frequently follows it in a sentence: *We sat watching the stars. Emily caught whatever it was you had.* (See p. 238.)
- An **indirect object** tells for or to whom something is done: *I lent Stan my car. Reiner bought us all champagne.* (See p. 240.)
- An **object of a preposition** usually follows a preposition and is linked by it to the rest of the sentence: *They are going to Rhode Island for the blues festival.* (See p. 245.)

object complement   See *complement.*

objective   See *case.*

opinion   A conclusion based on facts; an arguable, potentially changeable claim. Claims of opinion form the backbone of any argument. (See p. 181.)

ordinal number   The type of number that shows order: *first, eleventh, twenty-fifth.* Contrast *cardinal number* (such as *one, twenty-five*).

paragraph   Generally, a group of sentences set off by a beginning indention and developing a single idea. That idea is often stated in a **topic sentence.** (See Chapter 4.)

parallelism   Similarity of grammatical form between two or more coordinated elements: *Rising prices and declining incomes left many people in bad debt and worse despair.* (See Chapter 25.)

paraphrase   The restatement of source material in one's own words and sentence structures, useful for borrowing the original author's line of reasoning but not his or her exact words. Paraphrases must always be acknowledged in source citations. (See pp. 618–20.)

parenthetical citation   In the text of a paper, a brief reference, enclosed in parentheses, indicating that material is borrowed and directing the reader to the source of the material. See also *citation.*

parenthetical expression   A word or construction that interrupts a sentence and is not part of its main structure, called *parenthetical* because it could (or does) appear in parentheses: *Childe Hassam (1859–1935) was an American painter and etcher. The book, incidentally, is terrible.* (See pp. 482–83.)

participial phrase   A word group consisting of a participle plus any objects or modifiers. See also *verbals and verbal phrases.*

participle   A verbal showing continuing or completed action, used as an adjective or part of a verb phrase but never as the main verb of a sentence or clause. (See p. 248.)

- A **present participle** ends in *-ing: My heart is breaking* (part of verb phrase). *I like to watch the rolling waves* (adjective).
- A **past participle** most commonly ends in *-d, -ed, -n,* or *-en* (*wished, shown, given*) but sometimes changes the spelling of the verb (*sung, done, slept*): *Jeff has broken his own record* (part of verb phrase). *The closed door beckoned* (adjective).

See also *verbals and verbal phrases.*

particle   A preposition or adverb in a two-word verb: *look up, catch on.* (See pp. 291–92.)

parts of speech   The classes into which words are commonly grouped according to their form, function, and meaning: nouns, pronouns, verbs, adjectives, adverbs, conjunctions, prepositions, and interjections. See separate entries for each part of speech.

passive voice   See *voice.*

past participle   See *participle.*

past perfect tense   See *tense.*

past tense   See *tense.*

patterns of development   Ways of thinking that can help you develop and organize ideas in essays and paragraphs. (See pp. 24–25 and 91–100.)

perfect tenses   See *tense.*

periodic sentence   A suspenseful sentence in which modifiers precede the main clause, which falls at the end: *Postponing decisions about family while striving to establish themselves in careers, many young adults are falsely accused of greed.* Contrast *cumulative sentence.* (See p. 388.)

person   The form of a verb or pronoun that indicates whether the subject is speaking, spoken to, or spoken about. In English only personal pronouns and verbs change form to indicate difference in person. In the **first person,** the subject is speaking: *I am* [or *We are*] *planning a party.* In the **second person,** the subject is being spoken to: *Are you coming?* In the **third person,** the subject is being spoken about: *She was* [or *They were*] *going.*

personal pronoun   See *pronoun.*

personification   See *figurative language.*

phrase   A group of related words that lacks a subject or a predicate or both and that acts as a single part of speech. See *absolute phrase, prepositional phrase, verbals and verbal phrases,* and *verb phrase.*

plagiarism   The presentation of someone else's ideas or words as if they were one's own. Whether accidental or deliberate, plagiarism is a serious and often punishable offense. (See pp. 629–37.)

plain case   Another term for the subjective case of nouns. See *case.*

plain form   The dictionary form of a verb: *make, run, swivel.* See also *verb forms.*

planning   See *developing (planning).*

plot   The pattern of events in a work of literature. (See p. 741.)

plural   More than one. See *number.*

point of view   The perspective or attitude of the narrator or speaker in a work of literature. See also *person.* (See p. 741.)

positive degree   See *comparison.*

possessive   See *case.*

predicate The part of a sentence that makes an assertion about the subject. A predicate must contain a finite verb and may contain modifiers, objects of the verb, and complements. The **simple predicate** consists of the verb and its helping verbs: *A wiser person would have made a different decision.* The **complete predicate** includes the simple predicate and any modifiers, objects, and complements: *A wiser person would have made a different decision.* See also *intransitive verb, linking verb,* and *transitive verb.* (See pp. 233–34, 238–41.)

predicate adjective See *complement.*

predicate noun (predicate nominative) See *complement.*

prefix A letter or group of letters (such as *sub, in, dis, pre*) that can be added at the beginning of a root or word to create a new word: *sub + marine = submarine; dis + grace = disgrace.* Contrast *suffix.*

premise Generally, a claim or assumption basic to an argument. In a deductive syllogism, one premise applied to another leads logically to a conclusion. See also *syllogism.* (See pp. 203–06.)

preposition A word that forms a noun or pronoun (plus any modifiers) into a prepositional phrase: *about love, down the steep stairs.* The common prepositions include these as well as *after, before, by, for, from, in, on, to,* and many others. (See p. 245.)

prepositional phrase A word group consisting of a preposition and its object, plus any modifiers. A prepositional phrase usually functions as an adjective (*The boy in green stood up*) or as an adverb (*He walked to the speaker's platform*). (See pp. 245–46.)

present participle See *participle.*

present perfect tense See *tense.*

present tense See *tense.*

pretentious writing Writing that is more elaborate than the writing situation requires, usually full of fancy phrases and showy words. (See pp. 513–14.)

primary source Firsthand information, such as an eyewitness account of events; a diary, speech, or other historical document; a work of literature or art; a report of a survey or experiment; and one's own interview, observation, or correspondence. Contrast *secondary source.* (See p. 565.)

principal clause A main or independent clause. See *clause.*

principal parts The plain form, past-tense form, and past participle of a verb. See *verb forms.* (See pp. 275–77.)

problem-solution organization The arrangement of material to state and explain a problem and then to propose and explain a solution. (See pp. 40–41, 81–82.)

process analysis The explanation of how something works or how to do something. (See pp. 25, 99–100.)

progressive tense See *tense.*

pronoun   A word used in place of a noun. There are eight types of pronouns:

- **Personal pronouns** refer to a specific individual or to individuals: *I, you, he, she, it, we, they.* (See p. 268.)
- **Indefinite pronouns,** such as *everybody* and *some,* do not refer to specific nouns (*Everybody speaks*). (See pp. 309–10.)
- **Relative pronouns**—*who, whoever, which, that*—relate groups of words to nouns or pronouns (*The book that won is a novel*). (See pp. 254, 268.)
- **Interrogative pronouns**—*who, whom, whose, which, what*—introduce questions (*Who will contribute?*).
- **Intensive pronouns**—personal pronouns plus *-self* or *-selves*—emphasize a noun or other pronoun (*He himself asked that question*). (See pp. 268, 875.)
- **Reflexive pronouns** have the same form as intensive pronouns. They indicate that the sentence subject also receives the action of the verb (*They injured themselves*). (See pp. 268, 875.)
- **Demonstrative pronouns** such as *this, that,* and *such* identify or point to nouns (*This is the problem*).
- **Reciprocal pronouns**—*each other* and *one another*—are used as objects of verbs when the subjects are plural (*They loved each other*).

proofreading   Reading and correcting a final draft for misspellings, typographical errors, and other mistakes. (See pp. 62–63.)

proper adjective   See *adjective.*

proper noun   See *noun.*

purpose   For a writer, the chief reason for communicating something about a subject to a particular audience. Purposes are both general (usually explanation or persuasion) and specific (taking into account the subject and desired outcome). (See pp. 13–15.)

quotation   Repetition of what someone has written or spoken. In **direct quotation (direct discourse)**, the person's words are duplicated exactly and enclosed in quotation marks: *Polonius told his son, Laertes, "Neither a borrower nor a lender be."* An **indirect quotation (indirect discourse)** reports what someone said or wrote but not in the exact words and not in quotation marks: *Polonius advised his son, Laertes, not to borrow or lend.*

rational appeal   See *appeals.*

reciprocal pronoun   See *pronoun.*

reflexive pronoun   See *pronoun.*

regional language   Expressions common to the people in a particular geographical area. (See p. 512.)

regular verb   A verb that forms its past tense and past participle by adding *-d* or *-ed* to the plain form: *love, loved, loved; open, opened, opened.* Contrast *irregular verb.* (See p. 278.)

relative clause   A subordinate clause beginning with a relative pronoun such as *who* or *that* and functioning as an adjective.

relative pronoun See *pronoun*.

restrictive element See *essential element*.

revising The stage of the writing process in which one considers and improves the meaning and underlying structure of a draft. Compare *developing (planning)* and *drafting*. (See pp. 48–54.)

rhetoric The principles for finding and arranging ideas and for using language in speech or writing to achieve the writer's purpose in addressing his or her audience.

rhetorical question A question asked for effect, with no answer expected. The person asking the question either intends to provide the answer or assumes it is obvious: *If we let one factory pollute the river, what does that say to other factories that want to dump wastes there?*

run-on sentence See *fused sentence*.

sans serif See *serifs*.

search engine A computer program that conducts Internet searches from keywords or directories. (See pp. 588–90.)

secondary source A source reporting or analyzing information in other sources, such as a critic's view of a work of art or a sociologist's summary of others' studies. Contrast *primary source*. (See p. 565.)

second person See *person*.

sentence A complete unit of thought, consisting of at least a subject and a predicate that are not introduced by a subordinating word. Sentences can be classed on the basis of their structure in one of four ways. A **simple sentence** contains one main clause: *I'm leaving.* A **compound sentence** contains at least two main clauses: *I'd like to stay, but I'm leaving.* A **complex sentence** contains one main clause and at least one subordinate clause: *If you let me go now, you'll be sorry.* A **compound-complex sentence** contains at least two main clauses and at least one subordinate clause: *I'm leaving because you want me to, but I'd rather stay.* (See pp. 265–66.)

sentence fragment A sentence error in which a group of words is set off as a sentence even though it begins with a subordinating word or lacks a subject or a predicate or both. (See Chapter 17.)

Fragment	She lost the race. Because she was injured. [*Because*, a subordinating conjunction, makes the underlined clause subordinate.]
Revised	She lost the race because she was injured.
Fragment	He could not light a fire. Thus could not warm the room. [The underlined word group lacks a subject.]
Revised	He could not light a fire. Thus he could not warm the room.

sentence modifier An adverb or a word or word group acting as an adverb that modifies the idea of the whole sentence in which it appears rather than any specific word: *In fact, people will always complain.*

series A sequence of three or more items of equal importance: *The children are named John, Hallie, and Nancy.* The items in a series are separated with commas. (See pp. 441–42.)

serifs   Small lines on the characters in type fonts, such as the lines along the bottom of this A. **Sans serif** type, such as Arial, does not have serifs. (See p. 117.)

server   A computer that links other computers in a network. Servers transfer data and store files.

setting   The place where the action of a literary work happens. (See p. 742.)

sexist language   Language expressing narrow ideas about men's and women's roles, positions, capabilities, or value. (See pp. 514–17.)

signal phrase   Words that indicate who is being quoted: *"In the future,"* *said Andy Warhol, "everyone will be world-famous for fifteen minutes."* (For punctuating signal phrases, see pp. 444–46. For using signal phrases to integrate quotations, see pp. 625–27.)

simile   See *figurative language.*

simple predicate   See *predicate.*

simple sentence   See *sentence.*

simple subject   See *subject.*

simple tense   See *tense.*

singular   One. See *number.*

slang   Expressions used by the members of a group to create bonds and sometimes exclude others. Most slang is too vague, short-lived, and narrowly understood to be used in any but very informal writing. (See p. 512.)

source   A place where information or ideas may be found: book, article, Web site, work of art, television program, and so on.

spam   To send an irrelevant and unsolicited electronic message to many recipients at once, such as all the subscribers to a discussion list.

spatial organization   In a description of a person, place, or thing, the arrangement of details as they would be scanned by a viewer—for instance, from top to bottom or near to far. (See pp. 39 and 79–80.)

specific   See *general and specific.*

split infinitive   The often awkward interruption of an infinitive and its marker *to* by an adverb: *Management decided to immediately introduce the new product.* (See pp. 367–68.)

squinting modifier   See *misplaced modifier.*

standard American English   The dialect of English used and expected by educated writers and readers in colleges and universities, businesses, and professions. (See pp. 132–34, 510–11.)

subject   In grammar, the part of a sentence that names something and about which an assertion is made in the predicate. The **simple subject** consists of the noun alone: *The quick brown fox jumps over the lazy dog.* The **complete subject** includes the simple subject and its modifiers: *The quick brown fox jumps over the lazy dog.* (See pp. 233–34.)

subject complement   See *complement.*

subjective   See *case.*

subjunctive See *mood.*

subordinate clause See *clause.*

subordinating conjunction See *conjunction.*

subordination The use of grammatical constructions to de-emphasize one element in a sentence by making it dependent on rather than equal to another element: *Although I left six messages for him, the doctor failed to call.* Contrast *coordination.* (See pp. 398–402.)

substantive A word or word group used as a noun.

suffix A **derivational suffix** is a letter or group of letters that can be added to the end of a root word to make a new word, often a different part of speech: *child, childish; shrewd, shrewdly; visual, visualize.* An **inflectional suffix** adapts a word to different grammatical relations: *boy, boys; fast, faster; tack, tacked.*

summary A condensation and restatement of source material in one's own words and sentence structures, useful in reading for comprehending the material (see pp. 140–42) and in research writing for presenting the gist of the original author's idea (pp. 617–18). Summaries appearing in a paper must always be acknowledged in source citations.

superlative See *comparison.*

syllogism A form of deductive reasoning in which two premises stating generalizations or assumptions together lead to a conclusion. *Premise:* Hot stoves can burn me. *Premise:* This stove is hot. *Conclusion:* This stove can burn me. See also *deductive reasoning.* (See pp. 203–06.)

symbolism The use of a concrete thing to suggest something larger and more abstract, as a red rose may symbolize passion or romance. (See p. 742.)

synchronous communication Real-time, simultaneous communication over the Internet, analogous to a telephone conversation. Instant messaging and MOOs are examples. (See p. 593.)

synonyms Words with approximately but not exactly the same meanings, such as *snicker, giggle,* and *chortle.* (See p. 520.)

syntax In sentences, the grammatical relations among words and the ways those relations are indicated.

synthesis Drawing connections among the elements within a work (such as the images in a poem) or among entire works (entire poems). Synthesis is an essential skill in critical thinking, reading, and writing (see pp. 161–62, 171) and in research writing (pp. 610–11).

tag question A question attached to the end of a statement and consisting of a pronoun, a helping verb, and sometimes the word *not: It isn't raining, is it? It is sunny, isn't it?*

template A word-processing form for a letter, memo, or other document. (See p. 116.)

tense The form of a verb that expresses the time of its action, usually indicated by the verb's inflection and by helping verbs.

- The **simple tenses** are the **present** (*I race, you go*), the **past** (*I raced, you went*), and the **future,** formed with the helping verb *will* (*I will race, you will go*).
- The **perfect tenses,** formed with the helping verbs *have* and *had,* indicate completed action. They are the **present perfect** (*I have raced, you have gone*), the **past perfect** (*I had raced, you had gone*), and the **future perfect** (*I will have raced, you will have gone*).
- The **progressive tenses,** formed with the helping verb *be* plus the present participle, indicate continuing action. They include the **present progressive** (*I am racing, you are going*), the **past progressive** (*I was racing, you were going*), and the **future progressive** (*I will be racing, you will be going*).

(See p. 293 for a list of tenses with examples.)

theme   The main idea of a work of literature. (See p. 742.)

thesis   The central, controlling idea of an essay, to which all assertions and details relate. (See p. 27.)

thesis statement   A sentence or more that asserts the central, controlling idea of an essay and perhaps previews the essay's organization. (See pp. 28–31.)

third person   See *person.*

thread   In an Internet discussion group, a series of messages on the same topic.

tone   The sense of a writer's attitudes toward self, subject, and readers revealed by words and sentence structures as well as by content. (See pp. 12, 188–89, 209–10, 741.)

topic   The subject of an essay or paragraph.

topic sentence   See *paragraph.*

transitional expression   A word or phrase, such as *thus* or *for example,* that links sentences and shows the relations between them. (See pp. 86–87 for a list.) The error known as a comma splice occurs when two main clauses related by a transitional expression are separated only by a comma. (See pp. 346–47.)

transitive verb   A verb that requires a direct object to complete its meaning. (See pp. 238–39.)

trite expressions (clichés)   Stale expressions that dull writing and suggest that the writer is careless or lazy. (See pp. 527–28.)

two-word verb   A verb plus a preposition or adverb that affects the meaning of the verb: *jump off, put away, help out.* (See pp. 291–92.)

unity   The quality of an effective essay or paragraph in which all parts relate to the central idea and to each other. (See pp. 41–42 and 72–75.)

upload   To transfer data or files from your local computer to another computer.

URL (uniform resource locator)   An address for a document on the World Wide Web. (See p. 603.)

variety Among connected sentences, changes in length, structure, and word order that help readers see the importance and complexity of ideas. (See Chapter 26.)

verb A word or group of words indicating the action or state of being of a subject. The inflection of a verb and the use of helping verbs with it indicate its tense, mood, voice, number, and sometimes person. See separate listings for each aspect and for *predicate*. (See Chapter 14.)

verbals and verbal phrases **Verbals** are verb forms used as adjectives (*swimming children*), adverbs (*designed to succeed*), or nouns (*addicted to running*). The verbals in the preceding examples are a participle, an infinitive, and a gerund, respectively. (See separate entries for each type.) Verbal phrases consist of verbals plus objects or modifiers: *Swimming fast, the children reached the raft. Willem tried to unlatch the gate. Running in the park is his only recreation.* (See pp. 249–50.)

A verbal is a **nonfinite verb:** it cannot serve as the only verb in the predicate of a sentence. For that, it requires a helping verb. (See p. 248.)

verb forms Verbs have five distinctive forms. The first three are the verb's **principal parts:**

- The **plain form** is the dictionary form: *live, swim.*
- The **past-tense form** adds *-d* or *-ed* to the plain form if the verb is regular: *live, lived.* If the verb is irregular, the plain form changes in some other way, such as *swim, swam.*
- The **past participle** is the same as the past-tense form for regular verbs. For irregular verbs, the past participle may differ (*swum*).
- The **present participle** adds *-ing* to the plain form: *living, swimming.*
- The *-s* **form** adds *-s* or *-es* to the plain form: *lives, swims.*

verb phrase A verb consisting of a helping verb and a main verb: *has started, will have been invited.* A verb phrase can serve as the predicate of a clause: *The movie has started.*

voice The form of a verb that tells whether the sentence subject performs the action or is acted upon. In the active voice the subject acts: *We made the decision.* In the passive voice the subject is acted upon: *The decision was made by us.* (See pp. 302–03.)

warrant A term used for *assumption* in argument. See *assumption*.

Web forum A discussion group on the Web, open to everyone and organized around subjects.

wizard A file on many word processors and most desktop publishers that guides the user in designing documents. (See p. 116.)

word order The arrangement of the words in a sentence, which plays a large part in determining the grammatical relation among words in English.

writing process The activities involved in producing a finished piece of writing. The overlapping stages of the process—developing or planning, drafting, and revising—vary among writers and even for the same writer in different writing situations. (See Chapters 1–3.)

writing situation The unique combination of writer, subject, audience, purpose, and other elements that defines an assignment or occasion and helps direct the writer's choices. (See pp. 4–6.)

Credits

Text and Illustrations

Photos

Index

Useful Lists and Summaries

Editing Symbols

Boldface numbers and letters refer to chapters and sections of the handbook.

ab	Faulty abbreviation, **35**		*p*	Error in punctuation, **27–32**
ad	Misused adjective or adverb, **16**		*. ? !*	Period, question mark, exclama-
agr	Error in agreement, **15**			tion point, **27**
ap	Apostrophe needed or misused, **30**		✎	Comma, **28**
appr	Inappropriate language, **37**		;	Semicolon, **29**
arg	Faulty argument, **9–11**		✐	Apostrophe, **30**
awk	Awkward construction		" "	Quotation marks, **31**
case	Error in case form, **13**		: — ( ) [ ] … /	Colon, dash, paren-
cap	Use capital letter, **33**			theses, brackets, ellipsis mark,
cit	Missing source citation or error in form of citation, **45**			slash, **32**
coh	Coherence lacking, **2c-4, 4b**		*par,* ¶	Start new paragraph, **4**
con	Be more concise, **39**		¶ *coh*	Paragraph not coherent, **4b**
coord	Coordination needed or faulty, **24a**		¶ *dev*	Paragraph not developed, **4c**
cs	Comma splice, **18a–b**		¶ *un*	Paragraph not unified, **4a**
d	Ineffective diction (word choice), **37–39**		*pass*	Ineffective passive voice, **14j**
des	Ineffective or incorrect document design, **5**		*pn agr*	Error in pronoun-antecedent agreement, **15b**
det	Error in use of determiner, **16h**		*ref*	Error in pronoun reference, **19**
dev	Inadequate development, **2, 4c**		*rep*	Unnecessary repetition, **39c**
div	Incorrect word division, **41d**		*rev*	Revise or proofread, **3**
dm	Dangling modifier, **21h**		*shift*	Inconsistency, **20**
eff	Ineffective sentence(s), **23–26**		*sp*	Misspelled word, **41**
emph	Emphasis lacking or faulty, **23**		*sub*	Subordination needed or faulty, **24b**
exact	Inexact language, **39**		*t*	Error in verb tense, **14g–h**
fp	Faulty predication, **22b**		*t seq*	Error in tense sequence, **14h**
frag	Sentence fragment, **17**		*trans*	Transition needed, **4b-6, 4e**
fs	Fused sentence, **18c**		*und*	Underline or italicize, **34**
gram	Error in grammar, **12–16**		*usage*	See Glossary of Usage, p. 864
hyph	Error in use of hyphen, **41d**		*var*	Vary sentence structure, **26**
inc	Incomplete construction, **22c–e**		*vb*	Error in verb form, **14a–f**
ital	Italicize or underline, **34**		*vb agr*	Error in subject-verb agreement, **15a**
k	Awkward construction		*w*	Wordy, **39**
lc	Use lowercase (small) letter, **33f**		*ww*	Wrong word, **38a**
log	Faulty logic, **9g, 10d**		//	Faulty parallelism, **25**
mech	Error in mechanics, **33–36**		#	Separate with a space
mixed	Mixed construction, **22a–b**		‿	Close up the space
mm	Misplaced modifier, **21a–g**		✄	Delete
mng	Meaning unclear		t̲h̲e̲	Capitalize, **33**
no cap	Unnecessary capital letter, **33f**		T̸he	Use a small letter, **33**
no ✎	Comma not needed, **28j**		t⤸e⤸b	Transpose letters or words
no ¶	No new paragraph needed, **4**		X	Obvious error
num	Error in use of numbers, **36**		⋀	Something missing, **22e**
			??	Document illegible or meaning unclear

Throughout this handbook, the symbol  signals topics for students whose first language or dialect is not standard American English. These topics can be tricky because they arise from rules in standard English that are quite different in other languages and dialects. Many of the topics involve significant cultural assumptions as well.

No matter what your language background, as a college student you are learning the culture of US higher education and the language that is used and shaped by that culture. The process is challenging, even for native speakers of standard American English. It requires not just writing clearly and correctly but also mastering conventions of developing, presenting, and supporting ideas. The challenge is greater if, in addition, you are trying to learn standard American English and are accustomed to other conventions. Several habits can help you succeed:

- **Read.** Besides course assignments, read newspapers, magazines, and books in English. The more you read, the more fluently and accurately you'll write.
- **Write.** Keep a journal in which you practice writing in English every day.
- **Talk and listen.** Take advantage of opportunities to hear and use English.
- **Ask questions.** Your instructors, tutors in the writing lab, and fellow students can clarify assignments and help you identify and solve writing problems.
- **Don't try for perfection.** No one writes perfectly, and the effort to do so can prevent you from expressing yourself fluently. View mistakes not as failures but as opportunities to learn.
- **Revise first; then edit.** Focus on each essay's ideas, support, and organization before attending to grammar and vocabulary. See the revision and editing checklists on pages 51 and 58–59.
- **Set editing priorities.** Concentrate first on any errors that interfere with clarity, such as problems with word order or subject-verb agreement. The following index can help you identify the topics you need to work on and can lead you to appropriate text discussions. The pages marked * include exercises for self-testing.